T0140120

Lecture Notes in Computer Science   13047

Formal Methods

Subline of Lectures Notes in Computer Science

More information about this subseries at http://www.springer.com/series/7408

Marieke Huisman · Corina Păsăreanu ·
Naijun Zhan (Eds.)

Formal Methods

24th International Symposium, FM 2021
Virtual Event, November 20–26, 2021
Proceedings

 Springer

Editors
Marieke Huisman (iD)
University of Twente
Enschede, The Netherlands

Corina Păsăreanu
NASA Ames Research Center
Moffett Field, CA, USA

Naijun Zhan (iD)
Institute of Software, Chinese Academy
of Sciences
Beijing, China

ISSN 0302-9743   ISSN 1611-3349 (electronic)
Lecture Notes in Computer Science
ISBN 978-3-030-90869-0   ISBN 978-3-030-90870-6 (eBook)
https://doi.org/10.1007/978-3-030-90870-6

LNCS Sublibrary: SL2 – Programming and Software Engineering

This Springer imprint is published by the registered company Springer Nature Switzerland AG
The registered company address is: Gewerbestrasse 11, 6330 Cham, Switzerland

Preface

This volume contains the papers presented at the 24th Symposium on Formal Methods (FM 2021), organized by the Institute of Software of the Chinese Academy of Sciences, China, and held online during November 20–26, 2021. In addition, these proceedings also contain nine papers selected by the Program Committee of the Industry Day (I-Day@FM21).

FM 2021 was organized under the auspices of Formal Methods Europe (FME), an independent association whose aim is to stimulate the use of, and research on, formal methods for software development. It has been almost 35 years since the first VDM symposium in 1987 brought together researchers with the common goal of creating methods to produce high-quality software based on rigor and reason. Since then the diversity and complexity of computer technology has changed enormously and the formal methods community has stepped up to the challenges those changes brought by adapting, generalizing, and improving the models and analysis techniques that were the focus of that first symposium. The papers in this proceedings reflect this progress, and demonstrate how formal methods have been successfully applied in many different application areas.

To establish the program of FM 2021, we assembled a Program Committee (PC) of 46 renowned scientists from all over the world. We received a total of 161 abstract submissions, which resulted in 131 full paper submissions from authors in 28 different countries. Each submission went through a rigorous review process in which the papers were reviewed by at least three PC members. Following a discussion phase lasting two weeks, we selected 33 full papers and two short tool papers, an acceptance rate of 26 %, for presentation during the symposium and inclusion in these proceedings. The symposium featured keynotes by Paula Herber (University of Münster, Germany), Assia Mahboubi (Inria, France), Clark Barrett (Stanford University, USA), and Mingsheng Ying (University of Technology Sydney, Australia). Paula Herber and Mingsheng Ying also contributed a paper to the proceedings. We hereby thank these invited speakers for having accepted our invitation. The program also featured an FME Fellowship Award Ceremony.

We are grateful to all involved in FM 2021. In particular, the PC members and sub-reviewers for their accurate and timely reviewing, all authors for their submissions, and all attendees of the symposium for their participation. We also thank all the other committees (I-Day, Doctoral Symposium, Journal First Track, Workshops, and Tutorials), listed on the following pages, and particularly the excellent local organization and publicity teams.

We are very grateful to our sponsors: the Chinese Academy of Sciences, and in particular its Institute of Software, and the National Natural Science Foundation of China. Finally, we thank Springer for publishing these proceedings in their FM subline and we acknowledge the support from EasyChair in assisting us in managing the complete process from submissions to these proceedings to the program.

August 2021

Marieke Huisman
Corina Păsăreanu
Naijun Zhan

Organization

General Chair

Huimin Lin — Institute of Software, Chinese Academy of Sciences, China

Program Chairs

Marieke Huisman — University of Twente, The Netherlands
Corina Păsăreanu — NASA, KBR, and CMU, USA
Naijun Zhan — Institute of Software, Chinese Academy of Sciences, China

Program Committee

Bernhard K. Aichernig — TU Graz, Austria
Christel Baier — TU Dresden, Germany
Maurice H. ter Beek — ISTI-CNR, Italy
Gustavo Betarte — Universidad de la República, Uruguay
Ivana Cerna — Masaryk University, Czech Republic
Pedro R. D'Argenio — Universidad Nacional de Córdoba and CONICET, Argentina
Alessandro Fantechi — Universita' di Firenze, Italy
Bernd Fischer — Stellenbosch University, South Africa
Martin Fränzle — Carl von Ossietzky Universität Oldenburg, Germany
Vijay Ganesh — University of Waterloo, Canada
Fatemeh Ghassemi — University of Tehran, Iran
Stefania Gnesi — ISTI-CNR, Italy
Ichiro Hasuo — National Institute of Informatics, Japan
Paula Herber — University of Münster, Germany
Peter Höfner — Australian National University, Australia
Marieke Huisman — University of Twente, The Netherlands
Nils Jansen — Radboud University, The Netherlands
Einar Broch Johnsen — University of Oslo, Norway
Jan Kofron — Charles University in Prague, Czech Republic
Dorel Lucanu — Alexandru Ioan Cuza University, Romania
Radu Mateescu — Inria, France
Anastasia Mavridou — SGT Inc. and NASA Ames Research Center, USA
Annabelle McIver — Macquarie University, Australia
Rosemary Monahan — Maynooth University, Ireland
Nina Narodytska — VMware Research, USA
David Naumann — Stevens Institute of Technology, USA

Jose Oliveira	University of Minho, Portugal
Jun Pang	University of Luxembourg, Luxembourg
Dave Parker	University of Birmingham, UK
Corina Păsăreanu	NASA, KBR, and CMU, USA
Gustavo Petri	ARM, UK
Jaco van de Pol	Aarhus University, Denmark
Akshay Rajhans	MathWorks, USA
Tamara Rezk	Inria, France
Partha Roop	University of Auckland, New Zealand
Jun Sun	Singapore Management University, Singapore
Elena Troubitsyna	KTH Royal Institute of Technology, Sweden
Sebastian Uchitel	University of Buenos Aires, Argentina, and Imperial College London, UK
Mattias Ulbrich	Karlsruhe Institute of Technology, Germany
Tarmo Uustalu	Reykjavik University, Iceland
Ji Wang	University of Defense Science and Technology, China
Michael Whalen	Amazon Inc. and the University of Minnesota, USA
Anton Wijs	Eindhoven University of Technology, The Netherlands
Jim Woodcock	University of York, UK
Naijun Zhan	Institute of Software, Chinese Academy of Sciences, China
Lijun Zhang	Institute of Software, Chinese Academy of Sciences, China

Journal-First Track Chair

Eerke Boiten	De Montfort University, UK

Journal-first Track Program Committee

Manfred Broy	TU Munich, Germany
Cliff Jones	University of Newcastle, UK
Augusto Sampaio	Universidade Federal de Pernambuco, Brazil

Industry Day Chairs

Erika Ábrahám	RWTH Aachen University, Germany
Yang Liu	Nanyang Technological University, Singapore

Industry Day Program Committee

Simon Barner	Fortiss, Germany
Nikolaj Bjorner	Microsoft, USA
Klaus Havelund	NASA's Jet Propulsion Laboratory, USA
Naiyong Jin	Synopsys Ltd. Co., USA
Einar Broch Johnsen	University of Oslo, Norway

Joseph Kiniry   Galois, USA
Thierry Lecomte   ClearSy, France
Carl Seger   Chalmers University of Technology, Sweden
Danielle Stewart   Adventium Labs, USA
Kenji Taguchi   CAV Technologies, Co. Ltd., Japan

Doctoral Symposium Chairs

Wolfgang Ahrendt   Chalmers University of Technology, Sweden
Ji Wang   University of Defense Science and Technology, China

Workshops Chairs

Carlo A. Furia   Università della Svizzera italiana, Switzerland
Lijun Zhang   Institute of Software, Chinese Academy of Sciences,
                            China

Tutorials Chairs

Luigia Petre   Åbo Akademi University, Finland
Tim A. C. Willemse   Eindhoven University of Technology, The Netherlands

Publicity Chairs

Eunsuk Kang   Carnegie Mellon University, USA
Jun Pang   University of Luxembourg, Luxembourg

Finance Chair

Shuling Wang   Institute of Software, Chinese Academy of Sciences,
                            China

Local Organizers

Naijun Zhan (Chair)   Institute of Software, Chinese Academy of Sciences,
                            China
Bai Xue   Institute of Software, Chinese Academy of Sciences,
                            China
Bohua Zhan   Institute of Software, Chinese Academy of Sciences,
                            China
Zhilin Wu   Institute of Software, Chinese Academy of Sciences,
                            China
Andrea Turrini   Institute of Software, Chinese Academy of Sciences,
                            China

David Jansen	Institute of Software, Chinese Academy of Sciences, China
Peng Wu	Institute of Software, Chinese Academy of Sciences, China

Web Team

Bohua Zhan	Institute of Software, Chinese Academy of Sciences, China
Bai Xue	Institute of Software, Chinese Academy of Sciences, China
Andrea Turrini	Institute of Software, Chinese Academy of Sciences, China
Shouyun Sun	Institute of Software, Chinese Academy of Sciences, China
Runqing Xu	Institute of Software, Chinese Academy of Sciences, China

FME Board

Ana Cavalcanti	University of York, UK
Nico Plat	Thanos, The Netherlands
Lars-Henrik Eriksson	Uppsala University, Sweden
Stefania Gnesi	ISTI–CNR, Italy
Einar Broch Johnsen	University of Oslo, Norway

Additional Reviewers

Akshay, S.
An, Jie
Annenkov, Danil
Arusoaie, Andrei
Ashok Kumar, Pavithra
Ashok, Dhananjay
Badings, Thom
Bannister, Callum
Barnat, Jiri
Basile, Davide
Benes, Nikola
Berani Abdelwahab, Erzana
Beringer, Lennart
Bhave, Devendra
Blatter, Lionel
Blicha, Martin
Bohrer, Brandon

Bouvier, Pierre
Broccia, Giovanna
Bromberger, Martin
Bursuc, Sergiu
Calegari, Daniel
Campo, Juan Diego
Carnevali, Laura
Cassez, Franck
Castellano, Ezequiel Gustavo
Castro, Pablo
Chen, Liqian
Chen, Zhenbang
Chiang, James
Chong, Nathan
Ciobaca, Stefan
Condurache, Rodica
Cubuktepe, Murat

Czibula, Gabriela
Demasi, Ramiro
Di Stefano, Luca
Din, Crystal Chang
Doko, Marko
Dort, Vlastimil
Dubut, Jérémy
Eberl, Manuel
Faghih, Fathiyeh
Fan, Chuchu
Farjudian, Amin
Farrell, Marie
Fernandes, Natasha
Firsov, Denis
Fiterau-Brostean, Paul
Georges, Aina Linn
van Glabbeek, Rob
Gori, Gloria
Graves, Laura
Guarnieri, Marco
van den Haak, Lars
Hahn, Ernst Moritz
Henrio, Ludovic
Hojjat, Hossein
Holík, Lukáš
Hou, Zhe
Jakobs, Marie-Christine
Jansen, David N.
Junges, Sebastian
Jälkö, Joonas
Kamburjan, Eduard
Khayam, Adam
Kirsten, Michael
Klaška, David
Kliber, Filip
Ko, Yoonseok
Kramer, Oliver
Kröger, Paul
Kura, Satoshi
Lang, Frederic
Lanzinger, Florian
LeCours, Andrew
Ledent, Philippe
Leslie-Hurd, Joe
Lopez Pombo, Carlos Gustavo
Luckcuck, Matt

Luna, Carlos
Maarand, Hendrik
Madeira, Alexandre
Martens, Jan
Masopust, Tomas
McDermott, Dylan
Menghi, Claudio
Mikulski, Lukasz
Moerman, Joshua
Monteiro, Felipe
Morgan, Carroll
Mukherjee, Soham
Mulligan, Dominic
Muroor-Nadumane, Ajay
Muskardin, Edi
Nagisetty, Vineel
Neves, Renato
Noble, John
Norrish, Michael
Novotný, Petr
Oliveira, Marcel Vinicius Medeiros
Osama, Muhammad
Paixao, Joao
Paoletti, Nicola
Pardubska, Dana
Parizek, Pavel
Petrocchi, Marinella
Pfeifer, Wolfram
Pferscher, Andrea
Proença, José
Pun, Violet Ka I
Putot, Sylvie
Putruele, Luciano
Quer, Stefano
Rogalewicz, Adam
Rossi, Matteo
Rusu, Vlad
Sabahi Kaviani, Zeynab
Sabouri, Hamideh
Sagonas, Kostis
Schiffl, Jonas
Scott, Joseph
Semini, Laura
Serwe, Wendelin
Shaik, Irfansha
Sharma, Vaibhav

Shi, Jianqi
Silveira, Adrian
Smith, Graeme
Soudjani, Sadegh
Sousa Pinto, Jorge
Steffen, Martin
Stolz, Volker
Struth, Georg
Suilen, Marnix
Tapia Tarifa, Silvia Lizeth
Tappler, Martin
Tiezzi, Francesco
Tiu, Alwen

Trtík, Marek
Turrini, Andrea
Tuttle, Mark
Usman, Muhammad
Weigl, Alexander
Wimmer, Ralf
Xiong, Shale
Xu, Ming
Yamada, Akihisa
Yang, Pengfei
Yin, Banghu
Zhan, Bohua
Zuliani, Paolo

Contents

Program Verification II

Automata

Analysis of Complex Systems

Probabilities

Industry Track Invited Papers

Industry Track

Invited Presentations

Combining Forces: How to Formally Verify Informally Defined Embedded Systems

Paula Herber$^{(\boxtimes)}$, Timm Liebrenz, and Julius Adelt

University of Münster, Einsteinstr. 62, 48149 Münster, Germany
{paula.herber,timm.liebrenz,julius.adelt}@uni-muenster.de

Abstract. Embedded systems are ubiquitous in our daily lives, and they are often used in safety-critical applications, such as cars, airplanes, or medical systems. As a consequence, there is a high demand for formal methods to ensure their safety. Embedded systems are, however, concurrent, real-time dependent, and highly heterogeneous. Hardware and software are deeply intertwined, and the digital control parts interact with an analogous environment. Moreover, the semantics of industrially used embedded system design languages, such as MATLAB/Simulink or SystemC, is typically only informally defined. To formally capture informally defined embedded systems requires a deep understanding of the underlying models of computation. Furthermore, a single formalism and verification tool are typically not powerful enough to cope with the heterogeneity of embedded systems. In this paper, we summarize our work on automated transformations from informal system descriptions into existing formal verification tools. We present ideas to combine the strengths of various languages, formalisms, and verification backends, and discuss promising results, challenges and limitations.

Keywords: Formalization · Embedded systems · Verification

1 Introduction

Embedded systems, i.e., digital systems that are embedded into a physical environment, are ubiquitious in our daily lives. Examples are the control system of a car, a train, or a cardiac stimulator. The increasing digitalization and automation of our society has boosted embedded devices during the last decades. With the current trend towards the internet of things (IoT), the amount of embedded devices is reaching astounding heights, and they are getting more and more complex and interconnected. At the same time, they are often used in safety-critical applications where faulty behavior might endanger human lives, e.g., in pacemakers, airplanes, autonomous robots, or self-driving cars, or in applications, where a failure may result in enormous financial losses, e.g., in Industry 4.0, intelligent manufacturing, or smart factories. To ensure the correctness of embedded systems for all possible input scenarios, formal methods are highly

© Springer Nature Switzerland AG 2021
M. Huisman et al. (Eds.): FM 2021, LNCS 13047, pp. 3–22, 2021.
https://doi.org/10.1007/978-3-030-90870-6_1

desirable. However, there are two major problems that often preclude formal models from being applied in industrial embedded systems: First, they require a full formalization of the system under verification, which is often not available and often difficult to derive because the semantics of industrially used design languages are only informally defined. Second, formal methods often do not scale well for larger systems.

In this invited paper, we discuss how these problems can be overcome and how the huge gap between theory and practice might be reduced. The key ideas of our approach are twofold: First, we believe that the acceptance of formal methods in industry can be significantly increased if the required formal models are automatically generated from the designs and models that are typically used in industry. Second, we believe that a combination of analysis and verification techniques from various communities can help to achieve the scalability required in industrial applications. In the last decade, we have provided a number of formalizations of two industrially used system design languages, namely SystemC and Simulink. Furthermore, we have more recently experimented with the combination of various analysis and verification techniques, to increase the scalability of automated verification techniques and the automation of interactive approaches. In this paper, we give a summary of our main results, and discuss key advantages, challenges, and open problems.

2   Related Work

There have been several approaches to enable formal verification for SystemC. Some of them only cope with a synchronous subset (e.g. [14,48,49]), others rely on a transformation of SystemC designs into some sort of state machine, as done in [17,18,20,21,24,28,45,50,53], or they use process algebras, petri-nets or a C representation for the verification of SystemC designs [8–10,13,22,29,41]. In [26,33], the authors present an approach to verify SystemC designs using symbolic simulation and partial order reduction. In [15,16], the authors present a combination of induction and bounded model checking to formally verify SystemC designs. However, all of these approaches do not combine verification backends. They can be combined with our approach, as each of them can be used to verify the submodels generated by our automated formalization and partitioning approach. In [31], the authors present an approach for automatic HW/SW partitioning, which enables the underlying verification method to analyze hardware parts more efficiently. However, they do not provide a compositional verification approach. In [34,51], the authors present an approach for component-based HW/SW co-verification. However, the approach requires that the designer specifies subsystems and properties that can be separately verified. In contrast to this, we decompose SystemC designs fully automatically.

There also exists a number of approaches to enable formal verification for Simulink. The Simulink Design Verifier [43] provides means to use model checking and abstract interpretation. However, only discrete system behavior is considered and the scalability is limited [25]. In [2,47], transformations from Simulink into the input languages of various verification tools are proposed. However, they are only applicable for purely discrete systems, and their scalability is limited. The tool CheckMate [7] enables modeling and verification of hybrid Simulink models using hybrid automata. However, this approach is only applicable for a special class of hybrid systems. A transformation of hybrid Simulink models in a specific hybrid automata dialect (SpaceEx) is presented in [44]. However, the state space increases exponentially in the number of concurrent blocks, and thus the approach does not scale well. In [6,54], the authors present the tool MARS, which is used in the verification of Simulink/Stateflow models. The tool automatically transforms a given model into Hybrid CSP and enables the verification with Hybrid Hoare Logic in the HHL Prover. By using Hybrid CSP as underlying formalism, the authors inherit compositionality from a highly expressive process algebra. However, both the property specification and the verification process with Hybrid CSP require a very high level of expertise.

3   Preliminaries

In this section, we briefly introduce two industrially widely used design languages for embedded systems, namely SystemC and Simulink. SystemC is control-flow oriented and most widely used for the design of integrated hardware/software systems, MATLAB/Simulink is data-flow oriented and most widely used for modeling and simulation of complex dynamic systems.

3.1   SystemC

SystemC is a system-level design language and a framework for HW/SW co-simulation. The semantics of SystemC is informally defined in an IEEE standard [27]. It is implemented as a C++ class library, which provides language elements for the description of hardware and software, and allows for modeling of both hardware and software components on various levels of abstraction. It also features an event-driven simulation kernel, which enables the simulation of the design. A SystemC design consists of a set of communicating processes, triggered by events and interacting through channels. Modules and channels represent structural information. SystemC also introduces an integer-valued time model with arbitrary time resolution. Figure 1a shows an excerpt of a SystemC *producer* module that writes to a FIFO buffer. The *produce* method (which is executed within an *SC_THREAD* process) contains an infinite loop where the producer writes a value to the fifo port every clock cycle. The execution of SystemC designs is controlled by a non-preemptive scheduler. Processes suspend themselves using *wait* statements, and resume execution when an event they are waiting for is triggered or a timing delay given in the *wait* statement expires. Like typical hardware description languages, SystemC supports the notion of delta-cycles, which impose a partial order on parallel processes.

3.2   Simulink

MATLAB/Simulink [42] is a data flow oriented modeling language, which extends classical block diagrams with means to model dynamic systems, e.g.

```
1    SC_MODULE(producer)
2    {
3        sc_fifo_out<int> fifo;
4        sc_clk_in clk;
5
6        void produce() {
7            int c = 0;
8            while(true) {
9                wait();
10               c = (c + 1);
11               fifo->write(c);
12           } }
13       SC_CTOR(producer) {
14           SC_THREAD(produce);
15           sensitive << clk; }
16   };
```

(a) Simple SystemC Module

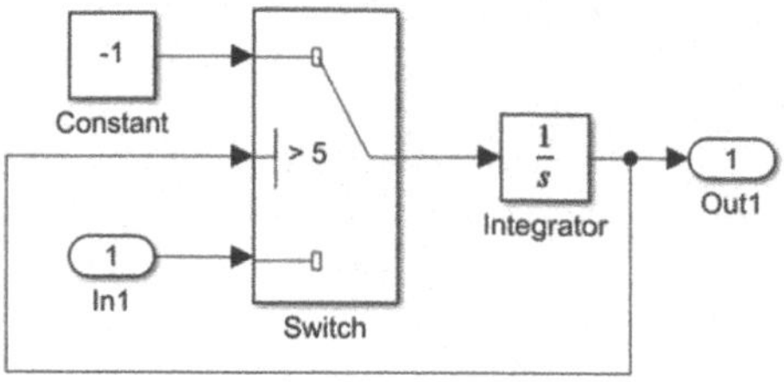

(b) Simple Simulink Model

Fig. 1. Example SystemC and Simulink models

differential equations and complex mathematical functions. With that, it enables the design and simulation of hybrid systems. The basic building blocks in Simulink are blocks, which belong to one or more of several groups, e.g., direct feed-through, time-discrete, time-continuous, and control flow blocks. Signals connect blocks and may carry discrete or continuous values.

Figure 1b shows a small example. The model provides the output of an *Integrator* block as output *Out1*. A *Switch* block controls the input for the integrator depending on its current value. If the value is larger than 5, a *Constant* of -1 is used as input. Otherwise, an input signal provided by the port *In1* is used. The input port *In1* and output port *Out1* connect the model to its environment.

4   Transformation-Based Formalization

The key concept behind our formalizations that enable us to formally verify informally defined embedded systems is shown in Fig. 2. For informal system models, we map the informally defined execution semantics into an existing formally well-defined language. From this semantic mapping, we derive transformation rules for relevant language constructs, and define predefined models for key components of the language definition that define its execution semantics, for example, for the SystemC scheduler and events. Based on our semantic mapping, we then develop fully-automatic transformations from industrially used system design languages into well-defined formal models. Our approach has three major advantages: First, with our semantic mapping, we define formal semantics for the informally defined industrial system design languages. Second, the transformation into formal models is performed fully-automatically, which means that we spare the designer the tedious task of creating a formal model. Third, we gain

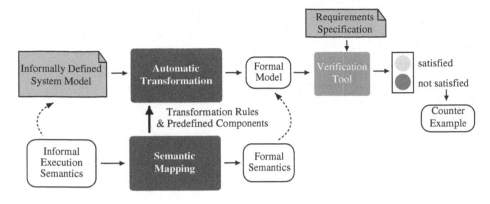

Fig. 2. Transformation-based formalization

access to existing and thus matured and sophisticated verification tools. For SystemC, we have developed transformations into the input languages of three powerful verification tools: the real-time model checker UPPAAL [3], which is especially well-suited for real-time systems and communication architectures, the bit-precise SMT solver UCLID [32], which is especially well-suited for hardware components, and the software model checker CPAchecker [4], which is especially well-suited for software model checking. For Simulink, we have developed transformations into the input languages of the bit-precise SMT solver UCLID [32] and of the interactive theorem prover for hybrid systems KeYmaera X [11]. For all our formalizations, the design is flattened before the transformation. Prefixing is used to keep the structure of the original design transparent to the designer. Note that, while some existing approaches prove the correctness of their transformations formally [52,54], the correctness of our transformations is not formally established. We state that our transformation rules *define* a formal semantics of the informally defined language constructs for SystemC and Simulink. We rely on these rules to capture the informally defined semantics correctly without a formal proof.

4.1   Formalization of SystemC

In the following, we present the key ideas of our transformations from SystemC to UPPAAL [20,21,24], from SystemC to CPAchecker [22] and from SystemC to UCLID [28]. As running example, we use the simple producer shown in Fig. 1a.

Assumptions. Our transformations cover a large subset of possible SystemC designs, but a few assumptions typically have to be fulfilled for a given SystemC design to enable its fully-automatic transformation into a formal representation:

(1) no dynamic variables or process creation are used
(2) no pointers, no side effects
(3) no recursion, no inheritance

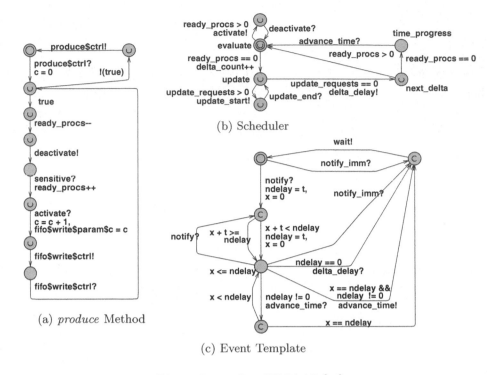

(a) *produce* Method

(b) Scheduler

(c) Event Template

Fig. 3. SystemC to UPPAAL [20]

(4) no external code or library calls

(5) data types are limited to boolean, fixed bit width integer, arrays and structs

(1) and (2) are relaxed for our transformations to UPPAAL and the CPAchecker. Still, there needs to be a statically computable upper bound on dynamic memory allocation and only simple pointer arithmetics are permitted. (4) can be skipped for our SystemC to UCLID transformation. However, unknown functions are then replaced by uninterpreted functions, so the properties to be verified may not depend on the execution of external code or library code.

SystemC to UPPAAL. The main idea of our transformation from SystemC to UPPAAL [20,21,24] is that we map each SystemC method to a single timed automaton and additionally provide predefined models of SystemC events, processes, and the SystemC scheduler. These predefined models execute the method automata according to the SystemC execution semantics. For our simple produce process from Fig. 1a, the transformation yields the timed automaton shown in Fig. 3a. The call-return semantics of a method call is modeled by just introducing a control channel that triggers the execution of the method, in our example *produce$ctrl*. The same channel is used to return control to the caller of the method if its execution terminates (which does not happen in our example). Conditional

```
1   void produce(int pid) {
2     switch(prod_produce_pc[pid]) {
3       case 1: goto Label1;
4       ...
5       case N: goto LabelN;
6     }
7     ...
8     state[pid] = SLEEP;
9     prod_produce_c[pid] = c;
10    prod_produce_pc[pid] = i;
11    return −1;
12    Labeli :
13    c = prod_produce_c[pid];
14  }
```

(a) Process Suspension

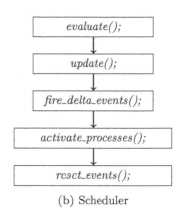

(b) Scheduler

Fig. 4. SystemC to CPAchecker [22]

control flow is modeled by using two outgoing transitions and UPPAAL conditions (in this example, the only condition is *true*). As UPPAAL supports C as a host language, many simple statements like assignments and arithmetic computations can just be copied to a transition. To model the concurrent, non-preemptive execution of processes within UPPAAL, we provide the scheduler model shown in Fig. 3b. The scheduler executes SystemC designs in three phases: *evaluate*, *update*, and *time_progress*. In the *evaluate* phase, processes that are ready to execute (i.e., waiting on the binary channel *activate*) are activated in non-deterministic order. On process suspension, the processes themselves decrement the number of processes that are ready to execute (*ready_procs−*), then first wait for the event that triggers them to resume execution (in our example: any event from the static sensitivity list, i.e. *sensitive*), and then for the scheduler to activate them again. Method calls (via a port or not) are executed by triggering the corresponding control channel, in our example *fifo$write$ctrl*, and then waiting for its return. Parameters are transfered by copying them to global variables. For calls *by-reference*, a pointer is transfered instead. Event notifications in SystemC correspond to a call to one of the *notify* methods. To model them in UPPAAL, we use a similar mechanism as for method calls, but do not wait for their return. Instead, the event notification is non-blocking and concurrently starts the notification process shown in Fig. 3c. In summary, an event waits for a given amount of time, a delta-cycle, or triggers processes that are sensitive to the event immediately by triggering the *wait* event. Pending notifications may be overwritten by notifications that expire earlier. The events synchronize with the scheduler and other events to make sure that time elapses uniformly.

SystemC to CPAchecker. The CPAchecker [4] is a configurable program analysis and model checking tool for sequential C code. Our key idea to transform

SystemC designs into the input language of the CPAchecker is mainly to transform SystemC designs into sequential C programs. To achieve this, we have defined the SystemC execution semantics in C [22]. Again, most interesting are the process suspension, event notification, and the non-preemptive scheduler. Our approach to model process suspension is illustrated in Fig. 4a, again for the running example from Fig. 1a. We introduce a global array that keeps track of the state of each process (referred to by its process id pid). If a process reaches a *wait* statement, i.e., should be suspended, we put the process to sleep by changing its state accordingly (Line 8), save all local variables, and then leave the process by recursively terminating all its methods. To resume process execution when a process is triggered again, we introduce a label at this point in the program and return to this label on process resumption. Note that to implement this, all methods start with a preamble that checks the current state of the associated process (given by a parameter pid, which is added to every method) and jump to the correct label. At process resumption, all local variables are restored. The behavior of the scheduler in each delta cycle is modeled as a sequence of C functions as shown in Fig. 4b. First, all processes that are ready to execute are executed in non-deterministic order (*evaluate*). Then, all update functions are executed (*update*), the events with delta-delayed notifications are set to *FIRED*, and in *activate_processes* processes are activated according to their sensitivities.

SystemC to UCLID. In UCLID [32], systems are specified using state machines, communication is modeled with shared variables, and case statements are used to model the control flow. To transform a given SystemC design into UCLID, we map each SystemC variable to one UCLID state machine, and translate all methods (resp. the state of their program counters) and all processes (resp. the process states) into state machines [28]. Finally, we formally define the SystemC execution semantics by modeling the scheduler, simulation time, and events as state machines. Then, we use k-inductive invariant verification to verify global safety properties with UCLID. This means that we first perform bounded model checking for k steps with the system in its initial state. Then, we verify that if the property holds for k steps, it also holds in step k + 1 from an arbitrary system state (i.e., with all variables set to a symbolic constant as initial value).

For our running example shown in Fig. 1a, our transformation yields the state machines shown in Fig. 5. The state machines representing the program counter (pc) of the *produce* method and the local variable c are shown in Fig. 5a. The pc is initially set to the beginning of the method in Line 7 ($l7$) and then to the next line in each step until it gets to the wait statement in Line 9 ($l9$). There, the execution is suspended until the process state machine (pm) is set to *running* again. For the program counter, we distinguish whether we just got to Line 9 ($l9\_wait$), which suspends execution, or are already waiting for an event ($l9$). This ensures that the scheduler can react to the changed process state before execution is resumed. The state machine for c models that c is initially set to zero and increased by 1 whenever the pc of the method gets to Line 10 ($l10$). The state machines representing the process and its sensitivity are shown in Fig. 5b. The static *sensitivity* of a process is set to true for one step whenever

```
ASSIGN
init[pc] := not_initialized;
next[pc] := case

   ...
   pc = init & pm.state = running : 17;
   pc = 17 : 18;
   pc = 18 & true : 19_wait;
   pc = 19_wait : 19;
   pc = 19 & pm.state = running : 110;
   pc = 110 : 111_call;
   pc = 111_call : 111;
   pc = 111 & fifo.write = done : 18;
   pc = 18 & ~(true) : done;
   default : pc;
esac;
ASSIGN
init[c] := (0 +_32 0);
next[c] := case
   pc = 17 : 0;
   pc = 110 : (c +_32 1);
   default : c;
esac;
```

(a) Method Transformation

```
DEFINE
sensitivity := case
                  clk_event.occurred : true;
                  default : false;
               esac;
ASSIGN
init[state] := no_init;
next[state] := case
   ipm.pc = init : initialized;
   state = initialized : runnable;
   scheduler.next = produce : running;
   ipm.pc = 19_wait : wait_s;
   state = wait_s & sensitivity : runnable;
   ipm.pc = done : terminated;
   ...
```

(b) Process Transformation

Fig. 5. SystemC to UCLID [28]

an event from the sensitivity list occurs. The state of the process is changed from *initialized* to *runnable* after an initialization phase and to *running* if the process is selected for execution by the scheduler. The process suspends itself and goes into a state where it waits for some event from the sensitivity list (*wait_s*) whenever the *wait* method is executed, which happens if the *pc* is set to *19_wait*.

Summary. All the transformations above encode the execution semantics of SystemC in the input language of a dedicated verification tool, and enable fully automatic transformation and verification of given SystemC designs via model checking, program analysis, or k-inductive invariant verification.

4.2 Formalization of Simulink

The idea that a formal model can automatically be derived from an informal design was also the main motivation for our work on the formalization of a subset of the Simulink modeling language. We have presented a fully-automatic transformation from discrete Simulink models into the input language of the UCLID SMT solver in [25]. Furthermore to overcome the restrictive assumptions that limit most existing work on the formal verification of Simulink models to time-discrete systems, we have presented a fully-automatic transformation from

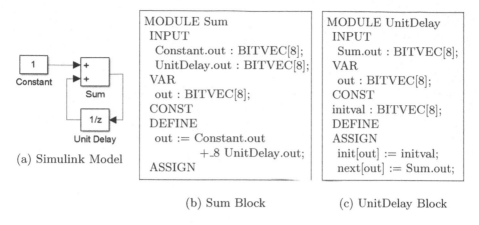

(a) Simulink Model

```
MODULE Sum
  INPUT
    Constant.out : BITVEC[8];
    UnitDelay.out : BITVEC[8];
  VAR
    out : BITVEC[8];
  CONST
  DEFINE
    out := Constant.out
           +_8 UnitDelay.out;
  ASSIGN
```

```
MODULE UnitDelay
  INPUT
    Sum.out : BITVEC[8];
  VAR
    out : BITVEC[8];
  CONST
    initval : BITVEC[8];
  DEFINE
  ASSIGN
    init[out] := initval;
    next[out] := Sum.out;
```

(b) Sum Block   (c) UnitDelay Block

Fig. 6. Simulink to UCLID [25]

hybrid Simulink models into the input language of KeYmaera X, namely the differential dynamic logic (d$\mathcal{L}$) [46], in [35].

Simulink to UCLID. The key idea of our semantic mapping from Simulink to UCLID [25] is that we map functional Simulink blocks into UCLID macros, and discrete Simulink blocks into state variables together with a transition relation that is derived from the semantics of the block, and we map the connections between blocks to shared variables. A simple example is shown in Fig. 6. For this example, the *Constant* block is translated to a variable with constant value, the UCLID specifications of *Sum* and *UnitDelay* are shown in Fig. 6b and Fig. 6c. The *Sum* block is a purely functional block and is transformed into a macro (*DEFINE*), which just corresponds to a term replacement. *UnitDelay* is a stateful block, and thus it is transformed into an initial assignment (*init*) together with a transition relation (*next*). Other logic or arithmetic blocks as well as stateful blocks are transformed analogously. Math functions (e.g. sine waves), Stateflow blocks and S-functions are transformed into uninterpreted functions together with a specification of bounds on the outputs. Our semantic mapping again enables us to transform given discrete Simulink models fully automatically into behaviorally equivalent UCLID specifications, which we can verify with the UCLID SMT solver using k-inductive invariant verification as described above.

Simulink to d$\mathcal{L}$. Differential Dynamic Logic (d$\mathcal{L}$) [46] is a formal logic for reasoning about properties of hybrid systems, e.g., with KeYmaera X [11]. The key idea of our transformation from Simulink to d$\mathcal{L}$ [35] is to define d$\mathcal{L}$ expressions that precisely capture the semantics of all Simulink blocks in a given model, connect them according to the signal lines, and expand control conditions such that assignments and evaluations are only performed if the control conditions are satisfied. To achieve this, we have introduced discrete state variables for time-discrete blocks that keep an inner state, continuous evolutions to model time-continuous blocks, and a sophisticated macro mechanism to represent stateless

```
 1  Integrator = INIT →
 2  [{ smallstep:=0;
 3      Out1:=Integrator;
 4      In1:=*;
 5      ?(In1 < IN_MAX & In1 > IN_MIN);
 6      {?(Integrator>5);
 7        {Integrator'=-1, smallstep'=1 & (Integrator>5 | smallstep <= ε)}
 8      ++ ?(Integrator<=5);
 9        {Integrator'=In1, smallstep'=1 & (Integrator<=5 | smallstep <= ε)}}
10  }*] (true)
```

Fig. 7. Simulink to d$\mathcal{L}$ [35]

behavior, e.g. port connections, arithmetic calculations, and, in particular, control flow. To capture the combined behavior of the whole model, we use a global simulation loop, which is modeled as a *nondeterministic repetition* in d$\mathcal{L}$. Note that our transformation from Simulink to d$\mathcal{L}$ requires that a given Simulink model uses no algebraic loops, no S-function blocks and no external scripts or libraries, and that there are some additional assumptions on the supported block set due to the current state of the implementation [35]. Figure 7 shows the d$\mathcal{L}$ model that results from a transformation of the Simulink model from the preliminaries (Fig. 1b). The switch block is expanded to the conditions and evolution domains in Lines 6–10. The integrator block from the original Simulink model is represented by its initial condition in Line 1 and the continuous evolutions in Line 7 and 10. The switch condition is added to the evolution domains to ensure that the control conditions are reevaluated whenever the threshold is crossed. The input block is represented by the nondeterministic assignment in Line 4 together with the condition in Line 5, as it may provide arbitrary inputs between *IN_MIN* and *IN_MAX*. The variable *smallstep* is introduced to the continuous evolutions and evolution domains to take the approximative character of Simulink simulations into account. By restarting the simulation loop and reevaluating all conditions with a delay of at most ϵ time units after the current condition is violated, small deviations in the switching behavior are allowed. Thus, e ensure that safety properties still hold if small delays in the switching behavior take place, for example due to numerical errors. Our transformation automatically generates a d$\mathcal{L}$ model from a given Simulink model, which can be verified using the interactive theorem prover KeYmaera X.

4.3   Experimental Results with Single Verification Tools

We have shown the applicability of our transformation with several case studies, some of them taken directly from the industry. For example, we have verified a SystemC implementation of the AMBA advanced high-performance bus, which is often used in ARM systems, using our SystemC to UPPAAL transformation [24]. In the case study, provided by Carbon Design Systems©, we have first detected a deadlock situation, which was possible in the rare case of a split transaction over the bus, where a variable reset was missing – a typical corner case which is difficult to find and was not detected in simulation and testing, as confirmed by Carbon Design Systems. With our transformation and verification approach, we have detected this bug in a few minutes and, thanks to the counter-example and structure-preservation of our transformation, could easily identify the source of the error. After fixing this and some smaller bugs, we have verified crucial properties of the AMBA AHB bus with up to 2 master and 2 slaves, for example that no deadlock is possible anymore, that only one master is active at a time, that a master that requests the bus gets it eventually granted, that transactions over the bus take at most 200 ms, that memory accesses are type safe and that no null pointer accesses may happen. We have also successfully verified reachability properties for an Anti Slip-Regulation and Anti-lock Braking System (ASR/ABS) using our SystemC to CPAChecker transformation [22], and safety properties for a universal asynchronous receiver transmitter (UART) implementation with our SystemC to UCLID transformation [28].

For our transformation from Simulink to UCLID, we have shown that the k-inductive invariant verification scales much better than the Simulink Design Verifier using an industrial case study provided by our partners from the automotive industry, namely a discrete variant of a multi-object distance warner [25]. For this case study, we have shown the absence of division-by-zero, overflows, and out-of-range assignments. Finally, we have verified various case studies using our Simulink to d$\mathcal{L}$ transformation and KeYmaera X. For example, we have verified the absence of overflows and functional properties, namely that a positive relative speed measurement causes an increase in the calculated distance, and vice versa for a negative relative speed, for a distance calculator that is part of the original hybrid version of the multi-object distance warner [35].

5   Combining Forces: Compositional Verification

So far, we have mainly targeted the informal semantics of industrially used design languages. To tackle the scalability problem, we have investigated the idea that the scalability of existing verification techniques can be significantly increased by combining static analysis, slicing, and various verification techniques. During our work with SystemC and Simulink, we have realized that some systems or components can be quite effectively verified with model checking, while others can be more effectively verified using counter-example guided abstraction refinement, or deductively with automatic or interactive theorem provers.

5.1   Combined Verification for SystemC

The key idea of our combined verification approach for SystemC is to decompose a given design into submodels that focus on certain aspects, for example the hardware part, the software part, or the communication architecture [19,23], as shown in Fig. 8. With novel dependency analysis and slicing techniques, we cut such submodels safely out of a complex design without compromising the

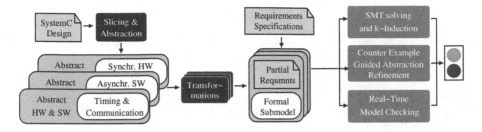

Fig. 8. Combined verification approach for SystemC [19, 23]

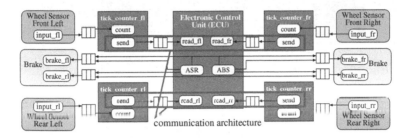

Fig. 9. ASR/ABS example system [23]

behavior with respect to some given properties. To achieve this, we automatically compute an over-approximation of the rest of the system by assigning random symbolic values to each variable that is written outside of a given submodel whenever this might happen [23, 40]. Each submodel together with the abstraction of the rest of the system is then verified with the verification technique that is best suited for it, for example, hardware parts with SMT solving, software parts with counter-example guided abstraction refinement and communication and timing with real-time model checking. As all submodels are safe abstractions, we thus achieve a modular, compositional verification approach.

As an example, we have used our ABS/ASR case study in [23]. Our automated partitioning approach performs a dependence analysis and then cuts the design into submodels such that there are no control or timing dependencies between the partitions. For data dependencies, we compute an abstract verification interface as a safe over-approximation for all variables that may be written outside of the partition. We use interval and timing analyses to get a tight over-approximation. For the ASR/ABS architecture, the communication architecture can be cut out of the overall system as shown in Fig. 9. The only data dependence is that the *tick* variables, which measure the speed at each wheel sensor, are sent over the bus. However, as an interval analysis reveals that the communication architecture is independent of their concrete value, the abstract verification interface consists of only one symbolic constant value representing an arbitrary value for each wheel: $IF = (ticks, \{\mathbb{I}(ticks) = \{(-\infty, \infty)\}\})$. We have successfully verified safety and timing properties of this submodel with UPPAAL.

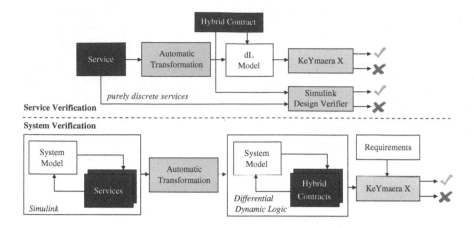

Fig. 10. Compositional verification approach for Simulink [36,37]

5.2 Compositional Verification for Simulink

Our verification approach for Simulink using d$\mathcal{L}$ and KeYmaera X is inherently compositional, as d$\mathcal{L}$ and KeYmaera X support contract-based verification. We have presented an approach to exploit this for Simulink using the concept of *service-based design and verification* [36,37,39]. The overall approach is shown in Fig. 10. The key idea is that we design or identify *services* within a Simulink model. A service encapsulates a group of Simulink blocks that provide a joint functionality into a customizable subsystem with a formally well-defined interface. Customizability is defined by a feature model. The formally well-defined interface must be manually provided by defining a hybrid contract in d$\mathcal{L}$ for each service. A hybrid contract abstractly defines the input-output behavior of a service in classical assume-guarantee style, i.e., it is defined as $hc = (\phi_{in}, \phi_{out})$, where ϕ_{in} are assumptions on input variables and ϕ_{out} are guarantees on trajectories and outputs. The manual definition of contracts requires high expertise and manual effort, but at the same time enables compositional verification: As shown in the upper part of Fig. 10, we can verify that each service adheres to its hybrid contract individually. To achieve this, we can either verify the service with fully automatic verification tools like the Simulink Design Verifier if the service is completely discrete, or we can use our transformation from Simulink to d$\mathcal{L}$ and KeYmaera X if the service contains both discrete and continuous behavior. For system verification, as shown in the lower part of Fig. 10, we can then automatically replace each service by its hybrid contract in the transformed d$\mathcal{L}$ model. This significantly simplifies the verification of safety properties of the overall system if the hybrid contracts are strong enough to capture the safety-relevant behavior of the relevant services and weak enough to provide abstraction. We have shown in [38] that this kind of abstraction is sound under certain assumptions that are ensured by the syntactical structure of a Simulink model.

As an example for our service-oriented verification approach, we have compositionally verified a generic infusion pump (GIP) in [37]. The Simulink model of the GIP consists of several subsystems, which we have encapsulated into services, for example, a pump controller, a warning generator, and a service that models the concentration of the drug in the bloodstream of the patient. For compositional verification, we have defined hybrid contracts for each service, and verified that each service adheres to its hybrid contract individually. For example, we have verified that the controller C does not pump whenever the drug concentration in the blood of the patient exceeds a critical value:

$$\phi_{in,C} \equiv (MedicationInBlood \geq MedCritical), \phi_{out,C} \equiv (PumpOut = 0)$$

For the overall GIP, a crucial system requirements is, for example, that the concentration of the drug in the bloodstream never exceeds a critical value. We have verified this by using our transformation from Simulink to d$\mathcal{L}$ together with our compositional approach. To this end, we have replaced all services with their respective hybrid contracts during the transformation from Simulink to d$\mathcal{L}$. We were able to verify our abstract GIP model containing the hybrid contracts instead of the concrete services in approximately 25 h using the interactive theorem prover KeYmaera X. In addition, we have also evaluated the combination of various verification techniques by verifying purely discrete services with the Simulink Design Verifier fully automatically and then verifying all other services and the overall system with KeYmaera X.

In [36], we have used our compositional verification approach for Simulink to verify safety properties of the full original hybrid version of the multi-object distance warner. Finally, we have also shown that our compositional verification approach can be used for intelligent embedded systems, if we find the right abstractions for learning components [1]. To enable the verification of Simulink models that are modeled with the Reinforcement Learning (RL) toolbox, we have proposed to capture the behavior of learning components with hybrid contracts and extended our Simulink to d$\mathcal{L}$ transformation with support for RL agents. To ensure that the RL agent adheres to its contract, we use runtime monitoring [12]. Using this approach, we have successfully verified that an autonomous robot that uses reinforcement learning and adheres to its hybrid contract avoids collisions with dynamically moving objects under all circumstances.[1]

6 Open Challenges

Although there can be seen quite some progress on the formal verification of informally defined embedded systems during the last decades, there remain a lot of open challenges. The major challenges that need to be solved to enable the formal verification of industrial embedded control systems are, in our opinion:

1. **Find the right abstractions, and make them reusable.** Both our combined verification approach for SystemC and the service-oriented verification

---

[1] Several of our case studies and our Simulink2dL transformation are freely available at https://www.uni-muenster.de/EmbSys/research/Simulink2dL.

approach for Simulink heavily rely on abstractions. In our SystemC verification approach, the abstractions are computed automatically, in the Simulink approach, the hybrid contracts that provide the abstraction are manually defined. In both cases, the major challenge is that the abstractions need to provide enough information about a submodel or service to verify desired safety properties. At the same time, they need to provide enough abstraction to ease system verification and to provide scalability. These are often conflicting goals, and few reusable patterns exist for the construction of the "right abstraction" for embedded control systems. Classic abstractions that often completely abstract from time or from the scheduling semantics do not work well for embedded systems, which heavily depend on the order of things, their timing, and their synchronization.

2. **Support for real real-time operating systems.** While powerful tools have been developed to verify (concurrent) software (e.g., VerCors [5], Frama-C [30]), they typically abstract from the execution environment completely. However, in embedded systems, timing and synchronization, typically controlled by a real-time operating system (RTOS), plays a crucial role for the correctness of the overall system. In industry, most companies use their own, individually implemented RTOS to provide interrupt handling, scheduling, and event mechanisms. To enable the integration of formal methods into industrial design processes, it would be highly desirable to provide formal models and abstractions that capture these mechanisms and can be adapted and reused for individual RTOS implementations.

3. **Integration of formal methods and testing** The acceptance of formal methods in industry is still comparatively low, while high costs of testing are generally accepted. A tighter integration of formal methods and testing has the potential not only to improve the testing process, but also to increase the acceptance of formal methods in industrial design processes. There exists a broad body of work on leveraging formal methods to automatically evaluate test results. However, it is still an open challenge how to systematically exploit the knowledge and expertise gained from formal verification (e.g., contracts and invariants) for simulation and testing.

7   Conclusion

In this paper, we have summarized our main results and contributions on the formal verification of systems that are designed in informal, industrially used design languages like SystemC or Simulink. We have presented the key ideas of our transformations from SystemC and Simulink into various formal languages, and briefly summarized some selected experimental results. Furthermore, we have presented approaches to overcome the scalability problems that arise if single verification techniques are used for heterogeneous embedded systems, and proposed systematic ways to increase the scalability of existing verification methods. Finally, we have discussed open challenges that, next to the missing formal descriptions and limited scalability, we believe to be key challenges for the formal verification of industrial embedded systems.

References

1. Adelt, J., Liebrenz, T., Herber, P.: Formal verification of intelligent hybrid systems that are modeled with Simulink and the reinforcement learning toolbox. In: Huisman, M., et al. (eds.) FM 2021, LNCS 13047, pp. 349–366. Springer, Heidelberg (2021)
2. Araiza-Illan, D., Eder, K., Richards, A.: Formal verification of control systems' properties with theorem proving. In: UKACC International Conference on Control (CONTROL), pp. 244–249. IEEE (2014)
3. Behrmann, G., David, A., Larsen, K.G.: A tutorial on UPPAAL. In: Bernardo, M., Corradini, F. (eds.) SFM-RT 2004. LNCS, vol. 3185, pp. 200–236. Springer, Heidelberg (2004). https://doi.org/10.1007/978-3-540-30080-9_7
4. Beyer, D., Keremoglu, M.E.: CPACHECKER: a tool for configurable software verification. In: Gopalakrishnan, G., Qadeer, S. (eds.) CAV 2011. LNCS, vol. 6806, pp. 184–190. Springer, Heidelberg (2011). https://doi.org/10.1007/978-3-642-22110-1_16
5. Blom, S., Huisman, M.: The VerCors tool for verification of concurrent programs. In: Jones, C., Pihlajasaari, P., Sun, J. (eds.) FM 2014. LNCS, vol. 8442, pp. 127–131. Springer, Cham (2014). https://doi.org/10.1007/978-3-319-06410-9_9
6. Chen, M., et al.: MARS: a toolchain for modelling, analysis and verification of hybrid systems. In: Hinchey, M.G., Bowen, J.P., Olderog, E.-R. (eds.) Provably Correct Systems. NMSSE, pp. 39–58. Springer, Cham (2017). https://doi.org/10.1007/978-3-319-48628-4_3
7. Chutinan, A., Krogh, B.H.: Computational techniques for hybrid system verification. IEEE Trans. Automa. Control. **48**(1), 64–75 (2003). IEEE
8. Cimatti, A., Micheli, A., Narasamdya, I., Roveri, M.: Verifying SystemC: a software model checking approach. In: Formal Methods in Computer-Aided Design (FMCAD), pp. 51–59. IEEE (2010)
9. Cimatti, A., Griggio, A., Micheli, A., Narasamdya, I., Roveri, M.: KRATOS – a software model checker for SystemC. In: Gopalakrishnan, G., Qadeer, S. (eds.) CAV 2011. LNCS, vol. 6806, pp. 310–316. Springer, Heidelberg (2011). https://doi.org/10.1007/978-3-642-22110-1_24
10. Cimatti, A., Narasamdya, I., Roveri, M.: Software model checking SystemC. IEEE Trans. Comput. Aided Des. Integr. Circ. Syst. **32**(5), 774–787 (2013)
11. Fulton, N., Mitsch, S., Quesel, J.-D., Völp, M., Platzer, A.: KeYmaera X: an axiomatic tactical theorem prover for hybrid systems. In: Felty, A.P., Middeldorp, A. (eds.) CADE 2015. LNCS (LNAI), vol. 9195, pp. 527–538. Springer, Cham (2015). https://doi.org/10.1007/978-3-319-21401-6_36
12. Fulton, N., Platzer, A.: Safe reinforcement learning via formal methods: toward safe control through proof and learning. In: Proceedings of the AAAI Conference on Artificial Intelligence, vol. 32 (2018)
13. Garavel, H., Helmstetter, C., Ponsini, O., Serwe, W.: Verification of an industrial SystemC/TLM model using LOTOS and CADP. In: IEEE/ACM International Conference on Formal Methods and Models for Co-Design (MEMOCODE 2009), pp. 46–55 (2009)
14. Große, D., Kühne, U., Drechsler, R.: HW/SW co-verification of embedded systems using bounded model checking. In: Great Lakes Symposium on VLSI, pp. 43–48. ACM Press (2006)
15. Große, D., Le, H.M., Drechsler, R.: Proving transaction and system-level properties of untimed SystemC TLM designs. In: MEMOCODE, pp. 113–122. IEEE (2010)

16. Große, D., Le, H.M., Drechsler, R.: Formal verification of SystemC-based cyber components. In: Jeschke, S., Brecher, C., Song, H., Rawat, D.B. (eds.) Industrial Internet of Things. SSWT, pp. 137–167. Springer, Cham (2017). https://doi.org/10.1007/978-3-319-42559-7_6
17. Habibi, A., Moinudeen, H., Tahar, S.: Generating finite state machines from SystemC. In: Design, Automation and Test in Europe, pp. 76–81. IEEE (2006)
18. Habibi, A., Tahar, S.: An approach for the verification of SystemC designs using AsmL. In: Peled, D.A., Tsay, Y.-K. (eds.) ATVA 2005. LNCS, vol. 3707, pp. 69–83. Springer, Heidelberg (2005). https://doi.org/10.1007/11562948_8
19. Herber, P.: The RESCUE approach - towards compositional hardware/software co-verification. In: International Conference on Embedded Software and Systems (ICESS 2014). pp. 721–724. IEEE (2014)
20. Herber, P., Fellmuth, J., Glesner, S.: Model checking SystemC designs using timed automata. In: International Conference on Hardware/Software Codesign and System Synthesis (CODES+ISSS), pp. 131–136. ACM press (2008)
21. Herber, P., Glesner, S.: A HW/SW co-verification framework for SystemC. ACM Trans. Embedd. Comput. Syst. (TECS) 12(1s), 1–23 (2013)
22. Herber, P., Hünnemeyer, B.: Formal verification of SystemC designs using the BLAST software model checker. In: ACESMB@ MoDELS, pp. 44–53 (2014)
23. Herber, P., Liebrenz, T.: Dependence analysis and automated partitioning for scalable formal analysis of SystemC designs. In: 18th ACM-IEEE International Conference on Formal Methods and Models for System Design (MEMOCODE), pp. 1–6. IEEE (2020)
24. Herber, P., Pockrandt, M., Glesner, S.: STATE - a SystemC to timed automata transformation engine. In: ICESS. IEEE (2015)
25. Herber, P., Reicherdt, R., Bittner, P.: Bit-precise formal verification of discrete-time MATLAB/Simulink models using SMT solving. In: International Conference on Embedded Software (EMSOFT), pp. 1–10. IEEE (2013)
26. Herdt, V., Le, H.M., Grosse, D., Drechsler, R.: Verifying SystemC using intermediate verification language and stateful symbolic simulation. IEEE Trans. Comput. Aided Des. Integr. Circ. Syst. 38(7), 1359–1372 (2018)
27. IEEE Standards Association: IEEE Std. 1666–2011, Open SystemC Language Reference Manual. IEEE Press (2011)
28. Jaß, L., Herber, P.: Bit-precise formal verification for SystemC using satisfiability modulo theories solving. In: Götz, M., Schirner, G., Wehrmeister, M.A., Al Faruque, M.A., Rettberg, A. (eds.) IESS 2015. IAICT, vol. 523, pp. 51–63. Springer, Cham (2017). https://doi.org/10.1007/978-3-319-90023-0_5
29. Karlsson, D., Eles, P., Peng, Z.: Formal verification of SystemC designs using a Petri-Net based representation. In: Design, Automation and Test in Europe (DATE), pp. 1228–1233. IEEE Press (2006)
30. Kirchner, F., Kosmatov, N., Prevosto, V., Signoles, J., Yakobowski, B.: Frama-C: a software analysis perspective. Formal Aspects of Comput. 27(3), 573–609 (2015). https://doi.org/10.1007/s00165-014-0326-7
31. Kroening, D., Sharygina, N.: Formal verification of SystemC by automatic hardware/software partitioning. In: Proceedings of MEMOCODE 2005, pp. 101–110. IEEE (2005)
32. Lahiri, S.K., Seshia, S.A.: The UCLID decision procedure. In: Alur, R., Peled, D.A. (eds.) CAV 2004. LNCS, vol. 3114, pp. 475–478. Springer, Heidelberg (2004). https://doi.org/10.1007/978-3-540-27813-9_40

33. Le, H.M., Grosse, D., Herdt, V., Drechsler, R.: Verifying SystemC using an intermediate verification language and symbolic simulation. In: Design Automation Conference (DAC), 2013 50th ACM/EDAC/IEEE, pp. 1–6. IEEE (2013)
34. Li, J., Sun, X., Xie, F., Song, X.: Component-based abstraction and refinement. In: Mei, H. (ed.) ICSR 2008. LNCS, vol. 5030, pp. 39–51. Springer, Heidelberg (2008). https://doi.org/10.1007/978-3-540-68073-4_4
35. Liebrenz, T., Herber, P., Glesner, S.: Deductive verification of hybrid control systems modeled in Simulink with KeYmaera X. In: Sun, J., Sun, M. (eds.) ICFEM 2018. LNCS, vol. 11232, pp. 89–105. Springer, Cham (2018). https://doi.org/10.1007/978-3-030-02450-5_6
36. Liebrenz, T., Herber, P., Glesner, S.: A service-oriented approach for decomposing and verifying hybrid system models. In: Arbab, F., Jongmans, S.-S. (eds.) FACS 2019. LNCS, vol. 12018, pp. 127–146. Springer, Cham (2020). https://doi.org/10.1007/978-3-030-40914-2_7
37. Liebrenz, T., Herber, P., Glesner, S.: Towards automated service-oriented verification of embedded control software modeled in Simulink. In: Margaria, T., Steffen, B. (eds.) ISoLA 2020, Part III. LNCS, vol. 12478, pp. 307–325. Springer, Cham (2020). https://doi.org/10.1007/978-3-030-61467-6_20
38. Liebrenz, T., Herber, P., Glesner, S.: Service-oriented decomposition and verification of hybrid system models using feature models and contracts. Sci. Comput. Program. **211**, 102694 (2021)
39. Liebrenz, T., Herber, P., Göthel, T., Glesner, S.: Towards service-oriented design of hybrid systems modeled in simulink. In: 2017 IEEE 41st Annual Computer Software and Applications Conference (COMPSAC), vol. 2, pp. 469–474. IEEE (2017)
40. Liebrenz, T., Klös, V., Herber, P.: Automatic analysis and abstraction for model checking HW/SW co-designs modeled in SystemC. In: ACM SIGAda Annual Conference on High Integrity Language Technology (HILT 2016). ACM (2016)
41. Man, K.L., Fedeli, A., Mercaldi, M., Boubekeur, M., Schellekens, M.: SC2SCFL: automated SystemC to $SystemC^{FL}$ translation. In: Vassiliadis, S., Bereković, M., Hämäläinen, T.D. (eds.) SAMOS 2007. LNCS, vol. 4599, pp. 34–45. Springer, Heidelberg (2007). https://doi.org/10.1007/978-3-540-73625-7_6
42. MathWorks: MATLAB Simulink. https://www.mathworks.com/products/simulink.html
43. MathWorks: White Paper: Code Verification and Run-Time Error Detection Through Abstract Interpretation. Technical report (2008)
44. Minopoli, S., Frehse, G.: SL2SX translator: from Simulink to SpaceEx models. In: 19th International Conference on Hybrid Systems: Computation and Control, pp. 93–98. ACM (2016)
45. Niemann, B., Haubelt, C., Oyanguren, M.U.: Formalizing TLM with communicating state machines. In: Huss, S.A. (ed.) Advances in Design and Specification Languages for Embedded Systems. Springer, Dordrecht (2007). https://doi.org/10.1007/978-1-4020-6149-3_14
46. Platzer, A.: Differential dynamic logic for hybrid systems. J. Autom. Reason. **41**(2), 143–189 (2008). https://doi.org/10.1007/s10817-008-9103-8
47. Reicherdt, R., Glesner, S.: Formal verification of discrete-time MATLAB/Simulink models using boogie. In: Giannakopoulou, D., Salaün, G. (eds.) SEFM 2014. LNCS, vol. 8702, pp. 190–204. Springer, Cham (2014). https://doi.org/10.1007/978-3-319-10431-7_14

48. Ruf, J., Hoffmann, D.W., Gerlach, J., Kropf, T., Rosenstiel, W., Müller, W.: The simulation semantics of SystemC. In: Design, Automation and Test in Europe, pp. 64–70. IEEE Press (2001)
49. Salem, A.: Formal semantics of synchronous SystemC. In: Design, Automation and Test in Europe (DATE). pp. 10376–10381. IEEE Computer Society (2003)
50. Traulsen, C., Cornet, J., Moy, M., Maraninchi, F.: A SystemC/TLM semantics in PROMELA and its possible applications. In: Bošnački, D., Edelkamp, S. (eds.) SPIN 2007. LNCS, vol. 4595, pp. 204–222. Springer, Heidelberg (2007). https://doi.org/10.1007/978-3-540-73370-6_14
51. Xie, F., Yang, G., Song, X.: Component-based hardware/software co-verification for building trustworthy embedded systems. J. Syst. Softw. 80(5), 643–654 (2007)
52. Yan, G., Jiao, L., Wang, S., Wang, L., Zhan, N.: Automatically generating SystemC code from HCSP formal models. ACM Trans. Softw. Eng. Methodol. (TOSEM) 29(1), 1–39 (2020)
53. Zhang, Y., Vedrine, F., Monsuez, B.: SystemC waiting-state automata. In: International Workshop on Verification and Evaluation of Computer and Communication Systems (2007)
54. Zou, L., Zhan, N., Wang, S., Fränzle, M.: Formal verification of Simulink/Stateflow diagrams. In: Finkbeiner, B., Pu, G., Zhang, L. (eds.) ATVA 2015. LNCS, vol. 9364, pp. 464–481. Springer, Cham (2015). https://doi.org/10.1007/978-3-319-24953-7_33

Model Checking for Verification
of Quantum Circuits

Mingsheng Ying[1,2,3]([⊠])

[1] Centre for Quantum Software and Information, University of Technology Sydney,
Ultimo, Australia
Mingsheng.Ying@uts.edu.au
[2] State Key Laboratory of Computer Science, Institute of Software,
Chinese Academy of Sciences, Beijing, China
[3] Department of Computer Science and Technology, Tsinghua University,
Beijing, China

Abstract. In this survey paper, we describe a framework for *assertion-based verification* of quantum circuits by applying *model checking* techniques for quantum systems developed in our previous work, in which:

- Noiseless and noisy quantum circuits are *modelled* as operator- and super-operator-valued transition systems, respectively, both of which can be further represented by tensor networks.
- Quantum *assertions* are specified by a temporal extension of Birkhoff-von Neumann quantum logic. Their semantics is defined based on the following design decision: they will be used in verification of quantum circuits by simulation on classical computers or human reasoning rather than by quantum physics experiments (e.g. testing through measurements);
- *Algorithms* for reachability analysis and model checking of quantum circuits are developed based on contraction of tensor networks. We observe that many optimisation techniques for computing relational products used in BDD-based model checking algorithms can be generalised for contracting tensor networks of quantum circuits.

Keywords: Quantum logic circuits · Verification · Assertion · Temporal logic · Model checking · Reachability · Tensor network

1 Introduction

Assertion-based verification (ABV) is a key methodology for functional verification of classical logic circuits and has been widely adopted in hardware industry. A major characteristic of ABV is that assertions are used for specifying design intent at a high level of abstraction and thus are ideal for using across multiple verification processes [10]. An example application procedure of ABV was described in [4] as follows:

© Springer Nature Switzerland AG 2021
M. Huisman et al. (Eds.): FM 2021, LNCS 13047, pp. 23–39, 2021.
https://doi.org/10.1007/978-3-030-90870-6_2

1. A specification language such as PSL (Property Specification Language, IEEE 1850 standard) or SVA (SystemVerilog Assertions) is used to write the *assertions* specifying the desired hardware properties.
2. Verification is performed by formal methods or in a dynamic manner where a *simulator* monitors the device under verification (DUV) and reports when and where assertions are violated.
3. The information on assertion violation can be used in the *debugging* process.

Verification of quantum circuits is emerging as an important issue duo to the rapid growth in the size of quantum computing hardware. A majority of the current research has been devoted to *equivalence checking* of *combinational* quantum circuits using various quantum generalisations of BDDs (Binary Decision Diagrams), such as QuIDD [24,25], and QMDD [6,22]. Recently, *sequential* circuit models are emerging to play an important role in quantum computing and information processing; examples include quantum memories [18], quantum feedback networks [12], and RUS (Repeat-Until-Success) quantum circuits [3]. A hardware description language was defined in [23] for specification of sequential quantum photonic circuits. An algorithm for equivalence checking of sequential quantum circuits is presented in [28]. One can expect that as more and more sophisticated quantum hardware be physically realisable, more and more complicated verification problems will appear for quantum circuits, and assertion-based verification (ABV) will become an indispensable technology in future design automation for quantum computing (QDA).

Model Checking Quantum Systems: Essentially, assertion-based verification (ABV) of logic circuits can be seen as an important application of temporal logic and model checking. Research on extending model checking for quantum system has been conducted in the last fifteen years. Early work aimed at verification of quantum communication protocols [1,8,11]. Targeting applications in analysis and verification of quantum programs [29], several model checking techniques for quantum automata, quantum Markov chains and super-operator valued Markov chains have been developed in [9,20,33,36] (see [31] for a more systematic exposition). However, a big gap between these quantum model checking techniques and their practical applications in verification of quantum circuits is still to be filled in. For near term applications, we believe that the following two challenges are crucial:

– *Challenge I* - *Finding compact representations of quantum circuits*: As a compact representation, BDDs have played a key role in successful applications of model checking in verification of classical circuits [5]. As pointed out before, several quantum generalisations of BDDs have been employed in equivalence checking of quantum circuits. On the other hand, tensor networks - a mathematical tool successfully applied in simulation of quantum physical system for decades - have been widely used in simulation of large quantum circuits on classical computers in the last few years [15,17,19,21,27]. These representations should be helpful in implementing a more efficient model checker for quantum circuits.

– **Challenge II** - *Identifying useful properties that can be checked by the current technology*: The previous research pursued theoretical generality and thus targeted checking general reachability and temporal logic properties of quantum systems. But a model checker (implemented on a classical computer) for such a purpose must be highly inefficient and only applicable to quantum circuits of very small sizes and depths. Thus, for realistic and in particular, near-term applications, we need to identify a class of simpler properties that can be efficiently checked by a current model checker for quantum systems.

In this survey paper, we describe a framework for *assertion-based verification* (ABV) of quantum circuits by applying *model checking* techniques for quantum systems developed in our previous work, in which quantum circuits are represented by tensor networks, and assertions about quantum circuits are specified using a simple temporal extension of Birkhoff-von Neumann quantum logic. The paper is organised as follows. Basic models of quantum circuits are reviewed in Sect. 2. To address Challenge I, we introduce tensor network representation of quantum circuits in Sect. 3. The reason for using tensor networks is that algorithms for reachability analysis and model checking of quantum circuits can be conveniently implemented by contraction of tensor networks. More importantly, we observe that many optimisation techniques for computing relational products used in BDD-based model checking algorithms can be generalised for contracting tensor networks of quantum circuits. Challenge II is gradually addressed in Sects. 4 to 6. In Sect. 4, we first show how a basic property, namely reachability, of quantum circuits can be checked. To specify more general properties, a simple temporal logic is defined in Sect. 5 as our assertion language. This language is chosen because it is actually useful for practical applications and at the same time, checking assertions written in it is much easier than for other assertion languages, as shown in Sect. 6. Furthermore, its semantics will be defined based on the following design decision: the target application is verification of quantum circuits by simulation on classical computers (or human reasoning) rather than by quantum physics experiments (e.g. testing through measurements). We hope that focusing on this more realistic target, a model checker can be built for practical use in verification and debugging of near term quantum hardware.

2 Quantum Logic Circuits

For convenience of the audience, let us start from a brief review of the basics of quantum computing, with the emphasis on several basic models of quantum circuits.

2.1 Combinational Quantum Circuits

Traditional combinational circuits are made from logic gates acting on wires. Combinational quantum circuits are quantum counterparts of them and made up of quantum (logic) gates, which are modelled by unitary operators.

Qubits (Quantum Bits): The quantum counterpart of a bit is a qubit. A state of a single qubit is represented by a 2-dimensional unit column vector $(\alpha, \beta)^T$, where T stands for transpose, and complex numbers α, β satisfy the normalisation condition $\|\alpha\|^2 + \|\beta\|^2 = 1$. It can be conveniently written in the Dirac's notation as $|\psi\rangle = \alpha|0\rangle + \beta|1\rangle$ with $|0\rangle = (1,0)^T$, $|1\rangle = (0,1)^T$ corresponding to classical bits 0 and 1, respectively. Intuitively, this qubit is in a superposition of 0 and 1. In general, we use $q, q_1, q_2, \ldots$ to denote qubit variables. Graphically, they can be thought of as wires in a quantum circuit. A state of n qubits $q_1, \ldots, q_n$ is then written as a 2^n-dimensional unit complex vector $(\alpha_0, \alpha_1, \ldots, \alpha_{2^n-1})^T$ or in the Dirac's notation:

$$|\psi\rangle = \sum_{x \in \{0,1\}^n} \alpha_x |x\rangle = \sum_{x_1, \ldots, x_n} \alpha_{x_1, \ldots, x_n} |x_1, \ldots, x_n\rangle \tag{1}$$

where its norm $\||\psi\rangle\| = \sqrt{\sum_x |\alpha_x|^2} = 1$, and we exchangeably use an n-bit string $x = x_1 \ldots x_n \in \{0,1\}^n$ and integer $x = \sum_{i=1}^n x_i \cdot 2^{i-1}$.

Quantum Gates: A gate on a single qubit is modelled by a 2×2 complex matrix U. In general, a gate on n qubits is described by a $2^n \times 2^n$ unitary matrix

$$U = (U_{x,y})_{x,y \in \{0,1\}^n} . \tag{2}$$

The output of U on an input $|\psi\rangle$ is quantum state $|\psi'\rangle$. Its mathematical representation as a vector is obtained by standard matrix multiplication $|\psi'\rangle = U|\psi\rangle$. To guarantee that $|\psi'\rangle$ is always unit, U must be unitary in the sense that $U^\dagger U = I$, where $U^\dagger$ is the adjoint of U obtained by transposing and then complex conjugating U. We often write $G \equiv U[q_1, \ldots, q_n]$ for gate U acting on qubits $q_1, \ldots, q_n$.

Example 1. *1. The following are several frequently used single-qubit gates:*

(a) Hadamard gate: $H = \frac{1}{\sqrt{2}} \begin{pmatrix} 1 & 1 \\ 1 & -1 \end{pmatrix}$;

(b) The Pauli matrices: $X = \begin{pmatrix} 0 & 1 \\ 1 & 0 \end{pmatrix}$, $Y = \begin{pmatrix} 0 & -i \\ i & 0 \end{pmatrix}$, $Z = \begin{pmatrix} 1 & 0 \\ 0 & -1 \end{pmatrix}$.

2. Let q_1, q_2 be qubits. Then CNOT (controlled-X) gate $C[q_1, q_2]$ is a two-qubit gate with q_1 as the control qubit and q_2 as the target qubit and defined by the 4×4 matrix $C = \begin{pmatrix} I & 0 \\ 0 & I \end{pmatrix}$, where I is the 2×2 identity matrix.

Combinational Quantum Circuits: A combinational quantum circuit is a sequence of quantum gates: $C \equiv G_1 \ldots G_m$, where $m \geq 1$ and $G_1, \ldots, G_m$ are quantum gates.

Example 2. *The quantum circuit $Z[q_1]H[q_2]C[q_1, q_2]Y[q_1]H[q_2]$ consisting of five quantum gates is visualised in Fig. 1.*

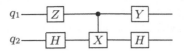

Fig. 1. A combinational quantum circuit.

2.2   Noisy Quantum Circuits

Fault-tolerant quantum computing is still out of the current technology's reach. To model noisy implementation of quantum circuits, we recall that a mixed state of an n-qubit system is an *ensemble* $\{(|\psi_i\rangle, p_i)\}$ of its pure states, meaning that this system is in state $|\psi_i\rangle$ with probability p_i. Mathematically, this mixed state can be described by a $2^n \times 2^n$ matrix, called a density matrix, $\rho = \sum_i p_i |\psi_i\rangle\langle\psi_i|$, where $\langle\psi_i|$ is the conjugate transpose of $|\psi_i\rangle$ and thus a 2^n-dimensional row vector. In particular, a pure state $|\psi\rangle$ can be identified with the outer product $|\psi\rangle\langle\psi|$. Then a noisy n-qubit gate can be modelled by a super-operator, often called a quantum channel in quantum information literature, which is a linear map $\mathcal{E} : \rho \to \mathcal{E}(\rho)$ from $2^n \times 2^n$ density matrices to themselves. A convenient way of representing $\mathcal{E}$ is the *Kraus operator-sum form*:

$$\mathcal{E}(\rho) = \sum_i E_i \rho E_i^\dagger \tag{3}$$

for any density matrix ρ, where $\{E_i\}$ is a set of $2^n \times 2^n$ matrices satisfying the normalisation condition $\sum_i E_i^\dagger E_i = I_{2^n}$. In particular, an idea n-qubit gate modelled by a unitary operator U can be seen as a super-operator $\mathcal{U} : \rho \mapsto U\rho U^\dagger$.

Example 3. *Several canonical noises on a single qubit are:*

1. *Bit flip: This noise flips the state of a qubit from $|0\rangle$ to $|1\rangle$ and vice versa with probability $1-p$, and is modelled by super-operator $\mathcal{N}_{bf}(\rho) = p\rho + (1-p)X\rho X$.*
2. *Phase flip: This noise changes the phase of a qubit (that is, applies phase operator Z on the qubit) with probability $1 - p$, and is modelled by the super-operator $\mathcal{N}_{pf}(\rho) = p\rho + (1 - p)Z\rho Z$.*
3. *Bit-phase flip: This noise applies Pauli operator Y on a qubit with probability $1 - p$: $\mathcal{N}_{bpf}(\rho) = p\rho + (1 - p)Y\rho Y$. Note that it is essentially a combination of a bit-flip and a phase flip because $Y = iXZ$.*

2.3   Dynamic Quantum Circuits

Quantum Measurement: The output of a combinational quantum circuit is a quantum state, which cannot be observed directly from the outside. To read out the outcome of computation, we have to perform a measurement at the end of the circuit. Mathematically, a quantum measurement on n qubits is described by a family $M = \{M_m\}$ of $2^n \times 2^n$ matrices such that $\sum_m M_m^\dagger M_m = I_{2^n}$, where m

denotes different possible outcomes. If one performs M on the qubits in state $|\psi\rangle$, then outcome m is obtained with probability $p_m = \|M_m|\psi\rangle\|^2$ and subsequently the state of these qubits will be changed to $\frac{M_m|\psi\rangle}{\sqrt{p_m}}$. More generally, if the n-qubit system is in a mixed state ρ, then outcome m is obtained with probability $p_m = \text{tr}(M_m^\dagger M_m \rho)$ and its state will be changed to $\frac{M_m \rho M_m^\dagger}{p_m}$. For example, the measurement in the computational basis is defined as $M = \{M_x : x \in \{0,1\}^n\}$ with $M_x = |x\rangle\langle x|$, and if it is performed on the qubits in a pure state (1), then outcome $x \in \{0,1\}^n$ is obtained with probability $|\alpha_x|^2$ and subsequently the qubits will be in basis state $|x\rangle$.

Dynamic Quantum Circuits: Quantum measurements are not only used for readout of the computational outcome at the end of a quantum circuit as described above. They may also occur at the middle of a quantum circuit where the measurement outcomes are used to conditionally control subsequent steps of the computation. This kind of circuits are called dynamic quantum circuits [7] and have been realised in several hardware platforms for quantum computing. Formally, they are inductively defined as follows (see [29], p. 38):

- (Noiseless or noisy) quantum gates are dynamic quantum circuits;
- If C_1, C_2 are dynamic quantum circuits, so is $C_1; C_2$; and
- If $M = \{M_m\}$ a measurement on qubits $q_1, ..., q_n$, and for each possible outcome m, C_m a dynamic quantum circuit , then **if** $(\llbracket m \cdot M[q_1, ..., q_n] = m \rightarrow C_m)$ **fi** is a dynamic quantum circuit. Intuitively, this conditional circuit performs measurement M on qubits $q_1, ..., q_n$, and then the subsequent computation is selected based on the measurement outcome: if the outcome is m, then the corresponding circuit C_m follows.

Quantum teleportation is a simple example of dynamic quantum circuits. Another example is the dynamic circuit for quantum phase estimation shown as Fig. 1 in [7].

Example 4. *Quantum teleportation is a protocol for transmitting quantum information (e.g. the exact state of an atom or photon) via only classical communication but with the help of previously shared quantum entanglement between the sender and receiver. It is one of the most surprising examples where entanglement helps to accomplish a certain task that is impossible in the classical world. The quantum circuit teleporting a single qubit is shown in Fig. 2.*

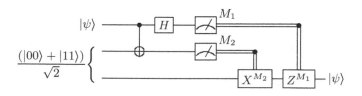

Fig. 2. Quantum teleportation circuit

2.4   Sequential Quantum Circuits

As is well-known, almost all practical digital devices contain (classical) sequential circuits. The output value of a combinational circuit is a function of only the current input value. In contrast, the output value of a sequential circuit depends on not only the external input value but also on the stored internal information. All quantum circuits considered in the previous subsections are combinational. However, several recent applications introduce a *sequential* model of quantum circuits, including quantum memories [18], quantum feedback networks [12], and RUS (Repeat-Until-Success) quantum circuits [3]. A synchronous model of sequential quantum circuit was defined in [28] and can be visualised as Fig. 3, which looks similar to its classical counterpart, except:

- The combinational part of a classical sequential circuit is modelled by a Boolean function; whereas the combinational part of a sequential quantum circuit is a unitary operator or a super-operator, depending on whether noise occurs in it.
- Certain measurements are needed at the end of qubits $q_1, ..., q_k$ to readout classical information from their outputs.

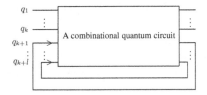

Fig. 3. A sequential quantum circuit

2.5   Quantum Transition Systems as a Model of Quantum Circuits

A classical circuit can be conveniently described by a transition relation [5]. Similarly, quantum circuits discussed above can be modelled by a quantum transition system defined as follows.

Definition 1 (Quantum Transition Systems). *A quantum transition system (QTS) for a circuit with n qubits consists of:*

1. a finite set L of locations, and an initial location $l_0 \in L$;
2. a set T of transitions:
   - *each transition $\tau \in T$ is a triple $\tau = \langle l, l', \mathcal{E} \rangle$, often written as $\tau = l \xrightarrow{\mathcal{E}} l'$ where $l, l' \in L$ are the pre- and post-locations of τ, respectively, and $\mathcal{E}$ is a super-operator on $2^n \times 2^n$ density matrices,*
   satisfying the normalisation condition: $\sum \{|\mathrm{tr}[\mathcal{E}(\rho)] : l \xrightarrow{\mathcal{E}} l' \in T|\} = 1$ for each $l \in L$ and $2^n \times 2^n$ density matrix ρ, where $\{|\cdot|\}$ stands for a multi-set, and trace $\mathrm{tr}(A)$ of a matrix A is the sum of the entries on the diagonal of A.

In particular, for a noiseless quantum circuit, every transition $l \xrightarrow{\mathcal{E}} l'$ is simply defined by a $2^n \times 2^n$ matrix E such that $\mathcal{E}(\rho) = E\rho E^\dagger$ for all density matrices ρ; for example, each quantum gate is defined as a unitary matrix U, and in a quantum measurement $M = \{M_m\}$, each branch corresponding to an outcome m can be described by the measurement operator M_m.

Example 5. *The circuit of quantum teleportation in Fig. 2 can be modelled by the QTS in Fig. 4, where quantum operations are visualised by edges; for example, $CX_{1,2}$ on edge $l_0 \to l_1$ denotes a CNOT on qubits 1 and 2, and $M_{2,1}$ on edge $l_2 \to l_4$ means that a measurement is performed on qubit 2 and outcome 1 is obtained.*

Remark 1. QTS's were first introduced in [9,14] where they are called quantum Markov chains. They were also used in defining invariants of quantum programs [34].

3   Tensor Network Representation of Quantum Circuits

In the last section, quantum circuits were defined in the traditional vector and matrix language of quantum mechanics. The shift from representing quantum circuits by matrices to tensor networks was proposed in [21] by identifying the following benefits in simulation of quantum circuits on classical computers: (i) quantum circuits can be arbitrarily partitioned into subcircuits; (ii) subcircuits can be simulated in arbitrary orders; and (iii) simulation results of subcircuits can be combined in arbitrary orders. From these benefits, the reader might already notice that the advantage of tensor network representation of quantum circuits over matrices is very much similar to that of BDD representation of classical circuits over truth tables (i.e. Boolean matrices). In this section, we briefly review the basic idea of tensor networks and show how they can be used to represent quantum circuits.

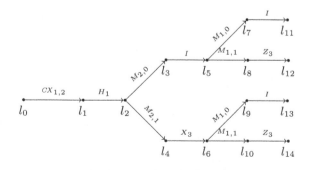

Fig. 4. A QST for quantum teleportation

3.1 Tensor Networks

A tensor is a multi-dimensional array of complex numbers. We only consider a special class of tensors suitable for representing quantum circuits. A tensor with an index set $\vec{q} = \{q_1, ..., q_n\}$ is a mapping $T : \{0,1\}^{\vec{q}} \to \mathbb{C}$. We often write $T = T_{\vec{q}}$ or $T_{q_1,...,q_n}$ to indicate the indices. For two tensors $T_{\vec{p},\vec{r}}$ and $T_{\vec{q},\vec{r}}$ sharing indices $\vec{r}$, their *contraction* is defined as a tensor $T_{\vec{p},\vec{q}} \stackrel{\triangle}{=} Contract(T_{\vec{p},\vec{r}}, T_{\vec{q},\vec{r}})$ by

$$T_{\vec{p},\vec{q}}(\vec{a}, \vec{b}) = \sum_{\vec{c} \in \{0,1\}^{\vec{r}}} T_{\vec{p},\vec{r}}(\vec{a}, \vec{c}) \cdot T_{\vec{q},\vec{r}}(\vec{b}, \vec{c}) \tag{4}$$

for any $\vec{a} \in \{0,1\}^{\vec{p}}$ and $\vec{b} \in \{0,1\}^{\vec{q}}$. Then a tensor network is a hyper-graph $H = (V, E)$, where a subset $E_0 \subseteq E$ is chosen as open edges, and each vertex $v \in V$ is associated with a tensor of which the hyper-edges incident to v are the indices. Thus, the hyper-edges between two vertices represent the indices shared by the two adjacent tensors. By contracting connected tensors in H, we can obtain a tensor T_H with E_0 as its index set. It is easy to see that T_H is independent of the order of contractions.

3.2 Representing Quantum States and Quantum Gates

The tensor representation of quantum states is straightforward. A pure state $|\psi\rangle$ of n qubits $q_1, ..., q_n$ given in Eq. (1) can be represented by a tensor $T_{|\psi\rangle} \stackrel{\triangle}{=} T_{q_1,...,q_n}$ with $T_{q_1,...,q_n}(x_1, ..., x_n) = \alpha_{x_1,...,x_n}$ for any $x_1, ..., x_n \in \{0,1\}$. Furthermore, a mixed state of n qubits $q_1, ..., q_n$ given as a $2^n \times 2^n$ density matrix $\rho = (\rho_{x,y})_{x,y \in \{0,1\}^n}$ can be represented by a tensor $T_\rho \stackrel{\triangle}{=} T_{q_1,...,q_n,q_1',...,q_n'}$, where for any $x, y \in \{0,1\}^n$:

$$T_{q_1,...,q_n,q_1',...,q_n'}(x, y) = \rho_{x,y}. \tag{5}$$

Similar to the tensor representation (5) of a density matrix, a (noise-less) quantum gate U on n qubits $q_1, ..., q_n$ given as unitary matrix (2) can be straightforwardly represented by a tensor $T_U \stackrel{\triangle}{=} T_{q_1,...,q_n,q_1',...,q_n'}$ with $T_{q_1,...,q_n,q_1',...,q_n'}(x, y) = U_{x,y}$ for any $x, y \in \{0,1\}^n$. To present a tensor representation of a noisy quantum gate $\mathcal{E}$ on n qubits $q_1, ..., q_n$, we assume that it is given in the Kraus representation (3), and define its matrix representation as

$$M_{\mathcal{E}} = \sum_i E_i \otimes E_i^* \stackrel{\triangle}{=} (M_{x,y,x',y'})_{x,y,x',y' \in \{0,1\}^n} \tag{6}$$

where E^* stands for the conjugate of E; that is, if $E = (E_{x,y})$, then $E^* = (E_{x,y}^*)$, and $E_{x,y}^*$ is the conjugate of complex number $E_{x,y}$ for any $x, y \in \{0,1\}^n$. Furthermore, if for each qubit q_i, we introduce a new copy p_i, then $M_{\mathcal{E}}$ can be represented by a tensor $T_{\mathcal{E}} \stackrel{\triangle}{=} T_{q_1,...,q_n,p_1,...,p_n,q_1',...,q_n',p_1',...,p_n'}$, where for any $x, y, x', y' \in \{0,1\}^n$:

$$T_{q_1,...,q_n,p_1,...,p_n,q_1',...,q_n',p_1',...,p_n'}(x, y, x', y') = M_{x,y,x',y'}. \tag{7}$$

3.3   Representing Quantum Circuits

Now we can present a tensor network representation of quantum circuits by assembling the ingredients given in the previous subsections. Suppose we are given a combinational or sequential quantum circuit C modelled as a quantum transition system. If we replace each (noiseless or noisy) gate in C by its tensor representation, then we obtain a tensor network representation of C. Furthermore, one can compute its tensor T_C by contraction (4). Moreover, if $|\psi\rangle$ or ρ is an input to C, then the tensor representation of output $C|\psi\rangle$ or $C(\rho)$ can be computed as contraction $Contract(T_{|\psi\rangle}, T_C)$ or $Contract(T_\rho, T_C)$, respectively. When computing the tensor of a noisy quantum circuit, it is often more efficient to use contraction in combination with the following lemma, which gives a way for computing the matrix representations of the sequential and parallel compositions of noisy quantum gates: the matrix representation of the sequential (respectively, parallel) composition of two noisy quantum gates is the multiplication (respectively, tensor product) of their matrix representation.

Lemma 1. *For any super-operators $\mathcal{E}$ and $\mathcal{F}$, we have $M_{\mathcal{E} \circ \mathcal{F}} = M_{\mathcal{F}} M_{\mathcal{E}}$ and $M_{\mathcal{E} \otimes \mathcal{F}} = M_{\mathcal{F}} \otimes M_{\mathcal{E}}$.*

3.4   Optimisations for Tensor Network Contraction

It is obvious that computation required in the contraction of tensor networks of quantum circuits tends to be exponential in the growth of the number of qubits and the depth of circuits. In the last few years, many optimisation techniques have been proposed in the tensor network-based algorithms for simulation of quantum circuits on classical computers [15,17,19,21,27]. The main reason for employing tensor networks rather than large matrices in simulation of quantum circuits is that tensor networks can exploit the regularity and locality in the structure of quantum circuits. Essentially, the basic idea is similar to that of optimisation strategies in BDD-based algorithms (although this similarity has not been explicitly pointed out in the literature). We believe that more BDD-optimisations can be adapted to computing tensor networks of quantum circuits, in particular when combined with their QST representations defined in Subsect. 2.5; for example, Lemma 1 enables us to generalise the partitioning technique in verification of classical circuits (see [5], Sect. V) to the case of noisy quantum circuits. For this purpose, we introduced a decision-diagram style data structure, called TDD (Tensor Decision Diagram), and showed that various operations of tensor networks essential in their applications can be conveniently implemented in TDDs [16].

4   Reachability Analysis of Quantum Circuits

We now start to consider the verification problem of quantum circuits. Many model checking problems about classical circuits (and other systems) can be reduced to a reachability problem. Reachability plays a similar role in model checking quantum systems [31]. In this section, as a basis of verification techniques for quantum circuits, let us focus on reachability of a simplest version of quantum transition systems, namely a *quantum Markov chain* [35], which is defined as a pair $\mathcal{C} = \langle \mathcal{H}, \mathcal{E} \rangle$, where $\mathcal{H}$ is a finite-dimensional Hilbert space as the system's state space, and $\mathcal{E}$ is a quantum operation (or super-operator) in $\mathcal{H}$ depicting transition of the system's state. Roughly speaking, if the initial state is ρ, then the quantum Markov chain behaves as follows: $\rho \to \mathcal{E}(\rho) \to \cdots \to \mathcal{E}^n(\rho) \to \mathcal{E}^{n+1}(\rho) \to \cdots$.

4.1   Adjacency and Reachability

As in the classical case, a graph structure is helpful for reachability analysis in quantum Markov chain $\mathcal{C}$. Let us first recall several notations needed to define such a graph structure. For any $X \subseteq \mathcal{H}$, let $\mathrm{span}(X)$ stand for the subspace spanned by X, i.e. the smallest subspace of $\mathcal{H}$ containing Y. The support $\mathrm{supp}(A)$ of an operator A on $\mathcal{H}$ is the subspace spanned by the eigenvectors of A associated with non-zero eigenvalues. For a family $\{X_i\}$ of subspaces of $\mathcal{H}_i$, we define their join as

$$\bigvee_i X_i = \mathrm{span}\left(\bigcup_i X_i\right). \tag{8}$$

In particular, we write $X_1 \vee X_2$ for the join of two subspaces X_1 and X_2. The image of a subspace X of $\mathcal{H}$ under $\mathcal{E}$ is defined as $\mathcal{E}(X) = \bigvee_{|\psi\rangle \in X} \mathrm{supp}(\mathcal{E}(|\psi\rangle\langle\psi|))$, where $|\psi\rangle\langle\psi|$ is the density operator corresponding to pure state $|\psi\rangle$.

Definition 2 (Adjacency Relation). *Let $|\varphi\rangle, |\psi\rangle \in \mathcal{H}$ be pure states and ρ, σ be mixed states (i.e. density matrices) in $\mathcal{H}$. Then*

1. *$|\varphi\rangle$ is adjacent to $|\psi\rangle$ in $\mathcal{C}$, written $|\psi\rangle \to |\varphi\rangle$, if $|\varphi\rangle \in \mathrm{supp}(\mathcal{E}(|\psi\rangle\langle\psi|))$.*
2. *$|\varphi\rangle$ is adjacent to ρ, written $\rho \to |\varphi\rangle$, if $|\varphi\rangle \in \mathcal{E}(\mathrm{supp}(\rho))$.*
3. *σ is adjacent to ρ, written $\rho \to \sigma$, if $\mathrm{supp}(\sigma) \subseteq \mathcal{E}(\mathrm{supp}(\rho))$.*

Then as in classical graph theory, a path from a state ρ to a state σ in $\mathcal{C}$ is a sequence $\rho_0 \to \rho_1 \to \cdots \to \rho_n$ $(n \geq 0)$ of adjacent states such that $\rho_0 = \rho$ and $\rho_n = \sigma$. For any two states ρ and σ, if there is a path from ρ to σ then we say that σ is reachable from ρ in $\mathcal{C}$.

Definition 3 (Reachable Subspace). *For any state ρ in $\mathcal{H}$, its reachable space in $\mathcal{C}$ is the subspace of $\mathcal{H}$ spanned by the states reachable from ρ:*

$$\mathcal{R}_\mathcal{C}(\rho) = \mathrm{span}\{|\psi\rangle \in \mathcal{H} : |\psi\rangle \text{ is reachable from } \rho \text{ in } \mathcal{C}\}.$$

The following theorem from [37] gives a useful characterisation of reachable subspaces. It is essentially a generalisation of Kleene closure in relational algebra.

Theorem 1. *Let $d = \dim \mathcal{H}$. Then for any state ρ in $\mathcal{H}$, we have:*

$$\mathcal{R}_{\mathcal{C}}(\rho) = \bigvee_{i=0}^{d-1} \text{supp}\left(\mathcal{E}^i(\rho)\right) = \text{supp}\left(\sum_{i=0}^{d-1} \mathcal{E}^i(\rho)\right) \qquad (9)$$

where $\mathcal{E}^i$ is the ith power of $\mathcal{E}$; that is, $\mathcal{E}^0 = \mathcal{I}$ (the identity operation in $\mathcal{H}$) and $\mathcal{E}^{i+1} = \mathcal{E} \circ \mathcal{E}^i$ for $i \geq 0$.

The reachable subspace $\mathcal{R}(\rho)$ can be viewed also as the least fixed point of quantum predicate transformer (see [30], Sect. 8.4) $T : \mathcal{S}(\mathcal{H}) \to \mathcal{S}(\mathcal{H})$ defined by $T(X) = \sup \rho \vee \mathcal{E}(X)$ for any $X \in \mathcal{S}(\mathcal{H})$.

4.2   Computing Reachable Subspaces

Based on Theorem 1, we can develop an algorithm for computing reachable subspaces in quantum Markov chain $\mathcal{C}$ using the tensor network representation of super-operator $\mathcal{E}$, with the help of the following:

Lemma 2. *Let $|\Psi\rangle = \sum_k |kk\rangle$ be the (unnormalised) maximally entangled state in $\mathcal{H} \otimes \mathcal{H}$. Then $(\mathcal{E}(A) \otimes I)|\Psi\rangle = M_{\mathcal{E}}(A \otimes I)|\Psi\rangle$, where I is the identity operator on $\mathcal{H}$.*

The basic idea of the algorithm is as follows. Define state $|\eta\rangle = \sum_{i=0}^{d-1} \mathcal{E}^i(\rho)$ in $\mathcal{H}$ and state $|\Phi\rangle = (\eta \otimes I)|\Psi\rangle$ in $\mathcal{H} \otimes \mathcal{H}$. Repeatedly using Lemma 2, we obtain:

$$|\Phi\rangle = \sum_{i=0}^{d-1} \left(\mathcal{E}^i(\rho) \otimes I\right)|\Psi\rangle = \sum_{i=0}^{d-1} M_{\mathcal{E}}^i(\rho \otimes I)|\Psi\rangle.$$

Thus, state $|\Phi\rangle$ can be computed by contracting the tensor network representations of $M_{\mathcal{E}}$, ρ and $|\Psi\rangle$. Finally, we can find the Schmidt decomposition of $|\Phi\rangle$: $|\Phi\rangle = \sum_j p_j |j\rangle \otimes |j'\rangle$, where $p_j > 0$ for all j. Then the reachable subspace $\mathcal{R}_{\mathcal{C}}(\rho) = \text{span}\{|j\rangle\}$ is computed. Of course, the optimisation techniques for contracting tensor networks discussed in Sect. 3.4 can be applied here and combined with Lemma 1 when $\mathcal{E}$ comes from (sequential and parallel) compositions of smaller super-operators on subsystems.

5   Temporal Quantum Logic

Now let us move on to consider the verification problem for a more general class of properties of quantum circuits. To specify these properties, we define an assertion language for quantum circuits in this section. We choose to simply use Birkhoff-von Neumann quantum logic [2] for specifying static behaviour of quantum circuits. To specify their behaviour over time, however, we need to introduce a temporal extension of Birkhoff-von Neumann logic. Several other temporal logics have been defined in the literature [1,9,26,33,38] that are able to specify some sophisticated properties of quantum circuits than this logic. But we decide to adopt this simple temporal logic because its model checking can be much more efficiently implemented and may find practical applications in the early stages of quantum design automation.

5.1   Birkhoff-von Neumann Quantum Logic

Birkhoff-von Neumann logic is a *propositional logic* for reasoning about (static properties of) quantum systems. We assume an alphabet consisting of:

- a set AP of atomic propositions, ranged over by metavariables $X, X_1, X_2, ...$; and
- propositional connectives $\neg$ (negation) and $\wedge$ (conjunction).

Given a Hilbert space $\mathcal{H}$ as the state space of the quantum circuit under consideration. We write $\mathcal{S}(\mathcal{H})$ for the set of its closed subspaces. It is well-known that $(\mathcal{S}(\mathcal{H}), \cap, \vee, \perp)$ is an orthomodular lattice with inclusion $\subseteq$ as its ordering, where $\cap, \vee$ and $\perp$ stand for intersection, join defined in Eq. (8), and orthocomplement, i.e. $X^{\perp} = \{|\psi\rangle : |\psi\rangle \text{ is orthogonal to all } |\varphi\rangle \in X\}$. Then atomic propositions are interpreted as subspaces of $\mathcal{H}$, i.e. elements of $\mathcal{S}(\mathcal{H})$, and connectives $\neg, \wedge$ are interpreted as $\perp$ and $\cap$, respectively. For each logical formula A, its semantics $[\![A]\!]$ is a subspace of $\mathcal{H}$, meaning that the circuit's current state is within the region $[\![A]\!]$, and $\neg A$ indicates that the probability that the circuit's state enters the region $[\![A]\!]$ is zero. We can define $\vee$ (disjunction) by $A \vee B := \neg(\neg A \wedge \neg B)$, and it is easy to see that $[\![A \vee B]\!] = [\![A]\!] \vee [\![B]\!]$ with the symbol $\vee$ in the right-hand side being join. Moreover, satisfaction of a proposition A by a pure state $|\psi\rangle$ or a mixed state ρ is simply defined as follows:

$$\varphi \models A \text{ iff } \varphi \in [\![A]\!], \qquad \rho \models A \text{ iff supp}(\rho) \subseteq [\![A]\!]. \qquad (10)$$

5.2   Computation Tree Quantum Logic

A temporal extension of quantum logic can be naturally defined. For the limitation of space, we only consider computation tree quantum logic CTQL. Its syntax is the same as that of classical computation tree logic CTL:

- State formulas: $\Phi ::= A \mid \exists\varphi \mid \forall\varphi \mid \neg\Phi \mid \Phi_1 \wedge \Phi_2$
- Path formulas: $\varphi ::= O\Phi \mid \Phi_1 U \Phi_2$

except that A stands here for a propositional formula in Birkhoff-von Neumann quantum logic rather than a classical (two-valued) proposition.

Simulation-Based Semantics: We define the semantics of CTQL with the following *design decision*: our verification of quantum circuits will be done by simulation on a classical computer. Therefore, no actual quantum measurement is performed for checking whether a quantum state $|\varphi\rangle$ or ρ is in a subspace X, i.e. $|\varphi\rangle \models X$ or $\rho \models X$ according to Eq. (10), and thus no quantum state decaying happens. Let $\mathcal{S} = \langle \mathcal{H}, L, l_0, \mathcal{T} \rangle$ be a QTS. Then a configuration of $\mathcal{S}$ is a pair (l, ρ), where $l \in L$ is a location and ρ is a quantum state in $\mathcal{H}$. We write $\mathcal{C}(\mathcal{S})$ for the set of configurations of $\mathcal{S}$. A sequence $\pi = (l_1, \rho_1)(l_2, \rho_2) \cdots (l_{i-1}, \rho_{i-1})(l_i, \rho_i) \cdots$ of configurations is a path in $\mathcal{S}$ if there exists a sequence $l_1 \xrightarrow{\mathcal{E}_1} l_2 \xrightarrow{\mathcal{E}_2} ... \xrightarrow{\mathcal{E}_{i-1}} l_i \xrightarrow{\mathcal{E}_i} \cdots$ of transitions such that $\rho_{i+1} = \mathcal{E}_i(\rho_i)$ for all i. We often write $\pi[i] = (l_{i+1}, \rho_{i+11})$ for $i \geq 1$. Then the satisfaction relation in CTL can be straightforwardly generalised to CTQL:

Definition 4. *1. Satisfaction $(l, \rho) \models \Phi$ for state formulas is defined as follows:*
  (a) $(l, \rho) \models A$ iff $\mathrm{supp}(\rho) \subseteq [\![A]\!]$;
  (b) $(l, \rho) \models \exists \varphi$ iff $\pi \models \varphi$ for some path π starting in (l, ρ);
  (c) $(l, \rho) \models \forall \varphi$ iff $\pi \models \varphi$ for all paths π starting in (l, ρ);
  (d) $(l, \rho) \models \neg \Phi$ iff $\rho \not\models \Phi$;
  (e) $(l, \rho) \models \Phi_1 \wedge \Phi_2$ iff $(l, \rho) \models \Phi_1$ and $(l, \rho) \models \Phi_2$.
2. Satisfaction $\pi \models \varphi$ for path formulas is defined as follows:
  (a) $\pi \models O\Phi$ iff $\pi[1] \models \Phi$;
  (b) $\pi \models \Phi_1 U \Phi_2$ iff there exists $i \geq 0$ such that $\pi[i] \models \Phi_2$ and $\pi[j] \models \Phi_1$ for all $0 \leq j < i$.
3. We say that S with initial state ρ satisfies Φ, written $(S, \rho) \models \Phi$, if $(l_0, \rho) \models \Phi$.

Remark 2. The above simulation-based semantics is fundamentally different from the measurement-based semantics of quantum temporal logics considered in the previous literature where the system's state is disturbed by a measurement, and the system's next step starts from the post-measurement state.

6   Model Checking Quantum Circuits

In this section, we show how model checking can be used in verification of the properties of quantum circuits specified in temporal logic CQTL introduced in the last section.

6.1   CTQL Model Checking

Indeed, classical CTL model checking techniques can be adapted to solve the following:

– **CTQL model checking problem:** Given a QTS $S = \langle \mathcal{H}, L, l_0, \mathcal{T} \rangle$, an initial state ρ and a CTQL state formula Φ. Check $(S, \rho) \models \Phi$?

The basic idea is to construct a classical transition system $\overline{S}_\rho$ from a QTS with an initial state ρ so that the above CTQL model checking problem is reduced to a CTL model checking problem. We construct $\overline{S}_\rho = \langle \mathcal{C}(S)_\rho, \Rightarrow, (l_0, \rho), L \rangle$ as follows:

– Transition relation $\Rightarrow$ between configurations $(l, \rho), (l', \rho') \in \mathcal{C}(S)$ is defined by

$$(l, \rho) \Rightarrow (l', \rho') \text{ iff for some } \mathcal{E}: l \xrightarrow{\mathcal{E}} l' \text{ and } \rho' = \mathcal{E}(\rho); \qquad (11)$$

– We define $\mathcal{C}(S)_\rho$ as the set of configurations reachable from (l_0, ρ) through $\Rightarrow$;
– Configuration (l_0, ρ) is defined as the initial state of $\overline{S}_\rho$;
– Propositional symbols A in CTQL are interpreted as propositions in Birkhoff-von Neumann quantum logic and thus their semantics $[\![A]\!]$ are subspaces of $\mathcal{H}$. However, in CTL for classical transition system $\overline{S}_\rho$, they are considered as classical two-valued propositions, and labelling function L interprets A as follows: for each $(l, \sigma) \in \mathcal{C}(S)_\rho$,

$$A \in L(l, \sigma), \text{ i.e. } (l, \sigma) \models A \text{ iff } \mathrm{supp}(\rho) \subseteq [\![A]\!]. \qquad (12)$$

The following simple lemma establishes a connection between CTQL for a QTS $\mathcal{S}$ and CTL for the classical transition system $\overline{\mathcal{S}}_\rho$ defined from $\mathcal{S}$ with an initial state ρ.

Lemma 3. *For any CTQL state formula Φ, any QTS $\mathcal{S}$ and any quantum state ρ in $\mathcal{S}$,*

$$(\mathcal{S}, \rho) \models \Phi \text{ iff } \overline{\mathcal{S}}_\rho \models \Phi. \tag{13}$$

Note that in the left-hand side of (13), Φ is treated as a CTQL formula, but in the right-hand side, it is seen as a CTL formula in which atomic propositions A are interpreted by labelling function L defined in Eq. (12).

Based on Lemma 3, whenever $\mathcal{C}(\mathcal{S})_\rho$ is finite, then CTL model checking algorithms together with computations of (11) and (12) can be used to check whether $\overline{\mathcal{S}}_\rho \models \Phi$ or not. However, it is possible that $\mathcal{C}(\mathcal{S})_\rho$ is infinite. In this case, we can apply bounded model checking to check the configurations reachable from (l_0, ρ) through $\leq k$ steps.

6.2   Assertion-Based Verification of Quantum Circuits

The above discussion indicates that assertions about quantum circuits written in CTQL can be verified by CTL model checking with some extra computations. It is well-known that a major practical hurdle in model checking applied to verifying classical circuits is the state space explosion problem. As one can imagine, this problem unavoidably occurs in the case of quantum circuits. The tensor network representation of quantum circuits discussed in Sect. 3, together with various partitioning techniques for quantum transition systems defined in Sect. 2.5 that exploit the locality in the circuits, can be a remedy to this issue. More explicitly, it is very helpful in computing reachable configurations $\mathcal{C}(\mathcal{S})_\rho$ and the labelling function (12). The symbolic representation of quantum circuits using matrix-valued Boolean expressions proposed in [32] should also be useful.

7   Conclusion

In this paper, we presented a framework for assertion-based verification of quantum circuits by model checking with the help of tensor networks. The verified properties are *qualitative* assertions written in a temporal extension of Birkhoff-von Neumann quantum logic. This modest aim of verifying only qualitative assertions is identified mainly for the reason that the verification algorithm can be more efficiently implemented and thus is actually useful in short-term practical applications. To check *quantitative* assertions (with probabilities) for quantum systems, some techniques have been developed in [9,31,36,38], but the involved computation are overwhelming. To remedy this seemingly inevitable inefficiency of verifying quantum circuits on classical computers, we also tried to develop quantum algorithms for model checking quantum systems [13].

Acknowledgment. This work has been partly supported by the National Key R&D Program of China (2018YFA0306701), the Australian Research Council (DP210102449) and the National Natural Science Foundation of China (61832015).

References

1. Baltazar, P., Chadha, R., Mateus, P.: Quantum computation tree logic: model checking and complete calculus. Int. J. Quant. Inf. **6**, 219–36 (2008)
2. Birkhoff, G., von Neumann, J.: The logic of quantum mechanics. Ann. Math. **37**, 823–843 (1936)
3. Bocharov, A., Roetteler, M., Svore, K.M.: Efficient synthesis of universal repeat-until-success quantum circuits. Phys. Rev. Lett. **114**, 080502 (2015)
4. Boule, M., Chenard, J.-S., Zilic, Z.: Assertion checkers in verification, silicon debug and in-field diagnosis. In: 8th IEEE International Symposium on Quality Electronic Design, pp. 613–620 (2007)
5. Burch, J.R., Clarke, E.D., Long, D.E., McMillan, K.L., Dill, D.L.: Symbolic model checking for sequential circuit verification. IEEE Trans. Comput. Aided Des. Integr. Circ. Syst. **13**, 401–424 (1994)
6. Burgholzer, L., Wille, R.: Advanced equivalence checking for quantum circuits. IEEE Trans. Comput. Aided Des. Integr. Circuits Syst. **40**(9), 1810–1824 (2021)
7. Corcoles, A.D., et al.: Exploiting dynamic quantum circuits in a quantum algorithm with superconducting qubits, arXiv: 2102:01682
8. Davidson, T.A., Gay, S.J., Mlnarik, H., Nagarajan, R., Papanikolaou, N.: Model checking for communicating quantum processes. Int. J. Unconv. Comput. **8**, 73–98 (2011)
9. Feng, Y., Yu, N.K., Ying, M.S.: Model checking quantum Markov chains. J. Comput. Syst. Sci. **79**, 1181–1198 (2013)
10. D Foster, H., Marschner, E.: Assertion-based verification, In: Lavagno, L., Martin, G.M., Markov, I.L., Scheffer, L.K. (eds.) Electronic Design Automation for IC System Design, Verification, and Testing, pp. 441-460. CRC Press (2016)
11. Gay, S.J., Nagarajan, R., Papanikolaou, N.: QMC: a model checker for quantum systems. In: Gupta, A., Malik, S. (eds.) CAV 2008. LNCS, vol. 5123, pp. 543–547. Springer, Heidelberg (2008). https://doi.org/10.1007/978-3-540-70545-1_51
12. Gough, J.E., James, M.R.: Quantum feedback network: Hamiltonian formulation. Commun. Math. Phys. **287**, 1109–1132 (2008). https://doi.org/10.1007/s00220-008-0698-8
13. Guan, J., Wang, Q.S., Ying, M.S.: An HHL-based algorithm for computing hitting probabilities of quantum random walks, Quantum Information & Computation (2021)
14. Gudder, S.: Quantum Markov chains. J. Math. Phys. **49**, 072105 (2008)
15. Häner, T., Steiger, D.S.: 0.5 petabyte simulation of a 45-qubit quantum circuit. In: Proceedings of the SC 2017, pp. 1–10 (2017)
16. Hong, X., Zhou, X.Z., Li, S.J., Feng, Y., Ying, M.S.: A tensor network based decision diagram for representation of quantum circuits, arXiv: 2009.02618
17. Huang, C.J.: et al.: Classical simulation of quantum supremacy circuits, arXiv:2005.06787
18. Kerckhoff, J., Nurdin, H.I., Pavlichin, D.S., Mabuchi, H.: Designing quantum memories with embedded control: photonic circuits for autonomous quantum error correction. Phys. Rev. Lett. **105**, 040502 (2010)

19. Li, R.L., Wu, B.J., Ying, M.S., Sun, X.M., Yang, G.W.: Quantum supremacy circuit simulation on Sunway TaihuLight. IEEE Trans. Parallel Distrib. Syst. **31**, 805–816 (2020)
20. Li, Y., Ying, M.: (Un)decidable problems about reachability of quantum systems. In: Baldan, P., Gorla, D. (eds.) CONCUR 2014. LNCS, vol. 8704, pp. 482–496. Springer, Heidelberg (2014). https://doi.org/10.1007/978-3-662-44584-6_33
21. Pednault, E., et al.: Breaking the 49-qubit barrier in the simulation of quantum circuits, arXiv:1710.05867
22. Seiter, J., Soeken, M., Wille, R., Drechsler, R.: Property checking of quantum circuits using quantum multiple-valued decision diagrams. In: Glück, R., Yokoyama, T. (eds.) RC 2012. LNCS, vol. 7581, pp. 183–196. Springer, Heidelberg (2013). https://doi.org/10.1007/978-3-642-36315-3_15
23. Tezak, N., Niederberger, A., Pavlichin, D.S., Sarma, G., Mabuchi, H.: Specification of photonic circuits using quantum hardware description language. Philos. Trans. R. Soc. A **370**, 5270–5290 (2012)
24. Viamontes, G.F., Markov, I.L., Hayes, J.P.: Improving gate-level simulation of quantum circuits. Quantum Inf. Process. **2**, 347–379 (2004). https://doi.org/10.1023/B:QINP.0000022725.70000.4a
25. Viamontes, G.F., Markov, I.L., Hayes, J.P.: Checking equivalence of quantum circuits and states. In: Proceedings of the ICCAD 2007, pp. 69–74 (2007)
26. Vigano, L., Volpe, M., Zorzi, M.: A branching distributed temporal logic for reasoning about entanglement-free quantum state transformations. Inf. Comput. **255**, 311–333 (2017)
27. Villalonga, B., et al.: A flexible high-performance simulator for verifying and benchmarking quantum circuits implemented on real hardware. NPJ Quantum Inf. **5**, 1–16 (2019). Art. no. 86
28. Wang ,Q.S., Ying, M.S.: Equivalence checking of sequential quantum circuits, arXiv:1811.07722
29. Ying, M.S.: Foundations of Quantum Programming. Morgan Kaufmann, Cambridge, MA, USA (2016)
30. Ying, M.S., Duan, R.Y., Feng, Y., Ji, Z.F.: Predicate transformer semantics of quantum programs. In: Mackie, I., Gay, S. (eds.) Semantic Techniques in Quantum Computation, pp. 311–360. Cambridge University Press (2010)
31. Ying, M.S., Feng, Y.: Model Checking Quantum Systems: Principles and Algorithms. Cambridge University Press, Cambridge, UK (2021)
32. Ying, M.S., Ji, Z.F.: Symbolic verification of quantum circuits, arXiv: 2010.03032
33. Ying, M.S., Li, Y.J., Yu, N.K., Feng, Y.: Model-checking linear-time properties of quantum systems. ACM Trans. Comput. Logic **15**, 1–31 (2014). Art. no. 22
34. Ying, M.S., Ying, S.G., Wu, X.D.: Invariants of quantum programs: characterisations and generation. In: POPL 2017, pp. 818–832 (2017)
35. Ying, M.S., Yu, N.K., Feng, Y., Duan, R.Y.: Verification of quantum programs. Sci. Comput. Program. **78**, 1679–1700 (2013)
36. Ying, S., Feng, Y., Yu, N., Ying, M.: Reachability probabilities of Quantum Markov chains. In: D'Argenio, P.R., Melgratti, H. (eds.) CONCUR 2013. LNCS, vol. 8052, pp. 334–348. Springer, Heidelberg (2013). https://doi.org/10.1007/978-3-642-40184-8_24
37. Yu, N., Ying, M.: Reachability and termination analysis of concurrent quantum programs. In: Koutny, M., Ulidowski, I. (eds.) CONCUR 2012. LNCS, vol. 7454, pp. 69–83. Springer, Heidelberg (2012). https://doi.org/10.1007/978-3-642-32940-1_7
38. Yu, N.K.: Quantum temporal logic, arXiv:1908.00158

Interactive Theorem Proving

Verifying Secure Speculation
in Isabelle/HOL

Matt Griffin🆔 and Brijesh Dongol$^{(\boxtimes)}$🆔

University of Surrey, Guildford, Surrey, UK
{matt.griffin,b.dongol}@surrey.ac.uk

Abstract. Secure speculation is an information flow security hyperproperty that prevents transient execution attacks such as Spectre, Meltdown and Foreshadow. Generic compiler mitigations for secure speculation are known to be insufficient for eliminating vulnerabilities. Moreover, these mitigation techniques often overprescribe speculative fences, causing the performance of the programs to suffer. Recently Cheang et al. have developed an operational semantics of program execution capable of characterising speculative executions as well as a new class of information flow hyperproperties named TPOD that ensure secure speculation. This paper presents a framework for verifying TPOD using the Isabelle/HOL proof assistant by encoding the operational semantics of Cheang et al. We provide translation tools for automatically generating the required Isabelle/HOL theory templates from a C-like program syntax, which speeds up verification. Our framework is capable of proving the existence of vulnerabilities *and* correctness of secure speculation. We exemplify our framework by proving the existence of secure speculation bugs in 15 victim functions for the MSVC compiler as well as correctness of some proposed fixes.

Keywords: Isabelle/HOL · Secure speculation · Formal verification · Spectre · Transient execution vulnerabilities · Hyperproperties

1 Introduction

Transient execution vulnerabilities, especially Spectre, remain an active area of research since their disclosure in 2018 [18]. Even with the availability of many (now mature) solutions, there is seemingly no decrease in the discovery of new variants, including "next generation attacks" [3,23]. Modern processors from nearly all vendors are susceptible, meaning that millions of devices are insecure. This problem is of high concern to cloud providers since vulnerabilities can leak sensitive information from system memory, including across hypervisor domains, which breaks virtual machine boundaries. Moreover, attacks can

Griffin is supported by funding from Amazon. Dongol is supported by EPSRC grants EP/V038915/1, EP/R032556/1, EP/R025134/2, VeTSS and ARC Discovery Grant DP190102142.

© Springer Nature Switzerland AG 2021
M. Huisman et al. (Eds.): FM 2021, LNCS 13047, pp. 43–60, 2021.
https://doi.org/10.1007/978-3-030-90870-6_3

be carried out using valid processor mechanisms, meaning that detecting an occurrence is extremely hard. A successful attack leaves almost no trace of its exploitation that could be discerned from normal operation.

The root of the problem lies within the design of modern microprocessors and the complexity of many interacting components. The combination of performance features such as speculative execution, branch prediction and out-of-order execution are exploited/misused to extract information through side channels such as the latency in memory access caused by the CPU cache. Interestingly, processors that exhibit these vulnerabilities are correct, at least according to their vendor's specifications. Moreover, exploited mechanisms, namely branch prediction and speculative execution, are key to high performance computation. This indicates weaknesses in the specifications themselves, primarily their non-determinism which affords flexibility at the permittance of undefined behaviour.

For some attacks (e.g., Meltdown [19] and Foreshadow [2]), the latest patches offer a combination of hardware- or microcode-based fixes, but older architectures remain vulnerable. Moreover, many attacks (e.g., those based on Spectre [18,23]) cannot be patched, even for the latest CPUs, since it is impossible to detect whether an arbitrary sequence of instructions is exploitable [17]. This suggests that a full solution to transient execution vulnerabilities will require a mix of hardware- and software-based solutions.

Existing mitigations (e.g., for Spectre) tend to be heavy handed, and thus, either incur performance penalties [21] or only target specific variants [15,26]. A compiler-based approach, developed by Microsoft (MSVC), designed to work with new specifications of the `lfence` instructions in x86 processors is known to over-prescribe speculation barriers, leading to performance concerns [17]. More seriously, these mitigations are known to be incomplete—13 victim functions presented for Spectre variant 1 (see §2.1) remain capable of bypassing MSVC mitigations [17].

The above motivates the need for formal proofs of correctness of secure speculation for the compiled assembly-level representation of programs. A significant step towards such proofs were taken by Cheang et al. [5], who developed an operational semantics of program execution capable of characterising speculative executions. They have coupled this with a new class of information flow hyperproperties [6] named *trace property-dependent observational determinism (TPOD)* with mechanisation in the UCLID5 model checker [25]. TPOD generalises observational determinism [20,24] to allow information flow from high to low states in the presence of speculation, succinctly characterising correctness of secure speculation.

Our paper comprises the following core contributions. **(1)** We build on the work of Cheang et al. [5] by encoding their operational semantics in the Isabelle/HOL proof assistant. **(2)** We couple our Isabelle/HOL mechanisation with a Hoare-style deductive verification technique, which we show is capable of reasoning about both the absence and presence of secure speculation. **(3)** We prove the existence of vulnerabilities for all 15 victim functions previously identified for MSVC [17], and correctness of two of the most interesting fixes. **(4)** We develop an automatic translation tool that generates associated Isabelle/HOL

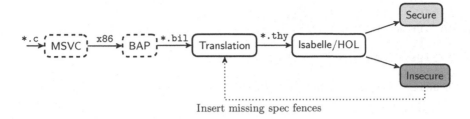

Fig. 1. Translation of C source programs to an Isabelle/HOL proof

```
1  void victim_function_v01(size_t x) {
2      if (x < array1_size) {
3          temp &= array2[array1[x] * 512];
4      }
5  }
```

Listing 1.1. Spectre bounds check bypass

theories for a given BIL[1] input, integrating into a verification workflow from C code to Isabelle/HOL proofs (see Fig. 1). **(5)** We develop theorems to identify programs that are guaranteed to satisfy TPOD, which reduces the proof burden. The tools and Isabelle/HOL mechanisation related to this paper may be found in [10].

Our mechanisation work uncovers minor issues in the operational semantics of Cheang et al. [5], which we revise in our operational semantics (see §3). Moreover, we treat speculative fences as dedicated instructions in program memory as opposed to abstract barriers, closely modelling a true mitigated program. Furthermore, we choose to clear speculative states on resolution for intuitive comparisons in proof conditions. We achieve similar verification scalability as the "havocing adversary" [5] through invariants and the discharge of trivial proof obligations, without the need for the Havoc instruction and adversary reduction lemmas.

2 Transient Execution Vulnerabilities

Transient execution vulnerabilities target performance features such as speculative execution and branch prediction. Since the first discovered attacks [18, 19] many such vulnerabilities have been uncovered, targetting specific hardware architectures. Some variants have been fixed via hardware and microarchitecture updates, e.g. Foreshadow [2] no longer affects Intel architectures since 9th Generation Coffee Lake [13]. However, many variants of Spectre remain unpatched and require software-based mitigation.

---

[1] BIL is an assembly intermediate language [1].

```
1 00001bbd: RAX := mem[array2, el]:u64
2 00001bc4: RDX := mem[array1, el]:u64
3 00001bdc: ... // some processing on the index of array1 RDX
4 00001c1c: RDX := mem[RDX, el]:u64
5 00001c54: ... // some processing on the index of array2 RAX
6 00001c6d: RDX := mem[RAX, el]:u64
```

Listing 1.2. Concise translation of line 3 in Listing 1.1 to assembly in BIL.

2.1 Spectre Variant 1: Bounds Check Bypass

Spectre mistrains the branch predictor so that mispredictions are made on branching statements. One such mistraining strategy targets the pattern history table (PHT), which is used to decide the direction (taken/not-taken) of a conditional branch. This vulnerability is classified as Spectre-PHT [3] and was first introduced as Spectre Bounds Check Bypass (BCB), aka variant 1, by Kocher et al. [18]. Consider the simple C program in Listing 1.1, which demonstrates the Spectre BCB vulnerability.

The function takes some untrusted input x and performs a bounds check to ensure that it is less that the size of array1 (array1_size). The value x indexes array1 and subsequently array2 through some transformation. The result is stored in temp before control is returned to the caller. The bounds check on line 2 is supposed to act as a guard between trusted and untrusted operations. Under normal execution, a caller would not be able to perform the memory reads and writes on line 3 if the guard does not hold. However, under speculative execution, the result of the branch condition on line 2 could be mispredicted, which can be reliably guaranteed if the branch predictor is mistrained.

If a misprediction occurs, the operations on line 3 will be executed speculatively with a value of x outside the prescribed bounds. This could lead to unconstrained reads from protected memory and differences in the speculative state across multiple executions. Note that the adversary cannot directly observe these differences as architectural changes are reverted when mispredictions are resolved. However, these changes persist in the *microarchitectural state* such as the various levels of the CPU cache.[2]

We demonstrate how reads can be unconstrained, by examining a subset of the assembly corresponding to the program in Listing 1.1. An excerpt of the BIL[3] instructions (resulting from compiling line 3) in the program using Microsoft's Visual C++ Compiler (MSVC) are shown in Listing 1.2. Instructions are shown on the right with addresses (in program memory) on the left.

---

[2] For this to be exploited we must have already "poisoned" the cache [18]. In this paper, assume cache poisoning to have occurred prior to execution of each program.

[3] BIL is an assembly intermediate language [1]. In general, we *must* reason about secure speculation in assembly language since compilers may optimise branch statements in high-level languages.

Assuming that the branch predictor has mispredicted the condition that x is less than the size of array1, the memory read at 00001c1c may load an unconstrained value v from memory into the register RDX, where v is being used as an address. As instruction 00001c1c is speculative, this read is permitted despite the fact that v is potentially a value in protected memory. This is the first indication of a vulnerability, even though the adversary cannot yet read v in the speculative state. However, the adversary can discover v through a side channel. In particular, the memory read at 00001c6d, ultimately accesses v,[4] which means that v will be brought into the cache. Even when the branch predictor resolves this misspeculation on x, v remains in the cache making the value susceptible to a timing attack [17,18]. Note that the purpose of array2 is to provide a mechanism for indexing addresses; the attacker is not aiming to steal secrets from array2 itself.

One way to fix this issue is via a *speculative fence*, specfence, which is an assembly instruction that resolves all branch predictions, in turn ensuring the absence of speculation at specific programmer-controlled locations. In Listing 1.2, a speculative fence is required prior to executing instruction 00001c6d, which is the instruction that loads v into the cache as an address. After introduction of a speculative fence immediately prior to 00001c6d, the misprediction on x will be resolved, preventing v from being loaded in the first place. However, determining precisely where speculative fences should be placed is difficult: underfencing leaves the code vulnerable, while overfencing negatively impact performance. Compilers cannot yet be trusted to reliably fence program code [17], pointing to a practical need for formal verification of specific programs.

2.2   TPOD

Properties involving speculative execution cannot be formalised over a single trace. Instead we require a more general class of properties called *hyperproperties* [6], which are properties over sets of traces. An example is *observational determinism* [20,24], which is a two-trace hyperproperty. It is well known that observational determinism allows one to establish *low equivalence*, which is an information flow property that holds iff from a *user state* (i.e., a *low state*) an observer cannot detect any difference in a *root state* (i.e., a *high state*). Operations are either untrusted and act on the low state, or are trusted and act on the high state.

It turns out *observational determinism* is not sufficient to characterise the types of properties described in §2.1 [5]. Instead, we require a more general condition called *trace property-dependent observational determinism (TPOD)*, which is a 4-safety hyperproperty. Unlike observational determinism, which precludes information flow from high to low states, TPOD allows information flow from a high state to a low state in the presence of misspeculation.

We describe TPOD directly in terms of its formal definition (see Fig. 2), but describe its components informally for now. The formal definitions of the

---

[4] Technically speaking, the value being accessed is the transformed value v * 512.

$$\forall \pi_1, \pi_2, \pi_3, \pi_4 \in \mathit{Tr}. \ \pi_1 \in T \wedge \pi_2 \in T \wedge \pi_3 \notin T \wedge \pi_4 \notin T \longrightarrow \qquad (1)$$

$$op_{\mathcal{L}}(\pi_1) = op_{\mathcal{L}}(\pi_2) = op_{\mathcal{L}}(\pi_3) = op_{\mathcal{L}}(\pi_4) \longrightarrow \qquad (2)$$

$$op_{\mathcal{H}}(\pi_1) = op_{\mathcal{H}}(\pi_3) \wedge op_{\mathcal{H}}(\pi_2) = op_{\mathcal{H}}(\pi_4) \longrightarrow \qquad (3)$$

$$\pi_1 \approx_{\mathcal{L}} \pi_2 \wedge \pi_3^0 \approx_{\mathcal{L}} \pi_4^0 \longrightarrow \qquad (4)$$

$$\pi_3 \approx_{\mathcal{L}} \pi_4 \qquad (5)$$

Fig. 2. Formal definition of TPOD

components comprising TPOD are given in §3.3. We use $s_1 \approx_{\mathcal{L}} s_2$ to denote that state s_1 and s_2 are low-equivalent. For traces π_1 and π_2, we use $\pi_1 \approx_{\mathcal{L}} \pi_2$ to denote that for all indices i, $\pi_1^i \approx_{\mathcal{L}} \pi_2^i$, where π_k^i is the state indexed i in π_k. We assume that Tr is the set of all traces of a program, and $T \subseteq \mathit{Tr}$ is the set of traces of the program with no misprediction. Moreover, $op_{\mathcal{L}}(\pi)$ returns the sequence of low-state (i.e., untrusted) instructions executed for each state of the trace, which may be null if the instruction is trusted. $op_{\mathcal{H}}(\pi)$ is similar, but returns the sequence of trusted instructions. A difference between $op_{\mathcal{L}}(\pi)$ and $op_{\mathcal{H}}(\pi)$ is that $op_{\mathcal{H}}(\pi)$ also returns the observable memory after each high instruction (see §3.3 for details).

By (1) we assume that π_1 and π_2 are traces with no misprediction (and hence no speculation) and π_3 and π_4 are traces with misprediction, and by (2) all four traces execute the same sequence of low instructions. By (3), traces π_1 and π_3 execute the same sequence of high instructions, as do π_2 and π_4. By (4), π_1 and π_2 are low equivalent, while π_3 and π_4 are initially low equivelent. Under these assumptions, we must show (5), which ensures that π_3 and π_4 (the traces with misprediction) are low equivalent. Note that π_1 and π_3 execute the same instructions with the same memory, but only π_3 can speculate. Similarly, for π_2 and π_4. Also note that there is no such constraint on π_1 and π_2 (and on π_3 and π_4), thus they could execute different instructions with different memory in the high state.

To see that TPOD does indeed capture the secure speculation properties of interest, consider a speculative execution of the program in Listing 1.2 up to instruction 00001c6d. We construct the four traces π_1-π_4 in parallel. Since we are considering a speculative execution, π_1 and π_2 will be *stuttering*, i.e., waiting at the mispredicted branch (see §3 below), while π_3 and π_4 are executing the program speculatively. Thus (1) holds. Further assume that conditions (2) and (3) hold, meaning that the operations executed until this point are equivalent as defined by (2) and (3). By (4), π_1 and π_2 are low equivalent, and since TPOD is prefix-closed [5] π_3 and π_4 must also be low equivalent. Upon executing 00001c6d, it will be possible for the system to load from different memory addresses, which violates low equivalence. This models the phenomenon where the adversary can identify a difference in the memory addresses accessed.

3   Operational Semantics

3.1   Syntax and Semantics

We model secure speculation using operational semantics for *speculative in-order* processors similar to Cheang et al. [5] with some modifications. We keep the proposed assembly intermediate representation (AIR), whose syntax for programs (*Prog*), instructions (*Instr*) and expressions (*Exp*) are given below. We let *Reg* and *Const* be the set of all registers and constants, respectively, and $\Diamond_u$ and $\Diamond_b$ be unary and binary operators.

$$Prog ::= Instr^* \qquad Exp ::= Const \mid Reg \mid \Diamond_u\ Exp \mid Exp\ \Diamond_b\ Exp$$
$$Instr ::= Reg := Exp \mid \mathsf{mem} := \mathsf{mem}[Exp \rightarrow Exp] \mid Reg := \mathsf{mem}[Exp]$$
$$\mid \mathsf{if}\ Exp\ \mathsf{goto}\ Addr_\Pi \mid \mathsf{goto}\ Addr_\Pi \mid \mathsf{specfence}$$

We let $Addr_\Pi, Addr_\mu \subseteq Const$ be the set of all program and memory addresses, respectively. The machine state is represented by $s = \langle \Pi, \Delta, \mu, pc, \omega, \beta, n \rangle$, where $\Pi : \mathbb{N} \rightarrow Addr_\Pi \rightarrow Instr$ is the *program memory* (mapping program addresses to instructions), $\Delta : \mathbb{N} \rightarrow Reg \rightarrow Val$ and $\mu : \mathbb{N} \rightarrow Addr_\mu \rightarrow Val$ are the *register* and *memory* states, $pc : \mathbb{N} \rightarrow Addr_\Pi$ is the *program counter*, $\omega \in (Addr_\Pi \times Addr_\mu)^*$ is the trace of *accessed program* and *memory addresses*, β is the *branch predictor*, and finally $n \in \mathbb{N}$ is the *speculation level*. Note that Δ, μ and pc are functions over the current speculation level, which discuss in detail below. We use Δ_n for $\Delta(n)$, where Δ_0 refers to the architectural state with no speculation (similarly μ_n, pc_n). We use dot notation (e.g., $s.\Pi$) to refer to components of s.

A program is *speculating* in state s (denoted in *speculating(s)* iff $s.n > 0$). Moreover, we use $\rho \doteq pc_n$ to refer to the current program counter, $\iota \doteq \Pi(\rho)$ to the current instruction. Following Cheang et al., we assume an evaluation function, where $[\![e]\!]_{\Delta_n}$ evaluates the expression e in the register state Δ_n. Semantics of expression evaluation are shown below.

$$\text{CONST} \frac{}{c = [\![c]\!]_{\Delta_n}} \qquad \text{REG} \frac{\Delta_n(r) = v}{v = [\![r]\!]_{\Delta_n}} \qquad \text{UNOP} \frac{v' = [\![e]\!]_{\Delta_n} \qquad v = \Diamond_u v'}{v = [\![\Diamond_u e]\!]_{\Delta_n}}$$

$$\text{BINOP} \frac{v_1 = [\![c_1]\!]_{\Delta_n} \qquad v_2 = [\![e_2]\!]_{\Delta_n} \qquad v = v_1 \Diamond_b v_2}{v = [\![e_1 \Diamond_b e_2]\!]_{\Delta_n}}$$

We now define the transition relation, which are shown in Fig. 3. Each state s already contains a mapping from s to the next instruction ($s.\iota$) to be executed. Thus, the transition relation is of the form $s \rightsquigarrow s'$, which advances the machine state from s to s' by either executing $s.\iota$ or resolving a misprediction in s. The rules use *uninterpreted predicates*, *mispred(n, β, pc)* and *resolve(n, β, pc)*, which model branch misprediction and resolution, respectively, and an *uninterpreted function*, *update(n, β, pc)*, which models branch prediction. The values of uninterpreted predicates and functions are non-deterministically selected and updated. Thus, in our verification, for any uninterpreted predicate or predicate, we must check both the true and false cases.

For a sequence $\sigma \in X^*$ and an element $x \in X$, we use $\sigma \cdot x$ for the sequence σ with x appended to the end. Thus $\omega \cdot \langle x, y \rangle$ denotes ω with the pair $\langle x, y \rangle$ appended to the end.

For space reasons, we only discuss the most important aspect of the transition relation here and ask the interested reader to consult the original paper for full details [5]. When executing a branch instruction, there are *four possible outcomes*, determined by the combination of the condition evaluation, $[\![e]\!]_{\Delta_n}$, and $mispred(n, \beta, pc)$. If $mispred(n, \beta, pc)$ holds we increment n, copy the values at n in the current Δ and μ to the next n and finally update pc.

An *execution* of a program is a sequence π generated using the transition rules in Fig. 3.

3.2 Adversary Model

In addition to the rules above, we require a model of the adversary's capabilities. Again, we follow Cheang et al. [5] and formalise an adversary model capable of reading from architectural registers and non-secret memory. To this end, we use a tuple $\mathcal{A} = \langle \mathcal{T}_\rho, \mathcal{EP}, \mathcal{S}_\mathcal{T}, \mathcal{U}_{rd}^\mu, \mathcal{U}_{wr}^\mu \rangle$, where $\mathcal{T}_\rho \subseteq Addr_\Pi$ refers to the *set of trusted instruction memory addresses*, $\mathcal{EP} : Addr_\Pi \in \mathcal{T}_\rho$ is the *trusted program's entrypoint*, $\mathcal{S}_\mathcal{T} \subseteq Addr_\mu$ is the *secret memory addresses*, $\mathcal{U}_{rd}^\mu \subseteq Addr_\mu$ and $\mathcal{U}_{wr}^\mu \subseteq Addr_\mu$ are the *adversary readable* and *writable addresses*.

In our development, we must define some restrictions on the adversary's capabilities. We assume that that adversary can only read from the addresses in the set $\mathcal{U}_{rd}^\mu$ and write to addresses in $\mathcal{U}_{wr}^\mu$. To enforce this we define the following state predicates. Note that we leave the state s implicit in the definitions.

$$conformantLoad_\mathcal{A} \doteq (\iota = \ r := \mathsf{mem}[e]) \longrightarrow [\![e]\!]_{\Delta_n} \in \mathcal{U}_{rd}^\mu$$
$$conformantStore_\mathcal{A} \doteq (\iota = \ \mathsf{mem} := \mathsf{mem}[e_1 \rightarrow e_2]) \longrightarrow [\![e_1]\!]_{\Delta_n} \in \mathcal{U}_{wr}^\mu$$

Both predicates are only required to hold if the program is not speculating or executing an untrusted instruction. Thus, we define $conformantLS_\mathcal{A} \doteq \rho \notin \mathcal{T}_\rho \wedge \neg \ speculating \longrightarrow conformantLoad_\mathcal{A} \wedge conformantStore_\mathcal{A}$.

A further constraint of the program memory is that any transition to an address in $\mathcal{T}_\rho$ must target an element in $\mathcal{EP}$. This is to prevent the bypass of speculative fences. The entrypoint from $\mathcal{EP}$ must exist at the boundary between an untrusted and trusted instruction. This is a property of an execution π, and is formalised by the following predicate:

$$conformantEP_\mathcal{A}(\pi) \doteq \forall i. \ \pi^i.\rho \notin \mathcal{T}_\rho \wedge \pi^{i+1}.\rho \in \mathcal{T}_\rho \longrightarrow \pi^{i+1}.\rho = \mathcal{EP}$$

The definitions above allow us to formalise the notion of a *conformant trace*, which is designed to remove spurious counterexamples. We specify that the initial state must not be speculating and satisfy some predicate $init(\pi^0)$. This is shown in the equation below:

$$conformant_\mathcal{A}(\pi) \doteq \neg speculating(\pi^0) \wedge init(\pi^0) \wedge$$
$$conformantEP_\mathcal{A}(\pi) \wedge (\forall i. \ conformantLS_\mathcal{A}(\pi^i))$$

We say any execution π that satisfies $conformant_\mathcal{A}(\pi)$ is a *trace* of the program.

$$\text{REGUPDATE}\dfrac{\begin{array}{ccc}\neg\ resolve(n,\beta,pc) & \iota = r := e & \Delta'_n = \Delta_n[r \mapsto [\![e]\!]_{\Delta_n}] \\ pc'_n = pc_n + 1 & & \omega' = \omega.\langle\rho,\bot\rangle\end{array}}{\langle\Pi,\Delta,\mu,pc,\omega,\beta,n\rangle \rightsquigarrow \langle\Pi,\Delta[n \mapsto D],\mu,pc',\omega',\beta,n\rangle}$$

$$\text{LOAD}\dfrac{\begin{array}{ccc}\neg\ resolve(n,\beta,pc) & \iota = r := \mathsf{mem}[e] & a = [\![e]\!]_{\Delta_n} \\ \Delta'_n = \Delta_n[r \mapsto \mu_n(a)] & pc'_n = pc_n + 1 & \omega' = \omega.\langle\rho,a\rangle\end{array}}{\langle\Pi,\Delta,\mu,pc,\omega,\beta,n\rangle \rightsquigarrow \langle\Pi,\Delta[n \mapsto D],\mu,pc',\omega',\beta,n\rangle}$$

$$\text{STORE}\dfrac{\begin{array}{ccc}\neg\ resolve(n,\beta,pc) & \iota = \mathsf{mem} := \mathsf{mem}[e_1 \to e_2] & a = [\![e_1]\!]_{\Delta_n} \\ \mu'_n = \mu_n[a \mapsto [\![e_2]\!]_{\Delta_n}] & pc'_n = pc_n + 1 & \omega' = \omega.\langle\rho,a\rangle\end{array}}{\langle\Pi,\Delta,\mu,pc,\omega,\beta,n\rangle \rightsquigarrow \langle\Pi,\Delta,\mu[n \mapsto D],pc',\omega',\beta,n\rangle}$$

$$\text{BRANCHT}\dfrac{\begin{array}{cccc}\neg\ resolve(n,\beta,pc) & \iota = \mathsf{if}\ e\ \mathsf{goto}\ c & \neg\ mispred(n,\beta,pc) & [\![e]\!]_{\Delta_n} \\ pc'_n = c & \omega' = \omega.\langle\rho,\bot\rangle & \beta' = update(n,\beta,pc)\end{array}}{\langle\Pi,\Delta,\mu,pc,\omega,\beta,n\rangle \rightsquigarrow \langle\Pi,\Delta,\mu,pc',\omega',\beta',n\rangle)}$$

$$\text{BRANCHF}\dfrac{\begin{array}{cccc}\neg\ resolve(n,\beta,pc) & \iota = \mathsf{if}\ e\ \mathsf{goto}\ c & \neg\ mispred(n,\beta,pc) & \neg[\![e]\!]_{\Delta_n} \\ pc'_n = pc_n + 1 & \omega' = \omega.\langle\rho,\bot\rangle & \beta' = update(n,\beta,pc)\end{array}}{\langle\Pi,\Delta,\mu,pc,\omega,\beta,n\rangle \rightsquigarrow \langle\Pi,\Delta,\mu,pc',\omega',\beta',n\rangle}$$

$$\text{MISPREDT}\dfrac{\begin{array}{cccc}\neg\ resolve(n,\beta,pc) & \iota = \mathsf{if}\ e\ \mathsf{goto}\ c & mispred(n,\beta,pc) & [\![e]\!]_{\Delta_n} \\ pc' = pc[n \mapsto c, n' \mapsto pc_n + 1] & \omega' = \omega.\langle\rho,\bot\rangle \\ \beta' = update(n,\beta,pc) & n' = n + 1\end{array}}{\langle\Pi,\Delta,\mu,pc,\omega,\beta,n\rangle \rightsquigarrow \langle\Pi,\Delta[n' \mapsto \Delta_n],\mu[n' \mapsto \mu_n],pc',\omega',\beta',n'\rangle}$$

$$\text{MISPREDF}\dfrac{\begin{array}{cccc}\neg\ resolve(n,\beta,pc) & \iota = \mathsf{if}\ e\ \mathsf{goto}\ c & mispred(n,\beta,pc) & \neg[\![e]\!]_{\Delta_n} \\ pc' = pc[n \mapsto pc_n + 1, n' \mapsto c] & \omega' = \omega.\langle\rho,\bot\rangle \\ \beta' = update(n,\beta,pc) & n' = n + 1\end{array}}{\langle\Pi,\Delta,\mu,pc,\omega,\beta,n\rangle \rightsquigarrow \langle\Pi,\Delta',\mu',pc',\omega',\beta',n'\rangle}$$

$$\text{GOTO}\dfrac{\begin{array}{ccc}\neg\ resolve(n,\beta,pc) & \iota = \mathsf{goto}\ c & pc'_n = c \\ \omega' = \omega.\langle\rho,\bot\rangle & \beta' = update(n,\beta,pc)\end{array}}{\langle\Pi,\Delta,\mu,pc,\omega,\beta,n\rangle \rightsquigarrow \langle\Pi,\Delta,\mu,pc',\omega',\beta',n\rangle}$$

$$\text{SPECFENCE}\dfrac{\begin{array}{cccc}\neg\ resolve(n,\beta,pc) & \iota = \mathsf{specfence} & \Delta' = \Delta \upharpoonright n' & \mu' = \mu \upharpoonright n' \\ pc' = \mathsf{if}\ n = 0\ \mathsf{then}\ pc[n \mapsto pc_n + 1]\ \mathsf{else}\ pc \upharpoonright 0 & \omega' = \omega.\langle\rho,\bot\rangle\end{array}}{\langle\Pi,\Delta,\mu,pc,\omega,\beta,n\rangle \rightsquigarrow \langle\Pi,\Delta',\mu',pc',\omega',\beta,0\rangle}$$

$$\text{RESOLVE}\dfrac{\begin{array}{ccc}resolve(n,\beta,pc) & \beta' = update(n,\beta,pc) & n' = n - 1\end{array}}{\langle\Pi,\Delta,\mu,pc,\omega,\beta,n\rangle \rightsquigarrow \langle\Pi,\Delta[n \mapsto \bot],\mu[n \mapsto \bot],pc[n \mapsto \bot],\omega,\beta',n'\rangle}$$

Fig. 3. Transition rules of the operational semantics, recall that ρ is defined to be pc_n. We define $A \upharpoonright a \doteq \lambda x.\ \mathsf{if}\ x = a\ \mathsf{then}\ A(a)\ \mathsf{else}\ \bot$.

3.3 Formalising TPOD

In this section, we formalise the components used in the definition of TPOD as given in §2.2. The presentation in §2.2 leaves the adversary implicit. Following §3.2, we have an explicit adversary model, thus formalise the components of TPOD in terms of this adversary.

The set of traces with no misprediction is defined as follows: $T \doteq \{\pi \in Tr \mid \forall i.\ \neg\ mispred(\pi^i.n, \pi^i.\beta, \pi^i.pc)\}$.

Next we define the low and high operations. Recall that $\mathcal{T}_\rho$ is the set of trusted instruction addresses with respect to an adversary $\mathcal{A}$. The low operations are given by $op_{\mathcal{L}}^{\mathcal{A}}(s) \doteq$ if $s.pc_0 \notin \mathcal{T}_\rho$ then $\Pi(s.pc_0)$ else $\bot$, where $s.pc_0$ is the architectural program counter for the current non-speculative instruction.

The high operations return both an instruction and the memory read. The instruction itself is given by $\mathrm{inst}_{\mathcal{T}}^{\mathcal{A}}(s) \doteq$ if $s.pc_0 \in \mathcal{T}_\rho$ then $\Pi[s.pc_0]$ else $\bot$ and the memory by $\mathcal{P}_{\mathcal{T}}^{\mathcal{A}}(s) \doteq \lambda a.$ if $a \notin \mathcal{S}_{\mathcal{T}}$ then $\mu_0(a)$ else $\bot$, recalling that $\mathcal{S}_{\mathcal{T}}$ denotes the secret memory addresses of $\mathcal{A}$. Moreover, we can determine the architectural memory using μ_0, which is the memory where no speculation is taking place. Formally, a high operation returns a tuple $op_{\mathcal{H}}^{\mathcal{A}}(s) \doteq \langle \mathrm{inst}_{\mathcal{T}}(s), \mathcal{P}_{\mathcal{T}}(s) \rangle$

We define low equivalence of two states s_1 and s_2 as follows:

$$s_1 \approx_{\mathcal{L}} s_2 \doteq (\neg speculating(s_1) \vee \neg speculating(s_2)) \wedge (op_{\mathcal{L}}(s_1) \neq \bot) \longrightarrow$$
$$(\forall a \in \mathcal{U}_{rd}^{\mu}.\ s_1.\mu_0(a) = s_2.\mu_0(a)) \wedge$$
$$s_1.\Delta_0 = s_2.\Delta_0 \wedge s_1.\beta = s_2.\beta \wedge s_1.\omega = s_2.\omega$$

Low-equivalence of traces is defined by pointwise lifting as discussed in §2.2.

4   Mechanisation Techniques

Our proofs are constructed using the proof assistant Isabelle/HOL, which overcomes the limitations of finite traces and the specific properties present in prior works, which used the UCLID5 model checker [25]. Our Isabelle/HOL theories act as a library, offering re-usability. The proofs themselves require very little human interaction.

Our workflow (see Fig. 1) is similar to that of Rasmussen [22], but we generate Isabelle/HOL theories instead of a UCLID5 representation. First, the C code is compiled to assembly. This step could target any compiler and architecture compatible with BAP [1]. In our work, we use the MSVC compiler to translate the C code into x86 assembly. Second the assembly code is fed into the Binary Analysis Platform (BAP) to generate the corresponding BIL [1]. Finally, we generate the optimised Isabelle/HOL theory for the given BIL. For this final translation step, we have developed an automatic translation tool from BIL to Isabelle/HOL that instantiates the theorems necessary to prove TPOD.

4.1   Program Specification

In our development, we provide an Isabelle/HOL representation of each BIL instruction (see Fig. 4 for an example). All data types are represented as uninterpreted 64-bit words, with expression evaluation handled by Isabelle/HOL's built-in Word_Lib theories. We define a well-formed predicate which ensures that the program memory is valid and verifiable. Well-formed predicates extend to other components of the system state, such as the program counter, trusted set of addresses, and entry point.

```
 1 definition "ex01_Π_vulnerable ≡ [
 2    0 ↦ RAX := mem[Const array1_size_addr , el]:u64,
 3    1 ↦ CF := (BinOp (Reg RDI) (air_lt) (Reg RAX)),
 4    2 ↦ when (Reg CF) goto (ProgramAddress 4),
 5    3 ↦ goto (ProgramAddress 19),
 6
 7    4 ↦ RAX := mem[Const array2_addr , el]:u64,
 8    5 ↦ RDX := mem[Const array1_addr , el]:u64,
 9    6 ↦ RCX := (Reg RDI),
10    7 ↦ RCX := (BinOp (Reg RCX) (air_shiftl) (Const 3)),
11    8 ↦ (V 274) := (Reg RCX),
12    9 ↦ RDX := (BinOp (Reg RDX) (+) (Reg (V 274))),
13   10 ↦ RDX := mem[Reg RDX, el]:u64,
14   11 ↦ RDX := (BinOp (Reg RDX) (air_shiftl) (Const 12)),
15   12 ↦ (V 284) := (Reg RDX),
16   13 ↦ RAX := (BinOp (Reg RAX) (+) (Reg (V 284))),
17   14 ↦ RDX := mem[Reg RAX, el]:u64,
18   15 ↦ RAX := mem[Const temp_addr , el]:u64,
19   16 ↦ RAX := (BinOp (Reg RAX) (AND) (Reg RDX)),
20   17 ↦ mem := mem with [Const temp_addr , el]:u64 <- (Reg RAX),
21   18 ↦ goto (ProgramAddress 19),
22
23   19 ↦ goto Halt
24 ]"
```

Fig. 4. Isabelle/HOL program memory for example 1

We have developed a set of theorems to discharge trivial cases automatically. Below, we describe the most interesting of such trivial programs for which a well formed TPOD proof obligation can be discharged without a complex stepwise, inductive proof. We ask the interested reader to consult our Isabelle/HOL theories [10] for other examples.

Theorem 1. *TPOD holds for any well-formed Π if any of the following hold:*

1. $\forall \iota \in \Pi . \ \iota \neq$ if e goto c,
2. $\forall \iota \in \Pi . \ \iota \notin \{r := \mathsf{mem}[e], \mathsf{mem} := \mathsf{mem}[e_1 \rightarrow e_2]\}$,
3. $\forall \rho \in \Pi . \ \rho \in \mathcal{T}_\rho.$

This theorem has been verified in Isabelle/HOL.

Intuitively speaking, condition 1 ensures that Π contains no branch instructions. TPOD assumes that we start in a state without speculation and branching introduces speculation. Therefore, if Π contains no branch instructions, there can be no speculation and no violation of TPOD. Condition 2 ensures that Π contains no load or store instructions. Recall that (4) in Fig. 2 assumes that the speculative traces are initially architecturally equivalent, thus the absence of memory operations prevents these traces from diverging. Condition 3 ensure that all instructions are trusted. Any two high states are trivially low equivalent to the adversary even if their states differ and would otherwise violate TPOD.

$$\frac{speculating\ s_s \qquad s_s \rightsquigarrow s'_s}{(s_{ns}, s_s) \rightsquigarrow_2 (s_{ns}, s'_s)} \qquad \frac{\neg\ speculating\ s_s \qquad s_s \rightsquigarrow s'_s \qquad s_{ns} \rightsquigarrow s'_{ns}}{(s_{ns}, s_s) \rightsquigarrow_2 (s'_{ns}, s'_s)}$$

$$\frac{(s_1, s_3) \rightsquigarrow_2 (s'_1, s'_3) \qquad (s_2, s_4) \rightsquigarrow_2 (s'_2, s'_4)}{(s_1, s_2, s_3, s_4) \rightsquigarrow_4 (s'_1, s'_2, s'_3, s'_4)}$$

Fig. 5. Transition rules for the states in the four traces of TPOD, where s_s and s_{ns} are states with and without speculation, respectively

4.2   Operational Semantics

We represent the operational semantics defined in §3 in our Isabelle/HOL theories using Hoare-style triples ($\{P\}\ S\ \{Q\}$), similar to those introduced in the Isabelle/HOL proofs for the seL4 kernel [16]. In our model, we define the precondition P and postcondition Q as state predicates and the statement S as a state transformer. Moreover, since the instructions to be executed can be determined from the pre-state s using $s.\iota$, we consider predicate transformers of the form $\{P\} \rightsquigarrow \{Q\}$. This expression of the operational semantics enables us to utilise intrinsic laws and properties of Hoare triples, such as strengthening, weakening and concatenation [14].

We introduce halting, defined by $halting \doteq pc_n \notin \Pi$ to describe a state with a program counter that does not point to an instruction in Π. At this point the program cannot advance and must resolve if speculating. We say a state s has terminated ($terminates(s)$) iff it is halting and not speculating such that $terminates(s) \doteq halting(s) \wedge \neg speculating(s)$. If the system terminates it will stutter, at which point we can trivially infer $\{P\} \rightsquigarrow \{P\}$.

As TPOD is a four-trace hyperproperty, we are required to transition each of the four system states simultaneously. This means that for a system with k transition rules, we must consider k^4 cases across all the four traces which quickly becomes intractable. Many of theses cases are spurious and cannot occur within a well-formed TPOD execution. For example, state pairs (s_1, s_3) and (s_2, s_4) are *operationally equivalent* if the execute the same low and high operations and therefore maintain the same architectural state. Operationally equivalent state pairs can be transitioned synchronously using a new transition rule $\rightsquigarrow_2$, which is defined using $\rightsquigarrow$ (see Fig. 5). This reduces the quadratic complexity of checking two traces to a linear check. This reduction can be performed on both speculating and non-speculating states, leading to a 4-way synchronous check $\rightsquigarrow_4$, which reduced k^4 interleavings to a linear check as well.

By the definition of low equivalence of states $s_a \approx_{\mathcal{L}} s_b$, s_a and s_b may have architectural differences iff these are high states or the program is speculating. Transitions only ever append to the set of program and memory addresses ω, an architectural system component verified in low equivalence. If at any point the predicate $violation_{\approx_{\mathcal{L}}}(s_a, s_b) \doteq s_a.\omega \preceq s_b.\omega \vee s_b.\omega \preceq s_a.\omega$ does not hold (where $\preceq$ denotes subsequence) then there exists no future transition in which $s_a.\omega = s_b.\omega$. Given a future transition in which we terminate in the low state s.t. $terminates(s) \wedge op_{\mathcal{L}}(s) \neq \bot$, we violate $s_a \approx_{\mathcal{L}} s_b$. In the case of the non speculative states s_1 and s_2 this will lead to an invalid trace, for the speculative states s_3 and s_4 this will violate TPOD.

We discuss execution traces in §4.3, and how we apply these predicates to catch invalid traces and violations of TPOD early.

4.3   Program Execution

Using concatenation rules for Hoare triples ($\{P\}$ S_1 $\{Q\} \wedge \{Q\}$ S_2 $\{R\}$ $\implies$ $\{P\}$ $S_1; S_2$ $\{R\}$) we construct an inductive predicate that defines a partial execution across four traces $execute(\pi_1, \pi_2, \pi_3, \pi_4)$ from any given system state given below. An execution is valid iff its traces are well-formed and each contain a single state, or the last two states in each trace are a valid transition. These execution traces are not required to satisfy the initial state requirements of the $conformant_A(\pi)$ predicate introduced in §3.2.

We use a predicate wfs to indicate that a state is well-formed. By showing that $\{wfs\} \rightsquigarrow \{wfs\}$ we build invariants that minimise spurious transitions and discharge trivially unreachable executions. This is extended to $\rightsquigarrow_2$ and $\rightsquigarrow_4$ for two and four-trace hyperproperties.

$execute(\pi_1, \pi_2, \pi_3, \pi_4) \doteq$

if $\pi_i = [s_i], i \in \{1, 2, 3, 4\}$ **then** $wfs4(s_1, s_2, s_3, s_4) \wedge violation_{\approx_{\mathcal{L}}}(s_1, s_2)$
else if $\pi_i = (\pi'_i[s_i])[s'_i], i \in \{1, 2, 3, 4\}$
then $(s_1, s_2, s_3, s_4) \rightsquigarrow_4 (s'_1, s'_2, s'_3, s'_4)$
$\wedge \ execute(\pi'_1[s_1], \pi'_2[s_2], \pi'_3[s_3], \pi'_4[s_4]) \wedge violation_{\approx_{\mathcal{L}}}(s_1, s_2)$

The theorem below, proven in Isabelle/HOL describes the trivial cases which when satisfied can discharge a proof of low equivalence $\pi_3 \approx_{\mathcal{L}} \pi_4$ across partial executions.

Theorem 2. *TPOD holds for any partial execution* $execute(\pi_1, \pi_2, \pi_3, \pi_4)$ *given any of the following hold:*

1. $\neg speculating(\pi_3^0) \wedge \neg speculating(\pi_4^0) \wedge \ \pi_3^0 \approx_{\mathcal{L}} \pi_4^0 \wedge$
   $((\forall i. \ \neg speculating(\pi_3^i)) \vee (\forall i. \ \neg speculating(\pi_4^i)))$,
2. $\forall i. \ op_{\mathcal{H}}(\pi_3^i) \neq \bot$,
3. $\forall i. \ speculating(\pi_3^i) \wedge speculating(\pi_4^i)$.

This theorem has been verified in Isabelle/HOL. Condition 1 inherently ensures that traces π_3 or π_4 do not speculate. Without speculation in traces π_3 and π_4 the architectural state remains constant and we satisfy low equivalence. Given we assume the initial states are not speculating and are architecturally equivalent we can infer for any i that $speculating(\pi_3^i)$ iff $speculating(\pi_4^i)$ as branch predictor will make the same prediction across all four traces. Therefore, we satisfy TPOD if π_3 or π_4 do not speculate. Conditions 2 and 3 ensures all states in a trace execute high operations or are speculative respectively. As the adversary cannot observe the trusted 'high' state or any speculative state then low equivalence will trivially hold, even if the architectural state is not equivalent.

We can join two partial executions given the first execution ends in four parallel states that transition (via $\leadsto_4$) to the initial four states in the second execution. This allows us to simplify TPOD proof obligations by joining trivially low equivalent partial executions with complex partial executions that require stepwise proofs. Using overloading, we also use $\cdot$ notation to mean sequence concatenation and sequence prepending.

$$\frac{execute(\pi_1[s_1], \pi_2[s_2], \pi_3[s_3], \pi_4[s_4]) \\ execute([s_1']\pi_1', [s_2']\pi_2', [s_3']\pi_3', [s_4']\pi_4') \\ (s_1, s_2, s_3, s_4) \leadsto_4 (s_1', s_2', s_3', s_4')}{execute(\pi_1 \cdot [s_1, s_1'] \cdot \pi_1', \pi_2 \cdot [s_2, s_2'] \cdot \pi_2', \pi_3 \cdot [s_3, s_3'] \cdot \pi_3', \pi_4 \cdot [s_4, s_4'] \cdot \pi_4')}$$

Finally, we define the predicate $execute_{TPOD}(\pi_1, \pi_2, \pi_3, \pi_4)$ which ensures a *full* and *conformant* (according to §3.2) execution of a program which eventually terminates in a low state. Given this, we can infer that if $\exists i.violation_{\approx_{\mathcal{L}}}(\pi_1^i, \pi_2^i)$ holds then our execution is invalid and if $\exists i.violation_{\approx_{\mathcal{L}}}(\pi_3^i, \pi_4^i)$ holds we violate $\pi_3 \approx_{\mathcal{L}} \pi_4$. It is sufficient to verify that TPOD holds for all execution traces that satisfy $execute_{TPOD}(\pi_1, \pi_2, \pi_3, \pi_4)$ to show that the program is secure in the context of TPOD.

5   Case Studies

Paul Kocher provided 15 victim functions [17] to test the effectiveness of MSVC's Spectre mitigations and placement of speculative fences, realised as `lfence` in Intel x86 and `CSDB` in ARM. These examples are variations on the vulnerable code discussed in §2.1. We have used our framework to show that all 15 examples contain secure speculation vulnerabilities prior to mitigation.

We also verify the correctness of Examples 1, 2 and 8 from [17]. Of these, Examples 1 and 2 compile to the same BIL, thus only require one proof in Isabelle/HOL. Example 8 uses a ternary operator to perform a bounds check, which changes the logical flow such that `array1` and `array2` are always indexed even if the program is out-of-bounds.

MSVC correctly identifies and fixes the secure speculation vulnerability in Examples 1 and 2 by placing a speculative fence immediately after the branch statement shown in Listing 1.3. However, placement of the speculative fence is not optimal. It occurs *prior* to either of the memory reads and any of the other non-vulnerable instructions. A more optimal solution is to move the `specfence` so that it is executed immediately before `00001c6d`. This optimised version of the program has also been proven correct using our Isabelle/HOL framework.

MSVC is unable to correctly place a `specfence` for the remaining 13 examples. We manually insert the necessary fences in Example 8, and prove that this modified program satisfies secure speculation.

```
 1  00000336:  when x >= array1_length goto %00000330
 2  00001bb8:  specfence // compiler generated (sub-optimal)
 3  00001bbd:  RAX := mem[array2, el]:u64
 4  00001bc4:  RDX := mem[array1, el]:u64
 5  00001bdc:  ... // some processing on the index of array1 RDX
 6  00001c1c:  RDX := mem[RDX, el]:u64
 7  00001c54:  ... // some processing on the index of array2 RAX
 8  00001c6d:  RDX := mem[RAX, el]:u64
 9  00001c54:  ... // some processing on the index of array2 RAX
10  00000330:  ... // end of program
```

Listing 1.3. Excerpt of MSVC solution in BIL. The placement of the **specfence** is sub-optimal and can be moved so that it is executed immediately before 00001c6d

6 Related Work

Proving correctness of secure speculation has received a lot of attention in recent years. Abstract models capable of describing Spectre-like attacks have been developed using CSP [7] and pomsets [8]. Such models are further removed from the original programs, and hence, additional work is required to link proofs with the programs themselves. In contrast, our workflow (Fig. 1) ensures that we verify the compiled assembly generated from the original program.

Correctness of secure speculation is of particular interest in the context of cryptographic code [4,11,28]. The properties of interest for cryptographic code are stronger than TPOD, making these proofs simpler since violations are easier to detect. We are interested in general programs making TPOD more applicable.

As far as we're aware, the novel TPOD is the only example of a hyper-property utilised in respect to secure speculation. TPOD is most comparable to observational determinism, which lacks the flexibility to sufficiently differentiate violations of secure speculation from correct behaviour.

Many of the analysis techniques have associated tools. For hardware, this includes SAT-based approaches [27] and Unique Program Execution Checking (UPEC) [9]. For languages, tools include those based on static analysis [4], static typing [28], concolic analysis [12] and model checking [5]. Such tools are fine-tuned to handle a specific property (often more restrictive than TPOD) with a fixed execution semantics, and there is no guarantee that tools themselves are correct. Our theorem proving-based approach is more transparent. Moreover, we also have flexibility to openly change the operational semantics (to incorporate other architectural features) and the properties being verified independently.

Our proofs do not yet consider more sophisticated behaviours, e.g., out-of-order executions, thus we do not yet check the full range of Spectre variants. However, the introduction of out-of-order executions introduces a large amount of non-determinism meaning existing tools (including [4,12,29]) become infeasible [12]. It will be interesting to see the impact of these (more permissive) behaviours for our current proof technique in future work.

7   Conclusions

This paper has presented a mechanisation of a recently developed operational semantics by Cheang et al. [5] in Isabelle/HOL. The mechanisation integrates with an existing workflow (Fig. 1) that allows one to trace the Isabelle/HOL theories back to original C programs. One of our core contributions is a translation tool that generates Isabelle/HOL theories for BIL representations of the C program. As discussed in §6 existing tools on verifying secure speculation are generally based on symbolic or static analysis of the programs, in contrast to our methods, which are based on Hoare-logic encodings within a deductive proof environment. Our mechanisation closely follows Cheang et al. [5], but it also reveals some minor issues in their presentation, and alternative characterisations for some aspects of the operational semantics, as discussed earlier.

The most challenging aspect of our development has been the state space explosion caused by the fact that for a state transition with k possible transition rules, since TPOD is a four-trace hyperproperty, a naive expansion would required one to consider k^4 cases for each step, which is infeasible. Our solution is described in §4.3. Further proof optimisation has been achieved by identifying programs and partial executions that that trivially satisfy TPOD, which allows one to discharge proofs of large sections of code automatically (see §4.3).

In future work, we will extend our approach to understand and verify the requirements of a Spectre-safe library as well as considering next generation Spectre vulnerabilities mitigated by recompilation. We also aim to move our approach forward with the modern web, e.g., WebAssembly, into our model and verifying that this too is secure against Spectre.

References

1. Brumley, D., Jager, I., Avgerinos, T., Schwartz, E.J.: BAP: a binary analysis platform. In: Gopalakrishnan, G., Qadeer, S. (eds.) Computer Aided Verification, CAV 2011. LNCS, vol. 6806, pp. 463–469. Springer, Heidelberg (2011). https://doi.org/10.1007/978-3-642-22110-1_37
2. Bulck, J.V., et al.: Foreshadow: extracting the keys to the Intel SGX kingdom with transient out-of-order execution. In: Enck, W., Felt, A.P. (eds.) USENIX Security Symposium, pp. 991–1008. USENIX Association (2018). https://www.usenix.org/conference/usenixsecurity18/presentation/bulck
3. Canella, C., et al.: Fallout: leaking data on meltdown-resistant CPUs. In: Cavallaro, L., Kinder, J., Wang, X., Katz, J. (eds.) CCS, pp. 769–784. ACM (2019). https://doi.org/10.1145/3319535.3363219
4. Cauligi, S., et al.: Constant-time foundations for the new spectre era. In: Donaldson, A.F., Torlak, E. (eds.) PLDI, pp. 913–926. ACM (2020). https://doi.org/10.1145/3385412.3385970
5. Cheang, K., Rasmussen, C., Seshia, S.A., Subramanyan, P.: A formal approach to secure speculation. In: CSF, pp. 288–303. IEEE (2019). https://doi.org/10.1109/CSF.2019.00027
6. Clarkson, M.R., Schneider, F.B.: Hyperproperties. J. Comput. Secur. **18**(6), 1157–1210 (2010). https://doi.org/10.3233/JCS-2009-0393

7. Colvin, R.J., Winter, K.: An abstract semantics of speculative execution for reasoning about security vulnerabilities. In: Sekerinski, E., et al. (eds.) Formal Methods. FM 2019 International Workshops, FM 2019. LNCS, vol. 12233, pp. 323–341. Springer, Cham (2020). https://doi.org/10.1007/978-3-030-54997-8_21
8. Disselkoen, C., Jagadeesan, R., Jeffrey, A., Riely, J.: The code that never ran: modeling attacks on speculative evaluation. In: IEEE S and P, pp. 1238–1255. IEEE (2019). https://doi.org/10.1109/SP.2019.00047
9. Fadiheh, M.R., Müller, J., Brinkmann, R., Mitra, S., Stoffel, D., Kunz, W.: A formal approach for detecting vulnerabilities to transient execution attacks in out-of-order processors. In: IEEE DAC, pp. 1–6. IEEE (2020). https://doi.org/10.1109/DAC18072.2020.9218572
10. Griffin, M., Dongol, B.: Isabelle files for Verifying Secure Speculation in Isabelle/HOL (2021). https://figshare.com/s/c185541c43a7cac258b6
11. Guanciale, R., Balliu, M., Dam, M.: Inspectre: breaking and fixing microarchitectural vulnerabilities by formal analysis. In: Ligatti, J., Ou, X., Katz, J., Vigna, G. (eds.) CCS, pp. 1853–1869. ACM (2020). https://doi.org/10.1145/3372297.3417246
12. Guarnicri, M., Köpf, B., Morales, J.F., Reineke, J., Sánchez, A.: Spectector: principled detection of speculative information flows. In: 2020 IEEE Symposium on Security and Privacy, SP 2020, San Francisco, CA, USA, 18–21 May 2020, pp. 1–19. IEEE (2020). https://doi.org/10.1109/SP40000.2020.00011
13. Intel: Transient execution attacks and related security issues by CPU. Tech. rep., Intel (2019). https://software.intel.com/security-software-guidance/processors-affected-transient-execution-attack-mitigation-product-cpu-model Accessed 5 May 2021
14. Kaldewaij, A.: Programming - the Derivation of Algorithms. Prentice Hall International Series in Computer Science. Prentice Hall, Hoboken (1990)
15. Kiriansky, V., Lebedev, I.A., Amarasinghe, S.P., Devadas, S., Emer, J.S.: DAWG: a defense against cache timing attacks in speculative execution processors. In: MICRO, pp. 974–987. IEEE Computer Society (2018). https://doi.org/10.1109/MICRO.2018.00083
16. Klein, G., et al.: seL4: formal verification of an OS kernel. In: Matthews, J.N., Anderson, T.E. (eds.) SOSP, pp. 207–220. ACM (2009). https://doi.org/10.1145/1629575.1629596
17. Kocher, P.: Spectre mitigations in microsoft's c/c++ compiler (2018). https://www.paulkocher.com/doc/MicrosoftCompilerSpectreMitigation.html. Accessed 5 May 2021
18. Kocher, P., et al.: Spectre attacks: exploiting speculative execution. In: IEEE S and P, pp. 1–19. IEEE (2019). https://doi.org/10.1109/SP.2019.00002
19. Lipp, M., et al.: Meltdown: reading kernel memory from user space. In: Enck, W., Felt, A.P. (eds.) USENIX Security Symposium, pp. 973–990. USENIX Association (2018). https://www.usenix.org/conference/usenixsecurity18/presentation/lipp
20. McLean, J.: Proving noninterference and functional correctness using traces. J. Comput. Secur. 1(1), 37–58 (1992). https://doi.org/10.3233/JCS-1992-1103
21. Prout, A., et al.: Measuring the impact of spectre and meltdown. In: IEEE HPEC, pp. 1–5. IEEE (2018). https://doi.org/10.1109/HPEC.2018.8547554
22. Rasmussen, C.: Secure Speculation: From Vulnerability to Assurances with UCLID5. Master's Thesis, EECS Department, University of California, Berkeley, May 2019. http://www2.eecs.berkeley.edu/Pubs/TechRpts/2019/EECS-2019-95.html

23. Ren, X., Moody, L., Taram, M., Jordan, M., Tullsen, D.M., Venkat, A.: I see dead μops: leaking secrets via Intel/AMD micro-op caches. In: ISCA (2021). https://www.cs.virginia.edu/venkat/papers/isca2021a.pdf

24. Roscoe, A.W.: CSP and determinism in security modelling. In: IEEE S and P, pp. 114–127. IEEE Computer Society (1995). https://doi.org/10.1109/SECPRI.1995.398927

25. Seshia, S.A., Subramanyan, P.: UCLID5: integrating modeling, verification, synthesis and learning. In: MEMOCODE, pp. 1–10. IEEE (2018). https://doi.org/10.1109/MEMCOD.2018.8556946

26. Taram, M., Venkat, A., Tullsen, D.M.: Context-sensitive fencing: securing speculative execution via microcode customization. In: Bahar, I., Herlihy, M., Witchel, E., Lebeck, A.R. (eds.) ASPLOS, pp. 395–410. ACM (2019). https://doi.org/10.1145/3297858.3304060

27. Trippel, C., Lustig, D., Martonosi, M.: Security verification via automatic hardware-aware exploit synthesis: the checkmate approach. IEEE Micro **39**(3), 84–93 (2019). https://doi.org/10.1109/MM.2019.2910010

28. Vassena, M., et al.: Automatically eliminating speculative leaks from cryptographic code with blade. In: Proceedings of the ACM Programming Language 5(POPL), 1–30 (2021). https://doi.org/10.1145/3434330

29. Wang, G., Chattopadhyay, S., Biswas, A.K., Mitra, T., Roychoudhury, A.: Kleespectre: detecting information leakage through speculative cache attacks via symbolic execution. ACM Trans. Softw. Eng. Methodol. **29**(3), 14:1–14:31 (2020). https://doi.org/10.1145/3385897

Two Mechanisations of WebAssembly 1.0

Conrad Watt[1]($\boxtimes$), Xiaojia Rao[2], Jean Pichon-Pharabod[1], Martin Bodin[2,3],
and Philippa Gardner[2]

[1] University of Cambridge, Cambridge, UK
conrad.watt@cl.cam.ac.uk
[2] Imperial College London, London, UK
[3] Inria, Rocquencourt, France

Abstract. WebAssembly (Wasm) is a new bytecode language supported
by all major Web browsers, designed primarily to be an efficient compilation target for low-level languages such as C/C++ and Rust. It is
unusual in that it is officially specified through a formal semantics. An
initial draft specification was published in 2017 [14], with an associated
mechanised specification in Isabelle/HOL published by Watt that found
bugs in the original specification, fixed before its publication [37].
The first official W3C standard, WebAssembly 1.0, was published
in 2019 [45]. Building on Watt's original mechanisation, we introduce
two mechanised specifications of the WebAssembly 1.0 semantics, written in different theorem provers: WasmCert-Isabelle and WasmCert-Coq.
Wasm's compact design and official formal semantics enable our mechanisations to be particularly complete and close to the published language
standard. We present a high-level description of the language's updated
type soundness result, referencing both mechanisations. We also describe
the current state of the mechanisation of language features not previously
supported: WasmCert-Isabelle includes a verified executable definition
of the instantiation phase as part of an executable verified interpreter;
WasmCert-Coq includes executable parsing and numeric definitions as
on-going work towards a more ambitious end-to-end verified interpreter
which does not require an OCaml harness like WasmCert-Isabelle.

Keywords: Mechanised specification · Type soundness · WasmCert

1 Introduction

WebAssembly (Wasm) is a new bytecode language, primarily designed as a compilation target for low-level languages such as C/C++ and Rust. It is supported
by all major Web browsers, allowing programs compiled to Wasm to be embedded in Web pages and executed client-side. Because a Web site may attempt
to execute arbitrary Wasm code in a visitor's browser, the language is designed
around strict principles of encapsulation. A Wasm program is made up of one
or more modules, which can only interact with the wider system through explicitly declared imports and exports. Moreover, the language defines a strict, static
type system, and all programs must be type-checked before execution.

© Springer Nature Switzerland AG 2021
M. Huisman et al. (Eds.): FM 2021, LNCS 13047, pp. 61–79, 2021.
https://doi.org/10.1007/978-3-030-90870-6_4

Wasm's official specification includes a formal semantics for the language, with a precise statement of the intended type soundness property. This formal approach to specification is unusual for a language created by industry. It was first published in an initial draft in 2017 [14], and then in the official standard, called WebAssembly 1.0 (Wasm 1.0), in 2019 [45].

Our goal is to develop a mechanised specification of Wasm 1.0 and verify the associated type soundness result. Many people have explored the mechanisation of real-world language specifications, especially using the Isabelle/HOL and Coq theorem provers; see Sect. 5 on related work. The accurate mechanisation of a standard can be difficult because the language may be huge and continually evolving (e.g. JavaScript [5]), underspecified (e.g. C [24]), and/or tricky to state precisely (e.g. relaxed memory concurrency [3]). Wasm 1.0 is an interesting target for mechanised specification because it is small, stable and formally specified.

We present two mechanised specifications of Wasm 1.0: WasmCert-Isabelle, written in the Isabelle/HOL theorem prover, and WasmCert-Coq, in the Coq theorem prover[1]. We prove type soundness for both specifications. Our work builds directly on Watt's mechanised specification in Isabelle/HOL of the 2017 draft semantics [37], which discovered and corrected bugs in the original specification and the statement of type soundness [37]. The Wasm 1.0 standard currently cites Watt's old work as the source of the language's type soundness proof [45]. Watt's mechanisation follows a methodology for establishing trust in mechanised specification, developed as part of the JSCert project, a Coq-mechanisation of JavaScript [5]. Watt's mechanised specification of Wasm's type checker and the runtime semantics is line-by-line close to the standard, an achievement made easier by Wasm's formal semantics. In addition, a separate type checker and executable interpreter are mechanised, with the type checker proven correct with respect to the mechanised type system, and the interpreter proven correct with respect to mechanised runtime semantics. These executable definitions are independently tested using the official test suite.

We pool our substantial experience with Wasm and mechanised language specification to develop our Wasm 1.0 mechanised specification. Our contributions are:

- WasmCert-Isabelle: our Isabelle/HOL mechanisation of the Wasm 1.0 semantics which extends and refactors the mechanisation of Watt [37], including the type soundness proof, type checker, and interpreter, to Wasm 1.0. This includes a number of editorial changes to the runtime semantics (Sect. 2), and an additional condition in the statement of type soundness (Sect. 3). We also give a verified mechanisation of the instantiation phase of the Wasm execution, which was not included in the 2017 draft semantics nor Watt's original mechanisation (Sect. 4). This work is also reported in Watt's PhD thesis [38].
- WasmCert-Coq: our fresh Coq mechanisation of the Wasm 1.0 semantics, which closely follows the structure of WasmCert-Isabelle. We include a mechanised proof of type soundness and document the common high-level proof

---

[1] Our mechanisations are distributed under open source licences on GitHub [36].

structure between the mechanisations (Sect. 3). We also include executable mechanisations of WebAssembly's numeric operations and binary decoding phase, which were not formalised in the 2017 draft semantics nor mechanised by Watt, and are not yet handled by WasmCert-Isabelle (Sect. 4). We also report on progress towards the verification of a more ambitious end-to-end executable interpreter which does not require an OCaml harness (see below).

We summarise our WasmCert-Isabelle and WasmCert-Coq specifications, contrasting them with Watt's original work. We mark ✗ to indicate a feature or proof which is not included, ✓ to mark a feature or proof which has been fully mechanised, ✓✓ to indicate that a feature is accompanied by a verified executable definition capable of OCaml extraction, and ✓✓+ to indicate additionally that the executable definition has been validated through full end-to-end execution of the Wasm 1.0 test suite.

	Watt 2018	WasmCert-Isabelle	WasmCert-Coq
Wasm 1.0 refactorings	✗	✓	✓
type system	✓✓+	✓✓+	✓✓
runtime semantics	✓✓+	✓✓+	✓✓
type soundness proof	✓	✓	✓
binary decoding	✗	✗	✓✓
numeric ops	✗	✗	✓✓
instantiation	✗	✓✓+	✓

The 2017 draft semantics and Watt's original mechanisation did not cover three main areas of the language: the binary decoding phase, where a Wasm program distributed as bytecode is decoded into the program AST; numeric operations, most notably floating-point operations; and the instantiation phase, which runs after decoding but prior to execution and performs linking and state allocation. Watt's extracted interpreter relied on an OCaml harness to fill in these three areas with unverified implementations. WasmCert-Isabelle continues to model the decoding phase and numeric operations as uninterpreted functions, but mechanises the Wasm 1.0 specification of instantiation and allocation, including a verified executable implementation, thus significantly reducing the size of the unverified OCaml harness. This implementation was non-trivial due to the standard's circular definition of instantiation (see Sect. 4). We validate WasmCert-Isabelle's extracted interpeter against the Wasm 1.0 official test suite [39].

WasmCert-Coq takes a more ambitious approach to its in-progress verified interpreter. It uses CompCert's mechanised int and float libraries [7,8] to implement Wasm 1.0 numerics, and the Parseque parser combinator library [1,2] to mechanise Wasm 1.0's binary decoding phase. It provides an executable interpreter and type checker, both proven correct with respect to the mechanised semantics. It includes a mechanisation of the instantiation phase and an associated mechanised implementation, not yet shown to be correct. We consider this proof to be high-priority future work, along with end-to-end testing using the Wasm 1.0 test suite.

2 Wasm 1.0 Core Semantics

We describe the runtime semantics and type system of Wasm 1.0, highlighting where Wasm 1.0 diverges from the draft formalisation [14] and summarising the WasmCert-Isabelle and WasmCert-Coq mechnaisations of this core semantics.

2.1 Core Concepts

Values. Wasm operations manipulate values of four fundamental *value types*: i32, i64, f32, and f64. These are 32- and 64-bit integers and floats, respectively. Every program value in Wasm has one of these types. Functions are not first-class, and must be called in a first-order, fully applied manner, with a limited mechanism for dynamic dispatch which incurs additional runtime checks.

The Stack. Wasm is a stack-based language. Each function call is associated with its own *value stack*, abstractly represented as a list of values, and operations within the call will push and pop values to/from the stack in the course of computation. Wasm's stack is governed by a course-grained dataflow type system similar to that of the Java Virtual Machine [22], which ensures that the shape of the stack is statically known at every program point. The value stack *only* contains values - the function's return address is not programmatically accessible.

Modules. The *module* is Wasm's unit of compilation. A module contains a list of Wasm function declarations, as well as declarations of "global" state which is accessible to any function (described below). Modules may share global state with each other through a system of explicit imports and exports.

Globals. Wasm modules may declare or import *global variables*. A global variable has a statically declared value type, and is accessible by any function within the module. A global variable may be exported, allowing it to be accessible through other modules. Individual Wasm functions may also declare *local variables*, which are scoped to their declaring function, and are either initialised with one of the function arguments, or default to 0 otherwise.

Memory. Wasm modules may declare or import a *memory*. A Wasm memory is a simple buffer of bytes. A value may be stored in memory: this converts the value to a list of bytes and stores it at a provided offset. Similarly, a value may be loaded from memory, by interpreting the list of bytes at a provided offset as a value of the requested type. Wasm guarantees that this process always succeeds and is stable in both directions - unlike C, values have no trap representations.

Table. Wasm modules may declare or import a function *table*. Functions stored in the table can be called by dynamic dispatch, although the function's type signature must be checked at runtime.

Control Flow. Within a function, Wasm does not provide any arbitrary goto instruction. Instead, Wasm provides explicit **block**, **loop**, and **if** labelled/scoped constructs, together with a **br** (break) instruction which may target any enclosing label. This style of control flow is sometimes called *semi-structured*, and is common in higher-level languages such as Java and JavaScript. Wasm's label constructs (**block**, **loop**, **if**) are explicitly type-annotated with the shape of the value stack at their beginning and end, to preserve the invariant that all control flow paths to a program point result in the same stack shape, and to simplify type checking. Control may only be transferred out of a function through a **call** to another function, or through a **return** to the calling function.

2.2 Abstract Syntax

We give a brief overview of Wasm's abstract syntax. In formal definitions, some components are greyed out (here is an example) to indicate that we do not describe them in detail. While we must partially elide some definitions for space reasons, they are included in full in our mechanisations, and the exhaustive pen-and-paper formalism can be found in the Wasm 1.0 specification [45].

Figure 1 contains the formal definitions of Wasm's core abstract syntax. In the abstract syntax it suffices to model static *immediates* as natural numbers, although they are often concretely restricted to a 32-bit range. Many parts of the Wasm state are referenced through immediates representing De Bruijn indices, rather than through explicit names. The four value types are self-explanatory. Function types are used by control constructs and functions in Wasm, which must be explicitly type-annotated to describe how the shape of the value stack changes across their execution. The pre-execution validation pass checks that these annotations are correct. An annotation *ft* describes the shape of the top of the stack before and after execution of the construct/function.

We briefly describe Wasm instructions. The (t.**const** c) instruction pushes the value c of type t onto the value stack. The *stackop* instructions provide pure operations for pushing and popping values to and from the value stack. For example, the **i32.add** instruction pops two i32 values from the stack and pushes the i32 result of their unsigned wrap-around addition. The validation pass ensures that instructions only pop values which are guaranteed to be on the stack at that program point.

The **local** and **global** instructions deal with accessing local and global variables. For example, (**local.get** i) pushes the current value of the i-th declared local variable of the function onto the stack, while (**global.set** i) pops a value from the stack and assigns it to the i-th declared global variable of the module.

The (t.**load**) instruction pops an i32 value from the stack to use as an index into the module's memory, and pushes a value of type t that is deserialised from the bytes at that location. The (t.**store**) instruction pops a value of type t and

$$
\begin{array}{lrcl}
\text{(immediates)} & i, min, max & ::= & nat \\
\text{(value types)} & t & ::= & \textsf{i32} \mid \textsf{i64} \mid \textsf{f32} \mid \textsf{f64} \\
\text{(func/block types)} & ft & ::= & t^* \to t^*
\end{array}
$$

$$
\begin{array}{lrcl}
\text{(instructions)} & e & ::= & t.\textbf{const}\ c \mid \textbf{i32.add} \mid other\ stackops \mid \\
& & & \textbf{local.\{get/set\}}\ i \mid \textbf{global.\{get/set\}}\ i \mid \\
& & & t.\textbf{load}\ flags \mid t.\textbf{store}\ flags \mid \\
& & & \textbf{memory.size} \mid \textbf{memory.grow} \mid \\
& & & \textbf{block}\ ft\ e^* \mid \textbf{loop}\ ft\ e^* \mid \textbf{if}\ ft\ e^*\ e^* \mid \\
& & & \textbf{br}\ i \mid \textbf{br\_if}\ i \mid \textbf{br\_table}\ i^+ \mid \\
& & & \textbf{call}\ i \mid \textbf{call\_indirect}\ i \mid \textbf{return}
\end{array}
$$

$$
\begin{array}{lrcl}
\text{(functions)} & func & ::= & \textbf{func}\ i\ t^*\ e^* \\
\text{(globals)} & glob & ::= & \textbf{glob mutable}^?\ t\ e_{\textsf{init}} \\
\text{(memories)} & mem & ::= & \textbf{mem}\ min\ max \\
\text{(tables)} & tab & ::= & \textbf{tab}\ min\ max
\end{array}
$$

(modules) $m ::=$
  { types :: ft^*, funcs :: $func^*$, globs :: $glob^*$, mems :: mem^*, tabs :: tab^*,
   data :: ... , elem :: ... , imports :: ... , exports :: ... }

WasmCert-Isabelle: `wasm_ast.thy` and `wasm_module.thy`
WasmCert-Coq: `datatypes.v`

Fig. 1. Wasm abstract syntax

an i32 index, and serialises the value into bytes at that location in memory. Both of these instructions have slight variant behaviours which are configured using intra-instruction flags, the details of which we elide. The indices provided to these instructions are dynamically bounds-checked against the size/length of the module's memory. The current size of memory can be explicitly checked through **memory.size**, and grown through **memory.grow**.

Wasm provides only *semi-structured* control flow constructs. Its **block**, **loop**, and **if** instructions define break targets. Code within the body of one of these constructs can target the construct with one of the **br** family of instructions, which works like the `break` instruction of a higher-level language, with **br_if** and **br_table** being forms of conditional break. Multiple nested constructs are allowed, with (**br** k) instruction breaking to the k-th enclosing label.

The (**call** k) instruction calls the k-th function declared or imported by the current module. The (**call_indirect** k) instruction is Wasm's dynamic dispatch call. It pops an i32 index j from the stack, and the function stored in the table at index j is called. The static index k references a type annotation declared by the module, and the dynamically indexed function is checked to have this type annotation. Execution is halted with an error if the check fails. The **return** instruction ends the current call, and returns control to the caller, possibly pushing values onto the caller's stack corresponding to the function's output type.

The top-level Wasm module contains the declarations of globally-scoped state (functions, globals, memories, tables). Functions must carry an explicit type annotation, which is encoded as an immediate i referencing a canonical list of function types held by the module. This indirection to a canonical list was newly introduced in Wasm 1.0 to shift the abstract syntax of the language to more closely mirror its bytecode format, which has a distinguished "types" declaration section. Globals must declare whether they are mutable, their value type, and an optional initialiser expression which is executed at start-up. Memories and tables must declare their minimum and maximum sizes (although currently only the memory can be grown, the table size will be used by future features [41]). Note that in Wasm 1.0 a module may only declare/import at most one memory and one table in total, although this restriction will be lifted in future.

2.3   Runtime Semantics

WebAssembly's runtime semantics is specified in terms of a small-step reduction of *configurations*. A Wasm configuration is of the form $S; F; e^*$, where S is the execution-wide *store*, F is the *frame* of the current function, and e^* is the code fragment comprising the list of intructions currently under execution.

(store) $S ::= \{ \text{ funcs} :: \mathit{finst}^*, \text{ globs} :: \mathit{ginst}^*, \text{ mems} :: \mathit{minst}^*, \text{ tabs} :: \mathit{tinst}^* \}$

(frame) $F ::= \{ \text{ locs} :: v^*, \text{ inst} ::= \mathit{inst} \}$

The store contains all the module state which has been created in the course of execution. Its fields hold the runtime representations of the globally-scoped state declared by the constituent modules of the executing program (see Sect. 2.2). We elide the precise definitions of these components, but their structures are runtime versions of the static declarations made by the module, as shown in Fig. 1. The frame holds information relevant to the currently executing function. It holds the current values of local variables (in a list representation), and the *instance*. The instance tracks which components of the store are in scope for the current function (because they were declared/imported by the function's enclosing module). We elide the further details of its formal structure.

The value stack is not given explicitly as part of Wasm's runtime configuration. Instead, the value stack is represented in each reduction rule through a leading list of **const** instructions. For example, the reduction rule for **i32.add** is:

$$S; F; (\textbf{i32.const } j)(\textbf{i32.const } k)(\textbf{i32.add}) \hookrightarrow S; F; (\textbf{i32.const } (j + k))$$

This reduction rule represents the consumption of two stack values j and k by the **i32.add** instruction, and the production of the stack value $j + k$. This computation leaves the store S and the frame F unchanged.

This configuration was refactored in the move from the draft specification to the Wasm 1.0 standard. Originally, the frame was not an explicit component of the configuration. Instead, all executing instances were held as an additional list field in the store, and reduction was parameterised by an integer indexing this list, denoting the instance used by the current executing code fragment.

Mechanisation. Our mechanisations of the Wasm 1.0 runtime semantics, the executable interpreter and the correctness proof can be found as follows:

Mechanisation of the reduction rules which define the runtime semantics:

WasmCert-{Isabelle/Coq}: `reduce in {wasm.thy/opsem.v}`

Mechanisation of an executable interpreter:
WasmCert-Isabelle: `wasm_interpreter.thy`
WasmCert-Coq: `interpreter_func.v`

Proof that the interpreter is sound with respect to the reduction rules:
WasmCert-Isabelle: `wasm_interpreter_properties.thy`
WasmCert-Coq: `interpreter_func_sound.v`

WasmCert-Isabelle's interpreter definitions and proofs are based on those of Watt [37]. We refactor the interpreter to use the Wasm 1.0 definition of configuration, as discussed above. Orthogonally, we significantly simplify the Isabelle/HOL proof of interpreter soundness, removing ∼800 lines of code from the original proof due to better use of high-level Isabelle tactics.

2.4   Validation

Wasm programs must be *validated* before they can be executed. The validation involves a type-checking pass which checks the correctness of function and block type annotations, and enforces the following properties for code in the module:

– Operations which pop from the value stack (such as **i32.add**) are guaranteed that the value stack will contain the values necessary to allow the pop;
– Operations which access state using a static index are checked to ensure that the index is in the bounds, e.g. every (**global.get** i) instruction is checked to ensure that at least $i + 1$ global variables have been declared/imported;
– **br** instructions must target an enclosing label construct, and the shape of the value stack at the point of the **br** must match construct's type annotation.

The typing judgement for a Wasm code fragment has the shape $C \vdash e^* : ft$, associating a list of Wasm expressions e^* with a function type ft in typing context C. The definition of the typing context and some selected typing rules are shown in Fig. 2. The typing context C tracks the types of state (e.g. global variables) which have been declared by the enclosing module and are available in the current environment, as well as currently in-scope label (for **br**) and return (for **return**) targets. We elide the full definitions of some fields of the typing context which are not required to understand the examples in this paper. The local component of the context C holds the types of the declared local variables as a list which is indexed by instructions such as **local.get**. The label component of C holds the list of break targets currently defined by the enclosing program context. Its structure is a list of stack types (list of list of value types). Each stack type represents the required shape of the stack at the point the break target is broken to. The syntax {label t_2^*} $\oplus C$ in the typing of **block** describes the addition of the entry t_2^* to the left of C's label list. When a **block** is targetted by **br**, execution jumps to the end of the block, so the block's output type is inserted into the label context. The **br** instruction counts outwards through enclosing contexts to determine its break target, and therefore requires its input type to match the required type of the k-th enclosing label. The return component of C functions similarly. When typing a function, the return component is set to the output type of the function, and is used for typing the **return** instruction. Note though that the return component is optional. When typing a top-level configuration, the return type is set to empty, to denote that the code inside cannot return out of the top level.

Mechanisation. Our mechanisations of the inductive typing rules of the Wasm type system (see Fig. 2) can be found as follows:

 WasmCert-Isabelle: `b_e_typing` in `wasm.thy`
 WasmCert-Coq: `be_typing` in `typing.v`

Mechanisation of an executable type checker:

 WasmCert-Isabelle: `wasm_checker.thy`
 WasmCert-Coq: `type_checker.v`

Proof that the type checker is correct with respect to the typing rules:

 WasmCert-Isabelle: `wasm_checker_properties.thy`
 WasmCert-Coq: `type_checker_reflects_typing.v`

$$C ::= \left\{ \begin{array}{l} \text{type} :: ft^*, \text{func} :: ft^*, \text{table} :: tt^*, \text{memory} :: mt^*, \text{global} :: gt^*, \\ \text{local} :: t^*, \text{label} :: (t^*)^*, \text{return} :: (t^*)^? \end{array} \right\}$$

$$\frac{}{C \vdash t.\textbf{const}\ c : \epsilon \to t} \qquad \frac{}{C \vdash \textbf{i32.add} : \text{i32 i32} \to \text{i32}} \qquad \frac{C.\text{local}[i] = t}{C \vdash \textbf{local.get}\ i : \epsilon \to t}$$

$$\frac{ft = t_1^* \to t_2^* \qquad \{\text{label}\ t_2^*\} \oplus C \vdash e^* : ft}{C \vdash \textbf{block}\ ft\ e^*\ \textbf{end} : ft} \qquad \frac{C.\text{label}[i] = t^*}{C \vdash \textbf{br}\ i : t_1^*\ t^* \to t_2^*}$$

Fig. 2. Selected typing rules.

3   Wasm 1.0 Type Soundness

The Wasm typing judgement described above is used by the standard as the basis of a standard statement of *syntactic type soundness* [46]. This involves defining an extended typing rule for runtime configurations [30] of the form $\vdash_c S; F; e^* : t^*$. This judgement associates a configuration with a stack type (using the typing judgement of Sect. 2.4 as we will see below), and the type soundness properties state that execution will either diverge, terminate with a runtime error (such as division by zero), or terminate with a value stack corresponding to the type t^*. Judgement definitions are found in our mechanisations here:

WasmCert-Isabelle: `wasm.thy`   WasmCert-Coq: `typing.v`

We give the high-level structure of important judgements, and the type sound-ness theorems. As previously mentioned, the formal definitions of the configura-tion and frame were refactored as part of the move from the draft specification to Wasm 1.0, with knock-on effects for the definitions of the associated judgements.

Configuration Validity. This is the top-level judgement in defining type sound-ness.

$$\frac{\vdash_s S : \mathsf{ok} \quad S; \epsilon \vdash_{\mathsf{loc}} F; e^* : t^*}{\vdash_c S; F; e^* : t^*}$$

Premise $\vdash_s S : \mathsf{ok}$ tracks well-formedness conditions on the store that must be preserved as language invariants (e.g. memories may not exceed their max size).

Local Validity. This types an instruction sequence under a given function frame.

$$\frac{S \vdash_f F : C \quad S; C \vdash e^* : \epsilon \to t^*}{S; \epsilon \vdash_{\mathsf{loc}} F; e^* : t^*}$$

The typing context C under which the instruction sequence is typed is deter-mined by the frame validity judgement defined below. Note that instruction sequence typing is defined via a slightly extended version of the judgement shown in Sect. 2.4, which is also parameterised by the store. This extension is necessary to type certain intermediate reducts which appear during execution.

Frame Validity. This judgement associates a frame with a type context.

$$\frac{(\,\mathsf{typeof}(v) = t_v\,)^n \quad F.\mathsf{locs} = v^n \quad S \vdash_i F.\mathsf{inst} : C}{S \vdash_f F : C[\mathsf{local} := t_v^n]}$$

The premise $S \vdash_i F.\mathsf{inst} : C$ builds an initial type context with the parts of the store that are in scope according to the instance component of frame F (full details elided). The context associated with the frame in the conclusion of the frame validity judgement is built from this initial type context, extended with the types of the local variables held by the frame. The premise $(\,\mathsf{typeof}(v) = t_v\,)^n$ abuses superscript notation to indicate that v^n is related to t_v^n by an element-wise mapping of the typeof relation.

Theorem 1 (preservation).
If $\vdash_c S; F; e^* : t^*$ and $S; F; e^* \hookrightarrow S'; F'; e'^*$, then $\vdash_c S'; F'; e'^* : t^*$ and $S \preceq_s S'$
WasmCert-Isabelle: `preservation` in `wasm_soundness.thy`
WasmCert-Coq: `t_preservation` in `type_preservation.v`

Theorem 2 (progress).
If $\vdash_c S; F; e^* : t^*$, then $\mathsf{is\text{-}terminal}(e^*) \lor \exists S' F' e'.\ S; F; e^* \hookrightarrow S'; F'; e'^*$.

WasmCert-Isabelle: `progress` in `wasm_soundness.thy`
WasmCert-Coq: `t_progress` in `type_progress.v`

The $\prec_s$ relation used when stating preservation is called *store extension*, and is an additional strengthening of the type soundness statement in the 1.0 specification, compared to that of Haas et al. [14]. Its presence in the preservation property enforces that the store cannot have elements removed as a result of execution (can only grow), and that previously allocated global state cannot change its type (even if the configuration would remain well-typed overall).

We first address the proof of the preservation property. In order for the induction to succeed, the inductive hypothesis must be strengthened so that instead of considering only the type preservation of a top-level configuration, we consider the type preservation of an arbitrary program fragment.

Lemma 1 (fragment preservation).
Assuming $S; F; e^* \hookrightarrow S'; F'; e'^*$
$\vdash_s S : ok$
$S \vdash_f F : C$
$S; C[\text{label} := l_{arb}, \text{return} := r_{arb}] \vdash e^* : tf$
we have $S \prec_s S'$
$\vdash_s S' : ok$
$S' \vdash_f F' : C$
$S'; C[\text{label} := l_{arb}, \text{return} := r_{arb}] \vdash e'^* : tf$

WasmCert-Isabelle: `types_preserved_e2` in `wasm_properties.thy`

WasmCert-Coq: `t_preservation_e`,
`reduce_inst_unchanged`, in `type_preservation.v`
`store_extension_reduce`

Note the inclusion of $S \prec_s S'$ in the conclusion, which as discussed is a new proof obligation introduced as part of the move to Wasm 1.0. The proof proceeds by induction on the definition of the reduction relation $\hookrightarrow$. The arbitrary label component l_{arb} appended to the type context C indicates that the code fragment e^* is potentially only well-typed when embedded inside some larger context of labelled control flow constructs (i.e. **block**, **loop**, **if**). The arbitrary return component r_{arb} indicates that the code is potentially only well-typed when embedded within a function definition with some arbitrary return type. We can then show that this stronger property implies the top-level preservation property. A similar generalisation must be made in proving the progress property:

Lemma 2 (fragment progress).
Assuming $S; C[\text{label} := l_{arb}, \text{return} := r_{arb}] \vdash e^* : t^* \to t'^*$
$C \vdash v^* : \epsilon \to t^*$
$\forall L^k. \; e^* \neq L^k[\textbf{return}]$
$\forall i \; L^k. \; e^* = L^k[\textbf{br } i] \implies i < k$
$\forall v'^*. \; e^* \neq v'^*$
$e^* \neq \textbf{trap}$
$\vdash_s S : ok$
$S \vdash_f F : C$
we have $\exists S' \; F' \; e'^*. \; S; F; v^* \; e^* \hookrightarrow S'; F'; e'^*$

WasmCert-Isabelle: progress_e in wasm_properties.thy
WasmCert-Coq: t_progress_e in type_progress.v

The proof proceeds by induction on the definition of expression typing. A number of restricting assumptions must be included, beyond those necessary for preservation, for the induction to succeed. Assumption $\forall L^k.\ e^* \neq L^k[\textbf{return}]$ restricts the induction to only consider program fragments which are not returning to a calling context. Assumption $\forall i\ L^k.\ e^* = L^k[\textbf{br}\ i] \implies i < k$ similarly restricts the induction to only consider program fragments which are breaking to a label within the program fragment itself, and not the label of any enclosing context. The L^k symbol denotes an evaluation context made up of k label constructs (**block**, **loop**, **if**). Failing to disregard these cases would make the induction hypothesis too weak, so they must be handled through separate proofs.

Lemma 3 (return progress).
  Assuming $S; \epsilon \vdash_{\textsf{loc}} F; e^* : t^*$ we have $\forall L^k.\ e^* \neq L^k[\textbf{return}]$
WasmCert-Isabelle: progress_e1 in wasm_properties.thy
WasmCert-Coq: s_typing_lf_br in type_progress.v

Lemma 4 (br progress).
  Assuming $S; \epsilon \vdash_{\textsf{loc}} F; e^* : t^*$ and $e^* = L^k[\textbf{br}\ i]$ we have $i < k$
WasmCert-Isabelle: progress_e2 in wasm_properties.thy
WasmCert-Coq: s_typing_lf_return in type_progress.v

These two lemmas are proven by induction on k, the label depth of the current evaluation context. The first lemma states that if the current frame has no return type set (denoted by ϵ), then the code fragment may not contain a **return** instruction. The second lemma states that a **br** instruction cannot attempt to jump outside the current frame, and so must target one of the labels inside the frame. These two lemmas show that the cases not handled by **fragment progess** are prevented by the type system from occurring at the top level of a program execution, so the lemmas together imply the top-level progress property.

4   Wasm 1.0 Full Semantics

The core runtime semantics and type checker for the W3C Wasm 1.0 standard, described in Sect. 2, is a refactoring of the 2017 draft semantics [14]. The full semantics of Wasm 1.0 significantly extends this draft semantics to include formal specifications of the binary decoding, the numerics and the instantiation phase. We describe our two mechanisations of these extensions: in Isabelle/HOL, we mechanise the instantiation using an OCaml harness for the binary encoding and numerics; and, in Coq, we mechanise the extentions in full, using established Coq libraries for the binary encoding and numerics. In this way, for the first time, we present a fully mechanised specification of the Wasm 1.0 standard.

Binary Decoding. Wasm modules are distributed in a bytecode format. Web browsers type check, compile, and instantiate Wasm code in a streaming manner as the files are downloaded to the user's browser [9]. Abstractly, it is specified that the Wasm binary format can be decoded into the module AST of Fig. 1, and subsequent phases of execution are defined over that AST [43]. In WasmCert-Coq, we make use of the Parseque [1] Coq library to mechanise the binary decoding phase of Wasm in an executable way. Parseque is more powerful than strictly necessary for our purposes. It is designed for parsing "complex recursive grammars" [2] whereas Wasm's binary grammar is fairly flat. However, using Parseque's *alternative* combinator gives us an off-the-shelf way to build an executable definition of the binary format which has close line-by-line correspondence to the Wasm 1.0 formal specification. Our Coq definitions (not including library code) come to ~800 lines of non-comment, non-whitespace code (`binary_format_parser.v`). We have not attempted an analogous mechanisation in WasmCert-Isabelle, although it would be interesting future work.

Numeric Operations. We provide executable numeric definitions in WasmCert-Coq by linking with CompCert's integer and float libraries. The Wasm specification defers many of the definitions of its floating point operations to the IEEE 754 floating point standard, which is also the basis of the CompCert mechanisation. Wasm 1.0 does, however, define its integer operations directly. We prove a number of "sanity lemmas" for the integer operations which check that CompCert's definitions match those of the Wasm 1.0 specification. Our Coq numeric definitions and proofs together (excluding library code) come to ~1500 lines of non-comment, non-whitespace code (`numerics.v`). As future work, we might exhaustively mechanise Wasm's integer operation specification, and prove it equivalent to the definitions of CompCert. WasmCert-Isabelle instead abstracts its numeric operations, and relies on an OCaml implementation of numerics provided by the WebAssembly Community Group [40] when extracting its interpreter.

Instantiation. Instantiation is a phase in the execution of a Wasm program which takes place after type-checking but before runtime evaluation. During instantiation, module imports are satisfied, and the state corresponding to module declarations (e.g. new memories, global variables) are created in the global store.

In the Wasm 1.0 standard [45], instantiation is fully formalised. The definition of instantiation is given by a large collection of inductive rules which do not directly describe an algorithm for instantiation. In essence, the specification defines a relational predicate which takes an initial state, a module to be instantiated, its provided imports, and an output state, and evaluates to true if and only if an instantiation operation in the initial state results in the output state. It does not give an algorithmic procedure for building the output state from the initial state. In fact, the standard's definition of instantiation contains deliberate circularities, which make direct execution of the definition unlikely.

An explanatory note in the standard indicates that a concrete implementation is expected to perform an additional pre-processing pass over the module to break this circularity [44].

The full definitions of module allocation and instantiation are too large and interconnected to other areas of the specification to summarise here, but we sketch the main source of definitional circularity in Fig. 3. The conclusion of the rule states that instantiating the *module* in global store S with the provided *imports* results in a global store S' (among other outputs which we elide for brevity). The store S' is obtained from the allocmodule abstract operation in the premise, which additionally requires the input v^*_{inits}, the values obtained by evaluating the global variable initialisers (see Sect. 2.2). However, the global initialisers are specified as being evaluated in the context of the global store S'. Therefore, the value of v^*_{inits} is defined as depending on the result of allocmodule, which itself takes v^*_{inits} as input—a circularity! In reality, the evaluation of the global initialisers only depends on a subset of the effects of allocmodule, in such a way that a concrete algorithm can pre-process the module to identify the parts of module allocation that global initialiser evaluation will depend on, perform part of the abstract allocmodule operation, evaluate global initialisers using the partial result, and then finish off the rest of the operation. This pre-pass is made simpler by the fact that the evaluation of a global initialiser is only allowed to depend on the values of imported (hence previously initialised) global variables. The specification deliberately chooses not to define this tiered process concretely.

$$\frac{\text{initialisers}(\textit{module}.\text{globs}) = e^*_{\text{inits}} \qquad S'; F; e^*_{\text{inits}} \hookrightarrow S'; F; v^*_{\text{inits}}}{\text{allocmodule}(S, \textit{module}, \textit{imports}, v^*_{\text{inits}}) = S' \dots}$$
$$\text{instantiate}(S, \textit{module}, \textit{imports}) = S' \dots$$

Fig. 3. Illustrating a circularity in the Wasm 1.0 instantiation definition.

In both WasmCert-Isabelle and WasmCert-Coq, we mechanise the standard's inductive definition of instantiation, and create an executable definition of instantiation which performs the pre-processing pass sketched by the standard's explanatory note to break the circularity of the instantiation definition. In WasmCert-Isabelle, we prove these two definitions equivalent. By integrating the executable definition with our verified interpreter, we eliminate a significant amount of Watt's original unverified OCaml harness [37]. The WasmCert-Isabelle definitions and proofs represent ~1650 lines of non-comment, non-whitespace code. WasmCert-Coq's definitions (currently without correctness proof) represent ~800 lines of non-comment, non-whitespace code.

WasmCert-Isabelle: `wasm_module.thy`, `wasm_module_checker.thy`, and `wasm_instantiation.thy`

WasmCert-Coq: `instantiation.v`

We also validate the WasmCert-Isabelle interpreter against the official Wasm 1.0 end-to-end test suite, containing ~17,810 tests, which we pass without error [39]. Testing the Coq-extracted interpreter end-to-end is left for future work.

5   Related Work

There is a wide body of existing work on the mechanised specification of programming language semantics [31]. It is usual for such specificication based on an interactive theorem prover to target an interesting language core or abstraction for mechanisation, due to the ambiguity, complexity, or size of the full language definition. In contrast, we are able to closely follow the *whole* of the Wasm 1.0 semantics directly, as stated in the standard, a task made tractable by its compact design and official formalisation. Xuan presents a partial Coq-mechanisation of Wasm in his M.Sc project, independently named WasmCert [15]. We have been given permission to use the WasmCert name. As already discussed, we build on Watt's Isabelle/HOL mechanisation [37].

Norrish presents a mechanisation of a fragment of C in HOL [26]. The CompCert project [23] has a mechanisation of a large fragment of C in Coq, called Clight [4], making simplifying assumptions regarding some details of the C memory model which are not relevent to the CompCert compilation correctness proof. Lee et al. mechanise in Twelf [29] an "internal language" with "equivalent expressive power" to Standard ML, the semantics of which they formalise via elaoration [21]. CakeML [19,35] includes a mechanised semantics in HOL4 for a large fragment of Standard ML (minus functors). OCaml Light [27] is a mechanised semantics in HOL4 of a core subset of OCaml. Jinja [18] and Java$_S$ [34] provide mechanised fragments of Java. JSCert [5] is a Coq-mechanised specification of a large subset of ECMAScript 5, handling all core constructs but leaving out "library objects" such as **Array** and **Number**. Guha et al. give a JavaScript semantics through elaboration to a mechanised semantics in Coq of a core calculus [13].

More lightweight approaches are possible: e.g. the K framework [32] used to define term-rewriting models of significant fragments of C [10], Java [6], JavaScript [28], and PHP [11]; Cerberus [24] which defines an elaboration semantics for a large fragment of C with a core calculus defined in the Lem specification language [25]; and JaVerT, an analysis tool for JavaScript programs [12,33], where the semantics of JavaScript is defined by a elaboration to a simpler intermediate language.

6   Conclusion and Future Work

We hope our mechanisation of Wasm 1.0 will replace Watt's mechanisation of the original Wasm draft [37] as the canonical source for the Wasm 1.0 type soundness proof. We also hope for further adoption of our work by the WebAssembly Community Group, with our mechanisations endorsed in the same way that certain developer tools and compilers for Wasm are already hosted under their official banner. Wasm 1.0 is in the process of being extended with a number of new feature proposals. We intend to keep our mechanisations abreast of these changes, and hope that early mechanisation will be valuable for in-progress features.

Our immediate future priority for WasmCert-Coq is to complete the final proofs and engineering to enable us to extract a verified end-to-end interpreter which does not use an unverified OCaml harness as is currently used in WasmCert-Isabelle. This would require us to complete the verification of the WasmCert-Coq instantiation implementation. We would also like to do independent testing of the end-to-end interpreter using the Wasm 1.0 test suite. Our priority for WasmCert-Isabelle is to mechanise Wasm's binary decoding phase and numeric operations, again with the aim of providing a verified end-to-end interpreter.

Our work opens the door to a number of applications. We are currently investigating the integration of WasmCert-Coq with the Iris framework [17], developing a higher-order mechanised program logic for a Wasm host language to explore language-interoperable reasoning. WasmCert-Coq could be linked to CompCert's IRs [8], to provide verified compilation both to and from Wasm. WasmCert-Isabelle could be linked to the Isabelle/HOL port of the CakeML verified compiler [16,20]. It could also be linked with a Java mechanisation such as Jinja [18], in order to investigate the expressivity of WebAssembly's hotly-debated in-progress extension of Garbage-Collected Types [42]. In summary, we believe that WasmCert-Isabelle and WasmCert-Coq each have the potential to become the foundation of many different mechanisation projects for Wasm 1.0.

Acknowledgement. Watt, Pichon-Pharabod, Bodin, and Gardner were supported by the EPSRC grant *REMS: Rigorous Engineering for Mainstream Systems* (EP/K008528/1). Watt and Pichon-Pharabod were supported by the VeTSS/NCSC grant *Mechanising Concurrent WebAssembly* (G105616 RI2).

Watt was supported by a Peterhouse Research Fellowship and a Google PhD Fellowship in Programming Technology and Software Engineering. Rao was supported by an Imperial College London, Department of Computing, Doctoral Scholarship Award. Pichon-Pharabod was supported by the ERC grant *Engineering with Logic and Verification: Mathematically Rigorous Engineering for Safe and Secure Computer Systems* (789108). Bodin and Gardner were supported by the EPSRC fellowship *VeTSpec: Verified Trustworthy Software Specification* (EP/R034567/1).

References

1. Allais, G.: Parseque (2017). https://github.com/gallais/parseque
2. Allais, G.: Agdarsec - total parser combinators. In: JFLA 2018 (2018)
3. Batty, M., Memarian, K., Nienhuis, K., Pichon-Pharabod, J., Sewell, P.: The problem of programming language concurrency semantics. In: Vitek, J. (ed.) ESOP 2015. LNCS, vol. 9032, pp. 283–307. Springer, Heidelberg (2015). https://doi.org/10.1007/978-3-662-46669-8_12
4. Blazy, S., Leroy, X.: Mechanized semantics for the Clight subset of the C language. J. Autom. Reason. **43**(3), 263–288 (2009). https://doi.org/10.1007/s10817-009-9148-3. https://hal.inria.fr/inria-00352524

5. Bodin, M., et al.: A trusted mechanised JavaScript specification. In: Proceedings of the 41st ACM SIGPLAN-SIGACT Symposium on Principles of Programming Languages, POPL 2014, pp. 87–100. Association for Computing Machinery, New York (2014). https://doi.org/10.1145/2535838.2535876

6. Bogdanas, D., Roşu, G.: K-Java: a complete semantics of Java. In: Proceedings of the 42nd Annual ACM SIGPLAN-SIGACT Symposium on Principles of Programming Languages, POPL 2015, pp. 445–456. Association for Computing Machinery, New York (2015). https://doi.org/10.1145/2676726.2676982

7. Boldo, S., Jourdan, J.H., Leroy, X., Melquiond, G.: Verified compilation of floating-point computations. J. Autom. Reason. **54**(2), 135–163 (2015). http://xavierleroy.org/publi/floating-point-compcert.pdf

8. Boldo, S., Melquiond, G.: Flocq: A unified library for proving floating-point algorithms in coq. In: 2011 IEEE 20th Symposium on Computer Arithmetic, pp. 243–252 (2011). https://doi.org/10.1109/ARITH.2011.40

9. Bynens, M.: Loading webassembly modules efficiently (2018). https://developers.google.com/web/updates/2018/04/loading-wasm

10. Ellison, C., Rosu, G.: An executable formal semantics of C with applications. In: Proceedings of the 39th Annual ACM SIGPLAN-SIGACT Symposium on Principles of Programming Languages, POPL 2012, pp. 533–544. Association for Computing Machinery, New York (2012). https://doi.org/10.1145/2103656.2103719

11. Filaretti, D., Maffeis, S.: An executable formal semantics of PHP. In: Jones, R. (ed.) ECOOP 2014. LNCS, vol. 8586, pp. 567–592. Springer, Heidelberg (2014). https://doi.org/10.1007/978-3-662-44202-9_23

12. Fragoso Santos, J., Maksimović, P., Sampaio, G., Gardner, P.: Javert 2.0: compositional symbolic execution for javascript. Proc. ACM Program. Lang. **3**(POPL) (2019). https://doi.org/10.1145/3290379

13. Guha, A., Saftoiu, C., Krishnamurthi, S.: The essence of JavaScript. In: D'Hondt, T. (ed.) ECOOP 2010. LNCS, vol. 6183, pp. 126–150. Springer, Heidelberg (2010). https://doi.org/10.1007/978-3-642-14107-2_7

14. Haas, A., et al.: Bringing the web up to speed with WebAssembly. In: Proceedings of the ACM SIGPLAN Conference on Programming Language Design and Implementation. ACM (2017)

15. Huang, X.: A mechanized formalization of the webassembly specification in coq. In: RIT Computer Science (2019)

16. Hupel, L., Zhang, Y.: Cakeml. Archive of Formal Proofs, March 2018. https://isa-afp.org/entries/CakeML.html. Formal proof development

17. Jung, R., Krebbers, R., Jourdan, J.H., Bizjak, A., Birkedal, L., Dreyer, D.: Iris from the ground up: a modular foundation for higher-order concurrent separation logic. J. Funct. Program. **28** (2018)

18. Klein, G., Nipkow, T.: A machine-checked model for a java-like language, virtual machine, and compiler. ACM Trans. Program. Lang. Syst. **28**(4), 619–695 (2006). https://doi.org/10.1145/1146809.1146811

19. Kumar, R., Myreen, M.O., Norrish, M., Owens, S.: CakeML: a verified implementation of ML. In: Proceedings of the 41st ACM SIGPLAN-SIGACT Symposium on Principles of Programming Languages, POPL 2014, pp. 179–191. Association for Computing Machinery, New York (2014). https://doi.org/10.1145/2535838.2535841

20. Kumar, R., Myreen, M.O., Norrish, M., Owens, S.: CakeML: a verified implementation of ML. In: Principles of Programming Languages (POPL), pp. 179–191. ACM Press (2014). https://doi.org/10.1145/2535838.2535841. https://cakeml.org/popl14.pdf

21. Lee, D.K., Crary, K., Harper, R.: Towards a mechanized metatheory of standard ML. In: Proceedings of the 34th Annual ACM SIGPLAN-SIGACT Symposium on Principles of Programming Languages, POPL 2007, pp. 173–184. Association for Computing Machinery, New York (2007). https://doi.org/10.1145/1190216.1190245

22. Leroy, X.: Java bytecode verification: an overview. In: Berry, G., Comon, H., Finkel, A. (eds.) CAV 2001. LNCS, vol. 2102, pp. 265–285. Springer, Heidelberg (2001). https://doi.org/10.1007/3-540-44585-4_26

23. Leroy, X.: Formal verification of a realistic compiler. Commun. ACM **52**(7), 107–115 (2009). https://doi.org/10.1145/1538788.1538814

24. Memarian, K., et al.: Into the depths of C: elaborating the de facto standards. In: Proceedings of the 37th ACM SIGPLAN Conference on Programming Language Design and Implementation, PLDI 2016, pp. 1–15. Association for Computing Machinery, New York (2016). https://doi.org/10.1145/2908080.2908081

25. Mulligan, D.P., Owens, S., Gray, K.E., Ridge, T., Sewell, P.: Lem: reusable engineering of real-world semantics. In: Proceedings of the 19th ACM SIGPLAN International Conference on Functional Programming, ICFP 2014, pp. 175–188. ACM, New York (2014). https://doi.org/10.1145/2628136.2628143

26. Norrish, M.: C formalised in HOL. Technical report (1998)

27. Owens, S.: A sound semantics for OCamllight. In: Drossopoulou, S. (ed.) ESOP 2008. LNCS, vol. 4960, pp. 1–15. Springer, Heidelberg (2008). https://doi.org/10.1007/978-3-540-78739-6_1

28. Park, D., Stefănescu, A., Roşu, G.: KJS: A complete formal semantics of JavaScript. In: Proceedings of the 36th ACM SIGPLAN Conference on Programming Language Design and Implementation, PLDI 2015, pp. 346–356. Association for Computing Machinery, New York (2015). https://doi.org/10.1145/2737924.2737991

29. Pfenning, F., Schürmann, C.: System description: twelf — a meta-logical framework for deductive systems. In: CADE 1999. LNCS (LNAI), vol. 1632, pp. 202–206. Springer, Heidelberg (1999). https://doi.org/10.1007/3-540-48660-7_14

30. Pierce, B.C.: Types and Programming Languages, 1st edn. The MIT Press, Cambridge (2002)

31. Ringer, T., Palmskog, K., Sergey, I., Gligoric, M., Tatlock, Z.: QED at large: a survey of engineering of formally verified software. Found. Trends Program. Lang. **5**(2-3), 102–281 (2019). https://doi.org/10.1561/2500000045

32. Rou, G., erbănută, T.F.: An overview of the K semantic framework. J. Logic Algebraic Program. **79**(6), 397–434 (2010). https://doi.org/10.1016/j.jlap.2010.03.012. http://www.sciencedirect.com/science/article/pii/S1567832610000160. Membrane computing and programming

33. Santos, J.F., Maksimović, P., Grohens, T., Dolby, J., Gardner, P.: Symbolic execution for JavaScript. In: Proceedings of the 20th International Symposium on Principles and Practice of Declarative Programming, PPDP 2018. Association for Computing Machinery, New York (2018). https://doi.org/10.1145/3236950.3236956

34. Syme, D.: Proving Java type soundness. In: Alves-Foss, J. (ed.) Formal Syntax and Semantics of Java. LNCS, vol. 1523, pp. 83–118. Springer, Heidelberg (1999). https://doi.org/10.1007/3-540-48737-9_3

35. Tan, Y.K., Owens, S., Kumar, R.: A verified type system for CakeML. In: Proceedings of the 27th Symposium on the Implementation and Application of Functional Programming Languages. IFL 2015. Association for Computing Machinery, New York (2015). https://doi.org/10.1145/2897336.2897344

36. WasmCert: WasmCert (2021). https://github.com/WasmCert
37. Watt, C.: Mechanising and verifying the WebAssembly specification. In: Proceedings of the 7th ACM SIGPLAN International Conference on Certified Programs and Proofs, CPP 2018, pp. 53–65. Association for Computing Machinery, New York (2018). https://doi.org/10.1145/3167082
38. Watt, C.: Mechanising and evolving the formal semantics of WebAssembly: The Web's new low-level language (2021, not yet published)
39. WebAssembly Community Group: tests (2020). https://github.com/WebAssembly/spec/tree/704d9d9e9c861fdb957c3d5e928f1d046a31497e/test
40. WebAssembly Community Group: Webassembly (2020). https://github.com/WebAssembly/spec/tree/704d9d9e9c861fdb957c3d5e928f1d046a31497e/
41. WebAssembly Community Group: bulk-memory-operations (2021). https://github.com/WebAssembly/bulk-memory-operations
42. WebAssembly Community Group: GC (2021). https://github.com/WebAssembly/gc
43. WebAssembly Working Group: Binary format (2019). https://www.w3.org/TR/2019/REC-wasm-core-1-20191205/#binary-format%E2%91%A0
44. WebAssembly Working Group: Instantiation (2019). https://www.w3.org/TR/2019/REC-wasm-core-1-20191205/#instantiation%E2%91%A1
45. WebAssembly Working Group: Webassembly core specification (2019). https://www.w3.org/TR/2019/REC-wasm-core-1-20191205/
46. Wright, A., Felleisen, M.: A syntactic approach to type soundness. Inf. Comput. 115(1), 38–94 (1994). https://doi.org/10.1006/inco.1994.1093

Neural Networks and Active Learning

Probabilistic Verification of Neural Networks Against Group Fairness

Bing Sun[1(✉)], Jun Sun[1], Ting Dai[2], and Lijun Zhang[3,4]

[1] Singapore Management University, Bras Basah, Singapore
bing.sun.2020@phdcs.smu.edu.sg
[2] Huawei, Changi, Singapore
[3] SKLCS, University of Chinese Academy of Science, Beijing, China
[4] Institute of Intelligent Software, Guangzhou, China

Abstract. Fairness is crucial for neural networks which are used in applications with important societal implication. Recently, there have been multiple attempts on improving fairness of neural networks, with a focus on fairness testing (e.g., generating individual discriminatory instances) and fairness training (e.g., enhancing fairness through augmented training). In this work, we propose an approach to formally verify neural networks against fairness, with a focus on independence-based fairness such as group fairness. Our method is built upon an approach for learning Markov Chains from a user-provided neural network (i.e., a feed-forward neural network or a recurrent neural network) which is guaranteed to facilitate sound analysis. The learned Markov Chain not only allows us to verify (with Probably Approximate Correctness guarantee) whether the neural network is fair or not, but also facilities sensitivity analysis which helps to understand why fairness is violated. We demonstrate that with our analysis results, the neural weights can be optimized to improve fairness. Our approach has been evaluated with multiple models trained on benchmark datasets and the experiment results show that our approach is effective and efficient.

1 Introduction

In recent years, neural network based machine learning has found its way into various aspects of people's daily life, such as fraud detection [25], facial recognition [47], self-driving [13], and medical diagnosis [56]. Although neural networks have demonstrated astonishing performance in many applications, there are still concerns on their dependability. One desirable property of neural networks for applications with societal impact is fairness [2]. Since there are often societal biases in the training data, the resultant neural networks might be discriminative as well. This has been demonstrated in [53]. Fairness issues in neural networks are often more 'hidden' than those of traditional decision-making software programs since it is still an open problem on how to interpret neural networks.

Recently, researchers have established multiple formalization of fairness regarding different sub-populations [9,21,24,28]. These sub-populations are often

© Springer Nature Switzerland AG 2021
M. Huisman et al. (Eds.): FM 2021, LNCS 13047, pp. 83–102, 2021.
https://doi.org/10.1007/978-3-030-90870-6_5

determined by different values of protected features (e.g., race, religion and ethnic group), which are application-dependent. To name a few, group fairness requires that minority members should be classified at an approximately same rate as the majority members [9,24], whereas individual discrimination (a.k.a. causal fairness) states that a machine learning model must output approximately the same predictions for instances which are the same except for certain protected features [21,28]. We refer readers to [51] for detailed definitions of fairness. In this work, we focus on an important class of fairness called independence-based fairness, which includes the above-mentioned group fairness.

Recently, there have been multiple attempts on analyzing and improving fairness of neural networks, with a focus on fairness testing (e.g., generating individual discriminatory instances) and fairness training (e.g., enhancing fairness through augmented training). Multiple attempts [4,27,54,58] have been made on testing machine learning models against individual discrimination, which aims to systematically generate instances that demonstrate individual discrimination. While these approaches have impressive performance in terms of generating such instances, they are incapable of verifying fairness. Another line of approaches is on fairness training [3,12,14,16,28,36], this includes approaches which incorporate fairness as an objective in the model training phase [3,12,16], and approaches which adopt heuristics for learning fair classifiers [36]. While the experiment results show that these approaches improve fairness to certain extent, they do not guarantee that the resultant neural networks are fair.

In this work, we investigate the problem of verifying neural networks against independence-based fairness. Our aim is to design an approach which allows us to (1) show evidence that a neural network satisfies fairness if it is the case; (2) otherwise, provide insights on why fairness is not satisfied and how fairness can be potentially achieved; (3) provide a way of improving the fairness of the neural network. At a high-level, our approach is designed as follows. Given a neural network (i.e., either a feed-forward or recurrent neural network), we systematically sample behaviors of the neural network (e.g., input/output pairs), based on which we learn a Markov Chain model that approximates the neural network. Our algorithm guarantees that probabilistic analysis based on the learned Markov Chain model (such as probabilistic reachability analysis) is probably approximately correct (hereafter PAC-correct) with respect to any computational tree logic (CTL [11]) formulae. With the guarantee, we are thus able to verify fairness property of the neural network. There are two outcomes. One is that the neural network is proved to be fair, in which case the Markov Chain is presented as an evidence. Otherwise, sensitivity analysis based on the Markov Chain is carried out automatically. Such analysis helps us to understand why fairness is violated and provide hints on how the neural network could be improved to achieve fairness. Lastly, our approach optimizes the parameters of the 'responsible' neurons in the neural network and improve its fairness.

We have implemented our approach as a part of the SOCRATES framework [45]. We apply our approach to multiple neural network models (including feed-forward and recurrent neural networks) trained on benchmark datasets which are the subject of previous studies on fairness testing. The experiment results show that our approach successfully verifies or falsifies all the models. It also confirms that fairness is a real concern and one of the networks (on the German Credit dataset) fails the fairness property badly. Through sensitivity analysis, our approach locates neurons which have the most contribution to the violation of fairness. Further experiments show that by optimizing the neural parameters (i.e., weights) based on the sensitivity analysis result, we can improve the model's fairness significantly whilst keeping a high model accuracy.

The remaining of the paper is organized as follows. In Sect. 2, we review relevant background and define our problem. In Sect. 3, we present each step of our approach in detail. In Sect. 4, we evaluate our approach through multiple experiments. We review related work in Sect. 5 and conclude in Sect. 6. For appendix, please refer to the extended version of this paper [50].

2 Preliminary

In this section, we review relevant background and define our problem.

Fairness. For classification problems, a neural network N learns to predict a target variable O based on a set of input features X. We write Y as the prediction of the classifier. We further write $F \subseteq X$ as a set of features encoding some protected characteristics such as gender, age and race. Fairness constrains how N makes predictions. In the literature, there are multiple formal definitions of fairness [9,21,24,28]. In this work, we focus on independence-based fairness, which is defined as follows.

Definition 1 (Independence-based Fairness (strict)). *A neural network N satisfies independence-based fairness (strict) if the protected feature F is statistically independent to the prediction Y. We write L as the prediction set and we have $\forall l \in L$, $\forall f_i, f_j \in F$ such that $i \neq j$,*

$$P(Y = l \mid F = f_i) = P(Y = l \mid F = f_j) \tag{1}$$

The definition states that, N's prediction is independent of the protected feature F. This definition is rather strict and thus unlikely to hold in practice. The following relaxes the above definition by introducing a positive tolerance ξ.

Definition 2 (Independence-based Fairness). *Let N be a neural network and ξ be a positive real-value constant. N satisfies independence-based fairness, with respect to ξ, if and only if, $\forall l \in L \; \forall f_i, f_j \in F$ such that $i \neq j$,*

$$\mid P(Y = l \mid F = f_i) - P(Y = l \mid F = f_j) \mid \; \leq \xi \tag{2}$$

Intuitively, the above definition states that N is fair as long as the probability difference is within the threshold ξ. In the following, we focus on Definition 2 as it is both more general and more practical compared to Definition 1.

Example 1. Let us take the network trained on the Census Income dataset [18] as an example. The dataset consists of 32k training instances, each of which contains 13 features. The task is to predict whether an individual's income exceeds $50K per year. An example instance x with a prediction y will be $x : \langle 3\ 5\ 3\ 0\ 2\ 8\ 3\ 0\ 1\ 2\ 0\ 40\ 0 \rangle$, $y : \langle 0 \rangle$. Note that all features are categorical (i.e., processed using binning). Among all features, gender, age and race are considered protected features. The model N trained based on the dataset is in the form of a six-layer fully-connected feed-forward neural network. The following is a fairness property defined based on the protected feature gender.

$$| P(Y = 1 \mid F = male) - P(Y = 1 \mid F = female) | \leq 0.1 \qquad (3)$$

Intuitively, the difference in the probability of predicting 1, for males and females, should be no more than 10%.

Our Problem. We are now ready to define our problem.

Definition 3 (The verification problem). *Let N be a neural network. Let ϕ be an independence-based fairness property (with respect to protected feature F and a threshold ξ). The fairness verification problem is to verify whether N satisfies ϕ or not.*

One way of solving the problem is through statistical model checking (such as hypothesis testing [40]). Such an approach is however not ideal. While it is possible to conclude whether N is fair or not (with certain level of statistical confidence), the result often provides no insight. In the latter case, we would often be interested in performing further analysis to answer questions such as whether certain feature or neuron at a hidden layer is particularly relevant to the fairness issue and how to improve the fairness. The above-mentioned approach offers little clue to such questions.

3   Our Approach

In this section, we present details of our approach. Our approach is shown in Algorithm 1. The first step is to learn a Markov Chain D which guarantees that probabilistic analysis such as probabilistic reachability analysis based on D is PAC-correct with respect to N. The second step is to apply probabilistic model checking [39] to verify D against the fairness property ϕ. In the third step, if the property ϕ is not verified, sensitivity analysis is performed on D which provides us information on how to improve N in terms of fairness. That is, we improve the fairness of the model by optimizing the neuron weights based on the sensitivity analysis results.

Note that our approach relies on building an approximation of the neural network in the form of Markov Chains. There are three reasons why constructing such an abstraction is beneficial. First, it allows us to reason about unbounded behaviors (in the case of a cyclic Markov Chains, which can be constructed from recurrent neural networks as we show below) which are known to be beyond the capability of statistical model checking [40]. Second, the Markov Chain model allows us to perform analysis such as sensitivity analysis (e.g., to identify neurons responsible for violating fairness) as well as predict the effect of changing certain probability distribution (e.g., whether fairness will be improved), which are challenging for statistical methods. Lastly, in the case that the fairness is verified, the Markov Chain serves as a human-interpretable argument on why fairness is satisfied.

In the following, we introduce each step in detail. We fix a neural network N and a fairness property ϕ of the form $|\, P(Y = l \,|\, F = f_i) - P(Y = l \,|\, F = f_j)\,| \leq \xi$. We use the neural network trained on the Census Income dataset (refer to Example 1) as a running example.

Algorithm 1: $verify\_repair(N, \phi, \mu\epsilon, \mu\delta)$

1 Fix the set of states S;
2 Learn DTMC D by
    $learn(N, S, \frac{\mu\epsilon}{2}, 1 - \sqrt{1 - \mu\delta})$;
3 Estimate $P(Y = l \,|\, F = f_i) \; \forall f_i \in F$;
4 Verify ϕ against ξ; **if** ϕ *is verified* **then**
5   **return** *"Verified" and D;*
6 **else**
7   Conduct sensitivity analysis on D;
8   Perform automatic repair of N;
9   **return** N';

Algorithm 2: $learn(N, S, \epsilon, \delta)$

1 $W := 0$;
2 $A_W := 0$;
3 **do**
4   generate new sample
        trace ω
5      $W := W + \omega$;
6   update $A_W(p, q)$ for all
        $p \in S$ and $q \in S$;
7   update $H(n)$;
8 **while** $\exists p \in S, n_p < H(n)$
   Output: A_W

3.1   Step 1: Learning a Markov Chain

In this step, we construct a Discrete-Time Markov Chain (DTMC) which approximates N (i.e., line 2 of Algorithm 1). DTMCs are widely used to model the behavior of stochastic systems [10], and they are often considered reasonably human-interpretable. Example DTMCs are shown in Fig. 1. The definition of DTMC is presented in [50]. Algorithm 2 shows the details of this step. The overall idea is to construct a DTMC, based on which we can perform various analysis such as verifying fairness. To make sure the analysis result on the DTMC applies to the original N, it is important that the DTMC is constructed in such a way that it preserves properties such as probabilistic reachability analysis (which is necessary for verifying fairness as we show later). Algorithm 2 is thus base on the recent work published in [10], which develops a sampling method for learning DTMC. To learn a DTMC which satisfies our requirements, we must answer three questions.

(1) What are the states S in the DTMC? The choice of S has certain consequences in our approach. First, it constrains the kind of properties that we are allowed to analyze based on the DTMC. As we aim to verify fairness, the states must minimally include states representing different protected features, and states representing prediction outcomes. The reason is that, with these

states, we can turn the problem of verifying fairness into probabilistic reachability analysis based on the DTMC, as we show in Sect. 3.2. What additionally are the states to be included depends on the level of details that we would like to have for subsequent analysis. For instance, we include states representing other features at the input layer, and states representing the status of hidden neurons. Having these additional states allows us to analyze the correlation between the states and the prediction outcome. For instance, having states representing a particular feature (or the status of a neuron of a hidden layer) allows us to check how sensitive the prediction outcome is with respect to the feature (or the status of a neuron). Second, the choice of states may have an impact on the cost of learning the DTMC. In general, the more states there are, the more expensive it is to learn the DTMC. In Sect. 4, we show empirically the impact of having different sizes of S. We remark that to represent continuous input features and hidden neural states using discrete states, we discretize their values (e.g., using binning or clustering methods such as *Kmeans* [42] based on a user-provided number of clusters). In our approach, for fairness verification only task, we include protected features and prediction outcomes. For sensitivity analysis task, we further include other features and hidden neural states.

(2) How do we identify the transition probability matrix? The answer is to repeatedly sample inputs (by sampling based on a prior probability distribution) and then monitor the trace of the inputs, i.e., the sequence of transitions triggered by the inputs. After sampling a sufficiently large number of inputs, the transition probability matrix then can be estimated based on the frequency of transitions between states in the traces. In general, the question of estimating the transition probability matrix of a DTMC is a well-studied topic and many approaches have been proposed, including frequency estimation, Laplace smoothing [10] and Good-Turing estimation [26]. In this work, we adopt the following simple and effective estimation method. Let W be a set of traces which can be regarded as a bag of transitions. We write n_p where $p \in S$ to denote the number transitions in W originated from state p. We write n_{pq} where $p \in S$ and $q \in S$ to be the number of transitions observed from state p to q in W. Let m be the total number of states in S. The transition probability matrix A_W (estimated based on W) is: $A_W(p,q) = \begin{cases} \frac{n_{pq}}{n_p} & \text{if } n_q \neq 0 \\ \frac{1}{m} & \text{otherwise} \end{cases}$. Intuitively, the probability of transition from state p to q is estimated as the number of transitions from p to q divided by the total number of transitions taken from state p observed in W. Note that if a state p has not been visited, $A_W(p,q)$ is estimated by $\frac{1}{m}$; otherwise, $A_W(p,q)$ is estimated by $\frac{n_{pq}}{n_p}$.

(3) How do we know that the estimated transition probability matrix is accurate enough for the purpose of verifying fairness? Formally, let A_W be the transition probability matrix estimated as above; and let A be the actual transition probability matrix. We would like the following to be satisfied.

$$P(Div(A, A_W) > \epsilon) \leq \delta \qquad (4)$$

where $\epsilon > 0$ and $\delta > 0$ are constants representing *accuracy* and *confidence*; $Div(A, A_W)$ represents the divergence between A and A_W; and P is the probability. Intuitively, the learned DTMC must be estimated such that the probability of the divergence between A_W and A greater than ϵ is no larger than the confidence level δ. In this work, we define the divergence based on the individual transition probability, i.e.,

$$P(\exists p \in S, \sum_{q \in S} |A(p,q) - A_W(p,q)| > \epsilon) \leq \delta \qquad (5)$$

Intuitively, we would like to sample traces until the observed transition probabilities $A_W(p,q) = \frac{n_{pq}}{n_p}$ are close to the real transition probability $A(p,q)$ to a certain level for all $p, q \in S$. Theorem 1 in the recently published work [10] shows that if we sample enough samples such that for each $p \in S$, n_p satisfies

$$n_p \geq \frac{2}{\epsilon^2} log(\frac{2}{\delta'}) \left[\frac{1}{4} - \left(max_q \left| \frac{1}{2} - \frac{n_{pq}}{n_n} \right| - \frac{2}{3} \epsilon \right)^2 \right] \qquad (6)$$

where $\delta' = \frac{\delta}{m}$, we can guarantee the learned DTMC is sound with respect to N in terms of probabilistic reachability analysis. Formally, let $H(n) = \frac{2}{\epsilon^2} log(\frac{2}{\delta'})[\frac{1}{4} - (max_q | \frac{1}{2} - \frac{n_{pq}}{n_p} | - \frac{2}{3} \epsilon)^2]$,

Theorem 1. *Let (S, I, A_W) be a DTMC where A_W is the transition probability matrix learned using frequency estimation based on n traces W. For $0 < \epsilon < 1$ and $0 < \delta < 1$, if for all $p \in S$, $n_p \geq H(n)$, we have for any CTL property ψ,*

$$P(|\gamma(A, \psi) - \gamma(A_W, \psi)| > \epsilon) \leq \delta \qquad (7)$$

where $\gamma(A_W, \psi)$ is the probability of A_W satisfying ψ.

Appendix A.3 in [50] provides the proof. Intuitively, the theorem provides a bound on the number of traces that we must sample in order to guarantee that the learned DTMC is PAC-correct with respect to any CTL property, which provides a way of verifying fairness as we show in Sect. 3.2.

We now go through Algorithm 2 in detail. The loop from line 3 to 8 keeps sampling inputs and obtains traces. Note that we use the uniform sampling by default and would sample according to the actual distribution if it is provided. Next, we update A_W as explained above at line 6. Then we check if more samples are needed by monitoring if a sufficient number of traces has been sampled according to Theorem 1. If it is the case, we output the DTMC as the result. Otherwise, we repeat the steps to generate new samples and update the model.

Example 2. In our running example, for simplicity assume that we select *gender* (as the protected feature) and the prediction outcome to be included in S and the number of clusters is set to 2 for both layers. Naturally, the two clusters identified for the protected feature are male and female (written as '*M*' and '*F*') and the two clusters determined for the outcome are ' $\leq 50K$' and ' $> 50K$'.

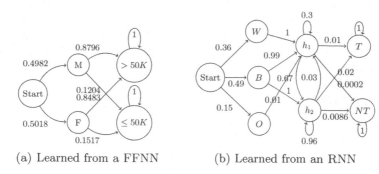

(a) Learned from a FFNN   (b) Learned from an RNN

Fig. 1. Sample learned DTMCs

A sample trace is $w = \langle Start, 'M', ' > 50K' \rangle$, where $Start$ is a dummy state where all traces start. Assume that we set accuracy $\epsilon = 0.005$ and confidence level $\delta = 0.05$. Applying Algorithm 2, 2.85K traces are generated to learn the transition matrix A_W. The learned DTMC D is shown in Fig. 1a.

3.2 Step 2: Probabilistic Model Checking

In this step, we verify N against the fairness property ϕ based on the learned D. Note that D is PAC-correct only with respect to CTL properties. Thus it is infeasible to directly verify ϕ (which is not a CTL property). Our remedy is to compute $P(Y = l \mid F = f_i)$ and $P(Y = l \mid F = f_j)$ separately and then verify ϕ based on the results. Because we demand there is always a state in S representing $F = f_i$ and a state representing $Y = l$, the problem of computing $P(Y = l \mid F = f_i)$ can be reduced to a probabilistic reachability checking problem ψ, i.e., the probability of reaching the state representing $Y = l$ from the state representing $F = f_i$. This can be solved using probabilistic model checking techniques. Probabilistic model checking [39] of DTMC is a formal verification method for analyzing DTMC against formally-specified quantitative properties (e.g., PCTL). Probabilistic model checking algorithms are often based on a combination of graph-based algorithms and numerical techniques. For straightforward properties such as computing the probability that a **U** (Until), **F** (Finally) or **G**(*Globally*) path formula is satisfied, the problem can be reduced to solving a system of linear equations [39]. We refer to the readers to [39] for a complete and systematic formulate of the algorithm for probabilistic model checking.

Example 3. Figure 1b shows a DTMC learned from a recurrent neural network trained on Jigsaw Comments dataset (refer to details on the dataset and network in Sect. 4.1). The protected features is *race*. For illustration purpose, let us consider three different values for *race*, i.e., White (W), Black (B) and Others (O). For the hidden layer cells, we consider LSTM cell 1 only and cluster its values into two groups, represented as two states h_1 and h_2. The output has two categories, i.e., Toxic (T) and Non-Toxic (NT). The transition probabilities are shown in the figure. Note that the DTMC is cyclic due to the recurrent hidden LSTM cells in the network. We obtained $P(Y = 'T' | F = 'W')$ by probabilistic model checking as discussed above. The resultant probability is 0.0263. Similarly, $P(Y = 'T' | F = 'B')$ and $P(Y = 'T' | F = 'O')$ are 0.0362 and 0.0112 respectively.

Next we verify the fairness property ϕ based on the result of probabilistic model checking. First, the following is immediate based on Theorem 1.

Proposition 1. Let $D = (S, I, A_W)$ be a DTMC learned using Algorithm 2. Let $P(Y = l | F = f_i)$ be the probability computed based on probabilistic model checking D and $P_t(Y = l | F = f_i)$ is the actual probability in N. We have

$$P\big(|P(Y = l | F = f_i) - P_t(Y = l | F = f_i)| > \epsilon\big) \leq \delta$$

Theorem 2. Let X be an estimation of a probability X_t such that $P(|X - X_t| > \epsilon) \leq \delta$. Let Z be an estimation of a probability Z_t such that $P(|Z - Z_t| > \epsilon) < \delta$ We have $P(|(X - Z) - (X_t - Z_t)| > 2\epsilon) \leq 2\delta$ δ^{η}.

Appendix A.4 in [50] provides the proof. Hence, given an expected accuracy $\mu\epsilon$ and a confidence level $\mu\delta$ on fairness property ϕ , we can derive ϵ and δ to be used in Algorithm 2 as: $\epsilon = \frac{\mu\epsilon}{2}$ and $\delta = 1 - \sqrt{1 - \mu\delta}$. We compute the probability of $P(Y = l | F = f_i)$ and $P(Y = l | F = f_j)$ based on the learned D (i.e., line 3 of Algorithm 1). Next, we compare $|P(Y = l | F = f_i) - P(Y = l | F = f_j)|$ with ξ. If the difference is no larger than ξ, fairness is verified. The following establishes the correctness of Algorithm 1.

Theorem 3. Algorithm 1 is PAC-correct with accuracy $\mu\epsilon$ and confidence $\mu\delta$, if Algorithm 2 is used to learn the DTMC D.

Appendix A.5 in [50] provides the proof.

The overall time complexity of model learning and probabilistic model checking is linear in the number of traces sampled, i.e., $\mathbf{O}(n)$ where n is the total number of traces sampled. Here n is determined by $H(n)$ as well as the probability distribution of the states. Contribution of $H(n)$ can be determined as $\mathbf{O}(\frac{\log m}{\mu\epsilon^2 \log \mu\delta})$ based on Eq. 6, where m is the total number of states. In the first case, for a model with only input features and output predictions as states, the probability of reaching each input states are statistically equal if we apply uniform sampling to generate IID input vectors. In this scenario the overall time complexity is $\mathbf{O}(\frac{m \log m}{\mu\epsilon^2 \log \mu\delta})$. In the second case, for a model with states representing the status of hidden layer neurons, we need to consider the probability for each hidden neuron states when the sampled inputs are fed into the network N. In the best case, the probabilities are equal, we denote m' as the maximum number of states in one layer among all layers included, the complexity is then $\mathbf{O}(\frac{m' \log m}{\mu\epsilon^2 \log \mu\delta})$. In the worst case, certain neuron is never activated (or certain predefined state is never reached) no matter what the input is. Since the probability distribution among the hidden states are highly network-dependent, we are not able to estimate the average performance.

Example 4. In our running example, with the learned A_W of D as shown in Fig. 1a, the probabilities as $P(Y = 1 \,|F = \text{`}F\text{'}) = 0.8483$ and $P(Y = 1\,|F = \text{`}M\text{'}) = 0.8796$. Hence, $|P(Y = 1|F = \text{`}F\text{'}) - P(Y = 1|F = \text{`}M\text{'})| = 0.0313$. Next, we compare the probability difference against the user-provided fairness criteria ξ. If $\xi = 0.1$, N satisfies fairness property. If $\xi = 0.02$, N fails fairness. Note that such a strict criteria is not practical and is used for illustration purpose only.

3.3 Step 3: Sensitivity Analysis

In the case that the verification result shows ϕ is satisfied, our approach outputs D and terminates successfully. We remark that in such a case D can be regarded as the evidence for the verification result as well as a human-interpretable explanation on why fairness is satisfied. In the case that ϕ is not satisfied, a natural question is: how do we improve the neural network for fairness? Existing approaches have proposed methods for improving fairness such as by training without the protected features [55] (i.e., a form of pre-processing) or training with fairness as an objective [16] (i.e., a form of in-processing). In the following, we show that a post-processing method can be supported based on the learned DTMC. That is, we can identify the neurons which are responsible for violating the fairness based on the learned DTMC and "mutate" the neural network slightly, e.g., adjusting its weights, to achieve fairness.

We start with a sensitivity analysis to understand the impact of each probabilistic distribution (e.g., of the non-protected features or hidden neurons) on the prediction outcome. Let F be the set of discrete states representing different protected feature values. Let I represent a non-protected feature or an internal neuron. We denote I_i as a particular state in the DTMC which represents certain group of values of the feature or neuron. Let l represent the prediction result that we are interested in. The sensitivity of I (with respect to the outcome l) is defined as follows.

$$sensitivity(I) = \sum_i reach(S_0, I_i) * reach(I_i, l) * \max_{\{f,g\} \subseteq F} \left(reach(f, I_i) - reach(g, I_i)\right)$$

where $reach(s, s')$ for any state s and s' represents the probability of reaching s' from s. Intuitively, the sensitivity of I is the summation of the 'sensitivity' of every state I_i, which is calculated as $\max_{f,g} \left(reach(f, I_i) - reach(g, I_i)\right)$, i.e., the maximum probability difference of reaching I_i from all possible protected feature states. The result is then multiplied with the probability of reaching I_i from start state S_0 and the probability of reaching l from I_i. Our approach analyzes all non-protected features and hidden neurons and identify the most sensitive features or neurons for improving fairness in step 4.

Example 5. In our running example, based on the learned DTMC D shown in Fig. 1a, we perform sensitivity analysis as discussed above. We observe that feature 9 (i.e., representing 'capital gain') is the most sensitive, i.e., it has the most contribution to the model unfairness. More importantly, it can be observed that the sensitivities of the neurons vary significantly, which is a good news as it suggests that for this model, optimizing the weights of a few neurons may be sufficient for achieving fairness. Figure 3 in Appendix A.6 in [50] shows the sensitively analysis scatter plot.

3.4 Step 4: Improving Fairness

In this step, we demonstrate one way of improving neural network fairness based on our analysis result, i.e., by adjusting weight parameters of the neurons identified in step 3. The idea is to search for a small adjustment through optimization techniques such that the fairness property is satisfied. In particular, we adopt the Particle Swarm Optimization (PSO) algorithm [37], which simulates intelligent collective behavior of animals such as flocks of birds and schools of fish. In PSO multiple particles are placed in the search space and the optimization target is to find the best location, where the fitness function is used to determine the best location. We omit the details of PSO here due to space limitation and present it in Appendix A.7 in [50].

In our approach, the weights of the most sensitive neurons are the subject for optimization and thus are represented by the location of the particles in the PSO. The initial location of each particle is set to the original weights and the initial velocity is set to zero. The fitness function is defined as follows.

$$fitness = Prob_{diff} + \alpha(1 - accuracy) \tag{8}$$

where $Prob_{diff}$ represents the maximum probability difference of getting a desired outcome among all different values of the sensitive feature; $accuracy$ is the accuracy of repaired network on the training dataset and constant parameter $\alpha \in (0, 1)$ determines the importance of the accuracy (relative to the fairness). Intuitively, the objective is to satisfy fairness and not to sacrifice accuracy too much. We set the bounds of weight adjustment to $(0, 2)$, i.e., 0 to 2 times of the original weight. The maximum number of iteration is set to 100. To further reduce the searching time, we stop the search as soon as the fairness property is satisfied or we fail to find a better location in the last 10 consecutive iterations.

Example 6. In our running example, we optimize the weight of ten most sensitive neurons using PSO for better fairness. The search stops at the 13rd iteration as no better location is found in the last 10 consecutive iterations. The resultant probability difference among the protected features dropped from 0.0313 to 0.007, whereas the model accuracy dropped from 0.8818 to 0.8606.

4   Implementation and Evaluation

Our approach has been implemented on top of SOCRATES [45], which is a framework for experimenting neutral network analysis techniques. We conducted our experiments on a machine with 1 Dual-Core Intel Core i5 2.9GHz CPU and 8GB system memory.

Table 1. Fairness verification results

Dataset	Feature	# States	# Traces	Max Prob. Diff.	Result	Time
Census	Race	8	12500	0.0588	PASS	4.13 s
Census	Age	12	23500	0.0498	PASS	6.31 s
Census	Gender	5	2850	0.0313	PASS	0.98 s
Credit	Age	11	22750	0.1683	Fail	6.72 s
Credit	Gender	5	2850	0.0274	PASS	1.01 s
Bank	Age	12	27200	0.0156	PASS	6.33 s
Jigsaw	Religion	10	35250	0.0756	PASS	29.6 m
Jigsaw	Race	7	30550	0.0007	PASS	27.3 m

4.1 Experiment Setup

In the following, we evaluate our method in order to answer multiple research questions (RQs) based on multiple neural networks trained on 4 datasets adopted from existing research [4,28,54,58], i.e., in addition to the *Census Income* [18] dataset as introduced in Example 1, we have the following three datasets. First is the *German Credit* [19] dataset consisting of 1k instances containing 20 features and is used to assess an individual's credit. Age and gender are the two protected features. The labels are whether an individual's credit is good or not. Second is the *Bank Marketing* [17] dataset consisting of 45k instances. There are 17 features, among which age is the protected feature. The labels are whether the client will subscribe a term deposit. Third is Jigsaw Comment [1] dataset. It consists of 313k text comments with average length of 80 words classified into toxic and non-toxic. The protected features analysed are race and religion.

Following existing approaches [4,28,54,58], we train three 6-layer feed-forward neural networks (FFNN) on the first three dataset (with accuracy 0.88, 1 and 0.92 respectively) and train one recurrent neural network, i.e., 8-cell Long Short Term Memory (LSTM), for the last dataset (with accuracy 0.92) and analyze their fairness against the corresponding protected attributes. For the LSTM model, we adopt the state-of-the-art embedding tool GloVe [44]. We use the 50-dimension word vectors pre-trained on Wikipedia 2014 and Gigaword 5 dataset.

Recall that we need to sample inputs to learn a DTMC. In the case of first three datasets, inputs are sampled by generating randomly values within the range of each feature (in IID manner assuming a uniform distribution). In the case of the Jigsaw dataset, we cannot randomly generate and replace words as the resultant sentence is likely invalid. Inspired by the work in [7,33,41], our approach is to replace a randomly selected word with a randomly selected synonym (generated by Gensim [46]).

4.2 Research Questions and Answers

RQ1: Is our Approach Able to Verify Fairness? We systematically apply our method to the above-mentioned neural networks with respect to each protected feature. Our experiments are configured with accuracy $\mu\epsilon = 0.01$, confidence level $\mu\delta = 0.1$ (i.e., $\epsilon = 0.005$, $\delta = 0.05$) and fairness criteria $\xi = 10\%$ (which is a commonly adopted threshold [6]). Furthermore, in this experiment, the states in the DTMC S are set to only include those representing the protected feature and different predictions. Table 1 summarizes the results. We successfully verify or falsify all models. Out of eight cases, the model trained on the German Credit dataset fails fairness with respect to the feature *age* (i.e., the maximum probability difference among different age groups is 0.1683 which is greater than $\xi = 10\%$). Furthermore, the model trained on the Jigsaw dataset shows some fairness concern with respect to the feature *religion* (although the probablity different is still within the threshold). This result shows that fairness violation could be a real concern.

RQ2: How Efficient is our Approach? We answer the question using two measurements. The first measurement is the execution time. The results are shown in the last column in Table 1. For the six cases of FFNN, the average time taken to verify a network is around 4.25 s, with a maximum of 6.72 s for the model trained on German Credit on feature *age* and a minimum of 0.98 s for the model trained on the Census Income dataset on feature *gender*. For the two cases of LSTM networks, the average time taken is 30 min. Compared with FFNN, verifying an LSTM requires much more time. This is due to three reasons. Firstly, as mentioned in Sect. 4.1, sampling texts requires searching for synonyms. This is non-trivial due to the large size of the dictionary. Secondly, during sampling, we randomly select instances from the training set and apply perturbation to them in order to generate new samples. However, most of the instances in the Jigsaw training set does not contain the sensitive word. This leads to an increased number of traces needed to learn a DTMC. Thirdly, the LSTM model takes much more time to make a prediction than that by FFNN in general. It is also observed that for all the cases, the execution time is proportional to the number of traces used in DTMC model learning (as discussed in our time complexity analysis). The other measurement is the number of traces that we are required to sample using Algorithm 2. For each model and protected feature, the number of traces generated in Algorithm 2 depends on number of categorical values defined for this protected feature and the number of predictions. That is, more

Table 2. Fairness improvement

Dataset	Max probability difference	Accuracy
German	$0.1683 \mapsto 0.1125$	$1.0 \mapsto 0.9450$
Census	$0.0588 \mapsto 0.0225$	$0.8818 \mapsto 0.8645$
Jigsaw	$0.0756 \mapsto 0.0590$	$0.9166 \mapsto 0.9100$

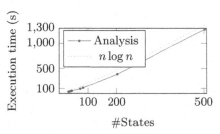

Fig. 2. Execution times vs number of states

categories and predictions result in more states in the learn a DTMC model, which subsequently lead to more traces required. Furthermore, the number of traces required also depends on the probabilistic distribution from each state in the model. As described in Algorithm 2, the minimum number of traces transiting from each state must be greater than $H(n)$. This is evidenced by results shown in Table 1, where the number of traces vary significantly between models or protected features, ranging from 2 K to 35 K. Although the number of traces is expected to increase for more complicated models, we believe that this is not a limiting factor since the sampling of the traces can be easily paralleled.

We further conduct an experiment to monitor the execution time required for the same neural network model with a different numbers of states in the learned DTMC. We keep other parameters (i.e., $\mu\epsilon$, $\mu\delta$ and ϕ) the same. Note that hidden neurons are not selected as states to reduce the impact of the state distribution. We show one representative result (based on the mode trained on the Census Income dataset with attribute *race* as the protected feature) in Fig. 2. As we can see the total execution time is bounded by $n \log n$ which tally with our time complexity analysis in Sect. 3.

RQ3: Is our Approach able to Improve Fairness and is the Sensitivity Analysis Useful? The question asks whether the sensitivity analysis results based on the learned DTMC can be used to improve fairness. To answer this question, we systematically perform sensitivity analysis (on both the input features and the hidden neurons) and optimize the weights of the neurons which are sensitive to fairness. We focus on three cases, i.e., the FFNN model trained on the German Credit model w.r.t *age* and on the Census Income model w.r.t *race* and the LSTM model trained on the Jigsaw comments w.r.t *religion*, as the maximum probability difference for these three cases (as shown in Table 1) is concerning (i.e., $> 5\%$). For the former two, we optimize the weights of the top-10 sensitive neurons (including the first layer neurons representing other features). For the LSTM model, we optimize top-3 sensitive cells (due to the small number of cells). Table 2 shows the fairness improvement as well as the drop in accuracy. It can be observed that in all three cases we are able to improve the fairness whilst maintaining the accuracy at a high-level. Note that the parameter α is set to 0.1 in these experiments and it can be used to achieve better fairness or accuracy depending the user requirement.

RQ4: How does our Approach Compare with Existing Alternatives? The most relevant tools that we identify are FairSquare [6] and VeriFair [9]. FairSquare and VeriFair use numerical integration to verify fairness properties of machine learning models including neural networks. FairSquare relies on constraint solving techniques and thus it is difficult to scale to large neural networks. VeriFair is based on adaptive concentration inequalities. We evaluate our approach against these two tools on all eight models. For FairSquare and VeriFair, we follow the setting of independent feature distribution and check for demographic parity [9]. For both tools, we set $c = 0.15$ as suggested and keep other parameters as default. As both FairSquare and VeriFair are designed to compare two groups of sub-populations, for those protected features that have more than two

Table 3. Comparison with FairSquare, VeriFair and Statistical Model Checking (SMC)

Dataset	Prot. Feat.	FairSquare		VeriFair		SMC		Ours	
		Result	Time	Result	Time	Result	Time	Result	Time
Census	Race	–	T.O.	Pass	2.33 s	Pass	0.81 s	Pass	0.93 s
Census	Age	–	T.O.	Pass	37.14 s	Pass	0.74 s	Pass	0.81 s
Census	Gender	–	T.O.	Pass	2.19 s	Pass	0.69 s	Pass	0.89 s
Credit	Age	–	T.O.	Pass	39.29 s	Pass	0.78 s	Pass	0.90 s
Credit	Gender	–	T.O.	Pass	8.23 s	Pass	0.70 s	Pass	0.82 s
Bank	Age	–	T.O.	Pass	245.34 s	Pass	0.66 s	Pass	0.97 s
Jigsaw	Religion	–	–	–	–	Pass	14.9 m	Pass	15.3 m
Jigsaw	Race	–	–	–	–	Pass	14.2 m	Pass	14.5 m

categories, we perform binning to form two groups. For the six FFNN models, we set timeout value to be $900s$ following the setting in VeriFair. As shown in Table 3, FairSquare is not able to scale for large neural network and for all FFNN models it fails to verify or falsify the model in time. Both VeriFair and our approach successfully verified all six FFNN models. But our approach completes the verification within 1s for all models while VeriFair takes 62 times more execution time than our approach on average. For the RNN models trained on Jigsaw dataset, neither FairSquare nor VeriFair is able to analyze them. FairSquare supports only loop-free models and, hence, it cannot handle RNN models. Although VeriFair is able to handle RNN networks in general, it does not support text classifiers. To evaluate the overhead introduced by constructing DTMCs in our approach, we further compare our approach with statistical model checking (SMC). In this experiment, we generate the same amount of samples as required by our approach for each scenario and directly perform statistical model checking. The result is shown in 3 column *SMC*. Compared with our approach, it is observed that most of the time were taken by sampling and inference and the overhead of building DTMCs is around 2.4% on average. Hence, compared with existing solutions, our approach is more efficient than FairSquare and VeriFair and can support RNN-based text classifiers. Furthermore, the overhead of constructing DTMCs is negligible.

5   Related Work

Neural network verification. There have been multiple approaches proposed to verify the robustness of neural networks utilizing various techniques, i.e., abstraction [23,29,48], SMT sovler [32,34,35], MILP and LP [22,52], symbolic execution [57] and many others [15,20,31,38]. Besides [6] and [9] that we addressed in RQ4, [28] and [43] studied fairness property of text classifiers. Unlike ours, they focus on text classifiers only and their performance on RNN is unknown.

Fairness testing and improvement. There have been an impressive line of methods proposed recently on machine learning model fairness testing and improvement. THEMIS [8, 27], AEQUITAS [54], Symbolic Generation (SG) [4] and ADF [58], are proposed to generate discriminatory instances for fairness testing. There are also existing proposals on fairness training [3, 12, 14, 16, 28, 36]. Our work instead focuses on post-processing where a trained model is repaired based on sensitivity analysis results to improve fairness.

Machine learning model repair. There have been multiple approaches proposed to repair machine learning models based on various technologies, i.e., [49] leverages SMT solving, [30] is based on advances in verification methods, [5] is guided by input population and etc. Unlike these methods, our work focuses on fairness repair and supports FFNN and RNN by design.

6 Conclusion

In this work, we proposed an approach to formally verify neural networks against fairness properties. Our work relies on an approach for leaning DTMC from given neural network with PAC-correct guarantee. Our approach further performs sensitivity analysis on the neural network if it fails the fairness property and provides useful information on why the network is unfair. This result is then used as a guideline to adjust network parameters and achieve fairness. Comparing with existing methods evaluating neural network fairness, our approach has significantly better performance in terms of efficiency and effectiveness.

Acknowledgements. We thank anonymous reviewers for their constructive feedback. This research is partly supported by Singapore Ministry of Education (project MOET 32020 − 0004) and Guangdong Science and Technology Department (Grant Number 2018B010107004).

References

1. https://www.kaggle.com/c/jigsaw-toxic-comment-classification-challenge
2. Draft ethics guidelines for trustworthy AI. Tech. rep., European Commission (2018)
3. Agarwal, A., Beygelzimer, A., Dudík, M., Langford, J., Wallach, H.M.: A reductions approach to fair classification. In: Dy, J.G., Krause, A. (eds.) Proceedings of the 35th International Conference on Machine Learning, ICML 2018, Stockholmsmässan, Stockholm, Sweden, 10-15 July 2018. Proceedings of Machine Learning Research, vol. 80, pp. 60–69. PMLR (2018). http://proceedings.mlr.press/v80/agarwal18a.html
4. Agarwal, A., Lohia, P., Nagar, S., Dey, K., Saha, D.: Automated test generation to detect individual discrimination in AI models. CoRR (2018). http://arxiv.org/abs/1809.03260
5. Albarghouthi, A., D'Antoni, L., Drews, S.: Repairing decision-making programs under uncertainty. In: Majumdar, R., Kunčak, V. (eds.) Computer Aided Verification, CAV 2017. LNCS, vol. 10426, pp. 181–200. Springer, Cham (2017). https://doi.org/10.1007/978-3-319-63387-9_9
6. Albarghouthi, A., D'Antoni, L., Drews, S., Nori, A.V.: Fairsquare: probabilistic verification of program fairness. Proc. ACM Program. Lang. 1(OOPSLA), 80:1–80:30 (2017). https://doi.org/10.1145/3133904

7. Alzantot, M., Sharma, Y., Elgohary, A., Ho, B., Srivastava, M.B., Chang, K.: Generating natural language adversarial examples. In: Proceedings of the 2018 Conference on Empirical Methods in Natural Language Processing (EMNLP 2018), Brussels, Belgium, pp. 2890–2896 (2018). https://doi.org/10.18653/v1/d18-1316
8. Angell, R., Johnson, B., Brun, Y., Meliou, A.: Themis: automatically testing software for discrimination. In: Proceedings of the 2018 ACM Joint Meeting on European Software Engineering Conference and Symposium on the Foundations of Software Engineering (ESEC/SIGSOFT FSE 2018), Lake Buena Vista, FL, USA, pp. 871–875 (2018). https://doi.org/10.1145/3236024.3264590
9. Bastani, O., Zhang, X., Solar-Lezama, A.: Probabilistic verification of fairness properties via concentration. PACMPL 3(OOPSLA), 118:1–118:27 (2019). https://doi.org/10.1145/3360544
10. Bazille, H., Genest, B., Jegourel, C., Sun, J.: Global PAC bounds for learning discrete time Markov chains. In: Lahiri, S.K., Wang, C. (eds.) Computer Aided Verification, CAV 2020. LNCS, vol. 12225, pp. 304–326. Springer, Cham (2020). https://doi.org/10.1007/978-3-030-53291-8_17
11. Ben-Ari, M., Pnueli, A., Manna, Z.: The temporal logic of branching time. Acta Informatica 20, 207–226 (1983). https://doi.org/10.1007/BF01257083
12. Berk, R., et al.: A convex framework for fair regression. CoRR abs/1706.02409 (2017). http://arxiv.org/abs/1706.02409
13. Bojarski, M., et al.: End to end learning for self-driving cars. CoRR (2016).http://arxiv.org/abs/1604.07316
14. Bolukbasi, T., Chang, K., Zou, J.Y., Saligrama, V., Kalai, A.T.: Man is to computer programmer as woman is to homemaker? debiasing word embeddings. In: Advances in Neural Information Processing Systems 29: Annual Conference on Neural Information Processing Systems 2016 (NeurIPS 2016), Barcelona, Spain, pp. 4349–4357 (2016). http://papers.nips.cc/paper/6228-man-is-to-computer-programmer-as-woman-is-to-homemaker-debiasing-word-embeddings
15. Bunel, R., Lu, J., Turkaslan, I., Torr, P.H.S., Kohli, P., Kumar, M.P.: Branch and bound for piecewise linear neural network verification. J. Mach. Learn. Res. 21, 42:1–42:39 (2020). http://jmlr.org/papers/v21/19-468.html
16. Cava, W.L., Moore, J.: Genetic programming approaches to learning fair classifiers. In: Proceedings of the 2020 Genetic and Evolutionary Computation Conference (2020)
17. Dua, D., Graff, C.: Bank marketing dataset at UCI machine learning repository (2017). https://archive.ics.uci.edu/ml/datasets/Bank+Marketing
18. Dua, D., Graff, C.: Census income dataset at UCI machine learning repository (2017). https://archive.ics.uci.edu/ml/datasets/adult
19. Dua, D., Graff, C.: German credit dataset at UCI machine learning repository (2017). https://archive.ics.uci.edu/ml/datasets/statlog+(german+credit+data)
20. Dvijotham, K.D., Stanforth, R., Gowal, S., Qin, C., De, S., Kohli, P.: Efficient neural network verification with exactness characterization. In: Globerson, A., Silva, R. (eds.) Proceedings of the Thirty-Fifth Conference on Uncertainty in Artificial Intelligence, UAI 2019, Tel Aviv, Israel, 22–25 July 2019. Proceedings of Machine Learning Research, vol. 115, pp. 497–507. AUAI Press (2019). http://proceedings.mlr.press/v115/dvijotham20a.html
21. Dwork, C., Hardt, M., Pitassi, T., Reingold, O., Zemel, R.S.: Fairness through awareness. In: Innovations in Theoretical Computer Science 2012, Cambridge, MA, USA, pp. 214–226 (2012). https://doi.org/10.1145/2090236.2090255
22. Ehlers, R.: Formal verification of piece-wise linear feed-forward neural networks. CoRR abs/1705.01320 (2017). http://arxiv.org/abs/1705.01320

23. Elboher, Y.Y., Gottschlich, J., Katz, G.: An abstraction-based framework for neural network verification. In: Lahiri, S.K., Wang, C. (eds.) CAV 2020. LNCS, vol. 12224, pp. 43–65. Springer, Cham (2020). https://doi.org/10.1007/978-3-030-53288-8_3

24. Feldman, M., Friedler, S.A., Moeller, J., Scheidegger, C., Venkatasubramanian, S.: Certifying and removing disparate impact. In: Proceedings of the 21th ACM SIGKDD International Conference on Knowledge Discovery and Data Mining, Sydney, NSW, Australia, pp. 259–268 (2015). https://doi.org/10.1145/2783258.2783311

25. Fu, K., Cheng, D., Tu, Y., Zhang, L.: Credit card fraud detection using convolutional neural networks. In: Hirose, A., Ozawa, S., Doya, K., Ikeda, K., Lee, M., Liu, D. (eds.) Neural Information Processing, ICONIP 2016. LNCS, vol. 9949, pp. 483–490. Springer, Cham (2016). https://doi.org/10.1007/978-3-319-46675-0_53

26. Gale, W.: Good-turing smoothing without tears. J. Quant. Linguist. 217–37 (1995)

27. Galhotra, S., Brun, Y., Meliou, A.: Fairness testing: testing software for discrimination. In: Proceedings of the 2017 11th Joint Meeting on Foundations of Software Engineering (ESEC/FSE 2017), Paderborn, Germany, pp. 498–510 (2017). https://doi.org/10.1145/3106237.3106277

28. Garg, S., Perot, V., Limtiaco, N., Taly, A., Chi, E.H., Beutel, A.: Counterfactual fairness in text classification through robustness. In: Proceedings of the 2019 AAAI/ACM Conference on AI, Ethics, and Society (AIES 2019), Honolulu, HI, USA, pp. 219–226 (2019). https://doi.org/10.1145/3306618.3317950

29. Gehr, T., Mirman, M., Drachsler-Cohen, D., Tsankov, P., Chaudhuri, S., Vechev, M.T.: AI2: safety and robustness certification of neural networks with abstract interpretation. In: 2018 IEEE Symposium on Security and Privacy, SP 2018, Proceedings, 21–23 May 2018, San Francisco, California, USA, pp. 3–18. IEEE Computer Society (2018). https://doi.org/10.1109/SP.2018.00058

30. Goldberger, B., Katz, G., Adi, Y., Keshet, J.: Minimal modifications of deep neural networks using verification. In: Albert, E., Kovács, L. (eds.) LPAR 2020: 23rd International Conference on Logic for Programming, Artificial Intelligence and Reasoning, Alicante, Spain, 22–27 May 2020. EPiC Series in Computing, vol. 73, pp. 260–278. EasyChair (2020). https://easychair.org/publications/paper/CWhF

31. Gross, D., Jansen, N., Pérez, G.A., Raaijmakers, S.: Robustness verification for classifier ensembles. In: Hung, D.V., Sokolsky, O. (eds.) Automated Technology for Verification and Analysis, ATVA 2020. LNCS, vol. 12302, pp. 271–287. Springer, Cham (2020). https://doi.org/10.1007/978-3-030-59152-6_15

32. Jacoby, Y., Barrett, C., Katz, G.: Verifying recurrent neural networks using invariant inference. In: Hung, D.V., Sokolsky, O. (eds.) Automated Technology for Verification and Analysis, ATVA 2020. LNCS, vol. 12302, pp. 57–74. Springer, Cham (2020). https://doi.org/10.1007/978-3-030-59152-6_3

33. Jia, R., Liang, P.: Adversarial examples for evaluating reading comprehension systems. In: Proceedings of the 2017 Conference on Empirical Methods in Natural Language Processing (EMNLP 2017), Copenhagen, Denmark, pp. 2021–2031 (2017). https://doi.org/10.18653/v1/d17-1215

34. Katz, G., Barrett, C., Dill, D.L., Julian, K., Kochenderfer, M.J.: Reluplex: an efficient SMT solver for verifying deep neural networks. In: Majumdar, R., Kunčak, V. (eds.) Computer Aided Verification, CAV 2017. LNCS, vol. 10426, pp. 97–117. Springer, Cham (2017). https://doi.org/10.1007/978-3-319-63387-9_5

35. Katz, G., et al.: The marabou framework for verification and analysis of deep neural networks. In: Dillig, I., Tasiran, S. (eds.) Computer Aided Verification, CAV 2019. LNCS, vol. 11561, pp. 443–452. Springer, Cham (2019). https://doi.org/10.1007/978-3-030-25540-4_26

36. Kearns, M.J., Neel, S., Roth, A., Wu, Z.S.: Preventing fairness gerrymandering: auditing and learning for subgroup fairness. In: Dy, J.G., Krause, A. (eds.) Proceedings of the 35th International Conference on Machine Learning, ICML 2018, Stockholmsmässan, Stockholm, Sweden, 10–15 July 2018. Proceedings of Machine Learning Research, vol. 80, pp. 2569–2577. PMLR (2018). http://proceedings.mlr.press/v80/kearns18a.html

37. Kennedy, J., Eberhart, R.: Particle swarm optimization. In: Proceedings of ICNN'95 - International Conference on Neural Networks, vol. 4, pp. 1942–1948 (1995). https://doi.org/10.1109/ICNN.1995.488968

38. Ko, C., Lyu, Z., Weng, L., Daniel, L., Wong, N., Lin, D.: POPQORN: quantifying robustness of recurrent neural networks. In: Chaudhuri, K., Salakhutdinov, R. (eds.) Proceedings of the 36th International Conference on Machine Learning, ICML 2019, 9–15 June 2019, Long Beach, California, USA. Proceedings of Machine Learning Research, vol. 97, pp. 3468–3477. PMLR (2019). http://proceedings.mlr.press/v97/ko19a.html

39. Kwiatkowska, M., Norman, G., Parker, D.: Advances and challenges of probabilistic model checking. In: 2010 48th Annual Allerton Conference on Communication, Control, and Computing, Allerton 2010 (2010). https://doi.org/10.1109/ALLERTON.2010.5707120

40. Legay, A., Delahaye, B., Bensalem, S., et al.: Statistical model checking: an overview. In: Barringer, H. (ed.) Runtime Verification, pp. 122–135. Springer, Berlin Heidelberg, Berlin, Heidelberg (2010)

41. Li, J., Ji, S., Du, T., Li, B., Wang, T.: Textbugger: generating adversarial text against real-world applications. In: 26th Annual Network and Distributed System Security Symposium (NDSS 2019), San Diego, California, USA (2019). https://www.ndss-symposium.org/ndss-paper/textbugger-generating-adversarial-text-against-real-world-applications/

42. Lloyd, S.P.: Least squares quantization in PCM. IEEE Trans. Inf. Theor. 28(2), 129–136 (1982). https://doi.org/10.1109/TIT.1982.1056489

43. Ma, P., Wang, S., Liu, J.: Metamorphic testing and certified mitigation of fairness violations in NLP models. In: Bessiere, C. (ed.) Proceedings of the Twenty-Ninth International Joint Conference on Artificial Intelligence, IJCAI 2020, pp. 458–465 (2020). https://doi.org/10.24963/ijcai.2020/64

44. Pennington, J., Socher, R., Manning, C.D.: Glove: global vectors for word representation. In: Proceedings of the 2014 Conference on Empirical Methods in Natural Language Processing (EMNLP 2014), 25–29 October 2014, Doha, Qatar, pp. 1532–1543 (2014). https://www.aclweb.org/anthology/D14-1162/

45. Pham, L.H., Li, J., Sun, J.: SOCRATES: towards a unified platform for neural network verification. CoRR abs/2007.11206 (2020). https://arxiv.org/abs/2007.11206

46. Řehůřek, R., Sojka, P.: Software framework for topic modelling with large Corpora. In: Proceedings of the LREC 2010 Workshop on New Challenges for NLP Frameworks, Valletta, Malta, pp. 45–50 (2010). http://is.muni.cz/publication/884893/en

47. Schroff, F., Kalenichenko, D., Philbin, J.: Facenet: a unified embedding for face recognition and clustering. In: IEEE Conference on Computer Vision and Pattern Recognition (CVPR 2015), Boston, MA, USA, pp. 815–823 (2015). https://doi.org/10.1109/CVPR.2015.7298682

48. Singh, G., Gehr, T., Püschel, M., Vechev, M.T.: An abstract domain for certifying neural networks. Proc. ACM Program. Lang. 3(POPL), 41:1–41:30 (2019). https://doi.org/10.1145/3290354

49. Sotoudeh, M., Thakur, A.: Correcting deep neural networks with small, generalizing patches. In: Workshop on Safety and Robustness in Decision Making (2019)

50. Sun, B., Sun, J., Dai, T., Zhang, L.: Probabilistic verification of neural networks against group fairness. CoRR abs/2107.08362 (2021). https://arxiv.org/abs/2107.08362

51. Thomas, P.S., da Silva, B.C., Barto, A.G., Giguere, S., Brun, Y., Brunskill, E.: Preventing undesirable behavior of intelligent machines. Science 366(6468), 999–1004 (2019). https://science.sciencemag.org/content/366/6468/999

52. Tjeng, V., Xiao, K.Y., Tedrake, R.: Evaluating robustness of neural networks with mixed integer programming. In: 7th International Conference on Learning Representations, ICLR 2019, New Orleans, LA, USA, 6–9 May 2019 (2019). https://openreview.net/forum?id=HyGIdiRqtm

53. Tramèr, F., et al.: Fairtest: discovering unwarranted associations in data-driven applications. In: 2017 IEEE European Symposium on Security and Privacy (EuroS and P 2017), Paris, France, pp. 401–416 (2017). https://doi.org/10.1109/EuroSP.2017.29

54. Udeshi, S., Arora, P., Chattopadhyay, S.: Automated directed fairness testing. In: Huchard, M., Kästner, C., Fraser, G. (eds.) Proceedings of the 33rd ACM/IEEE International Conference on Automated Software Engineering, ASE 2018, Montpellier, France, 3–7 September 2018, pp. 98–108. ACM (2018). https://doi.org/10.1145/3238147.3238165

55. Veale, M., Binns, R.: Fairer machine learning in the real world: mitigating discrimination without collecting sensitive data. Big Data Soc. 4 (2017)

56. Vieira, S., Pinaya, W.H., Mechelli, A.: Using deep learning to investigate the neuroimaging correlates of psychiatric and neurological disorders: methods and applications. Neurosci. Biobehav. Rev. 74, 58–75 (2017). https://doi.org/10.1016/j.neubiorev.2017.01.002

57. Wang, S., Pei, K., Whitehouse, J., Yang, J., Jana, S.: Formal security analysis of neural networks using symbolic intervals. In: Enck, W., Felt, A.P. (eds.) 27th USENIX Security Symposium, USENIX Security 2018, Baltimore, MD, USA, 15–17 August 2018, pp. 1599–1614. USENIX Association (2018). https://www.usenix.org/conference/usenixsecurity18/presentation/wang-shiqi

58. Zhang, P., et al.: White-box fairness testing through adversarial sampling. In: Proceedings of the 42th International Conference on Software Engineering (ICSE 2020), Seoul, South Korea (2020)

BanditFuzz: Fuzzing SMT Solvers with Multi-agent Reinforcement Learning

Joseph Scott[1]([✉]) [iD], Trishal Sudula[1] [iD], Hammad Rehman[1] [iD],
Federico Mora[2] [iD], and Vijay Ganesh[1] [iD]

[1] University of Waterloo, Waterloo, ON, Canada
{joseph.scott,trishal.sudula,harehman,vijay.ganesh}@uwaterloo.ca
[2] University of California, Berkeley, USA
fmora@berkeley.edu

Abstract. We present BanditFuzz, a multi-agent reinforcement learning
(RL) guided performance fuzzer for state-of-the-art Satisfiability Modulo Theories (SMT) solvers. BanditFuzz constructs inputs that expose
performance issues in a set of target solvers relative to a set of reference
solvers, and is the first performance fuzzer that supports the entirety of
the theories in the SMT-LIB initiative. Another useful feature of Bandit-
Fuzz is that users can specify the size of inputs they want, thus enabling
developers to construct very small inputs that zero-in on a performance
problem in their SMT solver relative to other competitive solvers. We
evaluate BanditFuzz across 52 logics from SMT-COMP '20 targeting
competition-winning solvers against runner-ups. We baseline BanditFuzz
against random fuzzing and a single agent algorithm and observe a significant improvement, with up to a 82.6% improvement in the margin of
PAR-2 scores across baselines on their respective benchmarks. Furthermore, we reached out to developers and contributors of the CVC4, Z3,
and Bitwuzla solvers and provide case studies of how BanditFuzz was
able to expose surprising performance deficiencies in each of these tools.

1 Introduction

In recent years, efficient Satisfiability Modulo Theories (SMT) solvers have dramatically impacted many areas of software engineering and security. Applications
of these tools range from program analysis [13,19,24], synthesis [39,44], model
checking [1,14,26], test case generation [12], and neural network verification [25],
to name just a few.

With efficient SMT solvers being the catalyst for numerous developments
in academia and industry, there is an insatiable demand for evermore powerful solvers. To this end, researchers have spent decades optimizing these tools.
Regrettably, despite these advances, SMT solvers are prone to hard-to-find performance deficiencies. While the worst-case complexity of the problems solved by

This work was supported in part by NSF grants CNS-1739816 and CCF-1837132, by
the DARPA LOGiCS project under contract FA8750-20-C-0156, by the iCyPhy center,
and by gifts from Intel, Amazon, and Microsoft.

© Springer Nature Switzerland AG 2021
M. Huisman et al. (Eds.): FM 2021, LNCS 13047, pp. 103–121, 2021.
https://doi.org/10.1007/978-3-030-90870-6_6

SMT solvers can be very high, they can be frustratingly slow on relatively simple formulas. Such performance deficiencies can be due to developer oversight (e.g., missing rewrite rules or unoptimized code and data structures) or the result of hard-to-entangle interactions of solver heuristics. If solvers are to continue to impact industry and fuel further research, it is imperative that there be an initiative to find and eliminate such performance deficiencies where possible.

In this paper, we make a case for the use of software performance fuzzing [28, 45,47] to systematically find such deficiencies in state-of-the-art SMT solvers. Software fuzzing techniques have had tremendous impacts in making SMT Solvers more robust [7,10,34,48,49], and there is no reason why performance fuzzers cannot have a similar impact. While it is still a relatively a new field, performance fuzzing is already showing promise in many domains despite the difficulty of the problem of finding suitable inputs that expose performance issues in programs-under-test [23,27].

This paper presents the BanditFuzz tool, a performance fuzzer that supports the entirety of the theories in SMT-LIB. We define the notion of "performance issue", in the SMT solver setting, in a relative sense. That is, we say that solver A is less performant on an input I relative to solver B, if solver B (that supports the same input language as A) can solve I significantly faster. This is very natural, since if both solvers-under-test are not able to solve an input, it doesn't unambiguously point to a performance issue in either. However, when one solver is significantly faster than a competing one on a given input, there is no question that the slower solver has a performance issue.

How BanditFuzz Works: The input to BanditFuzz is a set of target solvers, a set of reference solvers, and a constraint (e.g., size of input desired, the input language of the solvers), and its output is a single benchmark or test input, such that a quantity we refer to as the "performance margin" between the target solver and reference solver is maximized (the tool is designed to be run over multiple processes to create a benchmark suite). Intuitively, the performance margin can be defined as difference between the runtimes (or PAR-2 scores [31]) of a target and a reference solver on a given input.

Internally, BanditFuzz uses a two-agent reinforcement learning (RL) method to mutate a randomly-generated input such that over time the performance margin between a target and a reference solver is maximized. More precisely, first an input benchmark is randomly-generated and queried across all solvers. One of the agents learns how to mutate a benchmark by inserting and replacing the grammatical constructs of the SMT-LIB language, respecting the size constraints set forth by the user. More precisely, this agent manages an exploration vs. exploitation trade-off between trying new grammatical constructs (explore) vs. inserting ones that have been shown to increase the performance margin (exploit). The other agent manages the exploration vs. exploitation trade-off between generating new inputs (explore) or mutating the best-observed input (exploit). Fuzzers, including single-agent RL fuzzers, are notorious for getting stuck in local minima [16,17,29,41]. This two-agent RL method, by contrast, may avoid getting stuck in local minima.

Contributions

Specifically, we make the following contributions in this paper:

1. **BanditFuzz: A Multi-agent RL Performance Fuzzing Algorithm.** To the best of our knowledge, BanditFuzz is the first multi-agent RL performance fuzzing algorithm for SMT solvers that supports the entirety of SMT-LIB. The BanditFuzz tool includes two agents, one which learns how to mutate the best observed input [42] and another to help prevent the tool getting stuck in a local minimum (Sect. 3).
2. **Empirical Evaluation.** We provide an implementation of the performance fuzzer BanditFuzz [42] and lift it to the entirety of the theories in the SMT-LIB initiative, namely, Arrays, Bit-Vectors, Booleans, Floating-Point, Integers, Reals, Strings, Uninterpreted Functions, and all combinations thereof in both quantified and quantifier-free logics (Sects. 3, 5, 6). To test Bandit-Fuzz, we perform an extensive empirical evaluation across all 52 logics that were tested in SMT-COMP '20, with the aim of finding benchmarks where competition winners are slow relative to runner up solvers. We provide to the community a set of 1500 benchmarks across all logics, exposing relative performance issues in state-of-the-art competition-winning SMT Solvers. To validate the efficiency of BanditFuzz, we baseline it against random fuzzing and observe BanditFuzz to consistently outperform random fuzzing by up to a 82.6% increase in `PAR-2` margins (Sects. 3 and 5).
3. **Case studies of BanditFuzz with Solver Developers.** To further demonstrate the usefulness of BanditFuzz, we include three case studies of Bandit-Fuzz being used by solver developers and contributors. Specifically, developers were able to use BanditFuzz to find performance issues in the Z3 [15], CVC4 [3], and Bitwuzla [32,33] SMT Solvers (Sect. 3).

The rest of this paper is structured as follows: Sect. 2 provides the necessary background on reinforcement learning, SMT, and software fuzzing. Section 3 gives a technical description of BanditFuzz. Section 5 describes how to use Bandit-Fuzz, Sect. 6 gives an experimental evaluation of BanditFuzz over 52 from the SMT-LIB community, Sect. 7 goes over case studies with solver developers using BanditFuzz, Sect. 8 mentions threats to the validity of BanditFuzz, and Sect. 10 concludes the paper and discusses future work.

2 Background on Reinforcement Learning

In this section, we provide the necessary background and terminology of Reinforcement Learning, Satisfiability Modulo Theories, and Software Fuzzing for this paper.

2.1   Reinforcement Learning

There is a large literature on reinforcement learning and we refer the reader to the book by Sutton et al., on this topic [46]. In RL, an agent navigates an environment by taking actions to maximize the received reward. The multi-armed bandit (MAB) problem is a well-known RL problem based on a Markov Decision Process with a single state and a finite set of actions A. Since there is only a single state, MABs can be solved using computationally cheap algorithms relative to algorithms for other RL problems [46]. The agent solving the MAB computes an approximation of the probability distribution of rewards R over A. In the context of MAB, actions are often referred to as arms (or bandits). The term 'bandit' comes from gambling, as the arm or lever of a slot machine is referred to as a one-armed bandit, and MABs refer to several slot machines. The goal of the MAB agent is to maximize its reward by playing a sequence of actions (e.g., selecting which band/lever to pull).

In practice, MAB problems are commonly modelled so rewards are sampled from an unknown Bernoulli distribution (e.g., rewards are in $\{0, 1\}$). The MAB agent attempts to approximate the expected value of reward from the Bernoulli distribution for each action in A. Over time, the agent uses these distributions to form a *policy* – a stochastic process of how to select actions from A. This policy must remain privy to the exploration/exploitation trade-off, i.e., an MAB algorithm selects every action an infinite number of times, but selects the action(s) with the highest expected reward more frequently.

There are several algorithms for the MAB problem. In this paper, we exclusively consider *Thompson Sampling*. In Thompson Sampling, an agent maintains a Beta distribution for each action in the action space A. Beta distributions are derived from Gamma distributions, and have a long history with numerous applications. We refer the reader to Gupta et al. on Beta and Gamma distributions [20]. In the context of Thompson Sampling, a Beta distribution acts as continuous model of the expected value of a Bernoulli distribution. It is maintained by two shape parameters α the samples of 1, and β the samples of 0, from the underlying Bernoulli distribution. The agent selects an action by sampling each action's Beta distribution and greedily picks the action based on the maximum over the sampled values. Upon taking the action, α is incremented on reward, otherwise β is incremented. For more on Thompson sampling we refer to Russo et al. [40].

2.2   Satisfiability Modulo Theories

Satisfiability Modulo Theories (SMT) solvers are decision problems on first-order theories such as integers, bit-vectors, arrays, floating-point, and strings that are particularly suitable for verification, program analysis, and testing. The SMT-LIB provides a standardized syntax and semantics for several first-order theories and logics [4]. In this paper, we use the following acronyms (given in brackets), optionally in combination, to refer to various SMT-LIB logics: Quantifier Free (QF), Theory of Arrays (A), Uninterpreted Functions (UF), Bit-Vectors (BV),

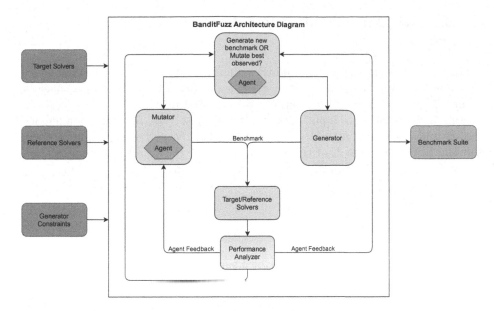

Fig. 1. Architecture Diagram of BanditFuzz. The BanditFuzz tool deploys two unique agents: one is a mutator agent that learns how to mutate the best observed input, while the other agent aims to assist in the prevention of getting stuck in local minima. Both agents learn an action selection policy in a feedback loop based on the empirically collected data over the course of running the target and reference solvers over the generated benchmarks.

Floating-Point (FP), Strings (S), Integers (I), Reals (R), or mixed (IR). Further, arithmetic over I and R can be linear (e.g., LIA, LRA), or nonlinear (e.g., NIA, NRA), or difference logics (IDL, RDL). For combinations of such, their order appears in the order they are written above. Each theory defines various operators/functions, predicates, terms, sorts, and generalized keywords (e.g., assert, check-sat, Int, Float32). For a full list of these, as well as more details on syntax and semantics, we refer to the SMT-LIB standard [4].

2.3   Software Fuzzing

Software fuzzing is a vast and active field of research. We refer to a recent survey that provides an overview of the field [28]. A *fuzzer* is a program that automatically generates inputs for a target program-under-test. A fuzzer is *blackbox* if it does not have access to the program-under-test. Fuzzers that are *model-based*, implement a *generator* which samples from the space of well-formed inputs. A *mutation* is a mapping from the space of inputs to the space of inputs.

3   BanditFuzz: A Multi-agent RL-Guided Performance Fuzzer

In this section, we describe the BanditFuzz fuzzing framework. BanditFuzz leverages reinforcement learning (RL) to guide a random fuzzer through a space of inputs. The architecture of BanditFuzz is presented in Fig. 1.

BanditFuzz takes as input a set T of target solvers, a set R of reference solvers and a set of constraints (e.g., size of the generated test input desired, and the SMT language L of the solvers in T and R (we refer to this as Generator Constraints in Fig. 1), and outputs a benchmark I that maximizes the performance margin between the solvers in T and R. The output of BanditFuzz is a benchmark or benchmark suite.

3.1   The Performance Margin

Formally, BanditFuzz solves a search problem to find a solver input I over the language L that maximizes the performance margin between T and R

$$\max_{I \in L} \phi(T, R, I)$$

where ϕ is a scoring function. In this paper, we will exclusively consider a scoring function of the PAR-2 score margin between the best performing target solver and worst performing reference solver. More formally, we score each input I with respect to T, R as follows:

$$\phi(T, R, I) = \min_{t \in T}(\texttt{PAR-2}(t, I)) - \max_{r \in R}(\texttt{PAR-2}(r, I))$$

where the PAR-2 function returns twice the wallclock timeout if the solver fails to solve the input, otherwise, the wallclock runtime. PAR-2 is a useful metric that quantifies a tools' performance over a benchmark suite and is used to determine winners in the SAT competitions [31]. These calculations correspond to the 'Performance Analyzer' in Fig. 1.

3.2   BanditFuzz: The Multi-agent RL-Based Fuzzing Algorithm

This tool paper presents an implementation of the BanditFuzz algorithm with three key improvements. First, BanditFuzz supports all theories in the SMT-LIB standard [4] and all their combined corresponding logics. The action set of the mutator agent is the set of grammatical constructs across all enabled logics.

The second major change is that this tool is now multi-agent. The BanditFuzz tool includes a second agent to assist in preventing the tool from getting stuck in local minima, which is a major problem in fuzzing in general [16,17,29,41]. A key contribution of this paper is an additional agent with the following **action set**: {Mutate the best observed benchmark, Randomly Sample from L}. The previous approach had a fixed alternation scheme of randomly sampling and mutating the best observed input, which posteriori, resulted in the algorithm frequently getting stuck in local minima, as it is oblivious to all previously collected empirical data. The second agent uses a similar **reward signal** if the most recent benchmark improves on the best observed benchmark, reward is received, otherwise no reward is received.

3.3   The Original BanditFuzz Algorithm vs. The Current Version

The original BanditFuzz fuzzing algorithm proposed by Scott et al. [42] is a mutational fuzzer that leverages single-agent RL method to find performance deficiencies in the quantifier-free floating-point and quantifier free-string logics. Specifically, the original algorithm learns how to make a *fuzzing mutation* (i.e., a minimal modification to an input seed). The key differences between their tool and the one presented here are the following: first, the current version of BanditFuzz uses a multi-agent RL method that avoids getting stuck in local minima that afflicted their tool, and second, the current version supports the entirety of SMT-LIB, whereas the previous one only supported floating-point and strings.

4   Implementation and Engineering

In this section, we discuss some of the implementation and the engineering of BanditFuzz. The BanditFuzz tool is written in Python3 and contains 5,000 lines of code. BanditFuzz is lightweight with minimal dependencies and can be installed in seconds.

Input/Output: Reference/Target solvers are provided to BanditFuzz as paths to an executable file which acts as an interface to the solver. These executable files will run internally within BanditFuzz during its main runtime loop. The generator constraints are command-line arguments bounding formula sizes with several theory specific constraints (e.g., bit-width, UF arity, etc.). The output of BanditFuzz is a directory of benchmarks with timing and memory analysis. A single run BanditFuzz will produce a single benchmark. To build a benchmark suite, BanditFuzz can safely be run in parallel and tested on several major cloud computing environments (e.g., AWS). We provide an interface that allows for this to be done via the command line.

Generator: The generator module is responsible for producing well-formed SMT-LIB inputs. Internally, BanditFuzz an Abstract Syntax Tree (AST) data structure to represent a benchmark. Each AST is asserted with root nodes of a boolean sort and positive arity. Each AST is populated by randomly sampling from the set constructs of the required sort with leaf nodes of variables or theory literals. All ASTs are full with respect to the maximum depth specified by the user.

Mutator: A mutator is a python method that takes as input a benchmark and a grammatical construct. The output is a perturbation of the input benchmark that contains a novel occurrence of the input construct. The mutator works by constructing the set nodes of the input construct's sort and then uniformly at random replaces the selected construct with the input construct. The mutator then applies a procedure to ensure the resulting benchmark remains well-formed as the node replacement may result in an arity change. This is done by deleting or generating new subtrees that are consistent with the generator constraints. Like the generator, the resulting AST from the mutator is full with respect to the maximum depth.

Agents: We use a context-free MAB approach in this paper for our agent, namely Thompson Sampling. However, in principle, this can be lifted to several more RL paradigms. Our agent implementation is lightweight and makes a single external API call (i.e., the NumPy beta distribution sampling method [21]). Furthermore, unlike several RL paradigms, our MAB solution only has a single hyper-parameter, the exponential decay of the observed empirical mean.

Performance Analyzer: We include a performance analyzer to monitor the subprocesses' resource consumption (e.g., wall-clock runtimes and memory). Processes are killed if they violate the user's constraints. When calling solvers, target solvers are run first under the provided constraints. Afterward, reference solvers are ran using a dynamic timeout scheme based best-observed performance margin. This prevents wasting time on the reference solvers when it is no longer possible for the current benchmark to have a higher margin than the best observed.

5   Using the BanditFuzz Fuzzing Framework

In this section, we demonstrate how to use BanditFuzz. The BanditFuzz package has two core tools:

- `smtfuzz` – A fuzzer (i.e., a tool that generates inputs to a program-under-test) for all SMT-LIB theories. In principle, this fuzzer can be used in any fuzzing context, but in this paper it is the core fuzzer in BanditFuzz's fuzzing algorithm.
- `banditfuzz` – An implementation of the BanditFuzz performance fuzzing algorithm. This program calls `smtfuzz` in a loop and inherits all of its command line arguments.

5.1   Using `smtfuzz`

The `smtfuzz` tool generates random Abstract Syntax Trees (ASTs) based on the enabled theories. `smtfuzz` is designed to be extremely flexible. Users can modify the problem size easily by setting the `--num-asserts` and `--depth` parameters to increase the number of assertions and size of each assertion respectively. The generator in `smtfuzz` supports all core theories in the SMT-LIB initiative [4]. Each theory can be enabled by setting its respective flag. `smtfuzz` will automatically set the problem's logic based on the enabled theories (Table 1 and Fig. 2).

Table 1. Sample of generator arguments for the BanditFuzz tool

Argument	Description
--num-asserts	Set the number of assertions in the generated benchmark
--depth	Set the depth of each asserting AST
--num-vars	The number of theory variables
-q --quantifiers	Enable quantifiers
-a --arrays	Enable arrays
-uf --uninterpreted-functions	Enable uninterpreted functions
-str --strings	Enable strings
-fp --floating-point	Enable floating-point
-bv --bit-vectors	Enable bit-vectors
-int --integer	Enable integers
-r --real	Enable reals
-8 -16 -32 -64 -128 -256	Bit width for bit-vectors and floating-point arithmetic
-l --linear	Enforce integer and real constraints to be linear

```
$ smtfuzz -qf -bv -fp - uf --num-asserts 1 --num-vars 1 --num-ufs 1
(set-logic QF_UFBVFP)
(declare-const bool_0 Bool)
(declare-const fp_0 (_ FloatingPoint 8 24))
(declare-const bv_0 (_ BitVec 32))
(declare-fun uf_0 (Bool (_ BitVec 32) Bool Bool (_ FloatingPoint 8 24)) Bool)
(assert (uf_0 (fp.isPositive (fp.roundToIntegral RTZ fp_0)) (bvsub (bvsmod bv_0
#x2ad75270 ) (bvxnor bv_0 #x3a990975 )) (fp.isNaN (fp.abs fp_0)) (bvuge (bvor bv_0
bv_0) (bvnor #x0a1b63c9  #x52911167 )) (fp.roundToIntegral RTN (fp.neg (fp #b1
#b11110100 #b11000100101000110101000)))))
(check-sat)
(exit)
```

Fig. 2. Example usage of **smtfuzz** to generate a benchmark in the logic of QF_UFBVFP

5.2   Using banditfuzz

The banditfuzz script is an implementation of the BanditFuzz algorithm and uses smtfuzz as its primary fuzzer. Furthermore, it has four key additional arguments:

1. **--target-solvers** – The set of executables that BanditFuzz will try to expose relative performance deficiencies on.
2. **--reference-solvers** – The set of reference executables that BanditFuzz will try to expose relative performance deficiencies with respect to.
3. **--query-timeout** – This parameter is the wallclock timeout of each query of a solver on an input benchmark.
4. **--global-timeout** – This parameter is the global timeout of banditfuzz. When this time is met, banditfuzz will return the benchmark that had the highest performance margin between the target solvers and the reference solvers.

6   Empirical Evaluation

In this section, we present an evaluation of BanditFuzz vs. standard performance fuzzing algorithms.

6.1   Experimental Setup

Experimental Objective: Here we describe our evaluation of BanditFuzz against random fuzzing and previous similar work by Scott et al. [42]. The objective of the experiment is as follows: given the same amount of resources, which of the three tools maximizes the performance margin for a given target solver vs. a set of reference solvers over all the 52 logics used in SMT-COMP '20. For target solvers, we choose the most performant solvers from SMT-COMP '20 competition, and as reference solvers we used the runner-up solver(s) from the same track in the competition. In the case where a solver was not able to run in our setup, often due to environmental hard-codings, we replace it with the next most performant alternative.

Baselines: As baselines, we use random fuzzing (i.e., `smtfuzz` from Sect. 5 in a loop) and the original performance fuzzer by Scott et al. [42] when possible since it is limited to floating-point and string logics. While there are many other fuzzers for SMT Solvers [10,34,48,49], they are mostly aimed at finding errors and not performance issues.

Other general purpose fuzzers like AFL [52] and PerfFuzz [27] are built around bit-string manipulation. We attempted to use these tools but, as we suspected, neither were able to produce a well-formed input given significant amounts of resources. Unfortunately, it is known that general purpose bit-string fuzzers do not to scale to programs with strict grammars like SMT Solvers, despite the fact that AFL has some capacity to add custom grammar [51].

Computational Environment: All experiments were performed on the Compute Canada computing service [2], a CentOS V7 cluster of Intel Xeon Processor E5-2683 running at 2.10 GHz with 8 GB of memory. Wallclock runtimes are rounded to the nearest second.

Generator: Fuzzers were set to generate benchmarks with 5 variables per sort, 5 assertions, and a maximum depth of 3 in logics that were neither just linear, just arrays, bit-vectors, nor just uninterpreted functions. Otherwise 10 variables, 10 assertions, and depth 5 was used. We use bit-widths of 64.

6.2   Results

Using the aforementioned experimental setup, we evaluated BanditFuzz against random fuzzing across 52 logics from the SMT-COMP '20. Tables 2, 3 summarizes our experimentation against random fuzzing across all 52. The first column in these tables denote the logic of the experiment, the second and third column denote the solver that was targeted and referenced respectively. The fourth and fifth column denotes the cumulative PAR-2 margin across 25 runs of random fuzzing and BanditFuzz respectively. The sixth column reports improvement of BanditFuzz over random fuzzing based on the absolute difference between their PAR-2 margins. We observe BanditFuzz to consistently outperform random fuzzing across all 52, with up to a 82.6% improvement in PAR-2 margin in the UFLIA logic.

To visually illustrate the benchmark testing suites generated by BanditFuzz, we include a cactus plot on the highly industrial logic of QF_BV in Fig. 3. A cactus plot is a visualization of a solver's performance on a benchmark suite the X-axis represents the number of benchmarks solved and the Y-axis represents time (in seconds) taken per benchmark. Every benchmark is the resultant of run a complete run of the tool. In SMT-COMP '20, the SMT Solver Bitwuzla had a strong performance, winning numerous gold medals including the QF_BV track over competing solvers CVC4, Z3, MathSAT, and Yices. However, the cactus plot clearly shows that Bitwuzla is least performant on the benchmarks produced by BanditFuzz by an extremely large margin.

In Table 4, we further compare against previous work by Scott et al. [42]. We baseline BanditFuzz against this work on the only two logics it supports, QF_S and QF_FP. We observe that BanditFuzz consistently outperforms against the baseline and achieves a maximum possible score in both logics, while the baseline fails to do so.

7   Case Studies with Solver Developers

In this section, we provide some case studies of BanditFuzz and how it enabled developers to find surprising performance deficiencies in state-of-the-art SMT solvers.

7.1   CVC4, Bitwuzla, and SymFPU

We contacted the developers of CVC4, Bitwuzla, and the SymFPU bit-blaster [9] for floating-point problems. While CVC4 and Bitwuzla have significantly different underlying bit-vector engines, they both utilize the SymFPU tool for bit-blasting floating-point operations. To this end, we proposed an experiment where we target both CVC4 and Bitwuzla (the target solvers) against Z3 (the reference).

The resulting benchmarks showcase performance issues in the SymFPU bit-blaster and possibly the CVC4 and Bitwuzla solvers themselves. We ran an analogous experiment to what was described in Sect. 6, with a 2400 s wallclock timeout over a 24 h period. BanditFuzz produced 25 benchmarks that significantly separated Bitwuzla and CVC4 from Z3 on the logic of QF_FP. On these benchmarks that BanditFuzz produced, Z3 had a PAR-2 score of 3,018 s, while CVC4 and Bitwuzla had 91,408 s and 120,000 s respectively[1].

---

[1] BitwuzlatimedoutonallbenchmarksproducedbyBanditFuzz.

Table 2. Table of results comparing BanditFuzz to Random fuzzing across logics of SMT-COMP '20. The improvement column is the percentage improvement of Bandit-Fuzz over Random Fuzzing. Rows are sorted alphabetically by logic.

Logic	Target	Reference	PAR-2 performance margin improvement on		
			Random	BanditFuzz	Baseline [%]
ABVFP	CVC4	Z3	2,716	5,579	105
ABVFPLRA	CVC4	Z3	21,376	60,000	181
ALIA	CVC4	Z3	4,238	11,340	168
ANIA	CVC4	Z3	34,883	60,000	72
AUFLIA	CVC4	Z3	34,229	60,000	75
AUFLIRA	CVC4	Z3	7,650	30,428	298
AUFNIA	CVC4	Z3	279	753	170
AUFNIRA	CVC4	Z3	7,967	16,949	113
BV	CVC4	Z3	50,561	60,000	19
BVFP	CVC4	Z3	319	758	138
BVFPLRA	CVC4	Z3	50,844	60,000	18
FP	CVC4	Z3	3,700	10,674	188
FPLRA	CVC4	Z3	15,325	49,528	223
LIA	CVC4	Z3	5,635	19,050	238
LRA	CVC4	Z3	11,184	25,560	129
NIA	CVC4	Z3	48,752	60,000	23
NRA	CVC4	Z3	27,066	60,000	122
QF_ABV	Bitwuzla	Yices2	16,280	45,814	181
QF_ABVFP	Bitwuzla	CVC4	48,484	60,000	24
QF_ABVFPLRA	CVC4	COLIBRI	1,652	4,431	168
QF_ALIA	Yices2	Z3	17,670	60,000	240
QF_ANIA	CVC4	Z3	34,444	60,000	74
QF_AUFBV	Yices2	Bitwuzla	5,375	14,704	174
QF_AUFLIA	Yices2	CVC4	21,836	56,345	158
QF_AUFNIA	CVC4	Z3	35,817	60,000	68
QF_AX	Yices2	CVC4	3,251	5,153	59

In discussions with Aina Niemetz and Mathias Preiner, members of CVC4 and Bitwuzla teams: "In general, the benchmarks produced by BanditFuzz can be super helpful for us to figure out what's missing in our solvers". For example, in their Bitwuzla tool, BanditFuzz found several benchmarks where the rewrite level (-rwl) was configured to be too high. Furthermore, Martin Brain, the author of SymFPU, said: "BanditFuzz is interesting because it gives us an abundant supply of something valuable but previously very rare; small benchmarks with significant performance differentials."

Table 3. Table of results comparing BanditFuzz to Random fuzzing across logics of SMT-COMP '20. The improvement column is the percentage improvement of Bandit-Fuzz over Random Fuzzing. Rows are sorted alphabetically by logic.

Logic	Target	Reference	PAR-2 performance margin improvement on		
			Random	BanditFuzz	Baseline [%]
QF_BV	Bitwuzla	CVC4	22, 142	52, 681	138
QF_BVFP	Bitwuzla	CVC4	29, 949	60, 000	100
QF_BVFPLRA	CVC4	COLIBRI	23, 053	55, 228	140
QF_FP	Bitwuzla	COLIBRI	37, 692	60, 000	59
QF_FPLRA	COLIBRI	CVC4	2, 030	4, 053	100
QF_LIA	CVC4	Yices2	3, 217	5, 399	68
QF_LIRA	Yices2	CVC4	1, 795	7, 584	323
QF_LRA	CVC4	Yices2	4, 571	14, 184	210
QF_NIA	CVC4	Yices2	32, 540	60, 000	84
QF_NIRA	CVC4	Yices2	8, 348	32, 509	289
QF_NRA	Yices2	CVC4	22, 861	60, 000	162
QF_S	CVC4	Z3str4	35172	60, 000	71
QF_SLIA	CVC4	Z3str4	3, 956	15, 381	289
QF_UF	Yices2	Z3	5, 607	15, 362	174
QF_UFBV	Yices2	Bitwuzla	34, 315	60, 000	75
QF_UFFP	Bitwuzla	COLIBRI	12, 909	20, 373	58
QF_UFLIA	Yices2	CVC4	1, 696	2, 428	43
QF_UFLRA	Yices2	Z3	8, 431	26, 529	215
QF_UFNIA	CVC4	Yices2	3, 864	13, 564	251
QF_UFNRA	Yices2	CVC4	53, 374	60, 000	12
UF	CVC4	Z3	3, 469	13, 368	285
UFBV	CVC4	Z3	37, 751	60, 000	59
UFLIA	CVC4	Z3	174	868	399
UFLRA	CVC4	Z3	1, 567	5, 159	229
UFNIA	CVC4	Z3	5, 671	17, 419	207
UFNRA	CVC4	Z3	17, 219	60, 000	248

7.2   Z3 String Solver

We also released the BanditFuzz tool to the developers of the Z3str4 string solver [5, 6], so that they could independently use it to expose performance issues in their solver. The Z3str4 team used BanditFuzz to find performance deficiencies in experimental builds of their solver, namely Z3str4-ACF and Z3str4-NCF (the target solvers) against CVC4 and Z3seq [15]. They were able to produce thousands of benchmarks demonstrating performance separations. Mitja Kulczynski, one of the authors of Z3str4, observed: "BanditFuzz is extremely easy to use! When targeting Z3str4-NCF, BanditFuzz was able to find benchmarks in the form of disjunctions over substring operations. While this issue was already known to us, BanditFuzz provided us with a benchmark suite to improve our tool.

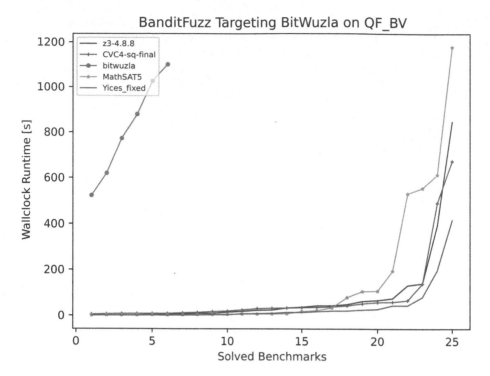

Fig. 3. Cactus plot for targeting Bitwuzla (winner of SMT-COMP '20 in the QF_BV division) against reference runner-up solvers that competed in the division. The X-axis represents the number of benchmarks solved and the Y-axis represents time (in seconds) taken.

Furthermore, when targeting Z3str4-ACF, BanditFuzz found a class of benchmarks of conjunctions of `str.at` where the solver was extremely slow. This was completely unknown to us!"

8   Threats to Validity

One major drawback of BanditFuzz and many other blackbox fuzzing approach is the inability to determine how many unique issues have been discovered. For example, in recent work by Winterer et al. [49] thousands of soundness bugs were reported, but upon inspection the total number of resolved issues was less. However, in our discussions with solver developers (Sect. 7), it was reported to us the benchmarks returned by BanditFuzz were not all of a common cause. In fact, in both case studies, while several of the discovered performance issues by BanditFuzz have been discussed and fixed by developers, several still have open issues.

With the recent advances in reinforcement learning, it is natural to wonder if the idea of BanditFuzz can be lifted to more powerful algorithms (e.g., deep

Q learning, actor critic, etc.). While these model-based techniques can be very powerful, relative to MAB algorithms, they require significantly more data to train effective agents (i.e., tens of thousands of steps on simple environments). As BanditFuzz aspires to generate benchmarks that take a significant amount of time to solve, a single environmental step can take several minutes.

9   Related Work

The work that is most similar to this paper is by Scott et al. [42]. In Sects. 1, 3, 6 of this paper we highlight the novel contributions on of this work. Specifically, our tool uses a multi-agent RL method over the single-agent by Scott et al., and hence has a lower propensity to get stuck in local minima. Additionally, we support all of SMT-LIB, while their tool only supports floating point and strings. Another closely related tool is PerfFuzz which is a bit-string performance fuzzer.

Table 4. Table of select results comparing BanditFuzz to the work of Scott et al. [42] across select logics. The improvement column is the percentage improvement of BanditFuzz over the baseline. (The previous code framework by Scott et al. [42] only supports two logics QF_FP and QF_S. When evaluating outside of these logics, we baseline by using the BanditFuzz code base with the second agent disabled.)

Logic	Target	Reference	PAR-2 performance margin improvement on		
			Scott et al. [42]	BanditFuzz	Baseline [%]
QF_FP	Bitwuzla	COLIBRI	51,893	60,000	14.4
QF_S	CVC4	Z3str4	53,231	60,000	11.9
ABVFPLRA	CVC4	Z3	46,237	60,000	25.9
ANIA	CVC4	Z3	54,120	60,000	10.3
AUFLIRA	CVC4	Z3	22,314	30,428	30.7
FP	CVC4	Z3	9,109	10,674	15.8
FPLRA	CVC4	Z3	31,808	49,528	43.5
LIA	CVC4	Z3	17,009	19,050	11.3
LRA	CVC4	Z3	16,098	25,560	45.4
NRA	CVC4	Z3	39,116	60,000	42.1
QF_ALIA	Yices2	Z3	35,912	60,000	50.2
QF_ANIA	CVC4	Z3	56,198	60,000	6.5
QF_AUFBV	Yices2	Bitwuzla	11,103	14,704	27.9
QF_BVFPLRA	CVC4	COLIBRI	47,180	55,228	15.7
QF_LIRA	Yices2	CVC4	3,152	7,584	82.6
QF_NIA	CVC4	Yices2	58,199	60,000	3.0
QF_NIRA	CVC4	Yices2	17,009	32,509	62.6
QF_NRA	Yices2	CVC4	42,188	60,000	34.9
QF_UFLRA	Yices2	Z3	22,092	26,529	18.3
QF_UFNIA	CVC4	Yices2	9,917	13,564	31.1
UFNIA	CVC4	Z3	14,282	17,419	19.8
UFNRA	CVC4	Z3	27,901	60,000	73.0

However, PerfFuzz is not grammar-aware and hence is unlikely to produce well-formed SMT formulas.

Fuzzing and Fuzzing SMT Solvers: Software fuzzing is a large field of research, and we refer to the survey by Manes et al. as a basis for the current research [28]. There are tools and fuzzers for finding bugs in specific SMT theories [7,10,11,30,30,35].

Machine Learning for Fuzzing: Bottinger et al. [8] introduce a deep Q learning algorithm for fuzzing model-free inputs. Godefroid et al. [18] use neural networks to learn an input grammar over complicated domains such as PDF and then use the learned grammar for model-guided fuzzing. Woo et al. [50] and Patil et al. [36] used MAB algorithms to select configurations of global hyper-parameters of fuzzing software. Rebert et al. [38] used MABs to select from a list of valid inputs seeds to fuzz on.

Machine Learning and SMT Solvers: Other works have leveraged machine learning to learn models relating to SMT solving performance. Healy et al. leveraged supervised learning for analyzing SMT solver performance in the context of software verification [22]. The MachSMT solver leverages machine learning SMT Solver algorithm selection [43] and the MelodySolver leverages reinforcement learning for online algorithm selection [37].

10   Conclusions

In this paper, we present BanditFuzz, a performance fuzzer for SMT Solvers. BanditFuzz is the first multi-agent RL-based performance fuzzer to support all of SMT-LIB and leverages reinforcement learning to find relative performance deficiencies in state-of-the-art SMT Solvers. We evaluated BanditFuzz across 52 logics from SMT-COMP '20 targeting competition-winning solvers against runner-up solvers. We compare BanditFuzz against random fuzzing and a single-agent tool with up to a 82.6% improvement in the margin of PAR-2 score on the UFLIA logic. We further provide several case studies demonstrating the utility of BanditFuzz to state-of-the-art SMT solver developers.

Acknowledgements. We would like to thank the following solver developers for their collaboration and feedback on BanditFuzz: Martin Brain, Aina Niemetz, and Mathias Preiner of the Bitwuzla and CVC4 teams, as well as Mitja Kulczynski and Murphy Berzish who developed Z3str4.

References

1. Armando, A., Mantovani, J., Platania, L.: Bounded model checking of software using SMT solvers instead of SAT solvers. Int. J. Softw. Tools Technol. Transf. **11**(1), 69–83 (2009)
2. Baldwin, S.: Compute Canada: advancing computational research. In: Journal of Physics: Conference Series, vol. 341, p. 012001. IOP Publishing (2012)

3. Barrett, C., et al.: CVC4. In: Gopalakrishnan, G., Qadeer, S. (eds.) CAV 2011. LNCS, vol. 6806, pp. 171–177. Springer, Heidelberg (2011). https://doi.org/10.1007/978-3-642-22110-1_14 http://www.cs.stanford.edu/ barrett/pubs/BCD+11.pdf
4. Barrett, C., Fontaine, P., Tinelli, C.: The satisfiability modulo theories library (SMT-LIB). www.SMT-LIB.org (2016)
5. Berzish, M., Ganesh, V., Zheng, Y.: Z3str3: a string solver with theory-aware heuristics. In: 2017 Formal Methods in Computer Aided Design (FMCAD), pp. 55–59. IEEE (2017)
6. Berzish, M., Mora, F., Kulczynski, M., Nowotka, D., Ganesh, V.: Z3str4 string solver: system description. In: SMT-COMP 2020 (2020)
7. Blotsky, D., Mora, F., Berzish, M., Zheng, Y., Kabir, I., Ganesh, V.: StringFuzz: a fuzzer for string solvers. In: Chockler, H., Weissenbacher, G. (eds.) CAV 2018, Part II. LNCS, vol. 10982, pp. 45–51. Springer, Cham (2018). https://doi.org/10.1007/978-3-319-96142-2_6
8. Böttinger, K., Godefroid, P., Singh, R.: Deep reinforcement fuzzing. arXiv preprint arXiv:1801.04589 (2018)
9. Brain, M., Schanda, F., Sun, Y.: Building better bit-blasting for floating-point problems. In: Vojnar, T., Zhang, L. (eds.) TACAS 2019, Part I. LNCS, vol. 11427, pp. 79–98. Springer, Cham (2019). https://doi.org/10.1007/978-3-030-17462-0_5
10. Brummayer, R., Biere, A.: Fuzzing and delta-debugging SMT solvers. In: Proceedings of the 7th International Workshop on Satisfiability Modulo Theories, pp. 1–5. ACM (2009)
11. Bugariu, A., Müller, P.: Automatically testing string solvers. In: International Conference on Software Engineering (ICSE), 2020. ETH Zurich (2020)
12. Cadar, C., Ganesh, V., Pawlowski, P.M., Dill, D.L., Engler, D.R.: Exe: automatically generating inputs of death. ACM Trans. Inf. Syst. Secur. (TISSEC) **12**(2), 10 (2008)
13. Calzavara, S., Grishchenko, I., Maffei, M.: Horndroid: practical and sound static analysis of android applications by SMT solving. In: 2016 IEEE European Symposium on Security and Privacy (EuroS&P), pp. 47–62. IEEE (2016)
14. Cordeiro, L., Fischer, B., Marques-Silva, J.: SMT-based bounded model checking for embedded ANSI-C software. IEEE Trans. Softw. Eng. **38**(4), 957–974 (2011)
15. de Moura, L., Bjørner, N.: Z3: an efficient SMT solver. In: Ramakrishnan, C.R., Rehof, J. (eds.) TACAS 2008. LNCS, vol. 4963, pp. 337–340. Springer, Heidelberg (2008). https://doi.org/10.1007/978-3-540-78800-3_24
16. Duchene, F.: Fuzz in the dark: genetic algorithm for black-box fuzzing. In: Black-Hat (2013)
17. Gerlich, R., Prause, C.R.: Optimizing the parameters of an evolutionary algorithm for fuzzing and test data generation. In: 2020 IEEE International Conference on Software Testing, Verification and Validation Workshops (ICSTW), pp. 338–345. IEEE (2020)
18. Godefroid, P., Peleg, H., Singh, R.: Learn&fuzz: machine learning for input fuzzing. In: Proceedings of the 32nd IEEE/ACM International Conference on Automated Software Engineering, pp. 50–59. IEEE Press (2017)
19. Gulwani, S., Srivastava, S., Venkatesan, R.: Program analysis as constraint solving. ACM SIGPLAN Not. **43**(6), 281–292 (2008)
20. Gupta, A.K., Nadarajah, S.: Handbook of Beta Distribution and its Applications. CRC Press, Boca Raton (2004)
21. Harris, C.R., et al.: Array programming with NumPy. Nature **585**(7825), 357–362 (2020)

22. Healy, A., Monahan, R., Power, J.F.: Predicting SMT solver performance for software verification. In: Dubois, C., Masci, P., Méry, D. (eds.) Proceedings of the Third Workshop on Formal Integrated Development Environment, F-IDE@FM 2016, Limassol, Cyprus, November 8, 2016. EPTCS, vol. 240, pp. 20–37 (2016). https://doi.org/10.4204/EPTCS.240.2
23. Jin, G., Song, L., Shi, X., Scherpelz, J., Lu, S.: Understanding and detecting real-world performance bugs. ACM SIGPLAN Not. **47**(6), 77–88 (2012)
24. Junker, M., Huuck, R., Fehnker, A., Knapp, A.: SMT-based false positive elimination in static program analysis. In: Aoki, T., Taguchi, K. (eds.) ICFEM 2012. LNCS, vol. 7635, pp. 316–331. Springer, Heidelberg (2012). https://doi.org/10.1007/978-3-642-34281-3_23
25. Katz, G., Barrett, C., Dill, D.L., Julian, K., Kochenderfer, M.J.: Reluplex: an efficient SMT solver for verifying deep neural networks. In: Majumdar, R., Kunčak, V. (eds.) CAV 2017, Part I. LNCS, vol. 10426, pp. 97–117. Springer, Cham (2017). https://doi.org/10.1007/978-3-319-63387-9_5
26. Komuravelli, A., Gurfinkel, A., Chaki, S.: SMT-based model checking for recursive programs. Form. Methods Syst. Des. **48**(3), 175–205 (2016)
27. Lemieux, C., Padhye, R., Sen, K., Song, D.: PerfFuzz: automatically generating pathological inputs. In: Proceedings of the 27th ACM SIGSOFT International Symposium on Software Testing and Analysis, pp. 254–265 (2018)
28. Manes, V.J., et al.: Fuzzing: art, science, and engineering. arXiv preprint arXiv:1812.00140 (2018)
29. Manès, V.J., Kim, S., Cha, S.K.: Ankou: guiding grey-box fuzzing towards combinatorial difference. In: Proceedings of the ACM/IEEE 42nd International Conference on Software Engineering, pp. 1024–1036 (2020)
30. Mansur, M.N., Christakis, M., Wüstholz, V., Zhang, F.: Detecting critical bugs in SMT solvers using blackbox mutational fuzzing. arXiv preprint arXiv:2004.05934 (2020)
31. Heule, M., Matti Järvisalo, M.S.: Sat race 2019 (2019). http://sat-race-2019.ciirc.cvut.cz/
32. Niemetz, A., Preiner, M.: Bitwuzla at the SMT-COMP 2020. CoRR abs/2006.01621 (2020). https://arxiv.org/abs/2006.01621
33. Niemetz, A., Preiner, M.: Ternary propagation-based local search for more bit-precise reasoning. In: 2020 Formal Methods in Computer Aided Design, FMCAD 2020, Haifa, Israel, September 21–24, 2020, pp. 214–224. IEEE (2020). https://doi.org/10.34727/2020/isbn.978-3-85448-042-6_29
34. Niemetz, A., Preiner, M., Biere, A.: Model-based API testing for SMT solvers. In: Proceedings of the 15th International Workshop on Satisfiability Modulo Theories, SMT, pp. 24–28 (2017)
35. Niemetz, A., Preiner, M., Biere, A.: Model-based API testing for SMT solvers. In: Brain, M., Hadarean, L. (eds.) Proceedings of the 15th International Workshop on Satisfiability Modulo Theories, SMT 2017), affiliated with the 29th International Conference on Computer Aided Verification, CAV 2017, Heidelberg, Germany, July 24–28, 2017, p. 10 (2017)
36. Patil, K., Kanade, A.: Greybox fuzzing as a contextual bandits problem. arXiv preprint arXiv:1806.03806 (2018)
37. Pimpalkhare, N., Mora, F., Polgreen, E., Seshia, S.A.: MedleySolver: online SMT algorithm selection. In: Li, C.-M., Manyà, F. (eds.) SAT 2021. LNCS, vol. 12831, pp. 453–470. Springer, Cham (2021). https://doi.org/10.1007/978-3-030-80223-3_31

38. Rebert, A., et al.: Optimizing seed selection for fuzzing. In: USENIX Security Symposium, pp. 861–875 (2014)
39. Reynolds, A., Deters, M., Kuncak, V., Tinelli, C., Barrett, C.: Counterexample-guided quantifier instantiation for synthesis in SMT. In: Kroening, D., Păsăreanu, C.S. (eds.) CAV 2015, Part II. LNCS, vol. 9207, pp. 198–216. Springer, Cham (2015). https://doi.org/10.1007/978-3-319-21668-3_12
40. Russo, D.J., Van Roy, B., Kazerouni, A., Osband, I., Wen, Z., et al.: A tutorial on Thompson sampling. Found. Trends® Mach. Learn. **11**(1), 1–96 (2018)
41. Saavedra, G.J., Rodhouse, K.N., Dunlavy, D.M., Kegelmeyer, P.W.: A review of machine learning applications in fuzzing. arXiv preprint arXiv:1906.11133 (2019)
42. Scott, J., Mora, F., Ganesh, V.: BanditFuzz: fuzzing SMT solvers with reinforcement learning. UWSpace. http://hdl.handle.net/10012/15753 (2020)
43. Scott, J., Niemetz, A., Preiner, M., Nejati, S., Ganesh, V.: MachSMT: a machine learning-based algorithm selector for SMT solvers. In: TACAS 2021, Part II. LNCS, vol. 12652, pp. 303–325. Springer, Cham (2021). https://doi.org/10.1007/978-3-030-72013-1_16
44. Srivastava, S., Gulwani, S., Foster, J.S.: From program verification to program synthesis. In: Proceedings of the 37th Annual ACM SIGPLAN-SIGACT Symposium on Principles of Programming Languages, pp. 313–326 (2010)
45. Sutton, M., Greene, A., Amini, P.: Fuzzing: Brute Force Vulnerability Discovery. Pearson Education, London (2007)
46. Sutton, R.S., Barto, A.G.: Reinforcement Learning: An Introduction. MIT Press, Cambridge (2018)
47. Takanen, A., Demott, J.D., Miller, C.: Fuzzing for Software Security Testing and Quality Assurance. Artech House, USA (2008)
48. Winterer, D., Zhang, C., Su, Z.: On the unusual effectiveness of type-aware operator mutations for testing SMT solvers. Proc. ACM Program. Lang. **4**(OOPSLA), 1–25 (2020)
49. Winterer, D., Zhang, C., Su, Z.: Validating SMT solvers via semantic fusion. In: PLDI, pp. 718–730 (2020)
50. Woo, M., Cha, S.K., Gottlieb, S., Brumley, D.: Scheduling black-box mutational fuzzing. In: Proceedings of the 2013 ACM SIGSAC Conference on Computer & Communications Security, pp. 511–522. ACM (2013)
51. Zalewski, M.: afl-fuzz: making up grammar with a dictionary in hand (2015). https://lcamtuf.blogspot.com/2015/01/afl-fuzz-making-up-grammar-with.html
52. Zalewski, M.: American Fuzzing Lop (2015)

Formally Verified Safety Net for Waypoint Navigation Neural Network Controllers

Alexei Kopylov[1], Stefan Mitsch[2], Aleksey Nogin[1(✉)], and Michael Warren[1]

[1] HRL Laboratories, LLC, Malibu, CA, USA
{akopylov,anogin,mawarren}@hrl.com
https://csrs.hrl.com/
[2] Carnegie Mellon University, Pittsburgh, PA, USA
smitsch@cs.cmu.edu

Abstract. This paper describes a formal model of a "location, heading and speed" waypoint navigation task for an autonomous ground vehicle—that is, a task of navigating the vehicle towards a particular location so that it has the desired heading and speed when in that location. Our novel way of modeling this task makes formal reasoning over controller correctness tractable. We state our model in differential dynamic logic (dL), which we then use to establish a formal definition of waypoint feasibility and formally verify its validity in the KeYmaera X interactive theorem prover. The formal machine-checked proof witnesses that for any waypoint we consider feasible, the vehicle can indeed be controlled to reach it within the prescribed error bound. We also describe how we use these formal definitions and theorem statements to inform training of neural network controllers for performing this waypoint navigation task. Note that in our approach we do not need to rely on the neural network controller always being perfect—instead, the formal model allows a synthesis of a correct-by-construction safety net for the controller that checks whether the neural network output is safe to act upon and present a safe alternative if it is not.

1 Introduction

Our work is motivated by the task of assuring that an autonomous ground vehicle will safely travel from a start point to a destination point. Specifically, we are working with the US Army Combat Capability Development Center (CCDC) Ground Vehicle Systems Center (GVSC) autonomous Polaris MRZR vehicle, which was originally developed and used as part of the Dismounted Soldier Autonomy Tools (DSAT) effort [18]. At the highest level, we consider this "start to destination" task as a combination of two subtasks. The first subtask, which is outside the scope of this paper, is to plan a safe path from start to destination, replanning as necessary when circumstances change. The second subtask, addressed in this paper, is to then control the vehicle in a way that can be

© Springer Nature Switzerland AG 2021
M. Huisman et al. (Eds.): FM 2021, LNCS 13047, pp. 122–141, 2021.
https://doi.org/10.1007/978-3-030-90870-6_7

assured to follow the planned path without deviating from it beyond some error margin.

Obviously, not every path can be followed with sufficient precision—for example, a path that requires a turn that is much sharper than the vehicle's minimum turning radius could not be feasibly followed without significant deviation. Moreover, we are not only interested in limiting ourselves to paths that are feasible from the point of view of the vehicle's mechanical limits—we are interested in limiting ourselves to paths for which we can *assure* that the vehicle will be able to follow successfully. The notion of a *feasible path* effectively becomes the contract between the two subtasks—in assuring the overall task, we need to assure that the path planning subtask will always output a path (including the relevant error margins) that is both safe and feasible, and then assure that the path navigation subtask is capable of navigating any such feasible path without exceeding the error margin. Our choice of focusing on the latter task first is motivated by the desire to find a formal notion of feasible paths that is both sufficiently liberal (provide flexibility in the solution of the former task), while at the same time conservative enough to support our assurance argument.

The benefit of a formally verified notion of feasible paths is that it allows us to use machine learning to aggressively optimize a path following controller: The current "baseline" path following controller on the MRZR is a pure pursuit controller that does not always follow complex paths accurately, typically limited to fairly low speeds, and according to the users "feels somewhat robotic". The goal is to replace the MRZR path following controller with a neural network based one that is capable of driving both more aggressively, yet more accurately, and with better control. To provide safety guarantees for this critical task despite using machine learning, we need to be able to assure that the neural network based controller can be trusted to not misbehave—even in unlikely corner cases that might have never been encountered during training and testing.

This paper presents the first iteration of our work on assuring a path following controller, where we make a number of simplifying assumptions *(i)* we use a point vehicle model with instantaneous steering,[1] *(ii)* control is instantaneous and can change the vehicle actuation at any time, that is, our model of control is event-based (e.g., we can control a vehicle when it reaches a safety region boundary) *(iii)* the vehicle is traversing even and flat terrain.

The goal is to first define a notion of feasible waypoint—those waypoints that we can assure the vehicle will be able to reach with some precision, given a particular starting state (or a particular set of possible starting states). Once we have a notion of a feasible waypoint, we can define a feasible path as a sequence of waypoints, such that the first waypoint in the sequence is feasible from the vehicle starting state, and for each non-final waypoint, reaching that waypoint (within a specified error margin) implies that the subsequent waypoint is feasible.

---

[1] As a consequence of instantaneous steering, the curvature of the vehicle's path is able to change instantaneously to any value in the feasible range (that is, between $-\frac{1}{R_{\min}}$ and $\frac{1}{R_{\min}}$, where $R_{\min}$ is the minimum turning radius of the vehicle).

In general, simply knowing the vehicle location is not enough to know whether the next waypoint will be feasible—at the very least, we need to know the vehicle heading and speed. Therefore, we specify waypoints in terms of *(i)* desired location *(ii)* desired heading *(iii)* maximal speed at waypoint (should also not be exceeded prior to reaching the waypoint, unless it is unavoidable due to excessive initial speed) *(iv)* error margin.

For the remainder of this paper, we focus on this specific subset of the general path following task—that of reaching a particular location, with desired heading at that location, and a speed limit at and prior to arrival at that location. We do not specifically restrict the route that the vehicle must take towards the desired location (it is the job of the route planner to place the waypoints close enough in those regions where the vehicle path needs to be tightly controlled), but prohibit the vehicle from driving "back"—that is, the angle between the vehicle's current heading and the desired heading at the waypoint must not exceed 180°.

Contributions. The main contributions of this work, summarized in Fig. 1, are the following. First, we develop a novel formalization of the "location, heading and speed" waypoint navigation task described above, expressing it in the differential dynamic logic (dL) modeling language [26, 27] inside the KeYmaera X interactive theorem prover [13]. Second, we deduce and express the notions of "safe" states—those vehicle states where reaching the waypoint (subject to an error bound) is feasible—and "safe" control actions—namely, those control actions that would allow the vehicle to correctly navigate towards the waypoint. Third, we create a sequence of formal proofs in KeYmaera X establishing the desired properties—namely, as long as the waypoint is not yet reached, for each safe state there is a safe control action and the use of any safe control actions implies to stay in the safe region until we reach the desired waypoint.

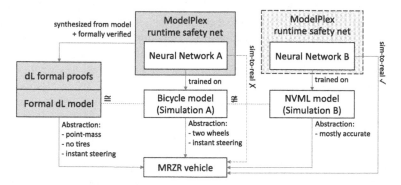

Fig. 1. Contributions overview: formal dL model, proofs, and runtime safety nets are formally verified; controllers are trained on simulations of varying fidelity, with varying sim-to-real success; verified safety net works well with the bicycle model simulation (fits closer to formal dL model), but additional work is needed to get to a formal model that closer matches the real vehicle.

We want to emphasize that we use theorem proving not merely as a tool to obtain a correctness proof about an already correct system; we use it to explore and understand a system in all its subtleties and with all its corner cases thoroughly, to structure the system analysis process, to discover properties of the system that are not or only partially known (e.g., loop invariants), to discover and fix correctness bugs in the process, and to link model and system execution formally. The proof then ensures that the conditions we identified are sufficient. They are not necessarily the weakest necessary conditions—in fact, our initial formulation proved to be too conservative in practice and we subsequently revised the formalization and proofs to relax the safety condition to be reasonable in practice. The safety conditions we derived and proved correct can now be used as a basis for designing and ensuring correctness of other system parts.

It is also important to emphasize that "safe" in our case does not just mean "safe for now"; instead it means that we have proven that as long as the starting state is "safe", and only "safe" control actions are taken, the vehicle will remain "safe" until the waypoint is reached. Once the theorem is completed, following the usual KeYmaera X methodology, we use the ModelPlex tool [24] to automatically extract a correct-by-construction runtime monitoring safety net from the proof. The monitoring condition extracted by ModelPlex is a Boolean combination of a number of (in)equalities, and therefore the computational cost of evaluating the monitor on measurements and control output is negligible.

Our final contribution is the manner in which our formulation of the waypoint navigation task informed training neural networks to perform the task. Note that in our approach we do not rely on the neural network controller always being correct—instead, the correct-by-construction safety net for the controller checks whether the neural network output is safe to act upon, and presents a safe alternative if not (again, "safe" in a sense that it can ensure the vehicle will stay safe in the future, not just safe right now). Also note that while our focus is on neural networks, the same safety net could be used with any other controller.

Paper Structure. The remainder of this paper is structured as follows. First, in Sect. 2 we provide background information on differential dynamic logic (dL) and the KeYmaera X interactive theorem prover. Then, in Sect. 3 we describe the dL formulations of waypoint feasibility and navigation. Next, in Sect. 4 we outline the formal proof of waypoint feasibility, implemented in and machine-checked by KeYmaera X. In Sect. 5, we describe how we use the dL formulation of the task to inform training of a neural network controller for performing the task. Finally, in Sect. 6 we discuss related work and next steps.

2   Background

We express our models in differential dynamic logic (dL) [26,27]. dL is a specification and verification language with logical formulas that express properties of hybrid systems written in a programming language. Hybrid programs support differential equations (ODEs) as program statements, which allows us to express

Table 1. Hybrid programs

Statement	Meaning
$x := e$	Assigns value of term e to x
$x := *$	Assigns an arbitrary real value to x
$?Q$	Stays in current state if formula Q is true
$\{x' = f(x)$ & $Q\}$	Continuous evolution for any duration $t \geq 0$ with Evolution domain constraint formula Q true throughout
$\alpha; \beta$	Executes β after α
$\alpha \cup \beta$	Executes either α or β, nondeterministically
α^*	Repeats α zero or more times

the control laws together with the entailed kinematics of the system and analyze control software for its correctness in terms of physical effects (e.g. collision avoidance). Proofs in differential dynamic logic are supported with the theorem prover KeYmaera X [13]. KeYmaera X is an LCF-style prover [22] with a small soundness-critical core of about 2000 LoC; the correctness of its core has been formally verified [4]. Table 1 summarizes the syntax and informal semantics of hybrid programs (detailed formal semantics are in [28]).

Typical control programs use assignments $x := e$ to compute intermediate or control output values. Random assignments $x := *$ choose any arbitrary real value for x and are often combined with tests $?Q$; for example, the program $x := *; ?0 \leq x < 5$ chooses any value in the half-open interval $[0, 5)$, the program $x := *; ?x^2 = y$ computes the square root of y. Tests $?Q$ control program execution: if the condition Q is true, program execution continues, otherwise it aborts (but may backtrack to another execution branch). Differential equations $x' = f(x)$ & Q follow a solution of $x' = f(x)$ for any duration as long as the constraint Q is true throughout. Note that even though the semantics is described in terms of solutions, in the proof calculus we do not rely on solving differential equations, but use invariance techniques for differential equations instead [30]. Sequential composition $\alpha; \beta$ first runs α and then β, non-deterministic choice $\alpha \cup \beta$ executes either α or β, and non-deterministic repetition α^* runs α any number of times (even zero). Other control instructions are expressible (e.g., if Q then α else β is expressed with $(?Q; \alpha) \cup (?\neg Q; \beta)$ with mutually exclusive conditions Q and $\neg Q$) and supported for convenience in the input syntax of KeYmaera X. It is good practice to avoid gaps in branch conditions (e.g., program $((?x \geq 5; x := 2) \cup (?x \leq 0; x := 2))^*$ gets stuck after at most one repetition of the loop).

Many models use a controller that runs periodically, following the shape

$$(u := \mathrm{ctrl}(x); t := 0; \{x' = f(x, u), t' = 1 \,\&\, t \leq T\})^* ,$$

where a discrete program outputs control input u (slight abuse of notation: ctrl may output non-deterministically chosen values) for a subsequent continuous model $x' = f(x, u)$ with a clock $t' = 1$, repeated in a loop (*). The continuous model runs for at most T time, as ensured by the time reset $t := 0$ and the constraint $t \leq T$, and then returns to $u := \text{ctrl}(x)$. Note that the loop may repeat any number of times and so our safety analysis will hold for unbounded time. The differential equations in interesting continuous models often have non-polynomial solutions or are not solvable at all, but can still be analyzed in dL [30] with some careful rephrasing of transcendental functions. To make up for the lack of decidability of transcendental and trigonometric functions in the underlying real arithmetic theory[2], we encode trigonometric functions with differential equations as illustrated in the following example of a point moving along a unit circle. A typical model represents the position along the circle with angle θ and computes the position of the point in cartesian coordinates (x, y) using trigonometric functions sin and cos: the differential equation $x' = \cos\theta, y' = \sin\theta, \theta' = \omega$ describes change in position (x, y) and change in angle θ with angular velocity ω. The symbolic solution of this differential equation again mentions sin and cos and so results in undecidable arithmetic. To avoid this, we follow [29] to axiomatize sin and cos with differential equations using additional symbols $d_x = \cos\theta$ and $d_y = \sin\theta$. We determine the derivatives of d_x and d_y using

$$d_x' = (\cos\theta)' = -\sin\theta \cdot \theta' = -d_y \cdot \omega$$
$$d_y' = (\sin\theta)' = \cos\theta \cdot \theta' = d_x \cdot \omega$$

and the resulting differential equation expands to $x' = d_x$, $y' = d_y$, $d_x' = -\omega d_y$, $d_y' = \omega d_x$, with the constraint $d_x^2 + d_y^2 = 1$ for the starting values, which no longer uses trigonometric functions. To prove properties of such differential equations (including proving that the $d_x^2 + d_y^2 = 1$ constraint is maintained), we use techniques in [30] instead of symbolic solutions.

We formalize properties with dL formulas per the following grammar where P, Q are formulas, $e, \tilde{e}$ are terms, x is a variable and α is a hybrid program:

$$P, Q ::= e \geq \tilde{e} \mid \neg P \mid P \wedge Q \mid P \vee Q \mid P \rightarrow Q \mid P \leftrightarrow Q \mid \forall x \, P \mid \exists x \, P \mid [\alpha]P$$

The operators of first-order real arithmetic are as usual with quantifiers ranging over the reals. For a hybrid program α and a dL formula P, $[\alpha]P$ is true *iff* P is true after all runs of α. It is particularly useful for expressing safety properties of the form $Q \rightarrow [\alpha]P$ with assumptions Q on the starting states of program α.

3   Modeling the Waypoint Navigation Task

Vehicle State. In a point-vehicle model, the state of a vehicle is defined by its position (x, y) and its velocity (v_x, v_y). We define the *left turning point* (l) and *right turning point* (r) as points that lie at equal distances from the center of the vehicle along a line transverse to the heading of the vehicle in left and right directions, respectively, and where the distance to the center is equal to the minimum radius of curvature $(R_{\min})$, as illustrated in Fig. 2.

---

[2] Some solvers, e.g. dReal [14], opt for δ-decidability to render transcendental functions decidable.

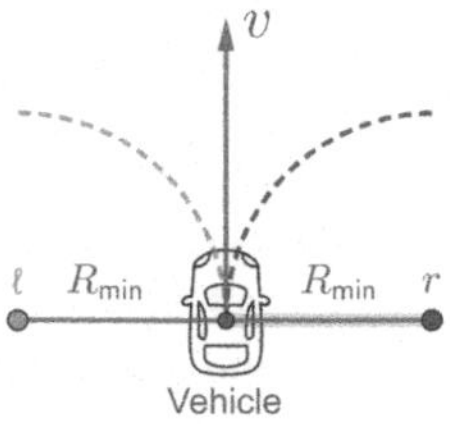

Fig. 2. Vehicle with left and right turning points.

Definition 1 (Vehicle State). *Coordinates of the left turning point l and right turning point r follow from vehicle position (x, y) and heading v, where (d_x, d_y) is a normalized direction of the vehicle:*

$$l_x = x - R_{min}d_y \qquad r_x = x + R_{min}d_y \qquad d_x = v_x/v \qquad v = \sqrt{v_x^2 + v_y^2}$$
$$l_y = y + R_{min}d_x \qquad r_y = y - R_{min}d_x \qquad d_y = v_y/v$$

It turns out that it is significantly easier to use (l_x, l_y, r_x, r_y, v) as coordinates of the state than the traditional (x, y, v_x, v_y). In this coordinate system the waypoint feasibility constraints become simpler and much easier to both visualize and reason about. Therefore in our model a state of the vehicle is a point *state* = (l_x, l_y, r_x, r_y, v) on a 4-dimensional manifold with condition:

$$\text{isWellformed}(state) ::= (l_x - r_x)^2 + (l_y - r_y)^2 = (2R_{\min})^2 \ .$$

Vehicle Control and Movement. We define a control action for the vehicle as a pair *control* = (a, κ), where a is the acceleration and κ is the curvature of the vehicle's path resulting from steering.

Definition 2 (Vehicle State Evolution). *The evolution of the vehicle state is specified by the following differential equations with control (a, κ):*

$$r'_x = v(l_y - r_y)(\mathrm{K} - \kappa)/2 \qquad l'_x = v(l_y - r_y)(\mathrm{K} + \kappa)/2 \qquad v' = a$$
$$r'_y = v(r_x - l_x)(\mathrm{K} - \kappa)/2 \qquad l'_y = v(r_x - l_x)(\mathrm{K} + \kappa)/2$$

Here $\mathrm{K} = \frac{1}{R_{min}}$ is the maximal curvature of a path the vehicle can take.

4   Proving Safety

4.1   Safe Starting States and Safe Actions

In Sect. 1 we outlined the notion of a *feasible waypoint*—that is a waypoint that, given a certain starting state, we can control the vehicle towards and can assure to reach within a given error bound. Here, we flip this relationship—rather than characterizing waypoints given a specific starting state, we will instead characterize starting states given a specific waypoint—namely a waypoint in the

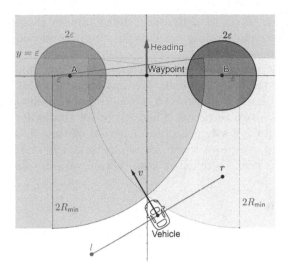

Fig. 3. Safety region for left and right turning centers of the vehicle starting state, when navigating to a waypoint at the origin. The state is considered to be safe when point l is outside of the light-red zone, point r is outside of the light-blue zone, and velocity v points upward. Dark red and dark blue circles are the destination zone: a vehicle is considered to have reached the waypoint when the point l is inside the dark-red circle and the point r inside the-dark blue circle.

origin $(0,0)$ with the desired heading along the y axis facing towards positive values of y (this specific choice does not introduce a loss of generality as we can always perform a coordinate transformation to move and rotate the waypoint). We will call a state *safe* if the waypoint remains feasible with that starting state, and for a particular safe state, a safe action is one that does not immediately take us out of a safe state.

We say that we have reached the waypoint if the turning points l and r each reach the small neighborhood of points A and B respectively, where A and B are the points that lie distance $R_{\texttt{min}}$ from the desired waypoint to the left and right (see Fig. 3).

Specifically, we require that each of $|l - A|$ and $|r - B|$ is $< 2\epsilon$ for some parameter ϵ, where $|\cdot|$ is Euclidean distance, and so a waypoint is considered reached by Definition 3.

Definition 3 (Waypoint reached). *For a waypoint at the origin, target region A for left turning point $l = (l_x, l_y)$ is at $(-R_{min}, 0)$ and target region B for right turning point $r = (r_x, r_y)$ is at $(R_{min}, 0)$, and so the waypoint is reached with tolerance ϵ when* Reached(*state*) *is satisfied:*

$$\text{Reached}(state) ::= (l_x + R_{min})^2 + l_y^2 < (2\epsilon)^2 \wedge (r_x - R_{min})^2 + r_y^2 < (2\epsilon)^2$$

Note, when $\epsilon \ll R_{\mathtt{min}}$, then Reached(*state*) implies that both the vehicle location and the vehicle heading are close to the desired ones, while allowing some trade-off between the two.

The rest of this section proceeds as follows. First, we define a safe region as a certain subset of the state manifold. We also define a set of safe actions as a subset of the set of possible controls (a, κ). To establish that our definitions are valid, we then prove two theorems. First, we prove that whenever we are in a safe state, and we take a safe action for a period of time δ, we will remain in a safe state. Second, we prove whenever we are in a safe state, then unless we already reached our goal, there exists a safe action we can take.

4.2   Safe Region

We define our state safety condition as a conjunction of three conditions:

$$\text{Safe}(\textit{state}) ::= \text{SafeDir}(\textit{state}) \wedge \text{SafeLeft}(\textit{state}) \wedge \text{SafeRight}(\textit{state}) \quad \text{where}$$

- SafeDir(*state*) $::= r_x \geq l_x$ captures the requirement that the vehicle is not allowed to drive "back",
- SafeLeft(*state*) is a proposition stating that the left turning point does not fall into the light red region shown in Fig. 3 and algebraically defined as a conjunction of the following clauses:
  - SafeFrontLineLeft(*state*) $::= l_y < \epsilon$
  - SafeCircleLeft(*state*) $::= l_y^2 + (l_x - R_{\mathtt{min}} - \epsilon)^2 \geq (2R_{\mathtt{min}})^2$
  - SafeBackLineLeft(*state*) $::= l_y \leq -2R_{\mathtt{min}} \vee l_x \leq R_{\mathtt{min}} + \epsilon$
- SafeRight(*state*) is a proposition defined symmetrically to SafeLeft(*state*), stating that the right turning point does not fall into the light blue region shown in Fig. 3.

4.3   Safe Action

For each of the clauses SafeX(*state*) in the definition of safe region, we define a condition for a safe action SafeControlX(*state*, *control*) such that whenever the vehicle is in a state that satisfies property SafeX(*state*) and we take a control action that satisfies SafeControlX(*state*, *control*) for a period of time δ according to this control, then SafeX will be true for the vehicle's end state. That is,

$$\text{SafeX}(\textit{state}) \wedge \text{SafeControlX}(\textit{state}, \textit{control}) \rightarrow [\text{Dynamics}]\,\text{SafeX}(\textit{state})$$

where Dynamics is a set of differential equations of Def. 2 augmented with a time limit δ until the next control action: $t' = 1 \& t < \delta$. For example, we define

$$
\begin{aligned}
&\text{SafeControlBackLineLeft}(\textit{state}, \textit{control}) ::= \\
&\quad \bigl(l_y \leq -2R_{\mathtt{min}} \wedge d_y(\mathrm{K} + \kappa)v\delta \leq -l_y\mathrm{K} - 2 - \Delta(\mathrm{K} + \kappa)v\delta\bigr) \\
&\quad \vee \left(l_x \leq R_{\mathtt{min}} + \epsilon \wedge \begin{pmatrix} d_x(\mathrm{K} + \kappa)v\delta \leq -(l_x - \epsilon)\mathrm{K} + 1 - \Delta(\mathrm{K} + \kappa)v\delta \\ \vee\, d_x(\mathrm{K} + \kappa)v\delta \leq -(l_x - \epsilon)\mathrm{K} + 1 \wedge (l_x - r_x)\kappa \leq 0 \end{pmatrix}\right)
\end{aligned}
$$

where $\Delta = |v\kappa|\delta$ is the maximum angle the vehicle can turn with steering κ at velocity v during the reaction time δ. Then we prove that

$$\text{SafeBackLineLeft}(state) \wedge \text{SafeControlBackLineLeft}(state, control) \rightarrow$$
$$[\text{Dynamics}]\,\text{SafeBackLineLeft}(state)$$

The proofs of these lemmas are based on the following fairly straightforward fact that requires some care to prove in KeYmaera X. Suppose we have a point (x, y) that is moving on a unit circle $x^2 + y^2 = 1$ by the dynamic given by equations: $x' = -y; y' = x$. If at the starting point $x \geq a + \delta$, and $x \geq a, y < 0$, $1 - 2\delta \geq a$, then after time δ we will have that $x \geq a$. In case of $x \geq a + \delta$, this is true simply because $x' \geq -1$ and this case is easy to prove in KeYmaera X as well. For the case of $x \geq a, y < 0, 1 - 2\delta \geq a$, this is true because the point is moving counterclockwise starting in the lower half of a circle and needs to move a distance of at least δ in order to cross the line $x = a$. This fact is key for establishing the various invariants, including those shown above, and was used many times in our proofs.

After proving such lemmas for all clauses we define SafeControl($state$, $control$) as a conjunction of these clauses.

Theorem 1. *Safe control keeps the vehicle in a safe state:*

$$\text{Safe}(state) \wedge \text{SafeControl}(state, control) \rightarrow [\text{Dynamics}]\,\text{Safe}(state)$$

Proof. By mechanized proof in KeYmaera X, splitting Safe into its conjuncts to apply lemmas. □

Theorem 2. *For every safe state, either the vehicle is at the destination, or there exists a control κ within the limits of maximum steering $K = \frac{1}{R_{min}}$ and a deadline D such that κ is safe up to deadline D:*

$$\text{Safe}(state) \rightarrow$$
$$\text{Reached}(state) \vee$$
$$\exists |\kappa| \leq K. \exists D > 0. \forall 0 < \delta \leq D.\ \text{SafeControl}(state, control)$$

Proof. By mechanized proof in KeYmaera X, along cases: a) not close to any of the bounds: go forward; b) close to a bound, then consider each of the following: go forward, or turn left, or turn right, or reached the waypoint, or unsatisfiable assumptions (case impossible). To formalize this proof in KeYmaera X, we used lemmas that allowed us to decompose statements under an existential quantifier:

$$\bigl(\exists D_1 > 0. \forall 0 < \delta \leq D_1.\ P(\delta)\bigr) \wedge \bigl(\exists D_2 > 0. \forall 0 < \delta \leq D_2.\ Q(\delta)\bigr)$$
$$\rightarrow \bigl(\exists D > 0. \forall 0 < \delta \leq D.\ P(\delta) \wedge Q(\delta)\bigr), \qquad \text{using } D = \min(D_1, D_2)$$
$$\bigl(\exists D > 0. \forall 0 < \delta \leq D.\ P(\delta)\bigr) \vee \bigl(\exists D > 0. \forall 0 < \delta \leq D.\ Q(\delta)\bigr)$$
$$\rightarrow \bigl(\exists D > 0. \forall 0 < \delta \leq D.\ P(\delta) \vee Q(\delta)\bigr).$$

These lemmas are used to prove statements of the form $\exists D > 0. \forall 0 < \delta \leq D.\ P(\delta)$ separately and construct the proofs by considering all cases. □

The two theorems together give us the desired safety property:

Corollary 1. *For each safe state there is a safe control action and we can use safe control actions to stay in the safe region, until we reach the desired waypoint.*

5 Training a Neural Network Controller

5.1 Controller Training

As we discussed in Sect. 4.1, we consider the waypoint reached, when points l and r that lie $R_{\min}$ to the left and right of the vehicle (where "left" and "right" are taken with respect to the vehicle heading) each get within ϵ of the corresponding points A and B that lie $R_{\min}$ to the left and right of the waypoint location (where "left" and "right" are taken with respect to the desired heading at the waypoint).

Reward Function. This definition informs a natural metric for how far the vehicle is from its goal—namely, $\sqrt{|l - A|^2 + |r - B|^2}$ (where $|\cdot|$ is the Euclidean distance). Similarly, to Def. 3 (Reached), this naturally combines the location and heading errors in the same metric.

We use this distance metric as a reward function to train neural network controllers for waypoint navigation. At each time step, the reward is computed as $-\sqrt{|l - A|^2 + |r - B|^2} - \lambda \max(0, v - v_{\max})$, where λ is a positive meta-parameter constant. That is, at every time step the controller is penalized proportional to its distance to the target, and is additionally penalized whenever its speed exceeds the speed limit $v_{\max}$.

Once the vehicle passes the $y = 0$ goal line, it is given a large reward if the waypoint is reached and a large penalty proportional to the distance to the waypoint—to encourage it to hit the waypoint as precisely as possible.

Training Parameters. We initially tried a number of algorithms for training the control NNs, including Trust Region Policy Optimization (TRPO) [32] and Constrained Policy Optimization (CPO) [1], but later settled on using a variation on the self-learned almost Lyapunov critics appoach [6], which is an extension of the Proximal Policy Optimization (PPO) algorithm [33]. We tried architectures with two and three dense hidden layers, and with hyperbolic tangent (tanh) and rectified linear unit (relu) activation functions, and eventually settled on using three hidden layers for the actor neural network, with 96, 32, and 16 nodes in each respectively, two hidden layers for the critic network, with 128 and 96 nodes in each respectively, relu activation for hidden layers, tanh activation for the output layer of the actor network, and softplus activation for the output layer of the critic network. In both cases, the chosen approach resulted in faster convergence as well as in faster and better-performing policies (as judged via a subjectively tuned combination of objective performance metrics).

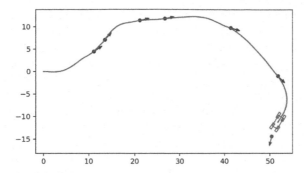

Fig. 4. Path of a simulated MRZR vehicle performing the waypoint+heading navigation task for a randomly chosen sequence of feasible waypoints, under an early neural
network policy trained using the TRPO algorithm and only feasible waypoints, trained
and tested in a simulator implementing a simple bicycle model of the vehicle, and a
brush tire model of tire-to-surface interactions (Simulation A in Fig. 1).

Lessons Learned from an Earlier Prototype. In an early prototype, we only
trained the controller on feasible waypoints. This worked well in simulation,
but once we integrated it with the autonomy software stack [18] on the MRZR
vehicle, it became obvious that an assured planner (the first subtask mentioned
earlier) is crucial to ensure that the vehicle is never asked to navigate towards
an infeasible waypoint. Without an assured planner, we must be prepared to
make a best effort to also reach infeasible waypoints, even if there is no longer
any assurance of success. Further analysis revealed that in the early prototype
the definition of feasible waypoint (or, equivalently, of safe starting state region)
was overly conservative, so that too many of the waypoints generated by the
(non-assured) planner were considered unsafe. As a consequence, we relaxed the
notion of waypoint feasibility to the one presented in this paper, formally verified
correctness of the relaxed definitions, and retrained the controllers.

5.2 Evaluating and Improving upon an Initial Controller

We initially trained and tested the neural network controller in a simulation
that used a simple bicycle model of the vehicle, with a model of tire-to-surface
interactions [2]. In that simulation environment, the neural network controller
appeared to work very well, successfully reaching over 99% of the feasible waypoints chosen at random (Fig. 4).

However, we soon discovered that the simulation used for initial training
(Simulation A in Fig. 1) of the controller was insufficiently representative of the
actual vehicle—e.g., the vehicle controls were more responsive and accurate in
simulation than on the actual MRZR vehicle. The behavior of our early controller
on the MRZR vehicle due to this mismatch can be seen in the video at https://
youtu.be/bE2UpKHxsLg.

In order to account for the above challenges, we replaced the vehicle model we
use for training the Neural Network with a model developed by CMU National

Robotics Engineering Center (NREC) and implemented in their NREC Vehicle Modeling Library (NVML) based on the Wheeled Mobile Robot Dynamics Engine (WMRDE) [34,35], instantiated and calibrated to provide an accurate model of MRZR (Simulation B in Fig. 1). We then also incorporated a variant of the Neural Lyapunov technique [6] to improve controller stability and speed up training convergence.

The resulting neural network (NN) controller appeared to perform well in practice. Anecdotally, the GVSC team evaluating the work reported that: *(i)* NN sticks closer to the planned path than the baseline; *(ii)* NN navigates the path more consistently than the baseline; *(iii)* With NN, the planner does not get "stuck" replanning as often; *(iv)* Baseline feels robotic, while NN feels like a student driver; *(v)* Baseline is crawling, while NN goes more reliably fast, but NN accelerates too aggressively at times and does not feel sufficiently "in control" at high speeds; *(vi)* NN feels more natural—when going slowly, it feels like it could safely go faster; and *(vii)* NN usually drives smoother around obstacles, compared to the baseline.

5.3   Controller Safety

While our goal is to train a trustworthy controller that can be assured to always output a safe action (e.g., ether using the Neural Lyapunov based barrier function technique [6,7], or using the dReal SMT solver [14] to verify the properties of the neural network), neither is necessary in order to be able to assure safe vehicle behavior. Even if the underlying neural network based controller is not trustworthy, our technique allows for the use of the ModelPlex tool [24], which is part of the KeYmaera X theorem prover, to create a safe-by-construction safety net for the controller that checks whether the neural network outputs satisfy the SafeControl property and are therefore formally verified safe to act upon or else presents a safe alternative action (see Fig. 1).

However, our dL formalization in KeYmaera X used a simple vehicle model with instantaneous steering (similar to that used in Simulation A from Fig. 1). As we discussed above, the actual MRZR does not behave close enough to that model, and we ended up having to train the neural network controller with a significantly different model (Simulation B). As a result, we could use (and indeed successfully tested) the ModelPlex-created safety wrapper in Simulation A, but that safety wrapper is unfortunately not yet applicable to the real vehicle.

6   Discussion

6.1   Conclusions and Next Steps

Our initial attempts to formalize the task using the traditional (x, y, v_x, v_y) representation of the state resulted in large formulas that took hours to even try to simplify in Mathematica, and so it was fairly hopeless to try reasoning about them in a theorem prover. Our turn center based model not only simplifies the

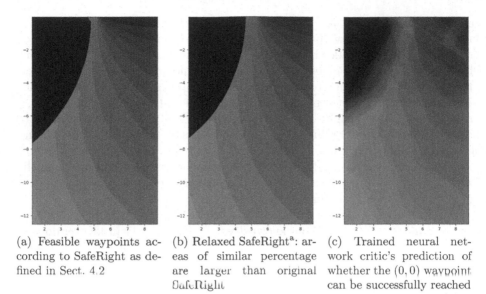

(a) Feasible waypoints according to SafeRight as defined in Sect. 4.2

(b) Relaxed SafeRight[a]: areas of similar percentage are larger than original SafeRight

(c) Trained neural network critic's prediction of whether the $(0,0)$ waypoint can be successfully reached

Fig. 5. SafeRight zone according to a verified formal model, a to-be-verified further relaxed formal model, and a neural network "critic"; $R_{\min}=5$, $\epsilon\approx0.17$, vehicle speed $0.5\,\mathrm{m/s}$, speed limit $0.5\,\mathrm{m/s}$ (deviation between simulator vehicle model for training the neural network and simplified formal model is smaller at low speed); color intensity of each point (r_x, r_y) indicates which percentage of orientations (i.e., starting configurations of fixed (r_x, r_y) and varying (l_x, l_y), so that the vehicle heading spans a range between $-90°$ and $90°$) would be safe; brighter is higher percentage. [a]Relaxed SafeRight: circle of radius $2R_{\min}-2\epsilon$ around destination point A excluded from safe zone and SafeFrontLineRight pushed back to 2ϵ.

formalization, but makes it modular and easier to work with—namely, it allows decomposing the Safe($state$) definition into three parts, each only referring to two of the coordinates—SafeDir only referring to r_x and l_x, SafeLeft only referring to l_x and l_y, and similarly SafeRight only referring to r_x and r_y. Such reduction in dimensionality is especially valuable given the doubly-exponential runtime complexity of deciding problems in real arithmetic [8]. This allowed us to separately reason about different components of the state and different parts of the Safe constraint. Furthermore, it allowed us to exploit the left-right symmetry: once the "left" parts of the relevant lemmas are proved, tactics for proving the corresponding "right" lemmas follow immediately by symmetry.

The ability of the turn center based formalization to provide a natural "distance to waypoint" metric combining both the location and heading requirements, as well as expressing a natural trade-off between the two, results in a synergy between the formal modeling and verification of the "location + heading" waypoint navigation task and training of the corresponding neural network based controllers, where the distance metric informs the reward function. The synergy could be leveraged further, by explicitly penalizing the controller for choosing actions that our definitions consider unsafe. The result of such a constrained training process would be a controller that learns to navigate without causing monitor violations. For now, we want to test the conservativeness of our formal models and allow the training process to explore and discover its own notion of safety—and indeed, the learned controllers tend to converge to notions of safety that are more aggressive than our formal models. In particular, our definition of SafeRight seems too conservative—it appears (although we have not been able to prove it just yet) that rather than excluding a circle of radius $2R_{\mathtt{min}}$ around $(-R_{\mathtt{min}} - \epsilon, 0)$ (light-blue quarter-circle in Fig. 3), it should be enough to only exclude a circle of radius $2R_{\mathtt{min}} - \epsilon$, or perhaps even just $2R_{\mathtt{min}} - 2\epsilon$ around the original point A (that is, $(-R_{\mathtt{min}} - \epsilon, 0)$), and similarly it might be safe to push back SafeFrontLineRight to 2ϵ. The corresponding SafeRight zone and the SafeRight zone as discovered by the neural network "critic" (using the bicycle model of the vehicle) are illustrated in Fig. 5.

The KeYmaera X proof outlined in this paper took several man-months to complete and is to the best of our knowledge the largest safety proof ever done in KeYmaera X. It is at least 4x larger (in both the number of the interactive proof steps and the number of the primitive proof steps) than a previous "location + curvature" waypoint navigation safety proof performed by a different subset of our team [5], which was about the same size as other the largest KeYmaera X safety proofs. Despite that complexity, we are optimistic that we will be able to tweak it to support a less conservative Safe(*state*) definition with relatively little effort since KeYmaera X translates interactive proof steps into proof tactics. However what we ultimately hope to be able to do is to state and prove similar safety theorems using more realistic vehicle models, with multiple wheels, friction, actuation delays, and uneven terrain. At present, it seems unlikely that this would be feasible using our current approach of manually stating the definition, manually discovering relevant invariants, and manually transforming real arithmetic statements until they become tractable for the state-of-the-art real arithmetic solvers used by KeYmaera X. Instead, we plan to explore a machine-learning approach, where some aspects of the problem and some proof details are discovered and approximated by neural networks (along the lines of how the neural network "critic" in Fig. 5 approximates our formal definition of SafeRight).

Another opportunity for future extension is to adapt the one-waypoint-at-a-time form of the navigation task to handle a sequence of multiple waypoints at once, which better resembles the current planner in the MRZR. While in our experience, the one-waypoint-at-a-time worked reasonably well (often better than the existing baseline implementation) even when used with a planner that generates waypoint sequences, we expect to be able to improve driving smoothness with a neural network controller that is provided with multiple waypoints.

6.2   Brief Comparison to Related Work

Formal verification of safety properties of robotic ground vehicles (see [21] for a comprehensive overview, or [11] for certification of autonomous systems) is roughly divided into methods based on reachability analysis and methods based on theorem proving: (online) reachability analysis [20,25] may support more complex differential equations at the expense of ignoring worst-case scenarios (e.g., [20] ignores the possibility of suddenly turning pedestrians), providing only bounded-time results and requiring online computation, which makes it challenging to use for training with reinforcement learning with large volumes of simulations. Verisig [17] translates neural network controllers with sigmoid/tanh activation functions into a hybrid systems model, combined with a plant model, and uses bounded-time reachability analysis for verification of the resulting closed-loop system. NNV [37] provides several reachability algorithms a variety of set representations to analyze stability and bounded-time safety of neural networks.

In contrast, we obtain unbounded-time results offline and verified monitoring conditions [24] that are fast to evaluate even in reinforcement learning settings. Unbounded-time results for waypoint navigation are also obtained in [5] for a point-robot with a focus on integrated safety and liveness properties, but without guarantees on the orientation of the robot. Ways to introduce sensor and actuator disturbance in unbounded-time safety models are discussed in [23]. In [31] a planner for ground vehicle motion is verified in Isabelle, but path tracking and control is not addressed.

Complementary approaches use synthesis from formal specifications to obtain correct-by-construction control or planning, e.g., [3,40,41]. Unlike in our approach, the safety arguments of synthesis do not transfer to learned controllers. Approaches for monitoring and falsification based on formal specifications in linear temporal logic (LTL), metric temporal logic (MTL), or signal temporal logic (STL) target bug finding and runtime safety, treating monitor specifications as trusted input to the monitoring tool. For example [38] tests the control choices of autonomous vehicles with machine-learning components in the loop; the PLANrm framework [15] uses MTL to inspect and modify plans; [39] generate barrier certificates from simulation to justify safety of learned controllers; [10] use falsification to find when control obtained through machine learning violates specifications; [9] monitor the assumptions used for model-checking a control software; [19] uses runtime monitors for fault disambiguation on mobile robots. Several runtime verification tools provide convenient integration with robotic platforms, e.g., [12,16,36]. This gives confidence in safety *if* the monitor specification is correct and "enough" simulations and tests are conducted.

In our approach, safety is formally guaranteed and the verified models presented here are the source for ModelPlex monitor generation by proof [24]; ModelPlex guarantees mutually satisfied assumptions: the offline proof justifies monitor correctness, while satisfied online monitors justify model correctness and provably detect when the assumptions of the offline model are no longer true in reality. All artifacts in the offline proof and in the monitor synthesis proofs, including invariant regions of differential equations, barrier certificates, and other properties of differential equations if they come up in proofs, are justified from axioms in differential dynamic logic [27] and its differential equation axioms [30].

Acknowledgment. This material is based upon work supported by the United States Air Force and DARPA under Contract No. FA8750-18-C-0092. Any opinions, findings and conclusions or recommendations expressed in this material are those of the authors and do not necessarily reflect the view of the United States Air Force and DARPA. Distribution Statement "A" (Approved for Public Release, Distribution Unlimited).

References

1. Achiam, J., Held, D., Tamar, A., Abbeel, P.: Constrained policy optimization. In: Proceedings of the 34th International Conference on Machine Learning, ICML 2017, Sydney, NSW, Australia, pp. 22–31 (2017). proceedings.mlr.press/v70/achiam17a.html
2. Ahn, E.: Towards Safe Reinforcement Learning in the Real World. Master's thesis, Carnegie Mellon University, cMU-RI-TR-19-56 (2019). www.ri.cmu.edu/wp-content/uploads/2019/08/MSR/Thesis/Edward/Ahn/2019.pdf
3. Alonso-Mora, J., DeCastro, J.A., Raman, V., Rus, D., Kress-Gazit, H.: Reactive mission and motion planning with deadlock resolution avoiding dynamic obstacles. Auton. Robot. **42**(4), 801–824 (2017). https://doi.org/10.1007/s10514-017-9665-6
4. Bohrer, B., Rahli, V., Vukotic, I., Völp, M., Platzer, A.: Formally verified differential dynamic logic. In: Proceedings of the 6th ACM SIGPLAN Conference on Certified Programs and Proofs. ACM (2017). https://doi.org/10.1145/3018610.3018616
5. Bohrer, B., Tan, Y.K., Mitsch, S., Sogokon, A., Platzer, A.: A formal safety net for waypoint following in ground robots. IEEE Robot. Automat. Lett. **4**(3), 2910–2917 (2019). https://doi.org/10.1109/LRA.2019.2923099
6. Chang, Y.C., Gao, S.: Stabilizing neural control using self-learned almost Lyapunov critics. In: Proceedings of the 2021 International Conference on Robotics and Automation (ICRA 2021) (2021). arxiv.org/abs/2107.04989
7. Chang, Y.C., Roohi, N., Gao, S.: Neural Lyapunov control (2020). arxiv.org/abs/2005.00611
8. Davenport, J.H., Heintz, J.: Real quantifier elimination is doubly exponential. J. Symb. Comput. **5**(1/2), 29–35 (1988). https://doi.org/10.1016/S0747-7171(88)80004-X
9. Desai, A., Saha, I., Yang, J., Qadeer, S., Seshia, S.A.: DRONA: a framework for safe distributed mobile robotics. In: Martínez, S., Tovar, E., Gill, C., Sinopoli, B. (eds.) Proceedings of the 8th International Conference on Cyber-Physical Systems, ICCPS 2017, Pittsburgh, Pennsylvania, USA, pp. 239–248. ACM (2017). https://doi.org/10.1145/3055004.3055022
10. Dreossi, T., Donzé, A., Seshia, S.A.: Compositional falsification of cyber-physical systems with machine learning Components. J. Autom. Reason. **63**(4), 1031–1053 (2019). https://doi.org/10.1007/s10817-018-09509-5
11. Fisher, M., Mascardi, V., Rozier, K.Y., Schlingloff, B.-H., Winikoff, M., Yorke-Smith, N.: Towards a framework for certification of reliable autonomous systems. Auton. Agents Multi-Agent Syst. **35**(1), 1–65 (2020). https://doi.org/10.1007/s10458-020-09487-2
12. Foughali, M., Bensalem, S., Combaz, J., Ingrand, F.: Runtime verification of timed properties in autonomous robots. In: 18th ACM/IEEE International Conference on Formal Methods and Models for System Design, MEMOCODE 2020, Jaipur, India, pp. 1–12. IEEE (2020). https://doi.org/10.1109/MEMOCODE51338.2020.9315156

13. Fulton, N., Mitsch, S., Quesel, J., Völp, M., Platzer, A.: Keymaera X: an axiomatic tactical theorem prover for hybrid systems. In: Felty, A.P., Middeldorp, A. (eds.) Automated Deduction - CADE-25 - 25th International Conference on Automated Deduction, Berlin, Germany, 2015, Proceedings. Lecture Notes in Computer Science, vol. 9195, pp. 527–538. Springer (2015). https://doi.org/10.1007/978-3-319-21401-6_36

14. Gao, S., Kong, S., Clarke, E.M.: dreal: An SMT solver for nonlinear theories over the reals. In: Bonacina, M.P. (ed.) Automated Deduction - CADE-24 - 24th International Conference on Automated Deduction, Lake Placid, NY, USA, 2013. Proceedings. Lecture Notes in Computer Science, vol. 7898, pp. 208–214. Springer (2013). https://doi.org/10.1007/978-3-642-38574-2_14

15. Hoxha, B., Fainekos, G.E.: Planning in dynamic environments through temporal logic monitoring. In: Magazzeni, D., Sanner, S., Thiébaux, S. (eds.) Planning for Hybrid Systems, Papers from the 2016 AAAI Workshop, Phoenix, Arizona, USA 2016. AAAI Workshops, vol. WS-16-12. AAAI Press (2016). www.aaai.org/ocs/index.php/WS/AAAIW16/paper/view/12556

16. Huang, J., Erdogan, C., Zhang, Y., Moore, B.M., Luo, Q., Sundaresan, A., Rosu, G.: ROSRV: runtime verification for robots. In: Bonakdarpour, B., Smolka, S.A. (eds.) Runtime Verification - 5th International Conference, RV 2014, Toronto, ON, Canada, 2014. Proceedings. Lecture Notes in Computer Science, vol. 8734, pp. 247–254. Springer (2014). https://doi.org/10.1007/978-3-319-11164-3_20

17. Ivanov, R., Carpenter, T.J., Weimer, J., Alur, R., Pappas, G.J., Lee, I.: Verifying the safety of autonomous systems with neural network controllers. ACM Trans. Embed. Comput. Syst. 20(1), 1–26 (2021). https://doi.org/10.1145/3419742

18. Kania, R., Frederick, P., Pritchett, W., Wood, B., Mentzer, C., Johnson, E.: Dismounted soldier autonomy tools (DSAT) – from conception to deployment. In: 2014 NDIA Ground Vehicles Systems Engineering and Technology Symposium (2014). gvsets.ndia-mich.org/publication.php?documentID=171

19. Kempa, B., Zhang, P., Jones, P.H., Zambreno, J., Rozier, K.Y.: Embedding online runtime verification for fault disambiguation on robonaut2. In: Bertrand, N., Jansen, N. (eds.) Formal Modeling and Analysis of Timed Systems - 18th International Conference, FORMATS 2020, Vienna, Austria, Proceedings. Lecture Notes in Computer Science, vol. 12288, pp. 196–214. Springer (2020). https://doi.org/10.1007/978-3-030-57628-8_12

20. Liu, S.B., Roehm, H., Heinzemann, C., Lütkebohle, I., Oehlerking, J., Althoff, M.: Provably safe motion of mobile robots in human environments. In: 2017 IEEE/RSJ International Conference on Intelligent Robots and Systems, IROS 2017, Vancouver, BC, Canada, pp. 1351–1357. IEEE (2017). https://doi.org/10.1109/IROS.2017.8202313

21. Luckcuck, M., Farrell, M., Dennis, L.A., Dixon, C., Fisher, M.: Formal specification and verification of autonomous robotic systems: a survey. ACM Comput. Surv. 52(5), 1–41 (2019). https://doi.org/10.1145/3342355

22. Milner, R.: LCF: a way of doing proofs with a machine. In: Becvár, J. (ed.) Mathematical Foundations of Computer Science 1979, Proceedings, 8th Symposium Lecture Notes in Computer Science. Olomouc, Czechoslovakia, vol. 74, pp. 146–159. Springer (1979). https://doi.org/10.1007/3-540-09526-8_11

23. Mitsch, S., Ghorbal, K., Vogelbacher, D., Platzer, A.: Formal verification of obstacle avoidance and navigation of ground robots. I. J. Robotics Res. 36(12), 1312–1340 (2017). https://doi.org/10.1177/0278364917733549

24. Mitsch, S., Platzer, A.: ModelPlex: verified runtime validation of verified cyber-physical system models. Formal Methods Syst. Design (1), 33–74 (2016). https://doi.org/10.1007/s10703-016-0241-z
25. Pan, Y., Lin, Q., Shah, H., Dolan, J.M.: Safe planning for self-driving via adaptive constrained ILQR. CoRR abs/2003.02757 (2020). arxiv.org/abs/2003.02757
26. Platzer, A.: Differential dynamic logic for hybrid systems. J. Autom. Reasoning **41**(2), 143–189 (2008). https://doi.org/10.1007/s10817-008-9103-8
27. Platzer, A.: A Complete Uniform Substitution Calculus for Differential Dynamic Logic. J. Autom. Reason. **59**(2), 219–265 (2016). https://doi.org/10.1007/s10817-016-9385-1
28. Platzer, A.: Logical Foundations of Cyber-Physical Systems. Springer (2018). https://doi.org/10.1007/978-3-319-63588-0
29. Platzer, A., Clarke, E.M.: Formal verification of curved flight collision avoidance maneuvers: a case study. In: Cavalcanti, A., Dams, D. (eds.) FM. LNCS, vol. 5850, pp. 547–562. Springer (2009). https://doi.org/10.1007/978-3-642-05089-3_35
30. Platzer, A., Tan, Y.K.: Differential equation invariance axiomatization. J. ACM **67**(1), 1–66 (2020). https://doi.org/10.1145/3380825
31. Rizaldi, A., Immler, F., Schürmann, B., Althoff, M.: A formally verified motion planner for autonomous vehicles. In: Lahiri, S.K., Wang, C. (eds.) Automated Technology for Verification and Analysis - 16th International Symposium, ATVA 2018, Los Angeles, CA, USA, 2018, Proceedings. Lecture Notes in Computer Science, vol. 11138, pp. 75–90. Springer (2018). https://doi.org/10.1007/978-3-030-01090-4_5
32. Schulman, J., Levine, S., Moritz, P., Jordan, M.I., Abbeel, P.: Trust region policy optimization. CoRR abs/1502.05477 (2015). arxiv.org/abs/1502.05477
33. Schulman, J., Wolski, F., Dhariwal, P., Radford, A., Klimov, O.: Proximal policy optimization algorithms (2017). arxiv.org/abs/1707.06347v2
34. Seegmiller, N.: Dynamic model formulation and calibration for wheeled mobile robots. Ph.D. thesis, Carnegie Mellon University, Pittsburgh, PA (2014). www.ri.cmu.edu/publications/dynamic-model-formulation-and-calibration-for-wheeled-mobile-robots/
35. Seegmiller, N., Kelly, A.: High-fidelity yet fast dynamic models of wheeled mobile robots. IEEE Trans. Robot. **32**(3), 614–625 (2016). https://doi.org/10.1109/TRO.2016.2546310
36. Shivakumar, S., Torfah, H., Desai, A., Seshia, S.A.: SOTER on ROS: a run-time assurance framework on the robot operating system. In: Deshmukh, J., Nickovic, D. (eds.) Runtime Verification - 20th International Conference, RV 2020, Los Angeles, CA, USA, 2020, Proceedings. Lecture Notes in Computer Science, vol. 12399, pp. 184–194. Springer (2020). https://doi.org/10.1007/978-3-030-60508-7_10
37. Tran, H., Yang, X., Lopez, D.M., Musau, P., Nguyen, L.V., Xiang, W., Bak, S., Johnson, T.T.: NNV: the neural network verification tool for deep neural networks and learning-enabled cyber-physical systems. In: Lahiri, S.K., Wang, C. (eds.) Computer Aided Verification - 32nd International Conference, CAV 2020, Los Angeles, CA, USA, 2020, Proceedings, Part I. Lecture Notes in Computer Science, vol. 12224, pp. 3–17. Springer (2020). https://doi.org/10.1007/978-3-030-53288-8_1
38. Tuncali, C.E., Fainekos, G., Prokhorov, D.V., Ito, H., Kapinski, J.: Requirements-driven test generation for autonomous vehicles with machine learning components. IEEE Trans. Intell. Veh. **5**(2), 265–280 (2020). https://doi.org/10.1109/TIV.2019.2955903

39. Tuncali, C.E., Kapinski, J., Ito, H., Deshmukh, J.V.: Reasoning about safety of learning-enabled components in autonomous cyber-physical systems. In: Proceedings of the 55th Annual Design Automation Conference, DAC 2018, San Francisco, CA, USA, pp. 1–6. ACM (2018). https://doi.org/10.1145/3195970.3199852
40. Wong, K.W., Ehlers, R., Kress-Gazit, H.: Resilient, provably-correct, and high-level robot behaviors. IEEE Trans. Robot. **34**(4), 936–952 (2018). https://doi.org/10.1109/TRO.2018.2830353
41. Wong, K.W., Finucane, C., Kress-Gazit, H.: Provably-correct robot control with ltlmop, OMPL and ROS. In: 2013 IEEE/RSJ International Conference on Intelligent Robots and Systems, Tokyo, Japan, p. 2073. IEEE (2013). https://doi.org/10.1109/IROS.2013.6696636

Model-Free Reinforcement Learning for Lexicographic Omega-Regular Objectives

Ernst Moritz Hahn[1], Mateo Perez[2], Sven Schewe[3], Fabio Somenzi[2], Ashutosh Trivedi[2(✉)], and Dominik Wojtczak[3]

[1] University of Twente, Enschede, The Netherlands
[2] University of Colorado Boulder, Boulder, USA
ashutosh.trivedi@colorado.edu
[3] University of Liverpool, Liverpool, UK

Abstract. We study the problem of finding optimal strategies in Markov decision processes with lexicographic ω-regular objectives, which are ordered collections of ordinary ω-regular objectives. The goal is to compute strategies that maximise the probability of satisfaction of the first ω-regular objective; subject to that, the strategy should also maximise the probability of satisfaction of the second ω-regular objective; then the third and so forth. For instance, one may want to guarantee critical requirements first, functional ones second and only then focus on the non-functional ones. We show how to harness the classic off-the-shelf model-free reinforcement learning techniques to solve this problem and evaluate their performance on four case studies.

1 Introduction

In the basic setting of model-free reinforcement learning (RL), the goal is to find a strategy that optimises the total accumulated (discounted) reward, given a single reward structure. However, this setting is seldom sufficient to concisely express real-world scenarios. On the one hand, it is often necessary to consider objectives for which it is not obvious how they could be expressed by a reward structure. On the other hand, in many cases multiple objectives are of interest, and not all of them are equally important.

This paper studies model-free RL for the lexicographic optimization of ω-regular objectives. That is, we are given k different ω-regular specifications, ordered by importance. We then optimise the probabilities of these specifications in the following way. An optimal strategy has to maximise the probability that first objective is achieved. The strategy then also has to maximise the probability

This work was supported by the Engineering and Physical Sciences Research Council through grant EP/P020909/1 and by the National Science Foundation through grant 2009022. ■ This project has received funding from the European Union's Horizon 2020 research and innovation programme under grant agreements No 101032464 (SyGaST), 864075 (CAESAR), and 956123 (FOCETA).

M. Huisman et al. (Eds.): FM 2021, LNCS 13047, pp. 142–159, 2021.
https://doi.org/10.1007/978-3-030-90870-6_8

that second objective holds among those strategies that achieve the maximum probability for the first objective. The next priority is then to maximise the third objective, and so forth.

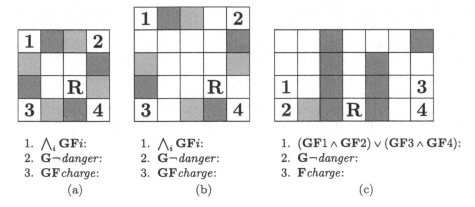

1. $\bigwedge_i \mathbf{GF}i$:
2. $\mathbf{G}\neg danger$:
3. $\mathbf{GF}\,charge$:

(a)

1. $\bigwedge_i \mathbf{GF}i$:
2. $\mathbf{G}\neg danger$:
3. $\mathbf{GF}\,charge$:

(b)

1. $(\mathbf{GF1} \wedge \mathbf{GF2}) \vee (\mathbf{GF3} \wedge \mathbf{GF4})$:
2. $\mathbf{G}\neg danger$:
3. $\mathbf{F}\,charge$:

(c)

Fig. 1. Robot case study: grid-world examples with multiple ω-regular objectives.

Consider a robot that moves around in a grid world. We depict three such scenarios of different sizes in Fig. 1. In each step, the robot can choose to go into one of four directions. If there is enough space, the robot might move one or two steps: With probability $\mathbf{p}$, the robot moves two steps into the chosen direction, while it moves only a single step into the selected direction with a probability of $1-\mathbf{p}$. If there is only room for one step, the robot deterministically moves one step. If there is no room for a step, then the robot doesn't move.

In the figure, the robot's initial position is marked with $\mathbf{R}$. Red fields are dangerous for the robot, while the green ones allow the robot to recharge its battery. Four fields are marked with **1** to **4**. For these scenarios (a)–(c), we have three different objectives expressed as LTL formulas. Among them 1. marks the objective with the highest priority, while 3. marks the objective with the lowest.

In scenario (a), the first priority of the robot is to visit all four numbered fields infinitely often, the second priority is never to enter a dangerous area, and the third priority is to visit some charging field infinitely often. In this scenario, it is possible to fulfil the primary objective with probability 1. However, the secondary objective can then not be fulfilled with any probability larger than 0: Due to its uncertain movements, the robot always has a chance to step into a dangerous field when trying to fulfil the primary objective. The third priority, however, can again be fulfilled with probability 1.

The objectives of scenario (b) are the same as for (a). However, because of the larger grid, the robot can stay out of danger while satisfying its primary objective; it can meet all three objectives with probability 1.

In scenario (c), the primary objective is to visit fields **1** and **2** infinitely often *or* to visit fields **3** and **4** infinitely often. The secondary objective is to avoid dangerous fields. The tertiary one is to eventually visit a charging field. Here, the robot can again fulfil its primary objective with probability 1. The secondary one can only be fulfilled with probability $1 - (\mathbf{p} \cdot (1 - \mathbf{p}))$: To fulfil its primary objective and then the secondary one, the best the robot can do is to move upwards and then to the right. If, by moving to the right, the robot first moves one field but then two fields, it will run into a dangerous field. When maximising the primary and secondary objectives, the tertiary objective can then only be fulfilled with probability $\mathbf{p} \cdot (1 - \mathbf{p})$, because trying to reach the charging field cannot be done without entering a dangerous field with at least probability $1 - \mathbf{p}$ (the chance of not "jumping" over the left barrier of red fields). Therefore, the tertiary objective is only pursued when the secondary objective has been missed.

The priorities play a key role here: For scenario (c), if the safety objective $\mathbf{G}\neg$danger were the most important, the robot would be able to completely avoid unsafe fields, fulfilling this objective with probability 1. However, the probability to fulfil the recurrence objective $(\mathbf{GF}1 \wedge \mathbf{GF}2) \vee (\mathbf{GF}3 \wedge \mathbf{GF}4)$ would be $\mathbf{p}$, because the robot can only reach the lower-right corner of the grid with probability $\mathbf{p}$ if it is to avoid danger at all cost.

Our Approach. Our approach is based on the following idea. We assume that each objective is given as a Good-for-MDPs (GFM) Büchi automaton [12]. We compose our model with the product of these Büchi automata. We obtain a Markov decision process (MDP) whose transitions are labeled with multiple separate Büchi conditions. Then, generalizing a method described in previous work [13], we transform different combinations of Büchi conditions into different rewards in a reduction to a weighted reachability problem that depends on the prioritisation. We end up with an MDP equipped with a standard scalar reward, to which general RL algorithms can be applied.

Naturally, in practice, we do not perform the composition of the MDP with the automata and the transformation into rewards before the RL process starts; indeed, the two steps are intertwined, such that we perform the composition on-the-fly, avoiding the costly construction of parts of the product automaton that would never be visited during RL.

Related Work. The study of the optimal control problems for MDPs under various performance objectives is the subject of [20]. For a given MDP and performance objective (total reward, discounted reward, and average reward), the optimal expected cost can be characterised using Bellman equations and an optimal strategy can be computed using dynamic programming (value iteration or policy iteration) or linear programming [20]. Chatterjee, Majumadar, and Henzinger [6] considered MDPs with multiple discounted reward objectives. In the presence of multiple objectives, the trade-off between different objectives can be characterised as Pareto curves. The authors of [6] showed that every Pareto-optimal point can be achieved by a memoryless strategy and the Pareto curve can be approximated in polynomial time. Moreover, the problem of checking the existence of a strategy that realises a value vector can be decided in polynomial time. These multi-objective optimization problems were studied in the context of multiple long-run average objectives by Chatterjee [5]. He showed that the Pareto curve can be approximated in polynomial time in the size of the MDP for irreducible MDPs and in polynomial space in the size of the MDP for general MDPs. Additionally, the problem of checking the existence of a strategy that guarantees values for different objectives to be equal to a given vector is in polynomial time for irreducible MDPs and in NP for general MDPs.

Verification of stochastic systems against ω-regular requirements has received considerable attention [2,17]. For systems modeled as MDPs and requirements expressed using ω-regular specifications, the key verification problem "probabilistic model-checking" is to compute optimal satisfaction probabilities and strategies. The probabilistic model checking problem can be solved [1] using graph-theoretic techniques (by computing so-called accepting end-component and then maximising the probability to reach states in such components) over the product of MDPs and ω-automata. Etessami et al. [7] were the first to study the multi-objective model-checking problem for MDPs with ω-regular objectives. Given probability intervals for the satisfaction of various properties, they developed a polynomial-time (in the size of the MDP) algorithm to decide the existence of such a strategy. They also showed that, in general, such strategies may require both randomization and memory. That paper also studies the approximation of the Pareto curve with respect to a set of ω-regular properties in time polynomial in the size of the MDP. Forejt et al. [9] studied quantitative multi-objective optimization over MDPs that combines ω-regular and quantitative objectives. Those algorithms are implemented in the probabilistic model checker PRISM [17].

RL is concerned with the optimal control of MDPs when the transition table and the reward structures are not known to the agents, but can be learned by interacting with the environment. In such a case, the aforementioned dynamic programming solutions are not applicable. RL [23] provides a framework to learn optimal strategies from repeated interactions with the environment. There are two main approaches to RL in MDPs: *model-free* approaches and *model-based* approaches. In a model-based approach, the learner interacts with the system to first estimate the transition probabilities and corresponding rewards, and then uses dynamic programming algorithms to compute optimal values and strategies. On the other hand, model-free RL [22] refers to a class of techniques that are asymptotically space-efficient because they do not construct a full model of the environment. These techniques include classic algorithms like Q-learning [24] as well as their extensions that use neural networks, like deep Q-learning [19].

RL has recently been applied to finding optimal control for ω-regular objectives [4,10–12,14–16,21], but all of theses papers deal with a single objective. Recently [3], the problem of maximising the probability of satisfying a safety condition together with an single ω-regular objective was considered and, as a secondary objective, the controller aims at maximising a discounted reward. Our approach is more flexible than [3] as we do not require that safety objectives be prioritised over liveness objectives.

2 Preliminaries

Nondeterministic Büchi Automata. A *nondeterministic Büchi automaton* is a tuple $\mathcal{A} = \langle \Sigma, Q, q_0, \Delta, \Gamma \rangle$, where Σ is a finite *alphabet*, Q is a finite set of *states*, $q_0 \in Q$ is the *initial state*, $\Delta \subseteq Q \times \Sigma \times Q$ is the set of transitions, and $\Gamma \subseteq Q \times \Sigma \times Q$ is the transition-based *acceptance condition*.

A *run* r of $\mathcal{A}$ on $w \in \Sigma^\omega$ is an ω-word $r_0, w_0, r_1, w_1, \ldots$ in $(Q \times \Sigma)^\omega$ such that $r_0 = q_0$ and, for $i > 0$, it is $(r_{i-1}, w_{i-1}, r_i) \in \Delta$. We write $\inf(r)$ for the set of transitions that appear infinitely often in the run r. A run r of $\mathcal{A}$ is *accepting* if $\inf(r) \cap \Gamma \neq \varnothing$. The *language*, $L_{\mathcal{A}}$, of $\mathcal{A}$ (or, *recognised* by $\mathcal{A}$) is the subset of words in Σ^ω that have accepting runs in $\mathcal{A}$. A language is ω-*regular* if it is accepted by a Büchi automaton.

An automaton $\mathcal{A} = \langle \Sigma, Q, q_0, \Delta, \Gamma \rangle$ is *deterministic* if $(q, \sigma, q'), (q, \sigma, q'') \in \Delta$ implies $q' = q''$ and is *complete* if, for all $\sigma \in \Sigma$ and $q \in Q$, there is a transition $(q, \sigma, q') \in \Delta$. A word has exactly one run in a deterministic, complete automaton.

Markov Decision Processes. A *Markov decision process (MDP)* $\mathcal{M}$ is a tuple $\langle S, s_0, A, T, \Sigma, L \rangle$ where S is a finite set of states, s_0 is a designated initial state, A is a finite set of *actions*, $T : S \times A \to \mathcal{D}(S)$, where $\mathcal{D}(S)$ is the set of probability distributions over S, is the *probabilistic transition (partial) function*, Σ is an alphabet, and $L : S \times A \times S \to \Sigma$ is the *labeling function* of the set of transitions. For a state $s \in S$, $A(s)$ denotes the set of actions available in s. For states $s, s' \in S$ and $a \in A(s)$, we have that $T(s,a)(s')$ equals $\Pr(s'|s, a)$.

A *run* of $\mathcal{M}$ is an ω-word $s_0, a_1, \ldots \in S \times (A \times S)^\omega$ such that $\Pr(s_{i+1}|s_i, a_{i+1}) > 0$ for all $i \geq 0$. A finite run is a finite such sequence. For a *run* $r = s_0, a_1, s_1, \ldots$ we define the corresponding labeled run as $L(r) = L(s_0, a_1, s_1), L(s_1, a_2, s_2), \ldots \in \Sigma^\omega$. We write $Runs(\mathcal{M})$ $(FRuns(\mathcal{M}))$ for the set of runs (finite runs) of $\mathcal{M}$ and $Runs_s(\mathcal{M})$ $(FRuns_s(\mathcal{M}))$ for the set of runs (finite runs) of $\mathcal{M}$ starting from state s. When the MDP is clear from the context we drop the argument $\mathcal{M}$.

A *strategy* in $\mathcal{M}$ is a function $\mu : FRuns \to \mathcal{D}(A)$ such that for all finite runs r we have $supp(\mu(r)) \subseteq A(\mathsf{last}(r))$, where $supp(d)$ is the support of d and $\mathsf{last}(r)$ is the last state of r. Let $Runs_s^\mu(\mathcal{M})$ denote the subset of runs $Runs_s(\mathcal{M})$ that correspond to strategy μ and initial state s. We say that a strategy μ is: *pure* if $\mu(r)$ assigns probability 1 to just one action in $A(\mathsf{last}(r))$ for all runs $r \in FRuns$; *stationary* if $\mathsf{last}(r) = \mathsf{last}(r')$ implies $\mu(r) = \mu(r')$ for all finite runs $r, r' \in FRuns$; and *finite-state* if there exists an equivalence relation $\sim$ on $FRuns$ with a finite index, such that $\mu(r) = \mu(r')$ for all finite runs $r \sim r'$.

The behavior of an MDP $\mathcal{M}$ under a strategy μ with starting state s is defined on a probability space $(Runs_s^\mu, \mathcal{F}_s^\mu, \Pr_s^\mu)$ over the set of infinite runs of μ from s. Given a random variable over the set of infinite runs $f : Runs \to \mathbb{R}$, we write $\mathbb{E}_s^\mu \{f\}$ for the expectation of f over the runs of $\mathcal{M}$ from state s that follow strategy μ. A *Markov chain* is an MDP whose set of actions is a singleton. For any MDP $\mathcal{M}$ and stationary strategy μ, let $\mathcal{M}_\mu$ be the Markov chain resulting from choosing the actions in $\mathcal{M}$ according to μ.

An *end-component* of an MDP is a set $C \subseteq S$ such that for every $s \in C$ we can pick an action $a_s \in A(s)$ in such a way that $\{s' \mid T(s, a_s)(s') > 0\} \subseteq C$ and the graph with vertices in C and edges in $E = \{(s, s') \mid s \in C$ and $T(s, a_s)(s') > 0\}$ is strongly connected. An end-component is *accepting* if at least one of such edges correspond to an accepting transition and is *maximal* if there does not exist an end-component $C' \supseteq C$. It is well-known (see, e.g., [1]) that for every strategy the union of the end-components is visited with probability 1 and once an end-component, C', is entered there is a pure finite-state strategy that visits its every edge infinitely many times while never leaving C'.

Syntactic and Semantic Satisfaction. Given an MDP $\mathcal{M}$ and an automaton $\mathcal{A} = \langle \Sigma, Q, q_0, \Delta, \Gamma \rangle$, we want to compute an optimal strategy satisfying the objective that the run of $\mathcal{M}$ is in the language of $\mathcal{A}$. We define the *semantic satisfaction* probability for $\mathcal{A}$ and a strategy μ from state s as:

$$\mathsf{PSem}_{\mathcal{A}}^{\mathcal{M}}(s, \mu) = \Pr_s^{\mu} \{ r \in Runs_s^{\mu}(\mathcal{M}) : L(r) \in L_{\mathcal{A}} \} \text{ and}$$
$$\mathsf{PSem}_{\mathcal{A}}^{\mathcal{M}}(s) = \sup_{\mu} \left(\mathsf{PSem}_{\mathcal{A}}^{\mathcal{M}}(s, \mu) \right).$$

A strategy μ_* is optimal for $\mathcal{A}$ if $\mathsf{PSem}_{\mathcal{A}}^{\mathcal{M}}(s, \mu_*) = \mathsf{PSem}_{\mathcal{A}}^{\mathcal{M}}(s)$.

When using automata for the analysis of MDPs, we need a syntactic variant of the acceptance condition. Given an MDP $\mathcal{M} = \langle S, s_0, A, T, \Sigma, L \rangle$ and an automaton $\mathcal{A} = \langle \Sigma, Q, q_0, \Delta, \Gamma \rangle$, the *product* $\mathcal{M} \times \mathcal{A} - \langle S \times Q, (s_0, q_0), A \times Q, T^{\times}, \Gamma^{\times} \rangle$ is an MDP augmented with an initial state (s_0, q_0) and accepting transitions $\Gamma^{\times}$. The function $T^{\times} : (S \times Q) \times (A \times Q) \to \mathcal{D}(S \times Q)$ is defined by

$$T^{\times}((s, q), (a, q'))((s', q')) = \begin{cases} T(s, a)(s') & \text{if } (q, L(s, a, s'), q') \in \Delta \\ 0 & \text{otherwise.} \end{cases}$$

Finally, $\Gamma^{\times} \subseteq (S \times Q) \times (A \times Q) \times (S \times Q)$ is defined by $((s, q), (a, q'), (s', q')) \in \Gamma^{\times}$ if, and only if, $(q, L(s, a, s'), q') \in \Gamma$ and $T(s, a)(s') > 0$. A strategy $\mu^{\times}$ on the product defines a strategy μ on the MDP with the same value, and vice versa. Note that for a stationary $\mu^{\times}$, the strategy μ may need memory. We define the *syntactic satisfaction* probabilities as

$$\mathsf{PSat}_{\mathcal{A}}^{\mathcal{M}}((s, q), \mu^{\times}) = \Pr_s^{\mu} \{ r \in Runs_{(s,q)}^{\mu^{\times}}(\mathcal{M} \times \mathcal{A}) : \inf(r) \cap \Gamma^{\times} \neq \varnothing \}$$
$$\mathsf{PSat}_{\mathcal{A}}^{\mathcal{M}}(s) = \sup_{\mu^{\times}} \left(\mathsf{PSat}_{\mathcal{A}}^{\mathcal{M}}((s, q_0), \mu^{\times}) \right) .$$

Note that $\mathsf{PSat}_{\mathcal{A}}^{\mathcal{M}}(s) = \mathsf{PSem}_{\mathcal{A}}^{\mathcal{M}}(s)$ holds for a deterministic $\mathcal{A}$. In general, $\mathsf{PSat}_{\mathcal{A}}^{\mathcal{M}}(s) \leqslant \mathsf{PSem}_{\mathcal{A}}^{\mathcal{M}}(s)$ holds, but equality is not guaranteed because the optimal resolution of nondeterministic choices may require access to future events.

An automaton $\mathcal{A}$ is *good for MDPs* (GFM), if $\mathsf{PSat}_{\mathcal{A}}^{\mathcal{M}}(s_0) = \mathsf{PSem}_{\mathcal{A}}^{\mathcal{M}}(s_0)$ holds for all MDPs $\mathcal{M}$ [12]. For an automaton to match $\mathsf{PSem}_{\mathcal{A}}^{\mathcal{M}}(s_0)$, its nondeterminism is restricted not to rely heavily on the future; rather, it must be possible to resolve the nondeterminism on-the-fly. In this paper we only consider GFM automata, which have this ability. Note that every LTL property and, more generally, every ω-regular objective can be expressed as a suitable GFM automaton [12].

For ω-regular objectives, optimal satisfaction probabilities and strategies can be computed using graph-theoretic techniques over the product structure. However, when the MDP transition structure is unknown, such techniques are not applicable. Model-free reinforcement learning overcomes this limitation.

3   From Lexicographic Objectives to Learning in 3.5 Steps

In this section, we provide a reduction from lexicographic ω-regular objectives to a payoff function (with hyperparameter) that can be wrapped for Q-learning (the additional half-step) in three steps. We assume that all properties are provided as good-for-MDP automata [12] based on which we construct an extended product automaton $\mathcal{P}$ in Subsect. 3.4.

3.1   Lexicographic ω-regular Objectives

For two k-dimensional vectors $v = (v_1, \ldots, v_k)$ and $v' = (v'_1, \ldots, v'_k)$, we say that v is larger in the *lexicographic order* than v', denoted by $v > v'$, if there exists $1 \leqslant i \leqslant k$ such that $v_i > v'_i$ and $v_j = v'_j$ for all $j < i$. We write $v \geqslant v'$ if $v > v'$ or $v = v'$. The problem we address is the following:

> *Given MDP $\mathcal{M}$ with unknown transition structure and k GFM Büchi automata $\mathcal{A}_1, \ldots, \mathcal{A}_k$ accepting ω-regular objectives $\varphi_1, \ldots, \varphi_k$, compute a strategy optimal for the* lexicographic ω-regular objective $(\mathcal{A}_1, \ldots, \mathcal{A}_k)$, *that is, a strategy that maximises according to the lexicographic order the vector* $(p_1, \ldots, p_k)$ *where* $p_i = \mathsf{PSem}_{\mathcal{A}_i}^{\mathcal{M}}(s_0)$ *is the probability that $\mathcal{M}$ satisfies φ_i.*

We adapt the model-free reinforcement learning (RL) framework to solve this problem. Bridging the gap between ω-regular specifications and model-free RL requires a translation from specifications to scalar rewards, such that a model-free RL algorithm maximising scalar rewards produces a strategy that maximises the probability to satisfy the specification. In this section we show how this can also be done for lexicographic ω-regular objectives.

3.2   Optimal Strategies for Lexicographic Objectives

Before turning to the reduction, we consider optimal strategies for the product of the MDP $\mathcal{M}$ and the automaton $\mathcal{P}$ that combines all the individual objectives. We also recapitulate what we need to achieve in $\mathcal{M} \times \mathcal{P}$ and what we can assume about optimal strategies (such that some optimal strategies will satisfy these assumptions).

Broadly speaking, the goal for each individual Büchi objective is to reach an end-component with an accepting transition for this objective, and to stay in this end-component forever, realizing this Büchi condition. maximising the probability of reaching such an end-component is the key objective, while, in the end-component, the strategy needs to make sure that some accepting transition is (almost surely) visited infinitely often.

For Büchi objectives with a lexicographic order, the reachability of a "good" end-component is the part that becomes lexicographic: the main objective is to maximise the chance of reaching an end-component, where the main objective is satisfied. Among all strategies that achieve this, we then maximise the chance of satisfying the secondary objective, and so forth.

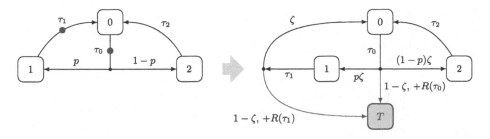

Fig. 2. Adding transitions to the target (T) in the augmented product MDP. The only edges that give non-zero reward are marked with a transition dependent $+R(\cdot)$ reward. In the original translation [11], all such rewards were equal to 1.

As we have Büchi objectives, it is in principle possible to only consider maximal end-components for this. While this cannot be a learning objective—as there is neither a concept of maximality in reinforcement learning, nor is learning such solutions a natural goal—it means that, whenever a state of $M \times P$ is in two end-components that satisfy the main and the secondary Büchi condition, then it is also in an end-component that satisfies both—for example, the union of the former two end-components. This prevents the interplay between these goals from becoming complex.

Once we have reached an end-component in $M \times P$ we want to stay in, the principle strategy is again to cover it, and thus to satisfy all objectives that this end-component satisfies almost surely.

3.3 Outline of Our Reduction

The reduction generalises the reduction from [11] for ω-regular objectives to reachability. The difference in the reduction is that it uses a *weighted* extension of reachability, i.e., different transitions to the target may be assigned different rewards. These weights are determined by the transition taken by an extended product automaton, which takes into account which set of individual objectives have recently been progressed towards by traversing accepting transitions of their corresponding GFM Büchi automata.

Broadly speaking, if we used this approach directly with a lexicographic order, it would translate a positional strategy that satisfies the individual properties with probabilities $(p_1, p_2, \ldots, p_k)$ to a "reachability" vector $(p'_1, p'_2, \ldots, p'_k)$, such that $p_i \leqslant p'_i \leqslant p_i + \varepsilon$, holds, where ε is bounded from above by $(1 - \zeta) \cdot E$, where ζ is the parameter from the reduction (Fig. 2), and E is the maximal (among pure positional strategies) expected number of accepting transitions visited before reaching an end-component that the strategy remains in.

Note that one cannot simply optimise the lexicographic value of $(p'_1, p'_2, \ldots, p'_k)$, as the noise in the assessment of the probability to meet the main objective, no matter how small, would outweigh all real differences in the probability of meeting the less relevant objectives. However, as the set of positional strategies is finite, there is a minimal difference $p_{min} > 0$ between the probabilities to achieve an individual objective by any two positional strategies with a different probability of meeting this objective.

Let $f_k = 1$, pick any $f_i \geqslant (1 + 1/p_{min})f_{i+1}$ for all $i < k$, and let $\overrightarrow{f} = (f_1, f_2, \ldots, f_k)$. Now, consider any two (pure and stationary) strategies that obtain probability vectors of satisfying the properties $\overrightarrow{p} = (p_1, p_2, \ldots, p_k)$ and $\overrightarrow{p}' = (p_1', p_2', \ldots, p_k')$, respectively, such that $\overrightarrow{p} > \overrightarrow{p}'$. We claim that the value of $\overrightarrow{p} \cdot \overrightarrow{f}^T$ is at least p_{min} higher than $\overrightarrow{p}' \cdot \overrightarrow{f}^T$. This is because, assuming that the i-th position is the first one where $\overrightarrow{p}$ and $\overrightarrow{p}'$ differ, we get:

$$\overrightarrow{p} \cdot \overrightarrow{f}^T - \overrightarrow{p}' \cdot \overrightarrow{f}^T \geqslant p_{min} f_i - \sum_{j>i} f_j$$

$$\geqslant p_{min}(1 + 1/p_{min})f_{i+1} - \sum_{j>i} f_j$$

$$= p_{min} f_{i+1} - \sum_{j>i+1} f_j \geqslant \ldots \geqslant p_{min} f_k = p_{min}.$$

Moreover, if $\sum_{i=1}^{k} f_i \cdot \varepsilon < p_{min}$, then using the weights of $\overrightarrow{f}$ for the reachability will guarantee that a strategy with a better performance obtains a better value and, in particular, only optimal strategies can obtain the highest value.

3.4   From Lexicographic Objectives to Lexicographic Büchi

In a first step, we discuss reductions from lexicographic ω-regular objectives, given as GFM Büchi automata, to GFM automaton with lexicographic Büchi objectives. In what follows, let $\mathbb{B} = \{0, 1\}$ be the set of Boolean values.

Lexicographic Büchi Objectives. We first have to give semantics for lexicographic Büchi objectives. For convenience in the proofs, we provide two: the *independent* semantics and the *infimum* semantics. We will show that we obtain the correct results, irrespective of which semantics we use, for the translations we suggest: both semantics provide the same value for the extended product automaton we define.

For this, we extend the usual product automaton by equipping the 'accepting transitions' Γ with a valuation function $v : \Gamma \to \mathbb{B}^k$, which maps each accepting transition to a k dimensional Boolean (0/1) vector different from the $\overrightarrow{0}$ vector, where each dimension refers to one of the k individual Büchi objectives.

The *infimum* semantics assigns to any run, r, the value according to the 'worst accepting transition' seen infinitely many times in r. Namely, to the set $I_A = \inf(r) \cap \Gamma$ of accepting transitions visited infinitely many times along r, it assigns the $\overrightarrow{0}$ vector if I_A is empty, and otherwise the lexicographically minimal vector in $\{v(t) \mid t \in I_A\}$.

The *independent* semantics intuitively treats all Büchi conditions independently: using it, a run would be assigned a Boolean vector $(b_1, b_2, \ldots, b_k)$, where $b_i = 1$ if there is a transition $t \in I_A$ such that the ith component of $v(t)$ is 1.

Reductions. We assume that the individual ω-regular objectives are given by k GFM Büchi automata $\mathcal{A}_1, \ldots, \mathcal{A}_k$, with $\mathcal{A}_i = (\Sigma, Q^i, q_0^i, \Delta^i, \Gamma^i)$. From these automata, we discuss a construction to an equivalent extended product automaton $\mathcal{P}$, where equivalence means that, for all finite-state strategies, the value that can be obtained using the k GFM automata for the properties, and the infimum and independent semantics for the two automata we construct provide the same results. Our construction builds an automaton $\mathcal{P} = (\Sigma, Q, q_0, \Delta, \Gamma, v)$, where

- $Q = \bigtimes_{i=1}^{k}(Q^i \times \mathbb{B})$
- $q_0 = (q_0^1, 0; q_0^2, 0; \ldots; q_0^k, 0)$
- $\Delta = \Gamma \cup \Delta'$, where the non-accepting transitions Δ' are defined independently for the k components: for the ith component,
  - $((q,0), \sigma, (q',0))$ is possible iff $(q, \sigma, q') \in \Delta^i \setminus \Gamma^i$ (i.e., iff (q, σ, q') is a non-accepting transition of $\mathcal{A}_i$),
  - $((q,0), \sigma, (q',1))$ is possible iff $(q, \sigma, q') \in \Gamma^i$ (i.e. iff, (q, σ, q') is an accepting transition of $\mathcal{A}_i$),
  - $((q,1), \sigma, (q',1))$ is possible iff $(q, \sigma, q') \in \Delta^i$ (i.e., iff (q, σ, q') is a transition of $\mathcal{A}_i$), and
- for all transitions $(q_1, b_1; \ldots; q_k, b_k; \sigma; q_1', b_1'; \ldots; q_k', b_k') \in \Delta'$ with $\sum_{i=1}^{k} b_k' \neq 0$, Γ contains a transition $t = (q_1, b_1; \ldots; q_k, b_k; \sigma; q_1', 0; \ldots; q_k', 0)$ (obtained by replacing all Boolean values in the target state by 0), with $v(t) = (b_1', b_2', \ldots, b_k')$; Γ contains no further transitions.

That is, Δ' simply collects the information, which of the individual accepting transitions has been seen since the last transition from Γ has been taken. Taking a transition from Γ then 'cashes in' on these transitions, while resetting the tracked values to 0.

As a minor optimisation, we remove the states $\bigtimes_{i=0}^{k-1} Q^i \times \{1\}$ together with the transitions that lead to them. This can be done as there is never a point in delaying to cash in on these transitions. Offering such additional choices that should never be taken would likely impede, rather than help, learning.

Equivalence. Recalling that pure finite-memory strategies suffice for MDPs with lexicographic Büchi objectives (follows from [7]), we now show equivalence.

Theorem 1. *Given an MDP $\mathcal{M}$ and k ω-regular objectives given as GFM Büchi automata $\mathcal{A}_1, \ldots, \mathcal{A}_k$, it holds that maximising these k objectives with lexicographic order, and maximising them with the automaton $\mathcal{P}$ from above with infimum or independent semantics provides the same result.*

Proof. We make use of the fact that pure finite-memory strategies suffice to obtain optimal control. We therefore fix an arbitrary finite-memory strategy μ for the control of the MDP $\mathcal{M}$ with lexicographic Büchi objectives, obtaining a Markov chain $\mathcal{M}_\mu$. Note that this is only a control for the MDP, not of the witness automaton $\mathcal{P}$.

We first turn any pure strategy for $\mathcal{P}$ with independent semantics into a strategy for the individual $\mathcal{A}_i$, which yields the same expected vector for every run (and thus the same probability vector). This is quite simple: every individual $\mathcal{A}_i$ can simply behave like its component in $\mathcal{P}$. On every run, if the ith component of the lexicographic vector is 1, then $\mathcal{A}_i$ has seen infinitely many accepting transitions.

Next, we turn k individual pure finite-memory strategies for the individual $\mathcal{A}_i$ into a strategy for $\mathcal{P}$ and evaluate it with the infimum semantics. For this, the automaton essentially follows the component strategies, and only has to additionally decide when to 'cash in.' $\mathcal{P}$ will make this choice whenever all individual automata have reached an end-component on the product of $\mathcal{M}_\mu$ and the automaton and, for all $\mathcal{A}_i$ that are in an accepting end-component, the Boolean store in the ith component is set to 1, or would have been set in this move. Note that this means that $v(t)$ in this case indicates all those components, for whom the individual $\mathcal{A}_i$ is in an accepting end-component whenever an accepting transition occurs. (In case that none of the $\mathcal{A}_i$ is in an accepting end-component, we do not use accepting transitions.)

Apart from this, it only uses accepting transitions when all Boolean values would otherwise be 1 (because then cashing in is forced).

With this strategy, the valuation can only differ from the individual valuations of the $\mathcal{A}_i$ if either (at least) one of the $\mathcal{A}_i$-s never reaches an end-component, or if it eventually reaches an accepting end-component, but only visits accepting transitions finitely often. As both of these events have probability 0, the expected vectors are the same for the individual $\mathcal{A}_i$ and for $\mathcal{P}$ with this strategy.

Finally, for every strategy the expected value for the independent semantics is at least as high as the value for the infimum semantics.   □

3.5   From Lexicographic Büchi to Weighted Büchi

We first observe that the previous theorem translates smoothly to a scalar version of the previous translation: we call a Büchi automaton *weighted* if it has a positive weight function $w : \Gamma \rightarrow \mathbb{R}$ instead of the lexicographic value function v. Similar to lexicographic Büchi, the value of a run is then 0 if no accepting transition occurs infinitely often. If accepting transitions do occur infinitely often, and they do occur in the order $t_1, t_2, t_3, \ldots \in \Gamma^\omega$, than the value of the run is $\liminf_{n \rightarrow \infty} (1/n) \sum_{i=1}^{n} w(t_i)$.

For any given linear function $f : \mathbb{R}^k \rightarrow \mathbb{R}$ with positive coefficients (i.e., linear functions that grow strictly monotonically in each dimension) that maps the k dimensional vectors to real numbers, we define $\mathcal{P}_f = (\Sigma, Q, q_0, \Delta, \Gamma, f \circ v)$ just like the automaton $\mathcal{P}$ from the previous subsection. The proof of Theorem 1 then trivially extends to the following theorem.

Theorem 2. *Given an MDP $\mathcal{M}$ and k lexicographic ω-regular objectives given as GFM Büchi automata $\mathcal{A}_1, \ldots, \mathcal{A}_k$, it holds that maximising these k objectives, weighted by some $f : \mathbb{R}^k \rightarrow \mathbb{R}$ with only positive coefficients, and maximising them with the automaton $\mathcal{P}_f$ provides the same result.*

Proof. The proof of Theorem 1 merely needs to be extended by the observation that, for every run r, with value b^+ in the independent semantics, b^- in the infimum semantics, and w_f in the weighted semantics, $f(b^+) \geqslant w_f \geqslant f(b^-)$ holds.

Recalling that the same expected vectors can be obtained using the individual $\mathcal{A}_i$, $\mathcal{P}$ with independent semantics, and $\mathcal{P}$ with infimum semantics, all these maximisations provide the same result. □

Lemma 1. *Let μ be any optimal finite-memory strategy for $\mathcal{M} \times \mathcal{P}_f$. Then $(\mathcal{M} \times \mathcal{P}_f)_\mu$ never has two transitions $t, t' \in \Gamma$ with $v(t) \neq v(t')$ in a end-component reachable from its initial state.*

Proof. Assuming such transitions t and t', the strategy can be improved by playing an adjusted strategy that mimics the strategy in the end-component (once reached), except that it only plays an accepting transition when all Boolean values that occur in this end-component in the independent semantics, are set. As this increases the expected reward, it contradicts the optimality of the end-component. □

This lemma also entails the existence of memoryless optimal strategies.

Observation. We now observe that, for carefully chosen f, optimizing the expected reward provides an optimal strategy for $\mathcal{P}$ (for both semantics). For a given MDP $\mathcal{M}$ and k GFM Büchi automata $\mathcal{A}_1, \ldots, \mathcal{A}_k$, there is a linear function f such that an optimal pure strategy for $\mathcal{M} \times \mathcal{P}_f$ is also optimal on $\mathcal{M} \times \mathcal{P}$. (Note that $\mathcal{M} \times \mathcal{P}$ and $\mathcal{M} \times \mathcal{P}_f$ have the same states and strategies, and that Lemma 1 entails that the value for both semantics of $\mathcal{P}$ is the same.) How to choose such weights was described in Sect. 3.3.

3.6   From Weighted Büchi to Weighted Reachability

Generalizing the construction for GFM Büchi automata from [11,12], we replace the *fixed* payoff of $+R(\cdot) = 1$ used in the gadget (cf. Fig. 2) by a *transition dependent* payoff $f(v(t))$. The gadget is otherwise unchanged: it takes the original transition with probability ζ, and moves, with a probability of $1 - \zeta$, to a sink state T—providing a payoff of $f(v(t))$—where the run ends. The payout on these transitions is the only reward that exists in this game, while ζ is a hyperparameter.

This has reduced the problem into a generalised reachability game, where a payout occurs only in the last step.

Theorem 3. *Given an MDP $\mathcal{M}$ and k lexicographic ω-regular objectives given as GFM Büchi automata $\mathcal{A}_1, \ldots, \mathcal{A}_k$, and an f that satisfies the condition from the observation above, there is a $\zeta_0 < 1$ such that, for all $\zeta \in [\zeta_0, 1)$, the optimal (pure positional) strategies obtained from replacing the accepting transitions in $\mathcal{M} \times \mathcal{P}_f$ by the gadget, are optimal for $\mathcal{M} \times \mathcal{P}_f$.*

Proof. We start with expanding the observation from Lemma 1 about end-components in optimal solutions to the weighted reachability objective obtained using this gadget: in both MDPs under consideration, $\mathcal{M} \times \mathcal{P}_f$ and the variation where accepting transitions are replaced by the gadget, there cannot be two

$t, t' \in \Gamma$ with $v(t) \neq v(t')$—if there were, the expected payoff could be improved as described in the proof of Lemma 1.

This leaves the expected difference to be purely down to the part *before* reaching an end-component. Moreover, for every positional strategy, the expected value of the undiscounted payoff is between the value obtained by removing the payoff for the gadgets not in an end-component, and increasing the payoff for these gadgets to the maximal payoff. As the expected difference between these extremes goes to 0 when ζ goes to 1, for sufficiently large $\zeta < 1$, optimal strategies for weighted reachability in the model with gadgets are also optimal for the mean payoff objective of $\mathcal{M} \times \mathcal{P}_f$. $\qquad\square$

Note that weighted reachability objectives always have optimal positional strategies. The theorems and the observation in this section show that, for suitable parameters, such an optimal positional strategy optimises the prioritised ω-regular objectives with lexicographic order.

Theorem 4. *Given an MDP $\mathcal{M}$ and k lexicographic ω-regular objectives given as GFM Büchi automata $\mathcal{A}_1, \ldots, \mathcal{A}_k$, a suitable linear function f, and a $\zeta < 1$ sufficiently close to 1, an optimal pure positional strategies for the MDP with weighted reachability objective obtained from replacing the accepting transitions in $\mathcal{M} \times \mathcal{P}_f$ by the gadget from this subsection provide an optimal control for $\mathcal{M}$ for the individual $\mathcal{A}_i$ with lexicographic order of relevance.*

3.7 Wrapping Up Weighted Reachability

We note that weighted reachability lacks the contraction property [20, 23], which makes it theoretically unsuitable for Q-learning. Learners often wrap reachability (and undiscounted payoff) into a discounted version thereof. This adds another parameter γ (the discount factor), which should be chosen significantly closer to 1 than ζ (e.g., $1 - (1 - \zeta)^2$).

4 Experimental Results

We refer to the gadget that keeps track of the accepting edges seen for each property as the tracker. We implemented the construction described in Sect. 3 on-the-fly, where we keep track of the states of the MDP, the automata, and the tracker, separately and compose them together at each timestep. The agent has additions actions to 'cash in' and to control any nondeterminism in the automata.

We ran Q-learning on a series of case studies that can be seen in Table 1. In Table 1, we list the name of the example, the property prioritisation order, the number of states in the MDP, the number of states in the product, the probability of satisfaction for each property under the learned strategy, and the time in seconds. We also report the values of the parameter f (which encodes the linear function for $\overrightarrow{f} = (f, 1)$ from Sect. 3.3 when we have two objectives, and for $\overrightarrow{f} = (f^2, f, 1)$ when we have three), the parameter ζ, the exploration

Table 1. Multiobjective Q-learning results. Blank entries indicate that the default value were used. The default values are: $f = 10$, $\zeta = 0.99$, $\epsilon = 0.1$, $\alpha = 0.1$, $\gamma = 0.999$, tol= 0.01, ep-l= 30, and ep-n= 20000. Parameters that were linearly decayed to zero over training are indicated with $\star$. For **Bridges** the sum of the probability of satisfaction of all properties is 6. Times are in seconds.

Name	Prop. ord.	States	Prod.	Prob.	Time	f	ζ	ϵ	α	tol	ep-l	ep-n
R 4×4	1,2,3	16	1024	1,0,1	6.37		0.7					65 k
R 4×4	2,1,3	16	1024	1,0,1	1.95		0.7		0.03			75 k
R 5×5	1,2,3	25	1600	1,1,1	12.49		0.5	0.2	0.4*	0	250	200 k
R 4×7	1,2,3	28	3584	1,0.75,0.25	23.18	20	0.9	0.2	0.9*	0	400	100 k
R 4×7	2,1,3	28	3584	1,0.5,0	10.62	20	0.7	0.2	0.15		200	200 k
Virus	1,2	809	58248	1,0	41.43		0.97	0.5	0.2		50	150 k
Virus	2,1	809	58248	1,0.25	191.97		0.97	0.5	0.9*		50	700 k
UAV	1,2	11448	732672	1,1	93.57	20		0.2			40	120 k
Bridges	1,...,7	19	5318784	—	3.55	1	0.9		0.2			30 k

rate ε, the learning rate α, the discount factor γ, the fraction under which action values are considered the same during model checking of the learned strategy, the value of the episode reset timer, and the number of training episodes. Parameters were tuned manually to minimise training time. In each case, the runtime for the experiment stays below 4 min. Next, we discuss these case studies.

4.1 Robot

For the robot example from the introduction in Fig. 1 with $\mathbf{p} = 0.5$, we have considered instances for the three scenarios discussed there, with different priorities of them. On examples R 4×4 and R 5×5 we initialise learning episodes randomly within the model to deepen exploration in order to achieve better performance. The results are in line with the analysis provided in the introduction.

Figure 3 shows an optimal strategy learned for the 4×7 Robot grid with property prioritisation order 2, 1, 3.

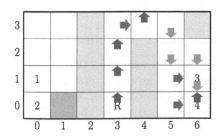

Fig. 3. Learned strategy on the 4×7 Robot grid with property prioritisation order 2, 1, 3. We show only reachable states and project the states in the product to the MDP. The 'cash in' action is not shown for clarity.

To avoid clutter, we show only states that are reachable under the learned strategy and do not show the 'cash in' action. Additionally, we project states in the product to the MDP. The robot starts in Row 0, Column 3 and moves up the column. Then, in Row 3, Column 3 it attempts to go across. With probability 0.5, it gets stuck in Row 3, Column 4. There are no safe actions from this field except to move north – keeping the robot in the same field. If it gets across to Row 3, Column 5, it moves down and visits the fields labeled 3 and 4.

4.2 Computer Virus

This case study (based on [18],[1]) considers the spread of a virus in a computer network. The structure of the model is sketched in Fig. 4. Circles represent network nodes, and lines between them indicate network connections, between which the virus can spread. An attack gets past the firewall with probability $p_{detect} = 0.5$. If past the firewall, an attack can then infect with probability $p_{infect} = 0.5$. The control of the attacks is centralised. A no operation action is always available. The instance coordinating the attack has the following objectives:

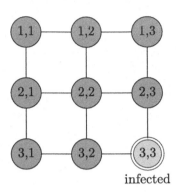

infected

Fig. 4. Virus case study

(v_1) $\mathbf{F} s_{3,2} = 2 \bigwedge \mathbf{G}((s_{3,2} = 2 \wedge s_{3,1} \neq 2) \implies \mathbf{XX} s_{3,1} = 2)$: eventually, node $(3,2)$ gets infected; and when $(3,2)$ is infected and $(3,1)$ is not, $(3,1)$ is infected within 2 steps.

(v_2) $\mathbf{F} s_{1,1} = 2 \bigwedge \mathbf{G}(s_{2,2} \neq 2 \wedge s_{2,3} \neq 2)$: eventually node $(1,1)$ gets infected while nodes $(2,2)$ and $(2,3)$ never get infected.

When the prioritisation order is 1, 2, then the optimal strategy crosses the barrier formed by nodes $(2,2)$ and $(2,3)$ in order to infect node $(3,1)$ before node $(3,2)$. When the prioritisation order is 2, 1, then the optimal strategy respects the barrier formed by nodes $(2,2)$ and $(2,3)$, and follows the path through node $(3,1)$ to $(1,1)$. This reduces the probability of satisfying v_1 from 1 to 0.25. This problem is particularly challenging because it requires discovering a long sequence of actions and the properties interfere with each other during learning.

4.3 Human-in-the-Loop UAV Mission Planning

This model (originally from [8],[2]) considers the control of an unmanned aerial vehicle (UAV) interacting with a human operator. The UAV operates on a network of roads. In this network, waypoints (w_i) are specified as well as restricted operation zones (roz_i). In specifications, waypoints serve as places that shall be visited (once or repeatedly), while restricted operation zones shall be avoided. In our experiments, we have used the following properties.

---

[1] http://prismmodelchecker.org/casestudies/virus.php.
[2] http://prismmodelchecker.org/casestudies/human-uav.php.

(u_1) $\bigwedge_i \mathbf{G} \neg roz_i$: UAV never visits a restricted operation zone
(u_2) $\mathbf{F}w_1 \wedge \mathbf{F}w_2 \wedge \mathbf{F}w_6$: UAV eventually visits w_1, w_2, and w_6

4.4   Seven Bridges of Königsberg

As a final example, we consider the classic problem of the seven bridges of Königsberg[3], in which one seeks a path that crosses each bridge exactly once. The model is deterministic and we have 7 properties of the form

$$(u_i) \ \mathbf{F}b_i \wedge \mathbf{G}(b_i \to \mathbf{XG} \neq b_i) \text{: cross bridge } i \text{ exactly once.}$$

where b_i indicates if one is on bridge i. Instead of applying a preference for each property, we set $f = 1$. In this setting, payoff is maximised when the sum of the probability of satisfaction of all properties is maximised, e.g., the agent maximises the expected number of bridges crossed exactly once. The RL agent successfully finds strategies to cross 6 bridges exactly once, the maximum number possible.

5   Conclusion

We have generalised recent work on applying model free reinforcement learning to finding optimal control for MDPs with ω-regular objectives to address the problem of controlling MDPs with multiple ω-regular objectives, and with a lexicographic order of importance: a main objective, a secondary objective, etc.

Starting with good-for-MDPs automata, the extension is surprisingly simple: it suffices to add a 'tracker' to the product of the individual automata, which memorises which of the individual Büchi conditions have occurred, and to allow the automaton to 'cash in' on these occurrences (while resetting the memory). How valuable the return is depends on the objectives, for which a good event (the passing of an individual Büchi transition) has been witnessed, where the main objective attracts a high reward and each consecutive objective obtains a small fraction of the reward assigned to the previous more important one.

Such a reward structure can be proven to work for reinforcement learning in essentially the same way as they have been proven to work for the simpler case of having a single objective (which is also a special case of our results).

This reduction is beautifully straightforward, and our experimental results show that it is also effective. This might look surprising: after all, the correctness proofs rely heavily on well chosen hyperparameters. Yet, in practice, the techniques have yet again shown to be robust: we could learn correct strategies reliably and efficiently.

---

[3] https://en.wikipedia.org/wiki/Seven_Bridges_of_Konigsberg.

References

1. de Alfaro, L.: Formal verification of probabilistic systems. Ph.D. thesis, Stanford University (1998)
2. Baier, C., Katoen, J.P.: Principles of Model Checking. MIT Press, Cambridge (2008)
3. Bozkurt, A.K., Wang, Y., Pajic, M.: Model-free learning of safe yet effective controllers. arXiv preprint arXiv:2103.14600 (2021)
4. Bozkurt, A.K., Wang, Y., Zavlanos, M.M., Pajic, M.: Control synthesis from linear temporal logic specifications using model-free reinforcement learning. In: 2020 IEEE International Conference on Robotics and Automation (ICRA), pp. 10349–10355 (2020). https://doi.org/10.1109/ICRA40945.2020.9196796
5. Chatterjee, K.: Markov decision processes with multiple long-run average objectives. In: Arvind, V., Prasad, S. (eds.) FSTTCS 2007: Foundations of Software Technology and Theoretical Computer Science, pp. 473–484. Springer, Heidelberg (2007)
6. Chatterjee, K., Majumdar, R., Henzinger, T.A.: Markov decision processes with multiple objectives. In: Durand, B., Thomas, W. (eds.) STACS 2006. LNCS, vol. 3884, pp. 325–336. Springer, Heidelberg (2006). https://doi.org/10.1007/11672142_26
7. Etessami, K., Kwiatkowska, M., Vardi, M.Y., Yannakakis, M.: Multi-objective model checking of Markov decision processes. In: Grumberg, O., Huth, M. (eds.) Tools and Algorithms for the Construction and Analysis of Systems, pp. 50–65. Springer, Heidelberg (2007)
8. Feng, L., Wiltsche, C., Humphrey, L.R., Topcu, U.: Controller synthesis for autonomous systems interacting with human operators. In: Bayen, A.M., Branicky, M.S. (eds.) Proceedings of the ACM/IEEE Sixth International Conference on Cyber-Physical Systems, ICCPS 2015, Seattle, WA, USA, 14–16, April, 2015, pp. 70–79. ACM (2015). https://doi.org/10.1145/2735960.2735973
9. Forejt, V., Kwiatkowska, M., Norman, G., Parker, D., Qu, H.: Quantitative multi-objective verification for probabilistic systems. In: Abdulla, P.A., Leino, K.R.M. (eds.) Tools and Algorithms for the Construction and Analysis of Systems, pp. 112–127. Springer, Heidelberg (2011)
10. Fu, J., Topcu, U.: Probably approximately correct MDP learning and control with temporal logic constraints. In: Robotics: Science and Systems, July 2014
11. Hahn, E.M., Perez, M., Schewe, S., Somenzi, F., Trivedi, A., Wojtczak, D.: Omega-regular objectives in model-free reinforcement learning. In: Vojnar, T., Zhang, L. (eds.) TACAS 2019. LNCS, vol. 11427, pp. 395–412. Springer, Cham (2019). https://doi.org/10.1007/978-3-030-17462-0_27
12. Hahn, E.M., Perez, M., Schewe, S., Somenzi, F., Trivedi, A., Wojtczak, D.: Good-for-mdps automata for probabilistic analysis and reinforcement learning. In: Tools and Algorithms for the Construction and Analysis of Systems (2020)
13. Hahn, E.M., Perez, M., Schewe, S., Somenzi, F., Trivedi, A., Wojtczak, D.: Faithful and effective reward schemes for model-free reinforcement learning of omega-regular objectives. In: Hung, D.V., Sokolsky, O. (eds.) ATVA 2020. LNCS, vol. 12302, pp. 108–124. Springer, Cham (2020). https://doi.org/10.1007/978-3-030-59152-6_6
14. Hasanbeig, M., Abate, A., Kroening, D.: Logically-correct reinforcement learning. CoRR abs/1801.08099 (2018). http://arxiv.org/abs/1801.08099

15. Hasanbeig, M., Abate, A., Kroening, D.: Certified reinforcement learning with logic guidance. arXiv:1902.00778 (2019)
16. Kretínský, J., Pérez, G.A., Raskin, J.: Learning-based mean-payoff optimization in an unknown MDP under omega-regular constraints. In: Schewe, S., Zhang, L. (eds.) 29th International Conference on Concurrency Theory, CONCUR 2018, 4–7, September, 2018, Beijing, China, vol. 118, pp. 8:1–8:18. LIPIcs, Schloss Dagstuhl - Leibniz-Zentrum für Informatik (2018). https://doi.org/10.4230/LIPIcs.CONCUR.2018.8
17. Kwiatkowska, M., Norman, G., Parker, D.: PRISM 4.0: verification of probabilistic real-time systems. In: Gopalakrishnan, G., Qadeer, S. (eds.) CAV 2011. LNCS, vol. 6806, pp. 585–591. Springer, Heidelberg (2011). https://doi.org/10.1007/978-3-642-22110-1_47
18. Kwiatkowska, M., Norman, G., Parker, D., Vigliotti, M.: Probabilistic mobile ambients. Theoretical Computer Science **410**(12–13), 1272–1303 (2009)
19. Mnih, V., et al.: Human-level control through deep reinforcement learning. Nature **518**(7540), 529–533 (2015)
20. Puterman, M.L.: Markov Decision Processes: Discrete Stochastic Dynamic Programming. Wiley, Hoboken (1994)
21. Sadigh, D., Kim, E., Coogan, S., Sastry, S.S., Seshia, S.A.: A learning based approach to control synthesis of Markov decision processes for linear temporal logic specifications. In: CDC, pp. 1091–1096, December 2014
22. Strehl, A.L., Li, L., Wiewiora, E., Langford, J., Littman, M.L.: PAC model-free reinforcement learning. In: International Conference on Machine Learning, ICM, pp. 881–888 (2006)
23. Sutton, R.S., Barto, A.G.: Reinforcement Learning: An Introduction, 2nd edn. MIT Press, Cambridge (2018)
24. Watkins, C.J., Dayan, P.: Q-learning. Mach. Learn. **8**(3–4), 279–292 (1992)

Logics and Theory

Efficient Algorithms for Omega-Regular Energy Games

Gal Amram[1], Shahar Maoz[1(✉)], Or Pistiner[1], and Jan Oliver Ringert[2]

[1] Tel Aviv University, Tel Aviv, Israel
maoz@cs.tau.ac.il
[2] Kings College London, London, UK

Abstract. ω-regular energy games are two-player ω-regular games augmented with a requirement to avoid the exhaustion of a finite resource, e.g., battery or disk space. ω-regular energy games can be reduced to ω-regular games by encoding the energy level into the state space. As this approach blows up the state space, it performs poorly. Moreover, it is highly affected by the chosen energy bound denoting the resource's capacity. In this work, we present an alternative approach for solving ω-regular energy games, with two main advantages. First, our approach is efficient: it avoids the encoding of the energy level within the state space, and its performance is independent of the engineer's choice of the energy bound. Second, our approach is defined at the logic level, not at the algorithmic level, and thus allows solving ω-regular energy games by seamless reuse of existing symbolic fixed-point algorithms for ordinary ω-regular games. We base our work on the introduction of *energy μ-calculus*, a multi-valued extension of game μ-calculus. We have implemented our ideas and evaluated them. The empirical evaluation provides evidence for the efficiency of our work.

1 Introduction

Energy games model a requirement to avoid the exhaustion of an initially available resource, e.g., disk space or battery capacity, and they have been studied extensively in the context of verification and synthesis, e.g., [11,19–21]. They are formalized as weighted two-player turn-based games with the quantitative objective to keep the *energy level*, the accumulated sum of an initial credit and weights of transitions traversed thus far, non-negative in each prefix of a play. As such, they induce a *decision problem* that checks for the existence of a finite initial credit sufficient for winning, and an *optimization problem* for the *minimum initial credit*. They may be viewed as safety games with an additional quantitative objective. Nevertheless, they have also been generalized to *ω-regular games with energy objectives* [20,21], which are the focus of our work.

The work [11] has introduced an *upper bound* c that specifies the maximal energy level allowed to be accumulated throughout a play. Intuitively, c denotes the capacity of the relevant resource. Given such finite bound c, ω-regular energy games can be reduced to ordinary ω-regular games via a *naive encoding*: one may introduce new system variables that encode the energy level, and add the requirement that these variables always represent a non-negative value. A major problem with this naive encoding approach is that it blows up the state space by a factor of c, even when it is not necessary. For illustration, assume the engineer sets an upper bound c, but the tightest bound sufficient

© Springer Nature Switzerland AG 2021
M. Huisman et al. (Eds.): FM 2021, LNCS 13047, pp. 163–181, 2021.
https://doi.org/10.1007/978-3-030-90870-6_9

for winning is $c_0 < c$. The naive encoding will still consider $\log(c)$ additional Boolean variables, although it is not required. Note that this scenario is realistic as it is difficult to estimate the tightest energy bound sufficient for winning.

In this work, we present an alternative approach for solving ω-regular energy games, with two main advantages. First, our approach is efficient: it avoids the encoding of the energy level within the state space, and its performance is independent of the engineer's choice of the capacity bound c. Second, our approach is defined at the logic level, not at the algorithmic level, and thus allows to solve ω-regular energy games by seamless reuse of existing symbolic fixed-point algorithms for ordinary ω-regular games.

Specifically, we introduce *energy μ-calculus*, a multi-valued extension of *game μ-calculus*, μ-calculus over symbolic game structures [10,23,35]. Game μ-calculus extends propositional logic with modal operators and least and greatest fixed-point operators. For every ω-regular condition φ, there exists a game μ-calculus formula that defines a symbolic fixed-point algorithm for computing the set of states that win φ [4].

Importantly, the standard game μ-calculus and our new energy μ-calculus share the same syntax, but they differ in their semantics. While a game μ-calculus formula characterizes a set of states, an energy μ-calculus formula, interpreted with an energy bound $c \in \mathbb{N}$, returns a function that maps states to $\{0, \dots, c\} \cup \{+\infty\}$. Intuitively, whereas a game μ-calculus formula computes the set of winning states, an energy μ-calculus formula computes a function that maps a state s to the minimal initial credit with which the system can win from s, while keeping the energy level non-negative, and further maps s to $+\infty$ if no such initial credit exists.

Remark 1. Although we focus on bounded energy games, our approach can be used to solve ω-regular energy games with no bound on the accumulated energy level (i.e., $c = +\infty$). In the technical report [7], we show that every ω-regular energy game admits a *sufficient finite bound* $c_f \in \mathbb{N}$ that can be calculated from the game parameters. That is, a bound c_f for which, if the system can win from state s with a bound $c = +\infty$, then it can also win with the bound $c = c_f$, and with the same initial credit. This fact is independent of the use of energy μ-calculus.

We have implemented and integrated both methods, naive encoding and energy μ-calculus, into Spectra, a specification language and GR(1) synthesis environment [1, 39]. GR(1) [10] is a popular assume-guarantee winning condition that, roughly speaking, expresses the schematic requirement: *"if assertions $a_1, \dots, a_m$ hold infinitely often, then assertions $g_1, \dots, g_n$ must hold infinitely often as well"*. As GR(1) subsumes other important ω-regular winning conditions, specifically safety, reachability, Büchi, and generalized Büchi [29], our implementation allows us to empirically evaluate the efficiency of our approach over different ω-regular energy games. Our implementation of naive encoding employs the standard Binary Decision Diagram [16] (BDD) based solver of Spectra. The efficient implementation of energy μ-calculus employs Algebraic Decision Diagrams (ADDs) [8,27]. While BDDs symbolically represent assertions and thus sets of states, ADDs extend BDDs to symbolically represent functions that map states to values (in our case, to energy levels). Both are implemented in the CUDD library [45].

The remainder of the paper is organized as follows. In Sect. 2 we present an example. In Sect. 3 we provide notations and relevant background. In Sect. 4 we present the semantics of energy μ-calculus and our main theorem. In Sect. 5 we present an empirical evaluation of our approach. Related work is discussed in Sect. 6 and Sect. 7 concludes. Proofs for all claims and extended discussions appear in a technical report [7].

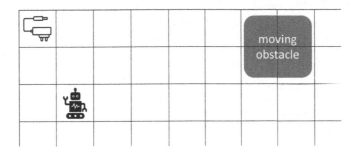

Fig. 1. An illustration of the energy augmented obstacle evasion example

2 An Illustrative Example

To demonstrate the differences between our approach and naive encoding, we consider an energy augmented variant of the obstacle evasion specification, a popular benchmark from the literature inspired by robotic mission planning [22,28,40]. Consider a single cell sized robot (the system) and a 2×2 cells sized obstacle (the environment), both moving on a 10×10 grid. The robot is smaller and more agile; it moves twice upon each step of the obstacle. The obstacle chases the robot (always tries to get closer to it), and the robot must evade the obstacle so that collision will never occur.

Importantly, in our energy augmented variant, the robot has a c-capacity battery. A charger placed in cell $(1,1)$ can charge the battery by m energy units, and each move of the robot consumes k energy units. Thus, in addition to satisfying the different winning conditions we list below, the robot should behave such that its battery is never empty, i.e., it keeps its energy non-negative at all times. See an illustration in Fig. 1, and an excerpt of a Spectra specification in Listing 1. The full specification is available from [2].

The above defines legal transitions for the players and thus defines a *game structure* and a safety game. That is, a game in which as long as the environment takes valid transitions, the system must take valid transitions as well. Hence, the winning condition for a safety game is merely (1) **true**. We further consider the following ω-regular winning conditions that we formulate in Linear Temporal Logic [43] (LTL).

(2) $\mathbf{F}(a)$, where a is the assertion: *the robot is at cell* $(10, 10)$. In words, the robot must visit cell $(10, 10)$.

(3) $\mathbf{GF}(a)$ where a is the assertion: *the robot is at cell* $(10, 10)$. In words, the robot must visit cell $(10, 10)$ infinitely often.

(4) $\bigwedge_{i=1}^{4} \mathbf{GF}(a_i)$ where a_i is the assertion: *the robot is at the i-th corner*. In words, the robot must visit all grid corners infinitely often.

(5) $\mathbf{GF}(b) \rightarrow \bigwedge_{i=1}^{4} \mathbf{GF}(a_i)$ where b is the assertion: *the obstacle is at most 4 cells away from the robot*, and each a_i is the assertion: *the robot is at the i-th corner*. In words, if, infinitely often, the obstacle is close to the robot (4 cells or less), then the robot must visit all corners infinitely often.

```
 1  spec MovingObstacle
 2
 3  env Int(1..9)[2] ob; //obstacle's location
 4  env boolean obWait;
 5  sys Int(1..10)[2] ro; // robot's location
 6
 7  asm initiallyObstacleAtLowerRightCorner: (ob[0]=9) & (ob
       [1]=9);
 8  asm initiallyObWaitFalse: !obWait;
 9  gar initiallyRobotAtZero: (ro[0]=1) & (ro[1]=1);
10
11  asm obWaitSwitches:
12  G (obWait -> next(!obWait)) & (!obsWait -> next(obsWait));
13  asm obstacleDoesNotMoveWhenWaits:
14  G obWait -> (next(ob[0])=ob[0] & next(ob[1])=ob[1]);
15  asm obstacleChasesRobot: // see full spec
16  asm ObstacleMovesToAdjacentCell: // see full spec
17
18  gar RobotMovesToAdjacentCell: // see full spec
19  gar RobotAvoidsObtacle: // see full spec
20  gar RobotDoesNotGetCaught: // see full spec
21
22  // Pay 5 energy units for every move of the robot
23  weight -5 ( ro[0]!=next(ro[0]) | ro[1]!=next(ro[1]) );
24  // Gain 35 energy units when moving to location (1,1)
25  weight 35 ( next(ro[0]=1 & ro[1]=1) );
```

Listing 1. Excerpt of Energy-enriched Obstacle Evasion specification in Spectra, with $k = 5$ and $m = 35$.

Formulas (1)–(5) are instances of safety, reachability, Büchi, generalized Büchi [29], and GR(1) [10] winning conditions, respectively, all of which are examples of ω-regular winning conditions.

Recall that we seek an efficient technique for solving ω-regular energy games that enables the reuse of existing algorithms. We turn to discuss how our approach addresses these two goals, using the energy-augmented obstacle evasion problem.

Efficiency of Energy μ-Calculus. In contrast to naive encoding, the algorithm that an energy μ-calculus formula prescribes considers only the intermediate energy values revealed during the computation. In particular, this implies that we avoid the encoding of the energy levels within the state space. For illustration, with energy μ-calculus, each of the energy-augmented obstacle evasion specifications employs a total of 17 variables, excluding reachability (winning condition (2)) that employs 18 variables (all specifications are available from [2]). However, the naive encoding approach adds $\lceil \log c \rceil$ variables to the specification, on top of these 17–18 variables. Note that with our approach, the number of variables is not dependent on the chosen bound c.

Furthermore, the described feature reduces the size of the data structures the solver employs. For illustration, assume that when solving the reachability game, some fixed-point iteration of the algorithm constructs an ADD that maps a state s to the energy value e. This means that, so far, the algorithm discovered that e energy units are sufficient for reaching cell $(10, 10)$ from s (ensuing iterations might improve this value). The corresponding iteration of a naive-encoding-based solver will create a BDD that accepts **all valuations** (s, e'), $e' \geq e$. Hence, naive encoding creates rather large BDDs that depend on the energy bound, which is costly. In contrast, the size of the ADD we use depends on the size of the range of the function it represents, i.e., we only consider the actual energy values revealed during the computation.

Algorithm 1 Büchi game solver	**Algorithm 2** energy Büchi game solver
1: $Z \leftarrow$ the state space	1: $Z \leftarrow$ mapping of all states to 0
2: **while** not reached fixed-point of Z **do**	2: **while** not reached fixed-point of Z **do**
3: $\quad recurr_a \leftarrow a \cap \lozenge Z$	3: $\quad recurr_a \leftarrow f_a \wedge \lozenge_{\mathbf{E}} Z$
4: $\quad Y \leftarrow \emptyset;$	4: $\quad Y \leftarrow$ mapping of all states to $+\infty$
5: $\quad$ **while** not reached fixed point of Y **do**	5: $\quad$ **while** not reached fixed-point of Y **do**
6: $\quad\quad Y \leftarrow recurr_a \cup \lozenge Y$	6: $\quad\quad Y \leftarrow recurr_a \vee \lozenge_{\mathbf{E}} Y$
7: $\quad Z \leftarrow Y$	7: $\quad Z \leftarrow Y$
8: **return** Z	8: **return** Z

Reuse of Existing Algorithms. In Sect. 4, we will prove that if a game μ-calculus formula ψ solves games with an ω-regular winning condition φ, then when interpreted according to the energy μ-calculus semantics, ψ computes a function that solves the minimum credit problem for the energy augmented game. That is, a function that maps a state s to the minimal initial credit with which the system wins from s.

To demonstrate this property, consider the Büchi condition $\mathbf{GF}(a)$ (winning condition (3) above). The following game μ-calculus formula solves Büchi games with target states a:

$$\psi_{\mathbf{GF}(a)} = \nu Z(\mu Y(a \wedge \lozenge Z) \vee \lozenge Y). \tag{1}$$

That is, $\psi_{\mathbf{GF}(a)}$ computes the set of all states from which the system can enforce infinitely many visits of the robot to cell $(10, 10)$.

Relying on our main theorem, we replace each occurrence of the modal operator $\lozenge$ in Eq. 1 with the new operator $\lozenge_{\mathbf{E}}$, and obtain the following energy μ-calculus formula that solves Büchi-energy games with target states a:

$$\psi_{\mathbf{GF}(a)}^{\mathbf{E}} = \nu Z(\mu Y(a \wedge \lozenge_{\mathbf{E}} Z) \vee \lozenge_{\mathbf{E}} Y). \tag{2}$$

That is, Eq. 2 defines the energy function that maps each state to the minimal initial credit sufficient for the system to reach cell $(10, 10)$ infinitely often, while keeping the energy level non-negative.

Most importantly, the above formulas induce algorithms. Algorithm 1 is a symbolic fixed-point algorithm that implements Eq. 1 according to the game μ-calculus' semantics following [10]. Likewise, Algorithm 2 is a symbolic fixed-point algorithm that implements Eq. 2 according to the energy μ-calculus' semantics. We see that energy μ-calculus allows the seamless reuse of existing game μ-calculus formulas and thus automatically transforms the fixed-point algorithms they prescribe into algorithms that take also the energy constraints into account. Indeed, our implementation, in Spectra, takes advantage of this seamless reuse. We use the same template code for both implementations.

3   Preliminaries

We provide relevant and concise definitions that are sufficient for the readability of the paper. Extended discussions and further definitions that are needed for the proof of our main theorem are given in the technical report [7].

For a set of Boolean variables $\mathcal{V}$, a *state* $s \in 2^{\mathcal{V}}$, is a truth assignment to $\mathcal{V}$, an *assertion* ϕ is a propositional formula over $\mathcal{V}$, $s \models \phi$ denotes that s satisfies ϕ, and $\mathcal{V}'$ denotes the set $\{v' \mid v \in \mathcal{V}\}$ of *primed* variables. We denote by $p(s) \in 2^{\mathcal{V}'}$ the *primed version* of the state $s \in 2^{\mathcal{V}}$, obtained by replacing each $v \in s$ with $v' \in \mathcal{V}'$. For $\mathcal{V} = \bigcup_{i=1}^{k} \mathcal{V}_i$ and truth assignments $s_i \in 2^{\mathcal{V}_i}$, we use $(s_1, \ldots, s_k)$ as an abbreviation for $s_1 \cup \ldots \cup s_k$. Thus, we may replace expressions, e.g., $s \in 2^{\mathcal{V}}$, $s \models \varphi$, $p(s)$, and $f(s)$ with $(s_1, \ldots s_k) \in 2^{\mathcal{V}}$, $(s_1, \ldots, s_k) \models \varphi$, $p(s_1, \ldots, s_k)$, and $f(s_1, \ldots, s_k)$, respectively. We denote by $s|_{\mathcal{Z}}$ the *projection* of $s \in 2^{\mathcal{V}}$ to $\mathcal{Z} \subseteq \mathcal{V}$, i.e., $s|_{\mathcal{Z}} := s \cap \mathcal{Z}$.

Games, Game Structures, and Strategies. We consider an infinite game played between an environment player (*env*) and a system player (*sys*) on a finite weighted directed graph as they move along its transitions. In each round of the game, the environment plays first by choosing a valid input, and the system plays second by choosing a valid output. Each such step consumes or reclaims energy, according to the weight function. The goal of the system is to satisfy the winning condition while keeping the energy level non-negative, regardless of the actions of the environment.

Formally, an energy game is symbolically represented by a *weighted game structure* (WGS) G^w, that extends a *game structure* (GS) G [10,42] with a weight function w^s. It consists of the following components:

- $\mathcal{V} = \{v_1, \ldots, v_n\}$: A finite set of Boolean variables.
- $\mathcal{X} \subseteq \mathcal{V}$: A set of *input variables* controlled by the *environment* player (*env*).
- $\mathcal{Y} = \mathcal{V} \setminus \mathcal{X}$: A set of *output variables* controlled by the *system* player (*sys*).
- ρ^e: An assertion over $\mathcal{V} \cup \mathcal{X}'$ that defines the environment's transitions. The environment uses ρ^e to relate a state over $\mathcal{V}$ to *possible next inputs* over $\mathcal{X}'$.
- ρ^s: An assertion over $\mathcal{V} \cup \mathcal{V}' = \mathcal{V} \cup \mathcal{X}' \cup \mathcal{Y}'$ that defines the system's transitions. The system uses ρ^s to relate a state over $\mathcal{V}$ and an input over $\mathcal{X}'$ to *possible next outputs* over $\mathcal{Y}'$.
- φ: The ω-regular winning condition of the system.
- w^s: a partial weight function, symbolically represented as pairs of the form (ρ, a) where ρ is an assertion over $\mathcal{V} \cup \mathcal{V}'$, and $a \in \mathbb{Z}$.

A state t is a *successor* of s if $(s, p(t)) \models \rho^e \wedge \rho^s$. The rounds of a game on G^w form a sequence of states $\sigma = s_0 s_1 \ldots$ called a *play*, which satisfies the following conditions: (1) *Consecution*: for each $i \geq 0$, s_{i+1} is a successor of s_i. (2) *Maximality*:

if σ is finite, then either it ends with a *deadlock for the environment*: $\sigma = s_0 \ldots s_k$, and there is no input value $s_\mathcal{X} \in 2^\mathcal{X}$ such that $(s_k, p(s_\mathcal{X})) \models \rho^e$, or it ends with a *deadlock for the system*: $\sigma = s_0 \ldots s_k s_\mathcal{X}$ where $s_\mathcal{X} \in 2^\mathcal{X}$, $(s_k, p(s_\mathcal{X})) \models \rho^e$, and there is no output $s_\mathcal{Y} \in 2^\mathcal{Y}$ such that $(s_k, p(s_\mathcal{X}), p(s_\mathcal{Y})) \models \rho^s$. A play σ wins w.r.t. φ if it ends in an environment deadlock, or it is infinite and satisfies φ.

A *strategy* for the system player is a function $g_{sys} : (2^\mathcal{V})^+ \times 2^\mathcal{X} \to 2^\mathcal{Y}$. Roughly speaking, the system employs a strategy g_{sys} to repeatedly choose outputs given the sequence of states traversed so far, and a new input. A strategy g_{sys} wins from state s w.r.t. energy bound c if for any play σ from s, consistent with the strategy, (1) σ wins for the system w.r.t. φ and (2) the energy level remains non-negative during the play, given that whenever it exceeds the upper bound c, it is truncated to c. For a WGS, G^w, we denote by W_{sys}^c the set of all states s such that there exists a strategy g_{sys} that wins from s. We omit c and write W_{sys} in case of a GS G.

Game μ-Calculus over Game Structures. We consider the logic of the game μ-calculus over GSs [10] below.

Definition 1 (game μ-calculus: syntax). *Let $\mathcal{V}$ be a set of Boolean variables, and let $Var = \{X, Y, \ldots\}$ be a set of relational variables. The formulas of game μ-calculus (in positive form) are built as follows:*

$$\psi ::= v \mid \neg v \mid X \mid \psi \vee \psi \mid \psi \wedge \psi \mid \Diamondwhite\psi \mid \Diamondblack\psi \mid \mu X\psi \mid \nu X\psi$$

where $v \in \mathcal{V}$, $X \in Var$, and μ and ν denote the least and greatest fixed-point operators, respectively.

We denote by $\mathcal{L}_\mu$ the set of all formulas generated by the grammar of Definition 1. We further denote by $\mathcal{L}_\mu^{sys}$ (resp. $\mathcal{L}_\mu^{env}$) the subset of $\mathcal{L}_\mu$ that consists of all formulas in which the modal operator $\Diamondblack$ (resp. $\Diamondwhite$) does *not* occur. We will refer to $\mathcal{L}_\mu^{sys}$ (resp. $\mathcal{L}_\mu^{env}$) formulas as *sys-μ* (resp. *env-μ*) formulas.

Given a game structure $G = \langle \mathcal{V}, \mathcal{X}, \mathcal{Y}, \rho^e, \rho^s, \varphi \rangle$ and a valuation $\mathcal{E} : Var \to (2^\mathcal{V} \to \{0, 1\})$, the semantics of a game μ-calculus formula ψ with variables from $\mathcal{V}$, $[\![\psi]\!]_\mathcal{E}^{G,1}$ is a subset of $2^\mathcal{V}$. Intuitively, $\Diamondwhite\psi$ (resp. $\Diamondblack\psi$) is the set of states from which the system (resp. environment) can force reaching a state in ψ's semantics in a single step. μ and ν are the least and greatest fixed-points, respectively. For a complete definition of the game μ-calculus semantics see, e.g., [10].

We say that a (closed) game μ-calculus formula ψ matches an ω-regular winning condition φ, if for every GS $G = \langle \mathcal{V}, \mathcal{X}, \mathcal{Y}, \rho^e, \rho^s, \varphi \rangle$, $[\![\psi]\!]^G = W_{sys}$. That is, ψ computes the set of states from which the system has a winning strategy. De Alfaro et al. [4] have shown that every ω-regular condition φ has a matching formula $\psi \in \mathcal{L}_\mu^{sys}$.

BDDs and ADDs. A Binary Decision Diagram (BDD) [16] is a DAG representation of an assertion. The non-leaves nodes of a BDD are labeled with variable names, and its edges and leaves are labeled with **true/false**. A BDD B represents an assertion ρ if

---

[1] If all of the relational variables in ψ are bound by fixed-point operators, i.e., ψ is a closed formula, we may omit $\mathcal{E}$ from the semantic brackets.

B's accepting branches (i.e. branches that end with a **true**-labeled leaf) correspond to the satisfying assignments of ρ. BDDs allow applying Boolean operators over assertions efficiently, and further satisfaction queries [17].

An Algebraic Decision Diagram (ADD) [8,27] is a DAG representation of a function that maps states to values. ADDs differ from BDDs in that their leaves are labeled with values from some domain ($\mathbb{Z}$, in our case).

Our implementation of energy μ-calculus relies on the use of ADDs.

4   Energy μ-Calculus over Weighted Game Structures

We are now ready to introduce *energy μ-calculus*, the underlying novel logic behind our efficient solution for ω-regular energy games. Energy μ-calculus is a multi-valued extension of the modal game μ-calculus over GSs [10,23]. We define its syntax and semantics, interpreted w.r.t. a finite upper bound c, and prove our main theorem: if ψ matches an ω-regular condition φ, then with the energy μ-calculus semantics, ψ solves energy φ-games.

Syntax of an Energy μ-Calculus Formula. Let $\mathcal{L}_{e\mu}$ denote the set of formulas generated by the following grammar:

Definition 2 (Energy μ-calculus: syntax). *Let $\mathcal{V}$ be a set of Boolean variables, and let $Var = \{X, Y, \ldots\}$ be a set of relational variables. The syntax of energy μ-calculus (in positive form) is as follows:*

$$\psi ::= v \mid \neg v \mid X \mid \psi \vee \psi \mid \psi \wedge \psi \mid \Diamond_{\mathbf{E}}\psi \mid \Box_{\mathbf{E}}\psi \mid \mu X\psi \mid \nu X\psi$$

where $v \in \mathcal{V}$ and $X \in Var$.

We denote by $\mathcal{L}_{e\mu}^{sys}$ (resp. $\mathcal{L}_{e\mu}^{env}$) the subset of $\mathcal{L}_{e\mu}$ that consists of all formulas in which $\Box_{\mathbf{E}}$ (resp. $\Diamond_{\mathbf{E}}$) does *not* occur. Further, let $\psi^{\mathbf{E}} \in \mathcal{L}_{e\mu}$ denote the energy μ-calculus formula obtained from $\psi \in \mathcal{L}_\mu$ by replacing all occurrences of $\Diamond$ and $\Box$ with $\Diamond_{\mathbf{E}}$ and $\Box_{\mathbf{E}}$, respectively. Here, we focus on $\mathcal{L}_{e\mu}^{sys}$ formulas as those solve energy ω-regular games for the system.[2]

$\mathcal{L}_{e\mu}^{sys}$ **Semantics Overview.** We now define the semantics of a formula $\psi^{\mathbf{E}} \in \mathcal{L}_{e\mu}^{sys}$. $\psi^{\mathbf{E}}$ is valuated w.r.t. a WGS $G^w = \langle \mathcal{V}, \mathcal{X}, \mathcal{Y}, \rho^e, \rho^s, \varphi, w^s \rangle$, and a finite upper bound $c \in \mathbb{N}$. We write $G^w(c)$ as a shorthand for the pair $\langle G^w, c \rangle$. The semantics $[\![\psi^{\mathbf{E}}]\!]^{G^w(c)}$ is an *energy function* that maps states of G^w to initial amounts of credit.[3] Hence, the range of the function $[\![\psi^{\mathbf{E}}]\!]^{G^w(c)}$ is the set of *energy credits* $E(c) := [0, c] \cup \{+\infty\}$, and thus $[\![\psi^{\mathbf{E}}]\!]^{G^w(c)}$ is an element of the set of *energy functions* $EF(c) := E(c)^{2^{\mathcal{V}}}$.

To define the semantics $[\![\psi^{\mathbf{E}}]\!]^{G^w(c)}$ in a precise manner, we need to define the semantics of the meet $\wedge$ and join $\vee$ operators, and of the *energy controllable predecessor* operator $\Diamond_{\mathbf{E}}$. We start with the meet and join operators.

---

[2] For a discussion of $\mathcal{L}_{e\mu}^{env}$ we refer the reader to [7].

[3] Assuming at this stage, for simplicity, that $\psi^{\mathbf{E}}$ has no free variables.

Meet $\wedge$ and join $\vee$ Semantics. The semantics of these operators is induced by a partial ordering of $EF(c)$, the set of energy functions, and a linear ordering of the set of c-bounded energy credits $E(c) = [0, c] \cup \{+\infty\}$. For $x, y \in E(c)$, we write $x \preceq y$ if $y \leq x$ (equivalently, $y = \min\{x, y\}$). Although seemingly unnatural, this design choice is not only technically justified (as we shall explain later), but also intuitive, considering our purposes, due to the next reasoning.

We study sufficient initial credits from the system's perspective. Hence, the $\leq$-smaller element y is preferable to the $\leq$-larger element x, and thus y is declared to be $\preceq$-larger. In particular, $+\infty$ is the $\preceq$-minimal (worst) element from the system's perspective, as it indicates that no initial credit is sufficient for winning. In summary, $x \preceq y$ if y is *better* (i.e. smaller) than x.

The ordering of $E(c)$ transfers to $EF(c)$. We say that $f \preceq g$ if for every state s, $f(s) \preceq g(s)$ (iff $f(s) \geq g(s)$). As for $E(c)$, this definition matches the intuition that g is better than f if it maps each state to a $\leq$-smaller credit. In particular, the minimal (worst) element is the function that maps each state to $+\infty$, denoted $f_{+\infty}$. This function indicates that the system cannot win from any state, regardless of its initial credit. Likewise, the maximal element is the function f_0 defined by $\forall s \in 2^{\mathcal{V}}(f_0(s) = 0)$. Now, the meet $\wedge$ (resp. join $\vee$) of two functions f and g is the maximal (resp. minimal) function that is $\preceq$-smaller (resp. $\preceq$-larger) than f and g:

$$f \wedge g = h \text{ such that } \forall s \in 2^{\mathcal{V}}(h(s) = \max\{f(s), g(s)\}),$$
$$f \vee g = h \text{ such that } \forall s \in 2^{\mathcal{V}}(h(s) = \min\{f(s), g(s)\}).$$

To avoid confusion, we clarify that max and min always relate to the natural ordering $\leq$. For example, $\max\{1, 4\} = 4$. We shall use the notations $\max_{\preceq}$ and $\min_{\preceq}$ to denote maximal and minimal elements w.r.t. the $\preceq$-ordering.

Energy Controllable Predecessor Semantics. We turn to discuss the semantics of the energy controllable predecessor operator $\ominus_{\mathbf{E}}$. Recall that we aim to use $\mathcal{L}_{e\mu}^{sys}$ formulas to compute the minimal initial credits with which the system can win w.r.t. the given ω-regular winning condition. Hence, given an energy function f, f, $\ominus_{\mathbf{E}}(f)$ is the energy function that maps each state s to the minimal credit with which the system can force reaching a state t, in a single step, with energy level at least $f(t)$. To define $\ominus_{\mathbf{E}}(f)$ properly, first, we analyze the next restricted case. We consider a single possible transition (s, t), and ask: if (s, t) is the ensuing step of the play, what credit is sufficient for the system to take this step and end with energy level at least $e = f(t)$? We denote this value by $\mathsf{EC}_c(s, t, e)$, and note that it depends on the weight function w^s, and on the transition relations ρ^e and ρ^s, as follows:

- If $(s, p(t|x)) \not\models \rho^e$, the step (s, t) is losing for the environment. Hence, all credits are sufficient and thus $\mathsf{EC}_c(s, t, e) = 0$ in this case.
- If $(s, p(t)) \models \rho^e \wedge \neg\rho^s$, the step (s, t) is losing for the system. Hence, all credits are insufficient and thus $\mathsf{EC}_c(s, t, e) = +\infty$ in this case.
- If $e = +\infty$, then no finite credit is sufficient. Hence, $\mathsf{EC}_c(s, t, e) = +\infty$ in this case.

- If $c + w^s(s, p(t)) < e$, then no c-bounded credit is sufficient to achieve energy level at least e. Hence, $\mathsf{EC}_c(s, t, e) = +\infty$ in this case as well.
- In any other case, any initial credit larger than $e - w^s(s, p(t))$ is sufficient. Hence, in any case not listed above, $\mathsf{EC}_c(s, t, e) = \max\{0, e - w^s(s, p(t))\}$.

The above single-step analysis enables us to define $\ominus_{\mathbf{E}}(f)$ properly. For a state s, we consider all possible inputs. For each input $t_{\mathcal{X}} \in 2^{\mathcal{X}}$, we find the best possible output $t_{\mathcal{Y}} \in 2^{\mathcal{Y}}$, i.e. the output that minimizes $\mathsf{EC}_c(s, t = (t_{\mathcal{X}}, t_{\mathcal{Y}}), f(t))$. Then, intuitively, we define $\ominus_{\mathbf{E}}(f)(s)$ to be the value obtained by the best output for the worst input, as we formally define below.

Definition 3 (Energy controllable predecessor operator). *For all WGSs $\langle G, w^s \rangle$, upper bounds $c \in \mathbb{N}$, energy functions $f \in EF(c)$, and states $s \in 2^{\mathcal{V}}$,*

$$ECpre_{sys}(f)(s) := \max_{t_{\mathcal{X}} \in 2^{\mathcal{X}}} [\min_{t_{\mathcal{Y}} \in 2^{\mathcal{Y}}} \mathsf{EC}_c(s, (t_{\mathcal{X}}, t_{\mathcal{Y}}), f(t_{\mathcal{X}}, t_{\mathcal{Y}}))]$$

where $\mathsf{EC}_c : 2^{\mathcal{V}} \times 2^{\mathcal{V}} \times E(c) \to E(c)$ and for all $s, t \in 2^{\mathcal{V}}$, and $e \in E(c)$,

$$\mathsf{EC}_c(s, t, e) = \begin{cases} 0, & \text{if } (s, p(t)) \not\models \rho^e \\ +\infty, & \text{if } (s, p(t)) \models \rho^e \land \neg \rho^s, \\ & \text{or } e = +\infty, \\ & \text{or } e - w^s(s, p(t)) > c \\ \max\{0, e - w^s(s, p(t))\}, & \text{otherwise} \end{cases}$$

Example 1. Consider the game structure depicted in Fig. 2, in which the environment player controls variable x and the system controls variable y. Take $c = 10$ and $g \in EF(c)$ such that[4]

$$g(!x, !y) = 0, \ g(x, !y) = 1, \text{ and } g(x, y) = g(!x, y) = +\infty.$$

What is $ECpre_{sys}(g)(!x, y)$?

There are two possible inputs, x and $!x$. For the input x we have:

- $\mathsf{EC}_c((!x, y), (x, y), g(x, y) = +\infty) = +\infty$.
- $\mathsf{EC}_c((!x, y), (x, !y), g(x, !y) = 1) = 4$.

And for the input $!x$:

- $\mathsf{EC}_c((!x, y), (!x, y), g(!x, y) = +\infty) = +\infty$.
- $\mathsf{EC}_c((!x, y), (!x, !y), g(!x, !y) = 0) = 1$.

Therefore,

$$ECpre_{sys}(g)(!x, y) = \max\{\min\{+\infty, 4\}, \min\{+\infty, 1\}\} = 4.$$

The value 4 is obtained as follows: the environment provides the input x, and thus the system can choose between $+\infty$ and 4. The system chooses the preferable energy amount 4, and correspondingly outputs $!y$. Consequently, $ECpre_{sys}(g)(!x, y) = \mathsf{EC}_c((!x, y), (x, !y), g(x, !y) = 1) = 4$.

---

[4] Standardly, we use $!x$ to denote that we assign the value **false** to x. Hence, as an example, $(!x, y)$ formally represents the state $\{y\}$.

Semantics of a $\psi^{\mathbb{E}} \in \mathcal{L}_{e\mu}^{sys}$ formula. We are finally ready to define the semantics of $\mathcal{L}_{e\mu}^{sys}$ formulas.

Definition 4 ($\mathcal{L}_{e\mu}^{sys}$: **semantics**). *The semantics* $[\![\psi^{\mathbb{E}}]\!]_{\mathcal{D}}^{G^w(c)} \in EF(c)$ *of* $\psi^{\mathbb{E}} \in \mathcal{L}_{e\mu}^{sys}$ *w.r.t. a WGS* $G^w = \langle \mathcal{V}, \mathcal{X}, \mathcal{Y}, \rho^e, \rho^s, \varphi, w^s \rangle$, *a finite upper bound* $c \in \mathbb{N}$, *and a valuation* $\mathcal{D} : Var \rightarrow EF(c)$ *over* $EF(c)$, *is inductively defined as follows:*[5]

- *For* $v \in \mathcal{V}$, $[\![v]\!]_{\mathcal{D}}^{G^w(c)} = f_v$ *and* $[\![\neg v]\!]_{\mathcal{D}}^{G^w(c)} = f_{\neg v}$ *where*
$$f_v(s) = \begin{cases} 0, & \text{if } s \vDash v \\ +\infty, & \text{if } s \nvDash v \end{cases}; f_{\neg v}(s) = \begin{cases} +\infty, & \text{if } s \vDash v \\ 0, & \text{if } s \nvDash v \end{cases}.$$

- *For* $X \in Var$, $[\![X]\!]_{\mathcal{D}}^{G^w(c)} = \mathcal{D}(X)$.
- $[\![\psi_1^{\mathbb{E}} \vee \psi_2^{\mathbb{E}}]\!]_{\mathcal{D}}^{G^w(c)} = [\![\psi_1^{\mathbb{E}}]\!]_{\mathcal{D}}^{G^w(c)} \vee [\![\psi_2^{\mathbb{E}}]\!]_{\mathcal{D}}^{G^w(c)}$.
- $[\![\psi_1^{\mathbb{E}} \wedge \psi_2^{\mathbb{E}}]\!]_{\mathcal{D}}^{G^w(c)} = [\![\psi_1^{\mathbb{E}}]\!]_{\mathcal{D}}^{G^w(c)} \wedge [\![\psi_2^{\mathbb{E}}]\!]_{\mathcal{D}}^{G^w(c)}$.
- $[\![\bigcirc_{\mathbb{E}} \psi^{\mathbb{E}}]\!]_{\mathcal{D}}^{G^w(c)} = ECpre_{sys}([\![\psi^{\mathbb{E}}]\!]_{\mathcal{D}}^{G^w(c)})$.
- $\left[\!\!\left[\begin{Bmatrix} \mu \\ \nu \end{Bmatrix} X \psi_1^{\mathbb{E}} \right]\!\!\right]_{\mathcal{D}}^{G^w(c)} = \begin{Bmatrix} lfp \\ gfp \end{Bmatrix} (\lambda f.[\![\psi_1^{\mathbb{E}}]\!]_{\mathcal{D}[X \mapsto f]}^{G^w(c)}) = \begin{Bmatrix} \max_{\preceq} \\ \min_{\preceq} \end{Bmatrix} [h_i]$,

where $\begin{Bmatrix} h_0 = f_{+\infty} \\ h_0 = f_0 \end{Bmatrix}$, $h_{i+1} = [\![\psi_1^{\mathbb{E}}]\!]_{\mathcal{D}[X \mapsto h_i]}^{G^w(c)}$, *and* $\mathcal{D}[X \mapsto h_i]$ *denotes the valuation that is like* $\mathcal{D}$ *except that it maps* X *to* h_i.

Note that the semantics is well-defined, as greatest and least fixed-points of $\lambda f.[\![\psi_1^{\mathbb{E}}]\!]_{\mathcal{D}[X \mapsto f]}^{G^w(c)}$ exist. This fact holds since $\mathcal{L}_{e\mu}^{sys}$ formulas are monotone: if $f \preceq g$, then $[\![\psi^{\mathbb{E}}]\!]_{\mathcal{D}[X \mapsto f]}^{G^w(c)} \preceq [\![\psi^{\mathbb{E}}]\!]_{\mathcal{D}[X \mapsto g]}^{G^w(c)}$.

As we mentioned earlier, we order $E(c)$ and $EF(c)$ by $\preceq$ (rather than by the seemingly more natural ordering $f \leq g \Leftrightarrow \forall s \in 2^{\mathcal{V}}(f(s) \leq g(s))$) due to a technical reason. This design choice maintains correspondence between the values of $\psi \in \mathcal{L}_{\mu}^{sys}$ and $\psi^{\mathbb{E}} \in \mathcal{L}_{e\mu}^{sys}$. Importantly, it keeps the classification of μ and ν formulas as liveness and safety properties [12]. For illustration, for $p \in \mathcal{V}$, consider the μ-formula $\psi_{\diamond p} := \mu X(p \vee \bigcirc X)$ that matches the p-states *reachability* winning condition [29]. If we had chosen to use $\leq$ instead of $\preceq$, we would have needed to take the ν-formula $\nu X(p \wedge \bigcirc_{\mathbb{E}} X)$ to solve energy augmented p-states reachability whereas, unnaturally, the formula $\mu X(p \vee \bigcirc_{\mathbb{E}} X)$ would match the p-states *safety* winning condition [29]. The ordering $\preceq$ enables our main result:

Theorem 1 ($\mathcal{L}_{e\mu}^{sys}$: **correctness**). *Let* $\psi_{\varphi} \in \mathcal{L}_{\mu}^{sys}$ *be a closed formula that matches the ω-regular winning condition φ of the WGS, $G^w = (G, w^s)$. Then, for all states $s \in 2^{\mathcal{V}}$: (1) if $[\![\psi_{\varphi}^{\mathbb{E}}]\!]^{G^w(c)}(s) \neq +\infty$ then $[\![\psi_{\varphi}^{\mathbb{E}}]\!]^{G^w(c)}(s)$ is the minimum initial credit for which the system wins from s w.r.t. c in G^w; (2) otherwise, s does not win for the system w.r.t. c.*

Note that Theorem 1 solves the *decision problem* ($s \in W_{sys}^c$ iff $[\![\psi_{\varphi}^{\mathbb{E}}]\!]^{G^w(c)}(s) \neq +\infty$), and the *minimum credit* problem (return $[\![\psi_{\varphi}^{\mathbb{E}}]\!]^{G^w(c)}(s)$).

---

[5] We may drop the valuation $\mathcal{D}$ from the semantic brackets for closed formulas.

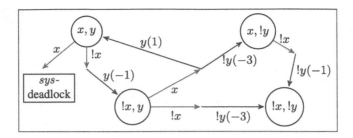

Fig. 2. A weighted game structure. The environment controls variable x (red arrows), and the system controls variable y (blue arrows). Edge-weights appear in parentheses. (Color figure online)

Complexity. A straightforward implementation of $[\![\psi_\varphi^{\mathbf{E}}]\!]^{G^w(c)}$ gives an algorithm to solve the decision and minimum credit problems in $O(((|2^{\mathcal{V}}|(c+1))^q)$ symbolic steps, where q is the largest number of nested fixed-point operators in the energy μ-calculus formula ψ_φ. Nevertheless, using the techniques proposed in [14] and [24] for faster computation of fixed-points, we can reduce this time complexity into $O(((|2^{\mathcal{V}}|(c+1))^{\lfloor d/2 \rfloor+1})$ symbolic steps, where d is the alternation depth of ψ_φ.[6] Although this worst-case time complexity is equal to the time complexity of the naive encoding approach, the evaluation we present in Sect. 5 shows that energy μ-calculus performs significantly better.

We conclude this section with an example for a valuation of an $\mathcal{L}_{e\mu}^{sys}$-formula.

Example 2 Consider again the game structure depicted in Fig. 2. The environment player controls variable x, and the system controls variable y. For illustration, from state (x, y), the environment can provide both possible inputs, x and $!x$. The system has no legal response for x (and thus it leads to a system-deadlock), but for the input $!x$, it can respond with y, which consumes 1 "energy units", but not with $!y$.

Consider the reachability winning condition with target $!x \wedge !y$. The game μ-calculus formula that matches our winning condition is $Z((!x \wedge !y) \vee \bigcirc(Z))$. We set an energy bound $c = 10$, and following Theorem 1 compute $[\![\mu Z((!x \wedge !y) \vee \bigcirc_{\mathbf{E}}(Z))]\!]^{G^w(10)}$. The fixed-point valuation is presented in the following table.

state	(x,y)	$(x,!y)$	$(!x,y)$	$(!x,!y)$
$g_0 = f_\infty$	$+\infty$	$+\infty$	$+\infty$	$+\infty$
$g_1 = (!x \wedge !y) \vee \bigcirc_{\mathbf{E}}(g_0)$	$+\infty$	$+\infty$	$+\infty$	0
$g_2 = (!x \wedge !y) \vee \bigcirc_{\mathbf{E}}(g_1)$	$+\infty$	1	$+\infty$	0
$g_3 = (!x \wedge !y) \vee \bigcirc_{\mathbf{E}}(g_2)$	$+\infty$	1	4	0
$g_4 = (!x \wedge !y) \vee \bigcirc_{\mathbf{E}}(g_3)$	$+\infty$	1	4	0

---

[6] The *alternation depth* [24,41] of a formula $\psi \in \mathcal{L}_\mu$ is the number of alternations between interdependent, nested least and greatest fixed-point operators in ψ. For the formal definition, see, e.g., [29, Chapter 10].

The computation reaches a fixed-point after three iterations, and thus g_3 maps each state to the minimal initial credit sufficient for the system to force reaching $(!x, !y)$. Note that the energy bound $c = 4$ is a sufficient bound and that $W_{sys}^4 = W_{sys}^{10}$. Yet, importantly, the unnecessarily high energy bound we chose, $c = 10$, does not cause an overhead, and we did not perform additional redundant computations.

5   Evaluation

To evaluate our approach for solving ω-regular energy games, we implemented it in the Spectra specification language and GR(1) synthesis environment [1,39], while modeling energy functions via ADDs, using the CUDD package [45].[7]

Adding support for energy μ-calculus in Spectra allowed us to evaluate our approach over different types of ω-regular winning conditions, since the GR(1) winning condition supported by Spectra subsumes safety, reachability, Büchi, and generalized Büchi. For illustration, GR(1) games are solved by the game μ-calculus formula $\nu Z(\bigwedge_{i=1}^{n} \mu Y(\bigvee_{j=1}^{m} \nu X((g_i \wedge \lozenge Z) \vee \lozenge Y \vee (\neg a_j \wedge \lozenge X))))$. A Büchi winning condition is a restricted GR(1) condition that merely requires: "g_1 holds infinitely often". Thus, with $m = 0$ and $n = 1$, the GR(1) game μ-calculus formula is contracted into $\nu Z(\mu Y((g \wedge \lozenge Z) \vee \lozenge Y))$, the game μ-calculus formula that matches the Büchi condition (recall Eq. 1).

We consider the following research questions:

RQ1. Is our approach better than naive encoding in terms of performance?
RQ2. Is the performance of our approach affected by the chosen energy bound?

Below we describe the experiments we performed to address **RQ1** and **RQ2**. All relevant materials and means to reproduce the experiments are available in [2].

Corpus. Our corpus for the experiments includes two families of specifications. First, we created specifications based on the energy augmented obstacle evasion problem we described in Sect. 2. Recall that each movement of the robot consumes k energy units and a charger in cell $(1, 1)$ charges the robot by m units. For each of the winning conditions from Sect. 2, safety, reachability, Büchi, generalized Büchi, and GR(1), and each energy bound $c = 10^2, \cdots, 10^6$, we created 30 realizable specifications by randomly choosing values for the parameters k and m. As c gets larger, we considered more possible values for k and m and thus created specifications with larger weights.

Second, we created energy-augmented specifications based on the arbiter problem from SYNTCOMP20.[8] The basic arbiter (the system) grants requests from 10 different clients (the environment). It can grant only a single request at each turn, and a request remains pending until it is granted.

---

[7] Our implementation, just like the standard realizability check of Spectra, uses the direct $O((|2^V|(c + 1))^q)$ time algorithm, rather than the $O((|2^V|(c + 1))^{\lfloor d/2 \rfloor + 1})$ approach. Note that a recent evaluation shows that, in practice, the later induces only a minor improvement, and can even be harmful for some instances [25].

[8] 2020 reactive synthesis competition http://www.syntcomp.org.

On top of the basic specification, we impose the following energy weights. $client_0$ is a preferable client. Hence, we penalize the arbiter by c energy units for the bad event: postponing a request by $client_0$. Furthermore, we penalize the arbiter by k energy units for the bad event: postponing a request by $client_i$, $i > 0$. Finally, we reward the arbiter by m energy units for the good event: granting a request from any client. See an excerpt of the Spectra specification in Listing 2. The full specification is available from [2].

```
1  spec Arbiter
2
3  env boolean[10] request;
4  sys Int(0..10) grant; //grant=10 denotes: no grant
5
6  asm reqUntilGrant:  G forall i in Int(0..9) .
7  (request[i] & grant!=i) -> (next(request[i]));
8
9  gar NoVacousGrants:
10 G forall i in Int(0..9) . (grant=i) -> request[i];
11
12 // Pay 100 for forcing client 0 to wait
13 weight -100 (request[0] & grant!=0);
14
15 // Pay 10 for forcing any other client to wait
16 weight -10 (request[1] & grant!=1);
17   // ... repeated for each client from 1 to 9 - see full spec
18 weight -10 (request[9] & grant!=9);
19
20 // Gain 90 for every grant granted
21 weight 90 (grant!=10);
```

Listing 2. Energy-enriched Arbiter specification in Spectra, with $c = 100$, $k = 10$, and $m = 90$.

We remark that our arbiter specification demonstrates a usage of energy that may seem different than the intuitive energy consumption and accumulation demonstrated in our obstacle evasion example. Here we use energy to synthesize a controller that must balance bad behaviors (that are perhaps unpreventable) with good behaviors. Otherwise, the controller will run out of "energy".

In addition to the basic safety arbiter specification (i.e., winning condition (1) **true**), we consider the following instances of reachability, Büchi, generalized Büchi, and GR(1).

(2) $\mathbf{F}(a)$ where a is: *only $client_0$ requests have been granted for 10 consecutive steps.*
(3) $\mathbf{GF}(a)$ where a is: *$client_0$ does not request, or its request is granted.*
(4) $\bigwedge_{i=0}^{9} \mathbf{GF}(a_i)$ where a_i is: *$client_i$ does not request, or its request is granted.*
(5) $\mathbf{GF}(b) \rightarrow \bigwedge_{i=0}^{9} \mathbf{GF}(a_i)$ where b is: *$client_0$ does not request*, and each a_i is the assertion: *$client_i$ does not request, or its request is granted.*

As in the obstacle evasion specifications, for each winning condition and energy bound $c = 10^2, \ldots, 10^6$, we created 30 realizable arbiter specifications by randomly choosing values for the parameters k and m. Again, as c gets larger, we considered more possible values for k and m and thus created specifications with larger weights.

Table 1. A comparison of median realizability checking running times (sec.) for naive encoding (NE) and for energy μ-calculus (EμC), over different ω-regular winning conditions and with growing energy bounds.

	Bound	10^2		10^3		10^4		10^5		10^6	
	Method	NE	EμC	NE	EμC	NE	EμC	NE	EμC	NE	EμC
Obstacle Evasion	`true`	3.5	1.6	5.6	1.7	6.7	1.8	76.9	1.7	timeout	1.6
	$\mathbf{F}(a)$	1.3	0.6	1.8	0.4	3.0	0.4	58.0	0.4	timeout	0.4
	$\mathbf{GF}(a)$	27.3	23.3	89.7	16.2	72.2	16.0	213.1	16.6	timeout	17.6
	$\wedge_{i=1}^{4}\mathbf{GF}(a_i)$	17.4	10.0	45.6	10.1	34.7	7.4	147.8	8.3	timeout	7.8
	$\mathbf{GF}(b) \rightarrow \wedge_{i=1}^{4}\mathbf{GF}(a_i)$	179.3	55.1	235.2	44.4	523.7	45.1	timeout	45.0	timeout	49.3
Arbiter	`true`	0.1	0.1	0.2	0.1	1.1	0.1	45.8	0.1	timeout	0.1
	$\mathbf{F}(a)$	1.9	0.3	5.7	0.2	21.1	0.2	90.0	0.2	timeout	0.2
	$\mathbf{GF}(a)$	0.1	0.1	0.2	0.1	1.1	0.1	47.0	0.1	timeout	0.1
	$\wedge_{i=0}^{9}\mathbf{GF}(a_i)$	1.7	0.7	8.1	0.5	28.2	1.0	130.3	0.6	timeout	0.5
	$\mathbf{GF}(b) \rightarrow \wedge_{i=0}^{9}\mathbf{GF}(a_i)$	0.3	0.1	0.5	0.1	1.5	0.1	53.3	0.1	timeout	0.1

Overall, our corpus includes 750 energy obstacle evasion specifications and 750 energy arbiter specifications.

Experiment Setup and Results. For each ω-regular winning condition (safety, reachability, Büchi, generalized Büchi, GR(1)) and for each energy bound ($c = 10^2, \ldots, 10^6$), we applied Spectra realizability check over the corresponding 30 specifications with each of the two methods, naive encoding (NE) and energy μ-calculus (EμC). We used a timeout of 10 min. We performed all experiments on a rather ordinary laptop with Intel i7-9750H processor, 32GB RAM, running windows 10, using a single processor.

Table 1 reports the median running times we obtained (in sec.). Columns titled NE present naive encoding results, and columns titled EμC present energy μ-calculus results. For example, for the 30 obstacle evasion specifications with Büchi winning condition and energy bound $c = 10^5$, the median running time of a realizability check is 213.1 s with naive encoding, and only 16.6 s with energy μ-calculus. Correspondingly, the cell on row 'Obstacle Evasion/$\mathbf{GF}(a)$', column '10^5/NE' reads 213.1, and on row 'Obstacle Evasion/$\mathbf{GF}(a)$', column '10^5/EμC' reads 16.6.

To compute the median values, we assigned timeout executions with a distinguished maximal value. Cells that read 'timeout' indicate that the distinguished maximal value is the median value, i.e., at least 15/30 executions failed to return within 10 min.

Observations. To answer **RQ1**, we see that our approach outperforms naive encoding by far. In all experiments, our approach presents better results than naive encoding, sometimes by several orders of magnitude.

To answer **RQ2**, we see that with energy μ-calculus, the increase in the energy bound had no effect on the performance of the realizability check. In contrast, with naive encoding, when increasing the bound, the realizability check is dramatically affected and quickly becomes infeasible.

Overall, while the naive encoding method reached the 10 min timeout for 365 (of the 1500) specifications, energy μ-calculus reached the timeout with only one of these 1500 specifications.

6 Related Work

Energy games were introduced in [19] and solved in [11,13,19]. To tackle ω-regular energy games, Chatterjee and Doyen studied energy parity games [20]. Of these, only [11] considers also a finite bound over the accumulated energy level, and none provides an implementation or an evaluation. Interestingly, essentially, the algorithms of [11,13,19] can be seen as a special case of our results, limited to safety games (i.e., applying the energy μ-calculus formula $\nu X(\bigcirc_{\mathbf{E}} X)$).

Multi-valued and quantitative extensions of the μ-calculus logic exist in the literature (e.g. [3,15,26,30,31]). Some extensions were introduced to solve generalizations of ω-regular games: probabilistic concurrent ω-regular games [6], and imperfect information ω-regular games [44]. Surprisingly, perhaps, none of these extensions subsumes energy μ-calculus. Some do not consider edge-weights [15,30,31]. Moreover, rather than addition of weights, the approach in [3] employs the max operator, and the approach in [26] employs weight multiplication.

ADDs have been used for the analysis of probabilistic models (e.g., [5,9,32,36, 37]). ADDs have also been studied in the context of game solving: an ADD-based parity solver is described in [18] and is implemented and evaluated in [33]; an ADD-based, symbolic fixed-point algorithm for (safety-only) energy games appears in [38].

7 Conclusion

We presented efficient means to solve ω-regular energy games, which relies on energy μ-calculus, a novel multi-valued extension of the modal game μ-calculus. Our technique avoids the encoding of the energy level within the state space, and allows the reuse of existing algorithms that solve ω-regular winning conditions.

We have implemented our technique in the Spectra specification language and synthesis environment. The experiments we presented provided evidence showing that energy μ-calculus is an efficient and scalable technique for solving energy games.

Future Work. Game μ-calculus has not only been used to compute the sets of the winning states, but also to synthesize winning strategies; see, e.g., [10,34]. Thus, in addition to solving the decision and the minimum credit problems, we believe that energy μ-calculus can augment game μ-calculus-based *strategy synthesis* with energy. That is, as future work, we consider how finite memory winning strategies may be extracted from the intermediate energy functions of the fixed-point iterations.

Acknowledgments. This project has received funding from the European Research Council (ERC) under the European Union's Horizon 2020 research and innovation programme (grant agreement No 638049, SYNTECH).

References

1. Spectra Website. http://smlab.cs.tau.ac.il/syntech/spectra/
2. Supporting Materials Website. http://smlab.cs.tau.ac.il/syntech/energyefficient/
3. de Alfaro, L., Faella, M., Stoelinga, M.: Linear and branching system metrics. IEEE Trans. Softw. Eng. **35**(2), 258–273 (2009). https://doi.org/10.1109/TSE.2008.106
4. de Alfaro, L., Henzinger, T.A., Majumdar, R.: From verification to control: dynamic programs for omega-regular objectives. In: 16th Annual IEEE Symposium on Logic in Computer Science, Boston, Massachusetts, USA, 16–19 June 2001, Proceedings, pp. 279–290. IEEE Computer Society (2001). https://doi.org/10.1109/LICS.2001.932504
5. de Alfaro, L., Kwiatkowska, M.Z., Norman, G., Parker, D., Segala, R.: Symbolic model checking of probabilistic processes using mtbdds and the kronecker representation. In: Tools and Algorithms for Construction and Analysis of Systems, 6th International Conference, TACAS 2000, Held as Part of the European Joint Conferences on the Theory and Practice of Software, ETAPS 2000, Berlin, Germany, 25 March–2 April 2000, Proceedings, pp. 395–410 (2000). https://doi.org/10.1007/3-540-46419-0_27
6. de Alfaro, L., Majumdar, R.: Quantitative solution of omega-regular games. J. Comput. Syst. Sci. **68**(2), 374–397 (2004). https://doi.org/10.1016/j.jcss.2003.07.009
7. Amram, G., Maoz, S., Pistiner, O., Ringert, J.O.: Energy mu-calculus: symbolic fixed-point algorithms for omega-regular energy games. CoRR abs/2005.00641 (2020). https://arxiv.org/abs/2005.00641
8. Bahar, R.I., et al.: Algebraic decision diagrams and their applications. Formal Methods Syst. Des. **10**(2/3), 171–206 (1997). https://doi.org/10.1023/A:1008699807402
9. Baier, C., Clarke, E.M., Hartonas-Garmhausen, V., Kwiatkowska, M.Z., Ryan, M.: Symbolic model checking for probabilistic processes. In: Automata, Languages and Programming, 24th International Colloquium, ICALP 1997, Bologna, Italy, 7–11 July 1997, Proceedings, pp. 430–440 (1997). https://doi.org/10.1007/3-540-63165-8_199
10. Bloem, R., Jobstmann, B., Piterman, N., Pnueli, A., Sa'ar, Y.: Synthesis of Reactive(1) Designs. J. Comput. Syst. Sci. **78**(3), 911–938 (2012). https://doi.org/10.1016/j.jcss.2011.08.007
11. Bouyer, P., Fahrenberg, U., Larsen, K.G., Markey, N., Srba, J.: Infinite runs in weighted timed automata with energy constraints. In: Cassez, F., Jard, C. (eds.) FORMATS 2008. LNCS, vol. 5215, pp. 33–47. Springer, Heidelberg (2008). https://doi.org/10.1007/978-3-540-85778-5_4
12. Bradfield, J., Stirling, C.: 12 modal mu-calculi. In: Patrick Blackburn, J.V.B., Wolter, F. (eds.) Handbook of Modal Logic, Studies in Logic and Practical Reasoning, vol. 3, pp. 721–756. Elsevier (2007). http://www.sciencedirect.com/science/article/pii/S1570246407800152
13. Brim, L., Chaloupka, J., Doyen, L., Gentilini, R., Raskin, J.: Faster algorithms for mean-payoff games. Formal Methods Syst. Des. **38**(2), 97–118 (2011). https://doi.org/10.1007/s10703-010-0105-x
14. Browne, A., Clarke, E.M., Jha, S., Long, D.E., Marrero, W.R.: An improved algorithm for the evaluation of fixpoint expressions. Theor. Comput. Sci. **178**(1–2), 237–255 (1997). https://doi.org/10.1016/S0304-3975(96)00228-9
15. Bruns, G., Godefroid, P.: Model checking with multi-valued logics. In: Díaz, J., Karhumäki, J., Lepistö, A., Sannella, D. (eds.) ICALP 2004. LNCS, vol. 3142, pp. 281–293. Springer, Heidelberg (2004). https://doi.org/10.1007/978-3-540-27836-8_26
16. Bryant, R.E.: Graph-based algorithms for boolean function manipulation. IEEE Trans. Comput. **35**(8), 677–691 (1986). https://doi.org/10.1109/TC.1986.1676819
17. Bryant, R.E.: Symbolic boolean manipulation with ordered binary-decision diagrams. ACM Comput. Surv. **24**(3), 293–318 (1992). https://doi.org/10.1145/136035.136043

18. Bustan, D., Kupferman, O., Vardi, M.Y.: A measured collapse of the modal μ-calculus alternation hierarchy. In: STACS 2004, 21st Annual Symposium on Theoretical Aspects of Computer Science, Montpellier, France, 25–27 March 2004, Proceedings, pp. 522–533 (2004). https://doi.org/10.1007/978-3-540-24749-4_46

19. Chakrabarti, A., de Alfaro, L., Henzinger, T.A., Stoelinga, M.: Resource interfaces. In: Alur, R., Lee, I. (eds.) EMSOFT 2003. LNCS, vol. 2855, pp. 117–133. Springer, Heidelberg (2003). https://doi.org/10.1007/978-3-540-45212-6_9

20. Chatterjee, K., Doyen, L.: Energy parity games. Theor. Comput. Sci. **458**, 49–60 (2012). https://doi.org/10.1016/j.tcs.2012.07.038

21. Chatterjee, K., Randour, M., Raskin, J.: Strategy synthesis for multi-dimensional quantitative objectives. Acta Inf. **51**(3–4), 129–163 (2014). https://doi.org/10.1007/s00236-013-0182-6

22. Ehlers, R., Raman, V.: Slugs: extensible GR(1) synthesis. In: Chaudhuri, S., Farzan, A. (eds.) CAV 2016. LNCS, vol. 9780, pp. 333–339. Springer, Cham (2016). https://doi.org/10.1007/978-3-319-41540-6_18

23. Emerson, E.A., Jutla, C.S.: Tree automata, mu-calculus and determinacy (extended abstract). In: 32nd Annual Symposium on Foundations of Computer Science, San Juan, Puerto Rico, 1–4 October 1991, pp. 368–377. IEEE Computer Society (1991). https://doi.org/10.1109/SFCS.1991.185392

24. Emerson, E.A., Lei, C.: Efficient model checking in fragments of the propositional mu-calculus (extended abstract). In: Proceedings of the Symposium on Logic in Computer Science (LICS 1986), Cambridge, Massachusetts, USA, 16–18 June 1986, pp. 267–278. IEEE Computer Society (1986). http://dblp2.uni-trier.de/rec/bib/conf/lics/EmersonL86

25. Firman, E., Maoz, S., Ringert, J.O.: Performance heuristics for GR(1) synthesis and related algorithms. Acta Informatica **57**(1–2), 37–79 (2020). https://doi.org/10.1007/s00236-019-00351-9

26. Fischer, D., Grädel, E., Kaiser, Ł: Model checking games for the quantitative μ-calculus. Theory Comput. Syst. **47**(3), 696–719 (2010). https://doi.org/10.1007/s00224-009-9201-y

27. Fujita, M., McGeer, P.C., Yang, J.C.: Multi-terminal binary decision diagrams: an efficient data structure for matrix representation. Formal Methods Syst. Des. **10**(2/3), 149–169 (1997). https://doi.org/10.1023/A:1008647823331

28. Galceran, E., Carreras, M.: A survey on coverage path planning for robotics. Robotics Auton. Syst. **61**(12), 1258–1276 (2013). https://doi.org/10.1016/j.robot.2013.09.004

29. Grädel, E., Thomas, W., Wilke, T. (eds.): Automata Logics, and Infinite Games. LNCS, vol. 2500. Springer, Heidelberg (2002). https://doi.org/10.1007/3-540-36387-4

30. Grumberg, O., Lange, M., Leucker, M., Shoham, S.: *Don't know* in the μ-calculus. In: Cousot, R. (ed.) VMCAI 2005. LNCS, vol. 3385, pp. 233–249. Springer, Heidelberg (2005). https://doi.org/10.1007/978-3-540-30579-8_16

31. Grumberg, O., Lange, M., Leucker, M., Shoham, S.: When not losing is better than winning: abstraction and refinement for the full μ-calculus. Inf. Comput. **205**(8), 1130–1148 (2007). https://doi.org/10.1016/j.ic.2006.10.009

32. Hermanns, H., Kwiatkowska, M.Z., Norman, G., Parker, D., Siegle, M.: On the use of MTBDDs for performability analysis and verification of stochastic systems. J. Log. Algebr. Program. **56**(1–2), 23–67 (2003). https://doi.org/10.1016/S1567-8326(02)00066-8

33. Jurdziński, M.: Small progress measures for solving parity games. In: Reichel, H., Tison, S. (eds.) STACS 2000. LNCS, vol. 1770, pp. 290–301. Springer, Heidelberg (2000). https://doi.org/10.1007/3-540-46541-3_24

34. Könighofer, R., Hofferek, G., Bloem, R.: Debugging formal specifications: a practical approach using model-based diagnosis and counterstrategies. STTT **15**(5–6), 563–583 (2013). https://doi.org/10.1007/s10009-011-0221-y

35. Kozen, D.: Results on the propositional μ-calculus. In: Proceedings of the 9th Colloquium on Automata, Languages and Programming, pp. 348–359. Springer, London (1982). http://dl.acm.org/citation.cfm?id=646236.682866

36. Kwiatkowska, M.Z., Norman, G., Parker, D.: Probabilistic symbolic model checking with PRISM: a hybrid approach. STTT **6**(2), 128–142 (2004). https://doi.org/10.1007/s10009-004-0140-2

37. Kwiatkowska, M., Norman, G., Parker, D.: PRISM 4.0: verification of probabilistic real-time systems. In: Gopalakrishnan, G., Qadeer, S. (eds.) CAV 2011. LNCS, vol. 6806, pp. 585–591. Springer, Heidelberg (2011). https://doi.org/10.1007/978-3-642-22110-1_47

38. Maoz, S., Pistiner, O., Ringert, J.O.: Symbolic BDD and ADD algorithms for energy games. In: Piskac, R., Dimitrova, R. (eds.) Proceedings Fifth Workshop on Synthesis, SYNT@CAV 2016, Toronto, Canada, 17–18 July 2016. EPTCS, vol. 229, pp. 35–54 (2016). https://doi.org/10.4204/EPTCS.229.5

39. Maoz, S., Ringert, J.O.: Spectra: a specification language for reactive systems. Softw. Syst. Model. (2021). http://link.springer.com/article/10.1007/s10270-021-00868-z

40. Neider, D., Topcu, U.: An automaton learning approach to solving safety games over infinite graphs. In: Chechik, M., Raskin, J.-F. (eds.) TACAS 2016. LNCS, vol. 9636, pp. 204–221. Springer, Heidelberg (2016). https://doi.org/10.1007/978-3-662-49674-9_12

41. Niwiński, D.: On fixed-point clones. In: Kott, L. (ed.) ICALP 1986. LNCS, vol. 226, pp. 464–473. Springer, Heidelberg (1986). https://doi.org/10.1007/3-540-16761-7_96

42. Piterman, N., Pnueli, A., Sa'ar, Y.: Synthesis of reactive(1) designs. In: Emerson, E.A., Namjoshi, K.S. (eds.) VMCAI 2006. LNCS, vol. 3855, pp. 364–380. Springer, Heidelberg (2005). https://doi.org/10.1007/11609773_24

43. Pnueli, A.: The temporal logic of programs. In: 18th Annual Symposium on Foundations of Computer Science, Providence, Rhode Island, USA, 31 October–1 November 1977, pp. 46–57. IEEE Computer Society (1977). https://doi.org/10.1109/SFCS.1977.32

44. Raskin, J., Chatterjee, K., Doyen, L., Henzinger, T.A.: Algorithms for omega-regular games with imperfect information. Logical Methods Comput. Sci. **3**(3) (2007). https://doi.org/10.2168/LMCS-3(3:4)2007

45. Somenzi, F.: CUDD: CU Decision Diagram Package Release 3.0.0 (2015). http://vlsi.colorado.edu/~fabio/CUDD/cudd.pdf

Generalizing Non-punctuality for Timed Temporal Logic with Freeze Quantifiers

Shankara Narayanan Krishna[1], Khushraj Madnani[2(✉)], Manuel Mazo Jr.[2], and Paritosh K. Pandya[1]

[1] IIT Bombay, Mumbai, India
{krishnas,pandya58}@cse.iitb.ac.in
[2] Delft University of Technology, Delft, The Netherlands
{k.n.madnani-1,m.mazo}@tudelft.nl

Abstract. Metric Temporal Logic (MTL) and Timed Propositional Temporal Logic (TPTL) are prominent real-time extensions of Linear Temporal Logic (LTL). In general, the satisfiability checking problem for these extensions is undecidable when both the future U and the past S modalities are used. In a classical result, the satisfiability checking for MTL[U,S], a non-punctual fragment of MTL[U,S], is shown to be decidable with EXPSPACE complete complexity. Given that this notion of non-punctuality does not recover decidability in the case of TPTL[U,S], we propose a generalization of non-punctuality called *non-adjacency* for TPTL[U,S], and focus on its 1-variable fragment, 1-TPTL[U,S]. While non-adjacent 1-TPTL[U,S] appears to be a very small fragment, it is strictly more expressive than MITL. As our main result, we show that the satisfiability checking problem for non-adjacent 1-TPTL[U,S] is decidable with EXPSPACE complete complexity.

1 Introduction

Metric Temporal Logic (MTL) and Timed Propositional Temporal Logic (TPTL) are natural extensions of Linear Temporal Logic (LTL) for specifying real-time properties [3]. MTL extends the U and S modalities of LTL by associating a timing interval with these. $a \cup_I b$ describes behaviours modeled as timed words consisting of a sequence of a's followed by a b which occurs at a time within (relative) interval I. On the other hand, TPTL uses freeze quantification to store the current time stamp. A Freeze quantifier with clock variable x has the form $x.\varphi$. When it is evaluated at a point i on a timed word, the time stamp τ_i at i is frozen in x, and the formula φ is evaluated using this value for x. Variable x is used in φ in a constraint of the form $T - x \in I$; this constraint, when evaluated at a point j, checks if $\tau_j - \tau_i \in I$, where τ_j is the time stamp at point j.

This work is partially supported by the European Research Council through the SENTIENT project (ERC-2017-STG #755953).

© Springer Nature Switzerland AG 2021
M. Huisman et al. (Eds.): FM 2021, LNCS 13047, pp. 182–199, 2021.
https://doi.org/10.1007/978-3-030-90870-6_10

For example, the formula $Fx.(a \wedge F(b \wedge T - x \in [1,2] \wedge F(c \wedge T - x \in [1,2])))$[1] asserts that there is a point in future where a holds and in its future within interval $[1,2]$, b and c occur, and the former occurs before the latter. This property is not expressible in MTL[U, S] [4,18]. Moreover, every property in MTL[U, S] can be expressed in 1-TPTL[U, S]. Thus, 1-TPTL[U, S] is strictly more expressive than MTL[U, S]. Unfortunately, both the logics have an undecidable satisfiability problem, making automated analysis for these logics theoretically impossible.

Exploring natural decidable variants of these logics has been an active area of research since the advent of these logics [2,8–10,21–23]. One line of work restricted itself to the future only fragments MTL[U] and 1-TPTL[U] which have both been shown to have decidable satisfiability over finite timed words, under a pointwise interpretation [7,17]. The complexity however is non-primitive recursive. Reducing the complexity to elementary has been challenging. One of the most celebrated of such logics is the Metric Interval Temporal Logic (MITL[U, S]) [1], a subclass of MTL[U, S] where the timing intervals are restricted to be non-punctual (i.e. intervals of the form $\langle x, y \rangle$ where $x < y$). The satisfiability checking for MITL formulae is decidable with EXPSPACE complete complexity [1]. While non-punctuality helps to recover the decidability of MTL[U, S], it does not help TPTL[U, S]. The freeze quantifiers of TPTL enables us to trivially express punctual timing constraints using only the non-punctual intervals: for instance the 1-TPTL formula $x.(aU(a \wedge T - x \in [1, \infty) \wedge T - x \in [0, 1]))$ uses only non-punctual intervals but captures the MTL formula $aU_{[1,1]}b$. Thus, a more refined notion of non-punctuality is needed to recover the decidability of 1-TPTL[U, S].

Contributions. With the above observations, to obtain a decidable class of 1-TPTL[U, S] akin to MITL[U, S], we revisit the notion of non-punctuality as it stands currently. As our first contribution, we propose *non-adjacency*, a refined version of non-punctuality. Two intervals, I_1 and I_2 are non-adjacent if the supremum of I_1 is not equal to the infimum of I_2. Non-adjacent 1-TPTL[U, S] is the subclass of 1-TPTL[U, S] where, every interval used in clock constraints within the same freeze quantifier is non-adjacent to itself and to every other timing interval that appears within the same scope. (Wlog, we consider formulae in negation normal form only.) The non-adjacency restriction disallows punctual timing intervals: every punctual timing interval is adjacent to itself. It can be shown (Theorem 2) that non-adjacent 1-TPTL[U, S], while seemingly very restrictive, is strictly more expressive than MITL and it can also express the counting and the Pnueli modalities [9]. Thus, the logic is of considerable interest in practical real-time specification. See the full version for an example.

Our second contribution is to give a decision procedure for the satisfiability checking of non-adjacent 1-TPTL[U, S]. We do this in two steps. 1) We introduce a logic PnEMTL which combines and generalises the automata modalities of [11, 22,23] and the Pnueli modalities of [9,10,21], and has not been studied before to the best of our knowledge. We show that a formula of non-adjacent 1-TPTL[U, S] can be reduced to an equivalent formula of non-adjacent PnEMTL (Theorem 5).

---

[1] Here T is a special symbol denoting the timestamp of the present point and x is the clock that was frozen when x. was asserted.

2) We prove that the satisfiability of non-adjacent PnEMTL is decidable with EXPSPACE complete complexity (Theorem 6). For brevity, some of the proof details are omitted here and can be found in the full version [13].

Related Work and Discussion. Much of the related work has already been discussed. MITL with counting and Pnueli modalities has been shown to have EXPSPACE-complete satisfiability [20,21]. Here, we tackle even more expressive logics: namely non-adjacent 1-TPTL[U, S] and non-adjacent PnEMTL. We show that EXPSPACE-completeness of satisfiability checking is retained in spite of the additional expressive power. These decidability results are proved by equi-satisfiable reductions to logic EMITL$_{0,\infty}$ of Ho [11]. As argued by Ho, it is quite practicable to extend the existing model checking tools like UPPAAL to logic EMITL$_{0,\infty}$ and hence to our logics too.

Addition of regular expression based modalities to untimed logics like LTL has been found to be quite useful for practical specification; even the IEEE standard temporal logic PSL has this feature. With a similar motivation, there has been considerable recent work on adding regular expression/automata based modalities to MTL and MITL. Raskin as well as Wilke added automata modalities to MITL as well as an Event-Clock logic *ECL* [22,23] and showed the decidability of satisfaction. The current authors showed that MTL[U, S$_{NP}$] (where U can use punctual intervals but S is restricted to non-punctual intervals), when extended with counting as well as regular expression modalities preserves decidability of satisfaction [12,14–16]. Recently, Ferrère showed the EXPSPACE decidability of MIDL which is LTL[U] extended with a fragment of timed regular expression modality [5]. Moreover, Ho has investigated a PSPACE-complete fragment EMITL$_{0,\infty}$ [11]. Our non-adjacent PnEMTL is a novel extension of MITL with modalities which combine the features of EMITL [11,22,23] and the Pnueli modalities [9,10,21].

2   Preliminaries

Let Σ be a finite set of propositions, and let $\Gamma = 2^\Sigma \setminus \emptyset$. A word over Σ is a finite sequence $\sigma = \sigma_1\sigma_2\ldots\sigma_n$, where $\sigma_i \in \Gamma$. A timed word ρ over Σ is a finite sequence of pairs $(\sigma, \tau) \in \Sigma \times \mathbb{R}_{\geq 0}$; $\rho = (\sigma_1, \tau_1)\ldots(\sigma_n, \tau_n) \in (\Sigma \times \mathbb{R}_{\geq 0})^*$ where $\tau_1 = 0$ and $\tau_i \leq \tau_j$ for all $1 \leq i \leq j \leq n$. The τ_i are called time stamps. For a timed or untimed word ρ, let $dom(\rho) = \{i | 1 \leq i \leq |\rho|\}$ where $|\rho|$ denotes the number of (event, timestamp) pairs composing the word ρ, and $\sigma[i]$ denotes the symbol at position $i \in dom(\rho)$. The set of timed words over Σ is denoted $T\Sigma^*$. Given a (timed) word ρ and $i \in dom(\rho)$, a pointed (timed) word is the pair ρ, i. Let $\mathcal{I}_{\text{int}}$ ($\mathcal{I}_{\text{nat}}$) be the set of open, half-open or closed time intervals, such that the end points of these intervals are in $\mathbb{Z} \cup \{-\infty, \infty\}$ ($\mathbb{N} \cup \{0, \infty\}$, respectively). We assume familiarity with LTL.

Metric Temporal Logic (MTL). MTL is a real-time extension of LTL where the modalities (U and S) are guarded with intervals. Formulae of MTL are built from Σ using Boolean connectives and time constrained versions U$_I$ and S$_I$ of the standard U, S modalities, where $I \in \mathcal{I}_{nat}$. Intervals of the form $[x, x]$ are called punctual; a non-punctual interval is one which is not punctual. Formulae in MTL are defined as follows. $\varphi ::= a \mid \top \mid \varphi \wedge \varphi \mid \neg\varphi \mid \varphi U_I \varphi \mid \varphi S_I \varphi$, where $a \in \Sigma$ and $I \in \mathcal{I}_{nat}$. For a timed word $\rho = (\sigma_1, \tau_1)(\sigma_2, \tau_2) \ldots (\sigma_n, \tau_n) \in T\Sigma^*$, a position $i \in dom(\rho)$, an MTL formula φ, the satisfaction of φ at a position i of ρ, denoted $\rho, i \models \varphi$, is defined below. We discuss the time constrained modalities.

- $\rho, i \models \varphi_1 U_I \varphi_2$ iff $\exists j > i$, $\rho, j \models \varphi_2$, $\tau_j - \tau_i \in I$, and $\rho, k \models \varphi_1 \forall i < k < j$,
- $\rho, i \models \varphi_1 S_I \varphi_2$ iff $\exists j < i$, $\rho, j \models \varphi_2$, $\tau_j - \tau_i \in I$, and $\rho, k \models \varphi_1 \forall j < k < i$.

The language of an MTL formula φ is defined as $L(\varphi) = \{\rho | \rho, 1 \models \varphi\}$. Using the above, we obtain some derived formulae: the *constrained eventual* operator $F_I\varphi \equiv trueU_I\varphi$ and its dual is $\mathcal{G}_I\varphi \equiv \neg F_I \neg\varphi$. Similarly $\mathcal{H}_I\varphi \equiv trueS_I\varphi$. The *next* operator is defined as $\oplus_I\varphi \equiv \perp U_I\varphi$. The non-strict versions of $F, \mathcal{G}$ are respectively denoted F^w and $\mathcal{G}^w$ and include the present point. Symmetric non-strict versions for past operators are also allowed. The subclass of MTL obtained by restricting the intervals I in the until and since modalities to **non-punctual intervals** is denoted MITL. We say that a formula φ is satisfiable iff $L(\varphi) \neq \emptyset$.

Theorem 1. *Satisfiability checking for* MTL[U, S] *is undecidable [2]. Satisfiability Checking for* MITL *is EXPSPACE-complete [1].*

Time Propositional Temporal Logic (TPTL). The logic TPTL also extends LTL using freeze quantifiers. Like MTL, TPTL is also evaluated on timed words. Formulae of TPTL are built from Σ using Boolean connectives, modalities U and S of LTL. In addition, TPTL uses a finite set of real valued clock variables $X = \{x_1, \ldots, x_n\}$. Let $\nu : X \to \mathbb{R}_{\geq 0}$ represent a valuation assigning a non-negative real value to each clock variable. The formulae of TPTL are defined as follows. Without loss of generality we work with TPTL in the negation normal form. $\varphi ::= a \mid \neg a \mid \top \mid \perp \mid x.\varphi \mid T - x \in I \mid x - T \in I \mid \varphi \wedge \varphi \mid \varphi \vee \varphi \mid \varphi U\varphi \mid \varphi S\varphi \mid \mathcal{G}\varphi \mid \mathcal{H}\varphi$, where $x \in X$, $a \in \Sigma$, $I \in \mathcal{I}_{int}$. Here T denotes the time stamp of the point where the formula is being evaluated. $x.\varphi$ is the freeze quantification construct which remembers the time stamp of the current point in variable x and evaluates φ.

For a timed word $\rho = (\sigma_1, \tau_1) \ldots (\sigma_n, \tau_n)$, $i \in dom(\rho)$ and a TPTL formula φ, we define the satisfiability relation, $\rho, i, \nu \models \varphi$ with valuation ν of all the clock variables. We omit the semantics of Boolean, U and S operators as they are similar to those of LTL.

- $\rho, i, \nu \models a$ iff $a \in \sigma_i$, and $\rho, i, \nu \models x.\varphi$ iff $\rho, i, \nu[x \leftarrow \tau_i] \models \varphi$
- $\rho, i, \nu \models T - x \in I$ iff $\tau_i - \nu(x) \in I$, and $\rho, i, \nu \models x - T \in I$ iff $\nu(x) - \tau_i \in I$
- $\rho, i, \nu \models \mathcal{G}\varphi$ iff $\forall j > i$, $\rho, j, \nu \models \varphi$, and
- $\rho, i, \nu \models \mathcal{H}\varphi$ iff $\forall j < i$, $\rho, j, \nu \models \varphi$

Let $\overline{0} = (0, 0, \ldots, 0)$ represent the initial valuation of all clock variables. For a timed word ρ and $i \in dom(\rho)$, we say that ρ, i satisfies φ denoted $\rho, i \models \varphi$ iff $\rho, i, \overline{0} \models \varphi$. The language of φ, $L(\varphi) = \{\rho | \rho, 1 \models \varphi\}$. The Pointed Language of φ is defined as $L_{pt}(\varphi) = \{\rho, i | \rho, i \models \varphi\}$. Subclass of TPTL that uses

only 1 clock variable (i.e. $|X| = 1$) is known as 1-TPTL. The satisfiability checking for 1-TPTL[U, S] is undecidable, which is implied by Theorem 1 and the fact that 1-TPTL[U, S] trivially generalizes MTL[U, S]. As an example, the formula $\varphi = x.(aU(bU(c \wedge T - x \in [1, 2])))$ is satisfied by the timed word $\rho = (a, 0)(a, 0.2)(b, 1.1)(b, 1.9)(c, 1.91)(c, 2.1)$ since $\rho, 1 \models \varphi$. The word $\rho' = (a, 0)(a, 0.3)(b, 1.4)(c, 2.1)(c, 2.5)$ does not satisfy φ. However, $\rho', 2 \models \varphi$: if we start from the second position of ρ', we assign $\nu(x) = 0.3$, and when we reach the position 4 of ρ' with $\tau_4 = 2.1$ we obtain $T - x = 2.1 - 0.3 \in [1, 2]$.

3   Introducing Non-adjacent 1-**TPTL** and **PnEMTL**

In this section, we define non-adjacent 1-TPTL and PnEMTL logics. Let x denote the unique freeze variable we use in 1-TPTL.

Non-Adjacent 1-TPTL is defined as a subclass of 1-TPTL where adjacent intervals within the scope of any freeze quantifier is disallowed. Two intervals $I_1, I_2 \in \mathcal{I}_{int}$ are non-adjacent iff $\sup(I_1) = \inf(I_2) \Rightarrow \sup(I_1) = 0$. A set $\mathcal{I}_{na}$ of intervals is non-adjacent iff any two intervals in $\mathcal{I}_{na}$ are non-adjacent. It does not contain punctual intervals other than $[0, 0]$ as every punctual interval is adjacent to itself. For example, the set $\{[1, 2), (2, 3], [5, 6)\}$ is not a non-adjacent set, while $\{[0, 0], [0, 1), (3, 4], [5, 6)\}$ is. Let $\mathcal{I}_{na}$ denote a set of non-adjacent intervals with end points in $\mathbb{Z} \cup \{-\infty, \infty\}$. See full version for an example specification using this logic. The freeze depth of a TPTL formula φ, $\mathsf{fd}(\varphi)$ is defined inductively. For a ptopositional formula $prop$, $\mathsf{fd}(prop) = 0$. Also, $\mathsf{fd}(x.\varphi) = \mathsf{fd}(\varphi) + 1$, and $\mathsf{fd}(\varphi_1 U \varphi_2) = \mathsf{fd}(\varphi_1 S \varphi_2) = \mathsf{fd}(\varphi_1 \wedge \varphi_2) = \mathsf{fd}(\varphi_1 \vee \varphi_2) = \mathsf{Max}(\mathsf{fd}(\varphi_1), \mathsf{fd}(\varphi_2)), \mathsf{fd}(\mathcal{G}(\varphi)) = \mathsf{fd}(\mathcal{H}(\varphi)) = \mathsf{fd}(\varphi)$.

Theorem 2. *Non-Adjacent 1-*TPTL[U, S] *is more expressive than* MITL[U, S]. *It can also express the Counting and the Pnueli modalities of [9, 10].*

The straightforward translation of MITL into TPTL in fact gives rise to non-adjacent 1-*TPTL* formula. Let $\widehat{I}$ abbreviate $T - x \in I$. E.g. MITL formula $aU_{[2,3]}(bU_{[3,4]}c)$ translates to $x.(aU(\widehat{[2, 3]} \wedge x.(bU(\widehat{[3, 4]} \wedge c))))$. It has been previously shown that $\mathsf{F}[x.(a \wedge \mathsf{F}(b \wedge \widehat{(1, 2)} \wedge \mathsf{F}(c \wedge \widehat{(1, 2)})))]$, which is in fact a formula of non-adjacent 1-*TPTL*, is inexpressible in MTL[U, S] [18]. The Pnueli modality $\mathsf{Pn}_I(\phi_1, \ldots, \phi_k)$ expresses that there exist positions $i_1 \leq \ldots \leq i_k$ within (relative) interval I where each i_j satisfies ϕ_j. This is equivalent to the non-adjacent 1-*TPTL* formula $x.(\mathsf{F}(\widehat{I} \wedge \phi_1 \wedge \mathsf{F}(\widehat{I} \wedge \phi_2 \wedge \mathsf{F}(\ldots))))$. Similarly the (simpler) counting modality can also be expressed.

Pnueli EMTL: There have been several attempts to extend logic MTL[U] with regular expression/automaton modalities [5, 11, 14, 23]. We use a generalization of these existing modalities to give the logic PnEMTL. For any finite automaton A, let $L(A)$ denote the language of A.

Given a finite alphabet Σ, formulae of PnEMTL have the following syntax:
$$\varphi ::= a \mid \varphi \wedge \varphi \mid \neg\varphi \mid \mathcal{F}_{I_1, \ldots, I_k}^k(\mathsf{A}_1, \ldots, \mathsf{A}_{k+1})(S) \mid \mathcal{P}_{I_1, \ldots, I_k}^k(\mathsf{A}_1, \ldots, \mathsf{A}_{k+1})(S)$$
where $a \in \Sigma$, $I_1, I_2, \ldots I_k \in \mathcal{I}_{nat}$ and $\mathsf{A}_1, \ldots \mathsf{A}_{k+1}$ are automata over 2^S where

S is a set of formulae from PnEMTL. $\mathcal{F}^k$ and $\mathcal{P}^k$ are the new modalities called future and past **Pnueli Automata** Modalities, respectively, where k is the arity of these modalities.

Let $\rho = (a_1, \tau_1), \ldots (a_n, \tau_n) \in T\Sigma^*$, $x, y \in dom(\rho)$, $x {\leq} y$ and $S = \{\varphi_1, \ldots, \varphi_n\}$ be a given set of PnEMTL formulae. Let S_i be the exact subset of formulae from S evaluating to true at ρ, i, and let $\mathsf{Seg}^+(\rho, x, y, S)$ and $\mathsf{Seg}^-(\rho, y, x, S)$ be the untimed words $S_x S_{x+1} \ldots S_y$ and $S_y S_{y-1} \ldots S_x$ respectively. Then, the satisfaction relation for ρ, i_0 satisfying a PnEMTL formula φ is defined recursively as follows:

- $\rho, i_0 {\models} \mathcal{F}^k_{I_1, \ldots, I_k}(\mathsf{A}_1, \ldots, \mathsf{A}_{k+1})(S)$ iff $\exists i_0 {\leq} i_1 {\leq} i_2 \ldots {\leq} i_k {\leq} n$ s.t.

$$\bigwedge_{w=1}^{k} [(\tau_{i_w} - \tau_{i_0} \in I_w) \wedge \mathsf{Seg}^+(\rho, i_{w-1}, i_w, S) \in L(\mathsf{A}_w)] \wedge \mathsf{Seg}^+(\rho, i_k, n, S) \in L(\mathsf{A}_{k+1})$$

- $\rho, i_0 \models \mathcal{P}^k_{I_1, I_2, \ldots, I_k}(\mathsf{A}_1, \ldots, \mathsf{A}_k, \mathsf{A}_{k+1})(S)$ iff $\exists i_0 {\geq} i_1 {\geq} i_2 \ldots {\geq} i_k {\geq} n$ s.t.

$$\bigwedge_{w=1}^{k} [(\tau_{i_0} - \tau_{i_w} \in I_w) \wedge \mathsf{Seg}^-(\rho, i_{w-1}, i_w, S) \in L(\mathsf{A}_w)] \wedge \mathsf{Seg}^-(\rho, i_k, n, S) \in L(\mathsf{A}_{k+1}).$$

Language of any PnEMTL formula φ, as $L(\varphi) = \{\rho | \rho, 1 \models \varphi\}$. The Pointed Language of φ is defined as $L_{pt}(\varphi) = \{\rho, i | \rho, i \models \varphi\}$. Given a PnEMTL formula φ, its arity is the maximum number of intervals appearing in any $\mathcal{F}, \mathcal{P}$ modality of φ. For example, the arity of $\varphi = \mathcal{F}^2_{I_1, I_2}(\mathsf{A}_1, \mathsf{A}_2, \mathsf{A}_3)(S_1) \wedge \mathcal{P}^1_{I_1}(\mathsf{A}_1, \mathsf{A}_2)(S_2)$ for some sets of formulae S_1, S_2 is 2. For the sake of brevity, $\mathcal{F}^k_{I_1, \ldots, I_k}(\mathsf{A}_1, \ldots, \mathsf{A}_k)(S)$ denotes $\mathcal{F}^k_{I_1, \ldots, I_k}(\mathsf{A}_1, \ldots, \mathsf{A}_k, \mathsf{A}_{k+1})(S)$ where automata A_{k+1} accepts all the strings over S. We define **non-adjacent** PnEMTL, as a subclass where every modality $\mathcal{F}^k_{I_1, \ldots, I_k}$ and $\mathcal{P}^k_{I_1, \ldots, I_k}$ is such that $\{I_1, \ldots, I_k\}$ is a non-adjacent set of intervals.

EMITL of [23] (and variants of it studied in [5, 11, 14, 15]) are special cases of the non-adjacent PnEMTL modality where the arity is restricted to 1 and the second automata in the argument accepts all the strings. Hence, automaton modality of [23] is of the form $\mathcal{F}_I(A)(S)$. Let EMITL$_{0,\infty}$ denote the logic EMITL extended with $\mathcal{F}$ and $\mathcal{P}$ modality where the timing intervals are restricted to be of the form $\langle l, \infty \rangle$ or $\langle 0, u \rangle$.

We conclude this section defining size of a temporal logic formula.

Size of Formulae. Size of a formula φ denoted by $|\varphi|$ is a measure of how many bits are required to store it. The size of a TPTL formula is defined as the sum of the number of U, S and Boolean operators and freeze quantifiers in it. For PnEMTL formulae, $|op|$ is defined as the number of Boolean operators and variables used in it. $|(\mathcal{F}^k_{I_1, \ldots, I_k}(\mathsf{A}_1, \ldots, \mathsf{A}_{k+1})(S))| = \sum_{\varphi \in S} (|\varphi|) + |\mathsf{A}_1| + \ldots + |\mathsf{A}_{k+1}|$ where $|A|$ denotes the size of the automaton A given by sum of number of its states and transitions.

4   Anchored Interval Word Abstraction

All the logics considered here have the feature that a sub-formula asserts timing constraints on various positions relative to an anchor position; e.g. the position of freezing the clock in TPTL. Such constraints can be symbolically represented as an interval word with a unique anchor position and all other positions carry a set of time intervals constraining the time stamp of the position relative to the time stamp of the anchor. See interval word κ in Fig. 1. We now define these interval words formally. Let $I_\nu \subseteq \mathcal{I}_{\mathsf{int}}$. An I_ν-interval word over Σ is a word κ of the form $a_1 a_2 \ldots a_n \in (2^{\Sigma \cup \{\mathsf{anch}\} \cup I_\nu})^*$. There is a unique $i \in dom(\kappa)$ called the *anchor* of κ and denoted by $\mathsf{anch}(\kappa)$. At the anchor position i, $a_i \subseteq \Sigma \cup \{\mathsf{anch}\}$, and $\mathsf{anch} \in a_i$. Let J be any interval in $\mathcal{I}_\nu$. We say that a point $i \in dom(\kappa)$ is a J-time restricted point if and only if, $J \in a_i$. i is called time restricted point if and only if either i is J-time restricted for some interval J in I_ν or $\mathsf{anch} \in a_i$.

From I_ν-interval word to Timed Words: Given a I_ν-interval word $\kappa = a_1 \ldots a_n$ over Σ and a timed word $\rho = (b_1, \tau_1) \ldots (b_m, \tau_m)$, the pointed timed word ρ, i is consistent with κ iff $dom(\rho) = dom(\kappa)$, $i = \mathsf{anch}(\kappa)$, for all $j \in dom(\kappa)$, $b_j = a_j \cap \Sigma$ and for $j \neq i$, $I \in a_j \cap I_\nu$ implies $\tau_j - \tau_i \in I$. Thus, κ and ρ, i agree on propositions at all positions, and the time stamp of a non-anchor position j in ρ satisfies every interval constraint in a_j relative to τ_i, the time stamp of anchor position. $\mathsf{Time}(\kappa)$ denotes the set of all the pointed timed words consistent with a given interval word κ, and $\mathsf{Time}(\Omega) = \bigcup_{\kappa \in \Omega} (\mathsf{Time}(\kappa))$ for a set of interval words Ω. Note that the "consistency relation" is a many-to-many relation.

Example. Let $\kappa = \{a, b, (-1, 0)\}\{b, (-1, 0)\}\{a, \mathsf{anch}\}\{b, [2, 3]\}$ be an interval word over the set of intervals $\{(-1, 0), [2, 3]\}$. Consider timed words ρ and ρ' s.t. $\rho = (\{a, b\}, 0)(\{b\}, .5), (\{a\}, .95)(\{b\}, 3)$, $\rho' = (\{a, b\}, 0)(\{b\}, 0.8)(\{a\}, 0.9) (\{b\}, 2.9)$.

Then $\rho, 3$ as well as $\rho', 3$ are consistent with κ while $\rho, 2$ is not. Likewise, for the timed word $\rho'' = (\{a, b\}, 0), (\{b\}, 0.5), (\{a\}, 1.1)(\{b\}, 3)$, $\rho'', 3$ is not consistent with κ as $\tau_1 - \tau_3 \notin (-1, 0)$, as also $\tau_4 - \tau_3 \notin [2, 3]$.

Let $I_\nu, I'_\nu \subseteq \mathcal{I}_{\mathsf{int}}$. Let $\kappa = a_1 \ldots a_n$ and $\kappa' = b_1 \ldots b_m$ be I_ν and I'_ν-interval words, respectively. κ is *similar* to κ', denoted by $\kappa \sim \kappa'$ if and only if,

(i) $dom(\kappa) = dom(\kappa')$, (ii) for all $i \in dom(\kappa)$, $a_i \cap \Sigma = b_i \cap \Sigma$, and (iii)$\mathsf{anch}(\kappa) = \mathsf{anch}(\kappa')$. Additionally, κ is *congruent* to κ', denoted by $\kappa \cong \kappa'$, iff $\mathsf{Time}(\kappa) = \mathsf{Time}(\kappa')$. I.e., κ and κ' abstract the same set of pointed timed words.

Collapsed Interval Words. The set of interval constraints at a position can be collapsed into a single interval by taking the intersection of all the intervals at that position giving a Collapsed Interval Word. Given an I_ν-interval word $\kappa = a_1 \ldots a_n$, let $\mathcal{I}_j = a_j \cap I_\nu$. Let $\kappa' = \mathsf{Col}(\kappa)$ be the word obtained by replacing $\mathcal{I}_j$ with $\bigcap_{I \in \mathcal{I}_j} I$ in a_j, for all $j \in dom(\kappa)$. Note that κ' is an interval word over $\mathsf{CL}(I_\nu) = \{I | I = \bigcap I', I' \subseteq I_\nu\}$. Note that if for any j, the set $\mathcal{I}_j$ contains two disjoint intervals (like $[1, 2]$ and $[3, 4]$) then $\mathsf{Col}(\kappa)$ is undefined. It is clear that $\mathsf{Time}(\kappa) = \mathsf{Time}(\kappa')$. An interval word κ is called *collapsed* iff $\kappa = \mathsf{Col}(\kappa)$.

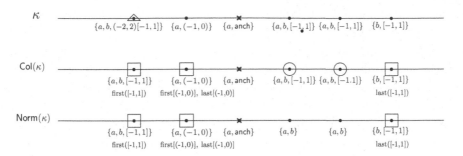

Fig. 1. Point within the triangle has more than one interval. The encircled points are intermediate points and carry redundant information. The required timing constraint is encoded by first and last time restricted points of all the intervals (within boxes).

Normalization of Interval Words. An interval I may repeat many times in a collapsed interval word κ. Some of these occurrences are redundant and we can only keep the first and last occurrence of the interval in the normalized form of κ. See Fig. 1. For a collapsed interval word κ and any $I \in I_\nu$, let $\mathsf{first}(\kappa, I)$ and $\mathsf{last}(\kappa, I)$ denote the positions of first and last occurrence of I in κ. If κ does not contain any occurrence of I, then both $\mathsf{first}(\kappa, I) = \mathsf{last}(\kappa, I) = \bot$. We define, $\mathsf{Boundary}(\kappa) = \{i | i \in dom(\kappa) \wedge \exists I \in I_\nu \text{ s.t. } (i = \mathsf{first}(\kappa, I) \vee i = \mathsf{last}(\kappa, I) \vee i = \mathsf{anch}(\kappa))\}$

The normalized interval word corresponding to κ, denoted $\mathsf{Norm}(\kappa)$, is defined as $\kappa_{nor} = b_1 \ldots b_m$, such that (i) $\kappa_{nor} \sim \mathsf{Col}(\kappa)$, (ii) for all $I \in \mathsf{CL}(I_\nu)$, $\mathsf{first}(\kappa, I) = \mathsf{first}(\kappa_{nor}, I)$, $\mathsf{last}(\kappa, I) = \mathsf{last}(\kappa_{nor}, I)$, and for all points $j \in dom(\kappa_{nor})$ with $\mathsf{first}(\kappa, I) < j < \mathsf{last}(\kappa, I)$, j is not a I-time constrained point. See Fig. 1. Hence, a normalized word is a collapsed word where for any $J \in \mathsf{CL}(I_\nu)$ there are at most two J-time restricted points. This is the key property which will be used to reduce 1-TPTL to a finite length PnEMTL formulae.

Lemma 1. $\kappa \cong \mathsf{Norm}(\kappa)$. *Note,* $\mathsf{Norm}(\kappa)$ *has at most* $2 \times |I_\nu|^2 + 1$ *restricted points.*

The proof follows from the fact that $\kappa \cong \mathsf{Col}(\kappa)$ and since $\mathsf{Col}(\kappa) \sim \mathsf{Norm}(\kappa)$, the set of timed words consistent with any of them will have identical untimed behaviour. For the timed part, the key observation is as follows. For some interval $I \in I_\nu$, let $i' = \mathsf{first}(\kappa, I), j' = \mathsf{last}(\kappa, I)$. Then for any ρ, i in $\mathsf{Time}(\kappa)$, points i' and j' are within the interval I from point i. Hence, any point $i' \leq i'' \leq j'$ is also within interval I from i. Thus, the interval I need not be explicitly mentioned at intermediate points. The full proof can be found in the full version.

5   1-TPTL to PnEMTL

In this section, we reduce a 1-TPTL formula into an equisatisfiable PnEMTL formula. First, we consider 1-TPTL formula with a single outermost freeze quantifier (call these simple TPTL formulae) and give the reduction. More complex formulae can be handled by applying the same reduction recursively as shown in the first step. For any set of formulae S, let $\bigvee S$ denote $\bigvee_{s \in S} s$. A TPTL formula is said to be *simple* if it is of the form $x.\varphi$ where, φ is a 1-TPTL formula with no freeze quantifiers. Let $\mathcal{I}_\nu \subseteq \mathcal{I}_{\text{int}}$. Let $\psi = x.\varphi$ be a simple $\mathcal{I}_\nu$-TPTL formula and let $\mathsf{CL}(\mathcal{I}_\nu) = I_\nu$. We construct a PnEMTL formula ϕ, such that $\rho, i \models \psi \iff \rho, i \models \phi$. We break this construction into the following steps:

1) We construct an LTL formula α s.t. $L(\alpha)$ contains only I_ν-interval words and $\rho, i \models \psi$ iff $\rho, i \in \mathsf{Time}(L(\alpha))$. Let A be the NFA s.t. $L(A) = L(\alpha)$. Let W be the set of all I_ν-interval words.

2) We partition W into finitely many types, each *type*, capturing a certain relative ordering between first and last occurrences of intervals from I_ν as well as anch. Let $\mathcal{T}(I_\nu)$ be the finite set of all types.

3) For each type $\mathsf{seq} \in \mathcal{T}$, we construct an NFA A_{seq} such that $L(A_{\mathsf{seq}}) = \mathsf{Norm}(L(A) \cap W_{\mathsf{seq}})$, where W_{seq} is the set of all the I_ν-interval words of type seq.

4) For every type seq, using the A_{seq} above, we construct a PnEMTL formula ϕ_{seq} such that, $\rho, i \models \phi_{\mathsf{seq}}$ if and only if $\rho, i \in \mathsf{Time}(L(A_{\mathsf{seq}}))$. The desired $\phi = \bigvee_{\mathsf{seq} \in \mathcal{T}(I_\nu)} \phi_{\mathsf{seq}}$. Hence, $L_{pt}(\phi) = \bigcup_{\mathsf{seq} \in \mathcal{T}} \mathsf{Time}(L(A_{\mathsf{seq}})) = \mathsf{Time}(L(A)) = L_{pt}(\psi)$.

1a) Simple TPTL to LTL over Interval Words: As above, $\psi = x.\varphi$. Consider an LTL formula $\alpha = \mathsf{F}[\mathsf{LTL}(\varphi) \wedge \mathsf{anch} \wedge \neg(\mathsf{F}(\mathsf{anch}) \vee \mathsf{P}(\mathsf{anch}))] \wedge \mathcal{G}(\bigvee \Sigma)$ over $\Sigma' = \Sigma \cup \mathcal{I}_\nu \cup \{\mathsf{anch}\}$, where $\mathsf{LTL}(\varphi)$ is the LTL formula obtained from φ by replacing clock constraints $T - x \in I$ with I and $x - T \in I$ with $-I$. Then all words in $L(\alpha)$ are $\mathcal{I}_\nu$-interval words.

Theorem 3. *For any timed word* ρ, $i \in dom(\rho)$, *and any clock valuation* v, $\rho, i, v \models \psi \iff \rho, i \in \mathsf{Time}(L(\alpha))$.

Proof Sketch. Note that for any timed word ρ and $i \in dom(\rho)$, $\rho, i, [x \leftarrow \tau_i] \models \varphi$ is equivalent to $\rho, i \models \psi$ since $\psi = x.\varphi$. Let κ be any $\mathcal{I}_\nu$-interval word over Σ with $\mathsf{anch}(\kappa) = i$. It can be seen that if $\kappa, i \models \mathsf{LTL}(\varphi)$ then for all $\rho, i \in \mathsf{Time}(\kappa)$ we have $\rho, i \models \psi$. Likewise, if $\rho, i \models \psi$ for a timed word ρ, then there exists some $\mathcal{I}_\nu$-interval word over Σ such that $\rho, i \in \mathsf{Time}(\kappa)$ and $\kappa, i \models \mathsf{LTL}(\varphi)$.

Illustrated on an example, if $\psi = x.\varphi$ and $\varphi = \mathsf{F}(x \in I \wedge a)$. Then $\rho, i \models \varphi$ iff there exists a point j within an interval I from i, where a holds. Now consider $\alpha = \mathsf{F}^w[(I \wedge a) \wedge \mathsf{anch} \wedge \neg(\mathsf{F}(\mathsf{anch}) \vee \mathsf{P}(\mathsf{anch}))] \wedge \mathcal{G}^w(\bigvee \Sigma)$ whose language consists of interval words κ such that there is a point ahead of the anchor point i where both a and I holds. Clearly, words in $\mathsf{Time}(\kappa)$ are such that they contain a point $j > i$ within an interval I from point i where a holds. Hence, $\rho, i \models \psi$ if and only if $\rho, i \in \mathsf{Time}(\{\kappa \mid \kappa, i \models \mathsf{LTL}(\varphi)\})$. Moreover, $\kappa \in L(\alpha)$ if and only if $\kappa, i \models \mathsf{LTL}(\varphi)$ and $\mathsf{anch}(\kappa) = i$. The full proof is in the full version.

1b) LTL to NFA over Collapsed Interval Words. It is known that for any $\mathsf{LTL}[\mathsf{U}, \mathsf{S}]$ formula, one can construct an equivalent NFA with at most exponential number of states [6]. We reduce the LTL formula α to an equivalent NFA $A_\alpha = (Q, \mathsf{init}, 2^{\Sigma'}, \delta', F)$ over I_ν-interval words, where $\Sigma' = 2^{\Sigma \cup I_\nu \cup \{\mathsf{anch}\}}$. From

A_α, we construct an automaton $A = (Q, \text{init}, 2^{\Sigma'}, \delta, F)$ s.t. $L(A) = \text{Col}(L(A_\alpha))$. Automaton A is obtained from A_α by replacing the set of intervals $\mathcal{I}$ on the transitions by the single interval $\bigcap \mathcal{I}$. In case $\exists I_1, I_2 \in \mathcal{I}$ s.t. $I_1 \cap I_2 = \emptyset$ (i.e. with contradictory interval constraints), the transition is omitted in A. This gives $L(A) = \text{Col}(L(A_\alpha))$.

2) Partitioning Interval Words. We discuss here how to partition W, the set of all collapsed I_ν-interval words, into finitely many classes. Each class is characterized by its **type** given as a finite sequences seq over $I_\nu \cup \{\text{anch}\}$. For any collapsed $w \in W$, its type seq gives an ordering between $\text{anch}(w)$, $\text{first}(w, I)$ and $\text{last}(w, I)$ for all $I \in I_\nu$, such that, any $I \in I_\nu$ appears at most twice and anch appears exactly once in seq. For instance, $\text{seq} = I_1 I_1 \text{anch} I_2 I_2$ is a sequence different from $\text{seq}' = I_1 I_2 \text{anch} I_2 I_1$ since the relative orderings between the first and last occurrences of I_1, I_2 and anch differ in both. Let the set of types $\mathcal{T}(I_\nu)$ be the set of all such sequences; by definition, $\mathcal{T}(I_\nu)$ is finite. Given $w \in W$, let $\text{Boundary}(w) = \{i_1, i_2, \ldots, i_k\}$ be the positions of w which are either $\text{first}(w, I)$ or $\text{last}(w, I)$ for some $I \in I_\nu$ or is $\text{anch}(w)$. Let $w \downarrow_{\text{Boundary}(w)}$ be the subword of w obtained by projecting w to the positions in $\text{Boundary}(w)$, restricted to the sub alphabet $2^{I_\nu} \cup \{\text{anch}\}$. For example, $w = \{a, I_1\}\{b, I_1\}\{c, I_2\}\{\text{anch}, a\}\{b, I_1\}\{b, I_2\}\{c, I_2\}$ gives $w \downarrow_{\text{Boundary}(w)}$ as $I_1 I_2 \text{anch} I_1 I_2$. Then w is in the partition W_{seq} iff $w \downarrow_{\text{Boundary}(w)} = \text{seq}$. Clearly, $W = \bigcup_{\text{seq} \in \mathcal{T}(I_\nu)} W_{\text{seq}}$. Continuing with the example above, w is a collapsed $\{I_1, I_2\}$-interval word over $\{a, b, c\}$, with $\text{Boundary}(w) = \{1, 3, 4, 5, 7\}$, and $w \in W_{\text{seq}}$ for $\text{seq} = I_1 I_2 \text{anch} I_1 I_2$, while $w \notin W_{\text{seq}'}$ for $\text{seq}' = I_1 I_1 \text{anch} I_2 I_2$.

3) Construction of NFA for each type: Let seq be any sequence in $\mathcal{T}(I_\nu)$. In this section, given $A = (Q, \text{init}, 2^{\Sigma'}, \delta, F)$ as constructed above, we construct an NFA $A_{\text{seq}} = (Q \times \{1, 2, \ldots |\text{seq}| + 1\} \cup \{\bot\}, (\text{init}, 1), 2^{\Sigma'}, \delta_{\text{seq}}, F \times \{|\text{seq}| + 1\})$ such that $L(A_{\text{seq}}) = \text{Norm}(L(A) \cap W_{\text{seq}})$. Thus, $\bigcup_{\text{seq} \in \mathcal{T}(I_\nu)} L(A_{\text{seq}}) = \text{Norm}(L(A))$. Thus, $\bigcup_{\text{seq} \in \mathcal{T}(I_\nu)} \text{Time}(L(A_{\text{seq}})) = \text{Time}(\text{Norm}(L(A))) = \text{Time}(L(A)) = L(\psi)$. Intuitively, the second element of the state makes sure that only normalized words of type seq are accepted. From (q, j), A_{seq} is allowed to read a set $S \subseteq \Sigma$ (containing no time interval or anch and hence an unrestricted point) or it can read a set $S \cup \{I\}$ where $S \subseteq \Sigma$ and $J = \text{seq}[j]$ (containing time interval/anchor $\text{seq}[j]$). In case of latter, the A_{seq} ends up with a state of the form $(q', j + 1)$ if and only if there is a transition in A of the form $q \xrightarrow{S \cup J} q'$. In case of the former, it non-deterministically proceeds to a state (q', j) if and only if, in automaton A, there is a transition of the form $q \xrightarrow{S} q'$ or $q \xrightarrow{S \cup J} q'$ where $\text{first}(J, w)$ has already been read and $\text{last}(J, w)$ is yet to be read in the future (that is, $\exists j'' j', j' < j \leq j'' \wedge \text{seq}[j'] = \text{seq}[j''] = J$). The detailed construction as well as the proof for Lemma 2 can be found in the full version. Let W_{seq} denote set of I_ν-interval words of type seq.

Lemma 2. $L(A_{\text{seq}}) = \text{Norm}(L(A) \cap W_{\text{seq}})$. *Hence,* $\bigcup_{\text{seq} \in \mathcal{T}(I_\nu)} L(A_{\text{seq}}) = \text{Norm}(L(A))$.

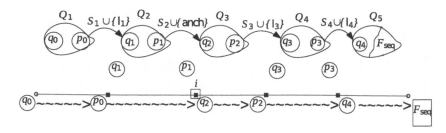

Fig. 2. Figure representing set of runs $A_{l_1 anch l_3 l_4}$ of type $Qseq$ where each $S_i \subseteq \Sigma$ and each sub-automaton Q_i has only transitions without any intervals. Here $Qseq = T_1 T_2 T_3 T_4$, for $1 \leq i \leq 4$, $T_i = (p_{i-1} \overset{S_i \cup \{I_i\}}{\rightarrow} q_i)$, $I_2 = \{anch\}$.

Our next step is to reduce the NFAs A_{seq} corresponding to each type seq to PnEMTL. The words in $L(A_{seq})$ are all normalized, and have at most $2|I_\nu| + 1$-time restricted points. Thanks to this, its corresponding timed language can be expressed using PnEMTL formulae with arity at most $2|I_\nu|$.

4) Reducing NFA of each type to PnEMTL: Next, for each A_{seq} we construct PnEMTL formula ϕ_{seq} such that, for a timed word ρ with $i \in dom(\rho), \rho, i \models \phi_{seq}$ iff $\rho, i \in Time(L(A_{seq}))$. For any NFA $N = (St, \Sigma, i, Fin, \Delta)$, $q \in Q$ $F' \subseteq Q$, let $N[q, F'] = (St, \Sigma, q, F', \Delta)$. For brevity, we denote $N[q, \{q'\}]$ as $N[q, q']$. We denote by $\mathsf{Rev}(N)$, the NFA N' that accepts the reverse of $L(N)$. The right/left concatenation of $a \in \Sigma$ with $L(N)$ is denoted $N \cdot a$ and $a \cdot N$ respectively.

Lemma 3. *We can construct a* PnEMTL *formula* ϕ_{seq} *with arity* $\leq |I_\nu|^2$ *and size* $\mathcal{O}(|A_{seq}|^{|seq|})$ *containing intervals from* I_ν *s.t.* $\rho, i \models \phi_{seq}$ *iff* $\rho, i \in \mathsf{Time}(L(A_{seq}))$.

Proof. Let seq $= I_1 I_2 \dots I_n$, and $I_j =$ anch for some $1 \leq j \leq n$. Let $\Gamma = 2^\Sigma$ and Qseq $= T_1 T_2 \dots T_n$ be a sequence of transitions of A_{seq} where for any $1 \leq i \leq n$, $T_i = p_{i-1} \overset{S_i'}{\rightarrow} q_i$, $S_i' = S_i \cup \{I_i\}$, $S_i \subseteq \Sigma$, $p_{i-1} \in Q \times \{i-1\}$, $q_i \in Q \times \{i\}$. Let $q_0 = (init, 1)$. We define R_{Qseq} as set of accepting runs containing transitions $T_1 T_2 \dots T_n$. Hence the runs in R_{Qseq} are of the following form:

$$T_{0,1} T_{0,2} \dots T_{0,m_0} T_1 T_{1,1} \dots T_{1,m_1} T_2 \cdots\cdots T_{n-1,1} T_{n-1,2} \dots T_n T_{n,1} \dots$$

T_{n+1} where the source of the transition $T_{0,1}$ is q_0 and the target of the transition T_{n+1} is any accepting state of A_{seq}. Moreover, all the transitions $T_{i,j}$ for $0 \leq i \leq n$, $1 \leq j \leq n_i$ are of the form $(p' \overset{S_{i,j}}{\rightarrow} q')$ where $S_{i,j} \subseteq \Sigma$ and $p', q' \in Q_{i+1}$. Hence, only $T_1, T_2, \dots T_n$ are labelled by any interval from I_ν. Moreover, only on these transitions the counter (second element of the state) increments. Let $\mathsf{A}_i = (Q_i, 2^\Sigma, q_{i-1}, \{p_{i-1}\}, \delta_{seq}) \equiv A_{seq}[q_{i-1}, p_{i-1}]$ for $1 \leq i \leq n$ and $\mathsf{A}_{n+1} = (Q_{n+1}, 2^\Sigma, q_n, F_{seq}, \delta_{seq}) \equiv A[q_n, F]$. Let $\mathcal{W}_{Qseq}$ be set of words associated with any run in R_{Qseq}. In other words, any word w in $\mathcal{W}_{Qseq}$ admits an accepting run on A which starts from q_0 reads letters without intervals (i.e., symbols of the form $S \subseteq \Sigma$) ends up at p_0, reads S_1', ends up at q_1 reads letters without intervals, ends up and p_1, reads S_2' and so on. Refer Fig. 2 for illustration. Hence, $w \in \mathcal{W}_{Qseq}$ if and only if $w \in L(\mathsf{A}_1) . S_1' . L(\mathsf{A}_2) . S_2' . \cdots . L(\mathsf{A}_n) . S_n' . L(\mathsf{A}_{n+1})$.

Let $\mathsf{A}'_k = S_{k-1} \cdot \mathsf{A}_k \cdot S_k$ for $1 \leq k \leq n+1$, with $S_0 = S_{n+1} = \epsilon^2$. Let $\rho = (b_1, \tau_1) \ldots (b_m, \tau_m)$ be a timed word over Γ. Then $\rho, i_j \in \mathsf{Time}(W_{Qseq})$

iff $\exists\ 0 \leq i_1 \leq i_2 \leq \ldots \leq i_{j-1} \leq i_j \leq i_{j+1} \leq \ldots \leq i_n \leq m$ s.t. $\bigwedge_{k=1}^{j-1} [(\tau_{i_k} - \tau_{i_j}) \in I_k) \wedge$

$\mathsf{Seg}^-(\rho, i_{k+1}, i_k, \Gamma) \in L(\mathsf{Rev}(\mathsf{A}'_k))] \wedge \bigwedge_{k=j}^{n} [(\tau_{i_k} - \tau_{i_j}) \in I_k) \wedge \mathsf{Seg}^+(\rho, i_k, i_{k+1}, \Gamma) \in$

$L(\mathsf{A}'_k)]$, where $i_0 = 0$ and $i_{n+1} = m$. Hence, by semantics of $\mathcal{F}^k$ and $\mathcal{P}^k$ modalities, $\rho, i \in \mathsf{Time}(W_{Qseq})$ if and only if $\rho, i \models \phi_{qseq}$ where $\phi_{qseq} = \mathcal{P}^j_{I_{j-1}, \ldots, I_1}(\mathsf{Rev}(\mathsf{A}'_1), \ldots, \mathsf{Rev}(\mathsf{A}'_j))(\Gamma) \wedge \mathcal{F}^{n-j}_{I_{j+1}, \ldots, I_n}(\mathsf{A}'_{j+1}, \ldots, \mathsf{A}'_{n+1})(\Gamma)$. Let State$-$seq be set of all possible sequences of the form Qseq. As A_{seq} accepts only words which has exactly n time restricted points, the number of possible sequences of the form Qseq is bounded by $|Q|^n$. Hence any word $\rho, i \in \mathsf{Time}(L(A_{seq}))$ iff $\rho, i \models \phi_{seq}$ where $\phi_{seq} = \bigvee_{qseq \in \text{State}-seq} \phi_{qseq}$. Disjuncting over all possible sequences $seq \in \mathcal{T}(I_\nu)$ we get formula ϕ and the following lemma.

Lemma 4. *Let $L(A)$ be the language of I_ν-interval words definable by a NFA A. We can construct a* PnEMTL *formula ϕ s.t. $\rho, i \models \phi$ iff $\rho, i \in \mathsf{Time}(L(A))$.*

Note that, if ψ is a simple 1-TPTL formula with intervals in $\mathcal{I}_\nu$, then the equivalent PnEMTL formula ϕ constructed above contains only interval in $\mathsf{CL}(\mathcal{I}_\nu)$. Hence, we have the following theorem.

Theorem 4. *For a simple non-adjacent 1-TPTL formula ψ containing intervals from $\mathcal{I}_\nu$, we can construct a non-adjacent* PnEMTL *formula ϕ, s.t. for any valuation v, $\rho, i, v \models \psi$ iff $\rho, i \models \phi$ where, $|\phi| = O(2^{Poly(|\psi|)})$ and arity of ϕ is $O(|\mathcal{I}_\nu|^2)$.*

This is a consequence of Theorem 3, Lemma 2 and Lemma 4. A formal proof appears in the full version For the complexity: The size LTL formula α constructed from ψ (in **1a**))) is linear in ψ. The translation from LTL formula α to NFA A has a complexity $\mathcal{O}(2^{|\alpha|}) = \mathcal{O}(2^{|\psi|})$. Let $I_\mu = \mathsf{CL}(\mathcal{I}_\nu)$. Hence, $|I_\mu| = \mathcal{O}(|\mathcal{I}_\nu|^2)$. The size of A_{seq} is $\mathcal{O}(|seq| \times 2^{(|\psi|)}) = \mathcal{O}(2^{Poly(|\psi|)})$ as $|seq| \leq 2 \times |I_\mu| = \mathcal{O}(|\mathcal{I}_\nu|^2) = \mathcal{O}(|\psi|^2)$. Next, $|\phi_{seq}| = \mathcal{O}(|A_{seq}|^{|seq|}) = \mathcal{O}(2^{Poly(|\psi|)})$. $|T(\mathcal{I}_\nu)| = O(2^{Poly(n)})$. Hence, $|\phi| = O(2^{Poly(n,|Q|)}) = O(2^{Poly(|A|)})$. Moreover, the arity of ϕ is also bounded by $2 \times |\mathsf{CL}(I_\nu)|$. Note that, $|\mathsf{CL}(I_\nu)| \leq |\mathcal{I}_\nu|^2$. Moreover, $\mathsf{CL}(I_\nu)$ is non-adjacent iff I_ν is. This result is lifted to a (non-simple) 1-TPTL formula ψ as follows: for each occurrence of a subformula $x.\varphi_i$ in ψ, introduce a new propositional variable a_i and replace $x.\varphi_i$ with a_i. After replacing all such, we are left with the outermost freeze quantifier. Conjunct $\bigwedge_{i=1}^{m} \mathcal{G}^w(a_i \leftrightarrow x.\varphi_i)$ to the replaced formula obtaining a simple 1-TPTL formula ψ', equisatisfiable to ψ. Apply the procedure above to each of the $m+1$ conjuncts of ψ' resulting in $m+1$ equivalent non-adjacent PnEMTL formulae φ'_i. The conjunction of φ'_i is the non-adjacent PnEMTL formula equisatisfiable with ψ, giving Theorem 5.

---

[2] We A'_k instead of A_k in the formulae below due to the strict inequalities in the semantics of PnEMTL modalities.

Theorem 5. *Any non-adjacent 1-TPTL formula ψ with intervals in $\mathcal{I}_\nu$, can be reduced to a non-adjacent PnEMTL, ϕ, with $|\phi| = 2^{Poly(|\psi|)}$ and arity of $\phi = O(|\mathcal{I}_\nu|^2)$ such that ψ is satisfiable if and only if ϕ is.*

6   Satisfiability Checking for Non-adjacent PnEMTL

Theorem 6. *Satisfiability Checking for non-adjacent PnEMTL and non- adjacent 1-TPTL are decidable with EXPSPACE complete complexity.*

The proof is via a satisfiability preserving reduction to logic $\text{EMITL}_{(0,\infty)}$ resulting in a formula whose size is at most exponential in the size of the input non-adjacent PnEMTL formula. Satisfiability checking for $\text{EMITL}_{0,\infty}$ is PSPACE complete [11]. This along with our construction implies an EXPSPACE decision procedure for satisfiability checking of non-adjacent PnEMTL. The EXPSPACE lower bound follows from the EXPSPACE hardness of sublogic MITL. The same complexity also applies to non-adjacent 1-TPTL, using the reduction in the previous section. We now describe the technicalities associated with our reduction. We use the technique of equisatisfiability modulo oversampling [12,16]. Let Σ and OVS be disjoint set of propositions. Given any timed word ρ over Σ, we say that a word ρ' over $\Sigma \cup \text{OVS}$ is an oversampling of ρ if $|\rho| \leq |\rho'|$ and when we delete the symbols in OVS from ρ' we get back ρ. Intuitively, OVS are set of propositions which are used to label oversampling points only. Informally, a formulae α is equisatisfiable modulo oversampling to formulae β if and only if for every timed word ρ excepted by β there exists an oversampling of ρ accepted by α and, for every timed word ρ' accepted by α its projection is accepted by α. Note that when $|\rho'| > |\rho|$, ρ' will have some time points where no proposition from Σ is true. These new points are called oversampling points. Moreover, we say that any point $i' \in dom(\rho')$ is an old point of ρ' corresponding to i iff i' is the ith point of ρ' when we remove all the oversampling points. For the rest of this section, let ϕ be a non-adjacent PnEMTL formula over Σ. We break down the construction of an $\text{EMITL}_{0,\infty}$ formula ψ as follows.

1) Add oversampling points at every integer timestamp using φ_{ovs} below,
2) Flatten the PnEMTL modalities to get rid of nested automata modalities, obtaining an equisatisfiable formula ϕ_{flat},
3) With the help of oversampling points, assert the properties expressed by PnEMTL subformulae ϕ_i of ϕ_{flat} using only EMITL formulae,
4) Get rid of bounded intervals with non-zero lower bound, getting the required $\text{EMITL}_{0,\infty}$ formula ψ_i. Replace ϕ_i with ψ_i in ϕ_{flat} getting ψ.

Let $\text{Last} = \mathcal{G}\bot$ and $\text{LastTS} = \mathcal{G}\bot \vee (\bot U_{(0,\infty)}\top)$. Last is true only at the last point of any timed word. Similarly, LastTS, is true at a point i if there is no next point $i + 1$ with the same timestamp τ_i. Let cmax be the maximum constant used in the intervals appearing in ϕ.

1) Behaviour of Oversampling Points. We oversample timed words over Σ by adding new points where only propositions from Int holds, where Int $\cap$

$\Sigma = \emptyset$. Given a timed word ρ over Σ, consider an extension of ρ called ρ', by extending the alphabet Σ of ρ to $\Sigma' = \Sigma \cup \text{Int}$. Compared to ρ, ρ' has extra points called *oversampling* points, where $\neg \bigvee \Sigma$ (and $\bigvee \text{Int}$) hold. These extra points are added at all integer timestamps, in such a way that if ρ already has points with integer time stamps, then the oversampled point with the same time stamp appears last among all points with the same time stamp in ρ'. We will make use of these oversampling points to reduce the PnEMTL modalities into $\text{EMITL}_{0,\infty}$. These oversampling points are labelled with a modulo counter $\text{Int} = \{\text{int}_0, \text{int}_1, \ldots, \text{int}_{\text{cmax}-1}\}$. The counter is initialized to be 0 at the first oversampled point with timestamp 0 and is incremented, modulo cmax, after exactly one time unit till the last point of ρ. Let $i \oplus j = (i + j)\%\text{cmax}$. The oversampled behaviours are expressed using the formula φ_{ovs}: $\{\neg F_{(0,1)} \bigvee \text{Int} \wedge$

$F_{[0,1)}\text{int}_0\} \wedge \{ \overset{\text{cmax}-1}{\underset{i=0}{\bigwedge}} \mathcal{G}^w\{(\text{int}_i \wedge F(\bigvee \Sigma)) \to (\neg F_{(0,1)}(\bigvee \text{Int}) \wedge F_{(0,1]}(\text{int}_{i\oplus 1} \wedge (\neg \bigvee \Sigma) \wedge$

$\text{LastTS}))\}$. to an extension ρ' given by $\text{ext}(\rho) = \rho'$ iff (i)ρ can be obtained from ρ' by deleting oversampling points and (ii)$\rho' \models \varphi_{\text{ovs}}$. Map ext is well defined as for any ρ, $\rho' = \text{ext}(\rho)$ if and only if ρ' can be constructed from ρ by appending oversampling points at integer timestamps and labelling k^{th} such oversampling point (appearing at time $k-1$) with $\text{int}_{k\%\text{cmax}}$.

2) Flattening. Next, we flatten ϕ to eliminate the nested $\mathcal{F}^k_{l_1,\ldots,l_k}$ and $\mathcal{P}^k_{l_1,\ldots,l_k}$ modalities while preserving satisfiability. Flattening is well studied [11,12,16,19]. The idea is to associate a fresh witness variable b_i to each subformula ϕ_i which needs to be flattened. This is achieved using the *temporal definition* $T_i = \mathcal{G}^w((\bigvee \Sigma \wedge \phi_i) \leftrightarrow b_i)$ and replacing ϕ_i with b_i in ϕ, $\phi''_i = \phi[b_i/\phi_i]$, where $\mathcal{G}^w$ is the weaker form of $\mathcal{G}$ asserting at the current point and strict future. Then, $\phi'_i = \phi''_i \wedge T_i \wedge \bigvee \Sigma$ is equisatisfiable to ϕ. Repeating this across all subformulae of ϕ, we obtain $\phi_{flat} = \phi_t \wedge T$ over the alphabet $\Sigma' = \Sigma \cup W$, where W is the set of the witness variables, $T = \bigwedge_i T_i$, ϕ_t is a propositional logic formula over W. Each T_i is of the form $\mathcal{G}^w(b_i \leftrightarrow (\phi_f \wedge \bigvee \Sigma))$ where $\phi_f = \mathcal{F}^n_{l_1,\ldots,l_n}(A_1,\ldots,A_{n+1})(S)$ (or uses $\mathcal{P}^n_{l_1,\ldots,l_n}$) and $S \subseteq \Sigma'$. For example, consider the formula $\phi = \mathcal{F}^2_{(0,1)(2,3)}(A_1,A_2,A_3)(\{\phi_1,\phi_2\})$, where $\phi_1 = \mathcal{P}^2_{(0,2)(3,4)}(A_4,A_5,A_6)(\Sigma)$, $\phi_2 = \mathcal{P}^2_{(1,2)(4,5)}(A_7,A_8,A_9)(\Sigma)$. Replacing the ϕ_1, ϕ_2 modality with witness propositions b_1, b_2, respectively, we get $\phi_t = \mathcal{F}^2_{(0,1)(2,3)}(A_1,A_2,A_3)(\{b_1,b_2\}) \wedge T$, where $T = \mathcal{G}^w(b_1 \leftrightarrow (\bigvee \Sigma \wedge \phi_1)) \wedge \mathcal{G}^w(b_2 \leftrightarrow (\bigvee \Sigma \wedge \phi_2))$, A_1, A_2, A_3 are automata constructed from A_1, A_2, A_3, respectively, by replacing ϕ_1 by b_1 and ϕ_2 by b_2 in the labels of their transitions. Hence, $\phi_{flat} = \phi_t \wedge T$ is obtained by flattening the $\mathcal{F}^k_{l_1,\ldots,l_k}, \mathcal{P}^k_{l_1,\ldots,l_k}$ modalities.

3) Obtaining equisatisfiable EMITL formula ψ_f for the PnEMTL formula ϕ_f in each $T_i = \mathcal{G}^w(b_i \leftrightarrow (\phi_f \wedge \bigvee \Sigma))$. The next step is to replace all the PnEMTL formulae occurring in temporal definitions T_i. We use oversampling to construct the formula ψ_f: for a timed word ρ over Σ, $i \in dom(\rho)$, there is an extension $\rho' = \text{ext}(\rho)$ over an extended alphabet Σ', and a point $i' \in dom(\rho')$ which is an old point corresponding to i such that $\rho', i' \models \psi_f$ iff $\rho, i \models \phi_f$. Consider $\phi_f = \mathcal{F}^n_{l_1,\ldots,l_n}(A_1,\ldots,A_{n+1})(S)$ where $S \subseteq \Sigma'$. Wlg, we assume:

- **[Assumption1]**: $\inf(l_1) \leq \inf(l_2) \leq \ldots \leq \inf(l_n)$ and $\sup(l_1) \leq \ldots \leq \sup(l_n)$. This is wlog, since the check for A_{j+1} cannot start before the check of A_j in case of $\mathcal{F}^n_{l_1,\ldots,l_n}$ modality (and vice-versa for $\mathcal{P}^n_{l_1,\ldots,l_n}$ modality) for any $1 \leq j \leq n$.

- **[Assumption 2]**: Intervals $l_1, \ldots l_{n-1}$ are bounded intervals. Interval l_n may or may not be bounded. This is also wlog[3].

Let $\rho = (a_1, \tau_1) \ldots (a_n, \tau_n) \in T\Sigma^*$, $i \in dom(\rho)$. Let $\rho' = \mathsf{ext}(\rho)$ be defined by $(b_1, \tau_1') \ldots (b_m, \tau_m')$ with $m \geq n$, and each τ_i' is a either a new integer times-tamp not among $\{\tau_1, \ldots, \tau_n\}$ or is some τ_j. Let i' be an old point in ρ' corresponding to i. Let $i_0' = i'$ and $i_{n+1}' = |\rho'|$. $\rho, i \models \phi_f$ iff $\mathsf{cond} \equiv \exists i' \leq$

$$i_1' \leq \ldots \leq i_{n+1}' \bigwedge_{g=1}^{n} (\tau_{i_g'}' - \tau_{i'}' \in I_g \wedge \rho', i_g' \models \bigvee \Sigma \wedge \mathsf{Seg}^+(\rho', i_{g-1}', i_g', S') \in L(A_g')) \wedge$$

$\mathsf{Seg}^+(\rho', i_n', i_{n+1}', S') \in L(A_{n+1}')$ where for any $1 \leq j \leq n+1$, A_j' is the automata built from A_j by adding self loop on $\neg \bigvee \Sigma$ (oversampling points) and $S' = S \cup \{\neg \bigvee \Sigma\}$. This self loop makes sure that A_j' ignores(or skips) all the over-sampling points while checking for A_j. Hence, A_j' allows arbitrary interleaving of oversampling points while checking for A_j. Hence, for any $g, h \in dom(\rho)$ with g', h' being old action points of ρ' corresponding to g, h, respectively, $\mathsf{Seg}^s(\rho, g, h, S) \in L(A_i)$ iff $\mathsf{Seg}^s(\rho', g', h', S \cup \{\neg \bigvee \Sigma\}) \in L(A_i')$ for $s \in \{+, -\}$. Note that the question, "$\rho, i \models \phi_f$?", is now reduced to checking cond on ρ'.

Checking the conditions for $\rho, i \models \phi_f$. Let $I_g = \langle l_g, u_g \rangle$ for any $1 \leq g \leq n$ (Here, $\langle \rangle$ denotes half-open, closed, or open). We discuss only the case where $\{I_1, \ldots, I_n\}$ are pairwise disjoint and $\inf(I_1) \neq 0$ in $\phi_f = \mathcal{F}^n_{l_1,\ldots,l_n}(A_1, \ldots, A_{n+1})(S)$. The case of overlapping intervals can be found in the full version. The disjoint interval assumption along with [Assumption 1] implies that for any $1 \leq g \leq n$, $u_{g-1} < l_g$. By construction of ρ', between i_{g-1}' and i_g', we have an oversampling point k_g. The point k_g is guaranteed to exist between i_{g-1}' and i_g', since these two points lie within two distinct non-overlapping, non-adjacent intervals l_{g-1} and l_g from i'. Hence their timestamps have different integral parts, and there is always a uniquely labelled oversampling point k_g with timestamp $\lceil \tau_{i_{g-1}'}' \rceil$ between i_{g-1}' and i_g' for all $1 \leq g \leq n$. Let for all $1 \leq g \leq n+1$, $A_g' = (Q_g, 2^S, init_g, F_g, \delta_g')$. Let the unique label for k_g be int_{j_g}. For any $1 \leq g \leq n$, we assert that the behaviour of propositions in S between points i_{g-1}' and i_g' (of ρ') should be accepted by A_g'. This is done by splitting the run at the oversampling point k_g(labelled as int_{j_g}) with timestamp $\tau_{k_g}' = \lceil \tau_{i_{g-1}'}' \rceil$, $i_{g-1}' < k_g < i_g'$.

(1) Concretely, checking for cond, for each $1 \leq g \leq n$, we start at i_{g-1}' in ρ', from the initial state $init_g$ of A_g, and move to the state (say q_g) that is reached at the closest oversampling point k_g. Note that we use only A_g (we disallow the $\neg \bigvee \Sigma$ self loops) to move to the closest oversampling point.

---

[3] Unbounded intervals can be eliminated using $\mathcal{F}^k_{l_1,l_2,\ldots,l_{k-2},[l_1,\infty)[l_2,\infty)}(A_1, \ldots, A_{k+1}) \equiv$ $\mathcal{F}^k_{l_1,l_2,\ldots,l_{k-2},[l_1,cmax)[l_2,\infty)}(A_1, \ldots, A_{k+1}) \vee \mathcal{F}^{k-1}_{l_1,l_2,\ldots,l_{k-2},[l_2,\infty)}(A_1, \ldots, A_{k-1}, A_k \cdot A_{k+1})$.

(2) Reaching q_g from $init_g$ we have read a behaviour between i'_{g-1} and k_g; this must to the full behaviour, and hence must also be accepted by A'_g (we use A'_g instead of A_g to ignore the oversampling points that could be encountered while checking the latter part). Towards this, we guess a point i'_g which is within interval I_g from i', such that, the automaton A'_g starts from state q_g reading int_{k_g} and reaches a final state in F_g at point i'_g. Then indeed, the behaviour of propositions from S between i'_{g-1} and i'_g respect A'_g, and also $\tau'_{i'_g} - \tau'_{i'} \in I_g$.

(1) amounts to $\mathsf{Seg}^+(\rho', i'_{g-1}, k_g, S) \in L(A_g[init_g, q_g]) \cdot int_{j_g}$. This is defined by the formula $\psi^+_{g-1, int_{j_g}, Q_g}$ which asserts $A_{g+1}[init_g, q_g] \cdot int_{j_g}$ from point i'_{g-1} to the next nearest oversampling point k_g where int_{j_g} holds.

(2) amounts to checking from point i, within interval I_g in its future, the existence of a point i'_g such that $\mathsf{Seg}^-(\rho', i'_g, k_g, S) \in L(\mathsf{Rev}(int_{j_g} \cdot A'_g[q_g, F_g]))$. This is defined by the formula $\varphi^-_{g, int_{j_g}, q_g}$ which asserts $\mathsf{Rev}(int_{j_g} \cdot A'_g[q_g, F_g])$, from point i'_g to an oversampling point k_q which is the earliest oversampling point s.t. $i'_{g-1} < k_g < i'_g$. For cond, we define the formula

$$\psi = \mathsf{F}_{[0,1)} int_{j_0} \wedge \bigvee_{g=1}^{n} [\psi^+_{g-1, int_{j_g}, q_g} \wedge \psi^-_{g, int_{j_g}, q_g}] \wedge \psi^+_n.$$

- For $1 \le g \le n$, $\psi^+_{g-1, int_{j_g}, q_g} = \mathsf{F}_{I_g}(\bigvee \Sigma \wedge \mathcal{F}(A_g[init_g, q_g] \cdot \{int_{j_g}\})(S \cup \{int_{j_g}\}))$,
- $\psi^+_n = \mathsf{F}_{I_n}(\bigvee \Sigma \wedge \mathcal{F}(A_{n+1} \cdot \{\mathsf{Last}\})(S \cup \{\mathsf{Last}\}))$, and
- For $1 \le g \le n$, $\psi^-_{g, int_{j_g}, q_g} = \mathsf{F}_{I_g}(\bigvee \Sigma \wedge \mathcal{P}(\mathsf{Rev}(int_{j_g} \cdot A_g[q_g, F_g]))(S \cup \{int_{j_g}\}))$.

Note that there is a unique point between i'_{g-1} and i'_g labelled int_{j_g}. This is because, $\tau'_{i'_g} - \tau'_{i'_{g-1}} < \tau'_{i'_g} - \tau'_{i'} \le \mathsf{cmax}$. Hence, we can ensure that the meeting point for the check (1) and (2) is indeed characterized by a unique label. Note that there is exactly one point labeled int_y from any point within future cmax or past cmax time units (by φ_{ovs}). This is the reason we used the counter modulo cmax to label the oversampling points. We encourage the readers to see the Fig. 3. The full EMITL formula ψ_f, is obtained by disjuncting over all n length sequences of states reachable at oversampling points k_g between i'_{g-1} and i'_g, and all possible values of the unique label $int_{j_g} \in \mathsf{Int}$ holding at point k_g.

4) Converting the EMITL to $\mathsf{EMITL}_{0,\infty}$: We use the reduction from EMITL to equivalent $\mathsf{EMITL}_{0,\infty}$ formula [16]. In ψ_f, only the F operators are timed with intervals of the form $\langle l, u \rangle$ where $l > 0$ and $u \ne \infty$, but the $\mathcal{F}_l$ and $\mathcal{P}_l$ modalities are untimed. We can reduce these time intervals into purely lower bound $(\langle l, \infty \rangle)$ or upper bound $(\langle 0, u \rangle)$ constraints using these oversampling points, preserving satisfiability, by reduction showed in [16] Chap. 5 lemma 5.5.2 Page 90–91.

The above 4 step construction shows that (i) the equisatisfiable $\mathsf{EMITL}_{0,\infty}$ formula ψ is of the size $(\mathcal{O}(|\phi|^{Poly(n)})$ where, n is the arity ϕ. (ii) For a non-adjacent 1-TPTL formula γ, applying the reduction in Sect. 5 yields ϕ of size $\mathcal{O}(2^{Poly|\gamma|})$ and, arity of $\phi = \mathcal{O}(|\gamma|^2)$. Also, after applying the reduction of Sect. 6 by plugging the value of $|\phi|$ from and its arity from (ii) in (i), we get the $\mathsf{EMITL}_{0,\infty}$ formula ψ of size $\mathcal{O}(2^{Poly(|\gamma|)*Poly(n)}) = \mathcal{O}(2^{Poly(|\gamma|)})$.

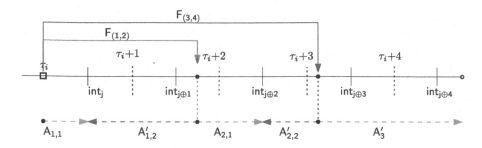

Fig. 3. Figure showing elimination of $\mathcal{F}^2$ modality from temporal definition of the form $\mathcal{G}^w(b \leftrightarrow \mathcal{F}^2_{(1,2),(3,4)}(A_1, A_2, A_3)(\Sigma')$. This is done by (i) checking for the first part of A_1, $A_{1,1}$, from present point to the next oversampling point at timestamp $\lceil \tau_i \rceil$, labelled, int_j, (ii) jumping to a non-deterministically chosen point within $(1, 2)$ and asserting the remaining part of A_1 skipping oversampling points, $A'_{1,2}$, in reverse till int_j, (iii) Following the steps similar to (i) and (ii) for checking A_2 but starting the check of first part of A_2 from the point chosen in (ii).

7   Conclusion

We generalized the notion of non-punctuality to non-adjacency in TPTL. We proved that satisfiabilty checking for non-adjacent 1-variable fragment of TPTL is EXPSPACE Complete. This gives us a strictly more expressive logic than MITL while retaining its satisfaction complexity. An interesting open problem is to compare the expressive power of non-adjacent 1-TPTL with that of MITL with Pnueli modalities (and hence Q2MLO) of [10]. We also leave open the satisfiabilty checking problem for non-adjacent TPTL with multiple variables.

References

1. Alur, R., Feder, T., Henzinger, T.: The benefits of relaxing punctuality. J. ACM **43**(1), 116–146 (1996)
2. Alur, R., Henzinger, T.A.: Real-time logics: complexity and expressiveness. Inf. Comput. **104**(1), 35–77 (1993)
3. Alur, R., Henzinger, T.A.: A really temporal logic. J. ACM **41**(1), 181–203 (1994)
4. Bouyer, P., Chevalier, F., Markey, N.: On the expressiveness of TPTL and MTL. In: Sarukkai, S., Sen, S. (eds.) FSTTCS 2005. LNCS, vol. 3821, pp. 432–443. Springer, Heidelberg (2005). https://doi.org/10.1007/11590156_35
5. Ferrère, T.: The compound interest in relaxing punctuality. In: Havelund, K., Peleska, J., Roscoe, B., de Vink, E. (eds.) FM 2018. LNCS, vol. 10951, pp. 147–164. Springer, Cham (2018). https://doi.org/10.1007/978-3-319-95582-7_9
6. Gastin, P., Oddoux, D.: LTL with past and two-way very-weak alternating automata. In: Rovan, B., Vojtáš, P. (eds.) MFCS 2003. LNCS, vol. 2747, pp. 439–448. Springer, Heidelberg (2003). https://doi.org/10.1007/978-3-540-45138-9_38
7. Haase, C., Ouaknine, J., Worrell, J.: On process-algebraic extensions of metric temporal logic. In: Roscoe, A.W., Jones, C.B., Wood, K.R. (eds.) Reflections on the Work of C.A.R. Hoare, pp. 283–300. Springer, London (2010). https://doi.org/10.1007/978-1-84882-912-1_13

8. Henzinger, T.A., Raskin, J.-F., Schobbens, P.-Y.: The regular real-time languages. In: Larsen, K.G., Skyum, S., Winskel, G. (eds.) ICALP 1998. LNCS, vol. 1443, pp. 580–591. Springer, Heidelberg (1998). https://doi.org/10.1007/BFb0055086
9. Hirshfeld, Y., Rabinovich, A.: An expressive temporal logic for real time. In: Královič, R., Urzyczyn, P. (eds.) MFCS 2006. LNCS, vol. 4162, pp. 492–504. Springer, Heidelberg (2006). https://doi.org/10.1007/11821069_43
10. Hirshfeld, Y., Rabinovich, A.: Expressiveness of metric modalities for continuous time. In: Grigoriev, D., Harrison, J., Hirsch, E.A. (eds.) CSR 2006. LNCS, vol. 3967, pp. 211–220. Springer, Heidelberg (2006). https://doi.org/10.1007/11753728_23
11. Ho, H.-M.: Revisiting timed logics with automata modalities. In: Ozay, N., Prabhakar, P. (eds.) Proceedings of the 22nd ACM International Conference on Hybrid Systems: Computation and Control, HSCC 2019, Montreal, QC, Canada, 16–18 April 2019, pp. 67–76. ACM (2019)
12. Madnani, K., Krishna, S.N., Pandya, P.K.: Partially punctual metric temporal logic is decidable. In: TIME, pp. 174–183 (2014)
13. Krishna, S.N., Madnani, K., Mazo Jr., M., Pandya, P.K.: Generalizing non-punctuality for timed temporal logic with freeze quantifiers. CoRR, abs/2105.09534 (2021)
14. Krishna, S.N., Madnani, K., Pandya, P.K.: Making metric temporal logic rational. In: Larsen, K.G., Bodlaender, H.L., Raskin, J.-F. (eds.) 42nd International Symposium on Mathematical Foundations of Computer Science, MFCS 2017, 21–25 August 2017 - Aalborg, Denmark. LIPIcs, vol. 83, pp. 77:1–77:14. Schloss Dagstuhl - Leibniz-Zentrum für Informatik (2017)
15. Krishna, S.N., Madnani, K., Pandya, P.K.: Logics meet 1-clock alternating timed automata. In: Schewe, S., Zhang, L. (eds.) 29th International Conference on Concurrency Theory, CONCUR 2018, 4–7 September 2018, Beijing, China. LIPIcs, vol. 118, pp. 39:1–39:17. Schloss Dagstuhl - Leibniz-Zentrum für Informatik (2018)
16. Madnani, K.N.: On decidable extensions of metric temporal logic. Ph.D. thesis, Indian Institute of Technology Bombay, Mumbai, India (2019)
17. Ouaknine, J., Worrell, J.: On the decidability of metric temporal logic. In: LICS, pp. 188–197 (2005)
18. Pandya, P.K., Shah, S.S.: On expressive powers of timed logics: comparing boundedness, non-punctuality, and deterministic freezing. In: Katoen, J.-P., König, B. (eds.) CONCUR 2011. LNCS, vol. 6901, pp. 60–75. Springer, Heidelberg (2011). https://doi.org/10.1007/978-3-642-23217-6_5
19. Prabhakar, P., D'Souza, D.: On the expressiveness of MTL with past operators. In: Asarin, E., Bouyer, P. (eds.) FORMATS 2006. LNCS, vol. 4202, pp. 322–336. Springer, Heidelberg (2006). https://doi.org/10.1007/11867340_23
20. Rabinovich, A.: Complexity of metric temporal logic with counting and pnueli modalities. In: FORMATS, pp. 93–108 (2008)
21. Rabinovich, A.: Complexity of metric temporal logics with counting and the pnueli modalities. Theor. Comput. Sci. **411**(22–24), 2331–2342 (2010)
22. Raskin, J.F.: Logics, automata and classical theories for deciding real time. Ph.D. thesis, Universite de Namur (1999)
23. Wilke, T.: Specifying timed state sequences in powerful decidable logics and timed automata. In: Formal Techniques in Real-Time and Fault-Tolerant Systems, Third International Symposium Organized Jointly with the Working Group Provably Correct Systems - ProCoS, Lübeck, Germany, 19–23 September, Proceedings, pp. 694–715 (1994)

Verified Quadratic Virtual Substitution for Real Arithmetic

Matias Scharager$^{(\boxtimes)}$, Katherine Cordwell , Stefan Mitsch ,
and André Platzer

Carnegie Mellon University, Pittsburgh, PA 15213, USA
{mscharag,kcordwel,smitsch,aplatzer}@cs.cmu.edu

Abstract. This paper presents a formally verified quantifier elimination
(QE) algorithm for first-order real arithmetic by linear and quadratic virtual substitution (VS) in Isabelle/HOL. The Tarski-Seidenberg theorem
established that the first-order logic of real arithmetic is decidable by QE.
However, in practice, QE algorithms are highly complicated and often
combine multiple methods for performance. VS is a practically successful
method for QE that targets formulas with low-degree polynomials. To
our knowledge, this is the first work to formalize VS for quadratic real
arithmetic including inequalities. The proofs necessitate various contributions to the existing multivariate polynomial libraries in Isabelle/HOL.
Our framework is modularized and easily expandable (to facilitate integrating future optimizations), and could serve as a basis for developing
practical general-purpose QE algorithms. Further, as our formalization
is designed with practicality in mind, we export our development to SML
and test the resulting code on 378 benchmarks from the literature, comparing to Redlog, Z3, Wolfram Engine, and SMT-RAT. This identified
inconsistencies in some tools, underscoring the significance of a verified
approach for the intricacies of real arithmetic.

Keywords: Virtual substitution · Quantifier elimination · Real-closed
fields · Theorem proving

1 Introduction

Quantifier elimination (QE) is the process of transforming quantified formulas
into logically equivalent quantifier-free formulas. In this paper, we consider QE
for the first-order logic of real arithmetic (FOL$_\mathbb{R}$), so quantifiers range over the
real numbers. The Tarski-Seidenberg theorem proves that QE is admissible for

This material is based upon work supported by the National Science Foundation under
Grant No. CNS-1739629, a National Science Foundation Graduate Research Fellowship under Grants Nos. DGE1252522 and DGE1745016, and by the AFOSR under
grant number FA9550-16-1-0288. Any opinions, findings, and conclusions or recommendations expressed in this material are those of the author(s) and do not necessarily
reflect the views of the National Science Foundation or of AFOSR.

© Springer Nature Switzerland AG 2021
M. Huisman et al. (Eds.): FM 2021, LNCS 13047, pp. 200–217, 2021.
https://doi.org/10.1007/978-3-030-90870-6_11

the theory of real-closed fields [25,29]. Real quantified statements arise in a number of application domains, including geometry, chemistry, life sciences, and the verification of cyber-physical systems (CPS) [27]. Many of the applications which require QE are safety-critical [18,19]; accordingly, it is crucial to have both efficient and formally verified support for QE to trust the resulting decisions.

Unfortunately, QE algorithms are quite intricate, which makes it difficult to formally verify their correctness. In practice, this necessitates the use of unverified tools. For example, the theorem prover KeYmaera X [8], which is designed to formally verify models of CPS (such as planes and surgical robots) uses Mathematica/Wolfram Engine and/or Z3 as blackbox solvers for QE. While these are admirable tools, they are unverified, and their use introduces a weak link [7] into what would otherwise be a (fully verified [1]) trustworthy proof.

To help fill this gap, we formally verify linear and quadratic *virtual substitution (VS)* due to Weispfenning [30,32], which focuses on QE for a quantified variable x occurring in polynomials $f(x)$ of at most degree 2 in x, although variations [12,31] handle higher degree polynomials. Linear and quadratic VS are of practical significance. They serve to improve QE [17] and SMT tools and are the basis of the experimentally successful [28] Redlog solver [6]. To our knowledge, ours is the first formally verified algorithm for VS with quadratic inequalities.

As we focus on correct and practical VS, we export our verified Isabelle/HOL code to SML for experimentation. We test our exported formalization of the equality VS algorithm (Sect. 3.2) and of the general VS algorithm (Sect. 3.3). We compare to four tools that implement real QE: Redlog, SMT-RAT [5], Z3 [14], and Wolfram Engine. With 304 examples, we solve more examples than SMT-RAT in quantifier elimination mode (solves 191) and come close to virtual substitution in Wolfram Engine (solves 322). The remaining tools solve almost all examples; this is to be expected given that those tools have been optimized and fine-tuned (some for decades) and use efficient general-purpose fallback QE algorithms when VS does not succeed. However, as we found 137 inconsistencies in other solvers, it is significant that ours is the only VS implementation with associated correctness proofs (assuming the orthogonal challenge of correct code generation from Isabelle [10]).

Our formalization is approximately 23,000 lines in Isabelle/HOL and is available on the Archive of Formal Proofs (AFP) [22].

2   Related Work

The fastest known QE algorithm is Cylindrical Algebraic Decomposition (CAD)[4], which has not yet been fully formally verified. There are few general-purpose formally verified QE algorithms, and there appears to exist a tradeoff between the practicality of an algorithm and the ease of formalization. Mahboubi and Cohen verified Tarski's original QE algorithm [3] and McLaughlin and Harrison have a proof-producing QE procedure based on Cohen-Hörmander [13]; unfortunately, Tarski's algorithm and Cohen-Hörmander both have non-elementary complexity, which limits the computational feasibility of these formalizations.

There has already been some work on formally verified VS: Nipkow [16] formally verified a VS procedure for *linear* equations and inequalities. The building blocks of $FOL_\mathbb{R}$ formulas, or "atoms", in Nipkow's work only allow for linear polynomials $\sum_i a_i x_i \sim c$, where $\sim \in \{=, <\}$, the x_i's are quantified variables and c and the a_i's are real numbers. These restrictions ensure that linear QE can always be performed, and they also simplify the substitution procedure and associated proofs. Nipkow additionally provides a generic framework that can be applied to several different kinds of atoms (each new atom requires implementing several new code theorems in order to create an exportable algorithm). While this is an excellent theoretical framework—we utilize several similar constructs in our formulation—we create an independent formalization that is specific to general $FOL_\mathbb{R}$ formulas, as our main focus is to provide an efficient algorithm in this domain. Specializing to one type of atom allows us to implement several optimizations, such as our modified DNF algorithm, which would be unwieldy to develop in a generic setting.

Chaieb [2] extends Nipkow's work to quadratic equalities. His formalizations are not publicly available, but he generously provided us with the code. While this was helpful for reference, we chose to build on a newer Isabelle/HOL polynomial library, and we focus on VS as an exportable standalone procedure, whereas Chaieb intrinsically links VS with an auxiliary QE procedure.

Other related work includes some unverified solvers. For example, some work has been done in constraint solving with falsification: RSolver [21] was designed for hybrid systems verification and can find concrete counterexamples for fully quantified existential QE problems on *compact* domains. dReal [9] is based on similar ideas and slightly relaxes the notion of satisfiability to δ-satisfiability. Constraint solving has also been considered in SMT-solving with Z3's nlsat [11], which uses CDCL to decide systems of nonlinear inequalities and equations.

3   The Virtual Substitution Algorithm

Informally (and broadly) speaking, VS discretizes the QE problem by solving for the roots of one or more low-degree polynomials $f_1(x), \ldots, f_n(x)$. VS focuses on these roots and the intervals around them to identify and substitute appropriate representative "sample points" for x into the rest of the formula. However, these sample points may contain fractions, square roots, and/or other extensions of the logical language, and so they must be substituted "virtually": That is, VS creates a formula *in* $FOL_\mathbb{R}$ *proper* that models the behavior of the direct substitution, which would be outside of $FOL_\mathbb{R}$. VS applies in two cases: an equality case and a general case. We formalize both, and discuss each in turn.

Remark 1. The VS algorithms need to work for *multivariate* polynomials. But as the VS correctness proofs show the equivalence is true for every real value of the free variables, they often implicitly treat all but one variable as having fixed (but arbitrary) real values. That is why most correctness lemmas (but not the top-level algorithmic constructions) suffice for *univariate* polynomials with *real coefficients*. We utilize this trick to simplify difficult proofs for general VS.

3.1 Example

Example 1. Say that we want to perform QE on the formula $\exists x.(x^2 = 2 \wedge xy^2 + 2y + 1 = 0)$. One might notice that $x^2 = 2$ forces $x = \pm\sqrt{2}$ and accordingly wish to substitute. Direct substitution yields the following expression: $(\sqrt{2}y^2 + 2y + 1 = 0 \vee -\sqrt{2}y^2 + 2y + 1 = 0)$. However, as its mention of the $\sqrt{\cdot}$ operator makes it an illegal $\text{FOL}_\mathbb{R}$ formula, we will need some further tricks.

Cleverly, VS finds that $\sqrt{2}y^2 + 2y + 1 = 0$ is logically equivalent to $y^2 \cdot (2y+1) \leq 0 \wedge 2y^4 - (2y+1)^2 = 0$, which is a $\text{FOL}_\mathbb{R}$ formula[1]. Similarly, VS identifies a $\text{FOL}_\mathbb{R}$ formula that is logically equivalent to $-\sqrt{2}y^2 + 2y + 1 = 0$. Then, VS returns the following quantifier-free $\text{FOL}_\mathbb{R}$ formula which is logically equivalent to $\exists x.(x^2 = 2 \wedge xy^2 + 2y + 1 = 0)$:

$$((y^2 \cdot (2y+1) \leq 0 \wedge 2y^4 - (2y+1)^2 = 0)$$
$$\vee\, (-y^2 \cdot (2y+1) \leq 0 \wedge 2y^4 - (2y+1)^2 = 0)).$$

Remark 2. If instead our starting formula were $\exists x.\exists y.(x^2 = 2 \wedge xy^2 + 2y + 1 = 0)$, where now y is quantified, then (following the same method as above) VS would identify the following logically equivalent $\text{FOL}_\mathbb{R}$ formula with fewer variables:

$$\exists y.((y^2 \cdot (2y+1) \leq 0 \wedge 2y^4 - (2y+1)^2 = 0)$$
$$\vee\, (-y^2 \cdot (2y+1) \leq 0 \wedge 2y^4 - (2y+1)^2 = 0)). \tag{1}$$

Unfortunately, here we are left with a quantified formula with no linear or quadratic equations or inequalities. As we are thus outside of the fragment of $\text{FOL}_\mathbb{R}$ that standard VS applies to, at this point we would want to outsource (1) to a general-purpose QE algorithm (like CAD) to eliminate the quantifier on y.

Example 1 was relatively simple, because it involved a quadratic equation with constant coefficients for x. However, nothing in our reasoning was limited to constant coefficients: To perform QE on $\exists x.(x^2 = c \wedge xy^2 + 2y + 1 = 0)$, where c is a polynomial in the variable z, we could handle substituting $x = \pm\sqrt{c}$ in the exact same way as for $x = \pm\sqrt{2}$, but the answer must distinguish the case of $c \geq 0$ symbolically. More difficult is the generalization to inequalities, which seemingly require uncountably infinitely many values to be virtually substituted. We first turn to the general equality case, and then discuss inequalities.

3.2 Equality Virtual Substitution Algorithm

Let a, b and c be arbitrary polynomials with real coefficients that do not mention the variable x. Consider the formula $\exists x.(ax^2 + bx + c = 0 \wedge F)$. There are three possible cases: Either $a \neq 0$, or $a = 0$ and b is nonzero, or all of a, b, c are zero

---

[1] Notice that if $y = 0$, then both $\sqrt{2}y^2 + 2y + 1 = 0$ and $y^2 \cdot (2y+1) \leq 0 \wedge 2y^4 - (2y+1)^2 = 0$ are false. If instead $y \neq 0$, then $\sqrt{2}y^2 + 2y + 1 = 0$ is true exactly when $\sqrt{2} = -(2y+1)/y^2$, or exactly when $-(2y+1)/y^2 \geq 0 \wedge 2y^4 - (2y+1)^2 = 0$, which is logically equivalent to $y^2 \cdot (2y+1) \leq 0 \wedge 2y^4 - (2y+1)^2 = 0$, as desired.

(so $ax^2 + bx + c = 0$ is uninformative). Letting F_x^r denote the substitution of $x = r$ for x in F, and solving for the roots of $ax^2 + bx + c$, we have the following:

$$\exists x.(ax^2 + bx + c = 0 \wedge F) \longleftrightarrow$$
$$\Big((a = 0 \wedge b = 0 \wedge c = 0 \wedge \exists x.F) \vee$$
$$(a = 0 \wedge b \neq 0 \wedge F_x^{-c/b}) \vee$$
$$(a \neq 0 \wedge b^2 - -4ac \geq 0 \wedge (F_x^{(-b+\sqrt{b^2--4ac})/(2a)} \vee F_x^{(-b-\sqrt{b^2--4ac})/(2a)}))\Big).$$

Conditions such as $b^2 - 4ac \geq 0$ are needed to ensure $(-b \pm \sqrt{b^2 - 4ac})/(2a)$ are well-defined; these are symbolic formulas unless a, b, c are concrete numbers.

Similarly as in Example 1, if we were to substitute $F_x^{-c/b}$, $F_x^{(-b+\sqrt{b^2-4ac})/(2a)}$, and $F_x^{(-b-\sqrt{b^2-4ac})/(2a)}$ directly (for polynomials a, b, and c that do not involve x), the resulting formula would no longer be in FOL$_\mathbb{R}$. Instead, VS avoids directly dividing polynomials or taking square roots with equivalent rewritings in FOL$_\mathbb{R}$. This involves two procedures: one for fractions, and one for square roots.

To virtually substitute a fraction p/q of polynomials where $q \neq 0$ into the atom $\sum_{i=0}^n a_i x^i \sim 0$, where $\sim \in \{=, <, \leq, \neq\}$ and each a_i is an arbitrary polynomial expression not involving x, it suffices to normalize the denominator of the LHS, with the caveat that we must not flip the direction of the inequality for $<$ and $\leq$ atoms by normalizing by a value that might be negative. When n is even, $q^n \geq 0$ under any possible valuation, so normalizing by q^n does not flip the inequality. Alternatively, if n is odd, $q^{n+1} \geq 0$. We formalize this in our `linear_substitution` function (see [23, Appendix A.1]).

Next, we consider substituting $x = \sqrt{c}$ into an atom $\sum_{i=0}^n a_i x^i \sim 0$, where c is an arbitrary polynomial expression not involving x that satisfies $c \geq 0$, each a_i is an arbitrary polynomial expression not involving x, and $\sim \in \{=, <, \leq, \neq\}$. Its direct substitution can be separated out into even and odd exponents:

$$\sum_{i=0}^n a_i \cdot (\sqrt{c})^i = \sum_{i=0}^{n/2} a_{2i} c^i + \sum_{i=0}^{n/2} a_{2i+1} c^i \sqrt{c}$$

Now our polynomial has the form $A + B\sqrt{c}$, where A and B and c are symbolic polynomial expressions not involving x. Then, we have the following cases:

$$A + B\sqrt{c} = 0 \longleftrightarrow AB \leq 0 \wedge A^2 - B^2 c = 0$$
$$A + B\sqrt{c} < 0 \longleftrightarrow (A < 0 \wedge B^2 c - A^2 < 0) \vee (B \leq 0 \wedge (A < 0 \vee A^2 - B^2 c < 0))$$
$$A + B\sqrt{c} \leq 0 \longleftrightarrow (A \leq 0 \wedge B^2 c - A^2 \leq 0) \vee (B \leq 0 \wedge A^2 - B^2 c \leq 0)$$
$$A + B\sqrt{c} \neq 0 \longleftrightarrow -AB < 0 \vee A^2 - B^2 c \neq 0$$

The equivalences for $=$ and $\neq$ atoms are derived from the observation that if $B \neq 0$, $A + B\sqrt{c} = 0$ can be solved to find $\sqrt{c} = -A/B$, which holds iff $A^2 = B^2 c$ and $-A/B \geq 0$. The inequality cases involve casework to determine when polynomial A is negative and dominates $B\sqrt{c}$ as $A^2 > B^2c$, and when B is negative and $B\sqrt{c}$ dominates A as $B^2c > A$. We formalize the VS procedure for quadratic roots in `quadratic_sub` (see [23, Appendix A.2]).

3.3 General Virtual Substitution Algorithm

As we have seen, QE very naturally leads to finitely many cases (discretizes) for formulas that involve quadratic equality atoms (we call this the *equality case*). The VS algorithm for the *general case*, which also handles inequality atoms, is more involved, because, unlike equalities, inequalities may have uncountably many solutions. General VS only directly applies to a very specific fragment of $FOL_{\mathbb{R}}$ formulas: conjunctions of polynomials that are at most quadratic in the variable of interest. However, we can extend general VS to apply to more formulas with the help of a disjunctive normal form (DNF) transformation.

As a simple example, consider the formula $\exists x.(p < 0 \land q < 0)$, where p and q are the univariate quadratic polynomials (in variable x) depicted in Fig. 1. Noting that the roots of p and q cannot possibly satisfy the strict inequalities, we partition the number line into ranges in between these zeros.

We recognize a key property: In each of the ranges between the roots of p, q, the signs of both p and q do not change. Since the ranges cover all roots of p, q, the truth value of the formula at a single point in a range is representative of the truth value of the formula on the entire range. To discretize the QE problem, we need only pick one sample point for each range.

Fig. 1. Two quadratics, their roots (black dots) and off-roots (red x's) (Color figure online)

However, we want to pick appropriate sample points *for any* possible p and q. The points we pick as representatives are called the off-roots, which occur ϵ units away from the roots, where $\epsilon > 0$ is arbitrarily small. We additionally need a representative for the leftmost range, which we represent with the point $-\infty$, where $-\infty$ is arbitrarily negative. Of course, we cannot directly substitute ϵ and $-\infty$: they are not real numbers! However, we can *virtually* substitute them.

Negative Infinity. Given any formula F, the VS of $-\infty$ should satisfy the equivalence $F_x^{-\infty} \longleftrightarrow \exists y. \forall x{<}y. F(x)$ (where y does not occur in F). Intuitively, this says that $-\infty$ acts as if it is arbitrarily negative (so less than the x component of all roots of the polynomials in F) and captures information for the leftmost range on the real number line in any valuation of the non-x variables.

If formula $\exists y. \forall x{<}y. ax^2 + bx + c = 0$ is true, where a, b, c are polynomials that do not involve x, then $ax^2 + bx + c = 0$ holds at infinitely many x; since nonzero polynomials have finitely many roots, this can only happen if ax^2+bx+c is the zero polynomial in x, i.e., it holds that:

$$(ax^2 + bx + c = 0)_x^{-\infty} \longleftrightarrow a = 0 \land b = 0 \land c = 0 \tag{2}$$

The negation of (2) captures the behavior of $\neq$ atoms. For $<$ atoms, note that the sign value at $-\infty$ is dominated by the leading coefficient, so:

$$(ax^2 + bx + c < 0)_x^{-\infty} \longleftrightarrow a < 0 \lor (a = 0 \land (b > 0 \lor (b = 0 \land c < 0)))$$

Finally, $(ax^2 + bx + c \leq 0)_x^{-\infty} \longleftrightarrow (ax^2 + bx + c = 0)_x^{-\infty} \lor (ax^2 + bx + c < 0)_x^{-\infty}$.

In Isabelle/HOL, we formalize that our virtual substitution of $-\infty$ satisfies the desired equivalence (on $\mathbb{R}$ using Remark 1) in the following lemma:

lemma `infinity_evalUni:` **shows** `"(∃y. ∀x<y. aEvalUni At x) =`
`(evalUni (substNegInfinityUni At) x)"`

To explain this lemma, we need to take a slight detour and discuss a few structural details of our framework (which is discussed in greater detail in Sect. 4). The datatype `atomUni` contains a triple of real numbers (which represent the coefficients of a univariate quadratic polynomial) and a sign condition:

datatype `atomUni = LessUni "real*real*real" | EqUni "real*real*real"`
`| LeqUni "real*real*real" | NeqUni "real*real*real"`

The `aEvalUni` function has type `atomUni ⇒ real ⇒ bool`; that is, it takes a sign condition with a triple of real numbers (a, b, c) and a real number x and evaluates whether $ax^2 + bx + c$ satisfies the sign condition. The `evalUni` function has type `atomUni fmUni ⇒ real ⇒ bool`, where an `atomUni fmUni` is a formula that involves conjunctions and disjunctions of elements of type `atomUni` (and "True" and "False"). That is, the `evalUni` function takes such a formula and a real number and evaluates whether the formula is true at the real number. Thus, `infinity_evalUni` states that, given `At` of type `atomUni`, with tuple (a, b, c) and sign condition $\sim \in \{<, =, \leq, \neq\}$, $At_x^{-\infty}$ holds iff $\exists y. \forall x < y. ax^2 + bx + c \sim 0$. This captures the desired equivalence.

Infinitesimals. Given arbitrary r (not containing x), VS for $r + \epsilon$ for variable x should capture the equivalence $F_x^{r+\epsilon} \longleftrightarrow \exists y > r. \forall x \in (r, y]. F(x)$, where F does not contain y. Intuitively, this says that (in any valuation of the non-x variables) $r + \epsilon$ captures information for the interval between r and the next greatest x-root.

For $=$ and $\neq$ atoms, we proceed in the same manner as we did with $-\infty$, as $(r, y]$ contains infinitely many points and only the zero polynomial has infinitely many solutions. As before, $\leq$ atoms turn into disjunctions of the inequality and equality representations at $r + \epsilon$. We are left only to consider $<$ atoms.

Consider $(p < 0)_x^{r+\epsilon}$ where $p = ax^2 + bx + c$ with polynomials a, b, c not containing x, and an arbitrary r not containing x. Notice that if $(p < 0)_x^r$, then because polynomials are continuous, we can choose a small enough y so that $\forall x \in (r, y]. p < 0$. If instead $(p = 0)_x^r$, then consider the partial derivative of p evaluated at r. If $\frac{\partial p}{\partial x}(r)$ is negative, then $\exists y > r. \forall x \in (r, y]. p < 0$ holds, because p is decreasing in x locally after $x = r$. If $\frac{\partial p}{\partial x}(r)$ is positive, then $\exists y > r. \forall x \in (r, y]. p < 0$

does not hold, because p is increasing in x after $x=r$. If $\frac{\partial p}{\partial x}(r)$ is zero, then to ascertain whether $\exists y > r. \forall x \in (r, y]. \ p < 0$, we will need to check higher derivatives.

This pattern forms the following recurrence, with the base case $(p < 0)_x^{r+\epsilon} = (p < 0)_x^r$ for polynomials p of degree zero:

$$(p < 0)_x^{r+\epsilon} \stackrel{\text{def}}{=} (p < 0)_x^r \vee \left((p = 0)_x^r \wedge ((\partial p / \partial x) < 0)_x^{r+\epsilon} \right)$$

We use the VS algorithm from Sect. 3.2 to characterize $(p < 0)_x^r$ and $(p = 0)_x^r$.

In Isabelle/HOL, we show that given a quadratic root r, the virtual substitution of $r + \epsilon$ satisfies the desired equivalence in the following theorem (on $\mathbb{R}$ using Remark 1; we have an analogous lemma for linear roots r):

lemma `infinitesimal_quad`:
  fixes *A B C D*:: `"real"`
  assumes `"D`$\neq$`0"`
  assumes `"C`$\geq$`0"`
  shows `"(`$\exists$`y::real>((A+B * sqrt(C))/(D)).`
    $\forall$`x::real` $\in$`{((A+B * sqrt(C))/(D))<..y}. aEvalUni At x)`
    `= (evalUni (substInfinitesimalQuadraticUni A B C D At) x)"`

Note that `{r<..y}` in Isabelle stands for the range $(r, y]$. This says that, given `At` of type `atomUni`, with tuple (a, b, c) and sign condition $\sim \in \{<, =, \leq, \neq\}$, `At`$_x^{r+\epsilon}$ holds iff $\exists y > r. \forall x \in (r, y]. ax^2 + bx + c \sim 0$, which is the desired equivalence.

The General VS Theorem. Now that we have explained virtually substituting $-\infty$ and infinitesimals, we are ready to state the general VS theorem.

Let F be a formula of the following shape, where each a_i, b_i, c_i, and d_i is a polynomial that is at most quadratic in variable x:

$$F = \left(\bigwedge a_i = 0 \right) \wedge \left(\bigwedge b_i < 0 \right) \wedge \left(\bigwedge c_i \leq 0 \right) \wedge \left(\bigwedge d_i \neq 0 \right).$$

Let $R(p)$ denote the set of symbolic expressions of the form $(g_1 + g_2 \sqrt{g_3})/g_4$ that, as in Sect. 3.2, are roots of the polynomial p in x, where the g_i's are polynomials not involving x. For the zero polynomial, let $R(0) = \emptyset$. Note that, as in Sect. 3.2, the g_i's come with certain well-definedness checks that we retain implicitly in the construction (for example, $g_4 \neq 0$ and $g_3 \geq 0$). We now define:

$$A = \bigcup R(a_i) \quad B = \bigcup R(b_i) \quad C = \bigcup R(c_i) \quad D = \bigcup R(d_i)$$

Then we obtain the following QE equivalence, where for simplicity we elide the relevant crucial well-definedness checks (cross-reference [19, Theorem 21.1]):

$$(\exists x.F) \longleftrightarrow F_x^{-\infty} \vee \bigvee_{r \in A \cup C} F_x^r \vee \bigvee_{r \in B \cup C \cup D} F_x^{r+\epsilon} \tag{3}$$

Intuitively, this formula states that if there is a particular x that satisfies F, then it must be the case that x is one of the equality roots from $A \cup C$, or that

x falls in one of the particular ranges (including $-\infty$ as a range) obtained by partitioning the number line by the roots in $B \cup C \cup D$.

Equation (3) can be optimized further by eliding C from the off-roots:

$$(\exists x.F) \longleftrightarrow F^{-\infty} \vee \bigvee_{r \in A \cup C} F_x^r \vee \bigvee_{r \in B \cup D} F_x^{r+\epsilon}. \tag{4}$$

Intuitively, this optimization holds because polynomials are continuous. More precisely, if F has the shape $F = (p \leq 0 \wedge G)$, and if r is an x-root of p, then r already satisfies $p \leq 0$ in any valuation of the non-x variables, so including $r + \epsilon$ as a sample point on account of $p \leq 0$ is redundant. It is possible that G contains some atom $q < 0$ or $q \neq 0$ where r is an x-root of q. In this case, $r + \epsilon$ will already be a sample point on account of q, and we do not need to add it in on account of p. Alternatively, if G does not contain such a q, then, in any valuation of the non-x variables, it is impossible for G to be satisfied by $r + \epsilon$ and not r, meaning that it is redundant to include $r + \epsilon$ as a sample point on account of G.

The general QE theorem is proved in Isabelle/HOL as the following, using Remark 1 to restrict to the univariate case and avoid well-definedness formulas:

```
theorem general_qe:
  defines "R ≡ {(=), (<), (≤), (≠)}"
  assumes "∀ rel∈R. finite (Atoms rel)"
  defines "F ≡ (λx. ∀rel∈R. ∀ (a,b,c)∈(Atoms rel). rel (a*x²+b*x+c) 0)"
  defines "Fε ≡ (λr. ∀rel∈R. ∀ (a,b,c)∈(Atoms rel). ∃y>r. ∀x∈{r<..y}.
    rel (a*x²+b*x+c) 0)"
  defines "F_inf ≡ (∀ rel∈R. ∀ (a,b,c)∈(Atoms rel). ∃x. ∀y<x.
    rel (a*y²+b*y+c) 0)"
  defines "roots ≡ (λ(a,b,c).
    if a=0 ∧ b≠0 then {-c/b} else
    if a≠0 ∧ b²-4*a*c≥0 then {(-b+sqrt(b²-4*a*c))/(2*a)}
      ∪ {(-b-sqrt(b²-4*a*c))/(2*a)} else {})"
  shows "(∃x. F(x)) = (F_inf ∨
              (∃r∈∪(roots ' (Atoms (=) ∪ Atoms (≤)))). F r) ∨
              (∃r∈∪(roots ' (Atoms (<) ∪ Atoms (≠)))). Fε r))"
```

Here, ' is the Isabelle/HOL syntax for mapping a function over a set. This theorem says that if a finite-length formula F is of the requisite shape, then there exists an x satisfying F iff F is satisfied at $-\infty$ (captured by F_{inf}), or there is a root r of one of the $=$ or $\leq$ atoms where F r holds, or if there is a root r of one of the $<$ or $\neq$ atoms where F_ε r holds. The proof is quite lengthy and involves a significant amount of casework; however, because we are working with univariate polynomials thanks to Remark 1, this casework mostly reduces to arithmetic computations and basic real analysis for univariate polynomials, and some of what we need, such as properties of discriminants and continuity properties of polynomials, is already formalized in Isabelle/HOL's standard library.

3.4   Top Level Algorithms

We develop several top-level algorithms that perform these VS procedures on multivariate polynomials; these are described in more detail in [23, Appendix B]. Crucially, each features its own proof of correctness. For example, for the *VSEquality* algorithm, which performs equality VS repeatedly, we have:

theorem *VSEquality_eval:* "$\forall$ *xs. eval (VSEquality φ) xs = eval φ xs*"

Here, the *eval* function expresses the truth value of the (multivariate) input formula given a valuation *xs*, represented as a list of real numbers. Since we quantify over all possible valuations and express that they are the same before and after running the algorithm, we prove the soundness of *VSEquality*. The correctness of this theorem only relies on Isabelle/HOL's trusted core.

As our algorithms are general enough to handle formulas with high degree polynomials where VS does not apply, we cannot assert that the result is quantifier free (it might not be). To demonstrate the practical usefulness of these algorithms, we export our code to SML and experimentally show that these algorithms solve many benchmarks. The code exports rely on the correctness of Isabelle/HOL's code export, which ongoing work is attempting to establish [10].

4   Framework

We turn to a discussion of our framework, which is designed with two key goals in mind: First, perform VS as many times as possible on any given formula. Second, reduce unwieldy multivariate proofs to more manageable univariate ones.

4.1   Representation of Formulas

We define our type for formulas in the canonical datatype *fm*:

datatype *(atoms: 'a) fm = TrueF | FalseF | Atom 'a*
  | And "'a fm" "'a fm" | Or "'a fm" "'a fm" | Neg "'a fm"
  | ExQ "'a fm" | AllQ "'a fm" | ExN "nat" "'a fm" | AllN "nat" "'a fm"

As in Nipkow's previous work [16], we use De Bruijn indices to express the variables: That is, the 0th variable represents the innermost quantifier, and variables greater than the number of quantifiers represent the free variables.

We have two constructors for each type of quantifier: *ExQ F* (resp. *AllQ F*) indicates a single existential (universal) quantifier, and *ExN n F* (resp. *AllN n F*) represents a *block* of *n* existential (universal) quantifiers. These representations are interchangeable and converted back and forth in our algorithm; we include the block representation for variable ordering heuristics (see [23, Appendix C.3]).

We utilize the multivariate polynomial library [26] to define our atoms:

datatype *atom = Less "real mpoly" | Eq "real mpoly" | Leq "real mpoly"*
  | Neq "real mpoly"

Each atom is normalized without loss of generality, so that the atom `Less p` means $p < 0$, `Eq p` means $p = 0$, and so on.

For example, the $\text{FOL}_{\mathbb{R}}$ formula $\forall x.((\exists y.xa = y^2 b) \wedge \neg(\forall y.5x^2 \leq y))$ is represented in our framework as follows, where `Const n` represents the constant $n \in \mathbb{R}$, and `Var i` represents the ith variable:

```
AllQ (And (ExQ (Atom (Eq (Var 1 * Var 2 - (Var 0)^2 * Var 3))))
          (Neg (AllQ (Atom (Leq (Const 5 * (Var 1)^2 - Var 0)))))).
```

Note that we could restrict ourselves to the $\top, \neg, \vee, \exists$ connectives and normalize $\leq$ and $\neq$ atoms to combinations of $<$ and $=$ atoms, and we could still express all of $\text{FOL}_{\mathbb{R}}$. We avoid this for two reasons: because it would linearly increase the size of the formula, and because we want to handle $\leq$ atoms in the optimized way discussed in Sect. 3.3 (see (4)). We do, however, allow for the normalization of $p = q$ into $p - q = 0$. This does not affect the size of the formula, and can afford simplifications: For example, $x^3 + x^2 + x + 1 = x^3$ becomes $x^2 + x + 1 = 0$.

4.2   Modified Disjunctive Normal Form

Nipkow's prior work [16] avoided incurring cases where linear VS does not apply by constraining atoms to be linear. In order to develop a general-purpose VS method which can be used, e.g., as a preprocessing method for CAD, we must reason about cases where VS fails to perform QE for a specific quantifier, and still continue the execution of the algorithm to the remaining quantifiers to simplify the formula as much as possible. To help with this, we implement a modified disjunctive normal form (DNF) that allows expressions to involve quantifiers.

Contextual Awareness. Let us analyze how to increase the informational content in a formula with respect to a quantified variable of interest.

Say we wish to perform VS to eliminate variable x in the formula $\exists x.F$, where F is not necessarily quantifier free. In linear time, we remove all negations from the formula by converting it into negation normal form. We can then normalize $\exists x.F$ into the following form, where the $A_{n,i}$'s are (quantifier-free) atoms:

$$\exists x. \bigvee_n \left(\bigwedge_i A_{n,i} \wedge \bigwedge_j (\forall y.F_{n,j}) \wedge \bigwedge_k (\exists z.F_{n,k}) \right).$$

This normalization procedure is similar to standard DNF, as it handles quantified formulas as if they were atomic formulas. We can distribute the existential quantifier across the disjuncts, which results in the equivalent formula:

$$\bigvee_n \exists x. \left(\bigwedge_i A_{n,i} \wedge \bigwedge_j (\forall y.F_{n,j}) \wedge \bigwedge_k (\exists z.F_{n,k}) \right). \tag{5}$$

Now we run the VS algorithm, i.e. the input to VS is a conjunction of atomic formulas and quantified formulas in the shape of (5). Notice that if equality

VS applies to atom $A_{n,i}$, then the relevant roots can be substituted into the quantified formulas $F_{n,j}$ and $F_{n,k}$, but roots from $F_{n,j}$ or $F_{n,k}$ cannot be substituted into $A_{n,i}$ since they feature quantified variables which are undefined in the broader context. So, our informational content is greatest when the number of $A_{n,i}$ atoms is maximized and the sizes of the $F_{n,j}$ and $F_{n,k}$ are minimized.

Innermost Quantifier Elimination. The innermost quantifier has an associated formula which is entirely quantifier free (and thus has no $F_{n,j}$ and $F_{n,k}$). As such, we opt to perform VS recursively, starting with the innermost quantifier and moving outwards, hoping that VS is successful and the quantifier-free property is maintained. This is not always optimal. Consider the following formula:

$$\exists x.(x = 0 \land \exists y. \; xy^3 + y = 0).$$

If we attempt to perform quadratic VS on the innermost y quantifier, it is cubic and will fail. However, performing VS on the x quantifier first fixes $x = 0$, which converts the cubic $xy^3 + y = 0$ equality into the linear $y = 0$. So, an (unoptimized) run of inside-out VS would produce $\exists y.y = 0$, and we could completely resolve the QE query by running VS again.

Reaching Under Quantifiers. We would like to recover usable information from the $F_{n,k}$ formulas to increase the informational content going into our QE algorithm. It would be ideal if we could "reach underneath" the existential binders and "pull out" the atoms from the formulas. We can achieve this through a series of transformations. Let k range from 0 to K_n. If we pull out each existential quantifier one by one, we get the following formula, which is equivalent to formula (5):

$$\bigvee_n \exists z_0. \cdots \exists z_{K_n}.\exists x.\left(\bigwedge_i A_{n,i} \land \bigwedge_j (\forall y.F_{n,j}) \land \bigwedge_k F_{n,k} \right)$$

This works because the rest of the conjuncts do not mention the quantified variable z_k and adjacent existential quantifiers can be swapped freely (without changing the logical meaning of the formula).

We can then recursively unravel the formulas $F_{n,k}$, moving as many existential quantifiers as possible to the front. Our implementation does this via a bottom-up procedure, starting underneath the innermost existential quantifier and building upwards, normalizing the formula into the form:

$$\bigvee_n \exists z_0. \cdots \exists z_{K_n}.\exists x.\left(\bigwedge_i A_{n,i} \land \bigwedge_j \forall y.F_{n,j} \right)$$

On paper, these transformations are simple as they involve named quantified variables; however, because our implementation uses a locally nameless form for quantifiers with DeBruijn indices, shifting an existential quantifier requires a "lifting" procedure $A{\uparrow}$ which increments all the variable indices in A by one. This allows for the following conversion: $A \land \exists z.F \longleftrightarrow \exists z.((A{\uparrow}) \land F)$.

4.3 Logical Evaluation

Our proofs show that the input formula and the output formula (after VS) are *logically equivalent*, i.e., have the same truth value under any valuation. This needs a method of "plugging in" the real-valued valuation into the variables of the polynomials. Towards this, we define the `eval` function, which accumulates new values into the valuation as we go underneath quantifiers, and the `aEval` function, which homomorphically evaluates a polynomial at a valuation.

When proving correctness, we focus our attention on one quantifier at a time. By Remark 1, correctness of general VS follows when considering a formula F with a single quantifier, where F contains only polynomials of at most degree two (otherwise general VS does not apply). With these restrictions, we can substitute a valuation into the non-quantified variables, transforming multivariate polynomials into univariate polynomials. For example, let a, b, and c be arbitrary multivariate polynomials that do not mention variable x. Let $\hat{p} = \gamma(p)$ denote the evaluation of polynomial p at valuation γ ($\hat{p}$ is a real number). We obtain the following conversion between multivariate and univariate polynomials:

$$\mathbf{eval}\ (ax^2 + bx + c = 0)\ \gamma \longleftrightarrow \mathbf{evalUni}\ (\hat{a}x^2 + \hat{b}x + \hat{c} = 0)\ \hat{x}$$

As such, we develop an alternative VS algorithm for univariate polynomials, where atoms are represented as triples of real-valued coefficients (as seen in Sect. 3.3), and show that under this specific valuation, the multivariate output is equivalent per valuation with the output of the univariate case. Thus, we finish the proof of the multivariate case by lifting the proof for the univariate case.

4.4 Polynomial Contributions

We build on the polynomials library [26], which was designed to support executable multivariate polynomial operations. This choice naturally comes with trade-offs, and a number of functions and lemmas that we needed were missing from the library. For example, we needed an efficient way to isolate the coefficient of a variable within a polynomial, which we define in the `isolate_variable_sparse` function. The following particularly critical lemma rewrites a multivariate polynomial in $\mathbb{R}[a_1, \ldots, a_n, x]$ as a nested polynomial $\mathbb{R}[a_1, \ldots, a_n][x]$, i.e., a univariate polynomial in x with coefficients that are polynomials in $\mathbb{R}[a_1, \ldots, a_n]$:

```
lemma sum_over_degree: "(p :: real mpoly)
  = (∑ i≤degree p x. isolate_variable_sparse p x i * Var x^i)"
```

This is needed rather frequently within VS, as we often seek to re-express polynomials with respect to a single quantified variable of interest, and although it is mathematically quite obvious, its verification was somewhat involved.

Additionally, to utilize the variables within polynomials as DeBruijn indices, we implemented various lifting and substitution operations. These include the `liftPoly` and `lowerPoly` variable reindexing functions. These and other contributions to the polynomials library are discussed in [23, Appendix B.4].

5   Experiments

The benchmark suite consists of 378 QE problems in category CADE09 collected from 94 examples [20], and category Economics with 45 QE problems [15].

CADE09 and Economics examples were converted into decision problems, powers were flattened to multiplications, and CADE09 were additionally rewritten to avoid polynomial division. For sanity checking, we also negated the CADE09 examples [20]. We run on commodity hardware.[2] The benchmark examples, as well as all scripts to rerun the experiments are in [24].

Tools. We compare the performance of *a)* our VSEquality (**E**), VSGeneral (**G**), VSLucky (**L**), and VSLEG (**LEG**) algorithms [23, Appendix B] to *b)* Redlog [6] snapshots 2021–04-13[3] (**R**$_t$) and 2021–07-16[4] (**R**$_\checkmark$, which includes bug fixes for contradictions we reported to Redlog developers), *c)* SMT-RAT 21.05[5] [5] quantifier elimination (**S-QE**$_\checkmark$) and satisfiability checking (**S-SAT**$_t$), *d)* the SMT solver Z3 4.8.10[6] [14] (**Z3**), and *e)* Wolfram Engine 12.3.1(**W-VS, W-QE**). All tools were run in Docker containers on Ubuntu 18.04 with 8GB of memory and 6 CPU cores. Tool syntax translations from SMT-LIB format were done prior to benchmarking: For our VS algorithms, examples were translated to SML data structures and compiled with MLton[7]; as a result, measurements do not include parsing. For W-VS and W-QE, examples were translated into Wolfram syntax, including configuration options restricting QE to quadratic virtual substitution in W-VS. For S-QE$_\checkmark$, check-sat was replaced with eliminate-quantifiers.

Results. Each example has a timeout of 30 s. Figure 2 summarizes the performance on the CADE09 and Economics examples in terms of the cumulative time needed to solve (return "true", "false", "sat", or "unsat") the fastest n problems with a logarithmic time axis: more problems solved and a flatter curve is better.

Wolfram Engine solves all problems in the CADE09 category, closely trailed by Redlog, Z3. The near constant computation time offset of Redlog in comparison to Z3, SMT-RAT, and Wolfram Engine may be attributable to the additional step of entering an SMT REPL. Our verified VSEquality (E), VSGeneral (G), VSLucky (L), and VSLEG (LEG) algorithms rank in performance between the basic quantifier elimination implementation in SMT-RAT (S-QE$_\checkmark$), virtual substitution in Wolfram Engine (W-VS), full SMT approaches (S-SAT$_t$, Z3), and combined virtual substitution plus CAD implementations (R$_\checkmark$, W-QE). The reduced startup time of our algorithms is attributable to the omitted parsing step. Overall, VSEquality and VSLucky solve examples fast, but the wider

---

[2] MacBook Pro 2019 with 2.6 GHz Intel Core i7 (model 9750H) and 32 GB memory (2667 MHz DDR4 SDRAM).

[3] https://sourceforge.net/projects/reduce-algebra/files/snapshot_2021-04-13/.

[4] https://sourceforge.net/projects/reduce-algebra/files/snapshot_2021-07-16/.

[5] https://github.com/ths-rwth/smtrat/releases/tag/21.05.

[6] https://github.com/Z3Prover/z3/releases/tag/z3-4.8.10.

[7] http://mlton.org/.

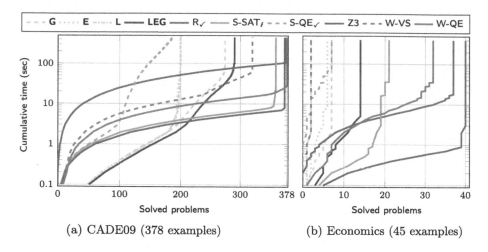

(a) CADE09 (378 examples)   (b) Economics (45 examples)

Fig. 2. Cumulative time to solve fastest n problems (flatter and more is better) (Color figure online)

applicability of VSGeneral and VSLEG allows them to solve considerably more examples. Though we have already implemented a number of optimizations for VS [23, Appendix C] we do not expect to outperform prior tools at this stage, as many of them have been optimized over a period of many years.

A comparison of duration per problem is in Fig. 3. Though there is considerable overlap between VSEquality, VSGeneral, and VSLucky, mutually exclusive sets of solved examples (and considerable performance differences on a number of examples) foreshadow the performance achievable with the combined VSLEG algorithm.

Contradictions. In Fig. 4, we compare the CADE09 results to the results on negated CADE09 examples to highlight *contradictions* between answers (e.g., both A and $\neg A$ are claimed to be true). Wolfram Engine and Z3 answer consistently on both formula sets, and solve (almost) all examples. Redlog, the main VS implementation, in R_f and previous versions in general does not perform well

Fig. 3. CADE09 duration per problem (color indicates duration, lighter is better) (Color figure online)

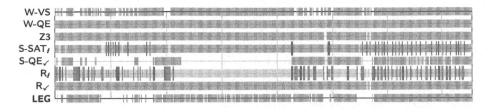

Fig. 4. CADE09 consistency comparison between original and negated formula: color indicates discrepancies within tools (green ■ : answer on original and negated formula agree, dark-blue ■ : only original solved, light-blue ▪ : only negated solved, red+long ■ : **contradictory** answers (both formulas unsat/proved or both sat/disproved), empty: both timeout/unknown) (Color figure online)

on the negated formulas and reports 96 contradictory answers; the contradictory examples were shared with the developers and triggered several bug fixes that are now available in $R_\checkmark$ (no contradictions found on the benchmark set). SMT-RAT performs better than $R_\sharp$ on the negated formulas, but in satisfiability mode contradicts itself on 41 examples by silently ignoring quantifiers in the input; in quantifier elimination mode, SMT-RAT supports quantifiers and does not report contradictions, but SMT-RAT then incurs a significant performance loss (S-SAT$_\sharp$ reports 359 answers while S-QE$_\checkmark$ only solves 187). No contradictions were found across tools, i.e., whenever a tool's answers were consistent internally, the answers agreed with those of other tools. Our VSLEG algorithm has similar performance for proving and disproving in terms of absolute number of solved examples, but combining proving and disproving would still solve more examples than just one question individually (as for S-QE$_\checkmark$ and W-VS).

In summary, the performance of our verified virtual substitution QE on the benchmark set is encouraging. The number of solved examples is close to other VS implementations (304 examples by our VSLEG vs. 322 by W-VS) and the cumulative solving time reveals that the majority of examples are solved fast.

6   Conclusion and Future Work

We verify linear and quadratic virtual substitution for real arithmetic; our algorithms are *provably correct* up to Isabelle/HOL's trusted core and code export. Developing practical verified VS in Isabelle/HOL required significant low-level improvements and extensions to Isabelle's multivariate polynomials library. Our extensive experiments both reveal the benefits of our current optimizations and indicate room for future improvements. Further optimizations to the polynomial libraries, such as efficient coefficient lookup for polynomials using red black trees, would be welcome. Expanding our framework to handle formulas that involve polynomial division would also be of practical significance. Continuing to develop our formalization with such improvements is of especial significance given that our experiments found long-standing errors in existing unverified real arithmetic tools. This demonstrates that, even if verification were not a virtue in and of itself, real arithmetic is so subtle that formal verification is the best way toward an implementation that is both useful and correct in practice.

Acknowledgment. We wish to thank Fabian Immler for his substantial contributions at CMU to the polynomial theories of Isabelle/HOL and regret that his current industry position precludes our ability to include him as a coauthor. Thank you also to the anonymous FM reviewers for their useful feedback.

References

1. Bohrer, B., Rahli, V., Vukotic, I., Völp, M., Platzer, A.: Formally verified differential dynamic logic. In: Bertot, Y., Vafeiadis, V. (eds.) CPP, pp. 208–221. ACM, New York (2017). https://doi.org/10.1145/3018610.3018616
2. Chaieb, A.: Automated methods for formal proofs in simple arithmetics and algebra. Ph.D. thesis, Technische Universität München (2008). mediatum.ub.tum.de/doc/649541/649541.pdf
3. Cohen, C., Mahboubi, A.: Formal proofs in real algebraic geometry: from ordered fields to quantifier elimination. Log. Methods Comput. Sci. **8**(1) (2012). https://doi.org/10.2168/LMCS-8(1:2)2012
4. Collins, G.E.: Quantifier elimination for real closed fields by cylindrical algebraic decomposition. In: Barkhage, H. (ed.) Automata Theory and Formal Languages. LNCS, vol. 33, pp. 134–183. Springer (1975). https://doi.org/10.1007/3-540-07407-4_17
5. Corzilius, F., Kremer, G., Junges, S., Schupp, S., Ábrahám, E.: SMT-RAT: an open source C++ toolbox for strategic and parallel SMT solving. In: Heule, M., Weaver, S.A. (eds.) SAT. LNCS, vol. 9340, pp. 360–368. Springer (2015). https://doi.org/10.1007/978-3-319-24318-4_26
6. Dolzmann, A., Sturm, T.: REDLOG: computer algebra meets computer logic. SIGSAM Bull. **31**(2), 2–9 (1997). https://doi.org/10.1145/261320.261324
7. Durán, A.J., Pérez, M., Varona, J.L.: The misfortunes of a trio of mathematicians using computer algebra systems. can we trust in them? Notices of the AMS **61**(10), 1249–1252 (2014). https://doi.org/10.1090/noti1173
8. Fulton, N., Mitsch, S., Quesel, J.D., Völp, M., Platzer, A.: KeYmaera X: An axiomatic tactical theorem prover for hybrid systems. In: Felty, A.P., Middeldorp, A. (eds.) CADE. LNCS, vol. 9195, pp. 527–538. Springer (2015). https://doi.org/10.1007/978-3-319-21401-6_36
9. Gao, S., Kong, S., Clarke, E.M.: dReal: An SMT solver for nonlinear theories over the reals. In: Bonacina, M.P. (ed.) CADE. LNCS, vol. 7898, pp. 208–214. Springer (2013). https://doi.org/10.1007/978-3-642-38574-2_14
10. Hupel, L., Nipkow, T.: A verified compiler from Isabelle/HOL to CakeML. In: Ahmed, A. (ed.) ESOP. LNCS, vol. 10801, pp. 999–1026. Springer (2018). https://doi.org/10.1007/978-3-319-89884-1_35
11. Jovanovic, D., de Moura, L.M.: Solving non-linear arithmetic. In: Gramlich, B., Miller, D., Sattler, U. (eds.) IJCAR. LNCS, vol. 7364, pp. 339–354. Springer (2012). https://doi.org/10.1007/978-3-642-31365-3_27
12. Košta, M.: New concepts for real quantifier elimination by virtual substitution. Ph.D. thesis, Universität des Saarlandes (2016)
13. McLaughlin, S., Harrison, J.: A proof-producing decision procedure for real arithmetic. In: Nieuwenhuis, R. (ed.) CADE. LNCS, vol. 3632, pp. 295–314. Springer (2005). https://doi.org/10.1007/11532231_22

14. de Moura, L.M., Bjørner, N.: Z3: an efficient SMT solver. In: Ramakrishnan, C.R., Rehof, J. (eds.) TACAS. LNCS, vol. 4963, pp. 337–340. Springer (2008). https://doi.org/10.1007/978-3-540-78800-3_24

15. Mulligan, C.B., Bradford, R.J., Davenport, J.H., England, M., Tonks, Z.: Quantifier elimination for reasoning in economics. CoRR (2018). arXiv:1804.10037

16. Nipkow, T.: Linear quantifier elimination. J. Autom. Reason. **45**(2), 189–212 (2010). https://doi.org/10.1007/s10817-010-9183-0

17. Passmore, G.O.: Combined decision procedures for nonlinear arithmetics, real and complex. Ph.D. thesis, School of Informatics, University of Edinburgh (2011)

18. Platzer, A.: Logical analysis of hybrid systems: proving theorems for complex dynamics. Springer, Heidelberg (2010). https://doi.org/10.1007/978-3-642-14509-4

19. Platzer, A.: Logical foundations of cyber-physical systems. Springer, Cham (2018). https://doi.org/10.1007/978-3-319-63588-0

20. Platzer, A., Quesel, J.D., Rümmer, P.: Real world verification. In: Schmidt, R.A. (ed.) CADE. LNCS, vol. 5663, pp. 485–501. Springer, Berlin (2009). https://doi.org/10.1007/978-3-642-02959-2_35

21. Ratschan, S., Smaus, J.: Verification-integrated falsification of non-deterministic hybrid systems. In: Cassandras, C.G., Giua, A., Seatzu, C., Zaytoon, J. (eds.) ADHS. IFAC Proceedings Volumes, vol. 39, pp. 371–376. Elsevier (2006). https://doi.org/10.3182/20060607-3-IT-3902.00068

22. Scharager, M., Cordwell, K., Mitsch, S., Platzer, A.: Verified quadratic virtual substitution for real arithmetic. Archive of Formal Proofs, Formal proof development (2021). https://www.isa-afp.org/entries/Virtual_Substitution.html

23. Scharager, M., Cordwell, K., Mitsch, S., Platzer, A.: Verified quadratic virtual substitution for real arithmetic. CoRR (2021). arXiv:2105.14183

24. Scharager, M., Cordwell, K., Mitsch, S., Platzer, A.: Verified quadratic virtual substitution for real arithmetic: benchmark examples and scripts. Zenodo (2021). https://doi.org/10.5281/zenodo.5189881

25. Seidenberg, A.: A new decision method for elementary algebra. Annals Math. **60**(2), 365–374 (1954)

26. Sternagel, C., Thiemann, R.: Executable multivariate polynomials. Archive of Formal Proofs, Formal proof development (2010). www.isa-afp.org/entries/Polynomials.html

27. Sturm, T.: A survey of some methods for real quantifier elimination, decision, and satisfiability and their applications. Math. Comput. Sci. **11**(3-4), 483–502 (2017). https://doi.org/10.1007/s11786-017-0319-z

28. Sturm, T.: Thirty years of virtual substitution: foundations, techniques, applications. In: Kauers, M., Ovchinnikov, A., Schost, É. (eds.) ISSAC, pp. 11–16. ACM (2018). https://doi.org/10.1145/3208976.3209030

29. Tarski, A.: A decision method for elementary algebra and geometry. RAND Corporation, Santa Monica (1951)

30. Weispfenning, V.: The complexity of linear problems in fields. J. Symb. Comput. **5**(1/2), 3–27 (1988). https://doi.org/10.1016/S0747-7171(88)80003-8

31. Weispfenning, V.: Quantifier elimination for real algebra - the cubic case. In: MacCallum, M.A.H. (ed.) ISSAC, pp. 258–263. ACM (1994). https://doi.org/10.1145/190347.190425

32. Weispfenning, V.: Quantifier elimination for real algebra - the quadratic case and beyond. Appl. Algebra Eng. Commun. Comput. **8**(2), 85–101 (1997). https://doi.org/10.1007/s002000050055

Business Processes Meet Spatial Concerns: The sBPMN Verification Framework

Rim Saddem-Yagoubi[1]([✉]), Pascal Poizat[2,3], and Sara Houhou[3,4,5]

[1] COSYS-ESTAS, Univ Gustave Eiffel, IFSTTAR, Univ Lille,
59650 Villeneuve d'Ascq, France
rim.saddem@ifsttar.fr
[2] Université Paris Lumières, Université Paris Nanterre, 92000 Nanterre, France
[3] Sorbonne Université, CNRS, LIP6, 75005 Paris, France
{pascal.poizat,sara.houhou}@lip6.fr
[4] Biskra University, LINFI Laboratory, Biskra, Algeria
[5] LIRMM, CNRS & Université de Montpellier, 34095 Cedex 5 Montpellier, France

Abstract. BPMN is the standard for business process modeling. It includes a rich set of constructs for control-flow, inter-process communication, and time-related concerns. However, spatial concerns are left apart while being essential to several application domains. We propose a comprehensive extension of BPMN to deal with this. Our proposal includes an integrated notation, a first-order logic semantics of the extension, and tool-supported verification means through the implementation of the semantics in TLA$^+$. Our tool support and our model database are open source and freely available online.

Keywords: Business processes · Spatial concerns · Formal semantics · Verification · Tool · BPMN · First-order logic · TLA$^+$

1 Introduction

The Business Process Model and Notation (BPMN) [11] is the de facto standard notation for the modeling of business processes. This rich notation includes features to support different aspects to be taken into account when designing a process model. This includes, among others, specifying the control flow, the inter-process communication, and time-related concerns.

Yet, a conventional process model may suit one's needs in a given context and not in other ones (think of rules for allowing, or not, attendance to conferences based on the COVID-related status of the hosting country). A context sensitive approach to business process modeling also offers the ability to adapt the process behaviours to changing contexts [14]. Coined by Schilit and Theimer [16] in 1994, the term "context" has been given a generic definition by Dey [6] in 2001 as *"any information that can be used to characterize the situation of an entity"*. Transferring this definition to the business process management domain, a useful

---

This work was supported by project PARDI ANR-16-CE25-0006.

M. Huisman et al. (Eds.): FM 2021, LNCS 13047, pp. 218–234, 2021.
https://doi.org/10.1007/978-3-030-90870-6_12

definition of a business process context could be *"the minimum set of variables containing all relevant information that impact the design and execution of a business process"* [13]. Saidani and Nurcan further identify in [14] four important kinds of contexts: location, time, resource, and organisation-related contexts. As a contextual factor, location is widely discussed as part of research related to mobile applications and it has wider implications for process management [13].

Without a first-class treatment for the location context in process modelling, one would have to rely on an abstraction of it, *e.g.*, using non-determinism to model conditional branching based on the current state of this context. This is known to yield over-approximation issues. For illustration purposes, let us suppose a process where a robot has to treat rooms in a power-plant or fields in a farm. For this, one relies on a looping workflow pattern, where the robot performs several tasks while there is still at least a place to deal with. Our case study, below, is an instance of this. With support for the location context, it is possible, first, to represent the state of the world (the power-plant rooms or the fields, and their status) and, second, to exit the loop when all places have been treated. Without this support, the fact that there is still, or not, a place to deal with would be modelled using non-determinism. One would then have a possible infinite run, where there is always a place left to treat, making it impossible to perform verification without using bounded analysis (up to some length of runs) or fairness constraints. In line with this, we focus here on the impact of the location-related context in the design and the execution of business processes.

Contributions. Our contributions in this direction are threefold. First, (1.) we propose an extension of the BPMN standard notation in order to take into account location-related (which we call spatial) concerns, (2.) we define a formal execution semantics for this extension, and (3.) we provide the process designers with tools for the automated verification of their extended process models.

With respect to (1.), we support the modeling of control flows based on location constraints, of process mobility, and of the action of processes on their environment. In this work we assume that only the processes at hand have the possibility to change this environment (*i.e.*, the environment cannot independently evolve). We made the choice to extract the specification of the location-related context into a specific structure that is then attached to the process model for verification. This makes the modelling of processes more generic, maintainable, and extensible as one can very simply change the context of use of a process to see the impact on its correctness. This structure, that we call *space structure*, describes all components of a location context: places (called basic locations), possible moves between places, and logical groups of places (called group locations) that can evolve over time and with the action of the processes. All our extensions rely on the standard BPMN extension mechanisms. The usual process design tools can hence be used to model extended processes (in practice, we use Camunda for this). Our extensions can be "forgotten" by verification or execution tools not supporting them. But using our own tooling (see below, 3.) the process designers will be able to go beyond standard BPMN verification and check also models in presence of location extensions.

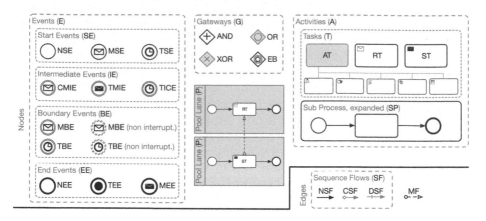

Fig. 1. BPMN subset being supported. Extension points are colored in green. (Color figure online)

With respect to (2.), we follow the approach in [8] and extend its first-order logic execution semantics for BPMN[1] towards taking into account our extensions. This is achieved structurally on the different extension constructs (space structure initial configuration, processes initial locations, extended inclusive and exclusive gateways, tasks for process mobility or for acting on the context).

With respect to (3.), our approach is based on two steps. An extended process model is first transformed into a TLA$^+$ representation of it. Then, given this representation and the TLA$^+$ implementation of the (2.) semantics, the model-checker from the TLA$^+$ tool-suite is used to perform verification of both standard process properties (safety, soundness) and location-related ones. Our tools and the models we use for evaluation are open source and available online [12].

BPMN Primer. The subset of BPMN that we support is given in Fig. 1. The main instrument to control the flow in processes are gateways. Parallel gateways (AND) require that all incoming flows are active and give control to all outgoing flows. Exclusive (XOR) and event-based (EB) gateways only require one of the incoming flows to be active and activate only one of the outgoing flows based either on a condition (for XOR) or some event (for EB, here message reception). The inclusive gateway (OR) has a more complex semantics. First, several outgoing flows can be activated at a time, based on conditions. Second, it requires that the maximum possible number of incoming flows are active (this may require waiting for some time before more incoming flows are activated, even if one is already active). Inter-process message-based communication can be achieved using send tasks (ST) or message throwing events (MEE at the end of a process, TMIE otherwise), and receive tasks (RT) or message catching events (MSE at the start of a process, CMIE otherwise). Activities are subject to boundary events either interrupting or not (the former interrupt the activity, the

---

[1] As far as time-related elements are concerned, we take the first, non-deterministic, semantics given in [8].

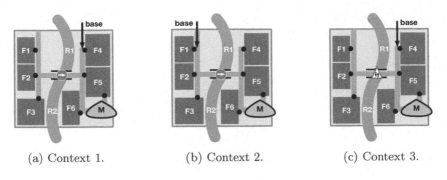

(a) Context 1.   (b) Context 2.   (c) Context 3.

Fig. 2. Case study – location contexts.

latter activate some flow branch without interrupting the activity). We refer the reader to [11] for more detailed information on the BPMN notation and to [8] for more discussion on the, complex, inclusive gateway.

Case Study. Figures 2 and 3 present the case study we use to illustrate our proposal and to perform verification. The outcomes of verification on more examples are synthesized in Sect. 3. This model is a simplified version of a collaborative process model where a controller (Controller), a crop planting robot (Planter), and a watering robot (Sprayer, not taken into account here) have to plant crops and water several fields spread over both banks of a river.

The context of the collaboration is the river and its banks, with three different instances given in Figs. 2a–2c. Places (basic locations) are either fields (F1 to F6), river (R1 and R2), bridge (B), or mountain (M). There is also the base (base) from which our collaboration peers will operate and move. Over these places we may define logical groups of locations (of simply, group locations) for the places where to plant crops (toPlant), the places to water (toWater), the places with crops (planted), and the watered places (watered). Finally, we have possible moves around the location context, based on roads and bridge. All together, basic locations, group locations, and possible moves, make up possible space structures to be associated to location-aware processes. Please note that in practice the location structures are of course not denoted using pictures but rather as a set of information extending the BPMN element for the process collaboration:

```
<bpmn:collaboration id="s006Robots2"><bpmn:extensionElements>
    <camunda:properties>
      <camunda:property name="base-locations"
                        value="[base,F1,F2,F3,F4,F5,F6,R1,R2,B,M]" />
      <camunda:property name="group-locations"
                        value="[toPlant,planted,toWater,watered]" />
      <camunda:property name="transitions"
                        value="[(base,F1),(F1,base),(F1,F2),(F2,F1),(F2,F3),...,(M,F6)]" />
      <camunda:property name="initial-space"
                        value="{toPlant:[F1,F2,F3,F4,F5,F6],
                                planted:[], toWater:[], watered:[]}" />
    </camunda:properties>
</bpmn:extensionElements></bpmn:collaboration>
```

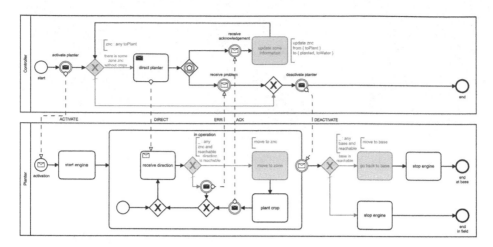

Fig. 3. Crop planting collaboration.

In Fig. 3 we have a BPMN collaboration that has been extended with the extensions we propose. In green we show which elements are extended (in addition to the whole collaboration, as seen before, and the processes' pool lanes extended to denote where the processes start). In blue we use notes to give, as comments, extensions that are indeed also stored as extension elements in the XML source BPMN file. We remind that since we use BPMN extension mechanisms, these extensions can be directly entered in BPMN design tools. The whole model (diagram and source file, with extensions) is available from [12].

The controller starts by activating the planter. It then checks if there are still some places where to plant crops. If so it sets znc to be any of these. In our extension checking some location-related constraint and setting accordingly a location variable is done at once using a *space condition*, znc: any toPlant (set znc to be any of the places in group toPlant). Then the controller sends a message to the planter ordering it to get there and waits to receive either an acknowledgement or the information that there is some problem. In the first case the controller registers that the place is now planted using an *update action*, removing znc from group toPlant and adding it to groups planted and toWater. If there is a problem, then the controller interrupts the planter and stops.

On its side, the planter starts upon activation by the controller and, after starting its engine, it enters the in operation sub-process. In this sub-process, it loops on receiving an order to move (it has then access to the shared znc information), checking if znc can be reached from its current location (using reachable, denoting places that are reachable, in the space condition _: any znc and reachable), and accordingly either moving to znc using a *move* action and sending an acknowledgement to the controller, or signalling a problem. Upon interruption by the controller, the loop stops and the planter tries to get back to the base (again, using a space condition to check if this is possible).

We were able to model spatial concerns in our collaboration. But what about correctness? Can the collaboration processes reach termination (black circles in the rightmost part of Fig. 3)? Are all fields planted at the end? Let us consider the contexts. If the planter starts on the right bank then the left one cannot be planted due to the one-way bridge (Fig. 2a). If the planter starts on the left bank (Fig. 2b) or if the bridge is two-way (Fig. 2c) then all fields can be planted.

This case study illustrates several points. First, a process model can operate on (or be adapted to) different space structures. Conversely, a space structure can be used with many processes (we have used one with several variants of the crop planting collaboration). This is made possible by separating the specifications of the context and of the processes, and then integrating them. Further, we have seen that, switch two variants of a process or two variants of a space structure and correctness may no longer hold. In the sequel we will see how to give a formal semantics to our extensions and support their verification using tools.

Outline. The formal part of the paper is developed in Sect. 2, addressing the presentation of the models underlying the semantics, and then the semantics itself. The implementation of the semantics in TLA$^+$, verification, and evaluation are then presented in Sect. 3. This section also includes a short introduction to the TLA$^+$ language and verification framework. Related work is given in Sect. 4, and we end with conclusions and perspectives in Sect. 5.

2   Formal Semantics

In this section, we first give the formal models for extended BPMN diagrams. Then, we present their formal semantics. It follows the "token game" given (in natural language) in Chap. 13 of the standard [11] and builds on the semantics for basic BPMN given in [8]. Hence, we will focus on points of extensions only.

2.1   Formal Models for Space BPMN

As we have seen earlier, space structures represent contexts with base locations, group locations, and possible moves. Hence the following definition.

Definition 1 (Space Structure). *A space structure is a tuple* $\mathbb{S} = (\mathbb{B}, \mathbb{G}, \rightarrow)$ *where* $\mathbb{B}$ *is the set of base locations,* $\mathbb{G}$ *is the set of group locations, and* $\rightarrow \subseteq \mathbb{B} \times \mathbb{B}$ *denotes all possible moves between base locations. Further, we require that* $\mathbb{B} \cap \mathbb{G} = \emptyset$ *and* $(b, b) \in \rightarrow$ *for every* b *in* $\mathbb{B}$.

Space structures may represent different kinds of location-based contexts such as countries and administrative or epidemiological statuses, offices and security levels, or agricultural environments as in our case study where, $\mathbb{B} = \{\mathsf{F1}, \dots, \mathsf{M}\}$, $\mathbb{G} = \{\mathsf{toPlant}, \mathsf{toWater}, \mathsf{planted}, \mathsf{watered}\}$, and $\{(\mathsf{F2}, \mathsf{F2}), (\mathsf{F2}, \mathsf{F5})\} \subset \rightarrow$. The set of all locations is denoted by $\mathbb{L} = \mathbb{B} \cup \mathbb{G}$, $\rightarrow^*$ denotes the transitive closure of $\rightarrow$, and $b_1 \rightarrow b_2$ denotes that $(b_1, b_2) \in \rightarrow$.

Notation. In the sequel, definitions are taken given a space structure $\mathbb{S} = (\mathbb{B}, \mathbb{G}, \rightarrow)$ and a set of variables V such that $V \cap \mathbb{L} = \emptyset$.

Space formulas are used to denote a subset of the base locations (see their interpretation in Def. 10). They are central to our extension as they are used both in conditions on conditional sequence flows (CSF) and in mobility actions.

Definition 2 (Space Formula). *The set of (space) formulas over* $\mathbb{S}$ *and* V, *denoted by* $Form$, *is the smallest set generated by* {true, v, b, g, not f, f_1 or f_2, here, reachable} *for* $v \in V$, $b \in \mathbb{B}$, $g \in \mathbb{G}$, *and* $f, f_1, f_2 \in Form$. *Further,* f_1 *and* f_2 *is defined as* not (not f_1 or not f_2).

Space actions are extensions of BPMN (abstract) tasks that can represent either a move or the update of the context by some process. Additionally, we use a specific **pass** action for tasks that are not related to the spatial concerns.

Definition 3 (Space Action). *The set of (space) actions over* $\mathbb{S}$ *and* V, *denoted by* $Action$, *is the smallest set generated by* {move(f), update(u, G^-, G^+), pass} *for* $f \in Form$, $u \in V$, $G^- \subseteq \mathbb{G}$, $G^+ \subseteq \mathbb{G}$, *and* $G^- \cap G^+ = \emptyset$.

Informally (the formal semantics is given in Def. 11), move(f) denotes that the process of interest moves to a location satisfying f and update(u, G^-, G^+) denotes the update of the context by removing some locations (retrieved by evaluating u) from all groups in G^- and adding them to all groups in G^+.

We may now give definitions for processes, which are represented using graphs with typed nodes and edges. Types correspond to the BPMN elements (see Fig. 1, *e.g.*, XOR for exclusive gateways): $T_{Nodes} = \{AT, RT, ST, NSE, MSE, TSE, CMIE, TMIE, TICE, MBE, TBE, NEE, TEE, MEE, AND, OR, XOR, EB, SP, P\}$ and $T_{Edges} = \{NSF, CSF, DSF, MF\}$. Definitions 4 and 5 are taken (and restructured) from [8]. Definition 6 integrates our extensions.

Definition 4 (Graph). *A graph is a tuple* $\rho = (N, E, source, target)$ *where* N *is the set of nodes,* E *(with* $N \cap E = \emptyset$*) is the set of edges, and* $source/target :$ $E \rightarrow N$ *denote the source/target of an edge.*

Definition 5 (BPMN Graph). *A BPMN graph is a tuple* $\widehat{\rho} = (\rho, cat_N, cat_E, R, \mathbb{M}, msg_t)$ *where* ρ *is a graph,* $cat_N : N \rightarrow T_{Nodes}$ *gives the type of a node* (N^T *denoting the set* $\{n \in N \mid cat_N(n) \in T\}$), $cat_E : E \rightarrow T_{Edges}$ *gives the type of an edge* (E^T *denoting the set* $\{e \in E \mid cat_E(e) \in T\}$), $R : N^{\{SP,P\}} \rightarrow 2^{N \cup E}$ *gives the set of nodes and edges which are directly contained in a container (process or sub-process),* $\mathbb{M}$ *is the set of message types, and* $msg_t : E^{\{MF\}} \rightarrow \mathbb{M}$ *gives the message associated to a message flow.*

Definition 6 (Space BPMN Graph). *A space BPMN graph is a tuple* $\rho^\circ = (\widehat{\rho}, \mathbb{S}, V, cvar, ckind, ccond, \prec, act)$ *where* $\widehat{\rho}$ *is a BPMN graph,* $\mathbb{S}$ *is a space structure,* V *is a set of variables,* $cvar : E^{\{CSF\}} \rightarrow V$, $ckind : E^{\{CSF\}} \rightarrow \{any, all\}$, *and* $ccond : E^{\{CSF\}} \rightarrow Form$ *are total functions that assign respectively a* *variable, a kind (denoting how to associate the interpretation of a space formula to a condition variable), and a space formula to each conditional edge, $\prec \subseteq E^{\{CSF\}} \times E^{\{CSF\}}$, is a relation ordering the conditional sequence flows outgoing from a conditional gateway, and $act : N^{\{AT\}} \to Action$ is a total function that assigns an action to each abstract task.*

2.2 Semantics for Space BPMN: States and Initial State

The semantics relies on the notion of *state* of the space BPMN graph, which is defined in terms of state markings, edge markings, and space configuration.

Notation. In the sequel, definitions are taken given a space BPMN graph $\rho^\circ = (\hat{\rho}, \mathbb{S}, V, cvar, ckind, ccond, \prec, act)$ with $\mathbb{S} = (\mathbb{B}, \mathbb{G}, \to)$ and $\mathbb{L} = \mathbb{B} \cup \mathbb{G}$.

Definition 7 (Space Configuration). *A (space) configuration c is a couple of substitutions (σ, subs), σ being a variable to base locations substitution ($\sigma : V \to 2^{\mathbb{B}}$) and subs being a group to base locations substitution (subs : $\mathbb{G} \to 2^{\mathbb{B}}$).*

The set of all configurations (of a space BPMN graph ρ°) is denoted by *Configs*. We note $\sigma^\perp$ the empty variable configuration ($\forall v \in V, \sigma^\perp(v) = \emptyset$). Given a configuration $c = (\sigma, \text{subs})$, $\sigma[v \mapsto B]$, denotes the update of σ by associating B to v (*i.e.*, $\sigma[v \mapsto B]$ is $\sigma(v')$ for each v' in $V \setminus \{v\}$ and B for v). Accordingly, subs$[g \mapsto B]$, denotes the update of subs by associating B to g.

Among the variables, we have process locations, *i.e.*, we have a variable $loc_p \in V$ for each p in $N^{\{P\}}$, and $\sigma(loc_p)$ gives the location of a process p. A configuration encompasses (in σ) the current values of variables – including the location of processes – and (in subs) the state of the relation between group and base locations. To become a state, a configuration is completed with the current marking of the BPMN graph nodes and edges.

Note that here we assume a model of shared variables (*e.g.* the znc variable in our example). This is driven by formalization convenience. Local variables with values exchanged using communication (messages) is part of our perspectives.

Definition 8 (State). *A state is a triple $s = (mn, me, c)$ where $mn : N \to \mathbb{N}$ (node marking), $me : E \to \mathbb{N}$ (edge marking), and c is a configuration.*

The set of all states (of a space BPMN graph ρ°) is denoted by *States*. One of them is the state in which the graph starts its execution: its initial state.

Definition 9 (Initial state). *The initial state of a space BPMN Graph ρ° is a state $s_o = (mn_0, me_0, c_0 = (\sigma_0, \text{subs}_0))$ such that only processes and their start events are marked ($\forall n \in N, mn_0(n) = 1$ if $\exists p \in N^{\{P\}}, n \in N^{\{NSE,MSE,TSE\}} \cap R(p)$, and 0 otherwise), no edge is marked ($\forall e \in E, me_0(e) = 0$), and σ_0 is set only for the start locations of processes ($\forall v \in V$, either $\exists p \in N^{\{P\}}, \exists loc_{p,0} \in \mathbb{B}, v = loc_p \land \sigma_0(v) = \{loc_{p,0}\}$ or $\sigma_0(v) = \emptyset$).*

The initial locations for processes (the $loc_{p,0}$) and subs$_0$ are *parameters of the model* and, hence, of its verification. In our example, for the context in Fig. 2b, we had all fields to plant and the planter starting in F1 (or in base, with base $\to$ F1). This means that the configuration in the initial state is such that $\sigma_0(loc_{\text{Planter}}) = \{\text{F1}\}$ (or $\{\text{base}\}$) and subs$_0(\text{toPlant}) = \{\text{F1}, \ldots, \text{F6}\}$.

2.3   Semantics for Space BPMN: Formulas and Actions

Having defined configurations, it is now possible to give a semantics to formulas and actions. Let us begin with the former.

Definition 10 (Formula Interpretation). *The interpretation of a formula f with reference to a configuration $c = (\sigma, \text{subs})$ and a process p, is denoted by $||f||_c^p$ ($|| \_ ||_-$: $Form \times N^{\{P\}} \times Configs \rightarrow 2^{\mathbb{B}}$) and defined as: $||\text{true}||_c^p = \mathbb{B}$ (all base locations), $||v||_c^p = \sigma(v)$ (value of a variable), $||b||_c^p = \{b\}$ (base location), $||g||_c^p = \text{subs}(g)$ (current locations of a group), $||\text{not } f||_c^p = \mathbb{B} \setminus ||f||_c^p$ (difference), $||f_1 \text{ or } f_2||_c^p = ||f_1||_c^p \cup ||f_2||_c^p$ (union), $||\text{here}||_c^p = \sigma(loc_p)$, and $||\text{reachable}||_c^p = \{b \in \mathbb{B} \mid \sigma(loc_p) \rightarrow^* b\}$ (reachable locations).*

In our example we use formula znc and reachable in the planter. Its interpretation is the intersection of $\sigma\{\text{znc}\}$ and of the locations that are reachable from the planter location. This is not empty only if znc is reachable, which is what we want to express. Let us now come to the actions.

Definition 11 (Actions Evaluation). *The evaluation of an action a over a configuration $c = (\sigma, \text{subs})$ and a process p is denoted by $[[a]]_c^p$ ($[[\_]]_-$: $Action \times N^{\{P\}} \times Configs \rightarrow Configs$) and defined as follows:*

- $[[\text{move}(f)]]_c^p = c'$ *where c' is c if $||f \text{ and reachable}||_c^p = \emptyset$ and c' is $(\sigma[loc_p \mapsto \{b\}], \text{subs})$ with $\{b \in ||f \text{ and reachable}||_c^p\}$ otherwise.*
- $[[\text{update}(u, G^-, G^+)]]_c^p = (\sigma, \text{subs}')$ *where $\text{subs}'(g)$ is $\text{subs}(g) \setminus \sigma(u)$ if $g \in G^-$, $\text{subs}(g) \cup \sigma(u)$ if $g \in G^+$, and $\text{subs}(g)$ otherwise (remind that $G^- \cap G^+ = \emptyset$)*
- $[[\text{pass}]]_c^p = c$

Action move(f) does nothing if f corresponds to no reachable locations satisfying it, otherwise one of the locations is chosen and the process location is updated accordingly. Action update(u, G^-, G^+) updates groups in G^- and G^+ respectively adding/removing locations in u. Action pass does nothing.

In our example the planter tries to move to its base at the end. Using condition _ : base and reachable, it checks before that this is indeed possible. Without checking this (suppose there is no exclusive gateway) trying move(base) if the base is not reachable would make the process block on this task.

2.4   Semantics for Space BPMN: Execution Semantics

In order to maintain traceability with the standard [11], we use a token-based approach. The movement of tokens is based on node types. We define an execution model based on two predicates (St, Ct) for each node type which correspond to, respectively, the enabling of the node to start its execution, and the enabling of the node to complete its execution. When not specified, the predicate is *true*.

The formal execution semantics is given in Table 1. The semantics of the elements in Fig. 1 and not in Table 1 is kept from [8]. We consider that mn and mn' (resp. me and me') denote two successive markings of a node (resp. edge)

Table 1. Space BPMN semantics (extensions to [8]).

$n \in N^{\{XOR\}}$	$Ct(n) \stackrel{def}{=} \exists ei \in in^{SF}(n), me(ei) \geq 1 \wedge me'(ei) = me(ei) - 1$ $\wedge \; \exists eo_1 \in out^{\{CSF\}}(n), \lVert ccond(eo_1) \rVert_c^{procOf(n)} \neq \emptyset$ $\wedge \; \forall eo_2 \in out^{\{CSF\}}(n), eo_2 \prec eo_1 \Rightarrow \lVert ccond(eo_2) \rVert_c^{procOf(n)} = \emptyset$ $\wedge \; me'(eo_1) = me(eo_1) + 1$ $\wedge \; \exists v \in V, v = cvar(eo_1)$ $\wedge \; ckind(v) = \mathsf{all}$ $\quad \Rightarrow \sigma' = \sigma[v \mapsto \lVert ccond(eo_1) \rVert_c^{procOf(n)}]$ $\wedge \; ckind(v) = \mathsf{any}$ $\quad \Rightarrow \exists x \in \lVert ccond(eo_1) \rVert_c^{procOf(n)}, \sigma' = \sigma[v \mapsto x]$ $\wedge \; \triangle(\{ei, eo_1\}) \wedge \Xi_{subs}$ $\vee \wedge \; \forall eo_1 \in out^{\{CSF\}}(n), \lVert ccond(eo_1) \rVert_c^{procOf(n)} = \emptyset$ $\wedge \; \exists eo_2 \in out^{\{DSF\}}(n), me'(eo_2) = me(eo_2) + 1$ $\wedge \; \triangle(\{ei, eo_2\}) \wedge \Xi_{subs}^{\sigma}$
$n \in N^{\{OR\}}$	$Ct(n) \stackrel{def}{=} In^+(n) \neq \emptyset$ $\wedge \; \forall ei \in In^+(n), me'(ei) = me(ei) - 1$ $\wedge \; \forall ez \in In^-(n),$ $\quad \forall ee \in (Pre_E(n, ez) \setminus ignore_E(n)), me(ee) = 0$ $\wedge \; \forall nn \in (Pre_N(n, ez) \setminus ignore_N(n)), mn(nn) = 0$ $\wedge \; \exists es \subseteq out^{\{CSF\}}(n) \wedge es \neq \emptyset$ $\wedge \; \nexists eo \in out^{\{CSF\}}(n) \setminus es, \lVert ccond(eo) \rVert_c^{procOf(n)} \neq \emptyset$ $\wedge \; \forall eo \in es, \lVert ccond(eo) \rVert_c^{procOf(n)} \neq \emptyset$ $\wedge \; me'(eo) = me(eo) + 1$ $\wedge \; \exists v \in V, v = cvar(eo)$ $\wedge \; ckind(v) = \mathsf{all}$ $\quad \Rightarrow \sigma' = \sigma[v \mapsto \lVert ccond(eo) \rVert_c^{procOf(n)}]$ $\wedge \; ckind(v) = \mathsf{any}$ $\quad \Rightarrow \exists x \in \lVert ccond(eo) \rVert_c^{procOf(n)}, \sigma' = \sigma[v \mapsto x]$ $\wedge \; \triangle(In^+(n) \cup es) \wedge \Xi_{subs}$ $\vee \wedge \; \forall eo_1 \in out^{\{CSF\}}(n), \lVert ccond(eo_1) \rVert_c^{procOf(n)} = \emptyset$ $\wedge \; \exists eo_2 \in out^{\{DSF\}}(n), me'(eo_2) = me(eo_2) + 1$ $\wedge \; \triangle(In^+(n) \cup \{eo_2\}) \wedge \Xi_{subs}^{\sigma}$
$n \in N^{\{AT\}}$	$St(n) \stackrel{def}{=} \exists ei \in in^{SF}(n), me(ei) \geq 1$ $\wedge \; me'(ei) = me(ei) - 1 \wedge \; mn'(n) = mn(n) + 1 \wedge \; \triangle(\{n, ei\}) \wedge \Xi_{subs}^{\sigma}$ $Ct(n) \stackrel{def}{=} mn(n) \geq 1$ $\wedge \; mn'(n) = mn(n) - 1$ $\wedge \; \forall eo \in out^{SF}(n), me'(eo) = me(eo) + 1$ $\wedge \; c' = [[act(n)]]_c^{procOf(n)}$ $\wedge \; act(n) = \mathsf{move}(f) \Rightarrow \lVert f \text{ and reachable} \rVert_c^{procOf(n)} \neq \emptyset$ $\wedge \; act(n) = \mathsf{pass} \wedge \triangle(\{n\} \cup out^{SF}(n)) \wedge \Xi_{subs}^{\sigma}$ $\vee \; act(n) = \mathsf{move}(f) \wedge \triangle(\{n\} \cup out^{SF}(n)) \wedge \Xi_{subs}$ $\vee \; act(n) = \mathsf{update}(u, G^-, G^+) \wedge \triangle(\{n\} \cup out^{SF}(n)) \wedge \Xi^{\sigma}$

in the execution semantics. Accordingly $c = (\sigma, subs)$ and $c' = (\sigma', subs')$ denote two successive configurations. $\triangle$ is a predicate that denotes marking equality but for nodes and edges given as parameter, $\triangle(X)$ means *"nothing changes but for*

X": $\triangle(X) \equiv \forall n \in N \setminus X, mn'(n) = mn(n) \wedge \forall e \in E \setminus X, me'(e) = me(e)$. In the same way, we define $\Xi^\sigma \equiv \sigma' = \sigma$, $\Xi_{\text{subs}} \equiv \text{subs}' = \text{subs}$, and $\Xi^\sigma_{\text{subs}} \equiv \Xi^\sigma \wedge \Xi_{\text{subs}}$.

In the semantics we use helper functions: $in/out : N \rightarrow 2^E$ give the incoming/outgoing edges of a node, $in(n) = \{e \in E \mid target(e) = n\}$ and $out(n) = \{e \in E \mid source(e) = n\}$. A family of functions in^T (resp. out^T) : $N \rightarrow 2^E$ is used to combine in (resp. out) with E^T, $in^T(n) = in(n) \cap E^T$ and $out^T(n) = out(n) \cap E^T$. The type set for sequence flows, SF, is defined as $\{NSF, CSF, DSF\}$. $procOf : N \rightarrow N^{\{P\}}$ gives the container process of a given node, $procOf(n) = p$ if and only if $n \in R^+(p)$, with R^+ being the transitive closure of R. Further, to deal with the complex semantics of the OR gateway, and formalize in a correct way its definition in [11], we use some more functions: $In^- : N \rightarrow E$ gives the unmarked incoming edges of a node: $In^-(n) = \{e \in in^{SF}(n) \mid me(e) = 0\}$. $In^+ : N \rightarrow E$ gives the marked incoming edges of a node: $In^+(n) \stackrel{def}{=} \{e \in in^{SF}(n) \mid me(e) \geq 1\}$. $Pre_N : N \times E \rightarrow 2^N$, gives the predecessor nodes of an edge such that n^{pre} is in $Pre_N(n, e)$ if there is a path from n^{pre} to e that never visits n. Accordingly, $Pre_E : N \times E \rightarrow 2^E$ gives predecessor edges. $ignore_E : N \rightarrow 2^E$ gives the predecessor edges of the marked incoming edges of a given node: $ignore_E(n) = \bigcup_{e^+ \in In^+(n)} Pre_E(n, e^+)$.

$ignore_N : N \rightarrow 2^N$ gives the predecessor nodes of the marked incoming edges of a given node: $ignore_N(n) = \bigcup_{e^+ \in In^+(n)} Pre_N(n, e^+)$.

Let us now describe Table 1.

Space Formulas and Gateways. Gateways are atomic hence define only the Ct predicate. A XOR gateway may complete by choosing one of its outgoing conditional flows eo_1 whose formula is satisfied (its interpretation, Def. 10, is not empty). In case there are several such transitions, we follow the BPMN standard and use ordering ($\prec$) so that only the first one is activated. If there is no such flow, the default sequence flow outgoing from the gateway (if it exists) is activated. When a conditional flow is activated, its variable is updated at the same time. Depending on the condition kind (any or all), either a single location from the formula interpretation or all of them are taken to update $\sigma(v)$.

An OR gateway has some differences $wrt.$ a XOR gateway. First it requires that no more ongoing flow ez can be activated before completing (lines 3–5 of Ct). Second, all outgoing conditional flows whose conditions are satisfied are activated (lines 6–8 of Ct are used to get the maximal set es of such flows).

Space Actions and Abstract Tasks. Actions are associated to abstract tasks which can start if at least one of their incoming flows is active. The completion of these tasks depends on the evaluation of their action (Def. 11) in order to change the configuration (c to c'), either σ for moves or subs for updates. For move(f), we require that there is at least one reachable location in the interpretation of f.

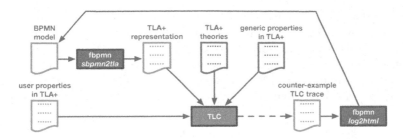

Fig. 4. Tool support (blue: model-specific, green: non model-specific).

3   Implementation and Verification

In this section, we present the implementation of our approach in a tool suite, sBPMN, enabling the verification of extended BPMN models and the animation of counter-examples. sBPMN is a part in a more general project about BPMN verification [12]. It works as presented in Fig. 4.

The user first designs an extended BPMN model using any modeler with support for BPMN extension mechanisms (we use Camunda). This model corresponds to Definition 5 with extensions information for Definition 6 (extensions to BPMN) and Definition 9 (initial state parameter). In practice, the space structure and the initial value of the subs relation are associated to the process diagram (as shown in page 5), initial locations are associated to processes, and conditional information and actions are associated respectively to conditional flows and to abstract tasks. A TLA$^+$ representation of this model is retrieved using the fbpmn command with option sbpmn2tla. Given this representation, the TLA$^+$ implementation of the semantics, and the TLA$^+$ encoding of generic and user given model-specific properties, the TLC model checker from the TLA$^+$ tool box (freely available at http://lamport.azurewebsites.net/tla/tla.html) is used to perform verification. If some properties are not satisfied, TLC outputs a counter-example trace that is then transformed using the fbpmn command with option log2html into an HTML+JS page enabling the user to animate the counter example on the BPMN model, step by step, to understand the error(s). We provide users with a script, sfbpmn-check, that performs all steps in Fig. 4 in a transparent way (see [12], under scripts/).

3.1   Implementing the Semantics and Encoding Models in TLA$^+$

TLA$^+$ [9] is a formal specification language based on untyped Zermelo-Fraenkel set theory for specifying data structures, and on the temporal logic of actions (TLA) for specifying dynamic behaviors. TLA$^+$ allows one to specify symbolic transition systems with variables and *actions*. An action is a transition predicate between a state and a successor state. It is an arbitrary first-order predicate with quantifiers, set and arithmetic operators, and functions, and where quoting denotes the value of variables in the successor state.

This is in phase with our St and Ct predicates. Further, the expression and action fragment of TLA$^+$ contains first-order logic, that we use to express the semantics. Hence, the encoding of the semantics in TLA$^+$ is straightforward (up to the TLA$^+$ concrete syntax of course). For example, the TLA$^+$ implementation for the semantics of XOR nodes is given in Fig. 5. The comprehensive TLA$^+$ theories for the semantics is available at [12] under `theories/stla`.

$$
\begin{array}{l}
\rule{4cm}{0.4pt}\text{ MODULE } XOR \rule{5cm}{0.4pt}\\[4pt]
xor\_complete(n) \triangleq \\
\quad \wedge\ CatN[n] = ExclusiveOr \\
\quad \wedge\ \exists\ ei \in intype(SeqFlowType,\, n): \\
\qquad \wedge\ edgemarks[ei] \geq 1 \\
\qquad \wedge\ edgemarks' = [edgemarks \text{ EXCEPT } ![ei] = @ - 1] \\
\quad \wedge\ \vee\ \exists\ eo1 \in outtype(\{ConditionalSeqFlow\},\, n): \\
\qquad\qquad \dots \\
\qquad \vee\ \wedge\ \forall\ eo1 \in outtype(\{ConditionalSeqFlow\},\, n): \\
\qquad\qquad evalF(sigma,\, subs,\, ProcessOf(n),\, cCond[eo1]) = \{\} \\
\qquad\quad \wedge\ \exists\ eo2 \ \in outtype(\{DefaultSeqFlow\},\, n): \\
\qquad\qquad edgemarks' = [edgemarks \text{ EXCEPT } ![eo2] = @ + 1] \\
\quad \wedge\ \text{UNCHANGED } nodemarks \wedge \text{UNCHANGED } subs \wedge \text{UNCHANGED } sigma
\end{array}
$$

Fig. 5. Semantics of XOR nodes in TLA$^+$ (part of).

3.2 Properties and Verification

TLC is an explicit-state model checker that checks both safety and liveness properties specified in LTL. This logic includes operators $\square$ and $\lozenge$ that respectively denote that, in all executions, a property F must always hold ($\square F$) or that it must hold at some instant in the future ($\lozenge F$). In our framework, properties are either properties that are generic to all process models, or user given properties specific to a given process model (see Fig. 6).

For the former, we reuse the TLA$^+$ implementation given in [8] for the properties defined by [5]: (1) safety, (2) soundness and (3) message-relaxed soundness. A collaboration is safe if no sequence flow holds more than one token. A collaboration is sound if all processes are sound and there are no undelivered messages, a process being sound if it can reach a state where nothing but its events are active. Finally, message-relaxed soundness is soundness without taking into account undelivered messages (tokens on message flows). For the model-specific properties, the user can rely on the elements in states (Def. 8), namely node and edge markings, variable substitution (including process locations) and group substitution. Examples of such properties are given in Fig. 6.

3.3 Experiments

Experiments were conducted on a 3.5 GHz Intel Core i7 processor (dual core) laptop with 16 GB of memory and running MacOS. Results for a selection of

```
┌─────────────────────────── MODULE Properties ───────────────────────────┐
```

$SafeCollaboration \triangleq$ generic property (1)
$\quad \Box(\forall e \in Edge : CatE[e] \in SeqFlowType \Rightarrow edgemarks[e] \leq 1)$

LOCAL $SoundProcessInt(p) \triangleq$
$\quad \wedge \quad \forall e \in Edge : source[e] \in ContainRel[p]$
$\qquad\qquad \wedge target[e] \in ContainRel[p] \Rightarrow edgemarks[e] = 0$
$\quad \wedge \quad \forall n \in ContainRel[p] :$
$\qquad\quad \vee CatN[n] \in StartEventType$
$\qquad\quad \vee nodemarks[n] = 0$
$\qquad\quad \vee nodemarks[n] = 1 \wedge CatN[n] \in EndEventType$

$SoundProcess(p) \triangleq \Diamond SoundProcessInt(p)$ generic property (2)

$SoundCollaboration \triangleq$
$\quad \Diamond\Box(\wedge \forall n \in Node : CatN[n] = Process \Rightarrow SoundProcessInt(n)$
$\qquad\quad \wedge \forall e \in Edge : CatE[e] \in MessageFlowType \Rightarrow edgemarks[e] = 0)$

$MessageRelaxedSoundCollaboration \triangleq$ generic property (3)
$\quad \Diamond\Box(\forall n \in Node : CatN[n] = Process \Rightarrow SoundProcessInt(n))$

$User1 \triangleq$ user specific property (4): always end at the base
$\quad \Diamond\Box(nodemarks["\text{PlanterEndInBase}"] \geq 1)$

$User2 \triangleq$ user specific property (5): always end with no place to plant
$\quad \Diamond\Box(subs["\text{toPlant}"] = \{\})$

```
└──────────────────────────────────────────────────────────────────────────┘
```

Fig. 6. Generic and model-specific properties in TLA$^+$.

models from our model database (available from [12], under models/) are presented in Table 2. The first column is the reference of the example in our model database. The characteristics of a model are: number of participants, number of nodes (incl. gateways), number of flow edges (sequence or message flows). When there is communication, we use a bag communication asynchronous model [8]. The results of the verification then follow. First, data on the resulting transition system are given: number of states, number of transitions, and depth (length of the longest sequence of transitions that the model checker had to explore). For each of the correctness properties presented above, we indicate if the model satisfies it. Lastly, the accumulated time for the verification of the properties is given (the time to transform BPMN models to TLA$^+$ transformation is negligible). We selected these five properties since they include BPMN specific generic ones [5], model-specific ones, and cover the safety vs liveness spectrum.

The first model, s004, is a single crop planting process with a loop (find a zone to be planted, move to it, plant it, and mark it to be sprayed) that exits when there are no such zones. Model s006 is our example given in Fig. 3. In this model (and other ones), the id of the end at base TEE is PlanterEndInBase and is used in verification (see property $User1$ in Fig. 6). Model s007 is a variant of model s006 where the context is updated in the planter rather than in the controller. Further, the planter uses the here space formula in the update action rather than znc. Model s008 is the full model (with processes inspired by s007),

Table 2. Experimental results (the space structure is the one in Fig. 2b).

Ref.	Characteristics			Com.	LTS size			Validity					Total
	Proc.	Nodes (gw.)	SF/MF	model	States	Trans.	Depth	(1)	(2)	(3)	(4)	(5)	time
s004	1	6 (1)	5/0	None	34	34	34	✓	✓	✓	✓	✓	<1 s
s006	2	32 (7)	30/5	Bag	276	437	118	✓	✓	✓	✗	✓	2 s
s007	2	31 (7)	29/5	Bag	67	104	31	✓	✓	✓	✓	✓	1 s
s008	3	67 (16)	74/10	Bag	4898	16263	53	✓	✓	✓	✓	✓	8 m 31 s
s009	2	33 (7)	31/5	Bag	296	472	123	✓	✓	✓	✗	✓	3 s

with both robots and two parallel robot-specific sub-processes in the controller. Finally, s009 is a variant of model s006 where the system does not stop upon an unreachable zone to plant, rather the zone is moved to a notTreated group.

Experiments show that our tool supports the verification of BPMN models with the different extensions we propose and is rather fast, even in presence of loops. Verification takes less than a few seconds for most models. It should be noted that property (1) being a safety property, it requires the whole state space to be constructed when the model satisfies the formula. With model s008 we can see the impact of non-determinism in the model, as we have both intra-process concurrency (two parallel sub-processes in the controller), inter-process concurrency (three peers with message communication), and existential quantification over the movements of the processes (planter and sprayer can move to several places each time). Still, verification is achieved in reasonable time.

4   Related Work

Context awareness and context modelling is widely studied in different domains such as Web systems, mobile applications, ubiquitous computing, and business process engineering [15]. Most approaches that support context awareness for Business Process Management (BPM) provide a categorization of contextual information [2,13–15]. Location is there stressed as an essential element.

A classification of contextual information into categories, that include geographical ones, is proposed in [2], with each category referring to multiple context values. The location model, in our work, is represented by the space structure. Many information reported in [1] were useful to identify its elements. Two kinds of coordinate systems, geometric and symbolic coordinates, are mentioned in [1]. Our space structure relies on the latter, with basic locations. According to [1], for symbolic coordinates and in order to allow spatial reasoning, explicit information about the spatial relations between pairs of symbolic coordinates has to be provided. This led in our approach to two instances of such relations: a static one, the → relation, and a dynamic one, the subs relation in configurations.

A survey on spatial models of context information is given in [1], yet without an appropriate model for locations in BPM. The only context modeling approach for BPM we are aware of is [15]. It includes location as a context entity with two attributes, zipcode and city. This is subsumed by our approach as these attributes, and their relations, can be represented using the $\rightarrow$ and subs relations.

Our space structure could be implemented with the data-related constructs of BPMN. Still, this would be cumbersome in comparison to a domain-specific extension like ours. This would also harm the separate reuse of contexts and process models which is made possible by our integration. While there are tools to animate BPMN models with data [4], there is a lack of tools for their verification. Choosing an intermediary expressiveness level, with just the data required for spatial concerns, made verification amenable in our approach. The approach presented in [3] presents interesting perspectives in terms of verification. This approach operates with to distinct databases: a static one (catalog) and an evolving one (repository). Since we deal with environments evolving as a result of the action of processes, we would have to study whether group locations could be treated as part of the catalog and the subs relation as part of the repository.

5   Conclusion and Perspectives

We have proposed a BPMN extension for spatial concerns. Its principles are indeed applicable to other notations such as UML activity diagrams. This widens the use of this family of notations to systems where mobile processes act on their environment. Through the definition of a first-order semantics, its implementation in TLA$^+$, and an automated model transformation, we made it possible to check both the usual process properties (safety, soundness) and context-specific properties. When properties are not satisfied by models, our tools generate counter-examples that are animated on the BPMN models. Our tools and model database are open source and available online at [12].

A first perspective of this work is to consider that the actions of processes can modify the possible moves in the spatial context. We already partially support this through the definition and updates of group locations, but modifying the $\rightarrow$ relation itself would add more expressiveness. By now, processes share the variables set by the evaluation of conditional flows. An extension would be to have also a local perspective of variables, and use message payloads to share them. Taking into account that the environment can evolve by itself (or under the action of processes not being modelled) is also an interesting perspective. This could be achieved, for example, with a specification of possible evolutions to be taken into account at verification time in conjunction with the properties of interest. Indeed, while we use here LTL (with TLA+ extensions to address model-specific properties), we could also study the use of LTL extensions to spatial concerns [7,10]. In this work, we base on the BPMN execution semantics given in [8] with the non-deterministic treatment for time-related elements given there. Another perspective concerns taking into account the second semantics for time given in [8], and study the interplay between time and space. A last perspective is to integrate an optimization aspect to the models, enabling processes to choose their path based on more complex, optimizing strategies, rather than on space formulas only.

Acknowledgements. The authors would like to thank Markus Alexander Kuppe and Philippe Quéinnec for their help with TLA$^+$ and the TLA$^+$ Toolbox.

References

1. Bettini, C., et al.: A survey of context modelling and reasoning techniques. Pervasive Mob. Comput. **6**(2), 161–180 (2010)
2. Born, M., Kirchner, J., Müller., J.P.: Context-driven business process modelling. In: Proceedings of the Joint Workshop on Advanced Technologies and Techniques for Enterprise Information Systems (2009)
3. Calvanese, D., Ghilardi, S., Gianola, A., Montali, M., Rivkin, A.: Formal modeling and SMT-based parameterized verification of data-aware BPMN. In: Proceedings of the International Conference on Business Process Management (2019)
4. Corradini, F., Muzi, C., Re, B., Rossi, L., Tiezzi, F.: MIDA: multiple instances and data animator. In: Proceedings of the International Conference on Business Process Management (2018)
5. Corradini, F., et al.: A classification of BPMN collaborations based on safeness and soundness notions. In: Proceedings of the International Workshop on Expressiveness in Concurrency and of the Workshop on Structural Operational Semantics (2018)
6. Dey, A.K.: Understanding and using context. Pers. Ubiquit. Comput. **5**(1), 4–7 (2001)
7. Haghighi, I., Jones, A., Kong, Z., Bartocci, E., Grosu, R., Belta, C.: Spatel: a novel spatial-temporal logic and its applications to networked systems. In: Proceedings of the International Conference on Hybrid Systems: Computation and Control (2015)
8. Houhou, S., Baarir, S., Poizat, P., Quéinnec, P., Kahloul, L.: A first-order logic verification framework for communication-parametric and time-aware BPMN collaboration. Inf. Syst. 101765 (2021, in press). https://doi.org/10.1016/j.is.2021.101765
9. Lamport, L.: Specifying Systems. The TLA+ Language and Tools for Hardware and Software Engineers, Addison-Wesley, Boston (2002)
10. Nenzi, L., Bortolussi, L., Ciancia, V., Loreti, M., Massink, M.: Qualitative and quantitative monitoring of spatio-temporal properties with SSTL. Log. Methods Comput. Sci. **14**(4), 1–38 (2018)
11. OMG Group: Business process modeling notation (2013). http://www.omg.org/spec/BPMN/2.0.2
12. Poizat, P., et al.: fbpmn repository (2021). https://github.com/pascalpoizat/fbpmn
13. Rosemann, M., Recker, J.: Context-aware process design exploring the extrinsic drivers for process flexibility. In: Proceedings of the CAISE 2006 Workshop on Business Process Modelling, Development, and Support (2006)
14. Saidani, O., Nurcan, S.: Towards context aware business process modelling. In: Proceedings of the CAiSE 2007 Workshop on Business Process Modeling, Development, and Support (2007)
15. Saidani, O., Rolland, C., Nurcan, S.: Towards a generic context model for BPM. In: Proceedings of the Annual Hawaii International Conference on System Sciences (2015)
16. Schilit, B.N., Theimer, M.M.: Disseminating active map information to mobile hosts. IEEE Netw. **8**(5), 22–32 (1994)

Program Verification I

Owicki-Gries Reasoning for C11
Programs with Relaxed Dependencies

Daniel Wright[1(✉)], Mark Batty[1], and Brijesh Dongol[2]

[1] University of Kent, Canterbury, UK
daw29@kent.ac.uk
[2] University of Surrey, Guildford, UK

Abstract. Deductive verification techniques for C11 programs have advanced significantly in recent years with the development of operational semantics and associated logics for increasingly large fragments of C11. However, these semantics and logics have been developed in a restricted setting to avoid the *thin-air-read* problem. In this paper, we propose an operational semantics that leverages an intra-thread partial order (called *semantic dependencies*) induced by a recently developed denotational event-structure-based semantics. We prove that our operational semantics is sound and complete with respect to the denotational semantics. We present an associated logic that generalises a recent Owicki-Gries framework for RC11 (repaired C11), and demonstrate the use of this logic over several example proofs.

1 Introduction

Significant advances have now been made on the semantics of (weak) memory models using a variety of axiomatic (aka declarative), operational and denotational techniques. Several recent works have therefore focussed on logics and associated verification frameworks for *reasoning* about program executions over weak memory models. These include specialised separation logics [9,11,15,26] and adaptations of classical Owicki-Gries reasoning [7,17]. At the level of languages, there has been a particular focus on C11 (the 2011 C/C++ standard).

Due to the complexity of C11 [4], many reasoning techniques have restricted themselves to particular fragments of the language by only allowing certain types of memory accesses and/or reordering behaviours. Several works (e.g., [7,10,15,17]) assume a memory model that guarantees that program order (aka sequenced-before order) is maintained [18]. While this restriction makes the logics and proofs of program correctness more manageable, it precludes reasoning

We thank Simon Doherty for discussions on an earlier version of this work. Wright is supported by VeTSS. Batty is supported by EPSRC grants EP/V000470/1 and EP/R032971/1, and the Royal Academy of Engineering. Dongol is supported by EPSRC grants EP/V038915/1, EP/R032556/1, EP/R025134/2, VeTSS and ARC Discovery Grant DP190102142.

M. Huisman et al. (Eds.): FM 2021, LNCS 13047, pp. 237–254, 2021.
https://doi.org/10.1007/978-3-030-90870-6_13

Init: x = y = r1 = r2 = 0

Thread 1	Thread 2
1: r1 := [x]	3: r2 := [y]
2: [y] := r1+1	4: [x] := 1
$\{r1 \in \{0,1\}\}$	$\{r2 \in \{r1+1,0\}\}$

$$\{r1 \neq 1 \vee r2 \neq 1\}$$

Fig. 1. Load-buffering with a semantic dependency

Init: x = y = r1 = r2 = 0

Thread 1	Thread 2
1: r1 := [x]	3: r2 := [x]
2: [y] := r1	4: [x] := r2
$\{r1 = 0\}$	$\{r2 = 0\}$

$$\{r1 = r2 = 0\}$$

Fig. 2. Load-buffering with two dependencies

about observable executions displaying certain real-world phenomena, e.g., those exhibited by the load-buffering litmus test under Power or ARMv7.

Load Buffering and The Thin Air Problem. C11 suffers from the *out of thin air* problem [5], where the language does not impose any ordering between a read and the writes that depend on its value. The intention is to universally permit aggressive compiler optimisation, but in doing so, this accidentally allows writes to take illogical values. The ARM and Power processors allow the relaxed outcome $r1 = 1$ and $r2 = 2$ in Fig. 1, where there is nothing to enforce the order of the load and store in the second thread [25]. In Fig. 2, each thread reads and then writes the value read – a data dependency from read to write. This dependency makes optimisation impossible, so the relaxed outcome $r1 = r2 = 1$ is forbidden on every combination of compiler and target processor. C++ erroneously allows the outcome $r1 = r2 = 1$, producing the value 1 "out of thin air".

Formally handling load buffering while avoiding out of thin air behaviours turns out to be an enormously complex task. Although several works [6,14,16, 19,23] have been dedicated to providing semantics for different variations of the load buffering example, many of these have also been shown to be inconsistent with expected behaviours under certain litmus tests [13,23]. This work builds on top of the recent MRD (Modular Relaxed Dependencies) semantics by Paviotti et al. [23]. MRD avoids thin air, and aims for compatibility with the existing ISO C and C++ standards.

A key component of MRD is the calculation of a *semantic dependency relation*, which describes when certain reorderings are disallowed. The program in Fig. 1 contains only the semantic dependency between lines 1 and 2, whereas the program in Fig. 2 contains semantic dependencies between lines 1 and 2, and lines 3 and 4. The program in Fig. 1 may therefore execute line 4 before line 3, while the program in Fig. 2 must execute both threads in order.

Contributions. Although precise, there is currently no direct mechanism for reasoning about programs under MRD because MRD is a denotational semantics defined over an event structure [27]. This paper addresses this gap by developing an operational semantics for MRD, which we then use as a basis for a deductive Owicki-Gries style verification framework. The key idea of our operational semantics is to take the semantic dependency relation as the only order in which programs must be executed, thereby allowing intra-thread reordering. This changes the fundamental meaning of sequential composition, allowing statements that occur "later" in the program to be executed early.

Our semantics is also designed to take non multi-copy atomicity into account, whereby writes are not propagated to all threads at the same time and hence may appear take effect out-of-order [1,2]. Note that this phenomenon is distinct from the reordering of operations within a thread (described above), and it is possible to separate the two. Here, we adapt the operational model of weak memory effects by Doherty et al. [10] so that it follows semantic dependency rather than the more restrictive thread order used in earlier works [7,10,15,17].

Finally, we develop a logic capable of reasoning about program executions that exhibit both of the phenomena described above. Our logic makes use of the technique by Dalvandi et al. [7] of including assertions that enable reasoning about the "views" of each thread. Since we have concurrent programs, the logic we develop incorporates Owicki-Gries style reasoning for programs, in which assertions are shown to be both locally correct and globally stable (interference free). However, unlike earlier works [7,17], since we relax thread order, the standard approach to Hoare-style proof decomposition is not possible.

Overview. This paper is organised as follows. We recap MRD in Sect. 2 and an operational semantics for RC11 in Sect. 3. Then in Sect. 4, we present a combined semantics, where program order in RC11 is replaced by a more relaxed order defined by MRD. A Hoare-like logic for reasoning about relaxed program execution together with Owicki-Gries-like rules for reasoning about interference is given in Sect. 5. We present an example proof in Sect. 6.

2   MRD and Semantic Dependencies

In this section, we review the MRD semantics for a simple C-like while language. This provides a mechanism for defining (in a denotational manner) a relaxed order in which statements within a thread are executed, which precludes development of a program logic.

Events and Actions. Weak memory literature uses a variety of terminology to refer to internal representations of changes to global memory, which complicates attempts to unify multiple models. In the following, we use *events* to refer to the objects created and manipulated by MRD, normally represented as integers. We use *actions* to refer to objects of the form i:R x v, i:W x v, referring to a read or write of value v at global location x arising from line i of the input program.

Program Syntax. We assume *shared variables* $x, y, z, \ldots$ from a set X, *registers* $r_1, r_2, \ldots$ from a set Reg, and *register files* $\rho : Reg \rightarrow Val$ mapping registers to values from a set Val. *Expressions* $e, e_1, e_2, \ldots$ are taken from a set E, whose syntax we do not specify, but which can be evaluated w.r.t. a register file using $eval \in E \times (Reg \rightarrow Val) \rightarrow Val$. Thus, $eval(e, \rho)$ is the value of e given the register values in ρ. For basic commands, we have variable assignments (or *stores*)

$[y] := e$ and register assignments (or *loads*) $r := [x]$. In this paper, we assume that stores and loads are *relaxed* [3,10,18] unless they are explicitly specified to be a releasing store (denoted $[y] :=^R e$) or an acquiring load (denoted $r :=^A [x]$). Finally, we assume a simple language of *programs*. The only unconventional aspect of this language is that we require each (variable or register) assignment be decorated with a unique *control label*. This allows a semantics which does not, in general, respect program order to refer to an individual statement without ambiguity. The syntax of commands (for a single thread) is defined by the following grammar, where B is an expression that evaluates to a boolean and i is a control label. Note that since guards are expressions, they must not mention any shared variables—any guard that relies on a shared memory variable must load its values into a local register prior to evaluating the guard.

$$ACom ::= i: \textbf{skip} \mid i: [x] :=^{[R]} e \mid i: r :=^{[A]} [x] \mid i: r := e$$
$$Com ::= ACom \mid Com; Com \mid \textbf{if } B \textbf{ then } Com \textbf{ else } Com \mid \textbf{while } B \textbf{ do } Com$$

We use $[x] :=^{[R]} e$ to denote that the releasing annotation R is optional (similarly $r :=^{[A]} [x]$ for the acquiring annotation A). For simplicity, we focus attention on the core atomic features of C11 necessary to probe the thin-air problem, and omit more complex instructions such as CAS, fences, non-atomic accesses and SC accesses [4].

We assume a top level parallel composition operator. Thus, a program is of the form $C_1 \| C_2 \| \ldots \| C_n$ where $C_i \in Com$. We further assume each atomic command $ACom$ in the program has a unique label across all threads.

Denotational MRD. For the purposes of this paper (i.e., the development of the operational semantics and associated program logic), the precise details of the MRD semantics [23] are unimportant. The most important aspect that we use is the set of *semantic dependency* relations that it generates, which precisely characterise the order in which atomic statements are executed.

In MRD, the *denotation* of a program P is returned by the semantic interpretation function $[\![P]\!]$. This gives a *coherent event structure* of the form:

$$(L, S, \vdash, \leq)$$

where

- $L = (E, \sqsubseteq, \#, Lab)$ is an *event structure* [27] equipped with a labelling function Lab from events (represented internally as integer identifiers) to actions. The set E contains all events in the structure, $a_1 \sqsubseteq a_2$ for $a_1, a_2 \in E$ iff a_1 is program ordered before a_2. Events in $\#$ cannot happen simultaneously, e.g., two reads of a variable returning different values are in conflict.
- $S = (A, \text{LK}, \text{RF}, \text{DP})$ is a set of *partial executions*, each of which represents a possible interaction of the program with the memory system. Each execution in S is a tuple of relations representing *lock/unlock order*, a *reads-from relation* and *dependency order* between operations of *that* execution, and the set of events to be executed. An execution is *complete* if every read in A is linked to a write to the same location of the same value by an RF edge.

- ⊢ is a *justification relation* used in the construction of the program's dependency relation.
- ≤ is the *preserved program order* (c.f., [2]), a subset of the program order of F that is respected by the memory model.

To develop our operational semantics, we only require some of these components. From S, we only require the dependency order. From the labelled event structure, we use the labelling function *Lab* to connect actions to events. From the coherent event structure, we use ≤ to enforce ordering alongside dependency order[1].

Example 1. The event structure in Fig. 3 represents the denotation of the program in Fig. 1. Note first that each store of a value into a register generates multiple events – one for each possible value. This is because MRD cannot make assertions about which values it may or may not observe during interpretation of the structure, it can only be provided with global value range restrictions prior to running. Instead, each read must indicate a write whose value it is observing during the axiomatic checks, subject to various coherence restrictions. A read will only appear in a *complete execution* if it can satisfy this requirement.

Events 2 and 4 are in *conflict* (drawn as a red zigzag) as they represent different potential values being read at line 1. Likewise, events 6, 8, and 10 represent different potential values at line 3. A single execution can observe events 2 and 6, but not events 2 and 4. Events 2 and 3 are in *program order* (represented by the black arrow). MRD generates a *dependency order* between events 2 and 3 and events 4 and 5 (represented by the yellow arrow). The read at line 1 is stored in register r1, which is in turn accessed by the write in line 2, leading to a data dependency. There is no semantic dependency between any events arising from lines 3 and 4, because there is no way for the value read at line 3 to influence the value written at line 4. This means that lines 1 and 2 must be executed in order, but line 4 is free to execute before line 3. For example, consider the traces H_1 and H_2 below.

$$H_1 = \text{Init} \quad 2{:}W\,y\,1 \quad 4{:}W\,x\,1 \quad 1{:}R\,x\,1 \quad 3{:}R\,y\,1$$
$$H_2 = \text{Init} \quad 1{:}R\,x\,1 \quad 4{:}W\,x\,1 \quad 2{:}W\,y\,1 \quad 3{:}R\,y\,1$$

For the program in Fig. 1, the trace H_1 is *disallowed* since in H_1, the operations at lines 2 and 1 are swapped in a manner inconsistent with the dependency order. The trace H_2 is *allowed*, since lines 3 and 4 are free to execute in any order.

3   Operational Semantics with Relaxed Write Propagation

To reason about the relaxed propagation of writes, Doherty et al. [10] build an operational semantics that is equivalent to a declarative (aka axiomatic)

---

[1] MRD also defines a set of axioms that describes when a particular execution is consistent with a denotation. We do not discuss these in detail here, but they are used in the soundness and completeness proofs.

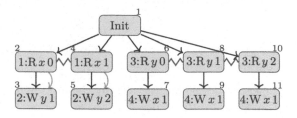

Fig. 3. Coherent event structure for the program in Fig. 1

semantics [18], which defines consistency of *tagged action graphs*. The operational semantics allows the stepwise construction of such graphs, in contrast to a declarative approach which only considers complete executions that are either accepted or rejected by the axioms of the memory model. We do not discuss the declarative semantics here, focusing instead on the operational model, which we generalise in Sect. 4. We also note that like other prior works [15,17,18], the existing operational semantics [10] assumes program order within a thread is maintained.

Formally, *tagged actions* are triples (g, a, t), where g is a tag (uniquely identifying the action); a is a read or write action (potentially annotated as a releasing write or acquiring read), and t is a thread (corresponding to the thread that issued the action). We let TA be the set of all tagged actions, $\mathsf{Wr}, \mathsf{Wr}_R, \mathsf{Rd}, \mathsf{Rd}_A \subseteq TA$ be the set of write, releasing write, read and acquiring reads, respectively. Note that Wr is the set of all writes, including those from Wr_R (similarly, Rd).

A *tagged action graph* is a tuple $(D, \mathsf{sb}, \mathsf{rf}, \mathsf{mo})$ where D is a set of tagged actions, which may correspond to read or write actions, and sb, rf and mo are relations over D. Here, sb is the *sequenced before* relation, where $b_1 \, \mathsf{sb} \, b_2$ iff b_1 and b_2 are tagged actions of the same thread and b_1 is executed before b_2. $\mathsf{rf} \subseteq \mathsf{Wr} \times \mathsf{Rd}$ is the *reads-from* relation [2] relating each write to the read that reads from that write. Finally, $\mathsf{mo} \subseteq \mathsf{Wr} \times \mathsf{Wr}$ denotes *modification order* (aka coherence order), which is the order in which writes occur in the system, and hence the order in which writes must be seen by all threads. Note that if $b_1 \, \mathsf{mo} \, b_2$, then b_1 and b_2 must act on the same variable. Moreover, $\mathsf{mo}|x$ is a total order, where $\mathsf{mo}|x$ is the relation mo restricted to writes of variable x.

We assume tagged action graphs are initialised with writes corresponding to the initialisation of the program, and relations sb, rf and mo are initially empty.

Following Lahav et al. [18], the so-called repairing or restricted C11 model (which is the model in [7,10,15]) instantiates sequence-before order to the *program order* relation [2]. This disallows statements within a thread from being executed out-of-order (although writes may be propagated to other threads in a relaxed manner). In Sect. 4, we present an alternative instantiation of sb using the semantic dependencies generated by MRD to enable out-of-order executions within a thread can be considered.

To characterise the operational semantics, we must define three further relations: *happens before*, denoted hb (which captures a notion of causality); *from read*, denoted fr (which relates each read to the write that overwrites the value read), and *extended coherence order*, denoted eco (which fixes the order of writes and reads). Formally we have:

$$\text{hb} = (\text{sb} \cup (\text{rf} \cap \text{Wr}_R \times \text{Rd}_A))^+ \qquad \text{fr} = (\text{rf}^{-1}; \text{mo}) \setminus Id \qquad \text{eco} = (\text{rf} \cup \text{mo} \cup \text{fr})^+$$

where Id is the identity relation, ; denotes relational composition, and $^+$ denotes transitive closure. Note that there is only a happens-before relation between a write-read pair related by rf if the write is releasing and the read is acquiring.

$$\text{READ} \frac{\begin{array}{cccc} b = (g, a, t) & g \notin tags(D) & a \in \{\text{i:R}\,x\,n, \text{i:R}^A\,x\,n\} \\ \sigma = (D, \text{sb}, \text{rf}, \text{mo}) & w \in OW_\sigma(t) & var(w) = x & wrval(w) = n \end{array}}{(D, \text{sb}, \text{rf}, \text{mo}) \overset{b}{\rightsquigarrow} (D \cup \{b\}, \text{sb} +_D b, \text{rf} \cup \{(w, b)\}, \text{mo})}$$

$$\text{WRITE} \frac{\begin{array}{ccc} b = (g, a, t) & g \notin tags(D) & a \in \{\text{i:W}\,x\,n, \text{i:W}^R\,x\,n\} \\ \sigma = (D, \text{sb}, \text{rf}, \text{mo}) & w \in OW_\sigma(t) & var(w) = x \end{array}}{(D, \text{sb}, \text{rf}, \text{mo}) \overset{b}{\rightsquigarrow} (D \cup \{b\}, \text{sb} +_D b, \text{rf}, \text{mo}[w, b])}$$

Fig. 4. Memory semantics

With these basic relations in place, we are now in a position to define the transition relation governing the operational rules for read and write actions. The rules themselves are given in Fig. 4. Assuming σ denotes the set of all tagged action graphs, each transition is a relation $\rightsquigarrow \subseteq \Sigma \times TA \times \Sigma$. We write $\sigma \overset{b}{\rightsquigarrow} \sigma'$ to denote $(\sigma, b, \sigma') \in \rightsquigarrow$.

To accommodate relaxed propagation of writes, the semantics allows different threads to have different views of the system, formalised by a set of *observable writes*. These are in turn defined in terms of a set of *encountered writes*, denoted $EW_\sigma(t)$, which are the writes that thread t is aware of (either directly or indirectly) in state σ:

$$EW_\sigma(t) = \{w \in \text{Wr} \cap D_\sigma \mid \exists b \in D_\sigma.\ tid(b) = t \wedge (w, b) \in \text{eco}_\sigma^?; \text{hb}_\sigma^?\}$$

Here $R^?$ is the reflexive closure of relation R and tid returns the thread identifier of the given tagged action. Thus, for each $w \in EW_\sigma(t)$, there must exist a tagged action b of thread t such that w is either eco-, hb- or eco; hb-prior to b. From these we determine the *observable writes*, which are the writes that thread t can observe in its next read. These are defined as:

$$OW_\sigma(t) = \{w \in \text{Wr} \cap D_\sigma \mid \forall w' \in EW_\sigma(t).\ (w, w') \notin \text{mo}_\sigma\}$$

$$\dfrac{n = eval(e, \gamma(t)) \quad a = \mathrm{i}{:}\mathrm{W}^{[R]}\, x\, n}{(i{:}\ [x] :=^{[R]} e, \gamma) \xrightarrow{\ a\ }_t (\mathbf{skip}, \gamma)} \qquad \dfrac{a = \mathrm{i}{:}\mathrm{R}^{[A]}\, x\, n \quad \rho' = \gamma(t)[r := n]}{(i{:}\ r :=^{[A]} [x], \rho) \xrightarrow{\ a\ }_t (\mathbf{skip}, \gamma[t := \rho'])}$$

$$\textsc{Prog} \dfrac{(P(t), \gamma) \xrightarrow{\ a\ }_t (C, \gamma')}{(P, \gamma) \xrightarrow{\ a\ }_t (P[t := C], \gamma')} \qquad \textsc{Full} \dfrac{b = (g, a, t) \qquad (P, \gamma) \xrightarrow{\ a\ }_t (P', \gamma') \qquad \sigma \xrightsquigarrow{\ b\ } \sigma'}{(P, (\sigma, \gamma)) \xRightarrow{\ b\ } (P', (\sigma', \gamma'))}$$

Fig. 5. Interpreted operational semantics of programs (sample)

Observable writes are writes that are not succeeded by any encountered write in modification order, i.e., the thread has not seen another write overwriting the value being read.

We now describe each of the rules in Fig. 4. Relations rf and mo are updated according to the write actions in D that are observable to the thread t executing the given action. A read action b may read from any write $w \in OW_\sigma(t)$. In the post state, we obtain a new tagged action set $D \cup \{b\}$, sequenced-before relation sb $+_D b$ (defined below) and reads-from relation rf $\cup \{(w, b)\}$. Relation mo is unmodified. Formally, sb $+_D b$ introduces b at the end of sb for thread t:

$$\mathsf{sb} +_D b = \mathsf{sb} \cup (\{b' \in D \mid tid(b') \in \{tid(b), 0\}\} \times \{b\})$$

Note that we assume that initialisation is carried out by a unique thread with id 0, and that we require the set D as an input to cope with initialisation where sb may be empty for the given thread.

The write rule is similar except that it leaves rf unchanged and updates mo to mo$[w, b]$. Given that $R[x]$ is the relational image of x in R, we define $R_{\Downarrow x} = \{x\} \cup R^{-1}[x]$ to be the set of all elements in R that relate to x (inclusive). The insertion of a tagged write action b directly after a w in mo is given by

$$\mathsf{mo}[w, b] = \mathsf{mo} \cup (\mathsf{mo}_{\Downarrow w} \times \{b\}) \cup (\{b\} \times \mathsf{mo}[w])$$

Thus, mo$[w, b]$ effectively introduces b immediately after the w in mo.

The final component of the operational semantics is a set of rules that link the program syntax in Sect. 2 with the memory semantics. In prior work, this was through a set of operational rules that generate the actions associated with each atomic statement, combined with the rules in Fig. 4 to formalise the evolution of states. A sample of these rules for reads and writes from memory are given in Fig. 5. These are then lifted to the level of programs using the rules PROG and FULL, where the transition rule $\xRightarrow{\ b\ }$ combines the thread-local semantics $\xrightarrow{\ a\ }_t$ and global-state semantics $\xrightsquigarrow{\ b\ }$. Note that we model parallel composition as functions from thread identifiers to commands, thus $P[t := C]$ represents the program, where the command for thread t is updated to C.

The rules in [10] generate actions corresponding to program syntax (i.e., $\xrightarrow{\ a\ }_t$) in *program order*. In this paper, we follow a different approach—the actions will be generated by (and executed in) the order defined by MRD. This therefore allows both reordering of program statements and relaxed write propagation.

4   Operational Semantics over MRD

Recall that the MRD semantic interpretation function $[\![P]\!]$ outputs a coherent event structure $\mu = (L, S, \vdash, \leq)$. In this section, we develop an operational semantics for traversing μ, while generating state configurations that model relaxed write propagation. In essence, this generalises the operational semantics in Sect. 3 so that threads are executed out-of-order, as allowed by MRD.

4.1   Program Futures

Defining our operational semantics over raw syntax would force us to evaluate statements in program order. Therefore we convert this syntax into a set of atomic statements. We call this the *atomic set* of C, written $\overline{C}$. MRD evaluates while loops using step-indexing, treating them as finite unwindings of **if-then-else** commands. For these, we generate a fresh unique label for each iteration of the while loop for each of the atomic commands within the loop body. Recall that the parallel composition of commands is modelled by a function from thread identifiers to (sequential) commands. The atomic set of a program P is therefore $\lambda t.\ \overline{P(t)}$.

To retain the ordering recognised during program execution, we introduce *futures*, which are sets of MRD events partially ordered by the semantic dependency and preserved program order relations. Essentially, instead of taking our operational steps in program order over the syntax, we can nondeterministically execute any statement which our futures tell us we have executed all necessary predecessors of.

For an execution $S = (A, \textsc{lk}, \textsc{rf}, \textsc{dp})$ of an event structure μ, we can construct an initial future $f = (A, \preceq)$, where $\preceq\ =\ \textsc{dp} \cup \leq_{|A}$ and $\leq_{|A}$ is the preserved program order $\leq$ (see Sect. 2) restricted to events in A. We say that an action a is *available* in a future $(K, \preceq)$ iff there exists some event g with label a such that $g \in K$ and g is minimal in $\preceq$, i.e., for all events $g' \in K$, $g' \npreceq g$. If a is available in f, then the *future of a in f*, denoted $a \triangleright f$, is the future

$$a \triangleright f \iff (K', \preceq_{|K'}) \qquad \text{where } K' = K \setminus \{g \mid \lambda_\mu(g) = a\}$$

We lift this to a set of futures F to describe the *candidate futures of a in F*, denoted $a \triangleright F$:

$$a \triangleright F = \{a \triangleright f \mid f \in F \wedge a \text{ available in } f\}$$

Note that a is *enabled* in F iff $a \triangleright F \neq \emptyset$.

Essentially, $a \triangleright F$ consumes an event g with label a from each of the futures in F provided a is available, discarding all futures in which a is not available. Intuitively, if an event is minimal in a program future then it may be executed immediately. If it is not minimal, its predecessors must be executed first.

4.2   Future-Based Transition Relation

Our operational semantics is defined by the transition relation in FUTURE-STEP given below, which generalises FULL in Fig. 5. The transition relation is defined over $(\overline{Q}, (\sigma, \gamma), F)$, where $\overline{Q}$ is the atomic set corresponding to the program text, (σ, γ) is a configuration and F is a set of *futures*. The rule generalises FULL in the obvious way, i.e., by evolving the configuration as allowed by $\xrightarrow{(g,a,t)}$ and $\xrightarrow{a}_t$ and consuming an available action a in F. Below, we use $\uplus$ to denote disjoint union and $f[k := v]$ to denote function updates where $f(k)$ is updated to v.

$$\text{FUTURE-STEP} \frac{\overline{Q}(t) = \overline{C} \uplus \{i\colon s\} \qquad a \triangleright F \neq \emptyset}{(i\colon s, \gamma) \xrightarrow{a}_t (\mathbf{skip}, \gamma') \qquad \sigma \xrightarrow{(g,a,t)} \sigma'}{(\overline{Q}, (\sigma, \gamma), F) \xLongrightarrow{\mu} (\overline{Q}[t := \overline{C}], (\sigma', \gamma'), a \triangleright F)}$$

Once a minimal action is chosen in a step of the operational semantics, it is checked for consistency and added to the set of executed events. The set of futures is pruned to remove the chosen event, and to exclude any futures that are incompatible with the chosen event. The operational semantics continues until it has consumed all of the futures.

   The following theorem establishes equivalence of our operational semantics and the MRD denotational semantics.

Theorem 1 (Soundness and Completeness). *Every execution generated by the MRD model can be generated by the operational semantics, and every final state generated by the operational semantics corresponds to a complete execution of the MRD semantics.*

4.3   Example

Recall the program in Fig. 1 and its event structure representation in Fig. 3. Let $\Delta_S = \{(x, x) \mid x \in S\}$ be the diagonal of set S. We first derive our set of futures from this structure:

$$\{2 \prec 3, 6, 7\} \qquad \{2 \prec 3, 8, 9\} \qquad \{2 \prec 3, 10, 11\}$$
$$\{4 \prec 5, 6, 7\} \qquad \{4 \prec 5, 8, 9\} \qquad \{4 \prec 5, 10, 11\}$$

where $\{2 \prec 3, 6, 7\}$ represents the future $(\{2, 3, 6, 7\}, 2 \prec 3 \cup \Delta_{\{2,3,6,7\}})$. The atomic set of the program is

$$\overline{P} = \left\{ \begin{array}{l} 1 \mapsto \{1\colon \mathtt{r1} := [\mathtt{x}], 2\colon [\mathtt{y}] := \mathtt{r1} + 1\}, \\ 2 \mapsto \{3\colon \mathtt{r2} := [\mathtt{y}], 4\colon [\mathtt{x}] := 1\} \end{array} \right\}$$

The initial configuration is (σ_0, γ_0), where $\sigma_0 = (\{(0_x, 0{:}\mathrm{W}\, x\, 0, 0), (0_y, 0{:}\mathrm{W}\, y\, 0, 0)\}, \emptyset, \emptyset, \emptyset)$ and $\gamma_0 = \{1 \mapsto \{r1 \mapsto 0\}, 2 \mapsto \{r2 \mapsto 0\}\}$, assuming the initialising thread has identifier 0.

   To find out which events we can execute, we check our futures set. We cannot execute events 3 or 5, which both have pre-requisite events that have not yet been executed. These events are the only available events generated by line 2, so we cannot attempt to execute line 2. We can, however, execute any other line. Suppose we execute line 4, which corresponds to $4 : [x] := 1$ in $\overline{P}(2)$. To use the transition relation $\overset{\mu}{\Longrightarrow}$, we need to do the following: (1) determine the corresponding action, a and new thread-local state using $\overset{a}{\longrightarrow}_2$; (2) generate a tagged action $b = (g, a, 2)$ for a fresh tag g and a new global state using $\overset{b}{\leadsto}$; and (3) check that a is available in the current set of futures.

For (1), we can only create one action $a = 4{:}W\,x\,1$ and the local state is unchanged. For (2), we generate a new global state using the WRITE rule in Fig. 4 (full details elided). For (3), we take our candidate futures $a \triangleright F$ by examining which MRD events have the label $4{:}W\,x\,1$—in this case events 7, 9, and 11. All futures can execute one of these events so the new future set contains all futures in F, each minus the set $\{7, 9, 11\}$.

5   Hoare Logic and Owicki-Gries Reasoning

Recall that the standard Owicki-Gries methodology [22] decomposes proofs of parallel programs into two cases:

- *local correctness* conditions, which define correctness of an assertion with respect to an individual thread, and
- *non-interference* conditions, which ensures stability of an assertion under the execution of statements in other threads.

The standard Owicki-Gries methodology has been shown to be applicable to a weak memory setting with relaxed write propagation (but without relaxed program order) [7]. Note that an alternative characterisation (also in a model without relaxed program order) has been given in [17][2]. Unfortunately, the unrestricted C11 semantics captured by MRD relaxes program order and hence sequential composition in order to allow behaviours such as those in Fig. 1, which requires a fundamental shift in Hoare-style proof decomposition. We show that the modular Owicki-Gries rules, for reasoning about concurrent threads remain unchanged.

Like Dalvandi et al. [7], we assume assertions are predicates over state configurations. In the current paper, the operational semantics is dictated by the set of futures generated by MRD, thus we require two modifications to the classical meaning. First, like prior work [7], we assume predicates are over state configurations, which include (local) register files and (shared) event graphs. This takes into account relaxed write propagation. Second, we introduce Hoare-triples with futures generated by MRD, which takes into account relaxed program execution.

In the development below, we refer to the *preprocessed form* of a program P given by $\mathcal{P}(P) = (\mu, \overline{P})$, where μ is the coherent event structure $[\![P]\!]$ and $\overline{P}$ the set normal form of P. We let F_μ be the initial set of futures corresponding to μ.

---

[2] This characterisation uses standard assertions but assumes a non-standard interpretation of Hoare-triples and introduces a stronger interference freedom check. In fact, for the model in [17], the introduction of auxiliary variables is unsound.

Definition 1 (Hoare triple). *Suppose X and Y are predicates over state configurations, P is a concurrent program, and $\mathcal{P}(P) = (\mu, \overline{P})$. The semantics of a Hoare triple is given by $\{X\}\ Init; P\ \{Y\}$, where*

$$\{X\}\ Init; P\ \{Y\}\ \ \widehat{=}\ \ (Init \Rightarrow X)\ \wedge$$
$$(\forall \mathbb{C}, \mathbb{C}'.\ X(\mathbb{C}) \wedge ((\overline{P}, \mathbb{C}, F_\mu) \xLongrightarrow{\mu}^* (\emptyset, \mathbb{C}', \emptyset))\ \Rightarrow\ Y(\mathbb{C}'))$$

That is, $\{X\}\ P\ \{Y\}$ holds iff for every pair of state configurations $\mathbb{C}, \mathbb{C}'$, assuming $X(\mathbb{C})$ holds and we execute $\overline{P}$ with respect to the future F_μ until $\overline{P}$ terminates in $\mathbb{C}'$, we have $Y(\mathbb{C}')$.

Although Definition 1 provides meaning for a Hoare triple, we still require a method for decomposing the proof outline. To this end, we introduce the concept of a *future predicate*, which is a predicate parameterised by both futures and configuration states. To make use of future predicates, we introduce a notion of a Hoare triple for programs in set normal form.

For the definitions below, assume P is a program and $\mathcal{P}(P) = (\mu, \overline{P})$. We say an atomic set $\overline{Q}$ is a *sub-program* of an atomic set $\overline{P}$ iff for all t, $\overline{Q}(t) \subseteq \overline{P}(t)$. We say a set of futures F' is a *sub-future* of set of futures F iff for each $f' \in F'$ there exists an $f \in F$ such that f' is an up-closed subset of f. For example, if $F = \{\{1 \prec 2, 3, 4\}, \{1 \prec 2, 3\}\}$, then $\{\{2, 4\}, \{1 \prec 2\}\}$ is a sub-future of F, but $\{\{1, 3\}\}$ is not. We say the sub-program $\overline{Q}$ corresponds to a sub-future F iff $labels(\overline{Q}) = labels(\{Lab_\mu[\pi_1 f] \mid f \in F\})$, where we assume $labels$ returns the set of all labels of its argument, π_1 is the project of the first component of the given argument, and $R[S]$ is the relational image of set S over relation R.

Definition 2 (Hoare triple (single step)). *Suppose I and I' are future predicates, P is a program and $\mathcal{P}(P) = (\mu, \overline{P})$. If G is a sub-future of F_μ, corresponding to a sub-program $\overline{Q}$ of $\overline{P}$, we define*

$$\{I\}_G\ \overline{Q}\ \{I'\}$$
$$\widehat{=} \forall \mathbb{C}, \mathbb{C}', G'.\ I(G)(\mathbb{C}) \wedge ((\overline{Q}, \mathbb{C}, G) \xLongrightarrow{\mu} (\overline{Q}', \mathbb{C}', G'))\ \Rightarrow\ I'(G')(\mathbb{C}')$$

We say I is *future stable* for $(F, \overline{P})$ iff for all sub-futures G of F with corresponding sub-programs $\overline{Q}$ of $\overline{P}$, we have $\{I\}_G\ \overline{Q}\ \{I\}$.

Lemma 1 (Invariant). *Suppose X and Y are configuration-state predicates, P is a program and $\mathcal{P}(P) = (\mu, \overline{P})$. If $X \Rightarrow I(F_\mu)$, $I(\emptyset) \Rightarrow Y$ and I is future stable for $(F_\mu, \overline{P})$, then $\{X\}Init; P\{Y\}$ provided $Init \Rightarrow X$.*

By construction, the sets of futures corresponding to different threads are disjoint, i.e., for each future $f \in F_\mu$, we have that $f = \bigcup_t f_{|t}$, where $f_{|t}$ denotes the future f restricted to events of thread t. The only possible inter-thread dependency in MRD is via the reads from relation [23], which does not contribute to the set of futures. This observation leads to a technique for an Owicki-Gries-like modular proof technique for decomposing the monolithic invariant I into an invariant per thread.

We define $F_{|t} = \{f_{|t} \mid f \in F\}$. Then, we obtain the following lemma for decomposing invariants in the same way as Owicki and Gries.

Lemma 2 (Owicki-Gries). *For each thread t, let I_t be a future predicate corresponding to t. If $Init \Rightarrow X$, $X \Rightarrow \forall t.\ I_t(F_{\mu|t})$, and $\forall t.\ I_t(\emptyset) \Rightarrow Y$, then $\{X\}P\{Y\}$ holds provided both of the following hold.*

1. *For all threads t, I_t is future stable for $(F_{\mu|t}, \overline{P})$.   (local correctness)*
2. *For all threads t_1, t_2 such that $t_1 \neq t_2$, sub-futures F_1 of $F_{\mu|t_1}$, and F_2 of $F_{\mu|t_2}$, if $\overline{Q}$ corresponds to F_2, then we have[3] $\{I_{t_1}(F_1) \wedge I_{t_2}\}_{F_2} \overline{Q} \{I_{t_1}(F_1)\}$.*

     (global correctness)

Thus, we establish $\{X\}P\{Y\}$ through a series of smaller proof obligations. We require that (1) the initialisation of the program guarantees X, (2) whenever X holds then for each thread t, I_t holds for the initial future $F_{\mu|t}$, (3) if $I_t(\emptyset)$ holds for all t, then the post-condition Y holds, (4) each I_t is maintained by the execution of each thread, and (5) I_t at each sub-future of t is stable with respect to steps of another thread.

6   A Verification Example

With the verification framework now in place, we present a correctness proof for the program in Fig. 1. The program and invariant are given in Fig. 6. First, in Sect. 6.1, we present assertions for reasoning about state-configurations.

6.1   View-Based Assertions

As we can see from Fig. 5, the states that we use are *configurations*, which are pairs of the form (σ, γ), where σ is an tagged action graph representing the shared state and γ is mapping from threads to register files representing the local state. Like prior work [7], we use assertions that describe the *views* of each thread, recalling that due to relaxed write propagation, the views of each thread may be different. Note that the formalisation of a state in prior work is a time-stamp based semantics [7]. Nevertheless, the principles for defining thread-view assertions also carry over to our setting of tagged action graphs.

In this paper, the programs we consider are relatively simple, and hence, we only use two types of view assertions: *synchronised view*, denoted $[x = v]_t$, which holds iff both thread t observes the last write to x and this write updates the value of x to v, and *possible view*, denoted $[x \approx v]_t$, which holds iff t may observe a write to x with value v. Formally, we define

$$[x = v]_t(\sigma, \gamma) \mathrel{\hat{=}} \exists w.\ OW_\sigma(t)_{|x} = \{w\} \wedge wrval(w) = v$$
$$[x \approx v]_t(\sigma, \gamma) \mathrel{\hat{=}} \exists w \in OW_\sigma(t)_{|x}.\ wrval(w) = v$$

where $OW_\sigma(t)|x$ denotes the writes in $OW_\sigma(t)$ restricted to the variable x. Recall that, by definition, for any state σ generated by the operational semantics, the last write to each variable in mo order is observable to every thread. Examples of these assertions in the context of an Owicki-Gries-style proof outline is given in Fig. 6.

---

[3] Technically speaking, each instance of $I_{t_1}(F_1)$ in the Hoare-triple is a function $\lambda x.\ I_{t_1}(F_1)$.

Init: $x = y = r1 = r2 = 0$
$$\{[x = 0]_1 \wedge [x = 0]_2 \wedge [y = 0]_1 \wedge [y = 0]_2 \wedge r1 = r2 = 0\}$$

Thread 1

$\{[y = 0]_2 \wedge r2 = 0$
$\quad \wedge (\forall i. \ i \notin \{0,1\} \Rightarrow [x \not\approx i]_1)\}_F$
1: r1 := [x]
$\{[y = 0]_2 \wedge r2 = 0 \wedge r1 \in \{0,1\}\}_{F_1}$
2: [y] := r1 + 1
$\{r1 \neq 1 \vee r2 \neq 1\}_{\emptyset}$

Thread 2

$\{[x = 0]_1 \wedge r1 = 0\}_G$
$\quad \{r1 = 0 \vee$
$\quad\quad (r1 = 1 \wedge (\forall i. \ i \notin \{0,2\} \Rightarrow [y \not\approx i]_2))\}_{G_4}$
3: r2 := [y]
$\{[x = 0]_1 \wedge r1 = 0\}_{G_3}$
4: [x] := 1
$\{r1 \neq 1 \vee r2 \neq 1\}_{\emptyset}$

$$\{r1 \neq 1 \vee r2 \neq 1\}$$

Fig. 6. Proof outline for load buffering with semantic dependencies

6.2   Example Proof

To reduce the domain of our future predicate, we collapse the event-based futures used by the operational semantics into sets of label-based futures. An event future F_E can be converted into a label future F_L by applying the labelling function to all events in F_E. This makes the futures $\{3\}$ and $\{5\}$ equivalent, as both are instances of $\{2:W\ y\ 2\}$, thus $I(\{3\}) = I(\{5\})$. This isn't always a valid step, as some events which share labels may not be related by $\preceq$ in the same way. Thus, the technique can only be used if the label-based representation describes exactly the futures generated by MRD, which is the case for our example.

We describe our initial set of label futures as $\{\{1_u < 2, 3_v, 4\} \mid u \in \{0,1\} \wedge v \in \{0,1,2\}\}$, using the notation $\{i_v\}$ to refer to an action with the line number i with a read that returns the value v. We verify that this is a valid step: all futures generated by MRD are described by these labels, and they do not describe any potential futures not generated by MRD. We partition this into $F = \{\{1_u < 2\} \mid u \in \{0,1\}\}$ and $G = \{\{3_v, 4\} \mid v \in \{0,1,2\}\}$ representing the future sets of threads 1 and 2, respectively. We let $F_1 = \{\{2\}\}$ be the future set after executing line 1, $G_3 = \{\{4\}\}$ be the future set after executing line 3 (reading some value for y), and $G_4 = \{\{3_v\} \mid v \in \{0,1,2\}\}$ be the future set after executing line 4.

Our future predicate I must output a configuration predicate for every sub-future of the initial set. Our partitioning fully describes these sub-futures, so we now attach our assertions to these futures.

To simplify the visualisation, we interleave the future predicate components with the program to provide Hoare-style pre/post-assertions, and place the assertion above a line of code if that line of code is contained in the applied future. We use indentation to denote that an assertion applies to more than one future. In this example G contains both lines 3 and 4, hence both lines are indented w.r.t. the first assertion in thread 2. We apply Lemma 2, and in the discussion below, we describe the local and global correctness checks.

For local correctness in thread 1, we must establish that $\{I\}_F\{1,2\}\{I\}_{\emptyset}$. By the definition of the future F, line 1 must be executed before line 2. This means we only need to verify that $\{I\}_F\{1\}\{I\}_{F_1}$ and $\{I\}_{F_1}\{2\}\{I\}_\emptyset$, which is identical to a standard Hoare logic proof and relatively uninteresting.

In thread 2, no order is imposed between lines 3 and 4. This means to establish local correctness we must check that:

- $\{I\}_G$ 3: `r2 := [y]` $\{I\}_{G_3}$
- $\{I\}_G$ 4: `[x] := 1` $\{I\}_{G_4}$
- $\{I\}_{G_3}$ 4: `[x] := 1` $\{I\}_\emptyset$
- $\{I\}_{G_4}$ 3: `r2 := [y]` $\{I\}_\emptyset$

The first three are trivial: line 3 modifies neither x nor $r1$ and line 4 does not modify $r1$. For the final step, the first disjunct of $\{I\}_{G_4}$ is the same as the first disjunct of $\{I\}_\emptyset$, and the second disjunct ensures that we cannot observe $r2 = 1$ after executing line 3.

For global correctness, we must check that every assertion in thread 1 continues to hold after every line of thread 2, and vice versa. These checks are also straightforward, so omit a detailed discussion. The only noteworthy aspect is that for line 3 (and similarly, line 4), our precondition is the conjunction $\{I\}_{G_4} \wedge \{I\}_G$, as both G and G_3 are subfutures corresponding to line 3.

The proof described above has actually been encoded and checked using our existing Isabelle/HOL development [7,8] by manually encoding the re-ordering in thread 2. We aim to develop full mechanisation support as future work.

7   Related Work

Work based on assumptions unsound in C++. Most logics for weak memory are based on simplifying assumptions that exclude thin air reads by ensuring program order is respected, even when no semantic dependency exists [7,10, 11,15,17]. These assumptions incorrectly exclude the relaxed outcome of load buffering tests like Fig. 1, introducing unsoundness when applied to languages like C++: compiling Fig. 1 for an ARM processor produces code that does exhibit the relaxed behaviour. The logic of Lundberg et al. [20] correctly discards many of this spurious program ordering, but it does not handle concurrency. We provide an operational semantics of C++ that solves the thin air problem, where prior attempts use simplifying assumptions like those of prior logics [7,21].

Thin-Air-Free Semantics. Each of the concurrency definitions that solves the out-of-thin-air problem is remarkably complex [6,14,16,19,23,24], and so too is MRD. We choose to base our logic on MRD because MRD's semantic dependency relation hides much of the complexity of the model that calculates it. Where previously we would rely on program ordering, now we consider the semantic dependency provided by MRD.

Logics for Thin-Air-Free Models. There are four logics built above concurrency models that solve the thin air problem: three of these are very simple and apply to only a handful of examples [13,14,16], and one is a separation logic built above the Promising Semantics [26]. Unfortunately, the Promising Semantics allows unwanted out-of-thin-air behaviour, forbidden by MRD [23], and as a result may not support type safety [13].

8   Conclusions and Future Work

The subtle behaviour of concurrent programs written in optimised languages necessitates good support for reasoning, but existing logics make unsound assumptions that rule out compiler optimisations, or use underlying concurrency models that admit out of thin air behaviour (see Sect. 7). We present a logic built above MRD. MRD has been recognised as a potential solution to the thin air problem in C and C++ by the ISO [12] and is the best guess at a C++ model that allows optimisation and forbids thin-air behaviours.

We follow a typical path for constructing a logic and start with an operational semantics that we show equivalent to MRD, and then as far a possible, follow the reasoning style of Owicki Gries. In each case, we diverge from a typical development because we cannot adopt program order into our reasoning system and instead must follow semantic dependency. Our logic supplants linear program order with a partial order, and where traditional pre- and post-conditions are indexed by the program counter, here we index them by their position in the partial order. This approach will work with any memory model that can provide a partially ordered structure over individual program actions.

The challenge in using the logic presented here is in managing the multitude of proof obligations that follow from the branching structure and lack of order in semantic dependency. This problem represents an avenue for further work: it may be possible to obviate the need for some of these additional proof obligations within the logic or to provide tools to more conveniently manage them.

References

1. Adve, S.V., Gharachorloo, K.: Shared memory consistency models: a tutorial. IEEE Comput. **29**(12), 66–76 (1996)
2. Alglave, J., Maranget, L., Tautschnig, M.: Herding cats: modelling, simulation, testing, and data mining for weak memory. ACM Trans. Program. Lang. Syst. **36**(2), 7:1–7:74 (2014)
3. Batty, M., Dodds, M., Gotsman, A.: Library abstraction for C/C++ concurrency. In: Giacobazzi, R., Cousot, R. (eds.) POPL, pp. 235–248. ACM (2013)
4. Batty, M., Owens, S., Sarkar, S., Sewell, P., Weber, T.: Mathematizing C++ concurrency. In: Ball, T., Sagiv, M. (eds.) POPL, pp. 55–66. ACM (2011)
5. Batty, M., Memarian, K., Nienhuis, K., Pichon-Pharabod, J., Sewell, P.: The problem of programming language concurrency semantics. In: Vitek, J. (ed.) ESOP 2015. LNCS, vol. 9032, pp. 283–307. Springer, Heidelberg (2015). https://doi.org/10.1007/978-3-662-46669-8_12
6. Chakraborty, S., Vafeiadis, V.: Grounding thin-air reads with event structures. Proc. ACM Program. Lang. **3**(POPL), 70:1–70:28 (2019). https://doi.org/10.1145/3290383

7. Dalvandi, S., Doherty, S., Dongol, B., Wehrheim, H.: Owicki-Gries reasoning for C11 RAR. In: Hirschfeld, R., Pape, T. (eds.) ECOOP. LIPIcs, vol. 166, pp. 11:1–11:26. Schloss Dagstuhl - Leibniz-Zentrum für Informatik (2020). https://doi.org/10.4230/LIPIcs.ECOOP.2020.11

8. Dalvandi, S., Dongol, B., Doherty, S.: Integrating Owicki-Gries for C11-style memory models into Isabelle/HOL. CoRR abs/2004.02983 (2020). https://arxiv.org/abs/2004.02983

9. Dang, H., Jourdan, J., Kaiser, J., Dreyer, D.: Rustbelt meets relaxed memory. Proc. ACM Program. Lang. **4**(POPL), 34:1–34:29 (2020), https://doi.org/10.1145/3371102

10. Doherty, S., Dongol, B., Wehrheim, H., Derrick, J.: Verifying C11 programs operationally. In: Hollingsworth, J.K., Keidar, I. (eds.) PPoPP, pp. 355–365. ACM (2019). https://doi.org/10.1145/3293883.3295702

11. Doko, M., Vafeiadis, V.: Tackling real-life relaxed concurrency with FSL++. In: ESOP, pp. 448–475 (2017)

12. Giroux, O.: ISO WG21 SG1 concurrency subgroup vote unanimously approved: OOTA is a major problem for C++, modular relaxed dependencies is the best path forward we have seen, and we wish to continue to pursue this direction (2010). https://github.com/cplusplus/papers/issues/554#issuecomment-551899923

13. Jagadeesan, R., Jeffrey, A., Riely, J.: Pomsets with preconditions: a simple model of relaxed memory. Proc. ACM Program. Lang. **4**(OOPSLA), 194:1–194:30 (2020). https://doi.org/10.1145/3428262

14. Jeffrey, A., Riely, J.: On thin air reads: Towards an event structures model of relaxed memory. Log. Methods Comput. Sci. **15**(1) (2019), https://doi.org/10.23638/LMCS-15(1:33)2019

15. Kaiser, J., Dang, H., Dreyer, D., Lahav, O., Vafeiadis, V.: Strong logic for weak memory: reasoning about release-acquire consistency in iris. In: ECOOP, pp. 17:1–17:29 (2017)

16. Kang, J., Hur, C., Lahav, O., Vafeiadis, V., Dreyer, D.: A promising semantics for relaxed-memory concurrency. In: Castagna, G., Gordon, A.D. (eds.) POPL, pp. 175–189. ACM (2017). http://dl.acm.org/citation.cfm?id=3009850

17. Lahav, O., Vafeiadis, V.: Owicki-Gries reasoning for weak memory models. In: Halldórsson, M.M., Iwama, K., Kobayashi, N., Speckmann, B. (eds.) ICALP 2015. LNCS, vol. 9135, pp. 311–323. Springer, Heidelberg (2015). https://doi.org/10.1007/978-3-662-47666-6_25

18. Lahav, O., Vafeiadis, V., Kang, J., Hur, C., Dreyer, D.: Repairing sequential consistency in C/C++11. In: Cohen, A., Vechev, M.T. (eds.) PLDI, pp. 618–632. ACM (2017)

19. Lee, S., Cho, M., Podkopaev, A., Chakraborty, S., Hur, C., Lahav, O., Vafeiadis, V.: Promising 2.0: global optimizations in relaxed memory concurrency. In: Donaldson, A.F., Torlak, E. (eds.) PLDI, pp. 362–376. ACM (2020). https://doi.org/10.1145/3385412.3386010

20. Lundberg, D., Guanciale, R., Lindner, A., Dam, M.: Hoare-style logic for unstructured programs. In: de Boer, F., Cerone, A. (eds.) Software Engineering and Formal Methods (2020)

21. Nienhuis, K., Memarian, K., Sewell, P.: An operational semantics for C/C++11 concurrency. In: OOPSLA, pp. 111–128. ACM (2016)

22. Owicki, S.S., Gries, D.: An axiomatic proof technique for parallel programs I. Acta Informatica **6**, 319–340 (1976). https://doi.org/10.1007/BF00268134

23. Paviotti, M., Cooksey, S., Paradis, A., Wright, D., Owens, S., Batty, M.: Modular relaxed dependencies in weak memory concurrency. In: Müller, P. (ed.) Programming Languages and Systems, pp. 599–625. Springer International Publishing, Cham (2020)
24. Pichon-Pharabod, J., Sewell, P.: A concurrency semantics for relaxed atomics that permits optimisation and avoids thin-air executions. In: Bodík, R., Majumdar, R. (eds.) Proceedings of the 43rd Annual ACM SIGPLAN-SIGACT Symposium on Principles of Programming Languages, POPL 2016, St. Petersburg, FL, USA, 20–22, January, 2016, pp. 622–633. ACM (2016). https://doi.org/10.1145/2837614.2837616
25. Podkopaev, A., Lahav, O., Vafciadis, V.: Bridging the gap between programming languages and hardware weak memory models. Proc. ACM Program. Lang. **3**(POPL), 69:1–69:31 (2019). https://doi.org/10.1145/3290382
26. Svendsen, K., Pichon-Pharabod, J., Doko, M., Lahav, O., Vafeiadis, V.: A separation logic for a promising semantics. In: Ahmed, A. (ed.) ESOP 2018. LNCS, vol. 10801, pp. 357–384. Springer, Cham (2018). https://doi.org/10.1007/978-3-319-89884-1_13
27. Winskel, G.: Event structures. In: Brauer, W., Reisig, W., Rozenberg, G. (eds.) ACPN 1986. LNCS, vol. 255, pp. 325–392. Springer, Heidelberg (1987). https://doi.org/10.1007/3-540-17906-2_31

Integrating ADTs in KeY and Their Application to History-Based Reasoning

Jinting Bian[1]([✉])(iD), Hans-Dieter A. Hiep[1](iD), Frank S. de Boer[1], and Stijn de Gouw[2](iD)

[1] CWI, Science Park 123, 1098 XG Amsterdam, The Netherlands
{j.bian,hdh,frb}@cwi.nl
[2] Open University, Heerlen, The Netherlands
sdg@ou.nl

Abstract. We discuss integrating abstract data types (ADTs) in the KeY theorem prover by a new approach to model data types using Isabelle/HOL as an interactive back-end, and translate Isabelle theorems to user-defined taclets in KeY. As a case study of this new approach, we reason about Java's `Collection` interface using histories, and we prove the correctness of several clients that operate on multiple objects, thereby significantly improving the state-of-the-art of history-based reasoning.

Open Science. Includes video material [4] and a source code artifact [5].

Keywords: Formal verification · Abstract data type · Program correctness · Java Collection Framework · KeY · Isabelle/HOL

1 Introduction

The overall aim of this paper is to put formal methods to work by the verification of software libraries which are the building blocks of millions of programs, and which run on the devices of billions of users every day. Our research agenda is to verify heavily used software libraries, such as the Java Collection Framework, since the verification effort weighs up against the potential impact of errors.

In [11] the use of formal methods led to the discovery of a major flaw in the design of TimSort, the default sorting method in many widely used programming languages, e.g. Java and Python, and platforms like Android. An improved version of TimSort was proven correct with the state-of-the-art theorem prover KeY [1]. The correctness proof of [11] convincingly illustrates the importance and potential of formal methods as a means of rigorously validating widely used software and improving it. In [17] this line of research has been further successfully extended by the verification of the basic methods of (a corrected version of) the `LinkedList` implementation of the Java Collection Framework, laying bare an integer overflow bug, using again the KeY theorem prover.

KeY is tailored to the verification of Java programs. In a proof calculus based on sequents, it symbolically executes fragments of the loaded program which are

M. Huisman et al. (Eds.): FM 2021, LNCS 13047, pp. 255–272, 2021.
https://doi.org/10.1007/978-3-030-90870-6_14

represented by modal operators of the underlying dynamic logic. KeY is based on the Java Modeling Language [7], JML for short, for the specification of class invariants, method contracts, and loop invariants. This specification language is intrinsically *state-based* and as such is not directly suitable for the specification of state-hiding *interfaces*. As such, the work described in [17] excludes the specification and verification of the `Collection#addAll(Collection)` method implemented by `LinkedList`, which adds all the elements of the collection that is passed as parameter. The difficulty lies in giving a specification of the interface, that works for all possible implementations (including `LinkedList` itself).

In recent previous work [16] the concept of a *history* as a sequence of method calls and returns has been introduced as a general methodology for specifying interfaces. As proof-of-concept, using the KeY theorem prover, this methodology has been applied to the core methods of Java's `Collection` interface and uses an encoding of histories as Java objects on the heap.

That encoding, however, made use of pure methods in specification and thus required extensive use of so-called *accessibility* clauses, which express the set of locations on the heap that a method may access during its execution. These accessibility clauses must be verified (with KeY). Furthermore, for recursively defined pure methods we also need to show *termination* and *determinism* [23]. Essentially, the associated verification conditions boil down to verifying that the method under consideration computes the same value starting in two heaps that are different except for the locations stated in the accessibility clause. To that end one has to symbolically execute the method more than once (in the two different heaps) and relate the outcome of the method starting in different heaps to one another. After such proof effort, accessibility clauses of pure methods can be used by the application of *dependency contracts*, that are used to establish that the outcome of a pure method in two heaps is the same if one heap is obtained from the other by assignments outside of the declared accessible locations.

The degree of automation in the proof search strategy with respect to pure methods, accessibility clauses and dependency contracts turned out to be rather limited in KeY. So, while the methodology works in principle, in practice, for advanced use, the pure methods were a source of large overhead and complexity in the proof effort.

This paper avoids this complexity by instead modeling histories as *Abstract Data Types*, ADTs for short. Elements of abstract data types are not present on the heap, avoiding the need to use dependency contracts for proving that heap modifications affect their properties. Since KeY has limited support for user-defined abstract data types, we introduce a general *workflow* which integrates the domain-specific theorem prover KeY and the general-purpose theorem prover Isabelle/HOL [25] for the specification of ADTs. We apply and discuss the application of this workflow to the Java `Collection` interface, including how we have now been able to specify and verify the `addAll` method. Furthermore, reasoning about advanced use cases involving multiple instances of the same interface is possible: we also have verified a method that compares *two* collections.

We assume the reader is somewhat familiar with KeY and/or Isabelle/HOL.

Related Work. The Java Collection Framework is among the most heavily-used software libraries in practice [8], and various case studies have focused on verifying parts of that framework [3,18,19]. Knüppel et al. [20] specified and verified several classes of the Java Collection Framework with standard JML state-based assertions, and found that specification was one of the main bottlenecks. One source of the complexity concerns framing: specifying and reasoning about properties and locations that do *not* change.

The idea presented in this paper of integrating Isabelle/HOL and KeY arises out of the need for user-defined data types usable within specifications. Other tools, such as Dafny [22] and Why3 [13], support user-defined data types in the specification language, contrary to JML as it is implemented by KeY. However, the former tools are not suitable to verify Java programs: for that, as far as the authors know, only KeY is suitable due to its modeling of the many programming features of the Java language present in real-world programs.

In state-based approaches, including the dynamic frames used in [20], frames inherently heavily depend on the chosen representation, i.e. at some point, the concrete fields that are touched or changed must be made explicit. The same holds for separation logic [26] approaches for Java [12]. Since interfaces do not have a concrete state-based representation, *a priori* specification of frames is not possible. Instead, for each class that implements the interface, further specifications must be provided to name the concrete fields. One can abstract from these concrete fields by using a footprint model method. However, the footprint model method itself also requires a dynamic frame, leading to recursion in dependency contracts [2]. Moreover, any specification that mentions (abstract or concrete) fields can be problematic for clients of the classes, since the representation is typically hidden from them (by means of an interface), which raises the question: how to verify clients that make use of interfaces?

The history-based approach in this paper (contrary to [16]) avoids framing entirely: there is no reference to an underlying state, as the complete behavior of an interface is captured by its history. Additionally, since we model such histories as elements of an ADT *separate from the sorts used by Java* in this paper, histories can not be touched by Java programs under verification themselves, and so we never have to use dependency contracts for reasoning about properties of histories. This allows us to avoid the verification bottleneck that arises in the approach of [16], which used an encoding of histories as ordinary Java objects living on the heap.

2   Integrating Abstract Data Types in KeY

Abstract data types were introduced in 1974 by Barbara Liskov and Stephen Zilles [24] to ease the programming task: instead of directly programming with concrete data representations, programmers would use a suitable abstraction that instead exposes an interface, thereby hiding the implementation details of a data type. In most programming languages, such interfaces only fix the signature of an abstract data type (e.g. Java's interface or Haskell's typeclass). Further research has lead to many approaches for specifying abstract data types, e.g. ranging from simple equational specifications, to axiomatizations in predicate logic. See for an extensive treatment of the subject the textbook [27].

In the context of our work, we need to distinguish the two levels in which abstract data types can appear: at the programming level, and at the specification level. In fact, Java supports abstract data types by means of its interfaces, and for example the Java Collection Framework provides many abstractions to ease the programming task. The specification language JML does support reasoning about the instances of such interfaces, but does not allow user-defined abstract data types on the specification level only The reason is that JML is designed to be "easier for programmers to learn and less intimidating than languages that use special-purpose mathematical notations" [21]. There are extensions to JML, e.g. [9], but this has not been implemented in KeY.

KeY extends JML in an important way: a number of built-in abstract data types at the specification level are provided in a type hierarchy [1, Section 2.4.1]. There is the abstract type of *sequences* that consists of finite sequences of arbitrary elements. Further, KeY provides the abstract data type of *integers* that comprises the mathematical integers (and not the integers modulo finite storage, as used in the Java language) to interpret JML's \bigint. Elements of these abstract types are not accessible by Java programs, and are not stored on the heap. It is possible to reason about elements of such abstract data types, since the KeY theorem prover allows to define their *theories* implemented by inference rules for deducing true statements involving these elements.

For introducing user-defined abstract data types, KeY does allow the specification of abstract data types by adding new inference rules: but it provides no guarantee that such user-defined theory is *consistent*. Thus, a small error in a user-defined abstract data type specification could lead to unsound proofs.

In contrast, Isabelle/HOL (Isabelle instantiated with Church's type theory) includes a definitional package for data types [6]. The definition mechanism provides so-called *freely generated* data types: the user provides some signature consisting of constants and function symbols and their types, and the system automatically derives (rather than postulate) characteristic theorems. Under the hood, each data type definition is associated to a Bounded Natural Functor (BNF) that admits a non-trivial initial algebra [28], but for our purposes we may simply trust that the system maintains consistency.

Our approach is to integrate the Isabelle/HOL theorem prover as an interactive back-end for KeY: this allows us to make use of the advanced capabilities of Isabelle to define data types, define functions, and prove general properties thereof, all while preserving consistency. We can then import these results from Isabelle in KeY to use them for proving the correctness of Java programs. The soundness of our approach crucially relies on the consistency of the imported Isabelle theory, and the soundness of the translation from statements in Isabelle/HOL to KeY taclets.

The overall approach can be summarized by a workflow diagram, see Fig. 1. Essentially, we will be following three steps:

1. We define data types and functions in Isabelle/HOL to logically model domain-specific knowledge of the Java program that we want to verify. These definitions can not refer to Java types directly, but can instead be defined using polymorphic type parameters.
2. We import the signature (sorts, function symbols) in KeY and write specifications of the Java program in JML. These specifications can make use of the imported function symbols by using a KeY-specific extension of JML.
3. We use the KeY system to perform symbolic execution of the Java program. This leads to proof obligations in which the imported symbols are uninterpreted, meaning that one is limited in reasoning about them in KeY. We then formulate a lemma that captures the expected property and prove it in Isabelle/HOL. If we succeed, the lemma is added to KeY by translating it back as an inference rule called a *taclet*. This step will be repeated many times, because we can not find all needed lemmas at once.

Below we give more detail on each of these main steps.

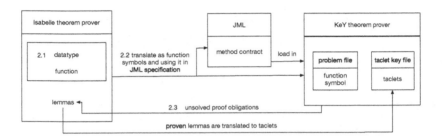

Fig. 1. The workflow of integrating ADTs in KeY.

Step 1. Formalizing ADTs in Isabelle/HOL. One defines data types and recursive functions in Isabelle/HOL in the usual manner: using the **datatype** and **fun** commands. There are a number of caveats when working in Isabelle, to ensure a smooth transfer of the theory to KeY.

– For data types that contain nested Java objects, we have to work around the limitation that the Java types are not available in Isabelle. This is a design choice of our approach, to keep Isabelle pure: we can instead introduce a polymorphic type parameter. Below we show how in our translation back to KeY, we put back the original types by instantiating the polymorphic type parameters by Java types which are available in KeY.
– Isabelle/HOL allows higher-order definitions, whereas the dynamic logic of KeY is first-order. Thus, for function symbols that we wish to import, we limit ourselves to first-order type signatures.

As a simple example, an element of the data type definition

$$\textbf{datatype } \alpha \; option = None \mid Some(\alpha)$$

in Isabelle/HOL is either 'nothing' or an element of type α. This introduces also
a constant $None : \alpha$ *option* and a unary function $Some : \alpha \Rightarrow \alpha$ *option*. One can
then define functions recursively over the structure of a user-defined data type.
This is illustrated in the next section.

Step 2. Using ADTs in JML Specifications. To declare new sorts and functions,
KeY uses an extensible formalism called *taclets* [14,15]. Taclets in KeY are stored
in plain-text files alongside Java sources and each contains the following sections:

  We introduce for each new type instantiation (where the type parameters are
  replaced by sorts) a corresponding logical sort with the desired name of the
  ADT. The syntactical notation uses a block section named \sorts.
– We declare the signatures of each function in a section named \functions.
  A function signature consists of the number and types of its parameters, and
  its return type. We erase the polymorphic type parameters, by replacing them
  by their instantiated sorts.
– We add axioms to specify properties of functions in a section named \axioms.

Listing 1 shows how to represent the above data type α *option* as a taclet. We
have instantiated the type parameter α with the Java Object sort.

```
\sorts { option; }
\functions { option Some(java.lang.Object);
             option None; ... }
\axioms { ... }
```

Listing 1. Declaring sorts and function symbols for new ADTs with KeY.

The new functions can then be used in JML specifications (such as method
contracts and class invariants) by prefixing their name with "\dl_". For example,
the function symbol *None* can be referred to in a JML contract by writing it
as \dl_None. To allow using the functions in JML specifications, axioms are
not (yet) needed. Therefore, in step two of our workflow we do not specify any
axioms. We describe adding axioms in more detail below, in step three.

Step 3. Translating Isabelle Theorems to KeY Taclets. We now focus on using
the new ADTs in proofs of Java programs with KeY. When one starts proving that a Java program satisfies its JML specification and that specification
contains function symbols declared as above, KeY treats them as uninterpreted
symbols (with unknown behavior, other than their signatures). Typically this is
insufficient to complete the proof: one needs specific properties that follow from
the underlying definition in Isabelle/HOL.

We can "import" such properties about the behavior of user-defined functions into KeY by defining inference rules in the axioms section of taclets. The
axioms are intended for basic facts that KeY can not derive from any other inference rules. We leverage Isabelle/HOL to prove the soundness and consistency
of the imported axioms. In essence, this provides a way to use Isabelle/HOL as
an interactive back-end to KeY. Our workflow supports a lazy approach that

minimizes the amount of work. We only add axioms about functions *when they are necessary*, i.e., when we are stuck in a proof situation that requires more knowledge of the function behavior.

Let us consider a concrete example that illustrates the above concepts. Suppose we have a proof obligation in KeY in which $Some(x) = Some(y)$ appears as an assumption (it occurs as an antecedent of an open goal sequent), and has $x = y$ as one of its conclusions (it appears as a succedent of the sequent). Without any axioms, KeY can not proceed in proving the goal. We thus formulate in Isabelle/HOL, abstracting from the particular sorts as they appear in KeY, the following lemma[1]

lemma *Some_injective* :: $Some(a) = Some(b) \leftrightarrow a = b$

which we easily verified using one of the characteristic theorems of the data type.

Our next objective is to import this lemma to KeY to make it available during the proving process. We do this by formulating the lemma as a taclet in the block `axioms`, see Listing 2.

```
\axioms {
  Some_injective {
    \schemaVar \term java.lang.Object o1, o2;
    \find(Some(o1) = Some(o2)) \replacewith(o1 = o2)
  }; }
```

Listing 2. Adding a taclet to KeY that expresses injectivity of the function *Some*.

This taclet states that the name of the inference rule is `Some_injective`. The keyword **find** states to which expressions or formulae the rule can be applied (on either side of the sequent). Two placeholder symbols called schema variables are used to stand for, in this case, the parameters of the `Some` function. These placeholders are instantiated when the inference rule is applied in a concrete proof. The `replacewith` clause states that the expression or formula in the find clause to which the rules is applied, is replaced after application by a new formula (in this case o1 = o2) in the resulting sequent. The **heuristics** clause indicates which of KeY's internal automated proof search strategies may use the rule.

One may also express side conditions on other formulas that need to be present in the sequent with the clause **assumes**, and variable conditions with the clause **varcond** (not shown in this example). A full exposition of the taclet language is out of scope of this article, we instead refer to [1, Section 4.3].

3 Case Study: History-Based Reasoning About `Collection`

In our case study, we apply histories to the specification of the `Collection` interface and verify clients of that interface with respect to this specification.

---

[1] A taclet which uses **find** and **replacewith** corresponds to a bi-implcation in Isabelle, since the term can appear on both sides of the sequent in KeY.

Histories are defined formally below as sequences of events, and a single event models a method call and its return. For each collection one may create new iterator objects as a view of its contents. Iterators require special treatment because their behavior relies on the history of other objects, such as the enclosing collection that *owns* the iterator. We therefore model iterators as sub-objects so that their history is recorded by the associated owning collection.

We thus introduce (in Isabelle/HOL) the following event data type:

$$\textbf{datatype}\,(\alpha, \beta)\; event = Add(\alpha, \textbf{bool}) \mid AddAll(\alpha\; elemlist, \textbf{bool}) \mid$$
$$Remove(\alpha, \textbf{bool}) \mid Contains(\alpha, \textbf{bool}) \mid IsEmpty(\textbf{bool}) \mid$$
$$Iterator(\beta) \mid IteratorNext(\beta, \alpha) \mid IteratorRemove(\beta) \mid \ldots$$

We focus here on the most important events only. The type parameters α and β correspond to (type abstractions of) the Java types `Object` and `Iterator`, respectively. We now introduce histories as sequences of events:

$$\textbf{datatype}\;(\alpha, \beta)\; history = Nil \mid Cons((\alpha, \beta)\; event, (\alpha, \beta)\; history)$$

As above, the type parameters α and β correspond to (type abstractions of) the Java types `Object` and `Iterator`.

Listing 3 illustrates the use of histories modeled as abstract data types and their functions in the interface specification of part of the **ensures** clause of the `addAll` method. It relates the multiplicities of elements of the argument collection with that of the receiving collection. Here, \dl_multiset(c.history(),o)) and \dl_multiset(history(),o), defined below, denote the multiplicity of an element o in the argument and receiving collection, respectively. The list el of type (where we overload *Nil* and *Cons*)

$$\textbf{datatype}\;\alpha\; elemlist = Nil \mid Cons(\alpha \times \textbf{bool}, \alpha\; elemlist)$$

associates a status flag to each occurrence of an element of the argument collection. This flag indicates whether the *receiving* collection's implementation actually *does* add the supplied element (e.g., a `Set` filters out duplicate objects but a `List` does not). Consequently, the multiplicity of the elements of the receiving collection is updated by how many times the object is actually added, denoted by \dl_multisetEl(el,o) (also defined below). The existential quantification of this list allows both for abstraction from the particular enumeration order of the argument collection and the implementation of the receiving collection as specified by the association of the Boolean values.

```
/*@ ...
  @ ensures (\exists elemlist el;
       (\forall Object o;
          \dl_occurs(el,o) == \dl_multiset(c.history(),o) &&
          \dl_multiset(history(),o) ==
          \dl_multiset(\old(history()),o) + \dl_multisetEl(el,o)));
  @*/
boolean addAll(Collection c);
```

Listing 3. The use of *multiset* and *elemlist* in the specification of `addAll`.

Using the data types above, we can now recursively define the crucial function *multiset*, that computes the multiplicity of an object given a particular history. Intuitively it represents the 'contents' of a collection at a particular instant.

fun $multiset : (\alpha, \beta)\ history \times \alpha \Rightarrow$ **int**

$multiset(Nil, x) = 0$

$multiset(Cons(Add(y, b), h), x) = multiset(h, x) + (x = y \wedge b\ ?\ 1 : 0)$

$multiset(Cons(AddAll(xs, b), h), x) = multiset(h, x) + multisetEl(xs, x)$

$multiset(Cons(Remove(y, b), h), x) = multiset(h, x) - (x = y \wedge b\ ?\ 1 : 0)$

$multiset(Cons(IteratorRemove(i), h), x)$
$\qquad\qquad = multiset(h, x) - (last(h, i) = Some(x)\ ?\ 1 : 0)$

$multiset(Cons(e, h), x) = multiset(h, x)$

The function *multisetEl* is defined as follows.

fun $multisetEl : \alpha\ elemlist \times \alpha \Rightarrow$ **int**

$multisetEl(Nil, x) = 0$

$multisetEl(Cons((y, b), t), x) = multisetEl(t, x) + (x = y \wedge b\ ?\ 1 : 0)$

For the full Isabelle theory of our case study (including the definition for *last*) we refer the reader to the artifact accompanying this paper [5]. This artifact includes the translation of the Isabelle theory to a signature that can be loaded in KeY (version 2.8.0), so that its function symbols are available in the JML specifications we gave for `Collection`. It also includes the taclets we imported from Isabelle, that we used to close the proof obligations generated by KeY.

3.1   Significant Improvement in Proof Effort

Using ADTs instead of encoding histories as Java objects results in significantly lower effort in defining functions for use in contracts and giving correctness proofs. This can be best seen by revisiting an example of our previous work [16] and comparing it to the proof effort required in the new approach using ADTs.

```
/*@ ...
  @ ensures (\forall Object o1; \dl_multiset(x.history(),o1) ==
        \dl_multiset(\old(x.history()),o1)); @*/
public static Object add_remove(Collection x, Object y) {
    if (x.add(y)) {
        x.remove(y);
    }
    return y;
}
```

Listing 4. Adding an object and if successful removing it again, leaves the contents of a `Collection` the same. See Table 1 for proof statistics and a link to the video.

The client code and its contract is given Listing 4, which has the same contract as in previous work, except we now use the imported functions we have defined in Isabelle instead of using pure methods and their dependency contracts.

In both the previous and this work, we specify the behavior of the client by ensuring that the 'contents' of the collection remains unmodified: we do so in terms of the multiset of the old history and the new history (after the add_remove method). During verification we make use of the contracts of methods add(Object) and remove(Object). These contracts specify their method behavior also in terms of the old and new history, relative to each call. Let h be the old history (before the call) and h' be the new history (after the call). Let y be the argument, the remove method contract specifies that $multiset(h', y) = multiset(h, y) - 1$ if the return value was true, and $multiset(h', y) = multiset(h, y)$ otherwise. Further, it ensures the return value is true if $multiset(h, y) > 0$. Also, $multiset(h', x) = multiset(h, x)$ holds for any object $x \neq y$. In similar terms, a contract is given for add that specifies that the multiplicity of the argument is increased by one, in case true is returned, and that regardless of the return value the multiplicity of the argument is positive after add.

We need to show that the multiplicity of the object y after the add method and the remove method is the same as before executing both methods. At this point, we can see a clear difference in verification effort required between the two approaches. In the previous approach, multiplicities are computed by a pure Java method Multiset that operates on an encoding of the history that lives on the heap. Since Java methods may diverge or use non-deterministic features, we need to show that the pure method behaves as a function: it terminates and is deterministic. Moreover, since we deal with effects of the heap, we also need to show that the computation of this pure method is not affected by calls of add or remove, which requires the use of a accessibility clause of the multiset method.

To make this explicit, Listing 5 shows a concrete example of a proof obligation from KeY that arose in the previous approach.

```
...
History.Multiset(h,y)@heap2 + 1 = History.Multiset(h,y)@heap1,
History.Multiset(h,y)@heap1 = History.Multiset(h,y)@heap + 1,
...
==>
History.Multiset(h,y)@heap2 = History.Multiset(h@heap,y)@heap2
```

Listing 5. Simplified proof obligation with histories as Java objects showing evaluation of the multiset function as a pure (Java) method in various heaps.

Informally, the proof obligation states that we must establish that the multiplicity of y after adding and removing object y (resulting in the heap named heap2) is equal to the multiplicity of y before both methods were executed (in the heap named heap). So we have to perform proof steps relating the result/behavior of the multiset method in different heaps. In practice, heap terms may grow very large (i.e. in a different, previous case study [10] we encountered heap terms that were several pages long) which further complicates reasoning.

By contrast, in the new ADT approach of this paper, we model multiset as a function without any dependency on the heap, and so we do not have to perform proof steps to relate the behavior of multiset in different heaps (the interpretation of multiset is fixed and does not change if the heap is modified). While the arguments of multiset may still depend on the heap (such as the history associated to an interface that lives on the heap), when we evaluate the argument to a particular value (such as an element of the history ADT) the behavior of the multiset function when given such values does not depend on the heap.[2] Moreover, by defining the function in Isabelle/HOL, we make use of its facilities to show that the function is well-defined (terminating and deterministic). In our case-study this is done fully automatically: contrary to the proofs of the same property in KeY in the previous approach. Thus, the new approach significantly reduces the total verification effort required.

The proof statistics of verifying this example are shown in Table 1. The previous approach (encoding histories as Java objects [16]) is marked, and includes the verification that the multiset pure method is terminating and deterministic and satisfies its equational specification (first row). This effort is completely eliminated in the new approach, since it can be done automatically using Isabelle/HOL. Furthermore, comparing the verification of the add_remove method in both approaches, it can be immediately seen that we no longer have to apply any dependency contract in the new approach. This improves two important factors of the total proof effort. Moreover, the previous approach was studied in the context of a simpler definition for histories (without modeling the addAll event), thus favoring the new approach even more. The non-marked rows, i.e. the new approach, are part of the accompanying artifact [5], and video files (no sound!) show a recording of the interactive proof sessions [4].

Table 1. Summary of proof statistics. **Nodes** and **Branches** measure the size of the proof tree, **I.step** counts the number of interactive steps performed by the user, **Q.inst** is the number of quantifier instantiations, Contract is the number of contracts applied, **Dep.** is the number of dependency contracts applied, **Loop inv.** is the number of loop invariants applied, and **Time** is the estimated time of completing the proof in the KeY theorem prover. The rows marked [†] come from the previous approach.

Name	Nodes	Branches	I.step	Q.inst	Contract	Dep.	Loop inv.	Time
Multiset[†]	54,857	1,053	52	476	39	0	0	72 min
add_remove[†]	3,936	79	44	5	2	23	0	11 min
add_remove	2,606	14	4	7	2	0	0	1 min
iterate_only[†]	8,549	58	53	0	4	12	1	15 min
iterate_only	3,447	15	0	2	3	0	1	1 min
iter_remove	5,003	20	5	0	4	0	1	3 min
all_contains	12,310	77	119	39	5	0	1	35 min
compare_two	28,585	147	371	84	6	0	1	75 min

---

[2] This can be compared to the expression $x + y$ in Java where x and y are fields: the value of x and y depends on the heap but the meaning of the '+' operation does not.

3.2   Advanced Use Cases

In this subsection we illustrate the benefits of our new approach in the verification of more complicated client programs that make use of the `Collection` interface. First we consider the following use case: iterating over the elements of a collection. An iterator is obtained as a view of the elements that a collection contains. It is possible to obtain multiple iterators, each with their own local view on a collection. The question arises: what happens when using an iterator when the collection it was obtained from is modified after its creation? In practice, a `ModificationException` is thrown. To ensure that the iterator methods are only called when the backing collection is not modified in the meantime, we introduce the notion of validity of an iterator. As already discussed above, we record the events of the iterators in the owning history, alongside other events that signal whether the owning collection is modified, so that indeed we *can* define a recursive function that determines whether an iterator is still valid. Another complex feature of the iterator is that it provides a parameterless `Iterator#remove()` method, producing no return value. Its intended semantics is to delete from the backing collection the element that was returned by a previous call to `Iterator#next()`, and invalidating all other iterators.

In the previous work [16], we did verify a client of iterator and showed its termination as shown in Listing 6: but we did not verify the pure methods (termination, determinism, equational specification) used in the specification that modeled the behavior of iterators. Functions like *size* of a history which computes the total number of elements contained by the collection, *iteratorSize* of a history and an iterator which computes the total number of elements already seen by the iterator, and the function *isIteratorValid* which depends on the functions *iteratorLast* (called *last* above), *iteratorHasNext*, and *iteratorVisited*.

The large number of auxiliary functions needed to model the behavior of iterators shows a verification bottleneck we encountered in the previous approach: modeling these as pure methods and verifying their properties takes roughly the same effort as required for *multiset*, per function! Using our new approach and the workflow above, we are able to define all functions and verify the properties necessary in completing the proof, thereby eliminating much proof effort.

```
public static boolean iterate_only(Collection x) {
    Iterator it = x.iterator();
    /*@ ...
      @ decreasing \dl_size(it.owner().history()) -
            \dl_iteratorSize(it.owner().history(),it); @*/
    while (it.hasNext()) {
        it.next();
    }
    return true;
}
```

Listing 6. Iterating over the collection. Why does it terminate?

Advancing further, we can verify a modifying iterator as is shown in Listing 7. This example shows an important aspect of our new approach: being able to use Isabelle/HOL to derive non-trivial properties of the functions we have defined.

```
/*@ ...
  @ ensures \dl_size(x.history()) == 0; @*/
public static boolean iter_remove(Collection x) {
    Iterator it = x.iterator();
    /*@ ...
      @ loop_invariant \dl_iteratorSize(it.owner().history(),it) == 0;
      @ decreasing \dl_size(it.owner().history()); @*/
    while (it.hasNext()) {
        it.next();
        it.remove();
    }
    return true;
}
```

Listing 7. Iterating over the collection and removing all its elements.

We iterate over a given collection and at each step we remove the last returned element by the iterator from the backing collection. Thus, after completing the iteration, when there are no next elements left, we expect to be able to prove that the backing collection is now empty. The crucial insight here is that, after we exit the loop, we know that **hasNext()** returned **false**. We modeled the outcome of the **hasNext()** method by defining a function *iteratorHasNext* of a history and an iterator. We established in Isabelle/HOL the (non-trivial) fact that if a valid iterator has no next elements then *iteratorSize* and *size* must be equal.

Following our workflow, we have proven this fact and imported it into KeY as a taclet, which is shown in Listing 8. Since it is a loop invariant that the size of the iterator remains zero (each time we remove an element through its iterator, it is not only removed from the backing collection but also from the elements seen by the iterator), we can thus deduce that finally the collection must be empty!

```
HasNext_size {
\schemaVar \term history h;
\schemaVar \term Iterator it;
\assumes(isIteratorValid(h,it) = TRUE, ... ==>)
\find(iteratorHasNext(h,it) = FALSE)
\replacewith(size(h) = iteratorSize(h,it))
\heuristics(concrete)
};
```

Listing 8. Taclet for showing the equality between *size* and *iteratorSize*.

Advancing even further, we have verified clients that operate on two collections at the same time. This is interesting, since both collections can be of a different implementation, and can potentially interfere with each other. The technique we applied here is to specify what properties remain *invariant* of histories of all other collections, e.g. that a call to a method of one collection does not change the history of any other collection. Since histories are not part of the heap, that a history remains invariant implies that all its (polymorphic) properties are invariant too. However, if a history contains some reference to an object on the heap, it can still be the case that properties of such an object have changed.

```
/*@ ...
  @ ensures \result = true; @*/
public static boolean all_contains(Collection x, Collection y) {
    x.addAll(y); Iterator it = y.iterator();
    /*@ ...
      @ loop_invariant (\forall Object o1;
            \dl_multiset(y.history(),o1) > 0 ==>
            \dl_multiset(x.history(),o1) > 0); @*/
    while(it.hasNext()) {
        if (!x.contains(it.next())) { return false; }
    }
    return true;
}
```

Listing 9. Using the addAll method and checking inclusion.

In the example given in Listing 9, we make use of the addAll method of the collection, adding elements of one collection to another. Clearly, during the addAll call, the collections interfere: collection x could obtain an iterator of collection y to add all elements of y to itself. So, in the specification of addAll we have not history invariance of y. Instead, we specify what properties of y's history remain invariant: in this case its multiset must remain invariant (assuming x and y are not aliases). The program first performs such addAll, and then iterates over the collection y that was supplied as argument. For each of the elements in the argument collection y, we check whether x did indeed add that element, by calling contains. We expect that after adding all elements, that all elements must (already) be contained. Indeed, we verified this propery.

The crucial property in this verification is shown as the loop invariant: all objects that are contained in collection y are also contained in collection x. This can be verified initially: the call to iterator does not change the multisets associated to the histories of x and y, and after the addAll method is called this inclusion is true. But why? As already explained above, in the specification of addAll, we state the existence of an element list: this is an enumeration of the contents of the argument collection y, but for each element also a Boolean flag that states whether x has decided to add those elements. Since this flag depends on the actual implementation of x, which is inaccessible to us, the contract of addAll existentially quantifies such element list. Thus, under the condition that for any element that was not yet contained in x at least one of the elements in the element list must have a **true** flag associated, we can deduce that the loop invariant holds initially. From the loop invariant, we can further deduce that the `contains` method never returns **false**, so the then-branch returning **false** is unreachable. Termination of the iterator can be verified as in the previous example. Hence, the whole client returns **true**.

The last example is the most complex: it is a method that compares two collections. Two collections are considered equivalent whenever they have the same multiplicities for all elements. The example shown in Listing 10 performs a destructive comparison: the collections are modified in the process. Thus, we have formulated in the contract that this method returns **true** if and only if the two collections were equivalent before calling the method.

```
/*@ ...
  @ requires x != y;
  @ ensures \result == true <==> (\forall Object o1;
        \dl_multiset(\old(x.history()),o1) ==
           \dl_multiset(\old(y.history()),o1)); @*/
public static boolean compare_two(Collection x, Collection y) {
    Iterator it = x.iterator();
    /*@ ...
      @ loop_invariant (\forall Object o1;
            \dl_multiset(\old(x.history()),o1) ==
              \dl_multiset(\old(y.history()),o1) <==>
            \dl_multiset(x.history(),o1) ==
              \dl_multiset(y.history(),o1)); @*/
    while (it.hasNext()) {
        if (!y.remove(it.next())) { return false; }
        else { it.remove(); }
    }
    return y.isEmpty();
}
```

Listing 10. Client side example for binary method.

We assume the collections are not aliases. The verification goes along the following lines: it is a loop invariant that the two collections were equivalent at the beginning of the method `compare_two` *if and only if* the two collections are equivalent in the current state. The invariant is trivially valid at the start of the method, and also at the start of the loop since the iterator does not change the multisets of either collection: the call on x explicitly specifies that x's multiset values are preserved, but moreover specifies the invariance of the history of any other collection (so also that of y). For each element of x, we try to remove it from y (which does not affect the iteration over x, since the removal of an element of y specifies that the history of any other collection is invariant). If that fails, then there is an element in x which is not contained in y, hence x and y are not equivalent, hence they were not equivalent. If removal did not fail, we also remove the element from x through its iterator: hence x and y are equivalent iff they were equivalent. At the end of the loop we know x is empty (a similar argument as seen in a previous example). If y is not empty then it had more elements than x, otherwise both are empty and were also equivalent at the start.

4 Conclusion

We showed how ADTs externally defined in Isabelle/HOL can be used in JML specifications and KeY proofs for Java programs. This provides a way to use Isabelle/HOL as an additional back-end for KeY, but also to enrich the specification language. We successfully applied our approach to define an ADT for histories of Java programs and specified and verified several client programs that use core methods of the main interface of the Java Collection Framework. Our method is sufficiently powerful to support programming to interfaces, binary methods, and iterators, the latter of which requires a notion of ownership as iterator behavior depends on the history of other objects, i.e. the enclosing collection and other iterators over that collection.

In a previous paper [16], we modeled the history as an ordinary Java class. That worked, but the modeling of histories in this paper, as an external ADT with functions, offers numerous benefits. Here, we avoid pure methods that rely on the heap, which give rise to additional proof obligations every time these pure methods are used in JML specifications. Also we significantly simplified reasoning about properties of user-defined functions themselves. For example, in our case study, we reduced proofs from the previous paper (in KeY) about *multiset* modeled as a pure method from 72 min of work, to a fully automated verification in Isabelle/HOL with *multiset* modeled as an ADT function.

This work has opened up the possibility to define many more functions on histories, thus furthering the ability to model complex object behavior: this we demonstrated by verifying complex client code using collections. Further, while KeY is tailored for proving properties of concrete Java programs, Isabelle/HOL has more powerful facilities for general theorem proving. Our approach allows leveraging Isabelle/HOL to guarantee, for example, meta-properties such as the consistency of axioms about user-defined ADT functions. Using KeY alone, this was problematic or even impossible.

A further next step in the history-based specification of interfaces and its application to the Java Collection Framework is the development of a general history-based *refinement* theory which allows to formally verify that a class *implements* a given interface, and, more specifically, that inherited methods are correct with respect to refinements of overridden methods. For example, the class `LinkedList` inherits from `AbstractSequentialList` which inherits from `AbstractList` and thus from `AbstractCollection`, that provides a partial implementation of the `Collection` interface. Thus, not all methods of the `Collection` interface are directly implemented by `LinkedList`, but inherited along the class hierarchy.

Acknowledgements. The authors wish to thank Mattias Ulbrich for pointing out a soundness issue in the taclet translation (see footnote 1) and his useful reference suggestion [9], and the anonymous referees for their comments and suggestions on how to improve this paper.

References

1. Ahrendt, W., Beckert, B., Bubel, R., Hähnle, R., Schmitt, P.H., Ulbrich, M.: Deductive Software Verification–The KeY, vol. 10001. LNCS. Springer, Cham (2016)
2. Banerjee, A., Naumann, D.A., Nikouei, M.: A logical analysis of framing for specifications with pure method calls. ACM Trans. Program. Lang. Syst. **40**(2) (2018)
3. Beckert, B., Schiffl, J., Schmitt, P.H., Ulbrich, M.: Proving JDK's dual pivot quicksort correct. In: Paskevich, A., Wies, T. (eds.) VSTTE 2017. LNCS, vol. 10712, pp. 35–48. Springer, Cham (2017). https://doi.org/10.1007/978-3-319-72308-2_3
4. Bian, J., Hiep, H.A.: Integrating ADTs in KeY and their application to history-based reasoning: video material. FigShare (2021). https://doi.org/10.6084/m9.figshare.c.5413263
5. Bian, J., Hiep, H.A., de Boer, F.S., de Gouw, S.: Integrating ADTs in KeY and their application to history-based reasoning: proof files. Zenodo (2021). https://doi.org/10.5281/zenodo.4744268
6. Biendarra, J., Blanchette, J.C., Desharnais, M., Panny, L., Popescu, A., Traytel, D.: Defining (co)datatypes and primitively (co)recursive functions in Isabelle/HOL (2016). https://isabelle.in.tum.de/doc/datatypes.pdf
7. Burdy, L., et al.: An overview of JML tools and applications. Int. J. Softw. Tools Technol. Transf. **7**(3), 212–232 (2005)
8. Costa, D., Andrzejak, A., Seboek, J., Lo, D.: Empirical study of usage and performance of Java collections. In: 8th Conference on Performance Engineering, pp. 389–400. ACM (2017)
9. Darvas, A., Müller, P.: Faithful mapping of model classes to mathematical structures. In: 2007 Conference on Specification and Verification of Component-Based Systems (SAVCBS), pp. 31–38. ACM (2007)
10. de Gouw, S., de Boer, F.S., Rot, J.: Proof pearl: the key to correct and stable sorting. J. Autom. Reason. **53**(2), 129–139 (2014)
11. de Gouw, S., Rot, J., de Boer, F.S., Bubel, R., Hähnle, R.: OpenJDK's Java.utils.Collection.sort() is broken: the good, the bad and the worst case. In: Kroening, D., Păsăreanu, C.S. (eds.) CAV 2015. LNCS, vol. 9206, pp. 273–289. Springer, Cham (2015). https://doi.org/10.1007/978-3-319-21690-4_16
12. Distefano, D., Parkinson, M.J.: jStar: towards practical verification for Java. In: 23rd Conference on Object-Oriented Programming, Systems, Languages, and Applications (OOPSLA), pp. 213–226. ACM (2008)
13. Filliâtre, J.-C., Paskevich, A.: Why3 — where programs meet provers. In: Felleisen, M., Gardner, P. (eds.) ESOP 2013. LNCS, vol. 7792, pp. 125–128. Springer, Heidelberg (2013). https://doi.org/10.1007/978-3-642-37036-6_8
14. Giese, M.: Taclets and the KeY prover. Electron. Notes Theor. Comput. Sci. **103**, 67–79 (2004)
15. Habermalz, E.: Ein dynamisches automatisierbares interaktives Kalkül für schematische theorie spezifische Regeln. Ph.D. thesis, University of Karlsruhe (2000)
16. Hiep, H.-D.A., Bian, J., de Boer, F.S., de Gouw, S.: History-based specification and verification of Java collections in KeY. In: Dongol, B., Troubitsyna, E. (eds.) IFM 2020. LNCS, vol. 12546, pp. 199–217. Springer, Cham (2020). https://doi.org/10.1007/978-3-030-63461-2_11
17. Hiep, H.-D.A., Maathuis, O., Bian, J., de Boer, F.S., van Eekelen, M., de Gouw, S.: Verifying OpenJDK's `LinkedList` using KeY. In: TACAS 2020. LNCS, vol. 12079, pp. 217–234. Springer, Cham (2020). https://doi.org/10.1007/978-3-030-45237-7_13

18. Huisman, M.: Verification of Java's AbstractCollection class: a case study. In: Boiten, E.A., Möller, B. (eds.) MPC 2002. LNCS, vol. 2386, pp. 175–194. Springer, Heidelberg (2002). https://doi.org/10.1007/3-540-45442-X_11

19. Huisman, M., Jacobs, B., van den Berg, J.: A case study in class library verification: Java's Vector class. Int. J. Softw. Tools Technol. Transf. 3(3), 332–352 (2001)

20. Knüppel, A., Thüm, T., Pardylla, C., Schaefer, I.: Experience report on formally verifying parts of OpenJDK's API with KeY. In: F-IDE 2018: Formal Integrated Development Environment, volume 284 of EPTCS, pp. 53–70. OPA (2018)

21. Leavens, G.T., Cheon, Y.: Design by contract with JML (2006). http://www.cs.utep.edu/cheon/cs3331/data/jmldbc.pdf

22. Leino, K.R.M.: Dafny: an automatic program verifier for functional correctness. In: Clarke, E.M., Voronkov, A. (eds.) LPAR 2010. LNCS (LNAI), vol. 6355, pp. 348–370. Springer, Heidelberg (2010). https://doi.org/10.1007/978-3-642-17511-4_20

23. Leino, K.R.M., Müller, P.: Verification of equivalent-results methods. In: Drossopoulou, S. (ed.) ESOP 2008. LNCS, vol. 4960, pp. 307–321. Springer, Heidelberg (2008). https://doi.org/10.1007/978-3-540-78739-6_24

24. Liskov, B., Zilles, S.: Programming with abstract data types. ACM SIGPLAN Not. 9(4), 50–59 (1974)

25. Nipkow, T., Paulson, L.C., Wenzel, M.: Isabelle/HOL: A Proof Assistant for Higher-Order Logic, vol. 2283. LNCS. Springer, Heidelberg (2002). https://doi.org/10.1007/3-540-45949-9

26. Reynolds, J.C.: Separation logic: a logic for shared mutable data structures. In: 17th Symposium on Logic in Computer Science (LICS), pp. 55–74. IEEE (2002)

27. Sannella, D., Tarlecki, A.: Foundations of Algebraic Specification and Formal Software Development. Monographs in Theoretical Computer Science. Springer, Heidelberg (2012). https://doi.org/10.1007/978-3-642-17336-3

28. Traytel, D., Popescu, A., Blanchette, J.C.: Foundational, compositional (co)datatypes for higher-order logic: category theory applied to theorem proving. In: 27th Symposium on Logic in Computer Science (LICS), pp. 596–605. IEEE (2012)

Identifying Overly Restrictive Matching Patterns in SMT-Based Program Verifiers

Alexandra Bugariu[(✉)], Arshavir Ter-Gabrielyan, and Peter Müller

Department of Computer Science, ETH Zurich, Zürich, Switzerland
{alexandra.bugariu,ter-gabrielyan,peter.mueller}@inf.ethz.ch

Abstract. Universal quantifiers occur frequently in proof obligations produced by program verifiers, for instance, to axiomatize uninterpreted functions and to express properties of arrays. SMT-based verifiers typically reason about them via E-matching, an SMT algorithm that requires syntactic matching patterns to guide the quantifier instantiations. Devising good matching patterns is challenging. In particular, overly restrictive patterns may lead to spurious verification errors if the quantifiers needed for a proof are not instantiated; they may also conceal unsoundness caused by inconsistent axiomatizations. In this paper, we present the first technique that identifies and helps the users remedy the effects of overly restrictive matching patterns. We designed a novel algorithm to synthesize missing triggering terms required to complete a proof. Tool developers can use this information to refine their matching patterns and prevent similar verification errors, or to fix a detected unsoundness.

Keywords: Matching patterns · Triggering terms · SMT · E-matching

1 Introduction

Proof obligations frequently contain universal quantifiers, both in the specification and to encode the semantics of the programming language. Most deductive verifiers [4,5,8,12,15,19,36] rely on SMT solvers to discharge the proof obligations via E-matching [14]. This SMT algorithm requires syntactic matching patterns of ground terms (called *patterns* in the following), to control the instantiations. The pattern $\{\mathtt{f}(x,y)\}$ in the formula $\forall x\colon \mathrm{Int}, y\colon \mathrm{Int} :: \{\mathtt{f}(x,y)\}\ (x = y) \wedge \neg\mathtt{f}(x,y)$ instructs the solver to instantiate the quantifier *only* when it finds a *triggering term* that matches the pattern, e.g., $\mathtt{f}(7,z)$. The patterns can be written manually or inferred automatically. However, devising them is challenging [20,23]. Too permissive patterns may lead to unnecessary instantiations that slow down verification or even cause non-termination (if each instantiation produces a new triggering term, in a so-called matching loop [14]). Overly restrictive patterns may prevent the instantiations needed to complete a proof; they cause two major problems in program verification, incompleteness and undetected unsoundness.

Incompleteness. Overly restrictive patterns may cause spurious verification errors when the proof of *valid* proof obligations fails. Figure 1 illustrates this

© Springer Nature Switzerland AG 2021
M. Huisman et al. (Eds.): FM 2021, LNCS 13047, pp. 273–291, 2021.
https://doi.org/10.1007/978-3-030-90870-6_15

```
function  len(x:  int):  int;
function  nxt(x:  int):  int;

axiom  (forall x:  int  ::  {len(nxt(x))}
          len(x) > 0 && (nxt(x) == x ==> len(x) == 1) &&
          (nxt(x) != x ==> len(x) == len(nxt(x)) + 1));

procedure  trivial()  { assert len(7) > 0;  }
```

Fig. 1. Example (in Boogie [7]) that leads to a spurious error. The assertion follows from the axiom, but the axiom does not get instantiated without a triggering term.

case. The integer x represents the address of a node, and the uninterpreted functions `len` and `nxt` encode operations on linked lists. The axiom defines `len`: its result is positive and the last node points to itself. The assertion directly follows from the axiom, but the proof fails because the proof obligation does not contain the triggering term `len(nxt(7))`; thus, the axiom does not get instantiated. However, realistic proof obligations often contain hundreds of quantifiers [33], which makes the manual identification of missing triggering terms extremely difficult.

Unsoundness. Most of the universal quantifiers in proof obligations appear in axioms over uninterpreted functions (to encode type information, heap models, datatypes, etc.). To obtain sound results, these axioms must be consistent (i.e., satisfiable); otherwise all proof obligations hold trivially. Consistency can be proved once and for all by showing the existence of a model, as part of the soundness proof. However, this solution is difficult to apply for those verifiers which generate axioms *dynamically*, depending on the program to be verified. Proving consistency then requires verifying the algorithm that generates the axioms for all possible inputs, and needs to consider many subtle issues [13,21,30].

A more practical approach is to check if the axioms generated for a given program are consistent. However, this check also depends on triggering: an SMT solver may fail to prove unsat if the triggering terms needed to instantiate the contradictory axioms are missing. The unsoundness can thus remain undetected.

For example, Dafny's [19] sequence axiomatization from June 2008 contained an inconsistency found only over a year later. A fragment of this axiomatization is shown in Fig. 2. It expresses that empty sequences and sequences obtained through the `Build` operation are well-typed (F_0–F_2), that the length of a type-correct sequence must be non-negative (F_3), and that `Build` constructs a new sequence of the required length (F_4). The intended behavior of `Build` is to update the element at index i_4 in sequence s_4 to v_4. However, since there are no constraints on the parameter l_4, `Build` can be used with a negative length, leading to a contradiction with F_3. This error cannot be detected by checking the satisfiability of the formula $F_0 \wedge \ldots \wedge F_4$, as no axiom gets instantiated.

This Work. For SMT-based deductive verifiers, discharging proof obligations and revealing inconsistencies in axiomatizations require a solver to prove unsat

$F_0: \forall t_0: \text{V} :: \{\text{Type}(t_0)\} \; t_0 = \text{ElemType}(\text{Type}(t_0))$

$F_1: \forall t_1: \text{V} :: \{\text{Empty}(t_1)\} \; \text{typ}(\text{Empty}(t_1)) = \text{Type}(t_1)$

$F_2: \forall s_2: \text{U}, i_2: \text{Int}, v_2: \text{U}, l_2: \text{Int} :: \{\text{Build}(s_2, i_2, v_2, l_2)\}$
$\qquad \text{typ}(\text{Build}(s_2, i_2, v_2, l_2)) = \text{Type}(\text{typ}(v_2))$

$F_3: \forall s_3: \text{U} :: \{\text{Len}(s_3)\} \; \neg(\text{typ}(s_3) = \text{Type}(\text{ElemType}(\text{typ}(s_3)))) \vee (0 \leq \text{Len}(s_3))$

$F_4: \forall s_4: \text{U}, i_4: \text{Int}, v_4: \text{U}, l_4: \text{Int} :: \{\text{Len}(\text{Build}(s_4, i_4, v_4, l_4))\}$
$\qquad \neg(\text{typ}(s_4) = \text{Type}(\text{typ}(v_4))) \vee (\text{Len}(\text{Build}(s_4, i_4, v_4, l_4)) = l_4)$

Fig. 2. Fragment of an old version of Dafny's sequence axiomatization. U and V are uninterpreted types. All the named functions are uninterpreted. To improve readability, we use mathematical notation throughout this paper instead of SMT-LIB syntax [10].

via E-matching. (Verification techniques based on proof assistants are out of scope.) Given an SMT formula for which E-matching yields *unknown* due to insufficient quantifier instantiations, our technique generates suitable triggering terms that allow the solver to complete the proof. These terms enable users to understand and remedy the revealed completeness or soundness issue. Since the SMT queries for the verification of different input programs are typically very similar, fixing such issues benefits the verification of many or even all future runs of the verifier.

Fixing the Incompleteness. For Fig. 1, our technique finds the triggering term `len(nxt(7))`, which allows one to fix the incompleteness. Tool *users* (who cannot change the axioms) can add the term to the program; e.g., adding `var t: int;` `t := len(nxt(7))` before the assertion has no effect on the execution, but triggers the instantiation of the axiom. Tool *developers* can devise less restrictive patterns. For instance, they can move the conjunct `len(x) > 0` to a separate axiom with the pattern `{len(x)}` (simply changing the axiom's pattern to `{len(x)}` would cause matching loops). Alternatively, tool developers can adapt the encoding to emit additional triggering terms enforcing certain instantiations [17,20].

Fixing the Unsoundness. In Fig. 2, our triggering term `Len(Build(Empty` `(typ(v)), 0, v, −1))` (for a fresh value v) is sufficient to detect the unsoundness (as shown in Appx. A of [11]). Tool developers can use this information to add a precondition to F_4, which prevents the construction of sequences with negative lengths.

Soundness Modulo Patterns. Figure 3 illustrates another scenario: Boogie's [7] map axiomatization is inconsistent by design at the SMT level [22], but this behavior cannot be exposed from Boogie, as the type system prevents the required instantiations. Thus it does not affect Boogie's soundness. It is nevertheless important to detect it because it could surface if Boogie was extended to support quantifier instantiation algorithms that are not based on E-matching (such as MBQI [16]) or first-order provers. They could *unsoundly* classify an incorrect program that uses this map axiomatization as correct. Since F_2 states

$F_0 : \forall kt_0 : V, vt_0 : V :: \{\texttt{Type}(kt_0, vt_0)\}\ \texttt{ValTypeInv}(\texttt{Type}(kt_0, vt_0)) = vt_0$

$F_1 : \forall m_1 : U, k_1 : U, v_1 : U :: \{\texttt{Select}(m_1, k_1, v_1)\}$
$\qquad \texttt{typ}(\texttt{Select}(m_1, k_1, v_1)) = \texttt{ValTypeInv}(\texttt{typ}(m_1))$

$F_2 : \forall m_2 : U, k_2 : U, x_2 : U, v_2 : U :: \{\texttt{Store}(m_2, k_2, x_2, v_2)\}$
$\qquad \texttt{typ}(\texttt{Store}(m_2, k_2, x_2, v_2)) = \texttt{Type}(\texttt{typ}(k_2), \texttt{typ}(v_2))$

$F_3 : \forall m_3 : U, k_3 : U, x_3 : U, v_3 : U, k_3' : U, v_3' : U :: \{\texttt{Select}(\texttt{Store}(m_3, k_3, x_3, v_3), k_3', v_3')\}$
$\qquad (k_3 = k_3') \lor (\texttt{Select}(\texttt{Store}(m_3, k_3, x_3, v_3), k_3', v_3') = \texttt{Select}(m_3, k_3', v_3'))$

Fig. 3. Fragment of Boogie's map axiomatization, which is sound only modulo patterns. U and V are uninterpreted types. All the named functions are uninterpreted.

that storing a key-value pair into a map results in a new map with a potentially *different* type, one can prove that two *different* types (e.g., Boolean and Int) are equal in SMT. This example shows that the problems tackled in this paper cannot be solved by simply switching to other instantiation strategies: these are not the preferred choices of most verifiers [4,5,8,12,15,19,36], and may produce unsound results for verifiers designed for E-matching with axiomatizations sound only modulo patterns.

Contributions. This paper makes the following technical contributions:

1. We present the first automated technique that allows the developers to detect *completeness* issues in program verifiers and *soundness* problems in their axiomatizations. Moreover, our approach helps them devise better triggering strategies for *all* future runs of their tool with E-matching.
2. We developed a novel algorithm for synthesizing the triggering terms necessary to complete unsatisfiability proofs using E-matching. Since quantifier instantiation is undecidable for first-order formulas over uninterpreted functions, our algorithm might not terminate. However, all identified triggering terms are indeed sufficient to complete the proof; there are no false positives.
3. We evaluated our technique on benchmarks with known triggering problems from four program verifiers. Our experimental results show that it successfully synthesized the missing triggering terms in 65,6% of the cases, and can significantly reduce the human effort in localizing and fixing the errors.

Outline. The rest of the paper is organized as follows: Sect. 2 gives an overview of our technique; the details follow in Sect. 3. In Sect. 4, we present our experimental results. We discuss related work in Sect. 5, and conclude in Sect. 6. Extensions of our algorithm, optimizations, more details about E-matching and the evaluation, and additional examples can be found in the extended version of our paper [11].

2   Overview

Our goal is to synthesize missing triggering terms, i.e., concrete instantiations for (a small subset of) the quantified variables of an input formula I, which are

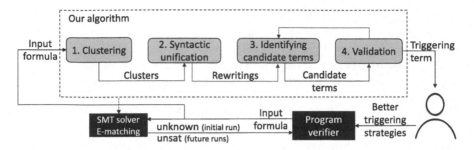

Fig. 4. Main steps of our algorithm that helps the developers of program verifiers devise better triggering strategies. Rounded boxes depict processing steps and arrows data.

necessary for the solver to prove its unsatisfiablity. Intuitively, these triggering terms include *counter-examples* to the satisfiability of I and can be obtained from a model of its negation. For example, $I = \forall n \colon \mathrm{Int} :: n > 7$ is unsatisfiable, and a counter-example $n = 6$ is a model of its negation $\neg I = \exists n \colon \mathrm{Int} :: n \le 7$.

However, this idea does not apply to formulas over uninterpreted functions, which are common in proof obligations. The negation of $I = \exists f, \forall n \colon \mathrm{Int} :: f(n, 7)$, where f is an uninterpreted function, is $\neg I = \forall f, \exists n \colon \mathrm{Int} :: \neg f(n, 7)$. This is a second-order constraint (it quantifies over functions), and cannot be encoded in SMT, which supports only first-order logic. We thus take a different approach.

Let F be a second-order formula. We define its *approximation* as:

$$F_\approx = F[\exists \overline{f} \; / \; \forall f] \tag{*}$$

where $\overline{f}$ are uninterpreted functions. The approximation considers only *one* interpretation, not *all* possible interpretations for each uninterpreted function.

We therefore construct a *candidate* triggering term from a model of $\neg I_\approx$ and check if it is sufficient to prove that I is unsatisfiable (due to the approximation, a model is no longer guaranteed to be a counter-example for the original formula).

The four main steps of our algorithm are depicted in Fig. 4. The algorithm is stand-alone, i.e., not integrated into, nor dependent on any specific SMT solver. We illustrate it on the inconsistent axioms from Fig. 5 (which we assume are part of a larger axiomatization). To show that $I = F_0 \wedge F_1 \wedge \ldots$ is unsatisfiable, the solver requires the triggering term $f(g(7))$. The corresponding instantiations of F_0 and F_1 generate contradictory constraints: $f(g(7)) \ne 7$ and $f(g(7)) = 7$. In the following, we explain how we obtain this triggering term systematically.

$$F_0: \quad \forall x_0 \colon \mathrm{Int} :: \{f(x_0)\} \;\; f(x_0) \ne 7$$
$$F_1: \quad \forall x_1 \colon \mathrm{Int} :: \{f(g(x_1))\} \;\; f(g(x_1)) = x_1$$

Fig. 5. Formulas that set contradictory constraints on the function f. Synthesizing the triggering term $f(g(7))$ requires theory reasoning and syntactic term unification.

Step 1: Clustering. As typical proof obligations or axiomatizations contain hundreds of quantifiers, exploring combinations of triggering terms for all of them does not scale. To prune the search space, we exploit the fact that I is unsatisfiable only if there exist instantiations of some (in the worst case all) of its *quantified* conjuncts F such that they produce contradictory constraints on some uninterpreted functions. (If there is a contradiction among the quantifier-free conjuncts, the solver will detect it directly.) We identify *clusters* C of formulas F that share function symbols and then process each cluster separately. In Fig. 5, F_0 and F_1 share the function symbol $\mathtt{f}$, so we build the cluster $C = F_0 \wedge F_1$.

Step 2: Syntactic Unification. The formulas within clusters usually contain uninterpreted functions applied to *different* arguments (e.g., $\mathtt{f}$ is applied to x_0 in F_0 and to $\mathtt{g}(x_1)$ in F_1). We thus perform syntactic unification to identify *sharing constraints* on the quantified variables (which we call *rewritings* and denote their set by R) such that instantiations that satisfy these rewritings generate formulas with common terms (on which they might set contradictory constraints). F_0 and F_1 share the term $\mathtt{f}(\mathtt{g}(x_1))$ if we perform the rewritings $R = \{x_0 = \mathtt{g}(x_1)\}$.

Step 3: Identifying Candidate Triggering Terms. The cluster $C = F_0 \wedge F_1$ from step 1 contains a contradiction if there exists a formula F in C such that: (1) F is unsatisfiable by itself, or (2) F contradicts at least one other formula from C.

To address scenario (1), we ask an SMT solver for a model of the formula $G = \neg C_\approx$, where $\neg C_\approx$ is defined in (*) above. After Skolemization, G is quantifier-free, so the solver is generally able to provide a model if one exists. We then obtain a candidate triggering term by substituting the quantified variables from the patterns of the formulas in C with their corresponding values from the model.

However, scenario (1) is not sufficient to expose the contradiction from Fig. 5, since both F_0 and F_1 are individually satisfiable. Our algorithm thus also derives *stronger* G formulas corresponding to scenario (2). That is, it will next consider the case where F_0 contradicts F_1, whose encoding into first-order logic is: $\neg F_{0\approx} \wedge F_1 \wedge \bigwedge R$, where R is the set of rewritings identified in step 2, used to connect the quantified variables. This formula is universally-quantified (since F_1 is), so the solver cannot prove its satisfiability and generate models. We solve this problem by requiring F_0 to contradict the *instantiation* of F_1, which is a weaker constraint. Let F be an arbitrary formula. We define its *instantiation* as:

$$F_{Inst} = F[\exists \overline{\mathbf{x}} \ / \ \forall \overline{\mathbf{x}}] \tag{**}$$

where $\overline{\mathbf{x}}$ are variables. Then $G = \neg F_{0\approx} \wedge F_{1Inst} \wedge \bigwedge R$ is equivalent to $(\mathtt{f}(x_0) = 7) \wedge (\mathtt{f}(\mathtt{g}(x_1)) = x_1) \wedge (x_0 = \mathtt{g}(x_1))$. (To simplify the notation, here and in the following formulas, we omit existential quantifiers.) All its models set x_1 to 7. Substituting x_0 by $\mathtt{g}(x_1)$ (according to R) and x_1 by 7 (its value from the model) in the patterns of F_0 and F_1 yields the candidate triggering term $\mathtt{f}(\mathtt{g}(7))$.

Step 4: Validation. Once we have found a candidate triggering term, we add it to the original formula I (wrapped in a fresh uninterpreted function, to make it

$$\text{I} ::= F \ (\wedge \ F)^* \qquad\qquad B ::= D \ (\vee \ D)^*$$
$$F ::= B \mid \forall \overline{x} \ :: \ \{P(\overline{x})\} \ B \qquad D ::= L \mid \neg L \mid \forall \overline{x} \ :: \ \{P(\overline{x})\} \ F$$

Fig. 6. Grammar of input formulas I. Inputs are conjunctions of formulas F, which are (typically quantified) disjunctions of literals (L or $\neg L$) or nested quantified formulas. Each quantifier is equipped with a pattern P. $\overline{x}$ denotes a (non-empty) list of variables.

available to E-matching, but not affect the input's satisfiability) and check if the solver can prove unsat. If so, our algorithm terminates successfully and reports the synthesized triggering term (after a minimization step that removes unnecessary sub-terms); otherwise, we go back to step 3 to obtain another candidate. In our example, the triggering term $f(g(7))$ is sufficient to complete the proof.

3 Synthesizing Triggering Terms

Next, we define the input formulas (Sect. 3.1), explain the details of our algorithm (Sect. 3.2) and discuss its limitations (Sect. 3.3). Appx. C and Appx. E of [11] present extensions that enable complex proofs and optimizations used in Sect. 4.

3.1 Input Formula

To simplify our algorithm, we pre-process the inputs (i.e., the proof obligations or the axioms of a verifier): we Skolemize existential quantifiers and transform all propositional formulas into *negation normal form* (NNF), where negation is applied only to literals and the only logical connectives are conjunction and disjunction; we also apply the distributivity of disjunction over conjunction and split conjunctions into separate formulas. These steps preserve satisfiability and the semantics of patterns (Appx. E of [11] addresses scalability issues). The resulting formulas follow the grammar in Fig. 6. Literals L may include interpreted and uninterpreted functions, variables and constants. Free variables are nullary functions. Quantified variables can have interpreted or uninterpreted types, and the pre-processing ensures that their names are globally unique. We assume that each quantifier is equipped with a pattern P (if none is provided, we run the solver to infer one). Patterns are combinations of *uninterpreted* functions and must mention *all* quantified variables. Since there are no existential quantifiers after Skolemization, we use the term *quantifier* to denote *universal quantifiers*.

3.2 Algorithm

The pseudo-code of our algorithm is given in Algorithm 1. It takes as input an SMT formula I (defined in Fig. 6), which we treat in a slight abuse of notation as both a formula and a set of conjuncts. Three other parameters allow us to customize the search strategy and are discussed later. The algorithm yields a triggering term that enables the unsat proof, or **None**, if no term was found. We assume here that I contains no nested quantifiers and present those later in this section.

Algorithm 1: Our algorithm for synthesizing triggering terms that enable unsatisfiability proofs. We assume that all quantified variables are globally unique and I does not contain nested quantifiers. The auxiliary procedures clustersRewritings and candidateTerm are presented in Algorithm 2 and Algorithm 3.

Arguments : I — input formula, also treated as set of conjuncts
σ — similarity threshold for clustering
δ — maximum depth for clustering
μ — maximum number of different models

Result: The synthesized triggering term or None, if no term was found

1 **Procedure** synthesizeTriggeringTerm

2   **foreach** depth $\in \{0, \ldots, \delta\}$ **do**

3   **foreach** $F \in$ I $\mid F$ is $\forall \overline{x} :: F'$ **do**

4   **foreach** $(C, R) \in$ clustersRewritings(I, F, σ, depth) **do**   // Steps 1, 2

5   Inst $\longleftarrow \{\}$

6   **foreach** $f \in C \mid f$ is $\forall \overline{x} :: D_0 \vee \ldots \vee D_n$ or $D_0 \vee \ldots \vee D_n$ **do**

7   Inst$[f] \longleftarrow \{(\bigwedge_{0 \le j < k} \neg D_j) \wedge D_k \mid 0 \le k \le n\}$

8   Inst$[F] \longleftarrow \{\neg F'\}$

9   **foreach** $H \in \bigtimes\{$Inst$[f] \mid f \in \{F\} \cup C\}$ **do**   // Cartesian product

10            $G \longleftarrow \bigwedge H \wedge \bigwedge R$

11   **foreach** m $\in \{0, \ldots, \mu - 1\}$ **do**

12   resG, model $\longleftarrow$ checkSat(G)

13   **if** resG $\neq$ SAT **then**

14   **break**   // No models if G is not SAT

15              $T \longleftarrow$ candidateTerm$(\{F\} \cup C$, R, model)   // Step 3

16   resl, _ $\longleftarrow$ checkSat(I $\wedge T$)   // Step 4

17   **if** resl = UNSAT **then**

18   **return** minimized(T) // Success

19              $G \longleftarrow G \wedge \neg$model   // Avoid this model next iteration

20   **return** None

The algorithm iterates over each *quantified* conjunct F of I (Algorithm 1, line 3) and checks if F is individually unsatisfiable (for depth = 0). For complex proofs, this is usually not sufficient, as I is typically inconsistent due to *a combination of* conjuncts ($F_0 \wedge F_1$ in Fig. 5). In such cases, the algorithm proceeds as follows:

Step 1: Clustering. It constructs clusters of formulas similar to F (Algorithm 2, line 4), based on their *Jaccard similarity index*. Let F_i and F_j be two arbitrary formulas, and S_i and S_j their respective sets of uninterpreted function symbols (from their bodies and the patterns). The Jaccard similarity index is defined as: $J(F_i, F_j) = \frac{|S_i \cap S_j|}{|S_i \cup S_j|}$ (the number of common uninterpreted functions divided by the total number). For Fig. 5, $S_0 = \{\mathtt{f}\}$, $S_1 = \{\mathtt{f}, \mathtt{g}\}$, $J(F_0, F_1) = \frac{|\{\mathtt{f}\}|}{|\{\mathtt{f}, \mathtt{g}\}|} = 0.5$.

Our algorithm explores the search space by iteratively expanding clusters to include transitively-similar formulas up to a maximum depth (parameter δ in Algorithm 1). For two formulas $F_i, F_j \in$ I, we define the similarity function as:

Algorithm 2: Auxiliary procedure for Algorithm 1, which identifies clusters of formulas similar to F and their rewritings. `sim` is defined in text (step 1). `unify` is a first-order unification algorithm (not shown); it returns a set of rewritings with restricted shapes, defined in text (step 2).

Arguments : I — input formula, also treated as set of conjuncts
F — quantified conjunct of I, i.e., $F \in I \mid F$ is $\forall \overline{x} :: F'$
σ — similarity threshold for clustering
depth — current depth for clustering
Result: A set of pairs, consisting of clusters and their corresponding rewritings

```
1  Procedure clustersRewritings
2      if depth = 0 then
3          return {(∅, ∅)}
4      simFormulas ⟵ {f | f ∈ I \ {F} and sim_I^depth(F, f, σ)}        // Step 1
6      rewritings ⟵ {}
7      foreach f ∈ simFormulas do
8          rws ⟵ unify(F, f)                                           // Step 2
9          if rws = ∅ and (f is ∀x̄ :: D₀ ∨ ... ∨ Dₙ) then
10             simFormulas ⟵ simFormulas \ {f}
11         rewritings[f] ⟵ rws
12     return {(C, R) | C ⊆ simFormulas and (∀r ∈ R, ∃f ∈ C : r ∈ rewritings[f])
                 and (∀x ∈ qvars(C): |{r | r ∈ R and x = lhs(r)}| ≤ 1)}
```

$$\text{sim}_I^\delta(F_i, F_j, \sigma) = \begin{cases} J(F_i, F_j) \geq \sigma, & \delta = 1 \\ \exists F_k : \text{sim}_{I \setminus \{F_i\}}^{\delta-1}(F_i, F_k, \sigma) \text{ and } J(F_k, F_j) \geq \sigma, & \delta > 1 \end{cases}$$

where $\sigma \in [0, 1]$ is a similarity threshold used to parameterize our algorithm.

The initial cluster (`depth = 1`) includes all the conjuncts of I that are *directly* similar to F. Each subsequent iteration adds the conjuncts that are directly similar to an element of the cluster from the previous iteration, that is, *transitively* similar to F. This search strategy allows us to gradually strengthen the formulas G (used to synthesize candidate terms in step 3) without overly constraining them (an over-constrained formula is unsatisfiable, and has no models).

Step 2: Syntactic Unification. Next (Algorithm 2, line 8) we identify *rewritings*, i.e., constraints under which two similar *quantified* formulas share terms. (Appx. D of [11] presents the quantifier-free case.) We obtain the rewritings by performing a *simplified* form of *syntactic term unification*, which reduces their number to a practical size. Our rewritings are *directed equalities*. For two formulas F_i and F_j and an uninterpreted function f they have one of the following two shapes:

(1) $x_i = rhs_j$, where x_i is a quantified variable of F_i, rhs_j are terms from F_j defined below, F_i contains a term $f(x_i)$ and F_j contains a term $f(rhs_j)$,
(2) $x_j = rhs_i$, where x_j is a quantified variable of F_j, rhs_i are terms from F_i defined below, F_j contains a term $f(x_j)$ and F_i contains a term $f(rhs_i)$,

where rhs_k is a constant c_k, a quantified variable x_k, or a composite function $(\mathtt{f} \circ \mathtt{g_0} \circ \ldots \circ \mathtt{g_n})(\overline{c_k}, \overline{x_k})$ occurring in the formula F_k and $\mathtt{g_0}, \ldots, \mathtt{g_n}$ are arbitrary (interpreted or uninterpreted) functions. That is, we determine the *most general unifier* [6] only for those terms that have uninterpreted functions as the outermost functions and quantified variables as arguments. The unification algorithm is standard (except for the restricted shapes), so it is not shown explicitly.

Since a term may appear more than once in F, or F unifies with multiple similar formulas through the same quantified variable, we can obtain *alternative rewritings* for a quantified variable. In such cases, we either duplicate or split the cluster, such that in each cluster-rewriting pair, each quantified variable is rewritten at most once (see Algorithm 2, line 12). In Fig. 7, both F_1 and F_2 are similar to F_0 (all three formulas share the uninterpreted symbol $\mathtt{f}$). Since the unification produces alternative rewritings for x_0 ($x_0 = x_1$ and $x_0 = x_2$), the procedure clustersRewritings returns the pairs $\{(\{F_1\}, \{x_0 = x_1\}), (\{F_2\}, \{x_0 = x_2\})\}$.

Step 3: Identifying Candidate Terms. From the clusters and the rewritings (identified before), we then derive *quantifier-free* formulas G (Algorithm 1, line 10), and, if they are satisfiable, construct the candidate triggering terms from their models (Algorithm 1, line 15). Each formula G consists of: (1) $\neg F_{\approx}$ (defined in (*), which is equivalent to $\neg F'$, since F has the shape $\forall \overline{x} :: F'$ from Algorithm 1, line 3), (2) the *instantiations* (see (**)) of all the similar formulas from the cluster, and (3) the corresponding rewritings R. (Since we assume that all the quantified variables are globally unique, we do not perform variable renaming for the instantiations).

If a similar formula has multiple disjuncts D_k, the solver uses short-circuiting semantics when generating the model for G. That is, if it can find a model that satisfies the first disjunct, it does not consider the remaining ones. To obtain more diverse models, we synthesize formulas that *cover* each disjunct, i.e., make sure that it evaluates to **true** at least once. We thus compute *multiple instantiations* of each similar formula, of the form: $(\bigwedge_{0 \le j < k} \neg D_j) \wedge D_k, \forall k: 0 \le k \le n$ (see Algorithm 1, line 7). To consider all the combinations of disjuncts, we derive the formula G from the Cartesian product of the instantiations (Algorithm 1, line 9). (To present the pseudo-code in a concise way, we store $\neg F'$ in the instantiations map as well (Algorithm 1, line 8), even if it does *not* represent the instantiation of F.)

In Fig. 8, F_1 is similar to F_0 and $R = \{x_0 = x_1\}$. F_1 has two disjuncts and thus two possible instantiations: $\mathsf{Inst}[F_1] = \{x_1 \ge 1, (x_1 < 1) \wedge (\mathtt{f}(x_1) = 6)\}$. The formula $G = (x_0 > -1) \wedge (\mathtt{f}(x_0) \le 7) \wedge (x_1 \ge 1) \wedge (x_0 = x_1)$ for the first instantiation is satisfiable, but none of the values the solver can assign to x_0

$$F_0 : \forall x_0 : \mathrm{Int} :: \{\mathtt{f}(x_0)\}\ \mathtt{f}(x_0) = 6$$
$$F_1 : \forall x_1 : \mathrm{Int} :: \{\mathtt{f}(x_1)\}\ \mathtt{f}(x_1) = 7$$
$$F_2 : \forall x_2 : \mathrm{Int} :: \{\mathtt{f}(x_2)\}\ \mathtt{f}(x_2) = 8$$

Fig. 7. Formulas that set contradictory constraints on the function $\mathtt{f}$. Synthesizing the triggering term $\mathtt{f}(0)$ requires clusters of similar formulas with alternative rewritings.

Algorithm 3: Auxiliary procedure for Algorithm 1, which constructs a triggering term from the given cluster, rewritings, and SMT model. dummy is a fresh function symbol, which conveys no information about the truth value of the candidate term; thus conjoining it to the input preserves (un)satisfiability.

Arguments : C — set of formulas in the cluster
R — set of rewritings for the cluster
model — SMT model, mapping variables to values
Result: A triggering term with no semantic information

1 **Procedure** candidateTerm
2   $P_0, \ldots, P_k \longleftarrow$ patterns(C)
3   **while** $R \neq \varnothing$ **do**
4   choose and remove $r \longleftarrow (x = rhs)$ from R
5    $P_0, \ldots, P_k \longleftarrow (P_0, \ldots, P_k)[\,rhs/x\,]$
6    $R \longleftarrow R\,[\,rhs/x\,]$
7   **foreach** $x \in$ qvars(C) **do**
8    $P_0, \ldots, P_k \longleftarrow (P_0, \ldots, P_k)[\,$model$(x)/x\,]$
9   **return** "dummy" + "(" + $P_0, \ldots, P_k$ + ")"

(which are all greater or equal to 1) are sufficient for the unsatisfiability proof to succeed. The second instantiation adds additional constraints: instead of $x_1 \geq 1$, it requires $(x_1 < 1) \wedge (\mathtt{f}(x_1) = 6)$. The resulting G formula has a unique solution for x_0, namely 0, and the triggering term $\mathtt{f}(0)$ is sufficient to prove unsat.

The procedure candidateTerm from Algorithm 3 synthesizes a candidate triggering term T from the model of G and the rewritings R. We first collect all the patterns of the formulas from the cluster C (Algorithm 3, line 2), i.e., of F and of its similar conjuncts (see Algorithm 1, line 15). Then, we *apply* the rewritings, in an arbitrary order (Algorithm 3, lines 3–6). That is, we substitute the quantified variable x from the left hand side of the rewriting with the right hand side term rhs and propagate this substitution to the remaining rewritings. This step allows us to include in the synthesized triggering terms additional information, which cannot be provided by the solver. Then (Algorithm 3, lines 7–8) we substitute the remaining variables with their *constant* values from the model (i.e., constants for built-in types, and fresh, unconstrained variables for uninterpreted types). The resulting triggering term is wrapped in an application to a fresh, uninterpreted function dummy to ensure that conjoining it to I does not change I's satisfiability.

$$F_0: \forall x_0: \mathrm{Int} :: \{\mathtt{f}(x_0)\} \; \neg(x_0 > -1) \vee (\mathtt{f}(x_0) > 7)$$
$$F_1: \forall x_1: \mathrm{Int} :: \{\mathtt{f}(x_1)\} \; \neg(x_1 < 1) \vee (\mathtt{f}(x_1) = 6)$$

Fig. 8. Formulas that set contradictory constraints on the function $\mathtt{f}$. Synthesizing the triggering term $\mathtt{f}(0)$ requires instantiations that cover all the disjuncts.

Step 4: Validation. We validate the candidate triggering term T by checking if $I \wedge T$ is unsatisfiable, i.e., if these particular interpretations for the uninterpreted functions generalize to all interpretations (Algorithm 1, line 16). If this is the case then we return the *minimized* triggering term (Algorithm 1, line 18). The `dummy` function has multiple arguments, each of them corresponding to one pattern from the cluster (Algorithm 3, line 9). This is an over-approximation of the required triggering terms (once instantiated, the formulas may trigger each other), so `minimized` removes redundant (sub-)terms. If T does not validate, we re-iterate its construction up to a bound μ and strengthen the formula G to obtain a different model (Algorithm 1, lines 19 and 11). Appx. B of [11] discusses heuristics for obtaining *diverse models*.

Nested Quantifiers. Our algorithm also supports nested quantifiers. Nested existential quantifiers in positive positions and nested universal quantifiers in negative positions are replaced in NNF by new, uninterpreted Skolem functions. Step 2 is also applicable to them: Skolem functions with arguments (the quantified variables from the outer scope) are unified as regular uninterpreted functions; they can also appear as *rhs* in a rewriting, but not as the left-hand side (we do not perform higher-order unification). In such cases, the result is imprecise: the unification of $f(x_0, \text{skolem}())$ and $f(x_1, 1)$ produces only the rewriting $x_0 = x_1$.

After pre-processing, the conjunct F and the similar formulas may still contain *nested universal quantifiers*. F is always negated in G, thus it becomes, after Skolemization, quantifier-free. To ensure that G is also quantifier-free (and the solver can generate a model), we extend the algorithm to *recursively instantiate* similar formulas with nested quantifiers when computing the instantiations.

3.3 Limitations

Next, we discuss the limitations of our technique, as well as possible solutions.

Applicability. Our algorithm effectively addresses a common cause of failed unsatisfiability proofs in program verification, i.e., missing triggering terms. Other causes (e.g., incompleteness in the solver's decision procedures due to undecidable theories) are beyond the scope of our work. Also, our algorithm is tailored to *unsatisfiability* proofs; satisfiability proofs cannot be reduced to unsatisfiability proofs by negating the input, because the negation cannot usually be encoded in SMT (as we have illustrated in Sect. 2).

SMT Solvers. Our algorithm synthesizes triggering terms as long as the SMT solver can find models for our quantifier-free formulas. However, solvers are incomplete, i.e., they can return *unknown* and generate only *partial models*, which are not guaranteed to be correct. Nonetheless, we also use partial models, as the validation step (step 4 in Fig. 4) ensures that they do not lead to false positives.

Patterns. Since our algorithm is based on patterns (provided or inferred), it will not succeed if they do not permit the necessary instantiations. For example, the formula $\forall x : \text{Int}, y : \text{Int} :: x = y$ is unsatisfiable. However, the SMT solver cannot automatically infer a pattern from the body of the quantifier, since equality is an interpreted function and must not occur in a pattern. Thus E-matching (and implicitly our algorithm) cannot solve this example, unless the user provides as pattern some uninterpreted function that mentions both x and y (e.g., $f(x,y)$).

Bounds and Rewritings. Synthesizing triggering terms is generally undecidable. We ensure termination by bounding the search space through various customizable parameters, thus our algorithm misses results not found within these bounds. We also only unify applications of uninterpreted functions, which are common in verification. Efficiently supporting interpreted functions (especially equality) is very challenging for inputs with a small number of types (e.g., from Boogie [7]).

Despite these limitations, our algorithm effectively synthesizes the triggering terms required in practical examples, as we experimentally show next.

4   Evaluation

Evaluating our work requires benchmarks with known triggering issues (i.e., for which E-matching yields *unknown*). Since there is no publicly available suite, in Sect. 4.1 we used manually-collected benchmarks from four verifiers [19,25,35,38]. Our algorithm succeeded for 65,6%. To evaluate its applicability to other verifiers, in Sect. 4.2 we used SMT-COMP [33] inputs. As they were not designed to expose triggering issues, we developed a filtering step (see Appx. F of [11]) to automatically identify the subset that falls into this category. The results show that our algorithm is suited also for [8,12,32]. Section 4.3 illustrates that our triggering terms are simpler than the unsat proofs produced by quantifier instantiation and refutation techniques, enabling one to fix the root cause of the revealed issues.

Setup. We used Z3 (4.8.10) [24] to infer the patterns, generate the models and validate the candidate terms. However, our tool can be used with any solver that supports E-matching and exposes the inferred patterns. We used Z3's NNF tactic to transform the inputs into NNF and locality-sensitive hashing to compute the clusters. We fixed Z3's random seeds to arbitrary values (sat.random_seed to 488, smt.random_seed to 599, and nlsat.seed to 611). We set the (soft) timeout to 600s and the memory limit to 6 GB per run and used a 1s timeout for obtaining a model and for validating a candidate term. The experiments were conducted on a Linux server with 252 GB of RAM and 32 Intel Xeon CPUs at 3.3 GHz.

4.1   Effectiveness on Verification Benchmarks with Triggering Issues

First, we used manually-collected benchmarks with known triggering issues from Dafny [19], F* [35], Gobra [38], and Viper [25]. We reconstructed 4, respectively 2 inconsistent axiomatizations from Dafny and F*, based on the changes from the repositories and the messages from the issue trackers; we obtained 11 inconsistent axiomatizations of arrays and option types from Gobra's developers and collected 15 incompleteness issues from Viper's test suite [3], with at least one assertion needed only for triggering. These contain algorithms for arrays, binomial heaps, binary search trees, and regression tests. The file sizes (minimum-maximum number of formulas or quantifiers) are shown in Table 1, columns 3–4.

Table 1. Results on verification benchmarks with known triggering issues. The columns show: the source of the benchmarks, the number of files (#), their number of conjuncts (#F) and of quantifiers (#$\forall$), the number of files for which five configurations (C0–C4) synthesized suited triggering terms, our results across all configurations, the number of unsat proofs generated by Z3 (with MBQI [16]), CVC4 (with enumerative instantiation [28]), and Vampire [18] (in CASC mode [34], using Z3 for ground theory reasoning).

Source	# min-max	#F min-max	#$\forall$ min-max	C0 default	C1 σ=0.1	C2 β=1	C3 type	C4 σ=0.1 $\wedge$ sub	Our work	Z3 MBQI	CVC4 enum inst	Vampire CASC $\wedge$ Z3
Dafny	4	6 - 16	5 - 16	1	1	1	1	0	1	1	0	2
F*	2	18 - 2388	15 - 2543	1	1	1	1	2	2	1	0	2
Gobra	11	64 - 78	50 - 63	5	10	1	7	10	11	6	0	11
Viper	15	84 - 143	68 - 203	7	5	3	5	5	7	11	0	15
Total	32							21 (65,6%)		19 (59,3%)	0 (0%)	30 (93,7%)

σ = similarity threshold; β = batch size; **type** = type-based constraints; **sub** = sub-terms   **C0**: $\sigma = 0.3$; $\beta = 64$; ¬**type**; ¬**sub**

Configurations. We ran our tool with five configurations, to also analyze the impact of its parameters (see Algorithm 1 and Appx. C of [11]). The default configuration C0 has: $\sigma = 0.3$ (similarity threshold), $\beta = 64$ (batch size, i.e., the number of candidate terms validated together), ¬type (no type-based constraints), ¬sub (no unification for sub-terms). The other configurations differ from C0 in the parameters shown in Table 1. All configurations use $\delta = 2$ (maximum transitivity depth), $\mu = 4$ (maximum number of different models), and 600s timeout per file.

Results. Columns 5–9 in Table 1 show the number of files solved by each configuration, column 10 summarizes the files solved by at least one. Overall, we found suited triggering terms for 65,6%, including all F* and Gobra benchmarks. An F* unsoundness exposed by all configurations in ≈60s is given in [11] (Fig. 9). It required two developers to be manually diagnosed based on a bug report [2]. A simplified Gobra axiomatization for option types, solved by C4 in ≈13s, is shown in [11] (Fig. 11). Gobra's team spent one week to identify some of the issues. As our triggering terms for F* and Gobra were similar to the manually-written ones, they could have reduced the human effort in localizing and fixing the errors.

Our algorithm synthesized missing triggering terms for 7 Viper files, including the array maximum example [1], for which E-matching could not prove that the maximal element in a strictly increasing array of size 3 is its last element. Our triggering term `loc(a,2)` (`loc` maps arrays and integers to heap locations) can be added by a *user* of the verifier to their postcondition. A *developer* can fix the root cause of the incompleteness by including a generalization of the triggering term to arbitrary array sizes: `len(a)!=0 ==> x==loc(a,len(a)-1).val`. Both result in E-matching refuting the proof obligation in under 0.1s. We also exposed another case where Boogie (used by Viper) is sound only modulo patterns (as in Fig. 3).

4.2   Effectiveness on SMT-COMP Benchmarks

Next, we considered 61 SMT-COMP [33] benchmarks from Spec# [8], VCC [32], Havoc [12], Simplify [14], and the Bit-Width-Independent (BWI) encoding [26].

Table 2. Results on SMT-COMP inputs. The columns have the structure from Table 1.

Source	# min-max	#F min-max	#∀ min-max	C0 default	C1 σ=0.1	C2 β=1	C3 type	C4 σ=0.1∧sub	Our work	Z3 MBQI	CVC4 enum inst	Vampire CASC∧Z3
Spec#	33	28 - 2363	25 - 645	16	16	14	16	15	16	16	0	29
VCC/Havoc	14	129 - 1126	100 - 1027	11	9	5	11	9	11	12	0	14
Simplify	1	256	129	0	0	0	0	0	0	1	0	0
BWI	13	189 - 384	198 - 456	1	1	2	1	1	2	12	0	12
Total	61			29 (47,5%)						41 (67,2%)	0 (0%)	55 (90,1%)

σ = similarity threshold; β = batch size; **type** = type-based constraints; **sub** = subterms   **C0:** $\sigma = 0.3$; $\beta = 64$; ¬**type**; ¬**sub**

Results. The results are shown in Table 2. Our algorithm enabled E-matching to refute 47.5% of the files, most of them from Spec# and VCC/Havoc. We manually inspected some BWI benchmarks (for which the algorithm had worse results) and observed that the validation step times out even with a much higher time-out. This shows that some candidate terms trigger matching loops and explains why C2 (which validates them individually) solved one more file. Extending our algorithm to avoid matching loops, by construction, is left as future work.

4.3   Comparison with Unsatisfiability Proofs

As an alternative to our work, tool developers could try to *manually* identify triggering issues from refutation proofs, but these do not consider patterns and are harder to understand. Columns 11–13 in Table 1 and Table 2 show the number of proofs produced by Z3 with MBQI [16], CVC4 [9] with enumerative instantiation [28], and Vampire [18] using Z3 for ground theory reasoning [27] and the CASC [34] portfolio mode with competition presets. CVC4 failed for all examples (it cannot construct proofs for quantified logics), Vampire refuted most of them. Our algorithm outperformed MBQI for F* and Gobra and had similar results for Dafny, Spec# and VCC/Havoc. All our configurations solved two VCC/Havoc files not solved by MBQI (Appx. D of [11] shows an example). Moreover, our triggering terms are much simpler and directly highlight the root cause of the issues. Compared to our generated term `loc(a,2)`, MBQI's proof for Viper's array maximum example has 2135 lines and over 700 reasoning steps, while Vampire's proof has 348 lines and 101 inference steps. Other proofs have similar complexity.

Vampire and MBQI cannot replace our technique: as most deductive verifiers employ E-matching, it is important to help the developers use the algorithm of their choice and return sound results even if they rely on patterns for soundness (as in Fig. 3). Our tool can also produce multiple triggering terms (see Appx. C of [11]), thus it can reveal *multiple* triggering issues for the same input formula.

5   Related Work

To our knowledge, no other approach automatically produces the information needed by developers to remedy the effects of overly restrictive patterns. Quantifier instantiation and refutation techniques (discussed next) can produce unsatisfiability proofs, but these are much more complex than our triggering terms.

Quantifier Instantiation Techniques. *Model-based quantifier instantiation* [16] (MBQI) was designed for sat formulas. It checks if the models obtained for the quantifier-free part of the input satisfy the quantifiers, whereas we check if the synthesized triggering terms obtained for some interpretation of the uninterpreted functions generalize to all interpretations. In some cases, MBQI can also generate unsatisfiability proofs, but they require expert knowledge to be understood; our triggering terms are much simpler. *Counterexample-guided quantifier instantiation* [29] is a technique for sat formulas, which synthesizes computable functions from logical specifications. It is applicable to functions whose specifications have explicit syntactic restrictions on the space of possible solutions, which is usually not the case for axiomatizations. Thus the technique cannot directly solve the complementary problem of proving soundness of the axiomatization.

E-matching-Based Approaches. Rümmer [31] proposed a *calculus* for first-order logic modulo linear integer arithmetic that integrates constraint-based free variable reasoning with E-matching. Our algorithm does not require reasoning steps, so it is applicable to formulas from all the logics supported by the SMT solver. *Enumerative instantiation* [28] is an approach that exhaustively enumerates ground terms from a set of ordered, quantifier-free terms from the input. It can be used to refute formulas with quantifiers, but not to construct proofs (see Sect. 4.3). Our algorithm derives quantifier-free formulas and synthesizes the triggering terms from their models, even if the input does not have a quantifier-free part. It uses also syntactic information to construct complex triggering terms.

Theorem Provers. First-order theorem provers (e.g., Vampire [18]) also generate refutation proofs. More recent works combine a superposition calculus with theory reasoning [27,37], integrating SAT/SMT solvers with theorem provers. We also use unification, but to synthesize triggering terms required by E-matching. However, our triggering terms are much simpler than Vampire's proofs and can be used to improve the triggering strategies for all future runs of the verifier.

6   Conclusions

We have presented the first automated technique that enables the developers of verifiers remedy the effects of overly restrictive patterns. Since discharging proof obligations and identifying inconsistencies in axiomatizations require an SMT solver to prove the unsatisfiability of a formula via E-matching, we developed a novel algorithm for synthesizing triggering terms that allow the solver to complete the proof. Our approach is effective for a diverse set of verifiers, and can significantly reduce the human effort in localizing and fixing triggering issues.

Acknowledgements. We would like to thank the reviewers for their insightful comments. We are also grateful to Felix Wolf for providing us the Gobra benchmarks, and to Evgenii Kotelnikov for his detailed explanations about Vampire.

References

1. Array maximum, by elimination (2021). http://viper.ethz.ch/examples/max-array-elimination.html
2. F* issue 1848 (2021). https://github.com/FStarLang/FStar/issues/1848
3. Viper test suite (2021). https://github.com/viperproject/silver/tree/master/src/test/resources
4. Amighi, A., Blom, S., Huisman, M.: Vercors: a layered approach to practical verification of concurrent software. In: PDP, pp. 495–503. IEEE Computer Society (2016). https://ieeexplore.ieee.org/abstract/document/7445381
5. Astrauskas, V., Müller, P., Poli, F., Summers, A.J.: Leveraging Rust types for modular specification and verification. In: Object-Oriented Programming Systems, Languages, and Applications (OOPSLA), vol. 3, pp. 147:1–147:30. ACM (2019). https://doi.org/10.1145/3360573
6. Baader, F., Snyder, W.: Unification theory. In: Robinson, J.A., Voronkov, A. (eds.) Handbook of Automated Reasoning, pp. 445–532. Elsevier and MIT Press (2001)
7. Barnett, M., Chang, B. Y.E., DeLine, R., Jacobs, B., Leino, K.R.M.: Boogie: a modular reusable verifier for object-oriented programs. In: de Boer, F.S., Bonsangue, M.M., Graf, S., de Roever, W.-P. (eds.) FMCO 2005. LNCS, vol. 4111, pp. 364–387. Springer, Heidelberg (2006). https://doi.org/10.1007/11804192_17
8. Barnett, M., Fähndrich, M., Leino, K.R.M., Müller, P., Schulte, W., Venter, H.: Specification and verification: the Spec# experience. Commun. ACM **54**(6), 81–91 (2011)
9. Barrett, C., et al.: CVC4. In: Gopalakrishnan, G., Qadeer, S. (eds.) CAV 2011. LNCS, vol. 6806, pp. 171–177. Springer, Heidelberg (2011). https://doi.org/10.1007/978-3-642-22110-1_14
10. Barrett, C., Fontaine, P., Tinelli, C.: The SMT-LIB Standard: Version 2.6. Technical report, Department of Computer Science, The University of Iowa (2017). www.SMT-LIB.org
11. Bugariu, A., Ter-Gabrielyan, A., Müller, P.: Identifying overly restrictive matching patterns in SMT-based program verifiers (extended version). Technical report, 2105.04385, arXiv (2021)
12. Chatterjee, S., Lahiri, S.K., Qadeer, S., Rakamarić, Z.: A reachability predicate for analyzing low-level software. In: Grumberg, O., Huth, M. (eds.) TACAS 2007. LNCS, vol. 4424, pp. 19–33. Springer, Heidelberg (2007). https://doi.org/10.1007/978-3-540-71209-1_4
13. Darvas, Á., Leino, K.R.M.: Practical reasoning about invocations and implementations of pure methods. In: Dwyer, M.B., Lopes, A. (eds.) FASE 2007. LNCS, vol. 4422, pp. 336–351. Springer, Heidelberg (2007). https://doi.org/10.1007/978-3-540-71289-3_26
14. Detlefs, D., Nelson, G., Saxe, J.B.: Simplify: a theorem prover for program checking. J. ACM **52**(3), 365–473 (2005). https://doi.org/10.1145/1066100.1066102
15. Eilers, M., Müller, P.: Nagini: a static verifier for Python. In: Chockler, H., Weissenbacher, G. (eds.) CAV 2018. LNCS, vol. 10981, pp. 596–603. Springer, Cham (2018). https://doi.org/10.1007/978-3-319-96145-3_33
16. Ge, Y., de Moura, L.: Complete instantiation for quantified formulas in satisfiabiliby modulo theories. In: Bouajjani, A., Maler, O. (eds.) CAV 2009. LNCS, vol. 5643, pp. 306–320. Springer, Heidelberg (2009). https://doi.org/10.1007/978-3-642-02658-4_25

17. Heule, S., Kassios, I.T., Müller, P., Summers, A.J.: Verification condition generation for permission logics with abstract predicates and abstraction functions. In: Castagna, G. (ed.) ECOOP 2013. LNCS, vol. 7920, pp. 451–476. Springer, Heidelberg (2013). https://doi.org/10.1007/978-3-642-39038-8_19

18. Kovács, L., Voronkov, A.: First-order theorem proving and VAMPIRE. In: Sharygina, N., Veith, H. (eds.) CAV 2013. LNCS, vol. 8044, pp. 1–35. Springer, Heidelberg (2013). https://doi.org/10.1007/978-3-642-39799-8_1

19. Leino, K.R.M.: Dafny: an automatic program verifier for functional correctness. In: Clarke, E.M., Voronkov, A. (eds.) LPAR 2010. LNCS (LNAI), vol. 6355, pp. 348–370. Springer, Heidelberg (2010). https://doi.org/10.1007/978-3-642-17511-4_20

20. Leino, K.R.M., Monahan, R.: Reasoning about comprehensions with first-order SMT solvers. In: Proceedings of the 2009 ACM Symposium on Applied Computing, SAC 2009, pp. 615–622. Association for Computing Machinery, New York (2009). https://doi.org/10.1145/1529282.1529411

21. Leino, K.R.M., Müller, P.: Verification of equivalent-results methods. In: Drossopoulou, S. (ed.) ESOP 2008. LNCS, vol. 4960, pp. 307–321. Springer, Heidelberg (2008). https://doi.org/10.1007/978-3-540-78739-6_24

22. Leino, K.R.M., Rümmer, P.: A polymorphic intermediate verification language: design and logical encoding. In: Esparza, J., Majumdar, R. (eds.) TACAS 2010. LNCS, vol. 6015, pp. 312–327. Springer, Heidelberg (2010). https://doi.org/10.1007/978-3-642-12002-2_26

23. Moskal, M.: Programming with triggers. In: SMT. ACM International Conference Proceeding Series, vol. 375, pp. 20–29. ACM (2009)

24. de Moura, L., Bjørner, N.: Z3: an efficient SMT solver. In: Ramakrishnan, C.R., Rehof, J. (eds.) TACAS 2008. LNCS, vol. 4963, pp. 337–340. Springer, Heidelberg (2008). https://doi.org/10.1007/978-3-540-78800-3_24

25. Müller, P., Schwerhoff, M., Summers, A.J.: Viper: a verification infrastructure for permission-based reasoning. In: Jobstmann, B., Leino, K.R.M. (eds.) VMCAI 2016. LNCS, vol. 9583, pp. 41–62. Springer, Heidelberg (2016). https://doi.org/10.1007/978-3-662-49122-5_2

26. Niemetz, A., Preiner, M., Reynolds, A., Zohar, Y., Barrett, C., Tinelli, C.: Towards bit-width-independent proofs in SMT solvers. In: Fontaine, P. (ed.) CADE 2019. LNCS (LNAI), vol. 11716, pp. 366–384. Springer, Cham (2019). https://doi.org/10.1007/978-3-030-29436-6_22

27. Reger, G., Bjorner, N., Suda, M., Voronkov, A.: AVATAR modulo theories. In: Benzmüller, C., Sutcliffe, G., Rojas, R. (eds) GCAI 2016. 2nd Global Conference on Artificial Intelligence. EPiC Series in Computing, vol. 41, pp. 39–52. EasyChair (2016). https://doi.org/10.29007/k6tp. https://easychair.org/publications/paper/7

28. Reynolds, A., Barbosa, H., Fontaine, P.: Revisiting enumerative instantiation. In: Beyer, D., Huisman, M. (eds.) TACAS 2018. LNCS, vol. 10806, pp. 112–131. Springer, Cham (2018). https://doi.org/10.1007/978-3-319-89963-3_7

29. Reynolds, A., Deters, M., Kuncak, V., Tinelli, C., Barrett, C.: Counterexample-guided quantifier instantiation for synthesis in SMT. In: Kroening, D., Păsăreanu, C.S. (eds.) CAV 2015. LNCS, vol. 9207, pp. 198–216. Springer, Cham (2015). https://doi.org/10.1007/978-3-319-21668-3_12

30. Rudich, A., Darvas, Á., Müller, P.: Checking well-formedness of pure-method specifications. In: Cuellar, J., Maibaum, T., Sere, K. (eds.) FM 2008. LNCS, vol. 5014, pp. 68–83. Springer, Heidelberg (2008). https://doi.org/10.1007/978-3-540-68237-0_7

31. Rümmer, P.: E-matching with free variables. In: Bjørner, N., Voronkov, A. (eds.) LPAR 2012. LNCS, vol. 7180, pp. 359–374. Springer, Heidelberg (2012). https://doi.org/10.1007/978-3-642-28717-6_28

32. Schulte, W.: VCC: contract-based modular verification of concurrent C. In: 31st International Conference on Software Engineering, ICSE 2009. IEEE Computer Society, January 2008. https://www.microsoft.com/en-us/research/publication/vcc-contract-based-modular-verification-of-concurrent-c/

33. SMT-COMP 2020: The 15th international satisfiability modulo theories competition (2020). https://smt-comp.github.io/2020/

34. Sutcliffe, G.: The CADE ATP system competition - CASC. AI Mag. **37**(2), 99–101 (2016)

35. Swamy, N., et al.: Dependent types and multi-monadic effects in F*. In: Proceedings of the 43rd Annual ACM SIGPLAN-SIGACT Symposium on Principles of Programming Languages, POPL 2016, pp. 256–270. Association for Computing Machinery, New York (2016). https://doi.org/10.1145/2837614.2837655

36. Swamy, N., Weinberger, J., Schlesinger, C., Chen, J., Livshits, B.: Verifying higher-order programs with the Dijkstra monad. In: Proceedings of the 34th annual ACM SIGPLAN conference on Programming Language Design and Implementation, PLDI 2013, pp. 387–398 (2013). https://www.microsoft.com/en-us/research/publication/verifying-higher-order-programs-with-the-dijkstra-monad/

37. Voronkov, A.: AVATAR: the architecture for first-order theorem provers. In: Biere, A., Bloem, R. (eds.) CAV 2014. LNCS, vol. 8559, pp. 696–710. Springer, Cham (2014). https://doi.org/10.1007/978-3-319-08867-9_46

38. Wolf, F.A., Arquint, L., Clochard, M., Oortwijn, W., Pereira, J.C., Müller, P.: Gobra: modular specification and verification of Go programs. In: Silva, A., Leino, K.R.M. (eds.) CAV 2021. LNCS, vol. 12759, pp. 367–379. Springer, Cham (2021). https://doi.org/10.1007/978-3-030-81685-8_17

Rely/Guarantee Reasoning for Multicopy Atomic Weak Memory Models

Nicholas Coughlin[1,2], Kirsten Winter[1,2], and Graeme Smith[1,2(✉)]

[1] Defence Science and Technology Group, Brisbane, Australia
[2] School of Information Technology and Electrical Engineering,
The University of Queensland, Brisbane, Australia
smith@itee.uq.edu.au

Abstract. Rely/guarantee reasoning provides a compositional approach to reasoning about concurrent programs. However, such reasoning traditionally assumes a sequentially consistent memory model and hence is unsound on modern hardware in the presence of data races. In this paper, we present a rely/guarantee-based approach for *multicopy atomic* weak memory models, i.e., where a thread's stores become observable to all other threads at the same time. Such memory models include those of the widely used x86-TSO and ARMv8 processor architectures, as well as the open-source RISC-V architecture. In this context, an operational semantics can be based on thread-local instruction reordering. We exploit this to provide an efficient compositional proof technique in which weak memory behaviour can be shown to preserve rely/guarantee reasoning on a sequentially consistent memory model. To achieve this, we introduce a side-condition, *reordering interference freedom*, reducing the complexity of weak memory to checks over pairs of reorderable instructions. To enable practical application, we also define a dataflow analysis capable of identifying a thread's reorderable instructions. All aspects of our approach have been encoded and proved sound in Isabelle/HOL.

1 Introduction

Reasoning about concurrent programs with interference over shared resources is a complex task. The interleaving of all thread behaviours leads to an exponential explosion in observable behaviour. Rely/guarantee reasoning [11] is one approach to reduce the complexity of the verification task. It enables reasoning about one thread at a time by considering an abstraction of the thread's environment given as a *rely condition* on shared resources. This abstraction is justified by proving that all other threads in the environment guarantee the assumed rely condition. The approach limits the interference between threads to the effects of the rely condition (specified as a relation over states) on a thread's state.

Xu et al. [34] show how rely/guarantee reasoning can be used to allow reasoning over individual threads in a concurrent program using Hoare logic [10]. We introduce a similar approach in [33] to allow thread-local reasoning, in the context of information flow security, using weakest precondition calculation [7].

© Commonwealth of Australia 2021
M. Huisman et al. (Eds.): FM 2021, LNCS 13047, pp. 292–310, 2021.
https://doi.org/10.1007/978-3-030-90870-6_16

These approaches work equally well for concurrent programs executed on weak memory models under the implicit assumption that the code is data-race free. This is a reasonable assumption given that most programmers avoid data races due to them leading to unexpected behaviour when the code's execution is optimised under the weak memory model of the compiler [4,12] or underlying hardware [3,6,27]. However, data races may be introduced inadvertently by programmers, or programmers may introduce data races for efficiency reasons, as seen in non-blocking algorithms [19]. These algorithms appear regularly in the low-level code of operating systems, e.g., seqlock [5] is used routinely in the Linux kernel, and software libraries, e.g., the Michael-Scott queue [18] is used as the basis for Java's ConcurrentLinkedQueue in java.util.concurrent.

There are a number of approaches for verifying concurrent code under weak memory models [1,2,9,14–16,30,31], which are centred around relations between instructions in multiple threads, thereby precluding the benefits of thread-local reasoning. Notable amongst these is the work by Abdulla et al. [1,2] which aims at automated tool support via stateless model checking and is based on the axiomatic semantic model of [3]. Instead of thread-local reasoning the approaches deal with execution graphs which include not only the interleaving behaviour of concurrent threads but also "parallelisation" of sequential code resulting from weak memory behaviour. Techniques to combat the resulting state-space explosion and improve scalability include elaborate solutions to dynamic partial order reduction, context bounds for a bug-finding technique [1] and (for a sound approach) coarsening the semantic model of execution graphs through reads-from equivalences [2].

Closer to our approach is the proof system for concurrent programs under the C11 memory model developed by Lahav et al. [16]. This proof system is based on the notion of Owicki-Gries reasoning with interference assertions between each line of code to capture potential interleavings. However, to achieve a thread-local approach the authors present their logic in a "rely/guarantee style" in which interference assertions are collected in "rely sets" whose stability needs to be guaranteed by the current thread. This leads to a fine-grained consideration of interference between threads whereas in standard rely/guarantee reasoning the interference is abstracted into a rely condition which summarises the effects of the environment. Moreover, similarly to [1,2] the semantic model is based on (an abstraction of) the axiomatic model in [3] so that the interference between threads includes additionally weak memory effects thereby further complicating the analysis over each instruction. A somewhat-related approach to capture assertions on thread interference is presented in [15] which computes the reads-from relation between threads which is then taken into a account by the thread-local static analyser.

Approaches that propose a purely thread-local analysis for concurrent code under weak memory models include the work by Ridge [24] and Suzanne et al. [29]. Both capture the weak memory model of x86-TSO [26] by modelling the concept of store buffers. This limits their applicability to that of this relatively simple memory model and prohibits adaption to weaker memory models.

In contrast, this paper defines a proof system for rely/guarantee reasoning that is parameterised by the weak memory model under consideration. We restrict our focus to those memory models that are *multicopy atomic*, i.e., where a thread's stores become observable to all other threads at the same time. This includes the memory models of x86-TSO [26], ARMv8 [23] and RISC-V [32] processor architectures, but not POWER [25], older ARM [8] processors nor C11 [4]. As shown by Colvin and Smith [6], multicopy atomic memory models can be captured in terms of instruction reordering. That is, they can be characterised by a reordering relation over pairs of instructions in a thread's code, indicating when two instructions may execute out-of-order[1]. This has been validated against the same sets of litmus test used to validate the widely accepted weak memory semantics of Alglave et al. [3], establishing a high degree of confidence in the correctness of the reordering semantics.

Consequently, the implications of weak memory can be captured thread-locally, enabling compositional reasoning. However, thread-local reasoning under such a semantics is non-trivial. Instruction reordering introduces interference within a single thread, similar to the effects of interference between concurrent threads and equally hard to reason about. For instance, a thread with n reorderable instructions may have $n!$ behaviours due to possible reordering. To tackle such complexity, we exploit the fact that many of these instructions will not influence the behaviour of others. We reduce the verification burden to a standard rely/guarantee judgement [34], over a sequentially consistent memory model, and a consideration of the pair-wise interference between reorderable instruction in a thread, totalling $n(n-1)/2$ pairs given n reorderable instructions. The resulting proof technique has been automated and shown to be sound on both a simple while language and an abstraction of ARMv8 assembly code using Isabelle/HOL [21] (see https://bitbucket.org/wmmif/wmm-rg).

We begin the paper in Sect. 2 with a formalisation of a basic proof system for rely/guarantee reasoning introduced in [34]. In Sect. 3, we abstractly introduce reordering semantics for weak memory models and our notion of *reordering interference freedom* which suffices to account for the effects of the weak memory model. Moreover, we discuss the practical implications of our approach. In Sect. 4 we present the instantiation of the approach with a simple language and demonstrate reasoning with an example. Our work on a more elaborate instantiation of ARMv8 assembly and the verification of a work-stealing deque developed for ARM [17] is available in the Isabelle/HOL theories. We conclude in Sect. 5.

2 Preliminaries

The language for our framework is purposefully kept abstract so that it can be instantiated for different programming languages. It consists of individual

---

[1] For non-multicopy atomic processors such as POWER and older versions of ARM, the semantics of Colvin and Smith additionally requires a *storage subsystem* to capture each thread's view of the global memory, resulting in a more complex semantics that cannot be fully captured by reordering.

instructions α, whose executions are atomic, and *commands* (or programs) c which are composed of instructions using sequential composition, nondeterministic choice, iteration, and parallel composition. Commands also include the empty program ϵ denoting termination.

$$c ::= \epsilon \mid \alpha \mid c_1 ; \ c_2 \mid c_1 \sqcap c_2 \mid c^* \mid c_1 \parallel c_2$$

Note that conditional instructions (like if-then-else and loops) and their evaluation are modelled via silent steps making a nondeterministic choice during the execution of a program (see Sect. 4).

A *configuration* of a program is a pair (c, σ), consisting of a command c to be executed and state σ (a mapping from variables to values) in which it executes. The behaviour of a component, or thread, in a concurrent program can be described via steps the program, including its environment, can perform during execution, each modelled as a relation between the configurations before and after the step. A *program step*, denoted as $(c, \sigma) \xrightarrow{ps} (c', \sigma')$, describes a single step of the component itself and changes the command (i.e., the remainder of the program). A program step may be an *action step* $(c, \sigma) \xrightarrow{as} (c', \sigma')$ which performs an instruction that also changes the state, or a *silent step*, $(c, \sigma) \rightsquigarrow (c', \sigma)$ which does not execute an instruction but makes a choice and thus changes the command only. Hence $\xrightarrow{ps} = (\xrightarrow{as} \cup \rightsquigarrow)$. An *environment step*, $(c, \sigma) \xrightarrow{es} (c, \sigma')$, describes a step of the environment (performed by any of the other concurrent components); it may alter the state but not the remainder of the program (of the component).

Program *execution* is defined via a small-step semantics over the command.

$$
\begin{aligned}
&\alpha \mapsto_\alpha \epsilon \\
&c_1 ; \ c_2 \mapsto_\alpha c_1' ; \ c_2 \text{ if } c_1 \mapsto_\alpha c_1' \\
&c_1 \parallel c_2 \mapsto_\alpha c_1' \parallel c_2 \text{ if } c_1 \mapsto_\alpha c_1' \text{ or } c_1 \parallel c_2 \mapsto_\alpha c_1 \parallel c_2' \text{ if } c_2 \mapsto_\alpha c_2'
\end{aligned}
\tag{1}
$$

The *semantics* of program steps is based on the evaluation of instructions. Each atomic instruction α has a relation over (pre- and post-) states $beh(\alpha)$, formalising its execution behaviour. A program step $(c, \sigma) \xrightarrow{as} (c', \sigma')$ requires an execution $c \mapsto_\alpha c'$ to occur such that the state is updated according to the executed instruction α, i.e.,

$$(c, \sigma) \xrightarrow{as} (c', \sigma') \Leftrightarrow \exists \alpha. \ c \mapsto_\alpha c' \wedge (\sigma, \sigma') \in beh(\alpha). \tag{2}$$

2.1 Rely/Guarantee Reasoning

A proof system for rely/guarantee reasoning in a Hoare logic style has been defined in [34]. Our approach largely follows its definitions, but includes a customisable verification condition, vc, with each instruction. This verification condition serves to capture the state an instruction must execute under to enforce properties such as the component's guarantee and can be considered part of the program's specification. For example, in an information flow security analysis (cf. [33]), it can be used to check that the value assigned to a publicly accessible variable is not classified. We define a Hoare triple as follows. For simplicity of presentation, we treat predicates as sets of states.

$$P\{\alpha\}Q \ \hat{=} \ P \subseteq vc(\alpha) \cap \{\sigma \mid \forall \sigma'. (\sigma, \sigma') \in beh(\alpha) \Rightarrow \sigma' \in Q\} \qquad (3)$$

The rely and guarantee conditions of a thread, denoted $\mathcal{R}$ and $\mathcal{G}$ respectively, are relations over (pre- and post-) states. The rely condition captures allowable environments steps and the guarantee constrains all program steps. A rely/guarantee pair $(\mathcal{R}, \mathcal{G})$ is wellformed when the rely condition is reflexive and transitive, and the guarantee condition is reflexive.

Given that $\mathcal{R}$ is transitive, stability of a predicate P under rely condition $\mathcal{R}$ is defined such that $\mathcal{R}$ maintains P.

$$stable_{\mathcal{R}}(P) \ \hat{=} \ P \subseteq \{\sigma \mid \forall \sigma'. (\sigma, \sigma') \in \mathcal{R} \Rightarrow \sigma' \in P\} \qquad (4)$$

The condition under which an instruction guarantees $\mathcal{G}$ is defined as

$$guar(\alpha, \mathcal{G}) \ \hat{=} \ vc(\alpha) \subseteq \{\sigma \mid \forall \sigma'. (\sigma, \sigma') \in beh(\alpha) \Rightarrow (\sigma, \sigma') \in \mathcal{G}\}. \qquad (5)$$

These ingredients allow us to introduce a rely/guarantee judgement. We do this on three levels: the instruction level $\vdash_a$, the component level $\vdash_c$, and the global level $\vdash$. On the instruction level the judgement requires that the pre- and post-condition are stable under $\mathcal{R}$. This ensures that these conditions, and hence the Hoare triple, hold despite any environmental interference. Additionally, the judgement requires that the instruction satisfies the guarantee $\mathcal{G}$.

$$\mathcal{R}, \mathcal{G} \vdash_a P\{\alpha\}Q \ \hat{=} \ stable_{\mathcal{R}}(P) \wedge stable_{\mathcal{R}}(Q) \wedge guar(\alpha, \mathcal{G}) \wedge P\{\alpha\}Q \qquad (6)$$

A rely/guarantee proof system on the component and global levels follows straightforwardly and is given in Fig. 1. At the component level, note the necessity for the invariant of the [Iteration] rule to be stable (such that it continues to hold amid environmental interference). At the global level, the rule for parallel composition [Par] includes a compatibility check ensuring that the guarantee for each component implies the rely conditions of the other component. A standard [Conseq] rule over global satisfiability is supported by the proof system, but omitted in Fig. 1.

Such rules are standard to rely/guarantee reasoning [34]. Our modification can be seen in can be seen in [Comp], in which global satisfiability is deduced from component satisfiability $\vdash_c$ plus an additional check on *reordering interference freedom*, $rif(\mathcal{R}, \mathcal{G}, c)$, which we introduce in Sect. 3.2. As a consequence, component-based reasoning in this proof system is based on standard rely/guarantee reasoning which can be conducted independently from the interference check.

Moreover, the proof system supports a notion of *auxiliary* variables, common to rely/guarantee reasoning [28, 34]. These variables increase the expressiveness of the specification ($\mathcal{R}, \mathcal{G}, P$ and Q) by representing properties of intermediate execution states. Auxiliary variables cannot influence program execution, as they are abstract, and their modification must be coupled with an instruction such that they are considered atomic.

$$[\text{Atom}]\frac{\mathcal{R},\mathcal{G} \vdash_a P\{\alpha\}Q}{\mathcal{R},\mathcal{G} \vdash_c P\{\alpha\}Q} \qquad [\text{Seq}]\frac{\mathcal{R},\mathcal{G} \vdash_c P\{c_1\}M \quad \mathcal{R},\mathcal{G} \vdash_c M\{c_2\}Q}{\mathcal{R},\mathcal{G} \vdash_c P\{c_1\,;c_2\}Q}$$

$$[\text{Choice}]\frac{\mathcal{R},\mathcal{G} \vdash_c P\{c_1\}Q \quad \mathcal{R},\mathcal{G} \vdash_c P\{c_2\}Q}{\mathcal{R},\mathcal{G} \vdash_c P\{c_1 \sqcap c_2\}Q} \qquad [\text{Iteration}]\frac{stable_\mathcal{R}(P) \quad \mathcal{R},\mathcal{G} \vdash_c P\{c\}P}{\mathcal{R},\mathcal{G} \vdash_c P\{c^*\}P}$$

$$[\text{Conseq}]\frac{P' \subseteq P \quad \mathcal{R}' \subseteq \mathcal{R} \quad \mathcal{G} \subseteq \mathcal{G}' \quad Q \subseteq Q' \quad \mathcal{R},\mathcal{G} \vdash_c P\{c\}Q}{\mathcal{R}',\mathcal{G}' \vdash_c P'\{c\}Q'}$$

$$[\text{Comp}]\frac{\mathcal{R},\mathcal{G} \vdash_c P\{c\}Q \quad rif(\mathcal{R},\mathcal{G},c)}{\mathcal{R},\mathcal{G} \vdash P\{c\}Q}$$

$$[\text{Par}]\frac{\mathcal{R}_1,\mathcal{G}_1 \vdash P_1\{c_1\}Q_1 \quad \mathcal{R}_2,\mathcal{G}_2 \vdash P_2\{c_2\}Q_2 \quad \mathcal{G}_2 \subseteq \mathcal{R}_1 \quad \mathcal{G}_1 \subseteq \mathcal{R}_2}{\mathcal{R}_1 \cap \mathcal{R}_2,\mathcal{G}_1 \cup \mathcal{G}_2 \vdash P_1 \cap P_2\{c_1 \,\|\, c_2\}Q_1 \cap Q_2}$$

Fig. 1. Proof rules for rely/guarantee reasoning

3   Weak Memory Models

Weak memory models are commonly defined to maintain sequentially consistent behaviour given the absence of data races, thereby greatly simplifying reasoning for the majority of programs. However, as we are interested in the analysis of racy concurrent code, it is necessary to reason on a semantics that fully captures the behaviours these models may introduce.

Colvin and Smith [6] show that weak memory behaviour for multicopy atomic processors such as x86-TSO, ARMv8 and RISC-V can be captured in terms of instruction reordering. A memory model, in these cases, is characterised by a reordering relation over pairs of instructions indicating whether the two instructions can execute out-of-order when they appear in a component's code. This complicates reasoning significantly. For example, one needs to determine whether an instruction α that is reordered to execute earlier in a program can invalidate verification conditions that are satisfiable under normal executions (following the program order without reordering). In that sense, we are facing not only interference between concurrent components (which can be visualised as *horizontal* interference) but also interference between the instructions within one component (which can be pictured as *vertical* interference).

3.1   Reordering Semantics

The reordering relation, $\hookrightarrow$, of a component is syntactically derivable based on the rules of the specific memory model (see Sect. 3.3). In ARMv8, for example, two instructions which do not access (write or read) a common variable are deemed semantically independent and can change their execution order. Moreover, weak memory models support various memory barriers that prevent particular forms of reordering. For example, a full fence prevents all reordering, while a control fence prevents speculative execution (for a complete definition refer to [6]).

Matters are complicated by the concept of *forwarding*, where an instruction that reads from a variable written in an earlier instruction might replace the reading access with the written value, hence shedding the dependence to the variable in common. This allows it to execute earlier, anticipating the write before it happens. For example $x := z; y := x$, where z cannot be modified by another component, can execute as $y := z; x := z$. We denote the instruction α with the value written in an earlier instruction β forwarded to it as $\alpha_{\langle\beta\rangle}$. Note that $\alpha_{\langle\beta\rangle} = \alpha$ whenever β does not write to a variable that is read by α.

Forwarding can span a series of instructions and can continue arbitrarily, with later instructions allowed to replace variables introduced by earlier forwarding modifications. The term $\gamma \prec c \prec \alpha$ denotes reordering of the instruction α prior to the command c, with the cumulative forwarding effects producing γ. $\alpha_{\langle\!\langle c\rangle\!\rangle}$ denotes the cumulative forwarding effects of the instructions in command c on α. We define both terms recursively over c.

$$\alpha_{\langle\beta\rangle} \prec \beta \prec \alpha \mathrel{\widehat{=}} \beta \hookleftarrow \alpha_{\langle\beta\rangle}$$
$$\alpha_{\langle\!\langle c_1 \,;\, c_2\rangle\!\rangle} \prec c_1 \,;\, c_2 \prec \alpha \mathrel{\widehat{=}} \alpha_{\langle\!\langle c_1 \,;\, c_2\rangle\!\rangle} \prec c_1 \prec \alpha_{\langle\!\langle c_2\rangle\!\rangle} \;\wedge\; \alpha_{\langle\!\langle c_2\rangle\!\rangle} \prec c_2 \prec \alpha \tag{7}$$

To capture the effects of reordering, we extend the definition of executions (1) with an extra rule that captures out-of-order executions: A step can execute an instruction whose original form occurs later in the program if reordering and forwarding can bring it (in its new form γ) to the beginning of the program.

$$c_1 \,;\, c_2 \mapsto_\gamma c_1 \,;\, c_2' \text{ if } \gamma \prec c_1 \prec \alpha \wedge c_2 \mapsto_\alpha c_2' \tag{8}$$

3.2   Reordering Interference Freedom

Our aim is to eliminate the implications of this reordering behaviour and, therefore, enable standard rely/guarantee reasoning despite a weak memory context. To achieve this, we note that a valid reordering transformation will preserve the thread-local semantics and, hence, will only invalidate reasoning when observed by the environment. Such interactions are captured either as invalidation of the component's guarantee $\mathcal{G}$ or new environment behaviours, as allowed by its rely condition $\mathcal{R}$. Consequently, reorderings may be considered benign if the modified variables are not related by $\mathcal{G}$ or $\mathcal{R}$.

We capture such benign reorderings via reordering interference freedom. Two instructions are said to be *reordering interference free* (*rif*) if we can show that reasoning over the instructions in their original (program) order is sufficiently strong to also include reasoning over their reordered behaviour. Consider the program text $\beta \,;\, \alpha$, where α can be forwarded and executed before β, resulting in an execution equivalent to $\alpha_{\langle\beta\rangle} \,;\, \beta$. Reordering interference freedom between α and β under given rely/guarantee conditions is then formalised as follows.

$$rif_a(\mathcal{R}, \mathcal{G}, \beta, \alpha) \mathrel{\widehat{=}} \forall P, Q, M.\; \mathcal{R}, \mathcal{G} \vdash_a P\{\beta\}M \wedge \mathcal{R}, \mathcal{G} \vdash_a M\{\alpha\}Q$$
$$\Rightarrow \exists M'.\; \mathcal{R}, \mathcal{G} \vdash_a P\{\alpha_{\langle\beta\rangle}\}M' \wedge \mathcal{R}, \mathcal{G} \vdash_a M'\{\beta\}Q \tag{9}$$

Importantly, rif_a is defined independently of the pre- and post-states of the given instructions, as can be seen by the universal quantification over P, M and Q in (9). This independence allows for the establishment of rif_a across a program via consideration of only pairs of reorderable instructions, rather than that of all execution traces under which they may be reordered. Such an approach dramatically reduces the complexity of reasoning in the presence of reordering, from one of $n!$ transformed programs for n reorderable instructions to $n(n-1)/2$ pairs. This can be seen in the case where all n instruction reorder, producing $n!$ permutations, whilst pairs need only consider the 2-combinations of n, equivalent to $n(n-1)/2$.

The definition of rif_a extends inductively over commands c with which α can reorder. Command c is *reordering interference free* from α under $\mathcal{R}$ and $\mathcal{G}$, if the reordering of α over each instructions of c is interference free, including those variants of α produced by forwarding.

$$rif_c(\mathcal{R}, \mathcal{G}, \beta, \alpha) = rif_a(\mathcal{R}, \mathcal{G}, \beta, \alpha)$$
$$rif_c(\mathcal{R}, \mathcal{G}, c_1\,;\,c_2, \alpha) = rif_c(\mathcal{R}, \mathcal{G}, c_1, \alpha_{\langle\!\langle c_2\rangle\!\rangle}) \wedge rif_c(\mathcal{R}, \mathcal{G}, c_2, \alpha) \qquad (10)$$

From the definition of executions including reordering behaviour given in (8) we have $c \mapsto_{\alpha_{\langle\!\langle r\rangle\!\rangle}} c' \Rightarrow r\,;\,\alpha \in prefix(c) \wedge \alpha_{\langle\!\langle r\rangle\!\rangle} \prec r \prec \alpha$, where $prefix(c)$ refers to the set of prefixes of c. Program c is *reordering interference free* if and only if all possible reorderings of its instructions over the respective prefixes are reordering interference free.

$$rif(\mathcal{R}, \mathcal{G}, c) \;\hat{=}\; \forall \alpha, r, c'.\, c \mapsto_{\alpha_{\langle\!\langle r\rangle\!\rangle}} c' \Rightarrow rif_c(\mathcal{R}, \mathcal{G}, r, \alpha) \wedge rif(\mathcal{R}, \mathcal{G}, c') \qquad (11)$$

As can be seen from the definitions, checking $rif(\mathcal{R}, \mathcal{G}, c)$ amounts to checking $rif_a(\mathcal{R}, \mathcal{G}, \beta, \alpha)$ for all pairs of instructions β and α that can reorder in c, including those pairs for which α is a new instruction generated through forwarding. Therefore one can reason about a component's code as follows.

1. Compute all pairs of reorderable instructions, i.e., each pair of instructions (β, α) such that there exists an execution trace where α reorders before β according to the memory model under consideration.
2. Demonstrate reordering interference freedom for as many of these pairs as possible (using $rif_a(\mathcal{R}, \mathcal{G}, \beta, \alpha)$).
3. If rif_a cannot be shown for some pairs, introduce memory barriers to prevent their reordering or modify the verification problem such that their reordering can be considered benign.
4. Verify the component in isolation, using standard rely/guarantee reasoning with an assumed sequentially consistent memory model.

We detail steps 1–3 in the following sections and assume the use of any standard rely/guarantee reasoning approach for step 4.

3.3 Computing All Reorderable Instructions

Pairs of potentially reorderable instructions can be identified via a dataflow analysis [13], similar to dependence analysis commonly used in compiler optimisation. However, rather than attempting to establish an absence of dependence, we are interested in demonstrating its presence, such that instruction reordering is not possible during execution. This notion of dependence is derived from the language's reordering relation, such that α is dependent on β iff $\beta \not\hookleftarrow \alpha$. All pairs of instructions for which a dependence cannot be established are assumed reorderable.

The approach is constructed as a backwards analysis over a component's program text, incrementally determining the instructions a particular instruction is dependent on and, inversely, those it can reorder before. Therefore, the analysis can be viewed as a series of separate analyses, one from the perspective of each instruction in the program text.

We describe one instance of this analysis for some instruction α. The analysis records a notion of α's cumulative dependencies, which simply begins as all instructions γ for which $\gamma \not\hookleftarrow \alpha$. The analysis commences at the instruction immediately prior to α in the program text and progresses backwards. For each instruction β we first determine if α depends on β by consulting α's cumulative dependencies. Given a dependence exists, α's cumulative dependencies are extended to include β's dependencies via a process we refer to as *strengthening*, such that the analysis may subsequently identify those instructions α is dependent on due to its dependence on β. If a dependence on β cannot be shown, the instructions are considered reorderable, subsequently requiring $rif_a(\mathcal{R}, \mathcal{G}, \beta, \alpha)$ to be shown. Moreover, a process of *weakening* is necessary to remove α's cumulative dependencies that β may resolve due to forwarding.

To illustrate the evolving nature of cumulative dependencies, consider the sequence β; γ; α where $\gamma \not\hookleftarrow \alpha$ and $\beta \not\hookleftarrow \gamma$ but $\beta \hookleftarrow \alpha$. The analysis from the perspective of α starts at γ and identifies a dependence, due to $\gamma \not\hookleftarrow \alpha$. Therefore, α gains γ's dependencies via strengthening. The analysis progresses to the next instruction, β, for which a dependence can be established due to α's cumulative dependencies including $\beta \not\hookleftarrow \gamma$. Consequently, despite no direct dependency between α and β, the sequence does not produce reordering pairs for α. Repeating this process for γ and β ultimately finds no reordering pairs over the entire sequence, resulting in no rif_a checks.

A realistic implementation of this analysis is highly dependent on the language's reordering relation. In most examples, this relation only considers the variables accessed by the instructions and special case behaviours for memory barriers, as illustrated by the instantiation in Sect. 4. Consequently, cumulative dependencies can be efficiently represented as sets of such information, for example capturing the variables read by α and those instructions it depends on. This representation lends itself to efficient set-based manipulations for strengthening and weakening.

The analysis has been implemented for both a simple while language and an abstraction of ARMv8 assembly, with optimisations to improve precision in each context. In particular, precision can be improved through special handling of the forwarding case as the effects of forwarding typically result in trivial rif_a checks. To illustrate, recall that forwarding will replace a load from a shared variable with a value written to the variable earlier in the program. As assembly instructions are typically limited to performing at most a single variable store or load at a time, forwarding will transform shared-variable loads into purely thread-local operations by eliminating the load. Consequently, the reordering of such an instruction with any further instructions is trivially free of interference, as the environment cannot observe or influence thread-local instructions.

Both the while language and ARMv8 implementations have been encoded and verified in Isabelle/HOL, along with proofs of termination (following the approach suggested in [20]).

Address Calculations. Dependence analysis is considerably more complex in the presence of address calculations. Under such conditions, it is not possible to syntactically identify whether two instructions access equivalent addresses, complicating an essential check to establishing dependence. Without sufficient aliasing information the analysis must over-approximate and consider the two addresses distinct, potentially introducing excess reordering pairs.

The precision of the analysis can be improved using an alias analysis to first identify equivalent address calculations, feeding such information into the dependency checks. Precision may also be improved by augmenting the interference check, rif_a, with any calculations that have been assumed to be distinct. For example, consider $[x] := e$; $[y] := f$, where $[v] := e$ represents a write to the memory address computed by the expression v. If an alias analysis cannot establish $x = y$, it is necessary to consider their interference. As they are assumed to reorder, a proof demonstrating $rif_a(\mathcal{R}, \mathcal{G}, [x] := e, [y] := f)$ can assume $x \neq y$. Such a property extends to any other comparisons with cumulative dependencies.

We have implemented such improvements in our analysis for ARMv8, relying on manual annotations to determine aliasing address calculations. These aliasing annotations are subsequently added to each instruction's verification condition to ensure they are sound.

3.4   Interference Checking

Given the set of reordering pairs, it is necessary to demonstrate rif_a on each to demonstrate freedom of reordering interference. Many rif_a properties can be shown trivially. For example, if one instruction does not access shared memory, rif_a can be immediately shown to hold as no interference via $\mathcal{R}$ could take place. Additionally, if the two instructions access distinct variables and these variables are not related by $\mathcal{R}$, then no interference would be observed.

If these shortcuts do not hold, then it is necessary to consider rif_a directly via manual verification. The property can be rephrased in terms of weakest precondition calculation [7], providing some automation.

3.5   Elimination of Reordering Interference

Step 3 of the process is intended to handle situations where rif_a cannot be shown for a particular pair of instructions. A variety of techniques can be applied in such conditions, depending on the overall verification goals. In some circumstances, a failure to establish rif_a indicates a problematic reordering such that the out-of-order execution of the instruction pair will violate any variation of the desired rely/guarantee reasoning. In such circumstances, it is necessary to prevent reordering through the introduction of a memory barrier.

As these barriers incur a performance penalty, this is not a suitable technique to correct all problematic pairs. Some reordering pairs can instead be resolved by demonstrating stronger properties during the standard rely/guarantee reasoning in step 4. We describe a series of techniques that can be employed to extract these stronger properties by modifying a program's verification conditions and/or abstracting over its behaviour. These techniques, while incomplete, are easily automated and cover the majority of cases.

Strengthening. Establishing rif_a may fail in cases where an instruction in a reordering pair modifies the other's verification condition. In such circumstances, it is possible to *strengthen* verification conditions such that the interference becomes benign by capturing both the in-order and out-of-order execution behaviours. Given a reordering pair (β, α), this is achieved by first determining the weakest P that solves $P\{\alpha_{\langle\beta\rangle}; \beta\}(true)$, representing the implications of each instruction's verification conditions when executed out-of-order. β's verification condition is then modified by conjoining this P to it, such that the constraints of the out-of-order execution are established during standard reasoning.

For example, consider the component $(y = 0)\{z := z + 1; \ x := y\}(true)$ where, due to a specialised analysis, the assignment to x has the verification condition $z = 1 \lor y = 0$ (and that for the assignment to z is $true$). Assume that $\mathcal{R}$ is the identity relation, i.e., no variables are changed by environment steps, and $\mathcal{G}$ is $true$. This component may be trivially verified when ignoring weak memory effects, as the verification condition for $x := y$ is transformed by $z := z + 1$ into $z = 0 \lor y = 0$, clearly implied by the specified precondition $y = 0$.

However, assuming the two assignments may be reordered, it is necessary to establish $rif_a(\mathcal{R}, \mathcal{G}, z := z + 1, x := y)$. Unfortunately, such a property does not hold. Recall that rif_a requires an out-of-order judgement for all valid in-order judgements under all possible pre- and postconditions. Therefore, we need only identify conditions that are valid for an in-order execution but invalid for the out-of-order to disprove rif_a. This can be seen with the precondition $z = 0$ and postcondition $true$, as we can establish an in-order judgement of $(z = 0)\{z := z + 1; \ x := y\}(true)$ via the same reasoning as above. This does not hold for the out-of-order case of $(z = 0)\{x := y; \ z := z + 1\}(true)$, as $z = 0$ does not imply $z = 1 \lor y = 0$.

Applying the strengthening approach, we compute P for the out-of-order execution as $z = 1 \lor y = 0$. The verification condition for $z := z + 1$ is then conjoined with this P to derive its new condition. As it was originally $true$, this trivial results in the verification condition becoming $z = 1 \lor y = 0$. With this new verification condition, we establish $\mathit{rif}_{\mathsf{a}}(\mathcal{R}, \mathcal{G}, z := z + 1, x := y)$, by invalidating the in-order judgement.

With rif established, the standard rely/guarantee reasoning in step 4 must demonstrate $(y = 0)\{z := z + 1;\ x := y\}(\mathit{true})$, with the strengthened verification condition for $z := z + 1$. This obviously holds given $y = 0$ initially.

Ignored Reads. An additional issue when correcting for $\mathit{rif}_{\mathsf{a}}$ derives from the quantification of the pre- and post-states. This quantification reduces the proof burden, such that only pairs of reorderable instruction must be considered, but can introduce additional proof effort where the precise pre- and post-states are well known and limited reordering takes place. For instance, consider the simple component $(\mathit{true})\{x := 1;\ z := y\}(x = 1)$ with a rely specification that will preserve the values of x and z always and the value of y given $x = 1$. The rely/guarantee reasoning to establish this judgement is trivial. However, the component will fail to demonstrate $\mathit{rif}_{\mathsf{a}}$ when considering the reordering of $x := 1$ and $z := y$, as their program order execution may establish the stronger $(\mathit{true})\{x := 1;\ z := y\}(x = 1 \land z = y)$, whereas the reordered cannot.

We employ two techniques to amend such situations. The most trivial is a weakening of the component's $\mathcal{R}$ specification to remove the relationship between y and x, as it is unnecessary for the component's verification. Otherwise, if this is not possible, the component can be abstracted to $(\mathit{true})\{x := 1;\ \mathsf{chaos}\ z\}(x = 1)$, where $\mathsf{chaos}\ v$ encodes a write of any value to the variable v. Consequently, the read of y is ignored. Both standard rely/guarantee reasoning and rif can be established for this modified component, subsequently enabling verification of the original via a refinement argument.

We propose the automatic detection of those reads that do not impact reasoning and, therefore, can be ignored when establishing rif. In general, such situations are rare as the analysis targets assembly code produced via compilation. Consequently, such unnecessary reads are eliminated via optimisation. Moreover, the $\mathcal{R}$ specification infrequently over-specifies constraints on the environment.

3.6   Soundness

Soundness of the proof system has been proven in Isabelle/HOL and is available in the accompanying theories at https://bitbucket.org/wmmif/wmm-rg.

3.7   Completeness

The proof system is incomplete due to the over-approximations required to reduce reasoning to pairs of reorderable instructions. This is by design, as the approach benefits significantly from such simplifications and the problematic cases appear rare, particularly when the techniques suggested in Sect. 3.5 are applied. As an illustration of these problematic cases, consider

$(P)\{x := v_1;\ y := v_2\}(\textit{true})$, where P is some precondition, the rely condition preserves the values of x and y, and the guarantee is $\textit{true}$. Moreover, assume the verification condition for $y := v_2$ requires $x \neq y$ and the instructions can reorder.

When considering both possible execution orderings a sufficient precondition P would be $x \neq y \wedge v_1 \neq y$, as this captures the constraints imposed by the single verification condition. However, the $\textit{rif}$ approach will introduce an additional, unnecessary condition to establish $\textit{rif}_a(\mathcal{R}, \mathcal{G}, x := v_1, y := v_2)$. First, observe that $x := v_1$ modifies the verification condition for $y := v_2$. Therefore, the verification condition for $x := v_1$ must be strengthened to $x \neq y$, following the same approach as the example in Sect. 3.5. However, the resulting instructions are still not interference free, as $y := v_2$ can now modify the new verification condition for $x := v_1$. This can be resolved through an additional application of strengthening, extending the verification condition for $x := v_1$ to $x \neq y \wedge x \neq v_2$. Consequently, the approach requires a precondition P stronger than $x \neq y \wedge v_1 \neq y \wedge x \neq v_2$, over-approximating the true requirements.

This failure can be attributed to the lack of delineation between the original components of a verification condition and those added due to strengthening, as interference checks on the latter are not necessary. We leave an appropriate encoding of such differences to future work.

4   Instantiating the Proof System

In this section, we illustrate instantiating the proof system with a simple while language. The Isabelle/HOL theories accompanying this work also include an instantiation for ARMv8 assembly which has been used to verify an implementation of the Chase-Lev work-stealing deque developed for ARM [17].

We distinguish three different types of state variables: global variables $\textit{Glb}$ and local variables $\textit{Loc}$, which are program variables, and global auxiliary variables $\textit{Aux}$. Local variables are unique to each thread and cannot be accessed by others.

Atomic instructions in our language comprise skips, assignments, guards, two kinds of fences, and coupling of an instruction with an auxiliary variable assignment and/or with a specific verification condition (similar to an assertion)

$$inst ::= \mathsf{nop} \mid v := e \mid \mathsf{guard}\ p \mid \mathsf{fence} \mid \mathsf{cfence} \mid \langle inst, a := e_a \rangle \mid \{\!| p_a |\!\} inst$$

where v is a program variable, e an expression over program variables, p a boolean expression over program variables, a an auxiliary variable, e_a an expression over program and auxiliary variables, p_a a boolean expression over program and auxiliary variables, and $\langle inst, a := e_a \rangle$ denotes the atomic execution of $inst$ followed by $a := e_a$.

Commands are defined over atomic instructions and their combinations

$$cmd ::= inst \mid cmd\ ;\ cmd \mid \mathsf{if}\ p\ \mathsf{then}\ cmd\ \mathsf{else}\ cmd \mid \mathsf{do}\ cmd\ \mathsf{while}(p, \textit{Inv})$$

where Inv denotes a loop invariant. Instructions instantiate individual instructions (i.e., α) in our abstract language. Sequential composition directly instantiates its abstract counterpart. Conditionals and loops are defined via the choice and iteration operator, i.e., if p then c_1 else c_2 is defined as (guard p); $c_1 \sqcap$ (guard $\neg p$); c_2, and do c while(p, Inv) as $(c;$ (guard $p))^*$; c; (guard $\neg p$), where the invariant Inv holds at the start of c's execution.

A reordering relation $\overset{inst}{\hookleftarrow}$ (and its inverse $\overset{inst}{\not\hookleftarrow}$) is defined over atomic instructions based on syntactic independence of reorderable instruction [6]. For all instructions α and β

fence $\overset{inst}{\not\hookleftarrow} \alpha$, $\quad \alpha \overset{inst}{\not\hookleftarrow}$ fence, $\quad$ guard $p \overset{inst}{\not\hookleftarrow}$ cfence,

cfence $\overset{inst}{\not\hookleftarrow} \alpha$ if $rd(\alpha) \not\subseteq Loc$,

guard $p \overset{inst}{\not\hookleftarrow} \alpha$ if $wr(\alpha) \in Glb \vee wr(\alpha) \in rd($guard $p) \vee rd($guard $p) \cap rd(\alpha) \not\subseteq Loc$,

and for all other cases,

$\beta \overset{inst}{\hookleftarrow} \alpha$ if $wr(\beta) \neq wr(\alpha) \wedge wr(\alpha) \notin rd(\beta) \wedge rd(\beta) \cap rd(\alpha) \subseteq Loc$.

where $wr(\alpha)$ is the program variable written by α and $rd(\alpha)$ the program variables read by α. Note that a cfence is used to prevent speculative reads of global variables when placed prior to the reading instruction and after a guard [6].

Forwarding a value to an assignment instruction in our language is defined as $(v_\alpha := e_\alpha[v_\beta \backslash e_\beta]) \prec (v_\beta := e_\beta) \prec (v_\alpha := e_\alpha)$ and to a guard as (guard $p[v_\alpha \backslash e_\alpha]) \prec (v_\alpha := e_\alpha) \prec$ (guard p) where $e[v \backslash e']$ replaces every occurrence of v in e by e'. The instruction after forwarding carries the same verification condition as the original instruction, i.e., $vc(\alpha_{\langle \beta \rangle}) = vc(\alpha)$.

Note that auxiliary variable updates and verification conditions do not influence the reordering relation, as they will not constrain execution behaviour. Both of these annotations remain linked to their respective instructions during reordering and forwarding.

4.1 Peterson's Mutual Exclusion Algorithm

We use Peterson's mutual exclusion algorithm [22] to demonstrate the workings of the instantiated proof system. The program (shown in Fig. 2) consists of two threads, each of which aims to get exclusive access to the shared variables when they are modified in the thread's critical section (which is represented by a placeholder in the figure). Fences have been added where required for the instantiated proof system.

In order to demonstrate our rely/guarantee reasoning, we define a rely condition for each thread that is reflected by the other thread's guarantee condition. These conditions refer to an auxiliary variable $a : Boolean$, which captures which thread can be in its critical section: when a is false, the left thread t_0 cannot be in its critical section, and when a is true, the right thread t_1 cannot be in its critical section. The rely/guarantee conditions can then be phrased as follows:

```
{  flag0 := true;                          {  flag1 := true;
   fence;                                      fence;
   ⟨turn := true, a := false⟩                  ⟨turn := false, a := true⟩
   fence;                                       fence;
   do                                           do
       ⟨r0 := flag1, a := a ∨ ¬flag1⟩;              ⟨r3 := flag0, a := a ∧ flag0⟩;
       r1 := turn;                                  r4 := ¬turn;
       while(r0 ∧ r1, flag0 ∧ (a ∨ turn));    ∥    while(r3 ∧ r4, flag1 ∧ (¬turn ∨ ¬a));
       ⦃ a ⦄ cfence;                               ⦃¬a⦄ cfence;
           critical_section;                           critical_section;
       ⦃ a ⦄ fence;                                ⦃¬a⦄ fence;
       flag0 := false;                             flag1 := false;
}                                           }
```

Fig. 2. Peterson's algorithm with fences to guarantee correctness under weak memory

$$\mathcal{R}_0 = \mathcal{G}_1 = \textit{flag0} = \textit{flag0}' \wedge ((\textit{flag0} \wedge a) \Rightarrow a') \wedge$$
$$(\textit{turn} = \textit{turn}' \vee (\textit{turn} \wedge \neg\textit{turn}' \wedge (\textit{flag0} \Rightarrow a')))$$
$$\mathcal{R}_1 = \mathcal{G}_0 = \textit{flag1} = \textit{flag1}' \wedge ((\textit{flag1} \wedge a') \Rightarrow a) \wedge$$
$$(\textit{turn} = \textit{turn}' \vee (\neg\textit{turn} \wedge \textit{turn}' \wedge (\textit{flag1} \Rightarrow \neg a')))$$

That is, $\mathcal{R}_0$ specifies that (i) the right thread t_1 does not modify $\textit{flag0}$, (ii) if t_0 is in the critical section, which is the case when $(\textit{flag0} \wedge a)$, t_1 cannot change a, and (iii) either $\textit{turn}$ remains unchanged or it is set to $\textit{false}$ in which case a cannot be falsified if t_0 has not exited its critical section, specified by $(\textit{flag0} \Rightarrow a')$. $\mathcal{R}_1$ can be explained similarly.

Reasoning over t_0's code c_0 requires showing that it is reordering interference free, $\textit{rif}(\mathcal{R}, \mathcal{G}, c_0)$, which holds if $\textit{rif}_a(\mathcal{R}, \mathcal{G}, \beta, \alpha)$ for all instructions α, β in c_0 such that $\beta \hookleftarrow \alpha$ (see (9)–(11)). As an example we discuss reordering interference freedom on the first two instructions of the original code (without **fence** instructions) $\textit{flag0} := \textit{true}$; $\langle \textit{turn} := \textit{true}, a := \textit{false} \rangle$ which are syntactically independent and, following the definition of $\overset{\textit{inst}}{\hookleftarrow}$, can execute out-of-order. To show $\textit{rif}_a$ requires proving that $\forall P, Q, M$.

$$\mathcal{R}, \mathcal{G} \vdash_a P\{\textit{flag0} := \textit{true}\}M \wedge \mathcal{R}, \mathcal{G} \vdash_a M\{\langle\textit{turn} := \textit{true}, a := \textit{false}\rangle\}Q \Rightarrow$$
$$\exists M'. \mathcal{R}, \mathcal{G} \vdash_a P\{\langle\textit{turn} := \textit{true}, a := \textit{false}\rangle\}M' \wedge \mathcal{R}, \mathcal{G} \vdash_a M'\{\textit{flag0} := \textit{true}\}Q.$$

Recall from (6) that the pre- and post-conditions of a Hoare triple are stable and that the instruction satisfies the component's guarantee. The latter holds for $\textit{flag0} := \textit{true}$ since $\mathcal{G}_0$ does not constrain $\textit{flag0}$, and for $\langle\textit{turn} := \textit{true}, a := \textit{false}\rangle$ since $\mathcal{G}_0$ always allows $\textit{turn}$ to stay true when it is true and change to true from false when a changes to false (since this makes $\textit{flag1} \Rightarrow \neg a'$ true).

Let Q be the predicate $\textit{flag0} \wedge (a \vee \textit{turn})$ which is stable under $\mathcal{R}_0$ ($\textit{flag0}$ cannot be changed, a cannot become false when $\textit{flag0}$ is true, and given that $\textit{flag0}$ is true $\textit{turn}$ can only become false when a becomes true). Then, via standard weakest precondition calculation, M could be $\textit{flag0}$ and P could be $\textit{true}$ each of which are also stable under $\mathcal{R}_0$. Hence, the antecedent of the implication holds. However, weakest precondition calculation for the same Q in the consequent requires that $M' \Rightarrow (a \vee \textit{turn})$. This can only be made stable by including $\textit{flag0}$ in M'. Hence, via weakest precondition calculation again, we require that $P \Rightarrow \textit{flag0}$. That is, the program would need to be initialised with $\textit{flag0}$ which is not suitable in the context of Peterson's algorithm (as $flag0$ should only be set when t_0 wants to enter the critical section [22]). Therefore, the analysis suggests including a fence instruction to prevent the reordering of the first and second instruction.

For all other reordering pairs in t_0 we follow similar reasoning (and similarly for the pairs of t_1), resulting in additional fence instructions being required, as shown in Fig. 2, to ensure the correct working of the algorithm. Note that fences are not required between the instructions in the loop bodies. While these instructions are reorderable under $\overset{inst}{\hookleftarrow}$, they can be proven to be reordering interference free. This is demonstrated in our Isabelle/HOL theories.

5   Conclusion

This paper presents a truly thread-local approach to reasoning about concurrent code on a range of weak memory models. It employs standard rely/guarantee reasoning to handle interference between threads, and a separate check of *reordering interference freedom* to handle interference within a thread due to weak memory behaviour.

Reordering interference freedom provides evidence that the weak memory model under consideration will not invalidate properties shown via standard rely/guarantee reasoning. It is a novel concept that hinges on a thread-local reordering semantics which can be defined for any *multicopy atomic* weak memory model, i.e., where a thread's stores become observable to all other threads at the same time. Such memory models include the widely used x86-TSO and ARMv8 processor architectures, and the open-source RISC-V architecture.

Importantly, our approach reduces the check of reordering interference to only pairs of instructions, thereby significantly reducing its complexity. Moreover, the computation of these pairs has been automated along with the validation of trivially benign reordering pairs. Consequently, the only additional manual burden is the establishment of freedom of reordering interference between instruction pairs exhibiting intricate interactions via rely/guarantee conditions. In situations where freedom of reordering interference cannot be shown, our approach includes methods to amend the program, to prohibit reordering behaviour, or modify its verification conditions, such that stronger arguments for reordering interference freedom may be shown.

The paper exemplifies an instantiation of the approach for a simple while language and memory model, and uses it to verify the mutual exclusion property of Peterson's algorithm. The approach is also instantiated to a more realistic assembly language, verifying a work-stealing deque developed specifically for ARM processors. These results, along with a soundness proof for our approach, have been encoded in Isabelle/HOL.

References

1. Abdulla, P.A., Atig, M.F., Bouajjani, A., Ngo, T.P.: Context-bounded analysis for POWER. In: Legay, A., Margaria, T. (eds.) TACAS 2017. LNCS, vol. 10206, pp. 56–74. Springer, Heidelberg (2017). https://doi.org/10.1007/978-3-662-54580-5_4
2. Abdulla, P.A., Atig, M.F., Jonsson, B., Lång, M., Ngo, T.P., Sagonas, K.: Optimal stateless model checking for reads-from equivalence under sequential consistency. Proc. ACM Program. Lang. 3(OOPSLA), 150:1–150:29 (2019)
3. Alglave, J., Maranget, L., Tautschnig, M.: Herding cats: modelling, simulation, testing, and data mining for weak memory. ACM Trans. Program. Lang. Syst. 36(2), 7:1–7:74 (2014)
4. Batty, M., Owens, S., Sarkar, S., Sewell, P., Weber, T.: Mathematizing C++ concurrency. In: Ball, T., Sagiv, M. (eds.) Proceedings of the 38th ACM SIGPLAN-SIGACT Symposium on Principles of Programming Languages, POPL 2011, pp. 55–66. ACM (2011)
5. Boehm, H.: Can seqlocks get along with programming language memory models? In: Zhang, L., Mutlu, O. (eds.) Proceedings of the 2012 ACM SIGPLAN workshop on Memory Systems Performance and Correctness: held in conjunction with PLDI 2012, pp. 12–20. ACM (2012)
6. Colvin, R.J., Smith, G.: A wide-spectrum language for verification of programs on weak memory models. In: Havelund, K., Peleska, J., Roscoe, B., de Vink, E. (eds.) FM 2018. LNCS, vol. 10951, pp. 240–257. Springer, Cham (2018). https://doi.org/10.1007/978-3-319-95582-7_14
7. Dijkstra, E.W., Scholten, C.S.: Predicate Calculus and Program Semantics. Springer, Heidelberg (1990). https://doi.org/10.1007/978-1-4612-3228-5
8. Flur, S., et al.: Modelling the ARMv8 architecture, operationally: concurrency and ISA. In: Bodík, R., Majumdar, R. (eds.) Proceedings of the 43rd Annual ACM SIGPLAN-SIGACT Symposium on Principles of Programming Languages, POPL 2016, pp. 608–621. ACM (2016)
9. Gavrilenko, N., Ponce-de-León, H., Furbach, F., Heljanko, K., Meyer, R.: BMC for weak memory models: relation analysis for compact SMT encodings. In: Dillig, I., Tasiran, S. (eds.) CAV 2019. LNCS, vol. 11561, pp. 355–365. Springer, Cham (2019). https://doi.org/10.1007/978-3-030-25540-4_19
10. Hoare, C.A.R.: An axiomatic basis for computer programming. Commun. ACM 12(10), 576–580 (1969)
11. Jones, C.B.: Specification and design of (parallel) programs. In: IFIP Congress, pp. 321–332 (1983)
12. Kang, J., Hur, C.K., Lahav, O., Vafeiadis, V., Dreyer, D.: A promising semantics for relaxed-memory concurrency. In: Castagna, G., Gordon, A.D. (eds.) Proceedings of the 44th ACM SIGPLAN Symposium on Principles of Programming Languages, POPL 2017, pp. 175–189. ACM (2017)
13. Kildall, G.A.: A unified approach to global program optimization. In: Proceedings of POPL, pp. 194–206. ACM (1973)
14. Kokologiannakis, M., Kaysin, I., Raad, A., Vafeiadis, V.: Persevere: persistency semantics for verification under ext4. Proc. ACM Program. Lang. 5(POPL), 1–29 (2021)
15. Kusano, M., Wang, C.: Thread-modular static analysis for relaxed memory models. In: Bodden, E., Schäfer, W., van Deursen, A., Zisman, A. (eds.) Proceedings of the 2017 11th Joint Meeting on Foundations of Software Engineering, ESEC/FSE 2017, pp. 337–348. ACM (2017)

16. Lahav, O., Vafeiadis, V.: Owicki-Gries reasoning for weak memory models. In: Halldórsson, M.M., Iwama, K., Kobayashi, N., Speckmann, B. (eds.) ICALP 2015. LNCS, vol. 9135, pp. 311–323. Springer, Heidelberg (2015). https://doi.org/10.1007/978-3-662-47666-6_25

17. Lê, N., Pop, A., Cohen, A., Zappa Nardelli, F.: Correct and efficient work-stealing for weak memory models. In: PPoPP 2013, pp. 69–80. ACM (2013)

18. Michael, M.M., Scott, M.L.: Simple, fast, and practical non-blocking and blocking concurrent queue algorithms. In: Burns, J.E., Moses, Y. (eds.) Proceedings of the Fifteenth Annual ACM Symposium on Principles of Distributed Computing, pp. 267–275. ACM (1996)

19. Moir, M., Shavit, N.: Concurrent data structures. In: Mehta, D.P., Sahni, S. (eds.) Handbook of Data Structures and Applications. Chapman and Hall/CRC (2004)

20. Nipkow, T., Klein, G.: Concrete Semantics - With Isabelle/HOL. Springer, Cham (2014). https://doi.org/10.1007/978-3-319-10542-0

21. Nipkow, T., Paulson, L.C., Wenzel, M.: Isabelle/HOL - A Proof Assistant for Higher-Order Logic. LNCS, vol. 2283. Springer, Heidelberg (2002). https://doi.org/10.1007/3-540-45949-9

22. Peterson, G.L.: Myths about the mutual exclusion problem. Inf. Process. Lett. 12(3), 115–116 (1981)

23. Pulte, C., Flur, S., Deacon, W., French, J., Sarkar, S., Sewell, P.: Simplifying ARM concurrency: multicopy-atomic axiomatic and operational models for ARMv8. PACMPL 2(POPL), 19:1–19:29 (2018)

24. Ridge, T.: A rely-guarantee proof system for x86-TSO. In: Leavens, G.T., O'Hearn, P., Rajamani, S.K. (eds.) VSTTE 2010. LNCS, vol. 6217, pp. 55–70. Springer, Heidelberg (2010). https://doi.org/10.1007/978-3-642-15057-9_4

25. Sarkar, S., Sewell, P., Alglave, J., Maranget, L., Williams, D.: Understanding POWER multiprocessors. In: Hall, M.W., Padua, D.A. (eds.) Proceedings of the 32nd ACM SIGPLAN Conference on Programming Language Design and Implementation, PLDI 2011, pp. 175–186. ACM (2011)

26. Sewell, P., Sarkar, S., Owens, S., Nardelli, F.Z., Myreen, M.O.: x86-TSO: a rigorous and usable programmer's model for x86 multiprocessors. Commun. ACM 53(7), 89–97 (2010)

27. Sorin, D.J., Hill, M.D., Wood, D.A.: A Primer on Memory Consistency and Cache Coherence. Synthesis Lectures on Computer Architecture. Morgan & Claypool Publishers (2011)

28. Stølen, K.: A method for the development of totally correct shared-state parallel programs. In: Baeten, J.C.M., Groote, J.F. (eds.) CONCUR 1991. LNCS, vol. 527, pp. 510–525. Springer, Heidelberg (1991). https://doi.org/10.1007/3-540-54430-5_110

29. Suzanne, T., Miné, A.: Relational thread-modular abstract interpretation under relaxed memory models. In: Ryu, S. (ed.) APLAS 2018. LNCS, vol. 11275, pp. 109–128. Springer, Cham (2018). https://doi.org/10.1007/978-3-030-02768-1_6

30. Turon, A., Vafeiadis, V., Dreyer, D.: GPS: navigating weak memory with ghosts, protocols, and separation. In: Black, A.P., Millstein, T.D. (eds.) Proceedings of the 2014 ACM International Conference on Object Oriented Programming Systems Languages & Applications, OOPSLA 2014, pp. 691–707. ACM (2014)

31. Vafeiadis, V., Narayan, C.: Relaxed separation logic: a program logic for C11 concurrency. In: Hosking, A.L., Eugster, P.T., Lopes, C.V. (eds.) Proceedings of the 2013 ACM SIGPLAN International Conference on Object Oriented Programming Systems Languages & Applications, OOPSLA 2013, pp. 867–884. ACM (2013)

32. Waterman, A., Lee, Y., Patterson, D.A., Asanovi, K.: The RISC-V instruction set manual. Volume 1: User-level ISA, version 2.2. Technical report EECS-2016-118, Department of Electrical Engineering and Computer Science, University of California, Berkeley (2016)
33. Winter, K., Coughlin, N., Smith, G.: Backwards-directed information flow analysis for concurrent programs. In: IEEE Computer Security Foundations Symposium (CSF 2021). IEEE Computer Society (2021)
34. Xu, Q., de Roever, W.P., He, J.: The rely-guarantee method for verifying shared variable concurrent programs. Formal Aspects Comput. 9(2), 149–174 (1997)

Hybrid Systems

Hybrid System Falsification for Multiple-Constraint Parameter Synthesis: A Gas Turbine Case Study

Sota Sato[1,4(✉)], Atsuyoshi Saimen[2], Masaki Waga[1,3], Kenji Takao[2],
and Ichiro Hasuo[1,4]

[1] National Institute of Informatics, Tokyo, Japan
{sotasato,hasuo}@nii.ac.jp
[2] ICT Solution Headquarters, Mitsubishi Heavy Industries, Ltd., Hyogo, Japan
{atsuyoshi_saimen,kenji_takao}@mhi.co.jp
[3] Graduate School of Informatics, Kyoto University, Kyoto, Japan
mwaga@fos.kuis.kyoto-u.ac.jp
[4] The Graduate University for Advanced Studies (SOKENDAI), Tokyo, Japan

Abstract. We report our experience of applying *hybrid system falsification*—an optimization-based method of finding a counterexample to a temporal-logic specification—to the parameter synthesis problem of an industrial gas turbine system model. We identified two major challenges unique to the target problem, namely 1) multiple requirements that are at odds, and 2) their geometric nature. These challenges are dealt with by the following two extensions of falsification, respectively: 1) the use of the *multiple constraint ranking* (MCR) method by de Paula Garcia et al., in combination with CMA-ES, for multiple requirements; and 2) the introduction of the *area modality*, following the logic *AvSTL* by Akazaki & Hasuo, for geometric requirements.

1 Introduction

We report our experience of using tools and techniques from *hybrid system falsification* for the purpose of synthesizing parameter values for a gas turbine system model. The latter is an industrial system model used in power plants. We also report two extensions of falsification techniques that we devised for the current industrial application. Overall, our experience demonstrates *the power of logic-based optimization techniques* developed in the formal methods community.

1.1 Parameter Synthesis for Power Plants

Synthesizing parameter values for optimal performance is a central task in the design of many systems; power plants are no exception. Moreover, the demand for uninterrupted service is extremely high for power plant systems. This results in the fact that power plant systems are under multiple requirements that are at

© Springer Nature Switzerland AG 2021
M. Huisman et al. (Eds.): FM 2021, LNCS 13047, pp. 313–329, 2021.
https://doi.org/10.1007/978-3-030-90870-6_17

odds. Parameter synthesis for power plant systems is therefore a delicate task, one that calls for careful balancing between different requirements.

We study the parameter synthesis for a *gas turbine* used in power plants.

One high-level requirement for this system is its *adaptability* to load changes. We study the particular case of *load rejection* in this paper: once the electricity demand drops, a gas turbine should swiftly respond and decrease its output.

Another high-level requirement is the *prevention of flame loss*. The decreasing output of a gas turbine can cause flame loss, after which it takes a lot of time, fuel, and effort to restart fire and make the system ready for high load again.

These high-level requirements are at odds with each other: quicker load rejection is more likely to cause flame loss. There are many other requirements, too, among which is the prevention of hardware wear for the long-term availability of the system's service.

1.2   Previous Approaches

Parameter synthesis for power plants is such a challenging task that it has been a subject of extensive research effort. When a *white-box model* is provided for the subject system—with the internal dynamics described in some explicit formalism such as ODEs—many mathematical programming techniques are readily applicable. See [4] for a survey.

However, in many cases, a white-box system model is not available. This is the case with our current case study: our gas turbine model is described in the industry-standard CPS modeling tool of Simulink; and techniques for white-box analysis of Simulink models are limited due to the difficulty of defining their semantics. See e.g. [5].

When a white-box system model is not available, one would rely on *black-box analysis* methods for parameter synthesis. In black-box analysis, optimal parameter values are picked by observing only the correspondence between parameter values and the system's output; this process does not use the internal dynamics or the system's operation principles. One major family of such methods is metaheuristics such as *stochastic optimization* and *evolutionary computation*. These methods can work on black-box models and thus apply to a wide range of problems, including power plant parameter synthesis. Application to gas turbine systems has been reported in [19,22].

The use of metaheuristics for gas turbine parameter synthesis still faces the following challenges: 1) a large number of requirements that are at odds (as we discussed in the above); 2) the size of the search space (models tend to have many parameters, e.g., 30 in our model); and 3) system models' complexity that makes their simulation costly. For these reasons, manual parameter synthesis relying on human expertise and trials-and-errors is still a norm in industry practice.

1.3   Hybrid System Falsification as Logic-Guided Metaheuristics

In this paper, therefore, we pursued the use of *hybrid system falsification* [10] for parameter synthesis for a gas turbine system. One can think of hybrid system falsification as *logic-guided metaheuristics*. Our experience reported below shows that the logical layer in falsification exposes many interfaces for further enhancement of optimization algorithms, eventually achieving improved optimization results.

Given a system model $\mathcal{M}$ and a specification φ (typically given in some temporal logic), the *falsification* problem is to find an execution trace of $\mathcal{M}$ that is a *counterexample*, in the sense that the trace does not satisfy φ. The methodology of optimization-based falsification solves the problem automatically, by first turning the logical specification φ into an objective function, and employing various optimization solvers (Fig. 1). Note that falsification is dual to synthesis—to falsify $\neg\psi$ is to satisfy φ—and thus can be used for synthesis.

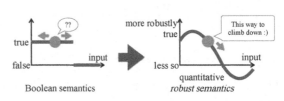

Fig. 1. Falsification by optimization

This workflow of optimization-based falsification has been used in academia and industry alike. Well-known implementations include Breach [8] and S-TaLiRo [2]. These tools have been applied to parameter synthesis as well [8,11].

1.4 Encountered Challenges and Countermeasures

In applying falsification to gas turbine parameter synthesis, we faced two significant challenges.

- **(Challenge 1: conjunctive synthesis)** Our specification φ—one that is desired to be satisfied—consists of multiple conjuncts that are at odds ($\varphi \equiv \varphi_1 \wedge \cdots \wedge \varphi_m$). This is a characteristic of power plant parameter synthesis as we discussed. Such conjunctive satisfaction is rarely pursued in the existing falsification literature such as [10].
- **(Challenge 2: geometric requirements)** Many of $\varphi_1, \ldots, \varphi_m$ are geometric conditions (Fig. 3 later) and we want to capture both *spatial* and *temporal* violation of them (Sect. 4.2). We found that the usual *robust semantics*—quantitative semantics that turns formulas into objective functions—fails to do so, yielding many plateaus and thus not many "hills to climb" to optimization solvers (Fig. 1).

We found that the above two challenges make the state-of-the-art falsification solver Breach [8] struggle. We, therefore, devised the following two extensions.

- **(Extension 1: multiple-constraint optimization by MCR)** For conjunctive synthesis, we used techniques for *multiple-constraint optimization*—specifically the *MCR* method [18], whose use for other problems is found in [21].
- **(Extension 2: area modality)** Following the logic AvSTL [1], we introduced a new modal operator that refines the operator $\lozenge$. Its robust semantics is sensitive to both spatial and temporal violation of requirements.

Table 1. Comparison of our approach (MCR+Area) with baselines

Approach	Solution quality	Automation	Cost
Manual synthesis	+	No	−− (7 person-days)
Breach [8]	−	Yes	+ (3 h)
MCR+Area (ours)	++	Yes	+ (3 h)

1.5   Experience and Lessons

Our extension of falsification successfully solved parameter synthesis. The performance comparison with two baselines—manual synthesis by engineers and Breach—is summarized in Table 1. Compared with the current industry norm (manual synthesis), our method brings more robust satisfaction of requirements (the "solution quality" column; see Fig. 3 and 5 for details), while it takes less effort (3 h of computation vs. 7 person-days).

We believe this successful experience points to the following lessons.

Firstly, the use of falsification should be in a broader range of industry domains. Case studies of falsification are mostly about synthesizing time-dependent *input signals* in transportation systems, such as automotive systems [9,13,16] and aircraft systems [6]. The current problem in the power plant domain has different characteristics (synthesizing static parameters, multiple requirements, etc.); our success shows falsification's applicability to such domains.

Secondly, the *power of logic* in optimization-based methods can be emphasized and further pursued. In the current work, temporal logic provides a useful interface to a rich body of optimization techniques, in the following two senses.

- The user can deploy advanced optimization techniques by only expressing desired properties as a logical formula. A falsification framework automatically translates the formula to objective functions and invokes optimization.
- The logical formalism exposes many possibilities for further enhancement of optimization, such as $\wedge$ for MCR and $\Diamond$ for the area modality in our case.

We believe that such an interplay between logic and optimization should be found in many places beyond falsification.

2   Our Problem: Synthesis of Gas Turbine Parameters Under Multiple Constraints

The target system is a real-world gas turbine product whose control design is not disclosed even to some of the authors. We worked on a black-box system model, specifically a Simulink model whose large part is given by machine code.

The problem is to synthesize the values of 30 parameters of the system, so that 1) the system satisfies two *mandatory* requirements, and 2) the system optimizes its performance characterized by three *desired* requirements.

2.1   The Target Gas Turbine Model

Before presenting ours, we introduce a mathematical formalization of system models in general. It is clear that Simulink models allow this formalization.

Definition 2.1 (system model). Let I, P, O be finite sets of *input, parameter,* and *output* variables, and T be a positive real number called a *horizon*. A *system model* is a function $\mathcal{M}$ that 1) takes an *input signal* $u\colon [0, T] \to \prod_{i \in I}[a_i, b_i]$ and 2) a *parameter valuation* $v \in \prod_{p \in P}[a_p, b_p]$, and 3) returns an *output signal* $\sigma\colon [0, T] \to \mathbb{R}^O$. Here the intervals $[a_i, b_i]$ and $[a_p, b_p]$ specify the *domains* of the values of the variables $i \in I$ and $p \in P$, respectively. For a signal σ and $t \in [0, T]$, σ^t is the *t-shift* of σ, that is, $\sigma^t(t') := \sigma(t + t')$. We can extend output signals for any $t > T$ by defining $\sigma(t) := \sigma(\inf\{t, T\})$.

The details of our gas turbine model are of a proprietary nature and thus are omitted. Nevertheless, we present some of its high-level characteristics that affect the difficulty of parameter synthesis.

Input signal. The model has no input variables, that is, $I = \emptyset$. (Precisely, the original gas turbine model has input but we fix an input signal.)

Parameter valuation. The model has 30 parameter variables $p_1, \ldots, p_{30} \in P$. What each parameter designates is not disclosed. The value domain $[a_p, b_p]$ is different for each parameter p: the largest domain is $[-20, 100]$ and the smallest is $[0.1, 10]$.

Output signal. The model has 4 output variables, $O = \{H_1, H_2, F, G\}$.

Implementation. The model is given by machine code that is obtained by compiling a Simulink model (it is therefore a black-box model). One feeds a parameter valuation v to the machine code, executes the code, and obtains an output signal σ.

Simulation time. The virtual simulation time—this is nothing but the horizon T in Definition 2.1—is 60 s.

Complexity of simulation. For 60 simulation seconds in the model, the *elapsed real time* is about 2.3 s in our environment (3.20 GHz Intel Core i7-8700, 16.0 GB RAM, MATLAB R2019b, and Breach 1.7.0.).

We cannot reveal the role of all parameters due to their proprietary nature; yet here are rough descriptions. Some parameters represent static parameters of the gas turbine; others represent time-dependent signals such as the degree of valve opening. For example, one time-dependent signal is represented by parameters $x_1, y_{A1}, \ldots, y_{A8}$ as shown in Fig. 2.

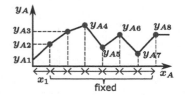

Fig. 2. Signal representation by parameters and interpolation

2.2   Requirements

The output signal σ of the model is subject to five requirements **Mand1**, **Mand2**, and **Desir1–Desir3**. The requirements refer to unsafe regions

Table 2. Our requirements **Mand1**, **Mand2**, and **Desir1–Desir3**, in the natural language

Mand1	Both of $H_1 \geq \Theta_4^1$ and $H_2 \geq \Theta_3^2$ must be true at a certain stage.
Mand2	The value of G must not reach Region 4, i.e., must keep $G \leq \Theta^g$.
Desir1	(H_1, H_2) should not reach Region 2 (defined in terms of Θ_j^i, see Fig. 3).
Desir2	H_2 should not reach Region 1, i.e., should keep $H_2 \leq \Theta_4^2$.
Desir3	F should not reach Region 3, i.e., should keep $F \leq \Theta^f$.

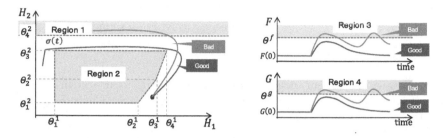

Fig. 3. The unsafe regions referred to in our requirements, with example signals

(Regions 1–4) that are defined by several constants, e.g., Θ^f. In this paper, we omit the concrete values of the constants (proprietary information), but the unsafe regions are illustratively shown in Fig. 3.

Table 2 shows the requirements. The two requirements **Mand1** and **Mand2** are *mandatory*; the other three requirements **Desir1–Desir3** are *desired*.

Violation of **Desir1–Desir3** is acceptable, but we aim at a smaller degree of violation. Note that there are both *spatial* and *temporal* violation of requirements. For example, for **Desir2**, the maximum of H_2 should better be small (spatial), while the time length of H going beyond Θ_4^2 should better be short (temporal).

Parameter synthesis of this degree of complexity is common in the power plant industry. An industrial norm is manual solution of such synthesis problems, where domain experts spend time in trying different parameter values, observing the corresponding outputs, and manually calibrating parameter values accordingly. Prior to the current work, such manual analysis was applied to our problem: it took seven person-days and relied much on the engineers' expert domain knowledge. The result of this manual synthesis is reported later in Sect. 5.

3   Synthesis by Optimization-Based Falsification

This section formulates our current synthesis problem in terms of optimization-based falsification with signal temporal logic (STL).

Table 3. Definition of robust semantics of STL

$$\llbracket \sigma, \top \rrbracket := \infty$$
$$\llbracket \sigma, \bot \rrbracket := -\infty$$
$$\llbracket \sigma, f(\boldsymbol{x}) > 0 \rrbracket := f(\sigma(0)(\boldsymbol{x}))$$
$$\llbracket \sigma, f(\boldsymbol{x}) < 0 \rrbracket := -f(\sigma(0)(\boldsymbol{x}))$$
$$\llbracket \sigma, \neg\varphi \rrbracket := -\llbracket \sigma, \varphi \rrbracket$$
$$\llbracket \sigma, \varphi_1 \vee \varphi_2 \rrbracket := \llbracket \sigma, \varphi_1 \rrbracket \sqcup \llbracket \sigma, \varphi_2 \rrbracket$$
$$\llbracket \sigma, \varphi_1 \wedge \varphi_2 \rrbracket := \llbracket \sigma, \varphi_1 \rrbracket \sqcap \llbracket \sigma, \varphi_2 \rrbracket$$

$$\llbracket \sigma, \varphi_1 \, \mathcal{U}_I \, \varphi_2 \rrbracket := \bigsqcup_{t \in I} (\llbracket \sigma^t, \varphi_2 \rrbracket \sqcap \bigsqcap_{t' \in [0,t)} \llbracket \sigma^{t'}, \varphi_1 \rrbracket)$$
$$\llbracket \sigma, \varphi_1 \, \mathcal{R}_I \, \varphi_2 \rrbracket := \bigsqcap_{t \in I} (\llbracket \sigma^t, \varphi_2 \rrbracket \sqcup \bigsqcup_{t' \in [0,t)} \llbracket \sigma^{t'}, \varphi_1 \rrbracket)$$
$$\llbracket \sigma, \Diamond_I \varphi \rrbracket := \bigsqcup_{t \in I} (\llbracket \sigma^t, \varphi \rrbracket)$$
$$\llbracket \sigma, \Box_I \varphi \rrbracket := \bigsqcap_{t \in I} (\llbracket \sigma^t, \varphi \rrbracket)$$

3.1 Signal Temporal Logic (STL)

We use *signal temporal logic (STL)* [17] to formally express the requirements of our synthesis problem (Sect. 2.2). Syntactically, the set **Fml** of *formulas* in STL is defined as follows, where f is a symbol representing a real-valued function $\mathbb{R}^n \to \mathbb{R}$, $\boldsymbol{x}$ is a tuple of the output variables O, and J is an interval in $\mathbb{R}_{\geq 0}$.

$$\mathbf{Fml} \ni \varphi ::= \top \mid \bot \mid f(\boldsymbol{x}) > 0 \mid \neg\varphi \mid \varphi \vee \varphi \mid \varphi \wedge \varphi \mid \varphi \, \mathcal{U}_J \, \varphi \mid \varphi \, \mathcal{R}_J \, \varphi \mid \Diamond_J \varphi \mid \Box_J \varphi$$

An example of such f is $f(x,y) = 4x - y - 3$; it denotes a function $\mathbb{R}^2 \to \mathbb{R}$.

In the Boolean semantics of STL in [17], a signal σ's satisfaction of a formula φ is given by a relation $\sigma \models \varphi$. To use optimization by hill-climbing, the truth value must be continuous rather than Boolean. See Fig. 1. We use the *robust semantics* of STL [12] that assigns a real value $\llbracket \sigma, \varphi \rrbracket \in \mathbb{R}$ to a signal σ and a formula φ. The robust semantics tells how robustly the formula φ is satisfied.

Definition 3.1 (robust semantics). Let $\sigma \colon \mathbb{R}_{\geq 0} \to \mathbb{R}^{\mathbf{Var}}$ be a signal and φ be a STL formula. We define the *robustness* $\llbracket \sigma, \varphi \rrbracket \in \mathbb{R} \cup \{\infty, -\infty\}$ by induction, as shown in Table 3. Here $\sqcap$ and $\sqcup$ denote infimums and supremums of (extended) real numbers, respectively, and $f(\sigma(0)(\boldsymbol{x}))$ denotes $f(\sigma(0)(x_1), \sigma(0)(x_2), \ldots, \sigma(0)(x_n))$.

We have following relation between the two semantics. See [12] for details.

$$\llbracket \sigma, \varphi \rrbracket > 0 \text{ implies } \sigma \models \varphi, \quad \text{and } \llbracket \sigma, \varphi \rrbracket < 0 \text{ implies } \sigma \not\models \varphi. \tag{1}$$

3.2 Optimization-Based Falsification

Problem 3.2 (falsification). The *falsification* problem is defined as follows.
Input a system model $\mathcal{M}$, and an STL formula φ (a specification);
Output an input signal u and a parameter valuation v s.t. $\mathcal{M}(u,v) \not\models \varphi$.

We note that our system model does not have input signals (Sect. 2.1).

The robust semantics of STL and (1) suggest a workflow to solve the falsification problem: we minimize $\llbracket \mathcal{M}(v), \varphi \rrbracket$, hoping that we eventually see $\llbracket \mathcal{M}(v), \varphi \rrbracket < 0$. This is the idea of optimization-based falsification; see [8]. The numerical optimization required here is amenable to various advanced algorithms including CMA-ES [15].

Table 4. STL formulas $\varphi_1^{\mathsf{Mand}}$, $\varphi_2^{\mathsf{Mand}}$, and $\varphi_1^{\mathsf{Desir}}, \ldots, \varphi_3^{\mathsf{Desir}}$. They formalize the informal requirements **Mand1**, **Mand2**, and **Desir1–Desir3** in Table 2

$\varphi_1^{\mathsf{Mand}}$ $\Diamond_{[0,60]}(H_1 \geq \Theta_4^1 \wedge H_2 \geq \Theta_3^2)$

$\varphi_2^{\mathsf{Mand}}$ $\Box_{[0,60]}(G \leq \Theta^g)$

$\varphi_1^{\mathsf{Desir}}$ $\Box_{[0,60]}\neg(H_1 > \Theta_1^1 \wedge H_2 < \Theta_3^2 \wedge H_2 > \Theta_1^2 \wedge H_2 > \alpha_1 H_1 + \beta_1 \wedge H_2 > \alpha_2 H_1 + \beta_2)$

$\varphi_2^{\mathsf{Desir}}$ $\Box_{[0,60]}(H_2 \leq \Theta_4^2)$

$\varphi_3^{\mathsf{Desir}}$ $\Box_{[0,60]}(F \leq \Theta^f)$

where $\alpha_1 = \frac{\Theta_3^2 - \Theta_2^2}{\Theta_4^1 - \Theta_3^1}$, $\alpha_2 = \frac{\Theta_2^2 - \Theta_1^2}{\Theta_3^1 - \Theta_2^1}$, $\beta_1 = -\alpha_1\Theta_3^1 + \Theta_2^2$, $\beta_2 = -\alpha_2\Theta_2^1 + \Theta_1^2$

3.3   Application to Our Synthesis Problem, and Challenges Therein

We can formalize the requirements **Mand1**, **Mand2**, **Desir1**, **Desir2**, and **Desir3** in Sect. 2.2 as STL formulas. Table 4 shows the resulting STL formulas $\varphi_1^{\mathsf{Mand}}$, $\varphi_2^{\mathsf{Mand}}$, $\varphi_1^{\mathsf{Desir}}$, $\varphi_2^{\mathsf{Desir}}$ and $\varphi_3^{\mathsf{Desir}}$.

We use optimization-based falsification to solve the problem introduced in Sect. 2. Our problem is parameter synthesis and to *satisfy* the formula

$$\varphi^{\mathsf{Req}} :\equiv \varphi_1^{\mathsf{Mand}} \wedge \varphi_2^{\mathsf{Mand}} \wedge \varphi_1^{\mathsf{Desir}} \wedge \varphi_2^{\mathsf{Desir}} \wedge \varphi_3^{\mathsf{Desir}} \ ;$$

but the satisfaction of φ^{Req} is equivalent to the *violation* of the formula

$$\neg\varphi^{\mathsf{Req}} \cong (\neg\varphi_1^{\mathsf{Mand}}) \vee (\neg\varphi_2^{\mathsf{Mand}}) \vee (\neg\varphi_1^{\mathsf{Desir}}) \vee (\neg\varphi_2^{\mathsf{Desir}}) \vee (\neg\varphi_3^{\mathsf{Desir}}) \ ,$$

enabling us to employ various falsification solvers.

However, we observed that the state-of-the-art tool Breach [8] struggles as reported in Sect. 5.2. We identified its reason with the two challenges discussed in Sect. 1; two extensions that cope with the challenges are introduced in the next section.

4   Falsification with MCR and the Area Modality

4.1   Multiple Constraint Ranking (MCR) for Conjunctive Synthesis

Due to the large number of specifications that are at odds with each other, our current problem exhibits an issue called the *scale problem* [23]. In Breach, falsification is performed by stochastic optimization of a single objective function. In our problem, the objective function is the robustness of the formula $\neg\varphi^{\mathsf{Req}} \cong (\neg\varphi_1^{\mathsf{Mand}}) \vee (\neg\varphi_2^{\mathsf{Mand}}) \vee (\neg\varphi_1^{\mathsf{Desir}}) \vee (\neg\varphi_2^{\mathsf{Desir}}) \vee (\neg\varphi_3^{\mathsf{Desir}})$. This objective function is given, according to the conventional robust semantics (see [12]), by the *supremum*

$$[\![\mathcal{M}(v), \neg\varphi^{\mathsf{Req}}]\!]$$
$$= [\![\mathcal{M}(v), \neg\varphi_1^{\mathsf{Mand}}]\!] \sqcup [\![\mathcal{M}(v), \neg\varphi_2^{\mathsf{Mand}}]\!] \sqcup [\![\mathcal{M}(v), \neg\varphi_1^{\mathsf{Desir}}]\!] \sqcup [\![\mathcal{M}(v), \neg\varphi_2^{\mathsf{Desir}}]\!] \sqcup [\![\mathcal{M}(v), \neg\varphi_3^{\mathsf{Desir}}]\!].$$

However, different output variables can have different scales (such as temperature vs. rpm), and so can the robustness values $[\![\mathcal{M}(v), \neg\varphi_i^{\mathsf{Mand}}]\!]$ or $[\![\mathcal{M}(v), \neg\varphi_j^{\mathsf{Desir}}]\!]$. In this case, the robustness of one disjunct $\neg\varphi_i^{\mathsf{Mand}}$ or $\neg\varphi_j^{\mathsf{Desir}}$ can mask the contribution of another disjunct. This is what is called the *scale problem* in [23].

For the scale problem, we used the technique in [21] of

- reducing conjunctive synthesis to *constrained optimization*, and
- using the *multiple constraint ranking (MCR)* method [18], a recent method for constrained optimization.

The main idea of the reduction to the constrained optimization is to deal with the different objectives ($\varphi_1^{\mathsf{Mand}}$, $\varphi_2^{\mathsf{Mand}}$, $\varphi_1^{\mathsf{Desir}}$, $\varphi_2^{\mathsf{Desir}}$ and $\varphi_3^{\mathsf{Desir}}$) separately, and to consider some of the objectives as constraints (rather than objectives). This is in contrast to the standard falsification algorithm, where the objectives are combined with $\vee$ and solved as a single object optimization problem. Recall, from Problem 3.2, that our ultimate goal is constraint satisfaction—we need the robustness of each objective $\neg\varphi_i^{\mathsf{Mand}}$ or $\neg\varphi_j^{\mathsf{Desir}}$ to be below 0, but we do not need to further minimize these values. These considerations lead to the following problem formalization.

Problem 4.1 (falsification by constrained optimization [21]). The *constrained optimization* problem is defined as follows.
Input functions f (*optimization target*) and $g_1, \ldots, g_k$ (*constraints*)
Output $\min_v f(v)$ subject to $g_i(v) < 0$, $i = 1, \ldots, k$

Our synthesis problem can be formulated in the above format:

$$\begin{aligned}
&\min_v \quad [\![\mathcal{M}(v), \neg\varphi_3^{\mathsf{Desir}}]\!] \\
&\text{subject to} \quad [\![\mathcal{M}(v), \neg\varphi_i^{\mathsf{Mand}}]\!] < 0, [\![\mathcal{M}(v), \neg\varphi_j^{\mathsf{Desir}}]\!] < 0 \quad (i, j \in \{1, 2\}).
\end{aligned} \quad (2)$$

In the formulation (2), the choice of $\neg\varphi_3^{\mathsf{Desir}}$ as the optimization target is arbitrary; other specifications could be used as well. We chose $\neg\varphi_3^{\mathsf{Desir}}$ since it is the hardest to falsify. In particular, we failed to find a parameter valuation v satisfying $[\![\mathcal{M}(v), \neg\varphi_3^{\mathsf{Desir}}]\!] < 0$, $[\![\mathcal{M}(v), \neg\varphi_1^{\mathsf{Mand}}]\!] < 0$, and $[\![\mathcal{M}(v), \neg\varphi_2^{\mathsf{Mand}}]\!] < 0$.

Now our goal is to solve Problem 4.1. We conducted literature survey, looking for an algorithm that

- solves the constrained optimization problem of the form of (2) (namely, *Known* as opposed to *Hidden*, *Simulation-based* as opposed to *A priori*, *Relaxable* as opposed to *Unrelaxable*, and *Quantifiable* as opposed to *Nonquantifiable*, according to the classification in [7]).
- works well with CMA-ES [3], the stochastic optimization algorithm that is seen as the most effective in hybrid system falsification.

We found that the *multiple constrained ranking (MCR)* [18] algorithm meets these requirements.

The MCR method [18] is a recent algorithm for constrained optimization. It is used in evolutionary computation (we use CMA-ES [3]). In selecting fittest

Table 5. Example; the values of f, g_1, g_2 for each individuals and their infimum

Individual	f	g_1	g_2	infimum
v_1	1400	59.9	-2	-2
v_2	-9	2	1	-9
v_3	-180	2	-1	-180

Table 6. Example; values of ranks and scoring function for each individuals

Individual	RObj_X	RCon_X^1	RCon_X^2	RVNum_X	F
v_1	1	1	3	2	7
v_2	2	1	1	1	5
v_3	3	1	2	2	8

individuals, MCR uses a ranking notion that is based on the following: 1) values of the optimization target, and 2) the violation of each constraint. Notably, when it combines different concerns, MCR does not combine values but it combines rankings. This way MCR avoids the scale problem; see [21, Tables 2–3] for illustration.

Before introducing MCR, we briefly explain the working of CMA-ES [14] with a fitness function f. CMA-ES is performed in an iterative manner, that is, repeating the following regenerational steps until termination. Let μ, λ be natural numbers ($\mu < \lambda$).

1. Generate *population* $X = v_1, v_2, \ldots, v_\lambda$ by sampling from a distribution on $\prod_{p \in P}[a_p, b_p]$ with distribution parameter θ.
2. Select μ individuals $u_{1:\lambda}, v_{2:\lambda}, \ldots v_{\mu:\lambda} \in X$ that is the fittest on f.
3. Update distribution parameter θ with the selected individuals.

For optimization problem without constraints, one can identify its objective function with fitness function f to solve that optimization problem with CMA-ES. MCR replaces a fitness function with the following *scoring function* $F_X(v)$ to adapt this regenerational steps with constrained optimization problem formulated in Problem 4.1.

A *scoring function* $F_X(v)$ is a function which gives a real value to each individual v among the population X.

$$F_X(v) = \begin{cases} \mathrm{RVNum}_X + \sum_{j=1}^k \mathrm{RCon}_X^j & \text{if no feasible solution in } X \\ \mathrm{RObj}_X + \mathrm{RVNum}_X + \sum_{j=1}^k \mathrm{RCon}_X^j & \text{otherwise} \end{cases}$$

$$\tag{3}$$

In MCR, the scoring function employs three kinds of ranks RObj_X, RCon_X^j and RVNum_X. RObj_X compares the value of the objective function f. This is the value of $[\![\mathcal{M}(v), \varphi_1]\!]$ in the setting of the problem (2). RCon_X^j ($j = 1, \ldots, k$) compares the violation degree of g_j, namely $0 \sqcup g_j(v)$. RVNum_X compares the number

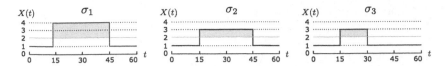

Fig. 4. Signals σ_1, σ_2, σ_3 (blue), and the threshold 2 (red). We have $[\![\sigma_1, \varphi_{\mathsf{Ar}}]\!] = 1$, $[\![\sigma_2, \varphi_{\mathsf{Ar}}]\!] = 0.5$, $[\![\sigma_3, \varphi_{\mathsf{Ar}}]\!] = 0.25$, while $[\![\sigma_1, \varphi_\diamond]\!] = 2$, $[\![\sigma_2, \varphi_\diamond]\!] = 1$, $[\![\sigma_3, \varphi_\diamond]\!] = 1$. (Color figure online)

of violated constraints. Note that the value of $F_X(v)$ depends on population X. Table 5 and Table 6 shows the behavior of theses ranks with its application to a simple example.

We note that MCR has been used for falsification in [21] by some of the authors. The experimental evaluation in [21] uses standard falsification benchmarks (automotive, etc.), while the point of the current paper is the method's effectivity in a real-world synthesis problem in a different industry domain.

4.2   Area Modality for Spatial and Temporal Robustness

In falsifying the specifications in Sect. 3.3, we want to measure the degree of violation in both *spatial* and *temporal* terms (cf. Sect. 2.2), in a refined way that would avoid plateaus in the robustness curve (cf. Sect. 1). To do so, we introduce a new modal operator called *area modality*. Its definition follows the format of the *averaged always* and *averaged eventually* operators in AvSTL [1], an extension of STL.

Definition 4.2 (the area modality Area). The *area modality* Area is a unary temporal operator. To introduce this, we extend the formulas **Fml** of STL as

$$\mathbf{Fml} \ni \varphi ::= \top \mid \bot \mid f(x) > 0 \mid \neg\varphi \mid \varphi \vee \varphi \mid \varphi \wedge \varphi \mid \varphi \,\mathcal{U}_J\, \varphi \mid \varphi \,\mathcal{R}_J\, \varphi \mid \Diamond_J \varphi \mid \Box_J \varphi \mid \mathsf{Area}_J \varphi.$$

In AvSTL [1], in defining the semantics of some modalities that use integrals, there is a need of separating *positive* and *negative robustness*. We therefore define the positive and negative semantics of the Area modality, respectively, as follows.

$$[\![\sigma, \mathsf{Area}_{[a,b]}\varphi]\!]^+ := \frac{1}{b-a} \int_a^b [\![\sigma^\tau, \varphi]\!]^+ d\tau, \quad [\![\sigma, \mathsf{Area}_{[a,b]}\varphi]\!]^- := \frac{1}{b-a} \int_a^b [\![\sigma^\tau, \varphi]\!]^- d\tau,$$

integrating the spatial robustness over time τ. The definition of the (positive and negative) robustness of the other operators are found in [1]; the positive one is largely the same as Table 3.

Unless otherwise specified, we let $[\![\sigma, \varphi]\!]$ stand for $[\![\sigma, \varphi]\!]^+$.

For example, consider the specification "X should be above 2" and the signals $\sigma_1, \sigma_2, \sigma_3$ in Fig. 4. It is intuitive that the three signals have different degrees of satisfaction. This intuitive difference is successfully captured by the formula $\varphi_{\mathsf{Ar}} \equiv \mathsf{Area}_{[0,60]}(X > 2)$, with the area modality measuring both spatial and

Table 7. The refined STL formulas φ_1^{Mand}, φ_2^{Mand}, and $(\varphi_1^{\text{Desir}})^{\text{Area}}, \ldots, (\varphi_3^{\text{Desir}})^{\text{Area}}$. The former two formulas φ_1^{Mand} and φ_2^{Mand} are same as original formulas in Table 4; the latter three formulas $(\varphi_1^{\text{Desir}})^{\text{Area}}, \ldots, (\varphi_3^{\text{Desir}})^{\text{Area}}$ are obtained by replacing the occurrences of $\square_J$ (that is equivalent to $\neg \Diamond_J \neg$) with $\neg \text{Area}_J \neg$.

φ_1^{Mand}	$\Diamond_{[0,60]}(H_1 \geq \Theta_4^1 \wedge H_2 \geq \Theta_3^2)$
φ_2^{Mand}	$\square_{[0,60]}(G \leq \Theta^g)$
$(\varphi_1^{\text{Desir}})^{\text{Area}}$	$\neg \text{Area}_{[0,60]}(H_1 > \Theta_1^1 \wedge H_2 < \Theta_3^2 \wedge H_2 > \Theta_1^2 \wedge$
	$H_2 > \alpha_1 H_1 + \beta_1 \wedge H_2 > \alpha_2 H_1 + \beta_2)$
$(\varphi_2^{\text{Desir}})^{\text{Area}}$	$\neg \text{Area}_{[0,60]}(\neg(H_2 > \Theta_4^2))$
$(\varphi_3^{\text{Desir}})^{\text{Area}}$	$\neg \text{Area}_{[0,60]}(\neg(F > \Theta^f))$

temporal satisfaction. The difference is not captured, however, by the STL formula $\varphi_\Diamond \equiv \Diamond_{[0,60]}(X > 2)$. Recall from [12] that the *eventually* operator $\Diamond$ has the robustness $[\![\sigma, \Diamond_{[a,b]}\varphi]\!] := \sup_{\tau \in [a,b]}[\![\sigma^\tau, \varphi]\!]$, which is sensitive to the vertical margin but disregards the temporal duration.

Our improvement of optimization-based falsification consists of replacing occurrences of $\Diamond$ in a specification with those of the Area modality. This is much like in [1]. Proposition 4.4 says that we do not miss target signals by this replacement.

Definition 4.3. A *positive context* is an STL formula with a hole $[]$ at a positive position. Formally, the set of positive contexts is defined as follows:

$$\mathcal{C} ::= [] \mid \neg(\neg \mathcal{C}) \mid \mathcal{C} \vee \varphi \mid \varphi \vee \mathcal{C} \mid \mathcal{C} \wedge \varphi \mid \varphi \wedge \mathcal{C} \mid \mathcal{C} \mathcal{U}_J \varphi \mid \varphi \mathcal{U}_J \mathcal{C} \mid \mathcal{C} \mathcal{R}_J \varphi \mid \varphi \mathcal{R}_J \mathcal{C}$$
$$\mid \text{Area}_J \mathcal{C} \quad \text{where } \varphi \text{ is a STL formula.}$$

For a positive context $\mathcal{C}$ and a STL formula φ, $\mathcal{C}[\varphi]$ denotes the formula obtained by substitution of φ for the hole $[]$ in $\mathcal{C}$.

The next result is shown easily by induction on the construction of $\mathcal{C}$.

Proposition 4.4. *Let $\mathcal{C}$ be a positive context. Then $[\![\sigma, \mathcal{C}[\text{Area}_J \varphi]]\!] > 0$ implies $[\![\sigma, \mathcal{C}[\Diamond_J \varphi]]\!] > 0$. Conversely, for any proper interval $J' \subseteq J$ such that σ is continuous on J', $[\![\sigma, \mathcal{C}[\Diamond_{J'} \varphi]]\!] > 0$ implies $[\![\sigma, \mathcal{C}[\text{Area}_J \varphi]]\!] > 0$.* □

Refinement of φ^{Req}. Now we turn back to our problem (Sect. 3.3). For refined sensitivity to spatial and temporal violation of our requirements (see Table 2), we can refine $\neg \varphi_1^{\text{Desir}}, \ldots, \neg \varphi_3^{\text{Desir}}$ of our original STL formulas (see Table 4) with the area modality Area. The refined formulas are shown in Table 7. Note that here we use the de Morgan-like law $\neg \square \neg \cong \Diamond$ and replace $\Diamond$ with Area.

By Proposition 4.4, falsifying $\neg \varphi^{\text{Req}} \cong (\neg \varphi_1^{\text{Mand}}) \vee (\neg \varphi_2^{\text{Mand}}) \vee (\neg \varphi_1^{\text{Desir}}) \vee (\neg \varphi_2^{\text{Desir}}) \vee (\neg \varphi_3^{\text{Desir}})$ is equivalent to the violation of $(\neg \varphi_1^{\text{Mand}}) \vee (\neg \varphi_2^{\text{Mand}}) \vee (\neg(\varphi_1^{\text{Desir}})^{\text{Area}}) \vee (\neg(\varphi_2^{\text{Desir}})^{\text{Area}}) \vee (\neg(\varphi_3^{\text{Desir}})^{\text{Area}})$.

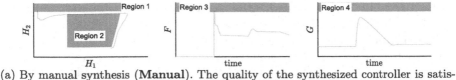

(a) By manual synthesis (**Manual**). The quality of the synthesized controller is satisfactory, although the trajectory touches Region 1,2 and 3.

(b) By original Breach (**Breach**). The quality of the synthesized controller is not satisfactory because (H_1, H_2) does not pass the top-right of Region 2, and the mandatory specification **Mand1** is violated. Moreover, F stays in Region 3 for a long period.

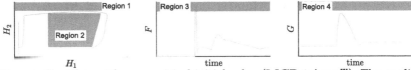

(c) By our algorithm with an empirical initial value (**MCR+Area^w**). The quality of the synthesized controller is satisfactory, although the trajectory touches Region 3.

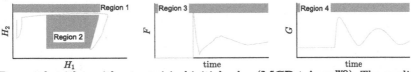

(d) By our algorithm without empirical initial value (**MCR+Area^{wo}**). The quality of the synthesized controller is satisfactory, although the trajectory touches Region 3.

Fig. 5. Comparison of the results of different approaches. The blue lines show the output signals. The red areas show the unsafe regions from Fig. 3. (Color figure online)

5   Experimental Evaluation

We used our extension of falsification discussed in Sect. 4 (henceforth referred to as **MCR+Area**) and successfully solved the gas turbine parameter synthesis problem. We report its result, comparing with two baselines: the manual synthesis by a domain expert (**Manual**), and the falsification solver Breach [8] (**Breach**).

The comparison is summarized in Table 1. For each approach, our evaluation of the quality of the synthesized parameter valuation was by 1) checking the satisfaction of the requirements in Sect. 2.2, and 2) interviewing a domain expert. We conducted the latter, too, since it is common that domain experts have implicit preferences that are not formalized or even communicated to us (namely those who work on parameter synthesis).

For the two automated approaches (**Breach** and **MCR+Area**), we used a machine with 3.20 GHz Intel Core i7-8700, 16.0 GB RAM, MATLAB R2019b, and Breach 1.7.0. Our approach **MCR+Area** is implemented on top of Breach 1.7.0. In each falsification trial, we ran optimization for three hours.

For **Manual**, as usual in industry practice, a domain expert started with an initial parameter valuation adapted from a similar product, and adjusted it manually through trials and errors. Machine support was limited to model simulation. In particular, **Manual** does not use formal logic.

5.1   Approach 1: Manual

The whole process of manual parameter synthesis took 7 days of the expert's effort. Note that machine support in this approach was limited to model simulation; observing performances and adapting valuations was done manually. In particular, this approach did not use formal logic. Figure 5a is the result. The output satisfies **Mand1** and **Mand2**. However, the plot of (H_1, H_2) violates **Desir1** and **Desir2** because it touches Regions 1–2. The plot of F also violates **Desir3** because it enters Region 3.

In the approach **Manual**, the quality of the solution was an acceptable one; however, it highly depends on the expert's domain knowledge. Moreover, the trial took much longer time (7 person-days).

5.2   Approach 2: Breach

We used Breach to assess the performance of existing falsification solvers for our problem (Sect. 2). We chose CMA-ES from the variety of optimization algorithms offered for Breach (CMA-ES is a popular choice [10]). The initial valuation was the same as **Manual**, adapting from a similar product.

Figure 5b shows the result. The output satisfies **Mand2**. However, the plot of (H_1, H_2) violates **Mand1**, failing to make a turn outside the upper-right corner of Region 2. Moreover, **Desir1** and **Desir2** are violated since the plot of (H_1, H_2) enters Regions 1 and 2. The plot of F enters Region 3, too, violating **Desir3**.

The **Breach** approach automatically solved the problem in three hours of computation without human intervention. However, the quality of the synthesized parameter valuation was low and did not meet practical demands.

5.3   Approach 3: MCR+Area with an Empirical Initial Valuation (MCR+Area^w)

In the first evaluation of our extension of falsification, we used the same initial parameter valuation as **Manual** and **Breach**—the empirical one obtained by adapting from a similar product.

To introduce Area modality, we feed **MCR+Area** with the refined specifications $\neg\varphi_1^{\mathsf{Mand}}$, $\neg\varphi_2^{\mathsf{Mand}}$, $\neg(\varphi_1^{\mathsf{Desir}})^{\mathsf{Area}}$, $\neg(\varphi_2^{\mathsf{Desir}})^{\mathsf{Area}}$, $\neg(\varphi_3^{\mathsf{Desir}})^{\mathsf{Area}}$ (Sect. 4.2).

We did not discriminate mandatory requirements (**Mand**) from desired ones (**Desir**) in this work. Extension of MCR to accommodate such discrimination is easily conceivable by adding weights to ranking scores. This is future work.

Figure 5c shows the result. The output satisfies **Mand1**, **Mand2**, **Desir1**, and **Desir2**. Only **Desir3** is slightly violated with F touching Region 3. The output of **MCR+Area** is significantly better than that of **Breach**: the former satisfies the two mandatory requirements, while **Breach** violates **Mand2**. **MCR+Area** is also better than **Manual**, satisfying more desired requirements. The interviewed domain expert confirmed the quality of the solution: it turned out that the solution satisfied their implicit preferences, too.

5.4   Approach 4: MCR+Area without Empirical Initial Valuation (MCR+Area^{wo})

We also evaluated **MCR+Area** without empirical initial valuation, using the middle point of the search space $\prod_{p \in P}[a_p, b_p]$ as the initial valuation. This way we excluded any form of human expertise (initial valuations or human intervention) from the process of synthesis.

The resulting output signal is depicted in Fig. 5d. The output still satisfies **Mand1**, **Mand2**, **Desir1**, and **Desir2**, and only **Desir3** is slightly violated. Therefore the quality of the solution of **MCR+Area^{wo}** is the same as that of **MCR+Area^{w}**, if measured in terms of the formal specifications.

However, the interviewed domain expert preferred the solution of **MCR+Area^{w}**, citing implicit preferences (besides those in Sect. 2.2) as reasons. Among them is that the values of a series of parameters $p_1, \ldots, p_8$ should not vary a lot since the parameters stand for the values of a single signal at different timepoints.

This experience demonstrates the worth of human expert knowledge: although automated approaches such as **MCR+Area** can answer what they are asked, there may be other implicit preferences that are addressed by previous human solutions.

We can also emphasize the worth of automated approaches in the iterative process of improving the parameter valuation. Since formal specifications are never complete, the iterative process will necessarily involve domain experts' reviews. In those steps, the solutions of automated approaches work as big hints. For example, in our case study, the solution of **MCR+Area^{wo}** helped the domain expert to explicate some implicit assumptions that would have been otherwise only in their mind.

6   Conclusions and Future Work

We applied hybrid system falsification to the parameter synthesis of an industrial gas turbine system, which is currently solved manually by a human expert. Our proposal **MCR+Area** performed better than the manual approach and the falsification solver Breach. This experience suggests that falsification as *logic-guided metaheuristics* has great potential for problems in various industry domains.

The discussion at the end of Sect. 5 envisages an iterative design process in which human domain experts and automated analysis tools (such as the one we presented) work together, using formal specifications and numeric synthesis results as communication media. In doing so, a major challenge is the fact that human experts are often not familiar with formal specification in a logical formalism. Tool support for formal specification, such as the one provided by the interactive tool STLInspector [20], should be pursued and integrated in a workflow.

Adoption of logic-based analysis tools in industry practice incurs considerable learning cost, and industry practitioners must be convinced that the cost will pay off. The current work serves this purpose by clearly exhibiting the value of logic-based automated tools (Table 1). It is our future work to further integrate the use of logic-based tools in industry practice and realize the above iterative design process in which human experts and automated tools closely collaborate.

Acknowledgments. This work is partially supported by JST ERATO HASUO Metamathematics for Systems Design Project (No. JPMJER1603), by JST ACT-X Grant No. JPMJAX200U, and by JST CREST Grant No. JPMJCR2012.

References

1. Akazaki, T., Hasuo, I.: Time robustness in MTL and expressivity in hybrid system falsification. In: Kroening, D., Păsăreanu, C.S. (eds.) CAV 2015. LNCS, vol. 9207, pp. 356–374. Springer, Cham (2015). https://doi.org/10.1007/978-3-319-21668-3_21
2. Annpureddy, Y., Liu, C., Fainekos, G., Sankaranarayanan, S.: S-TaLiRo: a tool for temporal logic falsification for hybrid systems. In: Abdulla, P.A., Leino, K.R.M. (eds.) TACAS 2011. LNCS, vol. 6605, pp. 254–257. Springer, Heidelberg (2011). https://doi.org/10.1007/978-3-642-19835-9_21
3. Auger, A., Hansen, N.: A restart CMA evolution strategy with increasing population size. In: Proceedings of CEC 2005, pp. 1769–1776 (2005)
4. Biegler, L.T.: An overview of simultaneous strategies for dynamic optimization. Chem. Eng. Process. Process Intensification **46**(11), 1043–1053 (2007). Special Issue on Process Optimization and Control in Chemical Engineering and Processing
5. Bouissou, O., Chapoutot, A.: An operational semantics for simulink's simulation engine. SIGPLAN Not. **47**(5), 129–138 (2012)
6. Delmas, R., Loquen, T., Boada-Bauxell, J., Carton, M.: An evaluation of Monte-Carlo tree search for property falsification on hybrid flight control laws. In: Zamani, M., Zufferey, D. (eds.) NSV 2019. LNCS, vol. 11652, pp. 45–59. Springer, Cham (2019). https://doi.org/10.1007/978-3-030-28423-7_3
7. Digabel, S.L., Wild, S.M.: A taxonomy of constraints in simulation-based optimization. arXiv preprint arXiv:1505.07881 (2015)
8. Donzé, A.: Breach, a toolbox for verification and parameter synthesis of hybrid systems. In: Touili, T., Cook, B., Jackson, P. (eds.) CAV 2010. LNCS, vol. 6174, pp. 167–170. Springer, Heidelberg (2010). https://doi.org/10.1007/978-3-642-14295-6_17
9. Eddeland, J.L., Donzé, A., Miremadi, S., Åkesson, K.: Industrial temporal logic specifications for falsification of cyber-physical systems. In: EPiC Series in Computing, vol. 74, pp. 267–274. EasyChair, September 2020. ISSN 2398-7340

10. Ernst, G., et al.: Arch-comp 2020 category report: falsification. In: Proceedings of ARCH 2020. EPiC Series in Computing, vol. 74, pp. 140–152. EasyChair (2020)
11. Fainekos, G., Hoxha, B., Sankaranarayanan, S.: Robustness of specifications and its applications to falsification, parameter mining, and runtime monitoring with S-TaLiRo. In: Finkbeiner, B., Mariani, L. (eds.) RV 2019. LNCS, vol. 11757, pp. 27–47. Springer, Cham (2019). https://doi.org/10.1007/978-3-030-32079-9_3
12. Fainekos, G.E., Pappas, G.J.: Robustness of temporal logic specifications for continuous-time signals. Theor. Comput. Sci. **410**(42), 4262–4291 (2009)
13. Gladisch, C., Heinz, T., Heinzemann, C., Oehlerking, J., Vietinghoff, A.V., Pfitzer, T.: Experience paper: search-based testing in automated driving control applications. In: 2019 34th IEEE/ACM International Conference on Automated Software Engineering (ASE), pp. 26–37, November 2019
14. Hansen, N.: The CMA evolution strategy: A tutorial. CoRR abs/1604.00772 (2016)
15. Hansen, N., Auger, A.: Principled design of continuous stochastic search: from theory to practice. In: Borenstein, Y., Moraglio, A. (eds.) Theory and Principled Methods for the Design of Metaheuristics. NCS, pp. 145–180. Springer, Heidelberg (2014). https://doi.org/10.1007/978-3-642-33206-7_8
16. Jin, X., Deshmukh, J.V., Kapinski, J., Ueda, K., Butts, K.: Powertrain control verification benchmark. In: Proceedings of the 17th International Conference on Hybrid Systems: Computation and Control, pp. 253–262. ACM, April 2014
17. Maler, O., Nickovic, D.: Monitoring temporal properties of continuous signals. In: Lakhnech, Y., Yovine, S. (eds.) FORMATS/FTRTFT -2004. LNCS, vol. 3253, pp. 152–166. Springer, Heidelberg (2004). https://doi.org/10.1007/978-3-540-30206-3_12
18. de Paula Garcia, R., de Lima, B.S.L.P., de Castro Lemonge, A.C., Jacob, B.P.: A rank-based constraint handling technique for engineering design optimization problems solved by genetic algorithms. Comput. Struct. **187**, 77–87 (2017)
19. Rezaie, A., Tsatsaronis, G., Hellwig, U.: Thermal design and optimization of a heat recovery steam generator in a combined-cycle power plant by applying a genetic algorithm. Energy **168**, 346–357 (2019)
20. Roehm, H., Heinz, T., Mayer, E.C.: STLInspector: STL validation with guarantees. In: Majumdar, R., Kunčak, V. (eds.) CAV 2017. LNCS, vol. 10426, pp. 225–232. Springer, Cham (2017). https://doi.org/10.1007/978-3-319-63387-9_11
21. Sato, S., Waga, M., Hasuo, I.: Constrained optimization for hybrid system falsification and application to conjunctive synthesis. IFAC-PapersOnLine **54**(5), 217–222 (2021). 7th IFAC Conference on Analysis and Design of Hybrid Systems ADHS 2021. ISSN 2405-8963. https://doi.org/10.1016/j.ifacol.2021.08.501
22. Valdés, M., Durán, M.D., Rovira, A.: Thermoeconomic optimization of combined cycle gas turbine power plants using genetic algorithms. Appl. Therm. Eng. **23**(17), 2169–2182 (2003)
23. Zhang, Z., Hasuo, I., Arcaini, P.: Multi-armed bandits for boolean connectives in hybrid system falsification. In: Dillig, I., Tasiran, S. (eds.) CAV 2019. LNCS, vol. 11561, pp. 401–420. Springer, Cham (2019). https://doi.org/10.1007/978-3-030-25540-4_23

Gaussian Process-Based Confidence Estimation for Hybrid System Falsification

Zhenya Zhang[1]([✉])(iD) and Paolo Arcaini[2](iD)

[1] Kyushu University, Fukuoka, Japan
[2] National Institute of Informatics, Tokyo, Japan

Abstract. Cyber-Physical Systems (CPSs) are widely adopted in safety-critical domains, raising great demands on their quality assurance. However, the application of formal verification is limited due to the continuous dynamics of CPSs. Instead, simulation-based falsification, which aims at finding a counterexample to refute the system specification, is a more feasible and hence actively pursued approach. Falsification adopts an optimization approach, treating *robustness*, given by the quantitative semantics of the specification language (usually Signal Temporal Logic (STL)), as the objective function. However, similarly to traditional testing, in the absence of found counterexamples, falsification does not give any guarantee on the system safety. To fill this gap, in this paper, we propose a *confidence measure* that estimates the probability that a formal specification is indeed not falsifiable, by relying on the information encapsulated in the simulation data collected during falsification. Methodologically, we approximate the robustness domain by feeding simulation data into a Gaussian Process (GP) Regression process; we then do a minimization sampling on the trained GP, and then estimate the probability that all the robustness values inferred from these sampled points are positive; we take this probability as the confidence measure. We experimentally study the properties of monotonicity and soundness of the proposed confidence measure. We also apply the measure to several state-of-the-art falsification algorithms to assess the maximum confidence they provide when they do not find a falsifying input, and the stability of such confidence across different repetitions.

Keywords: Confidence estimation · Hybrid system falsification · Gaussian process regression · Surrogate model

1 Introduction

Cyber-Physical Systems (CPS) are characterized by the combination of physical systems having continuous dynamics, and discrete digital controllers; for this,

Zhenya Zhang is supported by JSPS KAKENHI Grant No.20H04168, 19K24348, 19H04086, and JST-Mirai Program Grant No. JPMJMI18BB, Japan. Paolo Arcaini is supported by ERATO HASUO Metamathematics for Systems Design Project (No. JPMJER1603), JST.

M. Huisman et al. (Eds.): FM 2021, LNCS 13047, pp. 330–348, 2021.
https://doi.org/10.1007/978-3-030-90870-6_18

they are also called *hybrid systems*. CPSs are often employed in safety-critical domains, making their quality assurance of paramount importance. However, the continuous dynamics of hybrid systems makes their automated formal verification extremely difficult, if not impossible. Therefore, academia and industry have been pursuing the more feasible approach of *falsification* [13, 22, 29, 30, 33, 36, 37] that, instead of trying to prove a formal specification, attempts to find a counterexample showing its violation. Specifically, given a *model* $\mathcal{M}$ taking input signal $\mathbf{u}$ and producing output signal $\mathcal{M}(\mathbf{u})$, and a formal specification φ (a temporal formula), the falsification problem consists in finding a *falsifying input*, i.e., an input signal $\mathbf{u}$ such that $\mathcal{M}(\mathbf{u})$ violates φ.

The common approach to solve the falsification problem is to turn it into an optimization problem (also called *optimization-based falsification*), by exploiting the quantitative *robust semantics* of temporal formulas [14, 19]. Robust semantics extends the classical Boolean satisfaction relation $\mathbf{w} \models \varphi$ by assigning a value $[\![\mathbf{w}, \varphi]\!] \in \mathbb{R} \cup \{\infty, -\infty\}$ (i.e., *robustness*) that tells not only whether φ is satisfied or violated (by the sign), but also *how robustly* the formula is satisfied or violated. Optimization-based falsification algorithms iteratively generate inputs with the aim of finding an input with negative robustness. Several optimization-based falsification algorithms have been developed [1, 3, 10, 13, 18, 29, 33, 35–38].

Given a specification φ, a falsification algorithm either returns an input signal falsifying φ, or it reports that the search was *unsuccessful* if no such input was found. As usual in testing (falsification is a particular type of search-based testing approach), in the latter case, we do not know whether the specification φ is really not falsifiable, or the algorithm did not explore the search space enough. In such a case, a practitioner would like to have some estimate of the real absence of a falsifying input (and so of the satisfaction of φ).

To this aim, in this paper, we propose a *confidence measure* for hybrid system falsification. The definition of the measure starts from the observation that, as output, a falsification algorithm also provides the set of input signals that have been sampled during the search, together with their corresponding robustness values. Starting from these data[1], we try to estimate the likelihood that no falsifying input exists in the unexplored search space. The construction of the confidence measure is as follows. We first train, using *Gaussian Process Regression* [31], a *Gaussian Process* (GP) from the falsification data, acting as a *surrogate model* of the real robustness function, i.e., it provides an *estimation* of the robustness. Then, we sample in the GP the points that have the minimum values, as these are the points that have the higher probability to identify negative robustness. We then compute the cumulative probability that these surrogate sampled data are all positive, i.e., that the approximated robustness is always positive, and so the specification is not falsified. We take this probability as the *confidence value* estimating how likely it is that the specification holds.

---

[1] Note that we assume that the confidence measure is computed starting from non-falsifying inputs only. The measure does not make sense if at least one falsifying input is used for its computation; in that case, there is no need of the confidence measure, as we know that the specification is falsifiable.

We performed a series of experiments to assess to what extent the proposed confidence measure guarantees some desired properties:

- *monotonicity*: the confidence measure should not decrease as new falsification data (i.e., inputs with corresponding robustness values) are being added. A monotonically increasing measure does not prematurely assess high confidence, and so it can be reliably used to decide whether enough falsification search has been performed; it can also be used as a *stopping criterion* during the falsification search itself. In classical coverage criteria for software testing, increasing monotonicity is implicitly guaranteed, because the test requirements are known in advance, and so any new test input can only increase the coverage (when an uncovered test requirement is covered) or at most leave it unchanged. For our confidence measure, increasing monotonicity cannot be guaranteed, as it is always possible to find a new input signal that drastically changes the derived Gaussian Process and so the computed confidence. However, we will experimentally show that the measure can efficiently account for the unexplored search space and that monotonicity is guaranteed to some extent.
- *soundness*: intuitively, the confidence should also depend on "how robustly" a specification holds. Given two specifications that are both non-falsifiable, the one that is more robust should lead to higher confidence than the less robust one. Take the example of a car system, and two specifications requiring that the "speed is always less than 120" and "speed is always less than 150"; intuitively, in the absence of a falsifying input, the confidence of the latter specification should not be lower than that of the former one (given that a falsification approach has been run for both with the same budget).

In the experiments, we will also use the confidence measure to assess the performance of existing falsification algorithms, which implement different search strategies. Namely, we will check the confidence provided by three falsification algorithms (Random search, CMAES, and MCTS) executed with the same budget; moreover, we will also check their *stability*, i.e., how much the confidence measure changes in repeated runs.

Paper Structure. Section 2 provides the necessary background. Section 3 introduces the problem and overviews the approach to compute the proposed confidence measure, whose phases are described in Sect. 4. Section 5 presents the experiments done to assess the measure. Finally, Sect. 6 reviews related work, and Sect. 7 concludes the paper.

2   Background

We here review the basic concepts and approaches of hybrid system falsification.

System Model. Let $T \in \mathbb{R}_{\geq 0}$ be a positive real. An *M-dimensional signal* with a time horizon T is a function $\mathbf{w} \colon [0, T] \to \mathbb{R}^M$. We treat the system model as a black box, i.e., its behaviors are only observed from inputs and their corresponding outputs. Formally, a *system model*, with M-dimensional input and

N-dimensional output, is a function $\mathcal{M}$ that takes an input signal $\mathbf{u}\colon [0,T] \to \mathbb{R}^M$ and returns a signal $\mathcal{M}(\mathbf{u})\colon [0,T] \to \mathbb{R}^N$. Here the common time horizon $T \in \mathbb{R}_{\geq 0}$ is arbitrary. The process of obtaining a system output signal $\mathcal{M}(\mathbf{u})$, given an input signal $\mathbf{u}$, is called *simulation*.

Specifications. In this work, we adopt *Signal Temporal Logic (STL)* as our specification language to formalize properties that should be satisfied by the system. We introduce the syntax and semantics in the following.

Definition 1 (STL syntax). We fix a set **Var** of variables. In Signal Temporal Logic (STL), *atomic propositions* and *formulas* are defined as follows, respectively: $\alpha ::\equiv f(x_1,\ldots,x_N) > 0$, and $\varphi ::\equiv \alpha \mid \bot \mid \neg\varphi \mid \varphi \wedge \varphi \mid \varphi\, \mathcal{U}_I\, \varphi$. Here f is an N-ary function $f\colon \mathbb{R}^N \to \mathbb{R}$, $x_1,\ldots,x_N \in \mathbf{Var}$, and I is a closed non-singular interval in $\mathbb{R}_{\geq 0}$, i.e. $I = [a,b]$ or $[a,\infty)$ where $a,b \in \mathbb{R}$ and $a < b$. Other common connectives such as $\to$, $\top$, $\square_I$ (always) and $\Diamond_I$ (eventually), are introduced as abbreviations: $\Diamond_I \varphi \equiv \top\, \mathcal{U}_I\, \varphi$ and $\square_I \varphi \equiv \neg\Diamond_I \neg\varphi$.

Definition 2 (Robust semantics). Let $\mathbf{w}\colon [0,T] \to \mathbb{R}^N$ be an N-dimensional signal, and $t \in [0,T)$. The *t-shift* $\mathbf{w}^t$ of $\mathbf{w}$ is the signal $\mathbf{w}^t\colon [0,T-t] \to \mathbb{R}^N$ defined by $\mathbf{w}^t(t') := \mathbf{w}(t + t')$. Let $\mathbf{w}\colon [0,T] \to \mathbb{R}^{|\mathbf{Var}|}$ be a signal, and φ be an STL formula. We define the *robustness* $[\![\mathbf{w},\varphi]\!] \in \mathbb{R} \cup \{\infty, -\infty\}$ as follows, by induction on the construction of formulas. $\sqcap$ and $\sqcup$ denote infimums and supremums of real numbers, respectively. Their binary version $\sqcap$ and $\sqcup$ denote minimum and maximum.

$$
\begin{aligned}
&[\![\mathbf{w}, f(x_1,\cdots,x_N) > 0]\!] \ := \ f\big(\mathbf{w}(0)(x_1),\cdots,\mathbf{w}(0)(x_N)\big)\\
&[\![\mathbf{w}, \bot]\!] \ := \ -\infty \qquad\qquad\qquad [\![\mathbf{w}, \neg\varphi]\!] \ := \ -[\![\mathbf{w},\varphi]\!]\\
&[\![\mathbf{w}, \varphi_1 \wedge \varphi_2]\!] \ := \ [\![\mathbf{w},\varphi_1]\!] \sqcap [\![\mathbf{w},\varphi_2]\!]\\
&[\![\mathbf{w}, \varphi_1\, \mathcal{U}_I\, \varphi_2]\!] \ := \ \bigsqcup_{t \in I \cap [0,T]}\big([\![\mathbf{w}^t,\varphi_2]\!] \sqcap \textstyle\bigsqcap_{t' \in [0,t)}[\![\mathbf{w}^{t'},\varphi_1]\!]\big)
\end{aligned}
$$

The original STL semantics is Boolean, given by a binary relation $\models$ between signals and formulas. The robust semantics refines the Boolean one as follows: $[\![\mathbf{w},\varphi]\!] > 0$ implies $\mathbf{w} \models \varphi$, and $[\![\mathbf{w},\varphi]\!] < 0$ implies $\mathbf{w} \not\models \varphi$, see [19, Prop. 16].

In the following, given a fixed specification φ, we denote as $\mathsf{R_u}$ the robustness of an input signal $\mathbf{u}$ to the specification φ, i.e., $\mathsf{R_u} = [\![\mathcal{M}(\mathbf{u}),\varphi]\!]$.

Falsification Approaches. Falsification consists in synthesizing input signals to find one that violates the system specification. The targets of falsification, i.e., input signals $\mathbf{u}\colon [0,T] \to \mathbb{R}^M$, are time-variant continuous functions. In practice, synthesizing such continuous signals is infeasible. Hence, practitioners employ parametrized representations to characterize the signals [13,16,26]; a commonly used representation is *piecewise constant*. A piecewise constant signal $\mathbf{u}\colon [0,T] \to \mathbb{R}^M$ has a hyperparameter c, such that during each interval $[\frac{(i-1)T}{c}, \frac{iT}{c}]$ ($i \in 1,\ldots,c$), $\mathbf{u}(t)$ is a constant. In this way, a finite number $c \cdot M$ of parameters is used to identify a signal $\mathbf{u}$. We will identify with Ω the $(c \cdot M)$-dimensional hyperrectangle identifying the *input space* (also *search space*) used for falsification.

Various approaches have been proposed to solve the falsification problem. The naive one is by *uniformly random sampling* input signals $\mathbf{u}$ in the input space Ω, and check if the corresponding output signal $\mathcal{M}(\mathbf{u})$ violates the specification φ. A more efficient but greedy algorithm is by exploiting the STL robust semantics and turning falsification into an optimization problem that minimizes the robustness $[\![\mathcal{M}(\mathbf{u}), \varphi]\!]$; the process stops when a negative robustness result $[\![\mathcal{M}(\mathbf{u}), \varphi]\!]$ is observed (i.e., a falsifying input $\mathbf{u}$ has been found), or the search budget (in terms of number of simulations) expires.

In order to solve the optimization problem, *stochastic optimization* algorithms, such as *hill climbing*, are employed, because they work efficiently with black box objective functions, like $[\![\mathcal{M}(\mathbf{u}), \varphi]\!]$ in our case. These algorithms adopt various metaheuristic strategies so that they can efficiently explore the search space and achieve optimal solutions. For instance, *CMAES* [23] is an evolutionary search-based method that focuses on exploitation. A more recent work *MCTS* [36] employs *Monte-Carlo Tree Search* to achieve a balance between exploration and exploitation of the search space. We refer readers to [8] for a more comprehensive survey of different optimization-based falsification algorithms. Also mature tools, such as Breach [13] and S-TaLiRo [3], have been developed.

3   Problem Definition and Overview of the Proposed Approach

In this work, we tackle the problem of characterizing the likelihood that a formal specification is indeed non-falsifiable, given that a falsification algorithm has tried to falsify it using a given set of input signals, all giving positive robustness.

Definition 3 (Confidence Estimation Problem). The *confidence estimation problem* is formally defined as follows:

- **Given:** a finite set $T = \{\langle \mathbf{u}_1^*, \mathsf{R}_{\mathbf{u}_1^*} \rangle, \dots, \langle \mathbf{u}_N^*, \mathsf{R}_{\mathbf{u}_N^*} \rangle\}$ of pairs, where each $\mathbf{u}_i^* \in \Omega$ is a point in the input space Ω, and $\mathsf{R}_{\mathbf{u}_i^*} \in \mathbb{R}_{\geq 0}$ is the robustness (a positive real) of $\mathbf{u}_i^*$.
- **Return:** the likelihood that, for all points $\mathbf{u}' \in \Omega$, it holds $\mathsf{R}_{\mathbf{u}'} > 0$.

This problem is in general undecidable: first, the robustness computation $\mathsf{R}(\mathbf{u}) = [\![\mathcal{M}(\mathbf{u}), \varphi]\!]$ relies on a black box model $\mathcal{M}$, in which the robustness values of unexplored points are not predictable (i.e., R is unknown); moreover, there are infinitely many unexplored points in the search space Ω, regardless of the size of T, since Ω is a continuous domain.

Overview of the Proposed Approach for Confidence Estimation. We provide an overview of the proposed approach in Fig. 1. We assume that a falsification algorithm has been run for some time with the aim of falsifying a given specification for a given system, without success (i.e., no falsifying input has been found). The proposed approach takes as input the produced falsification data T, consisting of a set of system inputs $\mathbf{u}^*$ and their robustness values $\mathsf{R}_{\mathbf{u}^*}$, as defined in Definition 3. These data, after being normalized, are fed into a Gaussian Process (GP) Regression process to train a GP as a surrogate of robustness

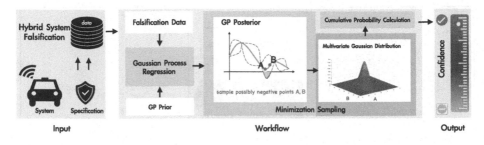

Fig. 1. The proposed GP regression-based confidence estimation approach for hybrid system falsification

function R. Using the obtained GP, we want to estimate the probability that there exists no point having negative robustness. First, we need to identify the points with lower values in the GP (so approximating lower robustness values), as these are those that can actually reduce the probability; to do this, we perform a global sampling method to collect a set of points that have low values, and then perform a local search starting from these points with the aim of finding points with even lower values. Starting from the found points, we apply an established method [6] to compute the probability that all these points still approximate positive robustness values. The approach outputs a confidence value $\mathsf{conf} \in [0, 1]$ that indicates *how likely* the system satisfies the system specification.

4   Confidence Estimation via Gaussian Process Regression

In this section, we explain all the phases of the process shown in Fig. 1. In Sect. 4.1, we first explain how we derive a Gaussian Process (GP) from the falsification data. Then, in Sect. 4.2, we describe how we sample from the obtained GP, and derive a confidence measure from the sampled data.

4.1   Building a Surrogate Model of the Robustness Function via Gaussian Process Regression

A *Gaussian Process* (GP) is a generalization of *Gaussian distribution* (a.k.a. *normal distribution*) from single/multiple variables to continuous domains [31]. While a Gaussian distribution characterizes the probability distribution of a finite set of variables, a GP models the distribution of infinite variables in a continuous domain, i.e., sampling from a GP derives a function instance in the domain. Formally, a GP over a continuous domain Ω is defined as a collection of random variables X_t indexed by $t \in \Omega$, such that any finite set $\mathsf{X} = \{X_t \mid t \in \Omega\}$ of those variables compose a *multivariate Gaussian distribution* $\mathsf{X} \sim \mathcal{N}(\mu, \Sigma)$, where μ and Σ are the *mean vector* and the *covariance matrix* of the distribution, respectively. The correlation between two variables $X_{t_i}, X_{t_j} \in \mathsf{X}$ is reflected by their covariance $\Sigma_{i,j}$—the larger $|\Sigma_{i,j}|$ is, the more highly X_{t_i} and X_{t_j} are

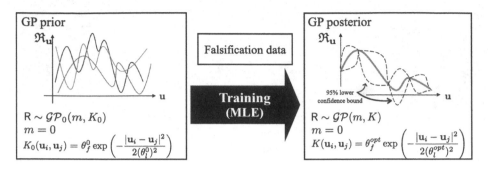

Fig. 2. Gaussian Process regression for the approximation of the robustness function

correlated. In a GP, the covariance between two variables X_{t_i} and X_{t_j} is dependent on the (Euclidean) distance of their indices t_i and t_j—the closer t_i and t_j are, the larger the covariance is. This is implemented by the *covariance function* (a.k.a. *kernel*) $K \colon \Omega \times \Omega \to \mathbb{R}$ of GP, whose complicated definition will be elaborated later.

GP regression consists in deciding the covariance function of a GP, by learning from the observed data, so that the distributions of unknown variables can be predicted, based on Bayes' rules [31, §2.1]. Unlike other regression frameworks (e.g., *deep learning*), the prediction for an unknown point made by the GP provides a *Gaussian distribution*, i.e., a *mean* and a *variance*, rather than a single value, so we can exploit this information to derive our confidence measure.

The prerequisite of GP regression is that the function that we want to approximate guarantees the following assumption [31].

Assumption 1. Two points that are geometrically closer in the input space have also closer output values.

In general, the assumption is reasonable for any robustness function, as a small tuning of input signals usually leads to a small change of the system outputs and so of the robustness value; such assumption is common in different works on testing of CPSs [2,9,32]. So, we can apply GP regression for approximating the robustness function. Figure 2 shows the GP regression we apply to learn a surrogate model for the robustness function R from the falsification data $T = \{\langle \mathbf{u}_1^*, \mathsf{R}_{\mathbf{u}_1^*} \rangle, \ldots, \langle \mathbf{u}_N^*, \mathsf{R}_{\mathbf{u}_N^*} \rangle\}$ in Definition 3. The process is elaborated in the following.

GP Prior. A GP is uniquely identified by a mean function m and a covariance function K, denoted as $\mathsf{R} \sim \mathcal{GP}(m, K)$. To determine m and K, a commonly-used approach is to first specify two parametrized function templates, and then fit the parameters based on training data. Conventionally, the mean function m can simply be a constant; here we use 0. The selection of the covariance function K is more sophisticated, as it is required to guarantee Assumption 1. Widely-used choices for K include *squared exponential kernel*, *Matérn kernel* and so on (see a discussion in [31, §4.2]). In this work, we follow a typical selection, namely, the *squared exponential kernel*, shown as follows:

$$K(\mathbf{u}_i, \mathbf{u}_j \mid \theta_f, \theta_l) = \theta_f \exp\left(-\frac{|\mathbf{u}_i - \mathbf{u}_j|^2}{2\theta_l^2}\right)$$

where $\theta_f, \theta_l \in \mathbb{R}$ are tunable hyperparameters. Initially (the left part of Fig. 2), these parameters have arbitrary values θ_f^0 and θ_l^0 and identify a function K_0; by this function, we obtain an initial *GP prior* $\mathsf{R} \sim \mathcal{GP}_0(m, K_0)$.

Training. The parameter tuning process aims at finding the optimal values θ_f^{opt}, θ_l^{opt} for θ_f, θ_l, such that, under θ_f^{opt} and θ_l^{opt}, the likelihood of the occurrence of the falsification data T (in Definition 3) is maximized. This method is referred to as *maximum likelihood estimation (MLE)*, shown as follows:

$$\theta_f^{opt}, \theta_l^{opt} = \arg\max_{\theta_f, \theta_l} P\left(\mathsf{R}_{\mathbf{u}_1^*}, \ldots, \mathsf{R}_{\mathbf{u}_N^*} \mid \theta_f, \theta_l\right) \tag{1}$$

where P is the *probability density function* of the multivariate Gaussian distribution of $[\mathsf{R}_{\mathbf{u}_1^*} \ldots \mathsf{R}_{\mathbf{u}_N^*}]$ (see [31, §2.2 and §5] for more details). This problem can be solved by a numerical optimization solver, such as *Quasi-Newton method* [7].

GP Posterior. Given the decision of hyperparameters θ_f and θ_l, we can fix our *GP posterior* for the robustness function R (the right part of Fig. 2) as $\mathsf{R} \sim \mathcal{GP}(m, K)$. By this, the posterior distribution of any unknown point $\mathbf{u} \in \Omega$ is inferred as follows, according to Bayes' rules [31, §2.2 and §A.2]:

$$\mathfrak{R}_{\mathbf{u}} \sim \mathcal{N}(\mu, \sigma^2) \qquad \mu = \Sigma_{\mathbf{u}} \Sigma_{\mathbf{u}^*}^{-1} \mathsf{R}_{\mathbf{u}^*} \quad \sigma^2 = K(\mathbf{u}, \mathbf{u}) - \Sigma_{\mathbf{u}} \Sigma_{\mathbf{u}^*}^{-1} \Sigma_{\mathbf{u}}^T \tag{2}$$

where $\Sigma_{\mathbf{u}} = \left[K(\mathbf{u}, \mathbf{u}_1^*) \ldots K(\mathbf{u}, \mathbf{u}_N^*)\right]$, $\Sigma_{\mathbf{u}^*} = \begin{bmatrix} K(\mathbf{u}_1^*, \mathbf{u}_1^*) & \cdots & K(\mathbf{u}_1^*, \mathbf{u}_N^*) \\ \vdots & \ddots & \vdots \\ K(\mathbf{u}_N^*, \mathbf{u}_1^*) & & K(\mathbf{u}_N^*, \mathbf{u}_N^*) \end{bmatrix}$, and

$\mathsf{R}_{\mathbf{u}^*} = \left[\mathsf{R}_{\mathbf{u}_1^*} \ldots \mathsf{R}_{\mathbf{u}_N^*}\right]$. $\mathfrak{R}_{\mathbf{u}}$ identifies the *inferred distribution* for the robustness of $\mathbf{u}$.

4.2 Confidence Estimation

In this section, we describe how we derive a *confidence measure* on the result of falsification, based on the surrogate GP posterior we obtained in Sect. 4.1. Accordingly, the problem introduced in Definition 3 is reformulated in terms of GP as follows:

Definition 4 (Confidence Estimation Based on GP Posterior)

- **Given:** the GP posterior $\mathsf{R} \sim \mathcal{GP}(m, K)$;
- **Return:** the likelihood that any inferred distribution $\mathfrak{R}_{\mathbf{u}}$ (for all $\mathbf{u} \in \Omega$) is positive.

The problem in Definition 4 asks for the *tail probability* of a given GP; the exact answer of the problem is hard in general, and is still actively pursued in the

---

Algorithm 1. Confidence estimation

Require: The $R \sim \mathcal{GP}(m, K)$ obtained in Sect. 4.1 and its input space Ω
Require: H: the number of points to randomly sample from $\mathcal{GP}$
Require: h: the number of top-h sampled points to use for local search, s.t. $h \ll H$
Ensure: conf: the confidence value that the specification holds

1: **function** ESTIMATECONFIDENCE($\mathcal{GP}$, Ω, H, h)
2:     collect a set U of $\mathbf{u} \in \Omega$ by randomly sampling H points in Ω
3:     sort all $\mathbf{u} \in U$ ascendingly by lowBound($\mathbf{u}$) and take the first h ones $\{\mathbf{u}_1, \ldots, \mathbf{u}_h\}$

4:     **for** $i \in \{1, \ldots, h\}$ **do**
5:         $\mathbf{u}'_i \leftarrow \arg\min_{\mathbf{u} \in \Omega} \mathsf{lowBound}(\mathbf{u})$ starting from $\mathbf{u}_i$ ▷ local search

6:     $\mathfrak{R}_{\mathbf{u}'_1}, \ldots, \mathfrak{R}_{\mathbf{u}'_h} \sim \mathcal{N}(\mu, \Sigma)$ s.t., $\begin{cases} \mu \leftarrow \Sigma_{\mathbf{u}} \Sigma_{\mathbf{u}*}^{-1} R_{\mathbf{u}*} \\ \Sigma \leftarrow K(\mathbf{u}, \mathbf{u}) - \Sigma_{\mathbf{u}} \Sigma_{\mathbf{u}*}^{-1} \Sigma_{\mathbf{u}}^T \end{cases}$ ▷ see Eq. 2

7:     **return** conf $\leftarrow$ MVNCDF$(\langle \mathfrak{R}_{\mathbf{u}'_1}, \ldots, \mathfrak{R}_{\mathbf{u}'_h} \rangle, [0, \infty))$

GP community [24,27,28]. Since our work mainly aims at giving a hint of *how likely* it is that there exists no counterexample in the falsification search space, an approximation of the tail probability is enough. In this section, we introduce a sampling-based approach to approximate the likelihood (i.e., the confidence measure) as defined in Definition 4.

The process of confidence estimation is shown in Algorithm 1.

It requires the GP posterior $\mathcal{GP}$ obtained in Sect. 4.1 with its input space Ω, and two natural numbers $H, h \in \mathbb{N}^+$ such that $h \ll H$. The algorithm consists in a *minimization sampling* phase, and a *cumulative probability calculation* phase; at the end, it returns a confidence value conf $\in [0, 1]$ that indicates how likely it is that there exists no counterexample in Ω. In the following, we elaborate on the process.

Minimization Sampling. The likelihood in Definition 4 is decided by its *dual problem*, i.e., the likelihood that there exists $\mathbf{u} \in \Omega$ whose $\mathfrak{R}_{\mathbf{u}}$ is negative. To answer this problem, we need to collect the points in Ω, whose inferred robustness values have a considerable probability to be negative, and then calculate their cumulative probability distribution. Since Ω is continuous, there could exist infinitely many such points, and hence it is impossible to involve all of them. However, our work mainly aims at giving an approximation of the likelihood, so it suffices to select a finite set of points from Ω as representatives for that class of points. To this aim, we construct a new function lowBound($\mathbf{u}$) $= \mu(\mathbf{u}) - 1.96\sigma(\mathbf{u})$, that is, the 95% lower confidence bound of the posterior distribution of $\mathfrak{R}_{\mathbf{u}}$ in Eq. 2 (see an illustration in the GP posterior in Fig. 2). Intuitively, if lowBound($\mathbf{u}$) is lower than 0, there is still a considerable probability that $\mathfrak{R}_{\mathbf{u}}$ is negative; otherwise, we consider that $\mathfrak{R}_{\mathbf{u}}$ is unlikely to be negative.

Therefore, this phase consists of an optimization process, taking lowBound($\mathbf{u}$) as the objective function to be minimized. In order to derive comprehensive and precise estimation, we adopt a hybrid optimization approach that combines global search and local search. First, in the global search, we perform a comprehensive random sampling in Ω (Line 2) and sort the H points ascendingly according to their 95% lower confidence bound lowBound(**u**) (Line 3); we select the first h sampled points to perform a further minimization process (Line 3). Namely, we take each of the h sampled points as a starting point to perform a local search, aiming at finding new points that have even lower confidence bound (Line 5); we use these points to construct a multivariate Gaussian distribution, based on the definition of GP (Line 6).

Cumulative Probability Calculation. Given the constructed multivariate Gaussian distribution $\mathfrak{R}_{\mathbf{u}_1'}, \ldots, \mathfrak{R}_{\mathbf{u}_k'} \sim \mathcal{N}(\mu, \Sigma)$ in Line 6, we can apply existing methods to calculate the probability that $\mathfrak{R}_{\mathbf{u}_1'}, \ldots, \mathfrak{R}_{\mathbf{u}_k'}$ are all positive. There have been a line of works doing this; in our work, we adopt the state-of-the-art, that is, a *minimax tilting*-based approach [6] to calculate the probability. The function MVNCDF in Line 7 shows the interface of [6]: it takes as input the multivariate Gaussian distribution, i.e., its mean and covariance matrix, and the range in which the distribution is expected to locate; it returns a value conf, that indicates how likely the multivariate Gaussian distribution distributes in the given range.

5 Experimental Evaluation

We here describe the experiments we conducted to evaluate the proposed confidence measure. We first present the experiments settings in Sect. 5.1; then, in Sect. 5.2, we analyze experimental results using a series of research questions.

5.1 Experiment Settings

As benchmarks, we selected three Simulink models and seven STL specifications defined for them, that are commonly used, in particular in falsification competitions [11,16,17]. Table 1 reports the benchmarks and the corresponding specifications. The specification ID identifies the corresponding model. A description of the models and of their specifications is as follows.

Table 1. Specifications. For each one, we list a set of parameters $\omega_1, \ldots, \omega_5$ for RQ2; the default parameter used in RQ1 and RQ3 is indicated by ω_d

Spec. ID	STL formula	ω_i $(i = 1, \ldots, 5)$	ω_d
AT1	$\Box_{[0,30]} \, (speed < \omega_i)$	{135, 140, 145, 150, 155}	ω_3
AT2	$\Box_{[0,10]} \, (speed < 50) \vee \Diamond_{[0,30]} \, (rpm > \omega_i)$	{500, 750, 1000, 1250, 1500}	ω_4
AT3	$\Box_{[0,29]}(speed < 100) \vee \Box_{[29,30]}(speed > \omega_i)$	{57, 59, 61, 63, 65}	ω_2
AT4	$\Box_{[0,30]}(rpm < 4770 \vee \Box_{[0,1]}(rpm > \omega_i))$	{200, 300, 400, 500, 600}	ω_1
FFR1	$\neg \, \Diamond_{[0,5]} \, x, y \in [3.9 + \omega_i, 4.1 - \omega_i] \wedge \dot{x}, \dot{y} \in [-0.5, 0.5]$	{0.01, 0.03, 0.05, 0.07, 0.09}	ω_1
FFR2	$\neg \Diamond_{[0,5]} \Box_{[0,2]}(x, y \in [1.5 + \omega_i, 1.7 - \omega_i])$	{0, 0.02, 0.04, 0.06, 0.08}	ω_2
AFC1	$\Box_{[11,50]}(controller\_mode = 1 \rightarrow \mu < \omega_i)$	{0.25, 0.3, 0.35, 0.4, 0.45}	ω_2

- *Automatic Transmission* (AT) [25] models an automotive system that has two input signals, *throttle* ∈ [0, 100] and *brake* ∈ [0, 325], and three outputs signals, *gear*, *speed*, and *rpm*. The specifications consider system safety: requirements on *speed* (AT1, AT3), on *rpm* (AT4), or their relation (AT2).
- *Free Floating Robot* (FFR) [9] models a robot operating in a 2D space. It has four input signals $u_1, u_2, u_3, u_4 \in [-10, 10]$ representing the boosters, and four output signals that represent the coordinates x, y of the robot position, and their one-order derivatives $\dot{x}, \dot{y}$. The specifications specify kinetic properties for the robot: FFR1 requires the robot to pass an area around the point (4, 4) under an input constraint, and FFR2 requires the robot to stay in a given area for at least 2 s.
- *Abstract Fuel Control* (AFC) [26] takes two input signals, *Pedal_Angle* ∈ [8.8, 70] and *Engine_Speed* ∈ [900, 1100], and outputs a ratio μ reflecting the deviation of *air-fuel-ratio* from its reference value. A requirement (AFC1) of the system is that μ shouldn't deviate too much from the reference value.

Specifications are parameterized by a parameter ω_i; we set it to five different values to have specifications of different complexity for the experiments.

Software and Hardware Specifications. Our experiments rely on Breach [13] to interface Simulink and compute STL robustness. The experiments have been executed on an AWS EC2 c4.2xlarge instance (2.9 GHz Intel Xeon E5-2666 v3, 15 GB RAM). The code and all the experimental results are available online at https://github.com/choshina/GPConfidence.

5.2 Evaluation

We assess the viability of the proposed confidence measure using three research questions, described as follows.

RQ1. Does the confidence measure monotonically increase?

As explained in Sect. 1, a confidence measure, in order to be reliable, should be monotonically increasing, i.e., it should not decrease as new falsification data is considered. As previously explained, this cannot be theoretically guaranteed by the proposed metric, as it is always possible to find a new input that drastically changes the learned GP. Therefore, we here want to assess to what extent the proposed metric is monotonically increasing. For each benchmark (using the default value ω_d), we have randomly sampled an increasing number of points in Ω; then, for each set of sampled points T, we have computed the minimum robustness and the confidence measure.

Figure 3 shows, for each benchmark, how the minimum robustness value (right axis and red plot) and the confidence measure (left axis and blue plot) change by increasing the size of T.[2] The plots show the intervals of sizes of T in which the confidence measure changes significantly, before stabilizing to a given

---

[2] Since computing the confidence measure can take up to 30 s, we have computed it only for some sizes of $|T|$.

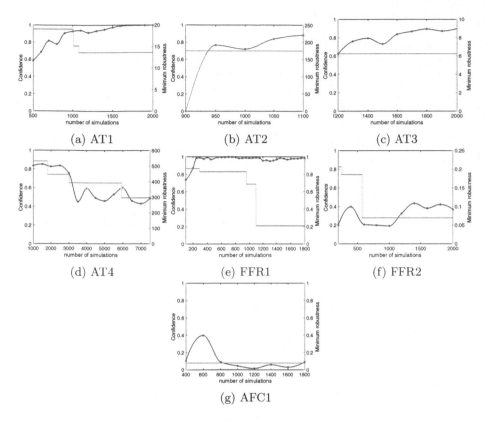

(a) AT1   (b) AT2   (c) AT3

(d) AT4   (e) FFR1   (f) FFR2

(g) AFC1

Fig. 3. RQ1 – Experimental results on monotonicity

value. We observe that, in most of the cases (i.e., AT1, AT2, AT3, FFR1, and FFR2), the measure is quite monotonic, with few oscillations for lower number of simulations (e.g., FFR2); these initial oscillations are expected, because the precision of the GP depends on the number of elements of the training data. For some cases, instead, the confidence measure remains high for some time at the beginning (i.e., AT4 and AFC1) and then stabilizes at a lower value. For AFC1, the reason is that the minimum robustness is always very low; so, with more observations, the GP learns such low robustness, and so the confidence on the absence of a falsifying input decreases. For AT4, the main decrease in confidence occurs due to big drops in minimum robustness. A way to increase the confidence also in the presence of low robustness would be to add more training data, so that the GP can get a better estimation; this is not applicable in our context, because we rely only on the falsification data. However, in the next research question, we show that the confidence metric is still reliable.

> **Answer to RQ1:** Most of the time, the confidence measure is reliable, as it does not decrease (significantly) with increasing number of simulations. However, in some cases, the measure is fluctuating for a lower number of simulations, due to big changes in minimum robustness.

RQ2. Is the confidence measure sound?

We claim that a confidence measure is sound if it is related to the difficulty of falsifying a specification, which can be assessed by the minimum robustness that is achieved by a falsification algorithm. Therefore, we expect that the lower the minimum robustness is, the lower the confidence should be. To assess to what extent the proposed confidence measure is sound, we compare the confidence results for the different instantiations of a specification type in Table 1; indeed, these represent similar problems that, however, can have different values of minimum robustness (as the specification is more or less demanding). Concretely, for each specification type and for each of the different values of the parameter ω_i, we have run random sampling for 2000 simulations, and we have collected the minimum robustness and the confidence measure over the simulations. Then, for each specification type, we have selected the minimum number of simulations for which, in at least one instantiation of ω_i, the confidence measure reaches 100% (or we select the maximum number 2000 if none of them reaches 100%), and we take this number of simulations to compare the results of the specification type: in this way, we can observe whether there are actually differences, and we avoid the saturation effect that may be obtained by using a lot of simulations in which the results converge to the same value.

Table 2 reports, for each specification type, results of the different instantiations, in terms of minimum robustness (minRob), confidence measure (conf), and confidence computation time (in secs); results are sorted increasingly by minRob.

Table 2. RQ2 – Experimental results on soundness. conf is in %; time is in secs.

	AT1				AT2				AT3				AT4		
ω_i	minRob	conf	time	ω_i	minRob	conf	time	ω_i	minRob	conf	time	ω_i	minRob	conf	time
ω_1	5.12	39.23	22.8	ω_5	33.42	0	30	ω_5	4.82	82.52	22.4	ω_3	355.44	56.59	29.9
ω_2	10.06	97.77	26.3	ω_4	34.55	0.01	33.4	ω_3	5.56	93.89	19.6	ω_4	445.41	87.62	30.9
ω_3	13.6	49.93	24.2	ω_3	43.72	0	27.9	ω_4	6.24	89.67	21.4	ω_5	466.57	85.86	26.6
ω_4	18.1	100	23.43	ω_2	250	26.33	29.3	ω_2	7.13	93.34	22.5	ω_2	473.54	90.79	30.6
ω_5	22.41	100	26.6	ω_1	500	88.92	29.7	ω_1	9.6	97.45	23.4	ω_1	608.4	91.99	28.5

	FFR1				FFR2				AFC1		
ω_i	minRob	conf	time	ω_i	minRob	conf	time	ω_i	minRob	conf	time
ω_5	0.21	99.28	20	ω_3	0.01	1.27	23.2	ω_1	0.03	1.84	0.3
ω_3	0.49	99.95	20.3	ω_1	0.02	11.17	21.2	ω_2	0.08	10.48	0.3
ω_2	0.5	90.84	21.5	ω_2	0.03	2.53	20.2	ω_3	0.13	99.95	0.2
ω_1	0.58	98.88	24.2	ω_4	0.07	47.23	16.8	ω_4	0.18	100	0.3
ω_4	0.64	92.37	23.1	ω_5	0.08	0.91	21.1	ω_5	0.23	100	0.3

We note that, overall, the metric is sound because, given a specification type, lower confidence values are obtained for lower robustness. Usually, large change in confidence occurs when there is a big percentage change in robustness, such as AT2, where the maximum value of minRob is 21.3% bigger than the minimum value, and the difference in confidence is 88.92 perc. points. In some cases, the variance of conf across the instantiations is not too high, as in AT3, AT4, and FFR1 (differences of 14.93, 35.4, and 9.11 perc. points); we notice that, in these cases, the percentage change of robustness is small (0.99%, 0.36%, and 2.04%).

Answer to RQ2: Overall, the confidence measure is sound as it is related to the difficulty of the specification, measured by the minimum robustness.

RQ3. What is the confidence provided by different falsification algorithms?

We are here interested in investigating what is the confidence provided by different falsification algorithms (i.e., implementing different search strategies) when they are not able to falsify. We took three representative algorithms: Random search that performs pure *exploration*, CMAES [23] that is a greedy approach that favours *exploitation*, and MCTS [36] that provides a balance between exploration and exploitation. We have applied the three algorithms (for 2000 simulations) to three benchmark specifications (AT3, FFR1, and AFC1 instantiated with ω_d as reported in Table 1); we repeated the experiments 10 times.

Figure 4 reports how the confidence measure changes across the 10 repetitions. We observe that higher confidence is usually obtained by Random: since it explores more, it can provide more distributed data for GP learning, so obtaining a better GP (with less uncertainty). On the contrary, CMAES obtains low confidence as it does not explore enough and so the GP learning does not have training data for large parts of the search space in which the uncertainty of the GP will be high. MCTS can obtain good results when it explores enough (as in

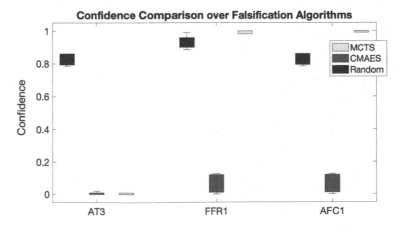

Fig. 4. Confidence comparison between different falsification algorithms

FFR1 and AFC1), but sometimes it can be too greedy (as in AT3) and so it obtains low confidence. Regarding the variance of the results, we observe that CMAES is the one with the highest variance, as different search trials can lead to different search paths and so different confidence values; also Random has some variance across the results, but not as much as CMAES. MCTS is the more stable approach, as the balance between exploration and exploitation leads most of the times to the same search paths, and so to the same confidence values.

Answer to RQ3: Falsification approaches that provide enough exploration lead to higher confidence. MCTS is the more stable algorithm.

---

6   Related Work

Gaussian processes and Gaussian process regression are widely applied in different contexts. In statistics, GP regression, usually referred to as *Kriging methods*, is used to build surrogate models for measuring the probability of rare events, e.g., [5,21,34]. These works usually develop new sampling techniques to derive rare events probability using limited numbers of observations, and have been widely applied in engineering domains. Theoretical explorations in tail probability of GPs have been heavily conducted in the statistics community [24,27,28]. In general, this is a hard problem and research efforts are still on-going; achievements so far usually limit GP to certain types, e.g., *Brownian motion*.

In falsification, GP regression has been mainly used for guiding the search process, and not for confidence estimation as done in this paper. Deshmukh et al. [9] apply *Bayesian optimization*, an optimization approach derived from GP regression, to falsification, and investigates a dimension reduction technique. Akazaki [2] uses it for the falsification of conditional properties $\Box_I \varphi_{cond} \rightarrow \varphi_{safe}$ in which the antecedent φ_{cond} must be satisfied in order to be able to violate the property; GP regression is used to guide the search towards input satisfying φ_{cond}. Silvetti et al. [32] use GP regression to approximate the STL semantics and so identify the inputs that have higher probability to have lower robustness. Apart from falsification, also in the more general context of search-based testing (SBT), the usage of GP regression has been recently advocated [20] for speeding up the search. However, to the best of our knowledge, no work in falsification or SBT uses GP regression for confidence estimation on the final result.

Our confidence measure has similarities with coverage criteria used in testing, as they both aim at giving a confidence on the absence of faults. The main difference is that coverage criteria fix a set of test requirements that need to be covered, and the coverage level acts as a confidence value; in our case, the confidence measure does not specify what needs to be covered, but implicitly considers the coverage of the input space. Coverage criteria have been proposed for falsification. Dokhanchi et al. [12] define coverage based on the blocks of Simulink models, and integrate the coverage level as part of the objective function of the falsification problem. Dreossi et al. [15] use "star discrepancy" as a measure of input space coverage, and use it to guide the falsification search. Adimoolam et al. [1] classify inputs according to their robustness values, and define coverage based on the clustered inputs. All these works use coverage as a means for guiding the search, but they do not explicitly use it as a confidence measure. Although our confidence measure is not a coverage criterion, it has some good properties as monotonicity that would allow to also use it as stopping criterion for falsification; this usage of the measure is part of our future work.

In the verification community, other approaches provide some type of confidence on the verification results. For example, in probabilistic model checking [4, Chapter 10], the probability that a given property holds can be estimated; the approach is, however, much different from ours, as it operates on much simpler models as Markov chains.

7   Conclusion

In this paper, we have proposed a confidence measure that, in case a falsification algorithm has terminated without returning any falsifying input, estimates the probability that the specification is indeed non-falsifiable. The measure is computed by first performing a Gaussian Process (GP) Regression process that learns the robustness function from the falsification data, and by then deriving from it the probability that no falsifying input exists.

In this work, we have considered one particular kernel function for GP; as future work, we plan to investigate whether other kernel functions provide better results. The proposed approach works better if the fitness landscape is smooth (see Assumption 1); however, in some cases, the fitness landscape of the robustness could be quite complicated, in particular when output signals of different magnitudes are used in the specification (called the *scale problem* in [37–39]); as future work, we plan to devise techniques that mitigate the scale problem, and so make it easier to learn the robustness function.

The approach is applicable to hybrid systems in which Assumption 1 holds, i.e., those for which the Gaussian approximation is suitable. While this usually holds for continuous dynamics, it may not hold when discrete modes (e.g., states of a hybrid automaton) are involved. As future work, we plan to perform a much larger empirical evaluation to try to properly characterize the systems in which the assumption holds, and so the confidence measure is more trustworthy.

References

1. Adimoolam, A., Dang, T., Donzé, A., Kapinski, J., Jin, X.: Classification and coverage-based falsification for embedded control systems. In: Majumdar, R., Kunčak, V. (eds.) CAV 2017. LNCS, vol. 10426, pp. 483–503. Springer, Cham (2017). https://doi.org/10.1007/978-3-319-63387-9_24
2. Akazaki, T.: Falsification of conditional safety properties for cyber-physical systems with Gaussian process regression. In: Falcone, Y., Sánchez, C. (eds.) RV 2016. LNCS, vol. 10012, pp. 439–446. Springer, Cham (2016). https://doi.org/10.1007/978-3-319-46982-9_27

3. Annpureddy, Y., Liu, C., Fainekos, G., Sankaranarayanan, S.: S-TaLiRo: a tool for temporal logic falsification for hybrid systems. In: Abdulla, P.A., Leino, K.R.M. (eds.) TACAS 2011. LNCS, vol. 6605, pp. 254–257. Springer, Heidelberg (2011). https://doi.org/10.1007/978-3-642-19835-9_21

4. Baier, C., Katoen, J.P.: Principles of Model Checking (Representation and Mind Series). The MIT Press (2008)

5. Balesdent, M., Morio, J., Marzat, J.: Kriging-based adaptive importance sampling algorithms for rare event estimation. Struct. Saf. **44**, 1–10 (2013)

6. Botev, Z.: The normal law under linear restrictions: simulation and estimation via minimax tilting. J. Roy. Stat. Soc. Ser. B (Stat. Methodol.) **1**(79), 125–148 (2017)

7. Broyden, C.G.: A class of methods for solving nonlinear simultaneous equations. Math. Comput. **19**(92), 577–593 (1965)

8. Corso, A., Moss, R.J., Koren, M., Lee, R., Kochenderfer, M.J.: A survey of algorithms for black-box safety validation. arXiv preprint arXiv:2005.02979 (2020)

9. Deshmukh, J., Horvat, M., Jin, X., Majumdar, R., Prabhu, V.S.: Testing cyber-physical systems through Bayesian optimization. ACM Trans. Embed. Comput. Syst. **16**(5s) (2017). https://doi.org/10.1145/3126521

10. Deshmukh, J., Jin, X., Kapinski, J., Maler, O.: Stochastic local search for falsification of hybrid systems. In: Finkbeiner, B., Pu, G., Zhang, L. (eds.) ATVA 2015. LNCS, vol. 9364, pp. 500–517. Springer, Cham (2015). https://doi.org/10.1007/978-3-319-24953-7_35

11. Dokhanchi, A., et al.: ARCH-COMP18 category report: results on the falsification benchmarks. In: 5th International Workshop on Applied Verification of Continuous and Hybrid Systems, ARCH18. EPiC Series in Computing, vol. 54, pp. 104–109. EasyChair (2018). https://doi.org/10.29007/t85q

12. Dokhanchi, A., Zutshi, A., Sriniva, R.T., Sankaranarayanan, S., Fainekos, G.: Requirements driven falsification with coverage metrics. In: Proceedings of the 12th International Conference on Embedded Software, EMSOFT 2015, pp. 31–40. IEEE Press (2015)

13. Donzé, A.: Breach, a toolbox for verification and parameter synthesis of hybrid systems. In: Touili, T., Cook, B., Jackson, P. (eds.) CAV 2010. LNCS, vol. 6174, pp. 167–170. Springer, Heidelberg (2010). https://doi.org/10.1007/978-3-642-14295-6_17

14. Donzé, A., Maler, O.: Robust satisfaction of temporal logic over real-valued signals. In: Chatterjee, K., Henzinger, T.A. (eds.) FORMATS 2010. LNCS, vol. 6246, pp. 92–106. Springer, Heidelberg (2010). https://doi.org/10.1007/978-3-642-15297-9_9

15. Dreossi, T., Dang, T., Donzé, A., Kapinski, J., Jin, X., Deshmukh, J.V.: Efficient guiding strategies for testing of temporal properties of hybrid systems. In: Havelund, K., Holzmann, G., Joshi, R. (eds.) NFM 2015. LNCS, vol. 9058, pp. 127–142. Springer, Cham (2015). https://doi.org/10.1007/978-3-319-17524-9_10

16. Ernst, G., et al.: ARCH-COMP 2020 category report: falsification. In: 7th International Workshop on Applied Verification of Continuous and Hybrid Systems (ARCH20), ARCH20. EPiC Series in Computing, vol. 74, pp. 140–152. EasyChair (2020). https://doi.org/10.29007/trr1

17. Ernst, G., et al.: ARCH-COMP 2019 category report: falsification. In: 6th International Workshop on Applied Verification of Continuous and Hybrid Systems, ARCH19. EPiC Series in Computing, vol. 61, pp. 129–140. EasyChair (2019). https://doi.org/10.29007/68dk

18. Ernst, G., Sedwards, S., Zhang, Z., Hasuo, I.: Fast falsification of hybrid systems using probabilistically adaptive input. In: Parker, D., Wolf, V. (eds.) QEST 2019. LNCS, vol. 11785, pp. 165–181. Springer, Cham (2019). https://doi.org/10.1007/978-3-030-30281-8_10

19. Fainekos, G.E., Pappas, G.J.: Robustness of temporal logic specifications for continuous-time signals. Theor. Comput. Sci. **410**(42), 4262–4291 (2009). https://doi.org/10.1016/j.tcs.2009.06.021

20. Feldt, R., Poulding, S.: Broadening the search in search-based software testing: it need not be evolutionary. In: Proceedings of the Eighth International Workshop on Search-Based Software Testing, SBST 2015, pp. 1–7. IEEE Press (2015)

21. Giordano, S., Gubinelli, M., Pagano, M.: Rare events of gaussian processes: a performance comparison between bridge Monte-Carlo and importance sampling. In: Koucheryavy, Y., Harju, J., Sayenko, A. (eds.) NEW2AN 2007. LNCS, vol. 4712, pp. 269–280. Springer, Heidelberg (2007). https://doi.org/10.1007/978-3-540-74833-5_23

22. Gladisch, C., Heinz, T., Heinzemann, C., Oehlerking, J., von Vietinghoff, A., Pfitzer, T.: Experience paper: search-based testing in automated driving control applications. In: Proceedings of the 34th IEEE/ACM International Conference on Automated Software Engineering. ASE 2019, pp. 26–37. IEEE Press (2019). https://doi.org/10.1109/ASE.2019.00013

23. Hansen, N., Müller, S.D., Koumoutsakos, P.: Reducing the time complexity of the derandomized evolution strategy with covariance matrix adaptation (CMA-ES). Evol. Comput. **11**(1), 1–18 (2003)

24. Harper, A.J.: Bounds on the suprema of Gaussian processes, and omega results for the sum of a random multiplicative function. Ann. Appl. Probab.**23**(2), 584–616 (2013). https://doi.org/10.1214/12-AAP847

25. Hoxha, B., Abbas, H., Fainekos, G.E.: Benchmarks for temporal logic requirements for automotive systems. In: 1st and 2nd International Workshop on Applied veRification for Continuous and Hybrid Systems, ARCH@CPSWeek 2014, Berlin, Germany, 14 April 2014 / ARCH@CPSWeek 2015, Seattle, USA, April 13, 2015. EPiC Series in Computing, vol. 34, pp. 25–30. EasyChair (2014)

26. Jin, X., Deshmukh, J.V., Kapinski, J., Ueda, K., Butts, K.: Powertrain control verification benchmark. In: Proceedings of the 17th International Conference on Hybrid Systems: Computation and Control, HSCC 2014, pp. 253–262. ACM (2014). https://doi.org/10.1145/2562059.2562140

27. Li, W.V., Shao, Q.M., et al.: Lower tail probabilities for gaussian processes. Ann. Probab. **32**(1A), 216–242 (2004)

28. Marcus, M.B., Shepp, L.A., et al.: Sample behavior of gaussian processes. In: Proceedings of the Sixth Berkeley Symposium on Mathematical Statistics and Probability, Volume 2: Probability Theory. The Regents of the University of California (1972)

29. Menghi, C., Nejati, S., Briand, L., Parache, Y.I.: Approximation-refinement testing of compute-intensive cyber-physical models: an approach based on system identification. In: Proceedings of the ACM/IEEE 42nd International Conference on Software Engineering. ICSE 2020, pp. 372–384. Association for Computing Machinery, New York (2020). https://doi.org/10.1145/3377811.3380370

30. Nejati, S., Gaaloul, K., Menghi, C., Briand, L.C., Foster, S., Wolfe, D.: Evaluating model testing and model checking for finding requirements violations in Simulink models. In: Proceedings of the 2019 27th ACM Joint Meeting on European Software Engineering Conference and Symposium on the Foundations of Software Engineering. ESEC/FSE 2019, pp. 1015–1025. Association for Computing Machinery, New York (2019). https://doi.org/10.1145/3338906.3340444

31. Rasmussen, C.E., Williams, C.K., Bach, F.: Gaussian Processes for Machine Learning. MIT Press (2006)

32. Silvetti, S., Policriti, A., Bortolussi, L.: An active learning approach to the falsification of black box cyber-physical systems. In: Polikarpova, N., Schneider, S. (eds.) IFM 2017. LNCS, vol. 10510, pp. 3–17. Springer, Cham (2017). https://doi.org/10.1007/978-3-319-66845-1_1

33. Yamagata, Y., Liu, S., Akazaki, T., Duan, Y., Hao, J.: Falsification of cyber-physical systems using deep reinforcement learning. IEEE Trans. Softw. Eng. (2020). https://doi.org/10.1109/TSE.2020.2969178

34. Zanette, A., Zhang, J., Kochenderfer, M.J.: Robust super-level set estimation using Gaussian processes. In: Berlingerio, M., Bonchi, F., Gärtner, T., Hurley, N., Ifrim, G. (eds.) ECML PKDD 2018. LNCS (LNAI), vol. 11052, pp. 276–291. Springer, Cham (2019). https://doi.org/10.1007/978-3-030-10928-8_17

35. Zhang, Z., Arcaini, P., Hasuo, I.: Hybrid system falsification under (in)equality constraints via search space transformation. IEEE Trans. Comput.-Aided Des. Integrated Circuits Syst. **39**(11), 3674–3685 (2020). https://doi.org/10.1109/TCAD.2020.3013073

36. Zhang, Z., Ernst, G., Sedwards, S., Arcaini, P., Hasuo, I.: Two-layered falsification of hybrid systems guided by Monte Carlo Tree Search. IEEE Trans. Comput.-Aided Des. Integrated Circuits Syst. **37**(11), 2894–2905 (Nov 2018). https://doi.org/10.1109/TCAD.2018.2858463

37. Zhang, Z., Hasuo, I., Arcaini, P.: Multi-armed bandits for Boolean connectives in hybrid system falsification. In: Dillig, I., Tasiran, S. (eds.) CAV 2019. LNCS, vol. 11561, pp. 401–420. Springer, Cham (2019). https://doi.org/10.1007/978-3-030-25540-4_23

38. Zhang, Z., Lyu, D., Arcaini, P., Ma, L., Hasuo, I., Zhao, J.: Effective hybrid system falsification using Monte Carlo tree search guided by QB-robustness. In: Silva, A., Leino, K.R.M. (eds.) CAV 2021. LNCS, vol. 12759, pp. 595–618. Springer, Cham (2021). https://doi.org/10.1007/978-3-030-81685-8_29

39. Zhang, Z., Lyu, D., Arcaini, P., Ma, L., Hasuo, I., Zhao, J.: On the effectiveness of signal rescaling in hybrid system falsification. In: Dutle, A., Moscato, M.M., Titolo, L., Muñoz, C.A., Perez, I. (eds.) NFM 2021. LNCS, vol. 12673, pp. 392–399. Springer, Cham (2021). https://doi.org/10.1007/978-3-030-76384-8_24

Formal Verification of Intelligent Hybrid Systems that are Modeled with Simulink and the Reinforcement Learning Toolbox

Julius Adelt[✉], Timm Liebrenz[✉], and Paula Herber[✉]

University of Münster, Einsteinstr. 62, 48149 Münster, Germany
{julius.adelt,timm.liebrenz,paula.herber}@uni-muenster.de

Abstract. Reinforcement Learning (RL) is a powerful technique to control autonomous hybrid systems (HSs) in dynamic and uncertain environments but makes it hard to guarantee their correct behavior in safety-critical applications. To formally guarantee safe behavior, a formal system description is required, which is often not available in industrial design processes and hard to obtain for the unpredictable, trial and error learning processes of RL. In this paper, we present an approach for semi-automatic deductive verification of intelligent HSs with embedded RL components modeled in Simulink together with the RL Toolbox. Our key ideas are threefold: First, we capture the safety-relevant behavior of RL components with hybrid contracts in differential dynamic logic. Second, we verify safety properties of the overall system with the RL component replaced by its contract deductively using the interactive theorem prover KeYmaera X. To make this possible, we precisely capture the semantics of industrially designed intelligent HSs by extending an existing transformation from Simulink to differential dynamic logic to support RL components. Third, we ensure that contracts are complied with at runtime by automatically deriving runtime monitors from our hybrid contracts. We demonstrate the practical applicability, scalability, and flexibility of our approach by verifying collision freedom of an autonomous intelligent robot in a factory setting.

Keywords: Formal verification · Theorem proving · Hybrid systems · Safe reinforcement learning · Hybrid contracts

1 Introduction

Hybrid systems (HSs) combine discrete and continuous behavior. They are increasingly applied in more and more complex scenarios, which feature dynamic and uncertain environments and make the application of machine learning methods like reinforcement learning (RL) desirable [1,10], for example, in smart factories or autonomous driving. At the same time, they often operate in safety-critical contexts where failures can endanger human lives and should be prevented under all circumstances.

© Springer Nature Switzerland AG 2021
M. Huisman et al. (Eds.): FM 2021, LNCS 13047, pp. 349–366, 2021.
https://doi.org/10.1007/978-3-030-90870-6_19

To cope with the complexity of HSs, modeling languages like MATLAB Simulink [23] have been proposed and widely adopted in industry. Simulink is a powerful tool for modeling, simulating and testing of dynamic, non-linear HSs. It comes with a graphical editor, a simulation environment, and enables automated code generation. Together with the RL Toolbox [24], it enables the intuitive definition of executable system descriptions of intelligent HSs.

RL is a class of machine learning techniques in which an agent learns a behavioral policy by gaining experience through interaction with its environment. It allows learning adaptable, intelligent controllers, which are often able to outperform manually designed controllers. However, RL components typically learn in a trial and error approach and are thus inherently unsafe components, which contradicts the safety-critical character of HSs. While there exist methods for safe RL that, e.g., apply domain knowledge to ensure that an RL components acts safely [1,9], these methods usually do not consider RL components as parts of a larger system. Furthermore, existing approaches to guarantee safe behavior of RL algorithms require a formal model, e.g., a Markov decision process or a description in formal logic. Such formal models are often not available in industrial design processes, and industrially used modeling languages like Simulink and the RL Toolbox do not have a formally defined semantics. There exist some approaches to overcome this problem for Simulink, but they do not consider RL.

In this paper, we present an approach for semi-automatic deductive verification of HSs with embedded RL components. We target intelligent HSs that are modeled with Simulink and its RL Toolbox. The key ideas of our approach are threefold: First, we capture the safety-relevant behavior of RL components with hybrid contracts [14] in differential dynamic logic ($d\mathcal{L}$) [19]. Thereby, we precisely capture the safe behavior of RL components, while providing "enough" abstraction to not unnecessarily hinder the learning experience of an RL controller. Second, we verify safety properties of the overall system with the RL component replaced by its contract deductively using the interactive theorem prover KeYmaera X. To precisely capture the semantics of intelligent Simulink models, we extend our previously proposed automatic Simulink to $d\mathcal{L}$ transformation [13] to reinforcement learning. Third, we ensure that contracts are complied with at runtime by automatically deriving runtime monitors from our hybrid contracts. The runtime monitors take the current system state as input and decide which of the possible actions of the RL component are safe w.r.t. the hybrid contracts. Note that our approach for runtime monitoring is inspired by and similiar to the approach presented in [9].

We illustrate our approach with an autonomous intelligent factory robot and verify that there are no collisions with moving obstacles. We evaluate in simulation experiments that our safe RL agent is still able to learn a useful policy, and show that the verification process scales well for an increasing number of obstacles and is flexible towards changes in the model.

The rest of this paper is structured as follows: In Sect. 2, we introduce preliminaries. In Sect. 3, we summarize related work. In Sect. 4, we introduce our approach. We present our evaluation results in Sect. 5 and conclude in Sect. 6.

2 Preliminaries

In this section, we introduce RL, Simulink, the RL Toolbox, d$\mathcal{L}$, and our previously proposed Simulink to d$\mathcal{L}$ transformation.

2.1 Reinforcement Learning

Reinforcement learning is a class of machine learning methods for learning in a trial and error approach by interacting with an environment through actions [21]. The mathematical basis for most RL algorithms are Markov decision processes (MDPs) [21]. An MDP is a tuple (S, A, R, p), where S is a set of possible states, A a set of possible actions, $R \subset \mathbb{R}$ a set of rewards, and p a probability distribution. In an MDP, an agent and an environment interact in discrete time steps, as shown in Fig. 1a. At each step t, the agent receives a current state $s_t \in S$ from the environment and chooses an action $a_t \in A$ to interact with it. The environment reacts with a new state $s_{t+1} \in S$ resulting from the applied action and a numeric reward $r_{t+1} \in R$. The probabilities of states s, actions a and rewards r at times t are given by random variables S_t, A_t and R_t. The expected reward r and next state s' resulting from the application of a in s can be expressed as the probability distribution $p(s', r|s, a) \doteq Pr\{S_t = s', \ R_t = r|S_{t-1} = s, \ A_{t-1} = a\}$, also called the dynamics of an MDP. The goal of an RL algorithm is to optimize the reward by learning a policy $\pi(a|s)$ that determines which actions to take in which states. To this end, RL algorithms collect knowledge about sequences of states and actions that lead to a high reward, often in a one-off training phase. RL algorithms primarily differ in the way the policy is learned and updated [21].

2.2 Simulink and the RL Toolbox

Simulink [23] is an industrially well established, graphical modeling language for HSs. Simulink models consist of blocks that are connected by signal lines. Signals can carry discrete or continuous values. The Simulink block library provides a large set of predefined blocks, ranging from arithmetics over control flow blocks to integrators and complex transformations. Together with the MATLAB library, linear and non-linear differential equations can be modeled and simulated. Simulink models can be parameterized by defining workspace variables.

Figure 1c shows a Simulink model of a simple vehicle that samples its position in discrete time intervals and stops if it exceeds a threshold. The position X_{out} of the vehicle is computed by an integrator block, which is fed by a velocity signal. The velocity depends on a switch block. If the current observed position is greater than a STOP constant, the vehicle stops, otherwise it may move with an arbitrary input velocity v_{in}. To model discrete sampling of the vehicles position, the model features a zero order hold X_{hold} before the switch.

The RL toolbox [24] provides an RL agent block, which enables the execution of pre- or user-defined RL algorithms. The RL agent acts in discrete sampling times. It takes observations s_t, rewards r_t, and a flag *isdone* as inputs and yields the action a_t chosen by the RL algorithm, as shown in Fig. 1b.

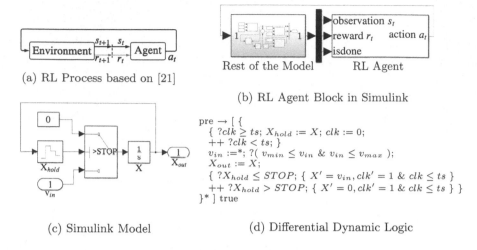

(a) RL Process based on [21]

(b) RL Agent Block in Simulink

(c) Simulink Model

(d) Differential Dynamic Logic

Fig. 1. Reinforcement Learning, Simulink, and d$\mathcal{L}$

2.3 Differential Dynamic Logic

Differential dynamic logic (d$\mathcal{L}$) [19] is a logic for specifying and reasoning about properties of hybrid programs (HPs). HPs are not directly executable, but provide means to formally model the possible behaviors of HSs.

$\alpha; \beta$ models a sequential composition of two HPs α and β. $\alpha \cup \beta$ (or $\alpha ++ \beta$) models a non-deterministic choice between α and β. A non-deterministic loop α^* executes α zero or more times. The HP $x := e$ evaluates the term e and assigns it to the variable x. $x := *$ denotes a non-deterministic assignment. $?\mathcal{Q}$ is a test, which checks whether the formula $\mathcal{Q}$ is fulfilled. Finally, $\{x'_1 = \theta_1, x'_2 = \theta_2, x'_n = \theta_3 \ \& \ \mathcal{Q}\}$ is a continuous evolution, which evolves a set of variables x, with a set of differential equations θ. A continuous evolution may progress for a non-deterministic duration as long as the evolution domain $\mathcal{Q}$ is satisfied.

d$\mathcal{L}$ provides two modalities for reasoning about reachable states of HPs. $[\alpha]\phi$ states that a formula ϕ holds in every state reachable by α. $\langle\alpha\rangle\phi$ states that there exists a state reachable by α in which ϕ holds. Specifications for HPs are defined as $pre \rightarrow [\alpha]post$ with precondition pre and postcondition $post$.

A d$\mathcal{L}$ specification can be deductively verified with the interactive theorem prover KeYmaera X [8]. In KeYmaera X, proofs are automatically stored in tactics, which can be rerun and customized. Interactive deductive reasoning avoids the state space explosion problem and can also be used for infinite-state systems, but requires high expertise and is associated with a steep learning curve [17].

2.4 Simulink2d$\mathcal{L}$ Transformation and Hybrid Contracts

The semantics of Simulink and the RL Toolbox are only informally defined by The MathWorks [23]. To precisely capture the semantics of intelligent HSs, we apply and extend our Simulink to d$\mathcal{L}$ transformation (Simulink2d$\mathcal{L}$)[1] proposed in [13,14] to also support the RL Toolbox. The Simulink2d$\mathcal{L}$ transformation yields a d$\mathcal{L}$ model of the form $pre \rightarrow [\alpha^*]true$, where α is the HP that respresents the combined semantics of individually transformed blocks, and α^* models a global simulation loop. The post condition $true$ may be replaced with the safety property of interest. Preconditions can also be strengthened or relaxed. Note that Simulink2d$\mathcal{L}$ provides an over-approximation of all possible behaviors of a given Simulink model that allows for arbitrarily small numerical errors. To account for this, we restrict ourselves to the use of the modality operator [ ].

Figure 1d shows a simplified d$\mathcal{L}$ model corresponding to the Simulink model depicted in Fig. 1c. The integrator block is captured by a continuous evolution. Depending on the control flow condition ($X_{hold} > STOP$), the X coordinate either evolves with 0 or the input velocity. The discrete sampling time is modeled using a clock variable. If the clock value reaches the sampling time, the clock is reset and the output is set to a new value. The input is modeled by a constrained non-deterministic assignment to consider every possible input scenario.

To handle larger Simulink models, the concept of *hybrid contracts* (HCs) and service-oriented verification has been proposed in [14]. There, Simulink blocks that provide a common functionality are grouped into services. The behavior of such services is abstractly defined in d$\mathcal{L}$ in an assume-guarantee style with $hc = (\phi_{in}, \phi_{out})$, where ϕ_{in} are assumptions on input variables and ϕ_{out} are guarantees on trajectories and outputs. With Simulink2d$\mathcal{L}$, KeYmaera X and HCs, services can be individually verified and then be replaced by their HC in the overall system verification. This enables compositional deductive verification.

3 Related Work

In the last decade, a variety of approaches have been proposed for the formal verification of Simulink. Aside from [14], which we apply and extend in this paper, there also exist other methods that transform Simulink models into formal representations to enable verification. In [2], Simulink models are transformed into the deductive verification platform Why3 [7]. In [11], safety properties for Simulink models are verified via the UCLID verification system [12]. In [20], Simulink models are transformed into Boogie [4] and verified with the Z3 solver [6]. However, contrary to [14], these approaches are limited to discrete subsets of Simulink and do not allow verifying safety properties of hybrid models. This is also true for the Simulink Design Verifier [22] tool provided by The MathWorks.

Formal verification methods that support continuous and hybrid behavior of Simulink models are rare. In [5], the authors propose the tool CheckMate for modeling hybrid automata in Simulink, which can then be formally verified. However, the approach uses specialized blocks and thus models are limited in expressibility compared to Simulink models used in industry. Models are verified by actively exploring the state space via reachability analysis. However, the state space grows exponentially with the number of concurrent blocks, which does

---

[1] https://www.uni-muenster.de/EmbSys/research/Simulink2dL.html.

not scale well for larger systems. The same is true for the transformation from Simulink to the hybrid automata dialect SpaceEx proposed in [15]. Furthermore, none of these methods enables verification of intelligent Simulink models.

Formal methods to ensure the safety of reinforcement learning have seen increased interest in recent years. In [10], Hartsell et al. propose a toolchain for designing HSs with machine learning components. However, while the toolchain provides support for formal verification of some learning components and arguing about acceptable levels of system safety through safety cases, it does not enable (semi-)automated formal verification of overall system properties. In [1], Alshiekh et al. propose the use of a shield, which substitutes unsafe for safe actions and is synthesized from a safety automaton and an abstraction of the environment. In [3] reinforcement learning is combined with safety guarantees by first identifying the safe state-space and then letting the learning algorithm only explore this safe state-space. In [9], Fulton and Platzer ensure the safety of an RL controller via verified runtime monitors based on a differential dynamic logic model. Our approach to ensure the safe behavior of an RL agent is inspired by and similar to this approach. These methods, however, require a formal model, which is often unavailable in industrial design processes. Furthermore, they typically verify the safe behavior of a central RL controller in a given environment and do not view RL as a part of a larger system that is to be developed and verified.

In [18], Phan et al. verify properties of a CPS consisting of unverified advanced controllers with a contract based approach. Contracts for unverified controllers are enforced by switching to pre-certified baseline controllers. However, their baseline controllers are verified manually and they neither provide ways to automatically formally capture nor to semi-automatically verify components together with the modeled environment.

4   Our Approach for Verifying Intelligent Hybrid Systems

In this section, we present our approach for scalable verification of intelligent HSs with embedded RL components. To support industrial design processes, we target intelligent HSs that are modeled with Simulink [23] and the RL Toolbox [24]. Our approach is depicted in Fig. 2. We assume that a given intelligent HS is modeled in Simulink together with the RL Toolbox, that is, it contains an RL agent block. As we adopt the service-oriented approach of [14], it may also contain other (non-intelligent) services that group Simulink blocks together. The key idea of our approach is threefold: ① We solve the problem of formally describing RL agents by capturing their safe behavior in a hybrid contract. This provides a formally well-defined basis for an RL agent's behavior in a HS. ② To overcome the problem that the Simulink semantics is only informally defined, we extend our previously proposed Simulink2d$\mathcal{L}$ transformation [14] to reinforcement learning (SimulinkRL2d$\mathcal{L}$). This enables the transformation of Simulink models with embedded RL components into a formal d$\mathcal{L}$ representation, and thus to use the interactive theorem prover KeYmaera X to verify safety properties deductively. If the verification fails, a counter-example can often be

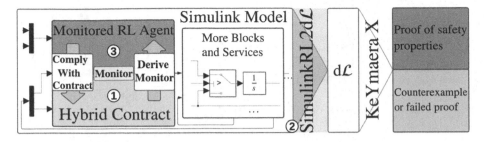

Fig. 2. Visualization of our approach

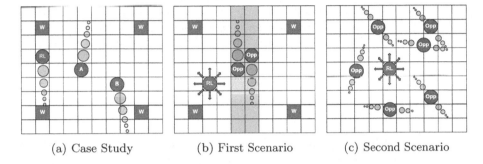

(a) Case Study   (b) First Scenario   (c) Second Scenario

Fig. 3. Scenarios of the case study

obtained, which may be used for debugging. ③ We ensure that the RL agent complies with its HC at simulation time by automatically generating runtime monitors from the HC that check the safety of actions. To illustrate our approach, we use a case study of a learning, autonomous ground robot, which interacts with other traffic participants in a factory setting.

4.1   Running Example: Autonomous Intelligent Robot in a Factory

Our case study consists of a RL ground robot (RL) and two opponents (A,B), which serve as moving obstacles in an abstract factory setting, as depicted in Fig. 3a. The traffic participants may move freely and are not restricted by the visualization as a gridmap. The RL robot is tasked with reaching workstations (W) while avoiding opponents. Positions of the traffic participants are two-dimensional vectors. We define the following abbreviations:

$$Pos_i = (X_i, Y_i) \tag{1}$$

$$d(Pos_i, Pos_j) = \sqrt{(X_i - X_j)^2 + (Y_i - Y_j)^2} \tag{2}$$

$$\hat{d}_{Opp} = \sqrt{(diff_{XOpp}^2 + diff_{YOpp}^2)} \tag{3}$$

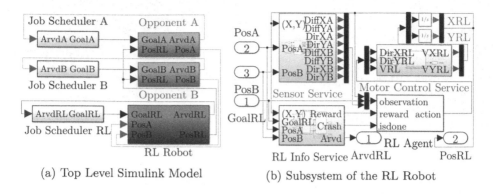

(a) Top Level Simulink Model   (b) Subsystem of the RL Robot

Fig. 4. Simulink model of our case study

where $i,j \in \{RL, A, B\}$, $Opp \in \{A, B\}$ and $diff_{XOpp}$ and $diff_{YOpp}$ are values from the RL robot's sensor (Fig. 4b). Our objective is to define a safe HC for the RL robot's agent and to verify that no collision with the opponents occurs.

Collision Avoidance Concept. We assume our map to be unbounded and that the two opponents are the only obstacles. The opponents and the RL robot feature discrete controllers (in case of the RL robot implemented as an RL agent), which periodically choose a direction and velocity. The movement is continuous. We abstract from acceleration and deceleration, however, harmful movement decisions cannot be corrected instantaneously due to the discrete decision making process together with the continuous movement.

Our collision avoidance concept is inspired by [16]. If the distance of an opponent to the RL robot falls below a safety threshold θ_{Opp}, the opponent evades actively. To ensure that an evasive move succeeds, we require the RL robot to always stop if it reaches θ_{Opp}. To ensure collision freedom as a system property, a safety distance $d_{min,Opp}$ must be maintained between each opponent and the RL robot at all times. We can formally define collision freedom as:

$$d(Pos_{RL}, Pos_A) > d_{min,A} \land d(Pos_{RL}, Pos_B) > d_{min,B}$$

Simulink Model. The top level model of our factory is shown in Fig. 4a. It consists of six main components: the *RL Robot*, the *Opponents A* and *B*, and *Job Schedulers*, which assign goals to the traffic participants. The RL robot is shown in Fig. 4b. The robot receives its current goal and the positions of the opponents, which are forwarded to a *Sensor Service*. The *Sensor Service* outputs the relative positions and movement directions of the opponents. Its implementation as a service allows refinement of the sensor model. The RL robot's goal is to learn to reach workstations (goals) efficiently, while avoiding opponents. For this purpose, it contains an *RL Agent* block, which makes discrete control decisions based on an RL algorithm defined with the RL Toolbox. In each sampling interval, the

RL agent outputs an action consisting of a direction vector and a velocity v_{RL}. The action is forwarded to the *Motor Control Service*, which forwards a velocity vector to integrator blocks. The *RL Info Service* provides the RL *Reward*, stops the simulation in case of a *Crash*, and signals arrival at a workstation (*Arvd*).

4.2   Defining the Safe Behavior of RL Agents with Hybrid Contracts

In our approach, we manually define an RL agent's safe behavior through a hybrid contract $hc = (\phi_{in}, \phi_{out})$ in d$\mathcal{L}$. The HC determines which actions are applicable under which observations. We define the assumptions as a d$\mathcal{L}$ formula $\phi_{in} = f(s_t, p)$ that expresses preconditions under which the RL agent guarantees its postconditions depending on the current system state $s_t \in S$ and the system parameters $p \in P$. The current system state is given by a vector of all inputs to the *observation* port of the RL agent block. The system parameters are given by workspace variables in MATLAB Simulink. Workspace variables are treated as symbolic constants in HCs. This enables the designer to prove safety properties for parameterized systems, e.g., with arbitrary safety distances. The guarantees $\phi_{out} = g(a_t, s_t, p)$ define a d$\mathcal{L}$ formula that expresses the postcondition of the RL agent in terms of safe actions $a_t \in A_{RL} \subseteq A_{d\mathcal{L}}$ depending on the current system state $s_t \in S$ and system parameters $p \in P$. Safe actions A_{safe} are a subset of all actions that are defined as outputs of the RL agent in the MATLAB implementation ($A_{safe} \subseteq A_{RL}$). The domain $A_{d\mathcal{L}}$ that represents possible actions in the HC may be larger than the valid action set of the RL agent ($A_{RL} \subseteq A_{d\mathcal{L}}$).

As an illustrating example, we provide a HC for the RL robot's agent. To avoid crashing, the RL robot needs to stop before reaching the opponents safety threshold (θ_{Opp}). The set of possible system states S observed by the RL agent is the cross product of its own position, the position of the goal, and the relative positions and directions of both opponents. The system parameters used in this model are the safety thresholds θ_{Opp}, sampling times ts_{RL}, and maximum velocities $v_{max,Opp}$. The set of possible actions of the RL agent $A_{RL} \subseteq \mathbb{R}$ is the cross product of possible output velocities v_{RL} and directions (dir_{XRL}, dir_{YRL}). The HC in Table 1 ensures the RL agent's safe behavior. The assumption restricts the system parameters to non-negative values. The guarantee allows the RL agent to choose only velocities v_{RL} as output actions a_t that do not decrease the perceived distance $\hat{d}_{Opp}$ beyond the safety threshold θ_{Opp} in one sampling time ts_{RL}, even if the opponent also decreases the distance with maximum velocity $v_{max,Opp}$. If $\hat{d}_{Opp}$ is less than any threshold θ_{Opp}, the agent must stop ($v_{RL} = 0$).

Describing the safe behavior of an RL agent with a HC provides a formal description of the RL behavior, which is compatible with the existing verification process of [14]. However, finding good HCs is one of the main challenges when using our approach. A HC should precisely capture the safety relevant behavior of an RL agent in d$\mathcal{L}$, it should provide enough abstraction to ease the verification process, and it should be as permissive as possible, i.e., it should not unnecessarily restrict the agent's available actions. The HC of our example is precise in that it ensures that the RL agent acts safely. At the same time, it abstracts from safety irrelevant information, such as the distance to the goals.

Table 1. Hybrid contract of the RL agent for each $Opp \in \{A, B\}$

Assumption	$ts_{RL} \geq 0 \wedge v_{max,Opp} \geq 0 \wedge \theta_{Opp} \geq 0$
Guarantee	$(v_{RL} > 0 \ \wedge \hat{d}_{Opp} - (v_{RL} + v_{max,Opp}) \cdot ts_{RL} > \theta_{Opp}) \vee v_{RL} = 0$

Furthermore, it enables a certain degree of freedom in the choice of actions, e.g., by not restricting the movement direction of the robot. Note, however, that the HC restricts the velocity of the RL robot independent of movement directions. This abstraction eases verification, but also limits the RL robot's behavior.

4.3 Transforming Safe RL Agents to d$\mathcal{L}$

To extend Simulink2d$\mathcal{L}$ to SimulinkRL2d$\mathcal{L}$, we provide a safe semantic translation for monitored RL agents as an additional transformation rule. Furthermore, we have added support for workspace variables via symbolic constants. To precisely capture the semantics of a safe RL agent and to embed it correctly into the surrounding Simulink model, we define the novel transformation rule from RL agent to d$\mathcal{L}$ shown in Fig. 5b. The transformed HP consists of a discrete block and a continuous evolution. The discrete HP selects a safe action according to the HC whenever the RL agent's sample time elapses. To model the sample time, we use a fresh clock variable clk, which ensures that the HC is evaluated at each discrete step. Our transformation of a monitored RL agent enables integration into the existing Simulink2d$\mathcal{L}$ approach of [13] and automated transformation of intelligent Simulink models into d$\mathcal{L}$. This captures their semantics formally.

In our running example, each of the services of the *RL Robot* (Fig. 4b) is replaced by a HC. Thereby, the HC of the *RL Agent* is transformed and embedded according to our transformation rule (Fig. 5b). Listing 1.1 shows a simplified version of the resulting HP, with only *Opponent A* considered. Note that the *RL Info Service* is omitted here, as its behavior is not relevant for collision freedom. The *Sensor Services* (Line 2–3) HC captures how the relative position of an opponent is calculated. Lines 4-8 show the transformed monitored RL agent, Lines 5-7 the embedded HC. The *Motor Control Service* (Lines 9-11) is captured by two HCs. These state that the norm of the output vector always equals the input velocity (Line 10), except for when the direction is (0,0) (Line 11).

Our SimulinkRL2d$\mathcal{L}$ transformation enables the automated translation of intelligent HSs that are modeled with Simulink and the RL Toolbox into d$\mathcal{L}$ specifications. Together with the concept of HCs and our monitoring-based safe RL approach, we can ensure safety properties of the overall system for all possible input scenarios and even for varying parameters.

4.4 Enforcing the Safe Behavior of RL Agents

To ensure that an RL agent acts safely at runtime, we propose to use runtime monitoring. Our HCs enable us to concisely and precisely define the set of safe

```
1   pre → [ { Pos_A := *; ... Pos_RL=(X_RL,Y_RL); /*Input and Output Assignments*/
2       diff_XA := *; diff_YA := *; dir_XA := *; dir_YA := *; ... /*Sensor HCs*/
3       ?true→(diff_XA = X_A − X_RL & diff_YA = Y_A − Y_RL); ...
4     { ?(clk ≥ ts_RL);
5         clk := 0; dir_XRL := *; dir_YRL := *; v_RL := *; /*Transformed Safe RL Agent*/
6         ?ts_RL ≥ 0 & v_max,A ≥ 0 & θ_A ≥ 0 & ... →
7             (v_RL > 0 & â_A − (v_RL + v_max,A) · ts_RL > θ_A & ... | v_RL = 0)
8       ++ ?(clk < ts_RL); }
9       v_XRL := *; v_YRL := *; /*Motor Control HCs*/
10      ?(v_RL ≥ 0 & (dir_XRL ≠ 0|dir_YRL ≠ 0)) → √(v²_XRL + v²_YRL) = v_RL;
11      ?(dir_XRL = 0 & dir_YRL = 0) → √(v²_XRL + v²_YRL) = 0;
12    { time' = 1, clk' = 1, X'_RL = v_XRL, Y'_RL = v_YRL & clk ≤ ts_RL } }* ] true
```

Listing 1.1. Simplified d$\mathcal{L}$ model of the RL robot (Colors correspond to Fig. 4b)

actions that may be chosen in a given system state. This enables us to automatically derive runtime monitors that check adherence of each action of the RL agent to the HCs in each system state, as it has also been proposed in [9].

Our safe RL approach with runtime monitoring is shown in Fig. 5a. The *learn* method is called by our safe RL agent in each sampling step in the training phase. After the training phase, the best known action a_t is still chosen from A_{safe}, but the RL knowledge representation is not updated further. The *learn* method receives the previous state s_{t-1} and action a_{t-1}, as well as the current state s_t and reward r_t from the surrounding Simulink model. The methods *update* and *choose* abstractly represent the underlying RL algorithm of the RL agent. The *update* method updates the knowledge that the RL algorithm uses for its decisions, e.g. a Q-table, with the experience gained from applying a_{t-1} in s_{t-1} and reaching state s_t with reward r_t. The set of safe actions A_{safe} is then determined by a contract monitor $CM : S \times A \times P \rightarrow Bool$ and the currently best possible action $a_t \in A_{safe}$ according to the RL algorithm is chosen (*choose*). We assume that the non-emptiness of the set A_{safe} is ensured by the developer. The contract monitor checks whether some action a is safe in a given state s_t with respect to the RL agent's HC under given system parameters p. It can automatically be derived from a given HC by transforming it to its HP form and using the code generation capabilities of KeYmaera X. If symbolic constants are used within the HC, parameterized monitors are generated, and arbitrary fixed values may be chosen for each simulation.

Note that in [9], the authors also restrict RL agent's to the behavior of a verified non-deterministic control policy via a controller monitor. Compared to the original approach of [9], however, we do not distinguish a model and a controller monitor because our monitored RL agent is fully verified together with its execution environment. Instead, we derive the safe actions directly from our HC and decide about the safety of actions using the observations and actions from our Simulink model with an embedded RL agent.

Input: last state s_{t-1}, last action
    a_{t-1}, reward r_t, current
    state s_t
Data: all actions A, safe actions
    A_{safe}
Output: safe action a_t
Function
    Learn($s_{t-1}, a_{t-1}, r_t, s_t, p$):
        update($s_{t-1}, a_{t-1}, r_t, s_t$);
        $A_{safe} = \{a \in A|CM(s_t, a, p)\}$;
        $a_t = \text{choose}(A_{safe})$;
        return a_t;
End

(a) Safe Simulink RL Agents: Learning

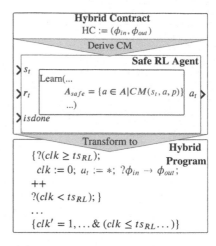

(b) Transformation of an RL Agent

Fig. 5. Safe reinforcement learning

5   Evaluation

To demonstrate the applicability of our approach, we 1) discuss the results from our running example. 2) To evaluate scalability, we add four additional opponents and re-verify the collision freedom property. 3) To show the flexibility of our approach, we add noise to the RL robot's sensors and show that such disturbances can be taken into account. 4) We illustrate the effective safety of our intelligent Simulink model by comparing the executions of a safe and an unsafe agent in simulation experiments. All models and proofs are available online.[2]

5.1   Case Study of an Autonomous Robot in a Factory

To verify collision freedom for our running example, we have defined HCs for the *RL Robot* and the *Opponents*, used our SimulinkRL2d$\mathcal{L}$ transformation, and KeYmaera X on the resulting d$\mathcal{L}$ model. Note that our Simulink model is parameterized in the sense that workspace variables are used for maximum velocities, minimal safety distances, and sampling times. The resulting proof holds for all possible input scenarios and parameters.

Both the RL robot and the opponent move continuously, but take discrete control decisions. The HCs for the RL robot and the opponents are shown in Table 2. $Pos_{old,i}$ denotes the last known position of a traffic participant i, δ the time that passed since the last loop iteration, and ts_{Opp} the sampling time of the opponents. The HC of the RL robot assumes that the movement of the opponents is restricted by their maximum velocity $v_{max,Opp}$ and guarantees that

---

Table 2. Hybrid contracts for the RL robot and the opponents

RL Robot	**Assumption**	$d(Pos_{old,Opp}, Pos_{Opp}) \leq v_{max,Opp} \cdot \delta$
	Guarantee	$d(Pos_{old,Opp}, Pos_{RL}) > \theta_{Opp} \vee Pos_{RL} = Pos_{old,RL}$
Opponent Evasion	**Assumptions**	$(d(Pos_{old,Opp}, Pos_{RL}) > \theta_{Opp} \vee Pos_{RL} = Pos_{old,RL}) \wedge$
		$\theta_{Opp} \geq d_{min,Opp} + v_{max,Opp} \cdot ts_{Opp} \wedge$
		$d(Pos_{old,Opp}, Pos_{RL}) > d_{min,Opp}$
	Guarantee	$d(Pos_{Opp}, Pos_{RL}) > d_{min,Opp}$
Opponent Velocity	**Assumption**	$true$
	Guarantee	$d(Pos_{Opp}, Pos_{old,Opp}) \leq v_{max,Opp} \cdot \delta$

it stops at a safe distance before any opponents threshold θ_{Opp}, as is ensured by the RL agent's HC at a lower level.

The first HC for the opponent (*Opponent Evasion*) guarantees that if the RL robot's new position is safe w.r.t. the opponents old position, the independently chosen new position of the opponent will also be safe. Note that as an assumption, the opponents threshold must leave enough room to detect an RL robot in time to ensure that if a threshold is violated at least one control decision is made by the opponent before it can collide. The second HC for the opponent (*Opponent Velocity*) guarantees that the opponent never moves faster than allowed by its maximum velocity. For brevity, we omitted the assumption of non-negative sampling times *ts* and velocities *v* in Table 2.

We have successfully verified that the RL robot and the opponents satisfy their HCs and that the overall system is collision free in KeYmaera X. Modeling and verifying the case study resulted in comparatively compact d$\mathcal{L}$ models. For example, the RL robot consists of 114, the opponents of 83, and the top level of our case study of 103 lines of d$\mathcal{L}$. The overall interactive verification time was approx. 20 person hours, mainly allocated to the opponent and the RL robot.

5.2 Collision Freedom with Additional Opponents

The required effort and expertise for interactive verification with KeYmaera X is considerable. However, one of the major advantages of our approach is that verified HCs can be reused in larger systems. Together with the deductive verification capabilities of KeYmaera X, this means that our approach scales well for a larger number of components. To demonstrate this, we have added four additional opponents and job schedulers to our case study, and verified the RL robot's HC for each opponent by applying tactical replacements. With that, we have verified the collision freedom property for the case study with six opponents in 20 additional minutes.

5.3 Collision Freedom with Additional Sensor Disturbances

Capturing the safe behavior of an RL agent through a HC enables us to take changes in a model into account. Also, service-oriented modeling and verification

Table 3. Modified hybrid contracts with noise

Modified Sensor	Assumption	$n_{min} \geq 0 \wedge n_{max} \geq n_{min} \wedge \hat{d}_{max} \geq 0$
	Guarantee	$n_{Opp} \geq n_{min} \wedge n_{max} \geq n_{Opp} \wedge$
		$(d(Pos_{Opp}, Pos_{RL}) \cdot n_{Opp} \leq \hat{d}_{max}$
		$\rightarrow \hat{d}_{Opp} = d(Pos_{Opp}, Pos_{RL}) \cdot n_{Opp}) \wedge$
		$(d(Pos_{Opp}, Pos_{RL}) \cdot n_{Opp} > \hat{d}_{max} \rightarrow \hat{d}_{Opp} = \hat{d}_{max})$
Modified RL Agent	Assumption	$n_{min} \geq 0 \wedge n_{max} \geq n_{min} \wedge n_{max} \geq 1 \wedge \hat{d}_{max} \geq 0$
	Guarantee	$\hat{d}_{Opp}/n_{max} - (v_{RL} + v_{max,Opp}) \cdot ts_{RL} > \theta_{Opp}$

enables us to make changes and to refine parts of a model with comparatively low additional verification effort. Overall, this results in a flexible approach, which enables us to reuse HCs and verification results if the model is changed.

To demonstrate this flexibility, we have modified the RL robot sensor by adding noise and a maximum measurable distance, and we have derived a new HC for the agent, as shown in Table 3. To introduce disturbance, we multiply the perceived distance $\hat{d}_{Opp}$ with a noise factor $n_{Opp} \geq 0$, which is generated from a uniform distribution. This stretches or shrinks the perceived distance to the opponent. We additionally limit the sensors range. If the perceived distance exceeds a maximum distance, $\hat{d}_{Opp}$ is set to $\hat{d}_{max}$. For $n_{Opp} > 1$, the perceived distance can exceed the actual distance. Given that the maximum possible noise factor n_{max} is known, however, we can compute the maximum distance as perceived distance relative to n_{max}.

5.4 Simulation Experiments

Our approach enables us to model and verify safe intelligent HSs. Furthermore, with the contract monitor, we can enforce safe behavior of an RL agent at simulation time. To illustrate that collisions are effectively prevented by our safety concept, we compare our monitored safe RL agent with a default RL agent in a first experiment. The default RL agent uses the same learning algorithm but does not implement a monitor to enforce safe behavior. In a second experiment, we demonstrate that our safety concept prevents collisions in dangerous scenarios even without a sophisticated RL algorithm. To this end, we compare a random agent that uses a safety monitor with a random agent that does not use such precautions in a totally chaotic environment.

Our first test scenario is depicted in Fig. 3b. It consists of four workstations and a road leading vertically through the factory. Two opponents (*Opp*) move up and down separate lanes of the road. The RL agents receive positive rewards for decreasing the distance to a workstation and for reaching a workstation. They are punished for colliding with an opponent or getting into an opponents safety threshold. Both agents use an approximate Q-learning algorithm with a custom approximation function. The function combines manually defined features, which describe implications of actions in certain states, for example, whether

Table 4. Simulation results

		Default RL agent	Safe RL agent		Default random	Safe random
Training	Crashes	0/250	0/250	**2 Opp**	753/1000 crashes	0/1000 crashes
Final simulation	First crash at	49689	no crash			
	Below threshold	8 times	25 times	**6 Opp**	965/1000 crashes	0/1000 crashes
	Goals reached	2945	4960			

the application of an action in the current state is likely to decrease the distance to the goal or whether it will likely decrease or increase the distance to the closest opponent. We have trained each agent for 250 episodes with a maximum of 120 steps each. After training, we have simulated both agents again for 100000 steps. The left half of Table 4 shows the results. The default agent crashed during the final simulation after 49689 steps. The safe RL agent never crashed neither in training nor in simulation and thus acted safely. However, although the safe agent was simulated for more than twice as long, it only reached 68% more goals. This indicates that the HC impedes its performance. For this scenario, we additionally observed the overhead induced by the runtime monitoring approach. The average runtime of the safe agent's *Learn* method, which uses the additional contract monitor as shown in Fig. 5a, exceeded the average runtime of the default agent's *Learn* method without monitoring by approximately 10%.

Our second test scenario is depicted in Fig. 3c. To model a chaotic environment, each opponent gets a random safe start position, and two random goals. These change in each training episode. The random agent uses a greedy policy with $\epsilon = 1$ in a chaotic environment, i.e., it can choose any action in any state. The safe random agent chooses randomly from the filtered set of actions allowed by its HC. We have simulated the models for both the default random agent as well as the safe random agent with two and six opponents for 1000 episodes with a maximum of 120 steps. The results are shown in the right half of Table 4. The safe random agent never crashed in any of the experiments. The default random agent crashed in a majority of episodes. This demonstrates that our safety concept is a decisive factor in ensuring collision freedom for the overall system.

6   Conclusion

In this paper, we have presented an approach for formal verification of industrially designed, intelligent hybrid systems with embedded RL components. To capture the safe behavior of RL components formally and abstractly, we propose to use hybrid contracts, which provide a flexible, formally well-defined interface for designing safe RL components and allow taking system parameters into account. To provide a formal semantics for intelligent HSs with RL components that are modeled with the industrially widely used modeling language Simulink and the RL Toolbox, we have extended our previously proposed Simulink2d$\mathcal{L}$ transformation [13] for RL components. This leads to a precise formal representation of an overall HS with embedded safe RL components in d$\mathcal{L}$, which can be formally verified with KeYmaera X. To ensure that RL agents comply with their hybrid contract at simulation time, we have proposed a runtime monitoring approach inspired by [9]. In contrast to [9], we use the observations and actions from a Simulink model, derive monitors directly from our hybrid contracts, and verify safety properties not only for the RL agent but for an overall intelligent system where the RL agent is only one component.

We have demonstrated the applicability, scalability and flexibility of our approach with a case study, in which we modeled an autonomous intelligent robot and its environment in an abstract factory setting and verified collision freedom. In simulation experiments, we have also shown that the verified intelligent robot with a monitored RL component behaves safely, while the inclusion of an unsafe agent leads to collisions with other traffic participants.

In future work, we plan to also verify intelligent HSs with zero crossing semantics. Furthermore, we also plan to investigate the cost of enforcing an agent's safe behavior through a contract in terms of performance. Finally, we also plan to investigate templates or contract design patterns. As one example, we believe that the safety distances we have used in this paper can be transferred to other applications, where a discrete controller keeps some variables in certain bounds. In such cases, the contract can be derived from the desired bounds plus the reaction time of the HS, as we did for our autonomous robot. To define templates for such scenarios would greatly ease the manual contract design and increase the reusability of existing specifications.

References

1. Alshiekh, M., Bloem, R., Ehlers, R., Könighofer, B., Niekum, S., Topcu, U.: Safe reinforcement learning via shielding. In: Proceedings of the AAAI Conference on Artificial Intelligence, vol. 32 (2018)
2. Araiza-Illan, D., Eder, K., Richards, A.: Formal verification of control systems properties with theorem proving. In: 2014 UKACC International Conference on Control, CONTROL 2014 - Proceedings, pp. 244–249. IEEE (2014)
3. Ashok, P., Křetínský, J., Larsen, K.G., Le Coënt, A., Taankvist, J.H., Weininger, M.: SOS: safe, optimal and small strategies for hybrid markov decision processes. In: Parker, D., Wolf, V. (eds.) QEST 2019. LNCS, vol. 11785, pp. 147–164. Springer, Cham (2019). https://doi.org/10.1007/978-3-030-30281-8_9
4. Barnett, M., Chang, B.-Y.E., DeLine, R., Jacobs, B., Leino, K.R.M.: Boogie: a modular reusable verifier for object-oriented programs. In: de Boer, F.S., Bonsangue, M.M., Graf, S., de Roever, W.-P. (eds.) FMCO 2005. LNCS, vol. 4111, pp. 364–387. Springer, Heidelberg (2006). https://doi.org/10.1007/11804192_17
5. Chutinan, A., Krogh, B.H.: Computational techniques for hybrid system verification. IEEE Trans. Autom. Control **48**(1), 64–75 (2003)
6. de Moura, L., Bjørner, N.: Z3: an efficient SMT solver. In: Ramakrishnan, C.R., Rehof, J. (eds.) TACAS 2008. LNCS, vol. 4963, pp. 337–340. Springer, Heidelberg (2008). https://doi.org/10.1007/978-3-540-78800-3_24

7. Filliâtre, J.-C., Paskevich, A.: Why3 — where programs meet provers. In: Felleisen, M., Gardner, P. (eds.) ESOP 2013. LNCS, vol. 7792, pp. 125–128. Springer, Heidelberg (2013). https://doi.org/10.1007/978-3-642-37036-6_8

8. Fulton, N., Mitsch, S., Quesel, J.-D., Völp, M., Platzer, A.: KeYmaera X: an axiomatic tactical theorem prover for hybrid systems. In: Felty, A.P., Middeldorp, A. (eds.) CADE 2015. LNCS (LNAI), vol. 9195, pp. 527–538. Springer, Cham (2015). https://doi.org/10.1007/978-3-319-21401-6_36

9. Fulton, N., Platzer, A.: Safe reinforcement learning via formal methods: toward safe control through proof and learning. In: Proceedings of the AAAI Conference on Artificial Intelligence, vol. 32 (2018)

10. Hartsell, C., et al.: Model-based design for CPS with learning-enabled components. In: Proceedings of the Workshop on Design Automation for CPS and IoT, pp. 1–9. DESTION '19, Association for Computing Machinery, New York, NY, USA (2019)

11. Herber, P., Reicherdt, R., Bittner, P.: Bit-precise formal verification of discrete-time MATLAB/Simulink models using SMT solving. In: International Conference on Embedded Software (EMSOFT), pp. 1–10. IEEE (2013)

12. Lahiri, S.K., Seshia, S.A.: The UCLID decision procedure. In: Alur, R., Peled, D.A. (eds.) CAV 2004. LNCS, vol. 3114, pp. 475–478. Springer, Heidelberg (2004). https://doi.org/10.1007/978-3-540-27813-9_40

13. Liebrenz, T., Herber, P., Glesner, S.: Deductive verification of hybrid control systems modeled in simulink with keymaera X. In: Sun, J., Sun, M. (eds.) ICFEM 2018. LNCS, vol. 11232, pp. 89–105. Springer, Cham (2018). https://doi.org/10.1007/978-3-030-02450-5_6

14. Liebrenz, T., Herber, P., Glesner, S.: A service-oriented approach for decomposing and verifying hybrid system models. In: Arbab, F., Jongmans, S.-S. (eds.) FACS 2019. LNCS, vol. 12018, pp. 127–146. Springer, Cham (2020). https://doi.org/10.1007/978-3-030-40914-2_7

15. Minopoli, S., Frehse, G.: SL2SX translator: from simulink to spaceex models. In: Proceedings of the 19th International Conference on Hybrid Systems: Computation and Control, pp. 93–98. HSCC '16, Association for Computing Machinery, New York, NY, USA (2016)

16. Mitsch, S., Ghorbal, K., Vogelbacher, D., Platzer, A.: Formal verification of obstacle avoidance and navigation of ground robots. Int. J. Robot. Res. **36**(12), 1312–1340 (2017)

17. Mitsch, S., Platzer, A.: The KeYmaera X Proof IDE - concepts on usability in hybrid systems theorem proving. Electronic Proceedings in Theoretical Computer Science, vol. 240 (2017)

18. Phan, D., et al.: A component-based simplex architecture for high-assurance cyber-physical systems. In: 2017 17th International Conference on Application of Concurrency to System Design (ACSD), pp. 49–58. IEEE (2017)

19. Platzer, A.: Differential dynamic logic for hybrid systems. J. Autom. Reason. **41**(2), 143–189 (2008)

20. Reicherdt, R., Glesner, S.: Formal verification of discrete-time MATLAB/Simulink models using boogie. In: Giannakopoulou, D., Salaün, G. (eds.) SEFM 2014. LNCS, vol. 8702, pp. 190–204. Springer, Cham (2014). https://doi.org/10.1007/978-3-319-10431-7_14

21. Sutton, R.S., Barto, A.G.: Reinforcement Learning: An Introduction, 2nd edn. The MIT Press Cambridge, Massachusetts London, England (2018)

22. The MathWorks: White Paper: Code Verification and Run-Time Error Detection Through Abstract Interpretation (2008)

23. The MathWorks: MATLAB Simulink (2021). www.mathworks.com/products/simulink.html
24. The MathWorks: Reinforcement Learning Toolbox (2021). https://www.mathworks.com/products/reinforcement-learning.html

Hybrid Systems Verification with Isabelle/HOL: Simpler Syntax, Better Models, Faster Proofs

Simon Foster[1]([✉]), Jonathan Julián Huerta y Munive[2], Mario Gleirscher[3], and Georg Struth[4]

[1] University of York, York, UK
`simon.foster@york.ac.uk`
[2] University of Copenhagen, Copenhagen, Denmark
[3] University of Bremen, Bremen, Germany
[4] University of Sheffield, Sheffield, UK

Abstract. We extend a semantic verification framework for hybrid systems with the Isabelle/HOL proof assistant by an algebraic model for hybrid program stores, a shallow expression model for hybrid programs and their correctness specifications, and domain-specific deductive and calculational support. The new store model yields clean separations and dynamic local views of variables, e.g. discrete/continuous, mutable/immutable, program/logical, and enhanced ways of manipulating them using combinators, projections and framing. This leads to more local inference rules, procedures and tactics for reasoning with invariant sets, certifying solutions of hybrid specifications or calculating derivatives with increased proof automation and scalability. The new expression model provides more user-friendly syntax, better control of name spaces and interfaces connecting the framework with real-world modelling languages.

1 Introduction

Deductive verification of hybrid systems with interactive proof assistants like Coq, HOL or Isabelle is currently gaining traction [1–8]. Such tools have reached a level of maturity, proof power and mathematical library support that makes the development of formal methods fast, dependable and competitive. With Isabelle/HOL, an impressive theory stack for ordinary differential equations (ODEs) [9] has been combined with algebras of programs and concrete hybrid program semantics into a semantic framework for reasoning about hybrid systems [5]. So far, the focus has been on the foundations, exploring Isabelle's mathematical and theory engineering facilities, supporting verification workflows for hybrid systems and formalising basic verification components for Isabelle.

Here we transform it towards a formal method. We supply a more refined hybrid program store model to reason about discrete and continuous, mutable and immutable, logical and program variables more locally using lenses [10] (Sect. 3). These allow us to refine the framework's deductive and calculational

© Springer Nature Switzerland AG 2021
M. Huisman et al. (Eds.): FM 2021, LNCS 13047, pp. 367–386, 2021.
https://doi.org/10.1007/978-3-030-90870-6_20

rules for hybrid systems, including inference rules à la differential dynamic logic (d$\mathcal{L}$) [11] (Sect. 5) and framing conditions for local reasoning about mutable continuous variables. We supply a new d$\mathcal{L}$-style ghost rule for invariant sets, a new frame rule à la separation logic, and more effective tactics, for instance for calculating framed Fréchet derivatives (Sect. 6). We use Isabelle's syntax translation mechanisms to create a more user-friendly specification language for the framework (Sect. 4). It is meant to be extensible to modelling languages such as Modelica and computer algebra systems such as Mathematica. These main contributions are explained through examples (Sect. 7). Additional contributions are highlighted throughout the text. Next we outline the main features of the framework to contextualise these contributions and prepare for the technical sections.

The framework [5] has been formalised as a shallow embedding within Isabelle. The benefits of shallowness are well documented [12,13]. A drawback addressed by our expression model is that syntactic properties of variables or expressions may be hard to capture. The framework is compositional with respect to three semantic layers: abstract algebras of programs are used for deriving structural program transformation laws and for verification condition generation (VCG) by equational reasoning. Isabelle's type polymorphism allows their instantiation, for example to state transformer semantics and further to concrete semantics of hybrid program stores—the level at which basic commands such as assignments are modelled. The store extension to hybrid programs is obtained by a state transformer semantics for continuous evolution commands. These commands specify ODEs via vector fields, and guards imposing boundary conditions on state spaces. The associated state transformer maps initial states of evolutions to their guarded orbits, or more general sets of reachable states. Our new hybrid store model supports general name spaces, dynamic stores and various implementations via functions, records or monads.

Users of the framework need to specify hybrid programs and partial correctness specifications with pre/postconditions and loop invariants. Two main workflows are then supported. If ODEs have unique solutions, one can certify them or even rely on automatic certification [14–16], then trigger automatic VCG and discharge the remaining proof obligations by reasoning about solutions in state spaces. More generally, one can assert invariant sets [17] for ODEs, trigger VCG and then reason about the invariants. So far, these two workflows have relied on Isabelle's internal support for equational reasoning, which seems natural for mathematicians or engineers. Here we make them more automatic by reasoning locally with certification conditions, invariant assertions or derivatives, and more structured by supporting data-level reasoning with invariants using d$\mathcal{L}$-style inference rules, for those who like this approach. Capturing fresh variables is instrumental for our new d$\mathcal{L}$-inspired ghost rule; projecting on mutable variables simplifies proof obligations and localises reasoning about them.

The framework has been tested successfully on a large set of hybrid verification benchmarks [18]. Our enhancements yield at least the same performance; initial case studies suggest a simplification of user interaction. More substantial experiments are left for future work. Our new components, integrated into a simplified version of the framework, can be found online[1].

2   Semantic Preliminaries

We first recall the basics of state and predicate transformers, the semantics of evolution commands and the set-up for our new hybrid store model [5, 10]. The semantics can be motivated using the hybrid program syntax of d$\mathcal{L}$ [11], $X :: = x := e \mid x' = f \& G \mid ?P \mid X ; X \mid X + X \mid X^*$. Beyond standard constructs of dynamic logic it features an *evolution command* $x' = f \& G$. It specifies a vector field $f : T \to \mathcal{S} \to \mathcal{S}$ with time domain T over a state space $\mathcal{S}$ and a *guard* $G : \mathcal{S} \to \mathbb{B}$, a predicate modelling boundary conditions.

State and Predicate Transformers. We model programs as *state transformers* $\alpha : \mathcal{S} \to \mathcal{PS}$, arrows of the Kleisli category of the powerset monad. (Forward) Kleisli composition $(\alpha \circ_K \beta) x = \bigcup \{ \beta y \mid y \in \alpha x \}$ models sequential composition, the program skip is the monadic unit $\eta_{\mathcal{S}} x = \{x\}$, abort is $\lambda x. \emptyset$, nondeterministic choice $\cup$ on functions and finite iteration $\alpha^* x = \bigcup_{i \in \mathbb{N}} \alpha^i x$, with powers defined using $\circ_K$. Tests and assertions are subidentities (functions $P \leq \eta_{\mathcal{S}}$, with $\leq$ extended pointwise) mapping any $x \in \mathcal{S}$ either to $\{x\}$ or $\emptyset$. They are isomorphic to sets and predicates, thus we abuse notation and use them interchangeably. Deterministic functions $\sigma : \mathcal{S} \to \mathcal{S}$ can be embedded into $\mathcal{S} \to \mathcal{PS}$ with the notation $\langle \sigma \rangle = \eta_{\mathcal{S}} \circ \sigma$. Backward diamond operators (disjunctive predicate transformers with contravariant composition) are Kleisli extensions of state transformers, forward box or *wlp* operators are their right adjoints on the boolean algebra of tests: $\mathit{wlp}\, \alpha\, Q = \{x \mid \alpha x \subseteq Q\}$ for any program α and test Q. We often write $\{P\}\, \alpha\, \{Q\}$ for partial correctness assertions $P \subseteq \mathit{wlp}\, \alpha\, Q$.

While the laws of propositional Hoare logic (ignoring assignments) are derivable in this semantics, equational VCG with $\mathit{wlp}\, (\alpha \circ_K \beta) = \mathit{wlp}\, \alpha \circ \mathit{wlp}\, \beta$ and $\mathit{wlp}\, (\text{if } P \text{ then } \alpha \text{ else } \beta)\, Q = (\overline{P} \cup \mathit{wlp}\, \alpha\, Q) \cap (P \cap \mathit{wlp}\, \beta\, Q)$ is more effective, while the standard Hoare rule can be used for loops decorated with invariants.

Continuous Dynamics. The evolution of continuous systems [17] is often modelled by *(local) flows* $\varphi : T \to \mathcal{S} \to \mathcal{S}$, where $T \subseteq \mathbb{R}$ models time and $\mathcal{S}$ a state space. Flows are assumed to be C^1-functions, and monoid actions if $T = \mathbb{R}$: $\varphi(t + t') = \varphi t \circ \varphi t'$ and $\varphi 0 = id_{\mathcal{S}}$. A *trajectory* $\varphi_s : T \to \mathcal{S}$ of φ at $s \in \mathcal{S}$ is then a curve $\varphi_s t = \varphi t s$, and its *orbit* at $s \in \mathcal{S}$ is given by state transformer $\gamma^\varphi : \mathcal{S} \to \mathcal{PS}, s \mapsto \mathcal{P} \varphi_s T$. It maps any state s to the set of states on the trajectory passing through it. Flows are typically solutions to *initial value problems* for systems of ODEs. These specify a *vector field* $f : T \to \mathcal{S} \to \mathcal{S}$ assigning vectors to points in space-time and an initial value $s \in \mathcal{S}$ at $t_0 \in T$. A

---

[1] github.com/isabelle-utp/Hybrid-Verification, also by clicking our 🐟 icons.

solution is then a C^1-function X that satisfies $X't = ft(Xt)$ and $Xt_0 = s$. For f continuous, existence of X is guaranteed by the Peano theorem. Yet f must be Lipschitz continuous to guarantee uniqueness via the Picard-Lindelöf theorem, which provides intervals $Us \subseteq T$ where solutions exist around t_0 for each $s \in S$ and gives rise to flows when $t_0 = 0$.

Semantics of Evolution Commands. Orbit maps $\gamma^\varphi : S \to PS$ are state transformers, but we generalise them to include guards and to depend on continuous vector fields. Our state transformer for evolution commands maps each $s \in S$ to the set of reachable states (or *generalised orbit*)

$$(x' = f\,\&\,G)\,s = \{Xt \mid t \in Us \wedge (\forall \tau \in \downarrow_{U\,s}\,t.\ G(X\tau)) \wedge X't = ft(Xt) \wedge Xt_0 = s\},$$

with $t_0 \in Us$ and where $\downarrow_{U\,s}\,t$ is the downward-closure of t in Us, often coinciding in applications with the interval $[t_0, t]$. The set Us constrains the domain of existence of the solutions X. If we know the flow φ for f, then this semantics reduces to $(x' = f\,\&\,G)\,s = \{\varphi t s \mid t \in Us \wedge (\forall \tau \in \downarrow_{U\,s}\,t.\ G(\varphi \tau s))\}$.

This state transformer maps any $s \in S$ to all reachable states along any solution to f. Thus $wlp\,(x' = f\,\&\,G)\,Q$ holds iff for every $t \in Us$, if $G(X\tau)$ holds for all $\tau \in \downarrow_{U\,s}\,t$, then $Q(Xt)$ holds as well. Computing wlps within the remits of Picard-Lindelöf is then straightforward: users only need to supply and certify the flow φ within the first workflow outlined in Sect. 1.

Invariant Sets. Instead of analytic solutions, one can use the generalised orbit semantics in combination with generalised invariant sets in the second workflow. Invariant sets [17] are preserved by the orbit map of the dynamical system. With guards, more generally, $I \subseteq S$ is an *invariant set* of $(x' = f\,\&\,G)$ whenever $(x' = f\,\&\,G)^\dagger\,I \subseteq I$, where $(-)^\dagger$ indicates Kleisli extension and yields a backward modal diamond operator. The adjunction mentioned translates this property into $I \subseteq wlp\,(x' = f\,\&\,G)\,I$, the standard format for invariance reasoning with predicate transformers [5]. Intuitively, such invariants characterise regions of the state space that contain all orbits that satisfy G and have a point inside them. It then suffices to assert suitable invariants in order to verify a correctness specification. We discuss invariance techniques for evolution commands in Sect. 5.

Lenses. Our algebraic model for hybrid stores is based on lenses [10,19], a tool for manipulating program stores or state spaces, which comes in many variants and guises [20–22], in support of algebraic reasoning about program variables and local reasoning about store shapes [23].

A *lens* $\lambda : V \Rightarrow S$ is a pair $(get_\lambda : S \to V, put_\lambda : V \to S \to S)$ such that

$$get_\lambda\,(put_\lambda\,v\,s) = v, \qquad put_\lambda\,v \circ put_\lambda\,v' = put_\lambda\,v, \qquad put_\lambda\,(get_\lambda s)\,s = s,$$

for all $v, v' \in V$ and $s \in S$. Lenses are arrows in a category [20], as outlined in Sect. 3 below. They admit many interpretations. Typically, S is a set of program stores. Yet $\mathcal{V}$ could be a smaller or simpler set of stores, $get\,s$ could forget part of $s \in \mathcal{S}$ and $put\,v\,s$ overwrite part of s with $v \in \mathcal{V}$. Otherwise, $\mathcal{V}$ could be a value domain, $get\,s$ could look up a value in s and $put\,v\,s$ could update s with v.

We use *variable lenses* $x : \mathcal{V} \Rightarrow \mathcal{S}$ to model program variables x, $get_x\,s$ to look up values in $\mathcal{V}$ in stores s and $put_x\,v\,s$ to update values in s by v. A variety of concrete store models can then be implemented using different variable lenses, such as partial functions and arrays [10,23]. A *variable assignment* $x := e$, with expression e represented semantically as a function $\mathcal{S} \rightarrow \mathcal{V}$, is then a state transformer $(x := e) = \langle \lambda s.\, put_x\,(e\,s)\,s \rangle$, and $wlp\,(x := e)\,Q = \lambda s.\, Q\,(put_x\,(e\,s)\,s)$. This suffices for VCG for hybrid programs without evolution commands.

3 Hybrid Store Components

Lenses enhance our hybrid store models in several ways. They provide an algebraic characterisation of observations and mutations of program variables, which can be instantiated with different concrete store types. They allow us to model frames—sets of mutable variables—and thus support local reasoning. They also allow us to project parts of the global store to vector spaces to describe continuous dynamics. These projections can be constructed using three lens combinators: composition, sum and quotient.

States and Variables. Many modelling and programming languages support modules with local variable and constant declarations. We have implemented an Isabelle command that automates the creation of hybrid stores.   🐿

```
dataspace sys =
    constants c₁::C₁..cₙ::Cₙ assumes a₁:P₁..aₙ:Pₙ variables x₁::T₁..xₙ::Tₙ
```

It has constants $c_i : C_i$, named constraints $a_i : P_i$ and state variables $x_i : T_i$. In its context, we can create local definitions, theorems and proofs, which are hidden, but accessible using its namespace. Internally, an Isabelle **locale** with fixed constants and assumptions is created. Each variable is a lens $x_i : T_i \Rightarrow \mathcal{S}$, using abstract store $\mathcal{S}$ with the lens axioms as locale assumptions. We also generate independence assumptions [10] that distinguish different variables semantically. Lenses $\lambda, \lambda' : \mathcal{V} \Rightarrow \mathcal{S}$ are *independent*, $\lambda \bowtie \lambda'$, if $put_\lambda\,u \circ put_{\lambda'}\,v = put_{\lambda'}\,v \circ put_\lambda\,u$, for all $u, v \in \mathcal{V}$, that is, these operations commute on all states.

Substitutions. We obtain more user-friendly program specifications with the notation $\sigma(x \rightsquigarrow e) = \lambda s.\, put_x\,(e\,s)\,(\sigma\,s)$. It allows describing assignments as sequences of updates: $[x_1 \rightsquigarrow e_1, x_2 \rightsquigarrow e_2, \cdots] = id(x_1 \rightsquigarrow e_1)(x_2 \rightsquigarrow e_2)\cdots$, for variable lenses $x_i : \mathcal{V}_i \Rightarrow \mathcal{S}$ and "expressions" $e_i : \mathcal{S} \rightarrow \mathcal{V}_i$. Implicitly, any variable y not mentioned in such a "substitution" $\sigma : \mathcal{S} \rightarrow \mathcal{S}$ is left unchanged: $y \rightsquigarrow y$. We further write $e[v/x] = e \circ [x \rightsquigarrow v]$, for $x : \mathcal{V} \Rightarrow \mathcal{S}$, $e : \mathcal{V}' \rightarrow \mathcal{S}$, and $v : \mathcal{V} \rightarrow \mathcal{S}$, for the application of substitutions to expressions. This yields standard notations for program specifications, e.g. $(x := e) = \langle [x \rightsquigarrow e] \rangle$ and *wlp* $\langle [x \rightsquigarrow e] \rangle \; Q = Q[e/x]$. Crucially, Isabelle's simplifier can reorder and reduce substitutions during VCG [10]. We can extract assignments for x writing $\langle \sigma \rangle_s x = \mathsf{get}_x \circ \sigma$ so that, e.g. $\langle [x \rightsquigarrow e_1, y \rightsquigarrow e_2] \rangle_s x$ reduces to e_1 when $x \bowtie y$.   &

Vectors and Matrices. We write $\lambda_1 \, \mathring{,} \, \lambda_2 : \mathcal{S}_1 \Rightarrow \mathcal{S}_3$, for $\lambda_1 : \mathcal{S}_1 \Rightarrow \mathcal{S}_2$, $\lambda_2 : \mathcal{S}_2 \Rightarrow \mathcal{S}_3$, for the forward composition and $1_\mathcal{S} : \mathcal{S} \Rightarrow \mathcal{S}$ for the units in the lens category, but do not show formal definitions [10]. Intuitively, $\mathring{,}$ selects a part of a larger store shape, as we will see.

Vectors and matrices are supported by HOL-Analysis. We supply notation `[[x11,...,x1n],...,[xm1,...,xmn]]` for matrices and means for accessing coordinates of vectors via hybrid program variables [24]. We view vectors in $\mathbb{R}^n$ as part of larger hybrid stores, hence as lenses $\mathbb{R}^n \Rightarrow \mathcal{S}$, and project onto coordinate v_k of any vector $\boldsymbol{v}$ in $\mathbb{R}^n$ using lens composition and a *vector lens* for v_k.   &

$$\Pi(k : [n]) = ((\lambda s. \, vec\text{-}nth \; s \; k) : A^n \to A, (\lambda v \; s. \, vec\text{-}upd \; s \; k \; v) : A \to A^n \to A^n),$$

where $[n] = \{1..n\}$, and A^n is isomorphic to $[n] \to A$. The lookup function *vec-nth* and update function *vec-upd* come from HOL-Analysis. Then, for example, $v_x = \Pi(1) \, \mathring{,} \, \boldsymbol{v}$ and $v_y = \Pi(2) \, \mathring{,} \, \boldsymbol{v}$ for $\boldsymbol{v} : \mathbb{R}^2 \Rightarrow \mathcal{S}$, using $\mathring{,}$ to first select the variable $\boldsymbol{v}$ and then the vector-part of the hybrid store. Obviously, $\Pi(i) \bowtie \Pi(j)$ iff $i \neq j$.

We can specify ODEs and flows via substitutions: $[\boldsymbol{p} \rightsquigarrow \boldsymbol{v}, \boldsymbol{v} \rightsquigarrow \boldsymbol{a}, \boldsymbol{a} \rightsquigarrow 0]$, e.g., specifies a vector field for lenses $\boldsymbol{p}, \boldsymbol{v}, \boldsymbol{a} : \mathbb{R}^2 \Rightarrow \mathcal{S}$. Though ostensibly syntactic objects, these substitutions are semantically functions $\mathcal{S} \to \mathcal{S}$, and consequently can be used with Isabelle's ODE components [25,26].

Frames. Lenses support algebraic manipulations of variable frames. A frame is a set of mutable variables by a program within some context. We first show how variable sets can be modelled via lens sums. Then we recall a predicate characterising immutable program variables [27]. More importantly, we derive a frame rule à la separation logic for local reasoning with framed variables.

Variable lenses can be combined into lenses for variable sets with *lens sum* [10] $\lambda_1 \oplus \lambda_2 : \mathcal{V}_1 \times \mathcal{V}_2 \Rightarrow \mathcal{S}$ defined for $\lambda_1 : \mathcal{V}_1 \Rightarrow \mathcal{S}$, $\lambda_2 : \mathcal{V}_2 \Rightarrow \mathcal{S}$ if $\lambda_1 \bowtie \lambda_2$ as $(\lambda(s_1, s_2). \, (\mathsf{get}_{\lambda_1} s_1, \mathsf{get}_{\lambda_2} s_2), (\lambda(v_1, v_2). \, \mathsf{put}_{\lambda_1} v_1 \circ \mathsf{put}_{\lambda_2} v_2))$. This combines two independent lenses, can model composite variables, e.g. $(x, y) = x \oplus y$, and is decomposed by the simplifier: $[(x, y) \rightsquigarrow (e_1, e_2)] = [x \rightsquigarrow e_1, y \rightsquigarrow e_2]$. We can also use it to specify finite sets: $\{x, y, z\}$ as $x \oplus (y \oplus z)$, yet each variable in the sum may have a different type, e.g. $\{v_x, \boldsymbol{p}\}$ is a valid and well-typed construction.   &

Lens sums are only associative and commutative up-to isomorphism of cartesian products. We need heterogeneous orderings and equivalences between lenses to capture this. We define a *lens preorder* [10], $\lambda_1 \preceq \lambda_2 \Leftrightarrow \exists \lambda_3. \, \lambda_1 = \lambda_3 \, \mathring{,} \, \lambda_2$ that captures the part-of relation between $\lambda_1 : \mathcal{V}_1 \Rightarrow \mathcal{S}$ and $\lambda_2 : \mathcal{V}_2 \Rightarrow \mathcal{S}$, e.g. $v_x \preceq \boldsymbol{v}$ and $\boldsymbol{p} \preceq \boldsymbol{p} \oplus \boldsymbol{v}$. *Lens equivalence* $\cong \; = \; \preceq \cap \succeq$ then identifies lenses with the same shape in the store. Then, for variable set lenses up-to $\cong$, $\oplus$ models $\cup$, and $\preceq$ models $\subseteq$ or $\in$. Since $\lambda_1 \preceq \lambda_1 \oplus \lambda_2$ and $\lambda_1 \oplus \lambda_2 \cong \lambda_2 \oplus \lambda_1$, with our variable set interpretation, we can show, e.g., that $x \in \{x, y, z\}$, $\{x, y\} \subseteq \{x, y, z\}$, and $\{x, y\} = \{y, x\}$. Hence we can use these lens combinators to construct and reason about variable frames.   🐾

Let $A : \mathcal{V} \Rightarrow \mathcal{S}$ be a lens modelling a variable set. For $s_1, s_2 \in \mathcal{S}$ let $s_1 \approx_A s_2$ hold if $s_1 = s_2$ up-to the values of variables in A, that is $get_A\ s_1 = get_A\ s_2$. For $\alpha : \mathcal{S} \to \mathcal{PS}$ define $\alpha\ \textit{nmods}\ A \Leftrightarrow \forall s_1 \in \mathcal{S},\ s_2 \in \alpha\ s_1 \Rightarrow s_1 \approx_A s_2$, i.e., the mutable variables in α are not in A. Then $(x := e)\ \textit{nmods}\ A$ whenever $x \bowtie A$ and, recursively, $(\alpha \,\fatsemi\, \beta)\ \textit{nmods}\ A$ and (if P then α else β) $\textit{nmods}\ A$ when $\alpha\ \textit{nmods}\ A$ and $\beta\ \textit{nmods}\ A$. Also, $A \preceq B$ and $\alpha\ \textit{nmods}\ B$ implies that $\alpha\ \textit{nmods}\ A$.   🐾

Similarly, we use lenses to describe when a variable does not occur freely in an expression or predicate as $A \,\sharp\, e \Leftrightarrow \forall v.\, e \circ (\textit{put}_A\ v) = e$ [10]. We also define $(-A) \,\sharp\, e \Leftrightarrow \forall s_1\, s_2\, v.\, e\, (\textit{put}_A\ v\ s_1) = e\, (\textit{put}_A\ v\ s_2)$ as the converse. We can now derive a frame rule for local reasoning: 🐾

$$\alpha\ \textit{nmods}\ A \wedge (-A) \,\sharp\, I \wedge \{P\}\ \alpha\ \{Q\} \Rightarrow \{P \wedge I\}\ \alpha\ \{Q \wedge I\}. \qquad (1)$$

Projections. Reasoning with frames often requires localising variables within the store. In Sect. 5 we partition the store into continuous and discrete parts and localise continuous variables to the former to compute derivatives. Formally, we may use a frame lens $A : \mathcal{C} \Rightarrow \mathcal{S}$ from global store $\mathcal{S}$ onto local store $\mathcal{C}$. Local reasoning within A uses the *lens quotient* [23] $\lambda /\!/ A$, which localises a lens $\lambda : T \Rightarrow \mathcal{S}$ to a lens $T \Rightarrow \mathcal{C}$. Assuming $\lambda \preceq A$, it yields $\lambda_1 : T \Rightarrow \mathcal{C}$ such that $\lambda = \lambda_1 \,\fatsemi\, A$. For example, $v_x /\!/ v = \Pi(1)$ with $\mathcal{C} = \mathbb{R}^n$.   🐾

4 Shallow Expressions Component   🐾

Next we present our new shallow expression component to support the intuitive expression syntax often used in programming languages and verification approaches semantically. We model expressions as functions $\mathcal{S} \to \mathcal{V}$ in Isabelle's own expression syntax, which is processed entirely in its meta-language (ML). We aim to suppress, e.g., λ-binders that typically pollute naive shallow expressions ($\lambda s.\ get_x\ s + get_y\ s$ versus $x + y$). Isabelle's syntax translations allow relating syntactic and semantic representations, and ultimately designing interfaces to modelling languages such as Modelica and MATLAB®.

Syntax Translation. Isabelle implements a multi-stage syntax pipeline. Unicode strings are parsed and transformed into "pre-terms" [28]: elements of the ML **term** type containing syntactic constants. These must be mapped to previously defined semantic constants by syntax translations, before they can be checked and certified in the Isabelle kernel. Printing reverses this pipeline, mapping terms to strings. The pipeline supports a host of syntactic constructions.

We reuse this pipeline with small modifications for our bidirectional expression transformation, including pretty printing. We subject pre-terms to a lifting process, which replaces their free variables and constants, and inserts store variables (s) and λ-binders. Its implementation uses the syntactic annotation $(t)_e$ to lift the syntactic term t to a semantic expression in the syntax translation rules

$$(t)_e \rightleftharpoons [(t)^e]_e, \quad (x)^e \rightleftharpoons \begin{cases} \lambda s.\, get_x\ s & \text{if } x \text{ is a lens,} \\ \lambda s.\, x & \text{otherwise,} \end{cases} \quad (f\ t)^e \rightleftharpoons \lambda s.\, f\ ((t)^e\ s),$$

where $p \rightleftharpoons q$ means that pre-term p is translated to term q, and q printed as p. Moreover, $[-]_e$ is a constant that marks lifted expressions that are embedded in terms. The pretty printer can then recognise a lifted term and print it.

Intuitively, $(t)_e$ is processed as follows. The syntax processor first parses a pre-term from string t. Then our parse translation traverses its syntax tree. Whenever it encounters a free variable x, the type system determines from the context whether it is a lens, in which case a get_x is inserted. Otherwise it is left unchanged as a logical variable. Function applications are left unchanged by $\rightleftharpoons$, except for expression constructs like $e[v/x]$. For program variables x and y and logical variable z, e.g., $((x + y)^2/z)_e \rightleftharpoons [\lambda s.\, (get_x\ s + get_y\ s)^2/z]_e$. Once an expression has been processed, the resulting λ-term is enclosed in $[-]_e$.

In assignments $x := e$ and substitutions $[x \rightsquigarrow e]$, e is lifted automatically without user annotations. We can also lift correctness specifications and allow intuitive parsing of assertions: $\{P\}\ \alpha\ \{Q\} \rightleftharpoons (P)_e \le wlp\,\alpha\,(Q)_e$.

Substitution. Though our expressions are functions, we can mimic syntactic evaluation of substitutions using the rule $(\lambda s.\, e(s))_e[v/x] = (\lambda s.\, e(put_x\ (v\ s)\ s))_e$. This pushes the substitution through the expression marker, by applying an update to the store. This rule preserves the lifted syntax, e.g. $((x+y)^2/c)_e[2 \cdot x/y]$ simplifies to $((3 \cdot x)^2/c)_e$. We can also use substitutions to determine whether a variable is used: $(x \,\sharp\, e) \Leftrightarrow \forall v.\, (e[v/x]) = e$, meaning e does not depend on x if substituting any value v for x leaves e (Sect. 3), e.g. $(5)_e[v/x] = (5)_e$, and thus $x \,\sharp\, 5$. Checking $\sharp$ is usually automatic. More generally, lenses allow simulating many standard syntactic manipulations semantically to support VCG.

5   Dynamical Systems Components

We extend previous components for continuous dynamics with function framing techniques that project to parts of the store as outlined in Sect. 3. This supports local reasoning where evolution commands modify only continuous variables and leave discrete ones—outside a frame—unchanged. We also introduce framed derivatives to calculate differential invariants, and we derive a ghost rule [11] that expands ODEs with fresh variables.

Framed Vector Fields. To localise variables to the continuous part C of hybrid store S, we use $\lambda : C \Rightarrow S$, with $\lambda = (put_\lambda : C \to S \to S, get_\lambda : S \to C)$, and assume C is a real normed vector space (e.g. $\mathbb{R}^n$). We can compose this data with any $f : S \to S$—*frame* it with λ—to $f_\lambda : S \to C \to C$ such that $f_\lambda s = get_\lambda \circ f \circ (\lambda v.\ put_\lambda v\ s)$. For $C \subseteq S$, $f_\lambda s$ is thus the restriction of f to C supplied with the full store s before restriction. For example for $S = \mathbb{R}^2 \times \mathbb{R}^2 \times S'$, $\lambda : \mathbb{R}^2 \times \mathbb{R}^2 \Rightarrow S = (\boldsymbol{p} \oplus \boldsymbol{v})$ frames $f : S \to S = [(\boldsymbol{p}, \boldsymbol{v}) \rightsquigarrow (\boldsymbol{v}, 0)]$, which behaves as the identity function on S', and thus $f_\lambda s : \mathbb{R}^2 \times \mathbb{R}^2 \to \mathbb{R}^2 \times \mathbb{R}^2$. Similarly, for a function $f : T \to S \to S$ and $s \in S$, the mapping $\lambda t.\ (f\ t)_\lambda s : T \to C \to C$ is the *framed vector field* f_λ for f and s. We can supply f as a substitution $\lambda t. [\boldsymbol{x} \rightsquigarrow e\ t]$ that describes the ODEs $\boldsymbol{x}'\ t = e\ t$ quite naturally, after framing.

Specifying Evolution Commands. Generalised orbits, the semantics for evolution commands $x' = f \,\&\, G$ in Sect. 2, are state transformers on real normed vector spaces C. We have formalised them as *g-orbital* [5]. Here we extend them to the full hybrid store S by introducing their framed version, *g-orbital-on* $\lambda\ f\ G\ U\ V\ t_0 : S \to \mathcal{P}\ S$, as the image under $(\lambda v.\ put_\lambda v\ s)$ of *g-orbital* applied to f_λ, U, V, t_0, $(\lambda v.\ G\ (put_\lambda v\ s))$, and $(get_\lambda\ s)$, where $V \subseteq C$ is the codomain of f_λ. The application of *g-orbital* to f_λ makes it a state transformer on C, while its image under $(\lambda v.\ put_\lambda v\ s)$ lifts it back to S. VCG with the first workflow and *g-orbital-on* then remains as outlined in Sects. 1 and 2: users must supply flows and constants for Lipschitz continuity in order to obtain *wlps*. We provide tactics that may automate this process in Sect. 6.

With Isabelle's syntax translations, we can specify *g-orbital-on* naturally as $\{x_1' = e_1, \cdots, x_n' = e_n \mid G \text{ on } U\ V @ t_0\}$, where each x_i is a summand of the lens $\{x_1, \cdots, x_n\}$. We use this notation in all our examples of Sect. 7. Users can thus declare the ODEs in evolution commands coordinate-wise with lifted expressions e_i ranging over S. The other parameters G, U, V and t_0 can be omitted, which defaults them to constantly $\mathtt{true}$, $\{t.\ t \geq 0\}$, C and 0, respectively. We can collapse further to $(x_1', \cdots, x_n') = (e_1, \cdots, e_n)$ or $\boldsymbol{x}' = \boldsymbol{e}$, and specify evolution commands using flows writing $\{\mathtt{EVOL}\ (x_1, \cdots, x_n) = (e_1\ \tau, \cdots, e_n\ \tau) \mid G\}$, which also carries a frame.

Framed Derivatives. Isabelle supports Fréchet derivatives and we are localising them by framing. These derivatives are defined for functions between normed vector spaces or Banach spaces. Recall that, for a Fréchet differentiable function $F : C \to T$ at $s \in C$, with $C \subseteq S$ open and C, T Banach spaces, its derivative $\boldsymbol{D}\,F\,s$ is a continuous linear operator in $C \to T$ [29]. If F is differentiable everywhere, $\boldsymbol{D}\,F : C \to L(C, T)$, where $L(C, T)$ is the subspace of continuous linear operators in $C \to T$. For finite-dimensional spaces, $\boldsymbol{D}\,F\,s$ is the Jacobian of F at s; compositions with unit vectors yield partial derivatives and the sum over these along the coordinates of a vector yield directional derivatives.

Fix $e : \mathcal{S} \to \mathcal{T}$ with restriction $e|_A^s : \mathcal{C} \to \mathcal{T} = e \circ (\lambda v.\ \mathsf{put}_A\ v\ s)$ differentiable everywhere, variable set lens A and function $f : \mathcal{S} \to \mathcal{S}$. The *Fréchet derivative* $\mathcal{D}_A^f(e) : \mathcal{S} \to \mathcal{T}$ *of* e *at* s *framed by* A *in direction* f is then defined as

$$\mathcal{D}_A^f(e)\, s = \boldsymbol{D}\ e|_A^s\, (\mathsf{get}_A\ s)\, (\mathsf{get}_A\ (f\ s)).$$

Here, $\mathsf{get}_A\ (f\ s)$ is a vector in $\mathcal{C}$. Intuitively, in the finite dimensional case, $\boldsymbol{D}\ e|_A^s\, (\mathsf{get}_A\ s) : \mathcal{C} \to \mathcal{S}$ corresponds to a Jacobian and $\mathsf{get}_A\ (f\ s)$ the vector associated by f to s in $\mathcal{C}$ along which the directional derivative is taken. From the user perspective, after framing, f supplies the vector field f_A representing the ODEs, s the values of the discrete variables, and e, the expression to differentiate.

Computing Framed Derivatives. We can calculate framed derivatives equationally. For lenses $x : V \Rightarrow \mathcal{S}$, $A : \mathcal{C} \Rightarrow \mathcal{S}$, function $f : \mathcal{S} \to \mathcal{S}$, and expressions $k, e_1, e_2 : \mathcal{S} \to T$, which become everywhere differentiable when framed by A,

$$\mathcal{D}_A^f(k) = 0 \qquad \text{if } A \sharp\ k, \tag{2}$$

$$\mathcal{D}_A^f(x) = 0 \qquad \text{if } x \bowtie A, \tag{3}$$

$$\mathcal{D}_A^f(x) = \langle f \rangle_s\ x \qquad \text{if } x \preceq A \text{ and } x /\!\!/ A \text{ is bounded linear}, \tag{4}$$

$$\mathcal{D}_A^f(e_1 + e_2) = (\mathcal{D}_A^f(e_1)) + (\mathcal{D}_A^f(e_2)), \tag{5}$$

$$\mathcal{D}_A^f(e_1 \cdot e_2) = (e_1 \cdot \mathcal{D}_A^f(e_2)) + (\mathcal{D}_A^f(e_1) \cdot e_2), \tag{6}$$

$$\mathcal{D}_A^f(e^n) = n \cdot (\mathcal{D}_A^f(e)) \cdot e^{(n-1)}, \tag{7}$$

$$\mathcal{D}_A^f(\ln(e)) = (\mathcal{D}_A^f(e))/e \qquad \text{if } e > 0. \tag{8}$$

Laws (2) and (5–8) are framed analogues of known derivative rules. Law (3), where our syntax translations allow us to write x instead of get_x, states that the derivative of a discrete variable is zero. Similarly, by law (4), that for a continuous variable is extracted from f as explained in Sect. 3. For this law, we need to show that $x \preceq A$ and that x localised to $\mathcal{C}$ by A ($x /\!\!/ A$) is Fréchet differentiable. For this, it suffices to assume that $\mathsf{get}_{x /\!\!/ A}$ is a bounded continuous linear operator. As an example, we can compute $\mathcal{D}_x^{[x \leadsto 1]}(x^2) = 2 \cdot (\mathcal{D}_x^{[x \leadsto 1]}(x)) \cdot x = 2 \cdot 1 \cdot x = 2x$. Lenses can modify the part of $\mathcal{S}$ described by $\mathcal{C}$, for instance, $\mathcal{D}_y^{[x \leadsto 1]}(x^2) = 2 \cdot (\mathcal{D}_y^{[x \leadsto 1]}(x)) \cdot x = 2 \cdot 0 \cdot x = 0$ if $y \bowtie x$. We can also take directions into account via the vector field: $\mathcal{D}_x^{[x \leadsto 2]}(x^2) = 2 \cdot (\mathcal{D}_x^{[x \leadsto 2]}(x)) \cdot x = 2 \cdot 2 \cdot x = 4x$.

Invariance Checking. The fact that I is an invariant for vector field f, as outlined in Sect. 2, has so far been modelled as *diff-inv*. We now supply a framed version *diff-inv-on* $I\ \lambda\ f\ U\ V\ t_0\ G$, replacing $\mathsf{g\text{-}orbital}$ with $\mathsf{g\text{-}orbital\text{-}on}$ in the definition of invariance, where again, $\lambda : \mathcal{C} \Rightarrow \mathcal{S}$ projects onto $\mathcal{C}$ and the others parameters also remain unchanged. The adjunction between backward diamonds and wlps still translates differential invariance to Hoare triples as in the discussion of invariant sets of Sect. 2:

$$\{I\} \{x' = e \mid G \text{ on } U V \text{ @ } t_0\} \{I\} \Leftrightarrow \text{diff-inv-on } I \, x \, (\lambda y. [x \rightsquigarrow e]) U V t_0 G. \quad (9)$$

This equivalence allows us to derive the d$\mathcal{L}$-style inference rules shown below. These are all proved as theorems using *diff-inv-on*, as are various rules for weakening and strengthening to support VCG.

$$\frac{G \Rightarrow \left(\mathcal{D}_x^{[x \rightsquigarrow e]} e_1\right) \propto^* \left(\mathcal{D}_x^{[x \rightsquigarrow e]} e_2\right)}{\{e_1 \propto e_2\} \{x' = e \mid G\} \{e_1 \propto e_2\}} \quad \propto \in \{=, \leq, <\} \quad (10)$$

$$\frac{\{I_1\} \{x' = e \mid G\} \{I_1\} \quad \{I_2\} \{x' = e \mid G \wedge I_1\} \{I_2\}}{\{I_1 \wedge I_2\} \{x' = e \mid G\} \{I_1 \wedge I_2\}} \quad (11)$$

$$\frac{x \sharp I \quad \{P\} \{x' = e \mid G\} \{Q\}}{\{P \wedge I\} \{x' = e \mid G\} \{Q \wedge I\}} \quad (12)$$

$$\frac{y \bowtie x \quad y \natural (G, e) \quad \{I\} \{(x, y)' = (e, k \cdot y) \mid G\} \{I\}}{\{\exists v. I[v/y]\} \{x' = e \mid G\} \{\exists v. I[v/y]\}} \quad (13)$$

Rule (10) performs differential induction on (in)equalities [30]. There, $\propto^*$ is $\leq$ if $\propto$ is $<$, and $\propto$ otherwise: if the framed derivatives of two expressions satisfy an (in)equality, then a corresponding (in)equality is an invariant. Boolean combinations of invariants reduce to basic ones where computations take place [5]. If Fréchet derivatives are not defined everywhere, we can still follow the procedure for invariant reasoning in [5]. Rule (11) is differential cut, framed but unchanged from [5] otherwise. It accumulates invariants in the guard sequentially during VCG. Framed differential weakening is also derived as before [5], but omitted for space reasons. Rule (12) is a frame rule that discharges invariants if they only refer to discrete variables, $x \sharp I$. For this we use the framing result $\{x' = e \mid G \text{ on } U V \text{ @ } t_0\} \text{ nmods} (-x)$, as variables outside of x do not change during evolution and hence, by (1) in Sect. 3, any I specified only over discrete variables is an invariant.

Finally, we have also derived (13), a framed variant of a differential ghost rule from d$\mathcal{L}$ [11]. In d$\mathcal{L}$, it expands the reasoning power with invariants [31]. It is used to transform an invariant for a vector field f into an invariant of f extended with a fresh variable y and its derivative. The extension makes the new invariant easy to prove with rules (10), (11) and (12). Formally, rule (13) says that I, with y abstracted, is an invariant for a system of ODEs with variables in x if it is also an invariant for the same system but with y as a fresh program variable, $x \oplus y$, satisfying $y' = k \cdot y$ for some constant k. Lens y must already exist in $\mathcal{S}$, but we can always expand the store with new variables [23]. We limit the derivative of y to be $k \cdot y$, but we will generalise in the future.

6 Reasoning Components

We have turned the results from Sects. 4 and 5 into automated proof methods for hybrid programs using Isabelle's Eisbach tool [32]. These increase proof automation for both our workflows relative to [5]. They use our baseline tactic *expr-auto*, which targets equalities and inequalities for shallow expressions.

hoare-wp-auto. First we supply a method for automated structural VCG. To discharge partial correctness specifications $\{P\}\ S\ \{Q\}$, it (1) computes *wlp S Q* by simplification, (2) reduces substitutions and side-conditions, and (3) applies *expr-auto* to the resulting proof goals. Loop invariant annotations are supported as usual, and are reduced by deduction when encountered. Our set-up ensures that the expression syntax is not expanded to HOL terms until step (3), which leads to readable data-level proof goals.   🪨

dInduct. To prove goals $\{I\}\ \{x' = e \mid G\}\ \{I\}$, it (1) applies rule 10 to get a framed derivative expression, and (2) calculates derivatives using Laws 2–8, substitution laws, and basic simplification laws. This yields derivative-free equality or inequality predicates. *dInduct* uses only the simplifier for calculating invariants, and so is both efficient and yields readable VCs. For cases requiring deduction, we supply *dInduct-auto*, which applies *expr-auto* after *dInduct*, plus further simplification lemmas from HOL-Analysis. Ultimately such heuristics should be based on decision procedures [33–36], as oracles or as verified components.   🪨

dInduct-mega. While *dInduct-auto* suffices for simpler examples, differential induction must often be combined with weakening and cut rules. The following steps are executed iteratively until all goals are proved or no rule applies: (1) try any fact labelled with attribute `facts`, (2) try differential weakening to prove the goal, (3) try differential cut (Law 11) to split it into two differential invariants, (4) try *dInduct-auto*. The rules are applied using backtracking, so that if one rule fails, another one is tried. This automatically discharges many differential invariants, as shown in Sect. 7.   🪨

local-flow. While the proof methods so far describe the second workflow using framed versions of the inference rule of d$\mathcal{L}$, the first workflow of the framework supports verification with certified solutions (flows), which can be supplied using a CAS. We have developed a proof method called *local-flow* for certifying that a flow is the unique solution to an ODE. To simplify finding suitable Lipschitz constants, we now supply a proof method *local-flow-auto* that tries several such constants, such as 0.5, 1 and 2. The Picard-Lindelöf theorem can then be used by *hoare-wp-auto* to replace any ODE system with its local flow.   🪨

7   Examples

Finally we illustrate the benefits of our extensions to the framework [5] by example. We illustrate the flexibility of our new store model, the user-friendliness of our new expression model, the local reasoning provided by frames and framed derivatives, and the automation supported by our proof methods.

Water Tank. First, we formalise the classic water tank example. We demonstrate the creation of hybrid stores using the **dataspace** command, user-friendly specification of hybrid programs using the shallow expression model, improved proof automation and local reasoning for continuous and discrete variables.

The water tank bounds the water level h: $H_l \leq h \leq H_u$. A controller turns a water pump on and off to regulate h. We specify the hybrid store as follows. &

```
dataspace water_tank = constants Hₗ::ℝ Hᵤ::ℝ cₒ::ℝ cᵢ::ℝ
  assumes co:"0 < cₒ" and ci:"cₒ < cᵢ" variables pmp::𝔹 h::ℝ hₘ::ℝ t::ℝ
```

Constants c_i and c_o indicate rates of in- and outflow (when the pump is on). Variable pmp models the water pump, h_m water level measurements, and t models time. Our new dataspace command generates lens laws for them, such as $h_m \bowtie t$. Previously, all program variables in our framework had to be real numbers. Now we separate between discrete and continuous variables in general name spaces.

With framed ODEs, we assign derivatives locally to variables h and t; the other variables are left implicitly immutable: &

```
abbreviation "dyn = IF pmp THEN {h' = -cₒ, t' = 1 | t ≤ (Hₗ hₘ)/( cₒ)]
                    ELSE {h' = cᵢ-cₒ, t' = 1 | t ≤ (Hᵤ-hₒ)/(cᵢ-cₒ)}"
```

The two ODEs model the dynamics when the inflow is on and off, respectively. The frame is inferred as $\{h,t\}$ and represented by the local lens $h \oplus t$. Consequently, h_m and pmp are immutable, as the following lemmas confirm: &

```
lemma nm: "dyn nmods {pmp, hₘ}" by (simp add: closure)
lemma "{pmp = X} dyn {pmp = X}" by (rule nmods_invariant[OF nm], unrest)
```

Specifically, pmp stays at its initial value X, which is recognised as a logical variable by our parser, since it is fresh. The first lemma is proved using modification, substitution, and lens laws. The second one is proved using local reasoning with our frame rule (1). &

Next, we can specify our controller:

```
abbreviation "ctrl ≡ (t,hₘ)::=(0,h); IF ¬pmp ∧ hₘ≤Hₗ+1 THEN pmp::=True
  ELSE IF pmp ∧ hₘ≥ Hᵤ-1 THEN pmp ::= False ELSE skip)"
```

This first part assigns 0 and h to t and h_m, respectively, to reset the time and measure the water level. Then, if the inflow is off and the height is getting close to the minimum, the inflow is enabled. Otherwise, if the level is getting near the maximum, it is disabled. If neither is true, then we skip.

With the second workflow, we discharge invariants for the tank dynamics using differential induction. This is automatic using a proof method called dProve. For illustration we first focus on the invariant when the inflow is enabled:

```
lemma "{0 ≤ t ∧ h = (cᵢ - cₒ)*t + hₘ ∧ Hₗ ≤ h ∧ h ≤ Hᵤ}
       {h' = cᵢ - cₒ, t' = 1 | t ≤ (Hᵤ - hₘ) / (cᵢ - cₒ)}
       {0 ≤ t ∧ h = (cᵢ - cₒ)*t + hₘ ∧ Hₗ ≤ h ∧ h ≤ Hᵤ}"
  using ci by dInduct_mega
```

This shows one verification step. We prove several invariants, using $c_i < c_o$. The key is to prove $h = (c_i - c_o) \cdot t + h_m$, which allows us to bound the change of the water level. Tactic *dInduct-mega* automates the proof with successive differential cuts. The system proof is concluded with *hoare-wp-auto* to verify the controller.

The overall verification is fully automatic using *dProve*:

```
lemma tank_correct:
 "{t = 0 ∧ h = h_m ∧ H_l ≤ h ∧ h ≤ H_u}
   LOOP ctrl ; dyn INV (0≤t ∧ h = ((pmp*c_i)-c_o)*t + h_m ∧ H_l≤h ∧ h≤H_u)
 {H_l ≤ h ∧ h ≤ H_u}" using ci co by dProve
```

We annotate an extended invariant for the controller and dynamics. Internally, the frame rule checks that both **pmp** and ¬**pmp** are invariants of **dyn**. The previous lemma is then not needed as *dProve* calls *dInduct-mega*.

We can alternatively verify the controller using the first workflow, with an analytic solution to the differential equations:

```
lemma lf:"local_flow_on [h↝k,t↝1] (h⊕t) UNIV UNIV (λτ.[h↝k*τ,t↝τ+t])"
 by local_flow_auto
```

```
lemma "{h_m≤h ∧ h≤h_M} LOOP ctrl;dyn INV (h_m≤h∧h≤h_M) {h_m≤h ∧ h≤h_M}"
 using tank_arith[OF _ co ci] by (hoare_wp_auto local_flow: lf)
```

We then certify the unique (framed) solution for the water tank vector field using *local-flow-auto*. The loop invariant does not need to refer to **pmp** or h_m, since these are discrete. The proof uses *hoare-wp-auto*, which is given the local flow proof `lf`, and so can internally replace the ODE with the flow.

Overall, with our support for local reasoning, we can verify the water tank with both workflows using a clear separation of discrete and continuous variables. The shallow expression model makes its presentation more user-friendly while our added tactics streamline its verification.

Exponential Decay. This example illustrates the differential ghost rule and the first workflow. The aim is to prove that $x > 0$ is an invariant of $f = [x \rightsquigarrow -x]$. This is not immediately obvious because the derivative of x is negative.

The proof using a differential ghost is as follows: $x > 0$ is equivalent to $xy^2 = 1$ for some $y : \mathbb{R}$. To show that this new property is an invariant for f, we use the ghost rule to expand the system of ODEs into $g = [x \rightsquigarrow -x, y \rightsquigarrow y/2]$, which retains the behaviour of x. Then, with our framed derivatives, $xy^2 = 1$ is an invariant because $\mathcal{D}^g_{\{x,y\}}(xy^2) = 2xy\mathcal{D}^g_{\{x,y\}}(y) + \mathcal{D}^g_{\{x,y\}}(x)y^2 = xy^2 - xy^2 = 0 = \mathcal{D}^g_{\{x,y\}}(1)$. The proof requires some interaction:

```
lemma dG_example: "{x > 0} {x' = -x} {x > 0}"
  apply (dGhost "y" "(x * y^2 = 1)_e" "1/2", expr_auto add: exp_arith)
  apply (dInduct_auto, simp add: power2_eq_square) done
```

The first line applies the differential ghost law, with the fresh variable y, the property $xy^2 = 1$, and the factor $1/2$ of $y \rightsquigarrow y/2$. This yields $0 < x \Leftrightarrow \exists v.\ xv^2 = 1$, which we prove using a lemma (`exp_arith`). The last line applies *dInduct-auto* and the fact *power2_eq_square* stating that $\forall x.\ x^2 = xx$ supplied by *sledgehammer* [34] to discharge the obligation $yy \neq y^2 \Rightarrow y = 0$.

For the first workflow, $x > 0$ is an invariant because the solution, $x\,t = x_0 e^{-t}$, is a positive exponential function for $x_0 > 0$. Note also that we can work with transcendental functions such as e^{-t} directly in specifications and proofs while this is not supported by the d$\mathcal{L}$ prover KeYmaera X [37]. The proof of invariance follows immediately from this fact and automatically with our tactic.

```
lemma flow_ex:"{x > 0} {x' = -x}{x > 0}" by (hoare_wp_auto local_flow: lf)
```

We again supply a certified solution using the theorem `lf` (omitted). Alternatively, if users wish to skip the certification and write the flow directly in the specification, this is also automated using the notation introduced in Sect. 5.

```
lemma "{x > 0} {EVOL x = x * exp (- τ)} {x > 0}" by hoare_wp_auto
```

Application of our new differential ghost rule shows that reasoning à la d$\mathcal{L}$ with our components is possible. Yet we provide users with the freedom of choice with alterative workflows that might be more natural for mathematicians or control engineers.

Autonomous Boat. Our final example [24] describes a controller for an autonomous boat using the second workflow. Beyond our previous examples, it demonstrates the use of vector variables, which are seamlessly integrated into our hybrid store model.

The boat's objective is to navigate along several way-points, while avoiding obstacles. It is manoeuvrable in $\mathbb{R}^2$ and has a rotatable thruster generating a positive propulsive force f with maximum f_{max}. The boat's state is determined by its position p, velocity v, and acceleration a:

```
dataspace AMV = constants S::ℝ fmax::ℝ assumes fmax:"fmax ≥ 0"
  variables p::"ℝ vec[2]" v::"ℝ vec[2]" a::"ℝ vec[2]" φ::ℝ s::ℝ
  wps::"(ℝ vec[2]) list" org::"(ℝ vec[2]) set" rs::ℝ rh::ℝ
```

This store model combines once again discrete and continuous variables. Here, ℝ vec[n] is a vector of dimension n. In the **dataspace**, we have a variable for linear speed s, and constant S is the maximum speed. We also model discrete variables for the way-point path (**wps**), the obstacle register (**org**), and requested speed and heading (**rs** and **rh**). Our dataspace allows us to declare a single variable $p : \mathbb{R}$ vec[2] and manipulate it using vector algebra and transcendental functions. The following axiom, relates s, ϕ with v and constrain s.

```
abbreviation "ax ≡ (s *ℝ [[sin(φ), cos(φ)]] = v ∧ 0 ≤ s ∧ s ≤ S)ᵉ"
```

This states that v is equal to s multiplied with the heading unit-vector using scalar multiplication ($*_R$) and our vector syntax, and $0 \leq s \leq S$. The kinematics $[p', v', a']^T$ is specified as follows: 🪨

abbreviation "ODE ≡ { p' = v, v' = a, a' = 0, ϕ' = ω,
                         s' = if s ≠ 0 then (v · a) / s else ‖a‖ | @ax }"

We also specify derivatives for ϕ and s. The former, ω, is the angular velocity, which has the value $arcos((v + a) \cdot v/(\|v + a\| \cdot \|v\|))$ when $\|v\| \neq 0$ and 0 otherwise. The linear acceleration (s') is calculated using the inner product of v and a. If the current speed is 0, then s' is simply $\|a\|$. All other variables in the store remain outside the evolution frame: 🪨

lemma "ODE nmods {rs, rh, wps, org}" **by** (simp add: closure)

Consequently, any invariant of the controller's discrete variables is also an invariant of the kinematics by local reasoning.

The controller for the AMV consists of three parts: **Navigation** for way-point following, **AP** the autopilot proportional controller, and **LRE** the safety controller. **Navigation** and **LRE** both supply requested headings and speeds to the **Autopilot**, which calculates an acceleration vector for the **ODE**. For reasons of space, we omit further details. We prove differential invariants of **ODE**:   🪨

lemma "{s^2 = v · v} ODE {s^2 = v · v}" **by** (dWeaken, metis orient_vec_mag_n)
lemma "{a = 0 ∧ v = V} ODE {a = 0 ∧ v = V}" **by** (dInduct_mega)
lemma "{(a = 0 ∧ s > 0) ∧ ϕ = X} ODE {ϕ = X}" **by** (dInduct_mega)

The first is discharged by differential weakening and a vector lemma. The second and third are discharged by *dInduct-mega*. These demonstrate our ability to form and prove differential invariants over vectors as well as scalars. We also reason about vectors algebraically without coordinate-wise decomposition. Since s and v are modified only by the ODE, we can also show that $s^2 = v \cdot v$ is an invariant of the other parts of the AMV's controller using our frame rule; e.g. $\{s^2 = v \cdot v\}$ **Autopilot** $\{s^2 = v \cdot v\}$. Moreover, this is also a system invariant. We check a final **ODE** invariant:

lemma "{a·v≥0 ∧ (a·v)^2 = (a·a)·(v·v)} ODE {a·v≥0 ∧ (a·v)^2 = (a·a)·(v·v)}"
  by (dInduct_mega, metis inner_commute)

This property tells us that if v and a have the same direction initially, i.e. $a \cdot v = \|a\| \cdot \|v\|$, then this will hold at any point in time. The boat may be linearly accelerating or decelerating, but is not turning during **ODE**. Method *dInduct-mega* yields a proof obligation relating to inner products, which is discharged with an automated proof.   🪨

This example further evidences the ability for local reasoning with our program store model. It allows us in particular to use a dataspace with previously unsupported types like vectors and lists. It also supports reasoning about invariants at the level of vectors instead of decomposing them into their coordinates.

8   Related Work, Conclusions, and Future Work

We have transformed an Isabelle framework for the verification of hybrid systems towards a formal method, using Isabelle's syntax translation mechanisms to interface with more user-friendly modelling and specification languages for hybrid programs. We have also shown how local reasoning about hybrid stores can be achieved using lenses, how this leads to better and more automatic tactics and to simpler verification conditions.

Deductive reasoning about hybrid systems is not new. There is substantial work supporting this activity through domain-specific decision procedures and techniques for finding and reasoning with invariants, which our work has so far ignored. With PVS, a formalisation for $d\mathcal{L}$-style verification by formalising semi-algebraic sets and real analytic functions is in its early steps [38]. With Coq, the ROSCoq framework [1] uses Coq's CoRN library of constructive real numbers to formalise a Logic of Events (LoE) to reason about hybrid systems. The VeriDrone project [2] uses the Coquelicot library for a variant of the temporal logic of actions. Both semantics are very different from our $d\mathcal{L}$-inspired one. Yet we view our work as rather complementary to $d\mathcal{L}$'s KeYmaera X tool [37], which brings the benefit of certified decision procedures for real arithmetic and a user-friendly interface. With Isabelle, a term checker for $d\mathcal{L}$ has been formalised as a deep embedding [39,40], but without aiming at verification components. A hybrid Hoare logic [3] for verifying hybrid CSP processes [41] has been formalised as a shallow embedding, but with a different semantics to our own Hoare logic [8]. The Refinement Calculus of Reactive Systems [42] allows verification of discrete time control laws in Simulink, also using predicate transformer semantics, but currently without support for continuous time.

Work remains to be done for transforming this framework into an industrial-strength formal method. This is supported by its openness and compositionality. Integrating a hybrid store and extant ODE components for Isabelle into the state transformer semantics, for instance, required little effort [5]; the same holds for our new lens-based hybrid store. Our new expression language could easily be replaced by Modelica syntax. In the future, one could use Isabelle's code generator for transforming hybrid programs into verified controller implementations. Solvers and decision procedures, which are indispensable for real-world applications, should be integrated either as oracles, for certification or as verified components, as already mentioned. Openness implies in particular that anyone interested in hybrid systems verification could extend, adapt and contribute to this framework. Its power is only limited by Isabelle's higher order logic and the mathematical and verification components that the community provides for it.

Acknowledgements. This work is funded by UKRI-EPSRC project CyPhyAssure (grant reference EP/S001190/1), Novo Nordisk Fonden Start Package Grant (NNF20OC0063462), the Assuring Autonomy International Programme (AAIP; grant CSI:Cobot), a partnership between Lloyd's Register Foundation and the University of York, and Labex DigiCosme through an invited professorship of the fourth author at the Laboratoire d'informatique de l'École polytechnique.

References

1. Anand, A., Knepper, R.: ROSCoq: robots powered by constructive reals. In: Urban, C., Zhang, X. (eds.) ITP 2015. LNCS, vol. 9236, pp. 34–50. Springer, Cham (2015). https://doi.org/10.1007/978-3-319-22102-1_3
2. Ricketts, D., Malecha, G., Alvarez, M.M., Gowda, V., Lerner, S.: Towards verification of hybrid systems in a foundational proof assistant. In: MEMOCODE, pp. 248–257. IEEE (2015)
3. Wang, S., Zhan, N., Zou, L.: An improved HHL prover: an interactive theorem prover for hybrid systems. In: Butler, M., Conchon, S., Zaïdi, F. (eds.) ICFEM 2015. LNCS, vol. 9407, pp. 382–399. Springer, Cham (2015). https://doi.org/10.1007/978-3-319-25423-4_25
4. Huerta y Munive, J.J., Struth, G.: Verifying hybrid systems with modal Kleene algebra. In: Desharnais, J., Guttmann, W., Joosten, S. (eds.) RAMiCS 2018. LNCS, vol. 11194, pp. 225–243. Springer, Cham (2018). https://doi.org/10.1007/978-3-030-02149-8_14
5. Huerta y Munive, J.J., Struth, G.: Predicate transformer semantics for hybrid systems: verification components for Isabelle/HOL. arXiv:1909.05618 [cs.LO] (2019)
6. Huerta y Munive, J.J.: Verification components for hybrid systems. Archive of Formal Proofs (2019)
7. Foster, S.: Hybrid relations in Isabelle/UTP. In: Ribeiro, P., Sampaio, A. (eds.) UTP 2019. LNCS, vol. 11885, pp. 130–153. Springer, Cham (2019). https://doi.org/10.1007/978-3-030-31038-7_7
8. Foster, S., Huerta y Munive, J.J., Struth, G.: Differential Hoare logics and refinement calculi for hybrid systems with Isabelle/HOL. In: Fahrenberg, U., Jipsen, P., Winter, M. (eds.) RAMiCS 2020. LNCS, vol. 12062, pp. 169–186. Springer, Cham (2020). https://doi.org/10.1007/978-3-030-43520-2_11
9. Immler, F., Traut, C.: The flow of ODEs: Formalization of variational equation and Poincaré map. J. Autom. Reasoning **62**(2), 215–236 (2019)
10. Foster, S., Baxter, J., Cavalcanti, A., Woodcock, J., Zeyda, F.: Unifying semantic foundations for automated verification tools in Isabelle/UTP. Science of Computer Programming, vol. 197, October 2020
11. Platzer, A.: Logical Foundations of Cyber-Physical Systems. Springer, Cham (2018). https://doi.org/10.1007/978-3-319-63588-0
12. Boulton, R.J., Gordon, A.D., Gordon, M.J.C., Harrison, J., Herbert, J., Tassel, J.V.: Experience with embedding hardware description languages in HOL. In: IFIP Transactions, vol. A-10, pp. 129–156, North-Holland (1992)
13. Wildmoser, M., Nipkow, T.: Certifying machine code safety: shallow versus deep embedding. In: Slind, K., Bunker, A., Gopalakrishnan, G. (eds.) TPHOLs 2004. LNCS, vol. 3223, pp. 305–320. Springer, Heidelberg (2004). https://doi.org/10.1007/978-3-540-30142-4_22
14. Huerta y Munive, J.J.: Affine systems of ODEs in Isabelle/HOL for hybrid-program verification. In: de Boer, F., Cerone, A. (eds.) SEFM 2020. LNCS, vol. 12310, pp. 77–92. Springer, Cham (2020). https://doi.org/10.1007/978-3-030-58768-0_5
15. Huerta y Munive, J.J.: Matrices for ODEs. Archive of Formal Proofs (2020)
16. Hickman, T., Laursen, C.P., Foster, S., Huerta y Munive, J.J.: Certifying differential equation solutions from computer algebra systems in Isabelle/HOL. arXiv:2102.02679 [cs.LO], February 2021
17. Teschl, G.: Ordinary Differential Equations and Dynamical Systems. AMS (2012)

18. Mitsch, S., Huerta y Munive, J.J., Jin, X., Zhan, B., Wang, S., Zhan, N.: ARCH-COMP20 category report: Hybrid systems theorem proving. ARCH **20**, 141–161 (2019)
19. Foster, S., Zeyda, F.: Optics. Archive of Formal Proofs, May 2017
20. Oles, F.: A Category-theoretic approach to the semantics of programming languages. Ph.D. thesis, Syracuse University (1982)
21. Back, R., von Wright, J.: Refinement Calculus–A Systematic Introduction. Springer, New York (1998). https://doi.org/10.1007/978-1-4612-1674-2
22. Foster, J.: Bidirectional programming languages. Ph.D. thesis, University of Pennsylvania (2009)
23. Foster, S., Baxter, J.: Automated algebraic reasoning for collections and local variables with lenses. In: Fahrenberg, U., Jipsen, P., Winter, M. (eds.) RAMiCS 2020. LNCS, vol. 12062, pp. 100–116. Springer, Cham (2020). https://doi.org/10.1007/978-3-030-43520-2_7
24. Foster, S., Gleirscher, M., Calinescu, R.: Towards deductive verification of control algorithms for autonomous marine vehicles. In: ICECCS. IEEE, October 2020
25. Immler, F., Hölzl, J.: Numerical analysis of ordinary differential equations in Isabelle/HOL. In: Beringer, L., Felty, A. (eds.) ITP 2012. LNCS, vol. 7406, pp. 377–392. Springer, Heidelberg (2012). https://doi.org/10.1007/978-3-642-32347-8_26
26. Hölzl, J., Immler, F., Huffman, B.: Type classes and filters for mathematical analysis in Isabelle/HOL. In: Blazy, S., Paulin-Mohring, C., Pichardie, D. (eds.) ITP 2013. LNCS, vol. 7998, pp. 279–294. Springer, Heidelberg (2013). https://doi.org/10.1007/978-3-642-39634-2_21
27. Foster, S., Nemouchi, Y., Gleirscher, M., Wei, R., Kelly, T.: Integration of formal proof into unified assurance cases with Isabelle/SACM. Formal Aspects of Computing (2021)
28. Kuncar, O., Popescu, A.: A consistent foundation for Isabelle/HOL. J. Autom. Reasoning **62**, 531–555 (2019)
29. Cheney, E.W.: Analysis for Applied Mathematics. Springer, New York (2001). https://doi.org/10.1007/978-1-4757-3559-8
30. Platzer, A.: The structure of differential invariants and differential cut elimination. Log. Meth. Comput. Sci. **8**(4), 1–38 (2012). https://doi.org/10.2168/LMCS-8(4:16)2012
31. Platzer, A., Tan, Y.K.: Differential equation axiomatization: the impressive power of differential ghosts. In: LICS, pp. 819–828. ACM (2018)
32. Matichuk, D., Murray, T.C., Wenzel, M.: Eisbach: a proof method language for Isabelle. J. Autom. Reasoning **56**(3), 261–282 (2016)
33. Hölzl, J.: Proving inequalities over reals with computation in Isabelle/HOL. In: PLMMS, pp. 38–45. ACM (2009)
34. Blanchette, J.C., Kaliszyk, C., Paulson, L.C., Urban, J.: Hammering towards QED. J. Formalized Reasoning **9**(1), 101–148 (2016)
35. Li, W., Passmore, G., Paulson, L.: Deciding univariate polynomial problems using untrusted certificates in Isabelle/HOL. J. Autom. Reasoning **62**, 29–91 (2019)
36. Cordwell, K., Yong, K.T., Platzer, A.: A verified decision procedure for univariate real arithmetic with the BKR algorithm. In Cohen, L., Kaliszyk, C. (eds.) ITP. Volume 193 of Leibniz International Proceedings in Informatics (LIPIcs), pp. 14:1–14:20. Schloss Dagstuhl - Leibniz-Zentrum für Informatik (2021)

37. Fulton, N., Mitsch, S., Quesel, J.-D., Völp, M., Platzer, A.: KeYmaera X: an axiomatic tactical theorem prover for hybrid systems. In: Felty, A.P., Middeldorp, A. (eds.) CADE 2015. LNCS (LNAI), vol. 9195, pp. 527–538. Springer, Cham (2015). https://doi.org/10.1007/978-3-319-21401-6_36

38. Slagel, J.T., White, L., Dutle, A.: Formal verification of semi-algebraic sets and real analytic functions. In: CPP, pp. 278–290. ACM (2021)

39. Bohrer, B., Rahli, V., Vukotic, I., Völp, M., Platzer, A.: Formally verified differential dynamic logic. In: CPP, pp. 208–221. ACM (2017)

40. Platzer, A.: Differential game logic. Archive of Formal Proofs (2019)

41. Liu, J., Lv, J., Quan, Z., Zhan, N., Zhao, H., Zhou, C., Zou, L.: A calculus for hybrid CSP. In: Ueda, K. (ed.) APLAS 2010. LNCS, vol. 6461, pp. 1–15. Springer, Heidelberg (2010). https://doi.org/10.1007/978-3-642-17164-2_1

42. Preoteasa, V., Dragomir, I., Tripakis, S.: Refinement calculus of reactive systems. In: International Conference on Embedded Systems (EMSOFT). IEEE, October 2014

Program Verification II

Z3str4: A Multi-armed String Solver

Federico Mora[1]($\boxtimes$), Murphy Berzish[2], Mitja Kulczynski[3], Dirk Nowotka[3], and Vijay Ganesh[2]

[1] University of California, Berkeley, USA
`fmora@cs.berkeley.edu`
[2] University of Waterloo, Waterloo, Canada
[3] Kiel University, Kiel, Germany

Abstract. We present Z3STR4, a new high-performance string SMT solver for a rich quantifier-free first-order theory of strings and length constraints. These kinds of constraints have found widespread application in analysis of string-intensive programs in general, and web applications in particular. Three key contributions underpin our solver: first, a novel length-abstraction algorithm that performs various string-length based abstractions and refinements along with a bit-vector backend; second, an arrangement-based solver with a bit-vector backend; third, an algorithm selection and constraint-sharing architecture which leverages the above-mentioned solvers along with the Z3 sequence (Z3seq) solver. We perform extensive empirical evaluation over 20 different industrial and randomly-generated benchmarks with over 120,000+ instances, and show that Z3STR4 outperforms the previous best solvers, namely, CVC4, Z3seq, and Z3str3 in both total solved instances and total runtime.

Keywords: SMT · String solvers · Program analysis

1 Introduction

Security and reliability of string-intensive programs, especially web applications, is a significant problem that has received considerable attention in recent years by both industrial and academic researchers. A variety of analysis, testing, and verification methods have been proposed to address this problem [4,11,15,19,25, 33,35,36,40], many of which depend on a string solver. As researchers continually improve their analysis tools and find new applications for string solvers, the demand for even more efficient solvers grows unabated.

To be used for these applications, string solvers must support a rich quantifier-free first-order theory T_S over string (a.k.a. word) equations, functions such as string concatenation and integer to string conversion, predicates such as string containment, and linear integer arithmetic over string length. Unfortunately, satisfiability problems for the theory T_S of strings (and its fragments) are generally hard. Specifically, the satisfiability problem for even the smallest interesting fragment of T_S, namely, the quantifier-free theory of word equations, is NP-hard and is in PSPACE [32]; the full theory T_S is undecidable [20]; and the

© Springer Nature Switzerland AG 2021
M. Huisman et al. (Eds.): FM 2021, LNCS 13047, pp. 389–406, 2021.
https://doi.org/10.1007/978-3-030-90870-6_21

question of decidability of the quantifier-free first-order theory of word equations and arithmetic over length remains open, despite many attempts to solve it over the last 50 years [31].

Despite their difficulty, much research has been done on practical algorithms for solving string constraints obtained from many real-world analysis, testing, verification, and synthesis applications [19,28,35,40]. Examples of such solvers include HAMPI [25], Stranger [42], Z3 sequence (Z3seq) [18], CVC4 [27], Norn [2], Trau [1], S3 [39], Z3str2 [43], and Z3str3 [9], each with varying strengths and weaknesses. Precisely because solving string formulas is believed to be hard in general, solver designers have come up with a diverse set of practical algorithms that incorporate a variety of tradeoffs. Some of these methods work well for pure word equations, but not so well for integer constraints over string length. Other methods work well for a mix of word equations and integer constraints, but perform poorly on more complicated constraints involving functions such as **substring** or predicates like **contains**. This diversity of algorithms presents an opportunity for effective *algorithm selection*.

Amadini [3] provides extensive documentation of this diversity, and classifies approaches to string constraint solving into three main categories: automata-based, word-based, and unfolding-based approaches. Automata-based approaches use finite automata to represent string variables and constraints. Word-based approaches reason about systems of word equations directly, while unfolding-based approaches expand string variables over the sequences of characters they represent. Solvers such as CVC4 [6], Z3str3 [9], and Z3seq [18] follow the word-based approach and implement a variety of algebraic proof rules, reductions, and axiomatizations for string formulas. Stranger [42] is an automata-based tool that uses reachability analysis together with finite automata representations of string constraints. The HAMPI tool [25] uses an unfolding-based approach, wherein the maximum length of each string variable is fixed *a priori* and solved using a reduction to bit-vector formulas.

We leverage this opportunity to apply algorithm selection for solvers, and introduce a new string solver, Z3STR4, that incorporates two novel solver algorithms and several optimization methods aimed at algorithm selection. Z3STR4 outperforms the previous best solvers, namely, CVC4, Z3seq, and the baseline Z3str3 overall on a diverse suite of 120,000+ industrial and randomly-generated instances from 20 different benchmarks (most of which were obtained from competing teams), on the basis of total number of instances solved and run time.

Contributions. We make the following contributions in this paper.

1. **A Length Abstraction Solver.** We present a length abstraction algorithm for solving string formulas based on abstractions and refinements of integer constraints. The algorithm iteratively refines an integer over-approximation of the input formula until it converges to the correct answer (See Subsect. 3.1).
2. **An Arrangement Solver with a Bit-Vector Backend.** We extend an existing arrangement method [9] for string solving via a conflict-driven clause learning-style abstraction-refinement string-to-bit-vector algorithm.

This hybrid approach combines the efficiency of an unfolding-based strategy with the ability of a word-based algorithm to reason about string terms of unbounded length (See Subsect. 3.1).

3. **Z3str4's Arm Selection Architecture.** We propose a variant of algorithm selection, *arm selection*, that selects sequences of algorithms to run on an input query. When one algorithm times out or gives up, the next algorithm is called immediately. Our arm selection method considers static and dynamic features. Additionally, algorithms within an arm can share constraints for additional performance benefits (See Subsect. 3.2).

4. **Extensive Experimental Results.** We combine the above-mentioned new methods as well as the Z3seq solver in an arm selection architecture, and call the resulting solver Z3STR4. We present an extensive experimental evaluation of Z3STR4 against three other state-of-the-art solvers, namely, CVC4, Z3seq, and Z3str3. Z3STR4 outperforms all these solvers overall. Results and code are available at `https://z3str4.github.io` (See Sect. 4).

We also performed extensive evaluations against other well-known solvers such as S3, S3P, Norn, Trau, Stranger, and Ostrich. Unfortunately, all these solvers suffer from either significant soundness issues (Trau, S3, Norn, Ostrich) producing incorrect results, robustness issues, or crashes (S3P, Trau, Norn, Ostrich), or do not support relevant functions/predicates or Boolean operators that are part of the SMT-LIB 2.6 standard (e.g., Stranger does not support arbitrary string disequalities). Hence, we report on them only very briefly in Sect. 4.

2   Formal Background

In this section, we provide a brief overview of the input language accepted by Z3STR4 and the logical theory T_S considered in this paper.

2.1   Logical Theory T_S

For further details on the syntax and semantics of this theory, we refer the reader to the SMT-LIB standard [8].

Syntax. The Z3STR4 solver accepts input in the SMT-LIB format [8] following the current published standard for the theory of strings, and can handle quantifier-free formulas over Boolean combinations of string, integer, and regular expression (regex) formulas and terms. Atomic formulas handled by the string solver include string equalities and disequalities, regular expression membership, and extended string predicates such as `contains`, `prefixof`, `suffixof`, etc. Atomic formulas over integers, which may include inequalities, are handled by Z3's arithmetic solver. Boolean combinations of atomic formulas are handled by Z3's core solver in conjunction with the string and arithmetic solvers in a DPLL(T)-style approach. A summary of the basic syntax of the theory T_S is presented in Fig. 1. (We note that while we do support regex constraints, we shall not discuss them any further in this paper.)

$$
\begin{aligned}
F &::= Atom \mid F \wedge F \mid F \vee F \mid \neg F \\
Atom &::= t_{str} = t_{str} \mid A_{int} \mid A_{ext} \mid A_{re} \\
A_{re} &::= t_{str} \in RE \\
A_{int} &::= t_{int} = t_{int} \mid t_{int} < t_{int} \\
A_{ext} &::= contains(t_{str}, t_{str}) \mid prefix(t_{str}, t_{str}) \mid suffix(t_{str}, t_{str}) \\
t_{int} &::= m \mid v \mid len(t_{str}) \mid t_{int} + t_{int} \mid m \cdot t_{int} \mid indexof(t_{str}, t_{str}, t_{int}) \mid \\
& \quad str.to\_int(t_{str}) \text{ where } m \in Con_{int} \text{ \& } v \in Var_{int} \\
t_{str} &::= s \mid v \mid t_{str} \cdot t_{str} \mid str.from\_int(t_{int}) \mid replace(t_{str}, t_{str}, t_{str}) \mid \\
& \quad charAt(t_{str}, t_{int}) \mid substr(t_{str}, t_{int}, t_{int}) \text{ where } s \in Con_{str} \text{ \& } v \in Var_{str}
\end{aligned}
$$

Fig. 1. The syntax of the quantifier-free first-order theory T_S.

Semantics. String terms are composed of a finite (possibly empty) ordered sequence of characters taken from a finite alphabet, such as ASCII or Unicode. The expression $t_{str} \cdot t_{str}$ denotes string concatenation. For a string term w, $len(w)$ denotes the length of w as an integer number of characters. The empty string denoted by ϵ has a length of 0. Operations that refer to the index of a particular character or substring within another string use a zero-based index, that is, the first character of a string has an index of zero. The term str.to_int interprets a string as an integer by treating it as a non-negative number in base 10, possibly with leading zeroes. If the string represents a negative number or contains non-digit characters, the value is taken as -1. The term str.from_int converts a non-negative integer to the shortest possible string representing it in base 10. If the integer is negative, the value is taken as the empty string. Z3STR4 supports constraints over regular expressions, but we do not focus on regular expressions in this paper and instead refer the interested reader to [10].

The satisfiability problem for the quantifier-free theory T_S is to decide whether there exists an assignment of some constant in Con_{str} to every string variable in Var_{str} and some constant in Con_{int} to every integer variable in Var_{int} such that the formula evaluates to true. A formula is *satisfiable* (SAT) if such an assignment exists, and is *unsatisfiable* (UNSAT) if no such assignment exists.

3   Z3STR4 Components and Architecture

In this section, we describe the architecture of Z3STR4 and each of its components. Input to the Z3STR4 solver is given as an SMT-LIB formula, and the output is one of SAT, UNSAT, or UNKNOWN. Z3STR4 is built on top of Z3 and reuses its parser and core architecture. Once parsed, the formula is passed to Z3STR4's arm selection procedure, which makes use of a series of "probes" to analyze the formula and decide which of its arms is most appropriate for the given input. Each arm can call the novel length abstraction solver, the updated arrangement solver, and/or Z3's existing sequence solver in some predetermined order, as shown in Fig. 2. Z3STR4 moves to the next solver in the predetermined

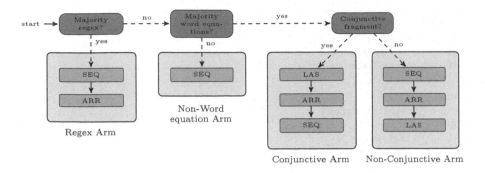

Fig. 2. Architecture of the Z3str4 tool. The red boxes indicate probes, and the blue boxes indicate algorithms. (Color figure online)

order when the current solver gives up. Solvers decide when to give up by using *dynamic difficulty estimation*, which we describe in Subsect. 3.2.

3.1 Novel Solver Algorithms in Z3str4

In this section, we describe the component algorithms of Z3STR4.

Z3str4's Length Abstraction Solver. We first describe a novel solving algorithm, called LAS, which uses an unfolding-based approach like HAMPI but overcomes the bounded length limitation by searching for length assignments. We begin with an overview of LAS's pseudocode in Algorithm 1, and then describe the subroutines it depends on in more detail. LAS takes in a conjunction ϕ of string literals, and returns either an assignment that satisfies ϕ or UNSAT. LAS begins by calling `MultisetCheck` at line 1. This subroutine can quickly determine UNSAT for many kinds of string constraints. If this check does not determine that the input is UNSAT, then LAS constructs θ_{lia}, an integer abstraction of ϕ, and enters its main solving loop. Every iteration of the loop updates θ_{lia}; the loop executes until either θ_{lia} is found to be UNSAT at line 5, or a satisfying string model is found at line 9. When θ_{lia} is SAT, we use a satisfying integer model, σ_{lia}, to reduce ϕ to a bit-vector query, θ_{bv}, and then check if θ_{bv} is SAT. If θ_{bv} is found to be SAT, at line 8, then we get a satisfying model, translate it to a satisfying string model, and return it as a solution. If θ_{bv} is found to be UNSAT, then we get an UNSAT core, update our length abstraction θ_{lia}, and repeat.

`MultisetCheck` is a heuristic that analyzes several static properties of atomic string formulas, and returns false if these formulas are UNSAT based on these properties. As an illustrative example, consider the word equation $0 \cdot X = X \cdot 1$. In order for this equation to be true, it is necessary that whatever value is assigned to X, the number of occurrences of each character on both sides must be equal. Since X appears on both sides exactly once, we can "cancel" it and

---

Algorithm 1: LAS Solver in Z3STR4

Data: Conjunction of theory literals ϕ
Result: Satisfying model or UNSAT

1 **if** ¬ `MultisetCheck`(ϕ) **then**
2 | **return** UNSAT
3 **end**
4 $\theta_{\text{lia}} \leftarrow$ `AbstractLengths`(ϕ)
5 **while** `LIACheck`$(\theta_{lia}) = SAT$ **do**
6 | $\sigma_{\text{lia}} \leftarrow$ `GetModel`(θ_{lia})
7 | $\theta_{\text{bv}} \leftarrow$ `ReduceToBV`(ϕ, σ_{lia})
8 | **if** `BVCheck`$(\theta_{bv}) = SAT$ **then**
9 | | **return** `TranslateModel`(`GetModel`(θ_{bv}))
10 | **else**
11 | | $\gamma_{\text{lia}} \leftarrow$ `Refine`(`GetUnsatCore`$(\theta_{bv}), \sigma_{lia})$
12 | | $\theta_{\text{lia}} \leftarrow \theta_{\text{lia}} \wedge \gamma_{\text{lia}}$
13 | **end**
14 **end**
15 **return** UNSAT

---

consider the remaining characters that appear in constant strings on each side. The left-hand side has a 0, but no 1s, and the right-hand side has a 1, but no 0s. From this we can conclude that the original equation must be false, since there is no way to assign X such that both sides have the same number of 0s or 1s. The `MultisetCheck` subroutine evaluates this heuristic by constructing the multisets of variables and characters that appear on each side of the equation and comparing them appropriately.

`AbstractLengths` takes the input query ϕ and returns an initial linear integer arithmetic length abstraction. The length abstraction contains simple length facts about the theory atoms in ϕ. For example, for the string equation $s = t$, we would assert $\text{len}(s) = \text{len}(t)$; for prefix$(s, t)$, we would assert $\text{len}(s) \leq \text{len}(t)$.

`ReduceToBV` takes a string formula f and an integer assignment σ (for string lengths and integer variables), and returns a bit-vector formula that is SAT iff $f \wedge \sigma$ is SAT. For example, given the formula $X = Y$, where X and Y are string variables, and the integer assignment $\sigma(\text{len}(X)) = 2 \wedge \sigma(\text{len}(Y)) = 2$, `ReduceToBV` would generate $X_1 = Y_1 \wedge X_2 = Y_2$, where all X_i and Y_i are 8-bit bit-vector variables. In this case, we say that the implied length constraint $\text{len}(X) = \text{len}(Y)$ *caused* the bit-vector equations $X_1 = Y_1$ and $X_2 = Y_2$. This bit-vector reduction is like that used by the HAMPI solver—we refer the reader to Ganesh et al. [25] for more details.

`LIACheck` and `BVCheck` take a linear integer arithmetic formula and bit-vector formula, respectively, and return either SAT or UNSAT. These two subroutines correspond to calling a linear integer arithmetic and bit-vector SMT solver, respectively. We implement this by calling a subsolver for the appropriate theory inside of Z3. For a concrete example, `BVCheck`$(X_1 = Y_1 \wedge X_2 = Y_2)$, where the input formula is as described above, would return SAT.

`GetModel` can only be used after a call to `LIACheck` or `BVCheck` that returned SAT. This subroutine returns a satisfying model from the previous solver. For example, calling `GetModel` after the call to `BVCheck` above, could return $\sigma_{bv}(X_1) = 11000001 \wedge \sigma_{bv}(X_2) = 11000010 \wedge \sigma_{bv}(Y_1) = 11000001 \wedge \sigma_{bv}(Y_2) = 11000010$. `TranslateModel` takes a bit-vector model and returns the corresponding string model. For example, given the bit-vector assignment σ_{bv}, `TranslateModel` would return $\sigma_s(X) = $ "ab" $\wedge \sigma_s(Y) = $ "ab".

`GetUnsatCore` can only be used after a call to `LIACheck` or `BVCheck` that returned UNSAT. This subroutine returns a conjunction of theory literals that is a subset of the input, and is UNSAT.

`Refine` takes the UNSAT core of a bit-vector reduction θ_{bv} and the integer model θ_{lia} that produced θ_{bv}, and returns a length constraint that will at least block the length assignment θ_{lia}. In many cases, `Refine` does better and blocks more than one assignment. This is formalized in Theorem 1. To get an intuition for how refine works, we first walk through an example. Consider the input query $X \cdot X \cdot Y = Y \cdot 1 \cdot 2 \cdot X \wedge Y = X \cdot 3$ with the length assignments $len(X) = 2$ and $len(Y) = 3$. In this case θ_{bv} would be

$$X_1 = Y_1 \wedge X_2 = Y_2 \wedge X_1 = Y_3 \wedge X_2 = 1 \wedge Y_1 = 2 \wedge Y_2 = X_1 \wedge Y_3 = X_2$$
$$\wedge Y_1 = X_1 \wedge Y_2 = X_2 \wedge Y_3 = 3$$

where X_i and Y_i are characters at position i of X and Y, respectively. An UNSAT core for θ_{bv} would be $X_2 = 1 \wedge Y_3 = X_2 \wedge Y_3 = 3$. Given this UNSAT core, `Refine` will generate the constraint $len(X \cdot X) \neq len(Y \cdot 1) \vee len(X \cdot X \cdot Y) \neq len(Y \cdot 1 \cdot 2 \cdot X) \vee len(Y) \neq len(X \cdot 3)$, which simplifies to $2 \cdot len(X) \neq len(Y)+1$ when taking into account the initial length abstraction. In other words, `Refine` creates a constraint that ensures that the same pairs of characters in an UNSAT core are never aligned again. These lessons are general when the bit-vector queries do not contain disjunctions and when the counterexamples fall on concatenation boundaries. If `Refine` is unable to learn a general lesson, as described in Theorem 1, it will negate θ_{lia}.

Theorem 1 (Simple, General Refine). *Let ϕ_{bv} be the bit-vector reduction of a word equation $X^1 \cdot ... \cdot X^n = Y^1 \cdot ... \cdot Y^m$ for some length assignment. Suppose $C := X_i = Y_j \wedge ... \wedge X_l = Y_k$ is a bit-vector UNSAT core for ϕ_{bv}, where every X_a and Y_b are the characters at positions $len(X^1 \cdot ... \cdot X^a)$ and $len(Y^1 \cdot ... \cdot Y^b)$ of the word equation, respectively, and let C_{len} be C but with every bit-vector equality replaced with the corresponding length constraint that caused each equality in ϕ_{bv}:*

$$C_{len} := len(X^1 \cdot ... \cdot X^i) = len(Y^1 \cdot ... \cdot Y^j) \wedge ... \wedge len(X^1 \cdot ... \cdot X^l) = len(Y^1 \cdot ... \cdot Y^k).$$

Then any lengths that satisfy C_{len} will cause an UNSAT bit-vector reduction.

Proof. Construct the same UNSAT core up to renaming of bit-vector variables. □

The main loop of Algorithm 1 returns UNSAT when there are no integer solutions to explore, and it returns SAT if a satisfying bit-vector model is found.

At a high-level, this algorithm is correct because **Refine** never blocks length assignments that could lead to a satisfying bit-vector reduction, and because every bit-vector model corresponds to a string model. Unfortunately, Algorithm 1 is not guaranteed to terminate.

Z3str4's Arrangement Solver with a Bit-vector Backend. The arrangement solver invoked by Z3STR4 is a variant of the one implemented in the Z3str3 solver [9]. The key modification is the introduction of a bit-vector backend which is invoked after arrangement reduction has finished. The bit-vector backend re-uses many of the components of LAS, but it follows the conflict-driven clause learning architecture of Z3str2 [43] and Z3str3.

Solving Strings via Arrangements. We briefly describe the arrangement solver for completeness, and refer the reader to previous papers [9,43] on this topic for a more thorough description. The core idea behind the arrangement technique is the reduction of string equations to simpler string equations until the formula is in "solved form": a conjunction of equations of the form $X = t$, where X is a string variable that appears in the input formula, t is a concatenation of string constants and possibly fresh string variables, and every variable in the input formula appears exactly once. See Section 4.3 of Ganesh et al. [21] for the complete, original definition of solved form. When considering an equality between strings, the arrangement technique introduces a disjunction of formulas describing the possible relationships between variables on the left-hand side and right-hand side of the equation. For example, for the equality $A \cdot B = X \cdot Y$, there are three possible relationships between A and X: either A and X have the same length, or A is shorter than X, or A is longer than X. The arrangement technique expresses the possible relationships with the following three implied formulas: either $A = X$ and $B = Y$, or $A \cdot X_1 = X$ and $B = X_1 \cdot Y$ for a fresh string variable X_1, or $A = X \cdot X_2$ and $X_2 \cdot B = Y$ for a fresh string variable X_2. These three formulas are asserted as a disjunction to the core solver, which chooses one branch to explore. The solver continues to reduce and explore the resulting formulas until either (1) it has reduced the entire formula to solved form or (2) it encounters an *overlap*. We describe the use of the novel bit-vector backend for both cases and define overlaps in the next two paragraphs.

ReduceToBV for Solved Form. The arrangement solver makes use of the same subroutines for reduction of strings to bit-vectors (**ReduceToBV**, **BVCheck**, **GetModel**, and **TranslateModel**) described for LAS. The bit-vector reduction is invoked after arrangement reduction completes and the integer constraints have been solved by Z3's arithmetic theory solver. That is, the bit-vector backend is used as the model construction algorithm once the solver has found a set of formulas in solved form. If the bit-vector reduction returns UNSAT, we block the corresponding assignment in Z3's core solver and instruct it to continue the search with a different length assignment or a different arrangement. This repeats until Z3STR4 converges to the correct answer and returns SAT, or the core solver finds a top-level conflict and returns UNSAT. Note that unlike LAS,

$$F \quad ::= Atom \mid F \wedge F \mid \neg G \mid A_{int} \vee A_{int} \mid \neg A_{int}$$
$$G \quad ::= G \vee G \mid \neg F$$
$$Atom ::= t_{str} = t_{str} \mid A_{int} \mid A_{ext}$$
$$A_{int} \quad ::= t_{int} = t_{int} \mid t_{int} < t_{int}$$
$$A_{ext} \quad ::= prefix(t_{str}, t_{str}) \mid suffix(t_{str}, t_{str})$$
$$t_{int} \quad ::= m \mid v \mid len(t_{str}) \mid t_{int} + t_{int} \mid m \cdot t_{int}$$
$$\text{where } m \in Con_{int} \ \& \ v \in Var_{int}$$
$$t_{str} \quad ::= s \mid v \mid t_{str} \cdot t_{str} \mid charAt(t_{str}, t_{int})$$
$$\text{where } s \in Con_{str} \ \& \ v \in Var_{str}$$

Fig. 3. Context-free grammar for conjunctive fragment.

which invokes the arithmetic solver as a procedure, the arrangement solver uses the string and integer theory integration approach described previously [43].

Reduce to BV for Overlaps. An important weakness of Z3str3's arrangement solver is that it cannot handle word equations which have the same variable occurring on both the left hand and right hand side of an equation, referred to as an overlapping variable. Consider the equation $0 \cdot X = X \cdot 0$. Z3str3's solver would detect the existence of an overlapping variable and return UNKNOWN. However, Z3STR4 easily handles such equations. Observe that once string variable lengths have been fixed, string equations can still be reduced to bit-vectors even if they contain overlapping variables. For example, again considering $0 \cdot X = X \cdot 0$, if the arithmetic solver proposes the candidate model $len(X) = 2$, the bit-vector reduction would reduce X to the 8-bit bit-vector characters $x_1 x_2$ and solve the bit-vector equation $0 x_1 x_2 = x_1 x_2 0$, finding it satisfiable with solution $X = 00$.

3.2 Algorithm Selection and Clause Sharing

We now describe how the component algorithms of Z3STR4 are combined using the arm selection procedure and the clause-sharing mechanism. The arm selection method uses static features of the instance to determine which of the three solver algorithms to invoke and in what order. Dynamic difficulty estimation determines when to move to the next solver in order.

Static Arm Selection. The input formula ϕ is first passed to Z3's simplifier and term rewriting procedure. The algorithm selection procedure then follows a three-tiered sequence of checks for static features, illustrated in Fig. 2. The order and choice of solvers to use was determined by a combination of empirical results and experimentation. First, if any regex constraints appear in the input formula ϕ, the arrangement solver is used. Otherwise, if a majority of top-level formulas in the input are *not* word equations, the sequence solver is used. Finally, the algorithm selection procedure calls the ConjunctiveFragment subroutine. This subroutine returns TRUE if the query is in the language generated by the grammar in Fig. 3, and FALSE otherwise. We call this language the conjunctive fragment. When a query is in the conjunctive fragment, we call LAS first, followed by the arrangement solver and the sequence solver. When a query is not in the conjunctive fragment, we call the sequence solver first, followed by the arrangement solver and the LAS solver.

The conjunctive fragment is effective because queries in the language are guaranteed to reduce to conjunctions of bit-vector equations when lengths are fixed (formalized in Theorem 2). This means that every iteration of LAS is quick (bit-vector solvers are efficient in this fragment), and LAS is more likely to learn general lessons (see Theorem 1).

Theorem 2 (Conjunctive Fragment). *Let L be the language generated by the grammar in Fig. 3. If $\varphi \in L$ is an input query, then LAS will always call* ReduceToBV *such that it produces a conjunction of bit-vector equations.*

Proof. LAS receives conjunctions of theory literals from the core solver (ϕ from Algorithm 1 is a solution to the Boolean abstraction of the input query φ). Show by induction on the grammar L that equality, prefix and suffix predicates must always appear under an even number of negations. Finally, show that theory literals that use these predicates will reduce to a conjunction of bit-vector equations iff they appear under an even number of negations.   □

Dynamic Difficulty Estimation. Rather than giving solvers a fixed time budget, we give up on them when it is unlikely that they will terminate. We call this process of monitoring the internal state of a solver and determining when to give up *dynamic difficulty estimation*. We incorporated dynamic difficulty estimation into the Z3 sequence solver and LAS.

At a high level, the Z3 sequence solver works as a sequence of checks: if a check fails, then a corresponding action is taken (for example, asserting an implied formula) and the process repeats; if all checks pass, then the query is solved. In total, the sequence solver has 20 of these checks. We observe that queries that are "easy" for the sequence solver rarely fail later checks. Our difficulty estimation monitor, therefore, keeps track of the current latest failing check, and we give up when the latest failing check is the ith check, where i can be specified as a solver parameter. Empirically, we find the best check to give up on to be the second to last check, branch_nqs. Additionally, we found that monitoring the number of automata propagations and calls to solve_eq performs similarly well.

LAS generates a bit-vector query that is solved by an external bit-vector solver. We measure two main aspects of LAS's state: the number of times ReduceToBV has been called, and the amount of time taken by each bit-vector check. We find that the benefit of each successive iteration diminishes rapidly, and that the time taken by the bit-vector solver tends to increase with each successive call (due to finding larger integer models). We fix the maximum number of iterations and the maximum time budget for a bit-vector check. When the solver exceeds either limit, we move to the next solver. Empirically, LAS solves most queries in the conjunctive fragment in under five iterations.

Constraint Sharing in Z3str4. When Z3STR4 switches from one solver to the next, it is useful to propagate information. This ensures that subsequent solvers will not get "stuck" exploring the same search space. We implemented a mechanism in Z3's SMT architecture wherein a theory solver can indicate during the search that one or more constraints are to be shared to future solvers in the event that it fails. Specifically, the LAS solver and arrangement solver both share blocked length assignments learned during the search. The only requirement for this to remain sound and complete is that each shared constraint must be implied by the original input formula and cannot contain any new variables that do not appear in the original formula.

4   Performance Evaluation

In this section, we report on the performance of Z3STR4 and how it compares against state-of-art solvers, CVC4, Z3seq, and Z3str3, over 20 different benchmark suites obtained from industrial applications as well as solver developers.

Description of Benchmark Suites. We evaluated Z3STR4 and competing solvers over 20 benchmark suites containing 120366 instances covering a wide range of applications. This is, to the best of our knowledge, the largest and most comprehensive collection of instances known for testing string solvers. Most of these suites were curated by solver developers or industrial users.

Of the 20 suites we used in our experimental evaluation, 16 are from various published sources, while one (BanditFuzz) is previously unpublished. The following benchmark suites come from well-known applications: Kaluza [35], PyEx [34], SMTLIB25 [7], PISA [37], IBM AppScan [43], Leetcode Strings [1], Sloth [22], Cashew [13], JOACO [38], Kausler [24]. The following suites were published by solver developers: Z3str3 Regression [9], Norn [2], Woorpje Word Equations [16], Trau Light [1], Stranger [42], StringFuzz [12], Automatark [10], stringfuzz-regex-generated [10], and stringfuzz-regex-transformed [10].

Competing String Solvers. We compared Z3STR4 against three leading string solvers, namely CVC4 [6], Z3str3 [9], and Z3seq [18].[1] We used the following criteria in determining which solvers to compare against: all of them had to be reasonably efficient on a diverse set of benchmarks, support the entirety of the string theory as standardized by the SMT-LIB initiative, be robust (have zero or very few crashes), and be reliable (have zero or very few wrong answers).

We also performed detailed evaluation of many other solvers, including S3, S3P [39], Norn [2], Trau, Z3-Trau [1], Ostrich [14], and Stranger [42]. Unfortunately, these solvers suffer from either significant soundness issues (S3, Norn, Trau, Ostrich), robustness issues (Trau, S3, Norn, Ostrich), or do not support string operations used in the benchmarks (Norn does not support the entire SMT-LIB input language; Ostrich does not support string length; Stranger does not support arbitrary string disequalities). Hence, we had to exclude them from our experimental evaluation. For example, Z3-Trau had more than 3,500 soundness errors and over 500 segmentation faults on our benchmarks.

---

[1] We used the binary version of CVC4 1.8 from cvc4.github.io. For Z3str3 and Z3seq, we used the commit #7e7360dd0c04cdee95c3f74a59908209742c5212 of the official repository of the Z3 solver (github.com/Z3Prover/z3).

Table 1. Cumulative results. Timeout = 20 s. Total time includes all solved, timeout, unknown and error instances. "Virtual Best Z3str4" represents perfect selection between Z3seq, LAS, and our novel arrangement solver. "Virtual Best Overall" represents perfect selection between CVC4, Z3seq, Z3str3, and Z3str4.

	CVC4	Z3seq	Z3str3	Z3str4	Virtual Best Z3str4	Virtual best overall
sat	68386	69853	59663	**71842**	74012	74096
unsat	43897	43783	41198	**44597**	44659	44923
unknown	**40**	50	949	170	454	113
timeout	8043	6680	18556	**3757**	1241	1234
soundness error	0	0	9	0	0	0
program crashes	0	0	0	0	0	0
Total correct	112283	113636	100852	**116439**	118671	119019
Time (s)	187941.021	176134.056	391379.159	**107456.964**	50996.414	44527.707
Time w/o timeouts (s)	27080.148	42534.056	**20259.159**	32316.964	23843.007	19289.888

Test Environment. All experiments were performed on a server running Ubuntu 18.04.4 LTS with two AMD EPYC 7742 processors and 2TB RAM using the ZaligVinder [26] benchmarking framework. We extended ZaligVinder with the ability to cross-validate models produced for SAT instances between solvers. The timeout for solving an instance was set at 20 s.

4.1 Overall Evaluation

Table 1 shows a summary of the results for all 20 benchmark sets, and is read as follows: the line "(un)sat" counts the number of instances classified (un)satisfiable, "Unknown" counts the number of instances where a solver returned UNKNOWN, and "Timeout" counts the number of instances where a solver exceeded its wall-time limit of 20 s. We also include the number of errors and crashes observed for each solver. "Total correct" counts the number of correctly classified instances. "Time" measures the total wall time to solve all instances, including timeouts, unknowns, and errors. The last line shows the total time excluding all timeouts. The rightmost columns of Table 1 present the "virtual best solvers:" hypothetical tools that always run the fastest solver for every query from an input set of solvers. The first virtual best solver, "Virtual Best Z3str4," selects between the algorithms within Z3STR4's portfolio (Z3seq, LAS, and our novel arrangement solver). The second virtual best solver, "Virtual Best Overall," depicts perfect selection among the state-of-the-art solvers (CVC4, Z3seq, Z3str3, and Z3str4). The same data is visually depicted as a cactus plot in Fig. 4. A detailed view containing the cumulative results for each benchmark group is available at https://z3str4.github.io.

Overall, Z3STR4 outperforms CVC4, Z3str3, and Z3seq, solving more instances and having a lower total solving time than every other solver and with no errors or crashes. Z3STR4 solves 4156 more cases than CVC4, 2803 more cases than Z3seq, and 15587 more cases than Z3str3. Including timeouts,

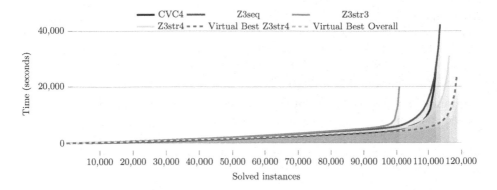

Fig. 4. Cactus plot of string solvers on all benchmarks. Timeout = 20 s. Timeout, unknown, and error instances excluded.

Z3STR4 is 75% faster than CVC4, 64% faster than Z3seq, and 264% faster than Z3str3. Z3STR4 approaches the overall virtual best solver in terms of number of queries solved (97.83%) and comes the closest in terms of total time taken (141%). Notably, our algorithm selection strategy approaches the optimal selection strategy for our portfolio of solvers ("Virtual Best Z3str4") and solves only 2232 fewer instances. The overall results indicate that Z3STR4 is highly effective at solving a wide variety of practical string instances.

4.2 Performance Analysis of Components of Z3STR4

To evaluate our architecture and to better understand our component algorithms, we categorize the queries by the arm they are assigned to and compare our component algorithms on the queries they are meant to do well on versus the queries they are not meant to do well on. There are 35345 regex queries, 42522 higher-order queries, 15113 conjunctive queries, and 23643 non-conjunctive queries. We exclude 3743 queries that are solved by the simplifier.

LAS Performance Analysis. We hypothesize that LAS will do comparatively better in the conjunctive fragment because it will learn more general lessons and its underlying bit-vector solver will be quicker every iteration. Empirically this hypothesis holds: LAS solves more queries per second compared to the arrangement solver in the conjunctive fragment (1128.5%) than it does outside the conjunctive fragment (904.6%). These high percentages are largely due to dynamic difficulty estimation, which lets LAS return unknown before wasting too much time on a query. Overall, we find that LAS is extremely effective in the conjunctive fragment, especially when used as the first solver in an arm.

Arrangement Solver Performance Analysis. The arrangement solver with our novel bit-vector backend significantly improves performance over the arrangement solver without the bit-vector backend, both in terms of time and number of instances solved. Without the bit-vector backend, the arrangement solver solves 72417 instances in 423949.163 s; with the bit-vector backend, the arrangement solver solves 107401 instances (148.3% of the queries without) in 262047.893 s (61.8% of the time without).

Sequence Solver Performance Analysis. Empirically, we find that the sequence solver is best when most constraints are not word equations. In this fragment, the sequence solver solves 39639 cases in 74565.085 s, while the next best solver, the arrangement solver, solves only 31376 (79.1%) in 220076.933 s (295.1% of the sequence solver's time).

Impact of Clause Sharing. Clause sharing significantly reduces the amount of time taken and slightly increases the number of solved instances. In particular, over all benchmarks, with clause sharing turned off, Z3STR4 solves 15 fewer cases and takes 2201.790 more seconds (102% of the time taken with clause sharing).

5 Related Work

Theory and Practice of String Solvers. Makanin showed in 1977 that the theory of quantifier-free word equations was decidable [30]. Plandowski later showed that this problem was in PSPACE [32]. Continuing the aforementioned thread of research, Ganesh et al. proved that satisfiability for quantified word equations with a single quantifier alternation is undecidable, as well as that satisfiability of the quantifier-free SMT-LIB theory of strings, including string-integer conversion, is also undecidable [20,21]. Many extensions to the theory of word equations have been shown to be undecidable [17,20,23,29,30,32].

HAMPI [25] is one of the first string solvers that used the idea of reducing fixed-length string constraints to bit-vectors. While highly effective, HAMPI does not support unbounded string variables, as many newer tools now do. Z3STR4's arrangement and length abstraction solvers use a similar reduction to bit-vectors, but do so in an abstraction refinement fashion that enables them to support constraints with arbitrary-length string variables. An interesting detail about Z3STR4's method for fixing string variable lengths is that it uses Z3's arithmetic solver to obtain length assignments for input string constraints that are consistent with input length constraints.

The Z3 theorem prover [18] is a DPLL(T)-based SMT solver for theory combinations over first-order logic. Z3 includes an arithmetic solver for linear integer arithmetic, and a sequence solver that supports word-based reasoning over strings. Z3STR4 uses Z3's sequence (Z3seq) solver as part of both arms considered during its algorithm selection. The Z3str3 solver [9] is based on Z3 and the previous Z3str2 solver [43]. It uses a reduction known as the arrangement technique to convert word equations into simpler formulas until a so-called "solved form" is reached. Z3STR4 uses a version of Z3str3 that has been extended with a string-to-bit-vector reduction, better heuristics for handling formulas with "overlapping variables" which Z3str3 (and Z3str2) have difficulties dealing with, and the ability to share certain learned clauses between invocations of the solver. The CVC4 solver [6] handles constraints over the theory of strings and arithmetic using an algebraic approach, and uses a similar DPLL(T) architecture to Z3. Norn [2] is an automata-based solver that solves integer arithmetic constraints using finite automata and then represents word equations with finite automata that have been restricted with respect to concrete length constraints. Stranger [42] is another automata-based approach, but based on a static analysis technique that determines possible solutions of a string variable while traversing an automaton. Ostrich [14] implements another technique using transducers to solving string constraints. A stand-alone solver named Trau [1] uses an approach which looks for simple patterns inside the input formula within a CEGAR framework.

Algorithm Selection for Solvers. SATZilla [41] is a portfolio-based algorithm selection strategy for Boolean SAT problems that uses many features of a SAT formula to predict the performance of each SAT solver in its portfolio and decide which solver to use for a given instance. SATZilla uses machine learning to train a predictive model of solver performance. FastSMT [5] uses machine learning to choose Z3 probes and tactics, a form of fine-grained method selection. After training on queries from one domain, the FastSMT generated strategy can be used to speed up the performance of Z3 on subsequent queries from that domain. FastSMT has been successfully applied to formulas which include bitvectors, integer arithmetic, and real arithmetic. We differ from FastSMT in that they are limited to existing probes, while we designed our own, and we also use dynamic information in addition to static features.

6 Conclusion and Future Work

We presented a new string solver, Z3STR4, which supports the entirety of the SMT-LIB standard for strings. Z3STR4 includes two novel algorithms for solving string constraints: a length abstraction algorithm and an arrangement solver with a string-to-bit-vector backend. Both of these algorithms use a variety of abstractions and refinements combined with a bit-vector reduction. We also describe an arm selection architecture which uses static features of an instance and dynamic information about solver state to get the best out of each algorithm. We demonstrated the performance of Z3STR4 over a comprehensive evaluation of 20 industrial and randomly-generated benchmarks and over 120,000 individual instances, showing that Z3STR4 outperforms leading string solvers.

As a future extension to this work, we plan to revisit the method by which algorithm selection is performed. Currently, the algorithm selection architecture is limited to choosing between fixed "arms" which have been hard-coded. Machine learning may give us the opportunity to learn a more sophisticated function for algorithm selection. Furthermore, we plan to improve the way in which constraints are shared between different algorithms within an arm by exploring the tradeoffs between constraint size and number of shared constraints.

Acknowledgments. We thank the anonymous reviewers whose comments and suggestions greatly improved our paper. This work was supported in part by NSF grants CNS-1739816 and CCF-1837132, by the DARPA LOGiCS project under contract FA8750-20-C-0156, by the iCyPhy center, and by gifts from Intel, Amazon, and Microsoft.

References

1. Abdulla, P.A., et al.: TRAU: SMT solver for string constraints. In: 2018 Formal Methods in Computer Aided Design (FMCAD), pp. 1–5. IEEE (2018)
2. Abdulla, P.A., et al.: Norn: an SMT solver for string constraints. In: Kroening, D., Păsăreanu, C.S. (eds.) CAV 2015. LNCS, vol. 9206, pp. 462–469. Springer, Cham (2015). https://doi.org/10.1007/978-3-319-21690-4_29
3. Amadini, R.: A survey on string constraint solving (2020)
4. Backes, J., et al.: Semantic-based automated reasoning for AWS access policies using SMT. In: Bjørner, N., Gurfinkel, A. (eds.) 2018 Formal Methods in Computer Aided Design, FMCAD 2018, Austin, TX, USA, 30 October–2 November 2018, pp. 1–9. IEEE (2018). https://doi.org/10.23919/FMCAD.2018.8602994
5. Balunovic, M., Bielik, P., Vechev, M.: Learning to solve SMT formulas. In: Bengio, S., Wallach, H., Larochelle, H., Grauman, K., Cesa-Bianchi, N., Garnett, R. (eds.) Advances in Neural Information Processing Systems, vol. 31, pp. 10337–10348. Curran Associates, Inc. (2018). http://papers.nips.cc/paper/8233-learning-to-solve-smt-formulas.pdf
6. Barrett, C., et al.: CVC4. In: Gopalakrishnan, G., Qadeer, S. (eds.) CAV 2011. LNCS, vol. 6806, pp. 171–177. Springer, Heidelberg (2011). https://doi.org/10.1007/978-3-642-22110-1_14
7. Barrett, C., Fontaine, P., Niemetz, A., Preiner, M., Schurr, H.J.: SMT-LIB benchmarks. https://clc-gitlab.cs.uiowa.edu:2443/SMT-LIB-benchmarks. commit 11f52315
8. Barrett, C., Fontaine, P., Tinelli, C.: The Satisfiability Modulo Theories Library (SMT-LIB). www.SMT-LIB.org (2016)
9. Berzish, M., Ganesh, V., Zheng, Y.: Z3str3: a string solver with theory-aware heuristics. In: 2017 Formal Methods in Computer Aided Design (FMCAD), pp. 55–59. IEEE (2017)
10. Berzish, M., et al.: An SMT solver for regular expressions and linear arithmetic over string length. In: Silva, A., Leino, K.R.M. (eds.) CAV 2021. LNCS, vol. 12760, pp. 289–312. Springer, Cham (2021). https://doi.org/10.1007/978-3-030-81688-9_14
11. Bjørner, N., Tillmann, N., Voronkov, A.: Path feasibility analysis for string-manipulating programs. In: Kowalewski, S., Philippou, A. (eds.) TACAS 2009. LNCS, vol. 5505, pp. 307–321. Springer, Heidelberg (2009). https://doi.org/10.1007/978-3-642-00768-2_27
12. Blotsky, D., Mora, F., Berzish, M., Zheng, Y., Kabir, I., Ganesh, V.: StringFuzz: a Fuzzer for string solvers. In: Chockler, H., Weissenbacher, G. (eds.) CAV 2018. LNCS, vol. 10982, pp. 45–51. Springer, Cham (2018). https://doi.org/10.1007/978-3-319-96142-2_6
13. Brennan, T., Tsiskaridze, N., Rosner, N., Aydin, A., Bultan, T.: Constraint normalization and parameterized caching for quantitative program analysis. In: Bodden, E., Schäfer, W., van Deursen, A., Zisman, A. (eds.) Proceedings of the 2017 11th Joint Meeting on Foundations of Software Engineering, ESEC/FSE 2017, Paderborn, Germany, 4–8 September 2017, pp. 535–546. ACM (2017). https://doi.org/10.1145/3106237.3106303

14. Chen, T., Hague, M., Lin, A.W., Rümmer, P., Wu, Z.: Decision procedures for path feasibility of string-manipulating programs with complex operations. In: Proceedings of the ACM on Programming Languages, vol. 3, no. POPL, pp. 1–30 (2019)

15. D'Antoni, L., Veanes, M.: The power of symbolic automata and transducers. In: Majumdar, R., Kunčak, V. (eds.) CAV 2017. LNCS, vol. 10426, pp. 47–67. Springer, Cham (2017). https://doi.org/10.1007/978-3-319-63387-9_3

16. Day, J.D., Ehlers, T., Kulczynski, M., Manea, F., Nowotka, D., Poulsen, D.B.: On solving word equations using SAT. In: Filiot, E., Jungers, R., Potapov, I. (eds.) RP 2019. LNCS, vol. 11674, pp. 93–106. Springer, Cham (2019). https://doi.org/10.1007/978-3-030-30806-3_8

17. Day, J.D., Ganesh, V., He, P., Manea, F., Nowotka, D.: The satisfiability of word equations: decidable and undecidable theories. In: Potapov, I., Reynier, P.-A. (eds.) RP 2018. LNCS, vol. 11123, pp. 15–29. Springer, Cham (2018). https://doi.org/10.1007/978-3-030-00250-3_2

18. de Moura, L., Bjørner, N.: Z3: an efficient SMT solver. In: Ramakrishnan, C.R., Rehof, J. (eds.) TACAS 2008. LNCS, vol. 4963, pp. 337–340. Springer, Heidelberg (2008). https://doi.org/10.1007/978-3-540-78800-3_24

19. Emmi, M., Majumdar, R., Sen, K.: Dynamic test input generation for database applications. In: ISSTA, pp. 151–162 (2007)

20. Ganesh, V., Berzish, M.: Undecidability of a theory of strings, linear arithmetic over length, and string-number conversion. CoRR arXiv:1605.09442 (2016). http://arxiv.org/abs/1605.09442

21. Ganesh, V., Minnes, M., Solar-Lezama, A., Rinard, M.: Word equations with length constraints: what's decidable? In: Biere, A., Nahir, A., Vos, T. (eds.) HVC 2012. LNCS, vol. 7857, pp. 209–226. Springer, Heidelberg (2013). https://doi.org/10.1007/978-3-642-39611-3_21

22. Holík, L., Janku, P., Lin, A.W., Rümmer, P., Vojnar, T.: String constraints with concatenation and transducers solved efficiently. In: PACMPL, vol. 2, no. POPL, pp. 4:1–4:32 (2018). https://doi.org/10.1145/3158092

23. Jez, A.: Recompression: a simple and powerful technique for word equations. In: Proceedings of STACS, LIPIcs, vol. 20, pp. 233–244 (2013)

24. Kausler, S., Sherman, E.: Evaluation of string constraint solvers in the context of symbolic execution. In: Proceedings of ASE - IEEE/ACM, pp. 259–270. ACM (2014)

25. Kiezun, A., Ganesh, V., Guo, P.J., Hooimeijer, P., Ernst, M.D.: HAMPI: a solver for string constraints. In: Proceedings of the Eighteenth International Symposium on Software Testing and Analysis, ISSTA 2009, pp. 105–116 (2009). https://doi.org/10.1145/1572272.1572286

26. Kulczynski, M., Manea, F., Nowotka, D., Poulsen, D.B.: The power of string solving: simplicity of comparison. In: Proceedings of AST (2020)

27. Liang, T., Reynolds, A., Tinelli, C., Barrett, C., Deters, M.: A DPLL(T) theory solver for a theory of strings and regular expressions. In: Biere, A., Bloem, R. (eds.) CAV 2014. LNCS, vol. 8559, pp. 646–662. Springer, Cham (2014). https://doi.org/10.1007/978-3-319-08867-9_43

28. Lin, A.W., Majumdar, R.: Quadratic word equations with length constraints, counter systems, and Presburger arithmetic with divisibility. In: Lahiri, S.K., Wang, C. (eds.) ATVA 2018. LNCS, vol. 11138, pp. 352–369. Springer, Cham (2018). https://doi.org/10.1007/978-3-030-01090-4_21

29. Lin, A.W., Barceló, P.: String solving with word equations and transducers: towards a logic for analysing mutation XSS. In: Bodík, R., Majumdar, R. (eds.) Proceedings of the 43rd Annual ACM SIGPLAN-SIGACT Symposium on Principles of Programming Languages, POPL 2016, St. Petersburg, FL, USA, 20–22 January 2016, pp. 123–136. ACM (2016). https://doi.org/10.1145/2837614.2837641

30. Makanin, G.: The problem of solvability of equations in a free semigroup. Math. Sbornik **103**, 147–236 (1977). English transl. in Math USSR Sbornik 32 (1977)

31. Matiyasevich, Y.: The connection between Hilbert's tenth problem and systems of equations between words and lengths. Semin. Math., V. A. Steklov Math. Inst., Leningrad **8**, 61–67 (1968). translation from Zap. Nauchn. Semin. Leningr. Otd. Mat. Inst. Steklov 8, 132–144 (1968)

32. Plandowski, W.: An efficient algorithm for solving word equations. In: Proceedings of the 38th Annual ACM Symposium on Theory of Computing STOC 2006, pp. 467–476 (2006). https://doi.org/10.1145/1132516.1132584

33. Redelinghuys, G., Visser, W., Geldenhuys, J.: Symbolic execution of programs with strings. In: Proceedings of the South African Institute for Computer Scientists and Information Technologists Conference, SAICSIT 2012, pp. 139–148 (2012). https://doi.org/10.1145/2389836.2389853

34. Reynolds, A., Woo, M., Barrett, C., Brumley, D., Liang, T., Tinelli, C.: Scaling Up DPLL(T) string solvers using context-dependent simplification. In: Majumdar, R., Kunčak, V. (eds.) CAV 2017. LNCS, vol. 10427, pp. 453–474. Springer, Cham (2017). https://doi.org/10.1007/978-3-319-63390-9_24

35. Saxena, P., Akhawe, D., Hanna, S., Mao, F., McCamant, S., Song, D.: A symbolic execution framework for JavaScript. In: Proceedings of the 2010 IEEE Symposium on Security and Privacy, SP 2010, pp. 513–528. IEEE Computer Society, Washington (2010). https://doi.org/10.1109/SP.2010.38

36. Sen, K., Kalasapur, S., Brutch, T., Gibbs, S.: Jalangi: a selective record-replay and dynamic analysis framework for JavaScript. In: Proceedings of the 2013 9th Joint Meeting on Foundations of Software Engineering, ESEC/FSE 2013, pp. 488–498. ACM, New York (2013). https://doi.org/10.1145/2491411.2491447

37. Tateishi, T., Pistoia, M., Tripp, O.: Path- and index-sensitive string analysis based on monadic second-order logic. ACM Trans. Softw. Eng. Methodol. **22**(4), 33:1–33:33 (2013). https://doi.org/10.1145/2522920.2522926

38. Thomé, J., Shar, L.K., Bianculli, D., Briand, L.: An integrated approach for effective injection vulnerability analysis of web applications through security slicing and hybrid constraint solving. IEEE TSE **46**(2), 163–195 (2018)

39. Trinh, M.T., Chu, D.H., Jaffar, J.: S3: a symbolic string solver for vulnerability detection in web applications. In: Proceedings of the 2014 ACM SIGSAC Conference on Computer and Communications Security, pp. 1232–1243 (2014)

40. Wassermann, G., Su, Z.: Sound and precise analysis of web applications for injection vulnerabilities. In: Ferrante, J., McKinley, K. (eds.) PLDI, pp. 32–41. ACM (2007)

41. Xu, L., Hutter, F., Hoos, H.H., Leyton-Brown, K.: SATzilla: portfolio-based algorithm selection for SAT. CoRR arXiv:1111.2249 (2011)

42. Yu, F., Alkhalaf, M., Bultan, T.: STRANGER: an automata-based string analysis tool for PHP. In: Esparza, J., Majumdar, R. (eds.) TACAS 2010. LNCS, vol. 6015, pp. 154–157. Springer, Heidelberg (2010). https://doi.org/10.1007/978-3-642-12002-2_13

43. Zheng, Y., et al.: Z3str2: an efficient solver for strings, regular expressions, and length constraints. Formal Meth. Syst. Des. **50**(2–3), 249–288 (2017)

Concise Outlines for a Complex Logic: A Proof Outline Checker for TaDA

Felix A. Wolf, Malte Schwerhoff[✉], and Peter Müller

Department of Computer Science, ETH Zurich, Zurich, Switzerland
{felix.wolf,malte.schwerhoff,peter.mueller}@inf.ethz.ch

Abstract. Modern separation logics allow one to prove rich properties of intricate code, e.g. functional correctness and linearizability of non-blocking concurrent code. However, this expressiveness leads to a complexity that makes these logics difficult to apply. Manual proofs or proofs in interactive theorem provers consist of a large number of steps, often with subtle side conditions. On the other hand, automation with dedicated verifiers typically requires sophisticated proof search algorithms that are specific to the given program logic, resulting in limited tool support that makes it difficult to experiment with program logics, e.g. when learning, improving, or comparing them. Proof outline checkers fill this gap. Their input is a program annotated with the most essential proof steps, just like the proof outlines typically presented in papers. The tool then checks automatically that this outline represents a valid proof in the program logic. In this paper, we systematically develop a proof outline checker for the TaDA logic, which reduces the checking to a simpler verification problem, for which automated tools exist. Our approach leads to proof outline checkers that provide substantially more automation than interactive provers, but are much simpler to develop than custom automatic verifiers.

1 Introduction

Standard separation logic enables the modular verification of heap-manipulating sequential [25,33] and data-race free concurrent programs [4,24]. More recently, numerous separation logics have been proposed that enable the verification of fine-grained concurrency by incorporating ideas from concurrent separation logic, Owicki-Gries [28], and rely-guarantee [15]. Examples include CAP [7], iCAP [40], CaReSL [42], CoLoSL [32], FCSL [37], GPS [43], RSL [45], and TaDA [35] (see Brookes et al. [3] for an overview). These logics are very expressive, but challenging to apply because they often comprise many complex proof rules. E.g. our running example (Fig. 1) consists of two statements, but requires over 20 rule applications in TaDA, many of which have non-trivial instantiations and subtle side conditions. This complexity seems inevitable for challenging verification problems involving, e.g. fine-grained concurrency or weak memory.

The complexity of advanced separation logics makes it difficult to develop proofs in these logics. It is, thus, crucial to have tools that check the validity

© Springer Nature Switzerland AG 2021
M. Huisman et al. (Eds.): FM 2021, LNCS 13047, pp. 407–426, 2021.
https://doi.org/10.1007/978-3-030-90870-6_22

of proofs and automate parts of the proof search. One way to provide this tool support is through *proof checkers*, which take as input a nearly complete proof and check its validity. They typically embed program logics into the higher-order logic of an interactive theorem prover such as Coq. Proof checkers exist, e.g. for RSL [45] and FCSL [37]. Alternatively, *automated verifiers* take as input a program with specifications and devise the proof automatically. They typically combine existing reasoning engines such as SMT solvers with logic-specific proof search algorithms. Examples are Smallfoot [2] and Grasshopper [31] for traditional separation logics, and Caper [8] for fine-grained concurrency.

Proof checkers and automated verifiers strike different trade-offs in the design space. Proof checkers are typically very expressive, enabling the verification of complex programs and properties, and produce foundational proofs. However, existing proof checkers offer little automation. Automated verifiers, on the other hand, significantly reduce the proof effort, but compromise on expressiveness and require substantial development effort, especially, to devise custom proof search algorithms.

It is in principle possible to increase the automation of proof checkers by developing proof tactics, or to increase the expressiveness of automated verifiers by developing stronger custom proof search algorithms. However, such developments are too costly for the vast majority of program logics, which serve mostly a scientific or educational purpose. As a result, adequate tool support is very rare, which makes it difficult for developers of such logics, lecturers and students, as well as engineers to apply, and gain experience with, such logics.

To remedy the situation, several tools took inspiration from the idea of *proof outlines* [1, 27], formal proof skeletons that contain the key proof steps, but omit most of the details. Proof outlines are a standard notation to present program proofs in publications and teaching material. *Proof outline checkers* such as Starling [46] and VeriFast [14] take as input a proof outline and then check automatically that it represents a valid proof in the program logic. They provide automation for proof steps for which good proof search algorithms exist, and can support expressive logics by requiring annotations for complex proof steps. Due to this flexibility, proof outline checkers are especially useful for experimenting with a logic, in situations where foundational proofs are not essential.

In this paper, we present Voila, a proof outline checker for TaDA [35], which goes beyond existing proof outline checkers and automated verifiers by supporting a substantially more complex program logic, handling fine-grained concurrency, linearizability, abstract atomicity, and other advanced features. We believe that our systematic development of Voila generalizes to other complex logics. Our contributions are as follows:

- The Voila *proof outline language*, which supports a large subset of TaDA and enables users to write proof outlines very similar to those used by the TaDA authors [34, 35] (Sect. 3).
- A systematic approach to automate the expansion of a proof outline into a full *proof candidate* via a normal form and heuristics (Sect. 5). Our approach automates most proof steps (20 out of 22 in the running example from Fig. 1).

- An encoding of the proof candidate into Viper [22], which checks its validity without requiring any TaDA-specific proof search algorithms (Sect. 6).
- The Voila proof outline checker, the *first* tool that supports specification for linearization points, provides a high degree of automation, and achieves good performance (Sect. 7). Our submission artifact with the Voila tool ready-to-use can be found at [49], and the Voila source repository is located at [48].

Outline. Section 2 gives an overview of the TaDA logic and illustrates our approach. Section 3 presents the Voila proof outline language, and Sect. 4 summarizes how we verify proof outlines. We explain how we automatically expand a proof outline into a proof candidate in Sect. 5 and how we encode a proof candidate into Viper in Sect. 6. In Sect. 7, we evaluate our technique by verifying several challenging examples, discuss related work in Sect. 8, and conclude in Sect. 9.

The full version of our paper [47] contains a substantial appendix with many further details, including: the full version and Viper encoding of our running example, with TaDA levels (omitted from this paper, but supported by Voila) and nested regions; additional inference heuristics; general Viper encoding scheme; encoding of a custom guard algebra; and a substantial soundness sketch.

2   Running Example and TaDA Overview

Figure 1 shows our running example: a TaDA proof outline for the lock procedure of a spinlock. As in the original publication [35], the outline shows only two out of 22 proof steps and omits most side conditions. We use this example to introduce the necessary TaDA background, explain TaDA proof outlines, and illustrate the corresponding Voila proof outline.

2.1   Regions and Atomicity

TaDA targets shared-memory concurrency with sequentially consistent memory. TaDA programs manipulate *shared regions*, data structures that are concurrently modified according to a specified *protocol* (as in rely-guarantee reasoning [15]). A shared region such as $\text{Lock}_r(x, s)$ is an abstraction over the region's content, analogous to abstract predicates [30] in traditional separation logic. In our example (lines 1–2), the lock owns memory location x (denoted by separation logic's points-to predicate $x \mapsto \_$), and its *abstract state* s is 0 or 1, indicating whether it is unlocked or locked. Here, the abstract state and the content of the memory location coincide, but they may differ in general. The subscript r uniquely identifies a region instance. Note that TaDA's region assertions are duplicable, such that multiple threads may obtain an instance of the Lock_r resource and invoke operations on the lock.

Lines 3–5 define the protocol for modifications of a lock as a labeled transition system. The labels are *guards* – abstract resources that restrict when a transition

$$
\begin{array}{ll}
1 & I(\mathbf{Lock}_r(x,0)) \triangleq x \mapsto 0 \\
2 & I(\mathbf{Lock}_r(x,1)) \triangleq x \mapsto 1 \\
\hline
3 & \mathrm{G} : 0 \rightsquigarrow 1 \\
4 & \mathrm{G} : 1 \rightsquigarrow 0 \\
\hline
5 & \mathrm{G} \bullet \mathrm{G} \text{ is undefined} \\
\hline
\end{array}
$$

```
 6   ∀s ∈ {0,1}.
 7   ⟨Lock_r(x, s) * [G]_r⟩
 8       r : s ∈ {0,1} ⇝ 1 ⊢
 9           {∃s ∈ {0,1}. Lock_r(x, s) * r ⤇ ♦}
10       do {
11           {∃s ∈ {0,1}. Lock_r(x, s) * r ⤇ ♦}

              ∀s ∈ {0,1}.
              ⟨x ↦ s⟩
              b := CAS(x, 0, 1);
              ⟨(x ↦ 1 * s = 0 * b = 1) ∨
               (x ↦ s * s ≠ 0 * b = 0)⟩

17           ⎧∃s ∈ {0,1}. Lock_r(x, s) *
18           ⎨((r ⤇ (0,1) * b = 1) ∨
19           ⎩(r ⤇ ♦ * b = 0))⎭
20       } while (b = 0);
21           {r ⤇ (0,1) * b = 1 * [G]_r}
22   ⟨Lock_r(x,1) * [G]_r * s = 0⟩
```

(left brace labels: **MAKEATOMIC** spanning lines 12–21, **UPDATEREGION** spanning lines 12–19)

Fig. 1. TaDA spinlock example with shared region Lock; adapted with only minor changes from TaDA [35]. The lock region (lines 1–2) comprises a single memory location, whose value is either 0 (available) or 1 (acquired). Guard G allows locking and unlocking (lines 3–4), and is unique (line 5). The proof outline (lines 6–22) shows a CAS-based lock operation with atomic specifications. An enclosing region (CAPLock in da Rocha Pinto et al. [35], verifiable by Voila and shown in the full paper [47] then establishes the usual lock semantics. Levels (denoted by λ in TaDA) are omitted from the discussion in this paper, but supported by Voila and included in the full paper [47].

may be taken. Here, guard G allows both locking and unlocking (lines 3–4), and is unique (line 5). Most lock specifications use duplicable guards to allow multiple threads to compete for the lock; in this example, the usual lock semantics is established by an enclosing region (CAPLock [35]; see the full paper [47]).

Lines 6–22 contain the proof outline for the lock procedure, which updates a lock x from an undetermined state – it can seesaw between locked and unlocked due to environment interference – to the locked state. Importantly, this update appears to be atomic to clients of the spinlock. These properties are expressed by the *atomic TaDA triple* (lines 6, 7, and 22)

$$
\forall s \in \{0,1\} \cdot \langle \mathtt{Lock}_r(x, s) * [\mathrm{G}]_r \rangle \ \mathtt{lock(x)} \ \langle \mathtt{Lock}_r(x, 1) * [\mathrm{G}]_r * s = 0 \rangle
$$

MAKEATOMIC $r \notin \mathcal{A}$ $\{(x,y) \mid x \in X, y \in Y\} \subseteq \mathcal{T}_R(G)^*$

$$\frac{r : x \in X \rightsquigarrow Y, \mathcal{A} \vdash \left\{\exists x \in X. \mathbf{R}_r^\lambda(\vec{z}, x) * r \mapsto \blacklozenge\right\} \mathbb{C} \left\{\exists x \in X, y \in Y. r \mapsto (x, y)\right\}}{\mathcal{A} \vdash \mathbb{W}x \in X. \left\langle \mathbf{R}_r^\lambda(\vec{z}, x) * [G]_r \right\rangle \mathbb{C} \left\langle \exists y \in Y. \mathbf{R}_r^\lambda(\vec{z}, y) * [G]_r \right\rangle}$$

UPDATEREGION

$$\frac{\mathcal{A} \vdash \mathbb{W}x \in X. \left\langle I(\mathbf{R}_r^\lambda(\vec{z}, x)) * P(x) \right\rangle \mathbb{C} \left\langle \exists y \in Y, w \in W. \begin{array}{c} I(\mathbf{R}_r^\lambda(\vec{z}, y)) * Q_1(x, y, w) \\ \vee\ I(\mathbf{R}_r^\lambda(\vec{z}\ x)) * Q_2(x, w) \end{array} \right\rangle}{\begin{array}{l} \mathbb{W}x \in X. \left\langle \mathbf{R}_r^\lambda(\vec{z}, x) * P(x) * r \mapsto \blacklozenge \right\rangle \\ r : x \in X \rightsquigarrow Y, \mathcal{A} \vdash \qquad\qquad\qquad \mathbb{C} \\ \left\langle \exists y \in Y, w \in W. \begin{array}{c} \mathbf{R}_r^\lambda(\vec{z}, y) * r \mapsto (x, y) * Q_1(x, y, w) \\ \vee\ \mathbf{R}_r^\lambda(\vec{z}, x) * r \mapsto \blacklozenge \qquad * Q_2(x, w) \end{array} \right\rangle \end{array}}$$

Fig. 2. Simplified versions of two key TaDA rules used in Fig. 1. MAKEATOMIC establishes an atomic triple (conclusion) for a linearizable block of code (premise), which includes checking that a state update complies with the region's transition system: $\mathcal{T}_R(G)^*$ is the reflexive, transitive closure of the transitions that G allows. UPDATERE-GION identifies a linearization point, for instance, a CAS statement. If successful, the diamond tracking resource $r \mapsto \blacklozenge$ is exchanged for the witness tracking resource $r \mapsto (x, y)$ to record the performed state update; otherwise, the diamond resource is kept, such that the operation can be attempted again.

Atomic triples (angle brackets) express that their statement is linearizable [13]. The abstract state of shared regions occurring in pre- and postconditions of atomic triples is interpreted relative to the linearization point, i.e. the moment in time when the update becomes visible to other threads (here, when the CAS operation on line 14 succeeds). The *interference context* $\mathbb{W}s \in \{0,1\}$ is a special binding for the abstract region state that forces callers to guarantee that the environment keeps the lock state in $\{0, 1\}$ until the linearization point is reached (a vacuous restriction in this case).

The precondition of the triple states that an instance of guard G for region r, $[G]_r$, is required to execute `lock(x)`. The postcondition expresses that, at the linearization point, the lock's abstract state was changed from unlocked ($s = 0$) to locked ($\text{Lock}_r(x, 1)$). In general, callers must assume that a region's abstract state may have been changed by the environment after the linearization point was reached; here, however, the presence of the unique guard $[G]_r$ enables the caller of `lock` to conclude (by the transition system) that the lock remains locked.

2.2 TaDA Proof Outline

Lines 6–22 of the proof outline in Fig. 1 show the main proof steps; Fig. 2 shows simplified versions of the applied key TaDA rules. MAKEATOMIC establishes an atomic triple by checking that a block of code is atomic w.r.t. a shared region abstraction (hence the change from non-atomic premise triple, written with curly braces, to an atomic conclusion triple). UPDATEREGION identifies the linearization point inside this code block. Rule MAKEATOMIC requires that the *atomicity context*, a set $\mathcal{A}$ of *pending updates*, of the premise triple includes any region updates performed by the statement of the triple (there can be at most one such update per region). In the proof outline, this requirement is reflected on line 8, which shows the intended update of the lock's state: $r : s \in \{0,1\} \rightsquigarrow 1$ (following TaDA publications, we omitted the tail of the atomicity context from the outline). MAKEATOMIC checks that the update is allowed by the region's transition system with the available guards (the rule's second premise in Fig. 2), but the check is omitted from the proof outline. Then MAKEATOMIC temporarily exchanges the corresponding guard $[G]_r$ for the *diamond tracking resource* $r \mapsto \blacklozenge$ (line 9), which serves as evidence that the intended update was not yet performed.

Inside the loop, an application of UPDATEREGION identifies the CAS (line 14) as the linearization point. The rule requires the diamond resource in its precondition (line 11), modifies the shared region (lines 12–16), and case-splits in its postcondition: if the update failed (line 19) then the diamond is kept for the next attempt; otherwise (line 18), the diamond is exchanged for the *witness tracking resource* $r \mapsto (0,1)$, which indicates that the region was updated from abstract state 0 to 1. At the end of MAKEATOMIC (lines 21–22), the witness resource is consumed and the desired abstractly atomic postcondition is established, stating that the shared region was updated from 0 to 1 at the linearization point.

2.3   Voila Proof Outline

Figure 3 shows the *complete* proof outline of our example in the Voila proof outline language, which closely resembles the TaDA outline from Fig. 1. In particular, the `region` declaration defines a region's interpretation, abstract state, and transition system, just like the initial declarations in Fig. 1. The subsequent proof outline for procedure `lock` annotates the same two rule applications as the TaDA outline and a very similar loop invariant. The Voila proof outline verifies automatically via an encoding into Viper, but the outline is expressed completely in terms of TaDA concepts; it does not expose any details of the underlying verification infrastructure. This means that our tool automatically infers the additional 20 rule applications, and all omitted side conditions, thereby closing the gap between the user-provided proof outline and a corresponding full-fledged proof.

3   Proof Outline Language

Proof outlines annotate programs with rule applications of a given program logic. These annotations indicate where to apply rules and how to instantiate their meta-variables. The goal of a proof outline is to convey the essential proof steps; ideally, consumers of such outlines can then construct a full proof with modest effort. Consumers may be human readers [27], or tools that automatically check the validity of a proof outline [14, 21, 46]; our focus is on the latter.

The key challenge of designing a proof outline language is to define annotations that accomplish this goal with low annotation overhead for proof outline

```
struct cell { int val; }

region Lock(id r, cell x)
  interpretation { x.val |-> ?v && (v == 0 || v == 1) }
  state { v }
  guards { unique G; }
  actions { G: 0 ~> 1; G: 1 ~> 0; }

abstract_atomic procedure lock(id r, cell x)
  interference ?s in Set(0, 1);
  requires Lock(r, x, s) && G@r;
  ensures  Lock(r, x, 1) && G@r && s == 0;
{
  bool b;
  make_atomic using Lock(r, x) with G@r {
    do
      invariant Lock(r, x);
      invariant !b ==> r |=> <D>;
      invariant  b ==> r |=> (0, 1);
    {
      update_region using Lock(r, x) {
        b := CAS(x, 0, 1);
      }
    } while (!b);
  }
}
```

Fig. 3. The Voila proof outline of our example, strongly resembling the TaDA proof outline from Fig. 1. id is the type of region identifiers; primitive types are passed by value, structs by reference. Logical variables are introduced using a question mark; e.g. x.val↦?v binds the logical variable v to the value of the location x.val. && denotes separating conjunction.

authors. To approach this challenge systematically, we classify the rules of the program logic (here: TaDA) into three categories: (1) For some rules, the program prescribes where and how to apply them, i.e. they do not require any annotations. We call such rules *syntax-driven rules*. An example in standard Hoare logic is the assignment rule, where the assignment statement prescribes how to manipulate the adjacent assertions. (2) Some rules can be applied and instantiated in many meaningful ways. For such rules, the author of the proof outline needs to indicate where or how to apply them through suitable annotations. Since such rules often indicate essential proof steps, we call them *key rules*. In proof outlines for standard Hoare logic, the while-rule typically requires an annotation *how* to apply it, namely the loop invariant. The rule of consequence typically requires an annotation *where and how* to apply it, e.g. to strengthen the precondition of a triple or to weaken its postcondition. (3) The effort of authoring a proof outline can be greatly reduced by applying some rules heuristically, based on information already present in the outline. We call such rules *bridge rules*. Heuristics reduce the annotation overhead, but may lead to incompleteness if they fail; a proof outline language may provide annotations to complement the heuristics in such situations, slightly blurring the distinction between key and bridge rules.

E.g. the Dafny verifier [20] applies heuristics to guess termination measures for loops, but also offers an annotation to provide a measure manually, if necessary.

The rule classification depends on the proof search capabilities of the verification tool that is used to check the proof outline. We use Viper [22], which provides a high degree of automation for standard separation logic and, thus, allows us to focus on the specific aspects of TaDA.

In the rest of this section, we give an overview of the Voila proof outline language and, in particular, discuss which TaDA rules are supported as syntax-driven, key, and bridge rules. Voila's grammar can be found in the full paper [47], showing that Voila strongly resembles TaDA, but requires fewer technical details.

Expressions and Statements. Voila supports all of TaDA's programming language constructs, including variables and heap locations, primitive types and operations thereon, atomic heap reads and writes, loops, and procedure calls. Consequently, Voila supports the corresponding syntax-driven TaDA rules.

Background Definitions. Voila's syntax for declaring regions and transitions closely resembles TaDA, but e.g. subscripts are replaced by additional parameters, such as the region identifier r. A region declaration defines the region's content via an **interpretation** assertion, and its value via a **state** function. The latter may refer to region parameters, as well as values bound in the interpretation, such as v in the example from Fig. 3. The region's transition system is declared by introducing the guards and the permitted *actions*, i.e. transitions. Voila includes several built-in guard algebras (adopted from Caper [8]); additional ones can be encoded, see the full paper [47]. A region declaration introduces a corresponding region predicate, which has an additional out-parameter that yields the region's abstract state (e.g. s in the precondition of procedure **lock** in Fig. 3), as defined by the **state** function. We omit this out-parameter when its value is irrelevant.

Specifications. Voila proof outlines require specifications for procedures, and invariants for loops; we again chose a TaDA-like syntax for familiarity. Explicit loop invariants are required by Viper, but also enable us to automatically instantiate certain bridge rules (see framing in Sect. 5).

Recall that specifications in TaDA are written as atomic or non-atomic triples, and include an interference context and an atomicity context. Voila simplifies the notation significantly by requiring these contexts only for abstractly-atomic procedure specifications; for all statements and rule applications, they are determined automatically, despite changing regularly during a proof. For procedures with abstractly-atomic behavior (modifier **abstract_atomic**), the interference context is declared through the **interference** clause. E.g. for procedure **lock** from Fig. 3, it corresponds to TaDA's interference context $\forall s \in \{0, 1\}$.

Key Rules. In addition to procedure and loop specifications, Voila requires user input only for the following fundamental TaDA rules: UPDATEREGION, MAKEATOMIC, USEATOMIC, and OPENREGION; applications of all other rules are automated. Since they capture the core ideas behind TaDA, these rules are among the most complex rules of the logic and admit a vast proof search space. Therefore, their annotation is essential, for both human readers [34,35] and automatic checkers. As seen in Fig. 3, the annotations for these key rules include only the used region and, for updates, the used guard; all other information present in the corresponding TaDA rules is derived automatically.

Bridge Rules. All other TaDA rules are applied automatically, and thus have no Voila counterparts. This includes all structural rules for manipulating triple atomicity (e.g. AWEAKENING1, AEXISTS), interference contexts (e.g. SUBSTITUTION, AWEAKENING2), and levels (e.g. AWEAKENING3). Their applications are heuristically derived from the program, applications of key rules, and adjacent triples. TaDA's frame rule is also automatically applied by leveraging Viper's built-in support for framing, combined with additional encoding steps to satisfy TaDA's frame stability side condition. Finally, TaDA entailments are bridge rules when they can be automated by the used verification tool. For Viper, this is the case for standard separation logic entailments, which constitute the majority of entailments to perform. To support TaDA's *view shifts* [6,34] – entailments similar to the classical rule of consequence, but involving arbitrary definitions of regions and guard algebras – Voila provides specialized annotations.

4   Proof Workflow

Our approach, and corresponding implementation, enables the following workflow: users provide a proof outline and possibly some annotations for complex entailments, but never need to insert any other rule. Hence, if the outline summarizes a valid proof, verification is automatic, without a tedious process of manually applying additional rules. If the outline is invalid, our tool reports which specification (e.g. loop invariant) it could not prove or which key rule application it could not verify, and why (e.g. missing guard).

Achieving this workflow, however, is challenging: by design, proof outlines provide the important proof steps, but are not complete proofs. Consider, e.g. the TaDA and Voila outlines from Fig. 1 and Fig. 3, respectively. Applying UPDATEREGION produces an atomic triple in its conclusion, whereas the while-rule requires a non-atomic triple for the loop body. A complete proof needs to perform the necessary adjustment through additional applications of bridge rules, which are not present in the proof outlines, and thus need to be inferred.

Our workflow is enabled by first expanding proof outlines into *proof candidates*, in two main steps: step 1 automatically inserts the applications of all syntax-driven rules; step 2 expands further by applying heuristics to insert bridge rule applications. The resulting proof candidate contains the applications of all rules of the program logic. Afterwards, we check that the proof candidate corresponds to a valid proof, by encoding it as a Viper program that checks whether all proof rules are applied correctly. Our actual implementation deviates slightly from this conceptual structure, e.g. because Viper does not require one to make the application of syntax-driven rules, framing, and entailment checking explicit.

5   Expanding Proof Outlines to Proof Candidates

Automatically expanding a proof outline is ultimately a proof search problem, with a vast search space in case of complex logics such as TaDA. Our choice of key rules (and corresponding annotations) reduces the search space, but it remains vast, due to TaDA's many structural rules that can be applied to almost all triples. To further reduce the search space, without introducing additional annotation overhead, we devised (and enforce) a *normal form* for proof candidate triples. Our normal form allows us to define *heuristics* for the application of bridge rules *locally*, based only on adjacent rule applications, without having to inspect larger proof parts. This locality reduces the search space substantially, and enables us to automatically close the gap between user-provided proof outline and finally verified proof candidate. In our running example, our heuristics infer 20 out of 22 rule applications.

It might be helpful to consider an analogy with standard Hoare logic: its rule of consequence can be applied to each Hoare triple. A suitable normal form could restrict proofs to use the rule of consequence only at the beginning of the program and for each loop (as in a weakest-precondition calculus). A heuristic can then infer the concrete applications, in particular, the entailments used in the rule application, treating the rule as a bridge rule.

Normal Form. Our normal is established by a combination of syntactic checks and proof obligations in the final Viper encoding. Its main restrictions are as follows: (1) All triples are either exclusively atomic or non-atomic, which enables us to infer the triple kinds from statements and key rule applications. Due to this restriction, Voila cannot express specifications that combine atomic and non-atomic behaviors. However, such specifications do not occur frequently (see Sect. 5.2.3 in [34] for an example) and could be supported via additional annotations. (2) All triple preconditions, as well as the postconditions of non-atomic triples, are *stable*, i.e. cannot be invalidated by (legal) concurrent operations. In contrast, TaDA requires stability only for certain assertions. Our stronger requirement enables us to *rely* on stability at various points in the proof instead of having to *check* it – most importantly, when Viper automatically applies its frame rule. To enforce this restriction, we eagerly stabilize assertions through suitable weakening steps. (3) In atomic triples, the state of every region is bound by exactly one interference quantifier ($\forall$), which simplifies the manipulation of interference contexts, e.g. for procedure calls. To the best of our knowledge, this restriction does not limit the expressiveness of Voila proofs. (4) Triples must hold for a *range* of atomicity contexts $\mathcal{A}$, rather than just a single context. This stronger proof obligation rules out certain applications of MakeAtomic – which we have seen only in contrived examples – but it increases automation substantially and improves procedure modularity.

By design, our normal form prevents Voila from constructing certain TaDA proofs. However, the only practical limitation is that Voila does not support TaDA's combination of atomic and non-atomic behavior in a single triple. As far as we are aware, all other normal form restrictions do not limit expressiveness for practical examples, or can be worked around in systematic ways.

Heuristics. We employ five main heuristics: to determine when to change triple atomicity, to ensure stable frames by construction, to compute atomicity context ranges, to compute levels, and to compute interference contexts in procedure body proofs. All heuristics are based on inspecting adjacent rule applications and their proof state. We briefly discuss the first three heuristics here, and refer readers to the full paper [47] for the remaining two heuristics. There, we give a more detailed explanation, and illustrate our heuristics in the context of our running example. (1) Changing triple atomicity corresponds to an application of (at least) TaDA rule AWEAKENING1, necessary when a non-atomic composite statement (e.g. the `while` statement in Fig. 1) has an abstract-atomic sub-statement (e.g. the atomic CAS in Fig. 1). We infer all applications of this rule. (2) A more complex heuristic is used in the context of framing: TaDA's frame rule requires the *frame*, i.e., the assertion preserved across a statement, to be stable. For simple statements such as heap accesses, it is sound to rely on Viper's built-in support for framing. For composite statements with arbitrary user-provided *footprints* (assertions such as a loop invariant describing which resources the composite statement may modify), we greedily infer frame rule applications that attempt to preserve all information outside the footprint. The inferred applications are later encoded in Viper such that the resulting frame is stable, by applying suitable weakening steps. (3) Atomicity context ranges are heuristically inferred from currently owned tracking resources and level information. Atomicity contexts are not manipulated by a specific TaDA rule, but they need to be instantiated when applying rules: most importantly, TaDA's procedure call rule, but also e.g. MAKEATOMIC and UPDATEREGION (see Fig. 2).

In our experience, our heuristics fail *only* in two scenarios: the first are contrived examples, concerned with TaDA resources in isolation, not properties of actual code – where they fail to expand a proof outline into a valid proof. More relevant is the second scenario, where our heuristics yield a valid proof that Viper then fails to verify because it requires entailments that Viper cannot discharge automatically. To work around such problems when they occur, Voila allows programmers to provide additional annotations to indicate where to apply complex entailments.

Importantly, a failure of our heuristics does not compromise soundness: if they infer invalid bridge rule applications, e.g. whose side conditions do not hold, the resulting invalid proof candidates are rejected by Viper in the final validation.

6 Validating Proof Candidates in Viper

Proof candidates – i.e. the user-provided program with heuristically inserted bridge rule applications – do not necessarily represent valid proofs, e.g. when users provide incorrect loop invariants. To check whether a proof candidate actually represents a valid proof, we need to verify (1) that each rule is applied correctly, in particular, that its premises and side conditions hold, and (2) that the property shown by the proof candidate entails the intended specification. To validate proof candidates automatically, we use the existing Viper tool [22]. In this section, we give a high-level overview of how we encode proof candidates into the Viper language.

Viper Language. Viper uses a variation of separation logic [29,38] whose assertions separate access permissions from value information: separation logic's points-to assertion x.f ↦ v is expressed as acc(x.f) && x.f == v, and separation logic predicates [30] are similarly split into a predicate (abstracting over permissions) and a heap-dependent function (abstracting over values). Well-definedness checks ensure that the heap is accessed only under sufficient permissions. Viper provides a simple imperative language, which includes in particular two statements to manipulate the verification state: **exhale** A asserts all logical constraints in assertion A, removes the permissions in A from the current state (or fails if the permissions are not available) and assigns non-deterministic values to the corresponding memory locations (to reflect that the environment could now modify them); **inhale** A analogously assumes constraints and adds permissions.

```
⟦region R(r: id, p̄: t̄)
  interpretation I
  state S
  guards G
  actions A⟧ ≜
predicate R(r: Ref, p̄:⟦t̄⟧) { ⟦I⟧ }

function R_State(r: Ref, p̄:⟦t̄⟧): T
  requires  R(r,p̄)
{ unfolding R(r,p̄) in ⟦S⟧ }

foreach g(p̄': t̄') ∈ G:
  predicate R_g(r: Ref, p̄':⟦t̄'⟧)
end

field diamond: Bool
```

```
field val: Int

predicate Lock(r: Ref, x: Ref) {
  acc(x.val) &&
  (x.val == 0 || x.val == 1)
}

function Lock_State
            (r: Ref, x: Ref): Int
  requires Lock(r, x)
{ unfolding lock(r, x) in x.val }

predicate Lock_G(r: Ref)

field diamond: Bool
```

Fig. 4. Excerpt of the Viper encoding of regions; general case (left), and for the lock region from Fig. 3 (right). The encoding function is denoted by double square brackets; overlines denote lists; *foreach* loops are expanded statically. Type T is the type of the state expression S, which is inferred. Actions A do not induce any global declarations. The elements of struct types and type **id** are encoded as Viper references (type Ref). The **unfolding** expression temporarily unfolds a predicate into its definition; it is required by Viper's backend verifiers. The struct type **cell** from Fig. 3 is encoded as a Viper reference with field **val** (in Viper, all objects have all fields declared in the program).

Regions and Assertions. TaDA's regions introduce various resources such as region predicates and guards. We encode these into Viper permissions and predicates as summarized in Fig. 4 (left). Each region R gives rise to a corresponding predicate, which is defined by the region interpretation. A region's abstract state may be accessed by a Viper function R_State, which is defined based on the region's state clause, and depends on the region predicate. Moreover, we introduce an abstract Viper predicate R_g for each guard g of the region.

These declarations allow us to encode most TaDA assertions in a fairly straightforward way. E.g. the assertion $Lock_r(x, s)$ from Fig. 1 is encoded as a combination of a region predicate and the function yielding its abstract state: Lock(r,x) && Lock_State(r,x) == s . We encode region identifiers as references in Viper, which allows us to use the permissions and values of designated fields to represent resources and information associated with a region instance. E.g. we use the permission acc(r.diamond) to encode the TaDA resource $r \mapsto \blacklozenge$.

Rule Applications. Proof candidates are tree structures, where each premise of a rule application R is established as the conclusion of another rule application, as illustrated on the right. To check the validity of a candidate, we check the validity of each rule application. For rules that are natively

$$\frac{\vdots}{\{\,P_p\,\}\,s\,\{\,Q_p\,\}}{\{\,P_c\,\}\,s\,\{\,Q_c\,\}}\ (R)$$
$$\vdots$$

supported by Viper (e.g. the assignment rule), Viper performs all necessary checks. Each other rule application is checked via an encoding into the following sequence of Viper instructions: (1) Exhale the precondition P_c of the conclusion to check that the required assertion holds. (2) Inhale the precondition P_p of the premise since it may be assumed when proving the premise. (3) After the code s of the premise, exhale the postcondition Q_p of the premise to check that it was established by the proof for the premise. (4) Inhale the postcondition Q_c of the conclusion. Steps 2 and 3 are performed for each premise of the rule. Moreover, we assert the side conditions of each rule. If a proof candidate is invalid, e.g. composes incompatible rules, one of the checks above fails and the candidate is rejected.

Using this encoding of rule applications as building blocks, we can assemble entire procedure proofs as follows: for each procedure, we inhale its precondition, encode the rule application for its body, and then exhale its postcondition.

Example: Stabilizing Assertions. Recall that an assertion A is stable if and only if the environment cannot invalidate A by performing any legal region updates. In practice, this means that the environment cannot hold a guard that allows it to change the state of a region in a way that violates A. The challenge of *checking* stability as a side-condition is to *avoid higher-order quantification* over region instances and guards, which is hard to automate. We address this challenge by eagerly *stabilizing* assertions in the Viper encoding, i.e. we weaken Viper's verification state such that the remaining information about the state is stable. We achieve this effect by first assigning non-deterministic values to the region state and then constraining these to be within the states permitted

Program	LOC	Stg	Wk	Cpr
SLock	15	2.6	2.1	1.4
TLock	23	21.8	8.1	2.4
TLockCl	16	2.9	2.6	0.5
CASCtr	25	3.9	2.7	1.5
BoundedCtr	24	8.1	5.1	63.1
IncDecCtr	28	4.2	3.1	2.9
ForkJoin	16	2.1	1.3	1.0
ForkJoinCl	28	2.9	2.3	1.6
BagStack	29	29.9	18.0	211.6
CounterCl	45	-	5.8	-

Program	Err	Stg	Wk	Cpr
CASCtr	L	1.5	1.9	1.5
	P	2.5	1.9	11.2
	C	1.5	1.2	0.5
	R	1.2	1.1	0.3
TLock	L	3.9	7.2	2.0
	P	7.2	3.4	2.4
	C	15.6	1.8	0.6
	R	4.1	1.8	0.7
TLockCl	P	2.9	2.6	143.4
	C	2.5	2.5	115.5
	R	1.8	1.7	5.0
BagStack	L	26.5	17.8	> 600
	P	27.9	17.7	> 600
	C	26.3	17.8	> 600
	R	14.4	9.2	216.6

Fig. 5. Timings in seconds for successful (left table) and failing (right table) verification runs; lines of code (LOC) are given for Voila programs and exclude proof annotations. *Stg/Wk* denote strong/weak Voila specifications; *Cpr* abbreviates Caper. Programs include spin and ticket locks, counters (*Ctr*), and client programs (*Cl*) using the proven specifications. Errors (*Err*) were seeded in loop invariants (*L*), postconditions (*P*), code (*C*), and region specifications (*R*).

by the region's transition system, taking into account the guards the environment could hold. The Viper code for stabilizing instances of Lock can be found in the full paper [47].

7   Evaluation

We evaluated Voila on nine benchmark examples from Caper's test suite, with the Treiber's stack [41] variant BagStack being the most complex example, and report verification times and annotation overhead. Each example has been verified in two versions: a version with Caper's comparatively *weak* non-atomic specifications, and another version with TaDA's *strong* atomic specifications; see Sect. 8 for a more detailed comparison of Voila and Caper. An additional example, CounterCl, demonstrates the encoding of a custom guard algebra not supported in Caper (see the full paper [47]). To evaluate performance stability, we seeded four examples with errors in the loop invariant, procedure postcondition, code, and region specification, respectively. Our benchmark suite is relatively small, but each example involves nontrivial specifications. To the best of our knowledge, no other (semi-)automated tool is able to verify similarly strong specifications.

Performance. Figure 5 shows the runtime for each example in seconds. All measurements were carried out on a Lenovo W540 with an Intel Core i7-4800MQ and 16 GB of RAM, running Windows 10 x64 and Java HotSpot JVM 18.9 x64; Voila was compiled using Scala 2.12.7. We used a recent checkout of Viper and Z3 4.5.0 x64 (we failed to compile Caper against newer versions of Z3). Each example was verified ten times (on a continuously-running JVM); after removing the highest and lowest measurement, the remaining eight values were averaged. Caper (which compiles to native code) was measured analogously.

Overall, Voila's verification times are good; most examples verify in under five seconds. Voila is slower than Caper and its logic-specific symbolic execution engine, but it exhibits stable performance for successful and failing runs, which is crucial in the common case that proof outlines are developed interactively, such that the checker is run frequently on incorrect versions. As demonstrated by the error-seeded versions of TLockCl and BagStack, Caper's performance is less stable.

Another interesting observation is that strong specifications typically do not take significantly longer to verify, although only they require the full spectrum of TaDA ingredients and make use of TaDA's most complex rules, MAKEATOMIC and UPDATEREGION. Notable exceptions are: BagStack, where only the strong specification requires sequence theory reasoning; and TLock and BoundedCtr, whose complex transition systems with many disjunctions significantly increase the workload when verifying atomicity rules such as MAKEATOMIC.

Automation. Voila's annotation overhead, averaged over the programs with *strong* specifications from Fig. 5, is 0.8 lines of proof annotations (not counting declarations and procedure specifications; neither for Caper) per line of code, which demonstrates the high degree of automation Voila achieves. Caper has an average annotation overhead of 0.13 for its programs from Fig. 5, but significantly weaker specifications. Verifying only the latter in Voila does not reduce annotation overhead significantly since Voila was designed to support TaDA's strong specifications. The overhead reported for encodings into interactive theorem provers such as Coq [10,17,18,45] is typically much higher, ranging between 10 and 20.

8 Related Work

We compare Voila to three groups of tools: automated verifiers, focusing on automation; proof checkers, focusing on expressiveness; and proof outline checkers, designed to strike a balance between automation and expressiveness. Closest to our work in the kind of supported logic is the automated verifier Caper [8], from which we drew inspiration, e.g. for how to specify region transition systems. Caper supports an improved version of CAP [7], a predecessor logic of TaDA. Caper's symbolic execution engine achieves an impressive degree of automation, which, for more complex examples, is higher than Voila's. Caper's automation also covers slightly more guard algebras than Voila. However, the automation comes at the price of expressiveness, compared to Voila: postconditions are often significantly weaker because the logic does not support linearizability (or any other notion of abstract atomicity). E.g. Caper cannot prove that the spinlock's unlock procedure actually releases the lock. As was shown in Sect. 7, Caper is typically faster than Voila, but exhibits less stable performance when a program or its specifications are wrong.

Other automated verifiers for fine-grained concurrency reasoning are Small-footRG [5], which can prove memory safety, but not functional correctness, and CAVE [44], which can prove linearizability, but cannot reason about non-linearizable code (which TaDA and Voila can). VerCors [26] combines a concurrent separation logic with process-algebraic specifications; special program annotations are used to relate concrete program operations to terms in the abstract process algebra model. Reasoning about the resulting term sequences is automated via model checking, but is non-modular. Summers et al. [39] present an automated verifier for the RSL family of logics [9,10,45] for reasoning about weak-memory concurrency. Their tool also encodes into Viper and requires very few annotations because proofs in the RSL logics are more stylized than in TaDA.

A variety of complex separation logics [9,10,12,16,19,23,37,43,45] are supported by proof checkers, typically via Coq encodings. As discussed in the introduction, such tools strike a different trade-off than proof outline checkers: they provide foundational proofs, but typically offer little automation, which hampers experimenting with logics.

Starling [46] is a proof outline checker and closest to Voila in terms of the overall design, but it focuses on proofs that are *easy* to automate. To achieve this, it uses a simple instantiation of the Views meta-logic [6] as its logic. Starling's logic does not enable the kind of strong, linearizability-based postconditions that Voila can prove (see the discussion of Caper above). Starling generates proof obligations that can be discharged by an SMT solver, or by GRASShopper [31] if the program requires heap reasoning. The parts of an outline that involve the heap must be written in GRASShopper's input language. In contrast, Voila does not expose the underlying system, and users can work on the abstraction level of TaDA.

VeriFast [14] can be seen as an outline checker for a separation logic with impressive features such as higher-order functions and predicates. It has no dedicated support for fine-grained concurrency, but the developers manually encoded examples such as concurrent stacks and queues. VeriFast favors expressiveness over automation: proofs often require non-trivial specification adaptations and substantial amounts of ghost code, but the results typically verify quickly.

9   Conclusion

We introduced Voila, a novel proof outline checker that supports most of TaDA's features, and achieves a high degree of automation and good performance. This enables concise proof outlines with a strong resemblance of TaDA.

Voila is the first deductive verifier that can reason automatically about a procedure's effect at its linearization point, which is essential for a wide range of concurrent programs. Earlier work either proves much weaker properties (the preservation of basic data structure invariants rather than the functional behavior of procedures) or requires substantially more user input (entire proofs rather than concise outlines).

We believe that our systematic approach to developing Voila can be generalized to other complex logics. In particular, encoding proof outlines into an existing verification framework allows one to develop proof outline checkers efficiently, without developing custom proof search algorithms. Our work also illustrates that an intermediate verification language such as Viper is suitable for encoding a highly specialised program logic such as TaDA. During the development of Voila, we uncovered and fixed several soundness and modularity issues in TaDA, which the original authors acknowledged and had partly not been aware of. We view this as anecdotal evidence of the benefits of tool support that we described in the introduction.

Voila supports the vast majority of TaDA's features; most of the others can be supported with additional annotations. The main exception are TaDA's hybrid assertions, which combine atomic and non-atomic behavior. Adding support for those is future work. Other plans include an extension of the supported logic, e.g. to handle extensions of TaDA [11,36].

Acknowledgements. We thank the anonymous referees of this paper, and earlier versions thereof, for suggesting many improvements to the explanation of our work. We are also thankful to Thomas Dinsdale-Young and Pedro da Rocha Pinto for instructive discussions about their work, TaDA, and for feedback on Voila.

References

1. Apt, K.R., de Boer, F.S., Olderog, E.: Verification of Sequential and Concurrent Programs. Texts in Computer Science. Springer, Cham (2009). https://doi.org/10.1007/978-1-84882-745-5
2. Berdine, J., Calcagno, C., O'Hearn, P.W.: Smallfoot: modular automatic assertion checking with separation logic. In: de Boer, F.S., Bonsangue, M.M., Graf, S., de Roever, W.-P. (eds.) FMCO 2005. LNCS, vol. 4111, pp. 115–137. Springer, Heidelberg (2006). https://doi.org/10.1007/11804192_6
3. Brookes, S., O'Hearn, P.W.: Concurrent separation logic. SIGLOG News **3**(3), 47–65 (2016)
4. Brookes, S.: A semantics for concurrent separation logic. In: Gardner, P., Yoshida, N. (eds.) CONCUR 2004. LNCS, vol. 3170, pp. 16–34. Springer, Heidelberg (2004). https://doi.org/10.1007/978-3-540-28644-8_2
5. Calcagno, C., Parkinson, M., Vafeiadis, V.: Modular safety checking for fine-grained concurrency. In: Nielson, H.R., Filé, G. (eds.) SAS 2007. LNCS, vol. 4634, pp. 233–248. Springer, Heidelberg (2007). https://doi.org/10.1007/978-3-540-74061-2_15
6. Dinsdale-Young, T., Birkedal, L., Gardner, P., Parkinson, M.J., Yang, H.: Views: compositional reasoning for concurrent programs. In: POPL, pp. 287–300. ACM (2013)
7. Dinsdale-Young, T., Dodds, M., Gardner, P., Parkinson, M.J., Vafeiadis, V.: Concurrent abstract predicates. In: D'Hondt, T. (ed.) ECOOP 2010. LNCS, vol. 6183, pp. 504–528. Springer, Heidelberg (2010). https://doi.org/10.1007/978-3-642-14107-2_24
8. Dinsdale-Young, T., da Rocha Pinto, P., Andersen, K.J., Birkedal, L.: CAPER - automatic verification for fine-grained concurrency. In: Yang, H. (ed.) ESOP 2017. LNCS, vol. 10201, pp. 420–447. Springer, Heidelberg (2017). https://doi.org/10.1007/978-3-662-54434-1_16

9. Doko, M., Vafeiadis, V.: A program logic for C11 memory fences. In: Jobstmann, B., Leino, K.R.M. (eds.) VMCAI 2016. LNCS, vol. 9583, pp. 413–430. Springer, Heidelberg (2016). https://doi.org/10.1007/978-3-662-49122-5_20
10. Doko, M., Vafeiadis, V.: Tackling real-life relaxed concurrency with FSL++. In: Yang, H. (ed.) ESOP 2017. LNCS, vol. 10201, pp. 448–475. Springer, Heidelberg (2017). https://doi.org/10.1007/978-3-662-54434-1_17
11. D'Osualdo, E., Farzan, A., Gardner, P., Sutherland, J.: TaDA live: compositional reasoning for termination of fine-grained concurrent programs. CoRR arXiv:1901.05750 (2019)
12. Frumin, D., Krebbers, R., Birkedal, L.: ReLoC: a mechanised relational logic for fine-grained concurrency. In: LICS, pp. 442–451. ACM (2018)
13. Herlihy, M., Wing, J.M.: Linearizability: a correctness condition for concurrent objects. ACM Trans. Program. Lang. Syst. 12(3), 463–492 (1990)
14. Jacobs, B., Smans, J., Philippaerts, P., Vogels, F., Penninckx, W., Piessens, F.: VeriFast: a powerful, sound, predictable, fast verifier for C and Java. In: Bobaru, M., Havelund, K., Holzmann, G.J., Joshi, R. (eds.) NFM 2011. LNCS, vol. 6617, pp. 41–55. Springer, Heidelberg (2011). https://doi.org/10.1007/978-3-642-20398-5_4
15. Jones, C.B.: Specification and design of (parallel) programs. In: IFIP Congress, pp. 321–332 (1983)
16. Jung, R., Krebbers, R., Jourdan, J., Bizjak, A., Birkedal, L., Dreyer, D.: Iris from the ground up: a modular foundation for higher-order concurrent separation logic. J. Funct. Program. 28, e20 (2018)
17. Kaiser, J., Dang, H., Dreyer, D., Lahav, O., Vafeiadis, V.: Strong logic for weak memory: reasoning about release-acquire consistency in Iris. In: ECOOP, LIPIcs, vol. 74, pp. 17:1–17:29. Schloss Dagstuhl - Leibniz-Zentrum fuer Informatik (2017)
18. Klein, G., et al.: seL4: formal verification of an OS kernel. In: SOSP, pp. 207–220. ACM (2009)
19. Krebbers, R., et al.: MoSeL: a general, extensible modal framework for interactive proofs in separation logic. PACMPL 2(ICFP), 77:1–77:30 (2018)
20. Leino, K.R.M.: Dafny: an automatic program verifier for functional correctness. In: Clarke, E.M., Voronkov, A. (eds.) LPAR 2010. LNCS (LNAI), vol. 6355, pp. 348–370. Springer, Heidelberg (2010). https://doi.org/10.1007/978-3-642-17511-4_20
21. Mooij, A.J., Wesselink, W.: Incremental verification of Owicki/Gries proof outlines using PVS. In: Lau, K.-K., Banach, R. (eds.) ICFEM 2005. LNCS, vol. 3785, pp. 390–404. Springer, Heidelberg (2005). https://doi.org/10.1007/11576280_27
22. Müller, P., Schwerhoff, M., Summers, A.J.: Viper: a verification infrastructure for permission-based reasoning. In: Jobstmann, B., Leino, K.R.M. (eds.) VMCAI 2016. LNCS, vol. 9583, pp. 41–62. Springer, Heidelberg (2016). https://doi.org/10.1007/978-3-662-49122-5_2
23. Nanevski, A., Ley-Wild, R., Sergey, I., Delbianco, G.A.: Communicating state transition systems for fine-grained concurrent resources. In: Shao, Z. (ed.) ESOP 2014. LNCS, vol. 8410, pp. 290–310. Springer, Heidelberg (2014). https://doi.org/10.1007/978-3-642-54833-8_16
24. O'Hearn, P.W.: Resources, concurrency and local reasoning. In: Gardner, P., Yoshida, N. (eds.) CONCUR 2004. LNCS, vol. 3170, pp. 49–67. Springer, Heidelberg (2004). https://doi.org/10.1007/978-3-540-28644-8_4
25. O'Hearn, P., Reynolds, J., Yang, H.: Local reasoning about programs that alter data structures. In: Fribourg, L. (ed.) CSL 2001. LNCS, vol. 2142, pp. 1–19. Springer, Heidelberg (2001). https://doi.org/10.1007/3-540-44802-0_1

26. Oortwijn, W., Blom, S., Gurov, D., Huisman, M., Zaharieva-Stojanovski, M.: An abstraction technique for describing concurrent program behaviour. In: Paskevich, A., Wies, T. (eds.) VSTTE 2017. LNCS, vol. 10712, pp. 191–209. Springer, Cham (2017). https://doi.org/10.1007/978-3-319-72308-2_12

27. Owicki, S.S.: Axiomatic proof techniques for parallel programs. Outstanding Dissertations in the Computer Sciences, Garland Publishing, New York (1975)

28. Owicki, S.S., Gries, D.: An axiomatic proof technique for parallel programs I. Acta Inf. **6**, 319–340 (1976)

29. Parkinson, M.J., Summers, A.J.: The relationship between separation logic and implicit dynamic frames. Logical Meth. Comput. Sci. **8**(3:01), 1–54 (2012)

30. Parkinson, M.J., Bierman, G.M.: Separation logic and abstraction. In: POPL, pp. 247–258. ACM (2005)

31. Piskac, R., Wies, T., Zufferey, D.: GRASShopper - complete heap verification with mixed specifications. In: Ábrahám, E., Havelund, K. (eds.) TACAS 2014. LNCS, vol. 8413, pp. 124–139. Springer, Heidelberg (2014). https://doi.org/10.1007/978-3-642-54862-8_9

32. Raad, A., Villard, J., Gardner, P.: CoLoSL: concurrent local subjective logic. In: Vitek, J. (ed.) ESOP 2015. LNCS, vol. 9032, pp. 710–735. Springer, Heidelberg (2015). https://doi.org/10.1007/978-3-662-46669-8_29

33. Reynolds, J.C.: Separation logic: a logic for shared mutable data structures. In: LICS, pp. 55–74. IEEE Computer Society (2002)

34. da Rocha Pinto, P.: Reasoning with time and data abstractions. Ph.D. thesis, Imperial College London, UK (2016)

35. da Rocha Pinto, P., Dinsdale-Young, T., Gardner, P.: TaDA: a logic for time and data abstraction. In: Jones, R. (ed.) ECOOP 2014. LNCS, vol. 8586, pp. 207–231. Springer, Heidelberg (2014). https://doi.org/10.1007/978-3-662-44202-9_9

36. da Rocha Pinto, P., Dinsdale-Young, T., Gardner, P., Sutherland, J.: Modular termination verification for non-blocking concurrency. In: Thiemann, P. (ed.) ESOP 2016. LNCS, vol. 9632, pp. 176–201. Springer, Heidelberg (2016). https://doi.org/10.1007/978-3-662-49498-1_8

37. Sergey, I., Nanevski, A., Banerjee, A.: Mechanized verification of fine-grained concurrent programs. In: PLDI, pp. 77–87. ACM (2015)

38. Smans, J., Jacobs, B., Piessens, F.: Implicit dynamic frames: combining dynamic frames and separation logic. In: Drossopoulou, S. (ed.) ECOOP 2009. LNCS, vol. 5653, pp. 148–172. Springer, Heidelberg (2009). https://doi.org/10.1007/978-3-642-03013-0_8

39. Summers, A.J., Müller, P.: Automating deductive verification for weak-memory programs. In: Beyer, D., Huisman, M. (eds.) TACAS 2018. LNCS, vol. 10805, pp. 190–209. Springer, Cham (2018). https://doi.org/10.1007/978-3-319-89960-2_11

40. Svendsen, K., Birkedal, L.: Impredicative concurrent abstract predicates. In: Shao, Z. (ed.) ESOP 2014. LNCS, vol. 8410, pp. 149–168. Springer, Heidelberg (2014). https://doi.org/10.1007/978-3-642-54833-8_9

41. Treiber, R.K.: Systems programming: coping with parallelism. Technical Report RJ 5118, IBM Almaden Research Center (1986)

42. Turon, A., Dreyer, D., Birkedal, L.: Unifying refinement and Hoare-style reasoning in a logic for higher-order concurrency. In: Morrisett, G., Uustalu, T. (eds.) International Conference on Functional Programming (ICFP), pp. 377–390. ACM (2013)

43. Turon, A., Vafeiadis, V., Dreyer, D.: GPS: navigating weak memory with ghosts, protocols, and separation. In: OOPSLA, pp. 691–707. ACM (2014)

44. Vafeiadis, V.: Automatically proving linearizability. In: Touili, T., Cook, B., Jackson, P. (eds.) CAV 2010. LNCS, vol. 6174, pp. 450–464. Springer, Heidelberg (2010). https://doi.org/10.1007/978-3-642-14295-6_40
45. Vafeiadis, V., Narayan, C.: Relaxed separation logic: a program logic for C11 concurrency. In: OOPSLA, pp. 867–884. ACM (2013)
46. Windsor, M., Dodds, M., Simner, B., Parkinson, M.J.: Starling: lightweight concurrency verification with views. In: Majumdar, R., Kunčak, V. (eds.) CAV 2017. LNCS, vol. 10426, pp. 544–569. Springer, Cham (2017). https://doi.org/10.1007/978-3-319-63387-9_27
47. Wolf, F.A., Schwerhoff, M., Müller, P.: Concise outlines for a complex logic: a proof outline checker for TaDA (full paper). CoRR arXiv:2010.07080 (2020)
48. Wolf, F.A., Schwerhoff, M., Müller, P.: The Voila source repository. https://github.com/viperproject/voila
49. Wolf, F.A., Schwerhoff, M., Müller, P.: Concise outlines for a complex logic: a proof outline checker for TaDA (2021). https://doi.org/10.5281/zenodo.5137791

Formal Verification of a JavaCard Virtual Machine with Frama-C

Adel Djoudi[1] ⓘ, Martin Hána[2] ⓘ, and Nikolai Kosmatov[3](✉) ⓘ

[1] Thales Digital Identity and Security, Meudon, France
adel.djoudi@thalesgroup.com
[2] Thales Digital Identity and Security, Prague, Czech Republic
martin.hana@thalesgroup.com
[3] Thales Research and Technology, Palaiseau, France
nikolai.kosmatov@thalesgroup.com

Abstract. Formal verification of real-life industrial software remains a challenging task. It provides strong guarantees of correctness, which are particularly important for security-critical products, such as smart cards. Security of a smart card strongly relies on the requirement that the underlying JavaCard virtual machine ensures necessary isolation properties. This case study paper presents a recent formal verification of a JavaCard Virtual Machine implementation performed by Thales using the Frama-C verification toolset. This is the first verification project for such a large-scale industrial smart card product where deductive verification is applied on the real-life C code. The target properties include common security properties such as integrity and confidentiality. The implementation contains over 7,000 lines of C code. After a formal specification in the ACSL specification language, over 52,000 verification conditions were generated and successfully proved. We present several issues identified during the project, illustrate them by representative examples and present solutions we used to solve them. Finally, we describe proof results, some lessons learned and desired tool improvements.

1 Introduction

Safety and security of critical software has become a major concern today. Formal software verification is able to rigorously demonstrate the absence of bugs and security flaws. It provides strong guarantees of correctness, which are particularly important for security-critical products, such as smart cards. However, formal verification of real-life industrial software still remains a challenging task.

Security of a smart card strongly relies on a set of isolation properties that must be ensured by the underlying JavaCard virtual machine. According to [20], "an applet shall not read, write, compare a piece of data belonging to an applet that is not in the same context, or execute one of the methods of an applet in another context without its authorization". The corresponding access rules are usually implemented by a specific access control mechanism ensuring necessary isolation, that is called a *firewall*.

This case study paper presents a recent formal verification of a JavaCard Virtual Machine (JCVM) implementation performed by Thales using the Frama-C

ⓒ Springer Nature Switzerland AG 2021
M. Huisman et al. (Eds.): FM 2021, LNCS 13047, pp. 427–444, 2021.
https://doi.org/10.1007/978-3-030-90870-6_23

verification platform [14]. It was realized for a Common Criteria EAL6 certification (for which the certificate was recently issued). Target properties include common security properties—such as integrity and confidentiality—that ensure the required access control rules. The perimeter of verification includes the majority of functions of the JCVM with over 7,000 lines of C code. They were formally annotated in the ACSL specification language [4], and verified using the WP and MetAcsl plugins of Frama-C. Overall, more than 52,000 proof goals (verification conditions) were generated and successfully proved. As far as we know, this is the first verification project for such a large-scale industrial smart card product where deductive verification is applied on the real-life C code.

Contributions. The contributions of the paper include a presentation of the formal verification case study fully realized in the industrial context. It took approximately 3 person-years. We present our specification and verification approach, emphasize some of the issues faced during the project and briefly explain how they were solved. The issues include bit-related operations, heterogeneous pointer casts, existential quantifiers, prover scalability and failures of automatic proof, expressing and efficient proof of global (e.g. security) properties, and code maintenance. While most solutions are not new, their accurate combination was essential for the proof. We also describe some extensions and improvements of Frama-C—some of which were key for the success of this project—identified during the project and implemented by its developers. Finally, we present our proof results, some lessons learned and the desired tool improvements. The source code of smart card products is highly sensitive and cannot be shared. To illustrate the implementation structure, a subset of properties and our verification approach, we use a toy example. Due to space limitations, some other specific aspects of this work (in particular, related to stack verification and the Common Criteria evaluation methodology) will be described in future publications.

Outline. Sections. 2 and 3 provide necessary background on Frama-C and JCVM. Our memory modeling approach using a companion ghost model is presented in Sect. 4. Section 5 describes the usage of lemmas and scripts to help the proof. Security property specification and verification with MetAcsl are presented in Sect. 6. Section 7 discusses code organization and maintenance. Our proof results, lessons learned and expected future improvements are presented in Sect. 8. Finally, Sects. 9 and 10 present related work and a conclusion.

2   Frama-C Verification Platform

This section briefly presents the verification tools used in this project. We assume that the reader is familiar with basic notions of contracts and deductive verification.

Frama-C [14] is a program verification platform for C code developed by CEA List with participation of INRIA. It offers several analyzers organized as plugins around a common kernel. Developed since 2008, Frama-C has been used in several academic and industrial projects and has a large community of developers and users. Today, thanks to an active development, rigorous validation process and a wide range of applications throughout the world, Frama-C is considered as a state-of-the-art verification toolset for C programs. Frama-C uses ACSL (ANSI C Specification Language) [4], a formal specification language for C programs. It allows the user to specify annotations as typed first-order logic formulas. In particular, a precondition (ACSL clause **requires**) of a function f defines a property expected to hold before any invocation of f. It is assumed on entry during the verification of f, but must be proved before any call of f during the verification of a caller. A postcondition (**ensures** clause) of f states a property that must hold after the function call. It must be proved during the verification of f but is assumed after the call to f in a caller. An **assigns** clause in the contract of f specifies the memory locations that can be modified by f. A **loop invariant** clause in a loop contract specifies a property that must hold before the loop and after every loop iteration. Local properties (ACSL clause **assert**) must hold at the point where they are inserted.

The WP plugin of Frama-C is dedicated to modular deductive verification of C code. It takes as input a C program and a (partial) formal specification expressed by ACSL annotations and tries to prove that the program respects the provided annotations. To do that, WP generates proof goals (or proof obligations, or verification conditions) that are then either proved by WP itself (thanks to its internal formula simplification engine called Qed [8]) or sent via the Why3 tool [12] to external provers (SMT solvers). In this work we use Alt-Ergo [7], chosen in agreement with the certification authority. If all proof goals generated for a given program with ACSL annotations are proved, the program is guaranteed to respect the given ACSL specification. In addition to the specified properties, to ensure that the program under verification represents no risk of provoking undefined behaviors (also called runtime errors), WP relies on the RTE plugin of Frama-C to generate additional assertions to exclude the risk of undefined behaviors. Their proof is an essential step, both for the soundness of verification and to avoid security vulnerabilities due to undefined behaviors. Finally, one can rely on the MetAcsl plugin [23–25] to verify some security properties. It allows the user to specify global properties and translates them into local assertions (for instance, for each reading or writing operation) that can then be verified by other tools (like WP).

3   Overview of JavaCard Virtual Machine

This section briefly presents JavaCard Virtual Machine (whose detailed understanding is not mandatory to follow the paper).

JavaCard Virtual Machine (JCVM) [22] is often part of a smart card architecture and plays an essential role in it: it executes JavaCard bytecode. Its main functional goal is to provide application interoperability, when the same JavaCard bytecode can be run without re-compilation on several smartcard architectures. JavaCard bytecode contains a sequence of opcodes, each defining a particular operation, e.g. allocation of a new object of a given class, arithmetic operation on the Java stack, writing into a heap object a value read from the Java stack, etc. Opcodes are read iteratively inside the main *dispatch loop*, which calls functions implementing particular opcodes.

We can distinguish 3 main memory locations managed by JCVM: Java stack, data heap and code area. Inside the code area, immutable information of the package(s) is stored during loading of application to the card, and is never modified later. It contains mainly package classes, including bytecode of their methods.

The data heap is used for storage of application data, namely class instances, arrays and (static) class variables. Three different types of memory are used to store heap data, depending on its life cycle: *transient deselect* data erased during owning application deselection, *transient reset* data erased only when the smart card is reset, and *persistent data* preserved anytime. The Java stack is a central location for data processing. In particular, its subpart, the operand stack, serves to realize arithmetic operations and for data exchange with the heap memory.

Next to functional aspects, JCVM also ensures security goals essential to the smart card ecosystem. As applications of different vendors can be loaded on the same smart card, it is crucial to guarantee isolation, in particular concerning the heap data. It is done by an oncard software component, JavaCard firewall [21].

A unique *context* value is assigned to each JavaCard binary (*CAP file*) during loading to the card. In general, the firewall blocks access to the data of another CAP file, except well-defined exceptions such as global arrays, ArrayViews or class variables. For simplicity, we ignore those exceptions in the examples in this paper. As a natural implementation choice, for each object on the heap (except class variables), the object owner context is stored inside the object header.

For illustration, we can list some examples of (simplified) security goals, which refine the general objective of CAP file data isolation, as defined in [20] (and quoted in Sect. 1), and distinguish confidentiality and integrity aspects.

$\mathcal{G}_{\text{integ}}^{\text{head}}$: Already allocated objects' headers cannot be modified during a VM run.
$\mathcal{G}_{\text{integ}}^{\text{data}}$: Elements of a (persistent or transient reset) array can be modified only if the accessing context is the owner of the accessed object.
$\mathcal{G}_{\text{conf}}^{\text{data}}$: Elements of a (persistent or transient reset) array can be read only if the accessing context is the owner of the accessed object.

There is an interplay between JCVM and another important security component of a smart card environment, Bytecode Verifier (BCV). As stated in [20], BCV must check any application prior to its execution to ensure its type security. On the other hand, (fully) defensive VMs ensure the discussed security properties even if the interpreted application is not verified by BCV. However, the toy example considered in this paper does not contain necessary sanity checks, so they rely on successful BCV checks. Thus, to enable its proof, we introduce hypotheses corresponding to particular BCV checks. For example, function updateJPC (modifying the Java program counter) will simply assume the updated code position stays within the method component of the CAP file.

The influence between JCVM and BCV is bidirectional. Indeed, BCV applies typed based simulation of bytecode, investigating all possible paths through the

```
1  typedef unsigned char u1; typedef unsigned short u2; typedef unsigned int u4;
2
3  // === Code model and current Java context ===
4  #define CODE_SIZE 10000
5  u1   Code[CODE_SIZE], *JPC; // Java code area and Java program counter
6  //@ ghost u4 gJPCOff;        // JPC offset in code area
7  u1   JCC;                    // Current Java context
8
9  // === Heap model ===
10 #define SEGM_SIZE 10000
11 #define MAX_OBJS  500
12 u1 ObjHeader[SEGM_SIZE];    // Object headers area
13 //Header(8B),Bytes:Contents: 0:Owner,1:Flags,2-3:Class,4-5:BodyOff,6-7:BodySize
14 #define GET_OWN(addr)   ( *((u1*)addr + 0) )
15 #define GET_FLAG(addr)  ( *((u1*)addr + 1) )
16 #define GET_OFF(addr)   ( (u2)((*((u1*)addr + 4))*256 + *((u1*)addr + 5)) )
17 #define GET_SIZE(addr)  ( (u2)((*((u1*)addr + 6))*256 + *((u1*)addr + 7)) )
18 u1 PersiData[SEGM_SIZE];    // Persistent objects data area
19 u1 TransData[SEGM_SIZE];    // Transient  objects data area
20
21 /*@ ghost // === Companion ghost memory view ===
22    u4 gNumObjs;              // Number of allocated objects
23    u1 gIsTrans  [MAX_OBJS]; // Nonzero for transient object
24    u4 gHeadStart[MAX_OBJS]; // Start offset of object header
25    u4 gDataStart[MAX_OBJS]; // Start offset of object data
26    u4 gDataEnd  [MAX_OBJS]; // End offset of object data
27    u4 gCurObj; */            // Currently considered object number
28
29 /*@ // === Validity predicates ===
30 predicate valid_code_model = 0 <= gJPCOff < CODE_SIZE &&
31    JPC == &Code[gJPCOff];
32 predicate valid_heap_model =
33    0 <= gNumObjs <= MAX_OBJS &&
34 // headers of allocated objects are within ObjHeader segment
35    (\forall integer i; 0 <= i < gNumObjs ==>
36      0 <= gHeadStart[i] <= SEGM_SIZE - 8 ) &&
37 // no overlapping between headers (each header has 8 bytes)
38    (\forall integer i,j; 0 <= i < j < gNumObjs ==>
39      (gHeadStart[i] >= gHeadStart[j]+8 || gHeadStart[j] >= gHeadStart[i]+8) ) &&
40 // IsTrans[i] encodes if i-th object's transient bit is set
41    (\forall integer i; 0 <= i < gNumObjs ==>
42      ( gIsTrans[i] <==> (GET_FLAG(ObjHeader+gHeadStart[i]) & 0x08) ) ) &&
43 // data of allocated objects is within a data segment
44    (\forall integer i; 0 <= i < gNumObjs ==>
45      gDataStart[i] == GET_OFF(ObjHeader+gHeadStart[i]) &&
46      gDataEnd[i] == gDataStart[i] + GET_SIZE(ObjHeader+gHeadStart[i]) - 1 &&
47      0 <= gDataStart[i] < gDataEnd[i] < SEGM_SIZE ) &&
48 // no overlapping between persistent object data
49    (\forall integer i,j; 0<=i<j<gNumObjs && !gIsTrans[i] && !gIsTrans[j] ==>
50      (gDataStart[i] > gDataEnd[j] || gDataStart[j] > gDataEnd[i]) ) &&
51 // no overlapping between transient object data
52    (\forall integer i,j; 0 <= i < j < gNumObjs && gIsTrans[i] && gIsTrans[j] ==>
53      (gDataStart[i] > gDataEnd[j] || gDataStart[j] > gDataEnd[i]) ); */
54
55 // Lines 56-66 give declarations of functions updateJPC, get_u1, get_u4, get_gu4.
```

Fig. 1. Illustrative example of JCVM: code and heap modeling.

code and checking its type safety [19]. As a hypothesis, BCV relies on the opcode specification [22] and its effect on the memory managed by JCVM (e.g. number of slots popped and pushed on the Java stack). It is therefore mandatory to check that JCVM respects this specification.

4   Memory Modeling and Companion Ghost Model

To illustrate our verification approach, we use a toy example of a JCVM, split into Figs. 1, 2, 3, 4 and 5, where we omit some less important fragments or empty lines. It is strongly simplified to fit the paper, and intentionally modified to avoid revealing real-life code features. It is of course too simple to provoke proof issues we faced on real-life code, but sufficient to explain when they occur and how we address them. We consider one JCVM run, in which allocated objects cannot be deleted, but new objects can be allocated. Figure 4 presents the dispatch loop that reads the next opcode and calls the relevant opcode function. An opcode function and a simple firewall function are shown in Fig. 3. We detail all components of the example below. In this section, we explain Fig. 1 and the C code of Fig. 3.

Line 1 in Fig. 1 defines unsigned integer types with 1, 2 and 4 bytes. Lines 3–7 show a simple code model, where Java program counter JPC will be assumed to refer inside the Code array as specified by the code model validity predicate on lines 30–31. This predicate will be maintained by most functions in our example. Here, *to facilitate the automatic proof, we avoid an existentially quantified offset* by introducing the offset gJPCOff as a *ghost* variable (i.e. used only in ACSL annotations). We start the names of ghost variables with a g.

Lines 9–27 show a simplified model of the heap, where we model only persistent and transient reset objects. We consider three separate memory segments: for objects headers, persistent object data and transient (reset) object data (cf. lines 12, 18–19). A header contains the object's owner context (1 byte), flags (1 byte), class reference (2 bytes), followed by the start offset of the object data (body) and its size, each over 2 bytes (cf. line 13). Macros on lines 14–17 extract some of these fields. The number of allocated objects is specified as a ghost variable gNumObjs, and the allocated objects are supposed be numbered starting from 0. For the i-th object, the offset of its header is modeled by a ghost array element gHeadStart[i], while gDataStart[i] and gDataSize[i] contain the offset and size of its body in one of the data segments. The ghost array element gIsTrans[i] is nonzero iff the i-th object has transient data.

The heap model validity predicate specifies first the value interval for the number of allocated objects (line 33). Lines 34–39 state that headers are within the bounds of the segment and do not overlap. Similarly, lines 43–53 state that object bodies are within the bounds of data segments and—when in the same segment—do not overlap. Thus, *we precisely model the heap memory using a companion ghost model*, some parts of which are not readily available in the C code. The heap validity predicate is maintained by most functions, including new object allocation.

Optimized code often uses bits, e.g. to encode various flags. Let us consider here only one bit: the *transient bit*, obtained from the flag byte with mask 0x08. If this bit is set, the object data is located in the transient segment (with the offset and size given in the header), otherwise in the persistent segment (with the offset and size given in the header). Its usage is well illustrated by function bastore (see lines 110–119 in Fig. 3). It writes a given value into a given object at a given offset. After calling the firewall to check the access, it tests the transient

```
67  /*@ // === A security property: object headers remain intact ===
68  predicate object_headers_intact{L1, L2} =
69    \forall integer i, off; 0 <= i < \at(gNumObjs,L1) &&
70      \at(gHeadStart[i],L1) <= off < \at(gHeadStart[i],L1) + 8 ==>
71      \at(ObjHeader[off],L1) == \at(ObjHeader[off],L2);
72
73  // === Memory footprint predicate and lemma example ===
74  predicate mem_model_footprint_intact{L1,L2} =
75    \at(gNumObjs,L1) <= \at(gNumObjs,L2) &&
76    ( \forall integer i; 0 <= i < \at(gNumObjs,L1) ==>
77      \at(gIsTrans[i],L1) == \at(gIsTrans[i],L2) &&
78      \at(gHeadStart[i],L1) ==\at(gHeadStart[i],L2) &&
79      \at(gDataStart[i],L1) ==\at(gDataStart[i],L2) &&
80      \at(gDataEnd[i],L1) ==\at(gDataEnd[i],L2) );
81
82  lemma vhm_preserved{L1,L2}: mem_model_footprint_intact{L1,L2} &&
83    object_headers_intact{L1,L2} && valid_heap_model{L1} &&
84    \at(gNumObjs,L1) == \at(gNumObjs,L2) ==> valid_heap_model{L2}; */
```

Fig. 2. Examples of a security property, a footprint-related predicate and a lemma.

bit to choose and write the target memory location before moving the program counter to a next opcode (using the function updateJPC, omitted here). The firewall function (see lines 93–97 in Fig. 3) allows the access if the current context is the object owner and the destination offset is in the bounds (cf. $\mathcal{G}_{\text{integ}}^{\text{data}}$, $\mathcal{G}_{\text{conf}}^{\text{data}}$ in Sect. 3). In the real-life code, several bits can be manipulated within the same function, leading to complex proof goals.

Straightforward specification of the code with bit-related operations does not scale well in our case study: automatic proof fails for many properties over the real-life code when numerous bits are involved, thus requiring extra assertions or interactive scripts. *To overcome proof scalability issues due to bit-level operations, we duplicate the bit-level information by boolean ghost variables and maintain their equivalence.* That is why we encode the transient bit of the i-th object as a ghost array element gIsTrans[i], as specified by lines 40–42. By expressing annotations using the resulting ghost variables (like on lines 49, 52, or as we will see later in Fig. 5) rather than the transient bit, we provide the provers with a parallel, companion view of bit-level information. It enhances their capacity of automatic proof in our project.

Heterogeneous pointer casts present another difficulty faced in our project. The definitions of macros of lines 16–17 in real-life code would use such casts:

```
#define GET_OFF(addr)  ( (u2)(*(u2*)(addr + 4)) )    // Before rewriting of casts
#define GET_SIZE(addr) ( (u2)(*(u2*)(addr + 6)) )    // Before rewriting of casts
```

To allow the proof with the Typed memory model of WP, we rewrite such casts equivalently as shown on lines 16–17. The equivalence of rewriting can be checked even by an exhaustive enumeration. The Typed memory model of WP [3] is both sound and efficient, but unable to support heterogeneous pointer casts. Lower-level models are either unsound or unable to reason efficiently on our case study. Introducing ghost variables to store the resulting casted values (cf. lines 45–46) and using those ghost variables in annotations (cf. line 91) also had a positive effect on the automatic proof.

Overall, the companion ghost model in our project has a twofold role: it allows us to conveniently express memory-related properties and facilitates automatic

```
86  /*@
87    requires vhm: valid_heap_model;
88    requires 0 <= gCurObj < gNumObjs && ObjRef == gHeadStart[gCurObj];
89    assigns \nothing;
90    ensures \result <==> ( GET_OWN(ObjHeader+ObjRef) == JCC &&
91      gDataStart[gCurObj] + DestOff <= gDataEnd[gCurObj] );
92  */
93  u1 firewall(u4 ObjRef, u4 DestOff){
94    if (GET_OWN(ObjHeader+ObjRef) == JCC && DestOff < GET_SIZE(ObjHeader+ObjRef))
95      return 1;
96    return 0;
97  }
98
99  /*@
100   requires vhm: valid_heap_model;
101   requires vcm: valid_code_model;
102   admit requires 0 <= gCurObj < gNumObjs && ObjRef == gHeadStart[gCurObj];
103   assigns  PersiData[0..(SEGM_SIZE-1)],TransData[0..(SEGM_SIZE-1)],JPC,gJPCOff;
104   assigns  JPC \from &Code[0]; // possible base address
105   ensures  vhm: valid_heap_model;
106   ensures  vcm: valid_code_model;
107   ensures  oh:  object_headers_intact{Pre,Post};
108   ensures  mmf: mem_model_footprint_intact{Pre,Post};
109 */
110 void bastore(u4 ObjRef, u4 DestOff, u1 Val)
111 {
112   if( ! firewall(ObjRef,DestOff) )                     // Check access and
113     return;                                            // exit if forbidden
114   if( GET_FLAG(ObjHeader+ObjRef) & 0x08 )              // If trans. bit set,
115     TransData[GET_OFF(ObjHeader+ObjRef) + DestOff] = Val;// write to trans.body
116   else                                                 // Otherwise
117     PersiData[GET_OFF(ObjHeader+ObjRef) + DestOff] = Val;// write to pers.body
118   updateJPC();
119 }
```

Fig. 3. firewall and bastore functions with their ACSL contracts.

reasoning for bit-level operations and heterogeneous casts rewritten with arithmetic operations.

5   Predicates, Lemmas and Scripts

This section details Figs. 2 and 4, as well as function contracts in Fig. 3.

The predicate on lines 68–71 of Fig. 2 states that the object headers of allocated objects do not change between labels (program points) L1, L2. The predicate on lines 74–80 states that the companion model does not change between labels L1, L2 for objects that existed at label L1, but new objects can have been allocated. As we said, we do not consider object deletion.

The C code of the dispatch loop in Fig. 4 reads the next opcode and chooses the opcode function to be called. The code of bastore function was presented in Sect. 4. We assume that baload is a similar function for reading a value, and other_opcode illustrates other opcodes. For simplicity, the Java stack and Java reference resolution are not modeled in this example, and the necessary arguments of bastore and baload are read as non-deterministic values (lines 185–186, 188–189). Here again, *to avoid an existential quantifier, we use a ghost variable* gCurObj *to represent the index of the object in our companion model.* We assume for simplicity as a precondition of bastore (cf. line 102 in Fig. 3)

```
120  //Lines 121-170 contain functions baload, other_opcode and a contract of main_loop
     ...
171  void main_loop(){
172  /*@
173    loop invariant vhm: valid_heap_model;
174    loop invariant vcm: valid_code_model;
175    loop invariant oh:  object_headers_intact{LoopEntry,Here};
176    loop invariant mmf: mem_model_footprint_intact{LoopEntry,Here};
177    loop invariant no:  gNumObjs >= \at(gNumObjs,LoopEntry);
178    loop assigns gNumObjs, ObjHeader[0..(SEGM_SIZE-1)],
179      gIsTrans[0..(MAX_OBJS-1)], gHeadStart[0..(MAX_OBJS-1)],
180      gDataStart[0..(MAX_OBJS-1)], gDataEnd[0..(MAX_OBJS-1)], gCurObj, JCC,
181      PersiData[0..(SEGM_SIZE-1)], TransData[0..(SEGM_SIZE-1)], JPC, gJPCOff;
182  */
183    while(1){
184      if(*JPC == 1)                                  // Assume code 1 is for BASTORE
185        /*@ ghost gCurObj=get_gu4(); */              // Assume arbitrary object index and
186        bastore(get_u4(),get_u4(),get_u1());         // header offset, body offset, value
187      else if(*JPC == 2)                             // Assume code 2 is for BALOAD
188        /*@ ghost gCurObj=get_gu4(); */              // Assume arbitrary object index and
189        baload(get_u4(),get_u4());                   // header offset, body offset
190      else if(*JPC == 3)                             // Assume code 3 is for exit
191        return;
192      else                                           // Other opcodes
193        other_opcode();
194    }
195  }
```

Fig. 4. The dispatch loop and its ACSL contract.

that the object reference is a valid object, therefore, it has an index in the companion model. The **admit** keyword[1] indicates that this annotation is assumed without proof. Heap and code validity are both pre- and postconditions (lines 100–101, 105–106). Line 103 indicates variables that the function is allowed to modify. Line 107 ensures security property $\mathcal{G}_{\text{integ}}^{\text{head}}$ of Sect. 3. Line 104 indicates base address(es) of memory locations pointer JPC can be assigned to refer to. This information is needed for a recent alias analysis in WP for pointers modified inside the function (see [3, Sect. 3.6]). Line 108 is explained below. The contract of firewall is straightforward.

The loop contract of the dispatch loop is similar to the contract of bastore, but also allows modifications of current context JCC, an allocation of new objects (line 177) and, therefore, modifications of the companion ghost model (lines 178–180). For simplicity, in properties on lines 175–177 we compare the state after each iteration (label Here, taken by default) to the start of the loop (label LoopEntry), i.e. to the objects allocated before the loop. To cover all objects allocated before the current iteration, similar properties comparing the start and the end of an iteration can be specified in the loop body.

The dispatch loop iterations can modify a large part of the memory in the real-life code, that decreases the capacity of automatic proof. To facilitate the proof, we introduce the memory model footprint preservation property for previously allocated objects (lines 73–80). It is used to state several preservation lemmas for complex properties (like on lines 82–84 in Fig. 2). They facilitate the automatic proof for the real-life code: non-modification of some variables is easier to prove

---

[1] It was recently added in the 23.0beta and 23.0 releases of Frama-C; it should be removed if an earlier release is used.

automatically than more complex properties, and helps to automatically deduce more complex properties using lemmas.

When automatic proof does not work, the interactive proof editor of WP [3] *is very helpful* to indicate some first proof steps—that can be recorded in a proof script—to help the automatic prover to finish the proof. For instance, for the lemma in Fig. 2, Alt-Ergo cannot perform the proof. The preservation of the loop invariant mmf in the dispatch loop is another unproved goal. Proof scripts can help to finish the proof. Typically, a script in our project includes unfolding some predicate definitions, splitting some proof goals and instantiating universally quantified goals with specific values.

Another issue was related to bit-level lemmas, not proved with Alt-Ergo, e.g.:

```
/*@ lemma dn: \forall u1 c; (c & 0x04)==0 && (c & 0x08)!=0 ==> (c & 0x0C)==0x08;*/
```

On our request, WP developers added new tactics so that now such lemmas are successfully proved after a few clics in the interactive proof editor of WP.

One scalability issue we met was related to the simplification engine Qed *of* WP: it could take about 40 min per property because of a very high number of branches (for 185 opcodes) in the dispatch loop. The solution we used was to deactivate some Qed simplifications (with option -wp-no-pruning) and to rewrite a long dispatch loop equivalently with shorter functions. *Another kind of code transformation was necessary to rewrite longjmp/setjmp instructions* present in the code but not yet supported by Frama-C. Apart from these two cases of transformations and a minor rewriting for heterogeneous pointer casts (see Sect. 4), *the real-life code was proved as is, without other code transformations.*

Overall, a careful combination of preservation properties, lemmas and interactive proof scripts helped us to successfully finish the proof.

6   Verification of Security Properties with MetAcsl

We saw that some security properties like $\mathcal{G}_{\text{integ}}^{\text{head}}$ can be specified in ACSL as an invariant property maintained by relevant functions and directly proved by WP. For other properties, like $\mathcal{G}_{\text{integ}}^{\text{data}}$ and $\mathcal{G}_{\text{conf}}^{\text{data}}$, it is not possible. Confidentiality properties cannot be currently verified by WP because there is no way supported by the tool to specify which variables (or memory locations) can be read and under which precise conditions. But even for an integrity property $\mathcal{G}_{\text{integ}}^{\text{data}}$, it is not easy to specify that modifications can only occur when allowed. The current context of the smart card can be changed (under certain conditions, that must of course be specified and verified as well). Hence $\mathcal{G}_{\text{integ}}^{\text{data}}$ cannot be specified as preservation of values during the dispatch loop: object data *can be modified* if the current context JCC was legally changed to the object owner. As various involved variables (in this example, object data and JCC) are changed in different functions under different specific conditions, it is extremely difficult to achieve a global view of what is really specified and verified. To solve this issue, we use the recent metaproperty-based approach and the MetAcsl plugin [23–25].

Figure 5 shows two metaproperties expressing $\mathcal{G}_{\text{integ}}^{\text{data}}$ and $\mathcal{G}_{\text{conf}}^{\text{data}}$ for persistent objects. Lines 198, 203 provide a name, the set of target functions (here, all

```
197  /*@ // === Metaproperties: persistent object data written/read only by owner ===
198  meta \prop,\name(meta_persi_objects_integrity),\targets(\ALL),\context(\writing),
199    ( \forall integer i; 0 <= i < gNumObjs && !gIsTrans[i] &&
200    ObjHeader[gHeadStart[i] + 0] != JCC ==>
201    \separated(\written,PersiData+(gDataStart[i]..gDataEnd[i])) );
202
203  meta \prop,\name(meta_persi_objects_confident),\targets(\ALL),\context(\reading),
204    ( \forall integer i; 0 <= i < gNumObjs && !gIsTrans[i] &&
205    ObjHeader[gHeadStart[i] + 0] != JCC ==>
206    \separated(\read,PersiData+(gDataStart[i]..gDataEnd[i])) ); */
```

Fig. 5. Metaproperties for persistent object data integrity/confidentiality.

functions) and the context—the situations in which it must apply. The first metaproperty has a writing context and applies whenever a variable is written. It means that whenever a variable (or memory location) is written, the predicate on lines 199–201 must hold, where \written refers to the written location. In other words, the written location must be *separated* (that is, disjoint) from the data of any persistent object if the current context is not its owner, as required by $\mathcal{G}_{\text{integ}}^{\text{data}}$. Similarly, the second metaproperty states that every read location must be separated (that is, disjoint) with the data of any persistent object if the current context is not its owner, as required by $\mathcal{G}_{\text{conf}}^{\text{data}}$. Metaproperties for transient objects are expressed similarly.

MetAcsl translates metaproperties into assertions at each relevant program point. For example, for the first metaproperty, an assertion of the provided predicate will be added before each writing operation, where \written will be replaced by the address of the written location. Those assertions can then be verified by WP. If all assertions are proved, the metaproperty is proved. Notice that these metaproperties directly ensure the security properties for all currently allocated objects (not only those allocated before the loop as for a loop invariant) since the predicate is inserted and evaluated at each relevant program location.

On our request, MetAcsl developers added an extremely useful feature: to translate a metaproperty into checks rather than asserts. In ACSL, the proof of a **check** is attempted, but it is not kept in the proof context for the following properties, contrary to an **assert**, that is proved and kept in the context. *Thanks to the translation of metaproperties into checks that do not overload proof contexts, the metaproperty-based approach scales very well,* despite a great number of generated annotations.

7   Specification Architecture and Effort

Maintenance Issue. ACSL annotations may become pervasive, difficult to track and to maintain, especially when the verification scope is meant to be extended. They require a *careful organization to ensure specification traceability and maintainability.* Function contracts are placed in header files with function declarations, security properties are grouped in a separate header file, etc.

Macros to Define Common Contracts. We leverage the pre-processing of C macros to organize a large part of function and loop contracts as macros.

Table 1. Specification effort for the real-life code.

Code subset	$\#_{opc}$	$\#_{fun}$	$\#_C$	User-provided ACSL					MetAcsl			RTE	
				Manual effort			Auto. prep.		Man.	Auto. trans.		Auto. gen.	
				$\#_{ghost}$	$\#_{ACSL}^{man}$	$\frac{\#_{ACSL}^{man}}{\#_C}$	$\#_{ACSL}^{pp}$	$\frac{\#_{ACSL}^{pp}}{\#_C}$	$\#_P$	$\#_{ACSL}^{meta}$	$\frac{\#_{ACSL}^{meta}}{\#_C}$	$\#_{ACSL}^{rte}$	$\frac{\#_{ACSL}^{rte}}{\#_C}$
Bastore	1	11	540	70	2,814	**5.21**	2,770	**5.12**	29	57,362	106.22	514	0.95
Sample 1	4	19	783	94	3,153	4.08	3,526	4.50	29	84,698	108.17	734	0.93
Sample 2	11	36	1,201	97	3,939	3.27	5,787	4.81	34	117,191	97.57	897	0.74
All	185	391	7,014	162	**12,432**	1.77	**35,480**	5.05	**36**	**396,603**	56.54	2,290	0.32

They are used to define common properties that occur in several contracts. For instance, one macro is used to gather all postconditions that apply to several opcode functions. Other examples of macros are some common preconditions, or common assigns clauses. *Macros reduce redundancy in specifications and facilitate updates and maintenance.* Note that specific clauses can still be added to opcode function contracts if required.

Macros to Reduce the VM to Particular Opcodes. We realize a rich set of macros to select a consistent minimal part of the C code and ACSL annotations for verification of properties for some code subsets: one opcode or a sample of opcodes. On a large project, running the proof on such a code subset is handy for getting faster results for a subset of opcodes and for proof debugging purposes.
Inventory of ACSL annotations. We distinguish several kinds of ACSL annotations in our project, depending whether they have been manually written by the user or automatically generated by MetAcsl, RTE or WP plugins:

- User-provided annotations: ACSL predicates and lemmas, function contracts, loop contracts, proof-guiding assertions and metaproperties.
- Automatically generated annotations, produced
  - by MetAcsl plugin according to user-defined metaproperties (cf. Sect. 6);
  - by RTE plugin to prevent undefined behaviors (cf. Sect. 2);
  - by WP plugin to detect ACSL specification inconsistencies, called *smoke tests* (optional) [3, Sect. 2.3.5]. Basically, they check if `false` is provable.

Target JCVM Code and Code Subsets. We verify the JCVM code that interprets 185 standard opcodes of the JavaCard platform [22]. To show our proof results, we consider four incrementally increasing subsets of C code: (i) the smallest subset required to interpret the bastore opcode; (ii) a subset required to interpret 4 opcodes (Sample 1); (iii) a subset for 11 opcodes (Sample 2); (iv) the whole code with all 185 opcodes (All). Columns $\#_{opc}$, $\#_{fun}$ and $\#_C$ of Table 1 show, respectively, the number of opcodes, functions and lines of C code in each subset. The whole code (All) submitted to our deductive verification contains 7,014 lines of C code. In addition to the 391 functions that are fully proved, it contains 23 stub functions (only specified in ACSL but not verified) to delimit the considered verification scope. They mainly include some specific functions exploring the hierarchy of classes and interfaces, functions for particular exception handler operations, and memory address resolution functions.

User-Provided ACSL Annotations. The core of our formal specification consists of manually written ACSL annotations. We show separately the amount (in lines of code (loc)) of ghost code and other annotations (except metaproperties), resp., in columns $\#_{ghost}$ and $\#^{man}_{ACSL}$ of Table 1. The amount of ghost code is relatively small (162 loc for All) compared to the project size. It mainly contains declaring and updating ghost variables. Column $\#^{pp}_{ACSL}$ shows the amount of ACSL annotations after preprocessing of the macros defining common contracts. We observe that the ratio of expanded ACSL annotations with respect to the C code (column $\#^{pp}_{ACSL}/\#_{C}$) is between 4.5 and 5.12 for all subsets. However the ratio of user-provided ACSL annotations with respect to the C code (column $\#^{man}_{ACSL}/\#_{C}$) shrinks drastically from 5.05 for Bastore to 1.77 for All. Indeed, macros help to reduce the number of lines of user-provided ACSL annotations from 35,480 to 12,432 for the whole C code. Hence, *the benefit of macros monotonically increases with the increase of redundant ACSL annotations for larger code subsets,* and the ratio of manually written annotations for the whole code becomes very reasonable. Macros save a lot of effort and enhance the readability and traceability of ACSL annotations. Notice though that this observation can be specific to our project, where some groups of opcodes have similar contracts.

MetAcsl Annotations. Column $\#_P$ in Table 1 gives the number of metaproperties (that varies since some of them cover different sets of functions). Column $\#^{meta}_{ACSL}$ shows the number of lines in annotations automatically generated from them by MetAcsl. Despite a very high number of ACSL annotations generated (396,603 loc for All, which is 56.54 times the original C code size), we had to write only 36 metaproperties with approximately 480 lines of ACSL. Note that the ratio of the size of generated ACSL annotations w.r.t the original code ($\#^{meta}_{ACSL}/\#_{C}$) decreases from 106.22 for Bastore to 56.54 for All, in particular, since All includes many simple, short opcode functions, for which MetAcsl generates less annotations.

RTE Annotations. The ratio of the size of generated RTE annotations w.r.t. the whole C code ($\#^{rte}_{ACSL}/\#_{C}$) is 0.32 (cf. Table 1), which is smaller compared to user-provided annotations (5.05) and MetAcsl-generated annotations (56.54). Is decreases for the same reason as for metaproperties.

8   Proof Results and Lessons Learned

8.1   Proof Results

Table 2 depicts proof results obtained by running Frama-C 22.0 (Titanium) on an Ubuntu virtual machine. It was used under VirtualBox on a host desktop PC running Windows 10 with Intel(R) core(TM) i7 CPU @ 2.00 GHz processor and 32.0 GB RAM. 8 processors and 24 GB were allocated to the virtual machine. Frama-C was run with option -wp-par 8 to optimally use the 8 allocated processors and a timeout for provers set to 100 s (option -wp-timeout 100). We used the Alt-Ergo solver, version 2.3.2. Overall, 52,198 proof goals have been proven within 3 h 28 m 07 s.

Table 2. Proof results for the real-life code.

Code subset	Prover	User-provided ACSL #Goals	MetAcsl #Goals	RTE #Goals	Total #Goals	Time
Bastore	Qed	1,019	3,304	106	4,429 (**77.92%**)	0h 47m 45s
	Script	78	131	1	210 (3.69%)	0h 11m 12s
	SMT	305	590	148	1,043 (18.35%)	0h 17m 23s
	All	1,402 (24.67%)	4,025 (**70.81%**)	255 (4.48%)	**5,684**	**0h 49m 37s**
Sample 1	Qed	1,491	5,037	120	6,648 (**79.76%**)	1h 00m 49s
	Script	111	149	7	267 (3.20%)	0h 13m 41s
	SMT	437	784	199	1,420 (17.03%)	0h 28m 24s
	All	2,039 (24.46%)	5,970 (**71.63%**)	326 (3.91%)	**8,335**	**0h 59m 59s**
Sample 2	Qed	2,413	6,884	126	9,423 (**79.43%**)	1h 04m 33s
	Script	144	257	20	421 (3.55%)	0h 18m 15s
	SMT	682	1,088	249	2,019 (17.01%)	0h 37m 01s
	All	3,239 (27.30%)	8,229 (**69.36%**)	395 (3.33%)	**11,863**	**1h 09m 47s**
All	Qed	18,925	22,361	168	41,454 (**79.42%**)	2h 58m 15s
	Script	330	212	30	572 (1.1%)	0h 44m 48s
	SMT	4,683	4,588	902	10,173 (19.49 %)	2h 36m 18s
	All	23,938 (**45.85%**)	27,435 (**52.55%**)	1,117 (2.13%)	**52,198**	**3h 28m 07s**

Results per Prover. The internal simplifier engine Qed of WP proves most proof goals (around 79%) with an average time of 257 ms per proved goal. The maximum time spent by Qed to prove one goal is 10.9 s. The SMT solver is able to discharge around 20% of proof goals with an average time of 974 ms per proved goal. The maximum time spent to prove one goal is 1 m 2 s. Last but not least, scripts prove the rest of the goals with an average time of 4 s 699 ms. The majority of scripts are necessary, but some scripts are introduced for time saving purpose, when a script-based proof is faster and more stable with a fixed timeout of 100 s.

Results per Annotation Kind. As discussed in Sect. 7, most lines of ACSL are generated by MetAcsl. Each ACSL annotation is usually encoded on several lines and several proof goals may be generated by WP for each ACSL annotation. This partially explains the difference of proportions between Tables 1 and 2: in Table 1, the ratio of the number of generated ACSL lines for MetAcsl w.r.t. the number of preprocessed user-provided ACSL lines ranges between 20 times for Bastore subset (57,362 vs 2,770) and 11 times for All (396,603 vs 35,480). However, in Table 2, the ratio of the number of generated goals for MetAcsl w.r.t. the number of goals for user-provided ACSL ranges between 3 times for Bastore subset (4,025 vs 1,402) and 1.1 times for All (27,435 vs 23,938). For the same reasons as explained in Sect. 7, the percentage of MetAcsl goals decreases from 70.81% for Bastore subset to 52.55% for All.

Overall Results Scalability. Results of Table 2 show that the proof scales well with an increasing number of proof obligations. Whereas the number of proof goals increases ten times from bastore subset to all opcodes subset, the proof time increased only four times. This is thanks to parallelisation of goal proofs in Frama-C. The distribution of proved goals over provers and ACSL annotation kinds is given in Table 2. Although scripts prove only 1% of goals for the whole program, they are very important to achieve a complete proof. They are also important to get a complete proof verdict in a reasonable time while the specification task is in progress and the verification engineers wait for the proof results. Without the 572 scripts, proved in 44 m 48 s, 16 extra hours will be necessary to get a complete proof verdict with a timeout of 100 s set for external provers.

8.2 Lessons Learned

Successful Industrial Application. Our application of deductive verification on a large industrial C program shows that formal verification of real-life industrial code has become feasible today. The proof of real-life code in our project requires a careful combination of several ingredients: companion ghost code, preservation properties, lemmas and proof scripts. This combination made it possible to efficiently reason about non-trivial code fragments involving bitwise operations without the use of external interactive tools (e.g. Coq) with a high level of automatic proof. The majority of proof goals (almost 99%) are proved automatically by the Qed simplification engine of WP and an automatic SMT solver. The remaining goals are successfully proved with proof scripts. MetAcsl proved to offer a convenient and efficient technique for specification and verification of security-related properties. An efficient support from the tool developers during the whole project was essential for its success. Some anomalies were reported and fixed, and several new features were requested and implemented. Examples of such features include the implementation of check-and-forget versions of all annotations (i.e. verified but not kept in the proof context), their usage for annotations generated by MetAcsl, as well as precise generation of memory model hypotheses necessary for a sound proof [3, Sect. 3.6].

Further Improvements. Creating and updating proof scripts in WP is a time-consuming task. Scripts are very sensitive to specification changes and require to be updated accordingly. Designing and applying custom, project-specific strategies possible in Frama-C—would at least partially address this issue and save efforts. Another issue we faced during this project is related to properties mixing casts and arithmetic operations between different integer types. Lemmas allowing to prove such properties should be either systematically activated in the tool or made applicable on request. Further improvements in the tool seem to be necessary to perform a proof of large programs, in particular, mixing complex logic properties and low-level operations. One future work direction is the development of collaborative memory models, capable to reason with different memory models on various parts of code (e.g. with and without low-level operations) and to soundly combine the results. Integrating more abstract levels of reasoning into source-code based deductive verification is also an interesting work perspective. Another work direction concerns a deeper proof parallelization. In our case study, doubling the number of processors dedicated to the proof computation from 8 to 16 cores does not seem to bring any benefit on the proof efficiency today since some parts of WP are not parallelized. A more efficient proof parallelization would facilitate industrial applications of the tool. Finally, scalability issues of the Qed simplification engine on very long functions—that we avoided by a code rewriting—should be further investigated.

9   Related Work

JavaCard Related Formal Verification. A classical approach of applying formal verification on JavaCard platform consists in building a high-level formal model of target sub-modules. Several case studies have adopted this approach. An executable formal semantics of the JCVM and BCV is proposed in [2] with 15,000 lines of Coq scripts. Authors of [17] describe a refinement-based approach, using the Coq proof assistant, to show that a native JavaCard API function fulfills its specification. In general, in such approaches, the traceability of formally proven properties may require a considerable effort to be justified because of the gap between the formal model and the source code. In our case, all specified features and properties are expressed as ACSL annotations directly on source code. An operational semantics of a language that models the JCVM behavior is proposed in [11,26]. It includes the basic structures needed to model object ownership and the JavaCard firewall. This is analogous to our formal specification. In addition, we perform a full proof of target security properties on a real-life JCVM implementation. Among tools devised and/or used for the purpose of providing formal guarantees about JavaCard platform security properties we can list: Key [16], KRAKATOA [15] and Caduceus [1].

Other Success Stories of Deductive Verification. Various verification case studies of real-life software have emerged in the last two decades, where code was annotated and verified, and often bugs were found [13]. A recent case study [18] presented formal verification of industrial safety-critical software for a traffic tunnel control system verification based on VerCors tool. Authors of [9] provide a feedback on their experience of using ACSL and Frama-C on a real-world example. Other case studies based on Frama-C present formal verification of kLIBC, a minimalistic C library [6], a unit-proof of almost 3315 C functions of an avionics software [5] and a verified RTE-free X.509 parser [10]. Proved properties tend to be shallower as the code becomes of a lower-level nature. In our work, we took on the challenge and managed to prove global critical security properties on large real-life C code.

10   Conclusion

In this paper, we have presented a formal verification case study fully realized in an industrial context for a certification purpose. It contributes to collect and publish best practices and specification patterns in formal verification. We believe this work will set up a new state of the art for applying deductive verification to prove global security properties directly on large security-critical code. We report detailed specification statistics and proof results that measure the specification effort and proof scalability. The reported lessons learned from this project open the door for further methodology and tool enhancements. As a future work, we plan to introduce deductive verification in a sustainable continuous integration process as both the code and its formal specification share the same codebase.

Acknowledgement. The authors thank the Frama-C team members for their reliable and efficient support. Many thanks to the anonymous reviewers for their helpful comments.

References

1. Andronick, J., Chetali, B., Paulin-Mohring, C.: Formal verification of security properties of smart card embedded source code. In: Fitzgerald, J., Hayes, I.J., Tarlecki, A. (eds.) FM 2005. LNCS, vol. 3582, pp. 302–317. Springer, Heidelberg (2005). https://doi.org/10.1007/11526841_21
2. Barthe, G., Dufay, G., Jakubiec, L., Serpette, B., de Sousa, S.M.: A formal executable semantics of the JavaCard platform. In: Sands, D. (ed.) ESOP 2001. LNCS, vol. 2028, pp. 302–319. Springer, Heidelberg (2001). https://doi.org/10.1007/3-540-45309-1_20
3. Baudin, P., Bobot, F., Correnson, L., Dargaye, Z., Blanchard, A.: WP Plug-in Manual (2020). https://frama-c.com/download/frama-c-wp-manual.pdf
4. Baudin, P., et al.: ACSL: ANSI/ISO C Specification Language, v1.16 (2020). http://frama-c.cea.fr/acsl.html
5. Brahmi, A., et al.: Industrial use of a safe and efficient formal method based software engineering process in avionics. In: Embedded Real Time Software and Systems (ERTS 2020) (2020)
6. Carvalho, N., da Silva Sousa, C., Pinto, J.S., Tomb, A.: Formal verification of kLIBC with the WP Frama-C plug-in. In: Badger, J.M., Rozier, K.Y. (eds.) NFM 2014. LNCS, vol. 8430, pp. 343–358. Springer, Cham (2014). https://doi.org/10.1007/978-3-319-06200-6_29
7. Conchon, S., et al.: The Alt-Ergo automated theorem prover. http://alt-ergo.lri.fr
8. Correnson, L.: Qed. Computing what remains to be proved. In: Badger, J.M., Rozier, K.Y. (eds.) NFM 2014. LNCS, vol. 8430, pp. 215–229. Springer, Cham (2014). https://doi.org/10.1007/978-3-319-06200-6_17
9. Dordowsky, F.: An experimental study using ACSL and Frama-C to formulate and verify low-level requirements from a DO-178C compliant avionics project. Electron. Proc. Theor. Comput. Sci. **187**, 28–41 (2015). https://doi.org/10.4204/EPTCS.187.3
10. Ebalard, A., Mouy, P., Benadjila, R.: Journey to a RTE-free X.509 parser. In: Symposium sur la sécurité des technologies de l'information et des communications (SSTIC 2019) (2019). https://www.sstic.org/media/SSTIC2019/SSTIC-actes/journey-to-a-rte-free-x509-parser/SSTIC2019-Article-journey-to-a-rte-free-x509-parser-ebalard_mouy_benadjila_3cUxSCv.pdf
11. Éluard, M., Jensen, T., Denne, E.: An operational semantics of the Java Card Firewall. In: Attali, I., Jensen, T. (eds.) E-smart 2001. LNCS, vol. 2140, pp. 95–110. Springer, Heidelberg (2001). https://doi.org/10.1007/3-540-45418-7_9
12. Filliâtre, J.-C., Paskevich, A.: Why3 — where programs meet provers. In: Felleisen, M., Gardner, P. (eds.) ESOP 2013. LNCS, vol. 7792, pp. 125–128. Springer, Heidelberg (2013). https://doi.org/10.1007/978-3-642-37036-6_8

13. Hähnle, R., Huisman, M.: Deductive software verification: from pen-and-paper proofs to industrial tools. In: Steffen, B., Woeginger, G. (eds.) Computing and Software Science. LNCS, vol. 10000, pp. 345–373. Springer, Cham (2019). https://doi.org/10.1007/978-3-319-91908-9_18
14. Kirchner, F., Kosmatov, N., Prevosto, V., Signoles, J., Yakobowski, B.: Frama-C: a software analysis perspective. Formal Aspects Comput. **27**(3), 573–609 (2015). https://doi.org/10.1007/s00165-014-0326-7
15. Marché, C., Paulin-Mohring, C., Urbain, X.: The KRAKATOA tool for certification of Java/JavaCard programs annotated in JML. J. Logic Algebraic Program. **58**(1–2), 89–106 (2004). https://doi.org/10.1016/j.jlap.2003.07.006
16. Mostowski, W.: Fully verified Java Card API reference implementation. In: 4th International Verification Workshop in connection with CADE-21. CEUR Workshop Proceedings, vol. 259. CEUR-WS.org (2007). http://ceur-ws.org/Vol-259/paper12.pdf
17. Nguyen, Q.-H., Chetali, B.: Certifying native Java Card API by formal refinement. In: Domingo-Ferrer, J., Posegga, J., Schreckling, D. (eds.) CARDIS 2006. LNCS, vol. 3928, pp. 313–328. Springer, Heidelberg (2006). https://doi.org/10.1007/11733447_23
18. Oortwijn, W., Huisman, M.: Formal verification of an industrial safety-critical traffic tunnel control system. In: Ahrendt, W., Tapia Tarifa, S.L. (eds.) IFM 2019. LNCS, vol. 11918, pp. 418–436. Springer, Cham (2019). https://doi.org/10.1007/978-3-030-34968-4_23
19. Oracle: Java Card 2.2 Off-Card Verifier, Whitepaper. Technical report, Oracle (2002)
20. Oracle: Java Card System - Open Configuration Protection Profile, Version 3.1. Technical report, Oracle (2020). https://www.bsi.bund.de/SharedDocs/Downloads/DE/BSI/Zertifizierung/Reporte/ReportePP/pp0099V2b_pdf.pdf;jsessionid=6C3F5A7FB5FA0D928A1C310C1C0EF1CE.internet462?__blob=publicationFile&v=1
21. Oracle: Java Card Platform: Runtime Environment Specification, Classic Edition, Version 3.1. Technical report, Oracle, February 2021. https://docs.oracle.com/javacard/3.1/related-docs/JCCRE/JCCRE.pdf
22. Oracle: Java Card Platform: Virtual Machine Specification, Classic Edition, Version 3.1. Technical report, Oracle, February 2021. https://docs.oracle.com/javacard/3.1/related-docs/JCVMS/JCVMS.pdf
23. Robles, V., Kosmatov, N., Prevosto, V., Rilling, L., Le Gall, P.: METAcSL: specification and verification of high-level properties. In: Vojnar, T., Zhang, L. (eds.) TACAS 2019. LNCS, vol. 11427, pp. 358–364. Springer, Cham (2019). https://doi.org/10.1007/978-3-030-17462-0_22
24. Robles, V., Kosmatov, N., Prevosto, V., Rilling, L., Le Gall, P.: Tame your annotations with METAcSL: specifying, testing and proving high-level properties. In: Beyer, D., Keller, C. (eds.) TAP 2019. LNCS, vol. 11823, pp. 167–185. Springer, Cham (2019). https://doi.org/10.1007/978-3-030-31157-5_11
25. Robles, V., Kosmatov, N., Prevosto, V., Rilling, L., Le Gall, P.: Methodology for specification and verification of high-level properties with MetAcsl. In: 9th IEEE/ACM International Conference on Formal Methods in Software Engineering (FormaliSE 2021), pp. 54–67. IEEE (2021). https://doi.org/10.1109/FormaliSE52586.2021
26. Siveroni, I.A.: Operational semantics of the Java Card Virtual Machine. J. Logic Algebraic Program. **58**(1–2), 3–25 (2004). https://doi.org/10.1016/j.jlap.2003.07.003

Verification of the Incremental Merkle Tree Algorithm with Dafny

Franck Cassez[✉][iD]

ConsenSys, New York, USA
franck.cassez@consensys.net

Abstract. The Deposit Smart Contract (DSC) is an instrumental component of the Ethereum 2.0 Phase 0 infrastructure. We have developed the first machine-checkable version of the incremental Merkle tree algorithm used in the DSC. We present our new and original correctness proof of the algorithm along with the Dafny machine-checkable version. The main results are: 1) a new proof of total correctness; 2) a software artefact with the proof in the form of the complete Dafny code base and 3) new provably correct optimisations of the algorithm.

1 Introduction

Blockchain-based decentralised platforms process transactions between parties and record them in an immutable distributed ledger. Those platforms were once limited to handle simple transactions but the next generation of platforms will routinely run *decentralised applications* (DApps) that enable users to make complex transactions (sell a car, a house or more broadly, swap assets) without the need for an institutional or governmental trusted third-party.

Smart Contracts. More precisely, the transactions are *programmatically* performed by *programs* called *smart contracts*. If there are real advantages having smart contracts act as third-parties to process transactions, there are also lots of risks that are inherent to computer programs: they can contain *bugs*. Bugs can trigger runtime errors like *division by zero* or *array-out-of-bounds*. In a networked environment these types of vulnerabilities can be exploited by malicious attackers over the network to disrupt or take control of the computer system. Other types of bugs can also compromise the business logic of a system, e.g., an implementation may contain subtle errors (e.g., using a += operator in C instead of =+) that make them deviate from the initial intended specifications.

Unfortunately it is extremely hard to guarantee that programs and henceforth smart contracts implement the correct business logics, that they are free of common runtime errors, or that they never run into a non-terminating

© Springer Nature Switzerland AG 2021
M. Huisman et al. (Eds.): FM 2021, LNCS 13047, pp. 445–462, 2021.
https://doi.org/10.1007/978-3-030-90870-6_24

computation.[1] There are notorious examples of smart contract vulnerabilities that have been exploited and publicly reported: in 2016, a *reentrance* vulnerability in the Decentralised Autonomous Organisation (DAO) smart contract was exploited to steal more than USD50 Million. There may be several non officially reported similar attacks that have resulted in the loss of assets.

The Deposit Smart Contract in Ethereum 2.0. The next generation of Ethereum-based networks, Ethereum 2.0, features a new *proof-of-stake* consensus protocol. Instead of miners used in Ethereum 1.x, the new protocol relies on *validators* to create and *validate* blocks of transactions that are added to the ledger. The protocol is designed to be fault-tolerant to up to 1/3 of Byzantine (i.e., malicious or dishonest) validators. To discourage validators to deviate from an honest behaviour, they have to *stake* some assets in Ether (a crypto-currency), and if they are dishonest they can be *slashed* and lose (part of) their stake. The process of staking is handled by the *Deposit Smart Contract (DSC)*: a validator sends a transaction ("stake some Ether") by *calling* the DSC. The DSC has a *state* and can update/record the history of deposits that have occurred so far.

As a result the DSC is a mission-critical component of Ethereum 2.0, and any errors/crashes could result in inaccurate tracking of the deposits or downtime which in turn may compromise the integrity/availability of the whole system.

This could be mitigated if the DSC was a simple piece of code, but, for performance reasons, it relies on sophisticated data structures and algorithms to maintain the list of deposits so that they can be communicated over the network efficiently: the history of deposits is summarised as a unique number, a *hash*, computed using a *Merkle* (or *Hash*) tree. The tree is built incrementally using the so-called *incremental Merkle tree algorithm*, and as stated in [21]:

> *"The efficient incremental algorithm leads to the DSC implementation being unintuitive, and makes it non-trivial to ensure its correctness."*

Related Work. In this context, it is not surprising that substantial efforts, auditing, reviewing [3], testing and formal verification [20,21] has been invested to guarantee the reliability and integrity (e.g., resilience to potential attacks) of the DSC. The DSC has been the focus of an end-to-end analysis [21], including the bytecode[2] that is executed on the Ethereum Virtual Machine (EVM). However, the *incremental Merkle tree algorithm* has not been *mechanically verified* yet, even though a pen and paper proof has been proposed [20] and *partially* mechanised using the K-framework [5]. An example of the limitations

---

[1] In the Ethereum ecosystem, programs can only use a limited amount of resources, determined by the *gas limit*. So one could argue that non-terminating computations are not problematic as they cannot arise: when the gas limit is reached a computation is aborted and has no side effects. It follows that a non-terminating computation (say an infinite loop due to a programming error) combined with a finite gas limit will abort and will result in the system being unable to successfully process some or all *valid* transactions and this is a serious issue.

[2] A limitation is that the bytecode is proved using a non-trusted manual specification.

of the mechanised part of the proof in [20] is that it does not contain a formal definition in K of Merkle trees. The mechanised sections (lemmas 7 and 9) pertain to some invariants of the algorithm but not to a proper correctness specification based on Merkle trees. The K-framework and KEVM, the formalisation of the EVM in K, has been used to analyse a number of other smart contracts [25]. There are several techniques and tools[3] e.g., [1,6,8,9,28], for auditing and analysing smart contracts written in Solidity (a popular language to write Ethereum smart contracts) or EVM bytecode, but they offer limited capabilities to verify complex functional requirements.

Interesting properties of incremental Merkle trees were established in [19] using the MONA prover. This work does not prove the algorithms in the DSC which are designed to minimise gas consumption and hence split into parts: insert a value in a tree, and compute the root hash. Moreover, some key lemmas in the proofs could not be discharged by MONA.

The gold standard in program correctness is a complete logical proof that can be *mechanically checked* by a prover. This is the problem we address in this paper: to design a *machine-checkable proof* for the DSC algorithms (not the bytecode) using the Dafny language and verifier. The DSC has been deployed in November 2020. To the best of our knowledge, our analysis, completed in October 2020, provided the first fully mechanised proof that the code logic was correct, and free of runtime errors. There seem to be few comparable case-studies of Dafny-verified (or other verification-aware programming languages like Whiley [23]) code bases. The most notorious and complex one is probably the IronFleet/IronClad [10] distributed system, along with some non-trivial algorithms like DPLL [2] or Red-Black trees [24], or operating systems, FreeR-TOS scheduler [16], and ExpressOS [15]. Other proof assistants like Coq [22], Isabelle/HOL [18] or Lean [17] have also been extensively used to write machine-checkable proofs of algorithms [7,12,26,27] and software systems [11,14].

Our Contribution. We present a thorough analysis of the incremental Merkle tree algorithm used in the DSC. Our results are available as software artefacts, written using the CAV-awarded Dafny[4] verification-aware programming language [13]. This provides a self-contained machine checkable and reproducible proof of the DSC algorithms. Our contribution is many-fold and includes:

- a *new original simple proof* of the incremental Merkle tree algorithm. In contrast to the previous non-mechanised proof in [20] we do not attempt to directly prove the existing algorithm, but rather to *design* and refine it. Our proof is *parametric* in the height of the tree, and *hash* functions;
- a *logical specification* using a formal definition of Merkle trees, and a *new functional version* of the algorithm that is proved correct against this specification; the functional version is used to specify the invariants for the proof of the imperative original version [4] of the algorithm;
- a repository[5] with the complete Dafny source code of the specification, the algorithms and the proofs, and comprehensive documentation;

---

[3] https://github.com/leonardoalt/ethereum_formal_verification_overview.

[4] https://github.com/dafny-lang/dafny.

[5] https://github.com/ConsenSys/deposit-sc-dafny.

- some new provably correct simplifications/optimisations;
- some reflections on the practicality of using a verification-aware programming language like Dafny and some lessons learned from this experience.

2   Incremental Merkle Trees

Merkle Trees. A *complete (or perfect) binary tree* is such that each non-leaf node has exactly two children, and the two children have the same *height*. An example of a complete binary tree is given in Fig. 1. A *Merkle (or hash) tree* is a complete binary tree the nodes of which are decorated with *hashes* (fixed-size bit-vectors). The hash values of the leaves are given and the hash values of the internal (non-leaf) nodes are computed by *combining* the values of their children with a binary function **hash**. It follows that a Merkle tree is a complete binary tree decorated with a *synthesised attribute* defined by a binary function.

Merkle trees are often used in distributed ledger systems to define a *property* of a collection of elements e.g., a list L of values. This property can then be used *instead of the collection itself* to verify,[6] using a mechanism called *Merkle proofs*, that data received from a node in the distributed system is not corrupted. This is a crucial optimisation as the size of the collection is usually large (typically up to 2^{32}) and using a compact representation is instrumental to obtain time and space efficient communication and a reasonable transactions' processing throughput.

> *In this work, we are not concerned with Merkle proofs but rather with the (efficient) computation of the* **hash** *attribute on a Merkle tree.*

The actual function used to compute the values of the internal nodes is not relevant in the incremental Merkle tree algorithms' functional logics and without loss of generality we may treat it as a parameter i.e., a given binary function.[7] In the sequel we assume that the decorations of the nodes are integers, and we use in the examples a simple function **hash** : Int × Int $\longrightarrow$ Int defined by $\textbf{hash}(x, y) = x - y - 1$ instead of an actual (e.g., **sha256**-based) hash function.

Properties of Lists with Merkle Trees. A complete binary tree of height[8] h has 2^h leaves and $2^{h+1} - 1$ nodes. Given a list L of integers (type Int) of size $|L| = 2^h$, we let $T(L)$ be the Merkle tree for L: the values of the leaves of $T(L)$, from left to right, are the elements of L and $T(L)$ is attributed with the **hash** function. The value of the attribute at the root of $T(L)$, the *root hash*, defines a property of the list L. It is straightforward to extend this definition to lists L of size $|L| \leq 2^h$ by right-padding the list with *zeroes* (or any other default values.) Given a list L of size $|L| \leq 2^h$, let $\overline{L}$ denote L right-padded with $2^h - |L|$ default values. The Merkle tree associated with L is $T(\overline{L})$, and the root hash of L is the root hash of $T(\overline{L})$. Computing the root hash of a tree $T(\overline{L})$ requires to traverse all the nodes of the tree and thus is *exponential* in the height of the tree.

---

[6] More precisely the verification result holds with high probability as the chosen hashing functions may (rarely) generate collisions.

[7] In the code base, the **hash** function is uninterpreted and its type is generic.

[8] The height is the length of the longest path from the root to any leaf.

The Incremental Merkle Tree Problem. A typical use case of a Merkle tree in the context of Ethereum 2.0 is to represent properties of lists that *grow monotonically*. In the DSC, a Merkle tree is used to record the list of validators and their stakes or deposits. A compact representation of this list, as the root hash of a Merkle tree, is communicated to the nodes in the network rather than the tree (or list) itself. However, as mentioned before, each time a new deposit is appended to the list, computing the new root hash using a standard synthesised-attribute computation algorithm requires exponential time in h. This is clearly impractical in a distributed system like Ethereum in which the height of the tree is 32 and the number of nodes is $2^{33} - 1$.

Given (a tree height) $h > 0$, L a list with $|L| < 2^h$, and e a new element to add to L, the incremental Merkle tree problem (IMTP) is defined as follows:[9]

*Can we find $\alpha(L)$ a **polynomial-space abstraction** of $T(L)$ such that we can compute in **polynomial-time**: 1) the root hash of $T(L)$ from $\alpha(L)$, and 2) the abstraction $\alpha(L + [e])$ from $\alpha(L)$ and e?*

Linear-time/space algorithms to solve the IMTP were originally proposed by V. Buterin in [4]. However, the correctness of these algorithms is not obvious. In the next section, we analyse the IMTP, and we present the main properties that enable us to *design* polynomial-time recursive algorithms and to *verify* them.

3   Recursive Incremental Merkle Tree Algorithm

In this section we present the main ideas of the *recursive* algorithms to insert a new value in a Merkle tree and to compute the new root hash (after a new value in inserted) by re-using (*dynamic programming*) previously computed results.

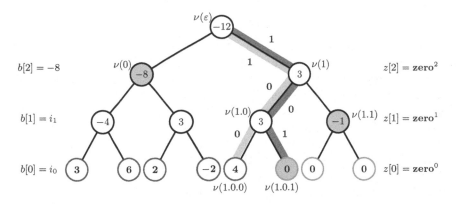

Fig. 1. A Merkle tree of height 3 for list $L_2 = [3, 6, 2, -2, 4]$ and $\mathbf{hash}(x, y) = x - y - 1$. The green path π_1 is encoded as 1.0.0 (from root to leaf) and the blue path π_2 as 1.0.1. The left and right siblings of π_1 are shaded. The values of the right siblings of π_1 at levels 0 and 1 are $z[0] = \mathbf{zero}^0 = 0$ and $z[1] = \mathbf{zero}^1 = \mathbf{hash}(0, 0) = -1$. i_0 and i_1 are arbitrary values. (Color figure online)

---

[9] Polynomial in the height of the tree h. The operator $+$ is list concatenation.

Notations. A *path* π from the root of a tree to a node can be defined as a sequence of bits (left or right) in $\{0,1\}^*$. In a Merkle tree of height h, the *length*, $|\pi|$, of π is at most h. $\nu(\pi)$ is the *node* at the end of π. If $|\pi| = h$ then $\nu(\pi)$ is a leaf. For instance $\nu(\varepsilon)$ is the root of the tree, $\nu(0)$ in Fig. 1 is the node carrying the value -8 and $\nu(1.0.0)$ is a leaf. The *right sibling of a left node* of the form $\nu(\pi.0)$ is the node $\nu(\pi.1)$. Left siblings are defined symmetrically. A node in a Merkle tree is associated with a *level* which is the distance from the node to a leaf in the tree. Leaves are at level 0 and the root is at level h. In a Merkle tree, level 0 has 2^h leaves that can be indexed left to right from 0 to $2^h - 1$. The *n-th leaf* of the tree for $0 \leq n < 2^h$ is the leaf at index n.

Computation of the Root Hash on a Path. We first show that the root hash can be computed if we know the values of the *siblings* of the nodes on *any* path, and the value at the end of the path. For instance, if we know the values of the left and right siblings (shaded nodes in Fig. 1) of the nodes on π_1 (green path in Fig. 1), and the value at the end of π_1, we can compute the root hash of the tree by propagating upwards the attribute **hash**. The value of the **hash** attribute at $\nu(1.0)$ is $\mathbf{hash}(4, \nu(1.0.1)) = 3$, at $\nu(1)$ it is $\mathbf{hash}(3, \nu(1.1)) = 3$ and at the root $\mathbf{hash}(\nu(0), \nu(1)) = \mathbf{hash}(-8, 3) = -12$.

Listing A.1. Recursive Algorithm to Compute the Root Hash.

```
computeRootUp(p:seq<bit>,left:seq<int>,right:seq<int>,seed:int):int
   requires |p| == |left| == |right| //  vectors have the same sizes
   decreases p
{
   if |p| == 0 then seed
   else if last(p) == 0 then // node at end of p is a left node
      computeRootUp(init(p),init(left),init(right),hash(seed,last(right)))
   else // node at end of p is a right node
      computeRootUp(init(p),init(left),init(right),hash(last(left),seed))
}
```

Algorithm `computeRootUp` (Listing A.1) computes[10] bottom-up in time linear in $|\mathbf{p}|$ the root hash with **left** the list of values of the left siblings (top-down) on a path **p** (top-down), **right** the values of the right siblings (top-down) and **seed** the value at $\nu(\mathbf{p})$. The generic version (uninterpreted hash function) of the algorithm is provided in the ComputeRootPath.dfy file.

For the green path $\mathbf{pi}_1 = [1,0,0]$ in Fig. 1, $\mathbf{left} = [-8, i_1, i_0]$, $\mathbf{right} = [-1, -1, 0]$ and the seed is 4. The evaluation of `computeRootUp` returns -12.

Given a path π, if the leaves on the right of $\nu(\pi)$ all have the default value 0, the values of the right siblings on the path π only depend on the *level* of the sibling in the tree. For example, the leaves on the right of π_1 (orange in Fig. 1) all have the default value 0. The root hash of a tree in which all the leaves have the same default value only depends on the level of the root: 0 at level 0, $\mathbf{hash}(0,0)$ at level 1, $\mathbf{hash}(\mathbf{hash}(0,0), \mathbf{hash}(0,0))$ at level 2 and so on. Let $\mathbf{zero}^l$ be defined by: $\mathbf{zero}^l = 0$ if $l = 0$ else $\mathbf{hash}(\mathbf{zero}_0^{l-1}, \mathbf{zero}_0^{l-1})$.

---

[10] For $l = l' + x$, $\mathtt{last}(l) = x$, $\mathtt{init}(l) = l'$, and for $l = x + l'$, $\mathtt{first}(l) = x$, $\mathtt{tail}(l) = l'$.

Given a path π, if all the leaves on the right of $\nu(\pi)$ have the default value, any right sibling value at level l on π is equal to $\mathbf{zero}^l$.

As an example in Fig. 1, the right siblings on $\pi_1 = 1.0.0$ have values 0 at level 0, node $\nu(1.0.1)$, and $\mathbf{hash}(0,0) = \mathbf{zero}^1 = -1$ at level 1, node $\nu(1.1)$. If a path p leads to a node with the default value 0 and all the leaves right of $\nu(\mathrm{p})$ have the default value 0, the root hash depends only on the values of the `left` and default `right` siblings. Hence the root hash can be obtained by `computeRootUp(p, left, right, 0)`. For the path `pi2` $= [1,0,1]$ (Fig. 1), `left` $= [-8, i_1, 4]$ and `right` $= [-1, -1, 0]$, `computeRootUp(pi2, left, right, 0)` returns -12.

As a result, to compute the root hash of a tree $T(\overline{L})$, we can use a compact abstraction $\alpha(L)$ of $T(\overline{L})$ composed of the left siblings vector b and the right siblings default values z (Fig. 1) of the path to the $|L|$-th leaf in $T(\overline{L})$.

Insertion: Update the Left Siblings. Assume π_1 is a path to the n-th leaf and $n < 2^h - 1$ (not the last leaf), where the next value v is to be inserted. As we have shown before, if we have b_1 holding the values of left siblings of π_1, z and v, we can compute the new attribute values of the nodes on π_1 and the new root hash after v is inserted. Let π_2 be the path to the $n+1$-th leaf. If we can compute the values b_2 of the left siblings of π_2 as a function of b_1, z and v, we have an efficient algorithm to *incrementally* compute the root hash of a Merkle tree: we keep track of the values of the left siblings b on the path to the next available leaf, and iterate this process each time a new value is inserted.

As $\nu(\pi_1)$ is not the last leaf, π_1 must contain at least one 0, and has the form[11] $\pi_1 = w.0.1^k$ with $w \in \{0,1\}^*, k \geq 0$. Hence, the path π_2 to the $n+1$-th leaf is $w.1.0^k$, arithmetically $\pi_2 = \pi_1 + 1$. An example of two consecutive paths is given in Fig. 1 with π_1 (green) and π_2 (blue) to the leaves at indices 4 and 5.

The related forms of π_1 (a path) and π_2 (the successor path) are useful to figure out how to incrementally compute the left siblings vector b_2 for π_2:

- as the initial prefix w is the same in π_1 and π_2, the values of the left siblings on the nodes of w are the same in b_1 and b_2;
- all the nodes in the suffix 0^k of π_2 are left nodes and have right siblings. It follows that the corresponding k values in b_2 are irrelevant as they correspond to right siblings, and we can re-use the corresponding b_1 values;
- hence b_2 is equal to b_1 except possibly for the level of the node at $\nu(w.0)$.

We now illustrate how to compute the new value in the vector b_2 on the example of Fig. 1. Let $\pi_1 = w.0$ and $\pi_2 = w.1$ with $w = 1.0$ and $|w| = 2$. For the top levels 2 and 1, b_2 is the same as b_1: $b_2[2] = b_1[2] = -8$ and $b_2[1] = b_1[1] = i_1$. For level 0, the level of the node $\nu(w.0)$, the value at $\nu(w.0) = \nu(1.0.0)$ becomes the left sibling of the node $\nu(1.0.1)$ on π_2 at this level. So the new value of the left sibling on π_2 is exactly the new value, 4, of the node $\nu(1.0.0)$ after 4 is inserted.

More generally, when computing the new root hash bottom-up on π_1, the first time we encounter a left node, at level d, we update the corresponding

---

[11] $x^k, x \in \{0,1\}$ denotes the sequence of k x's.

value of b with the computed value of the attribute on π_1 at level d. Algorithm[12] insertValue in Listing A.2 computes, in linear-time, the list of values of the left siblings (top-down) of the path $p + 1$ using as input the list (top-down) of values left (resp. right) siblings left (resp. right) of p and seed the new value inserted at $\nu(p)$. The generic (non-interpreted hash) algorithm is provided in the NextPathInCompleteTreesLemmas.dfy file.

Listing A.2. Recursive Algorithm to Compute the New Left Siblings.

```
insertValue(p:seq<bit>,left:seq<int>,right:seq<int>,seed:int):seq<int>
  requires |left| == |right| == |p| >= 1
  decreases p
{
  if |p| == 1 then   // note that first(p) == last(p) in this case
    if first(p) == 0 then [seed] else left
  else if last(p) == 0 then // we encounter a left node. Stop recursion.
    init(left) + [seed]
  else // right node, move up on the path.
    insertValue(init(p),init(left),init(right),hash(last(left),seed))
      + [last(left)]
}
```

We illustrate how the algorithm insertValue works with the example of Fig. 1. Assume we insert the seed 4 at the end of the (green) path pi1 = [1,0,0]. The left (resp. right) siblings' values are given by left = $[-8, i_1, i_0]$ (resp. right = $[-1, -1, 0]$). insertValue computes the values of the left siblings on the (blue) path pi2 = [1,0,1] after 4 is inserted at the end of π_1: the first call terminates the algorithm and returns $[-8, i_1, 4]$ which is the list of left siblings that are needed on π_2.

In the next section we describe how to verify the recursive algorithms and the versions implemented in the DSC.

4 Verification of the Algorithms

In order to verify the implemented (imperative style/Solidity) versions of the algorithms of the DSC, we first prove total correctness of the recursive versions (Sect. 3) and them use them to prove the code implemented in the DSC.

In this section, the Dafny code has been simplified and sometimes even altered while retaining the main features, for the sake of clarity. The code in this section may not compile. We provide the links to the files with the full code in the text and refer the reader to those files.

Correctness Specification. The (partial) correctness of our algorithms reduces to checking that they compute the same values as the ones obtained with a synthesised attribute on a Merkle tree. We have specified the data types Tree, MerkleTree and CompleteTrees and the relation between Merkle trees and lists of values. The definitions are provided in the trees folder.

---

[12] + stands for list concatenation.

The root hash of a `MerkleTree` t is t.rootv. The (specification) function `buildMerkle(h, L, hash)` returns a `MerkleTree` of height h, the leaves of which are given by the values (right-padded) $\overline{L}$, and the values on the internal nodes agree with the definition of the synthesised attribute **hash**, i.e., what we previously defined in Sect. 2 as $T(\overline{L})$. It follows that `buildMerkle(h, L, hash).rootv` is the value of the root hash of a Merkle tree with leaves $\overline{L}$.

Total Correctness. The total correctness proof for the `computeRootUp` function amounts to showing that 1) the algorithm always terminates and 2) the result of the computation is the same as the hash of the root of the tree. In Dafny, to prove termination, we need to provide a ranking function (strictly decreasing and bounded from below.) The length of the path p is a suitable ranking function (see the **decreases** clause in Listing A.1) and is enough for Dafny to prove termination of `computeRootUp`.

We establish property 2) by proving a *lemma* (Listing A.3): the preconditions (**requires**) of the lemma are the assumptions, and the postconditions (**ensures**) the intended property. The body of the lemma (with a non-interpreted hash function) which provides the machine-checkable proof is available in the computeRootPath.dfy file.

Listing A.3. Correctness Proof Specification for `ComputeRootUp`.

```
lemma computeRootUpIsCorrectForTree(
  p:seq<bit>,r:Tree<int>,left:seq<int>,right:seq<int>,seed:int)
  //  size of p is the height of the tree r
  requires |p| == height(r)
  //  r is a Merkle tree for attribute hash
  requires isCompleteTree(r)
  requires isDecoratedWith(hash,r)
  //  the value at the end of the path p in r is seed
  requires seed == nodeAt(p,r).v
  //  vectors of same sizes
  requires |right| == |left| == |p|
  // Left and right contain values of left and right siblings of p in r.
  requires forall i :: 0 <= i < |p| ==>
    //  the value of the sibling of the node at p[..i] in r
    siblingValueAt(p,r,i + 1) ==
    //  are stored in left and right
    if p[i] == 0 then right[i] else left[i]
  //  Main property: computeRootUp computes the hash of the root of r
  ensures r.rootv == computeRootUp(p,left,right,seed)
```

Lemma `computeRootUpIsCorrectForTree` requires that the tree r is a Merkle tree, and that the lists `left` (resp. `right`) store the values of left (resp. right) siblings of the nodes on a path p. Moreover, the value at the end of p should be **seed**. Under these assumptions the conclusion (**ensures**) is that `computeRootUp` returns the value of the root hash of r.

The proof of lemma `computeRootUpIsCorrectForTree` requires a few intermediate sub-lemmas of moderate difficulty. The main step in the proof is to establish an equivalence between a bottom-up computation `computeRootUp` and the top-down definition of (attributed) Merkle trees. All the proofs are by induction on the tree or the path. The complete Dafny code for this algorithm is available in computeRootPath.dfy file.

Termination for `insertValue` is proved by using a ranking function (decreases clause in Listing A.2). The functional correctness of `insertValue` reduces to proving that, assuming `left` (resp. `right`) contains the values of the left (resp. right) siblings of the nodes on p, then `insertValue(p, left, right, seed)` returns the values of the nodes that are left siblings on the successor path. The code for this lemma is in the NextPathInCompleteTreesLemmas.dfy file. The main proof is based on several sub-lemmas that are not hard conceptually but cannot be easily discharged using solely the built-in Dafny induction strategies. They require some intermediate proof hints (verified calculations) to deal with all the nodes on the path p.

Listing A.4. ComputeRootUpWithIndex.

```
computeRootUpWithIndex (
    h : nat , k : nat , left : seq<int> , right : seq<int> , seed : int ) : int
  requires  | left | == | right | == h
  // the index is in the range of indices for a tree of height h
  requires  k < power2(h)
  // Indexed algorithm computes the same value as computeRootUp
  ensures  computeRootUpWithIndex(h,k, left , right ,f, seed )  ==
      // natToBitList(k,h) is the binary encoding of k over h bits
      computeRootUp( natToBitList(k,h) , left , right ,f, seed )
  // ranking function
  decreases h
{
  if h == 0 then seed
  else if k % 2 == 0 then //  left node
  computeRootUpWithIndex(h−1,k/2, init ( left ) , init ( right ) , hash ( seed , last ( right )))
  else //  right node
  computeRootUpWithIndex(h−1,k/2, init ( left ) , init ( right ) , hash ( last ( left ) , seed ))
}
```

Index Based Algorithms. The algorithms that implement the DSC do not use a bitvector to encode a path, but rather, a *counter* that records the number of values inserted so far and the height of the tree. In order to prove the algorithms actually implemented in the DSC, we first recast the `computeRootUp` and `insertValue` algorithms to use a counter and the height h of a tree. In this step, we use a parameter k that is the index of the next available leaf where a new value can be inserted. The leaves are indexed left to right from 0 to $2^h - 1$ and hence k is the number of values that have been inserted so far. It follows that the leaves with indices $k \le i \le 2^h - 1$ have the default value. The correspondence between the bitvector encoding of the path to the leaf at index k and the value k is straightforward: the encoding of the path p is the value of k in binary over h bits. We can rewrite left `computeRootUp` to use k and h (`computeRootUpWithIndex`, Listing A.4) and prove it computes the same value as `computeRootUp`. A similar proof can be established for the `insertValue` algorithm. The index based algorithms and the proofs that they are equivalent (compute the same values as) to `computeRootUp` and `insertValue` are available in the IndexBasedAlgorithm.dfy file. Dafny can discharge the equivalence proofs with minimal proof hints using the builtin induction strategies.

Total Correctness of the Algorithms Implemented in the DSC. In this section we present the final proof of (total) correctness for the algorithms implemented in the DSC (Solidity-like version.) Our proof establishes that the imperative versions, with while loops and dynamic memory allocation (for arrays) are correct, terminate and are memory safe.

The DSC is an object and has a state defined by a few variables: count is the number of inserted values (initially zero), branch is a vector that stores that value of the left siblings of the path leading to the leaf at index count, and zero_hashes is what we previously defined as z. The algorithm that computes the root hash of the Merkle tree in the DSC is get_deposit_root(). get_deposit_root() does not have any *seed* parameter as it computes the root hash using the default value (0). The correctness proof of get_deposit_root() uses the functional (proved correct) algorithm computeRootUpWithIndex as an invariant. Listing A.5 is a simplified version (for clarity) of the full code available in the DepositSmart.dfy file.

Listing A.5. Implemented Version of computeRootUp.

```
method get_deposit_root() returns (r:int)
    // The result of get_deposit_root_() is the root value of the Merkle tree
    // values is a ghost variable and records all the inserted values
    ensures r == buildMerkle(values, TREE_HEIGHT, hash).rootv
{
    // Store the expected result in a ghost variable.
    ghost var e := computeRootUpWithIndex(TREE_HEIGHT, count, branch, zero_hashes, 0);
    // Start with default value for r.
    r := 0;
    var h := 0;
    var size := count;
    while h < TREE_HEIGHT
        // Main invariant:
        invariant e == computeRootUpWithIndex(
            TREE_HEIGHT - h, size,
            take(branch, TREE_HEIGHT - h), take(zero_hashes, TREE_HEIGHT - h), r)
    {
        if size % 2 == 1 {
            r := hash(branch[h], r);
        } else {
            r := hash(r, zero_hashes[h]);
        }
        size := size / 2;
        h := h + 1;
    }
}
```

The algorithm that inserts a value v in the tree is deposit(v) in the implemented version of the DSC. Listing A.6 is an optimised version of the original algorithm. The simplification is explained in Sect. 5. The correctness of the algorithm is defined by ensuring that, if at the beginning of the computation the vectors branch (resp. zero_hashes) contain values of the left (resp. right) siblings of the path leading to the leaf at index count, then at the end of the computation, after v is inserted, this property still holds. The proof of this invariant requires a number of proof hints for Dafny to verify it. We use the functional version of the algorithm to specify a loop invariant (not provided in Listing A.6).

The termination proof is easy using `size` as the decreasing ranking function. However, a difficulty in this proof is memory safety, i.e. to guarantee that the index i used to access `branch[i]` is within the range of the indices of `branch`.

We have also proved the initialisation functions `init_zero_hashes()` and the DSC `constructor`. The full code of the imperative version of the DSC is available in the DepositSmart.dfy file.

Listing A.6. The `deposit` method.

```
method deposit(v: int)
  // The tree cannot be full
  requires count < power2(TREE_HEIGHT) - 1
  // branch and zero_hashes hold the values of the siblings
  requires areSiblingsAtIndex(|values|,
    buildMerkle(values, TREE_HEIGHT, hash), branch, zero_hashes)
  // Correctness property
  ensures areSiblingsAtIndex(|values|,
    buildMerkle(values, TREE_HEIGHT, hash), branch, zero_hashes)
{
  var value := v;
  var size : nat := count;
  var i : nat := 0;
  // Store the expected result in e.
  ghost var e := computeLeftSiblingsOnNextpathWithIndex(
    TREE_HEIGHT, old(size), old(branch), zero_hashes, v);
  while size % 2 == 1
    // Main invariant:
    invariant e ==
    computeLeftSiblingsOnNextpathWithIndex(
        TREE_HEIGHT - i, size,
        take(branch, TREE_HEIGHT - i),
        take(zero_h, TREE_HEIGHT - i), value) + drop(branch, TREE_HEIGHT - i)
    decreases size
  {
    value := f(branch[i], value);
    size := size / 2;
    i := i + 1;
  }
  // 0 <= i < |branch| and no there is no index-out-of-bounds error
  branch[i] := value;
  count := count + 1;
  values := values + [v];
}
```

5   Findings and Lessons Learned

Methodology. In contrast to the previous attempts to analyse the DSC, we have adopted a textbook approach and used standard algorithms' design techniques (e.g., dynamic programming, refinement, recursion.) This has several advantages over a direct proof (e.g., [20]) of the imperative code including:

– the design of simple algorithms and proofs;
– recursive and language-agnostic recursive versions of the algorithms;
– new and provably correct simplifications/optimisations.

Algorithmic Considerations. Our implementations and formal proofs have resulted in the identification of two previously unknown/unconfirmed optimisations. First, it is not necessary to initialise the vector of left siblings, b, and the algorithms are correct for any initial value of this vector.

Second, the original version of the `deposit` algorithm (which we have proved correct too) has the form[13] given in Listing A.7. Our formal machine-checkable proof revealed[14] that indeed the condition C1 is always true and the loop always terminates because C2 eventually becomes true. As witnessed by the comment after the loop in the Solidity code of the DSC, this property was expected but not confirmed and the Solidity contract authors did not take the risk to simplify the code. Our result shows that the algorithm can be simplified to `while not(C2) do ... od`.

Listing A.7. Solidity Version of the DSC Deposit Function.

```
deposit( ... )
{
  while C1 do
    if C2 return;
    ...
  od
  // As the loop should always end prematurely with the 'return' statement,
  // this code should be unreachable. We assert 'false' just to be safe.
  assert(false);
}
```

This is interesting not only from a safety and algorithmic perspectives, but also because it reduces the computation cost (in gas/Ether) of executing the `deposit` method. This simplification proposal is currently being discussed with the DSC developer, however the currently deployed version still uses the non-optimised code.

Verification Effort. The verification effort for this project is 12 person-weeks resulting in 3500 lines of code and 1000 lines of documentation. This assumes familiarity with program verification, Hoare logic and Dafny. Table 1 provides some insights into the code base. Note that in Table 1 we do not report on the verification time (e.g. time spent in Z3) as it is known to be an irrelevant metrics in Dafny/Z3: implemented optimisations may use clever cashing hash tables and even a name change can drastically impact the verification. What Dafny/Z3 guarantees is that the *result* of the verification is the sound but not that the verification time is stable.

---

[13] The complete Solidity source code is freely available on GitHub at https://github.com/ethereum/eth2.0-specs/blob/dev/solidity_deposit_contract/deposit_contract.sol.

[14] This finding was not uncovered in any of the previous audits/analyses.

The filenames in green are the ones that require the less number of hints for Dafny to check a proof. In this set of files the hints mostly consist of simple *verified calculations* (e.g., empty sequence is a neutral element for lists [] + 1 == 1 + [] == 1.) Most of the results on sequences (**helpers** package) and simplifications of sequences of bits (**seqofbits** package) are in this category and require very few hints. This also applies for the proofs[15] of the **algorithms** package, e.g., proving that the versions using the index of a leaf instead of the binary encoding of a path are equivalent.

The filenames in orange require some non-trivial proof hints beyond the implicit induction strategies built in Dafny. For instance in NextPathInCompleteTrees.dfy and PathInCompleteTrees.dfy, we had to provide several annotations and structure for the proofs. This is due to the fact that the proofs involve properties on a Merkle tree t_1 and its *successor* t_2 (after a value is inserted) which is a new tree, and on a path π_1 in t_1 and its successor π_2 in t_2.

The filenames in red require a lot of hints. For the files in the **synthattribute** package it is mostly calculation steps. Some steps are not absolutely necessary but adding them reduces the verification time by on order of magnitude (on our system configuration, MacBookPro 16 GB RAM). The hardest proof is probably the correctness of the **deposit** method in DepositSmart.dfy. The proof requires non trivial lemmas and invariants. The difficulty stems from a combination of factors: first the while loop of the algorithm (Listing A.6) maintains a constraint between **size** and **i**, the latter being used to access the array elements in **branch**. Proving that there is no array-of-bounds error (i.e., i is within the size of **branch**) requires to prove some arithmetic properties. Second, the proof of the main invariant (Listing A.6) using the functional specification **computeLeftSiblingsOnNextpathWithIndex** is complex and had to be structured around additional lemmas.

Overall, almost 90% of the lines of code are (non-executable) proofs, and function definitions used in the proofs. The verified algorithms implemented in the DSC functional are provided in **DepositSmart.dfy** and account for less than 10% of the code.

Considering the criticality of the DSC (it processes millions of ETH), 12 person-weeks can be considered a moderate effort well worth the investment: the result is an unparalleled level of trustworthiness that can inspire confidence in the Ethereum platform. According to our experts (ConsenSys Diligence) in the verification of Smart Contracts, the size of such an effort is realistic and practical considering the level of guarantees provided. The only downside is the level of verification expertise required to design the proofs.

The trust base in our work is composed of the Dafny verification engine (verification conditions generator) and the SMT-solver Z3.

Dafny Experience. Dafny has excellent documentation, support for data structures, functional (side-effect free) and object-oriented programming. The automated verification engine has a lot of built-in strategies (e.g., induction, calcula-

---

[15] The file **CommuteProof.dfy** in this package is not needed for the main proof but was originally used and provides an interesting result, so it is still in code base.

Table 1. Dafny Code Statistics. #Loc (resp. #Doc) is the number of Lines of Code (resp. Documentation), Lemmas is the number of proofs broken down in difficulty levels, Methods the number of executable methods/function methods. Colour scheme easy/few proof hints, moderate, hard/detailed proof hints.

src/dafny/**package**/file.dfy	#LoC	Lemmas	Methods	#Doc	(#Doc/#LoC in %)
smart					
DepositSmart.dfy	163	1 + 1	1 + 3	92	56
smart/algorithms					
CommuteProof.dfy	73	2	0	31	42
IndexBasedAlgorithm.dfy	96	3	2	59	61
MainAlgorithm.dfy	66	2	0	38	58
OptimalAlgorithm.dfy	24	2	0	15	62
Sub-total	**259**	2 + **7**	**2**	**143**	**55**
smart/helpers					
Helpers.dfy	51	5	1	10	20
SeqHelpers.dfy	137	10	6	34	25
smart/paths					
NextPathInCompleteTrees.dfy	262	1 + 2	2	99	38
PathInCompleteTrees.dfy	408	2 + 13	0	60	15
Sub-total	**670**	3 + **15**	**2**	**159**	**24**
smart/seqofbits					
SeqOfBits.dfy	527	19	0	100	19
smart/synthattribute					
ComputeRootPath.dfy	305	2 + 9	0	116	38
GenericComputation.dfy	148	6	0	75	51
RightSiblings.dfy	210	1 + 2 + 2	1	57	27
Siblings.dfy	124	1 + 1	0	31	25
SiblingsPlus.dfy	556	2 + 2	0	52	9
Sub-total	**1343**	4 + 4 + **20**	**1**	**331**	**25**
smart/trees					
CompleteTrees.dfy	89	8	1	19	21
MerkleTrees.dfy	208	6	3	101	49
Trees.dfy	91	3	5	41	45
Sub-total	**388**	**17**	**9**	**161**	**41**
src/dafny					
TOTAL	**3538**	5 + 9 + **94**	1 + **24**	**1030**	**29**

tions) and a good number of specifications are proved fully automatically without providing any hints. The Dafny proof strategies and constructs that we mostly used are *verified calculations* and *induction*. The side-effect free proofs seem to be handled much more efficiently (time-wise) than the proofs using mutable data structures.

In the current version we have used the `autocontracts` attribute for the DSC object which is a convenient way of proving memory safety using a specific invariant (given by the `Valid` predicate). This could probably be optimised as

Dafny has some support to specify precisely the side-effects using *frames* (based on *dynamic framing*).

Overall, Dafny is a practical option for the verification of mission-critical smart contracts, and a possible avenue for adoption could be to extend the Dafny code generator engine to support Solidity, a popular language for writing smart contracts for the Ethereum network, or to automatically translate Solidity into Dafny. We are currently evaluating these options with our colleagues at ConsenSys Diligence, as well as the benefits of our technique to the analysis of other critical smart contracts.

The software artefacts including the implementations, proofs, documentation and a Docker container to reproduce the results are freely available as a GitHub repository at https://github.com/ConsenSys/deposit-sc-dafny.

Acknowledgements. I wish to thank Suhabe Bugrara, ConsenSys Mesh, for helpful discussions on the DSC's previous work and the anonymous reviewers of a preliminary version of this paper.

References

1. Amani, S., Bégel, M., Bortin, M., Staples, M.: Towards verifying ethereum smart contract bytecode in Isabelle/HOL. In: Andronick, J., Felty, A.P. (eds.) Proceedings of the 7th ACM SIGPLAN International Conference on Certified Programs and Proofs, CPP 2018, Los Angeles, CA, USA, 8–9 January 2018, pp. 66–77. ACM (2018). https://doi.org/10.1145/3167084

2. Andrici, C., Ciobâcă, Ş.: Verifying the DPLL algorithm in Dafny. In: Marin, M., Craciun, A. (eds.) Proceedings Third Symposium on Working Formal Methods, FROM 2019, EPTCS, Timişoara, Romania, 3–5 September 2019, vol. 303, pp. 3–15 (2019). https://doi.org/10.4204/EPTCS.303.1

3. Bugrara, S.: A review of the deposit contract (2020). https://github.com/suhabe/eth-deposit-contract-vyper-review/blob/master/EthDepositContractVyperReview.pdf

4. Buterin, V.: Progressive Merkle tree. https://github.com/ethereum/research/blob/master/beacon_chain_impl/progressive_merkle_tree.py

5. Chen, X., Roşu, G.: $\mathbb{K}$—a semantic framework for programming languages and formal analysis. In: Bowen, J.P., Liu, Z., Zhang, Z. (eds.) SETSS 2019. LNCS, vol. 12154, pp. 122–158. Springer, Cham (2020). https://doi.org/10.1007/978-3-030-55089-9_4

6. ConsenSys Diligence: Mythx. https://mythx.io/

7. de Gouw, S., Rot, J., de Boer, F.S., Bubel, R., Hähnle, R.: OpenJDK's Java.utils.Collection.sort() is broken: the good, the bad and the worst case. In: Kroening, D., Păsăreanu, C.S. (eds.) CAV 2015. LNCS, vol. 9206, pp. 273–289. Springer, Cham (2015). https://doi.org/10.1007/978-3-319-21690-4_16

8. Hajdu, Á., Jovanović, D.: SOLC-VERIFY: a modular verifier for solidity smart contracts. In: Chakraborty, S., Navas, J.A. (eds.) VSTTE 2019. LNCS, vol. 12031, pp. 161–179. Springer, Cham (2020). https://doi.org/10.1007/978-3-030-41600-3_11

9. Hajdu, Á., Jovanovic, D., Ciocarlie, G.F.: Formal specification and verification of solidity contracts with events (short paper). In: Bernardo, B., Marmsoler, D. (eds.) 2nd Workshop on Formal Methods for Blockchains, FMBC@CAV 2020, OASIcs, Los Angeles, California, USA (Virtual Conference), 20–21 July 2020, vol. 84, pp. 2:1–2:9. Schloss Dagstuhl - Leibniz-Zentrum für Informatik (2020). https://doi.org/10.4230/OASIcs.FMBC.2020.2

10. Hawblitzel, C., et al.: IronFleet: proving practical distributed systems correct. In: Miller, E.L., Hand, S. (eds.) Proceedings of the 25th Symposium on Operating Systems Principles, SOSP 2015, Monterey, CA, USA, 4–7 October 2015, pp. 1–17. ACM (2015). https://doi.org/10.1145/2815400.2815428

11. Klein, G., et al.: seL4: formal verification of an OS kernel. In: Matthews, J.N., Anderson, T.E. (eds.) Proceedings of the 22nd ACM Symposium on Operating Systems Principles 2009, SOSP 2009, Big Sky, Montana, USA, 11–14 October 2009, pp. 207–220. ACM (2009). https://doi.org/10.1145/1629575.1629596

12. Lammich, P.: Efficient verified implementation of Introsort and Pdqsort. In: Peltier, N., Sofronie-Stokkermans, V. (eds.) IJCAR 2020. LNCS (LNAI), vol. 12167, pp. 307–323. Springer, Cham (2020). https://doi.org/10.1007/978-3-030-51054-1_18

13. Leino, K.R.M.: Accessible software verification with Dafny. IEEE Softw. **34**(6), 94–97 (2017). https://doi.org/10.1109/MS.2017.4121212

14. Leroy, X.: A formally verified compiler back-end. J. Autom. Reason. **43**(4), 363–446 (2009). https://doi.org/10.1007/s10817-009-9155-4

15. Mai, H., Pek, E., Xue, H., King, S.T., Madhusudan, P.: Verifying security invariants in expressos. In: Sarkar, V., Bodík, R. (eds.) Architectural Support for Programming Languages and Operating Systems, ASPLOS 2013, Houston, TX, USA, 16–20 March 2013, pp. 293–304. ACM (2013). https://doi.org/10.1145/2451116.2451148

16. Matias, M.: Program verification of FreeRTOS using Microsoft Dafny. Cleveland State University (2014). https://books.google.com.au/books?id=A_iyoQEACAAJ

17. de Moura, L., Kong, S., Avigad, J., van Doorn, F., von Raumer, J.: The lean theorem prover (system description). In: Felty, A.P., Middeldorp, A. (eds.) CADE 2015. LNCS (LNAI), vol. 9195, pp. 378–388. Springer, Cham (2015). https://doi.org/10.1007/978-3-319-21401-6_26

18. Nipkow, T., Paulson, L.C., Wenzel, M.: Isabelle/HOL — A Proof Assistant for Higher-Order Logic, LNCS, vol. 2283. Springer, Heidelberg (2002). https://doi.org/10.1007/3-540-45949-9

19. Ogawa, M., Horita, E., Ono, S.: Proving properties of incremental Merkle trees. In: Nieuwenhuis, R. (ed.) CADE 2005. LNCS (LNAI), vol. 3632, pp. 424–440. Springer, Heidelberg (2005). https://doi.org/10.1007/11532231_31

20. Park, D., Zhang, Y.: Formal verification of the incremental Merkle tree algorithm (2020). https://github.com/runtimeverification/verified-smart-contracts/blob/master/deposit/formal-incremental-merkle-tree-algorithm.pdf

21. Park, D., Zhang, Y., Rosu, G.: End-to-end formal verification of Ethereum 2.0 deposit smart contract. In: Lahiri, S.K., Wang, C. (eds.) CAV 2020. LNCS, vol. 12224, pp. 151–164. Springer, Cham (2020). https://doi.org/10.1007/978-3-030-53288-8_8

22. Paulin-Mohring, C.: Introduction to the Coq proof-assistant for practical software verification. In: Meyer, B., Nordio, M. (eds.) LASER 2011. LNCS, vol. 7682, pp. 45–95. Springer, Heidelberg (2012). https://doi.org/10.1007/978-3-642-35746-6_3

23. Pearce, D.J., Utting, M., Groves, L.: An introduction to software verification with Whiley. In: Bowen, J.P., Liu, Z., Zhang, Z. (eds.) SETSS 2018. LNCS, vol. 11430, pp. 1–37. Springer, Cham (2019). https://doi.org/10.1007/978-3-030-17601-3_1

24. Peña, R.: An assertional proof of red-black trees using Dafny. J. Autom. Reason. **64**(4), 767–791 (2020). https://doi.org/10.1007/s10817-019-09534-y
25. Runtime Verification Inc.: Formally verified smart contracts. https://github.com/runtimeverification/verified-smart-contracts
26. Sternagel, C.: Proof pearl-a mechanized proof of GHC's Mergesort. J. Autom. Reason. **51**(4), 357–370 (2013). https://doi.org/10.1007/s10817-012-9260-7
27. Wimmer, S., Lammich, P.: Verified model checking of timed automata. In: Beyer, D., Huisman, M. (eds.) TACAS 2018. LNCS, vol. 10805, pp. 61–78. Springer, Cham (2018). https://doi.org/10.1007/978-3-319-89960-2_4
28. Wüstholz, V., Christakis, M.: Harvey: a greybox fuzzer for smart contracts, pp. 1398–1409. Association for Computing Machinery, New York (2020). https://doi.org/10.1145/3368089.3417064

Automata

Congruence Relations for Büchi Automata

Yong Li[1], Yih-Kuen Tsay[2], Andrea Turrini[1,3], Moshe Y. Vardi[4],
and Lijun Zhang[1,3,5(✉)]

[1] State Key Laboratory of Computer Science, Institute of Software,
Chinese Academy of Sciences, Beijing, China
zhanglj@ios.ac.cn
[2] National Taiwan University, Taipei, Taiwan
[3] Institute of Intelligent Software, Guangzhou, China
[4] Rice University, Houston, USA
[5] University of Chinese Academy of Sciences, Beijing, China

Abstract. We revisit congruence relations for Büchi automata, which
play a central role in automata-based formal verification. The size of the
classical congruence relation is in $3^{\mathcal{O}(n^2)}$, where n is the number of states
of the given Büchi automaton. We present improved congruence relations
that can be exponentially coarser than the classical one. We further give
asymptotically *optimal* congruence relations of size $2^{\mathcal{O}(n \log n)}$. Based on
these optimal congruence relations, we obtain an *optimal* translation
from a Büchi automaton to a family of deterministic finite automata
(FDFA), which can be made to accept either the original language or its
complement. To the best of our knowledge, our construction is the *first
direct* and *optimal* translation from Büchi automata to FDFAs.

1 Introduction

Congruence relations for nondeterministic Büchi automata (NBAs) [6] are fundamental for Büchi complementation, a key operation used in the formal verification framework based on automata theory [14]. To formally verify whether the behavior of a system A satisfies a given specification B, one usually reduces this problem to a language-containment problem between the NBAs A and B; this containment problem is then reduced to the nonemptiness of the intersection of A and the complement of B. The first complementation construction for Büchi automata, proposed by Büchi [6] and widely known as Ramsey-based Büchi complementation (RBC), relies on a congruence relation with a $2^{2^{\mathcal{O}(n)}}$ blow-up, where n is the number of states of the input automaton. One can associate each equivalence class of the congruence relation with a state of the complementary automaton, similarly to the characterization provided by the Myhill-Nerode theorem for regular languages [22]. The blow-up of the congruence relation of RBC was later reduced by Sistla *et al.* [21] to $3^{\mathcal{O}(n^2)}$, without providing an explicit formal notion of congruence relation, which was later formalized by Thomas [22].

© Springer Nature Switzerland AG 2021
M. Huisman et al. (Eds.): FM 2021, LNCS 13047, pp. 465–482, 2021.
https://doi.org/10.1007/978-3-030-90870-6_25

Notably, current practical approaches to the containment checking for NBAs are based on the classical congruence relation given in [21,22], even though it has a larger blow-up ($3^{\mathcal{O}(n^2)}$ vs. $2^{\mathcal{O}(n \log n)}$) than other optimal complementation constructions, such as the *rank-based* complementation [15]. In fact, RABIT, the state-of-the-art tool for checking language-containment between NBAs, is also based on the classical congruence relation of [21,22] and has integrated various state-space pruning techniques for RBC, proposed in [1,2,8].

In another line of work, *families of deterministic finite automata* (FDFAs) [3] have been proposed for representing ω-regular languages, as an alternative to NBAs. By modelling a given system and specification as FDFAs, the formal verification problem can be reduced to a containment problem between two FDFAs, which can be done in polynomial time [3], in contrast to PSPACE-completeness for NBAs [14]. It has been shown that an FDFA can be induced from a congruence relation defined over a given ω-regular language, where each state of the FDFA corresponds to an equivalence class of the congruence relation [4].

In this work we show that RBC and FDFAs have an intimate connection: congruence relations for NBAs constitute the underlying concept that connects them. This connection gives us the possibility to further tighten the congruence relations for both RBC and FDFAs (see Sects. 3.2 and 4). In fact, the state-space pruning techniques developed in [1,2] for RBC [21,22] are inherently heuristics for identifying subsumption and simulation relations between congruence relations of RBC. Therefore, in order to further theoretically or empirically improve model-checking algorithms based on RBC or FDFAs, it is important to understand congruence relations for both FDFAs and RBC and, hopefully, make their congruence relations coarser. This motivates our search for better congruence relations for NBAs.

Contribution. We focus here on an in-depth study of congruence relations for NBAs and their connection to FDFAs. First, we show how to improve the classical congruence relation $\backsim$ with a blow-up of $3^{\mathcal{O}(n^2)}$, defined by the classical RBC, to congruence relations that can be exponentially tighter (Theorem 3), but can never be larger than the classical congruence relation $\backsim$ (Theorem 2). Notably, the improved congruence relations only have a blow-up of $\mathcal{O}(n^2)$ when dealing with deterministic Büchi automata (Theorem 4). Second, we further propose congruence relations for NBAs with a blow-up of only $2^{\mathcal{O}(n \log n)}$ (Lemma 11), which is then proved to be optimal (Theorem 7). Finally, we show that our congruence relations define an FDFA recognizing $\Sigma^\omega \backslash \mathcal{L}(\mathcal{A})$ from an NBA $\mathcal{A}$. In particular, if $\mathcal{A}$ has n states, then our optimal congruence relations yield an FDFA $\mathcal{F}$ with an optimal complexity $2^{\mathcal{O}(n \log n)}$. Thus, to the best of our knowledge, we present the *first direct* translation from an NBA to an FDFA with *optimal* complexity. Missing proofs can be found in [18].

2   Preliminaries

Fix an *Alphabet* Σ. A *word* is a finite or infinite sequence of letters in Σ; ϵ denotes the empty word. Let Σ^* and Σ^ω denote the set of all finite and infinite words (or ω-words), respectively. In particular, we let $\Sigma^+ = \Sigma^* \backslash \{\epsilon\}$. A *finitary language* is a subset of Σ^*; an ω-*language* is a subset of Σ^ω. Let L be a finitary language (resp., ω-langu003age); the complementary language of L is $\Sigma^* \backslash L$ (resp., $\Sigma^\omega \backslash L$). Let ρ be a sequence; we denote by $\rho[i]$ the i-th element of ρ and by $\rho[i..k]$ the subsequence of ρ starting at the i-th element and ending at the k-th element inclusively when $i \leq k$, and the empty sequence ϵ when $i > k$. Given a finite word u and a word w, we denote by $u \cdot w$ (uw, for short) the concatenation of u and w. Given a finitary language L_1 and a finitary/ω-language L_2, the concatenation $L_1 \cdot L_2$ ($L_1 L_2$, for short) of L_1 and L_2 is the set $L_1 \cdot L_2 = \{\, uw \mid u \in L_1, w \in L_2 \,\}$ and L_1^ω the infinite concatenation of L_1.

NBAs. A (nondeterministic) automaton is a tuple $\mathcal{A} = (Q, I, \delta, F)$, where Q is a finite set of states, $I \subseteq Q$ is a set of initial states, $\delta \colon Q \times \Sigma \to 2^Q$ is a transition function, and $F \subseteq Q$ is a set of accepting states. We extend δ to sets of states, by letting $\delta(S, a) = \bigcup_{q \in S} \delta(q, a)$. We also extend δ to words, by letting $\delta(S, \epsilon) = S$ and $\delta(S, a_1 a_2 \cdots a_k) = \delta(\delta(S, a_1), \cdots, a_k)$, where we have $k \geq 1$ and $a_i \in \Sigma$ for $i \in \{1, \cdots, k\}$. An automaton on finite words is called a *nondeterministic finite automaton* (NFA), while an automaton on ω-words is called a *nondeterministic Büchi automaton* (NBA). An NFA $\mathcal{A}$ is said to be a *deterministic* finite automaton (DFA) if $|I| = 1$ and for each $q \in Q$ and $a \in \Sigma$, $|\delta(q, a)| \leq 1$. Deterministic Büchi automata (DBAs) are defined similarly.

A *run* of an NFA/NBA $\mathcal{A}$ on a finite word u of length $n \geq 0$ is a sequence of states $\rho = q_0 q_1 \cdots q_n \in Q^+$, such that for every $0 < i \leq n$, $q_i \in \delta(q_{i-1}, u[i])$. We write $q_0 \xrightarrow{u} q_n$ if there is a run from q_0 to q_n over u and by $q_0 \xRightarrow{u} q_n$ if such a run also visits an accepting state. Obviously, we have that $q \xrightarrow{\epsilon} q$ for all $q \in Q$ and $q \xRightarrow{\epsilon} q$ for all $q \in F$. A finite word $u \in \Sigma^*$ is *accepted* by an NFA $\mathcal{A}$ if there is a run $q_0 \cdots q_n$ over u such that $q_0 \in I$ and $q_n \in F$. Similarly, an ω-*run* of $\mathcal{A}$ on an ω-word w is an infinite sequence of states $\rho = q_0 q_1 \cdots$ such that $q_0 \in I$ and for every $i > 0$, $q_i \in \delta(q_{i-1}, w[i])$. Let $Inf(\rho)$ be the set of states that occur infinitely often in the run ρ. An ω-word $w \in \Sigma^\omega$ is *accepted* by an NBA $\mathcal{A}$ if there exists an ω-run ρ of $\mathcal{A}$ over w such that $Inf(\rho) \cap F \neq \emptyset$. The *finitary language* recognized by an NFA $\mathcal{A}$, denoted by $\mathcal{L}_*(\mathcal{A})$, is defined as the set of finite words accepted by it. Similarly, we denote by $\mathcal{L}(\mathcal{A})$ the ω-*language* recognized by an NBA $\mathcal{A}$, i.e., the set of ω-words accepted by $\mathcal{A}$. NFAs/DFAs accept exactly *regular* languages while NBAs recognize exactly ω-*regular* languages. The complementary automaton of an NBA $\mathcal{A}$ accepts the complementary language of $\mathcal{L}(\mathcal{A})$, i.e., $\Sigma^\omega \backslash \mathcal{L}(\mathcal{A})$.

Congruence Relations. A *right congruence* (RC) relation is an equivalence relation $\backsim$ over Σ^* such that $x \backsim y$ implies $xv \backsim yv$ for all $v \in \Sigma^*$. A *congruence relation* is an equivalence relation $\backsim$ over Σ^* such that $x \backsim y$ implies $uxv \backsim uyv$ for every $x, y, u, v \in \Sigma^*$. We denote by $|\backsim|$ the index of $\backsim$, i.e., the number of equivalence classes of $\backsim$. A *finite congruence relation* is a congruence relation with a finite index. We denote by $\Sigma^*/_\backsim$ the set of equivalence classes of Σ^* under $\backsim$; we use $\Sigma^+/_\backsim$ to denote the same set of equivalence classes excluding ϵ. Given $x \in \Sigma^*$, we denote by $[x]_\backsim$ the equivalence class of $\backsim$ that x belongs to.

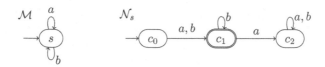

Fig. 1. An example of FDFA $\mathcal{F} = (\mathcal{M}, \{\mathcal{N}_s\})$ which is not saturated.

For a given right congruence $\backsim$ of a regular language L, it is well-known that the Myhill-Nerode theorem [19,20] defines a unique minimal DFA D of L, in which each state of D corresponds to an equivalence class defined by $\backsim$ over Σ^*. Therefore, we can construct a DFA $\mathcal{D}[\backsim]$ from $\backsim$ in a standard way.

Definition 1 ([19,20]). *Let $\backsim$ be a right congruence of finite index. The DFA $\mathcal{D}[\backsim]$ without accepting states induced by $\backsim$ is a tuple $(S, s_0, \delta_\mathcal{D}, \emptyset)$ where $S = \Sigma^*/_\backsim$, $s_0 = [\epsilon]_\backsim$, and for each $u \in \Sigma^*$ and $a \in \Sigma$, $\delta_\mathcal{D}([u]_\backsim, a) = [ua]_\backsim$.*

The DFA $\mathcal{D}[\backsim]$ is parametric on $\backsim$, indicating that it is induced by the right congruence relation $\backsim$. We may just write $\mathcal{D}$ if $\backsim$ is clear from the context.

UP-Words. The ω-regular languages accepted by NBAs can also be recognized by FDFAs by means of their *ultimately periodic words* (UP-words) [3]. A UP-word w is an ω-word of the form uv^ω, where $u \in \Sigma^*$ and $v \in \Sigma^+$. Thus $w = uv^\omega$ can be represented as a pair of finite words (u, v), called a *decomposition* of w. A UP-word can have multiple decompositions: for instance (u, v), (uv, v), and (u, vv) are all decompositions of uv^ω. For an ω-language L, let $\mathrm{UP}(L) = \{ uv^\omega \in L \mid u \in \Sigma^* \land v \in \Sigma^+ \}$ denote the set of all UP-words in L. The set of UP-words of an ω-regular language L can be seen as the fingerprint of L, as stated below.

Theorem 1 ([7]). *(1) Every non-empty ω-regular language L contains at least one UP-word. (2) Let L and L' be two ω-regular languages. Then $L = L'$ if and only if $\mathrm{UP}(L) = \mathrm{UP}(L')$.*

FDFAs. Based on Theorem 1, Angluin *et al.* introduced in [3] the notion of FDFAs as another type of automata to recognize ω-regular languages.

Definition 2 (FDFAs [3]). *An FDFA is a pair $\mathcal{F} = (\mathcal{M}, \{\mathcal{N}_q\})$ consisting of a leading DFA $\mathcal{M}$ and of a progress DFA $\mathcal{N}_q$ for each state q in $\mathcal{M}$.*

Intuitively, the leading DFA $\mathcal{M}$ of $\mathcal{F} = (\mathcal{M}, \{\mathcal{N}_q\})$ for an ω-regular language L consumes the finite prefix u of a UP-word $uv^\omega \in \mathrm{UP}(L)$, reaching some state q, and for each state q of $\mathcal{M}$, the progress DFA $\mathcal{N}_q$ accepts the period v of uv^ω. An example of FDFA $\mathcal{F}$ is depicted in Fig. 1 where the leading DFA $\mathcal{M}$ has only the state s and the progress DFA associated with s is $\mathcal{N}_s$. Note that the leading DFA $\mathcal{M}$ of every FDFA does not make use of accepting states.

Let $\mathcal{D}$ be a DFA with initial state q_0 and transition function δ. Given a word $u \in \Sigma^*$, we often use $\mathcal{D}(u)$ as a shorthand for $\delta(q_0, u)$. Each FDFA $\mathcal{F}$ characterizes a set of UP-words $\mathrm{UP}(\mathcal{F})$ by following the acceptance condition.

Definition 3 (FDFA Acceptance). *Let $\mathcal{F} = (\mathcal{M}, \{\mathcal{N}_q\})$ be an FDFA and w be a UP-word. A decomposition (u, v) of w is normalized with respect to $\mathcal{F}$ if $\mathcal{M}(u) = \mathcal{M}(uv)$.[1] A decomposition (u, v) is accepted by $\mathcal{F}$ if (u, v) is normalized and we have $v \in \mathcal{L}_*(\mathcal{N}_q)$ where $q = \mathcal{M}(u)$. The UP-word w is accepted by $\mathcal{F}$ if there exists a decomposition (u, v) of w accepted by $\mathcal{F}$.*

Note that the normalized decomposition (u, v) is defined with respect to $\mathcal{F}$. We usually omit $\mathcal{F}$ and just say (u, v) is normalized when $\mathcal{F}$ is clear from the context. Consider again the FDFA $\mathcal{F}$ from Fig. 1: $(aba)^\omega$ is not accepted since no decomposition of $(aba)^\omega$ is accepted, while $(ab)^\omega$ is accepted since the decomposition (ab, ab) of $(ab)^\omega$ is such that $\mathcal{M}(ab \cdot ab) = \mathcal{M}(ab) = s$ and $ab \in \mathcal{L}_*(\mathcal{N}_s)$.

One can observe that the normalized decomposition $(ab, abab)$ of $(ab)^\omega$ is not accepted by $\mathcal{F}$, despite that (ab, ab) is accepted by $\mathcal{F}$. In the following, we define a class of FDFAs that *saturates* every accepting normalized decomposition $(ab, (ab)^k)$ of $(ab)^\omega$ (where $k \geq 1$) if (ab, ab) is accepted, which is important for FDFAs to recognize ω-regular languages [3,17].

Definition 4 (Saturation of FDFAs [3]). *Let $\mathcal{F} = (\mathcal{M}, \{\mathcal{N}_q\})$ be an FDFA and w be a UP-word in $UP(\mathcal{F})$. We say $\mathcal{F}$ is saturated if for all normalized decompositions (u, v) and (u', v') of w, either both (u, v) and (u', v') are accepted by $\mathcal{F}$ or both are not.*

Intuitively, for a saturated FDFA $\mathcal{F}$, a UP-word w is accepted by $\mathcal{F}$ if and only if all normalized decompositions (u, v) of w are accepted by $\mathcal{F}$. From a saturated FDFA $\mathcal{F}$, one can construct an equivalent NBA $\mathcal{A}$ that recognizes $UP(\mathcal{F})$ in polynomial time.

Lemma 1 (Polynomial Translation from FDFAs to NBAs [3,17]). *Let $\mathcal{F} = (\mathcal{M}, \{\mathcal{N}_q\})$ be a saturated FDFA with n states. Then, one can construct an NBA $\mathcal{A}$ with $\mathcal{O}(n^3)$ states such that $UP(\mathcal{F}) = UP(\mathcal{L}(\mathcal{A}))$.*

Note that an FDFA that is *not* saturated does not necessarily recognize an ω-regular language (cf. [17]), let alone permit an equivalent translation to NBAs.

In the remainder of the paper, we fix an NBA $\mathcal{A} = (Q, I, \delta, F)$, unless explicitly stated otherwise, where $\mathcal{A}$ has n states, i.e., $n = |Q|$. We call a state in an FDFA a *macrostate* to distinguish it from states of $\mathcal{A}$.

3 Improved Congruence Relations for NBAs

In this section we present congruence relations that can be used to construct NBAs accepting the language of a given NBA $\mathcal{A}$ or its complement. We first review in Sect. 3.1 the classical congruence relations defined in [21,22] and then give improved congruence relations in Sect. 3.2.

---

[1] We use the normalized decomposition of UP-words defined in [17], which is different from the one given in [3]. Ours is a definition for a UP-word, while their definition is applied to a decomposition. However, this difference does not affect the definition of a saturated FDFA to be given later.

3.1 Classical Congruence Relations

As mentioned in the introduction, the index of the congruence relation of RBC proposed by Büchi [6] is doubly exponential in the size of $\mathcal{A}$. Sistla, Vardi, and Wolper [21] showed how to improve RBC with a subset construction that was later presented by Thomas [22] as the following congruence relation $\backsim_{\mathcal{A}}$.

Definition 5 ([21,22]). *In the RBC construction, for all $u_1, u_2 \in \Sigma^*$, we have $u_1 \backsim_{\mathcal{A}} u_2$ if for all $q, r \in Q$, (1) $q \xrightarrow{u_1} r$ iff $q \xrightarrow{u_2} r$ and (2) $q \overset{u_1}{\Rightarrow} r$ iff $q \overset{u_2}{\Rightarrow} r$.*

It is easy to verify that $\backsim_{\mathcal{A}}$ is a (right-)congruence relation: given two finite words u_1 and u_2 such that $u_1 \backsim_{\mathcal{A}} u_2$, we have that $x u_1 y \backsim_{\mathcal{A}} x u_2 y$ holds for all $x, y \in \Sigma^*$. Moreover, we have that $\backsim_{\mathcal{A}}$ is of finite index, as stated by the next lemma. To simplify the notation, we just write $\backsim$ instead of $\backsim_{\mathcal{A}}$ as $\mathcal{A}$ is fixed.

Lemma 2 ([21,22]). *Let $\backsim$ be as given in Definition 5. Then $|\backsim| \leq 3^{n^2}$.*

Since the congruence relation $\backsim$ is defined by reachability between states, the result follows from the fact that we can map each of the n^2 pairs of states (q, r) to either both $q \overset{u}{\Rightarrow} r$ and $q \xrightarrow{u} r$, just $q \xrightarrow{u} r$, or none of them. Thus we have $|\backsim| = |\Sigma^*/_\backsim| \leq 3^{n^2}$. We can also establish a lower bound for $\backsim$, by means of a family of DBAs inspired by the proof of [4, Theorem 2].

Lemma 3. *There is a family of DBAs $\{\mathcal{C}_n\}_{n \in \mathbb{N}}$ such that each DBA $\mathcal{C}_n$ has $n + 2$ states and the corresponding $\backsim_{\mathcal{C}_n}$ is such that $|\backsim_{\mathcal{C}_n}| \geq n!$.*

An important property we want to have is that the congruence relation $\backsim$ captures correctly the language of the NBA it corresponds to. This means that $\backsim$ must not relate words in $\mathcal{L}(\mathcal{A})$ with those in $\Sigma^\omega \backslash \mathcal{L}(\mathcal{A})$, that is, for each $[u]_\backsim \in \Sigma^*/_\backsim$ and $[v]_\backsim \in \Sigma^+/_\backsim$, either $[u]_\backsim [v]_\backsim^\omega \subseteq \mathcal{L}(\mathcal{A})$ or $[u]_\backsim [v]_\backsim^\omega \subseteq \Sigma^\omega \backslash \mathcal{L}(\mathcal{A})$. Moreover, $\backsim$ should cover the whole Σ^ω, that is, it saturates $\mathcal{L}(\mathcal{A})$, $\Sigma^\omega \backslash \mathcal{L}(\mathcal{A})$, and Σ^ω. This is formalized by the following *saturation lemma* of the congruence relation $\backsim$, which is a known result from [21] that we adapt to our notation.

According to [21,22], given two classes $[u]_\backsim \in \Sigma^*/_\backsim, [v]_\backsim \in \Sigma^+/_\backsim$, the ω-language $[u]_\backsim [v]_\backsim^\omega$ is called *proper* if $[u]_\backsim [v]_\backsim \subseteq [u]_\backsim$ and $[v]_\backsim [v]_\backsim \subseteq [v]_\backsim$.

Lemma 4 (Saturation Lemma [21,22])

1. *For $[u]_\backsim \in \Sigma^*/_\backsim, [v]_\backsim \in \Sigma^+/_\backsim$, if $[u]_\backsim [v]_\backsim^\omega$ is proper, then either $[u]_\backsim [v]_\backsim^\omega \cap \mathcal{L}(\mathcal{A}) = \emptyset$ or $[u]_\backsim [v]_\backsim^\omega \subseteq \mathcal{L}(\mathcal{A})$.*
2. *$\Sigma^\omega = \bigcup \{ [u]_\backsim [v]_\backsim^\omega \mid [u]_\backsim \in \Sigma^*/_\backsim \wedge [v]_\backsim \in \Sigma^+/_\backsim \wedge [u]_\backsim [v]_\backsim^\omega$ is proper$\}$.*
3. *$\Sigma^\omega \backslash \mathcal{L}(\mathcal{A}) = \bigcup \{ [u]_\backsim [v]_\backsim^\omega \mid [u]_\backsim \in \Sigma^*/_\backsim \wedge [v]_\backsim \in \Sigma^+/_\backsim \wedge [u]_\backsim [v]_\backsim^\omega \cap \mathcal{L}(\mathcal{A}) = \emptyset \wedge [u]_\backsim [v]_\backsim^\omega$ is proper$\}$.*

Thus, it suffices to just consider proper languages to get the languages Σ^ω (cf. Item (2) of Lemma 4) and $\Sigma^\omega \backslash \mathcal{L}(\mathcal{A})$ (cf. Item (3) of Lemma 4). This means that the congruence relation $\backsim$ allows us to obtain $\mathcal{L}(\mathcal{A})$ (resp., $\Sigma^\omega \backslash \mathcal{L}(\mathcal{A})$) by identifying the exact set of proper languages that are inside $\mathcal{L}(\mathcal{A})$ (resp., outside $\mathcal{L}(\mathcal{A})$). In the remainder of the paper, we show that we can obtain similar saturation lemmas (cf. Lemma 7 and Lemma 13) for the congruence relations we are going to propose to obtain $\mathcal{L}(\mathcal{A})$ or the complementary language $\Sigma^\omega \backslash \mathcal{L}(\mathcal{A})$.

3.2   Improved Congruence Relations for NBAs

In this section, we introduce the relations $\backsim^i$ and $\approx_u$, for $u \in \Sigma^*$, that can never have larger index than that of the classical congruence relation $\backsim$ (cf. Lemma 5) while possibly being exponentially coarser than $\backsim$ (cf. Theorem 3). When restricted to DBAs, we reduce the worst-case blow-up from $\Omega(n!)$ (cf. Lemma 3) to $\mathcal{O}(n^2)$ (cf. Theorem 4). Still, they capture correctly $\mathcal{L}(\mathcal{A})$ and $\Sigma^\omega \backslash \mathcal{L}(\mathcal{A})$ (cf. Lemma 7).

We improve the classical congruence relation $\backsim$ given in Sect. 3.1 based on the following key observations: (1) we can use different congruence relations to process the finite prefix u and the periodic word v of a UP-word uv^ω, separately, in a manner similar to FDFAs; (2) the assumption $[v]_\backsim [v]_\backsim \subseteq [v]_\backsim$ of proper languages is not necessary, according to [21]; (3) inspired by [5], we can consider only reachable states in $\mathcal{A}$, which allows us to use just *right congruences* instead of congruences such as $\backsim$. We defer the comparison of our work with [5] to Remark 2.

Instead of considering every pair of states (q, r) of $\mathcal{A}$ to define the congruence relation $\backsim$ (cf. Definition 5), we process the finite prefixes u by a simple subset construction over the states of $\mathcal{A}$, obtaining the following relation $\backsim^i$ that is obviously a right congruence.

Definition 6 (RC $\backsim^i$). *For $u_1, u_2 \in \Sigma^*$, we have $u_1 \backsim^i u_2$ if and only if $\delta(I, u_1) = \delta(I, u_2)$.*

As one can expect, by relaxing the conditions on the relation $\backsim^i$, we reduce how large its index can be, from 3^{n^2} (cf. Lemma 3) to 2^n, showing also that $\backsim^i$ is a right congruence of finite index.

Lemma 5. *Let $\backsim^i$ be the right congruence in Definition 6. Then $|\backsim^i| \leq 2^n$.*

Differently from $\backsim$ (see, e.g., Lemma 4), we will use $\backsim^i$ only to process the finite prefix u of a UP-word uv^ω; to process the period v, we now introduce the right congruence $\approx_u$, by considering only states reachable from $\delta(I, u)$.

Definition 7 (RC $\approx_u$). *For $u, v_1, v_2 \subset \Sigma^*$, we have $v_1 \approx_u v_2$ if for all states $q \in \delta(I, u)$ and $r \in Q$ of $\mathcal{A}$, (1) $q \xrightarrow{v_1} r$ iff $q \xrightarrow{v_2} r$ and (2) $q \overset{v_1}{\Rightarrow} r$ iff $q \overset{v_2}{\Rightarrow} r$.*

Compared to Definition 5, we only take into account the states that can be reached from $\delta(I, u)$, as opposed to the whole set Q. In this way we obtain a right congruence relation that is coarser than $\backsim$ for the periodic finite words.

Theorem 2. *Let $\backsim$ be the congruence relation in Definition 5. For each $u, v_1, v_2 \in \Sigma^*$, we have that $v_1 \backsim v_2$ implies that $v_1 \approx_u v_2$.*
Similarly, $u_1 \backsim u_2$ implies that $u_1 \backsim^i u_2$ for all $u_1, u_2 \in \Sigma^*$.

Although the right congruence relation $\approx_u$ is coarser than its predecessor $\backsim$, it has the same upper bound for its index (cf. Lemma 2).

Lemma 6. *Given $u \in \Sigma^*$, let $\approx_u$ be as defined in Definition 7. Then $|\approx_u| \leq 3^{n^2}$.*

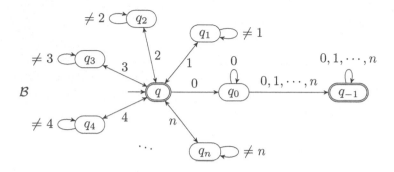

Fig. 2. The family of NBAs $\{\mathcal{B}_n\}_{n \in \mathbb{N}}$ over the alphabet $\{0, 1, \cdots, n\}$ with $n+3$ states for which $|\frown|$ is at least $n!$ while $|\approx_u|$ is at most $(n+3)+2$ for each $u \in \Sigma^*$; the initial state is q and $F = \{q, q_{-1}\}$. We remark that this NBA is inspired by a DBA from [4]. However, our NBA is not deterministic.

Despite this common upper bound, $|\approx_u|$ can be exponentially smaller than $|\frown|$, as witnessed by the family of NBAs $\{\mathcal{B}_n\}_{n \in \mathbb{N}}$ depicted in Fig. 2.

Theorem 3. *Given $u \in \Sigma^*$, let $\frown$ be the congruence relation in Definition 5 and $\approx_u$ be the right congruence in Definition 7. There is a family of NBAs $\{\mathcal{B}_n\}_{n \in \mathbb{N}}$ with $n+3$ states for which $|\frown| \geq n!$ and $|\approx_u| \leq (n+3)+2$.*

The idea underlying this result is that in $\frown^i$, there are at most $n+4$ equivalence classes, which correspond to the singletons $\{r\}$ with $r \in Q$ and the set $\{q_{-1}, q_0\}$. For each of these classes, say $[u]_{\frown^i} = [1]_{\frown^i}$, the associated classes $[v]_{\approx_u}$ can correspond to at most $(n+3)+2$ configurations of (accepting) runs, like $\{q_1 \xrightarrow{v} q_1\}$ and $\{q_1 \xrightarrow{v} q_0, q_1 \overset{v}{\Rightarrow} q_0, q_1 \xrightarrow{v} q_{-1}, q_1 \overset{v}{\Rightarrow} q_{-1}\}$. On the other hand, since $\frown$ must take care of both prefixes and periods, different permutations of $\{1, \cdots, n\}$ taken as prefixes cannot be equivalent, thus $|\frown| \geq n!$. We refer to [18, proof of Theorem 3] for more detailed reasoning and explanations.

When working with DBAs, the overall index of the right congruence relations $\bigcup_{u \in \Sigma^*}\{\approx_u\}$ can be exponentially tighter than that of $\frown$ (cf. Lemma 3).

Theorem 4. *Let $\mathcal{A}$ be a DBA with n states. Then $\Sigma_{[u]_{\frown^i} \in \Sigma^*/_{\frown^i}} |\approx_u| \in \mathcal{O}(n^2)$.*

Similarly to Lemma 4, the saturation lemma for $\frown$, the right congruences $\frown^i$ and $\approx_u$ with $u \in \Sigma^*$ also allow us to recognize *exactly* $\mathcal{L}(\mathcal{A})$ or its complement $\Sigma^\omega \backslash \mathcal{L}(\mathcal{A})$: for these relations we have again that the ω-language $[u]_{\frown^i}[v]^\omega_{\approx_u}$ with $uv \frown^i u$ is either completely inside $\mathcal{L}(\mathcal{A})$ or outside $\mathcal{L}(\mathcal{A})$, even if we drop the requirement $[v]_{\approx_u}[v]_{\approx_u} \subseteq [v]_{\approx_u}$.

Lemma 7 (Saturation Lemma for $(\frown^i, \bigcup_{u \in \Sigma^*}\{\approx_u\})$)

1. *For $u \in \Sigma^*, v \in \Sigma^+$, if $uv \frown^i u$, then either $[u]_{\frown^i}[v]^\omega_{\approx_u} \cap \mathcal{L}(\mathcal{A}) = \emptyset$ or $[u]_{\frown^i}[v]^\omega_{\approx_u} \subseteq \mathcal{L}(\mathcal{A})$.*
2. *$\Sigma^\omega = \bigcup\{[u]_{\frown^i}[v]^\omega_{\approx_u} \mid [u]_{\frown^i} \in \Sigma^*/_{\frown^i} \wedge [v]_{\approx_u} \in \Sigma^+/_{\approx_u} \wedge uv \frown^i u\}$.*

3. $\Sigma^\omega \backslash \mathcal{L}(\mathcal{A}) = \bigcup \{ [u]_{\backsim^i} [v]^\omega_{\approx_u} \mid [u]_{\backsim^i} \in \Sigma^* /_{\backsim^i} \wedge [v]_{\approx_u} \in \Sigma^+ /_{\approx_u} \wedge uv \backsim^i u \wedge [u]_{\backsim^i} [v]^\omega_{\approx_u} \cap \mathcal{L}(\mathcal{A}) = \emptyset \}$.

By definition of $\backsim^i$ and $\approx_u$, if $uv \backsim^i u$, then the set of states $\delta(I, u)$ is visited infinitely often when reading the word $w = uv^\omega$; it also implies $uv^j \backsim^i u$ for each $j \geq 0$. Moreover, if $w \in \mathcal{L}(\mathcal{A})$, then there is a run of $\mathcal{A}$ over w that is accepting, i.e., the run visits infinitely often states in F. This happens when dealing with v^ω, since u is a finite word; thus $\mathcal{A}$ visits an accepting state when reading v on the way from $\delta(I, u)$ to $\delta(\delta(I, u), v) = \delta(I, u)$.

These properties allow us to prove Item (1), i.e., that if $w \in [u]_{\backsim^i} [v]^\omega_{\approx_u} \cap \mathcal{L}(\mathcal{A})$, then for each word $w' \in [u]_{\backsim^i} [v]^\omega_{\approx_u}$ we have $w' \in \mathcal{L}(\mathcal{A})$, because w' can be written as $w' = u' \cdot v'_1 \cdot v'_2 \cdots$ with $u' \in [u]_{\backsim^i}$ and $v'_j \in [v]_{\approx_u}$ for each $j \geq 1$. Thus for w' we have that $\mathcal{A}$ visits infinitely often the set $\delta(I, u'v'_j) = \delta(I, u') = \delta(I, u)$ while visiting an accepting state on the way from $\delta(I, u')$ to $\delta(\delta(I, u'), v'_j) = \delta(I, u')$ since $v \approx_u v'_j$. Item (2) holds by considering only the UP-words (cf. Theorem 1), for which we have that for each $w = u'v'^\omega \subset \mathrm{UP}(\Sigma^\omega)$, we can construct a decomposition $(u = u'v'^h, v = v'^k)$ of w with $u \backsim^i uv$ for some $h, k \geq 1$ since $\backsim^i$ is of finite index. By combining Items (1) and (2), to obtain $\Sigma^\omega \backslash \mathcal{L}(\mathcal{A})$, we can just take the union of all languages $[u]_{\backsim^i} [v]^\omega_{\approx_u}$ such that $[u]_{\backsim^i} [v]^\omega_{\approx_u} \cap \mathcal{L}(\mathcal{A}) = \emptyset$.

4   Optimal Congruence Relations for NBAs

The right congruence relations we introduced in Sect. 3.2, despite improving $\backsim$, still lead to a blow-up of $3^{O(n^2)}$ (cf. Lemma 6). The main cause of the exponent n^2 is that it is possible for each of the n states to be a predecessor of a state r over the word v. To avoid having to consider all such precedessors, we look for specific representatives, in order to reduce the blow-up. Inspired by [9,10], we introduce a *preorder* on the states based on the transition structure of $\mathcal{A}$; we then use the preorder to select the representatives. In particular, if the predecessors of r can be reduced to only one representative for a given v, we obtain that the blow-up reduces to $2^{O(n \log n)}$. The representative we are going to use is the maximal equivalence class induced by the preorder among at most n equivalence classes. Breuers *et al.* [5] also proposed a preorder-based optimization to improve RBC; see Remark 2 for a detailed comparison.

In the remainder of this section, we present a preorder $\preceq_u$ inspired by [9,10] on the set of states $\delta(I, u)$, $u \in \Sigma^*$, yielding optimal congruence relations for NBAs. The preorder $\preceq_u$ over the set of states $\delta(I, u)$ is defined by comparing the finite runs of $\mathcal{A}$ over u from the initial states to those states.

Fix a finite word u; given a run π of $\mathcal{A}$ over u, recall that $\pi[i]$ denotes the i-th element (i.e. state) of π. For each run π, we define the function $\mathbb{1}_F(\pi) = \mathbb{1}_F(\pi[1]) \mathbb{1}_F(\pi[2]) \ldots$ where $\mathbb{1}_F(s) = 1$ if $s \in F$ and 0 if $s \notin F$. In other words, each run π can be encoded as a binary sequence. Given two runs π, π' of $\mathcal{A}$ over u, the two runs π and π' can be ordered by the lexicographical order with 1 being larger than 0; formally, we say that π' is *greater* than π, denoted by $\pi' > \pi$, if there is a prefix $\alpha 1$ of $\mathbb{1}_F(\pi')$ such that $\alpha 0$ is a prefix of $\mathbb{1}_F(\pi)$. That is, π' is greater than π if there is an integer $1 \leq j \leq |u|+1$ such that $\pi'[j] \in F$, $\pi[j] \notin F$, and $\pi'[i] \in F \iff \pi[i] \in F$ for all $1 \leq i < j$ (i does not exist when $j = 1$).

Let $\Pi_{u,q}$ be the set of runs of $\mathcal{A}$ over u starting from I with the last state being q. For each state $q \in \delta(I, u)$, there may be several runs in $\Pi_{u,q}$; the set of *maximal* runs in $\Pi_{u,q}$ is defined as $\max(\Pi_{u,q}) = \{ \pi' \in \Pi_{u,q} \mid \forall \pi \in \Pi_{u,q}, \pi \not> \pi' \}$. The following result is a direct consequence of the definition above.

Proposition 1. *For two runs $\pi_q, \pi'_q \in \max(\Pi_{u,q})$, for each $1 \leq i \leq |u| + 1$ we have that $\pi_q[i] \in F \iff \pi'_q[i] \in F$.*

That is, all runs in $\max(\Pi_{u,q})$ have the same image under $\mathbb{1}_F$.

In the following, we define the preorder $\preceq_u$ on the set of states $P = \delta(I, u)$ by comparing the sets of maximal runs $\max(\Pi_{u,q})$ and $\max(\Pi_{u,r})$ for $q, r \in P$.

Definition 8 (Preorder $\preceq_u$). *Given $u \in \Sigma^*$,*

- *if $u = \epsilon$, then for $q, r \in I = \delta(I, u)$, we define $q \preceq_\epsilon r$ if and only if $q \in F \implies r \in F$ holds. Therefore, $q \prec_\epsilon r$ if and only if $q \notin F$ and $r \in F$;*
- *when $u \in \Sigma^+$, for $q, r \in \delta(I, u)$, $q \preceq_u r$ if the runs $\pi_q \in \max(\Pi_{u,q})$ are not greater than the runs $\pi_r \in \max(\Pi_{u,r})$. In particular, $q \prec_u r$ if the runs $\pi_r \in \max(\Pi_{u,r})$ are greater than the runs $\pi_q \in \max(\Pi_{u,q})$.*

One can verify that $\preceq_u$ is a binary relation that is reflexive (i.e., for each $q \in Q$, $q \preceq_u q$) and transitive (i.e., for each $q, r, s \in Q$, $q \preceq_u r$ and $r \preceq_u s$ implies $q \preceq_u s$), so it is a preorder; we also have $q \prec_u r$ whenever $q \preceq_u r$ and $r \not\preceq_u q$ and we write $q \simeq_u r$ whenever $q \preceq_u r$ and $r \preceq_u q$. Intuitively, we have $q \prec_u r$ if there is a run from an initial state to r on u that sees an accepting state earlier than all paths from the initial states to q on u. That is, there is a prefix $\alpha 1$ of $\mathbb{1}_F(\pi_r)$ for a run π_r to r such that $\alpha 0$ is a prefix of $\mathbb{1}_F(\pi_q)$ for all runs π_q to q.

Due to Proposition 1, if there is a run $\pi_r \in \max(\Pi_{u,r})$ greater than a run in $\max(\Pi_{u,q})$, then all runs in $\max(\Pi_{u,r})$ are greater than the runs in $\max(\Pi_{u,q})$.

Example 1. Consider the NBA $\mathcal{B}_n$ depicted in Fig. 2 and let $P = \delta(\{q\}, 00) = \{q_{-1}, q_0\}$; we have $q_0 \prec_{00} q_{-1}$ on this set since there is a run from the initial state q to q_{-1} that sees the accepting state q_{-1} after inputting the second 0, while all runs from q to q_0 on 00 do not visit an accepting state right after inputting the second 0.

Remark 1. The preorder $\preceq_u$ in Definition 8 shares the same idea of comparing the maximal runs with the *lexicographical order* of vertices at the same level of the run direct acyclic graph (DAG) over an ω-word w used in [10]; see [18, Appendix B] for a detailed comparison between their and our works. The difference between our work and the work in [10] is that the latter applies this idea to Slice-based [12] and Rank-based complementation algorithms [16] while ours is designed for RBC. A similar idea was also used in [9] for determinizing NBAs.

As an immediate consequence of Definition 8, given two states $q, r \in \delta(I, u)$ such that $q \preceq_u r$, we have that a run from an initial state to q that visits an accepting state mandates that there must be a run from an initial state to r that also visits accepting states.

Corollary 1. *Let $q, r \in \delta(I, u)$, with $q \preceq_u r$. Then $\iota_q \overset{u}{\Rightarrow} q$ for some initial state $\iota_q \in I$ implies $\iota_r \overset{u}{\Rightarrow} r$ for some initial state $\iota_r \in I$.*

Let $P = \delta(I, u)$. The preorder $\preceq_u$ defines a partition of P in which states in the same set are equivalent under $\preceq_u$. By abuse of terminology, we call the set $[r]_{\preceq_u} = \{ r' \in P \mid r' \simeq_u r \}$ the equivalence class of $r \in P$ under $\preceq_u$; we denote by $P/_{\preceq_u}$ the set of all such equivalence classes. Since every two states $q, r \in P$ are *comparable* under $\preceq_u$, we define the maximal equivalence class of P under $\preceq_u$ as $\max_{\preceq_u}(P) = \max(P/_{\preceq_u}) = \{ r \in P \mid r' \preceq_u r \text{ for all } r' \in P \}$; moreover, the equivalence classes in $P/_{\preceq_u}$ can be linearly ordered by $[r]_{\preceq_u} \trianglelefteq_u [r']_{\preceq_u} \iff r \preceq_u r'$; so we have $[r]_{\preceq_u} \triangleleft_u [r']_{\preceq_u}$ if $[r]_{\preceq_u} \trianglelefteq_u [r']_{\preceq_u}$ and $[r'] \npreceq_u [r]_{\preceq_u}$. Here $\trianglelefteq_u$ is a partial order, not a preorder, which implies that $[r]_{\preceq_u} = [r']_{\preceq_u}$ if and only if $[r]_{\preceq_u} \trianglelefteq_u [r']_{\preceq_u}$ and $[r']_{\preceq_u} \trianglelefteq_u [r]_{\preceq_u}$. In the remainder of this section, by abuse of terminology, we just use $P/_{\preceq_u}$ to denote the preordered set of equivalence classes of P under $\preceq_u$, i.e., $P/_{\preceq_u}$ not just represents a set of equivalence classes but also linearly orders those equivalence classes with $\trianglelefteq_u$.

An interesting property of the states $\mathcal{A}$ visits on the maximal runs from the initial states I to a state $q \in \delta(I, uv)$ over the finite word uv is that they are step by step all equivalent under the preorder with respect to the prefix of uv. Let $\max(\Pi_{uv,q})|_u = \{ \pi[|u| + 1] \mid \pi \in \max(\Pi_{uv,q}) \}$, i.e., the set of states reached from the initial states after inputting u on the maximal runs to q over uv.

Lemma 8. *Given $u, v \in \Sigma^*$ and $q \in \delta(I, uv)$, let $[p]_{\preceq_u} = \max_{\preceq_u}\{ [p']_{\preceq_u} \in \delta(I, u)/_{\preceq_u} \mid p' \overset{v}{\rightarrow} q \}$. Then for each $q' \in [q]_{\preceq_{uv}}$, $\max(\Pi_{uv,q'})|_u \subseteq [p]_{\preceq_u}$.*

By definition of $[q]_{\preceq_{uv}}$, all the maximal runs from the initial states to the states in $[q]_{\preceq_{uv}}$ have the same image under $\mathbb{1}_F$. As a consequence, the states on these runs reached after reading u must belong to the same equivalence class $[p]_{\preceq_u}$ under $\preceq_u$, which is also the maximal equivalence class under $\preceq_u$ that reaches $[q]_{\preceq_{uv}}$. If this would not be the case, then we would be able to find runs to $[q]_{\preceq_{uv}}$ greater than the current maximal runs by visiting $[p]_{\preceq_u}$.

A useful property of these maximal runs is that they share visits to accepting states; more precisely, if one of the maximal runs on a word uv to a state $q_1 \in [q]_{\preceq_{uv}}$ visits an accepting state while reading v, then so do all other maximal runs on the same word to some other state $q_2 \in [q]_{\preceq_{uv}}$. The motivation for this is again the maximality of the runs: if one run visits an accepting state while another does not, then the former is greater than the latter, which implies that the latter cannot be maximal. This property is formalized below.

Lemma 9. *Let $u, v \in \Sigma^*$ and $q \in \delta(I, uv)$. For each $q_1, q_2 \in [q]_{\preceq_{uv}}$, $p_1 \in \max(\Pi_{uv,q_1})|_u$, and $p_2 \in \max(\Pi_{uv,q_2})|_u$, we have $p_1 \overset{v}{\Rightarrow} q_1$ if and only if $p_2 \overset{v}{\Rightarrow} q_2$.*

Similarly to Lemma 8, a consequence of Lemma 9 is that, for a given finite word u and $q_1 \simeq_u q_2$, the maximal runs in $\max(\Pi_{u,q_1})$ and in $\max(\Pi_{u,q_2})$ visit accepting states at the same moment, i.e., they have the same image under $\mathbb{1}_F$.

The preorder $\preceq_u$ enjoys several properties about the states and maximal runs of $\mathcal{A}$ for the given finite word u. Thus, instead of tracing only the set of reachable states, as done by the right congruence $\backsim^i$ (cf. Definition 6), we also trace the reachable states $\delta(I, u)$ with the preorder $\preceq_u$ to get the right congruence $\backsim^o$.

Definition 9 (RC $\backsim^o$). *For $u_1, u_2 \in \Sigma^*$, we have $u_1 \backsim^o u_2$ if and only if $\delta(I, u_1)/_{\preceq_{u_1}} = \delta(I, u_2)/_{\preceq_{u_2}}$.*

Example 2. Consider again the NBA $\mathcal{B}_n$ depicted in Fig. 2: we can represent $\delta(I, 00)/_{\preceq_{00}}$ as the ordered sequence of sets $\langle \{q_0\}, \{q_{-1}\} \rangle$ since we have $\{q_0\} \lhd_{00} \{q_{-1}\}$. Analogously, $\delta(I, 000)/_{\preceq_{000}}$ can also be represented as $\langle \{q_0\}, \{q_{-1}\} \rangle$ while $\delta(I, 001)/_{\preceq_{001}}$ as $\langle \{q_{-1}\} \rangle$. We can see that $00 \backsim^o 000$ since $\delta(I, 00)/_{\preceq_{00}} = \delta(I, 000)/_{\preceq_{000}} = \langle \{q_0\}, \{q_{-1}\} \rangle$ while $000 \not\backsim^o 001$ as $\delta(I, 001)/_{\preceq_{001}} = \langle \{q_{-1}\} \rangle$.

Since each equivalence class $[u]_{\backsim^o}$, $u \in \Sigma^*$, can be uniquely encoded as the set $\delta(I, u)/_{\preceq_u}$, i.e., an ordered sequence of sets over Q, by [10] we have that the number of possible ordered sequences of sets over Q is $\mathcal{O}((\frac{n}{e \ln n})^n) \approx (0.53n)^n \leq n^n$. Thus we have the following upper bound for $\backsim^o$, so it is of finite index.

Lemma 10. *Let $\backsim^o$ be the right congruence in Definition 9. Then $|\backsim^o| \leq n^n$.*

Given their definitions, it is clear that $\backsim^i$ is coarser than $\backsim^o$, thus $|\backsim^i| \leq |\backsim^o|$. Nonetheless, the right congruence $\backsim^o$ allows us to define a novel right congruence relation $\approx_u^o$ of index $2^{\mathcal{O}(n \log n)}$, for a given $u \in \Sigma^*$.

Definition 10 (RC $\approx_u^o$). *Given $u, v_1, v_2 \in \Sigma^*$, we say $v_1 \approx_u^o v_2$ if and only if (1) $uv_1 \backsim^o uv_2$ and (2) for all states $q \in P'$, for $S_1 = \max_{\preceq_u}\{ [p]_{\preceq_u} \in P/_{\preceq_u} \mid p \xrightarrow{v_1} q \}$ and $S_2 = \max_{\preceq_u}\{ [p]_{\preceq_u} \in P/_{\preceq_u} \mid p \xrightarrow{v_2} q \}$, we have (i) $S_1 = S_2$ and (ii) $p_1 \xRightarrow{v_1} q$ for $p_1 \in \max(\Pi_{uv_1, q})|_u$ if and only if $p_2 \xRightarrow{v_2} q$ for some $p_2 \in \max(\Pi_{uv_2, q})|_u$ where $P = \delta(I, u)$ and $P' = \delta(I, uv_1) = \delta(I, uv_2)$.*

Note that the equality $\delta(I, uv_1) = \delta(I, uv_2)$ holds because, under the assumption $uv_1 \backsim^o uv_2$, we have that the sets of equivalence classes $\delta(I, uv_1)/_{\preceq_{u_1}}$ and $\delta(I, uv_2)/_{\preceq_{u_2}}$ are equal according to the definition of $\backsim^o$, which then implies that $\delta(I, uv_1)$ and $\delta(I, uv_2)$ must be equal as well.

Definition 10 formalizes the following idea for recognizing the ω-words accepted and rejected by $\mathcal{A}$. Since we want to use $(\backsim^o, \cup_{u \in \Sigma^*}\{\approx_u^o\})$ to characterize $\mathcal{L}(\mathcal{A})$ and $\Sigma^\omega \backslash \mathcal{L}(\mathcal{A})$, i.e., to establish its saturation lemma in line with $\backsim$ (cf. Lemma 4) and $(\backsim^i, \cup_{u \in \Sigma^*}\{\approx_u\})$ (cf. Lemma 7), under the assumption that $uv_1 \backsim^o u$ and $u \backsim^o uv_2$, we need to guarantee that if $v_1 \approx_u^o v_2$, then $uv_1^\omega \in \mathcal{L}(\mathcal{A})$ if and only if $uv_2^\omega \in \mathcal{L}(\mathcal{A})$. To achieve this, the first condition we impose (cf. Item (1) of Definition 10) is to visit infinitely often the same states over the ω-words uv_1^ω and uv_2^ω, so we require $uv_1 \backsim^o uv_2$. The second condition is to guarantee that the images under $\mathbb{1}_F$ of the maximal runs over uv_1^k and uv_2^k, $k \geq 1$, either both contain only 0s, or both contain some 1; by this, when extending to infinite words, the images of uv_1^ω and uv_2^ω under $\mathbb{1}_F$ will both have infinitely many 1s or none of them does. This ensures that $uv_1^\omega \in \mathcal{L}(\mathcal{A})$ if and only if $uv_2^\omega \in \mathcal{L}(\mathcal{A})$. To guarantee having the property above, we first require that the maximal equivalence classes from each state $q \in \delta(I, u)$ over both finite words v_1 and v_2 have to be the same (cf. Condition (2)-(i), together with Lemma 8); then, we demand that they share the visits to accepting states (cf. Condition (2)-(ii) and Lemma 9).

Example 3. Consider again Example 1 and let $u = \epsilon$, $v_1 = 00$, and $v_2 = 000$. We now check whether $00 \approx_\epsilon^o 000$. Clearly $\epsilon \cdot 00 \leadsto^o \epsilon \cdot 000$ since $00 \leadsto^o 000$. We can represent $\delta(I, \epsilon)/_{\preceq_\epsilon}$ as $\langle \{q\} \rangle$, a singleton, hence, we have $S_1 = S_2 = \{q\}$, thus we satisfy Condition (2)-(i) of Definition 10. To fulfill Condition (2)-(ii), we first have $P' = \{q_{-1}, q_0\}$. We also have $\max(\Pi_{\epsilon \cdot 00, q_{-1}}) = \{qq_0q_{-1}\}$, $\max(\Pi_{\epsilon \cdot 00, q_0}) = \{qq_0q_0\}$, $\max(\Pi_{\epsilon \cdot 000, q_{-1}}) = \{qq_0q_{-1}q_{-1}\}$, and $\max(\Pi_{\epsilon \cdot 000, q_0}) = \{qq_0q_0q_0\}$. For state $q_{-1} \in P'$, Condition (2)-(ii) is satisfied since qq_0q_{-1} and $qq_0q_{-1}q_{-1}$ both visit accepting states. For state $q_0 \in P'$, Condition (2)-(ii) is also fulfilled as qq_0q_0 and $qq_0q_0q_0$ both visit accepting state q. Therefore, we conclude that $00 \approx_\epsilon^o 000$ holds. Clearly $000 \not\approx_\epsilon^o 001$ since we already know that $\epsilon \cdot 000 \not\leadsto^o \epsilon \cdot 001$.

As desired before Definition 10, the index of $\approx_u^o$ is indeed in $2^{\mathcal{O}(n \log n)}$.

Lemma 11. *Given $u \in \Sigma^*$, let $\approx_u^o$ be the right congruence from Definition 10. Then $|\approx_u^o| \leq n^n \times (n+1)^n \times 2^n \in 2^{\mathcal{O}(n \log n)}$.*

The upper bound for $|\approx_u^o|$ derives from the encoding we use for $[v]_{\approx_u^o}$. $[v]_{\approx_u^o}$ is mapped to the pair $\langle \delta(I, uv)/_{\preceq_{uv}}, f \rangle$ where the function f keeps track of the satisfaction of the states $q \in Q$ of the conditions in Definition 10, i.e., whether $q \in \delta(I, uv)$ and whether Conditions (2)-(i) and (2)-(ii) are satisfied for such states. The codomain of f has size $2n + 1 < 2(n+1)$, so the possible different functions f are $(2(n+1))^n = 2^n \times (n+1)^n$, while by [10] the possible sets $\delta(I, uv)/_{\preceq_{uv}}$ are n^n, hence $|\approx_u^o| \leq n^n \times (n+1)^n \times 2^n \in 2^{\mathcal{O}(n \log n)}$.

Similarly to Lemma 4, if we restrict ourselves to DBAs, then $|\approx_u^o|$ is exponentially better than the bound $2^{\mathcal{O}(n \log n)}$ we have for general NBAs.

Lemma 12. *Let $\mathcal{A}$ be a DBA with n states. Then $\Sigma_{[u]_{\leadsto^o} \in \Sigma^*/_{\leadsto^o}} |\approx_u^o| \in \mathcal{O}(n^2)$.*

This result follows from the fact that, $\mathcal{A}$ being deterministic, there are at most n classes $[u]_{\leadsto^o} \in \Sigma^*/_{\leadsto^o}$. By taking the same encoding as in Lemma 11, this time the index of $\approx_u^o$ is at most $2n$, and so the result follows.

Similarly to the other (right) congruence relations we considered, i.e., $\leadsto$ (cf. Lemma 4) and $(\leadsto^i, \cup_{u \in \Sigma^*} \{\approx_u\})$ (cf. Lemma 7), $(\leadsto^o, \cup_{u \in \Sigma^*} \{\approx_u^o\})$ also enjoys its saturation lemma. As stated below, $(\leadsto^o, \cup_{u \in \Sigma^*} \{\approx_u^o\})$ is able to recognize exactly $\mathcal{L}(\mathcal{A})$ and $\Sigma^\omega \setminus \mathcal{L}(\mathcal{A})$; a core property to obtain this is again that the ω-languages $[u]_{\leadsto^o}[v]_{\approx_u^o}^\omega$ are included either in $\mathcal{L}(\mathcal{A})$ or in its complement $\Sigma^\omega \setminus \mathcal{L}(\mathcal{A})$.

Lemma 13 (Saturation Lemma for $(\leadsto^o, \cup_{u \in \Sigma^*} \{\approx_u^o\})$)

1. *For $u \in \Sigma^*$ and $v \in \Sigma^+$, if $uv \leadsto^o u$, then either $[u]_{\leadsto^o}[v]_{\approx_u^o}^\omega \cap \mathcal{L}(\mathcal{A}) = \emptyset$ or $[u]_{\leadsto^o}[v]_{\approx_u^o}^\omega \subseteq \mathcal{L}(\mathcal{A})$.*
2. $\Sigma^\omega = \bigcup \{ [u]_{\leadsto^o}[v]_{\approx_u^o}^\omega \mid [u]_{\leadsto^o} \in \Sigma^*/_{\leadsto^o} \wedge [v]_{\approx_u^o} \in \Sigma^+/_{\approx_u^o} \wedge uv \leadsto^o u \}$.
3. $\Sigma^\omega \setminus \mathcal{L}(\mathcal{A}) = \bigcup \{ [u]_{\leadsto^o}[v]_{\approx_u^o}^\omega \mid [u]_{\leadsto^o} \in \Sigma^*/_{\leadsto^o} \wedge [v]_{\approx_u^o} \in \Sigma^+/_{\approx_u^o} \wedge uv \leadsto^o u \wedge [u]_{\leadsto^o}[v]_{\approx_u^o}^\omega \cap \mathcal{L}(\mathcal{A}) = \emptyset \}$.

The proof for this saturation lemma follows the same steps as for the other two saturation lemmas, with the appropriate adaptations that take into consideration the differences in the definitions of the right congruences.

Remark 2. In their work [21], Sistla *et al.* constructed an NBA $\mathcal{B}_{u,v}$ for each proper language $Y_{u,v} = [u]_\backsim [v]_\backsim^\omega$ such that $Y_{u,v} \cap \mathcal{L}(\mathcal{A}) = \emptyset$. Each $\mathcal{B}_{u,v}$ can be constructed with two copies of the DFA $\mathcal{M}[\backsim]$ induced by $\backsim$ (cf. Definition 1), where the first copy processes the finite prefix u while the second copy is modified to accept the word v^ω. According to [21], the resulting NBA $\mathcal{A}^c$ has $3^{\mathcal{O}(n^2)}$ states. Breuers *et al.* [5] also proposed a subset construction for improving RBC for complementing NBAs; in particular, they used the subset construction to process the finite prefix u of a UP-word uv^ω in $\Sigma^\omega \backslash \mathcal{L}(\mathcal{A})$. On the other hand, they still used the classical congruence relation $\backsim$ for recognizing the periodic word v of uv^ω. Differently from the algorithms proposed in [5,21], we exploit the right congruences $\approx_u$ or $\approx_u^o$ instead of the congruence $\backsim$ for accepting the period v of uv^ω; this can result in a considerable decrease of the index of the relation (cf. Theorem 3), which influences the number of states of the automata we build from these relations. The part for accepting v in [5] has also been optimized with a preorder and its size is also reduced to $2^{\mathcal{O}(n \log n)}$. While leading to the same upper bound, there is a difference on the automata needed to process the period v: for a given u, the construction given in [5] uses more than one automaton for recognizing v; instead, our approach needs one automaton, because the equivalence class $[u]_{\backsim^o}$ of $\backsim^o$ only relates with one right congruence relation $\approx_u^o$. This allows us to represent $(\backsim^o, \bigcup_{u \in \Sigma^*} \{\approx_u^o\})$ as an FDFA, as we explain in Sect. 5.

5   Connection to FDFAs

In this section, we highlight the deep connection between the congruence relations of NBAs and FDFAs. This connection allows us to use the right congruences $(\backsim^o, \bigcup_{u \in \Sigma^*} \{\approx_u^o\})$ we introduced in Sect. 4 to construct an FDFA $\mathcal{F}$ with *optimal* complexity that accepts $\Sigma^\omega \backslash \mathcal{L}(\mathcal{A})$. As a byproduct of this connection, we are able to prove Theorem 7; in other words, one cannot find congruence relations of index less than $2^{\mathcal{O}(n \log n)}$ that recognize $\Sigma^\omega \backslash \mathcal{L}(\mathcal{A})$.

We now introduce the construction of FDFAs from the right congruences. Since $\backsim^o$ (resp., $\backsim^i$) and $\approx_u^o$ (resp., $\approx_u$) with $u \in \Sigma^*$ are right congruences of finite index, by means of Definition 1 they can be used to define the transition structures of the DFAs of an FDFA $\mathcal{F}$ recognizing $\Sigma^\omega \setminus \mathcal{L}(\mathcal{A})$. Moreover, by Lemma 13 (resp., Lemma 7), we can identify the accepting macrostates of the progress DFAs. We now give the construction of the FDFA $\mathcal{F}$ with $\backsim^o$ and $\approx_u^o$. The construction of the FDFA with $\backsim^i$ and $\approx_u$ is similar.

Definition 11. *The FDFA $\mathcal{F}$ is a tuple $(\mathcal{M}[\backsim^o], \{\mathcal{N}_u[\approx_u^o]\})$ where*

- $\mathcal{M}[\backsim^o]$ *is the DFA induced by $\backsim^o$ according to Definition 1;*
- *for each macrostate $[u]_{\backsim^o}$ of $\mathcal{M}[\backsim^o]$, the progress DFA $\mathcal{N}_u[\approx_u^o]$ is constructed as in Definition 1 parameterized with $\approx_u^o$. The accepting macrostates of*

$\mathcal{N}_u[\approx_u^o]$ are the equivalence classes $[v]_{\approx_u^o}$ of $\approx_u^o$ such that $uv \leadsto^o u$ and $[u]_{\leadsto^o}[v]_{\approx_u^o}^\omega \cap \mathcal{L}(\mathcal{A}) = \emptyset$.

The FDFA constructed according to Definition 11 has the desired properties we are looking for: it accepts $\Sigma^\omega \setminus \mathcal{L}(\mathcal{A})$ and has only $2^{\mathcal{O}(n \log n)}$ macrostates.

Theorem 5. *Let $\mathcal{F}$ be the FDFA constructed from $\mathcal{A}$ in Definition 11. Then (1) $UP(\mathcal{F}) = UP(\Sigma^\omega \setminus \mathcal{L}(\mathcal{A}))$; (2) $\mathcal{F}$ is saturated; and (3) $\mathcal{F}$ has $2^{\mathcal{O}(n \log n)}$ macrostates.*

The three results stated in Theorem 5 follow by the definition of $\mathcal{F}$ and the properties of $(\leadsto^o, \bigcup_{u \subset \Sigma^*} \{\approx_u^o\})$: Result (1) is a direct consequence of Definition 11; Result (2) is implied by the saturation lemma for $(\leadsto^o, \bigcup_{u \in \Sigma^*} \{\approx_u^o\})$ (cf. Item (1) of Lemma 13); and Result (3) by the indexes of $(\leadsto^o, \bigcup_{u \in \Sigma^*} \{\approx_u^o\})$ and the construction of the DFAs of $\mathcal{F}$. It is easy to see that one can also construct an FDFA accepting $\mathcal{L}(\mathcal{A})$ by setting the accepting macrostates of $\mathcal{N}_u[\approx_u^o]$ to be the equivalence classes $[v]_{\approx_u^o}$ such that $uv \leadsto^o u$ and $[u]_{\leadsto^o}[v]_{\approx_u^o}^\omega \cap \mathcal{L}(\mathcal{A}) \neq \emptyset$.

We are now able to formalize the optimality of our FDFA construction of $\mathcal{F}$ based on $(\leadsto^o, \bigcup_{u \in \Sigma^*} \{\approx_u^o\})$. The upper bound is due to Theorem 5; the matching lower bound comes from the well-known fact [23] that there exists a family of NBAs $\{\mathcal{A}_n\}_{n \in \mathbb{N}}$ whose complementary NBAs $\{\mathcal{A}_n^c\}_{n \in \mathbb{N}}$ have $2^{\Omega(n \log n)}$ states, so the same lower bound must hold for FDFAs since there are polynomial-time translations from FDFAs to NBAs (cf. Lemma 1).

Theorem 6. *The construction of FDFAs in Definition 11 with the right congruence relations $(\leadsto^o, \bigcup_{u \in \Sigma^*} \{\approx_u^o\})$ from $\mathcal{A}$ is asymptotically optimal.*

Remark 3. Here we discuss related works on FDFAs. As mentioned before, there are polynomial-time translations from FDFAs to NBAs [3,7]. The opposite translation is more challenging: the direct translations from an n-states NBA, proposed in [7] and in [13], produce an FDFA with $\mathcal{O}(4^{n^2+n})$ states and an FDFA with $\mathcal{O}(3^{n^2+n})$ states, respectively. Our construction in Definition 11 replaced with $(\leadsto^i, \bigcup_{u \in \Sigma^*} \{\approx_u\})$ can even be exponentially better than these two translations; due to lack of space, the detailed reasoning can be found in [18, Appendix C]. The translation based on an intermediate determinization of NBAs to deterministic Parity automata given in [3] also yields an FDFA with the optimal complexity $2^{\mathcal{O}(n \log n)}$. Our construction (cf. Definition 11), however, is the *first direct* and *optimal* translation from an NBA to an FDFA without involving determinization of NBAs. Like in [13], our congruence relation-based translation also reveals that FDFAs are actually being applied in the language-containment checking of NBAs (cf. [1,2,11]). The specialized translation for DBAs proposed in [3] can be used to convert a DBA $\mathcal{A}$ with n states to a saturated FDFA $\mathcal{F}'$ with $n + n \times 2n \in \mathcal{O}(n^2)$ macrostates such that $UP(\mathcal{F}') = UP(\Sigma^\omega \setminus \mathcal{L}(\mathcal{A}))$; we remark that our construction for FDFAs in Sect. 5 degenerates to their construction when the given NBA $\mathcal{A}$ is deterministic. Given an ω-regular language L, Angluin and Fisman [4] directly operate on the language L and give congruence relations for constructing FDFAs of L. In contrast, our work takes an NBA $\mathcal{A}$

as input and defines congruence relations for recognizing $\Sigma^\omega \backslash \mathcal{L}(\mathcal{A})$ based on the transitions of $\mathcal{A}$.

We now formalize the main result of this paper as Theorem 7, which is a direct consequence of Theorem 6 since the constructed FDFA has the same number of macrostates as the index the congruence relations $(\backsim^o, \bigcup_{u \in \Sigma^*} \{\approx_u^o\})$ (cf. Definition 11).

Theorem 7. *The right congruence relations $(\backsim^o, \bigcup_{u \in \Sigma^*} \{\approx_u^o\})$ given in Definitions 9 and 10, respectively, are asymptotically optimal among all right congruence relations $(\backsim, \bigcup_{u \in \Sigma^*} \{\approx_u\})$ such that for each $u \in \Sigma^*$ and $v \in \Sigma^+$, if $uv \backsim u$, then either $[u]_\backsim [v]_{\approx_u}^\omega \cap \mathcal{L}(\mathcal{A}) = \emptyset$ or $[u]_\backsim [v]_{\approx_u}^\omega \subseteq \mathcal{L}(\mathcal{A})$.*

6   Concluding Remarks

In this work, we considered congruence relations for NBAs and we have proposed coarser relations than the classical one; we have further given asymptotically *optimal* right congruences for NBAs. To the best of our knowledge, we have given the *first direct* translation from an NBA to an FDFA with *optimal* complexity, based on our optimal right congruences.

We have shown that congruence relations relate tightly the classical RBC and FDFAs. Congruence relations are known to be able to yield the minimal DFAs for given regular languages by the Myhill-Nerode Theorem, by identifying equivalent states [19,20]. The classical congruence relation $\backsim$ has already been exploited to avoid exploration of redundant states, which explains why RBC is suitable for developing state-space pruning techniques [1,2,11]. We believe that the congruence relations we introduced in this work may further enable the reduction of the state space in practical NBA complementation construction. In future work, we plan to study whether subsumption and simulation techniques, similar to the ones developed in [1,2] for the classical congruence relation, can also be proposed for our right congruences, in the context of language-containment checking between two NBAs.

As mentioned in the introduction, formal verification based on NBAs is PSPACE-complete, which is computationally expensive. An alternative and also cheaper method is to model the system and the specification as FDFAs, so that the model-checking problem can be reduced to a containment problem between two FDFAs, which can be done in polynomial time [3]. We believe that our work benefits the community with a deep understanding of the relationship between NBAs and FDFAs, which may help with the modelling of systems as FDFAs and enhance the possibility of the use of FDFAs in formal verification.

Acknowledgements. We would like to thank the anonymous reviewers for their valuable suggestions and comments about this paper. Work supported in part by the Guangdong Science and Technology Department (Grant No. 2018B010107004), NSF grants IIS-1527668, CCF-1704883 and IIS-1830549, and an award from the Maryland Procurement Office.

References

1. Abdulla, P.A., et al.: Simulation subsumption in Ramsey-based Büchi automata universality and inclusion testing. In: Touili, T., Cook, B., Jackson, P. (eds.) CAV 2010. LNCS, vol. 6174, pp. 132–147. Springer, Heidelberg (2010). https://doi.org/10.1007/978-3-642-14295-6_14

2. Abdulla, P.A., et al.: Advanced Ramsey-based Büchi automata inclusion testing. In: Katoen, J.-P., König, B. (eds.) CONCUR 2011. LNCS, vol. 6901, pp. 187–202. Springer, Heidelberg (2011). https://doi.org/10.1007/978-3-642-23217-6_13

3. Angluin, D., Boker, U., Fisman, D.: Families of DFAs as acceptors of ω-regular languages. Log. Methods Comput. Sci. **14**(1), 1–21 (2018)

4. Angluin, D., Fisman, D.: Learning regular omega languages. Theor. Comput. Sci. **650**, 57–72 (2016)

5. Breuers, S., Löding, C., Olschewski, J.: Improved Ramsey-based Büchi complementation. In: FOSSACS, pp. 150–164 (2012)

6. Büchi, J.R.: On a decision method in restricted second order arithmetic. In: Proceedings of the International Congress on Logic, Method, and Philosophy of Science 1960, pp. 1–12. Stanford University Press (1962)

7. Calbrix, H., Nivat, M., Podelski, A.: Ultimately periodic words of rational ω-languages. In: Brookes, S., Main, M., Melton, A., Mislove, M., Schmidt, D. (eds.) MFPS 1993. LNCS, vol. 802, pp. 554–566. Springer, Heidelberg (1994). https://doi.org/10.1007/3-540-58027-1_27

8. Clemente, L., Mayr, R.: Efficient reduction of nondeterministic automata with application to language inclusion testing. Logic. Methods Comput. Sci. **15**(1), 12:1-12:73 (2019)

9. Fogarty, S., Kupferman, O., Vardi, M.Y., Wilke, T.: Profile trees for Büchi word automata, with application to determinization. Inf. Comput. **245**, 136–151 (2015)

10. Fogarty, S., Kupferman, O., Wilke, T., Vardi, M.Y.: Unifying Büchi complementation constructions. Logic. Methods Comput. Sci. **9**(1), 1–22 (2013)

11. Fogarty, S., Vardi, M.Y.: Efficient Büchi universality checking. In: Esparza, J., Majumdar, R. (eds.) TACAS 2010. LNCS, vol. 6015, pp. 205–220. Springer, Heidelberg (2010). https://doi.org/10.1007/978-3-642-12002-2_17

12. Kähler, D., Wilke, T.: Complementation, disambiguation, and determinization of Büchi automata unified. In: Aceto, L., Damgård, I., Goldberg, L.A., Halldórsson, M.M., Ingólfsdóttir, A., Walukiewicz, I. (eds.) ICALP 2008, Part I. LNCS, vol. 5125, pp. 724–735. Springer, Heidelberg (2008). https://doi.org/10.1007/978-3-540-70575-8_59

13. Kuperberg, D., Pinault, L., Pous, D.: Coinductive algorithms for Büchi automata. In: Hofman, P., Skrzypczak, M. (eds.) DLT 2019. LNCS, vol. 11647, pp. 206–220. Springer, Cham (2019). https://doi.org/10.1007/978-3-030-24886-4_15

14. Kupferman, O., Vardi, M.Y.: Verification of fair transition systems. In: Alur, R., Henzinger, T.A. (eds.) CAV 1996. LNCS, vol. 1102, pp. 372–382. Springer, Heidelberg (1996). https://doi.org/10.1007/3-540-61474-5_84

15. Kupferman, O., Vardi, M.Y.: Model checking of safety properties. Form. Methods Syst. Des. **19**(3), 291–314 (2001)

16. Kupferman, O., Vardi, M.Y.: Weak alternating automata are not that weak. ACM Trans. Comput. Logic **2**(3), 408–429 (2001)

17. Li, Y., Chen, Y.F., Zhang, L., Liu, D.: A novel learning algorithm for Büchi automata based on family of DFAs and classification trees. In: TACAS, pp. 208–226. Springer (2017). https://doi.org/10.1007/978-3-662-54577-5_12

18. Li, Y., Tsay, Y.K., Turrini, A., Vardi, M.Y., Zhang, L.: Congruence relations for Büchi automata. CoRR abs/2104.03555 (2021)
19. Myhill, J.: Finite automata and the representation of events. In: Technical Report WADD TR-57-624, pp. 112–137 (1957)
20. Nerode, A.: Linear automaton transformations. Am. Math. Soc. **9**, 541–544 (1958)
21. Sistla, A.P., Vardi, M.Y., Wolper, P.: The complementation problem for Büchi automata with applications to temporal logic. Theor. Comput. Sci. **49**(2–3), 217–237 (1987)
22. Thomas, W.: Automata on infinite objects. In: Handbook of Theoretical Computer Science, Volume B: Formal Models and Semantics, pp. 133–191. Elsevier and MIT Press (1990)
23. Yan, Q.: Lower bounds for complementation of ω-automata via the full automata technique. Logic. Methods Comput. Sci. **4**(1:5), 1–20 (2008)

Featured Team Automata

Maurice H. ter Beek[1]([✉])(iD), Guillermina Cledou[2]([✉])(iD), Rolf Hennicker[3],
and José Proença[4]([✉])(iD)

[1] ISTI–CNR, Pisa, Italy
`maurice.terbeek@isti.cnr.it`
[2] HASLab, INESC TEC, University of Minho, Braga, Portugal
`mgc@inesctec.pt`
[3] Ludwig-Maximilians-Universität München, Munich, Germany
[4] CISTER, ISEP, Polytechnic Institute of Porto, Porto, Portugal
`pro@isep.ipp.pt`

Abstract. We propose featured team automata to support variability
in the development and analysis of teams, which are systems of reactive components that communicate according to specified synchronisation types. A featured team automaton concisely describes a family of
concrete product models for specific configurations determined by feature
selection. We focus on the analysis of communication-safety properties,
but doing so product-wise quickly becomes impractical. Therefore, we
investigate how to lift notions of receptiveness (no message loss) to the
level of family models. We show that featured (weak) receptiveness of featured team automata characterises (weak) receptiveness for all product
instantiations. A prototypical tool supports the developed theory.

1 Introduction

Team automata, originally introduced in the context of computer supported
cooperative work to model groupware systems [26], are formalised as a theoretical framework to study synchronisation mechanisms in system models [9].
Team automata represent an extension of I/O automata [12]. Their distinguish-
ing feature is the loose nature of synchronisation according to which, in principle, any number of component automata can participate in the synchronised
execution of a shared communicating action, either as a sender or as a receiver.
Team automata can determine specific synchronisation policies defining when
and which actions are executed and by how many components. Synchronisation types classify the policies realisable in team automata (e.g., peer-to-peer
or broadcast communication) in terms of ranges for the number of sender and
receiver components that can participate in a synchronisation [6]. In extended
team automata (ETA) [11], synchronisation type specifications (STS) individually assign a synchronisation type to each communicating action. Such a specification uniquely determines a *team* and gives rise to communication requirements
to be satisfied by the team.

For systems composed by components communicating via message exchange,
it is desirable to guarantee absence of communication failures, like message loss

© Springer Nature Switzerland AG 2021
M. Huisman et al. (Eds.): FM 2021, LNCS 13047, pp. 483–502, 2021.
https://doi.org/10.1007/978-3-030-90870-6_26

(typically output not received as input, violating receptiveness) or indefinite waiting (typically for input that never arrives, violating responsiveness). This requires knowledge of the synchronisation policies to establish the compatibility of communicating components [15,23,30]; for team automata this was first studied for full synchronous products of component automata in [16]. Subsequently, a generic procedure to derive requirements for receptiveness and responsiveness for each synchronisation type was defined, and communication-safety of (extended) team automata was expressed in terms of compliance with such requirements [6,11]. A team automaton is called compliant with a given set of communication requirements if in each reachable state the requirements are met (i.e. the communication is safe). If the required communication cannot occur immediately, but only after some arbitrary other actions have been executed, the team automaton is called weakly compliant (akin to weak compatibility [5,29] or agreement of lazy request actions [3]).

Many of today's software systems are highly configurable, variant-rich systems, developed as a software product line (SPL) with a notion of variability in terms of features that conceptualise pieces of system functionality or aspects that are relevant to the stakeholders [1]. Formal models of SPL behaviour are studied extensively. Such variability-rich behavioural models are often based on the superimposition of multiple product models in a single family model, equipped with feature-based variability such that each product model corresponds to a different configuration. Arguably the best known models are featured transition systems (fTSs) [19–21] and modal transition systems [27,28], possibly with variability constraints [2,10], but also I/O automata [30,31], Petri nets [34,35] and contract automata [3,4] have been equipped with variability. An fTS is a labelled transition system (LTS) whose transitions are annotated with feature expressions that are Boolean expressions over features, which condition the presence of transitions in product models, and a feature model, which determines the set of valid product models (configurations) of the family model. The analysis of family models is challenging due to their innate variability, since the number of possible product models may be exponential in the number of features. In particular for larger models, enumerative product-by-product analysis becomes unfeasible; thus, dedicated family-based analysis techniques and tools, which exploit variability in terms of features, have been developed [13,14,17,18,21,22,24,25,37,38].

Motivation. fTSs have mostly been studied in the context of families of configurable components. Less attention has been paid on their parallel execution, in particular in the context of systems of reactive, concurrently running components, where interaction is a crucial issue, often realised by message exchange. For this, we need i) to discriminate between senders and receivers and thus between input and output actions in fTSs, and ii) a flexible synchronisation mechanism, not necessarily peer-to-peer, for sets of fTSs, called (featured) systems. In particular, the type of synchronisation should remain variable, depending on selected features (products). Important questions for analysis of such systems concern behavioural compatibility (communication-safety). As mentioned above, compositionality and communication-safety have been studied extensively in the literature for a variety of formal (automata-based) models, but—to the best of our knowledge—not considering variability. Thus, we need a means to define and verify communication-safety for systems of fTSs, ideally performing analyses on the level of featured systems such that the respective properties are automatically guaranteed for any product instantiation. In this paper, we focus on the property of (weak) receptiveness.

Running Example. We consider a configurable access management system consisting of a server and users who can either login with secure authentication or without (open access). Concrete automata capturing user and server behaviour are specified as family models whose product models correspond to configurations with or without secure authentication.

Figure 1 shows two fTSs: a family model of user components (Fig. 1a) and a family model of server components (Fig. 1b), as well as a feature model $fm = 🔒 \oplus 🔓$. The feature model expresses an exclusive choice of two features, 🔒 and 🔓, representing access with or without secure authentication, respectively, and defines two valid products (sets of features): {🔒} and {🔓}. The idea is that the server must confirm login access only for secure authentication. Thus, each transition is annotated with a constraint, denoted by a feature expression in square brackets (e.g., [🔒]), to indicate the product(s) that allow this transition.

A user starts in the initial state 0, indicated by the incoming arrow, in which only the action *join!* can be executed. Depending on the specific product, this results in a move to state 1 (if feature {🔒} is present) or to state 2 (if {🔓} is present). From state 2, a user can move back to state 0 by executing action *leave!*, in either product, as enabled by the transition constraint [⊤] (denoting

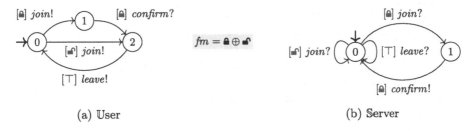

Fig. 1. Family models of users $\mathbb{U}$ and servers $\mathbb{S}$ and a shared feature model fm

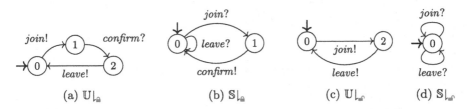

Fig. 2. Product models of users and servers (projections of the models in Fig. 1)

truth value true). In state 1, which is only present for the product with secure authentication, the user waits for explicit confirmation of login access from the server.

Figures 2a and 2c show the LTSs representing the user product models, which result from projecting the user (fTS) in Fig. 1a onto its set of valid products. Similarly, Figs. 2b and 2d show the LTSs of the server product models, projecting the server (fTS) onto its two valid products.

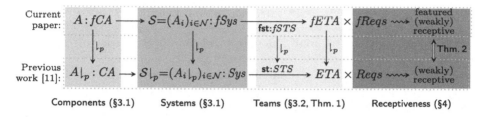

Fig. 3. Overview of this paper, using a valid product p

Contribution. Figure 3 illustrates the contents and contributions of this paper, which we now explain and relate to the literature mentioned above. In particular, we extend [11], by enriching ETA with variability, proposing a new model called *featured* ETA (fETA) to allow the specification of—and reasoning on—a family of ETA parameterised by a set of features. We define *projections* $\lfloor_p$ (for any valid product p) to relate the featured setting of this paper to that without in [11].

First, we extend *component automata* (CA), the building blocks of (extended) team automata, with variability, resulting in fTSs with input and output actions, called *featured* CA (fCA). Basically, CA are LTSs that distinguish between input and output actions (and internal actions, omitted in this paper) and which capture the behaviour of a component. The fTSs in the running example are fCA in which input and output actions are appended by ! and ?, respectively. Multiple CA can run in parallel to form a *system* (*Sys* in Fig. 3) of the CA; we propose a *featured* system (fSys) to consist of fCA instead of CA.

Given a system and a *synchronisation type specification* (STS), it is possible to generate an ETA and derive *receptiveness requirements* (Reqs), and study whether the ETA is (weakly) compliant with all such Reqs, in which case it is called *(weakly) receptive*. An ETA is an LTS that restricts how CA in the system can communicate based on the STS. We propose a *featured* STS (fSTS) to parameterise an STS with variability, giving rise to the aforementioned fETA and *featured* Reqs (fReqs). If the fETA is featured (weakly) compliant with all such fReqs, it is called *featured (weakly) receptive*.

While the extension from CA to fCA (and from systems to featured systems) is rather straightforward, fETA are not simple extensions of ETA: the fSTSs giving rise to fETA are a nontrivial extension of the STSs for ETA, partially due to the variability in synchronisation types. Our first result (Theorem 1) confirms the soundness of our extension. Our main result (Theorem 2) is that featured (weak) receptiveness induces and reflects (weak) receptiveness of product models, i.e. a fETA is featured (weakly) receptive if and only if all ETA obtained by product projections are (weakly) receptive.

Outline. Section 2 provides some basic definitions concerning variability. Section 3 lifts the theory of team automata to that of featured team automata, and Sect. 4 does the same for receptiveness requirements and compliance. We present a prototypical implementation of the developed theory in Sect. 5, and Sect. 6 concludes the paper and provides some ideas for future work. The proofs of our results can be found in a companion report [7, Appendix A].

2   Variability

This section provides definitions of the basic notions concerning variability, viz. *features, feature expressions, feature models*, and fTSs.

A *feature*, ranged over by f, is regarded as a Boolean variable that represents a unit of variability. This paper assumes a finite set of features F. A *product*, ranged over by $p \subseteq F$, is a finite subset of selected features. In the context of SPLs, a product can be interpreted as a configuration used to derive concrete software systems. A *feature expression* ψ over a set of features F, denoted $\psi \in FE(F)$, is a Boolean expression over features with the usual Boolean connectives and constants $\top$ and $\bot$ interpreted by the truth values true and false. A product p satisfies a feature expression ψ, denoted $p \models \psi$, if and only if ψ is evaluated to $\top$ if $\top$ is assigned to every feature in p and $\bot$ to the features not in p. A feature expression ψ is *satisfiable* if there exists a product p such that $p \models \psi$. A *feature model fm* $\in FE(F)$ is a feature expression that determines the set of products for which concrete systems of an SPL can be derived. We use $[\![fm]\!]$ to denote the set of products that satisfy the feature model $fm \in FE(F)$.

Notation. For any product $p \subseteq F$, its view as a feature expression is $\chi_p = \bigwedge_{f \in p} f \wedge \bigwedge_{f \in F \backslash p} \neg f$. p is the unique product with $p \models \chi_p$. A set P of products is characterised by the feature expression $\chi_P = \bigvee_{p \in P} \chi_p$. Clearly, for any product p, $p \in P$ iff $p \models \chi_P$. Note that the conjunctions and disjunctions are finite, since F is finite. Moreover, $\bigwedge_{i \in \emptyset} \psi_i$ stands for $\top$ and $\bigvee_{i \in \emptyset} \psi_i$ stands for $\bot$.

A *featured transition system* (fTS) is a tuple $A = (Q, I, \Sigma, E, F, fm, \gamma)$ such that (Q, I, Σ, E) is an LTS with a finite set of states Q, a set of initial states $I \subseteq Q$, a finite set of actions Σ, and a transition relation $E \subseteq Q \times \Sigma \times Q$. F is a finite set of features, $fm \in FE(F)$ is a feature model and $\gamma : E \to FE(F)$ is a mapping assigning feature expressions to transitions. A product $p \subseteq F$ is *valid* for the feature model fm, if $p \in [\![fm]\!]$. The mapping γ expresses *transition constraints* for the realisation of transitions. A transition $t \in E$ is *realisable* for a valid product p if $p \models \gamma(t)$.

An fTS A can be *projected* to a valid product p by using γ to filter realisable transitions, resulting in the LTS $A\!\restriction_p = (Q, I, \Sigma, E\!\restriction_p)$, where $E\!\restriction_p = \{t \in E \mid p \models \gamma(t)\}$. Such a projection is also called product model or configuration. Hereafter, we will generally write projections using superscripts, e.g. A^p to denote $A\!\restriction_p$.

Notation. Given an LTS or an fTS A, we write $q \xrightarrow{a}_A q'$, or shortly $q \xrightarrow{a} q'$, to denote $(q, a, q') \in E$. For $\Gamma \subseteq \Sigma$, we write $q \xrightarrow{\Gamma}{}^* q'$ if there exist $q \xrightarrow{a_1} q_1 \xrightarrow{a_2} \cdots \xrightarrow{a_n} q'$ for some $n \geq 0$ and $a_1, \ldots, a_n \in \Gamma$. An action a is *enabled* in A at state $q \in Q$, denoted $a\,\mathbf{en}_A@q$, if there exists $q' \in Q$ such that $q \xrightarrow{a} q'$. A state $q \in Q$ is *reachable* if $q_0 \xrightarrow{\Sigma}{}^* q$ for some $q_0 \in I$.

3   Team Automata with Variability

This section proposes to integrate variability in the modelling of teams of reactive components which communicate according to specified synchronisation policies. For this purpose we define *featured CA*, *featured systems*, and *featured ETA*, and compare them to their featureless counterparts. Throughout this section we will use grey backgrounds to highlight extensions with features.

3.1   Featured Component Automata and Featured Systems

A *featured component automaton* (fCA) is an fTS $A = (Q, I, \Sigma, E, F, fm, \gamma)$ such that $\Sigma = \Sigma^? \uplus \Sigma^!$ consists of disjoint sets $\Sigma^?$ of *input actions* and $\Sigma^!$ of *output actions*. For simplicity, we do not consider internal actions here. For easier readability, input actions will be shown with suffix "?" and output actions with suffix "!". fCA extend *component automata* (CA) [9,11] with features and feature models. The running example in Sect. 1 contains examples of fCA.

A *featured system* (fSys) is a pair $\mathcal{S} = (\mathcal{N}, (A_i)_{i \in \mathcal{N}})$, where $\mathcal{N}$ is a finite, nonempty set of component names and $(A_i)_{i \in \mathcal{N}}$ is an $\mathcal{N}$-indexed family of fCA $A_i = (Q_i, I_i, \Sigma_i, E_i, F, fm, \gamma_i)$ over a shared set of features F and feature model fm. Composition of feature models is out of the scope of this paper, but note that multiple approaches exist in the literature, e.g., using conjunction or disjunction of feature models [19,20,36].

Featured systems extend *systems of CA* [11] by using fCA instead of CA as system components. An fSys $\mathcal{S} = (\mathcal{N}, (A_i)_{i \in \mathcal{N}})$ induces: the set of system states $Q = \prod_{i \in \mathcal{N}} Q_i$ such that, for any $q \in Q$ and for all $i \in \mathcal{N}$, $q_i \in Q_i$; the set of initial states $I = \prod_{i \in \mathcal{N}} I_i$; the set of system actions $\Sigma = \bigcup_{i \in \mathcal{N}} \Sigma_i$; the set of system labels $\Lambda \subseteq 2^{\mathcal{N}} \times \Sigma \times 2^{\mathcal{N}}$ defined as $\Lambda = \{(S, a, R) \mid \emptyset \neq S \cup R \subseteq \mathcal{N}, \forall_{i \in S} \cdot a \in \Sigma_i^!, \forall_{i \in R} \cdot a \in \Sigma_i^?\}$; and the set of system transitions $E \subseteq Q \times \Lambda \times Q$ defined as $E = \{q \xrightarrow{(S,a,R)} q' \mid \forall_{i \in (S \cup R)} \cdot q_i \xrightarrow{a}_{A_i} q_i', \forall_{j \in \mathcal{N} \setminus (S \cup R)} \cdot q_j = q_j'\}$.

A transition labelled by a *system label* denotes the atomic execution of an action a by a set of components in which a is enabled. More concretely, for a system label $(S, a, R) \in \Lambda$, S represents the set of *senders* and R the set of *receivers* that synchronise on an action $a \in \Sigma$. Since, by definition of system labels, $S \cup R \neq \emptyset$, at least one component participates in any system transition. The transitions of a system capture all possible synchronisations of shared actions of its components, even when only one component participates. Given a system transition $t = q \xrightarrow{(S,a,R)} q'$, we write $t.a$ for a, $t.S$ for S and $t.R$ for R.

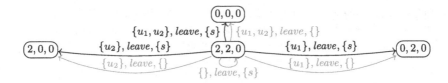

Fig. 4. Some system transitions of $\mathcal{S}_@$

For ease of presentation, we assume in this paper that systems are closed. This means that any system action $a \in \Sigma$ occurs in (at least) one of its components as an input action and in (at least) one of its components as an output action.

The *projection* of an fSys $\mathcal{S} = (\mathcal{N}, (A_i)_{i \in \mathcal{N}})$ to a product $p \in \llbracket fm \rrbracket$ is the system $\mathcal{S}^p = (\mathcal{N}, (A_i^p)_{i \in \mathcal{N}})$.

Example 1. We consider an fSys $\mathcal{S}_@$ with three components, two users and one server following the running example in Sect. 1. Formally, $\mathcal{S}_@ = (\mathcal{N}, (A_i)_{i \in \mathcal{N}})$, where $\mathcal{N} = \{u_1, u_2, s\}$ are component names, A_{u_1}, A_{u_2} are copies of the fCA $\mathbb{U}$ in Fig. 1a, and A_s is a copy of the fCA $\mathbb{S}$ in Fig. 1b.

The system states are tuples (p, q, r) with user states $p \in Q_{u_1}$ and $q \in Q_{u_2}$, and server state $r \in Q_s$. $\mathcal{S}_@$ has an initial state $(0, 0, 0)$, a total of 18 states ($3 \times 3 \times 2$), actions $\Sigma = \{join, leave, confirm\}$, and a total of 142 system transitions. Some of these (with action *leave*) are depicted in Fig. 4; the transitions marked in grey will be discarded based on synchronisation restrictions in the next section.

The projection of $\mathcal{S}_@$ to the valid product $\{\text{🔒}\}$, respecting the shared feature model $\text{🔒} \oplus \text{🔓}$, is the system $\mathcal{S}_@^{\text{🔒}} = (\mathcal{N}, \{A_{u_1}^{\text{🔒}}, A_{u_2}^{\text{🔒}}, A_s^{\text{🔒}}\})$, such that $A_{u_1}^{\text{🔒}}, A_{u_2}^{\text{🔒}}$ are copies of $\mathbb{U}\vert_{\text{🔒}}$ in Fig. 2a and $A_s^{\text{🔒}}$ is a copy of $\mathbb{S}\vert_{\text{🔒}}$ in Fig. 2b. Similarly, for product $\{\text{🔓}\}$, we get the projected system $\mathcal{S}_@^{\text{🔓}} = (\mathcal{N}, \{A_{u_1}^{\text{🔓}}, A_{u_2}^{\text{🔓}}, A_s^{\text{🔓}}\})$. $\triangleright$

3.2   Featured Team Automata

Featured team automata (fETA) are the key concept to model families of teams. They are constructed over an fSys $\mathcal{S}$ together with a specification of synchronisation types expressing desirable synchronisation constraints. This section first formalises the latter and then fETA as fTSs.

A *synchronisation type* $(s, r) \in \mathsf{Intv} \times \mathsf{Intv}$ is a pair of intervals s and r which determine the number of senders and receivers that can participate in a communication. Each interval is written $[min, max]$, with $min \in \mathbb{N}$ and $max \in \mathbb{N} \cup \{*\}$. We use $*$ to denote 0 or more participants, and write $x \in [n, m]$ if $n \leq x \leq m$ and $x \in [n, *]$ if $x \geq n$. For a system transition t, we define $t \models (s, r)$ if $|t.S| \in s \wedge |t.R| \in r$.

A *featured synchronisation type specification* (fSTS) over an fSys $\mathcal{S}$, is a total function, $\mathbf{fst} : \llbracket fm \rrbracket \times \Sigma \to \mathsf{Intv} \times \mathsf{Intv}$, mapping each product $p \in \llbracket fm \rrbracket$ and action $a \in \Sigma$ to a synchronisation type. Thus, an fSTS is parameterised by (valid) products and therefore supports variability of synchronisation conditions.

fSTSs are extensions of synchronisation type specifications (STSs) in [11]; an STS $\mathbf{st} : \Sigma \to \mathsf{Intv} \times \mathsf{Intv}$ maps actions to bounds of senders and receivers. For any product $p \in [\![fm]\!]$, an fSTS $\mathbf{fst}$ can be projected to an STS $\mathbf{fst}^p$ such that $\mathbf{fst}^p(a) = \mathbf{fst}(p, a)$ for all $a \in \Sigma$.

Example 2. The definition of $\mathbf{fst}_@$ corresponds to an fSTS for the fSys $\mathcal{S}_@$ in Example 1:

$$\mathbf{fst}_@(p, confirm) = ([1,1],[1,1]) \text{ for } p \in \{\{\mathbf{\triangle}\},\{\mathbf{\triangleleft}\}\} \tag{1}$$

$$\mathbf{fst}_@(\{\mathbf{\triangle}\}, a) = ([1,1],[1,1]) \text{ for } a \in \{join, leave\} \tag{2}$$

$$\mathbf{fst}_@(\{\mathbf{\triangleleft}\}, a) = ([1,*],[1,1]) \text{ for } a \in \{join, leave\} \tag{3}$$

Intuitively, independently of the selected product, users can receive *confirm*ation from the server in a *one-to-one* fashion (1). If secure authentication $\mathbf{\triangle}$ is required, one user can *join/leave* by synchronising exclusively with one server (2). If open access $\mathbf{\triangleleft}$ is required, multiple users can *join/leave* at the same time (3).   ▷

Given an fSys $\mathcal{S} = (\mathcal{N}, (A_i)_{i \in \mathcal{N}})$ and an fSTS $\mathbf{fst}$ over $\mathcal{S}$, the *featured team automaton* fETA generated by $\mathcal{S}$ and $\mathbf{fst}$, written $\mathbf{fst}[\mathcal{S}]$, is the fTS $(Q, I, \Sigma, E, F, fm, \gamma)$ where Q, I, Σ, E, F, and fm are determined by $\mathcal{S}$. It remains to construct the mapping $\gamma : E \to FE(F)$, which constrains system transitions by feature expressions. The definition of γ is derived from both the transition constraints γ_i of every A_i and from $\mathbf{fst}$. It is motivated by the fact that a system transition $t = q \xrightarrow{(S,a,R)} q' \in E$ should be realisable for those products $p \in [\![fm]\!]$ for which both of the following conditions hold:

1. In each component A_i, with $i \in (S \cup R)$, the local transition $q_i \xrightarrow{a}_{A_i} q_i'$ is realisable for p. This means $p \models \hat{\gamma}(t)$, where $\hat{\gamma}(t) = \bigwedge_{i \in (S \cup R)} \gamma_i(q_i \xrightarrow{a}_{A_i} q_i')$.
2. For any action $a \in \Sigma$, the number of senders $|S|$ and receivers $|R|$ fits the synchronisation type $\mathbf{fst}(p, a)$. This means $p \models \chi_{P(\mathbf{fst},t)}$, where $\chi_{P(\mathbf{fst},t)}$ (cf. Sect. 2) is the feature expression characterising the set of products $P(\mathbf{fst}, t) = \{p \in [\![fm]\!] \mid t \models \mathbf{fst}(p, t.a)\}$.

In summary, for any $t = q \xrightarrow{(S,a,R)} q' \in E$, we define $\gamma(t) = \hat{\gamma}(t) \wedge \chi_{P(\mathbf{fst},t)}$. Note that, since $P(\mathbf{fst}, t)$ is a subset of $[\![fm]\!]$, it holds $\models \chi_{P(\mathbf{fst},t)} \to fm$ and hence $\models \gamma(t) \to fm$. In cases where $P(\mathbf{fst}, t) = [\![fm]\!]$, $\chi_{P(\mathbf{fst},t)}$ and fm are equivalent and then we will often use $\gamma(t) = \hat{\gamma}(t) \wedge fm$.

Recall that an fTS can be projected to products (as defined in Sect. 2) and therefore also the fETA $\mathbf{fst}[\mathcal{S}]$ can be projected to a valid product $p \in [\![fm]\!]$ yielding the LTS $\mathbf{fst}[\mathcal{S}]^p$. Thus any fETA $\mathbf{fst}[\mathcal{S}]$ specifies a family of product models.

Example 3. Consider the fSys $\mathcal{S}_@$ and the fSTS $\mathbf{fst}_@$ from Example 2, here and in the following examples simply called $\mathbf{fst}$, as well as the generated fETA $\mathbf{fst}[\mathcal{S}_@]$.

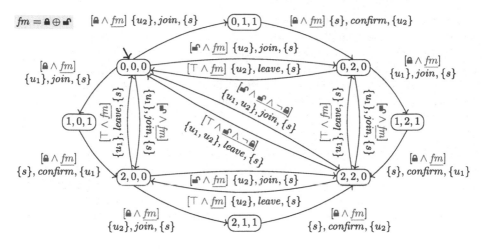

Fig. 5. Generated fETA $\mathsf{fst}_@[\mathcal{S}_@]$

There are many system transitions, for instance

$$t_1 = (0,0,0) \xrightarrow{(\{u_1,u_2\},join,\{s\})} (2,2,0) \text{ and}$$

$$t_2 = (0,0,0) \xrightarrow{(\{u_1,u_2\},join,\{s\})} (1,1,1).$$

For t_1, we have $\hat{\gamma}(t_1) = \bigwedge_{i\in\{1,2\}} \gamma_{u_i}(0 \xrightarrow{join}_{A_{u_i}} 2) \wedge \gamma_s(0 \xrightarrow{join}_{A_s} 0) = \mathbf{\hat{a}} \wedge \mathbf{\hat{a}} \wedge \mathbf{\hat{a}}$. Since $\{\mathbf{\hat{a}}\}$ is the only valid product p such that $t_1 \models \mathsf{fst}(p,join) = ([1,*],[1,1])$—note that only for open access more than one user can join simultaneously—we have $\chi_{P(\mathsf{fst},t_1)} = \mathbf{\hat{a}} \wedge \neg \mathbf{\hat{a}}$ (where $P(\mathsf{fst},t_1) = \{\{\mathbf{\hat{a}}\}\}$). Thus, in summary, $\gamma(t_1) = (\mathbf{\hat{a}} \wedge \mathbf{\hat{a}} \wedge \mathbf{\hat{a}}) \wedge (\mathbf{\hat{a}} \wedge \neg \mathbf{\hat{a}})$. Hence t_1 can only be realised for open access.

For t_2, we have $\hat{\gamma}(t_2) = \mathbf{\hat{a}} \wedge \mathbf{\hat{a}} \wedge \mathbf{\hat{a}}$ and $\chi_{P(\mathsf{fst},t_2)} = \mathbf{\hat{a}} \wedge \neg \mathbf{\hat{a}}$ as before, since $\{\mathbf{\hat{a}}\}$ is the only product p such that $t_2 \models \mathsf{fst}(p,join)$. Therefore, $\gamma(t_2) = (\mathbf{\hat{a}} \wedge \mathbf{\hat{a}} \wedge \mathbf{\hat{a}}) \wedge (\mathbf{\hat{a}} \wedge \neg \mathbf{\hat{a}})$, which reduces to $\bot$ and thus is not realisable by any product.

Figure 5 shows the full generated fETA $\mathsf{fst}[\mathcal{S}_@]$, after removing all unreachable states and all non-realisable transitions t, i.e. $\forall_{p\in[\![fm]\!]} \cdot p \not\models \gamma(t)$. For each transition t in Fig. 5 we present $\gamma(t)$ as a conjunction of (a semantics-preserving simplification of) $\hat{\gamma}(t)$ and an underlined $\chi_{P(\mathsf{fst},t)}$ or $fm = \mathbf{\hat{a}} \oplus \mathbf{\hat{a}}$ if $P(\mathsf{fst},t) = [\![fm]\!]$. The latter is the case in all transitions in which only one user participates. If two users join or leave simultaneously, then $\chi_{P(\mathsf{fst},t)}$ is always $\mathbf{\hat{a}} \wedge \neg \mathbf{\hat{a}}$ as explained above for t_1. (Further reductions are possible for the conjoined $\gamma(t)$.)   ▷

3.3   fETA Versus ETA

fETA are not simple extensions of extended team automata (ETA) introduced in [11]. An ETA is an LTS $\mathsf{st}[\mathcal{S}]$ generated over a system $\mathcal{S}$ of CA by an STS st that explicitly filters the system transitions that satisfy the synchronisation types determined by **st**. Concretely, an ETA **st**$[\mathcal{S}]$ is the LTS $(Q, I, \Sigma, \mathbf{st}[E])$, where Q, I, Σ, and E are induced by $\mathcal{S}$, and $\mathbf{st}[E] = \{t \in E \mid t \models \mathbf{st}(t.a)\}$.

Observe that an STS thus restricts the set of system transitions of a system $\mathcal{S}$, such that the ETA **st**$[\mathcal{S}]$ has only a subset of the transitions of $\mathcal{S}$. Instead, an fSTS and the local transition constraints of the components $\mathcal{A}_i$ impose transition constraints γ on the system transitions of an fSys $\mathcal{S}$ such that the fETA **fst**$[\mathcal{S}]$ has all transitions of $\mathcal{S}$, but appropriately constrained such that many of them will not be realisable anymore for concrete products.

The next theorem shows that, for any valid product p, the projection onto p of the fETA **fst**$[\mathcal{S}]$, generated over the fSys $\mathcal{S}$ by the fSTS **fst**, is the same as the ETA over the projected system $\mathcal{S}^p$ generated by the projected STS **fst**^{p}. This result justifies the soundness of the definition of a generated fETA, in particular of its transition constraint γ. It also shows that the diagram in Fig. 3 commutes.

Theorem 1. *Let $\mathcal{S}$ be an fSys with feature model fm, let **fst** be an fSTS, and let $p \in [\![fm]\!]$ be a valid product. Then:*

$$\mathbf{fst}[\mathcal{S}]^p = \mathbf{fst}^p[\mathcal{S}^p].$$

4   Receptiveness

As explained in Sect. 3 and formalised in Theorem 1, a fETA **fst**$[\mathcal{S}]$ can be projected to a product $p \in [\![fm]\!]$, thus yielding an ETA (i.e. a team) $\mathbf{fst}[\mathcal{S}]^p = \mathbf{fst}^p[\mathcal{S}^p]$. Any such ETA describes the behaviour of a concrete system $\mathcal{S}^p$ whose components (the team members) are coordinated by the synchronisation type specification $\mathbf{st} = \mathbf{fst}^p$. This section analyses communication-safety of such families of ETA. Our aim is to provide criteria on the level of fETA that guarantee communication-safety properties for all ETA obtained by projection (cf. Sect. 4.3).

4.1   Receptiveness for ETA

We focus on the property of receptiveness, which has been studied before in the literature [15,23,30], mainly in the context of peer-to-peer communication. An extension to multi-component communications was studied in [16] and in [11], where also a notion of responsiveness not considered here was introduced. The idea of receptiveness is as follows: whenever, in a reachable state q of an ETA $\mathbf{st}[\mathcal{S}]$, a group of components J is (locally) enabled to perform an output action a such that its synchronous execution is in accordance with the synchronisation type $\mathbf{st}(a)$, we get a receptiveness requirement, written as $\mathbf{rcp}(J, a)@q$. The ETA is *compliant* with this requirement if J can find partners in the team which synchronise with the components in J by taking (receiving) a as input. If reception is immediate, we talk about receptiveness; if the other components first perform some intermediate actions before accepting a, we talk about weak receptiveness.

Formally, receptiveness requirements, compliance, and receptiveness are defined as follows and illustrated in Example 4. We assume a given ETA

$\mathsf{st}[\mathcal{S}] = (Q, I, \Sigma, \mathsf{st}[E])$ generated by the STS st over a system $\mathcal{S} = (\mathcal{N}, (A_i)_{i \in \mathcal{N}})$ of CA A_i.

A *receptiveness requirement* (Req) is an expression $\mathsf{rcp}(J, a)@q$, where $q \in Q$ is a reachable state of $\mathsf{st}[\mathcal{S}]$, $a \in \Sigma$ is an action, and $\emptyset \neq J \subseteq \mathcal{N}$ is a set of component names such that $\forall_{j \in J} \cdot a \in \Sigma_j^! \wedge a \; \mathsf{en}_{A_j}@q_j$ and $\mathsf{st}(a) = (s, r) \Rightarrow |J| \in s \wedge 0 \notin r$. The last condition requires that i) the number of components in J fits the number of allowed senders according to the synchronisation type of a, and ii) at least one receiver must exist according to the synchronisation type of a.[1] Hence our subsequent compliance and receptiveness notions, taken from [11] and formalising the informal explanations above, depend strongly on the synchronisation types of actions.

The ETA $\mathsf{st}[\mathcal{S}]$ is *compliant* with a Req $\mathsf{rcp}(J, a)@q$ if the following holds:

$$\exists_{R \neq \emptyset \text{ and } q' \in Q} \cdot q \xrightarrow{(J,a,R)}_{\mathsf{st}[\mathcal{S}]} q'.$$

The ETA $\mathsf{st}[\mathcal{S}]$ is *weakly compliant* with a Req $\mathsf{rcp}(J, a)@q$ if

$$\exists_{R \neq \emptyset \text{ and } \hat{q}, q' \in Q} \cdot q \xrightarrow{\Lambda_{\backslash J}}^*_{\mathsf{st}[\mathcal{S}]} \hat{q} \xrightarrow{(J,a,R)}_{\mathsf{st}[\mathcal{S}]} q',$$

where $\Lambda_{\backslash J}$ denotes the set of system labels in which no component of J participates. Indeed, only when state $\hat{q}$ is reached, the components of J can actively get rid of their output.

The ETA $\mathsf{st}[\mathcal{S}]$ is *(weakly) receptive* if it is (weakly) compliant with *all* Reqs for $\mathsf{st}[\mathcal{S}]$.

Example 4. Let ETA $\mathsf{fst}^{\oplus}[\mathcal{S}_{\oplus}^{\oplus}]$ be generated by the STS $\mathsf{fst}^{\oplus}$ (i.e. the projection of fst from Example 3 to $\{\oplus\}$) over the system $\mathcal{S}_{\oplus}^{\oplus} = (\mathcal{N}, \{A_{u_1}^{\oplus}, A_{u_2}^{\oplus}, A_s^{\oplus}\})$ of Example 1, with $\mathsf{fst}^{\oplus}(join) = \mathsf{fst}^{\oplus}(confirm) = \mathsf{fst}^{\oplus}(leave) = ([1,1], [1,1])$. In the initial global state $(0, 0, 0)$ both users are enabled to execute output action *join*, but not simultaneously. Hence, we get two Reqs $\mathsf{rcp}(\{u_i\}, join)@(0, 0, 0)$, one for each $i \in \{1, 2\}$. The ETA $\mathsf{fst}^{\oplus}[\mathcal{S}_{\oplus}^{\oplus}]$ is compliant with both Reqs because $(0, 0, 0) \xrightarrow{(\{u_1\}, join, \{s\})}_{\mathsf{fst}^{\oplus}[\mathcal{S}_{\oplus}^{\oplus}]} (1, 0, 1)$ and $(0, 0, 0) \xrightarrow{(\{u_2\}, join, \{s\})}_{\mathsf{fst}^{\oplus}[\mathcal{S}_{\oplus}^{\oplus}]} (0, 1, 1)$. Now assume that user $A_{u_1}^{\oplus}$ joins. Then $\mathsf{fst}^{\oplus}[\mathcal{S}_{\oplus}^{\oplus}]$ ends up in state $(1, 0, 1)$, where user $A_{u_2}^{\oplus}$ may decide to join, i.e. there is a Req $\mathsf{rcp}(\{u_2\}, join)@(1, 0, 1)$. But the server is not yet ready for $A_{u_2}^{\oplus}$ as it first needs to send a confirmation to $A_{u_1}^{\oplus}$. Therefore $\mathsf{fst}^{\oplus}[\mathcal{S}_{\oplus}^{\oplus}]$ is not compliant with $\mathsf{rcp}(\{u_2\}, join)@(1, 0, 1)$, but it is weakly compliant with this Req. We can show that the ETA $\mathsf{fst}^{\oplus}[\mathcal{S}_{\oplus}^{\oplus}]$ is either compliant or weakly compliant with any Req and therefore it is weakly receptive.

Next, consider ETA $\mathsf{fst}^{\odot}[\mathcal{S}_{\oplus}^{\odot}]$ generated by the STS $\mathsf{fst}^{\odot}$ over the system $\mathcal{S}_{\oplus}^{\odot} = (\mathcal{N}, \{A_{u_1}^{\odot}, A_{u_2}^{\odot}, A_s^{\odot}\})$ of Example 1 with $\mathsf{fst}^{\odot}(join) = \mathsf{fst}^{\odot}(leave) = ([1, *], [1, 1])$. In state $(0, 0, 0)$, both users are enabled to output *join*. Therefore, according to the sending multiplicity $[1, *]$ of $\mathsf{fst}^{\odot}(join)$, there are three Reqs for that state, among which $\mathsf{rcp}(\{u_1, u_2\}, join)@(0, 0, 0)$. Note that $\mathsf{fst}^{\odot}[\mathcal{S}_{\oplus}^{\odot}]$ is compliant with

---

[1] Otherwise, the components in J could simply output a without reception.

this Req due to the team transition $(0,0,0) \xrightarrow{(\{u_1,u_2\},join,\{s\})}_{\textbf{fst}^{\textbf{a}}[\mathcal{S}_{\textbf{@}}^{\textbf{a}}]} (1,1,1)$. In fact, the ETA $\textbf{fst}^{\textbf{a}}[\mathcal{S}_{\textbf{@}}^{\textbf{a}}]$ is compliant with all Reqs and therefore it is receptive. ▷

4.2 Featured Receptiveness for fETA

We now turn to fETA and discuss how the notions of receptiveness requirements, compliance, and receptiveness can be transferred to the feature level. We assume a given fETA $\textbf{fst}[\mathcal{S}] = (Q, I, \Sigma, E, F, fm, \gamma)$ generated by the fSTS $\textbf{fst}$ over an fSys $\mathcal{S} = (\mathcal{N}, (A_i)_{i \in \mathcal{N}})$, with fCA A_i. The crucial difference with the case of ETA is that fETA are based on syntactic specifications modelling families of teams. Hence a Req $\textbf{rcp}(J, a)@q$ formulated for an ETA cannot be formulated for a fETA as it is. Instead, it must take into account the valid products p of the family for which the requirement is meaningful. For this purpose, we propose to complement $\textbf{rcp}(J, a)@q$ by a syntactic application condition, resulting in a *featured receptiveness requirement* (fReq), written as $[\textbf{prod}(J, a, q)]\,\textbf{rcp}(J, a)@q$. Herein $\textbf{prod}(J, a, q)$ is a feature expression, which characterises the set of valid products for which the Req $\textbf{rcp}(J, a)@q$ is applicable for $\textbf{fst}[\mathcal{S}]^p$. The expression $\textbf{prod}(J, a, q) = \textbf{fe}(J, a, q) \wedge \chi_{P(\textbf{fst}, J, a)} \wedge \chi_{P(q)}$ consists of the following parts:

1. $\textbf{fe}(J, a, q) = \bigwedge_{j \in J} \bigvee \gamma_j(q_j \xrightarrow{a}_{A_j} q_j')$ combines the feature expressions of all transitions of components A_j ($j \in J$) with action a and starting in the local state q_j. For any fCA A_j, the disjunction $\bigvee \gamma_j(q_j \xrightarrow{a}_{A_j} q_j')$ ranges over the feature expressions of all local transitions of A_j starting in q_j and labelled with a. Hence, if there are more such transitions it is sufficient if one of them is realised (in a projection of A_j). Thus $\textbf{fe}(J, a, q)$ characterises those products p for which outgoing transitions with output a are realisable in the local states q_j of A_j and hence enabled in q_j in the projected component A_j^p.
2. $\chi_{P(\textbf{fst}, J, a)}$ is the feature expression which characterises (cf. Sect. 2) the set $P(\textbf{fst}, J, a) = \{p \in \llbracket fm \rrbracket \mid \textbf{fst}(p, a) = (s, r) \Rightarrow |J| \in s \wedge 0 \notin r\}$. This is the set of all products p such that $\textbf{fst}(p, a)$ allows $|J|$ as number of senders and requires at least one receiver.
3. $\chi_{P(q)}$ is the feature expression which characterises the set $P(q)$ of products for which state q is reachable by transitions of $\textbf{fst}[\mathcal{S}]$ whose constraints are satisfied by p, i.e. $P(q) = \{p \in \llbracket fm \rrbracket \mid \exists_{q_0 \in I} \cdot q_0 \xrightarrow{l_1}_{\textbf{fst}[\mathcal{S}]} q_1 \xrightarrow{l_2} \ldots \xrightarrow{l_n}_{\textbf{fst}[\mathcal{S}]} q_n = q$ for some $n \geq 0$, and $p \models \gamma(q_{i-1} \xrightarrow{l_i}_{\textbf{fst}[\mathcal{S}]} q_i)$ for $i = 1, \ldots, n\}$.

In summary, an fReq for $\textbf{fst}[\mathcal{S}]$ has the form $[\textbf{prod}(J, a, q)]\,\textbf{rcp}(J, a)@q$, where $q \in Q$ is a reachable state of $\textbf{fst}[\mathcal{S}]$, $a \in \Sigma$, $\emptyset \neq J \subseteq \mathcal{N}$ is a set of component names such that $\forall_{j \in J} \cdot a \in \Sigma_j^! \wedge a\ \textbf{en}_{A_j}@q_j$, and $\textbf{prod}(J, a, q)$ is a satisfiable feature expression as defined above. Note that $\models \textbf{prod}(J, a, q) \rightarrow fm$, because $P(\textbf{fst}, J, a)$ in item 2 (and also $P(q)$ in item 3) is a subset of $\llbracket fm \rrbracket$.

The following lemma provides a formal relation between Reqs and fReqs.

Lemma 1. *For all products p it holds: $[\textbf{prod}(J, a, q)]\,\textbf{rcp}(J, a)@q$ is an fReq for $\textbf{fst}[\mathcal{S}]$ and $p \models \textbf{prod}(J, a, q)$ iff $p \in \llbracket fm \rrbracket$ and $\textbf{rcp}(J, a)@q$ is a Req for $\textbf{fst}[\mathcal{S}]^p$.*

Example 5. Figure 6 shows an excerpt of the fETA $\mathbf{fst}[\mathcal{S}_@]$ in Fig. 5 depicting the fReqs for states $(0,0,0)$, $(0,1,1)$, and $(0,2,0)$. First note that an output of *join* is enabled at local state 0 in both components A_{u_1} and A_{u_2}. For $\mathbf{rcp}(\{u_1\}, join)$ at state $(0,0,0)$ we get $\mathbf{fe}(\{u_1\}, join, (0,0,0)) = 🔒 \vee 🔓$ according to the constraints of both *join* transitions in A_{u_1}. Moreover, $P(\mathbf{fst}, \{u_1\}, join) = \{\{🔒\}, \{🔓\}\} = [\![fm]\!]$ and therefore $\chi_{P(\mathbf{fst},\{u_1\},join)}$ is equivalent to *fm*. Also $P(0,0,0) = \{\{🔒\}, \{🔓\}\}$ since state $(0,0,0)$ is reachable in both products. So $\mathbf{prod}(\{u_1\}, join, (0,0,0)) = (🔒 \vee 🔓) \wedge fm \wedge fm$, which reduces to $fm = 🔒 \oplus 🔓$. Thus we get the fReq $[🔒 \oplus 🔓]\,\mathbf{rcp}(\{u_1\}, join)$ at $(0,0,0)$. The case of $\{u_2\}$ is analogous.

Considering a possible simultaneous output of *join* by u_1 and u_2 we get $\mathbf{fe}(\{u_1, u_2\}, join, (0,0,0)) = (🔒 \vee 🔓) \vee (🔒 \vee 🔓)$. And we get $P(\mathbf{fst}, \{u_1, u_2\}, join) = \{\{🔓\}\}$, since only for the product $\{🔓\}$ a synchronisation of several users is allowed. Therefore $\chi_{P(\mathbf{fst},\{u_1,u_2\},join)} = 🔓 \wedge \neg 🔒$. As above, $\chi_{P(0,0,0)} = fm$. Thus $\mathbf{prod}(\{u_1, u_2\}, join, (0,0,0)) = (🔒 \vee 🔓) \wedge (🔓 \wedge \neg 🔒) \wedge fm$, which reduces to $🔓 \wedge \neg 🔒$. Hence we get the fReq $[🔓 \wedge \neg 🔒]\,\mathbf{rcp}(\{u_1, u_2\}, join)$ at $(0,0,0)$.

An interesting case is $[🔒 \wedge \neg 🔓]\,\mathbf{rcp}(\{u_1\}, join)$ at $(0,1,1)$. Here $\mathbf{fe}(\{u_1\}, join, (0,1,1))$ is again $🔒 \vee 🔓$ and $\chi_{P(\mathbf{fst},\{u_1\},join)}$ is equivalent to *fm*. However, the state $(0,1,1)$ is only reachable in the product $\{🔒\}$, i.e. $P(0,1,1) = \{\{🔒\}\}$. Therefore, $\chi_{P(0,1,1)} = 🔒 \wedge \neg 🔓$. In summary, $\mathbf{prod}(\{u_1, u_2\}, join, (0,1,1)) = (🔒 \wedge 🔓) \wedge fm \wedge (🔒 \wedge \neg 🔓)$, which reduces to $(🔒 \wedge \neg 🔓)$. The other fReqs are computed similarly. $\triangleright$

Next, we define featured compliance with an fReq. We use a logical formulation which, as we shall see, captures compliance for the whole family of products.

The fETA $\mathbf{fst}[\mathcal{S}]$ is *featured compliant* with an fReq $[\psi]\,\mathbf{rcp}(J, a)@q$ if for some $n \geq 1$ and for $k = 1, \dots, n$ there exist transitions $t^k = q \xrightarrow{(J, a, R^k)}_{\mathbf{fst}[\mathcal{S}]} q^k$ with $R^k \neq \emptyset$ such that $\models \psi \to \bigvee_{k \in \{1,\dots,n\}} \gamma(t^k)$.

The definition of featured compliance can be unfolded by considering all $p \in [\![fm]\!]$. This shows the relationship to the compliance notion for ETA.

Lemma 2. *Let* $[\psi]\,\mathbf{rcp}(J, a)@q$ *be an fReq for the fETA* $\mathbf{fst}[\mathcal{S}]$. *Then:*

$$\begin{bmatrix} \mathbf{fst}[\mathcal{S}] \text{ is featured compliant} \\ \text{with } [\psi]\,\mathbf{rcp}(J, a)@q \end{bmatrix} \Leftrightarrow \begin{bmatrix} \forall_{p \subseteq F \text{ with } p \models \psi} \cdot \ \exists_{R \neq \emptyset \text{ and } q' \in Q} \cdot \\ q \xrightarrow{(J, a, R)}_{\mathbf{fst}[\mathcal{S}]} q' \text{ and } p \models \gamma(q \xrightarrow{(J, a, R)}_{\mathbf{fst}[\mathcal{S}]} q') \end{bmatrix}$$

The next definition generalises featured compliance to featured weak compliance. It is a technical but straightforward extension that transfers the concept of weak receptiveness to the featured level.

The fETA $\mathbf{fst}[\mathcal{S}]$ is *featured weakly compliant* with an fReq $[\psi]\,\mathbf{rcp}(J, a)@q$ if for some $n \geq 1$ and for $k = 1, \dots, n$ there exist sequences σ^k of transitions

$$\sigma^k = q_0^k \xrightarrow{(S_0^k, a_0^k, R_0^k)}_{\mathbf{fst}[\mathcal{S}]} q_1^k \ \cdots \ q_{m_k}^k \xrightarrow{(S_{m_k}^k, u, R_{m_k}^k)}_{\mathbf{fst}[\mathcal{S}]} q_{m_k+1}^k$$

with $q_0^k = q, m_k \geq 0$, $(S_i^k \cup R_i^k) \cap J = \emptyset$ for $i = 0, \dots, m_{k-1}$, $R_i^k \neq \emptyset$ for $i = 0, \dots, m_k$, and $S_{m_k}^k = J$ such that

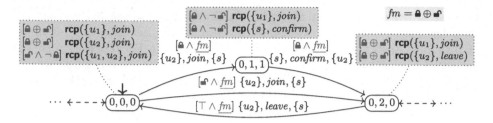

Fig. 6. Part of $\mathbf{fst}[\mathcal{S}_@]$ from Fig. 5 enriched with Reqs

$$\models \psi \rightarrow \bigvee_{k \in \{1,\dots,n\}} \bigwedge_{i \in \{0,\dots,m_k\}} \gamma(q_i^k \xrightarrow{(S_i^k, a_i^k, R_i^k)}_{\mathbf{fst}[\mathcal{S}]} q_{i+1}^k).$$

We remark that Lemma 2 can be extended in a straightforward way to characterise featured weak compliance.

The fETA $\mathbf{fst}[\mathcal{S}]$ is *featured (weakly) receptive* if it is featured (weakly) compliant with all fReqs for $\mathbf{fst}[\mathcal{S}]$.

Example 6. We consider some fReqs for the fETA $\mathbf{fst}[\mathcal{S}_@]$ as depicted in Fig. 6. The first fReq is $[🔒 \oplus 🔓]\, \mathbf{rcp}(\{u_1\}, join)@(0,0,0)$. As we can see in Fig. 5, there are two transitions, say t_1, t_2, in $\mathbf{fst}[\mathcal{S}_@]$ with source state $(0,0,0)$ and label $(\{u_1\}, join, \{s\})$, such that $\gamma(t_1) = 🔒 \wedge fm$ and $\gamma(t_2) = 🔓 \wedge fm$. Hence, for checking featured compliance with this fReq we have to prove:

$$\models 🔒 \oplus 🔓 \rightarrow (🔒 \wedge fm) \vee (🔓 \wedge fm).$$

But this is easy, since the conclusion is equivalent to $fm = 🔒 \oplus 🔓$. To achieve this it is essential to have the disjunction of $\gamma(t_1)$ and $\gamma(t_2)$ in the conclusion.

As a second fReq we consider $[🔓 \wedge \neg 🔒]\, \mathbf{rcp}(\{u_1, u_2\}, join)@(0,0,0)$. As we can see in Fig. 5, there is one transition in $\mathbf{fst}[\mathcal{S}_@]$ with source state $(0,0,0)$ and label $(\{u_1, u_2\}, join, \{s\})$, which has the transition constraint $🔓 \wedge \neg 🔒$. Featured compliance with this fReq holds trivially, since

$$\models 🔓 \wedge \neg 🔒 \rightarrow 🔓 \wedge \neg 🔒.$$

As a last example, consider the (fReq) $[🔒 \wedge \neg 🔓]\, \mathbf{rcp}(\{u_1\}, join)@(0,1,1)$. In state $(0,1,1)$, no transition with action $join$ can be performed by the fETA $\mathbf{fst}[\mathcal{S}_@]$. Therefore featured compliance does not hold. However, featured weak compliance holds for the following reasons. We take $n = 1$ (in the definition of featured weak compliance) and select, in Fig. 5, the transition sequence

$$(0,1,1) \xrightarrow{[🔒 \wedge fm](\{s\}, confirm, \{u_2\})} (0,2,0) \xrightarrow{[🔒 \wedge fm](\{u_1\}, join, \{s\})} (1,2,1).$$

Then, we get the following proof obligation (conjoining the constraints of the two consecutive transitions in the conclusion): $\models (🔒 \wedge \neg 🔓) \rightarrow (🔒 \wedge fm) \wedge (🔒 \wedge fm)$. Obviously, this holds since the conclusion reduces to $🔒 \wedge \neg 🔓$. We can show that the fETA $\mathbf{fst}[\mathcal{S}_@]$ is either featured compliant or featured weakly compliant with any fReq and therefore it is featured weakly receptive.   ▷

4.3   From Featured Receptiveness to Receptiveness

This section presents our main result. We show that instead of checking product-wise each member of a family of product configurations for (weak) receptiveness, it is sufficient to verify once featured (weak) receptiveness for the family model. We can even show that this technique is not only sound but also complete in the sense, that if we disprove featured (weak) receptiveness on the family level, then there will be a product for which the projection is not (weakly) receptive.

Theorem 2. *Let S be an fSys with feature model fm, let* **fst** *be an fSTS, and let* **fst**$[S]$ *be its generated fETA. Then:*

$$\Big[\mathbf{fst}[S] \text{ is featured (weakly) receptive}\Big] \Leftrightarrow \Big[\forall_{p \in [\![fm]\!]} \cdot \mathbf{fst}[S]^p \text{ is (weakly) receptive}\Big]$$

Example 7. In Example 6 we showed that the fETA **fst**$[S_@]$ is featured weakly receptive. Therefore, by applying Theorem 2, we know that for both products $\{\mathbf{a}\}$ and $\{\mathbf{a}\}$, the ETA **fst**$^a[S_@^a]$ and **fst**$^a[S_@^a]$ are weakly receptive (a result which we checked product-wise in Example 4).   ▷

Note on Complexity. Note that an fReq for **fst**$[S]$ necessarily involves a syntactic application condition, which is a feature expression that characterises the set of valid products p for which the featureless Req is applicable for **fst**$[S]^p$. Part of this feature expression is a characterisation $\chi_{P(q)}$ of the set $P(q)$ of products for which state q is reachable by transitions of **fst**$[S]$ whose constraints are satisfied by p, which requires a reachability check for q. This may seem computationally expensive. However, it has been shown that static analysis of properties of fTSs that concern the reachability of states and transitions in valid products (LTSs) is feasible in reasonable time even for fTSs of considerable size, by reducing the analysis to SAT solving [8]. In fact, while SAT solving is NP-complete, SAT solvers are effectively used for static analysis of feature models with hundreds of thousands of clauses and tens of thousands of variables [32,33]. Finally, we note that the results presented in this section are still sound, but not complete, without the aforementioned characterisation of $P(q)$.

5   Tool Support

We implemented a prototypical tool to specify and analyse fETA. This requires to define an fSys over a set of fCA, a shared feature model, and an fSTS. The tool can be used online and downloaded at https://github.com/arcalab/team-a. The interface is organised by 5 widgets (illustrated in Fig. 7): ① a text editor to specify a fETA, using a dedicated domain-specific language; ② an fTS view of the fETA, together with the fReqs generated automatically for each state, similar to Fig. 6; ③ a set of example fETA; ④ a view of each individual fCA, similar to Fig. 1; and ⑤ some statistics of the various models, including the number of states, transitions, features, and products.

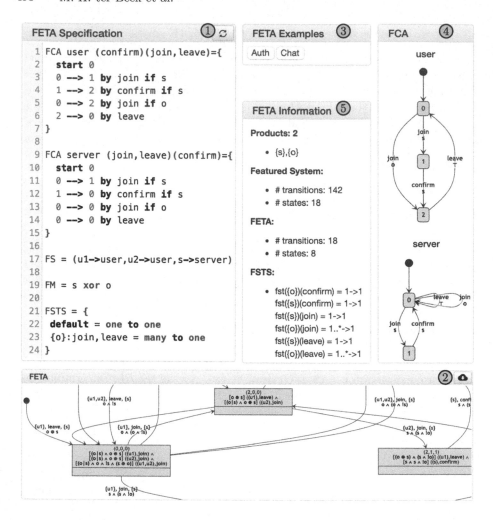

Fig. 7. Screenshots of the widgets in the online tool for (fETA)

The tool is written in Scala and it uses the Play Framework to generate an interactive website using a client-server architecture. The Scala code is compiled into JavaScript using `Scala.js` to run on the client side, and into JVM binaries that run on the server side. The server side is currently needed to use an off-the-shelf Java library, `Sat4j`, to find all products that satisfy a feature model.

6   Conclusion

We introduced featured team automata to specify and analyse systems of featured component automata and to explore composition and communication-safety. We showed that family-based analysis of receptiveness (no message loss) suffices to study receptiveness of product configurations. We implemented our theory in a prototypical tool.

In the future, we intend to extend our theory to address i) responsiveness, i.e. no indefinite waiting for input, and ii) compositionality, i.e. extend fETA to composition of systems (that behaves well with fSTSs) and investigate conditions under which communication safety is preserved by fETA composition. Moreover, we will further develop the tool and analyse the practical impact of fETA on the basis of larger case studies. This involves a thorough study of the efficiency of featured receptiveness checking compared to product-wise checking of receptiveness. Finally, we aim to implement a family-based analysis algorithm that computes, for a given fETA, the set of all product configurations that yield communication-safe systems.

Acknowledgements. Ter Beek received funding from the MIUR PRIN 2017FTXR7S project IT MaTTerS (Methods and Tools for Trustworthy Smart Systems). Cledou and Proença received funding from the ERDF – European Regional Development Fund through the Operational Programme for Competitiveness and Internationalisation – COMPETE 2020 Programme – and by National Funds through the Portuguese funding agency, FCT – Fundação para a Ciência e a Tecnologia (project DaVinci, POCI-01-0145-FEDER-029946, PTDC/CCI-COM/29946/2017). Proença also received National Funds through FCT/MCTES, within the CISTER Research Unit (UIDP/UIDB/04234/2020); by the Norte Portugal Regional Operational Programme – NORTE 2020 (project REASSURE, NORTE-01-0145-FEDER-028550) under the Portugal 2020 Partnership Agreement, through ERDF the FCT; and European Funds through the ECSEL Joint Undertaking (JU) under grant agreement No. 876852 (project VALU3S).

References

1. Apel, S., Batory, D., Kästner, C., Saake, G.: Feature-Oriented Software Product Lines: Concepts and Implementation. Springer, Heidelberg (2013). https://doi.org/10.1007/978-3-642-37521-7
2. Asirelli, P., ter Beek, M.H., Fantechi, A., Gnesi, S.: Formal description of variability in product families. In: Proceedings of the 15th International Software Product Lines Conference (SPLC), pp. 130–139. IEEE (2011). https://doi.org/10.1109/SPLC.2011.34
3. Basile, D., et al.: Controller synthesis of service contracts with variability. Sci. Comput. Program. **187**, 102344 (2020). https://doi.org/10.1016/j.scico.2019.102344
4. Basile, D., Di Giandomenico, F., Gnesi, S., Degano, P., Ferrari, G.L.: Specifying variability in service contracts. In: Proceedings of the 11th International Workshop on Variability Modelling of Software-Intensive Systems (VaMoS), pp. 20–27. ACM (2017). https://doi.org/10.1145/3023956.3023965
5. Bauer, S.S., Mayer, P., Schroeder, A., Hennicker, R.: On weak modal compatibility, refinement, and the MIO workbench. In: Esparza, J., Majumdar, R. (eds.) TACAS 2010. LNCS, vol. 6015, pp. 175–189. Springer, Heidelberg (2010). https://doi.org/10.1007/978-3-642-12002-2_15

6. ter Beek, M.H., Carmona, J., Hennicker, R., Kleijn, J.: Communication requirements for team automata. In: Jacquet, J.-M., Massink, M. (eds.) COORDINATION 2017. LNCS, vol. 10319, pp. 256–277. Springer, Cham (2017). https://doi.org/10.1007/978-3-319-59746-1_14

7. ter Beek, M.H., Cledou, G., Hennicker, R., Proença, J.: Featured Team Automata. arXiv:2108.01784 (August 2021)

8. ter Beek, M.H., Damiani, F., Lienhardt, M., Mazzanti, F., Paolini, L.: Efficient static analysis and verification of featured transition systems. Empir. Softw. Eng. **10** (2021). https://doi.org/10.1007/s10664-020-09930-8

9. ter Beek, M.H., Ellis, C.A., Kleijn, J., Rozenberg, G.: Synchronizations in team automata for groupware systems. Comput. Sup. Coop. Work **12**(1), 21–69 (2003). https://doi.org/10.1023/A:1022407907596

10. ter Beek, M.H., Fantechi, A., Gnesi, S., Mazzanti, F.: Modelling and analysing variability in product families: model checking of modal transition systems with variability constraints. J. Log. Algebr. Methods. Program. **85**(2), 287–315 (2016). https://doi.org/10.1016/j.jlamp.2015.11.006

11. ter Beek, M.H., Hennicker, R., Kleijn, J.: Compositionality of safe communication in systems of team automata. In: Pun, V.K.I., Stolz, V., Simao, A. (eds.) ICTAC 2020. LNCS, vol. 12545, pp. 200–220. Springer, Cham (2020). https://doi.org/10.1007/978-3-030-64276-1_11

12. ter Beek, M.H., Kleijn, J.: Modularity for teams of I/O automata. Inf. Process. Lett. **95**(5), 487–495 (2005). https://doi.org/10.1016/j.ipl.2005.05.012

13. ter Beek, M.H., van Loo, S., de Vink, E.P., Willemse, T.A.C.: Family-based SPL model checking using parity games with variability. In: FASE 2020. LNCS, vol. 12076, pp. 245–265. Springer, Cham (2020). https://doi.org/10.1007/978-3-030-45234-6_12

14. ter Beek, M.H., de Vink, E.P., Willemse, T.A.C.: Family-based model checking with mCRL2. In: Huisman, M., Rubin, J. (eds.) FASE 2017. LNCS, vol. 10202, pp. 387–405. Springer, Heidelberg (2017). https://doi.org/10.1007/978-3-662-54494-5_23

15. Carmona, J., Cortadella, J.: Input/output compatibility of reactive systems. In: Aagaard, M.D., O'Leary, J.W. (eds.) FMCAD 2002. LNCS, vol. 2517, pp. 360–377. Springer, Heidelberg (2002). https://doi.org/10.1007/3-540-36126-X_22

16. Carmona, J., Kleijn, J.: Compatibility in a multi-component environment. Theor. Comput. Sci. **484**, 1–15 (2013). https://doi.org/10.1016/j.tcs.2013.03.006

17. Češka, M., Jansen, N., Junges, S., Katoen, J.-P.: Shepherding hordes of Markov chains. In: Vojnar, T., Zhang, L. (eds.) TACAS 2019, Part II. LNCS, vol. 11428, pp. 172–190. Springer, Cham (2019). https://doi.org/10.1007/978-3-030-17465-1_10

18. Chrszon, P., Dubslaff, C., Klüppelholz, S., Baier, C.: ProFeat: feature-oriented engineering for family-based probabilistic model checking. Form. Asp. Comput. **30**(1), 45–75 (2017). https://doi.org/10.1007/s00165-017-0432-4

19. Classen, A.: Modelling and Model Checking Variability-Intensive Systems. Ph.D. thesis, University of Namur (2011). http://hdl.handle.net/2078.2/90863

20. Classen, A., Cordy, M., Schobbens, P.Y., Heymans, P., Legay, A., Raskin, J.F.: Featured transition systems: foundations for verifying variability-intensive systems and their application to LTL model checking. IEEE Trans. Softw. Eng. **39**(8), 1069–1089 (2013). https://doi.org/10.1109/TSE.2012.86

21. Classen, A., Heymans, P., Schobbens, P.Y., Legay, A., Raskin, J.F.: Model checking lots of systems: efficient verification of temporal properties in software product lines. In: Proceedings of the 32nd International Conference on Software Engineering (ICSE), pp. 335–344. ACM (2010). https://doi.org/10.1145/1806799.1806850

22. Damiani, F., Schaefer, I.: Family-based analysis of type safety for delta-oriented software product lines. In: Margaria, T., Steffen, B. (eds.) ISoLA 2012, Part I. LNCS, vol. 7609, pp. 193–207. Springer, Heidelberg (2012). https://doi.org/10.1007/978-3-642-34026-0_15

23. de Alfaro, L., Henzinger, T.A.: Interface automata. In: Proceedings of the 8th European Software Engineering Conference held jointly with 9th ACM SIGSOFT International Symposium on Foundations of Software Engineering (ESEC/FSE), pp. 109–120. ACM (2001). https://doi.org/10.1145/503209.503226

24. Dimovski, A.S.: CTL* family-based model checking using variability abstractions and modal transition systems. Int. J. Softw. Tools Technol. Transf. **22**(1), 35–55 (2019). https://doi.org/10.1007/s10009-019-00528-0

25. Dimovski, A.S., Al-Sibahi, A.S., Brabrand, C., Wąsowski, A.: Efficient family-based model checking via variability abstractions. Int. J. Softw. Tools Technol. Transf. **19**(5), 585–603 (2016). https://doi.org/10.1007/s10009-016-0425-2

26. Ellis, C.A.: Team automata for groupware systems. In: Proceedings of the 1st International ACM SIGGROUP Conference on Supporting Group Work (GROUP), pp. 415–424. ACM (1997). https://doi.org/10.1145/266838.267363

27. Fantechi, A., Gnesi, S.: A behavioural model for product families. In: Proceedings of the 6th Joint Meeting of the European Software Engineering Conference and the ACM SIGSOFT International Symposium on Foundations of Software Engineering (ESEC/FSE), pp. 521–524. ACM (2007). https://doi.org/10.1145/1287624.1287700

28. Fischbein, D., Uchitel, S., Braberman, V.A.: A foundation for behavioural conformance in software product line architectures. In: Proceedings of the ISSTA Workshop on Role of Software Architecture for Testing and Analysis (ROSATEA), pp. 39–48. ACM (2006). https://doi.org/10.1145/1147249.1147254

29. Hennicker, R., Bidoit, M.: Compatibility properties of synchronously and asynchronously communicating components. Log. Methods Comput. Sci. **14**(1), 1–31 (2018). https://doi.org/10.23638/LMCS-14(1:1)2018

30. Larsen, K.G., Nyman, U., Wąsowski, A.: Modal I/O automata for interface and product line theories. In: De Nicola, R. (ed.) ESOP 2007. LNCS, vol. 4421, pp. 64–79. Springer, Heidelberg (2007). https://doi.org/10.1007/978-3-540-71316-6_6

31. Lauenroth, K., Pohl, K., Töhning, S.: Model checking of domain artifacts in product line engineering. In: Proceedings of the 24th International Conference on Automated Software Engineering (ASE), pp. 269–280. IEEE (2009). https://doi.org/10.1109/ASE.2009.16

32. Liang, J.H., Ganesh, V., Czarnecki, K., Raman, V.: SAT-based Analysis of large real-world feature models is easy. In: Proceedings of the 19th International Software Product Line Conference (SPLC), pp. 91–100. ACM (2015). https://doi.org/10.1145/2791060.2791070

33. Mendonça, M., Wąsowski, A., Czarnecki, K.: SAT-based analysis of feature models is easy. In: Proceedings of the 13th International Software Product Line Conference (SPLC), pp. 231–240. ACM (2009)

34. Muschevici, R., Proença, J., Clarke, D.: Feature nets: behavioural modelling of software product lines. Softw. Syst. Model. **15**(4), 1181–1206 (2015). https://doi.org/10.1007/s10270-015-0475-z

35. Muschevici, R., Proença, J., Clarke, D.: Modular modelling of software product lines with feature nets. In: Barthe, G., Pardo, A., Schneider, G. (eds.) SEFM 2011. LNCS, vol. 7041, pp. 318–333. Springer, Heidelberg (2011). https://doi.org/10.1007/978-3-642-24690-6_22

36. Schobbens, P., Heymans, P., Trigaux, J.C., Bontemps, Y.: Feature diagrams: a survey and a formal semantics. In: Proceedings of the 14th IEEE International Conference on Requirements Engineering (RE), pp. 136–145. IEEE (2006). https://doi.org/10.1109/RE.2006.23
37. Thüm, T., Apel, S., Kästner, C., Schaefer, I., Saake, G.: A classification and survey of analysis strategies for software product lines. ACM Comput. Surv. **47**(1), 6 (2014). https://doi.org/10.1145/2580950
38. Thüm, T., Schaefer, I., Hentschel, M., Apel, S.: Family-based deductive verification of software product lines. In: Proceedings of the 11th International Conference on Generative Programming and Component Engineering (GPCE), pp. 11–20. ACM (2012). https://doi.org/10.1145/2371401.2371404

From Partial to Global Assume-Guarantee Contracts: Compositional Realizability Analysis in FRET

Anastasia Mavridou[1]($\boxtimes$), Andreas Katis[1], Dimitra Giannakopoulou[2],
David Kooi[3], Thomas Pressburger[2], and Michael W. Whalen[4]

[1] KBR, NASA Ames Research Center, Moffett Field, CA, USA
[2] NASA Ames Research Center, Moffett Field, CA, USA
{anastasia.mavridou,andreas.katis,dimitra.giannakopoulou,
tom.pressburger}@nasa.gov
[3] University of California, Santa Cruz, CA, USA
dkooi@ucsc.edu
[4] University of Minnesota, Minneapolis, MN, USA
whalen@cs.umn.edu

Abstract. Realizability checking refers to the formal procedure that aims to determine whether an implementation exists, always complying to a set of requirements, regardless of the stimuli provided by the system's environment. Such a check is essential to ensure that the specification does not allow behavior that can force the system to violate safety constraints. In this paper, we present an approach that decomposes realizability checking into smaller, more tractable problems. More specifically, our approach automatically partitions specifications into sets of non-interfering requirements. We prove that checking whether a specification is realizable reduces to checking that each partition is realizable. We have integrated realizability checking and implemented our decomposition approach within the open-source Formal Requirements Elicitation Tool (FRET). A FRET user may check the realizability of a specification monolithically or compositionally. We evaluate our approach by comparing monolithic and compositional checking and showcase the strengths of our decomposition approach on a variety of industrial-level case studies.

1 Introduction

Defining requirements for a complex system is a challenging, error-prone task. The focus of this paper is on ensuring consistency of system component requirements, thus building a solid foundation for subsequent system-level analysis [4,12,13,55]. For *reactive* systems, which interact with an uncontrollable environment, consistency must be established for all reasonable inputs from the environment, leading to the notion of realizability [50]. Realizability checking, however, comes with challenges. While optimal algorithms exist for finite state

© Springer Nature Switzerland AG 2021
M. Huisman et al. (Eds.): FM 2021, LNCS 13047, pp. 503–523, 2021.
https://doi.org/10.1007/978-3-030-90870-6_27

problems over subsets of Linear Temporal Logic specifications (LTL) [18,49], scalability issues can make the analysis impractical for realistic systems, and the use of infinite data types can render the entire problem undecidable [20,29].

This work makes the following contributions for checking realizability:

1. a novel compositional theoretical framework to check realizability of a global contract through smaller, more tractable parts, named *partial contracts*;
2. an algorithm that identifies, for a global system contract, equivalent partial contracts that can be checked for realizability instead of the global one;
3. implementation of our framework in the open-source Formal Requirements Elicitation Tool FRET [23], and its evaluation on industrial-level projects.

Partial contracts describe requirements that observe only a subset of a global system state. Partial-contract realizability then introduces the notion of realizability of a system with respect to a set of partial contracts. We show that partial-contract realizability is equivalent to checking that every partial contract is realizable, when partial contracts are non-interfering, meaning that they observe disjoint sets of system state variables. Finally, we provide conditions under which checking realizability of a global contract is equivalent to partial-contract realizability. This equivalence enables us to: 1) ensure realizability of a global contract by checking that each one of its partial contracts is realizable, and 2) when a partial contract is unrealizable, conclude that the global contract is also unrealizable.

Our decomposition algorithm automatically computes partial contracts that fit the conditions of our theory, based on the notion of connected components for undirected graphs. The evaluation of our compositional approach showcases several benefits as compared to monolithic realizability analysis. Decomposition is key for both scalability and performance of realizability analysis. Moreover, when both monolithic and compositional analyses fail to complete, compositional analysis may still be able to return results for some of the partial contracts. Finally, for unrealizable contracts, our approach is able to attribute the causes of unrealizability to partial contracts, which are generally easier to debug.

Specification decomposition has also been studied, independently, in a recent work by Finkbeiner et al. [17], in the context of reactive synthesis. Even though the theoretical formulation of the two works is different due to the respective settings in which they have been developed, they explore similar avenues. We dedicate Subsect. 6.2 of our evaluation section to providing a detailed comparison of the two approaches.

2   Liquid Mixer System Example

We use as running example the controller of a liquid mixing system [35] (see Fig. 1), whose behavior must satisfy the 12 requirements shown in Table 1. To relate our approach with the EARS-CTRL approach presented in [35], we took the 12 requirements expressed in EARS-CTRL and translated them into FRETISH, the requirements language of FRET.

Table 1. Liquid mixer system requirements in English and FRETISH.

Req ID	Original Requirement Text	Requirement in FRETish
[LM-001]	While not liquid level 1 is reached, when start button is pressed the liquid mixer controller shall open valve 0	when start_button the liquid_mixer shall immediately satisfy if ! liquid_level_1 then valve_0
[LM-002]	When liquid level 1 is reached occurs, the liquid mixer controller shall close valve 0	when liquid_level_1 the liquid_mixer shall immediately satisfy ! valve_0
[LM-003]	While not liquid level 2 is reached, when liquid level 1 is reached the liquid mixer controller shall open valve 1 until emergency button is pressed.	when liquid_level_1 the liquid_mixer shall until emergency_button satisfy if ! liquid_level_2 then valve_1
[LM-004]	When liquid level 2 is reached occurs, the liquid mixer controller shall close valve 1.	when liquid_level_2 the liquid_mixer shall immediately satisfy ! valve_1
[LM-005]	When liquid level 2 is reached occurs, the 60 sec timer shall start.	when liquid_level_2 the liquid_mixer shall immediately satisfy timer_60sec_start
[LM-006]	When liquid level 2 is reached happens, liquid mixer controller shall start stirring motor until 60 second timer expires or emergency button is pressed.	when liquid_level_2 the liquid_mixer shall until (timer_60sec_expire | emergency_button) satisfy stirring_motor
[LM-007]	When 60 second timer expires occurs, the 120 sec timer shall start.	when timer_60sec_expire the liquid_mixer shall immediately satisfy timer_120sec_start
[LM-008]	When 60 second timer expires happens, the liquid mixer controller shall open valve 2 until 120 sec timer expires or emergency button is pressed.	when timer_60sec_expire the liquid_mixer shall until (timer_120sec_expire | emergency_button) satisfy valve_2
[LM-009]	When emergency button is pressed occurs, the liquid mixer controller shall close valve 0.	when emergency_button the liquid_mixer shall immediately satisfy ! valve_0
[LM-010]	When emergency button is pressed occurs, the liquid mixer controller shall close valve 1.	when emergency_button the liquid_mixer shall immediately satisfy ! valve_1
[LM-011]	When emergency button is pressed occurs, the liquid mixer controller shall close valve 2.	when emergency_button the liquid_mixer shall immediately satisfy ! valve_2
[LM-012]	When emergency button is pressed occurs, the liquid mixer controller shall stop stirring motor.	when emergency_button the liquid_mixer shall immediately satisfy ! stirring_motor

A FRETISH requirement consists of up to six fields: scope, condition, component*, shall*, timing, and response*. Mandatory fields are indicated by an asterisk. component specifies the component that the requirement refers to. shall is used to express that the component's behavior must conform to the requirement. response is a Boolean condition that the component's behavior must satisfy. scope specifies the period when the requirement holds. The optional condition field is a Boolean expression that further constrains when the response shall occur. The timing field, e.g., *always*, *after N time units*, specifies when the response shall happen, subject to condition and scope.

The original text of the Liquid Mixer requirements and their FRETISH versions are shown in Table 1. We used the following variables to write requirement **[LM-001]** in FRETISH: 1) *liquid_level_1* that evaluates to true when liquid level 1 is reached; 2) *start_button* that becomes true when the start button is pressed; 3) *valve_0* that evaluates to true while valve 0 is open. This requirement refers to the liquid_mixer component. We

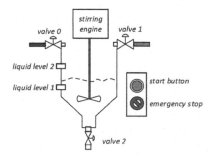

Fig. 1. Liquid mixing system (figure taken from Lúcio et al. [35]).

omit the **scope**, which means that the requirement holds during the entire execution. FRET conditions trigger a requirement when their corresponding boolean expression becomes true from false. In this case, every time *start_button* becomes true (from false) the response if ! *liquid_level_1* then *valve_0* must hold.

3   Background on Realizability

This section provides background on modeling requirements as Assume-Guarantee contracts and on the notion of realizability.

3.1   Assume-Guarantee (AG) Contracts

We rely on the notion of AG contracts as defined by previous work on JSYN and JSYN-VG [20,29]. We use two types *state* and *inputs* for a transition system (I, T) where predicate $I(s) : state \rightarrow bool$ denotes the set of initial states, and predicate $T(s, a, s') : state \times inputs \times state \rightarrow bool$ is the system's transition relation from states s to primed states s', given inputs a. State variables represent both internal and output variables of the system.

A contract (A, G) for system (I, T) consists of an assumption predicate $A(s, a) : state \times inputs \rightarrow bool$ and a guarantee G, made up of two predicates: $G_I(s) : state \rightarrow bool$ and $G_T(s, a, s') : state \times inputs \times state \rightarrow bool$, capturing initial-state and transitional guarantees, respectively. In practice, as described in Sect. 5, A and G may be expressed as sets of predicates, with A and G corresponding to their conjunctions. Note that, any behavior following an environmental input that violates the contract's assumptions is unrestricted by the contract.

Consider the FRETISH liquid mixer system requirements of Table 1. The state variables are: {*stirring_motor, valve_0, valve_1, valve_2, timer_60sec_start, timer_120sec_start*}. The input variables are: {*emergency_button, start_button, liquid_level_1, liquid_level_2, timer_60sec_expire, timer_120sec_expire*}. All variables involved in this system are of type boolean. Let us take input variable *liquid_level_1*, for example. We use *liquid_level_1* and !*liquid_level_1* to represent a true or false valuation for it.

The liquid mixer system does not involve any assumptions or initial guarantees, so for all s, a, $A(s, a) = true$ and $G_I(s) = true$. Moreover, $G_T(s, a, s') = true$ if and only if the transition satisfies all requirements of Table 1, i.e., their conjunction. The FRET tool automatically produces requirement formalizations in a variety of languages, as well as generates and exports analysis code, e.g., CoCoSpec[1] code [40]. For the purposes of this work, we have extended the code generation functionality of FRET to support Lustre code that is digested by the JSYN and JSYN-VG procedures of the JKIND model checker. The generated Lustre code captures the transition relation of an AG contract.

---

[1] CoCoSpec [9] is a contract-based extension of the Lustre synchronous language.

3.2 Realizability

An AG contract is *realizable* if there exists a system implementation that satisfies the contract guarantees for all assumption-complying stimuli provided by the environment. As mentioned above, any behavior following an environmental input that violates the contract's assumptions is unrestricted by the contract.

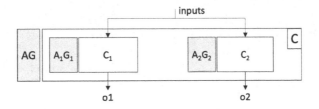

Fig. 2. Partial assume-guarantee contracts.

Definition 1 (Viability of an AG contract). *A set of viable [20] system responses is defined coinductively, as the greatest fixed point of the following equation:*

$$\mathsf{Viable}_{AG}(s) = \forall a.\ (A(s, a) \Rightarrow \exists s'.\ G_T(s, a, s') \land \mathsf{Viable}_{AG}(s'))$$

Realizability of a contract (A, G) is then defined as follows:

Definition 2 (Realizability of an AG contract).

$$\mathsf{Realizable}_{AG} \stackrel{\text{def}}{=} \exists s.\ G_I(s) \land \mathsf{Viable}_{AG}(s)$$

For realizability checking, we use a combination of two off-the-shelf algorithms, namely JSyn [20,30] and JSyn-vg [29]. These algorithms are automated; the engineer does not need to be actively involved during analysis. Moreover, both algorithms are agnostic with respect to the theories that may be exercised within the specification, allowing for a wide range of supported expressions. As of this paper, JSyn and JSyn-vg employ techniques that perform over the theories of Linear Integer and Real Arithmetic (LIRA). Since the input specification can admit infinite theories, the overall problem of realizability checking is undecidable. Problem decomposition is therefore an attractive means of dividing the original challenge into subproblems of smaller size. Nevertheless, decomposition over quantified formulas is not straightforward.

4 Decomposing Realizability

Our theory of compositional realizability checking is based on the notion of partial contracts, i.e., contracts that observe only part of the state of a target system. We use the example of Fig. 2 to provide intuition for the concepts that we present. In the example, a component C, is made up of components C_1 and

C_2, each with their individual contracts (A_1, G_1) and (A_2, G_2). Note that we do not consider the case where C_1 and C_2 communicate with each other; in other words, outputs[2] of C_1 do not intersect with input variables of C_2, and vice versa. Note also that we study the simple case where the components share inputs. We can generalize this case later. In the context of component C, contracts (A_1, G_1) and (A_2, G_2) are partial contracts, as defined below.

Let us assume a set of types $T = \{T_1, \ldots, T_k\}$ and a set of typed state variables $SV = \{s_1 : T_1, \ldots, s_k : T_k\}$. Let $STATES \stackrel{\text{def}}{=} T_1 \times \ldots \times T_k$. We use k-dimensional vectors $(v(s_1), \ldots, v(s_k))$ to represent states that range over $STATES$, where $v(s_i) \in T_i$ is the valuation of variable s_i.

For a state $s = (v(s_1), \ldots, v(s_k)) \in STATES$, and a subset $SV_i \subseteq SV$ over some of its state variables:

$$s@SV_i \stackrel{\text{def}}{=} (v(s_j) \mid s_j \in SV_i)$$

In other words, operator @ maps a state vector s to a sub-vector based on the subset of variables in SV_i. We can extend this operation to sets of states:

$$STATES@SV_i \stackrel{\text{def}}{=} \{s_i \mid \exists s \in STATES.\ s_i = s@SV_i\}.$$

Let (I, T) be a transition system over SV, with $I(s) : STATES \to bool$ and $T(s, a, s') : STATES \times inputs \times STATES \to bool$. In Sect. 3, we defined AG contracts (A, G) over the states and inputs of a system. In this section, we consider partial contracts (A_i, G_i) that only refer to some state variables $SV_i \subseteq SV$ of the system, i.e.:

$$A_i : STATES@SV_i \times inputs \to bool$$
$$G_{Ii} : STATES@SV_i \to bool$$
$$G_{Ti} : STATES@SV_i \times inputs \times STATES@SV_i \to bool$$

In our example of Fig. 2, contracts (A_1, G_1) and (A_2, G_2) are partial contracts for component C, because they relate to its sub-components, and as such, they each observe a subset of C's state variables, namely o_1, and o_2, respectively. As our goal is contract decomposition for realizability, we are particularly interested to discover conditions under which contracts (A_1, G_1) and (A_2, G_2) can be equivalently represented by a global contract (A, G) where $A = A_1 \wedge A_2$ and $G = G_1 \wedge G_2$, meaning that $G_I = G_{I1} \wedge G_{I2}$ and $G_T = G_{T1} \wedge G_{T2}$. We have identified two challenges in addressing this goal: guarantee and assumption interference.

Subcontracts sharing state variables may cause guarantee interference. In our example, imagine that o_1 and o_2 are the same variable. Then finding an implementation for (A_1, G_1) and an implementation for (A_2, G_2) does not mean that there exists one for (A, G), since these implementations may be based on conflicting valuations for the common output. Because of guarantee interference,

---

[2] Note that output and internal variables are considered state variables.

checking realizability of a global contract by checking realizability of its partial contracts may be too optimistic, in the sense that it may return false positives.

In previous work, we proposed a decomposition approach based on connected components to avoid common state variables [33]. This approach was applied to requirements expressed as sets of guarantees, i.e., they were not taking AG contracts into account. In terms of assumptions, we observe that common input and state variables may create assumption interference. In our example, let i be an input variable, and let $A_1 = (i > 0)$ and $A_2 = (i < 3)$. When $i = 5$, A_1 holds but A_2 does not. Realizability of (A_1, G_1) will still require an implementation that conforms to G_1 for $i = 5$, but realizability of (A, G) will not, because A_2 is violated. Because of assumption interference, checking realizability of a global contract by checking realizability of its partial contracts may be too pessimistic, in the sense that it may return false negatives.

This work builds upon our previous work [33] by examining how to decompose global contracts in the presence of assumptions. Let $AG_1^n \stackrel{\text{def}}{=} \{(A_i, G_i) : i = 1, \ldots, n\}$ represent a set of n partial AG contracts for a system over $STATES$ and $inputs$. We start by introducing a notion of realizability $\mathsf{PRealizable}_{AG_1^n}$ for AG_1^n. Theorem 1 then shows that in the context of contracts that do not share state, $\mathsf{PRealizable}_{AG_1^n}$ is equivalent to ensuring that every subcontract (A_i, G_i) is realizable. Finally, Theorem 2 uses these results to decompose the realizability of a contract (A, G) into realizability of subcontracts. Due to space limitations, the proofs of Theorems 1 and 2 are provided in [22].

We first extend the notions of viability and realizability presented in Sect. 3 for a set of partial contracts AG_1^n as follows.

Definition 3 (Partial-contract viability). *A set of viable system responses with respect to a set of partial contracts is defined coinductively, as the greatest fixed point of the following equation:*

$\mathsf{PViable}_{AG_1^n}(s) = \forall a : inputs.$

$(\vee_{i=1}^n A_i(s@SV_i, a)) \Rightarrow$

$\exists s'.[(\wedge_{i=1}^n (A_i(s@SV_i, a) \Rightarrow G_{Ti}(s@SV_i, a, s'@SV_i))) \wedge \mathsf{PViable}_{AG_1^n}(s')]$

Intuitively, each partial contract (A_i, G_i) imposes constraints on how a subset of the state variables must evolve. When at least one assumption $A_i(s@SV_i, a)$ holds, then constraints are imposed on the state transition. Note that when a system consists of a single contract (A_1, G_1) where $SV_1 = SV$, Definition 3 becomes equivalent to Definition 1.

We define realizability of a set of partial contracts AG_1^n as:

Definition 4 (Partial-contract Realizability).

$\mathsf{PRealizable}_{AG_1^n} \stackrel{\text{def}}{=} \exists s. \wedge_{i=1}^n G_{Ii}(s@SV_i) \wedge \mathsf{PViable}_{AG_1^n}(s)$

Following our observations of [33], we call a *non-interfering contract set over* SV, a set of partial contracts (A_i, G_i) over SV_i iff the sets SV_i partition SV. In other words, the partial contracts have no common state variables and together they cover SV. For non-interfering contract sets, realizability can be decomposed, following Theorem 1 below.

Theorem 1. *Let AG_1^n be a non-interfering contract set. Then:*

$$(\wedge_{i=1}^n \text{Realizable}_{A_i G_i}) \Leftrightarrow \text{PRealizable}_{AG_1^n}$$

In other words, for non-interfering contract sets, partial-contract realizability is equivalently decomposed into realizability of the individual partial contracts. It remains to discover conditions under which partial-contract realizability coincides with global contract realizability. By comparing the definitions of Viable_{AG} and $\text{PViable}_{AG_1^n}$, a main difference that stands out is $\wedge_{i=1}^n A_i$ vs $\vee_{i=1}^n A_i$. So we examine the case where $\wedge_{i=1}^n A_i \equiv \vee_{i=1}^n A_i$, which is equivalent to $A_1 \equiv A_2 \equiv \ldots \equiv A_n$ (from Boolean algebra). Additionally, since $A = \wedge_{i=1}^n A_i$, it follows that $A \equiv A_1 \equiv A_2 \equiv \ldots \equiv A_n$. Since the partial contracts (A_i, G_i) are non-interfering, they are defined over state variable sets SV_i that partition SV. For all the assumptions A_i to be equivalent under all circumstances, these assumptions, including assumption A, must be independent of state. An assumption $A(s, a) : state \times inputs \rightarrow bool$ is considered *independent of state*, iff $\forall s_1, s_2 \in state, \forall a \in inputs. A(s_1, a) = A(s_2, a)$. We abbreviate $A(*, a)$ by $A(a)$. The following theorem captures these observations.

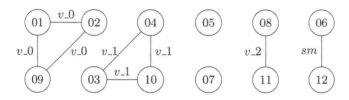

Fig. 3. `liquid_mixer` connected components. We use the last two digits of req. names, and abbreviate `valve_x` to `v_x`, `stirring_motor` to `sm`.

Theorem 2. *Let (A, G) be an AG contract over state variable set SV, with A independent of state, and let (A, G_i) with $i = 1 \ldots n$, be a non-interfering contract set over state variable sets SV_i, where $G = \wedge_{i=1}^n G_i$ (i.e., $G_I = \wedge_{i=1}^n G_{Ii}$ and $G_T = \wedge_{i=1}^n G_{Ti}$). Then $\text{Realizable}_{AG} \equiv (\wedge_{i=1}^n \text{Realizable}_{AG_i})$.*

5   Connected Components

In this section, we present one approach to automatically decomposing an assume-guarantee contract (A, G) into an equivalent set of partial contracts (A, G_i) per the conditions of Theorem 2. As discussed, Theorem 2 requires the assumption A to be independent of state. Consequently, to obtain non-interfering contracts, we only need to consider guarantees.

More specifically, we decompose an assume-guarantee contract that fits the conditions of Theorem 2 by splitting the guarantees G based on the notion of connected components [25,54] for undirected graphs. As seen in Fig. 3, the connected components of a graph essentially represent separated pieces of the graph. Two vertices belong to the same connected component if and only if there exists some path between them.

As discussed in Sect. 3, AG contracts (A, G) are typically expressed as sets of assumption and guarantee predicates, with A and G corresponding to their respective conjunctions. More formally, let R_{GI} and R_{GT} be sets of predicates that define G, meaning that $G_I = \bigwedge_{R_i \in R_{GI}} R_i$, and $G_T = \bigwedge_{R_i \in R_{GT}} R_i$. We use the set $R = R_{GI} \cup R_{GT}$ to represent all guarantee predicates involved in G, without differentiating between initial state and transitional guarantees. We refer to elements of set R as requirements.

A *requirements graph* for R is an undirected graph (V, E), which is built as follows. Each vertex in V corresponds to a requirement in R. If the state variables referenced by two requirements overlap, their corresponding vertices in the graph are connected by an edge in E. By computing connected components in R, we are able to decompose the original specification into partial contracts.

Figure 3 illustrates the connected components for the liquid mixer system. The components partition the requirement state variables, namely *valve_0*, *valve_1*, *valve_2*, *timer_60sec_start* (referenced only by [**LM-005**]), *timer_120sec_start* (referenced only by [**LM-007**]), and *stirring_motor*. Let us now formally present our connected component approach.

Let R be the set of requirements in an AG contract (A, G) over state variables in SV, as described previously. For $R_i \in R$, we use SV_{Ri} to denote the state variables that are referenced by requirement R_i. For initial state guarantees, this means that $\forall s_1, s_2 \in STATES. (s_1@SV_{Ri} = s_2@SV_{Ri}) \Rightarrow R_i(s_1) = R_i(s_2)$. For each R_i we can therefore define the predicate $R_i@SV_{Ri}$ that behaves as R_i, but has lower dimensionality when $SV_{Ri} \subset SV$:

$$\forall s_i \in STATES@SV_{Ri}.$$
$$R_i@SV_{Ri}(s_i) \stackrel{\text{def}}{=} \exists s \in STATES. ((s@SV_{Ri} = s_i) \wedge R_i(s)).$$

The above notations and definitions naturally extend to transitional guarantees.

Definition 5 (Requirements Graph). *A requirements graph RG is an undirected graph whose vertices are requirements $R_i \in R$ and with an edge (R_i, R_j) between every pair of requirements R_i and R_j that share at least one state variable; that is, $SV_{Ri} \cap SV_{Rj} \neq \varnothing$. Notice that we do not consider input variables for the construction of this graph.*

Definition 6 (State-Connected Component (SCC)). *Let R be a set of requirements, and RG be its corresponding requirements graph. A State-Connected Component is a tuple $C = (R_c, SV_c)$ where*

- *$R_c \subseteq R$ is the set of requirements in a connected component of RG; that is, there is a connected path of edges between each pair of requirements in R_c and no superset of R_c also has this property.*

- SV_c is the set of state variables that are mentioned in any requirement in R_c; that is, $SV_c = \bigcup_{R_i \in R_c} SV_{Ri}$.

State-connected components can be computed with a connected component algorithm. For example, our framework implements Tarjan's classic connected components algorithm [25] with an $O(|V| + |E|)$ complexity. State-connected components can then be used to create AG contracts as follows.

Definition 7 (Connected AG Contract). *Let* (A, G) *be an AG contract over state variables* SV, *where* A *is independent of state. Let* $R = R_{GI} \sqcup R_{GT}$ *be the contract's set of requirements, with its corresponding requirements graph* RG. *Each state-connected component* $C = (R_c, SV_c)$ *in* RG *defines a Connected AG Contract* (A_c, G_c), *as follows:*

- $\forall s \in STATES@SV_c, \forall a \in inputs.\ A_c(s, a) = A(a)$.
- $G_{Ic} = \bigwedge_{Ri \in (R_c \cap R_{GI})} Ri@SV_c$ *is* G_c's *initial-state guarantee predicate.*
- $G_{Tc} = \bigwedge_{Ri \in (R_c \cap R_{GT})} Ri@SV_c$ *is* G_c's *transitional guarantee predicate.*

Table 2. Case studies statistics. The "Monolithic" and "Total SCC" columns record the monolithic and compositional (SCC) analysis time in seconds. SCC times are denoted by "N/A" if decomposition was not successful.

Project	Benchmark	#Reqs	#SCCs	Realizable?		Monolithic		Total SCC	
				JSYN	JSYN-VG	JSYN	JSYN-VG	JSYN	JSYN-VG
Example	liquid_mixer	12	6	✗	✗	0.50	10.27	2.47	5.85
GPCA	Infusion_Manager	26	1	✗	✗	0.40	10.76	N/A	N/A
QFCS	FCC	9	7	✔	?	53.31	T/O	4.12	T/O + 6.38
QFCS	FCC (inlined)	79	38	✔	✔	1.11	T/O	13.10	16.41
QFCS	OSAS	10	2	✗	✗	1.82	T/O	2.96	T/O + 1.12
QFCS	OSAS (inlined)	190	21	✗	✗	1.32	T/O	10.83	640.89
LMCPS	AP	13	3	?	?	0.40	T/O	1.42	T/O + 8.68
LMCPS	FSM	13	3	✗	✗	0.42	1524.82	3.51	6.74
LMCPS	EB	5	2	?	?	1.41	1.01	1.62	1.39
LMCPS	NN	4	1	?	?	55.80	269.87	N/A	N/A
LMCPS	REG	10	5	?	✔	286.14	99.52	422.52	5.72
LMCPS	TSM	6	1	✗	✔	3.33	242.67	N/A	N/A

✔: realizable ✗: unrealizable ?: unknown T/O: timeout (12 h)

By construction, the state variables over which individual connected AG contracts are defined partition the set of system state variables. Hence, connected AG contracts are partial contracts that can be used to decompose realizability checking, according to Theorem 2.

Of the 6 connected components in liquid_mixer (Fig. 3), only 1 was found to be unrealizable, consisting of requirements [**LM-001**], [**LM-002**] and [**LM-009**]. Thus, we were able to localize and identify the conflict between [**LM-001**] and [**LM-009**], a result consistent with the findings by Lúcio et al. [35].

6   Case Studies

We applied our compositional approach on three multi-component, industrial-level projects[3]. The different components/benchmarks and number of requirements of each project are shown in Table 2. Next, we describe each project.

Generic Infusion Pump (GPCA): The Generic Infusion Pump Research Project [2] is a joint effort by the United States Food and Drug Administration (USFDA), Hutchison China MediTech (Chi-Med), CIMIT [1] and ten universities to identify best software engineering practices in the development of medical devices. The Generic Patient Controlled Analgesic (GPCA) infusion pump has been previously developed and formally analyzed using the AGREE framework [45,46]. This study used the **Infusion_Manager** subcomponent, previously shown unrealizable by Gacek et al. [20] through the use of the JSYN algorithm. The subcomponent contains 12 requirements.

We first translated the original specification into FRETISH, and created 26 (as opposed to 12) requirements. This difference is mainly due to our choice of using FRET's inherent support for modes through the **scope** field. The original contract used a single variable $Current\_System\_Mode$ with 8 different values to model the 8 component modes. In FRET, it is more natural to use 8 different mode variables instead, and avoid mixing properties of different modes in a single requirement. As an example, consider the following requirement:

$$\mathbf{G1} \stackrel{\text{def}}{=} (Current\_System\_Mode' \geq 0)\ (Current\_System\_Mode' \leq 8)$$
$$\land\ (Current\_System\_Mode' = 0 \Rightarrow\ Commanded\_Flow\_Rate' = 0)$$
$$\land\ (Current\_System\_Mode' = 1 \Rightarrow\ Commanded\_Flow\_Rate' = 0)$$

which gets decomposed into three requirements $\mathbf{G1_1}$, $\mathbf{G1_2}$, and $\mathbf{G1_3}$, corresponding to the first, second and third line in the original contract[4]. Requirement $\mathbf{G1_1}$ ensures that the system is in at least one of the 8 modes at any time. Requirements $\mathbf{G1_2}$ and $\mathbf{G1_3}$ define component behavior when in mode 0 and 1, respectively. We added requirements to ensure mutual exclusion between modes, something that was not needed with a single mode variable. We used KIND 2 [10] to show equivalence between our requirements and the original specification.

NASA's Quad-Redundant Flight Control System (QFCS): QFCS is a component in NASA's Transport Class Model aircraft simulation [26]. It is composed of four cross-checking flight control computers (FCC), and contains specifications regarding the control laws and sensing properties of the aircraft. It has been used in the past for the purposes of requirements analysis within the Assume-Guarantee Reasoning Framework (AGREE) [12], both in terms of compositional verification [3] as well as realizability checking and synthesis through JKIND [20,29]. Compared to the latter work, our compositional approach yields

---

[3] Datasets are available upon request. Please email the authors.

[4] We discuss requirements in the original contract notation to make it easy to relate to Gacek et al. [20].

new information, that would otherwise be impossible to derive using the monolithic algorithms in JKIND. We present new results on the FCC (9 requirements) and Output Signal Analysis and Selection (OSAS, 10 requirements) contracts. For this case study, we did not write the requirements in FRET but directly used the provided Lustre specifications to perform decomposition and analysis.

Lockheed Martin CPS Challenge Problems (LMCPS): LMCPS is a set of industrial Simulink model benchmarks and natural language requirements [15,16]. They consist of a set of problems inspired by flight control and vehicle management systems, which are representative of flight critical systems. LMCPS was created by Lockheed Martin Aeronautics to evaluate and improve the state-of-the-art in formal method toolsets. There are two recent research works that study the formalization of the LMCPS requirements and their analysis against the Simulink models. Nejati et al. [47] perform model testing and checking, while Mavridou et al. [42] perform requirement specification and model checking. However, none of these works check consistency or realizability. To perform realizability analysis, we used the FRETISH form of the requirements [41].

We present results for several LMCPS challenges[5]: 1) 6DoF with DeHavilland Beaver Autopilot (AP): a simulation of the DeHavilland Beaver airplane with autopilot (13 requirements); 2) Finite State Machine (FSM): an abstraction of an advanced autopilot system (13 requirements); 3) Effector Blender (EB): a control allocation method that calculates the optimal effector configuration (5 requirements); 4) Feedforward Cascade Connectivity Neural Network (NN): a predictor neural network (4 requirements); 5) Control Loop Regulators (REG): a regulator's inner loop architecture (10 requirements); 6) Triplex Signal Monitor (TSM): a redundancy management system (6 requirements).

6.1   Analysis Outcomes and Lessons Learned

In Table 2 we summarize analysis outcomes and performance times of the Infusion Manager example, and the GPCA, QFCS, and LMCPS projects. For each project, we computed the number of SCCs and applied monolithic and compositional realizability analysis by using both the JSYN and JSYN-VG algorithms. The experiments were run on an Ubuntu VM, 4.5 GB RAM, i5-8365U, 4 cores@1.60 GHz. Next, we discuss in detail the analysis results and provide insights.

No Decomposition: Our decomposition method returned a single SCC for the LMCPS NN, LMCPS TSM, and the Infusion_Manager specifications. One reason that contributed to the unsuccessful decomposition was that requirements were connected through mode variables. In the future, we plan to study whether large mode-related specifications can be analyzed modularly, by studying the mode-transition logic separately from the intra-mode requirements.

---

[5] For brevity, we omit challenges for which our work did not yield new information. Additional analysis results can be found in a supplementary technical report [33].

Challenges in Realizability Analysis: The nested quantifiers in Definition 2 can be particularly challenging for state-of-the art solvers. Furthermore, infinite-state problems are undecidable in general, and the corresponding solvers are not complete. Additionally, many of the LMCPS specifications contain non-linear expressions that are not entirely supported by SMT solvers. For instance, the EB challenge returned "unknown" due to non-linearities for both JSYN and JSYN-VG and we were not able to get a result even after decomposing the specification into 2 SCCs. Similarly, in the AP challenge, the monolithic JSYN approach returned "unknown" due to non-linearities, while JSYN-VG timed out. Even though, the monolithic approach did not yield results for AP, by decomposing the specification we were able to get more meaningful results as explained next.

Successful Decomposition: Several of our case studies demonstrated how decomposition can effectively reduce problem complexity, surpass some of the aforementioned challenges, and lead to significant performance benefits.

– LMCPS AP: Our SCC algorithm decomposed the specification into 3 SCCs. It is worth noting that while we were able to verify realizability of the two SCCs in less than 8.7 s, JSYN-VG was not able to solve the last SCC and timed-out due to non-linear expressions. Despite not getting a conclusive answer, decomposition helped us identify and successfully check linear fragments of the specification. AP showcases how partial results can be retrieved via decomposition, while identifying fragments for which the solvers fail due to problem complexity.

– LMCPS FSM: Monolithic realizability analysis returned unrealizable with both JSYN and JSYN-VG. Decomposition returned 3 SCCs. One was realizable while the other two were unrealizable. This helped us localize the causes of unrealizability within the corresponding SCCs. Additionally, decomposing our original specification allowed us to reduce the total analysis time from 1524.82 s to less than 7 s with JSYN-VG.

– LMCPS REG: This challenge is highly decomposable: for 10 requirements our decomposition approach returned 5 SCCs. REG was proven realizable by JSYN-VG through monolithic checking in 99.52 s, while compositional checking needed a total time of only 5.72 s. On the contrary, JSYN timed out during both the monolithic check and when checking each SCC independently.

– QFCS: The FCC contract contains only 9 requirements, yet JSYN required 53.31 s to declare it as realizable while JSYN-VG could not solve the same problem, even for a timeout value of 12 h. Using our decomposition method, we partitioned the contract into 7 SCCs, 6 of which contain a single requirement, with the seventh containing 3. We then ran a realizability check over each component individually. The decomposition step resulted in a dramatic performance improvement: JSYN required only 4.12 s to solve the entire problem, and JSYN-VG solved the six singletons in 6.38 s, and timed out for the seventh SCC (FCC-7).

Requirement Granularity: To better identify why FCC-7 was so hard to solve, we examined the requirement definitions: the majority of the requirements in the project (i.e., both FCC and OSAS) are big conjunctions, where each conjunct corresponds to the application of user-defined, reusable predicate templates, over a disjoint set of state variables (FCC contains 6 templates in total, OSAS contains

9). For example, requirement **GUARANTEE6** in FCC is defined as[6]:

$$\textbf{GUARANTEE6} \stackrel{\text{def}}{=} range(valid\_acts.TL, acts\_out.TL', 0.0, 50.0) \wedge \ldots$$
$$\ldots \wedge range(valid\_acts.STEER, acts\_out.STEER', 0.0, 50.0),$$

where each conjunct is the application of the template *range* over pairs of variables from *valid_acts* and *acts_out*. While using big conjunctions was, as commented by the project authors, "out of convenience", it unsurprisingly resulted in performance overhead, as the monolithic algorithms needed to consider all of the conjuncts at the same time (the solver query has 1481 variables), even though each conjunct can be considered as a separate requirement, and therefore be a candidate for decomposition.

As such, we split the initial 9 requirements of FCC into subrequirements: for each requirement, and for each application of a template, we derived a subrequirement. The resulting FCC contract, i.e., FCC (inlined) in Table 2, consists of 79 requirements. The monolithic JSYN run improved significantly (1.11 s), but JSYN-VG still timed out. Decomposing the new contract resulted in 38 SCCs, which we individually checked for realizability (30 variables per SCC query, on average). While the compositional run for JSYN was a bit slower (13.10 s total, ∼0.34 s per SCC), JSYN-VG was finally able to determine the contract as realizable, requiring in total only 16.41 s (∼0.43 s per SCC).

Similarly, we decomposed the original OSAS contract into 2 SCCs, one of which was a singleton. To our surprise, the singleton was unrealizable, and further inspection revealed the cause: the corresponding requirement was declared as a guarantee, yet contained no state variables. Such a guarantee would always be unrealizable as the system cannot control inputs. As with FCC, templates are heavily used in OSAS. Deriving new requirements out of templates resulted in a new contract, i.e., OSAS (inlined), with 190 requirements, and 21 SCCs (the monolithic query contained 3035 variables, versus the 151 per SCC query). Through the decomposition, we were able to determine the contract as unrealizable by using both JSYN and JSYN-VG.

To sum up, our compositional approach helped us understand that requirement templates can negatively impact analysis performance and decomposition (e.g., 21 vs. 2 SCCs in OSAS). The QFCS case study stands out from the rest since we did not enter the requirements in FRET but instead directly used the provided Lustre specifications. From our experience, it is not common in practice to write such long requirements (as the ones provided in Lustre) in FRET; usually FRETISH sentences are relatively short. For example, take the GPCA case study, for which we created 26 FRETISH requirements as opposed to the initial 12 requirements. As shown via the inlined requirements, shorter requirements may enable finer decomposition and thus, return meaningful results.

Algorithm Trade-Offs: Although the JSYN algorithm is not sound for unrealizability results, it returned a result in several cases (e.g., FCC, OSAS) for which JSYN-VG needed more time or even timed out. We thus realised that the two

---

[6] We have shortened the element names in the requirement to reduce the overall size.

algorithms can be combined together with our compositional approach to optimize performance. To this end, JSYN can be used for returning fast sound realizable results, while JSYN-VG can be effectively used in the compositional context to determine sound unrealizability without timing out (e.g., `OSAS (inlined)`).

To conclude, our compositional approach helped us gain significant insights into the challenges of realizability analysis and possible ways to overcome these. For example, we understood that the granularity level of specifications plays an important role since shorter formulas usually enable finer decomposition. Additionally, we realized that decomposition can be particularly helpful for the analysis of specifications that are challenging for state-of-the-art solvers, such as specifications with nested quantifiers and non-linear expressions. In general, our compositional approach helps us overcome challenges in realizability checking since it reduces problem complexity and achieves significant performance gains.

6.2 Comparison of Decomposition with Finkbeiner et al. [17]

Finkbeiner et al. recently proposed, in an independent effort to ours, two approaches towards specification decomposition for reactive synthesis. Most relevant to our work is a decomposition algorithm for LTL specifications where, given an LTL formula, each conjunct of its CNF equivalent occurs in exactly one subspecification. Similarly to our work, this is achieved by partitioning the original specification based on dependencies between system variables.

One notable difference between the two approaches is the level at which they are performed. We perform decomposition at the level of FRET requirements, rather than their corresponding LTL formulas. One of the reasons for this choice is that FRET interacts with users at the level of requirements, which promotes diagnosis and repair. Moreover, as observed in our experiments, when expressing requirements in the FRET environment, users tend to write small requirements as opposed to conjoining multiple ones in a single FRETish sentence. Nevertheless, the FRET formula generation algorithms [24] may create large formulas. It would be interesting to explore if we can obtain additional gains by performing decomposition at the level of formulas using Finkbeiner et al.'s algorithms. In fact, we could try to apply Finkbeiner et al.'s algorithms on the connected components identified by our algorithm for further decomposition.

To compare the approaches we used ten benchmarks from the SYNT-COMP 2020 competition [27][7], for which the decomposition proposed by Finkbeiner et al. yielded exemplary results [17]. Since neither JSYN nor JSYN-VG support liveness properties, a direct comparison regarding realizability results is not possible. As such, we focused on comparing the quality

Table 3. Comparison with Finkbeiner et al. [17]. Iden stands for identical.

Benchmark	#SCCs	#Specs [17]	Iden?
Cockpitboard	8	8	✔
Gamelogic	4	4	✔
LedMatrix	3	3	✔
Radarboard	11	11	✔
zoo10	1	2	✘
generalized_buffer_2	2	2	✔
generalized_buffer_3	2	2	✔
shift_8	8	8	✔
shift_10	10	10	✔
shift_12	12	12	✔

---

[7] SYNTCOMP 2020 benchmarks: https://github.com/SYNTCOMP/benchmarks.

of decomposition. As shown in Table 3, our decomposition procedure yielded identical results with Finkbeiner et al. for all but the zoo10 benchmark[8]. We attribute the discrepancy to an optimization in the algorithm by Finkbeiner et al., which yields two subspecifications whose assumptions are not equivalent to each other. It is currently unclear to us whether this decomposition is compatible with our formal framework, and we plan on revisiting this in future work.

7   Related Work

Realizability checking of specifications is a well-established field of research in formal methods, and is strongly tied to the area of *reactive synthesis*. Pnueli and Rosner were the first to show that the complexity of the problem is double-exponential (2-EXPTIME) for propositional specification [50], while further advancements in the General Reactivity of Rank 1 (GR(1)) fragment of LTL showed that a polynomial time algorithm exists [6,49]. In the context of propositional logic, various tools have been proposed towards the realizability analysis of reactive systems, some of which follow a user-guided approach [53], while others serve as general requirements analysis and debugging frameworks [5,14,37]. Our work addresses the same problem, but in the context of potentially infinite-state specifications, where scalability is a major concern.

Specification decomposition is also a research problem of relevance to formal methods and more specifically formal verification, with previous work on procedures that factorize the specification into smaller problems [7,21,48]. The same also applies in the context of synthesis where compositional techniques have been proposed, taking advantage of Binary Decision Diagrams, And-Inverter Graphs and Extended Finite-State Machines to restructure the original problem into factored formulas [8,28,43,56]. In comparison to this work, our proposed algorithm to compute SCCs is orthogonal and does not rely on solvers to perform the decomposition. Furthermore, our approach is not affected by the order in which specification elements are processed and as such does not require the application of sophisticated ordering heuristics [44,56].

The diagnosis of unrealizable specifications has also been extensively explored, primarily in the context of computing minimal sets of conflicting specification elements, commonly referred to as *unrealizable cores*. In this paper, we rely on the model-based diagnosis technique proposed by Kónighofer et al. [32] to compute all minimal unrealizable cores. The technique is modular with respect to the way that a single minimal conflict is computed, allowing for different implementations to be considered. FRET supports both delta debugging [57] and a linear algorithm proposed by Cimatti et al. [11] to compute minimal conflicts. By default, we use delta debugging as it has been shown to perform better, on average. Recently, Maoz et al. proposed QUICKCORE for computing unrealizable cores, with optimizations based on specific properties of GR(1) specifications [39]. Within the context of GR(1) specifications, QUICKCORE was shown

---

[8] The authors provided us with their resulting subspecifications.

to perform better than delta debugging. In the future, we intend to evaluate the applicability of QUICKCORE within FRET.

Akin to realizability checking, prior work exists in other aspects of requirement analysis, such as *rt-inconsistency* [34,51,52], *well-separation* [31,36] and *inherent vacuity* [19,38]. Note that in the case of rt-inconsistency, an unrealizable contract is also rt-inconsistent but not necessarily vice-versa. It would be interesting to explore whether SCC computation could also benefit these types of analysis.

8   Conclusion

We presented a new realizability analysis framework, developed as an extension of FRET. Our partial contracts approach can be applied as a preprocessing step on a variety of realizability analysis tools, by taking advantage of a specification's modularity over disjoint subsets of requirements. We evaluated our approach with state-of-the-art infinite-state realizability algorithms on several industrial case studies. We obtained encouraging results in reducing problem complexity and significantly improving analysis performance.

We focused on conditions under which the realizability of a global contract can equivalently be decomposed into the realizability of its partial contracts. In the future, we plan to study if it is possible to relax the requirement of equivalent partial contract assumptions in Theorem 2. It is worthwhile noting that, for non-interfering contract sets, partial contract realizability always implies global contract realizability, but not vice versa. So to establish a positive realizability result, we can relax the conditions for decomposition, at the expense of losing the capability to call unrealizability. We plan to explore such trade-offs in practice.

References

1. Consortia for improving medicine within innovation and technology. https://cimit.org/home
2. Generic infusion pump research project. https://rtg.cis.upenn.edu/gip/
3. Backes, J., Cofer, D., Miller, S., Whalen, M.W.: Requirements analysis of a quad-redundant flight control system. In: Havelund, K., Holzmann, G., Joshi, R. (eds.) NFM 2015. LNCS, vol. 9058, pp. 82–96. Springer, Cham (2015). https://doi.org/10.1007/978-3-319-17524-9_7
4. Benveniste, A., et al.: Contracts for system design (2018)
5. Bloem, R., et al.: RATSY – a new requirements analysis tool with synthesis. In: Touili, T., Cook, B., Jackson, P. (eds.) CAV 2010. LNCS, vol. 6174, pp. 425–429. Springer, Heidelberg (2010). https://doi.org/10.1007/978-3-642-14295-6_37
6. Bloem, R., Jobstmann, B., Piterman, N., Pnueli, A., Sa'ar, Y.: Synthesis of reactive (1) designs. J. Comput. Syst. Sci. **78**(3), 911–938 (2012)
7. Burch, J.R., Clarke, E.M., Long, D.E.: Representing circuits more efficiently in symbolic model checking. In: Proceedings of the 28th ACM/IEEE Design Automation Conference, pp. 403–407. Association for Computing Machinery, New York (1991). https://doi.org/10.1145/127601.127702

8. Chakraborty, S., Fried, D., Tabajara, L.M., Vardi, M.Y.: Functional synthesis via input-output separation. In: 2018 Formal Methods in Computer Aided Design (FMCAD), pp. 1–9. IEEE (2018)
9. Champion, A., Gurfinkel, A., Kahsai, T., Tinelli, C.: CoCoSpec: a mode-aware contract language for reactive systems. In: De Nicola, R., Kühn, E. (eds.) SEFM 2016. LNCS, vol. 9763, pp. 347–366. Springer, Cham (2016). https://doi.org/10.1007/978-3-319-41591-8_24
10. Champion, A., Mebsout, A., Sticksel, C., Tinelli, C.: The KIND 2 model checker. In: Chaudhuri, S., Farzan, A. (eds.) CAV 2016, Part II. LNCS, vol. 9780, pp. 510–517. Springer, Cham (2016). https://doi.org/10.1007/978-3-319-41540-6_29
11. Cimatti, A., Roveri, M., Schuppan, V., Tchaltsev, A.: Diagnostic information for realizability. In: Logozzo, F., Peled, D.A., Zuck, L.D. (eds.) VMCAI 2008. LNCS, vol. 4905, pp. 52–67. Springer, Heidelberg (2008). https://doi.org/10.1007/978-3-540-78163-9_9
12. Cofer, D., Gacek, A., Miller, S., Whalen, M.W., LaValley, B., Sha, L.: Compositional verification of architectural models. In: Goodloe, A.E., Person, S. (eds.) NFM 2012. LNCS, vol. 7226, pp. 126–140. Springer, Heidelberg (2012). https://doi.org/10.1007/978-3-642-28891-3_13
13. Damm, W., Hungar, H., Josko, B., Peikenkamp, T., Stierand, I.: Using contract-based component specifications for virtual integration testing and architecture design. In: 2011 Design, Automation & Test in Europe, pp. 1–6. IEEE (2011)
14. Ehlers, R., Raman, V.: Slugs: extensible GR(1) synthesis. In: Chaudhuri, S., Farzan, A. (eds.) CAV 2016, Part II. LNCS, vol. 9780, pp. 333–339. Springer, Cham (2016). https://doi.org/10.1007/978-3-319-41540-6_18
15. Elliott, C.: On example models and challenges ahead for the evaluation of complex cyber-physical systems with state of the art formal methods V&V, Lockheed Martin Skunk Works. In: Laboratory, A.F.R. (ed.) Safe & Secure Systems and Software Symposium (S5) (2015)
16. Elliott, C.: An example set of cyber-physical V&V challenges for S5, Lockheed Martin Skunk Works. In: Laboratory, A.F.R. (ed.) Safe & Secure Systems and Software Symposium (S5) (2016)
17. Finkbeiner, B., Geier, G., Passing, N.: Specification decomposition for reactive synthesis. In: Dutle, A., Moscato, M.M., Titolo, L., Muñoz, C.A., Perez, I. (eds.) NFM 2021. LNCS, vol. 12673, pp. 113–130. Springer, Cham (2021). https://doi.org/10.1007/978-3-030-76384-8_8
18. Firman, E., Maoz, S., Ringert, J.O.: Performance heuristics for GR (1) synthesis and related algorithms. Acta Informatica $57(1)$, 37–79 (2020)
19. Fisman, D., Kupferman, O., Sheinvald-Faragy, S., Vardi, M.Y.: A framework for inherent vacuity. In: Chockler, H., Hu, A.J. (eds.) HVC 2008. LNCS, vol. 5394, pp. 7–22. Springer, Heidelberg (2009). https://doi.org/10.1007/978-3-642-01702-5_7
20. Gacek, A., Katis, A., Whalen, M.W., Backes, J., Cofer, D.: Towards realizability checking of contracts using theories. In: Havelund, K., Holzmann, G., Joshi, R. (eds.) NFM 2015. LNCS, vol. 9058, pp. 173–187. Springer, Cham (2015). https://doi.org/10.1007/978-3-319-17524-9_13
21. Geist, D., Beer, I.: Efficient model checking by automated ordering of transition relation partitions. In: Dill, D.L. (ed.) CAV 1994. LNCS, vol. 818, pp. 299–310. Springer, Heidelberg (1994). https://doi.org/10.1007/3-540-58179-0_63
22. Giannakopoulou, D., Katis, A., Mavridou, A., Pressburger, T.: Compositional realizability checking within FRET. NASA Technical Memorandum (March 2021). https://ti.arc.nasa.gov/publications/20210013008/download/, 32 p

23. Giannakopoulou, D., Pressburger, T., Mavridou, A., Rhein, J., Schumann, J., Shi, N.: Formal requirements elicitation with FRET. In: Joint Proceedings of REFSQ-2020 Workshops, Doctoral Symposium, Live Studies Track, and Poster Track co-located with the 26th International Conference on Requirements Engineering: Foundation for Software Quality (REFSQ 2020), Pisa, Italy, March 24, 2020. CEUR Workshop Proceedings, vol. 2584. CEUR-WS.org (2020). http://ceur-ws.org/Vol-2584/PT-paper4.pdf

24. Giannakopoulou, D., Pressburger, T., Mavridou, A., Schumann, J.: Automated formalization of structured natural language requirements. Inf. Softw. Technol. **137**, 106590 (2021). https://doi.org/10.1016/j.infsof.2021.106590, https://www.sciencedirect.com/science/article/pii/S0950584921000707

25. Hopcroft, J., Tarjan, R.: Algorithm 447: efficient algorithms for graph manipulation. Commun. ACM **16**(6), 372–378 (1973)

26. Hueschen, R.M.: Development of the transport class model (TCM) aircraft simulation from a sub-scale generic transport model (GTM) simulation (2011)

27. Jacobs, S., et al.: The first reactive synthesis competition (syntcomp 2014). Int. J. Softw. Tools Technol. Transf. **19**(3), 367–390 (2017)

28. John, A.K., Shah, S., Chakraborty, S., Trivedi, A., Akshay, S.: Skolem functions for factored formulas. In: 2015 Formal Methods in Computer-Aided Design (FMCAD), pp. 73–80. IEEE (2015)

29. Katis, A., et al.: Validity-guided synthesis of reactive systems from assume-guarantee contracts. In: Beyer, D., Huisman, M. (eds.) TACAS 2018, Part II. LNCS, vol. 10806, pp. 176–193. Springer, Cham (2018). https://doi.org/10.1007/978-3-319-89963-3_10

30. Katis, A., Gacek, A., Whalen, M.W.: Towards synthesis from assume-guarantee contracts involving infinite theories: a preliminary report. In: 4th International Conference on Formal Methods in Software Engineering (FormaliSE), pp. 36–41. IEEE (2016)

31. Klein, U., Pnueli, A.: Revisiting synthesis of GR(1) specifications. In: Barner, S., Harris, I., Kroening, D., Raz, O. (eds.) HVC 2010. LNCS, vol. 6504, pp. 161–181. Springer, Heidelberg (2011). https://doi.org/10.1007/978-3-642-19583-9_16

32. Könighofer, R., Hofferek, G., Bloem, R.: Debugging formal specifications: a practical approach using model-based diagnosis and counterstrategies. Int. J. Softw. Tools Technol. Transf. **15**(5–6), 563–583 (2013)

33. Kooi, D., Mavridou, A.: Integrating realizability checking in FRET. NASA Technical Memorandum (June 2019). https://ntrs.nasa.gov/api/citations/20190033980/downloads/20190033980.pdf, 28 p

34. Langenfeld, V., Dietsch, D., Westphal, B., Hoenicke, J., Post, A.: Scalable analysis of real-time requirements. In: 2019 IEEE 27th International Requirements Engineering Conference (RE), pp. 234–244 (2019). https://doi.org/10.1109/RE.2019.00033

35. Lúcio, L., Rahman, S., Cheng, C.-H., Mavin, A.: Just formal enough? Automated analysis of EARS requirements. In: Barrett, C., Davies, M., Kahsai, T. (eds.) NFM 2017. LNCS, vol. 10227, pp. 427–434. Springer, Cham (2017). https://doi.org/10.1007/978-3-319-57288-8_31

36. Maoz, S., Ringert, J.O.: On well-separation of GR (1) specifications. In: Proceedings of the 2016 24th ACM SIGSOFT International Symposium on Foundations of Software Engineering, pp. 362–372 (2016)

37. Maoz, S., Ringert, J.O.: Spectra: a specification language for reactive systems. arXiv preprint arXiv:1904.06668 (2019)

38. Maoz, S., Shalom, R.: Inherent vacuity for GR (1) specifications. In: Proceedings of the 28th ACM Joint Meeting on European Software Engineering Conference and Symposium on the Foundations of Software Engineering, pp. 99–110 (2020)
39. Maoz, S., Shalom, R.: Unrealizable cores for reactive systems specifications. In: 2021 IEEE/ACM 43rd International Conference on Software Engineering (ICSE), pp. 25–36. IEEE (2021)
40. Mavridou, A., Bourbouh, H., Garoche, P.L., Giannakopoulou, D., Pressburger, T., Schumann, J.: Bridging the gap between requirements and simulink model analysis. In: Joint Proceedings of REFSQ-2020 Workshops, Doctoral Symposium, Live Studies Track, and Poster Track co-located with the 26th International Conference on Requirements Engineering: Foundation for Software Quality (REFSQ 2020), Pisa, Italy, March 24, 2020. CEUR Workshop Proceedings, vol. 2584. CEUR-WS.org (2020). http://ceur-ws.org/Vol-2584/PT-paper9.pdf
41. Mavridou, A., Bourbouh, H., Garoche, P.L., Hejase, M.: Evaluation of the FRET and CoCoSim tools on the ten Lockheed Martin cyber-physical challenge problems. Tech. rep., NASA (October 2019). 84 p
42. Mavridou, A., et al.: The ten Lockheed Martin cyber-physical challenges: formalized, analyzed, and explained. In: Proceedings of the 2020 28th IEEE International Requirements Engineering Conference (2020)
43. Mohajerani, S., Malik, R., Fabian, M.: A framework for compositional synthesis of modular nonblocking supervisors. IEEE Trans. Autom. Control **59**(1), 150–162 (2013)
44. Mohajerani, S., Malik, R., Fabian, M.: Compositional synthesis of supervisors in the form of state machines and state maps. Automatica **76**, 277–281 (2017)
45. Murugesan, A., Sokolsky, O., Rayadurgam, S., Whalen, M., Heimdahl, M., Lee, I.: Linking abstract analysis to concrete design: a hierarchical approach to verify medical CPS safety. In: Proceedings of ICCPS 2014 (April 2014)
46. Murugesan, A., Whalen, M.W., Rayadurgam, S., Heimdahl, M.P.: Compositional verification of a medical device system. In: ACM International Conference on High Integrity Language Technology (HILT) 2013. ACM (November 2013)
47. Nejati, S., Gaaloul, K., Menghi, C., Briand, L.C., Foster, S., Wolfe, D.: Evaluating model testing and model checking for finding requirements violations in Simulink models. In: Proceedings of the 2019 27th ACM Joint Meeting on European Software Engineering Conference and Symposium on the Foundations of Software Engineering, pp. 1015–1025 (2019)
48. Pan, G., Vardi, M.Y.: Symbolic techniques in satisfiability solving. In: Giunchiglia, E., Walsh, T. (eds.) SAT 2005. Springer, Dordrecht (2005). https://doi.org/10.1007/978-1-4020-5571-3_3
49. Piterman, N., Pnueli, A., Sa'ar, Y.: Synthesis of reactive(1) designs. In: Emerson, E.A., Namjoshi, K.S. (eds.) VMCAI 2006. LNCS, vol. 3855, pp. 364–380. Springer, Heidelberg (2005). https://doi.org/10.1007/11609773_24
50. Pnueli, A., Rosner, R.: On the synthesis of a reactive module. In: Proceedings of the 16th ACM SIGPLAN-SIGACT Symposium on Principles of Programming Languages, pp. 179–190. ACM (1989)
51. Post, A., Hoenicke, J., Podelski, A.: rt-inconsistency: a new property for real-time requirements. In: Giannakopoulou, D., Orejas, F. (eds.) FASE 2011. LNCS, vol. 6603, pp. 34–49. Springer, Heidelberg (2011). https://doi.org/10.1007/978-3-642-19811-3_4
52. Roth, S.: Erweiterte Konsistenzanalyse für Anforderune (Checking Extended Consistency for Requirements). Master's thesis, Karlsruhe Institute of Technology (2011). see Section 3.2

53. Ryzhyk, L., Chubb, P., Kuz, I., Le Sueur, E., Heiser, G.: Automatic device driver synthesis with termite. In: Proceedings of the ACM SIGOPS 22nd Symposium on Operating Systems Principles, pp. 73–86. ACM (2009)
54. Skiena, S.S.: The Algorithm Design Manual: Text, vol. 1. Springer, Heidelberg (1998). https://doi.org/10.1007/978-1-84800-070-4
55. Stachtiari, E., Mavridou, A., Katsaros, P., Bliudze, S., Sifakis, J.: Early validation of system requirements and design through correctness-by-construction. J. Syst. Softw. 145, 52–78 (2018)
56. Tabajara, L.M., Vardi, M.Y.: Factored Boolean functional synthesis. In: 2017 Formal Methods in Computer Aided Design (FMCAD), pp. 124–131. IEEE (2017)
57. Zeller, A., Hildebrandt, R.: Simplifying and isolating failure-inducing input. IEEE Trans. Softw. Eng. 28(2), 183–200 (2002)

Fingerprinting Bluetooth Low Energy Devices via Active Automata Learning

Andrea Pferscher$^{(\boxtimes)}$ and Bernhard K. Aichernig⑩

Institute of Software Technology, Graz University of Technology, Graz, Austria
{apfersch,aichernig}@ist.tugraz.at

Abstract. Active automata learning is a technique to automatically infer behavioral models of black-box systems. Today's learning algorithms enable the deduction of models that describe complex system properties, e.g., timed or stochastic behavior. Despite recent improvements in the scalability of learning algorithms, their practical applicability is still an open issue. Little work exists that actually learns models of physical black-box systems. To fill this gap in the literature, we present a case study on applying automata learning on the Bluetooth Low Energy (BLE) protocol. It shows that not the size of the system limits the applicability of automata learning. Instead, the interaction with the system under learning, is a major bottleneck that is rarely discussed. In this paper, we propose a general automata learning architecture for learning a behavioral model of the BLE protocol implemented by a physical device. With this framework, we can successfully learn the behavior of five investigated BLE devices. The learned models reveal several behavioral differences. This shows that automata learning can be used for fingerprinting black-box devices, i.e., identifying systems via their specific learned models. Based on the fingerprint, an attacker may exploit vulnerabilities specific to a device.

Keywords: Active automata learning · Model inference · Learning-based testing · Fingerprinting · Bluetooth Low Energy · IoT

1 Introduction

Bluetooth is a key communication technology in many different fields. Currently, it is assumed that 4.5 billion Bluetooth devices are shipped annually and that the number will grow to 6.4 billion by 2025 [9]. This growth mainly refers to the increase of peripheral devices that support Bluetooth Low Energy (BLE). With BLE, Bluetooth became also accessible for low-energy devices. Hence, BLE is a vital technology in the Internet of Things (IoT).

The amount of heterogeneous devices in the IoT makes the assurance of dependability a challenging task. Additionally, the insight into IoT components is frequently limited. Therefore, the system under test must be considered as a black-box. Enabling in-depth testing of black-box systems is difficult, but can

© Springer Nature Switzerland AG 2021
M. Huisman et al. (Eds.): FM 2021, LNCS 13047, pp. 524–542, 2021.
https://doi.org/10.1007/978-3-030-90870-6_28

be achieved with model-based testing techniques. Garbelini et al. [17] successfully used a generic model of the BLE protocol to detect security vulnerabilities of BLE devices via model-based fuzzing. However, their work states that the creation of such a comprehensive model was challenging since the BLE protocol has high degrees of freedom. In practice, the creation of such a model is an error-prone process and is usually not feasible.

To overcome the problem of model availability, learning-based testing techniques have been proposed [4]. In learning-based testing, we use automata learning algorithms to automatically infer a behavioral model of a black-box system. The learned model could then be used for further verification. Motivated by promising results of learning-based testing, various automata learning algorithms have been proposed to extend learning for more complex system properties like timed [6,32] or stochastic behavior [30]. However, few of these algorithms have been evaluated on systems in practice.

In this paper, we present a case study that applies active automata learning on real physical devices. Our objective is to learn the behavioral model of the BLE protocol implementation. For this, we propose a general automata-learning framework that automatically infers the behavioral model of BLE devices. Our presented framework uses state-of-the-art automata learning techniques. We adapt these algorithms considering practical challenges that occur in learning real network components.

In our case study, we present our results on learning five different BLE devices. Based on these results, we stress two different findings. First, we observe that the implementations of the BLE stacks differ from device to device. Using this observation, we show that active automata learning can be used to identify black-box systems. That is, our proposed framework generates a fingerprint of a BLE device. Second, the presented performance metrics show that not only does the system's size influences the performance of the learning algorithm. Additionally, the creation of a deterministic learning setup creates a significant overhead which has an impact on the efficiency of the learning algorithm, since we have to repeat queries and wait for answers.

The contribution of this paper is threefold: First, we present our developed framework that enables learning of BLE protocol implementations of peripheral devices. Second, we present the performed case study that evaluates our framework on real physical devices. The framework including the learned models is available **online**[1] [22]. Third, we propose how our presented technique can be used to fingerprint black-box systems.

The paper is structured as follows. Section 2 discusses the used modeling formalism, active automata learning, and the BLE protocol. In Sect. 3, we propose our learning architecture, followed by the performed evaluation based on this framework in Sect. 4. Section 5 discusses related work and Sect. 6 concludes the paper.

---

[1] https://github.com/apferscher/ble-learning.

2 Preliminaries

2.1 Mealy Machines

Mealy machines represent a neat modeling formalism for systems that create observable outputs after an input execution, i.e., reactive systems. Moreover, many state-of-the-art automata learning algorithms and frameworks [18,20] support Mealy machines. A Mealy machine is a finite state machine, where the states are connected via transitions that are labeled with input actions and the corresponding observable outputs. Starting from an initial state, input sequences can be executed and the corresponding output sequence is returned. Definition 1 formally defines Mealy machines.

Definition 1 (Mealy machine). *A Mealy machine is a 6-tuple* $\mathcal{M} = \langle Q, q_0, I, O, \delta, \lambda \rangle$ *where*

- Q *is the finite set of states*
- q_0 *is the initial state*
- I *is the finite set of inputs*
- O *is the finite set of outputs*
- $\delta : Q \times I \rightarrow Q$ *is the state-transition function*
- $\lambda : Q \times I \rightarrow O$ *is the output function*

To ensure learnability, we require $\mathcal{M}$ to be deterministic and input-enabled. Hence, δ and λ are total functions. Let S be the set of observable sequences, where a sequence $s \in S$ consists of consecutive input/output pairs $(i_1, o_1), \ldots,$ $(i_i, o_i), \ldots, (i_n, o_n)$ with $i_i \in I$, $o_i \in O$, $i \leq n$ and $n \in \mathbb{N}$ defining the length of the sequence. We define $s_I \in I^*$ as the corresponding input sequence of s, and $s_O \in O^*$ maps to the output sequence. We extend δ and λ for sequences. The state transition function $\delta^* : Q \times I^* \rightarrow Q$ gives the reached state after the execution of the input sequence and the output function $\lambda^* : Q \times I^* \rightarrow O^*$ returns the observed output sequence. We define two Mealy machines $\mathcal{M} = \langle Q, q_0, I, O, \delta, \lambda \rangle$ and $\mathcal{M}' = \langle Q', q_0', I, O, \delta', \lambda' \rangle$ as equal if $\forall s_i \in I^* : \lambda^*(q_0, s_i) = \lambda'^*(q_0', s_i)$, i.e. the execution of all input sequences lead to equal output sequences.

2.2 Active Automata Learning

In automata learning, we learn a behavioral model of a system based on a set of execution traces. Depending on the generation of these traces, we distinguish between two techniques: *passive* and *active* learning. Passive techniques reconstruct the behavioral model from a given set of traces, e.g., log files. Consequently, the learned model can only be as expressive as the provided traces. Active techniques, instead, actively query the system under learning (SUL). Hence, actively learned models are more likely to cover rare events that cannot be observed from ordinary system monitoring.

Many current active learning algorithms build upon the L^* algorithm proposed by Angulin [7]. The original algorithm learns the minimal deterministic finite automaton (DFA) of a regular language. Angluin's seminal work introduces the minimally adequate teacher (MAT) framework, which comprises two members: the *learner* and the *teacher*. The learner constructs a DFA by questioning the teacher, who has knowledge about the SUL. The MAT framework distinguishes between *membership* and *equivalence* queries. Using membership queries, the learner asks if a word is part of the language, which can be either answered with *yes* or *no* by the teacher. Based on these answers, the learner constructs an initial behavioral model. The constructed hypothesis is then provided to the teacher in order to ask if the DFA conforms to the SUL, i.e. the learner queries equivalence. The teacher answers to equivalence queries either with a counterexample that shows non-conformance between the hypothesis and the SUL or by responding *yes* to affirm conformance. In the case that a counterexample is responded, the learner uses this counterexample to pose new membership queries and construct a new hypothesis. This procedure is repeated until a conforming hypothesis is proposed.

The L^* algorithm has been extended to learn Mealy machines of reactive systems [19,21,27]. To learn Mealy machines, membership queries are replaced by output queries. For this, the learner asks for the output sequence on a given sequence of inputs. We assume that the teacher has access to the SUL in order to execute inputs and observe outputs.

In practice, we cannot assume a *perfect* teacher who provides the shortest counterexample that shows non-conformance between the hypothesis and the SUL. To overcome this problem, we use conformance testing to substitute equivalence queries. For this, we need to define a conformance relation between the hypothesis and the SUL based on testing. Tretmans [33] introduces an implementation relation $\mathcal{I}$ **imp** $\mathcal{S}$, which defines conformance between an implementation $\mathcal{I}$ and a specification $\mathcal{S}$. In model-based testing, $\mathcal{I}$ would be a black-box system and $\mathcal{S}$ a formal specification in terms of a model, e.g., a Mealy machine. Furthermore, he denotes that $\mathcal{I}$ **passes** t if the execution of the test t on $\mathcal{I}$ leads to the expected results. Based on a test suite $T_\mathcal{S}$ that adequately represents the specification $\mathcal{S}$, Tretmans defines the conformance relation as follows.

$$\mathcal{I} \text{ imp } \mathcal{S} \Leftrightarrow \forall t \subset T_\mathcal{S} : \mathcal{I} \textbf{ passes } t \tag{1}$$

Informally, $\mathcal{I}$ conforms to $\mathcal{S}$, if $\mathcal{I}$ passes all test cases. We apply this conformance relation for conformance testing during learning. In learning, we try to verify if the learned hypothesis $\mathcal{H}$ conforms to the black-box SUL $\mathcal{I}$, i.e., if the relation $\mathcal{H}$ **imp** $\mathcal{I}$ is satisfied. Furthermore, we assume that $\mathcal{I}$ can be represented by the modeling formalism of $\mathcal{H}$. Based on the definition of equivalence of Mealy machines, Tappler [29] stresses that $\mathcal{I}$ **imp** $\mathcal{H} \Leftrightarrow \mathcal{H}$ **imp** $\mathcal{I}$ holds. Therefore, we can define the conformance relation for learning Mealy machines based on a test suite $T \subseteq I^*$ as follows.

$$\mathcal{H} \text{ imp } \mathcal{I} \Leftrightarrow \forall t \in T : \lambda^*_\mathcal{H}(q_0^\mathcal{H}, t) = \lambda^*_\mathcal{I}(q_0^\mathcal{I}, t) \tag{2}$$

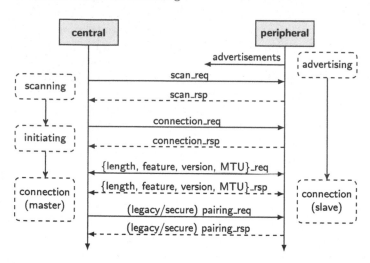

Fig. 1. Communication between a BLE central and peripheral to establish connection. The sequence diagram is adapted from [17].

2.3 Bluetooth Low Energy

The BLE protocol is a lightweight alternative to the classic Bluetooth protocol, specially designed to provide a low-energy alternative for IoT devices. The Bluetooth specification [10] defines the connection protocol between two BLE devices according to different layers of the BLE protocol stack. Based on the work of Garbelini et al. [17], Fig. 1 shows the initial communication messages of two connecting BLE devices on a more abstracted level. We distinguish between the *peripheral* and the *central* device. In the remainder of this paper, we refer to the central device simply as *central* and to the peripheral device as *peripheral*. The peripheral sends advertisements to show that it is available for connection with a central. According to the BLE specification, the peripheral is in the *advertising* state. If the central scans for advertising devices it is in the *scanning* state. For this, the central sends a scan request (scan_req) to the peripheral, which response with a scan response (scan_rsp). In the next step, the central changes from the *scanning* to the *initiating* state by sending the connection request (connection_req). If the peripheral answers with a connection response (connection_rsp), the peripheral and central enter the *connection* state. The BLE specification defines now the central as *master* and the peripheral as *slave*. After the connection, the negotiation on communication parameters starts. Both the central and peripheral can request features or send control packages. These request and control packages include maximum package length, maximum transmission unit (MTU), BLE version, and feature exchanges. As noted by Garbelini et al. [17], the order of the feature requests is not defined in the BLE specification and can differ for each device. After this parameter negotiation, the pairing procedure starts by sending a pairing request (pairing_req) from the central to the peripheral, answered by a pairing response (pairing_rsp). The

BLE protocol distinguishes two pairing procedures: *legacy* and *secure* pairing. In the remainder of this paper, we will only consider *secure* pairing requests.

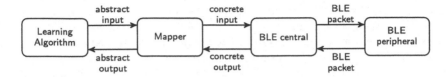

Fig. 2. Similar to the interface of Tappler et al. [31] we create a learning architecture to execute abstract queries on the BLE peripheral.

3   Learning Setup

Our objective is to learn the behavioral model of the BLE protocol implemented by the peripheral device. The learning setup is based on active automata learning, assuming that unusual input sequences reveal characteristic behavior that enables fingerprinting. According to Sect. 2.3, we can model the BLE protocol as a reactive system. Tappler et al. [31] propose a learning setup for network components. Following a similar architecture, we propose a general learning framework for the BLE protocol. Figure 2 depicts the four components of the learning interface: learning algorithm, mapper, BLE central and BLE peripheral.

The applied *learning algorithm* is an improved variant of the L^* algorithm. Since L^* is based on an exhaustive input exploration in each state, we assume that it is beneficial for fingerprinting. Rivest and Schapire [24] proposed the improved L^* version that contains an advanced counterexample processing. This improvement might reduce the number of required output queries. Considering that the BLE setup is based on Python, we aim at a consistent learning framework integration. At present, AALPY [20] is a novel active learning library that is also written in Python. AALPY implements state-of-the-art learning algorithms and conformance testing techniques, including the improved L^* variant that is considered here. Since the framework implements equivalence queries via conformance testing, we assume that the conformance relation defined in Eq. 2 holds. To create a sufficient test suite, we combine random testing with state coverage. The applied test-case generation technique generates for each state in the hypothesis n_{test} input traces. The generated input traces of length n_{len} comprise the input prefixes to the currently considered state concatenated with a random input sequence.

Learning physical devices via a wireless network connection introduces problems that hamper the straightforward application of the learning algorithm. We observe two main problems: package loss and non-deterministic behavior. Both problems required adaptions of the AALPY framework. Package loss might be critical for packages that are necessary to establish a connection. To overcome unexpected connection losses, we assume that the scanning and connection requests are always answered by corresponding responses of the peripheral. If we do not receive such a response, we assume that the request was lost and report a connection error. In the case of a connection error, we repeat the performed output query. To guarantee termination, the query is only repeated up to n_{error} times. After n_{error} repetitions, we abort the learning procedure.

We pursue an akin procedure for non-deterministic behavior. Non-determinism might occur due to the loss or delay of responses. In Sect. 4, we discuss further causes of non-deterministic behavior that we experienced during learning. If we observe non-determinism, we repeat the output query. Again we define an upper limit for a repeating non-deterministic behavior by a maximum of n_{nondet} query executions.

The applied learning algorithm requires that the SUL is resettable since it is expected that every output query is executed from the initial state of the SUL. The learning library AALPY can perform resetting actions before and after the output query execution. We denote the method that is called *before* executing the output query as **pre** and the method *after* the output query as **post**. We assume that the peripheral can be reset by the central by sending a scan_req. To ensure a proper reset before executing the output query, a scan request is performed in the **pre** method.

Besides the reset, we have to consider that some peripherals might enter a standby state in which they stop advertising. This could be the case, e.g., if the peripheral does not receive any expected commands from the central after a certain amount of time. The main problem of a peripheral entering the standby state is that the central might not be able to bring back the peripheral to the advertising state. To prevent the peripheral from entering the standby state, we send keep-alive messages in the **pre** and **post** method. These keep-alive messages include a connection request followed by a scan request. To ensure a proper state before executing the output query, we check for connection errors during the keep-alive messages as previously described.

The *mapper* component serves as an abstraction mechanism. Considering a more universal input and output alphabet, we learn a behavioral model on a more abstract level. The learning algorithm, therefore, generates output queries that comprise abstract input sequences. The mapper receives these abstract inputs and translates them to concrete inputs that can be executed by the central. After the central received a concrete input action, the central returns the corresponding concrete output. This concrete output is then taken by the mapper and translated to a more abstract output that is used by the learning algorithm to construct the hypothesis.

The abstracted input alphabet to learn the behavior of the BLE protocol implementations is defined by $I^A = \{$scan_req, connection_req, length_req, length_rsp, feature_req, feature_rsp, version_req, mtu_req, pairing_req$\}$. The abstract inputs of I^A are then translated to concrete BLE packages that can be sent by the central to the peripheral. For example, the abstract input length_req is translated to a BLE control package including a corresponding valid command of the BLE protocol stack. For the construction of the BLE packages we use the Python library SCAPY [26]. In SCAPY syntax the BLE package for the length_req can be defined as BTLE/BTLE_DATA/BTLE_CTRL/LL_LENGTH_REQ(*params*).

Considering the input/output definition of reactive systems, it may be unusual to include responses in the input alphabet. For our setup, we included the feature and length response as inputs. In Sect. 2.3, we explained that after the connection request of the central, also the peripheral might send control packages or feature requests. To explore more behavior of the peripheral, we have to reply to received requests from the peripheral. In a learning setup, the inputs feature_rsp and length_rsp are responses from the central to received outputs from the peripheral that contain requests. For learning an expressive behavioral model, we consider responses to feature and length requests, i.e. feature_rsp and length_rsp, as additional inputs.

Regarding translation of outputs, the mapper returns the received BLE packages conforming to the SCAPY syntax. One exception applies to the response on scan_req, where two possible valid responses are mapped to one scan response (ADV). In the BLE protocol it is possible that one input might lead to multiple responses that are distributed via individual BLE packages. For the creation of a single output, the mapper collects several responses in a set. The collected outputs in the set are then concatenated in alphabetical order to one output string. This creates deterministic behavior, even though packages might be received in a different order. We repeat the collection of BLE package responses at least $n_{\min}^{\mathrm{rsp}}$ times. If after $n_{\min}^{\mathrm{rsp}}$ responses no convincing response has been returned, we continue listening for responses. We define a response as *convincing*, if the received package contains more than a BLE data package, i.e. BTLE/BTLE_DATA. However, the maximum number of listening attempts is limited by $n_{\max}^{\mathrm{rsp}}$. If we do not receive any BLE package after $n_{\max}^{\mathrm{rsp}}$, the mapper returns the empty output which is denoted by the string EMPTY. As previously mentioned, the assumption of an empty response is not valid for scan and connection requests. In the case of $n_{\max}^{\mathrm{rsp}}$ empty responses, we perform the described connection-error handling.

The *BLE central* component comprises the adapter implementation and the physical central device. We use the Nordic nRF52840 USB dongle as central. Our learning setup requires to stepwise send BLE packages to the peripheral device. For this, our implementation follows the setup proposed by Garbelini et al. [17]. We use their provided firmware for the Nordic nRF52840 System on a Chip (SoC) and adapted their driver implementation to perform single steps of the BLE protocol.

The *BLE peripheral* represents the black-box device that we want to learn, i.e., the SUL. We assume that the peripheral is advertising and only interacts with our central device. For learning, we require that the peripheral is resettable and that the reset can be initiated by the central. After a reset, the peripheral should be again in the advertising state.

4 Evaluation

We evaluated the proposed automata learning setup for the BLE protocol in a case study consisting of five different BLE devices. The learning framework is available **online**[2] [22]. The repository contains the source code for the BLE learning framework, the firmware for the Nordic nRF52840 Dongle and Nordic nRF52840 Development Kit, the learned automata, and the learning results.

Table 1. Evaluated BLE devices

Company (Board)	SoC	Application
Cypress (CY8CPROTO-063-BLE)	CYBLE-416045-02	Find Me Target
Nordic (decaWave DWM1001-DEV)	nRF52832	Nordic GATTS
Texas Instruments (LAUNCHXL-CC2640R2)	CC2640R2	Project Zero
Texas Instruments (LAUNCHXL-CC2650)	CC2650	Project Zero
Cypress (Raspberry Pi 4 Model B)	CYW43455	BlueZ GATT Server[a]

[a] https://scribles.net/creating-ble-gatt-server-uart-service-on-raspberry-pi/

4.1 BLE Devices

Table 1 lists the five investigated BLE devices. In the remainder of this section, we refer to the BLE devices by their SoC identifiers. All evaluated SoCs support the Bluetooth v5.0 standard [10]. To enable a BLE communication, we deployed and ran an example of a BLE application on the SoC. The considered BLE applications were either already installed by the semiconductor manufacturer or taken from examples in the semiconductor's specific software development kits. In the case of the CYW43455 (Raspberry Pi), an example code from the internet was used.

4.2 BLE Learning

For our learning setup, we used the Python learning library AALPY [20] (version 1.0.1). For the composition of the BLE packages, we used a modified version of the Python library SCAPY [26] (version 2.4.4). The used modifications are now available on SCAPY v2.4.5. All experiments were performed with Python 3.9.0 on an Apple MacBook Pro 2019 with an Intel Quad-Core i5 operating at 2.4 GHz and with 8 GB RAM. As BLE central device, we used the Nordic nRF52840 Dongle. The deployed firmware for the USB dongle was taken from the SWEYNTOOTH repository [16].

Learning the communication protocol in use by interacting with a non-simulated physical device may cause unexpected behavior, e.g., the loss of transmitted packages. This erroneous behavior can cause missing responses or non-deterministic behavior. To adapt the AALPY framework for such a real-world

---

[2] https://github.com/apferscher/ble-learning

setup, we modified the implementation of the equivalence oracle and the used caching mechanism. These modifications of our framework handle connection errors and non-deterministic outputs according to our explanation in Sect. 3. For this, we set the maximum number of consecutive connection errors $n_{error} = 20$ and the number of consecutive non-deterministic output queries to $n_{nondet} = 5$. Our experiments show that this parameters setup created a stable and fast learning setup.

For conformance testing, we copied the class `StatePrefixEqOracle` from AALPY and added our error handling behavior. The number of performed queries per state is set to $n_{test} = 10$ and the number of performed inputs per query is set to $n_{len} = 10$. We stress that the primary focus of this paper was to generate a fingerprint of the investigated BLE SoCs. Therefore, it was sufficient to perform a lower number of conformance tests. However, we recommend increasing the number of conformance tests if a more accurate statement about conformance of the model to the SUL is required.

Table 2. Learning results of four out of five evaluated BLE SoCs

	CYBLE-416045-02	nRF52832	CC2650	CYW43455
# States	3	5	5	11
Total time in minutes (min)	25.86	151.47	49.63	209.43
Learning (min)	20.42	85.43	36.57	159.66
Conformance checking (min)	5.44	66.04	13.06	49.77
# Output Queries	243	406	405	891
# Output Query Steps	729	1461	1458	4131
# Conformance Tests	30	50	50	111
# Conformance Test Steps	330	580	580	1403
# Connection Errors	555	913	910	2071
# Non-Deterministic Queries	0	1	0	0

In Sect. 3, we explained that a sent BLE message could lead to multiple responses. These responses can be distributed over several BLE packages. Hence, our central listens for a minimum number of responses n_{min}^{rsp}, but stops listening after n_{max}^{rsp} attempts. For our learning setup, we set for all SoCs $n_{min}^{rsp} = 20$ and $n_{max}^{rsp} = 30$. Experiments during our evaluation show that this setup enables stable and fast learning for all SoCs. However, we decided to create a different parameter setup for the scan request. The parameter setup depends on the purpose of the request. We distinguish between two cases. In the first case, we perform the scan request to reset the SUL. On the one hand, we want to continue fast if we receive a response, therefore, $n_{min}^{rsp} = 5$. On the other hand, we want to be sure that the SUL is properly reset, therefore $n_{max}^{rsp} = 100$. The second case occurs during learning where the scan request is included as an input action in an output query. For this purpose, we decrease the parameters to $n_{\min}^{\text{rsp}} = 5$ and $n_{\max}^{\text{rsp}} = 20$, since the query is repeated in case of a missing response.

Table 2 shows learning results for four out of the five investigated SoCs. Results of CC2640R2 are not included, since we were not able to learn a deterministic model of CC2640R2 using the defined input alphabet. We discuss possible reasons for the non-deterministic behavior later. For all other SoCs, we learned a deterministic Mealy machine using the complete input alphabet.

We required for each SUL one learning round, i.e. we did not find a counterexample to conformance between the initially created hypothesis and the SUL. The learned behavioral models range from a simpler structure with only three states (CYBLE-416045-02) to more complex behavior that can be described by eleven states (CYW43455).

The learning of the largest model regarding the number of states (CYW43455) took approximately 3.5 h, whereas the smallest model (CYBLE-416045-02) could be learned in less than half an hour. We observed that the total runtime for SoCs with a similar state space (nRF52832 and CC2650) significantly differs. The results presented in Table 2 show that learning the nRF52832 took three times as long as learning the CC2650, where both learned models have five states. The difference in runtime indicates that the scalability of active automata learning does not merely depends on the input alphabet size and state space of the SUL. Rather, we assume that the overhead to create a deterministic learning setup, e.g. repeating queries or waiting for answers, also influences the efficiency of active automata learning.

Conforming to the state space, the number of performed output queries and steps increases. Rather unexpected, also the number of connection errors seems to align with the complexity of the behavioral model. Therefore, we assume that message loss regularly occurs in our learning setup. The comparison between the number of performed output queries, including conformance tests, and the observed connection errors show that more connection errors occur than output queries are performed. Since an output query would have been repeated after a connection error, we assume that we observe more connection errors in the resetting procedure. This creates our conjecture that a decent error-handling resetting procedure is required to ensure that the SUL is reset to the initial state before the output query is executed. Furthermore, we observe fewer connection errors and non-determinism during the output queries. Hence, we assume that our proposed learning setup appropriately resets the SUL.

Figure 3 shows the learned model of the nRF52832 and Fig. 4 of the CC2650. To provide a clear and concise representation, we merged and simplified transitions. The unmodified learned models of all SoCs considered in this case study are available online[3]. The comparison between the learned models of the nRF52832 (Fig. 3) and the CC2650 (Fig. 4) shows that even models with the same number of states describe different BLE protocol stack implementations. We highlighted in red for both models the transitions that show a different behavior on the input length_rsp. The nRF52832 responds to an unrequested length response

---

[3] https://github.com/apferscher/ble-learning.

only with a BLE data package and then completely resets the connection procedure. Therefore, executing an unexpected length response on the nRF52832 leads to the initial state akin to the performance of a scan request. The CC2650, instead, reacts to an unrequested length response with a response containing the package LL_UNKNOWN_RSP and remains in the same state.

Using the learning setup of Sect. 3, we could not learn the CC2640R2. Independent from the adaption of our error handling parameters, we always observed non-deterministic behavior. More interestingly, the non-deterministic behavior could repeatedly be observed on the following output query.

connection_req · pairing_req · length_rsp · length_req · feature_req

In earlier stages of the learning procedure, we observed the following output sequence after the execution of the inputs.

LL_LENGTH_REQ·SM_PAIRING_RSP·BTLE_DATA·LL_LENGTH_RSP·LL_FEATURE_RSP

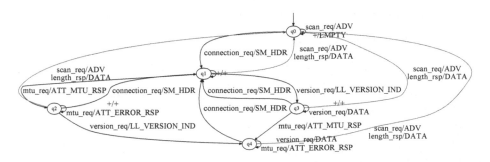

Fig. 3. Simplified learned model of the nRF52832. Inputs are lowercased and outputs are capitalized. For a clear presentation, received outputs are abbreviated, and input and outputs are summarized by the +-symbol.

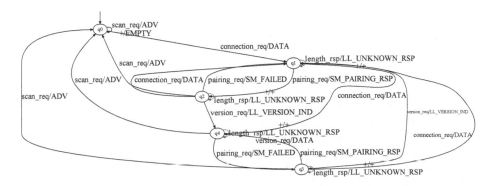

Fig. 4. Simplified learned model of the CC2650.

Table 3. The non-deterministic behavior of the CC2640R2 BLE SoC disabled learning considering the entire input alphabet. The table shows the results of learning with a reduced input alphabet.

	no pairing_req	no length_req	no feature_req
# States	6	11	11
Total time (min)	54.17	88.76	87.15
Learning time (min)	40.83	61.57	60.28
Conformance checking time (min)	13.34	27.19	26.87
# Output Queries	390	705	704
# Output Query Steps	1499	3141	3136
# Conformance Tests	61	110	110
# Conformance Test Steps	710	1370	1370
# Connection Errors	978	1657	1628
# Non-Deterministic Queries	7	1	0

Later in learning, we never again received any feature response for the input feature_req if we executed this output query. The observed outputs always corresponded to the following sequence.

LL_LENGTH_REQ · SM_PAIRING_RSP · BTLE_DATA · LL_LENGTH_RSP · BTLE_DATA

If we remove one of the inputs pairing_req, length_req or feature_req, our learning setup successfully learned a deterministic model. Table 3 shows the learning results for the CC2640R2 with the adapted input alphabets. Compared to the results in Table 2, we observe more non-deterministic behavior, which led to repetitions of output queries.

4.3   BLE Fingerprinting

The comparison of the learned models shows that all investigated SoCs behave differently. Therefore, it is possible to uniquely identify the SoC. The advantage of active automata learning, especially using L^*-based algorithms, is that every input is queried in each state to uniquely identify a state of the model. The collected query information can then be used to fingerprint the system. A closer look at the models shows that even short input sequences sufficiently fingerprint the SoC.

In our BLE learning setup, we noticed that for each learned model, an initial connection request leads to a new state. Table 4 shows the observable outputs for each input after performing the initial connection request connect_req, i.e., the table shows the outputs that identify the state for the corresponding SoC. We determine that the set of observable outputs after an initial connection request is different for every SoC.

A closer look at the observable outputs shows that a combination of only two observable outputs is enough to identify the SoC. We highlight in Table 4 two

Table 4. The investigated SoCs can be identified by only a single model state that is reached after performing an initial connection request. The columns of the table present the outputs that are observed when the input (row) is executed in the connection state. The observable outputs show that only two inputs are required to distinguish the SoCs.

	CYBLE-416045-02	nRF52832	CC2640R2	CC2650	CYW43455
scan_req	ADV	ADV	ADV	ADV	ADV
connect_req	BTLE_DATA	SM_HDR/RAW	LL_LENGTH_REQ	BTLE_DATA	LL_FEATURE_REQ
length_req	LL_UNKNOWN_RSP	LL_LENGTH_RSP	LL_LENGTH_RSP	LL_UNKNOWN_RSP	LL_LENGTH_RSP
length_rsp	LL_UNKNOWN_RSP	BTLE_DATA	BTLE_DATA	LL_UNKNOWN_RSP	LL_REJECT_RSP
feature_req	LL_FEATURE_RSP	LL_FEATURE_RSP	LL_FEATURE_RSP	LL_FEATURE_RSP	LL_FEATURE_RSP
feature_rsp	**LL_REJECT_RSP**	**LL_UNKNOWN_RSP**	**BTLE_DATA**	**BTLE_DATA**	**LL_LENGTH_REQ**
version_req	**LL_VERSION_IND**	**LL_VERSION_IND**	**BTLE_DATA**	**LL_VERSION_IND**	**LL_VERSION_IND**
mtu_req	ATT_MTU_RSP	ATT_MTU_RSP	ATT_MTU_RSP	ATT_MTU_RSP	BTLE_DATA
pairing_req	SM_FAILED	SM_PAIRING	SM_PAIRING	SM_PAIRING	BTLE_DATA

possible output combinations that depict the fingerprint of a SoC. We note that also other output combinations are possible. We can now use the corresponding inputs to generate a single output query that uniquely identifies one of our investigated SoCs. Under the consideration that a scan request resets the SoC, we define the fingerprinting for the five SoCs output query as follows.

scan_req · connection_req · feature_rsp · scan_req · connection_req · version_req

The execution of this output query leads to a different observed output sequence for each of the five investigated SoCs. For example, the corresponding output sequence for the nRF52832 is

ADV · SM_HDR · LL_UNKNOWN_RSP · ADV · SM_HDR · LL_VERSION_IND,

whereas the sequence for the CC2650 is

ADV · BTLE_DATA · BTLE_DATA · ADV · BTLE_DATA · LL_VERSION_IND.

The proposed manual analysis serves as a proof of concept that active automata learning can be used for fingerprinting BLE SoCs. Obviously, the found input sequences for fingerprinting are only valid for the given SoCs. For other SoCs, a new model should be learned to identify a possibly extended set of input sequences for fingerprinting. We note that this fingerprinting sequence could also be found rather fast by random test execution. The advantage of using automata learning for fingerprinting is that the models only have to be created once. Based on these behavioral models, we could create new fingerprinting sequences if we consider further SoCs. For this, is not required to test the prior investigated SoCs. However, we recommend replacing the manual analysis with an automatic conformance testing technique between the models akin to Tappler et al. [31].

5   Related Work

Celosia and Cunche [11] also investigated fingerprinting BLE devices, however, their proposed methodology is based on the Generic Attribute Profile (GATT), whereas our technique also operates on different layers, e.g. the Link Layer (LL), of the BLE protocol stack. Their proposed fingerprinting method is based on a large dataset containing information that can be obtained from the GATT profile, like services and characteristics.

Argyros et al. [8] discuss the combination of active automata learning and differential testing to fingerprint the SULs. They propose a framework where they first learn symbolic finite automata of different implementations and then automatically analyze differences between the learned models. They evaluated their technique on implementations of TCP, web application firewalls, and web browsers. A similar technique was proposed by Tappler et al. [31] investigating the Message Queuing Telemetry Transport (MQTT) protocol. However, their motivation was not to fingerprint MQTT brokers, but rather test for inconsistencies between the learned models. These found inconsistencies show discrepancies to the MQTT specification. Following an akin idea, but motivated by security testing, several communication protocols like TLS [25], TCP [13], SSH [15] or DTLS [14] have been learning-based tested. In the literature, these techniques are denoted as protocol state fuzzing. To the best of our knowledge, none of these techniques interacted with an implementation on an external physical device, but rather interacted via localhost or virtual connections with the SULs.

One protocol state fuzzing technique on physical devices was proposed by Stone et al. [28]. They detected security vulnerabilities in the 802.11 4-Way handshake protocol by testing Wi-Fi routers. Aichernig et al. [3] propose an industrial application for learning-based testing of measurement devices in the automotive industry. Both case studies emphasize our observation that nondeterministic behavior hampers the inference of behavioral models via active automata learning. Other physical devices that have been learned are bank cards [1] and biometric passports [2]. The proposed techniques use a USB-connected smart card reader to interact with the cards. Furthermore, Chalupar et al. [12] used Lego® to create an interface to learn the model of a smart card reader.

6   Conclusion

Summary. In this paper, we presented a case study on learning-based testing of the BLE protocol. The aim of this case study was to evaluate learning-based testing in a practical setup. For this, we proposed a general learning architecture for BLE devices. The proposed architecture enabled the inference of a model that describes the behavior of a BLE protocol implementation. We evaluated our presented learning framework in a case study consisting of five BLE devices. The results of the case study show that the active learning of a behavioral model is possible in a practicable amount of time. However, our evaluation showed that adaptions to state-of-the-art learning algorithms, such as including error-handling procedures, were required for successful model inference. The learned models depicted that implementations of the BLE stack vary significantly from device to device. This observation confirmed our hypothesis that active automata learning enables fingerprinting of black-box systems.

Discussion. We successfully applied active automata learning to reverse engineer the behavioral models of BLE devices. Despite the challenges in creating a reliable and general learning framework to learn a physical device, the BLE interface creation only needs to be done once. Our proposed framework, which is also publicly available [22], can now be used for learning the behavioral models of many BLE devices. Our presented learning results show that in practice the scalability of active automata learning not only depends on the efficiency of the underlying learning algorithm but also on the overhead due to SUL interaction. All of the learned models show behavioral differences in the BLE protocol stack implementations. Therefore, we can use active automata learning to fingerprint the underlying SoC of a black-box BLE device. The possibility to fingerprint the BLE could be a possible security issue, since it enables an attacker to exploit specific vulnerabilities, e.g. from a BLE vulnerability collection like SWEYNTOOTH [17]. Compared to the BLE fingerprinting technique of Celosia and Cunche [11], our proposed technique is data and time efficient. Instead of collecting 13 000 data records over five months, we can learn the models within hours.

Future Work. To the best of our knowledge, the learned models do not show any security vulnerabilities. However, for future work, we plan to consider further levels of the BLE protocol stack, e.g., the encryption-key exchange in the pairing procedure. Considering these levels of the BLE stack might reveal security issues. Related work [13,14,25,28] has shown that automata learning can successfully be used to detected security vulnerabilities. Therefore, learning the security-critical behavior of the BLE protocol might be interesting for further security analysis and testing.

Our proposed method was inspired by the work of Garbelini et al. [17], since their presented fuzz-testing technique demonstrated that model-based testing is applicable to BLE devices. Instead of creating the model manually, we showed that learning a behavioral model of the BLE protocol implemented on a physical device is possible. For future work, it would be interesting to use our learned models to generate test cases for fuzzing. We are currently working on extending our proposed learning framework for learning-based fuzzing of the BLE protocol. For this, we follow a similar technique that we proposed on fuzzing the MQTT protocol via active automata learning [5].

We find that the non-deterministic behavior of the BLE devices hampered the learning of deterministic models. Instead of workarounds to overcome non-deterministic behavior, we could learn a non-deterministic model. We already applied non-deterministic learning on the MQTT protocol [23]. Following a similar idea, we could learn a non-deterministic model of the BLE protocol.

Acknowledgment. This work is supported by the TU Graz LEAD project "Dependable Internet of Things in Adverse Environments" and by the Austrian Research Promotion Agency (FFG), project "LearnTwins". We would like to thank Maximilian Schuh for providing support for the BLE devices and the authors of the SWEYNTOOTH paper for creating an open-source BLE interface. Furthermore, we thank the anonymous reviewers for their useful remarks.

References

1. Aarts, F., de Ruiter, J., Poll, E.: Formal models of bank cards for free. In: Sixth IEEE International Conference on Software Testing, Verification and Validation, ICST 2013 Workshops Proceedings, Luxembourg, Luxembourg, 18–22 March 2013, pp. 461–468. IEEE Computer Society (2013). https://doi.org/10.1109/ICSTW.2013.60

2. Aarts, F., Schmaltz, J., Vaandrager, F.: Inference and abstraction of the biometric passport. In: Margaria, T., Steffen, B. (eds.) ISoLA 2010. LNCS, vol. 6415, pp. 673–686. Springer, Heidelberg (2010). https://doi.org/10.1007/978-3-642-16558-0_54

3. Aichernig, B.K., Burghard, C., Korošec, R.: Learning-based testing of an industrial measurement device. In: Badger, J.M., Rozier, K.Y. (eds.) NFM 2019. LNCS, vol. 11460, pp. 1–18. Springer, Cham (2019). https://doi.org/10.1007/978-3-030-20652-9_1

4. Aichernig, B.K., Mostowski, W., Mousavi, M.R., Tappler, M., Taromirad, M.: Model learning and model-based testing. In: Bennaceur, A., Hähnle, R., Meinke, K. (eds.) Machine Learning for Dynamic Software Analysis: Potentials and Limits. LNCS, vol. 11026, pp. 74–100. Springer, Cham (2018). https://doi.org/10.1007/978-3-319-96562-8_3

5. Aichernig, B.K., Muškardin, E., Pferscher, A.: Learning-based fuzzing of IoT message brokers. In: 14th IEEE Conference on Software Testing, Verification and Validation, ICST 2021, Porto de Galinhas, Brazil, April 12–16, 2021, pp. 47–58. IEEE (2021). https://doi.org/10.1109/ICST49551.2021.00017

6. Aichernig, B.K., Pferscher, A., Tappler, M.: From passive to active: learning timed automata efficiently. In: Lee, R., Jha, S., Mavridou, A., Giannakopoulou, D. (eds.) NFM 2020. LNCS, vol. 12229, pp. 1–19. Springer, Cham (2020). https://doi.org/10.1007/978-3-030-55754-6_1

7. Angluin, D.: Learning regular sets from queries and counterexamples. Inf. Comput. **75**(2), 87–106 (1987). https://doi.org/10.1016/0890-5401(87)90052-6

8. Argyros, G., Stais, I., Jana, S., Keromytis, A.D., Kiayias, A.: Sfadiff: automated evasion attacks and fingerprinting using black-box differential automata learning. In: Weippl, E.R., Katzenbeisser, S., Kruegel, C., Myers, A.C., Halevi, S. (eds.) Proceedings of the 2016 ACM SIGSAC Conference on Computer and Communications Security, Vienna, Austria, 24–28 October 2016, pp. 1690–1701. ACM (2016). https://doi.org/10.1145/2976749.2978383

9. Bluetooth SIG: Market update. https://www.bluetooth.com/wp-content/uploads/2021/01/2021-Bluetooth_Market_Update.pdf. Accessed 6 June 2021

10. Bluetooth SIG: Bluetooth core specification v5.2. Standard (2019). https://www.bluetooth.com/specifications/specs/core-specification/

11. Celosia, G., Cunche, M.: Fingerprinting Bluetooth-Low-Energy devices based on the generic attribute profile. In: Liu, P., Zhang, Y. (eds.) Proceedings of the 2nd International ACM Workshop on Security and Privacy for the Internet-of-Things, IoT S&P@CCS 2019, London, UK, 15 November 2019, pp. 24–31. ACM (2019). https://doi.org/10.1145/3338507.3358617

12. Chalupar, G., Peherstorfer, S., Poll, E., de Ruiter, J.: Automated reverse engineering using Lego®. In: Bratus, S., Lindner, F.F. (eds.) 8th USENIX Workshop on Offensive Technologies, WOOT 2014, San Diego, CA, USA, 19 August 2014. USENIX Association (2014). https://www.usenix.org/conference/woot14/workshop-program/presentation/chalupar

13. Fiterău-Broştean, P., Janssen, R., Vaandrager, F.: Combining model learning and model checking to analyze TCP implementations. In: Chaudhuri, S., Farzan, A. (eds.) CAV 2016. LNCS, vol. 9780, pp. 454–471. Springer, Cham (2016). https://doi.org/10.1007/978-3-319-41540-6_25

14. Fiterau-Brostean, P., Jonsson, B., Merget, R., de Ruiter, J., Sagonas, K., Somorovsky, J.: Analysis of DTLS implementations using protocol state fuzzing. In: Capkun, S., Roesner, F. (eds.) 29th USENIX Security Symposium, USENIX Security 2020, 12–14 August 2020, pp. 2523–2540. USENIX Association (2020). https://www.usenix.org/conference/usenixsecurity20/presentation/fiterau-brostean

15. Fiterau-Brostean, P., Lenaerts, T., Poll, E., de Ruiter, J., Vaandrager, F.W., Verleg, P.: Model learning and model checking of SSH implementations. In: Erdogmus, H., Havelund, K. (eds.) Proceedings of the 24th ACM SIGSOFT International SPIN Symposium on Model Checking of Software, Santa Barbara, CA, USA, 10–14 July 2017, pp. 142–151. ACM (2017). https://doi.org/10.1145/3092282.3092289

16. Garbelini, M.E., Wang, C., Chattopadhyay, S., Sun, S., Kurniawan, E.: SweynTooth - unleashing mayhem over bluetooth low energy. https://github.com/Matheus-Garbelini/sweyntooth_bluetooth_low_energy_attacks. Accessed 5 May 2021

17. Garbelini, M.E., Wang, C., Chattopadhyay, S., Sun, S., Kurniawan, E.: Sweyntooth: unleashing mayhem over Bluetooth Low Energy. In: Gavrilovska, A., Zadok, E. (eds.) 2020 USENIX Annual Technical Conference, USENIX ATC 2020, 15–17 July 2020, pp. 911–925. USENIX Association (2020). https://www.usenix.org/conference/atc20/presentation/garbelini

18. Isberner, M., Howar, F., Steffen, B.: The open-source LearnLib. In: Kroening, D., Păsăreanu, C.S. (eds.) CAV 2015. LNCS, vol. 9206, pp. 487–495. Springer, Cham (2015). https://doi.org/10.1007/978-3-319-21690-4_32

19. Margaria, T., Niese, O., Raffelt, H., Steffen, B.: Efficient test-based model generation for legacy reactive systems. In: Ninth IEEE International High-Level Design Validation and Test Workshop 2004, Sonoma Valley, CA, USA, November 10–12, 2004, pp. 95–100. IEEE Computer Society (2004). https://doi.org/10.1109/HLDVT.2004.1431246, https://ieeexplore.ieee.org/xpl/conhome/9785/proceeding

20. Muškardin, E., Aichernig, B.K., Pill, I., Pferscher, A., Tappler, M.: AALpy: an active automata learning library. In: Hou, Z., Ganesh, V. (eds.) ATVA 2021. LNCS, vol. 12971, pp. 67–73. Springer, Cham (2021). https://doi.org/10.1007/978-3-030-88885-5_5

21. Niese, O.: An integrated approach to testing complex systems. Ph.D. thesis, Technical University of Dortmund, Germany (2003). https://d-nb.info/969717474/34

22. Pferscher, A.: Fingerprinting Bluetooth Low Energy via active automata learning. https://github.com/apferscher/ble-learning. Accessed 10 May 2021

23. Pferscher, A., Aichernig, B.K.: Learning abstracted non-deterministic finite state machines. In: Casola, V., De Benedictis, A., Rak, M. (eds.) ICTSS 2020. LNCS, vol. 12543, pp. 52–69. Springer, Cham (2020). https://doi.org/10.1007/978-3-030-64881-7_4

24. Rivest, R.L., Schapire, R.E.: Inference of finite automata using homing sequences. Inf. Comput. **103**(2), 299–347 (1993). https://doi.org/10.1006/inco.1993.1021

25. de Ruiter, J., Poll, E.: Protocol state fuzzing of TLS implementations. In: Jung, J., Holz, T. (eds.) 24th USENIX Security Symposium, USENIX Security 2015, Washington, D.C., USA, August 12–14, 2015, pp. 193–206. USENIX Association (2015). https://www.usenix.org/conference/usenixsecurity15/technical-sessions/presentation/de-ruiter

26. S, R.R., R, R., Moharir, M., G, S.: Scapy - a powerful interactive packet manipulation program. In: 2018 International Conference on Networking, Embedded and Wireless Systems (ICNEWS), pp. 1–5 (2018). https://doi.org/10.1109/ICNEWS.2018.8903954
27. Shahbaz, M., Groz, R.: Inferring mealy machines. In: Cavalcanti, A., Dams, D.R. (eds.) FM 2009. LNCS, vol. 5850, pp. 207–222. Springer, Heidelberg (2009). https://doi.org/10.1007/978-3-642-05089-3_14
28. McMahon Stone, C., Chothia, T., de Ruiter, J.: Extending automated protocol state learning for the 802.11 4-Way handshake. In: Lopez, J., Zhou, J., Soriano, M. (eds.) ESORICS 2018. LNCS, vol. 11098, pp. 325–345. Springer, Cham (2018). https://doi.org/10.1007/978-3-319-99073-6_16
29. Tappler, M.: Learning-based testing in networked environments in the presence of timed and stochastic behaviour. Ph.D. thesis, TU Graz (2019). https://mtappler.files.wordpress.com/2019/12/thesis.pdf
30. Tappler, M., Aichernig, B.K., Bacci, G., Eichlseder, M., Larsen, K.G.: L^*-based learning of Markov decision processes. In: ter Beek, M.H., McIver, A., Oliveira, J.N. (eds.) FM 2019. LNCS, vol. 11800, pp. 651–669. Springer, Cham (2019). https://doi.org/10.1007/978-3-030-30942-8_38
31. Tappler, M., Aichernig, B.K., Bloem, R.: Model-based testing IoT communication via active automata learning. In: ICST 2017, Tokyo, Japan, March 13–17, 2017, pp. 276–287. IEEE (2017). https://doi.org/10.1109/ICST.2017.32
32. Tappler, M., Aichernig, B.K., Larsen, K.G., Lorber, F.: Time to learn – learning timed automata from tests. In: André, É., Stoelinga, M. (eds.) FORMATS 2019. LNCS, vol. 11750, pp. 216–235. Springer, Cham (2019). https://doi.org/10.1007/978-3-030-29662-9_13
33. Tretmans, J.: Model based testing with labelled transition systems. In: Hierons, R.M., Bowen, J.P., Harman, M. (eds.) Formal Methods and Testing. LNCS, vol. 4949, pp. 1–38. Springer, Heidelberg (2008). https://doi.org/10.1007/978-3-540-78917-8_1

Analysis of Complex Systems

Trace Abstraction-Based Verification for Uninterpreted Programs

Weijiang Hong[1,2], Zhenbang Chen[1(✉)], Yide Du[1], and Ji Wang[1,2(✉)]

[1] College of Computer, National University of Defense Technology, Changsha, China
{hongweijiang17,zbchen,dyd1024,wj}@nudt.edu.cn
[2] State Key Laboratory of High Performance Computing,
National University of Defense Technology, Changsha, China

Abstract. The verification of uninterpreted programs is undecidable in general. This paper proposes to employ counterexample-guided abstraction refinement (CEGAR) framework for verifying uninterpreted programs. Different from the existing interpolant-based trace abstraction, we propose a congruence-based trace abstraction method for infeasible counterexample paths to refine the program's abstraction model, which is designed specifically for uninterpreted programs. Besides, we propose an optimization method that utilizes the decidable verification result for coherent uninterpreted programs to improve the CEGAR framework's efficiency. We have implemented our verification method and evaluated it on two kinds of benchmark programs. Compared with the state-of-the-art, our method is more effective and efficient, and achieves 3.6x speedups on average.

Keywords: Uninterpreted programs · CEGAR · Trace abstraction

1 Introduction

Uninterpreted programs [15] belong to a class of programs in which there are uninterpreted functions [12]. An uninterpreted function f only has a function signature (*i.e.*, function name, and the types of input and output) but no other definitions. f only satisfies the common property, *i.e.*, given the same input, f produces the same output. Uninterpreted programs are motivated in many scenarios of program analysis and verification. For example, suppose we want to verify a partial program in which some functions are not defined. We can over-approximate the program by considering the undefined functions as uninterpreted functions. Even for well-defined programs, we can carry out a pre-analysis of a function by considering all the called functions in f as uninterpreted functions. Specially, the solving of the SMT formulas in the theory of equality and uninterpreted functions is decidable and has a PSPACE complexity [11]. However, the verification problem of uninterpreted programs is generally undecidable [15], because of the loop structures.

Weijiang Hong and Zhenbang Chen contributed equally to this work and are cofirst authors.

© Springer Nature Switzerland AG 2021
M. Huisman et al. (Eds.): FM 2021, LNCS 13047, pp. 545–562, 2021.
https://doi.org/10.1007/978-3-030-90870-6_29

There exists a sub-class of uninterpreted programs (called *coherent* uninterpreted programs) whose verification problem is decidable and PSPACE-complete [15]. As far as we know, there exist no verification methods designed specifically for the general uninterpreted programs. In this paper, we propose to leverage the idea of counterexample-guided abstraction refinement (CEGAR) [6] to verify safety properties of uninterpreted programs. Although the existing CEGAR-based verification methods, such as [8] and [1], are also applicable for uninterpreted programs, we argue that more efficient CEGAR-based verification for uninterpreted programs can be achieved by employing the abstraction and refinement methods designed specifically for uninterpreted programs.

Leveraging the decidable result of coherent program verification in [15], we propose in this paper a trace abstraction [8] based CEGAR framework to verify uninterpreted programs. Different from the traditional SMT-based trace feasibility checking [5] and interpolant-based trace abstraction [8], our framework provides a new congruence-based method for abstracting the infeasible counterexample traces. The congruence-based method directly captures the core invariant features (*i.e.*, equality and congruence closure [18]) of uninterpreted programs and improves the efficiency of trace abstraction-based refinement. Besides, based on the observation that some parts (even the ones containing complex loops) of an uninterpreted program are *coherent* [15] and can be efficiently verified, we propose an optimization for the CEGAR framework that verifies the program's coherent part first and then employs the CEGAR-based procedure to verify the remaining part, which can further improve the verification's efficiency.

The main contributions of this paper are as follows:

- We propose a CEGAR-based verification framework for uninterpreted programs. The framework verifies the program's coherent part first and then employs the CEGAR-based procedure to verify the non-coherent part.
- We propose a new congruence-based trace abstraction method which utilizes the verification method of coherent programs for checking the trace feasibility and constructing the trace abstraction.
- We have implemented our CEGAR framework for Boogie uninterpreted programs. The experimental results on several benchmarks indicate that: compared with the *state-of-the-art* work [7], *i.e.*, ULTIMATE, our method achieves in average 3.6x speedup for the verified programs.

Related Work. Our work is closely related to the existing work for uninterpreted programs. In [15], the decidability result of coherent uninterpreted programs is discovered, which inspires our work. Following the work [15], Mathur *et al.* extend the decidable result to the programs with memory allocations [17]. In [20], La Torre *et al.* prove that the verification of coherent concurrent programs is decidable. Krogmeier *et al.* in [13] investigate the synthesis problem of uninterpreted programs and propose a decidable synthesis procedure for coherent uninterpreted programs. Besides, Mathur *et al.* in [16] study the verification problem of uninterpreted programs under different types of data models. Different from these approaches, we consider the verification problem of general uninterpreted programs. Another line is CEGAR-based program verification methods [1,3,4,8], which differ in the target programs, abstraction models, and refinement methods. Our work for uninterpreted programs is in the style of trace abstraction-based refinement [8]. Unlike the interpolant-based trace abstraction method [3,4,8–10], our abstraction is congruence-based and provides a new mechanism for the trace abstraction of uninterpreted programs.

Structure. The remainder of this paper is organized as follows. A brief summary of the backgrounds and an illustration of our method are presented in Sect. 2. The verification framework's details will be presented in Sect. 3. The evaluation of our method and its results are presented in Sect. 4. Finally, Sect. 5 concludes the paper.

2 Background and Illustration

This section briefly introduces uninterpreted programs. Then, we use a motivation example to illustrate our trace abstraction based verification method.

2.1 Uninterpreted Programs

Syntax Let Σ be a *finite* symbolic set, and $\mathbb{C} \subseteq \Sigma$ the constant set. The syntax of uninterpreted programs is defined in Fig. 1, where $c \in \mathbb{C}, x, y, f \in \Sigma$, and $\bar{z}$ denotes a tuple of symbols.

$$\langle stmt \rangle ::= \mathbf{skip} \mid x := c \mid x := y \mid x := f(\bar{z})$$
$$\mid \mathbf{assume}(\langle cond \rangle) \mid \mathbf{assert}(\langle cond \rangle)$$
$$\mid \langle stmt \rangle \, \mathbf{;} \, \langle stmt \rangle$$
$$\mid \mathbf{if} \, (\langle cond \rangle) \, \mathbf{then} \, \langle stmt \rangle \, \mathbf{else} \, \langle stmt \rangle$$
$$\mid \mathbf{while} \, (\langle cond \rangle) \, \langle stmt \rangle$$

$$\langle cond \rangle ::= x = y \mid \langle cond \rangle \wedge \langle cond \rangle \mid \neg \langle cond \rangle$$

Fig. 1. The syntax of uninterpreted programs.

For the *atomic* statements, the statement **skip** does nothing and is the unit statement. $x := c$ is the constant assignment statement. $x := y$ is the assignment statement. $x := f(\bar{z})$ assigns the term of the uninterpreted function f to variable x. The term accepts the tuple $\bar{z}$. The assume statement $\mathbf{assume}(\langle cond \rangle)$ blocks the program states that does not satisfy $\langle cond \rangle$; otherwise, it is a **skip**. The assertion statement $\mathbf{assert}(\langle cond \rangle)$ requires that all the states reaching the statement should satisfy $\langle cond \rangle$. There are three compositive statements: sequential composition, if-then-else branch composition, and while loop composition. For conditions, there is only one atomic condition, *i.e.*, equality. It indicates that x is equal to y. Then, for the sake of brevity, we only include the conjunction and negation operations. Note that there only exist symbols in uninterpreted programs. Besides, we can also represent other kinds of relations as functions.

$$\frac{\mathcal{P} = \mathbf{skip}}{\langle \mathcal{M}, \mathcal{S} \rangle \rightarrow_{\mathcal{P}} \langle \mathcal{M}, \mathcal{S} \rangle} \qquad \frac{\mathcal{P} = x := c}{\langle \mathcal{M}, \mathcal{S} \rangle \rightarrow_{\mathcal{P}} \langle \mathcal{M}, \mathcal{S}[x \mapsto \mathcal{I}(c)] \rangle}$$

$$\frac{\mathcal{P} = x := y}{\langle \mathcal{M}, \mathcal{S} \rangle \rightarrow_{\mathcal{P}} \langle \mathcal{M}, \mathcal{S}[x \mapsto \mathcal{S}(y)] \rangle} \qquad \frac{\mathcal{P} = x := f(\bar{z}) \quad (\mathcal{S}(\bar{z}), v) \in \mathcal{I}(f)}{\langle \mathcal{M}, \mathcal{S} \rangle \rightarrow_{\mathcal{P}} \langle \mathcal{M}, \mathcal{S}[x \mapsto v] \rangle}$$

$$\frac{\mathcal{P} = \mathbf{assume}~(\mathcal{C}) \quad \langle \mathcal{M}, \mathcal{S} \rangle \models \mathcal{C}}{\langle \mathcal{M}, \mathcal{S} \rangle \rightarrow_{\mathcal{P}} \langle \mathcal{M}, \mathcal{S} \rangle} \qquad \frac{\mathcal{P} = \mathbf{assume}~(\mathcal{C}) \quad \langle \mathcal{M}, \mathcal{S} \rangle \models \neg \mathcal{C}}{\langle \mathcal{M}, \mathcal{S} \rangle \rightarrow_{\mathcal{P}} \langle \mathcal{M}, \mathsf{Blocked} \rangle}$$

$$\frac{\mathcal{P} = \mathbf{assert}~(\mathcal{C}) \quad \langle \mathcal{M}, \mathcal{S} \rangle \models \mathcal{C}}{\langle \mathcal{M}, \mathcal{S} \rangle \rightarrow_{\mathcal{P}} \langle \mathcal{M}, \mathcal{S} \rangle} \qquad \frac{\mathcal{P} = \mathbf{assert}~(\mathcal{C}) \quad \langle \mathcal{M}, \mathcal{S} \rangle \models \neg \mathcal{C}}{\langle \mathcal{M}, \mathcal{S} \rangle \rightarrow_{\mathcal{P}} \langle \mathcal{M}, \mathsf{Failed} \rangle}$$

$$\frac{\mathcal{P} = \mathcal{P}_1 \,\text{\textsemicolon}\, \mathcal{P}_2 \quad \langle \mathcal{M}, \mathcal{S} \rangle \rightarrow_{\mathcal{P}_1} \langle \mathcal{M}, \mathcal{S}_1 \rangle \quad \langle \mathcal{M}, \mathcal{S}_1 \rangle \rightarrow_{\mathcal{P}_2} \langle \mathcal{M}, \mathcal{S}_2 \rangle}{\langle \mathcal{M}, \mathcal{S} \rangle \rightarrow_{\mathcal{P}} \langle \mathcal{M}, \mathcal{S}_2 \rangle}$$

$$\frac{\mathcal{P} = \mathbf{if}~(\mathcal{C})~\mathbf{then}~\mathcal{P}_1~\mathbf{else}~\mathcal{P}_2 \quad \langle \mathcal{M}, \mathcal{S} \rangle \models \mathcal{C} \quad \langle \mathcal{M}, \mathcal{S} \rangle \rightarrow_{\mathcal{P}_1} \langle \mathcal{M}, \mathcal{S}_1 \rangle}{\langle \mathcal{M}, \mathcal{S} \rangle \rightarrow_{\mathcal{P}} \langle \mathcal{M}, \mathcal{S}_1 \rangle}$$

$$\frac{\mathcal{P} = \mathbf{if}~(\mathcal{C})~\mathbf{then}~\mathcal{P}_1~\mathbf{else}~\mathcal{P}_2 \quad \langle \mathcal{M}, \mathcal{S} \rangle \models \neg \mathcal{C} \quad \langle \mathcal{M}, \mathcal{S} \rangle \rightarrow_{\mathcal{P}_2} \langle \mathcal{M}, \mathcal{S}_2 \rangle}{\langle \mathcal{M}, \mathcal{S} \rangle \rightarrow_{\mathcal{P}} \langle \mathcal{M}, \mathcal{S}_2 \rangle}$$

$$\frac{\mathcal{P} = \mathbf{while}~(\mathcal{C})~\mathcal{P}_1 \quad \langle \mathcal{M}, \mathcal{S} \rangle \models \neg \mathcal{C}}{\langle \mathcal{M}, \mathcal{S} \rangle \rightarrow_{\mathcal{P}} \langle \mathcal{M}, \mathcal{S} \rangle}$$

$$\frac{\mathcal{P} = \mathbf{while}~(\mathcal{C})~\mathcal{P}_1 \quad \langle \mathcal{M}, \mathcal{S} \rangle \models \mathcal{C} \quad \langle \mathcal{M}, \mathcal{S} \rangle \rightarrow_{\mathcal{P}_1} \langle \mathcal{M}, \mathcal{S}_1 \rangle \quad \langle \mathcal{M}, \mathcal{S}_1 \rangle \rightarrow_{\mathcal{P}} \langle \mathcal{M}, \mathcal{S}_2 \rangle}{\langle \mathcal{M}, \mathcal{S} \rangle \rightarrow_{\mathcal{P}} \langle \mathcal{M}, \mathcal{S}_2 \rangle}$$

Fig. 2. Semantics rules for uninterpreted programs.

Semantics. The semantics of an uninterpreted program is defined *w.r.t.* a data model $\mathcal{M} = (\mathcal{U}, \mathcal{I})$ for interpretation, where $\mathcal{U}$ is the universal element set for interpretation, and $\mathcal{I}$ interprets the symbols in Σ. Specifically, $\mathcal{I}$ interprets a symbol in $\mathbb{C}$ to an element in $\mathcal{U}$, and a function f as a relation of $\mathcal{U}$. Given a data model $\mathcal{M}$, the semantics of an uninterpreted program $\mathcal{P}$ is defined as a state transition graph. Each state $\mathcal{S} : \Sigma \rightarrow \mathcal{U}$ maps a symbol to an element in the universal set of the data model. The initial state is an empty map. Figure 2 gives the transition rules for the semantics, where $\mathsf{Blocked}$ and Fail are the special blocked and failed terminated states, respectively. $\mathcal{S}[x \mapsto e]$ is $\mathcal{S} \cup \{(x, e)\}$ if $x \notin dom(\mathcal{S})$; otherwise, it is defined as follows.

$$\mathcal{S}[x \mapsto e](y) = \begin{cases} e & y = x \\ \mathcal{S}(y) & otherwise \end{cases} \tag{1}$$

For the sake of brevity, we extend $\mathcal{S}$ to tuples and use $\mathcal{S}(\bar{z})$ to denote the value tuple of $\bar{z}$. For example, $\mathcal{S}((x, y))$ is $(\mathcal{S}(x), \mathcal{S}(y))$. Besides, we define state $\mathcal{S}$ satisfies a condition $\mathcal{C}$, *i.e.*, $\mathcal{S} \models \mathcal{C}$, as follows.

$$\begin{aligned} \mathcal{S} &\models x = y \quad \textbf{iff}~\mathcal{S}(x) = \mathcal{S}(y) \\ \mathcal{S} &\models \mathcal{C}_1 \wedge \mathcal{C}_2~\textbf{iff}~\mathcal{S} \models \mathcal{C}_1 \wedge \mathcal{S} \models \mathcal{C}_2 \\ \mathcal{S} &\models \neg \mathcal{C} \quad\quad \textbf{iff}~\mathcal{S} \not\models \mathcal{C} \end{aligned} \tag{2}$$

We use $\langle \mathcal{M}, \mathcal{S}_1 \rangle \rightsquigarrow_{\mathcal{P}} \langle \mathcal{M}, \mathcal{S}_2 \rangle$ to represent that state $\mathcal{S}_2$ can be reached from state $\mathcal{S}_1$ during the execution of $\mathcal{P}$ under the data model $\mathcal{M}$.

Verification Problem. In this paper, we only consider the verification of uninterpreted programs *w.r.t.* reachability properties. There are assertions in the program. Each assertion can be specified by **assert**($\langle cond \rangle$), which requires that $\langle cond \rangle$ holds for the program in terms of any data models. We define $\mathcal{P}$ satisfies the assertions as follows.

$$\forall \mathcal{M} \bullet \langle \mathcal{M}, \emptyset \rangle \not\rightarrow_{\mathcal{P}} \langle \mathcal{M}, \mathsf{Fail} \rangle \tag{3}$$

It means that the Fail state is not reachable during the execution of $\mathcal{P}$ under *any data model*. In general, the verification problem of uninterpreted programs is undecidable [15]. Recently, a fragment of uninterpreted programs, called *coherent uninterpreted programs* [15], has been discovered, and its verification problem is decidable and has a PSPACE-complete time complexity.

Coherent Uninterpreted Programs. The coherence is defined in a purely symbol-oriented manner. Each variable of the program is supposed to have an initial term. The statements in the program are interpreted as term rewritings. For example, if y's current term is t_y, $x := f(y)$ assigns term $f(t_y)$ to x. Then, along with the program's execution, the congruence closure relation [18] *w.r.t.* equality can also be inferred. The relation can be used to reason the equality or dis-equality of the program variables, which supports proving the program's assertions. Specifically, the coherent uninterpreted program requires that all of its traces satisfy the following two properties.

- **Memoizing:** whenever a term t is recomputed, there must be a variable x whose term value is equal to t *w.r.t.* the congruence closure relation.
- **Early assumes: assume**($x = y$) statement appears before the assignments of the variables whose term values are equal (also *w.r.t.* the congruence closure relation) to a super-term of x's term or y's term.

If an uninterpreted program $\mathcal{P}$ satisfies these two conditions, *i.e.*, $\mathcal{P}$ is coherent, the congruence closure relations that can be concluded from $\mathcal{P}$ are *complete*, which is the key to ensure the verification's completeness. Then, $\mathcal{P}$'s verification can be reduced to an emptiness checking problem of a finite state automata (FSA), which is the intersection of $\mathcal{P}$'s execution automata $\mathcal{A_P}$ (sound approximation) and another FSA $\mathcal{A_U}$ for checking feasibility. $\mathcal{A_U}$ ensures the soundness and completeness of the feasibility checking for its coherent traces. Therefore, this verification method for coherent uninterpreted programs is sound and complete. More details can be found in [15].

2.2 Trace Abstraction Based CEGAR

Trace abstraction based CEGAR first abstracts a program $\mathcal{P}$ by an FSA $\mathcal{A}$, which is an over-approximation of $\mathcal{P}$. Then, a counter-example trace t is extracted from $\mathcal{A}$ if any counter-example traces exist. If t is feasible, a real counter-example is found; otherwise, t will be abstracted to an FSA $\mathcal{A}_c$, in which all the accepted traces are not feasible. Then, the abstraction $\mathcal{A}$ is refined to $\mathcal{A} \cap \neg \mathcal{A}_c$. If $\mathcal{A}$ contains no counter-example traces, $\mathcal{P}$ is verified to satisfy the assertions; otherwise, the trace abstraction based refinement continues.

Figure 3(a) shows an example program $\mathcal{P}$ to demonstrate our framework. For this program, the assertion in the last line is truly a fact. However, the program is not a coherent uninterpreted program. The **assume** statement in the **else** branch does not satisfy the requirement of *early assumes*, because $f(t)$ may be already computed and dropped in before while loop. Thus, we cannot use the verification method in [15] to verify this program. Besides, if we use ULTIMATE [7], *i.e.*, a state-of-the-art verification tool implementing trace abstraction based CEGAR [8], to verify the program, the refinement process does not terminate.

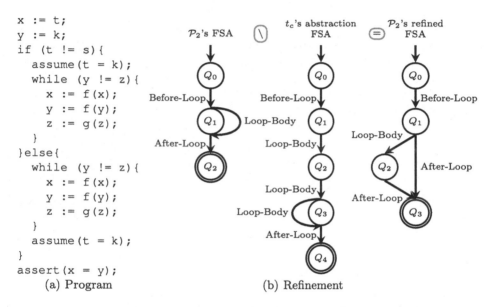

```
x := t;
y := k;
if (t != s){
    assume(t = k);
    while (y != z){
        x := f(x);
        y := f(y);
        z := g(z);
    }
}else{
    while (y != z){
        x := f(x);
        y := f(y);
        z := g(z);
    }
    assume(t = k);
}
assert(x = y);
```
(a) Program

(b) Refinement

Fig. 3. A motivation example, where Before-Loop, Loop-Body and After-Loop represent $x := t \, \mathring{,} \, y := k \, \mathring{,} \, \textbf{assume}(t = s)$, $\textbf{assume}(y \neq z) \, \mathring{,} \, x := f(x) \, \mathring{,} \, y := f(y) \, \mathring{,} \, z := g(z)$, and $\textbf{assume}(y = z) \, \mathring{,} \, \textbf{assume}(t = k) \, \mathring{,} \, \textbf{assume}(x \neq y)$, respectively.

Notice that $\mathcal{P}$ can be separated into two sub-programs $\mathcal{P}_1$ and $\mathcal{P}_2$, which corresponds to the **true** and **false** branch cases, respectively. $\mathcal{P}_1$ is a coherent program, but $\mathcal{P}_2$ is not, because $\mathcal{P}_2$ violates the requirement of *early assumes*. We use $\mathcal{P}_2$ to demonstrate our CEGAR procedure. $\mathcal{P}_2$'s FSA is the first one in Fig. 3(b), where each state represents the one after the transition of a sequence of statements (for the sake of brevity). Note that the statement $\textbf{assert}(x = y)$ will be replaced by $\textbf{assume}(x \neq y)$, and the verification problem *w.r.t.* $\textbf{assert}(x = y)$ will be converted into a reachability problem *w.r.t.* $\textbf{assume}(x \neq y)$. Then, suppose we get a counterexample trace t in which the loop body is executed *three* iterations. t is not a coherent trace, but any finite trace is k-coherent [15].

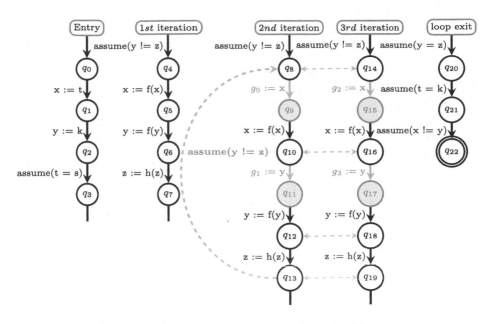

Fig. 4. The demonstration of abstracting infeasible trace.

So we translate t to a coherent trace t_c by adding k ghost variables. Figure 4 shows the trace t_c, which is divided into several segments. The gray states (q_9, q_{11}, q_{15} and q_{17}) and transitions are related to ghost variables. Then, along with t_c, we can compute the congruence closure relation based state transitions. Each state consists of three parts: an equality relation E of variables, a dis-equality relation D, and a set F of function relations. For example, after executing the first two statements, q_2's E is as follows.

$$\{(x, x), (x, t), (t, x), (y, y), (y, k), (k, y), (z, z), (t, t), (k, k), (s, s)\}$$

q_2's D is $\emptyset$ and q_2's F is $\{R_f, R_g\}$, where both R_f and R_g are the relation $\{([v]_E, \mathsf{Undef}) \mid v \in \{x, y, z, s\}\}$, in which $[v]_E$ represents v's equivalent set $w.r.t.$ q_2's E, and Undef means that the input's value is undefined.

If there exist two variables that have a relation in both one state's E and D, the state is *inconsistent*. If a trace can result in an inconsistent state, the trace is *infeasible*. In total, there are 23 states along the coherent trace t_c. State q_{22} is inconsistent, because x and y are equal but also in the dis-equality relation of q_{22} (implied by the last statement **assume**$(x \neq y)$). Hence, t_c is infeasible.

So we abstract t_c to refine $\mathcal{P}_2$'s FSA. The abstraction for t_c is as follows. We first remove the transitions and the states related to ghost variables and remove the ghost variables' definitions from each state. For t_c, we remove q_9, q_{11}, q_{15} and q_{17} and their incoming transitions (*i.e.*, the gray states and transitions in Fig. 4). Then, we scan the remaining states and transitions and try to match the equal states. Two states are equal if they have the same E and D. Figure 4 shows the pairs of equivalent states by ◂----▸. Because each state in the second iteration has a corresponding equivalent state in the third iteration, we can add a transition (dotted line) from q_{13} to q_8. This abstraction ensures that each trace in the abstraction is infeasible, because the core reason of inconsistency is **assume**($t = k$) and **assume**($x \neq y$). Same as t_c, any trace in the abstraction can always be transferred to a coherent trace, whose last state is inconsistent.

The abstraction's FSA is the second FSA in Fig. 3(b), in which the loop body is executed two or more iterations. We refine P_2's FSA (*i.e.*, the first one in Fig. 3(b)) by removing the traces in t_c's abstraction. The result is the third FSA in Fig. 3(b), in which only two traces exist. These two traces are also infeasible. Therefore, P_2 is proved to satisfy the assertion by three rounds of refinement.

Optimization We can use the aforementioned CEGAR-based procedure to verify the whole program in Fig. 3(a), which takes 8 rounds of refinement to complete the verification. Instead of doing that, by observing that $\mathcal{P}_1$ is a coherent program, we verify $\mathcal{P}_1$ by employing the verification method in [15] and then employ the CEGAR-based procedure to verify $\mathcal{P}_2$, which significantly reduces the refinement rounds. In contrast, the optimized verification only needs 3 rounds of refinement. Such optimization effectively improves the verification's efficiency.

3   Verification Framework

Fig. 5 shows our verification framework. There are two stages in the framework. In the first stage, the framework partitions $\mathcal{P}$ into different parts. For the coherent parts, the framework verifies them by the verification method in [15]. Now, our framework only partitions each if-then-else branch statement into two parts. The loop statement is atomic and will not be partitioned.

The second stage verifies the remaining parts via CEGAR-based procedure. The framework constructs the FSA abstracting $\mathcal{A}_u$ for each sub-program $\mathcal{P}_u$. If there exists an accepted trace t, *i.e.*, a statement sequence driving from an initial state to an accepted state of $\mathcal{A}_u$, the framework employs a congruence-based method based on [15] to check t's feasibility (Sect. 3.1). If t is feasible, a real counterexample is found, and the framework terminates. Otherwise, the framework constructs an FSA $\mathcal{A}_t$ that abstracts the infeasible trace t (Sect. 3.2). In principle, all the traces in $\mathcal{A}_t$ are infeasible and equivalent with t w.r.t. t's core reason for infeasibility. Then, $\mathcal{A}_u$ is refined by removing the traces in $\mathcal{A}_t$, *i.e.*, $\mathcal{A}_u = \mathcal{A}_u \cap \neg \mathcal{A}_t$. If there is no accepted trace in $\mathcal{A}_u$, $\mathcal{P}_u$ is verified to satisfy the property. Otherwise, the iteration will continue from $\mathcal{A}_u$ until the verification succeeds (*i.e.*, find a real counterexample or prove all $\mathcal{P}_u$s' satisfaction to the property) or timeout.

3.1   Congruence-Based Feasibility Checking

We use congruence-based term state transitions to check a coherent trace's feasibility [15]. Each term state represents the current equality, dis-equality and function relations. Each term state is formally defined as follows.

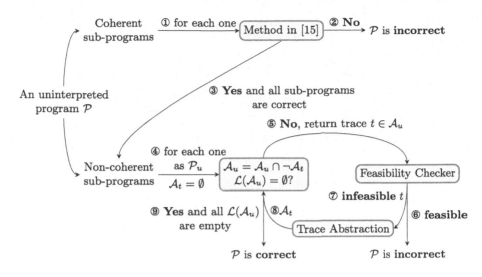

Fig. 5. Verification framework.

Definition 1. *Given an uninterpreted program $\mathcal{P}$ and its variable set V, a term state S is defined as a triple (E, D, F), where*

- *$E \subseteq V \times V$ is the equality relation, and we use $[V]_E \subseteq 2^V$ to represent the set of V's equivalent classes w.r.t. E.*
- *$D \subseteq [V]_E \times [V]_E$ is the dis-equality relation.*
- *F is the set of function definitions, and each function $f : [V]_E \times \ldots \times [V]_E \to [V]_E$ defines a relation between equivalent variable classes w.r.t. E.*

We use $[x]_E$ to represent x's equivalent variable class w.r.t. E. A state $S = (E, D, F)$ is *inconsistent* when the following condition holds.

$$\exists x, y \in V \bullet (x, y) \in E \wedge ([x]_E, [y]_E) \in D \tag{4}$$

Two states S_1 and S_2 are equivalent (denoted by $S_1 \equiv S_2$) if they have the same E and D. The beginning term state S_{ini} is $(\mathsf{ID}_V, \emptyset, F_{\mathsf{Undef}})$, where ID_V is $\{(x, x) \mid x \in V\}$, *i.e.*, any variable should be equal to itself, and each function in F_{Undef} gives Undef for any inputs. Then, given a coherent trace $t = \langle stmt_1, \ldots, stmt_n \rangle$ of the program $\mathcal{P}$, we can derive t's state transitions starting from S_{ini} by the rules in Fig. 6, wherein the following definitions are used. We use $E[x := y]$ below to denote changing x's equivalent elements to those that are equivalent with y, wherein $E \downarrow_V$ represents E's projection on the variable set V.

$$E[x := y] ::= E \downarrow_{V \setminus \{x\}} \cup \{(x, y'), (y', x) \mid (y, y') \in E\} \cup \{(x, x)\} \tag{5}$$

$D[x, E']$ below represents redefining D w.r.t. a new equality relation E' and removing x related dis-equality relations.

$$D[x, E'] ::= \{([x_1]_{E'}, [x_2]_{E'}) \mid \{x_1, x_2\} \subseteq V \setminus \{x\} \wedge ([x_1]_E, [x_2]_E) \in D\} \tag{6}$$

$$\frac{Stmt = \mathbf{skip}}{(E, D, F) \rightarrow_{Stmt} (E, D, F)}$$

$$\frac{Stmt = x := y \wedge E' = E[x := y]}{(E, D, F) \rightarrow_{Stmt} (E', D[x, E'], F[x, E'])}$$

$$\frac{Stmt = x := f(z) \wedge F[\![f]\!]([z]_E) = [y]_E \wedge E' = E[x := y]}{(E, D, F) \rightarrow_{Stmt} (E', D[x, E'], F[x, E'])}$$

$$\frac{Stmt = x := f(z) \wedge F[\![f]\!]([z]_E) = \mathsf{Undef} \wedge E' = E \downarrow_{V \backslash \{x\}} \cup \{(x, x)\}}{(E, D, F) \rightarrow_{Stmt} (E', D[x, E'], F[x, E', f(z)])}$$

$$\frac{\begin{array}{c} Stmt = \mathbf{assume}(x = y) \wedge E' = \mathsf{LCC}(E, F, x, y) \wedge \\ D' = \{([x_1]_{E'}, [x_2]_{E'}) \mid ([x_1]_E, [x_2]_E) \in D\} \end{array}}{(E, D, F) \rightarrow_{Stmt} (E', D', F[E'])}$$

$$\frac{Stmt = \mathbf{assume}(x \neq y)}{(E, D, F) \rightarrow_{Stmt} (E, D \cup \{([x]_E, [y]_E), ([y]_E, [x]_E)\}, F)}$$

Fig. 6. Transition rules for term states, where $\mathsf{LCC}(E, F, x, y)$ represents the congruence closure of E after adding the equality between x and y to E. Note that, $x := c$ can be replaced by $x := x_c$ where x_c is a never-used variable and its initial term is c. $\mathbf{assert}(\langle cond \rangle)$ has been replaced by $\mathbf{assume}(\neg \langle cond \rangle)$ during verification.

We use $F[\![f]\!]$ to represent the function f in F and $F[E']$ defined as follows to represent redefining the functions in F w.r.t. the equality relation E'.

$$F[E'][\![f]\!]([x_1]_{E'}, \ldots, [x_n]_{E'}) ::= \begin{cases} [u]_{E'} & [u]_E = F[\![f]\!]([x_1]_E, \ldots, [x_n]_E) \\ \mathsf{Undef} & \text{otherwise} \end{cases} \quad (7)$$

Then, based on $F[E']$, we define $F[x, E']$ to represent redefining the functions in F w.r.t. E' when x is assigned with another variable or constant. The function relations defined on x are modified to Undef.

$$F[x, E'][\![f]\!]([x_1]_{E'}, \ldots, [x_n]_{E'}) ::= \begin{cases} F[E'][\![f]\!]([x_1]_{E'}, \ldots, [x_n]_{E'}) & x \notin \{u, x_1, \ldots, x_n\} \\ \mathsf{Undef} & \text{otherwise} \end{cases} \quad (8)$$

Besides, if x is assigned with an uninterpreted function expression $f(z)$ and z's value defined by f is Undef, the functions in F are redefined as follows.

$$F[x, E', f(z)][\![g]\!]([y]_{E'}) ::= \begin{cases} F[x, E'][\![g]\!]([y]_{E'}) & g \neq f \\ [x]_{E'} & g = f \wedge x \notin \{y\} \wedge y \in [z]_E \\ [u]_{E'} & g = f \wedge x \notin \{u, y\} \wedge \\ & [u]_E = F[\![f]\!]([y]_E) \\ \mathsf{Undef} & \text{otherwise} \end{cases} \quad (9)$$

For the functions other than f, the definitions are the same as those in $F[x, E']$; otherwise, the values of z's equivalent variables (not including x) are $[x]_{E'}$, and f's relations defined on x are modified to Undef.

We use $S_1 \rightsquigarrow_t S_2$ to represent that S_2 can be reached after executing the trace t starting from S_1. Then, a trace t is *infeasible* (denoted as $\mathsf{infeasible}(t)$)

if an *inconsistent* state S_{inc} can be reached from the beginning state S_{ini}, *i.e.*, where $t_1 \preceq t$ represents that t_1 is a prefix of t.

$$\exists t_1 \bullet t_1 \preceq t \wedge S_{ini} \leadsto_{t_1} S_{inc} \tag{10}$$

Example. Suppose that the current term state (E, D, F) is as follows, where $V = \{x, y, z\}$ and there is only one uninterpreted function f.

$$E = \{(x, x), (y, y), (z, z), (y, z), (z, y)\} \qquad D = \{([x]_E, [y]_E)\}$$

$$F[\![f]\!] = \{f([x]_E) = [y]_E, f([y]_E) = \mathsf{Undef}, f([z]_E) = \mathsf{Undef}\}$$

Then, after executing $x := f(z)$, we can obtain the next term state (E', D', F') (denoted as S'), *i.e.*, $(E, D, F) \rightarrow_{x := f(z)} (E', D', F')$, which is as follows according to the forth rule in Fig. 6.

$$E' = E \downarrow_{V \setminus \{x\}} \cup \{(x, x)\} = \{(y, y), (z, z), (y, z), (z, y), (x, x)\}$$

$$D' = D[x, E'] = \{([x_1]_{E'}, [x_2]_{E'}) \mid \{x_1, x_2\} \subseteq \{y, z\} \wedge ([x_1]_E, [x_2]_E) \in D\} = \{\}$$

$$F' = F[x, E', f(z)]$$

$F[x, E', f(z)]$ defines f as follows.

$$F[x, E', f(z)][\![f]\!]([x]_{E'}) = \mathsf{Undef} \text{ because } x \in \{x\}$$
$$F[x, E', f(z)][\![f]\!]([y]_{E'}) = [x]_{E'} \text{ because } x \notin \{y\} \wedge y \in [z]_E$$
$$F[x, E', f(z)][\![f]\!]([z]_{E'}) = [x]_{E'} \text{ because } x \notin \{z\} \wedge z \in [z]_E$$

3.2 Trace Abstraction

Based on an infeasible coherent trace t_c, we can abstract t_c to an FSA, which represents the equivalent infeasible traces of t_c. Algorithm 1 shows the details of trace abstraction. The inputs are an infeasible trace t_c and the program $\mathcal{P}$, and the output is the abstraction FSA $\mathcal{A}_t$. The algorithm removes the useless states and transitions and generalizes the loop bodies with the same state transitions.

First, the algorithm constructs an initial automata to accept the infeasible coherent trace t_c (Lines 2 – 5). Especially, the statements after the inconsistent state S_m make self loops on S_m (Line 4). Then, it recognizes those *ghost* variables P_v in $\mathcal{P}$ and t_c, including $\mathcal{P}$'s observing variables [14] and the variables added to t_c for making t_c coherent (Line 7). The algorithm removes each state's relations that are related to P_v (Line 8). After that, the states brought by ghost variables are removed (Line 9), like the states (q_9, q_{11}, q_{15} and q_{17}) in Fig. 4. The transitions of the remaining states that are connected by those deleted states are established (Line 11). So far, the algorithm removes all the useless states.

Next, the algorithm matches the states that are the entry state of the same loop body (denoted by $\mathsf{LES}(S_i, S_j)$) and have the same state transitions in the loop body, which is defined as follows.

$$\begin{aligned}
\mathsf{match}(S_i, S_j) ::= \mathsf{LES}(S_i, S_j) \wedge & \\
\exists k \bullet \forall 0 \leq m \leq k \bullet S_{i+m} \equiv S_{j+m} \wedge & \\
\forall 1 \leq n \leq k \bullet stmt_{i+n} = stmt_{j+n} &
\end{aligned} \tag{11}$$

Algorithm 1: Generalize(t_c, $\mathcal{P}$)

Input: An infeasible coherent trace $t_c = \langle stmt_1, ..., stmt_n \rangle$ and t_c's transitions are
$S_0 \rightarrow_{stmt_1} S_1 ... \rightarrow_{stmt_m} S_m$, where S_0 is S_{ini}, S_m is inconsistent, and $m \leq n$.
Output: The generalization automata $\mathcal{A}_t = (\Sigma, S, T, S_I, S_F)$
1: // Automata initialization
2: $\Sigma \leftarrow \{stmt_1, ..., stmt_m, ..., stmt_n\}$
3: $S \leftarrow \{S_0, S_1, ..., S_m\}$
4: $T \leftarrow \{(S_i, stmt_{i+1}, S_{i+1}) \mid 0 \leq i \leq m-1\} \cup \{(S_m, stmt_{j+1}, S_m) \mid m \leq j \leq n-1\}$
5: $S_I, S_F \leftarrow S_0, S_m$
6: // Ghost elimination
7: $P_v \leftarrow$ ghostVariables($\mathcal{P}, t_c$)
8: $S \leftarrow \{S_i \downarrow_{V \backslash P_v} \mid 0 \leq i \leq m\}$ //$S_i \downarrow_V$ represents S_i's projection on V
9: $S \leftarrow S \backslash \{S_i \mid S_i \in S \wedge \exists S_j \in S \bullet S_j \equiv S_i \wedge j < i\}$
10: // Connect these states interrupted by the states brought by ghost variables
11: $T \leftarrow T \cup \{(S_i, stmt_j, S_j) \mid S_i \in S \wedge j = \underset{k > i \wedge S_k \in S}{\arg\min} \ k\}$
12: // Loop construction
13: **for** $\mathcal{E} \in [S]_{\text{match}}$ **do**
14:    $i, j \leftarrow \underset{S_k \in \mathcal{E}}{\arg\min} k$, $\underset{k > i \wedge S_k \in \mathcal{E}}{\arg\min} \ k$ //Get the first and second entry states in $\mathcal{E}$
15:    $\mathcal{C} \leftarrow$ getCondition($stmt_{i+1}$)   // Get the S_i's loop condition $\mathcal{C}$
16:    $e \leftarrow \underset{k > i \wedge S_{k-1} \rightarrow_{\text{assume}(\neg \mathcal{C})} S_k}{\arg\min} k$ // Get the state S_e after exiting the loop
17:    $T \leftarrow T \backslash \{(S_f, stmt, S_t) \mid S_t = S_j\}$ // Remove the transitions to S_j
18:    $T \leftarrow T \backslash \{(S_f, stmt, S_t) \mid S_t = S_e\}$ // Remove the transitions to S_e
19:    $T \leftarrow T \cup \{(S_{j-1}, \text{assume}(\mathcal{C}), S_i)\}$ // Generalize by adding a loop
20:    $T \leftarrow T \cup \{(S_{j-1}, \text{assume}(\neg \mathcal{C}), S_e)\}$ // Add the edge for exiting the loop
21: **end for**
22: $\mathcal{A}_t \leftarrow (\Sigma, S, T, S_I, S_F)$ // $\mathcal{A}_t$'s unreachable states and transitions are removed
23: **return** $\mathcal{A}_t$

For example, match(S_8, S_{14}) holds in Fig. 4. If match(S_i, S_j) and match(S_j, S_k) hold, then $\{S_i, S_j, S_k\}$ constitutes an equivalent state class with respect to match.

After that, for each equivalent state class in $[S]_{\text{match}}$, the algorithm keeps just one loop body (*i.e.*, the first one) and generalizes the trace by introducing a loop in the FSA (Lines $14 - 20$). The algorithm get the first and second entry states (S_i, S_j) in each equivalent state class and the corresponding state S_e after exiting the loop (Lines $14 - 16$). Based on these information, the algorithm constructs a loop. For example, in Fig. 4, (S_i, S_j, S_e) can be (S_8, S_{14}, S_{20}). This loop construction advanced by cutting and adding the corresponding edges and states (Lines $17 - 20$). We do this for each equivalent state class to complete the generalization of the loop bodies.

Finally, the algorithm removes the unreachable states and transitions in the FSA (Line 22) (omitted for the sake of space). The following theorem ensures the correctness of the trace abstraction algorithm.

Theorem 1 (Soundness). *Given an infeasible coherent trace t_c of the uninterpreted program $\mathcal{P}$, each accepted trace of* Generalize($t_c, \mathcal{P}$) *is also infeasible.*

Proof. The key point of proof is that each generalization step in Algorithm 1 does not introduce any feasible accepted traces. We prove by contradiction.

- *Automata initialization:* For Lines $2 \sim 5$ in Algorithm 1, the traces accepted by automata are in the form of $\langle stmt_1, ..., stmt_m, ... \rangle$. If there exists a feasible trace $t = \langle stmt_1, ..., stmt_m, ..., stmt_l \rangle$, then it requires that all the states reached by the trace should be consistent, which is not true since t will enter the inconsistent state S_m after executing $\langle stmt_1, ..., stmt_m \rangle$. Therefore, *Automata initialization* does not introduce accepted traces.
- *Ghost elimination:* For Lines $7 \sim 11$ in Algorithm 1, the only difference between the accepted trace t before this step and the accepted trace t' after this step is that t' does not contain the statements related to these ghost variables. If there exists a t' that is feasible, the corresponding t must be feasible since the ghost variables only observe the program states and do not change the trace's feasibility. However, t obtained by *Automata initialization* should be an infeasible trace, which results in a conflict. Therefore, *Ghost elimination* does not introduce accepted traces.
- *Loop construction*: Similar to ghost elimination, the difference between the accepted trace t before loop construction and the accepted trace t' after this step is that t' may have different copies of loop bodies. According to the match's definition, the executions of these loop bodies do not change the state that exits the loop, which implies that t and t' have the same feasibility. If t' is feasible, the corresponding t must be feasible. However, t obtained by *Ghost elimination* should be an infeasible trace, which results in a conflict. Therefore, *Loop construction* does not introduce any accepted traces either.

In total, $\mathsf{Generalize}(t_c, \mathcal{P})$ does not introduce any feasible accepted traces.

4   Evaluation

We have implemented our method as a prototype[1] in Python. Our prototype supports the uninterpreted programs in Boogie language [2]. We evaluate our method's effectiveness and efficiency by applying the prototype on verifying *general* uninterpreted programs. Since there is no standard benchmark of uninterpreted programs, we designed a program generator to generate Boogie uninterpreted programs automatically. The generator composes the component programs randomly by branch operator. The types of the component programs are as follows: the ones satisfying *memoizing* or not, the ones satisfying *early assumes* or not, the ones containing *if-else* or not, and the ones containing *while* or not. The generator covers the representative cases of uninterpreted programs.

We compare our prototype with the state-of-the-art tool ULTIMATE [7] on the benchmark programs in terms of effectiveness and efficiency. We use 10 minutes as the time threshold for each verification task. All the experiments were carried out on a machine with eight cores and 8G memory, and the operating system is Ubuntu 18.04.

---

[1] Our implementation and benchmark are available at the GitHub repository https://github.com/Verifier4UP/Trace-Refinement-based-Verification.

Table 1. The experimental results, where TO stands for timeout and the grey cell means that the corresponding tool performs better. The first column lists the benchmark programs and the second column shows the Lines of Code (LoC) of each program. The third and fourth columns show the results of ULTIMATE. The columns between fifth and ninth show the results of our method. The columns named **Result** show the verification results. The columns named **Time** show the time of verification. The column **Partition** shows the time for partition in our method. The column **C(#)** shows the time of verifying coherent sub-programs and the number of coherent sub-programs. The column **NC(#)** shows the time of verifying non-coherent sub-programs and the number of non-coherent sub-programs.

Program	LoC	ULTIMATE		Our Method				
		Result	Time	Result	Time	Partition	C(#)	NC(#)
benchmark0	41	incorrect	1.816	incorrect	1.424	0.175	0.04(2)	1.209(10)
benchmark1	43	correct	1.958	correct	1.162	0.137	0.086(6)	0.938(12)
benchmark2	54	TO	TO	correct	33.647	0.612	0.245(12)	32.79(15)
benchmark3	49	TO	TO	correct	10.101	0.248	0.115(8)	9.738(10)
benchmark4	41	incorrect	1.606	incorrect	0.212	0.178	0.034(3)	0(9)
benchmark5	46	TO	TO	correct	3.010	0.138	0.076(6)	2.796(12)
benchmark6	42	TO	TO	correct	2.011	0.176	0.038(4)	1.797(8)
benchmark7	52	TO	TO	correct	15.395	0.387	0.327(6)	14.682(12)
benchmark8	44	incorrect	1.593	incorrect	0.091	0.077	0.014(3)	0(9)
benchmark9	40	incorrect	1.582	incorrect	0.066	0.045	0.021(4)	0(4)
benchmark10	46	incorrect	1.796	incorrect	0.200	0.186	0.014(5)	0(13)
benchmark11	54	TO	TO	correct	9.522	0.605	0.608(15)	8.308(12)
benchmark12	37	incorrect	1.589	incorrect	0.089	0.076	0.013(3)	0(5)
benchmark13	39	incorrect	1.559	incorrect	0.115	0.101	0.014(2)	0(6)
benchmark14	50	correct	46.887	correct	254.083	214.727	39.356(8)	0(0)
benchmark15	41	incorrect	1.587	incorrect	0.107	0.094	0.013(6)	0(6)
benchmark16	40	correct	95.587	correct	0.842	0.19	0.219(7)	0.433(1)
benchmark17	47	incorrect	1.562	incorrect	9.650	0.105	0.034(3)	9.51(9)
benchmark18	46	incorrect	1.585	incorrect	73.801	60.686	13.054(4)	0.061(4)
benchmark19	49	correct	1.909	correct	186.273	172.073	14.2(12)	0(0)
benchmark20	37	incorrect	1.614	incorrect	1.139	0.07	0.054(4)	1.014(4)
benchmark21	39	incorrect	1.645	incorrect	1.404	0.05	0.043(3)	1.311(5)
benchmark22	48	incorrect	1.613	incorrect	0.165	0.143	0.022(6)	0(2)
benchmark23	54	TO	TO	correct	3.191	0.325	0.212(12)	2.655(15)
benchmark24	41	incorrect	1.592	incorrect	0.211	0.199	0.011(4)	0(8)
benchmark25	44	incorrect	1.56	incorrect	9.361	0.167	0(0)	9.193(12)
benchmark26	47	TO	TO	correct	1.723	0.202	0.179(10)	1.342(8)
benchmark27	48	incorrect	1.627	incorrect	0.231	0.198	0.033(5)	0(13)
benchmark28	45	incorrect	1.674	incorrect	0.298	0.206	0.092(7)	0(5)
benchmark29	45	TO	TO	correct	1.843	0.073	0.065(6)	1.705(6)
benchmark30	57	correct	1.748	correct	31.438	26.878	2.906(10)	1.654(8)
benchmark31	39	incorrect	1.589	incorrect	0.071	0.045	0.026(2)	0(6)
benchmark32	41	incorrect	1.588	incorrect	3.836	0.218	0.036(2)	3.583(10)
benchmark33	46	incorrect	1.556	incorrect	0.152	0.139	0.013(3)	0(9)
benchmark34	55	TO	TO	correct	9.955	0.456	0.091(6)	9.408(21)
benchmark35	51	incorrect	1.606	incorrect	60.027	41.231	18.776(9)	0.021(3)
benchmark36	43	incorrect	1.619	incorrect	0.121	0.107	0.014(6)	0(6)
benchmark37	41	incorrect	1.598	incorrect	1.466	0.118	0.103(6)	1.244(6)
benchmark38	49	TO	TO	correct	2.138	0.203	0.11(6)	1.826(12)
benchmark39	47	TO	TO	correct	3.380	0.127	0.086(6)	3.167(12)
benchmark40	42	TO	TO	correct	1.662	0.129	0.067(5)	1.465(7)
benchmark41	41	incorrect	1.586	incorrect	0.281	0.242	0.039(8)	0(4)
benchmark42	22	correct	1.645	correct	0.023	0.007	0.005(2)	0.011(1)
benchmark43	46	incorrect	1.626	incorrect	33.946	32.568	1.379(8)	0(0)
benchmark44	40	correct	1.914	correct	2.064	0.087	0.066(2)	1.911(6)
benchmark45	53	TO	TO	correct	18.148	0.379	0.083(5)	17.686(13)
benchmark46	28	TO	TO	correct	0.185	0.029	0.031(2)	0.124(1)
benchmark47	46	correct	1.806	correct	1.736	0.149	0.146(9)	1.441(9)
benchmark48	53	correct	1.899	correct	27.209	23.601	3.608(12)	0(0)
benchmark49	44	TO	TO	correct	10.421	0.176	0.156(4)	10.089(4)

4.1   Effectiveness & Efficiency

Table 1 shows the experimental results. In the total 50 programs (half correct and half incorrect), our tool completes the verification tasks of 50 programs (100%), while ULTIMATE completes the verification of 34 programs (68%), which indicates the effectiveness of our method. For the 34 programs verified by both our method and ULTIMATE, our method performed better on 23 programs (67.6%). On average, our method achieves 3.6x speedups for the verified programs, indicating that our method is efficient. The speedup calculation is as follows, where $T(\texttt{Ours})$ and $T(\texttt{ULTIMATE})$ are the verification time of our prototype and ULTIMATE, respectively.

$$speedup = \begin{cases} \frac{T(\texttt{ULTIMATE})}{T(\texttt{Ours})}, & T(\texttt{ULTIMATE}) > T(\texttt{Ours}) \\ 0, & T(\texttt{ULTIMATE}) = T(\texttt{Ours}) \\ -\frac{T(\texttt{Ours})}{T(\texttt{ULTIMATE})}, & T(\texttt{ULTIMATE}) < T(\texttt{Ours}) \end{cases} \qquad (12)$$

For the programs on which ULTIMATE performs better than us (*e.g.*, benchmark14), our method usually spends much time on the coherence checking in the program partition, whose complexity is the same as verifying coherent programs.

4.2   The Results of Different Trace Abstraction Methods

The CEGAR module in our framework plays an important role in tackling with non-coherent programs. To further inspect our trace abstraction method's effectiveness, we compare the verification performance under three different configurations: partition with congruence-based CEGAR module, partition with interpolant-based CEGAR module (ULTIMATE), and ULTIMATE. We only conduct this experiment on the 25 correct programs in the above benchmark. The reason is that for the incorrect programs, the running under different configurations might terminate early by finding different true counterexamples.

As shown in Fig. 7, our method, that is, partition with congruence-based CEGAR module, performs better on 17 programs while the other two perform better on 2 and 6 programs, respectively. This result indicates that for small programs (the sub-programs after the partition), the congruence-based trace abstraction is more efficient than the interpolant-based trace abstraction. Besides, the program partition and the congruence-based trace abstraction are both necessary.

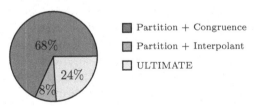

Fig. 7. The influence of different configurations. The percentage indicates the ratio of programs in which the corresponding configurations performs better.

4.3   The Results on SV-COMP Benchmark

To further evaluate the performance of the congruence-based verification and the trace abstraction in our method, we selected 46 benchmark C programs from the *loops* category of SV-COMP[2] [19] and manually transformed them into Boogie programs. In these C programs, there are only equality and disequality constraints, and the expressions can be modeled as uninterpreted functions. Besides, these programs can no longer be partitioned into sub-programs, which means that the whole program is either coherent or non-coherent. We compare our prototype and ULTIMATE on these benchmark programs.

Figure 8 shows the results, where the x-axis displays the indexes of the programs, and the y-axis shows the speedup value (calculated by Eq. 12) of the verification time. In the total 46 programs, our method performs better on 44 programs (95.7%) than ULTIMATE. On average, our method achieves 1.90x speedups. Besides, for the 29 coherent programs, our method achieves 2.13x speedups on average; for the remaining 17 non-coherent programs, our method achieves 1.52x speedups on average. These results indi-

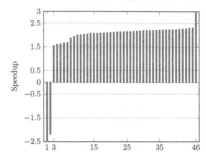

Fig. 8. The evaluation results on SV-COMP benchmark.

cate that the congruence-based verification method and the congruence-based trace abstraction method are effective and efficient on the benchmark.

5   Conclusion and Future Work

This paper applies a CEGAR framework for verifying uninterpreted programs. With the help of program partition, we partition an uninterpreted program into coherent and non-coherent sub-programs. Then, for the coherent sub-programs, we verify them by the method in [15]. For the remaining sub-programs, we propose a congruence-based trace abstraction method to carry out the CEGAR loop. We have implemented our method, and the experimental results indicate that our method is more effective and efficient than the state-of-the-art.

The future work lies in several directions: (1) extend our verification framework to other uninterpreted programs, such as the ones in [17] that have dynamic memory allocations; (2) enhance the trace abstraction method further, *e.g.*, by automated synthesized loop invariants; (3) more extensive evaluation on more uninterpreted programs.

Acknowledgments. This research was supported by National Key R&D Program of China (No. 2017YFB1001802) and the NSFC Programs (No. 62172429, 61632015, 62032024, and 61690203).

Author contributions. Weijiang Hong and Zhenbang Chen contributed equally to this work and are co-first authors.

---

[2] SV-COMP is one of the most popular benchmarks for software verification.

References

1. Ball, T., Majumdar, R., Millstein, T.D., Rajamani, S.K.: Automatic predicate abstraction of C programs. In: Burke, M., Soffa, M.L. (eds.) Proceedings of the 2001 ACM SIGPLAN Conference on Programming Language Design and Implementation (PLDI), Snowbird, Utah, USA, 2001, pp. 203–213. ACM (2001). https://doi.org/10.1145/378795.378846
2. Boogie Language: www.microsoft.com/en-us/research/project/boogie-an-intermediate-verification-language/
3. Cassez, F., Jensen, P.G., Larsen, K.G.: Verification and parameter synthesis for real-time programs using refinement of trace abstraction. Fundam. Informaticae 178(1–2), 31–57 (2021). https://doi.org/10.3233/FI-2021-1997
4. Cassez, F., Ziegler, F.: Verification of concurrent programs using trace abstraction refinement. In: Davis, M., Fehnker, A., McIver, A., Voronkov, A. (eds.) LPAR 2015. LNCS, vol. 9450, pp. 233–248. Springer, Heidelberg (2015). https://doi.org/10.1007/978-3-662-48899-7_17
5. Christ, J., Hoenicke, J., Nutz, A.: SMTInterpol: an interpolating SMT solver. In: Donaldson, A., Parker, D. (eds.) SPIN 2012. LNCS, vol. 7385, pp. 248–254. Springer, Heidelberg (2012). https://doi.org/10.1007/978-3-642-31759-0_19
6. Clarke, E., Grumberg, O., Jha, S., Lu, Y., Veith, H.: Counterexample-guided abstraction refinement. In: Emerson, E.A., Sistla, A.P. (eds.) CAV 2000. LNCS, vol. 1855, pp. 154–169. Springer, Heidelberg (2000). https://doi.org/10.1007/10722167_15
7. Heizmann, M., et al.: Ultimate automizer with SMTInterpol. In: Piterman, N., Smolka, S.A. (eds.) TACAS 2013. LNCS, vol. 7795, pp. 641–643. Springer, Heidelberg (2013). https://doi.org/10.1007/978-3-642-36742-7_53
8. Heizmann, M., Hoenicke, J., Podelski, A.: Refinement of trace abstraction. In: Palsberg, J., Su, Z. (eds.) SAS 2009. LNCS, vol. 5673, pp. 69–85. Springer, Heidelberg (2009). https://doi.org/10.1007/978-3-642-03237-0_7
9. Heizmann, M., Hoenicke, J., Podelski, A.: Nested interpolants. In: Hermenegildo, M.V., Palsberg, J. (eds.) Proceedings of the 37th ACM SIGPLAN-SIGACT Symposium on Principles of Programming Languages, POPL 2010, Madrid, Spain, pp. 471–482. ACM (2010). https://doi.org/10.1145/1706299.1706353
10. Hoder, K., Kovács, L., Voronkov, A.: Playing in the grey area of proofs. In: Field, J., Hicks, M. (eds.) Proceedings of the 39th ACM SIGPLAN-SIGACT Symposium on Principles of Programming Languages, POPL 2012, Philadelphia, Pennsylvania, USA, pp. 259–272. ACM (2012). https://doi.org/10.1145/2103656.2103689
11. Kozen, D.: Automata and computability. Undergraduate texts in computer science, Springer (1997)
12. Kroening, D., Strichman, O.: Decision procedures - an algorithmic point of view, 2nd Edn. Texts in Theoretical Computer Science. An EATCS Series, Springer (2016). https://doi.org/10.1007/978-3-662-50497-0
13. Krogmeier, P., et al.: Decidable synthesis of programs with uninterpreted functions. In: Lahiri, S. K., Wang, C. (eds.) CAV 2020. LNCS, vol. 12225, pp. 634–657. Springer, Cham (2020). https://doi.org/10.1007/978-3-030-53291-8_32
14. Leino, K., Rustan, M..: Dafny: an automatic program verifier for functional correctness. In: Clarke, E.M., Voronkov, A. (eds.) LPAR 2010. LNCS (LNAI), vol. 6355, pp. 348–370. Springer, Heidelberg (2010). https://doi.org/10.1007/978-3-642-17511-4_20

15. Mathur, U., Madhusudan, P., Viswanathan, M.: Decidable verification of uninter-preted programs. In: Proceedings ACM Programing. Language 3(POPL), pp. 1–29 (2019). https://doi.org/10.1145/3290359
16. Mathur, U., Madhusudan, P., Viswanathan, M.: What's decidable about program verification modulo axioms?. In: TACAS 2020. LNCS, vol. 12079, pp. 158–177. Springer, Cham (2020). https://doi.org/10.1007/978-3-030-45237-7_10
17. Mathur, U., Murali, A., Krogmeier, P., Madhusudan, P., Viswanathan, M.: Decid-ing memory safety for single-pass heap-manipulating programs. In: Proceedings ACM Programming Language 4(POPL), 1–29 (2020). https://doi.org/10.1145/3371103
18. Nelson, G., Oppen, D.C.: Fast decision procedures based on congruence closure. J. ACM **27**(2), 356–364 (1980). https://doi.org/10.1145/322186.322198
19. SV-benchmarks: github.com/sosy-lab/sv-benchmarks
20. Torre, S.L., Madhusudan, P.: Reachability in concurrent uninterpreted programs. In: Chattopadhyay, A., Gastin, P. (eds.) 39th IARCS Annual Conference on Foun-dations of Software Technology and Theoretical Computer Science, FSTTCS 2019, Bombay, India. LIPIcs, vol. 150, pp. 1–16. Schloss Dagstuhl - Leibniz-Zentrum für Informatik (2019). https://doi.org/10.4230/LIPIcs.FSTTCS.2019.46

HStriver: A Very Functional Extensible Tool for the Runtime Verification of Real-Time Event Streams

Felipe Gorostiaga[1,2,3]([✉]) [iD] and César Sánchez[1] [iD]

[1] IMDEA software institute, Madrid, Spain
{felipe.gorostiaga,cesar.sanchez}@imdea.org
[2] Universidad Politécnica de Madrid, Madrid, Spain
[3] CIFASIS, Rosario, Argentina

Abstract. We present HStriver, an extensible stream runtime verification tool for event streams. The tool consists of a runtime verification engine for (1) real-time events streams where individual observations and verdicts can occur at arbitrary times, and (2) rich data in the observations and verdicts. This rich setting allows, for example, encoding as HStriver specifications quantitative semantics of logics like STL, including different notions of robustness.

The keystone of stream runtime verification (SRV) is the clean separation between temporal dependencies and data computations. To encode the data values and computations involved in the monitoring process we borrow (almost) arbitrary data-types from Haskell. These types are transparently lifted to the specification language and incorporated in the engine, so they can be used as the types of the inputs (observations), outputs (verdicts), and intermediate streams. The resulting extensible language is then embedded, alongside the temporal evaluation engine (which is agnostic to the types) into Haskell as an embedded Domain Specific Langauge (eDSL). Morever, the availability of functional features in the specification language enables the direct implementation of desirable features in HStriver like parametrization (using functions that return stream specifications), etc. The resulting tool is a flexible and extensible stream runtime verification engine for real-time streams. We illustrate the use of the tool on many sophisticated real-time specifications, including realistic signal temporal logic (STL) properties of existing designs.

1 Introduction

Runtime Verification [4,25,29] is a lightweight dynamic technique for systems reliability that studies (1) how to generate monitors from formal specifications, and (2) algorithms to monitor the system under analysis, by processing one trace

The tool is available open source at http://github.com/imdea-software/hstriver. This work was funded in part by the Madrid Regional Government under project "S2018/TCS-4339 (BLOQUES-CM)", by Spanish National Project "BOSCO (PGC2018-102210-B-100)".

© Springer Nature Switzerland AG 2021
M. Huisman et al. (Eds.): FM 2021, LNCS 13047, pp. 563–580, 2021.
https://doi.org/10.1007/978-3-030-90870-6_30

at a time. Early RV formal specification languages were based on temporal logics like past LTL [31] adapted to finite traces [7,13,26], regular expressions [36], rewriting [34], fix-point logics [1], rule based languages [3]. In these languages, verdicts (and many times observations) are Boolean, because these logics were borrowed from static verification—where decidability is crucial.

Stream runtime verification (SRV) [12,35] attempts to generalize these monitoring algorithms to richer datatypes, including in observations and verdicts, which allows the computation of quantitative values and summaries, the computation of witnesses, models or the collection of representative data, etc. The keystone of SRV is to cleanly separate the temporal engine from the individual data operations, abstracting the temporal monitoring algorithms which can then be instantiated with generic data types. SRV offers declarative specifications where offset expressions allow accessing streams at different moments in time, including future instants. The first SRV developments [12] were based on similarly synchronous languages—like Esterel [8] or Lustre [21]. These languages force causality because their intention is to describe systems and not observations or monitors, while SRV removes the causality assumption allowing the reference to future values. Synchronous SRV languages have been extended in recent years to event-based systems for monitoring real-time event streams [10,15,18,20,28]. Most SRV efforts to date, synchronous and event-based, have focused on efficiently implementing the temporal engine, only offering a handful of hard-wired data-types. However, in practice, adding a new datatype requires modifying the parser, the internal representation and the runtime system, which becomes a cumbersome activity. More importantly, these tools are shipped as monolithic tools with a few hard-wired datatypes which the user of the tool cannot extend.

In this paper we describe the tool HStriver, an extensible implementation of an event-based SRV language. The core language is based on [18], and enables the extensions to arbitrary datatypes, implemented as an embedded DSL in Haskell. There are other RV tools implemented as eDSLs [2,24,37] but a main novelty of HStriver is the use of *lift deep embedding*, that allows borrowing Haskell types transparently and embedding the resulting language back into Haskell [9].

Most of the HStriver datatypes were introduced after the temporal engine was completed without any re-implementation, so users of the tool can also extend the datatypes easily. The second contribution of HStriver is the implementation of a novel efficient asynchronous engine for the temporal part, described in Sect. 2. Implementing HStriver as a Haskell eDSL enables the use of higher-order functions which in turn allows writing code that produces stream declarations from stream declarations, enabling features like stream parametrization, which requires costly ad-hoc implementations in previous tools. This is used to package HStriver libraries that describe logics like STL, etc. with Boolean and quantitative semantics in a few lines.

Related work. There have been runtime verification tools for the monitoring of event-based streams (see [14] for a survey). R2U2 [33] is based on a variation of metric interval temporal logic (MITL) for finite (real-time) traces. Since R2U2 uses logic as a specification formalism, the observations and verdicts are based on Boolean values. BeepBeep [22,23] is a framework to build runtime verification tools based on connecting streaming blocks. Even though BeepBeep could be used as a programming framework for tools like HStriver, in comparison to HStriver, BeepBeep lacks semantics both in terms of the data-types, the assumptions on the temporal domain and lacks a way to compute the resources needed. MonPoly [5,6] is a monitoring tool based on first-order MITL. Even though the tool can produce witnesses for the quantifiers, in comparison with SRV, FO-MITL cannot compute values of arbitrary data-types like the computation of statistics and quantitative semantics of logics. Copilot [32] is a Haskell implementation that offers a collection of building blocks to transform streams, but Copilot does not offer explicit time accesses and offsets (and in particular future accesses). Also, Copilot is based on synchronous time. The closest tools to HStriver are RTLola [15,16] and TeSSLa [10] which are SRV tools extending Lola [12] with capabilities to real-time event streams. The main difference are that RTLola and TeSSLa come with a predefined collection of data-types, while HStriver enjoys the Haskell capabilities to import and create new types without changing HStriver. Also, HStriver incorporates an asynchronous pull engine and borrows flexible data-types and functional features from the host language. Additionally, HStriver allows event-generation, while RTLola is restricted to be event-driven or periodic events. Compared with TeSSLa, HStriver is an explicit timed language while TeSSLa uses stream transformers.

The main contributions of this tool paper are (1) to describe the implementation of HStriver, an SRV tool for real-time event streams using a lift deep embedding in Haskell; (2) the novel pull algorithm to implement an asynchronous temporal engine and; (3) to illustrate many of the HStriver features by example. The rest of the paper is structured as follows. Section 2 introduces SRV and describes the internals of HStriver, Sect. 3 illustrates many features by example, and finally Sect. 4 concludes.

2   The HStriver Tool

SRV generalizes monitoring algorithms to arbitrary data, where data-types are abstracted using multi-sorted first-order interpreted signatures. These data-types are called *data theories* in the SRV terminology. The signatures are interpreted in the sense that every functional symbol f used to build terms of a given type is accompanied with an evaluation function f (the interpretation) that allows the computation of values (given values of the arguments). In the context of event-streams, a specification not only needs to declare the values of output streams (based on input and output streams) but also the temporal instants at which there are events in the output streams.

The temporal core of the tool HStriver is based on the Striver specification language [18]. A specification $\langle I, O, E \rangle$ consists of (1) a set of typed input stream variables I, which correspond to the input observations; (2) a set of typed output stream variables O which represent outputs of the monitor and intermediate observations; and (3) defining equations, which associate every output $y \in O$

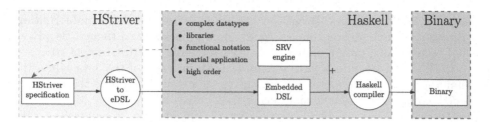

Fig. 1. Software Architecture of HStriver.

with two stream expressions: T_y, which describes when there is an event in y, and E_y which describes what the value is whenever there is an event. Tick expressions T_y are built from constant time-instants, and the union, and shift and delays of the ticking instants of other streams. Stream Expressions E_y are built from constant values, function symbols and offset expressions that allow referring to the previous and next-events in streams, according to the time-stamps of events. The online algorithm proposed in [18] is a *push* algorithm that processes input events in the order of their time-stamps and produces output events also in time order. The algorithm implemented in HStriver is a much more efficient *pull* algorithm, which attempts to compute events in output streams fetching the necessary events from other streams. We have empirically shown that HStriver is capable of processing tens of thousands of events per second [17].

HStriver Architecture. The architecture of HStriver follows the same approach as the tool HLola [19] and is shown in Fig. 1. An HStriver specification defines event streams using the syntax described below as well as Haskell datatypes and type members. A specification can also borrow Haskell notation and features such as list comprehension and let-clauses (represented by the red dashed arrow in Fig. 1). Then, a very simple translator generates Haskell code from the source specification. This translator does not parse and interpret the totality of the source code, but only performs simple rewritings introduced to make the specification cleaner. The resulting Haskell code is then combined with the execution engine described below, written in Haskell, and compiled using the GHC to obtain the binary for the specification monitor. In this manner, the HStriver tool can be easily extended with new data-theories, and Haskell programs can use HStriver specifications as part of their code.

The Language. A stream declaration in an HStriver specification can be either:

- An input declaration, which is bound to a name and a type using the following syntax:
  input <TypeConstraints>? <Type> <name> **<ArgType argame>***, or
- An output declaration, which is bound to a name, a *TickExpression te* assigned to the field **ticks** and a *ValueExpression ve* assigned to the field **val**, using the following syntax:

```
output <TypeConstraints>? <Type> <name> <ArgType argame>* :
  ticks = te
  val = ve
```

where **<TypeConstraints>** is an optional set of constraints over the polymorphic types handled by the stream and expressed in Haskell notation, and **<ArgType argame>*** is an optional list of arguments. We can use **define** instead of **output** to define intermediate streams, whose values are not reported by the monitor but can be used by other streams. We can replace the last **:** with a **=** to define an output stream as the copy of another stream instead of indicating its *Tick* and *Value Expressions*.

The types of the streams have to be Haskell **Typeable** types, which is a very general class of types, enough for our the purpose of SRV data theories. The types of **input** streams have to be parseable from JSON using the Haskell aeson library (i.e., they have to be an instance of the **FromJSON** class), and the output streams have to be serializable to JSON using the aeson library (this is, they have to implement the **ToJSON** class). Also, the current HStriver frontend imposes some minor syntactic restrictions (the work reported in this tool paper focuses on an efficient implementation with rich data theories, while ongoing work includes bringing the specification language closer to Striver).

The *TickExpression* of an output stream indicates when it might produce an event, and is defined by the following recursive datatype:

- A single point in time t, which we write {t},
- The instants at which stream s contains an event, written ticksOf s
- The instants of the events of s shifted by a constant c, written shift $c\ s$,
- The instants at which a stream of type **TimeDiff** ("Time Difference") s contains an event, delayed by the value in the event (unless s contains a new event meanwhile), which we write delay s, or
- The union of two *TickExpressions* te_1 and te_2, which we write te_1 U te_2

The *ValueExpression* of an output stream indicates if the stream will contain an event at a ticking point, and with which value. A *TickExpression* also "carries" the values of all events that made the stream wake up to facilitate the computation of the *ValueExpression*. The *ValueExpression* is defined as follows:

- The constructor **'** x encapsulates an element x from a data-theory. This constructor represents the *lift* stage of the *lift-deep embedding* technique [9].
- Function application is juxtaposition, has the greatest precedence and is automatically lifted for *ValueExpressions*. Parentheses are used to impose a different association between functions and values.
- The value cv contains the value carried by the tick expression.
- The constructor :=> is used to refrain from producing a value: it will return the value at the right hand of the operator provided that the expression at the left hand side holds, and will not produce a value otherwise.

Two additional constructors allow accessing timestamps and values of different streams:

- We use `timeOf` te to access the timestamp of a *TauExpression* (explained below) *te*, and
- We use the projection constructor *s*[*te*|_] to access the value of a stream *s* in a *TauExpression te*, either (1) providing a default value *v* with the same type as *s* in case the tau expression *te* falls off the trace as in *s*[*te*|*v*]; or (2) with no default value, delegating the obligation to check if the expression falls off the trace to the surrounding expression, as in *s*[*te*|?]; or (3) with no default value, indicating that the inner *TauExpression* does not fall off the trace, as in *s*[*te*|].

Finally, the datatype for *TauExpression*, which allows offsets in time:

- The value t represents the current time.
- The constructor *s* « *te* allows us to refer to the last event in stream *s* strictly before the value of the *TauExpression te*.
- The constructor *s* <~ *te* is like « but also considers the current t.
- The constructors » and ~> are the future duals of « and <~ respectively.

Sometimes, the offset expressions can allow us to express bounds on the time which enable a more efficient implementation (very useful to capture logics like STL). We rewrite the stream accesses to make them more compact and improve legibility. Thus, *s*[*s* « *te*|_] becomes *s*[<*te*|_], *s*[*s* <~ *te*|_] becomes *s*[~*te*|_], *s*[*s* » *te*|_] becomes *s*[*te*>|_], and *s*[*s* ~> *te*|_] becomes *s*[*te*~|_].

The language HStriver offers the possibility to work with two temporal domains: **Double** and **UTC**. The former uses the Haskell type `Double` as the time domain, while the latter uses `Data.Time` from package `time`.

We specify the time domain for a specification with the directive **time domain** followed by either **Double** or **UTC**. HStriver libraries and theories are imported with **use library/theory** `Name`, which allows the access to functions and streams from the imported file by prepending the name of the library or theory as in `Name.member`.

The main difference between a **library** and a **theory** file is that the former contains utilities for streams manipulation and definitions, while a theory is agnostic of the Striver concepts and comprises functions and constants from a specific application domain. Data theories, as described in Sect. 2, are implemented directly in the host language, which lets us use native types and functions, as well as third parties out of the shelf, and even define our own custom types and functions as data theories. In this manner, the syntactic name of a Haskell function definition (or its lambda expression in the case of anonymous functions) make up the functional symbols used to build terms, while their semantics in the Haskell language are the functions interpretations. This characteristic of the language shows the extensibility of the language in terms of data theories.

We can also import arbitrary Haskell libraries with the directive **use haskell** `Name`. Finally, we can access functions and constants in the Haskell Prelude by prepending P to their names.

Example 1. In this example we show the definition of an *output* stream *stock* to calculate the stock of a certain product based on two input event streams:

sale that represents the sales of such product, and arrival which represents the arrivals of the same product. The output stream stock is defined to tick when either sale or arrival (or both) tick. The value carried by the tick expression is of type (Maybe Int, Maybe Int) and represents the units of the product sold and received at a given point in time. Notice that at least one of the members will be a Just value.

```
time domain Double
use haskell Data.Maybe

input Int sale
input Int arrival

output Int stock:
  ticks = ticksOf sale U ticksOf arrival
  val = let
    (msal, marr) = cv
    sal = 1'(fromMaybe 0) msal
    arr = 1'(fromMaybe 0) marr
    in
    stock[<t|0] - sal + arr
```

In HStriver we can also define a stream as the transformation of another stream, which does not require the explicit definition of a *TickExpression* and a *ValueExpression*. We call this feature *Stream aliasing*. HStriver also allows the static parameterization of streams, which lets us reuse stream definitions and instantiate these for different parameters in static time. These two features are shown in the following example.

Example 2. The following specification generalizes Ex. 1 for multiple products. It uses the delay operator to set up a timer and raise an alarm in case the stock of any product has been low for too long.

```
time domain Double
use library Utils
use haskell Data.Maybe

#HASKELL
data Product = ProductA | ProductB | ProductC deriving (Show, Eq)
#ENDOFHASKELL

input Int sale <Product p>
input Int arrival <Product p>

define Int stock <Product p>:
  ticks = ticksOf (sale p) U ticksOf (arrival p)
  val = let
    (msal, marr) = cv
    sal = 1'(fromMaybe 0) msal
    arr = 1'(fromMaybe 0) marr
    in
    stock p [<t|0] - sal + arr

define Bool low_stock <Product p> = Utils.strMap "low" (lowval p) (stock p)
```

```
define Bool cp_low_stock <Product p> = Utils.changePointsOf (low_stock p)
define TimeDiff alarm_timer <Product p>:
  ticks = ticksOf (cp_low_stock p)
  val = if cv then tolerance p else (-1)

define () alarm <Product p>:
  ticks = delay (alarm_timer p)
  val = '()

output () any_alarm:
  ticks = ticksOf (alarm ProductA) U ticksOf (alarm ProductB)
        U ticksOf (alarm ProductC)
  val = '()

- Alternative alarm:
define TimeDiff alarm_timer2 <Product p>:
  ticks = ticksOf (cp_low_stock p) U ticksOf (arrival p)
  val = let
    (mls, marr) = cv
    ls = 1'fromJust mls
    in if (1'isJust marr) || not ls then (-1) else tolerance p
```

The Engine. In earlier work [18] we proposed an online monitoring algorithm, limited to past offsets only, that processes input events in strictly increasing time, producing outputs also in increasing time. We call this a *push* approach, because input events are pushed into the monitor. Instead, the implementation of HStriver follows a novel *pull* approach: the engine computes events for the output streams, which requires pulling events from other streams, and eventually pulling events from inputs. The performance of both execution approaches is similar for the common fragment of the language (i.e., the past-only fragment of Striver). Using a pull procedure, we gain expressivity in exchange for a somewhat more complex execution design. In this section we explain the pull algorithm in detail.

Input events are read from named pipes in JSON format. The main algorithm maintains the following *state* that updated at each step in the computation: (1) one *Leader* for each stream declared, and (2) one *Pointer* from one stream to another for every timeOf or projection used.

The task of the *Leader* is to fetch the next event in a stream when required. The *Leader* for an input stream will pull the next input event, while the *Leader* for an output stream will use its definition to calculate the next event, pulling from the pointers in the value and tick expressions if necessary. Leaders can also discover the lack of events, which is useful data for referring streams, and is necessary to prevent the system from hanging trying to calculate a real event.

A *Pointer* represents a relevant position in the sequence of events of a stream. Pointers advance from past to future over the events of a stream. The events in the past of a pointer have already been used, while the events in the future will be used later in the computation. When a Pointer needs an event that has not yet been computed, it will use the corresponding Leader to fetch it. When all the pointers of a stream pass beyond an event, this event can be forgotten. For example, the Leader for the stream `any_alarm` in Example 2 maintains one pointer to each of the three `alarm` streams to determine when to generate the unit value. In particular, `any_alarm` will pull from every `alarm` stream at the beginning and then keep pulling from the pointer at the minimum position. Each of the `alarm` streams also maintains a pointer to its corresponding `alarm_timer`, to calculate if the corresponding `stock` is low for too long, so it produces a unit value. In particular, the leader will pull from `alarm_timer` one event to check the next timestamp and value; and one more to determine whether the timer is reset or not. The engine maintains an extra pointer for every output stream, which it uses to pull events and print them. The diagram on the right shows how the pointers are updated every

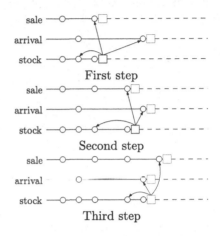

time the output stream `stock` is pulled. The big box of each stream represents its Leader. Everything at the right of the leader has not yet been discovered, hence the dashed line. The leader of the stream `stock` maintains one pointer to the last event of each other stream, plus an extra pointer to its own last event (not considering the event that is being computed).

2.1   How to Run HStriver

To compile an HStriver specification or library we execute the **hstriverc** program —which is shipped with the tool— with a set of filenames, of which at most one can be a runnable specification, while the rest have to be library definitions. This will produce an executable monitor, with the name specified using the flag -o *filename*, or **a.out** if no output filename was specified.

To run our **monitor** over input data, it has to be executed with a parameter indicating the directory where the input data is located as its parameter: **monitor** *dir*. For every non-parameterized input stream *s*, the **monitor** will read its events from the file *dir/s.*`json`. For a parameterized input stream *s* with parameters $arg_0 \ldots arg_n$, the **monitor** will read the events for the instantiated input streams from the files *dir/*arg_0*/.../*arg_n*.*`json`. The input events have to be of the form {"Time": *ts*, "Value": *val*}, where *val* is the value of the stream at the instant *ts*, and there has to be one event per line, with a monotonically increasing timestamp. The monitor will then produce a list of events with the form {"Id": *id*, "Time": *ts*, "Value": *val*}, where *val* is the value of the stream *id* at the instant *ts*.

Note that the input files can be named pipes, which will be consumed when it is necessary to compute the next output event, following the pull model explained in Sect. 2, effectively allowing the monitor to be run over data generated in real time. Also notice that it is easy to write a wrapper that acts as a sink for different input events and dispatches every event to its corresponding named pipe, if necessary.

Take for example the specification in Ex. 1, whose definition is in the file stock.hstriver, and suppose we want to execute with the input streams in the directory ins in the working directory. Then, we need to run:

```
$ hstriverc -o monitor stock.hstriver
$ ./monitor ins
```

There need to be two input stream files in the directory ins: ins/sale.json and ins/arrival.json. The monitor will print the events of stock to the standard output progressively when the information is available in the input stream files.

To run the specification in Ex. 2, where paramstock.hstriver contains the definitions and the input streams are in the sub-directory paramins of the current directory, we need to run

```
$ hstriverc -o monitor paramstock.hstriver
$ ./monitor paramins
```

and there need to be two directories in the directory ins: ins/sale and ins/arrival, with three input files inside each of them, namely

ins/sale/ProductA.json,   ins/arrival/ProductA.json
ins/sale/ProductB.json,   ins/arrival/ProductB.json
ins/sale/ProductC.json, and   ins/arrival/ProductC.json

The monitor will print an event whenever there is a shortage of any product.[1]

3   Example Specifications and Libraries

In this section we show a selection of HStriver specifications, each of which illustrates a particular interesting feature of the language.

3.1   Example: Clock

The specification below demonstrates the use of the delay operator to define a specification with no input streams and one output streams clock, which generates a unit value at each instant multiple of 5. In this specific case, we could have used the shift operator instead with identical results. This example illustrates that HStriver is not only event-driven, and can generate ticks at instants where no input streams have an event.

```
time domain Double
output TimeDiff clock:
  ticks = {0} U delay clock
  val = 5
```

---

[1] See the tool webpage https://software.imdea.org/hstriver to find example specifications along with input and output data.

TeSSLa [10] can also implement this feature but most other systems, like RTLola [16] can only tick at periodic instants or at points at which inputs have events.

3.2   Libraries

We can use HStriver to collect reusable code and stream transformers in libraries (that do not have output streams). Libraries are declared with the directive **library** Name. Specifications can then import the definitions in the library to aid the stream definitions. Some libraries are time domain agnostic and do not require the definition of a time domain. We leverage the modules system of the host language to implement this feature. The libraries definitions contain many definitions of stream declarations from stream declarations, which shows the high-order nature of HStriver. Here we show the implementation of the library Utils, which contains useful stream operators that are used extensively in the rest of the examples.

```
library Utils
define (...) => b strMap <String funame> <(a->b) f> <Stream a s>:
  ticks = ticksOf s
  val = 1'f cv

define (Streamable a) => a filter <String funame> <(a->Bool) f> <Stream a x>:
  ticks = ticksOf x
  val = (1'f cv) :=> cv

define (Eq a, Streamable a) => a changePointsOf <Stream a s>:
  ticks = ticksOf s
  val = let
    prevMVal = s[<t|?]
    noprev = prevMVal === '-out
    prevVal = 1'getEvent prevMVal
    update = prevVal /== cv
    in noprev || update :=> cv
    where
    getEvent (Ev x) = x

define Streamable a => a firstEvOf <Stream a s>:
  ticks = ticksOf s
  val = let
    _this = firstEvOf s
    isfirst = timeOf (_this « t) === '-infty
    in isfirst :=> cv

define Streamable a => a shift <TimeDiff n> <Stream a x>:
  ticks = shift n x
  val = cv
```

We also show part of the implementations of the library STL which implements the operators of the Signal Temporal Logic STL [30], a temporal logic widely used to describe system properties of continuous signals, which are represented as timestamped event streams.

```
library STL
use library Utils
use haskell Data.Maybe
define Bool until <(TimeDiff, TimeDiff) (a,b)> <Stream Bool x> <Stream Bool y>:
  ticks = shift (-a) y U shift (-b) y U shift (-b) x U ticksOf x
  val = let
    tnow = 1'T now
    yT = filterId y
    min_yT = if Utils.shift (-a) y [~t|False] then tnow
             else timeOf (Utils.shift (-a) yT »_(b-a) t)
    xF = filterNot x
    min_xF = if not (x [~t|False]) then tnow else timeOf (xF »_b t)
    plus x tim = 2'timeDiffPlus x 'tim
    in
    min_yT 'plus' a <= tnow 'plus' b && min_yT 'plus' a <= min_xF

define TimeDiff alwaysaux <TimeDiff n> <Stream Bool x>:
  ticks = ticksOf x
  val = let
    nextx = 1'unT (timeOf (x»t))
    frontier = 2'tDiffAdd nextx 'n
    in
    not cv :=> if not (x [t>|False]) then (-1) else 2'tDiff frontier now

define Bool statealways <TimeDiff n> <Stream Bool x>:
  ticks = let aaux = alwaysaux n x in delay aaux U ticksOf aaux
  val = 1'isNothing (snd cv)

define Bool always <(TimeDiff, TimeDiff) (a,b)> <Stream Bool x>:
  ticks = shift (-a) (statealways (b-a) x) U {0}
  val = let
    _this = always (a,b) x
    in 2'fromMaybe (_this [<t|True]) (fst cv)

define Bool eventually <(TimeDiff, TimeDiff) (a,b)> <Stream Bool x> =
  neg (always (a,b) (neg x))
```

This snippet illustrates the definitions of the $\mathcal{U}_{[a,b]}$ as until, $\Phi_{[a,b]}$ as always and $\Psi_{[a,b]}$ as eventually. These definitions are parametrized by the interval bounds and the streams of the sub-expressions.

3.3   STL

The next example illustrates a simple STL specification: if the input speed becomes toofast, then speed will decelerate continuously until reaching an admissible speed (speedok) within 0.5 time units (represented by the stream slow_down). This example shows a straightforward use of the STL library to define temporal properties as streams.

```
time domain Double

use library STL
use library Utils

const max_speed = 5
const ok_speed = 4

input Double speed

define Bool toofast = Utils.strMap "toofast" (P.>max_speed) speed

define Bool speedok = Utils.strMap "speedok" (P.<=ok_speed) speed

define Bool decel:
  ticks = ticksOf speed
  val = cv > speed[t>|0]

define Bool slow_down = STL.until (0,5) decel speedok

output Bool ok:
  ticks = ticksOf toofast U ticksOf slow_down
  val = toofast [~t|False] 'implies' slow_down [~t|True]
```

3.4   Example: Cost Computation

The following example calculates the accumulated energy cost incurred by a monitor, based on a cost model for (a) waking up, (b) processing an event, (c) going to sleep, (d) being idle, (e) being awake, and also a patience parameter, which models how long to wait for a new event before going to sleep. This specification contains the definition of an output stream which is the quantitative result of a progressive computation, as opposed to typical Boolean output streams. In this example the event production is unpredictable and not governed by a predefined ratio[2]. This example uses custom datatype definitions, and event generation at instants where there is no input event.

```
time domain Double
use haskell Data.Maybe

input () wakeup

define TimeDiff sleep_delayer:
  ticks = ticksOf wakeup
  val = 'patience

define () sleep:
  ticks = delay sleep_delayer
  val = '()

define RunMode runMode:
  ticks = ticksOf wakeup U ticksOf sleep
  val = if 1'isJust (fst cv) then 'Alert else 'Sleeping
```

---

[2] The full code or all examples and libraries in this section can be found in https://software.imdea.org/hstriver.

```
output Cost cost:
  ticks = ticksOf runMode
  val = let
    previousRunMode = runMode[<t|Alert]
    currentRunMode = cv
    costOfTransitioning = 2'transitionCost previousRunMode currentRunMode
    getTimeT (T x) _ = x
    getTimeT _ y = y
    prevt = 2'getTimeT (timeOf (runMode « t)) now
    timediff = 1'(round.realToFrac) (2'tDiff now prevt)
    accum = cost [<t|0] + timediff * ('runCostPerSecond previousRunMode)
  in
  accum + costOfTransitioning
```

3.5   Example: PowerTrain

Our third example makes a heavy use of the STL library to implement STL properties for the verification of a powertrain control verification from [27], where input signals change asynchronously.

```
time domain Double
use library STL

input Double verification
input Double mode
input Double pedal
```

- phi = []_(taus ,simTime)(((low/\<>_(0, h) high)
-    \/ (high/\<>_(0,h) low)) -> []_[eta, zeta_min] (utr /\utl))

```
const ut2 = 0.02
output Bool opt2 =
  STL.always (taus, simTime) (((low 'conj' STL.eventually (0,h) high)
    'disj' (high 'conj' STL.eventually (0,h) low))
    'strImplies' STL.always (eta, zeta_min) (utl ut2 'conj' utr ut2))
```

- phi = <>_[simTime,simTime] utr

```
const ut3 = 0.05
output Bool opt3 = STL.eventually (simTime, simTime) (utr ut3)
```

- phi = []_(taus,simTime) utr

```
const ut4 = 0.1
output Bool opt4 = STL.always (taus, simTime) (utr ut4)
```

As in [27] we use input data computed from a MatLab simulation of the powertrain. This example shows how to import and use the STL operators to describe properties. We have aimed to keep the syntax of the original properties.

3.6   Example: Smart Home

This example is a smart home specification that uses the Orange4Home dataset [11]. The following monitor calculates how much time residents spend watching TV per day, assessing that every day the people living the house should not watch more than three hours of TV (exceeded3hPerDay). More interesting is exceededAvgPlus30m, which states that residents should not watch thirty minutes more than the total average of TV watched historically. This threshold is dynamic, and requires declaring intermediate quantitative streams that compute the average and current day TV time.

```
time domain UTC

use library Utils
use haskell Data.Time

input TVStatus livingroom_tv_status
input TVStatus office_tv_status

define Bool any_tv_on:
  ticks = ticksOf office_tv_on U ticksOf livingroom_tv_on
  val = office_tv_on [~t|False] || livingroom_tv_on [~t|False]

output Bool exceeded3hPerDay:
  ticks = ticksOf any_tv_on
  val = howMuchTvToday[~t|] > 3*60*instantsPerMinute

define Int totalTVTime:
  ticks = ticksOf any_tv_on
  val = totalTVTime [<t|0] + if any_tv_on[~t|] then 1 else 0

define Int avgTvPast:
  ticks = ticksOf any_tv_on
  val = if isNewDay[~t|] then 2'div (totalTVTime[~t|]) (countDays[~t|])
    else avgTvPast [<t|0]

output Bool exceededAvgPlus30m:
  ticks = ticksOf any_tv_on
  val = howMuchTvToday[~t|] > avgTvPast[~t|] + 30 * instantsPerMinute
```

4   Conclusion

We have a presented HStriver, a stream runtime verification tool for real-time event-streams, implemented as an eDSL with Haskell as the host language, based on a technique called lift-deep embedding. The architecture of HStriver lets us use Haskell tools straightforwardly to aid improving the confidence on the correctness of the implementation with respect to the semantics of Striver, for example using unit tests, end-to-end tests and tools like Quickcheck and LiquidHaskell, as displayed in [9]. In this seminal paper we have focused on functionality, but future work includes the certification of HStriver, which is a more accessible endeavor for a concise language with a few constructs with clean semantics as Striver than for a general purpose language. HStriver has been used in (non-critical) UAV missions, where garbage collection is forbidden for critical applications, but we are exploring the generation of Misra-C from (a restricted set of) HStriver specifications. Also, future work includes a frontend that allows adapting the input syntax to particular use cases, offering a friendly syntax and the necessary types and features from HStriver.

References

1. Barringer, H., Goldberg, A., Havelund, K., Sen, K.: Rule-based runtime verification. In: Proceedings of the 5th Int'l Conference on Verification, Model Checking and Abstract Interpretation (VMCAI'04). LNCS, vol. 2937, pp. 44–57. Springer (2004). https://doi.org/10.1007/978-3-540-24622-0_5
2. Barringer, H., Havelund, K.: Tracecontract: A scala DSL for trace analysis. In: Proceedings of the 17th Int'l Symposium on Formal Methods (FM'11). LNCS, vol. 6664, pp. 57–72. Springer (2011). https://doi.org/10.1007/978-3-642-21437-0_7
3. Barringer, H., Rydeheard, D., Havelund, K.: Rule systems for run-time monitoring: from eagle to ruleR. In: Proceedings of the 7th Int'l Workshop on Runtime Verification (RV'07). LNCS, vol. 4839, pp. 111–125. Springer (2007). https://doi.org/10.1007/978-3-540-77395-5_10
4. Bartocci, E., Falcone, Y. (eds.): Lectures on Runtime Verification. LNCS, vol. 10457. Springer, Cham (2018). https://doi.org/10.1007/978-3-319-75632-5
5. Basin, D., Klaedtke, M.H.F., Zalinescu, E.: MONPOLY: monitoring usage-control policies. In: Proceedings of the 2nd Int'l Conference on Runtime Verification (RV'11). LNCS, vol. 7186, pp. 360–364. Springer (2011). https://doi.org/10.1007/978-3-642-29860-8_27
6. Basin, D.A., Klaedtke, F., Zalinescu, E.: The MonPoly monitoring tool. In: Proceedings of the Int'l Workshop on Competitions, Usability, Benchmarks, Evaluation, and Standardisation for Runtime Verification Tools (RV-CUBES), pp. 19–28. Kalpa Publications in Computing, EasyChair (2017). https://doi.org/10.29007/89hs
7. Bauer, A., Leucker, M., Schallhart, C.: Runtime verification for LTL and TLTL. ACM Trans. Softw. Eng. Methodol. **20**(4), 14 (2011). https://doi.org/10.1145/2000799.2000800
8. Berry, G.: Proof, language, and interaction: essays in honour of Robin Milner, chap. The foundations of Esterel, pp. 425–454. MIT Press (2000). https://doi.org/10.7551/mitpress/5641.001.0001
9. Ceresa, M., Gorostiaga, F., Sánchez, C.: Declarative stream runtime verification (hLola). In: Proceedings of the 18th Asian Symposium on Programming Languages and Systems (APLAS'20). LNCS, vol. 12470, pp. 25–43. Springer (2020). https://doi.org/10.1007/978-3-030-64437-6_2
10. Convent, L., Hungerecker, S., Leucker, M., Scheffel, T., Schmitz, M., Thoma, D.: TeSSLa: temporal stream-based specification language. In: Proceedings of SBMF'18. LNCS, vol. 11254. Springer (2018). https://doi.org/10.1007/978-3-030-03044-5_10
11. Cumin, J., Lefebvre, G., Ramparany, F., Crowley, J.: A dataset of routine daily activities in an instrumented home. In: Ubiquitous Computing and Ambient Intelligence, pp. 413–425. Springer International Publishing, Cham (2017). https://doi.org/10.1007/978-3-319-67585-5_43
12. D'Angelo, B., Sankaranarayanan, S., Sánchez, C., Robinson, W., Finkbeiner, B., Sipma, H.B., Mehrotra, S., Manna, Z.: LOLA: runtime monitoring of synchronous systems. In: Proceedings of the 12th Int'l Symposium of Temporal Representation and Reasoning (TIME'05), pp. 166–174. IEEE CS Press (2005). https://doi.org/10.1109/TIME.2005.26
13. Eisner, C., Fisman, D., Havlicek, J., Lustig, Y., McIsaac, A., Campenhout, D.V.: Reasoning with temporal logic on truncated paths. In: Proceedings of the 15th Int'l Conference on Computer Aided Verification (CAV'03). LNCS, vol. 2725, pp. 27–39. Springer (2003). https://doi.org/10.1007/978-3-540-45069-6_3

14. Falcone, Y., Krstic, S., Reger, G., Traytel, D.: A taxonomy for classifying runtime verification tools. In: Proceedings of the 18th Int'l Conference on Runtime Verification (RV'18). LNCS, vol. 11237, pp. 241–262. Springer (2018). https://doi.org/10.1007/978-3-030-03769-7_14

15. Faymonville, P., Finkbeiner, B., Schledjewski, M., Schwenger, M., Stenger, M., Tentrup, L., Hazem, T.: StreamLAB: stream-based monitoring of cyber-physical systems. In: Proceedings of the 31st Int'l Conference on Computer-Aided Verification (CAV'19). LNCS, vol. 11561, pp. 421–431. Springer (2019). https://doi.org/10.1007/978-3-030-25540-4_24

16. Faymonville, P., Finkbeiner, B., Schwenger, M., Torfah, H.: Real-time stream-based monitoring. CoRR abs/1711.03829 (2017). arxiv.org/abs/1711.03829

17. Gorostiaga, F., Danielsson, L.M., Sánchez, C.: Unifying the time-event spectrum for stream runtime verification. In: Proceedings of 20th Int'l Conference on Runtime Verification (RV'20). LNCS, vol. 12399, pp. 462–481. Springer (2020). https://doi.org/10.1007/978-3-030-60508-7_26

18. Gorostiaga, F., Sánchez, C.: Striver: Stream runtime verification for real-time event-streams. In: Proceedings of the 18th Int'l Conference on Runtime Verification (RV'18). LNCS, vol. 11237, pp. 282–298. Springer (2018). https://doi.org/10.1007/978-3-030-03769-7_16

19. Gorostiaga, F., Sánchez, C.: HLola: a very functional tool for extensible stream runtime verification. In: Proceedings of the 27th Int'l Conference on Tools and Algorithms for the Construction and Analysis of Systems (TACAS'21). Part II, pp. 349–356. LNCS, Springer (2021). https://doi.org/10.1007/978-3-030-72013-1_18

20. Gorostiaga, F., Sánchez, C.: Stream runtime verification of real-time event streams with the Striver language. Int. J. Softw. Tools Technol. Transfer **23**(2), 157–183 (2021). https://doi.org/10.1007/s10009-021-00605-3

21. Halbwachs, N., Caspi, P., Pilaud, D., Plaice, J.: Lustre: a declarative language for programming synchronous systems. In: Proceedings of the 14th ACM Symposium on Principles of Programming Languages, pp. 178–188. ACM Press (1987). https://doi.org/10.1145/41625.41641

22. Hallé, S.: When RV meets CEP. In: Proceedings of RV'16. LNCS, vol. 10012, pp. 68–91. Springer (2016). https://doi.org/10.1007/978-3-319-46982-9_6

23. Hallé, S., Khoury, R.: Event stream processing with BeepBeep 3. In: Proceedings of the Int'l Workshop on Competitions, Usability, Benchmarks, Evaluation, and Standardisation for Runtime Verification Tools (RV-CUBES), pp. 81–88. Kalpa Publications in Computing, EasyChair (2017). https://doi.org/10.29007/4cth

24. Havelund, K.: Rule-based runtime verification revisited. Int. J. Softw. Tools Technol. Transfer **17**(2), 143–170 (2014). https://doi.org/10.1007/s10009-014-0309-2

25. Havelund, K., Goldberg, A.: Verify your runs. In: Proceedings of VSTTE'05, pp. 374–383. LNCS 4171, Springer (2005). https://doi.org/10.1007/978-3-540-69149-5_40

26. Havelund, K., Roşu, G.: Synthesizing monitors for safety properties. In: Proceedings of the 8th Int'l Conference on Tools and Algorithms for the Construction and Analysis of Systems (TACAS'02). LNCS, vol. 2280, pp. 342–356. Springer-Verlag (2002). https://doi.org/10.1007/3-540-46002-0_24

27. Jin, X., Deshmukh, J.V., Kapinski, J., Ueda, K., Butts, K.: Powertrain control verification benchmark. In: Proceedings of the 17th Int'l Conference on Hybrid systems: Computation and Control (HSCC'14), pp. 253–262. ACM (2014). https://doi.org/10.1145/2562059.2562140

28. Leucker, M., Sánchez, C., Scheffel, T., Schmitz, M., Schramm, A.: TeSSLa: runtime verification of non-synchronized real-time streams. In: Proceedings of the 33rd Symposium on Applied Computing (SAC'18). ACM (2018). https://doi.org/10.1145/3167132.3167338

29. Leucker, M., Schallhart, C.: A brief account of runtime verification. J. Logic Algebr. Progr. **78**(5), 293–303 (2009). https://doi.org/10.1016/j.jlap.2008.08.004

30. Maler, O., Nickovic, D.: Monitoring temporal properties of continuous signals. In: Proceedings of FORMATS/FTRTFT 2004. LNCS, vol. 3253, pp. 152–166. Springer (2004). https://doi.org/10.1007/978-3-540-30206-3_12

31. Manna, Z., Pnueli, A.: Temporal Verification of Reactive Systems. Springer-Verlag (1995). https://doi.org/10.1007/978-1-4612-4222-2

32. Pike, L., Goodloe, A., Morisset, R., Niller, S.: Copilot: a hard real-time runtime monitor. In: Proceedings of the 1st Int'l Conference on Runtime Verification (RV'10). LNCS, vol. 6418, pp. 345–359. Springer (2010). https://doi.org/10.1007/978-3-642-16612-9_26

33. Reinbacher, T., Rozier, K.Y., Schumann, J.: Temporal-logic based runtime observer pairs for system health management of real-time systems. In: Proceedings 20th International Conference on Tools and Algorithms for the Construction and Analysis of Systems (TACAS'14). LNCS, vol. 8413, pp. 357–372. Springer (2014). https://doi.org/10.1007/978-3-642-54862-8_24

34. Roşu, G., Havelund, K.: Rewriting-based techniques for runtime verification. Autom. Softw. Eng. **12**(2), 151–197 (2005). https://doi.org/10.1007/s10515-005-6205-y

35. Sánchez, C.: Online and offline stream runtime verification of synchronous systems. In: Proceedings of the 18th Int'l Conference on Runtime Verification (RV'18). LNCS, vol. 11237, pp. 138–163. Springer (2018). https://doi.org/10.1007/978-3-030-03769-7_9

36. Sen, K., Roşu, G.: Generating optimal monitors for extended regular expressions. In: Electronic Notes in Theoretical Computer Science, vol. 89. Elsevier (2003). https://doi.org/10.1016/S1571-0661(04)81051-X

37. Stolz, V., Huch, F.: Runtime verification of concurrent Haskell programs. Electron. Notes Theor. Comput. Sci. **113**, 201–216 (2005). https://doi.org/10.1016/j.entcs.2004.01.026

CABEAN 2.0: Efficient and Efficacious Control of Asynchronous Boolean Networks

Cui Su[1] and Jun Pang[1,2]

[1] Interdisciplinary Centre for Security, Reliability and Trust,
University of Luxembourg, Esch-sur-Alzette, Luxembourg
{cui.su,jun.pang}@uni.lu
[2] Faculty of Science, Technology and Medicine, University of Luxembourg,
Esch-sur-Alzette, Luxembourg

Abstract. We present a new version of the software, CABEAN, integrating six source-target control methods and three target control methods for the reprogramming of asynchronous Boolean networks. The source-target control methods compute the minimal one-step and sequential control strategies that can guide the dynamics of a Boolean network from a source attractor to the desired target attractor with instantaneous, temporary, or permanent perturbations. The target control methods further identify efficacious interventions that can drive the network from any initial state to the desired target attractor with these three types of perturbations. These control methods have been applied to various real-life biological networks to demonstrate their efficacy and efficiency.

Keywords: Boolean networks · Cell reprogramming · Network control · Target control · Attractors · Software tool

1 Introduction

Cell reprogramming harnesses the power of somatic cells to treat diseases featured by a deficiency of certain cells or diseased cells [11,12,44]. It reprograms abundant somatic cells to deficient or damaged cells, in order to restore functions of diseased organs in the human body. Therefore, cell reprogramming sheds light on the development of tissue engineering and regenerative medicine.

One of the significant hurdles for the application of cell reprogramming lies in the identification of efficacious intervention targets, whose perturbations can engender desired changes. Experimental approaches select promising combinations of targets, perturb them and monitor if the perturbation triggers desired changes. Such "trial and error" approaches can be costly and require long-time commitment, which render them inefficient [9]. Advances in sequencing techniques and the availability of wealthy data on gene expression profiles promote the shift from experimental approaches to the computational predictions based on mathematical modelling of biological systems. Mathematical models allow us to discover different combinations of targets by providing a broad view of the

© Springer Nature Switzerland AG 2021
M. Huisman et al. (Eds.): FM 2021, LNCS 13047, pp. 581–598, 2021.
https://doi.org/10.1007/978-3-030-90870-6_31

whole biological system. In this way, we can systematically make predictions and speed up the development of cell reprogramming, as such predictions are much faster and cheaper than experimental approaches. Moreover, it has great promise to discover novel intervention targets for cell reprogramming.

Several modelling frameworks have been developed for modelling biological systems, and Boolean networks are chosen as the representative of biological networks, thanks to its simplicity and qualitative nature with the ability of dealing with large-scale networks. Boolean networks, first introduced by Kauffman [14], are a well-established modelling framework for gene regulatory networks and their associated signalling pathways. In Boolean networks, molecular species, such as genes and transcription factors, are described as Boolean variables. Each Boolean variable is associated with a Boolean function, which determines the evolution of the variable. Boolean functions characterise activation or inhibition regulations between the molecular species (i.e., nodes in the networks). The states of a Boolean network are binary strings, where every bit of the string represents the state of a molecular species – '0' for inactive (or absent) and '1' for active (or present). The dynamics of a Boolean network is assumed to evolve in discrete time steps, moving from one state to the next, under one of the updating schemes, such as the *synchronous* or *asynchronous* updating scheme. Under the synchronous scheme, all the variables update their values simultaneously at each time step, while under the asynchronous scheme, only one variable is randomly selected to update its value at each time step. The asynchronous updating scheme is considered more realistic than the synchronous one, since it captures the phenomenon that biological processes occur at different classes of time scales [49]. Therefore, we focus on asynchronous Boolean networks. The steady-state behaviour of a Boolean network is described as *attractors*, to one of which the system eventually settles down. Attractors are hypothesised to characterise cellular phenotypes [13].

In the context of Boolean networks, cell reprogramming amounts to driving the network dynamics from a source state to a desired attractor of the network. The realisation of the transition needs to respect certain constraints to ensure the feasibility of the identified perturbations. The original version of the software CABEAN [36] supports six methods [24, 32, 33, 38, 40] for the *source-target control* of Boolean networks—to identify one-step or sequential control strategies that guide the network dynamics from a source attractor to a target attractors with instantaneous, temporary or permanent perturbations. The source-target control methods implemented in CABEAN guarantee the minimality of the identified control strategies in terms of the number of required perturbations, even though this makes the control problem sometimes computationally difficult [22, 23],

In this paper, we present an extension and a new version of CABEAN with three new appealing methods for *target control* of Boolean networks—to identify a set of nodes, whose perturbations drive the network from *any initial state* to the desired target attractor. The motivation of target control is that cells typically exist as a mixture of different cell types. There is a surge to identify effective perturbations that can reprogram any cells to the desired cell type. Another new functionality of CABEAN 2.0 is that it allows users of the software tool to encode a phenotype based on the expressions of a subset of nodes (the marker nodes). The phenotype serves as the desired target, which is considered more realistic in biological experiments than specifying a target attractor. CABEAN 2.0 is able to identify the target control strategies towards the desired phenotype, which may correspond to one or more attractors of a given Boolean network.

Structure of the Paper. After the introduction, methods for controlling complex networks and Boolean networks, and related software tools are summarised in Sect. 2. Section 3 contains preliminary notions of asynchronous Boolean networks. Section 4 continues to present the control methods implemented in the tool CABEAN, with a focus on the newly extended functionalities. Evaluation of the three new methods for the target control of Boolean networks on a number of real-life biological networks is presented in Sect. 5. In Sect. 6, implementation details of CABEAN are given and an example is also given to illustrate the usage of the new functionalities of the software tool. Section 7 concludes the paper with future developments of the tool.

2   Related Work

Control Methods for Complex Networks. Several important methods have been developed for the control of complex networks [4,6,7,10,19,27,42,47]. However, these methods do not directly apply to Boolean networks. Methods based on the semi-tensor product (STP) have been proposed to solve different control problems for Boolean control networks (BCNs) under the synchronous updating scheme [3,17,21,43,45,48,50,52]. For synchronous Boolean networks, Kim *et al.* [15] developed a method to compute a small fraction of nodes, called "control kernels", whose modulation can govern the dynamics of the network; and Moradi *el al.* [28] developed an algorithm guided by forward dynamic programming to solve the control problem. Lin *et al.* [18] proposed a Max-SAT based automatic test pattern generate to identify faulty genes that cause undesired behaviours of GRNs and to identify the best drug selection for cancer treatment. Their algorithm considers synchronous Boolean networks under a stuck-at fault model. Murrugarra *el al.* [30] proposed a method for identifying intervention targets based on algebraic techniques for synchronous Boolean networks. None of the above-mentioned methods is applicable to asynchronous Boolean networks.

Control Methods for Asynchronous Boolean Networks. Recently, Mandon *et al.* [22,23] proposed several methods to encode all possible control strategies into the transition system for the control of asynchronous Boolean networks. The size of the resulting *perturbed transition graph* grows exponentially in the number of perturbations, which renders these methods inefficient. The algorithm Kali [34] predicts perturbations to reduce the reachability of undesired attractors that are linked to pathological phenotypes for both synchronous and asynchronous Boolean networks. However, Kali can only estimate the attractors and their basins of a Boolean network in an approximate way. Therefore, the predictions of Kali might not be fully accurate. Fontanals *et al..* [8] proposed a method based on trap space to deal with the temporary target control of asynchronous Boolean networks. This method requires the preservation of the target attractors during control, which could be eased since the control will eventually be released to retrieve the original transition system where the desired attractor is in. The stable motifs-based control method (SMC) [46] predicts a set of transient perturbations that can guide the dynamics from any initial states to the desired target attractor. Based on the functional information of the network, SMC has a substantial improvement in computing the number of perturbations, but it does not guarantee to find the minimal number of perturbations. Details on comparing SMC with the target control methods implemented in CABEAN 2.0 can be found in [37,39]. In general, the target control methods CABEAN 2.0 are more efficient and can produce more and effective control strategies than SMC.

Software Tools. A number of software tools have been developed for the analysis of logical models of Biological networks. ACTONETLIB [1] implements a method based on abductive reasoning to identify a minimal set of causal topological actions that cause expected changes at stable states for BCNs. The caspo toolbox [41], CANA [5] and PyBoolNet [16] are all Python packages. In particular, the caspo toolbox [41] provides a work-flow to study logical networks families of three-valued semantics under the synchronous updating scheme. CANA [5] focuses on quantifying redundancy and control of synchronous Boolean networks, PyBoolNet [16] integrates methods for manipulating Boolean networks, such as generation, visualisation, and attractor detection. BoolNet [31] is a powerful R package, which provides functions for reconstruction, generalisation, and attractor identification for synchronous, asynchronous, and probabilistic Boolean networks. Although BoolNet and PyBoolNet can handle asynchronous Boolean networks, neither of them supports the identification of intervention targets for modulating the dynamics.

3   Preliminaries

A *Boolean network* is a tuple $\mathsf{BN} = (X, F)$, where $X = \{x_1, x_2, \ldots, x_n\}$, such that $x_i \in X$ is a Boolean variable and $F = \{f_1, f_2, \ldots, f_n\}$ is a set of Boolean functions over X. A *state* s of BN is an element in $\{0, 1\}^n$. Let $S = \{0, 1\}^n$ denote the set of all states of BN. For two states $s, s' \in S$, the *Hamming distance* between s and s' will be denoted as $hd(s, s')$ and $\arg(hd(s, s')) \subseteq \{1, 2, \ldots, n\}$ will denote the set of indices in which s and s' differ. These two notions can be lifted to a set of states. For two subsets $S', S'' \subseteq S$, the Hamming distance between S' and S'' is defined as the minimum of the Hamming distances between all the states in S' and all the states in S''. We let $\arg(hd(S', S''))$ denote the set of subsets of $\{1, 2, \ldots, n\}$ such that $I \in \arg(hd(S', S''))$ if and only if I is a set of indices of the variables that realise this Hamming distance.

We assume that a Boolean network $\mathsf{BN} = (X, F)$ evolves in discrete time steps. It starts from an initial state and its state changes in every time step based on the Boolean functions F and the updating schemes. Different updating schemes lead to different dynamics of the network [26,51]. Suppose $s_0 \in S$ is an

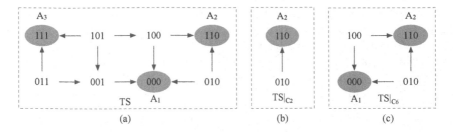

Fig. 1. (a) The transition system for Example 1; (b) the transition system under control $C_2 = \{x_2 = 1, x_3 = 0\}$ for Example 2; and (c) the transition system under control $C_6 = \{x_3 = 0\}$ for Example 3.

initial state of BN. We use $\wp(S)$ to denote the power set of S. The *asynchronous evolution* of BN is a function $\xi_{BN} : \mathbb{N} \to \wp(S)$ such that $\xi_{BN}(0) = \{s_0\}$ and for every $j \geq 0$, if $s \in \xi_{BN}(j)$ then $s' \in \xi_{BN}(j+1)$ is a possible *next state* of s iff either $hd(s, s') = 1$ and there exists i such that $s'[i] = f_i(s) = 1 - s[i]$, or $hd(s, s') = 0$ and there exists i such that $s'[i] = f_i(s) = s[i]$. It is worth noting that the asynchronous dynamics is non-deterministic. At each time step, only one node is randomly selected to update its value based on its Boolean function. A different choice may lead to a different next state $s' \in \xi(j+1)$. The *transition system* of a Boolean network BN, denoted as TS, is a tuple $(S, \to_{BN})$, where the vertices are the set of states S and for any two states s and s' there is a directed edge from s to s', denoted $s \to s'$, iff s' is a possible next state of s according to the asynchronous evolution function ξ of BN.

A *path* ρ from a state s to a state s' is a (possibly empty) sequence of transitions from s to s' in TS. Thus, $\rho = s_0 \to s_1 \to \ldots \to s_k$, where $s_0 = s$ and $s_k = s'$. A path from a state s to a subset S' of S is a path from s to any state $s' \in S'$. For a state $s \in S$, $reach_{TS}(s)$ denotes the set of states s' such that there is a path from s to s' in TS and can be defined as the fixed point of the successor operation which is often denoted as $post^*_{TS}$. An *attractor* A of TS is a minimal non-empty subset of states of S such that for every $s \in A$, $reach_{TS}(s) = A$.

Attractors are hypothesised to characterise steady-state behaviours of the network. Any state, which is not in an attractor, is a *transient state*. An attractor A of TS is said to be *reachable* from a state s if $reach(s) \cap A \neq \emptyset$. The network starting from any initial state $s_0 \in S$ will eventually end up in one of the attractors of TS and remain there forever unless perturbed externally. Thus, it is easy to observe that any attractor of TS is a *bottom strongly connected component* of TS. Each attractor has a *weak basin* and a *strong basin*. The weak basin of an attractor A with respect to TS is defined as $bas^W_{TS}(A) = \{s \in S \mid reach_{TS}(s) \cap A \neq \emptyset\}$, which equals the fixed point of the predecessor operation on A and is often denoted as $pre^*_{TS}(A)$. The strong basin of A with respect to TS is defined as $bas^S_{TS}(S') = \{s \in S \mid \forall \rho = s_0 \to s_1 \to \ldots \in P_\infty(s), \exists j \geq 0, s_j \in S'\}$.

Intuitively, the weak basin of A includes all the states from which there exists a path to A. It is possible that there also exist paths from a state in the weak basin of A to some other attractor $A' \neq A$ of TS. However, the notion of the strong basin of an attractor does not allow this. Any path from a state in the strong basin of A will eventually reach A and cannot reach any other distinct attractor $A' \neq A$ of TS.

Example 1. To illustrate the notions of Boolean networks, let us consider a Boolean network $\mathsf{BN} = (X, F)$, where $X = \{x_1, x_2, x_3\}$, $F = \{f_1, f_2, f_3\}$, and $f_1 = x_2$, $f_2 = x_1$ and $f_3 = x_2 \wedge x_3$. Its transition system under the asynchronous updating is given in Fig. 1(a) with self-loops omitted. This network consists of three attractors A_1, A_2 and A_3, plotted as grey nodes. For attractor A_1, its strong basin consists of two states (000) and (001). The weak basin of A_1 includes six states, $\{000, 001, 101, 011, 100, 010\}$ and from any of these states, there exists at least one path to A_1.

4   Functionalities

We describe the main functionalities of the software tool CABEAN, implementing six source-target control methods and three target control methods for the reprogramming of asynchronous Boolean networks. First, we define what types of control, in terms of node perturbations, can be applied to Boolean networks. We then proceed with briefly describing the main ideas of the implemented control methods.

Control in Boolean Networks. Let BN be a given Boolean network, S be the set of states of BN and $\mathcal{A}$ be the set of attractors of BN. A *control strategy* (*control* for short) C is a tuple $\mathsf{C} = (\mathbb{0}, \mathbb{1})$, where $\mathbb{0}, \mathbb{1} \subseteq \{1, 2, \ldots, n\}$ and $\mathbb{0}$ and $\mathbb{1}$ are mutually disjoint (possibly empty) sets of indices of nodes of a Boolean network BN. The application of a control C inhibits the nodes in $\mathbb{0}$, i.e., the values of these nodes are set (perturbed) to be 0, and overexpresses the nodes in $\mathbb{1}$, i.e., the values of these nodes are set (perturbed) to be 1. Formally, given a state $s \in S$, the *application of a control* C to a state s, denoted $\mathsf{C}(s)$, is defined as the state $s' \in S$ such that $s'[i] = 0$ for $i \in \mathbb{0}$ and $s'[i] = 1$ for $i \in \mathbb{1}$. State s' is called the intermediate state w.r.t. C.

The control can be applied to the network for different periods of time: (a) *instantaneous control*—the control is applied instantaneously (only one time step); (b) *temporary control*—the control is applied for a finite number of time steps and then released; and (c) *permanent control*—the control is applied for all the following time steps, i.e., the parameters are changed for all the following steps. Next, we formulate the problems of *source-target control* and *target control* of Boolean networks.

Source-Target Control. Given a source attractor A_s and a target attractor A_t of TS, to drive the network from A_s to A_t is called *source-target control*.

A source-target control C is called *one-step source-target control* if C drives the network from A_s to A_t in one step as shown in Fig. 2a. When the control

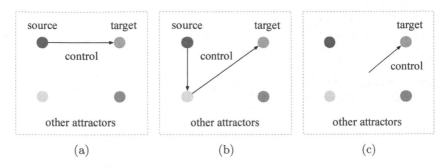

Fig. 2. Schematic illustration for source-target control and target control of Boolean networks: (a) one-step source-target control; (b) sequential source-target control; and (c) target control.

C is the instantaneous, temporary or permanent control, we call it respectively *one-step instantaneous, temporary or permanent control* (OI, OT, or OP). To minimise experimental costs, it is often important to find the minimal solution, denoted as $C_{min}^{A_s \rightarrow A_t}$, which solves the source-target control of driving the network from A_s to A_t. The minimal OI control [32,33] perturbs the network from s in A_s to a state s' in the strong basin of A_t, denoted $bas_{TS}^S(A_t)$, where s and s' are a pair of states that realise the minimal Hamming distance between A_s and $bas_{TS}^S(A_t)$.

The minimal OT (temporary) and OP (permanent) controls [40] have extended effects on the network dynamics. The minimal OT control explores the weak basin of A_t, $bas_{TS}^W(A_t)$ from the one that has the shortest Hamming distance to A_s. It searches for a state s', such that after applying the corresponding control $C^{A_s \rightarrow s'}$ for a sufficient period of time, BN will surely reach a state s'' in $bas_{TS}^S(A_t)$. Once BN is in s'', $C^{A_s \rightarrow s'}$ can be released. To apply $C^{A_s \rightarrow s'}$ will not harm the inevitable reachability of A_t since there only exist paths to A_t from s''. The minimal OP control looks for a state s' in $bas_{TS}^W(A_t)$, such that the application of the control $C^{A_s \rightarrow s'}$ preserves A_t and s' can only reach A_t and cannot reach any other attractors.

Besides the one-step source-target control, to identify a sequence of perturbations to drive the network from A_s to A_t in a stepwise manner is called *sequential control*. As shown in Fig. 2b, it is more practical to concentrate on the sequential control through other attractors, called *attractor-based sequential control*: to find a sequence of attractors of TS, i.e. $\Phi = \langle A_1, A_2, \ldots, A_m \rangle$, where $A_1 = A_s, A_m = A_t, A_i \neq A_j$ for any $i,j \in [1,m]$ and $2 \leq m \leq |\mathcal{A}|$, such that after the application of a sequence of minimal one-step controls $\langle C_{min}^{A_1 \rightarrow A_2}, C_{min}^{A_2 \rightarrow A_3}, \ldots, C_{min}^{A_{m-1} \rightarrow A_m} \rangle$, the network always eventually reaches A_m, i.e. A_t. Similarly, when the control $C_{min}^{A_i \rightarrow A_j}$, $A_i, A_j \in \Phi$ is the instantaneous, temporary or permanent control, we call it *attractor-based sequential instantaneous, temporary or permanent control* (ASI, AST or ASP), respectively. The ASI, AST and ASP control methods [24,38] are based on the three one-step control methods [32,33,40]. Given a source attractor A_s, a target attractor A_t and a threshold k of perturbations, the sequential control methods find an intermediate attractor A, such that $C_{\min}^{A \to A_t}$ needs no more than $k-1$ perturbations. Then, the control paths are extended by taking A as a new target attractor and find a new intermediate attractor A' such that $C_{\min}^{A' \to A} + C_{\min}^{A \to A_t} \leq k$. This procedure is repeated until all the sequential control paths with at most k perturbations are found.

The first version of CABEAN (version 1.0) has implemented the above six methods for the minimal one-step and attractor-based source-target control of Boolean networks (see Table 1). To avoid duplication, we refer to [36] for instructions and to [24,33,38,40] for case studies and evaluations of the source-target control methods.

Target Control. As illustrated in Fig. 2c, when the source is not given, to identify a subset of nodes, the perturbations of which can stir the dynamics of a Boolean network from any state $s \in S$ to the target attractor A_t, is called *target control* of Boolean networks.

The application of a control C can be lifted to a subset of states $S' \subseteq S$. Given a control $C = (\mathbb{0}, \mathbb{1})$, $C(S') = S''$, where $S'' = \{s'' \in S | s'' = C(s'), s' \in S'\}$. Set S'' includes all the intermediate states with respect to the control C and the subset of states S'. In the case of target control, since we assume a given Boolean network can be in any initial state, we simply focus on applying a control, i.e., a number of node perturbations, on S. When perturbations are applied instantaneously, temporarily or permanently, we call them *instantaneous target control* (ITC), *temporary target control* (TTC) or *permanent target control* (PTC) [37,39], respectively.

The three target control methods, ITC, TTC and PTC, are based on the computation of the strong basin and the weak basin of the target attractor A_t and the notion of *schema*. A schema is a subset S' of S, such that there exists a triple $M = (\mathbb{0}, \mathbb{1}, \mathbb{D})$, where $\mathbb{0} \cup \mathbb{1} \cup \mathbb{D} = \{1, 2, \ldots, n\}$, $\mathbb{0}, \mathbb{1}$ and $\mathbb{D}$ are mutually disjoint (possibly empty) sets of indices of nodes of BN. The projection of S' onto the set $\mathbb{0}$ is a $|\mathbb{0}|$-bit string of zeros and the projection of S' onto the set $\mathbb{1}$ is a $|\mathbb{1}|$-bit string of ones. Let $\mathbb{D}$ denote the remaining set of nodes (i.e., don't-care-set), $X \setminus (\mathbb{0} \cup \mathbb{1})$. The projection of S' to $\mathbb{D}$ consists of all combinations of binary strings of $|\mathbb{D}|$ bits. Since the total number of nodes $n = |\mathbb{0}| + |\mathbb{1}| + |\mathbb{D}|$ is fixed, a larger schema implies more elements in $\mathbb{D}$ and fewer elements in $\mathbb{0} \cup \mathbb{1}$.

Similar to the instantaneous source-target control (OI), in order to ensure the inevitable reachability of a target attractor A_t, the ITC method drives the network BN from any initial state to the strong basin of A_t, $bas_{TS}^S(A_t)$. ITC divides $bas_{TS}^S(A_t)$ into a set of schemata and each schema leads to an ITC strategy. Thanks to the sustained effects of temporary and permanent perturbations, TTC and PTC can drive BN to the weak basin of A_t, $bas_{TS}^W(A_t)$. In a similar way, they partition $bas_{TS}^W(A_t)$ into a set of schemata, which results in a set of potential control strategies. Every subset of the candidate control sets is optimised and verified based on the constraints for temporary and permanent control [37].

Intuitively, in order to guarantee the inevitable reachability of A_t, by the time we release the control, we need to verify (1) whether the network has

Table 1. Control methods integrated in CABEAN.

	Source-target control		Target Control
	Minimal One-step Control (OI, OT, OP)	Attractor-based Sequential Control (ASI, AST, ASP)	(ITC, TTC, PTC)
Instantaneous	✓ (version 1.0)	✓ (version 1.0)	✓ (version 2.0)
Temporary	✓ (version 1.0)	✓ (version 1.0)	✓ (version 2.0)
Permanent	✓ (version 1.0)	✓ (version 1.0)	✓ (version 2.0)

to reach a state s in the strong basin of A_t, i.e. $bas_{TS}^S(A_t)$, from which there only exist paths to A_t. Furthermore, we need to ensure (2) that any possible intermediate state $s' \in C(S)$ is in the strong basin of the remaining strong basin (i.e., $bas_{TS}^S(A_t) \cap C(S)$) in the transition system under control, so that the network will always evolve to the remaining strong basin. Once the network actually reaches the remaining strong basin (i.e., $bas_{TS}^S(A_t) \cap C(S)$), the control can then be released and the network will evolve spontaneously towards the target attractor A_t.[1]

Next, we elaborate the three target control methods with the network BN given in Example 1.

Example 2. For attractor A_2 of BN given in Example 1, its strong basin contains only one state (110), which is a schema. Thus, the ITC for A_2 is $C_1 = \{x_1 = 1, x_2 = 1, x_3 = 0\}$. The application of C_1 drives BN from any state directly to A_2. The weak basin of A_2, $bas_{TS}^W(A_2) = \{010, 110, 100, 101\}$, can be divided into two schemata $\{100, 101\}$ and $\{010, 110\}$, represented as '*10' and '10*'. The two schemata give rise to two candidate control sets: $C_2 = \{x_2 = 1, x_3 = 0\}$ and $C_3 = \{x_1 = 1, x_2 = 0\}$. After the step of verifying these two sets, control C_2 is both a TTC and a PTC for A_2, but C_3 is neither a TTC nor a PTC for A_2. The application of C_2 reshapes the transition system (under the control of C_2) to a new one as shown in Fig. 1(b) and BN is driven from any initial state to a state in the transition system in Fig. 1(b), from which the network will eventually stabilise to A_2. Similarly, we know that $C_4 = \{x_1 = 0, x_2 = 0\}$ is an ITC for A_1 and $C_5 = \{x_1 = 0\}$ is both a TTC and a PTC for A_1.

CABEAN 2.0 now integrates the three target control methods, and detailed description of the methods are referred to [37, 39].

Cell Phenotype as Control Target. Another new and interesting feature of CABEAN 2.0 is that it supports the target control of a desired phenotype. In practice, it is rarely feasible to have *complete observability* of a biological network. *Partial observability* empowers us to distinguish a phenotype based on the expressions of the marker nodes contained in the network.

---

[1] We refer to [40] for the precise formulation of the verification conditions and the correctness proof.

Table 2. An overview of the biological networks.

Network	# nodes	# edges	# singleton attractors	# cyclic attractors
yeast	10	28	12	1
ERBB	20	52	3	0
HSPC-MSC	26	81	2	2
tumour	32	158	9	0
hematopoiesis	33	88	5	0
PC12	33	62	7	0
bladder	35	116	3	1
PSC-bFA	36	237	4	0
co-infection	52	136	30	0
MAPK	53	105	12	0
CREB	64	159	8	0
HGF	66	103	10	0
bortezomib	67	135	5	0
T-diff	68	175	12	0
HIV1	136	327	8	0
CD4+	188	380	6	0
pathway	321	381	3	1

In general, one phenotype may correspond to one or more attractors in the Boolean network, being a model of the underlying biological network. To meet these practical needs, CABEAN 2.0 implements the new functionality to compute both the source-target and the target control of a desired phenotype (i.e., for all the methods in Table 1). It encodes the phenotype according to the input specification file, groups the attractors associated with the phenotype as a new target, and computes the control strategies for this new target. CABEAN 2.0 merges the attractors of the same phenotype first and then perform the computation for the merged attractor. In this way, it potentially can discover smaller and even new control strategies than solving the control problem by enumerate the attractors contained in the phenotype. One example is given as follows.

Example 3. For BN in Example 1, let us consider the phenotype P, where x_3 has a value of 0. P corresponds to two attractors, A_1 and A_2. That is, $P = \{000, 110\}$. CABEAN explores the strong basin and the weak basin of P to search for solutions of ITC, TTC and PTC. For instance, $C_6 = \{x_3 = 0\}$ is neither a TTC for A_1 nor a TTC for A_2. But the temporary inhibition of x_3, C_6 transforms the transition system to Fig. 1(c) and it will surely guide BN to P.

5   Evaluation

In this section, we present an overview of the evaluation of the target control methods (ITC, TTC and PTC) on a number of real-life biological networks to

Table 3. The minimal number of perturbations computed by the control methods ITC, TTC, and PTC for the biological networks.

Network	The minimal number of perturbations		
	ITC	TTC	PTC
yeast	10	5	5
ERBB	10	2	2
HSPC-MSC	2	2	2
hematopoiesis	5	3	3
PC12	12	3	3
bladder	14	2	2
PSC-bFA	11	1	2
co-infection	19	5	5
MAPK	24	4	4
CREB	3	3	3
HGF	22	4	4
bortezomib	3	1	1
T-diff	20	4	4
HIV1	3	3	3
CD4+	7	3	3
pathway	2	2	2

demonstrate their efficacy and efficiency.[2] In Table 2, we present information on the number of nodes, the number of edges and the number of singleton and cyclic attractors for each of these networks. Further details on the networks are referred to the original works where the Boolean networks were originally presented (see the corresponding references of the networks in [39]).

Efficacy. Table 3 gives the minimal number of perturbations computed by the target control methods (ITC, TTC and PTC) for one of the attractors of the networks. It is clear to see that ITC always requires more perturbations than the other two methods due to its instantaneous effect of the perturbations. In Table 3, ITC often needs to perturb around 10 to 20 nodes, whereas TTC and PTC can achieve the inevitable reachability of target attractors with at most 5 perturbations. Since it is difficult to realise the instantaneous perturbation of a number of nodes simultaneously, this makes ITC less practical and less attractive for real-life applications. Thus, TTC and PTC, which employ temporary or permanent perturbations, are more preferable than ITC.

Efficiency. Table 4 summarises the computational time for computing the target control strategies for *all* the attractors of the networks. All the experiments are

---

[2] We refer to [24,33,38,40] for case studies and evaluations of the source-target control methods implemented in CABEAN 1.0.

Table 4. Computational time of the control methods ITC, TTC, and PTC for the biological networks. The symbol '*' means that the corresponding method failed to finish its computation for the network within 12 h.

Network	Computational time (seconds)		
	ITC	TTC	PTC
yeast	0.028	0.987	0.933
ERBB	0.055	0.117	0.163
HSPC-MSC	0.097	0.101	0.109
hematopoiesis	0.374	139.859	72.793
PC12	0.149	17.653	22.189
bladder	0.302	2.426	7.997
psc-bFA	36.77	3,732.780	9,296.740
co-infection	6,294.290	*	*
MAPK	4.608	22.218	45.504
CREB	7.962	8.277	8.693
HGF	19.925	1,437.290	201.363
bortezomib	15.605	*	*
T-diff	21.581	29,738.500	*
HIV1	302.8	323.666	379.127
CD4+	549.878	1,982.450	21,358.400
pathway	445.251	4,435.590	10,038.600

performed on a high-performance computing (HPC) platform, which contains CPUs of Intel Xeon Gold 6132 @2.6 GHz.

From Table 4, we clearly observe that ITC is the most efficient one, but it requires more perturbations (see the above discussion and Table 3). The efficiency of these target control methods are influenced by many factors, including the network size, the network density, the number of attractors and the number of required node perturbations. For instance, for the co-infection network and the model of bortezomib responses, TTC and PTC were able to identify target control efficiently for some of the attractors, but failed for the other attractors of these two networks. One reason is that the target control of those attractors require many perturbations, thus it takes a considerable amount of time to verify all the subsets of the schemata (see Sect. 4). This can be improved if it is sufficient to provide only some of the solutions instead of all the solutions.

In summary, we conclude that the target control methods (ITC, TTC and PTC) scale well for Boolean networks of a few hundreds of nodes and they are able to identify a rich set of solutions with a small number of node perturbations.

6   Implementation

CABEAN 2.0 implements the six source-target control methods and the three target control methods (see Table 1) in C and C++, based on the CUDD package [35], the model checker MCMAS [20], and the tool ASSA-PBN [26]. There are two main factors resulting in a high efficiency of CABEAN 2.0. First, both the transition system and transition relations of Boolean networks are encoded as binary decision diagrams (BDDs). BDDs are introduced by Bryant [2] to represent Boolean functions, and they have an advantage of memory efficiency to alleviate the state space explosion. Realisation of the control methods implemented in CABEAN 2.0 depends on the efficiency of BDD operations. Second, the methods are based on the efficient decomposition-based strong basin computation [32,33], which adapts the divide and conquer strategy and thus scales well for large Boolean networks.

In the following, we use the Boolean network BN given in Example 1 to demonstrate the new features of CABEAN 2.0, including the three target control methods and the encoding of a phenotype. For a detailed and complete user guide of CABEAN, we refer to the website of the software tool.[3]

Model Files. CABEAN 2.0 supports two formats for the model file, including the BoolNet and ISPL (Interpreted Systems Programming Language) format of the software MCMAS [20]. Further details on the syntax of the two formats can be found at the website of the tool. Other formats, such as SBML-qual, Petri net, GINsim, can be converted to the BoolNet format using the BioLQM toolkits.[4]

Target Control of an Attractor. CABEAN 2.0 integrates the decomposition-based attractor detection method [25] to compute attractors of a Boolean network. Prior to the computation of target control strategies, CABEAN 2.0 computes all the exact attractors of the given network and prints them in lexicographic order. Users can then specify the index of an attractor as the desired attractor for the target control of the network.

The target control is computed using the following command line:

./cabean -compositional 2 -control <Control method> -tin <index of the target attractor> <model file>

The option '-compositional 2' indicates that the decomposition-based methods [25,33] are used for attractor detection and the strong basin computation; the option '-control <Control method>' selects one of the target methods, ITC, TTC or PTC; and the option '-tin <index of the target attractor>' sets the index of the target attractor.

Suppose we want to compute TTC for A_1 and A_2 for BN in Example 1. The outputs of CABEAN 2.0 are given below. The results show that the network will stabilise in A_1 with the temporary inhibition of A_1 and it will settle down to A_2 from any initial state with the temporary control of $\{x2 = 1 \; x3 = 0\}$. These results are consistent with Example 2.

---

[3] https://satoss.uni.lu/software/CABEAN/.

[4] BioLQM is available at http://colomoto.org/biolqm/.

```
**************************************************
TARGET ATTRACTOR #1
**************************************************
Control set 1: x1=0
**************************************************
TARGET ATTRACTOR #2
**************************************************
Control set 1: x2=1 x3=0
```

Target Control of a Phenotype. The target control of a phenotype can be computed using the following command line:

./cabean -compositional 2 -control <Control method> -tmarker <specification file> <model file>

Instead of setting the index of a target attractor, we need to specify a phenotype with an input file. For example, the phenotype P in Example 3 is specified as the following:

```
nodes, value
x3, 0
```

The computed TTC of P is given below. The line 'TARGET ATTRACTOR #1, #2' indicates that attractors A_1 and A_2 agree with the phenotype P. The results show that temporary inhibition of x_1, x_2 or x_3 guarantees the inevitable reachability of P. In Example 3, we have explained the case of $C_6 = \{x_3 = 0\}$.

```
**************************************************
TARGET ATTRACTOR #1 #2
**************************************************
Control set 1: x1=0
Control set 2: x2=0
Control set 3: x3=0
```

7   Conclusion

Motivated by the important and appealing application of cell reprogramming in biology, recent years have seen a rapid development of a number of computational methods for the control of gene regulatory networks modelled as Boolean networks. In this paper, we have presented a new release of CABEAN (version 2.0) that integrates three new target control methods for asynchronous Boolean networks. These methods identify a set of nodes, whose instantaneous, temporary or permanent perturbations can drive a Boolean network from any initial state to a desired attractor or a phenotype.

CABEAN 2.0 has assembled a variety of control methods (see Table 1) that manipulate the dynamics of a Boolean network in different ways. All these methods focus on identifying which nodes in the Boolean network to be perturbed in order to drive the network's dynamics into a desired attractor. A node perturbation corresponds to the removal or blocking of a particular gene in a gene regulatory network. However, in complex diseases it is more common that several subtle changes affect interactions between genes [29]. This suggests perturbations at the edge level, i.e., targeting selected interactions between genes. Currently, new methods are under development for the control of Boolean networks with edgetic perturbations, which will be eventually integrated into CABEAN as well. In future, we also plan to provide a graphical user interface (GUI) for the convenience of users.

Acknowledgements. This work was supported by the project SEC-PBN funded by University of Luxembourg and the ANR-FNR project AlgoReCell (grant No. INTER/ANR/15/11191283).

References

1. Biane, C., Delaplace, F.: Causal reasoning on Boolean control networks based on abduction: theory and application to cancer drug discovery. IEEE/ACM Trans. Comput. Biol. Bioinf. **16**(5), 1574–1585 (2018)
2. Bryant, R.E.: Symbolic verification of MOS circuits. In: Proceedings the 1985 Chapel Hill Conference on Very Large Scale Integration, pp. 419–438. Computer Science Press (1985)
3. Chen, H., Liang, J., Wang, Z.: Pinning controllability of autonomous Boolean control networks. Sci. China Inf. Sci. **59**(7), 1–14 (2016). https://doi.org/10.1007/s11432-016-5579-8
4. Cornelius, S.P., Kath, W.L., Motter, A.E.: Realistic control of network dynamics. Nat. Commun. **4**(1), 1–9 (2013)
5. Correia, R.B., Gates, A.J., Wang, X., Rocha, L.M.: CANA: a python package for quantifying control and canalization in Boolean networks. Front. Physiol. **9**, 1046 (2018)
6. Czeizler, E., Gratie, C., Chiu, W.K., Kanhaiya, K., Petre, I.: Target controllability of linear networks. In: Bartocci, E., Lio, P., Paoletti, N. (eds.) CMSB 2016. LNCS, vol. 9859, pp. 67–81. Springer, Cham (2016). https://doi.org/10.1007/978-3-319-45177-0_5
7. Fiedler, B., Mochizuki, A., Kurosawa, G., Saito, D.: Dynamics and control at feedback vertex sets. I: informative and determining nodes in regulatory networks. J. Dyn. Differ. Equ. **25**(3), 563–604 (2013)
8. Cifuentes Fontanals, L., Tonello, E., Siebert, H.: Control strategy identification via trap spaces in Boolean networks. In: Abate, A., Petrov, T., Wolf, V. (eds.) CMSB 2020. LNCS, vol. 12314, pp. 159–175. Springer, Cham (2020). https://doi.org/10.1007/978-3-030-60327-4_9
9. Gam, R., Sung, M., Prasad Pandurangan, A.: Experimental and computational approaches to direct cell reprogramming: recent advancement and future challenges. Cells **8**(10), 1189 (2019)

10. Gao, J., Liu, Y.Y., D'Souza, R.M., Barabási, A.L.: Target control of complex networks. Nat. Commun. **5**, 5415 (2014)
11. Grath, A., Dai, G.: Direct cell reprogramming for tissue engineering and regenerative medicine. J. Biol. Eng. **13**(1), 14 (2019)
12. Gurdon, J.B.: The developmental capacity of nuclei taken from intestinal epithelium cells of feeding tadpoles. Development **10**(4), 622–640 (1962)
13. Huang, S.: Genomics, complexity and drug discovery: insights from Boolean network models of cellular regulation. Pharmacogenomics **2**(3), 203–222 (2001)
14. Kauffman, S.: Homeostasis and differentiation in random genetic control networks. Nature **224**, 177–178 (1969)
15. Kim, J., Park, S.M., Cho, K.H.: Discovery of a kernel for controlling biomolecular regulatory networks. Sci. Rep. **3**, 2223 (2013)
16. Klarner, H., Streck, A., Siebert, H.: PyBoolNet: a python package for the generation, analysis and visualization of Boolean networks. Bioinformatics **33**(5), 770–772 (2017)
17. Liang, J., Chen, H., Lam, J.: An improved criterion for controllability of Boolean control networks. IEEE Trans. Autom. Control **62**(11), 6012–6018 (2017)
18. Lin, P.C.K., Khatri, S.P.: Application of Max-SAT-based ATPG to optimal cancer therapy design. BMC Genomics **13**(S6), S5 (2012)
19. Liu, Y.Y., Slotine, J.J., Barabási, A.L.: Controllability of complex networks. Nature **473**, 167–173 (2011)
20. Lomuscio, A., Qu, H., Raimondi, F.: MCMAS: an open-source model checker for the verification of multi-agent systems. Int. J. Softw. Tools Technol. Transfer **19**(1), 9–30 (2017)
21. Lu, J., Zhong, J., Ho, D.W., Tang, Y., Cao, J.: On controllability of delayed Boolean control networks. SIAM J. Control. Optim. **54**(2), 475–494 (2016)
22. Mandon, H., Haar, S., Paulevé, L.: Relationship between the reprogramming determinants of boolean networks and their interaction graph. In: Cinquemani, E., Donzé, A. (eds.) HSB 2016. LNCS, vol. 9957, pp. 113–127. Springer, Cham (2016). https://doi.org/10.1007/978-3-319-47151-8_8
23. Mandon, H., Haar, S., Paulevé, L.: Temporal reprogramming of boolean networks. In: Feret, J., Koeppl, H. (eds.) CMSB 2017. LNCS, vol. 10545, pp. 179–195. Springer, Cham (2017). https://doi.org/10.1007/978-3-319-67471-1_11
24. Mandon, H., Su, C., Haar, S., Pang, J., Paulevé, L.: Sequential reprogramming of boolean networks made practical. In: Bortolussi, L., Sanguinetti, G. (eds.) CMSB 2019. LNCS, vol. 11773, pp. 3–19. Springer, Cham (2019). https://doi.org/10.1007/978-3-030-31304-3_1
25. Mizera, A., Pang, J., Qu, H., Yuan, Q.: Taming asynchrony for attractor detection in large Boolean networks. IEEE/ACM Trans. Comput. Biol. Bioinf. **16**(1), 31–42 (2019)
26. Mizera, A., Pang, J., Su, C., Yuan, Q.: ASSA-PBN: a toolbox for probabilistic Boolean networks. IEEE/ACM Trans. Comput. Biol. Bioinf. **15**(4), 1203–1216 (2018)
27. Mochizuki, A., Fiedler, B., Kurosawa, G., Saito, D.: Dynamics and control at feedback vertex sets. II: a faithful monitor to determine the diversity of molecular activities in regulatory networks. J. Theor. Biol. **335**, 130–146 (2013)
28. Moradi, M., Goliaei, S., Foroughmand-Araabi, M.H.: A Boolean network control algorithm guided by forward dynamic programming. PLoS ONE **14**(5), e0215449 (2019)
29. Mosca, R., et al.: dSysMap: exploring the edgetic role of disease mutations. Nat. Methods **12**(3), 167–168 (2015)

30. Murrugarra, D., Veliz-Cuba, A., Aguilar, B., Laubenbacher, R.: Identification of control targets in Boolean molecular network models via computational algebra. BMC Syst. Biol. **10**(1), 94 (2016)

31. Müssel, C., Hopfensitz, M., Kestler, H.A.: BoolNet-an R package for generation, reconstruction and analysis of Boolean networks. Bioinformatics **26**(10), 1378–1380 (2010)

32. Paul, S., Su, C., Pang, J., Mizera, A.: A decomposition-based approach towards the control of Boolean networks. In: Proceedings of 9th ACM Conference on Bioinformatics, Computational Biology, and Health Informatics, pp. 11–20. ACM Press (2018)

33. Paul, S., Su, C., Pang, J., Mizera, A.: An efficient approach towards the source-target control of Boolean networks. IEEE/ACM Trans. Comput. Biol. Bioinf. **17**(6), 1932–1945 (2020)

34. Poret, A., Guziolowski, C.: Therapeutic target discovery using Boolean network attractors: improvements of kali. R. Soc. Open Sci. **5**(2), 171852 (2018)

35. Somenzi, F.: CUDD: CU Decision diagram package (release 2.5.1) (2015). http://vlsi.colorado.edu/fabio/CUDD/

36. Su, C., Pang, J.: CABEAN: a software for the control of asynchronous Boolean networks. Bioinformatics **37**(6), 879–881 (2020)

37. Su, C., Pang, J.: A dynamics-based approach for the target control of Boolean networks. In: Proceedings of 11th ACM Conference on Bioinformatics, Computational Biology, and Health Informatics, pp. 50:1–50:8. ACM Press (2020)

38. Su, C., Pang, J.: Sequential temporary and permanent control of boolean networks. In: Abate, A., Petrov, T., Wolf, V. (eds.) CMSB 2020. LNCS, vol. 12314, pp. 234–251. Springer, Cham (2020). https://doi.org/10.1007/978-3-030-60327-4_13

39. Su, C., Pang, J.: Target control of asynchronous Boolean networks. arXiv preprint arXiv:2101.00644 (2021)

40. Su, C., Paul, S., Pang, J.: Controlling large boolean networks with temporary and permanent perturbations. In: ter Beek, M.H., McIver, A., Oliveira, J.N. (eds.) FM 2019. LNCS, vol. 11800, pp. 707–724. Springer, Cham (2019). https://doi.org/10.1007/978-3-030-30942-8_41

41. Videla, S., Saez-Rodriguez, J., Guziolowski, C., Siegel, A.: caspo: a toolbox for automated reasoning on the response of logical signaling networks families. Bioinformatics **33**(6), 947–950 (2017)

42. Wang, L.Z., Su, R.Q., Huang, Z.G., Wang, X., Wang, W.X., Grebogi, C., Lai, Y.C.: A geometrical approach to control and controllability of nonlinear dynamical networks. Nat. Commun. **7**(1), 1–11 (2016)

43. Wu, Y., Sun, X.M., Zhao, X., Shen, T.: Optimal control of Boolean control networks with average cost: a policy iteration approach. Automatica **100**, 378–387 (2019)

44. Yamanaka, S.: Strategies and new developments in the generation of patient-specific pluripotent stem cells. Cell Stem Cell **1**(1), 39–49 (2007)

45. Yue, J., Yan, Y., Chen, Z., Jin, X.: Identification of predictors of Boolean networks from observed attractor states. Math. Methods Appl. Sci. **42**(11), 3848–3864 (2019)

46. Zañudo, J.G.T., Albert, R.: Cell fate reprogramming by control of intracellular network dynamics. PLOS Comput. Biol. **11**(4), e1004193 (2015)

47. Zañudo, J.G.T., Yang, G., Albert, R.: Structure-based control of complex networks with nonlinear dynamics. Proc. Natl. Acad. Sci. **114**(28), 7234–7239 (2017)

48. Zhao, Y., Kim, J., Filippone, M.: Aggregation algorithm towards large-scale Boolean network analysis. IEEE Trans. Autom. Control **58**(8), 1976–1985 (2013)

49. Zheng, D., Yang, G., Li, X., Wang, Z., Liu, F., He, L.: An efficient algorithm for computing attractors of synchronous and asynchronous Boolean networks. PLoS ONE **8**(4), e60593 (2013)
50. Zhong, J., Liu, Y., Kou, K.I., Sun, L., Cao, J.: On the ensemble controllability of Boolean control networks using STP method. Appl. Math. Comput. **358**, 51–62 (2019)
51. Zhu, P., Han, J.: Asynchronous stochastic Boolean networks as gene network models. J. Comput. Biol. **21**(10), 771–783 (2014)
52. Zhu, Q., Liu, Y., Lu, J., Cao, J.: Further results on the controllability of Boolean control networks. IEEE Trans. Autom. Control **64**(1), 440–442 (2018)

Dynamic Reconfiguration via Typed Modalities

Ionuţ Ţuţu[1,3(✉)], Claudia Elena Chiriţă[2], and José Luiz Fiadeiro[3]

[1] Simion Stoilow Institute of Mathematics of the Romanian Academy,
Bucharest, Romania
ionut.tutu@imar.ro
[2] School of Informatics, University of Edinburgh, Edinburgh, UK
cchirita@ed.ac.uk
[3] School of Science and Engineering, University of Dundee, Dundee, UK
jfiadeiro@dundee.ac.uk

Abstract. Modern software systems are increasingly exhibiting dynamic-reconfiguration features analogous to naturally occurring phenomena where the architecture of a complex changes dynamically, at run time, on account of interactions between its components. This has led to a renewed interest in modal logics for formal system development, building on the intuitive idea that system configurations can be regarded as local models of a Kripke structure, while reconfigurations are captured by accessibility relations. We contribute to this line of research by advancing a modal logic with varying quantification domains that employs typed modalities and dedicated modal operators to specify and reason about a new generation of Kripke structures, called dynamic networks of interactions, that account for the context of a system's dynamics, identifying which actants have triggered a reconfiguration and what are its outcomes. To illustrate the expressiveness of the formalism, we provide a specification of the biological process of membrane budding, which we then analyse using a sound and complete proof-by-translation method that links dynamic networks of interactions with partial first-order logic.

Keywords: Reconfigurable systems · Modal logic · Typed modalities · Standard translation · Partial first-order logic

1 Introduction

The process of dynamic reconfiguration is central to understanding the way modern software systems operate. For instance, in service-oriented computing, where software applications need to evolve in response to changing requirements or environmental conditions, reconfigurability accounts for run-time architectural transformations [12]; therefore, the process is closely related to self-adaptability – a key feature of the systems operating today in cyberspace. Dynamic reconfigurability is also one of the main processes that drive the functioning of cyber-physical systems. In actor-network theory – a modelling framework for cyber-physical-system protocols that we have recently formalized in [13] in connection with

© Springer Nature Switzerland AG 2021
M. Huisman et al. (Eds.): FM 2021, LNCS 13047, pp. 599–615, 2021.
https://doi.org/10.1007/978-3-030-90870-6_32

Robin Milner's bigraphs [22] – the topology of a network is modified dynamically, during its execution, as a result of interactions taking place between actors.

The topic is duly receiving growing attention in the formal-methods literature, notably through new mathematical models as well as specification and reasoning tools based on modal and hybrid(ized) logics that explore the intrinsic connection between reconfigurability and Kripke structures (e.g., [8,10,18,21]). In their most basic form, hybrid logics enrich ordinary modal logics with nominals – designating states in Kripke structures – and a local-satisfaction operator that enables a change of perspective from the state under consideration to another state that is named (e.g., [1,4]). Our work on actor-network theory [13,30] highlighted two important limitations of the hybrid-logic approach: it offers no support for tracking, which means that even though reconfigurations are triggered by specific interactions between network components, there is no way to pin down the components involved in an interaction or to track them through the reconfiguration; moreover, the systems thus modelled are closed, meaning that reconfigurations can alter the locality or inter-connectivity of network components but they cannot add or remove components to or from a given configuration. This has a significant impact on the specification capabilities of the approach.

In this work, we set out to address those limitations by introducing a modal logic for reconfigurable systems with two new features: (a) it makes use of typed modalities where inner and outer types indicate which network components have triggered a reconfiguration and what the outcomes are; and (b) it allows for varying quantification domains – in lieu of the more conventional constant domains – thus enabling the modelling of open systems. The first feature, in particular, is a notable departure from ordinary modal logics because the accessibility relations of Kripke structures, whilst still capturing reconfigurations, no longer link network configurations directly; instead, they define inter-network connections between different states or instances of the components involved in reconfigurations.

The paper is structured as follows. In Sect. 2, we highlight some of the challenges raised by dynamic reconfigurations on conventional modal-logic frameworks; for that purpose, we present a case study based on the biological process of membrane budding [19], which is paradigmatic for open systems. In Sect. 3, we introduce a new kind of Kripke structures – called dynamic networks of interactions – that underlie the modal-logic formalism proposed in this paper, which we then apply to the case study. Finally, in Sect. 4, we outline a sound and complete proof-by-translation technique for dynamic networks of interactions and we put it to use in order to analyse the membrane-budding process.

2   Membrane Budding

Dynamic networks of interactions can be broadly described as networks whose configurations change dynamically, at run time, as a result of interactions taking place among their components. Where examples abound in computer-based or software-enabled systems such as cyber-physical systems, to help us develop an intuitive understanding of the nature of such reconfigurations we look instead at membrane budding – a biological process that is emblematic of eukaryotic cells through which protein and lipid molecules are transported between organelles such as the endoplasmic reticulum and the Golgi complex. Biological processes are being used, more and more, for developing new modes of computation (e.g., [20,25]), and mathematical modelling techniques play an important part in reasoning about such processes; our running example serves both purposes.

In a nutshell, membrane budding facilitates the transport of cargo molecules along intracellular pathways by enclosing them in carrier vesicles, which in turn develop during the budding process through the deformation of the donor organelle's membrane. As a reference, we consider the simplified model of membrane budding from [19]. The biological model explains (a) the assembly of protein coats on the membrane of a source organelle, (b) the formation of a bud as a result of interactions between coat proteins and the membrane, (c) the detachment of the bud from the organelle, hence forming a vesicle, (d) the uncoating of the vesicle, and finally (e) the fusion with the membrane of the target organelle.

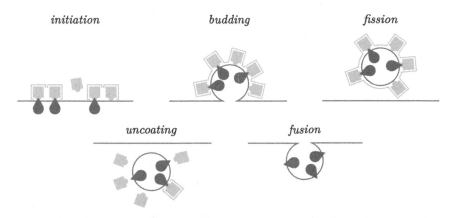

Fig. 1. The five stages of the membrane-budding process   black lines represent membranes of organelles, buds, or vesicles; yellow squares represent proteins; blue drops represent cargo molecules; and yellow contours around proteins represent coats (Color figure online)

The entire process is depicted in Fig. 1, and unfolds as follows. The first stage – called *initiation* (cf. [19, Table 2]) – begins with a set of reactions that lead to the recruitment of specific proteins (represented in our figure as yellow squares); those proteins eventually bind to the donor membrane (represented as the lower black line), cluster into coats, and capture cargo molecules (represented as blue drops) from the underlying membrane. The second stage – *coat propagation*, or *budding* – corresponds to a deformation of the membrane under the effect of the coat assembly. The third stage – *vesicle formation*, or *fission* – is triggered by the completion of the coat, which depends on the kinds of proteins involved, and consists in the detachment of the bud from the membrane by scission. The last two stages – *uncoating* and *fusion* – occur at the arrival of the vesicle in the proximity of the target organelle. The vesicle then loses its coat and fuses with the membrane, thus completing the delivery of its cargo molecules.

Using Modalities to Capture Reconfigurations. Dynamic networks of interactions similar to the ones arising in membrane budding are essentially discrete reconfigurable systems; hence, it is natural to formalize them as Kripke structures whose states/worlds correspond to network configurations (specific arrangements of organelles, proteins, cargo molecules, etc., at a given time) and whose transitions capture reconfigurations (like those occurring during budding or fission). This opens the possibility to use standard modal-logic formalisms as in [7,11,18,21,30], among other, to specify and reason about reconfigurations.

The modal-logic approach to dynamic reconfigurations ordinarily relies on the use of logical systems that blend features of a base logic (in our case, of many-sorted first-order logic with equality) with features that are conventionally attributed to modal logic such as possible-worlds semantics and the use of modal operators. We use base-logic sentences to specify relationships between network components in a given configuration, and modal-logic operators to describe the effects of reconfigurations. To illustrate the modus operandi, consider the binding of proteins to organelles during the initiation stage of membrane budding. Whenever a free (i.e., unbound) protein p is close enough to an organelle o, binding p to o results in a new configuration where p is part of a coat c formed on the membrane of o. Formally, we could write:

$$\text{close-enough}(p, o) \land \text{free}(p) \Rightarrow [\text{bind}] \exists c \cdot \text{part-of}(p, c) \land \text{brane}(c) = \text{brane}(o)$$

where close-enough, free, part-of, and brane are relation/operation symbols from a base first-order signature (suitably axiomatized, as we discuss in Sect. 3), and bind is a modality. This sentence is a typical example of the use of modal logic to formalize pre/post-conditions in program specification and verification [24]: the consequent $\exists c \cdot \text{part-of}(p, c) \land \text{brane}(c) = \text{brane}(o)$ captures the effect of any reconfiguration performed by the action (modality) bind on any configuration that satisfies the antecedent $\text{close-enough}(p, o) \land \text{free}(p)$.

However, this usage of modalities is not adequate for our purposes because it fails to capture all bind-reconfigurations of interest whilst allowing other – biologically inconsistent – reconfigurations to occur. That is because the ramifications of the above axiomatization are global: under the usual semantics of the modal-logic operator [bind], given that variables p and o are implicitly universally quantified, bind-reconfigurations simultaneously affect *all* organelles o (in any configuration) and *all* unbound proteins p that are sufficiently close to o. Therefore, proteins that are sufficiently close to several organelles will necessarily end up being bound to all of them in the same resulting configuration – which is discordant with the biological model of membrane budding that we intend to formalize.

Another drawback of conventional modal-logic approaches to reconfigurable systems is that they make use of constant quantification domains (were variables such as p, o, and c in the sentence above are instantiated). That is, conventionally, reconfigurations cannot create or remove network components; their effects are limited to changing the states of components or the way they relate to other components. In regard to membrane budding, this constraint is admissible for proteins, whose states may change from free to bound, or vice versa; however, it is not admissible for coats, which are created during initiation and removed during the uncoating stage – nor for buds or vesicles, which have a similar transitory nature. Returning to the sentence above, the consequent variable c ought to refer to a newly generated coat that could not have existed in the configuration where p and o are instantiated (because p is unbound in that configuration).

Towards Typed Modalities and Varying Domains. In light of the discussion above, the next section brings forward a new modal-logic formalism that is specifically adapted to support the development/specification and analysis of dynamic networks of interactions. There are two major attributes that differentiate the formalism we propose from previous modal-logic approaches:

1. It makes use of typed modalities and generalized modal operators that account for the context in which reconfigurations take place.
2. It features varying quantification domains in order to accommodate open systems where components are created or removed on the fly as needed.

The second attribute belongs to an area of modal logic that has received considerable attention (e.g., [2,4,14,16]) mainly through exploring specific choices of kinds of first-order symbols and of Kripke structures; for instance, in [14], every individual (network component) needs to exist in some local domain, while [4] admits only constant-operation symbols and flexible predicates. Our contribution is in facilitating the full, unhindered use of many-sorted first-order logic in conjunction with modal operators; this can be seen as a varying-domain counterpart of the work reported in [11], which employs shared quantification domains.

Typed modalities are, to the best of our knowledge, a new development. They provide a mechanism that supports tracking – reminiscent of [22, Chapter 11] – so that one can identify, for every reconfiguration, which actants (network components) have triggered it and what are its specific outcomes. For instance, the bind-reconfigurations that we have considered thus far are triggered by interactions between proteins p and organelles o, and their outcomes are specific coats c that arise once p is attached to the membrane of o. Therefore, we can regard bind as a modality that is typed by proteins, organelles, and coats.

3   Logical Support for Dynamic Networks of Interactions

In order to address the concerns raised in Sect. 2, we propose a dedicated logical system, hereafter referred to as DNI, that supports the formal development of dynamic networks of interactions. We present the logic in familiar fashion, focusing on *signatures* (organized collections of non-logical symbols), *models* (Kripke structures over which the symbols declared in signatures are given semantics), *sentences* (built from symbols declared in signatures), and *satisfaction relations* (establishing which sentences hold at given configurations of a network).

First-Order-Logic Preliminaries. DNI combines first-order quantifiers with features specific to modal and, in particular, hybrid logics [1]. To establish the terminology and notations used throughout the paper, we recall a few basic notions pertaining to first-order logic in an algebraic setting – see [11,17] for more details.

By *first-order signature* we mean a triple $\Sigma = \langle S, F, P \rangle$, where S is a set of *sorts* (which we typically denote by s), F is an $S^* \times S$-indexed family of sets of *operation symbols* $\sigma \colon u \to s$ (named σ, having *arity* u and *sort* s), and P is an S^*-indexed family of sets of *predicate symbols* $\pi \colon u$ (named π, of *arity* u). An $\langle S, F, P \rangle$-*model* is a structure M that interprets: every sort s in S as a set M_s, called the *carrier set* of s in M; every finite sequence of sorts $u = s_1 \cdots s_n$ as the Cartesian product $M_{s_1} \times \cdots \times M_{s_n}$; every operation symbol $\sigma \colon u \to s$ in F as a function $M_\sigma \colon M_u \to M_s$; and every predicate symbol $\pi \colon u$ in P as a subset $M_\pi \subseteq M_u$. In relation to the syntax of first-order logic, we consider *terms* built, inductively, from operation symbols, including constants. We use terms to form *equational atoms* $t_1 = t_2$, where t_1 and t_2 are terms of the same sort, and *relational atoms* $\pi(t)$, where π is a predicate symbol and t is a *tuple of terms* corresponding to the arity of π. Full first-order sentences are obtained from equational and relational atoms using Boolean connectives and quantifiers (over variables which we treat as new constant-operation symbols).

The presentation of DNI makes use of first-order signature extensions, model reducts, and closed submodels. We say that a signature Σ' *extends* Σ, and we write $\Sigma \subseteq \Sigma'$ when every sort and every operation/predicate symbol in Σ belongs to Σ' as well. In particular, for every set X of variables (distinct from the constant-operation symbols in Σ), we obtain the extension $\Sigma(X)$ by adding the variables in X to Σ as new constant-operation symbols. For every Σ'-model M' we define the *reduct* $M'\!\restriction_\Sigma$ as the Σ-model M obtained from M' by 'forgetting' the interpretation of all symbols in Σ' that do not belong to Σ – and in that case we also say that M' is a Σ'-*expansion* of M. Lastly, we say that M is a *closed submodel* of D, and we write $M \subseteq D$, when $M_s \subseteq D_s$ for every sort s in Σ, $M_\sigma(a) = D_\sigma(a)$ for every operation symbol $\sigma \colon u \to s$ and every tuple of arguments $a \in M_u$, and $M_\pi = D_\pi \cap M_u$ for every predicate symbol $\pi \colon u$.

DNI-*signatures.* Depending on where and how they are meant to be interpreted, we distinguish between (*a*) symbols that are meant to be interpreted only globally, at network level, irrespective of configurations, (*b*) symbols that are evaluated only locally, at every configuration of a network, yielding interpretations that may vary from one configuration to another, and (*c*) symbols that are evaluated both globally and locally, in which case we require their interpretations to agree. In keeping with standard modal-logic terminology, we refer to the symbols belonging to the first and third category as *rigid*, and to those in the second category as *flexible*. In addition, we refer to symbols that belong to the third category as *shared* to indicate that their interpretation is jointly defined across configurations.

Besides first-order symbols, DNI-signatures make use of *nominals* – as in hybrid logic [1] – through which specific configurations can be designated and of *typed modalities* with *inner* and *outer types* that match the triggers and outcomes of their corresponding reconfigurations.

Formally, a DNI-*signature* is a tuple $\Xi = \langle \Delta, \Omega, N, \Lambda \rangle$ consisting of:

- first-order signatures Δ and Ω over the same set S of sorts; Δ comprises the global, and thus *rigid*, symbols of Ξ, while Ω comprises the local symbols of Ξ; the symbols in $\Sigma = \Delta \cap \Omega$ are *shared*, and those in $\Omega \setminus \Sigma$ are *flexible*;
- a set N of *nominals*, or *configuration designators*; and
- an $S^* \times S^*$-indexed family Λ of sets of *modalities*; given two sequences of sorts $u, v \in S^*$, we typically write $\lambda \colon u \times v$ for $\lambda \in \Lambda_{u,v}$ and we say that u is the *inner type* and v is the *outer type* of λ.

Example 1. For membrane budding, we define a DNI-signature with seven sorts:

> **sorts** Organelle, Brane, Protein, Cargo, Coat, Bud, Vesicle

These correspond, in order, to organelles, membranes (of organelles, but also of buds or vesicles), proteins, cargo molecules, coats, buds, and vesicles.

Intuitively, coats are clusters of proteins bound to a given membrane; as such, we define two rigid operations: just, which is used to form simple coats out of single, isolated proteins, and add, which is used to enlarge existing coats.

> **rigid ops** just: Protein $\to$ Coat
> add: Protein Coat $\to$ Coat

These operations are rigid but not shared because, when applied to proteins and coats in a configuration w, they may evaluate to coats that do not belong to w. For instance, if a protein p is unbound in w, then the coat just(p) cannot belong to w – because that would imply that p is bound to a membrane.

We also consider two membership predicates: part-of to determine whether a protein belongs to a coat, and enclosed to determine whether a cargo molecule is surrounded by a given membrane. The first one is shared because coats are intended to be uniquely determined by the proteins of which they are formed (independently of the configuration where said proteins and coats are located), while the second is flexible because the cargo molecules enclosed in a membrane may vary from one configuration to another as a result of their transport.

shared pred part-of: Protein Coat
flexible pred enclosed: Cargo Brane

Some entities have corresponding membranes. This is obvious for organelles, buds, and vesicles, but it also holds for coats, which are necessarily bound to specific membranes. We capture these attributes by overloading the operation symbol brane. For the first three cases, we declare brane as a shared symbol because the membranes of organelles, buds, and vesicles are fixed and defined at every configuration; for the latter case, brane is flexible because the membrane of a coat varies depending on the organelle on which the coat is located.

shared op brane: $s \to$ Brane, where $s \in \{$Organelle, Bud, Vesicle$\}$
flexible op brane: Coat $\to$ Brane

We use an additional predicate to indicate if a protein is close enough to an organelle in order to be bound. This predicate is flexible because the position of a protein relative to an organelle may change from one configuration to another. For example, a protein that is attached (and thus close enough) to an organelle during the initiation stage will no longer be so during fission.

flexible pred close-enough: Protein Organelle

Similar predicates are used to indicate if a cargo molecule is close enough to a protein (in order to be captured) or if two proteins belonging to different coats are close enough to enable the two coats to merge into a bigger cluster.

The modal part of the signature consists of seven modalities: bind for binding a protein to an organelle, thus producing a coat; merge for merging two neighbouring coats into a bigger coat; capture, thorough which a cargo molecule is captured by a protein (bound to the membrane enclosing that molecule); etc.

modalities bind: Protein Organelle × Coat;   merge: Coat Coat × Coat;
                capture: Cargo Protein × ε;   bud: Coat × Bud;
                split: Bud × Vesicle;   uncoat: Protein Vesicle × ε;
                fuse: Vesicle Organelle × ε.

Some of the modalities listed above, such as capture and uncoat, have empty outer types, which we indicate by ε; this means that their corresponding reconfigurations have no specific outcomes other than the (implicit) change of configuration.

Dynamic networks. A $\varXi$-model, or network, $\langle D, W, M \rangle$ consists of:

- a first-order Δ-model D, called the *global domain* of the network;
- a *Kripke frame* W; we denote by $|W|$ the set of *possible worlds* or *configurations* of W, and by $W_i \in |W|$ and $W_\lambda \subseteq |W| \times |W|$ the interpretations of nominals $i \in N$ and modalities λ in Λ (regardless of their inner/outer types);
- for every $w \in |W|$, a *local Ω-model* M_w such that $M_w{\restriction}_\Sigma \subseteq D{\restriction}_\Sigma$;[1]

---

[1] Recall that, in the context of DNI, we denote by Σ the intersection $\Delta \cap \Omega$.

– for every $(w, w') \in W_\lambda$ with $\lambda \colon u \times v$, a relation $M_{w\lambda w'} \subseteq M_{w,u} \times M_{w',v}$ between elements in M_w corresponding to the sorts in u (triggering actants for λ) and elements in $M_{w'}$ corresponding to the sorts in v (outcomes of λ).

Signature Extensions and Network Reducts. The formalism we propose makes use of two kinds of variables: rigid first-order variables for referencing network components or data, and nominal variables (inherited from ordinary hybrid logic) for referencing configurations. Both kinds of symbols need to be distinct from the constants and nominals declared in the signature under consideration.

For every DNI-signature $\Xi = \langle \Delta, \Omega, N, \Lambda \rangle$ over a set S of sorts, and every S-sorted set X of first-order variables and set K of nominal variables, we obtain an extended signature $\Xi(X; K) = \langle \Delta(X), \Omega, N \uplus K, \Lambda \rangle$ and thus the inclusion $\Xi \subseteq \Xi(X; K)$ by adding the first-order variables in X to Δ as new rigid constants and the nominal variables in K to N as new nominals. If $X = \emptyset$, we denote the extended signature by $\Xi(K)$; similarly, if $K = \emptyset$, we use the notation $\Xi(X)$.

Similarly to first-order logic, every $\Xi(X; K)$-network $\langle D', W', M' \rangle$ can be reduced to a Ξ-network $\langle D, W, M \rangle = \langle D', W', M' \rangle {\upharpoonright}_\Xi$ simply by forgetting the interpretation of the newly added symbols from X and K. That is, $\langle D, W, M \rangle$ is a network with the same carrier sets and possible worlds as $\langle D', W', M' \rangle$, and which interprets all first-order and modal symbols in Ξ just as $\langle D', W', M' \rangle$.

Sentences. The terms over a DNI-signature Ξ are built by freely putting together operation symbols from the two first-order signatures that underlie it. To that end, we define DNI-*terms* over Ξ as first-order terms over the compound signature $\Delta \cup \Omega$. For every sort s in Ξ, we denote by $T_{\Xi,s}$ the set of Ξ-terms of sort s, and for every sequence of sorts $u = s_1 \cdots s_n$, we denote by $T_{\Xi,u}$ the Cartesian product $T_{\Xi,s_1} \times \cdots \times T_{\Xi,s_n}$. We further inherit from first-order logic both *equational atoms* $t_1 = t_2$, where t_1 and t_2 are Ξ-terms of the same sort, and *relational atoms* $\pi(t)$, where $\pi \colon u$ is a relation symbol (with arity u) in $\Delta \cup \Omega$ and $t \in T_{\Xi,u}$ is a tuple of Ξ-terms corresponding to the sorts in u.

Core DNI-*sentences* over Ξ are defined according to the following grammar:

$$\rho ::= e \mid \flat l \mid i \mid \neg\rho \mid \rho \wedge \rho \mid @i \cdot \rho \mid [t \, \lambda \, z]\rho' \mid \forall X; K \cdot \rho^\dagger$$

where (a) e is either an equational or a relational atom over Ξ; (b) $\flat$ is a *local-membership* operator and l is a Ξ-term; (c) i is a nominal, which, together with e and $\flat l$, is also considered an atomic sentence; (d) @ is a special *local-satisfaction* operator – as in hybrid logics; (e) $\lambda \colon u \times v$ is a modality, t is a tuple of terms corresponding to the sorts in u, z is a tuple of first-order variables corresponding to the sorts in v, and ρ' is a sentence over the extended signature $\Xi(z)$; and lastly, (f) X is a finite set of first-order variables, K is a finite set of nominal variables, and $\rho^\dagger$ is a sentence over the extended signature $\Xi(X; K)$. When either X or K is empty, we denote $\forall X; K \cdot \rho^\dagger$ by $\forall K \cdot \rho^\dagger$ or $\forall X \cdot \rho^\dagger$, respectively.

For convenience, other logical connectives can be defined in terms of the basic ones in the usual manner. We denote disjunctions by $\rho_1 \vee \rho_2$, implications by $\rho_1 \Rightarrow \rho_2$, equivalences by $\rho_1 \Leftrightarrow \rho_2$, possibility statements by $\langle t \lambda z \rangle \rho$, and existentially quantified sentences by $\exists X; K \cdot \rho$ – together with the simplified forms $\exists X \cdot \rho$ and $\exists K \cdot \rho$, as described above. In addition, we consider *locally quantified sentences* $\forall \flat X \cdot \rho$ and $\exists \flat X \cdot \rho$, where $\forall \flat X \cdot \rho$ stands for $\forall X \cdot \bigwedge \{\flat x \mid x \in X\} \Rightarrow \rho$ and $\exists \flat X \cdot \rho$ stands for $\exists X \cdot \bigwedge \{\flat x \mid x \in X\} \wedge \rho$ – this matches the usual notion of *actualist quantification* from first-order modal logic [14]. Lastly, the *store* operator $\downarrow k \cdot \rho$ used in hybrid logics can be defined as $\forall \{k\} \cdot k \Rightarrow \rho$.

The Satisfaction Relation. As with any modal logic, we distinguish between local – i.e., at configuration level – and global satisfaction of sentences by models (networks); the former takes precedence. To define satisfaction, we need to take a closer look at the way operation and relation symbols of a DNI-signature Ξ are interpreted locally, at given configurations of a network $\langle D, W, M \rangle$.

Interpretation of Terms. For every configuration $w \in |W|$, every rigid operation $\sigma \colon u \to s$ is interpreted as a function $\langle D, W, M \rangle_\sigma^w \colon D_u \to D_s$ defined by $\langle D, W, M \rangle_\sigma^w(a) = D_\sigma(a)$ for all $a \in D_u$. In contrast, every flexible operation $\sigma \colon u \to s$ is interpreted as a partial function $\langle D, W, M \rangle_\sigma^w \colon D_u \nrightarrow D_s$, where $\langle D, W, M \rangle_\sigma^w(a)$ is defined and equal to $M_{w,\sigma}(a)$ if and only if $a \in M_{w,u}$.

The interpretation of operation symbols generalizes to DNI-terms in a straight-forward inductive way: given an operation symbol $\sigma \colon u \to s$ and a tuple of terms $t \in T_{\Xi,u}$, the interpretation of the compound term $\sigma(t)$ at a configuration w, denoted $\langle D, W, M \rangle_{\sigma(t)}^w$, is defined and equal to $\langle D, W, M \rangle_\sigma^w(\langle D, W, M \rangle_t^w)$ if and only if the interpretation of t is defined at w and it belongs to the domain of $\langle D, W, M \rangle_\sigma^w$. Whenever we write $\langle D, W, M \rangle_t^w$, we implicitly assume that (the interpretation of) t is defined at w in the network $\langle D, W, M \rangle$.

Interpretation of Relation Symbols. Interpreting relation symbols is significantly simpler: if $\pi \colon u$ is a rigid relation symbol, we define $\langle D, W, M \rangle_\pi^w$ as D_π; otherwise (i.e., when $\pi \colon u$ is flexible), we define it as $M_{w,\pi} \subseteq D_u$.

The *local-satisfaction relations* of DNI are defined inductively, as follows:

- $\langle D, W, M \rangle \vDash_\Xi^w t_1 = t_2$ if $\langle D, W, M \rangle_{t_1}^w = \langle D, W, M \rangle_{t_2}^w$, meaning that both terms are defined at w, and their interpretations are equal;
- $\langle D, W, M \rangle \vDash_\Xi^w \pi(t)$ if $\langle D, W, M \rangle_t^w \in \langle D, W, M \rangle_\pi^w$;
- $\langle D, W, M \rangle \vDash_\Xi^w \flat l$ if $\langle D, W, M \rangle_l^w \in M_{w,s}$, when l is a Ξ-term of sort s;
- $\langle D, W, M \rangle \vDash_\Xi^w i$ if $w = W_i$, when i is a nominal;
- $\langle D, W, M \rangle \vDash_\Xi^w \neg \rho$ if $\langle D, W, M \rangle \nvDash_\Xi^w \rho$;
- $\langle D, W, M \rangle \vDash_\Xi^w \rho_1 \wedge \rho_2$ if $\langle D, W, M \rangle \vDash_\Xi^w \rho_1$ and $\langle D, W, M \rangle \vDash_\Xi^w \rho_2$;
- $\langle D, W, M \rangle \vDash_\Xi^w @i \cdot \rho$ if $\langle D, W, M \rangle \vDash_\Xi^{W_i} \rho$;

- $\langle D, W, M \rangle \vDash_{\Xi}^{w} [t \lambda z] \rho'$ if $\langle D', W, M \rangle \vDash_{\Xi(z)}^{w'} \rho'$ for all transitions $(w, w') \in W_{\lambda}$ and all expansions $\langle D', W, M \rangle$ of $\langle D, W, M \rangle$ along the signature inclusion $\Xi \subseteq \Xi(z)$ such that $(\langle D, W, M \rangle_{t}^{w}, \langle D', W, M \rangle_{z}^{w'}) \in M_{w \lambda w'}$;
- $\langle D, W, M \rangle \vDash_{\Xi}^{w} \forall X; K \cdot \rho^{\dagger}$ if $\langle D^{\dagger}, W^{\dagger}, M^{\dagger} \rangle \vDash_{\Xi(X;K)}^{w} \rho^{\dagger}$ for all expansions $\langle D^{\dagger}, W^{\dagger}, M^{\dagger} \rangle$ of $\langle D, W, M \rangle$ along the signature inclusion $\Xi \subseteq \Xi(X; K)$.

Global satisfaction equates to local satisfaction at all possible worlds. More precisely, a Ξ-network $\langle D, W, M \rangle$ *globally satisfies* a DNI-sentence ρ, which we denote by $\langle D, W, M \rangle \vDash_{\Xi} \rho$, when $\langle D, W, M \rangle \vDash_{\Xi}^{w} \rho$ for all $w \in |W|$.

Example 2. We are now ready to outline the DNI-specification of membrane budding, which consists in a set E_{MB} of sentences written over the signature Ξ_{MB} introduced in Example 1. As usual, the semantics of the specification is given by the class of all Ξ_{MB}-networks that globally satisfy all sentences in E_{MB}.

We organize the specification in two categories of sentences:

1. Static constraints, which are meant to ensure that the configurations we specify are coherent with the biological model of membrane budding. Here, we include, for example, the relationship between proteins and coats, which is partly described in sentences (1) and (2) below, and what it means for a protein to be free, according to sentence (3). To keep the notations short within formulae, we write variables without their corresponding sorts; we let c range over coats, p and q range over proteins, and o over organelles.

$$\forall \{c\} \cdot \exists \{p\} \cdot \mathsf{part\text{-}of}(p, c) \tag{1}$$

$$\forall \{p, q\} \cdot \mathsf{part\text{-}of}(p, \mathsf{just}(q)) \Leftrightarrow p = q \tag{2}$$

$$\forall \flat \{p\} \cdot \mathsf{free}(p) \Leftrightarrow \neg \exists \flat \{c\} \cdot \mathsf{part\text{-}of}(p, c) \tag{3}$$

2. Sentences dealing with the dynamic aspects of membrane budding. In this case, for every kind of reconfiguration, we present both *progress axioms*, indicating under which conditions a reconfiguration may occur, and *effect axioms*, which describe the changes induced by that particular type of reconfiguration. To illustrate, we look once again at bind-reconfigurations, for which the sentences (4) and (5) below capture the notions of progress and effect.

$$\forall \flat \{p, o\} \cdot (\langle p, o \ \mathsf{bind} \ c \rangle \ true) \Leftrightarrow \mathsf{close\text{-}enough}(p, o) \land \mathsf{free}(p) \tag{4}$$

$$\forall \flat \{p, o\} \cdot [p, o \ \mathsf{bind} \ c] c = \mathsf{just}(p) \land \mathsf{brane}(c) = \mathsf{brane}(o) \tag{5}$$

Note that, unlike p and o, which are bound by $\forall \flat$, the variable c is bound by the modal operators $\langle p, o \ \mathsf{bind} \ c \rangle$ and $[p, o \ \mathsf{bind} \ c]$. This is useful because we expect c, on the one hand, to be interpreted in the new configuration generated as a result of binding p to o – instead of where p and o interact – and on the other hand, to be tracked through reconfigurations along with the specific protein p and organelle o that have led to its formation.

Typed modalities – and their corresponding modal operators, as in (4) and (5) – also provide a scope for addressing the property of binding proteins to organelles discussed in Sect. 2, which we can rewrite as follows:

$$\forall b \{p, o\} \cdot \text{close-enough}(p, o) \wedge \text{free}(p)$$
$$\Rightarrow [p \, o \text{ bind } c] \text{ part-of}(p, c) \wedge \text{brane}(c) = \text{brane}(o). \quad (6)$$

This sentence is a consequence of the above axiomatization of membrane budding. More specifically, one can easily see that any network that satisfies (2) and (5) satisfies (6) too. We make this relationship precise in Sect. 4, where we also outline a general and fully automated technique for checking entailment.

The entire DNI-specification of membrane budding, which covers many more static constraints and requirements of the biological model as well as a full description of each of the seven types of reconfigurations, is available in [29].

4   A Proof-by-translation Technique for DNI

In order to check properties of dynamic networks of interactions, we employ a proof-by-translation technique whereby both the specification of the system that we intend to analyse and the property to be checked are translated to other logical systems for which tool support for formal verification has already been developed. In our case, the logical system of reference into which we translate DNI-specifications is (many-sorted) partial first-order logic (PFOL) [6].

The main feature of PFOL is that it accommodates both total and partial operations. Hence, a PFOL-signature can be broadly described as a first-order signature $\langle S, F, P \rangle$ where F is partitioned in two families TF and PF of sets of total- and partial-operation symbols, respectively. We denote such signatures by $\langle S, TF, PF, P \rangle$. Models and sentences are defined in a similar manner to ordinary first-order logic, except that *(a)* the operation symbols in PF are interpreted as partial rather than total functions, and *(b)* quantifiers apply only to total first-order variables. The notion of satisfaction of a sentence by a model needs to be adapted accordingly, but only for equational and relational atoms. We take the *existential* approach by which a PFOL-model M satisfies an equational atom $t_1 = t_2$ when the interpretations M_{t_1} and M_{t_2} are both defined and are equal; likewise, M satisfies $\pi(t)$ when M_t is defined and $M_t \in M_\pi$.

The gist of the translation of DNI into PFOL lies in making network configurations explicit and in encoding typed modalities as many-sorted relations:

– every DNI-signature $\Xi = \langle \Delta, \Omega, N, \Lambda \rangle$ is encoded as a PFOL-signature $\Phi(\Xi) = \langle S_\Xi, TF_\Xi, PF_\Xi, P_\Xi \rangle$ together with a set Γ_Ξ of $\Phi(\Xi)$-sentences;
– every Ξ-sentence ρ is translated to a PFOL-sentence $\alpha(\rho)$ over $\Phi(\Xi)$; and
– every $\Phi(\Xi)$-model M' that satisfies Γ_Ξ is reduced to a Ξ-network $\beta(M')$.[2]

---

[2] Technically, the maps α and β are both indexed by the DNI-signature under consideration, but we put this detail aside in order to reduce the notational burden.

The Encoding of Signatures. We let $S_\Xi = S \cup \{\varkappa\}$, where S is the set of sorts of Ξ and $\varkappa$ is a new sort, distinct from those in S, that corresponds to configurations. Now suppose that $\Delta = \langle S, F_\Delta, P_\Delta \rangle$ and $\Omega = \langle S, F_\Omega, P_\Omega \rangle$. The remaining components of $\Phi(\Xi)$ are defined as follows:

$$TF_\Xi = F_\Delta \uplus \{i\colon \varepsilon \to \varkappa \mid i \in N\} \qquad \text{(encoding nominals as constants of sort } \varkappa)$$
$$PF_\Xi = \{\sigma\colon \varkappa u \to s \mid (\sigma\colon u \to s) \in F_\Omega\} \qquad \text{(making configs explicit for local operations)}$$
$$P_\Xi = \{\text{loc}\colon \varkappa s \mid s \in S\} \qquad \text{(encoding the 'locality' of network components)}$$
$$\uplus P_\Delta \uplus \{\pi\colon \varkappa u \mid (\pi\colon u) \in P_\Omega\} \qquad \text{(making configs explicit for local predicates)}$$
$$\uplus \{\lambda\colon \varkappa u \varkappa v \mid (\lambda\colon u \times v) \in \Lambda\} \qquad \text{(encoding typed modalities as relations)}$$

The set Γ_Ξ of $\Phi(\Xi)$-sentences contains axioms ensuring, for example, that local operations are well defined (in 7, which applies to all symbols $\sigma\colon u \to s$ in F_Ω), that shared operations indeed agree on shared local components (in 8, which applies to symbols $\varsigma\colon u \to s$ in $F_\Delta \cap F_\Omega$), and that transitions involve triggers that are local to their source configuration and outcomes that are local to their target configuration (in 9, for all modalities $\lambda\colon u \times v$ in Λ). To that end, we let k and k' be variables of sort $\varkappa$, x and y be tuples of variables corresponding to arities u and v, respectively, and we write $\text{loc}(k, x)$ in place of $\text{loc}(k, x_1) \wedge \cdots \wedge \text{loc}(k, x_n)$ when $x = (x_1, \ldots, x_n)$. Similar axioms to (7) and (8) are added for local and for shared predicates. We also use the derived PFOL-atom $\text{def}\, t$, which stands for $t = t$, indicating that (the interpretation of) the term t is defined.

$$\forall \{k, x\} \cdot \big(\text{def}\, \sigma(k, x) \Rightarrow \text{loc}(k, x)\big) \wedge \big(\text{loc}(k, x) \Rightarrow \text{loc}(k, \sigma(k, x))\big) \tag{7}$$
$$\forall \{k, x\} \cdot \text{loc}(k, x) \Rightarrow \varsigma(k, x) = \varsigma(x) \tag{8}$$
$$\forall \{k, k', x, y\} \cdot \lambda(k, x, k', y) \Rightarrow \text{loc}(k, x) \wedge \text{loc}(k', y) \tag{9}$$

The Translation of Sentences. We let $\alpha(\rho) = \forall \{k\} \cdot \alpha(k, \rho)$, where $\alpha(k, \rho)$ is defined inductively on the structure of the DNI-sentence ρ, as follows:

- $\alpha(k, t_1 = t_2) = \big(\alpha(k, t_1) = \alpha(k, t_2)\big)$, where $\alpha(k, \sigma(t)) = \sigma(k, \alpha(k, t))$ if σ is a local operation symbol, and $\alpha(k, \sigma(t)) = \sigma(\alpha(k, t))$ if σ is not local;[3]
- $\alpha(k, \pi(t)) = \pi(k, \alpha(k, t))$ if π is local, and $\alpha(k, \pi(t)) = \pi(\alpha(k, t))$ otherwise;
- $\alpha(k, \flat l) = \text{loc}(k, \alpha(k, l))$;
- $\alpha(k, i) = (k = i)$, when i is a nominal;
- $\alpha(k, \neg \rho) = \neg \alpha(k, \rho)$ and $\alpha(k, \rho_1 \wedge \rho_2) = \alpha(k, \rho_1) \wedge \alpha(k, \rho_2)$;
- $\alpha(k, @i \cdot \rho) = \alpha(i, \rho)$;
- $\alpha(k, [t \lambda z]\rho') = \forall \{k', z\} \cdot \lambda(k, \alpha(k, t), k', z) \Rightarrow \alpha(k', \rho')$;
- $\alpha(k, \forall X; K \cdot \rho^\dagger) = \forall (X \cup K) \cdot \alpha(k, \rho^\dagger)$.

---

[3] When $t = (t_1, \ldots, t_n)$ is a tuple of terms, by $\alpha(k, t)$ we mean $(\alpha(k, t_1), \ldots, \alpha(k, t_n))$.

The Reduction of Models. Suppose M' is a PFOL-model of $\Phi(\Xi)$ that satisfies Γ_Ξ. We define $\beta(M')$ as the Ξ-network $\langle D, W, M \rangle$ given by:

- $D = M'{\restriction}_\Delta$ – for this purpose, notice that Δ is a subsignature of $\Phi(\Xi)$;
- $|W| = M'_\varkappa$, $W_i = M'_i$ for all nominals $i \in N$, and $W_\lambda = \{(w, w') \mid (w, a, w', a') \in M'_\lambda$ for some $a \in M'_u$ and $a' \in M'_v\}$ for all modalities $\lambda \colon u \times v$;
- for every $w \in |W|$, $M_{w,s} = \{a \in M'_s \mid (w, a) \in M'_{\text{loc}:\varkappa s}\}$ for all sorts $s \in S$, $M_{w,\sigma}(a) = M'_\sigma(w, a)$ for all operation symbols $\sigma \colon u \to s$ in Ω and $a \in M_{w,u}$, and $M_{w,\pi} = \{a \in M_{w,u} \mid (w, a) \in M'_\pi\}$ for all predicate symbols $\pi \colon u$ in Ω;
- for every modality $\lambda \colon u \times v$ and every transition $(w, w') \in W_\lambda$, we have $M_{w\lambda w'} = \{(a, a') \in M_{w,u} \times M_{w',v} \mid (w, a, w', a') \in M'_\lambda\}$.

It is straightforward to check now, based on our initial assumption that M' satisfies the constraints in Γ_Ξ, that $\beta(M')$ is indeed a well defined Ξ-network.

Proposition 1. *For every Ξ-sentence ρ and model M' that satisfies Γ_Ξ[4],*

$$M' \vDash^{\text{PFOL}}_{\Phi(\Xi)} \alpha(\rho) \quad \text{if and only if} \quad \beta(M') \vDash^{\text{DNI}}_\Xi \rho.$$

That is, the syntactic and the semantic components of the proposed encoding of DNI into PFOL are mutually coherent. Moreover, it is easy to see that the encoding is *conservative* in the sense that for every Ξ-network $\langle D, W, M \rangle$ there exists a $\Phi(\Xi)$-model M' such that $\beta(M') = \langle D, W, M \rangle$ – by which we also mean that M' satisfies all sentences in Γ_Ξ. Used in conjunction with Proposition 1, being conservative ensures that the semantic entailment relations of DNI are indistinguishable from the semantic entailment relations of its encoding in PFOL. We write $E \vDash^{\text{DNI}}_\Xi \rho$ to indicate that ρ is a semantic consequence of E; i.e., ρ holds in all networks of interactions that globally satisfy all sentences in E.

Proposition 2. *For every set E of Ξ-sentences and every Ξ-sentence ρ,*

$$E \vDash^{\text{DNI}}_\Xi \rho \quad \text{if and only if} \quad \alpha(E) \cup \Gamma_\Xi \vDash^{\text{PFOL}}_{\Phi(\Xi)} \alpha(\rho).$$

A Preliminary Analysis of Membrane Budding. The practical significance of Proposition 2 is that any sound and complete syntactic entailment system for PFOL yields a sound and complete syntactic entailment system for DNI, which enables us to conduct proofs in DNI using syntactic entailment systems and supplementary tools 'borrowed' from PFOL – cf. [5].

We use this result to analyse the specification of membrane budding developed in Examples 1 and 2, checking whether it guarantees the property (6) of binding proteins to organelles that we originally discussed in Sect. 2. We can even strengthen the requirement by asking for the coat c to be newly generated through binding. For this purpose, we rewrite the proof goal as follows:

---

[4] Here, we annotate the double-turnstile symbols with DNI and PFOL in order to distinguish between the two types of satisfaction relation used in the statement.

$E_{\mathsf{MB}} \models\ \downarrow\! k \cdot \forall b\,\{p, o\} \cdot \mathsf{close\text{-}enough}(p, o) \land \mathsf{free}(p)$

$\qquad \Rightarrow [p\,o\ \mathsf{bind}\ c]\ \mathsf{part\text{-}of}(p, c) \land @k \cdot \neg b c \land \mathsf{brane}(c) = \mathsf{brane}(o).$

The actual proof is performed, according to Proposition 2, in two stages: first we translate the proof goal to PFOL, then we use HETS [23] along with automated first-order theorem provers such as E [28], SPASS [31], and Vampire [26] to further analyse it – the way we combine provers is similar to the Sledgehammer tool [3] for Isabelle/HOL. The same technology is employed to check a much more complex requirement, namely that cargo molecules can indeed be transported between organelles through the stages of membrane budding. Using typed modalities, this property can be formalized as a DNI-sentence of the form:

$$\mathsf{enclosed}(x, \mathsf{brane}(os)) \Rightarrow \langle p_j\ os\ \mathsf{bind}\ c_j \rangle \ldots \langle p_1\ x\ \mathsf{capture} \rangle \ldots \langle c_1\ c_2\ \mathsf{merge}\ c \rangle \ldots$$
$$\langle c\ \mathsf{bud}\ b \rangle \ldots [b\ \mathsf{split}\ v] \ldots \langle p_j\ v\ \mathsf{uncoat} \rangle \ldots \langle v\ ot\ \mathsf{fuse} \rangle \mathsf{enclosed}(x, \mathsf{brane}(ot))$$

where x is a variable of sort Cargo, os and ot are variables of sort Organelle (corresponding to the source and target organelle, respectively), p_j are variables of sort Protein, c and c_j are variables of sort Coat, b is a Bud and, lastly, v is a Vesicle. The full formalization of this requirement is available in [29].

5   Conclusions

In this paper, we have presented an extension of the conventional modal-logic approach to reconfigurable systems, giving prominence to the interactions that trigger reconfigurations (through typed modalities) and to the structural changes that they induce (through varying quantification domains and flexible attributes). In addition, we have shown how the standard translation of modal into first-order logic can be adapted for dynamic networks of interactions, providing in this way a sound and complete proof-by-translation technique for specifications and properties written using the formalism advanced in Sect. 3. To illustrate the contributions of our work, we have formalized the biological process of membrane budding – a non-trivial example of reconfigurable system that raises significant challenges to previously developed modal specification languages.

The full analysis of membrane budding, which we have only touched upon in this paper, has revealed the need for further enhancements of our specification and verification technology. The proof goals we considered in Sect. 4 are pairs consisting of a monolithic theory presentation (say, of membrane budding) and a DNI-property whose entailment is scrutinized. Because we rely on automated theorem provers, this approach works well for simple verification tasks, but it quickly becomes impractical in large-scale case studies. To carry out the analysis of membrane budding in [29], we made use of standard modularization techniques from institution theory [27] both at the specification and at the verification stage; the original analysis task is thus reduced to smaller proof goals, which are easier to discharge automatically. We aim to further investigate the institution-theoretic foundations of this method in the context of DNI.

In the long run, through DNI we seek to develop a formal specification framework based on modal logic and typed modalities for reasoning about systems that exhibit interactive behaviour and whose configurations change dynamically as a result of interactions. Besides modal logic and its hybrid variants, there are numerous other approaches to reconfigurable systems based on graph or term rewriting, action calculi, tile logic [15] and, notably, bigraphs [22] – which inspired us to study membrane budding in the first place. Therefore, another natural next step is to study the relationship between DNI and logics such as BiLog [9], which are effective at capturing bigraphs and their substructures.

References

1. Blackburn, P.: Representation, reasoning, and relational structures: a hybrid logic manifesto. Logic J. IGPL **8**(3), 339–365 (2000)
2. Blackburn, P., Marx, M.: Tableaux for quantified hybrid logic. In: Egly, U., Fermüller, C.G. (eds.) TABLEAUX 2002. LNCS (LNAI), vol. 2381, pp. 38–52. Springer, Heidelberg (2002). https://doi.org/10.1007/3-540-45616-3_4
3. Blanchette, J.C., Böhme, S., Paulson, L.C.: Extending Sledgehammer with SMT solvers. J. Autom. Reasoning **51**(1), 109–128 (2013)
4. Braüner, T.: First-order hybrid logic: introduction and survey. Logic J. IGPL **22**(1), 155–165 (2014)
5. Cerioli, M., Meseguer, J.: May I borrow your logic? (Transporting logical structures along maps). Theor. Comput. Sci. **173**(2), 311–347 (1997)
6. Cerioli, M., Mossakowski, T., Reichel, H.: From total equational to partial first-order logic. In: Algebraic Foundations of Systems Specification, pp. 31–104. IFIP State-of-the-Art Reports. Springer, Cham (1999). https://doi.org/10.1007/978-3-642-59851-7_3
7. Clarke, D.: A basic logic for reasoning about connector reconfiguration. Fundamenta Informaticae **82**(4), 361–390 (2008)
8. Codescu, M.: Hybridisation of institutions in Hets. In: CALCO 2019. LIPIcs, vol. 139, pp. 17:1–17:10. Schloss Dagstuhl - Leibniz-Zentrum für Informatik (2019)
9. Conforti, G., Macedonio, D., Sassone, V.: Static BiLog: a unifying language for spatial structures. Fundamenta Informaticae **80**(1–3), 91–110 (2007)
10. Diaconescu, R.: Introducing H, an institution-based formal specification and verification language. Logica Universalis **14**(2), 259–277 (2020)
11. Diaconescu, R., Madeira, A.: Encoding hybridized institutions into first-order logic. Math. Struct. Comput. Sci. **26**(5), 745–788 (2016)
12. Fiadeiro, J.L., Lopes, A.: A model for dynamic reconfiguration in service-oriented architectures. Softw. Syst. Model. **12**(2), 349–367 (2013)
13. Fiadeiro, J.L., Țuțu, I., Lopes, A., Pavlovic, D.: Logics for actor networks: a two-stage constrained-hybridisation approach. J. Logical Algebraic Meth. Program. **106**, 141–166 (2019)
14. Fitting, M., Mendelsohn, R.L.: First-Order Modal Logic. Kluwer Academic Publishers, Boston (1998)

15. Gadducci, F., Montanari, U.: Comparing logics for rewriting: rewriting logic, action calculi and tile logic. Theor. Comput. Sci. **285**(2), 319–358 (2002)
16. Garson, J.W.: Quantification in modal logic. In: Gabbay, D.M., Guenthner, F. (eds.) Handbook of Philosophical Logic, vol. 3. Springer, Cham (2001). https://doi.org/10.1007/978-94-017-0454-0_3
17. Goguen, J.A., Burstall, R.M.: Institutions: abstract model theory for specification and programming. J. ACM **39**(1), 95–146 (1992)
18. Hennicker, R., Madeira, A., Knapp, A.: A hybrid dynamic logic for event/data-based systems. In: Hähnle, R., van der Aalst, W. (eds.) FASE 2019. LNCS, vol. 11424, pp. 79–97. Springer, Cham (2019). https://doi.org/10.1007/978-3-030-16722-6_5
19. Kirchhausen, T.: Three ways to make a vesicle. Nature reviews. Mol. Cell Biol. **1**, 187–198 (2000)
20. Krivine, J., Milner, R., Troina, A.: Stochastic bigraphs. In: MFPS 2008. Electronic Notes in Theoretical Computer Science, vol. 218, pp. 73–96. Elsevier (2008)
21. Madeira, A., Neves, R., Barbosa, L.S., Martins, M.A.: A method for rigorous design of reconfigurable systems. Sci. Comput. Program. **132**, 50–76 (2016)
22. Milner, R.: The Space and Motion of Communicating Agents. Cambridge University Press, Cambridge (2009)
23. Mossakowski, T., Maeder, C., Lüttich, K.: The heterogeneous tool set (Hets). In: The 4th International Verification Workshop. CEUR Workshop Proceedings, vol. 259. CEUR-WS.org (2007)
24. Pratt, V.R.: Semantical considerations on Floyd-Hoare logic. In: 17th Annual Symposium on Foundations of Computer Science, pp. 109–121. IEEE Computer Society (1976)
25. Regot, S., Macía, J., Conde-Pueyo, N., Furukawa, K., Kjellén, J., Peeters, T., Hohmann, S., de Nadal, E., Posas, F., Solé, R.V.: Distributed biological computation with multicellular engineered networks. Nature **469**(7329), 207–211 (2011)
26. Riazanov, A., Voronkov, A.: The design and implementation of Vampire. AI Commun. **15**(2–3), 91–110 (2002)
27. Sannella, D., Tarlecki, A.: Foundations of Algebraic Specification and Formal Software Development. Monographs in Theoretical Computer Science. An EATCS Series, Springer, Heidelberg (2011). https://doi.org/10.1007/978-3-642-17336-3
28. Schulz, S., Cruanes, S., Vukmirović, P.: Faster, higher, stronger: E 2.3. In: Fontaine, P. (ed.) CADE 2019. LNCS (LNAI), vol. 11716, pp. 495–507. Springer, Cham (2019). https://doi.org/10.1007/978-3-030-29436-6_29
29. Țuțu, I., Chiriță, C.E., Fiadeiro, J.L.: A DNI-specification of membrane budding. Ontohub (2021). https://ontohub.org/dni
30. Țuțu, I., Chiriță, C.E., Lopes, A., Fiadeiro, J.L.: Logical support for bike-sharing system design. In: ter Beek, M.H., Fantechi, A., Semini, L. (eds.) From Software Engineering to Formal Methods and Tools, and Back. LNCS, vol. 11865, pp. 152–171. Springer, Cham (2019). https://doi.org/10.1007/978-3-030-30985-5_10
31. Weidenbach, C., Dimova, D., Fietzke, A., Kumar, R., Suda, M., Wischnewski, P.: SPASS version 3.5. In: Schmidt, R.A. (ed.) CADE 2009. LNCS (LNAI), vol. 5663, pp. 140–145. Springer, Heidelberg (2009). https://doi.org/10.1007/978-3-642-02959-2_10

Probabilities

On Lexicographic Proof Rules for Probabilistic Termination

Krishnendu Chatterjee[1], Ehsan Kafshdar Goharshady[2], Petr Novotný[3],
Jiří Zárevúcky[3], and Đorđe Žikelić[1(✉)]

[1] IST Austria, Klosterneuburg, Austria
{krishnendu.chatterjee,djordje.zikelic}@ist.ac.at
[2] Ferdowsi University of Mashhad, Mashhad, Iran
e.kafshdargoharshady@mail.um.ac.ir
[3] Masaryk University, Brno, Czech Republic
{petr.novotny,xzarevuc}@fi.muni.cz

Abstract. We consider the almost-sure (a.s.) termination problem for probabilistic programs, which are a stochastic extension of classical imperative programs. Lexicographic ranking functions provide a sound and practical approach for termination of non-probabilistic programs, and their extension to probabilistic programs is achieved via lexicographic ranking supermartingales (LexRSMs). However, LexRSMs introduced in the previous work have a limitation that impedes their automation: all of their components have to be non-negative in all reachable states. This might result in LexRSM not existing even for simple terminating programs. Our contributions are twofold: First, we introduce a generalization of LexRSMs which allows for some components to be negative. This standard feature of non-probabilistic termination proofs was hitherto not known to be sound in the probabilistic setting, as the soundness proof requires a careful analysis of the underlying stochastic process. Second, we present polynomial-time algorithms using our generalized LexRSMs for proving a.s. termination in broad classes of linear-arithmetic programs.

Keywords: Probabilistic programs · Termination · Martingales

1 Introduction

The extension of classical imperative programs with randomization gives rise to probabilistic programs (PPs) [45], which are used in multitude of applications, including stochastic network protocols [7,39,56,75], randomized algorithms [32,66], security [9,10], machine learning, and planning [25,41,44,50, 73,74,77]. The analysis of PPs is an active research area in formal methods [1,18,20,21,33,51,52,69,70,78]. PPs can be extended with nondeterminism to allow over-approximating program parts that are too complex for static analysis [30,59].

© Springer Nature Switzerland AG 2021
M. Huisman et al. (Eds.): FM 2021, LNCS 13047, pp. 619–639, 2021.
https://doi.org/10.1007/978-3-030-90870-6_33

For non-probabilistic programs, the *termination* problem asks whether a given program *always* terminates. While the problem is well-known to be undecidable over Turing-complete programs, many sound automated techniques that work well for practical programs have been developed [27,28]. Such techniques typically seek a suitable *certificate* of termination. Particularly relevant certificates are *ranking functions (RFs)* [15,26,37,71,72,76] mapping program states into a well-founded domain, forcing a strict decrease of the function value in every step. The basic ranking functions are 1-dimensional, which is often insufficient for complex control-flow structures. Lexicographic ranking functions (LexRFs) are multi-dimensional extensions of RFs that provide an effective approach to termination analysis [2,15–17,29,43]. The literature typically restricts to linear LexRFs for linear-arithmetic (LA) programs, as LA reasoning can be more efficiently automated compared to non-linear arithmetic.

For probabilistic programs, the termination problem considers aspects of the probabilistic behaviors as well. The most fundamental is the *almost-sure (a.s.)* termination problem, which asks whether a given PP terminates with probability 1. One way of proving a.s. termination is via *ranking supermartingales (RSMs)*, a probabilistic analogue of ranking functions named so due to the connection with (super)martingale stochastic processes [80]. There is a rich body of work on 1-dimensional RSMs, while the work [1] introduces lexicographic RSMs. In probabilistic programs, a transition τ available in some state s yields a probability distribution over the successor states. The conditions defining RSMs are formulated in terms of the expectation operator $\mathbb{E}^\tau$ of this distribution. In particular, *lexicographic ranking supermartingales* (LexRSMs) of [1] are functions f mapping program states to $\mathbb{R}^d$, such that for each transition τ there exists a component $1 \le i \le d$, satisfying, for any reachable state s at which τ is enabled, the following conditions *P-RANK* and *S-NNEG* (with f_i the i-component of f and $s \models G(\tau)$ denoting the fact that s satisfies the guard of τ):

1. $P\text{-}RANK(f,\tau) \equiv s \models G(\tau) \Rightarrow \left(\mathbb{E}^\tau[f_i(s')] \le f_i(s) - 1 \text{ and } \mathbb{E}^\tau[f_j(s')] \le f_j(s) \right.$
   for all $1 \le j < i$).
2. $S\text{-}NNEG(f,\tau) \equiv s \models G(\tau) \Rightarrow \left(f_j(s) \ge 0 \text{ for all } 1 \le j \le d \right)$.

(We use the standard primed notation from program analysis, i.e. s' is the probabilistically chosen successor of s when performing τ.) The *P-RANK* condition enforces an expected decrease in lexicographic ordering, while *S-NNEG* stands for "strong non-negativity". Proving the soundness of LexRSMs for proving a.s. termination is highly non-trivial and requires reasoning about complex stochastic processes [1]. Apart from the soundness proof, [1] also presents an algorithm for the synthesis of linear LexRSMs.

While LexRSMs improved the applicability of a.s. termination proving, their usage is impeded by the *restrictiveness of strong non-negativity* due to which a linear LexRSM might not exist even for simple a.s. terminating programs. This is a serious drawback from the automation perspective, since even if such a program admits a non-linear LexRSM, efficient automated tools that restrict to linear-arithmetic reasoning would not be able to find it.

$\ell_0:$ **while** $y \geq 0$ **do**
$\qquad x := y;$
$\ell_1:$ $\qquad$ **while** $x \geq 0$ **do**
$\qquad\qquad x := x - 1 + Norm(0, 1)$
$\qquad$ **od**;
$\qquad y := y - 1$
$\quad$ **od**

$\ell_0:$ **while** $x \geq 0$ **do**
$\qquad$ **if** $y \geq 0$ **then**
$\qquad\qquad y := y + Uni[-7, 1]$
$\qquad$ **else**
$\qquad\qquad x := x + Uni[-7, 1];$
$\ell_1:$ $\qquad\qquad y := y + Uni[-7, 1]$
$\qquad$ **fi** **od**

(a) $\qquad\qquad\qquad\qquad\qquad\qquad\qquad$ (b)

Fig. 1. Motivating examples. $Norm(\mu, \sigma)$ samples from the normal distribution with mean μ and std. deviation σ. $Uni[a, b]$ samples uniformly from the interval $[a, b]$. Location labels are the "ℓ_i": one location per loop head and one additional location in (b) so as to have one assignment per transition (a technical requirement for our approach). A formal representation of the programs via *probabilistic control flow graphs* is presented later, in Sect. 4.

Consider the program in Fig. 1a. By employing simple random-walk arguments, we can manually prove that the program terminates a.s. A linear LexRSM proving this needs to have a component containing a positive multiple of x at the head of the inner while-loop (ℓ_1). However, due to the sampling from the normal distribution, which has unbounded support, the value of x inside the inner loop cannot be bounded from below. Hence, the program does not admit a linear LexRSM. In general, LexRSMs with strong non-negativity do not handle well programs with unbounded-support distributions.

Now consider the program in Fig. 1b. It can be again shown that this PP terminates a.s.; however, this cannot be witnessed by a linear LexRSM: to rank the "if-branch" transition, there must be a component with a positive multiple of y in ℓ_0. But y can become arbitrarily negative within the else branch, and cannot be bounded from below by a linear function of x.

Contribution: Generalized Lexicographic RSMs. In the non-probabilistic setting, strong non-negativity can be relaxed to *partial non-negativity* (*P-NNEG*), where only the components which are to the left of the "ranking component" i (inclusive) need to be non-negative (Ben-Amram–Genaim RFs [12]). We show that in the probabilistic setting, the same relaxation is possible under additional *expected leftward non-negativity* constraint *EXP-NNEG*. Formally, we say that f is a *generalized lexicographic ranking supermartingale* (GLexRSM) if for any transition τ there is $1 \leq i \leq d$ such that for any reachable state s at which τ is enabled we have $P\text{-}RANK(f, \tau) \wedge P\text{-}NNEG(f, \tau) \wedge EXP\text{-}NNEG(f, \tau)$, where

$$P\text{-}NNEG(f, \tau) \quad \equiv \quad s \models G(\tau) \Rightarrow \big(f_j(s) \geq 0 \text{ for all } 1 \leq j \leq i\big)$$

$$EXP\text{-}NNEG(f, \tau) \quad \equiv \quad s \models G(\tau) \Rightarrow \big(\mathbb{E}^\tau[f_j(s') \cdot \mathbb{I}_{<j}(s')] \geq 0 \text{ for all } 1 \leq j \leq i\big),$$

with $\mathbb{I}_{<j}$ being the indicator function of the set of all states in which a transition ranked by a component $< j$ is enabled.

We first formulate GLexRSMs as an abstract proof rule for general stochastic processes. We then instantiate them into the setting of probabilistic programs and define *GLexRSM maps,* which we prove to be sound for proving a.s. termination. These results are general and *not specific* to linear-arithmetic programs.

Contribution: Polynomial Algorithms for Linear GLexRSMs.

1. For linear arithmetic PPs in which sampling instructions use bounded-support distributions we show that the problem LINGLEXPP of deciding whether a given PP with a given set of *linear invariants* admits a linear GLexRSM is decidable in polynomial time. Also, our algorithm computes the witnessing linear GLexRSM whenever it exists. In particular, our approach proves the a.s. termination of the program in Fig. 1b.
2. Building on results of item 1, we construct a sound polynomial-time algorithm for a.s. termination proving in PPs that *do perform* sampling from *unbounded-support* distributions. In particular, the algorithm proves a.s. termination for our motivating example in Fig. 1a.

Related Work. Martingale-based termination literature mostly focused on 1-dimensional RSMs [18,20,21,23,36,40,42,48,60,61,63]. RSMs themselves can be seen as generalizations of Lyapunov ranking functions from control theory [14,38]. Recently, the work [49] pointed out the unsoundess of the 1-dimensional RSM-based proof rule in [36] due to insufficient lower bound conditions and provided a corrected version. On the multi-dimensional front, it was shown in [36] that requiring components of (lexicographic) RSMs to be nonnegative only at points where they are used to rank some enabled transition (analogue of Bradley-Manna-Sipma LexRFs [15]) is unsound for proving a.s. termination. This illustrates the intricacies of dealing with lower bounds in the design of a.s. termination certificates. Lexicographic RSMs with strong non-negativity were introduced in [1]. The work [24] produces an ω-regular decomposition of program's control-flow graph, with each program component ranked by a different RSM. This approach does not require a lexicographic ordering of RSMs, but each component in the decomposition must be ranked by a single-dimensional non-negative RSM. RSM approaches were also used for cost analysis [6,69,79] and additional liveness and safety properties [8,19,23].

Logical calculi for reasoning about properties of probabilistic programs (including termination) were studied in [34,35,54,55] and extended to programs with non-determinism in [46,52,58,59,70]. In particular [58,59,61] formalize RSM-like proof certificates within the *weakest pre-expectation (WPE)* calculus [64,65]. The power of this calculus allows for reasoning about complex programs [61, Sect. 5], but the proofs typically require a human input. Theoretical connections between martingales and the WPE calculus were recently explored in [47]. There is also a rich body of work on analysis of probabilistic functional programs, where the aim is typically to obtain a general type system [4,31,53,57] for reasoning about termination properties (automation for discrete probabilistic term rewrite systems was shown in [5]).

As for other approaches to a.s. termination, for *finite-state programs* with nondeterminism a sound and complete method was given in [33], while [62] considers a.s. termination proving through abstract interpretation. The work [51] shows that proving a.s. termination is harder (in terms of arithmetical hierarchy) than proving termination of non-probabilistic programs.

The computational complexity of the construction of lexicographic ranking functions in non-probabilistic programs was studied in [11,12].

Paper Organization. The paper is split in two parts: the first one is "abstract", with mathematical preliminaries (Sect. 2) and definition and soundness proof of abstract GLexRSMs (Sect. 3). We also present an example showing that "GLexRSMs" without the expected leftward non-negativity constraint are not sound. The second part covers application to probabilistic programs: preliminaries on the program syntax and semantics (Sect. 4), a GLexRSM-based proof rule for a.s. termination (Sect. 5), and the outline of our algorithms (Sect. 6).

2   Mathematical Preliminaries

We use boldface notation for vectors, e.g. $\mathbf{x}$, $\mathbf{y}$, etc., and we denote an i-th component of a vector $\mathbf{x}$ by $\mathbf{x}[i]$. For an n-dimensional vector $\mathbf{x}$, index $1 \leq i \leq n$, and number a we denote by $\mathbf{x}(i \leftarrow a)$ a vector $\mathbf{y}$ such that $\mathbf{y}[i] = a$ and $\mathbf{y}[j] = \mathbf{x}[j]$ for all $1 \leq j \leq n$, $j \neq i$. For two real numbers a and b, we use $a \cdot b$ to denote their product.

We assume familiarity with basics of probability theory [80]. A *probability space* is a triple $(\Omega, \mathcal{F}, \mathbb{P})$, where Ω is a *sample space*, $\mathcal{F}$ is a *sigma-algebra* of measurable sets over Ω, and $\mathbb{P}$ is a *probability measure* on $\mathcal{F}$. A *random variable (r.v.)* $R \colon \Omega \to \mathbb{R} \cup \{\pm\infty\}$ is an $\mathcal{F}$-*measurable* real-valued function (i.e. $\{\omega \mid R(\omega) \leq x\} \in \mathcal{F}$ for all $x \in \mathbb{R}$) and we denote by $\mathbb{E}[R]$ its *expected value*. A *random vector* is a vector whose every component is a random variable. We denote by $\mathbf{X}[j]$ the j-component of a random vector $\mathbf{X}$. A (discrete time) *stochastic process* in a probability space $(\Omega, \mathcal{F}, \mathbb{P})$ is an infinite sequence of random vectors in this space. We will also use random variables of the form $R \colon \Omega \to A$ for some finite or countable set A, which easily translates to the real-valued variables.

Let $(\Omega, \mathcal{F}, \mathbb{P})$ be a probability space and let X be a random variable. A *conditional expectation* of X given a sub-sigma algebra $\mathcal{F}' \subseteq \mathcal{F}$ is any real-valued random variable Y s.t.: i) Y is $\mathcal{F}'$-measurable; and ii) for each set $A \in \mathcal{F}'$ it holds that $\mathbb{E}[X \cdot \mathbb{I}(A)] = \mathbb{E}[Y \cdot \mathbb{I}(A)]$. Here, $\mathbb{I}(A) \colon \Omega \to \{0,1\}$ is an *indicator function* of A, i.e. function returning 1 for each $\omega \in A$ and 0 for each $\omega \in \Omega \setminus A$.

It is known [3] that a random variable satisfying the properties of conditional expectation exists whenever a) $\mathbb{E}[\|X\|] < \infty$, i.e. X is *integrable*, or b) X is real-valued and nonnegative (though these two conditions are not necessary). Moreover, whenever the conditional expectation exists it is also known to be a.s. unique. We denote this a.s. unique conditional expectation by $\mathbb{E}[X|\mathcal{F}']$. It holds that for any $\mathcal{F}'$-measurable bounded r.v. Z, we have $\mathbb{E}[X \cdot Z|\mathcal{F}'] = \mathbb{E}[X|\mathcal{F}'] \cdot Z$, whenever the former conditional expectation exists [80, Theorem 9.7(j)].

A *filtration* in $(\Omega, \mathcal{F}, \mathbb{P})$ is an increasing (w.r.t. set inclusion) sequence $\{\mathcal{F}_t\}_{t=0}^{\infty}$ of sub-sigma-algebras of $\mathcal{F}$. A *stopping time* w.r.t. a filtration $\{\mathcal{F}_t\}_{t=0}^{\infty}$ is a random variable T taking values in $\mathbb{N} \cup \{\infty\}$ s.t. for every t the set $\{T = t\} = \{\omega \in \Omega \mid T(\omega) = t\}$ belongs to $\mathcal{F}_t$. Intuitively, T returns a time step in which some process should be "stopped", and the decision to stop is made solely on the information available at the current step.

3   Generalized Lexicographic Ranking Supermartingales

In this section, we introduce *generalized lexicographic ranking supermartingales (GLexRSMs)*: an abstract concept that is not necessarily connected to PPs, but which is crucial for the soundness of our new proof rule for a.s. termination.

Definition 1 (Generalized Lexicographic Ranking Supermartingale).
Let $(\Omega, \mathcal{F}, \mathbb{P})$ be a probability space and let $(\mathcal{F}_t)_{t=0}^{\infty}$ be a filtration of $\mathcal{F}$. Suppose that T is a stopping time w.r.t. $\mathcal{F}$. An n-dimensional real valued stochastic process $(\mathbf{X}_t)_{t=0}^{\infty}$ is a generalized lexicographic ranking supermartingale for T (GLexRSM) if:

1. *For each $t \in \mathbb{N}_0$ and $1 \leq j \leq n$, the random variable $\mathbf{X}_t[j]$ is $\mathcal{F}_t$-measurable.*
2. *For each $t \in \mathbb{N}_0$, $1 \leq j \leq n$, and $A \in \mathcal{F}_{t+1}$, the conditional expectation $\mathbb{E}[\mathbf{X}_{t+1}[j] \cdot \mathbb{I}(A) \mid \mathcal{F}_t]$ exists.*
3. *For each $t \in \mathbb{N}_0$, there exists a partition of the set $\{T > t\}$ into n subsets $L_1^t, \ldots, L_n^t$, all of them $\mathcal{F}_t$-measurable (i.e., belonging to $\mathcal{F}_t$), such that for each $1 \leq j \leq n$*
   - $\mathbb{E}[\mathbf{X}_{t+1}[j] \mid \mathcal{F}_t](\omega) \leq \mathbf{X}_t[j](\omega)$ *for each $\omega \in \cup_{j'=j}^{n} L_{j'}^t$,*
   - $\mathbb{E}[\mathbf{X}_{t+1}[j] \mid \mathcal{F}_t](\omega) \leq \mathbf{X}_t[j](\omega) - 1$ *for each $\omega \in L_j^t$,*
   - $\mathbf{X}_t[j](\omega) \geq 0$ *for each $\omega \in \cup_{j'=j}^{n} L_{j'}^t$,*
   - $\mathbb{E}[\mathbf{X}_{t+1}[j] \cdot \mathbb{I}(\cup_{j'=0}^{j-1} L_{j'}^{t+1}) \mid \mathcal{F}_i](\omega) \geq 0$ *for each $\omega \in \cup_{j'=j}^{n} L_{j'}^t$, with $L_0^{t+1} = \{T \leq t+1\}$.*

Intuitively, we may think of each $\omega \in \Omega$ as a trajectory of process that evolves over time (in the second part of our paper, this will be a probabilistic program run). Then, $\mathbf{X}_t$ is a vector function depending on the first t time steps (each $\mathbf{X}_t[j]$ is $\mathcal{F}_t$-measurable), while T is the time at which the trajectory is stopped. Then in point 3 of the definition, the first two items encode the expected (conditional) lexicographic decrease of $\mathbf{X}_t$, the third item encodes non-negativity of components to the left (inclusive) of the one which "ranks" ω in step t, and the last item encodes the expected leftward non-negativity (sketched in Sect. 1). For each $1 \leq j \leq n$ and time step $t \geq 0$, the set L_j^t contains all $\omega \in \{T > t\}$ which are "ranked" by the component j at time t. An *instance* of an n-dimensional GLexRSM $\{\mathbf{X}_t\}_{t=0}^{\infty}$ is a tuple $(\mathbf{X}_{t=0}^{\infty}, \{L_1^t, \ldots, L_n^t\}_{t=0}^{\infty})$, where the second component is a sequence of partitions of Ω satisfying the condition in Definition 1. We say that $\omega \in \Omega$ has *level j* in step t of the instance $((\mathbf{X}_t)_{t=0}^{\infty}, (L_1^t, \ldots, L_n^t)_{t=0}^{\infty})$ if $T(\omega) > t$ and $\omega \in L_j^t$. If $T(\omega) \leq t$, we say that the level of ω at step t is 0.

We now state the main theorem of this section, which underlies the soundness of our new method for proving almost-sure termination.

Theorem 1. *Let $(\Omega, \mathcal{F}, \mathbb{P})$ be a probability space, $(\mathcal{F}_t)_{t=0}^{\infty}$ a filtration of $\mathcal{F}$ and T a stopping time w.r.t. $\mathcal{F}$. If there is an instance $((\mathbf{X}_t)_{t=0}^{\infty}, (L_1^t, \ldots, L_n^t)_{t=0}^{\infty})$ of a GLexRSM over $(\Omega, \mathcal{F}, \mathbb{P})$ for T, then $\mathbb{P}[T < \infty] = 1$.*

In [1], a mathematical notion of LexRSMs is defined and a result for LexRSMs analogous to our Theorem 1 is established. Thus, the first part of our proof mostly resembles the proof of Theorem 3.3. in [1], up to the point of defining the stochastic process $(Y_t)_{t=0}^{\infty}$ in Eq. (1). After that, the proof of [1] crucially relies on nonnegativity of each $\mathbf{X}_t[j]$ and Y_t at every $\omega \in \Omega$ that is guaranteed by LexRSMs, and it cannot be adapted to the case of GLexRSMs. Below we first show that, for GLexRSMs, $\mathbb{E}[Y_t] \geq 0$ for each $t \geq 0$, and then we present a very elegant argument via the Borel-Cantelli lemma [80, Theorem 2.7] which shows that this boundedness of expectation is sufficient for the theorem claim to hold.

Proof (Sketch of Proof of Theorem 1). We proceed by contradiction. Suppose that there exists an instance of a GLexRSM but that $\mathbb{P}[T = \infty] > 0$. First, we claim that there exists $1 \leq k \leq n$ and $s, M \in \mathbb{N}_0$ such that the set B of all $\omega \in \Omega$ for which the following properties hold has positive measure, i.e. $\mathbb{P}[B] > 0$: (1) $T(\omega) = \infty$, (2) $\mathbf{X}_s[k](\omega) \leq M$, (3) for each $t \geq s$, the level of ω at step t is at least k, and (4) the level of ω equals k infinitely many times. The claim is proved by several applications of the union bound, see the extended version of the paper [22].

Since B is defined in terms of tail properties of ω ("level is at least k *infinitely many times*") it is not necessarily $\mathcal{F}_t$-measurable for any t. Hence, we define a stochastic process $(Y_t)_{t=0}^{\infty}$ such that each Y_t is $\mathcal{F}_t$-measurable, and which satisfies the desirable properties of $(\mathbf{X}_t[k])_{t=0}^{\infty}$ on B.

Let $D = \{\omega \in \Omega \mid \mathbf{X}_s[k](\omega) \leq M \wedge \omega \in \cup_{j=k}^{n} L_j^s\}$. Note that D is $\mathcal{F}_t$-measurable for $t \geq s$. We define a stopping time F w.r.t. $(\mathcal{F}_t)_{t=0}^{\infty}$ via $F(\omega) = \inf\{t \geq s \mid \omega \notin \cup_{j'=k}^{n} L_{j'}^t\}$; then a stochastic process $(Y_t)_{t=0}^{\infty}$ via

$$
Y_t(\omega) = \begin{cases} 0, & \text{if } \omega \notin D, \\ M, & \text{if } \omega \in D, \text{ and } t < s, \\ \mathbf{X}_t[k](\omega), & \text{if } \omega \in D, \ t \geq s \text{ and } F(\omega) > t, \\ \mathbf{X}_{F(\omega)}[k](\omega), & \text{else.} \end{cases} \tag{1}
$$

A straightforward argument (presented in the extended version of the paper [22]) shows that for each $t \geq s$ we have $\mathbb{E}[Y_{t+1}] \leq \mathbb{E}[Y_t] - \mathbb{P}[L_k^t \cap D \cap \{F > t\}]$. By a simple induction we obtain:

$$
\mathbb{E}[Y_s] \geq \mathbb{E}[Y_t] + \sum_{r=s}^{t-1} \mathbb{P}[L_k^r \cap D \cap \{F > r\}]. \tag{2}
$$

Now, we show that $\mathbb{E}[Y_t] \geq 0$ for each $t \in \mathbb{N}_0$. The claim is clearly true for $t < s$, so suppose that $t \geq s$. We can then expand $\mathbb{E}[Y_t]$ as follows

$$\mathbb{E}[Y_t] = \mathbb{E}[Y_t \cdot \mathbb{I}(F = s)] + \sum_{r=s+1}^{t} \mathbb{E}[Y_t \cdot \mathbb{I}(F = r)] + \mathbb{E}[Y_t \cdot \mathbb{I}(F > t)]$$

$(Y_s \geq 0$ as $D \subseteq \cup_{j=k}^{n} L_j^s$ and $Y_t(\omega) \geq 0$ whenever $F(\omega) > t)$

$$\geq \sum_{r=s+1}^{t} \mathbb{E}[Y_t \cdot \mathbb{I}(F = r)] = \sum_{r=s+1}^{t} \mathbb{E}[Y_t \cdot \mathbb{I}(\{F = r\} \cap D)]$$

$(Y_t(\omega) = \mathbf{X}_{F(\omega)}[k](\omega)$ whenever $\omega \in D$, $t \geq s$ and $F(\omega) \leq t)$

$$= \sum_{r=s+1}^{t} \mathbb{E}[\mathbf{X}_r[k] \cdot \mathbb{I}(\cup_{j=0}^{k-1} L_j^r) \cdot \mathbb{I}(\{F > r - 1\} \cap D)]$$

(properties of cond. exp. & $\mathbb{I}(\{F > r - 1\} \cap D)$ is $\mathcal{F}_{r-1}$-measurable)

$$= \sum_{r=s+1}^{t} \mathbb{E}\left[\mathbb{E}[\mathbf{X}_r[k] \cdot \mathbb{I}(\cup_{j=0}^{k-1} L_j^r) \mid \mathcal{F}_{r-1}] \cdot \mathbb{I}(\{F > r - 1\} \cap D)\right] \geq 0$$

$(\mathbb{E}[\mathbf{X}_r[k] \cdot \mathbb{I}(\cup_{j=0}^{k-1} L_j^r) \mid \mathcal{F}_{r-1}](\omega) \geq 0$ for $\omega \in \{F > r - 1\} \subseteq \cup_{j=k}^{n} L_j^{r-1})$.

Plugging into Eq. (2) that $\mathbb{E}[Y_t] \geq 0$, we get $\mathbb{E}[Y_s] \geq \sum_{r=s}^{t-1} \mathbb{P}[L_k^r \cap D \cap \{F > r\}]$ for each $t \geq s$. By letting $t \to \infty$, we conclude $\mathbb{E}[Y_s] \geq \sum_{r=s}^{\infty} \mathbb{P}[L_k^r \cap D \cap \{F > r\}]$. As $Y_s \leq M$ and $Y_s = 0$ outside D, we know that $\mathbb{E}[Y_s] \leq M \cdot \mathbb{P}[D]$. We get

$$\sum_{r=s}^{\infty} \mathbb{P}[L_k^r \cap D \cap \{F = \infty\}] \leq \sum_{r=s}^{\infty} \mathbb{P}[L_k^r \cap D \cap \{F > r\}] \leq M \cdot \mathbb{P}[D] < \infty.$$

By the Borel-Cantelli lemma, $\mathbb{P}[L_k^r \cap D \cap \{F = \infty\}$ for infinitely many $r] = 0$. But the event $\{L_k^r \cap D \cap \{F = \infty\}$ for infinitely many $r\}$ is precisely the set of all runs $\omega \in \Omega$ for which (1) $T(\omega) = \infty$ (as ω never has level zero by $\omega \in L_k^r$ for inf. many k), (2) $\mathbf{X}_s[k](\omega) \leq M$, (3) for each $r \geq s$ the level of ω at step t is at least k, and (4) the level of ω is k infinitely many times. Hence, $B = \{L_k^r \cap D \cap \{F = \infty\}$ for infinitely many $r\}$ and $\mathbb{P}[B] = 0$, a contradiction.   □

GLexRSMs would be unsound without the expected leftward nonnegativity.

Example 1. Consider a one-dimensional stochastic process $(Y_t)_{t=0}^{\infty}$ s.t. $Y_0 = 1$ with probability 1 and then the process evolves as follows: in every step t, if $Y_t \geq 0$, then with probability $p_t = \frac{1}{4} \cdot \frac{1}{2^t}$ we put $Y_{t+1} = Y_t - \frac{2}{p_t}$ and with probability $1 - p_t$ we put $Y_{t+1} = Y_t + \frac{1}{1-p_t}$. If $Y_t < 0$, we put $Y_{t+1} = Y_t$. The underlying probability space can be constructed by standard techniques and we consider the filtration $(\mathcal{F}_t)_{t=0}^{\infty}$ s.t. $\mathcal{F}_t$ is the smallest sub-sigma-algebra making Y_t measurable. Finally, consider the stopping time T returning the first point in time when $Y_t < 0$. Then $T < \infty$ if and only if the process ever performs the

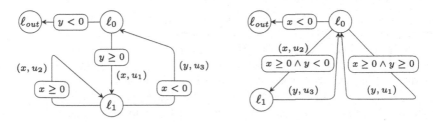

Fig. 2. The pCFGs of the programs presented in Fig. 1. Guards are shown in the rounded boxes, (absence of a box = guard is *true*). The update tuples are shown using variable aliases instead of indexes for better readability. On the left, we have $u_1 = y, u_2 = x - 1 + Norm(0,1)$, and $u_3 = y - 1$. On the right, we have $u_1 = y + Uni[-7,1], u_2 = x + Uni[-7,1]$, and $u_3 = y + Uni[-7,1]$

update $Y_{t+1} = Y_t - \frac{2}{p_t}$, but the probability that this happens is bounded by $\frac{1}{4} + \frac{3}{4} \cdot \frac{1}{8} + \frac{3}{4} \cdot \frac{7}{8} \cdot \frac{1}{16} + \cdots < \frac{1}{4} \sum_{t=0}^{\infty} \frac{1}{2^t} = \frac{1}{2} < 1$. At the same time, putting $L_1^t = \{Y_t \geq 0\}$ we get that the tuple $((Y_t)_{t=0}^{\infty}, (L_1^t)_{t=0}^{\infty})$ satisfies all conditions of Definition 1 apart from the last bullet of point 3.

4 Program-Specific Preliminaries

Arithmetic *expressions* in our programs are built from constants, program variables and standard Borel-measurable [13] arithmetic operators. We also allow sampling instructions to appear on right-hand sides of variable assignments as linear terms. An expression with no such terms is called *sampling-free*. We allow sampling from both discrete and continuous distributions. We denote by $\mathcal{D}$ the set of distributions appearing in the program with each $d \in \mathcal{D}$ assumed to be *integrable*, i.e. $\mathbb{E}_{X \sim d}[\|X\|] < \infty$. This is to ensure that expected value of each d over any measurable set is well-defined and finite.

A *predicate* over a set of variables V is a Boolean combination of *atomic predicates* of the form $E \leq E'$, where E, E' are sampling-free expressions whose all variables are from V. We denote by $\mathbf{x} \models \Psi$ the fact that the predicate Ψ is satisfied by substituting values of $\mathbf{x}$ for the corresponding variables in Ψ.

We represent probabilistic programs (PPs) via the standard concept of *probabilistic control flow graphs (pCFGs)* [1,21,23]. Formally, a (pCFG) is a tuple $\mathcal{C} = (L, V, \Delta, Up, G)$ where L is a finite set of *locations*; $V = \{x_1, \ldots, x_{|V|}\}$ is a finite set of *program variables*; Δ is a finite set of *transitions*, i.e. tuples of the form $\tau = (\ell, \delta)$, where ℓ is a location and δ is a distribution over *successor locations*. Δ is partitioned into two disjoint sets: Δ_{PB} of probabilistic branching transitions for which $|supp(\delta)| = 2$, and Δ_{NPB} of remaining transitions for which $|supp(\delta)| = 1$. Next, Up is a function assigning to each transition in Δ_{NPB} either the element $\perp$ (representing no variable update) or a tuple (i, u), where $1 \leq i \leq |V|$ is a *target variable index* and u is an *update element*, which can be either an expression (possibly involving a single sampling instruction), or a bounded interval $R \subseteq \mathbb{R}$ representing a nondeterministic update. Finally, G is a function assigning a predicate (a *guard*) over V to each transition in Δ_{NPB}. Figure 2 presents the pCFGs of our two motivating examples in Fig. 1.

Transitions in Δ_{PB} correspond to the "probabilistic branching" specified by the **if prob(p) then**... **else**... construct in imperative-style source code [1]. A program (pCFG) is *linear* (or *affine*) if all its expressions are *linear*, i.e. of the form $b + \sum_{i=1}^{n} a_i \cdot Z_i$ for constants $a_1, \ldots, a_n, b$ and program variables/sampling instructions Z_i. we assume that parameters of distributions are constants, so they do not depend on program variable values, a common assumption in martingale-based automated approaches to a.s. termination proving [1,18,21,24,49].

A *state* of a pCFG $\mathcal{C}$ is a tuple $(\ell, \mathbf{x})$, where ℓ is a location of $\mathcal{C}$ and $\mathbf{x}$ is a $|V|$-dimensional vector of *variable valuations*. A transition τ is *enabled* in $(\ell, \mathbf{x})$ if τ is outgoing from ℓ and $\mathbf{x} \models G(\tau)$. A state $c' = (\ell', \mathbf{x}')$ is a *successor* of a state $c = (\ell, \mathbf{x})$ if it can result from c by performing a transition τ enabled in c (see the extended version of the paper [22] for a formal definition).

A *finite path* of length k in $\mathcal{C}$ is a finite sequence $(\ell_0, \mathbf{x}_0) \cdots (\ell_k, \mathbf{x}_k)$ of states such that $\ell_0 = \ell_{init}$ and for each $0 \leq i < k$ the state $(\ell_{i+1}, \mathbf{x}_{i+1})$ is a successor of $(\ell_i, \mathbf{x}_i)$. A *run* in $\mathcal{C}$ is an infinite sequence of states whose every finite prefix is a finite path. We denote by $Fpath_{\mathcal{C}}$ and $Run_{\mathcal{C}}$ the sets of all finite paths and runs in $\mathcal{C}$, respectively. A state $(\ell, \mathbf{x})$ is *reachable* if there is, for some $\mathbf{x}_{init}$, a finite path starting in $(\ell_{init}, \mathbf{x}_{init})$ and ending in $(\ell, \mathbf{x})$.

The nondeterminism is resolved via schedulers. A *scheduler* is a function σ assigning: i) to every finite path ending in a state s, a probability distribution over transitions enabled in s; and ii) to every finite path that ends in a state in which a transition τ with a nondeterministic update $Up(\tau) = (i, R)$ is enabled, an integrable probability distribution over R. To make the program dynamics under a given scheduler well-defined, we restrict to *measurable* schedulers. This is standard in probabilistic settings [67,68] and hence we omit the formal definition.

We use the standard Markov Decision Process (MDP) semantics of pCFGs [1,21,52]. Each pCFG $\mathcal{C}$ induces a sample space $\Omega_{\mathcal{C}} = Run_{\mathcal{C}}$ and the standard *Borel* sigma-algebra $\mathcal{F}_{\mathcal{C}}$ over $\Omega_{\mathcal{C}}$. Moreover, a pCFG $\mathcal{C}$ together with a scheduler σ, initial location ℓ_{init}, and initial variable valuation $\mathbf{x}_{init}$ uniquely determine a probability measure $\mathbb{P}^{\sigma}_{\ell_{init}, \mathbf{x}_{init}}$ in the probability space $(\Omega_{\mathcal{C}}, \mathcal{F}_{\mathcal{C}}, \mathbb{P}^{\sigma}_{\ell_{init}, \mathbf{x}_{init}})$ capturing the rather intuitive dynamics of the programs execution: we start in state $(\ell_{init}, \mathbf{x}_{init})$ and in each step, a transition τ enabled in the current state is selected (using σ if multiple transitions are enabled). If $Up(\tau) = (i, u)$, then the value of variable x_i is changed according to u. The formal construction of $\mathbb{P}^{\sigma}_{\ell_{init}, \mathbf{x}_{init}}$ proceeds via the standard *cylinder construction* [3, Theorem 2.7.2]. We denote by $\mathbb{E}^{\sigma}_{\ell_{init}, \mathbf{x}_{init}}$ the expectation operator in the probability space $(\Omega_{\mathcal{C}}, \mathcal{F}_{\mathcal{C}}, \mathbb{P}^{\sigma}_{\ell_{init}, \mathbf{x}_{init}})$.

We stipulate that each pCFG has a special *terminal location* ℓ_{out} whose all outgoing transitions must be self-loops. We say that a run ϱ *terminates* if it contains a configuration whose first component is ℓ_{out}. We denote by *Terminates* the set of all terminating runs in $\Omega_{\mathcal{C}}$. We say that a program represented by a pCFG $\mathcal{C}$ terminates *almost-surely (a.s.)* if for each measurable scheduler σ and each initial variable valuation $\mathbf{x}_{init}$ it holds that $\mathbb{P}^{\sigma}_{\ell_{init}, \mathbf{x}_{init}}[\textit{Terminates}] = 1$.

5   GLexRSMs for Probabilistic Programs

In this section, we define a syntactic proof rule for a.s. termination of PPs, showing its soundness via Theorem 1. In what follows, let $\mathcal{C}$ be a pCFG.

Definition 2 (Measurable Map). *An n-dimensional measurable map (MM) is a vector $\boldsymbol{\eta} = (\eta_1, \ldots, \eta_n)$, where each η_i is a function mapping each location ℓ to a real-valued Borel-measurable function $\eta_i(\ell)$ over program variables. We say that $\boldsymbol{\eta}$ is a* linear expression map *(LEM) if each η_i is representable by a linear expression over program variables.*

The notion of pre-expectation was introduced in [55], was made syntactic in the Dijkstra wp-style in [64], and was extended to programs with continuous distributions in [18]. It formalizes the "one-step" expectation operator $\mathbb{E}^\tau$ we used on an intuitive level in the introduction. In the extended version of the paper [22], we generalize the definition of pre-expectation presented in [18] in order to allow taking expectation over subsets of successor states $\mathcal{C}$ (a necessity for handling the *EXP-NNEG* constraint). We say that a set S of states in $\mathcal{C}$ is *measurable*, if for each location ℓ in $\mathcal{C}$ we have that $\{\mathbf{x} \in \mathbb{R}^{|V|} \mid (\ell, \mathbf{x}) \in S\} \in \mathcal{B}(\mathbb{R}^{|V|})$, i.e. it is in the Borel sigma-algebra of $\mathbb{R}^{|V|}$. Furthermore, we also differentiate between the *maximal* and *minimal pre-expectation*, which may differ in the case of non-deterministic assignments in programs and intuitively are equal to the maximal resp. minimal value of the next-step expectation over all non-deterministic choices. Let η be a 1-dimensional MM, $\tau = (\ell, \delta)$ a transition and S be a measurable set of states in $\mathcal{C}$. We denote by $\text{max-pre}^\tau_{\eta,S}(s)$ the *maximal pre-expectation* of η in τ given S (i.e. the maximal expected value of η after making a step from s computed over successor states belonging to S), and similarly we denote by $\text{min-pre}^\tau_{\eta,S}$ the *minimal pre-expectation* of η in τ given S.

As in the case of non-probabilistic programs, termination certificates are supported by program invariants over-approximating the set of reachable states. An *invariant* in $\mathcal{C}$ is a function I which to each location ℓ of $\mathcal{C}$ assigns a Borel-measurable set $I(\ell) \subseteq \mathbb{R}^{|V|}$ such that for any state $(\ell, \mathbf{x})$ reachable in $\mathcal{C}$ it holds that $\mathbf{x} \in I(\ell)$. If each $I(\ell)$ is given by a conjunction of linear inequalities over program variables, we say that I is a *linear invariant*.

GLexRSM-Based Proof Rule for Almost-Sure Termination. Given $n \in \mathbb{N}$, we call a map $\text{lev} : \Delta \to \{0, 1, \ldots, n\}$ a *level map*. For $\tau \in \Delta$ we say that $\text{lev}(\tau)$ is its level. The level of a state is the largest level of any transition enabled at that state. We denote by $S_{\text{lev}}^{\leq j}$ the set of states with level $\leq j$.

Definition 3 (GLexRSM Map). *Let $\boldsymbol{\eta}$ be an n-dimensional MM and I an invariant in $\mathcal{C}$. We say that $\boldsymbol{\eta}$ is a* generalized lexicographic ranking supermartingale map *(GLexRSM map) supported by I, if there is a level map $\text{lev} : \Delta \to \{0, 1, \ldots, n\}$ such that $\text{lev}(\tau) = 0$ iff τ is a self-loop transition at ℓ_{out}, and for any transition $\tau = (\ell, \delta)$ with $\ell \neq \ell_{out}$ the following conditions hold:*

1. $P\text{-}RANK(\boldsymbol{\eta}, \tau) \equiv \mathbf{x} \in I(\ell) \cap G(\tau) \Rightarrow \left(max\text{-}pre^{\tau}_{\eta_{\mathsf{lev}(\tau)}}(\ell, \mathbf{x}) \leq \eta_{\mathsf{lev}(\tau)}(\ell, \mathbf{x}) - 1 \wedge \right.$
   $max\text{-}pre^{\tau}_{\eta_j}(\ell, \mathbf{x}) \leq \eta_j(\ell, \mathbf{x})$ for all $1 \leq j < \mathsf{lev}(\tau))$;
2. $P\text{-}NNEG(\boldsymbol{\eta}, \tau) \equiv \mathbf{x} \in I(\ell) \cap G(\tau) \Rightarrow \left(\eta_j(\ell, \mathbf{x}) \geq 0 \text{ for all } 1 \leq j \leq \mathsf{lev}(\tau)\right)$;
3. $EXP\text{-}NNEG(\boldsymbol{\eta}, \tau) \equiv \mathbf{x} \in I(\ell) \cap G(\tau) \Rightarrow min\text{-}pre^{\tau}_{\eta_j, S^{\leq j-1}_{\mathsf{lev}}}(\ell, \mathbf{x}) \geq 0$ for all
   $1 \leq j \leq \mathsf{lev}(\tau)$.

A *GLexRSM map* $\boldsymbol{\eta}$ is linear *(or LinGLexRSM map)* if it is also an LEM.

Theorem 2 (Soundness of GLexRSM-maps for a.s. Termination). *Let $\mathcal{C}$ be a pCFG and I an invariant in $\mathcal{C}$. Suppose that $\mathcal{C}$ admits an n-dimensional GLexRSM map $\boldsymbol{\eta}$ supported by I, for some $n \in \mathbb{N}$. Then $\mathcal{C}$ terminates a.s.*

The previous theorem, proved in the extended version of the paper [22], instantiates Theorem 1 to probability spaces of pCFGs. The instantiation is *not* straightforward. To ensure that a scheduler cannot "escape" ranking by intricate probabilistic mixing of transitions, we prove that it is sufficient to consider *deterministic* schedulers, which do not randomization among transitions. Also, previous martingale-based certificates of a.s. termination [1,21,36,40] often impose either nonnegativity or integrability of random variables defined by measurable maps in programs to ensure that their conditional expectations exist. We show that these conditional expectations exist even without such assumptions and in the presence of nondeterminism. This generalizes the result of [18] to PPs with nondeterminism.

Remark 1 (Comparison to [49]). The work [49] considers a modular approach. Given a loop whose body has already been proved a.s. terminating, they show that the loop terminates a.s. if it admits a 1-dimensional MM satisfying *P-RANK* for each transition in the loop, *P-NNEG* for the transition entering the loop, and the "*bounded expected difference*" property for all transitions. Hence, their approach is suited mainly for programs with incremental variable updates.

Modularity is also a feature of the approaches based on the weakest preexpectation calculus [58,59,61].

6 Algorithm for Linear Probabilistic Programs

We now present two algorithms for proving a.s. termination in linear probabilistic programs (LinPPs). The first algorithm considers LinPPs with sampling from bounded-support distributions, and we show that the problem of deciding the existence of LinGLexRSM maps for such LinPPs is decidable. Our second algorithm extends the first algorithm into a sound a.s. termination prover for general LinPPs. In what follows, let $\mathcal{C}$ be a LinPP and I a linear invariant in $\mathcal{C}$.

6.1 Linear Programs with Distributions of Bounded Support

Restricting to linear arithmetic is standard in automated a.s. termination proving, allowing to encode the existence of the termination certificate into systems of linear constraints [1,18,21,24]. In the case of LinGLexRSM maps, the difficulty lies in encoding the *EXP-NNEG* condition, as it involves integrating distributions in variable updates which cannot always be done analytically. We show, however, that for LinPPs with bounded-support sampling, we can define another condition which is easier to encode and which can replace *EXP-NNEG*. Formally, we say that a distribution $d \in \mathcal{D}$ has a *bounded support*, if there exists $N(d) \geq 0$ such that $\mathbb{P}_{X \sim d}[|X| > N(d)] = 0$. Here, we use $\mathbb{P}_{X \sim d}$ to denote the probability measure induced by a random variable X with the probability distribution d. We say that a LinPP has the *bounded support property (BSP)* if all distributions in the program have bounded support. For instance, the program in Fig. 1b has the BSP, whereas the program in Fig. 1a does not. Using the same notation as in Definition 3, we put:

$$W\text{-}EXP\text{-}NNEG(\boldsymbol{\eta}, \tau) \equiv \mathbf{x} \in I(\ell) \cap G(\tau) \Rightarrow \forall 1 \leq j \leq \mathsf{lev}(\tau) \text{ min-pre}_{\eta_j}^{\tau}(\ell, \mathbf{x}) \geq 0.$$

(The 'W' stands for "weak.") Intuitively, *EXP-NNEG* requires nonnegativity of the expected value of η_j when integrated over successor states of level smaller than j, whereas the condition *W-EXP-NNEG* requires nonnegativity of the expected value of η_j when integrated over all successor states. Since η_j is non-negative at successor states of level at least j, this new condition is weaker than *EXP-NNEG*. Nevertheless, the following lemma shows that in order to decide existence of LinGLexRSM maps for programs with the BSP, we may w.l.o.g. replace *EXP-NNEG* by *W-EXP-NNEG* for all transitions but for those of probabilistic branching. The proof of the lemma can be found in the extended version of the paper [22].

Lemma 1. *Let $\mathcal{C}$ be a LinPP with the BSP and I be a linear invariant in $\mathcal{C}$. If a LEM $\boldsymbol{\eta}$ satisfies conditions P-RANK and P-NNEG for all transitions, EXP-NNEG for all transitions in Δ_{PB} and W-EXP-NNEG for all other transitions, then $\boldsymbol{\eta}$ may be increased pointwise by a constant value in order to obtain a LinGLexRSM map.*

Algorithmic Results. Let $\mathrm{LINGLexPP}^{\mathrm{BOUNDED}}$ be the set of pairs $(\mathcal{C}, I)$ of a pCFG $\mathcal{C}$ representing a LinPP with the BSP and a linear invariant I in $\mathcal{C}$, such that $\mathcal{C}$ admits a LinGLexRSM map supported by I.

Theorem 3. *There is a polynomial-time algorithm deciding if a tuple $(\mathcal{C}, I)$ belongs to $\mathrm{LINGLexPP}^{\mathrm{BOUNDED}}$. Moreover, if the answer is yes, the algorithm outputs a witness in the form of a LinGLexRSM map of minimal dimension.*

The algorithm behind Theorem 3 is a generalization of algorithms in [1,2] finding LinLexRFs in non-probabilistic programs and LinLexRSM maps in PPs, respectively. Suppose that we are given a LinPP $\mathcal{C} = (L, V, \Delta, Up, G)$ with the BSP and a linear invariant I. Our algorithm stores a set $\mathcal{T}$ initialized to all transitions in $\mathcal{C}$. It then proceeds in iterations to compute new components of the witness. In each iteration it searches for a LEM η which is required to

1. be nonnegative on each $\tau = (\ell, \delta) \in \mathcal{T}$, i.e. $\forall \mathbf{x}. \mathbf{x} \in I(\ell) \cap G(\tau) \Rightarrow \eta(\ell, \mathbf{x}) \geq 0$;

2. be unaffecting on each $\tau = (\ell, \delta) \in \mathcal{T}$, i.e. $\forall \mathbf{x}. \mathbf{x} \in I(\ell) \cap G(\tau) \Rightarrow$ max-pre$_\eta^\tau(\ell, \mathbf{x}) \leq \eta(\ell, \mathbf{x})$;

3. have nonnegative minimal pre-expectation for each $\tau = (\ell, \delta) \in \mathcal{T} \setminus \Delta_{PB}$, i.e. $\forall \mathbf{x}. \mathbf{x} \in I(\ell) \cap G(\tau) \Rightarrow$ min-pre$_\eta^\tau(\ell, \mathbf{x}) \geq 0$;

4. if S is the set of states in $\mathcal{C}$ whose all enabled transitions have been removed from $\mathcal{T}$ in the previous algorithm iterations, $\forall \tau = (\ell, \delta) \in \mathcal{T} \cap \Delta_{PB}, \forall \mathbf{x}. \mathbf{x} \in I(\ell) \cap G(\tau) \Rightarrow$ pre$_{\eta, S}^\tau(\ell, \mathbf{x}) \geq 0$; and

5. 1-rank the maximal number of transitions in $\tau \in \mathcal{T}$, i.e. $\forall \mathbf{x}. \mathbf{x} \in I(\ell) \cap G(\tau) \Rightarrow$ max-pre$_\eta^\tau(\ell, \mathbf{x}) \leq \eta(\ell, \mathbf{x}) - 1$ for as many $\tau = (\ell, \delta)$ as possible.

This is done by fixing an LEM template for each location ℓ in $\mathcal{C}$, and converting the above constraints to an equivalent linear program $\mathcal{LP}_\mathcal{T}$ in template variables via Farkas' lemma (FL). The FL conversion (and its extension to strict inequalities [21]) is standard in termination proving and encoding conditions 1–3 and 5 above is analogous to [1,2], hence we omit the details. We show how condition 4 can be encoded via linear constraints in the extended version of the paper [22], along with the algorithm pseudocode and the proof of its correctness. In each algorithm iteration, all transitions that have been 1-ranked are removed from $\mathcal{T}$ and the algorithm proceeds to the next iteration. If all transitions are removed from $\mathcal{T}$, the algorithm concludes that the program admits a LinGLexRSM map (obtained by increasing the constructed LEM by a constant defined in the proof of Lemma 1). If in some iteration a new component which 1-ranks at least 1 transition in $\mathcal{T}$ cannot be found, the program does not admit a LinGLexRSM map.

We conclude by showing that our motivating example in Fig. 1b admits a LinGLexRSM map supported by a very simple linear invariant. Thus, by completeness, our algorithm is able to prove its a.s. termination.

Example 2. Consider the program in Fig. 1b with a linear invariant $I(\ell_0) = true$, $I(\ell_1) = x \geq -7$. Its a.s. termination is witnessed by a LEM $\eta(\ell_0, (x, y)) = (1, x+7, y+7)$, $\eta(\ell_1, (x, y)) = (1, x+8, y+7)$ and $\eta(\ell_{out}, (x, y)) = (0, x+7, y+7)$. Since $\Delta_{PB} = \emptyset$ here, and since *P-RANK*, *P-NNEG* and *W-EXP-NNEG* are satisfied by η, by Lemma 1, $\mathcal{C}$ admits a LinGLexRSM map supported by I.

6.2 Algorithm for General LinPPs

While imposing *W-EXP-NNEG* lets us avoid integration in LinPPs with the BSP, this is no longer the case if we discard the BSP.

Intuitively, the problem in imposing the condition *W-EXP-NNEG* instead of *EXP-NNEG* for LinPPs without the BSP, is that the set of states of smaller level over which *EXP-NNEG* performs integration might have a very small probability, however the value of the LinGLexRSM component on that set is negative and arbitrarily large in absolute value. Thus, a naive solution for general LinPPs would be to "cut off" the tail events where the LinGLexRSM component can become arbitrarily negative and over-approximate them by a constant value in order to obtain a piecewise linear GLexRSM map. However, this might lead to the jump in maximal pre-expectation and could violate *P-RANK*.

Algorithm 1: Algorithm for proving a.s. termination in LinPP*.

    input : A LinPP* $\mathcal{C}$, linear invariant I.
    output: An LEM satisfying the conditions of Lemma 2, if it exists

1   $\mathcal{T} \longleftarrow$ all transitions in $\mathcal{C}$; $d \longleftarrow 0$
2   **while** $\mathcal{T}$ *is non-empty* **do**
3   construct $\mathcal{LP}_{\mathcal{T}}^{\text{unb}}$
4   **if** $\mathcal{LP}_{\mathcal{T}}^{\text{unb}}$ *is feasible* **then**
5         $d \longleftarrow d + 1$; $\eta_d \longleftarrow$ LEM defined by the optimal solution of $\mathcal{LP}_{\mathcal{T}}^{\text{unb}}$
6         $\mathcal{T} \longleftarrow \mathcal{T} \backslash \{\tau \in \mathcal{T} \mid \tau \text{ is 1-ranked by } \eta_d\}$

7   **else**
8   found $\longleftarrow$ false
9   **for** $\tau_0 \in \mapsto^{unb} \cap\, \mathcal{T}$ **do**
10   construct $\mathcal{LP}_{\mathcal{T}}^{\tau_0,\text{unb}}$
11   **if** $\mathcal{LP}_{\mathcal{T}}^{\tau_0,\text{unb}}$ *is feasible* **then**
12               $d \longleftarrow d + 1$; found $\longleftarrow$ true
13               $\eta_d \longleftarrow$ LEM defined by the optimal solution of $\mathcal{LP}_{\mathcal{T}}^{\tau_0,\text{unb}}$
14               $\mathcal{T} \longleftarrow \mathcal{T} \backslash \{\tau \in \mathcal{T} \mid \tau \text{ is 1-ranked by } \eta_d\}$

15   **if** *not found* **then return** No LEM as in Lemma 2

16 **return** $(\eta_1, \ldots, \eta_d)$

In what follows, we consider a slight restriction on the syntax of LinPPs that we consider, and introduce a new condition on LEMs that allows the over-approximation trick mentioned above while ensuring that the *P-RANK* condition is not violated. We consider the subclass LinPP* of LinPPs in which no transition of probabilistic branching and a transition with a sampling instruction share a target location. This is a very mild restriction (satisfied, e.g. by our motivating example in Fig. 1b) which is enforced for technical reasons arising in the proof of Lemma 2. Each LinPP can be converted to satisfy this property by adding a **skip** instruction in the program's source code where necessary. Second, using the notation of Definition 3, we define the new condition *UNBOUND* as follows:

$UNBOUND(\boldsymbol{\eta}, \tau) \equiv$ if $Up(\tau) = (i, u)$ with u containing a sampling from a distribution of unbounded support, and ℓ' is the target location of τ, then the
coefficient of the variable with index i in $\eta_j(\ell')$ is 0 for all $1 \leq j < \mathsf{lev}(\tau)$.

The following technical lemma is an essential ingredient in the soundness proof of our algorithm for programs in LinPP*. Its proof can be found in the extended version of the paper [22].

Lemma 2. *Let $\mathcal{C}$ be a LinPP* and I be a linear invariant in $\mathcal{C}$. If a LEM $\boldsymbol{\eta}$ satisfies P-RANK and P-NNEG for all transitions, EXP-NNEG for all transitions of probabilistic branching, W-EXP-NNEG for all other transitions, as well as UNBOUND, then $\mathcal{C}$ admits a piecewise linear GLexRSM map supported by I.*

Algorithm. The new algorithm shares an overall structure with the algorithm from Sect. 6.1. Thus, we only give a high level overview and focus on novel aspects. The algorithm pseudocode is presented in Algorithm 1.

The condition *UNBOUND* is encoded by modifying the templates for the new LEM components. Let $\mapsto^{\text{unb}}$ be the set of transitions in $\mathcal{C}$ containing sampling from unbounded support distributions, and for any such transition τ let ℓ'_τ be its target location. Then for any set of transitions $\mathcal{T}$, construct a linear program $\mathcal{LP}_{\mathcal{T}}^{\text{unb}}$ analogously to $\mathcal{LP}_{\mathcal{T}}$ in Sect. 6.1, additionally enforcing that for each $\tau \in \mapsto^{\text{unb}} \cap \mathcal{T}$, the coefficient of the variable updated by τ in the LEM template at ℓ'_τ is 0. Algorithm 1 first tries to prune as many transitions as possible by repeatedly solving $\mathcal{LP}_{\mathcal{T}}^{\text{unb}}$ and removing ranked transitions from $\mathcal{T}$, see lines 3–6. Once no more transitions can be ranked, the algorithm tries to rank new transitions by allowing non-zero template coefficients previously required to be 0, while still enforcing *UNBOUND*. For a set of transitions $\mathcal{T}$ and for $\tau_0 \in \mapsto^{\text{unb}} \cap \mathcal{T}$, we construct a linear program $\mathcal{LP}_{\mathcal{T}}^{\tau_0,\text{unb}}$ analogously to $\mathcal{LP}_{\mathcal{T}}^{\text{unb}}$ but allowing a non-zero coefficient of the variable updated by τ_0 at ℓ'_{τ_0}. However, we further impose that the new component 1-ranks any other transition in $\mapsto^{\text{unb}} \cap \mathcal{T}$ with the target location ℓ'_{τ_0}. This new linear program is solved for all $\tau_0 \in \mapsto^{\text{unb}} \cap \mathcal{T}$ and all 1-ranked transitions are removed from $\mathcal{T}$, as in Algorithm 1, lines 7–15. The process continues until all transitions are pruned from $\mathcal{T}$ or until no remaining transition can be 1-ranked, in which case no LEM as in Lemma 2 exists.

Theorem 4. *Algorithm 1 decides in polynomial time if a LinPP* $\mathcal{C}$ admits an LEM which satisfies all conditions of Lemma 2 and which is supported by I. Thus, if the algorithm outputs an LEM, then $\mathcal{C}$ is a.s. terminating and admits a piecewise linear GLexRSM map supported by I.*

The proof of Theorem 4 can be found in the extended version of the paper [22]. We conclude by showing that Algorithm 1 can prove a.s. termination of our motivating example in Fig. 1a.

Example 3. Consider the program in Fig. 1a with a linear invariant $I(\ell_0) = true$, $I(\ell_1) = y \geq 0$. The LEM defined via $\eta(\ell_0, (x, y)) = (1, 2y + 2, x + 1)$, $\eta(\ell_1, (x, y)) = (1, 2y + 1, x + 1)$ and $\eta(\ell_{out}, (x, y)) = (0, 2y + 2, x + 1)$ satisfies *P-RANK*, *P-NNEG* and *W-EXP-NNEG*, which is easy to check. Furthermore, the only transition containing a sampling instruction is the self-loop at ℓ_1 which is ranked by the third component of η. As the coefficients of x of the first two components at ℓ_1 are equal to 0, η also satisfies *UNBOUND*. Hence, η satisfies all conditions of Lemma 2 and Algorithm 1 proves a.s. termination.

7   Conclusion

In this work we present new lexicographic termination certificates for probabilistic programs. We also show how to automate the search for the new certificate within a wide class of probabilistic programs. An interesting direction of future work would be automation beyond linear arithmetic programs.

Acknowledgements. This research was partially supported by the ERC CoG 863818 (ForM-SMArt), the Czech Science Foundation grant No. GJ19-15134Y, and the European Union's Horizon 2020 research and innovation programme under the Marie Skłodowska-Curie Grant Agreement No. 665385.

References

1. Agrawal, S., Chatterjee, K., Novotný, P.: Lexicographic ranking supermartingales: an efficient approach to termination of probabilistic programs. PACMPL **2**(POPL), 34:1–34:32 (2018)
2. Alias, C., Darte, A., Feautrier, P., Gonnord, L.: Multi-dimensional rankings, program termination, and complexity bounds of flowchart programs. In: Cousot, R., Martel, M. (eds.) SAS 2010. LNCS, vol. 6337, pp. 117–133. Springer, Heidelberg (2010). https://doi.org/10.1007/978-3-642-15769-1_8
3. Ash, R., Doléans-Dade, C.: Probability and Measure Theory. Harcourt/Academic Press, Boston (2000)
4. Avanzini, M., Dal Lago, U., Ghyselen, A.: Type-based complexity analysis of probabilistic functional programs. In: 2019 34th Annual ACM/IEEE Symposium on Logic in Computer Science (LICS), pp. 1–13 (2019). https://doi.org/10.1109/LICS.2019.8785725
5. Avanzini, M., Lago, U.D., Yamada, A.: On probabilistic term rewriting. Sci. Comput. Program. **185**, 102338 (2020). https://doi.org/10.1016/j.scico.2019.102338
6. Avanzini, M., Moser, G., Schaper, M.: A modular cost analysis for probabilistic programs. In: Proceedings of the ACM on Programming Languages, vol. 4 ((Proceedings of OOPSLA 2020)), pp. 1–30 (2020)
7. Baier, C., Katoen, J.P.: Principles of Model Checking. The MIT Press, Cambridge (2008)
8. Barthe, G., Espitau, T., Ferrer Fioriti, L.M., Hsu, J.: Synthesizing probabilistic invariants via Doob's decomposition. In: Chaudhuri, S., Farzan, A. (eds.) CAV 2016. LNCS, vol. 9779, pp. 43–61. Springer, Cham (2016). https://doi.org/10.1007/978-3-319-41528-4_3
9. Barthe, G., Gaboardi, M., Grégoire, B., Hsu, J., Strub, P.Y.: Proving differential privacy via probabilistic couplings. In: Proceedings of the 31st Annual ACM/IEEE Symposium on Logic in Computer Science, pp. 749–758, LICS 2016. ACM, New York, NY, USA (2016). https://doi.org/10.1145/2933575.2934554
10. Barthe, G., Gaboardi, M., Hsu, J., Pierce, B.: Programming language techniques for differential privacy. ACM SIGLOG News **3**(1), 34–53 (2016)
11. Ben-Amram, A.M., Genaim, S.: On the linear ranking problem for integer linear-constraint loops. In: Proceedings of the 40th Annual ACM SIGPLAN-SIGACT Symposium on Principles of Programming Languages, pp. 51–62, POPL 2013. ACM, New York, NY, USA (2013). https://doi.org/10.1145/2429069.2429078
12. Ben-Amram, A.M., Genaim, S.: Complexity of Bradley-Manna-Sipma lexicographic ranking functions. In: Kroening, D., Păsăreanu, C.S. (eds.) CAV 2015. LNCS, vol. 9207, pp. 304–321. Springer, Cham (2015). https://doi.org/10.1007/978-3-319-21668-3_18
13. Billingsley, P.: Probability and Measure, 3rd edn. Wiley, New York (1995)
14. Bournez, O., Garnier, F.: Proving positive almost-sure termination. In: RTA, pp. 323–337 (2005)

15. Bradley, A.R., Manna, Z., Sipma, H.B.: Linear ranking with reachability. In: Computer Aided Verification, 17th International Conference, CAV 2005, Edinburgh, Scotland, UK, 6–10 July 2005, Proceedings, pp. 491–504 (2005). https://doi.org/10.1007/11513988_48

16. Brockschmidt, M., Cook, B., Fuhs, C.: Better termination proving through cooperation. In: Computer Aided Verification - 25th International Conference, CAV 2013, Saint Petersburg, Russia, July 13–19, 2013, Proceedings, pp. 413–429 (2013). https://doi.org/10.1007/978-3-642-39799-8_28

17. Brockschmidt, M., Cook, B., Ishtiaq, S., Khlaaf, H., Piterman, N.: T2: temporal property verification. In: Chechik, M., Raskin, J.-F. (eds.) TACAS 2016. LNCS, vol. 9636, pp. 387–393. Springer, Heidelberg (2016). https://doi.org/10.1007/978-3-662-49674-9_22

18. Chakarov, A., Sankaranarayanan, S.: Probabilistic program analysis with martingales. In: CAV 2013, pp. 511–526 (2013)

19. Chakarov, A., Voronin, Y.-L., Sankaranarayanan, S.: Deductive proofs of almost sure persistence and recurrence properties. In: Chechik, M., Raskin, J.-F. (eds.) TACAS 2016. LNCS, vol. 9636, pp. 260–279. Springer, Heidelberg (2016). https://doi.org/10.1007/978-3-662-49674-9_15

20. Chatterjee, K., Fu, H., Goharshady, A.K.: Termination analysis of probabilistic programs through Positivstellensatz's. In: CAV, pp. 3–22 (2016)

21. Chatterjee, K., Fu, H., Novotný, P., Hasheminezhad, R.: Algorithmic analysis of qualitative and quantitative termination problems for affine probabilistic programs. ACM Trans. Program. Lang. Syst. **40**(2), 7:1–7:45 (2018). https://doi.org/10.1145/3174800

22. Chatterjee, K., Goharshady, E.K., Novotný, P., Zárevúcky, J., Žikelić, D.: On lexicographic proof rules for probabilistic termination (2021). https://arxiv.org/abs/2108.02188

23. Chatterjee, K., Novotný, P., Žikelić, D.: Stochastic invariants for probabilistic termination. In: Proceedings of the 44th ACM SIGPLAN Symposium on Principles of Programming Languages, pp. 145–160, POPL 2017. ACM, New York, NY, USA (2017). https://doi.org/10.1145/3009837.3009873

24. Chen, J., He, F.: Proving almost-sure termination by omega-regular decomposition. In: Proceedings of the 41st ACM SIGPLAN International Conference on Programming Language Design and Implementation, PLDI 2020, London, UK, June 15–20, 2020, pp. 869–882 (2020). https://doi.org/10.1145/3385412.3386002

25. Claret, G., Rajamani, S.K., Nori, A.V., Gordon, A.D., Borgström, J.: Bayesian inference using data flow analysis. In: Joint Meeting on Foundations of Software Engineering, pp. 92–102. ACM (2013)

26. Colón, M., Sipma, H.: Synthesis of linear ranking functions. In: Tools and Algorithms for the Construction and Analysis of Systems, 7th International Conference, TACAS 2001 Held as Part of the Joint European Conferences on Theory and Practice of Software, ETAPS 2001 Genova, Italy, April 2–6, 2001, Proceedings, pp. 67–81 (2001). https://doi.org/10.1007/3-540-45319-9_6

27. Cook, B., Podelski, A., Rybalchenko, A.: Termination proofs for systems code. SIGPLAN Not. **41**(6), 415–426 (2006)

28. Cook, B., Podelski, A., Rybalchenko, A.: Proving program termination. Commun. ACM **54**(5), 88–98 (2011)

29. Cook, B., See, A., Zuleger, F.: Ramsey vs. lexicographic termination proving. In: Piterman, N., Smolka, S.A. (eds.) TACAS 2013. LNCS, vol. 7795, pp. 47–61. Springer, Heidelberg (2013). https://doi.org/10.1007/978-3-642-36742-7_4

30. Cousot, P., Cousot, R.: Abstract interpretation: a unified lattice model for static analysis of programs by construction or approximation of fixpoints. In: Conference Record of the Fourth ACM Symposium on Principles of Programming Languages, Los Angeles, California, USA, January 1977, pp. 238–252 (1977). https://doi.org/10.1145/512950.512973

31. Dal Lago, U., Faggian, C., Rocca, S.R.D.: Intersection types and (positive) almost-sure termination. Proc. ACM Program. Lang. **5**(POPL), 1–32 (2021). https://doi.org/10.1145/3434313

32. Dubhashi, D., Panconesi, A.: Concentration of Measure for the Analysis of Randomized Algorithms, 1st edn. Cambridge University Press, New York (2009)

33. Esparza, J., Gaiser, A., Kiefer, S.: Proving termination of probabilistic programs using patterns. In: CAV 2012, pp. 123–138 (2012)

34. Feldman, Y.A.: A decidable propositional dynamic logic with explicit probabilities. Inf. Control **63**(1), 11–38 (1984)

35. Feldman, Y.A., Harel, D.: A probabilistic dynamic logic. In: Proceedings of the Fourteenth Annual ACM Symposium on Theory of Computing, pp. 181–195. ACM (1982)

36. Fioriti, L.M.F., Hermanns, H.: Probabilistic termination: soundness, completeness, and compositionality. In: Proceedings of the 42nd Annual ACM SIGPLAN-SIGACT Symposium on Principles of Programming Languages, POPL 2015, Mumbai, India, January 15–17, 2015, pp. 489–501 (2015). https://doi.org/10.1145/2676726.2677001

37. Floyd, R.W.: Assigning meanings to programs. Math. Aspects Comput. Sci. **19**, 19–33 (1967)

38. Foster, F.G.: On the stochastic matrices associated with certain queuing processes. Ann. Math. Stat. **24**(3), 355–360 (1953)

39. Foster, N., Kozen, D., Mamouras, K., Reitblatt, M., Silva, A.: Probabilistic NetKAT. In: Thiemann, P. (ed.) ESOP 2016. LNCS, vol. 9632, pp. 282–309. Springer, Heidelberg (2016). https://doi.org/10.1007/978-3-662-49498-1_12

40. Fu, H., Chatterjee, K.: Termination of nondeterministic probabilistic programs. In: Enea, C., Piskac, R. (eds.) VMCAI 2019. LNCS, vol. 11388, pp. 468–490. Springer, Cham (2019). https://doi.org/10.1007/978-3-030-11245-5_22

41. Ghahramani, Z.: Probabilistic machine learning and artificial intelligence. Nature **521**(7553), 452–459 (2015)

42. Giesl, J., Giesl, P., Hark, M.: Computing expected runtimes for constant probability programs. In: Fontaine, P. (ed.) Automated Deduction - CADE 27, pp. 269–286. Springer, Cham (2019)

43. Gonnord, L., Monniaux, D., Radanne, G.: Synthesis of ranking functions using extremal counterexamples. In: Proceedings of the 36th ACM SIGPLAN Conference on Programming Language Design and Implementation, pp. 608–618, PLDI 2015. ACM, New York, NY, USA (2015). https://doi.org/10.1145/2737924.2737976

44. Gordon, A.D., Aizatulin, M., Borgstrom, J., Claret, G., Graepel, T., Nori, A.V., Rajamani, S.K., Russo, C.: A model-learner pattern for Bayesian reasoning. ACM SIGPLAN Not. **48**(1), 403–416 (2013)

45. Gordon, A.D., Henzinger, T.A., Nori, A.V., Rajamani, S.K.: Probabilistic programming. In: Proceedings of the on Future of Software Engineering, pp. 167–181. ACM (2014)

46. Gretz, F., Katoen, J.P., McIver, A.: Operational versus weakest pre-expectation semantics for the probabilistic guarded command language. Perform. Eval. **73**, 110–132 (2014)

47. Hark, M., Kaminski, B.L., Giesl, J., Katoen, J.: Aiming low is harder: induction for lower bounds in probabilistic program verification. Proc. ACM Program. Lang. **4**(POPL), 37:1–37:28 (2020). https://doi.org/10.1145/3371105

48. Huang, M., Fu, H., Chatterjee, K.: New approaches for almost-sure termination of probabilistic programs. In: Ryu, S. (ed.) Programming Languages and Systems, pp. 181–201. Springer, Cham (2018)

49. Huang, M., Fu, H., Chatterjee, K., Goharshady, A.K.: Modular verification for almost-sure termination of probabilistic programs. Proc. ACM Program. Lang. **3**(OOPSLA), 129:1–129:29 (2019). https://doi.org/10.1145/3360555

50. Kaelbling, L.P., Littman, M.L., Moore, A.W.: Reinforcement learning: a survey. JAIR **4**, 237–285 (1996)

51. Kaminski, B.L., Katoen, J.P., Matheja, C.: On the hardness of analyzing probabilistic programs. Acta Informatica **56**(3), 1–31 (2018)

52. Kaminski, B.L., Katoen, J., Matheja, C., Olmedo, F.: Weakest precondition reasoning for expected runtimes of randomized algorithms. J. ACM **65**(5), 30:1–30:68 (2018). https://doi.org/10.1145/3208102

53. Kobayashi, N., Lago, U.D., Grellois, C.: On the termination problem for probabilistic higher-order recursive programs. Log. Methods Comput. Sci. **16**(4), 2:1–2:57 (2020). https://lmcs.episciences.org/6817

54. Kozen, D.: Semantics of probabilistic programs. J. Comput. Syst. Sci. **22**(3), 328–350 (1981). https://doi.org/10.1016/0022-0000(81)90036-2

55. Kozen, D.: A probabilistic PDL. In: Proceedings of the Fifteenth Annual ACM Symposium on Theory of Computing, pp. 291–297, STOC 1983. ACM, New York, NY, USA (1983). https://doi.org/10.1145/800061.808758

56. Kwiatkowska, M., Norman, G., Parker, D.: PRISM 4.0: verification of probabilistic real-time systems. In: Gopalakrishnan, G., Qadeer, S. (eds.) CAV 2011. LNCS, vol. 6806, pp. 585–591. Springer, Heidelberg (2011). https://doi.org/10.1007/978-3-642-22110-1_47

57. Lago, U.D., Grellois, C.: Probabilistic termination by monadic affine sized typing. ACM Trans. Program. Lang. Syst. **41**(2), 10:1–10:65 (2019). https://doi.org/10.1145/3293605

58. McIver, A., Morgan, C.: Developing and reasoning about probabilistic programs in pGCL. In: PSSE, pp. 123–155 (2004)

59. McIver, A., Morgan, C.: Abstraction, Refinement and Proof for Probabilistic Systems. Monographs in Computer Science. Springer, New York (2005). https://doi.org/10.1007/b138392

60. McIver, A., Morgan, C.: A new rule for almost-certain termination of probabilistic and demonic programs. CoRR abs/1612.01091 (2016). http://arxiv.org/abs/1612.01091

61. McIver, A., Morgan, C., Kaminski, B.L., Katoen, J.: A new proof rule for almost-sure termination. PACMPL **2**(POPL), 33:1–33:28 (2018). https://doi.org/10.1145/3158121

62. Monniaux, D.: An abstract analysis of the probabilistic termination of programs. In: Cousot, P. (ed.) SAS 2001. LNCS, vol. 2126, pp. 111–126. Springer, Heidelberg (2001). https://doi.org/10.1007/3-540-47764-0_7

63. Moosbrugger, M., Bartocci, E., Katoen, J.-P., Kovács, L.: Automated termination analysis of polynomial probabilistic programs. In: ESOP 2021. LNCS, vol. 12648, pp. 491–518. Springer, Cham (2021). https://doi.org/10.1007/978-3-030-72019-3_18

64. Morgan, C., McIver, A.: pGCL: formal reasoning for random algorithms (1999)

65. Morgan, C., McIver, A., Seidel, K.: Probabilistic predicate transformers. ACM Trans. Program. Lang. Syst. (TOPLAS) **18**(3), 325–353 (1996)
66. Motwani, R., Raghavan, P.: Randomized Algorithms. Cambridge University Press, New York (1995)
67. Neuhäußer, M.R., Katoen, J.-P.: Bisimulation and logical preservation for continuous-time Markov decision processes. In: Caires, L., Vasconcelos, V.T. (eds.) CONCUR 2007. LNCS, vol. 4703, pp. 412–427. Springer, Heidelberg (2007). https://doi.org/10.1007/978-3-540-74407-8_28
68. Neuhäußer, M.R., Stoelinga, M., Katoen, J.-P.: Delayed nondeterminism in continuous-time Markov Decision Processes. In: de Alfaro, L. (ed.) FoSSaCS 2009. LNCS, vol. 5504, pp. 364–379. Springer, Heidelberg (2009). https://doi.org/10.1007/978-3-642-00596-1_26
69. Ngo, V.C., Carbonneaux, Q., Hoffmann, J.: Bounded expectations: resource analysis for probabilistic programs. In: PLDI 2018, pp. 496–512 (2018)
70. Olmedo, F., Kaminski, B.L., Katoen, J.P., Matheja, C.: Reasoning about recursive probabilistic programs. In: Proceedings of the 31st Annual ACM/IEEE Symposium on Logic in Computer Science, pp. 672–681, LICS 2016. ACM, New York, NY, USA (2016). https://doi.org/10.1145/2933575.2935317
71. Podelski, A., Rybalchenko, A.: A complete method for the synthesis of linear ranking functions. In: 5th International Conference on Verification, Model Checking, and Abstract Interpretation, VMCAI 2004, Venice, January 11–13, 2004, Proceedings, pp. 239–251 (2004). https://doi.org/10.1007/978-3-540-24622-0_20
72. Podelski, A., Rybalchenko, A.: Transition invariants. In: Proceedings of the 19th Annual IEEE Symposium on Logic in Computer Science, pp. 32–41, LICS 2004. IEEE Computer Society, Washington, DC, USA (2004). https://doi.org/10.1109/LICS.2004.50
73. Roy, D., Mansinghka, V., Goodman, N., Tenenbaum, J.: A stochastic programming perspective on nonparametric Bayes. In: Nonparametric Bayesian Workshop, International Conference on Machine Learning, vol. 22, p. 26 (2008)
74. Ścibior, A., Ghahramani, Z., Gordon, A.D.: Practical probabilistic programming with monads. ACM SIGPLAN Not. **50**(12), 165–176 (2015)
75. Smolka, S., Kumar, P., Foster, N., Kozen, D., Silva, A.: Cantor meets Scott: semantic foundations for probabilistic networks. In: POPL 2017, pp. 557–571 (2017)
76. Sohn, K., Gelder, A.V.: Termination detection in logic programs using argument sizes. In: Proceedings of the Tenth ACM SIGACT-SIGMOD-SIGART Symposium on Principles of Database Systems, May 29–31, 1991, Denver, Colorado, USA, pp. 216–226 (1991). https://doi.org/10.1145/113413.113433
77. Thrun, S.: Probabilistic robotics. Commun. ACM **45**(3), 52–57 (2002)
78. Wang, D., Hoffmann, J., Reps, T.W.: PMAF: an algebraic framework for static analysis of probabilistic programs. In: PLDI 2018, pp. 513–528 (2018)
79. Wang, P., Fu, H., Goharshady, A.K., Chatterjee, K., Qin, X., Shi, W.: Cost analysis of nondeterministic probabilistic programs. In: PLDI 2019, pp. 204–220 (2019)
80. Williams, D.: Probability with Martingales. Cambridge Mathematical Textbooks, Cambridge University Press, Cambridge (1991)

Fuel in Markov Decision Processes (FiMDP): A Practical Approach to Consumption

František Blahoudek[1], Murat Cubuktepe[2], Petr Novotný[3], Melkior Ornik[4], Pranay Thangeda[4(✉)], and Ufuk Topcu[2]

[1] Brno University of Technology, Brno, Czech Republic
[2] The University of Texas at Austin, Austin, USA
{mcubuktepe,utopcu}@utexas.edu
[3] Masaryk University, Brno, Czech Republic
petr.novotny@fi.muni.cz
[4] University of Illinois Urbana-Champaign, Urbana, USA
{mornik,pranayt2}@illinois.edu

Abstract. Consumption Markov Decision Processes (CMDPs) are probabilistic decision-making models of resource-constrained systems. We introduce FiMDP, a tool for controller synthesis in CMDPs with LTL objectives expressible by deterministic Büchi automata. The tool implements the recent algorithm for polynomial-time controller synthesis in CMDPs, but extends it with many additional features. On the conceptual level, the tool implements heuristics for improving the expected reachability times of accepting states, and a support for multi-agent task allocation. On the practical level, the tool offers (among other features) a new strategy simulation framework, integration with the Storm model checker, and FiMDPEnv - a new set of CMDPs that model real-world resource-constrained systems. We also present an evaluation of FiMDP on these real-world scenarios.

1 Introduction

Planning the motion of an agent operating in a stochastic environment described by a discrete-time *Markov decision process* (MDP) is a classical problem of stochastic control [3,20]. In each step, the agent selects an action to perform, the outcome of which is given by a probability distribution over successor states depending on the current state and the selected action. Such a framework finds immediate use in planning for robots and autonomous vehicles operating on complex terrain, as well as operations on a financial market [7,12,16].

This work was partially supported by NASA under Early Stage Innovations grant No. 80NSSC19K0209, and by DARPA under grant No. HR001120C0065. Petr Novotný was supported by the Czech Science Foundation grant No. GJ19-15134Y and František Blahoudek was supported by the Czech Ministry of Education, Youth and Sports ERC CZ project LL1908.

© Springer Nature Switzerland AG 2021
M. Huisman et al. (Eds.): FM 2021, LNCS 13047, pp. 640–656, 2021.
https://doi.org/10.1007/978-3-030-90870-6_34

Constructing control strategies that enable the agent to reach a particular target state with maximum probability has been the focus of substantial previous work on MDPs [4,14,22]. Moving forward from simple reachability tasks, linear temporal logic (LTL) [19] serves as a convenient way to describe a wide class of missions for such an agent [2,11]. LTL specifications can describe the desired spatiotemporal features of the agent's path like "visit area A before visiting either area B or C, while never visiting area D". The synthesis of optimal control strategies for such specifications has also been studied previous work (e.g. [2,22]); a standard method is to monitor the agent's progress at its mission by a deterministic automaton, thus posing mission success as producing an accepting path in the synchronous product of the automaton and the MDP.

The motivation for this paper is to practically enable planning for resource-constrained agents. Such agents maintain a limited amount of some critical resource (e.g. energy needed to operate) at every time step. The resource is consumed in each time step (with the amount depending on the current state and action) and can be replenished at particular *reload states*. The agent's specification is to satisfy its mission while retaining a positive amount of the resource throughout its operation.

A naive planning approach for resource-constrained agents is (i) to append the resource level as a part of the agent's state and (ii) to enrich the mission specification defined on the agent's states by "always *resource* > 0". This method multiplies the size of the agent's state space by the number of the possible resource levels which significantly adds to the computational burden of planning. (In particular, it leads to an *exponential* time complexity if the agent's resource capacity is specified in binary).

Our recent paper [5] introduces a formalism of *consumption Markov decision processes* which avoids encoding the resource levels into states. Instead, the consumption of the resource is defined as a special cost. It is then up to the agents to monitor their own resource levels and choose actions also with respect to their current remaining amount of the resource. This is exactly what *counter strategies* introduced in the same paper do. They use counters to monitor the resource level and *action selectors* to choose actions to play in a state depending on the resource level. As a result, an agent can exhibit two or more behaviors in one state. For instance, the agent may elect to go to a reload state when the resource level is too low to complete the mission without reloading, while it may proceed with the mission without reloading when it has a sufficient resource level. The decision does not have to be specified for each resource level, but rather for *intervals* of resource levels. Using this insight, [5] proves that counter strategies with polynomial-sized representation are sufficient for guaranteeing mission success with probability 1, and that the associated qualitative synthesis problem can be solved in *polynomial* time. Hence, consumption MDPs and counter strategies provably quicken the qualitative controller synthesis for resource-constrained agents.

The algorithms presented in [5] were implemented in a prototype implementation. After more than a year of additional development, in this paper we introduce FIMDP (Fuel in Markov Decision Processes): a tool for design and analysis of consumption MDPs, and for synthesis of resource-aware control strategies for them. We designed FIMDP with two goals in mind: practicality and education.

The practical purpose of the tool is to provide high-quality results for interesting planning problems in reasonable time. Therefore, we have extended the previous work by (i) constructing novel heuristics that produce strategies that not only satisfy the mission almost surely, but also attempt to complete the mission in a short time, (ii) enabling support of missions specified by deterministic Büchi automata or by the corresponding fragment of linear temporal logic, (iii) enabling an interface with well-established modeling languages like PRISM [17] and JANI [8], and (iv) given a set of targets and homogeneous agents, providing a polynomial-time algorithm that computes a target allocation and assignment to minimize the resource capacity of each agent. We also show that the tool translates the theoretical gains of the new formalism to practice: FIMDP provides the ability to synthesize resource-aware strategies for significantly larger state spaces than the state-of-the-art model checker STORM [15].

To be educational, the tool makes the framework of consumption MDPs accessible by (i) having a simple user interface, (ii) possessing an ability to read models in existing modeling languages, (iii) constructing visual representations of the models and results, and (iv) supporting simulations of the synthesized strategies. These components help the users to understand the key concepts of the novel formalism without being exposed to the entire technical machinery behind the framework.

FIMDP comes bundled with FIMDPENV: a set of environments inspired by real world that are built on top of consumption MDPs. FIMDPENV interfaces with FIMDP for strategy synthesis, and simulates the strategies in a visually vivid manner. This feature allows the user to easily modify the high-level parameters of the mission at hand, such as the mission specification, as necessary.

FIMDP is available at https://github.com/FiMDP/FiMDP. FIMDPENV is available at https://github.com/FiMDP/FiMDPEnv. We created a series of tutorials available at https://github.com/FiMDP/tutorials to get started with the tool. These tutorials, presented in interactive Jupyter notebooks, are designed to provide the user with an in-depth understanding of the key features offered by the tool.

The next section defines consumption MDPs and the necessary notation. Section 3 summarizes the features of FIMDP and explains the novel functionality not available before. More details about FIMDP follow in Sect. 4 and Sect. 5 presents FIMDPENV. Finally, Sect. 6 empirically compares strategy synthesis for consumption MDPs in FIMDP and STORM, and also shows the effect of the novel heuristics on the quality of the synthesized control strategies.

2   Consumption Markov Decision Processes

Notation. The set of all non-negative integers is denoted by $\mathbb{N}$. If $\mathcal{X}$ is a set, the set of all infinite sequences of elements in $\mathcal{X}$ is denoted by $\mathcal{X}^\omega$. The set of all subsets of $\mathcal{X}$ is denoted by $2^{\mathcal{X}}$. Notation $\mathbb{P}(X)$ denotes the probability of an event X in an appropriate event space.

Throughout this section, we follow the framework introduced in [5]. In order to model the agent's resource consumption and capacity, we first amend the definition of a standard Markov decision process [20] by defining a *consumption Markov decision process*.

Definition 1 (CMDP). *A consumption Markov decision process (CMDP) is a tuple $\mathcal{M} = (S, A, P, C, R, cap)$ where:*

- *S is a finite set of states,*
- *A is a finite set of actions,*
- *$P : S \times A \times S \to [0,1]$ is a transition probability function which satisfies $\sum_{s' \in S} P(s, a, s') = 1$ for all $s \in S$, $a \in A$,*
- *$C : S \times A \to \mathbb{N}$ is a consumption function,*
- *$R \subseteq S$ is a set of reload states, and*
- *$cap \in \mathbb{N}$ is a resource capacity.*

The CMDP $\mathcal{M}$ evolves in discrete time steps. In each time step $t \in \mathbb{N}$, the agent's state is denoted by s_t and its *resource level* by r_t. The agent chooses an action a_t with consumption not higher than r_t. Based on a_t, the agent transitions to state s_{t+1} that is chosen randomly using the transition probability function P: state s_{t+1} is a random variable such that $\mathbb{P}(s_{t+1} = s' | s_t, a_t) = P(s_t, a_t, s')$. The dynamics of the resource level are given by the following equation.

$$r_{t+1} = \begin{cases} cap & \text{if } s_{t+1} \in R \\ r_t - C(s_t, a_t) & \text{otherwise} \end{cases} \tag{1}$$

In other words, when an agent reaches a reload state, its resource is reloaded to the full capacity cap. Otherwise, the resource level is reduced by $C(s_t, a_t)$. This means that r_t is uniquely defined at every time t by the initial resource level r_0 and the history of states and actions.

We introduce the notion of a *path* as a finite or infinite state-action sequence

$$\Phi = s_0 a_0 s_1 a_1 s_2 a_2 s_3 \cdots \in (S \times A)^{\omega} \bigcup \left(\bigcup_{n \in \mathbb{N}} (S \cdot A)^n \right) \times S.$$

The length of a path Φ is ∞ if $\Phi \in (S \times A)^{\omega}$, and n if $\Phi \in (S \times A)^n \times S$. We call an infinite path a *run*, and a finite path a *history*.

A *strategy* for an agent operating on $\mathcal{M}$ is a function $\sigma : \mathcal{H}(\mathcal{M}) \to A$, where $\mathcal{H}(\mathcal{M})$ is the set of all histories on $\mathcal{M}$. In other words, an agent can decide its next action based on all previous states and actions, and thus, by (1), possibly also based on its resource level. *Positional strategies* (or *memoryless strategies*) known from regular MDPs base their decision solely on the current state. *Counter strategies* extend positional strategies by taking also the current resource level into consideration. A counter strategy consists of a counter that keeps track of the resource level r_t, and an *action selector* that maps the current state and resource level into the action to play.

An action selector is a function $sel: S \times \{0, 1, \ldots, cap\} \to A$ which we effectively represent using intervals. In particular, for every state s we define values $0 = p_1^s < p_2^s < \ldots < p_{k_s}^s < cap + 1 = p_{k_s+1}^s$ and actions $a_1^s, \ldots, a_{k_s}^s \in A$. Then for given state s and resource level r the value $sel(s, r)$ is a_j^s if $p_j^s \leq r < p_{j+1}^s$.

A CMDP is *decreasing* if and only if each cycle either contains a reload state or has non-zero consumption. This means that the agent is forced to visit reload states in a decreasing CMDP. From now on, we only consider decreasing CMDPs.

Labeled Consumption Markov Decision Processes. In [5], we have only considered reachability or Büchi objectives defined explicitly using a set F of *accepting* or *target* states. To extend the range of possible mission specifications, we introduce a *labeling function* $L : S \to 2^{AP}$ which assigns to each state a set of *atomic propositions*. Atomic propositions are features relevant to the agent's objective. For instance, we can encode the set of accepting states F from above by setting $L(s) = \{F\}$ if $s \in F$ and define $L(s) = \emptyset$ otherwise.

Each path Φ naturally induces a sequence of labels $L(s_0)L(s_1)L(s_2)\ldots$. These sequences can be evaluated against specifications describing the agent's objective given as an automaton or as a formula of Linear temporal logic (LTL) [19]. We refer the reader to [2] for precise definitions. In this paper, we consider properties that can be expressed via *deterministic Büchi automata (DBA)* or via formulas from the *recurrence* fragment of the Manna-Pnueli hierarchy for LTL [18]. This fragment is strong enough to express many useful properties like "keep visiting states labeled by F while never seeing label *exit* before label *landed*", and each recurrence formula can be translated into an equivalent DBA.

3 Features of FiMDP

In this section, we first briefly review the theoretical foundations of FiMDP, as introduced in [5]. We then present FiMDP's main features, focusing on the novel features that distinguish it from the prototype artifact of [5].

3.1 Theoretical Foundations

FiMDP is a tool for qualitative analysis and controller synthesis in CMDPs. As such, it builds on the polynomial-time synthesis algorithm for CMDPs presented in [5]. We are given a CMDP $\mathcal{M} = (S, A, P, C, R, cap)$ and a set of accepting states $F \subseteq S$. The task is to compute a strategy σ which is *safe* (i.e., ensures that the resource level never drops below zero) and almost surely satisfies the Büchi objective given by F. More precisely, for every initial state s, the algorithm computes the minimal initial resource level $min\text{-}lev(s) \in \{0, \ldots, cap\} \cup \{\infty\}$ such that there exists a strategy σ ensuring the following properties:

a) for all $t \in \mathbb{N}$, $\mathbb{P}^\sigma(r_t < 0 \mid s_0 = s, r_0 = min\text{-}lev(s)) = 0$; and
b) $\mathbb{P}^\sigma(s_t \in F$ *for infinitely many* $t \mid s_0 = s, r_0 = min\text{-}lev(s)) = 1$;

where $\mathbb{P}^\sigma$ is the probability measure induced by σ over the runs in $\mathcal{M}$. If $min\text{-}lev(s) = \infty$, the objective is unachievable from s; we say that s is a *losing* state and the algorithm reports all such states. We call all the other states *winning*. The rationale behind the minimal resource levels is that due to the monotonicity inherent to the resource constraints, a strategy that satisfies a) and b) satisfies the same conditions for any initial resource level $r_0 \geq min\text{-}lev(s)$. In [5], it was also proved that there exists a polynomial-sized counter strategy σ that satisfies both a) and b) in every winning state. The algorithm presented in [5] also computes such a strategy.

The computation of both the minimal resource levels and the corresponding strategy σ proceeds in two phases. In the first phase, the algorithm solves the *positive reachability* problem. The problem consists of computing the minimal resource levels $min\text{-}pos\text{-}reach(s) \in \{0, \ldots, cap\} \cup \{\infty\}$ and a strategy π which, given the initial resource level $min\text{-}pos\text{-}reach(s)$, reaches an accepting state with a positive probability while preventing resource exhaustion:

a') for all $t \in \mathbb{N}$, $\mathbb{P}^\pi(r_t < 0 \mid s_0 = s, r_0 = min\text{-}pos\text{-}reach(s)) = 0$; and
b') there exists $t \in \mathbb{N}$ s.t. $\mathbb{P}^\pi(s_t \in F \mid s_0 = s, r_0 = min\text{-}pos\text{-}reach(s)) > 0$.

The corresponding algorithm iterates a suitable Bellman functional in a process analogous to value iteration. Note that the agent using π might eventually run in a situation where $r_t < min\text{-}pos\text{-}reach(s_t)$.

The values $min\text{-}pos\text{-}reach$ are the key for building the desired strategy σ out of π. Imagine a strategy that behaves like π and at the same time it keeps the resource level high enough so that r_t never drops below $min\text{-}pos\text{-}reach(s_t)$. If that is possible, we have always a positive probability of reaching F (the property b')) and thus the agent will eventually reach F. And since even when reaching F at time t_F we have that $r_{t_F} \geq min\text{-}pos\text{-}reach(s_{t_F})$, it will be reached again, and so on *ad infinitum*. Thus, the Büchi property b) is satisfied.

There is a small caveat in this approach: unlike π, the strategy σ needs to avoid states that are losing for the positive reachability problem at all costs. Thus it might differ from π and as such it might lose property b'). To solve this, we remove the losing states from the given CMDP, compute a new π and $min\text{-}pos\text{-}reach$ in this reduced CMDP and repeat this until all states of the reduced CMDP are winning. In such case, π actually satisfies both b') and b) and we have our σ for the Büchi objective.

3.2   New Features

The algorithm that rests at the heart of FiMDP has polynomial complexity and its prototype scaled well in the somewhat lightweight experiments of [5]. FiMDP extends this algorithmic core with further heuristics and additional functionality that greatly enhances its practical capabilities. We present these new features in the remainder of this section.

Labeled CMDPs, Deterministic Büchi Automata and LTL. The algorithm in [5] synthesizes a resource-constrained strategy for almost-sure satisfaction of a Büchi objective, where the accepting states have to be explicitly specified as a part of the MDP. FiMDP now fully supports CMDPs with states labeled by sets of atomic propositions. Given such a labeled CMDP $\mathcal{M}$ and a deterministic Büchi automaton $\mathcal{A}$ over the same atomic propositions, FiMDP can synthesize a resource-aware strategy that produces (for a suitable initial level of resource) runs whose labeling is almost surely accepted by $\mathcal{A}$. To achieve this, FiMDP follows the classical approach of constructing and analyzing the product $\mathcal{M} \otimes \mathcal{A}$ via the standard *synchronous parallel composition* technique [2].

Obviously, the counter strategy synthesized for $\mathcal{M} \otimes \mathcal{A}$ operates correctly only on this product, which might be impractical. For the convenience of users, FiMDP provides a capability to synthesize a counter strategy that stores $\mathcal{A}$ in its memory. This means, the strategy tracks in memory both the resource level (using a counter) and the progress in $\mathcal{A}$, and makes decisions based on the current state, the current resource level, and the current state of the automaton. As a result, the users can run these strategies on their original model. Another advantage of these strategies is that the potentially large object for $\mathcal{M} \otimes \mathcal{A}$ can be discarded from memory right after the analysis.

The product-based approach extends naturally to the recurrence fragment of linear temporal logic. Given a formula φ of this fragment and a labeled CMDP $\mathcal{M}$, FiMDP can compute the values $min\text{-}lev_\varphi$ and synthesize a strategy σ, which operates on $\mathcal{M}$ and which has the following properties:

a) for all $t \in \mathbb{N}$, $\mathbb{P}^\sigma(r_t < 0 \mid s_0 = s, r_0 = min\text{-}lev_\varphi(s)) = 0$; and
b) $\mathbb{P}^\sigma(\varphi$ is satisfied by the sample run $\mid s_0 = s, r_0 = min\text{-}lev_\varphi(s)) = 1$.

This capability is justified by the fact that each formula of the recurrence fragment can be translated to an equivalent DBA [18]. FiMDP uses the Spot library [10] for this translation and then employs the product approach described above. The user requires just one line of code with FiMDP to run this pipeline and get a strategy without ever being exposed to the product construction.

Strategies and Simulations Framework. The core algorithm for strategy synthesis does not compute the strategies (objects with memory) directly. It produces action selectors, the integral parts of counter strategies. The strategy simply asks the selector, what should be the next action given its current state of memory. As we saw in the labeled framework, altering the type of the strategy's memory (and of the selector) might result in more useful strategy representations. FiMDP provides an interface for objects representing strategies that completely hides the implementation details of the strategy from the users. A built-in strategy *simulator* uses the interface to create sample paths created by given strategies. Moreover, following this interface, users can define their own types of strategies and test them using the infrastructure of FiMDP.

Integration with Storm. FiMDP is now integrated with the state-of-the-art probabilistic model checker Storm [15] through its Python interface Stormpy. The integration works in two ways. First, we can translate a CMDP from FiMDP into Storm's data structures as an equivalent MDP that has the energy constraints encoded in states and actions. Second, we define CMDPs as a special case of MDPs with cost (for consumption) and labels (for reload states) and FiMDP can read all such MDPs from STORM into its own data structure as CMDPs. STORM's ability to read PRISM and JANI models extends thereby allowing us to read CMDPs expressed in the two languages into FiMDP. We implemented a direct support for reading PRISM files, including a convenient interface for parametric models, e.g., models with undefined constants.

Heuristics for Expected Reachability Time. The basic synthesis algorithm of [5] ensures that an accepting state is eventually reached with probability 1 (and then again and again, *ad infinitum*). However, it is purely qualitative and ignores the precise transition probabilities during strategy synthesis. Further, it does not take into account the expected number of steps to reach an accepting state, hereinafter referred to as the expected reachability time (ERT), a parameter of significant practical importance: e.g. from a patrolling unmanned vehicle we expect that it visits all the checkpoints in a reasonable amount of time. In order to tackle this issue, FiMDP employs two heuristics proposed in [6]: the *goal leaning* heuristic and its extension, the *threshold* heuristic with a *threshold* $0 \leq \delta \leq 1$ parameter. Both heuristics modify only the way in which the strategy π and the values *min-pos-reach* are computed.

Optimal Allocation in Multi-agent Scenarios. In many scenarios, we can use multiple agents to reach a set of accepting states instead of a single agent. Utilizing multiple agents instead of a single agent may significantly reduce the expected number of steps to reach all targets and the required energy capacity of each agent. Given a consumption MDP, a set of target states, and a set of homogeneous agents with fixed initial states, we compute a target allocation and an assignment of targets to agents. The objective is to minimize the *resource capacity* of the agents while ensuring that each target state is infinitely often visited by an agent with probability 1. We utilize a reduction to a new combinatorial optimization problem called *minimal-cost SCC matching* defined on graphs with edges denoting the minimal capacity needed to reach one target from another [9]. We first compute a decomposition of this graph into its strongly connected components (SCCs) using a binary search over the values for the resource capacity. We then assign each SCC to an agent to minimize the resource capacity of each agent. Our recent work [9] showed that this problem belongs to P, and our algorithm can solve this problem in polynomial time.

4   FiMDP: What Is Under the Hood and How to Drive It

FiMDP is written in Python 3 as a library with an interface suitable for the interactive environment of Jupyter notebooks. The basic functionality is accessible without any dependencies, and three third-party libraries are used for more involved features: Spot [10] with its Python bindings is needed for using the Büchi-automata-based and LTL specifications, STORM [15] with STORMPY is needed to read models described in PRISM or JANI languages, and finally GraphViz [13] is used to render visualizations in Jupyter notebooks.

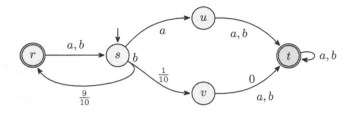

Fig. 1. Example CMDP. The doubly circled states r and t are reload states, s is the initial state, the green-shaded state t is an accepting state. We have two actions, a and b. The only probabilistic effect arises when playing b in s, where $P(s, b, r) = \frac{9}{10}$ and $P(s, b, v) = \frac{1}{10}$. We specify the consumption as $C(v, a) = C(v, b) = 0$ while $C(q, c) = 1$ for all states $q \neq v$ and all actions $c \in \{a, b\}$ (not shown in the figure). (Color figure online)

Threshold Example

```
[1]:  import fimdp
      fimdp.setup()

      mdp = fimdp.ConsMDP()
      mdp.new_states(5, names=["r", "s", "u", "v", "t"])
      mdp.set_reload([0, 4])
      # action: src_state, dst_distribution, label, consumption
      mdp.add_action(0, {1:1}, "a,b", 1); mdp.add_action(1, {2:1}, "a", 1)
      mdp.add_action(1, {3:.1, 0:.9},"b",1); mdp.add_action(2, {4:1}, "a,b", 1)
      mdp.add_action(3, {4:1}, "a,b", 0); mdp.add_action(4, {4:1}, "a,b", 1);
```

```
[2]:  targets = [mdp.state_with_name("t")]; capacity = 3
      solver = fimdp.energy_solvers.GoalLeaningES(mdp, capacity, targets, threshold=0.2)
      solver.get_min_levels(fimdp.objectives.BUCHI)
      solver.show()
```

```
[3]:  s = mdp.state_with_name("s")
      print(solver.get_selector(fimdp.objectives.BUCHI)[s])

      {
          1 - 1: b,
          2+: a
      }
```

Fig. 2. FiMDP in a Jupyter notebook. The notebook demonstrates the analysis of the threshold example. Reload states are doubly-circled and the accepting state t is green. (Color figure online)

Figure 2 represents a simple use case in Jupyter notebook. In cell `[1]` we build the CMDP from Fig. 1 and in cell `[2]` we compute and visualize the vector *min-lev* for the Büchi objective on the state t; for each state p, the value *min-lev*(p) is shown as the little green number next to the state's name. Finally, in cell [3] we show that the threshold heuristic indeed chooses action a for all resource levels ≥ 2, and the action b for the resource level equal to 1.

The package is built in a modular fashion; we describe the most important modules from the perspective of users. Figure 2 already uses three of them. The data structures for CMDPs and counter strategies are implemented in fimdp.core. To synthesize a strategy, the tool also uses one of the solvers implemented in fimdp.energy_solvers for one of the objectives defined in fimdp.objectives.

Labeled CMDPs, their product with DBAs, and strategies that keep track of an automaton in their memory are implemented in the module fimdp.labeled. Apart from the main symbolic algorithm sketched in Sect. 3, FiMDP allows to encode the energy constraints of a given CMDP into states and actions of a regular MDP that is equivalent to the CMDP via the fimdp.explicit module. Finally, such an MDP can be translated to the data structures of STORMPY with a function of the module responsible for the STORMPY integration: fimdp.io.

Solvers. Solvers are objects that do the main work. We need to supply a CMDP $\mathcal{M}$, the desired capacity[1], and the set of target states in order to create the solver. Additionally, solvers can accept specific parameters. For example, the GoalLeaningES solver accepts the parameter threshold in cell [2] of Fig. 2. FiMDP currently offers three solver classes (the ES in the names refers to *energy solver*). BasicES implements the algorithms as presented in [5]. GoalLeaningES implements both heuristics presented in Sect. 3; in fact, the goal-leaning heuristic is now implemented as the special case of the threshold heuristic with threshold=0. Finally, LeastFixpointES can solve the *safety* problem, e.g. never deplete the energy, more efficiently than BasicES on certain classes of CMDPs.

After we create a solver object, we can call the following three functions: compute, get_min_levels, and get_selector. All these functions take an objective (from fimdp.objectives) as a parameter and do what their names suggest.

Strategies and Simulators. After we call solver.get_selector, we can feed the selector to the constructor of CounterStrategy. We also need to initialize the initial memory of the strategy (init_energy in case of counter strategies) and set the initial state of the history. Then, strategy.next_action() returns the action picked by the strategy for the history it saw so far. The strategy then needs to know how the outcome of this action is resolved, e.g. what is the next state of the history. It accepts the information via the function strategy.update_state. Finally, in order to run the strategy again from the same initial conditions, we can call strategy.reset().

Given an initialized strategy and a number of steps n, the class Simulator from the fimdp.core module queries the strategy n times for an action to play and resolves the outcomes of these actions based on the transition probability

---

[1] Unlike the definition of CMDP in this paper, the implementation keeps the capacity outside of the CMDP object. That enables us to compare strategies built for different capacities without modification of the CMDP object.

function. The generated history is accessible by `simulator.state_history` and `simulator.action_history`.

Storm, PRISM, and JANI Models. FIMDP can both read and create CMDPs expressed in STORM's data structures. In the first direction, function `fimdp.io.encode_to_stormpy` takes a CMDP and capacity, builds a product CMDP in which the energy constraints are also encoded in states and actions, and converts this product to the `SparseMdp` object of STORM. Alternatively, we can create an MDP with the same state-space as the input CMDP, with the consumption expressed as an action-based reward called `consumption`, and with the reload states labeled by `reload`.

In the other directions, we can read such MDPs with `consumption` reward and `reload` label from STORM to FIMDP via the `storm_sparsemdp_to_consmdp` function. We can read similarly encoded models expressed in the PRISM language by `fimdp.io.prism_to_cmdp`. The function accepts a filename, and possibly a dictionary `constants` in which we can set values to constants left undefined in PRISM parametric models.

Data Structures. To follow the main design goals—simple user interface and easy exploration of the CMDP formalism—FIMDP works with explicitly encoded models. The class that represents CMDPs is called `fimdp.core.ConsMDP`. The states of a CMDP are represented implicitly by integers, and the actions are stored as a list of `ActionData` objects. An additional list maps each state s to the first action of s. Finally, all actions that start in s are linked by a nested list (linked by an attribute of `ActionData`) that is used for effective iterations over them. As seen in Fig. 2, FIMDP offers a convenient interface that hides this representation from the users.

The selected data structure enables interactive building of the CMDPs, simple modifications and processing of actions. It however incurs the price of higher memory requirements in comparison to sparse-matrix based representations of MDPs. As CMDPs can be substantially smaller than their equivalent MDP counterparts, the higher memory consumption is not a considerable limitation. Using the nested linked list enables the tool to quickly iterate the outgoing actions of one state without the need for sorting or other limitations of sparse matrices.

5   FIMDPENV: Environments for FIMDP

This section presents FIMDPENV, an open-source Python package containing environments that model real-world consumption Markov decision processes. In particular, we detail two environments that model (i) the stochastic dynamics of one or more unmanned underwater vehicles (UUVs) operating with limited onboard energy storage capacity, and, (ii) the stochastic energy consumption of an autonomous electric vehicle (AEV) operating in the busy streets of Manhattan, New York. All environments in FIMDPENV are based on real-world data and are designed to show the utility and scalability of our tool. In addition to these two environments discussed in detail below, adding more relevant environments is a part of our release roadmap.

5.1   UUV Environment

The UUV environment models the high-level dynamics of unmanned underwater vehicles (UUVs) operating in environments with stochastic ocean currents. We discretize the area of interest into two-dimensional grid-world environment where the cells form the state space and the UUV is expected to take high-level control decisions in each cell. The action space is comprised of two different classes of actions; the *weak* actions consume less energy but have stochastic outcomes whereas the *strong* actions have deterministic outcomes with the downside of significantly higher energy consumption. In the context of the UUV, the strong actions can model an additional actuator that can be used to correct the UUV course even in the presence of stronger currents. The environment offers up to 16 actions in total with weak and strong variants for each of the 8 directions: East, North-East, North, North-West, West, South-West, South, and South-East. While the ocean currents are stochastic, any data on mean flow velocity and UUV heading velocity available to the user can be readily incorporated into the environment [1]. Often, the UUVs with limited onboard energy storage capability, are expected to safely reload at predetermined locations while pursuing their objective of exploring given targets of interest.

The environment can be accessed by creating instances of one of the two classes in the `UUVEnv` module, `SingleAgentEnv` and `Synchronous MultiAgentEnv` where the former models a single agent operating in the grid-world whereas the latter models a user-specified number of agents acting synchronously in the environment. We now discuss the required inputs and the functionality provided for the single-agent environment with the understanding that the discussion extends to the multi-agent environment where the vector inputs provide information related to multiple agents. The user needs to specify the desired grid size, the reload states, the target states, and the energy capacity of the agents as required inputs. In addition, the users can also optionally specify the initial state, the size of the action space, and the UUV velocity. To run simulations on an instance of the environment, the user needs to generate a counter strategy using the `create_counterstrategy(solver, objective)` method by specifying the solver and objective to use. The state of an instance can also be updated using the `step()` method in one-step increments while the `reset()` can be used to reset the internal state of the environment. We refer the reader to the documentation for further details.

5.2   AEV Environment

The AEV environment, introduced in [5], models the routing problem of an autonomous vehicle operating on a street network. For our study, we consider the area in the middle of Manhattan, from 42nd to 116th Street. The user can specify their own region of interest by providing appropriate data. Intersections in the street network and directions of feasible movement form the state and action spaces of the MDP. We use intersections in the proximity of real-world fast charging stations [21] in the area of interest as the set of reload states.

After the AEV picks a direction, it reaches the next intersection in that direction deterministically with a stochastic energy consumption. As described in [5], we estimate the energy consumption distribution using the distribution of velocity on different road segments and discretize it into three possible values (c_1, c_2, c_3) reached with corresponding probabilities (p_1, p_2, p_3). We then model the transition from one intersection to another using additional dummy states creating a CMDP with 7378 states and 8473 actions.

The environment can be accessed by creating an instance of the `AEVEnv` class in the `AEVEnv` module of FIMDPENV. The required inputs are similar to the UUV environment with the exception of reload states which are already provided in the environment. The user needs to specify the starting and destination states of the AEV along with its energy capacity. While we consider a simple routing problem in this environment, a similar structure can also be used to model a variety of resource allocation and navigation problems in stochastic environments.

6   Evaluation

In this section, we first compare the time needed by FIMDP for strategy synthesis for a given CMDP, to the time needed by Storm to solve the equivalent problem with the energy constraints encoded in the state space of a regular MDP. Then we demonstrate the effect of the goal-leaning and the threshold heuristics on the expected reachability time.

6.1   Analyzing CMDPs in FIMDP and Storm

STORM is an open-source, state-of-the-art probabilistic model checker designed to be efficient in terms of time and memory. This section reveals whether the theory behind FIMDP can beat the efficient implementation of STORM.

We use the UUV environment described in Sect. 5 to generate CMDPs for grid-worlds of varying sizes and capacities. We measure the time FIMDP needs to analyze such CMDPs and to synthesize the corresponding strategy for the given Büchi objective. We also transform the CMDP into the equivalent MDP with the energy constraints encoded in states and actions. We then measure the time that STORMPY needs to finish `stormpy.model_checking(mdp, prop)` for this MDP and the qualitative Büchi property expressed in PCTL [2] as:
`prop = 'Pmax>=1 [G Pmax>=1 [F "target" & Pmax>=1 [F "reload"]]]'`

The computation time for different test scenarios, averaged over multiple runs, is presented in Fig. 3. The plots present the variation of average computation time with both capacity and size of the grid-world, both of which together define the overall size of the model. We can observe that FIMDP outperforms STORM in terms of computation time in all test cases with the exception of small problems where STORM, owing to its efficient C++ implementation, is faster. The advantage of FIMDP lies in the fact that the state-space of CMDPs (and also the time needed for their analysis) does not grow with rising capacity.

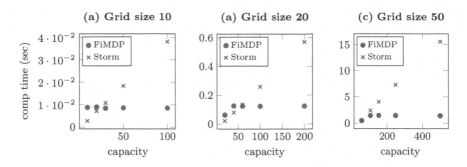

Fig. 3. Mean computation times for solving the CMDP model of the UUV environment with varying capacities proportional to the size of the grid-world. Each subplot in the figure corresponds to a different size of the grid-world.

6.2 Goal-Leaning Solvers

This section investigates the novel heuristics from a practical, optimal decision-making perspective. We utilize the UUV environment discussed in Sect. 5. The test scenario contains a single reload state and a single target, where the objective of the agent is to travel from its initial state to the target state and keep enough energy to be able to come back to the reload state. We consider agents with three different strategies generated by the solvers of FiMDP and measure the expected reachability time (ERT) introduced in Sect. 3 using 10,000 independent runs with a simulation horizon of 10,000. The agent following a counter strategy generated by the **BasicES** solver (no heuristic) never reached the target within the simulation horizon, since the probability of reaching the target between two visits to the reload state was too small. The agent with a strategy generated by the **GoalLeaningES** solver with no threshold (goal-leaning heuristic) needed about 124 time steps on average to reach the target. Finally, the agent following a strategy generated by **GoalLeaningES** with threshold 0.1 needed 62 time steps on average. Table 1 summarizes the ERT values for the discussed three solvers.

The goal-leaning solver ensures that the agent heads towards the target with high probability; only at the one place in the middle between the goal and the reload state, this agent picks a "wrong" action. The additional threshold eliminates this drawback and thus ensures that the agent always proceeds in a near-optimal fashion leading to a significant improvement in the ERT.

Table 1. Comparison of different energy solvers

Solver	Expected reachability time
BasicES	–
GoalLeaningES with threshold 0	124
GoalLeaningES with threshold 0.1	62

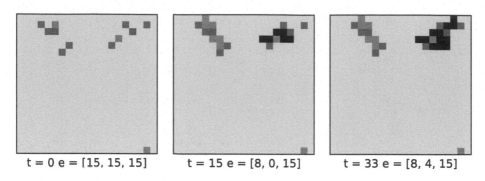

t = 0 e = [15, 15, 15]   t = 15 e = [8, 0, 15]   t = 33 e = [8, 4, 15]

Fig. 4. Demonstration of the multi-agent allocation algorithm with 3 agents (blue cells), 7 targets (green cells) and 2 reload states (red cells). The images provide snapshots of the current and historical locations of the agents at different time instances. We denote the trajectory of two different agents with black and gray cells. Note that the agent at the bottom right of the grid is not allocated to any target and therefore takes no action to transition into different cells in the grid. (Color figure online)

6.3   Multi-agent Allocation

In this section, we demonstrate the multi-agent allocation algorithm in the UUV environment, as in the previous subsection. This test scenario consists of allocating seven targets to three agents to satisfy a Büchi objective and then return to their initial location. As previously mentioned in Sect. 5, the allocation algorithm from [9] computes a target allocation and assignment to an agent to minimize the resource capacity of each agent, while satisfying the Büchi objective. Figure 4 shows a situation where the required capacity increases if all agents are required to allocate some of the target locations. In Fig. 4 we illustrate the initial locations of the agents and targets (left), the time-step (indicated with t) where the current energy level (the vector e) of one of the agents is minimal (middle), and the final time-step where all targets are visited by some agent.

The capacity required with the assignment (and the corresponding strategy) computed by the optimal allocation in this multi-agent scenario is 15. On the other hand, if we require to allocate some of the target locations to each agent, the minimal required capacity is 54, which is about four times larger compared to the optimal allocation. Such an allocation may induce a shorter time to visit all locations by using all agents. However, the difference in the required capacity highlights the tradeoffs between computing an allocation and a strategy that induces a trajectory with minimal time and energy capacity. We also estimate the expected time to visit all target locations using the allocation by simulating the strategies in the underlying consumption MDP. We run 10000 simulations with this strategy. On average, the strategy synthesized by using `GoalLeaningES` solver with threshold 0.3 needed 32.3 steps on average.

7 Conclusion

We introduced FiMDP, a tool for strategy synthesis in consumption MDPs with deterministic Büchi LTL objectives. The tool provides a robust framework for modeling, synthesis, simulation, and analysis of discrete resource-constrained stochastic systems. Our experiments show that FiMDP can efficiently handle models of real-world scenarios.

References

1. Al-Sabban, W.H., Gonzalez, L.F., Smith, R.N.: Extending persistent monitoring by combining ocean models and Markov decision processes. In: 2012 Oceans, pp. 1–10 (2012)
2. Baier, C., Katoen, J.P.: Principles of Model Checking. MIT Press, Cambridge (2008)
3. Bertsekas, D.P.: Dynamic Programming and Optimal Control, 3rd edn, Vol. II. Athena Scientific (2007). ISBN 1886529302
4. Bharadwaj, S., Le Roux, S., Pérez, G.A., Topcu, U.: Reduction techniques for model checking and learning in MDPs. In: 26th International Joint Conferences on Artificial Intelligence, pp. 4273–4279 (2017)
5. Blahoudek, F., Brázdil, T., Novotný, P., Ornik, M., Thangeda, P., Topcu, U.: Qualitative controller synthesis for consumption Markov decision processes. In: 32nd International Conference on Computer-Aided Verification, vol. II, pp. 421–447 (2020)
6. Blahoudek, F., Novotný, P., Ornik, M., Thangeda, P., Topcu, U.: Efficient strategy synthesis for MDPs with resource constraints (2021)
7. Brechtel, S., Gindele, T., Dillmann, R.: Probabilistic decision-making under uncertainty for autonomous driving using continuous POMDPs. In: 17th International IEEE Conference on Intelligent Transportation Systems, pp. 392–399 (2014)
8. Budde, C.E., Dehnert, C., Hahn, E.M., Hartmanns, A., Junges, S., Turrini, A.: JANI: quantitative model and tool interaction. In: Legay, A., Margaria, T. (eds.) TACAS 2017. LNCS, vol. 10206, pp. 151–168. Springer, Heidelberg (2017). https://doi.org/10.1007/978-3-662-54580-5_9
9. Cubuktepe, M., Blahoudek, F., Topcu, U.: Polynomial-time algorithms for multi-agent minimal-capacity planning (2021)
10. Duret-Lutz, A., Lewkowicz, A., Fauchille, A., Michaud, T., Renault, É., Xu, L.: Spot 2.0 — a framework for LTL and ω-automata manipulation. In: Artho, C., Legay, A., Peled, D. (eds.) ATVA 2016. LNCS, vol. 9938, pp. 122–129. Springer, Cham (2016). https://doi.org/10.1007/978-3-319-46520-3_8
11. Fainekos, G.E., Kress-Gazit, H., Pappas, G.J.: Temporal logic motion planning for mobile robots. In: IEEE International Conference on Robotics and Automation, pp. 2020–2025 (2005)
12. Feinberg, E.A., Shwartz, A.: Handbook of Markov Decision Processes: Methods and Applications. Springer, Cham (2012)
13. Gansner, E.R., North, S.C.: An open graph visualization system and its applications to software engineering. Softw. Pract. Exp. **30**(11), 1203–1233 (2000)
14. Hartmanns, A., Junges, S., Katoen, J.-P., Quatmann, T.: Multi-cost bounded reachability in MDP. In: Beyer, D., Huisman, M. (eds.) TACAS 2018. LNCS, vol. 10806, pp. 320–339. Springer, Cham (2018). https://doi.org/10.1007/978-3-319-89963-3_19

15. Hensel, C., Junges, S., Katoen, J.P., Quatmann, T., Volk, M.: The probabilistic model checker storm. Int. J. Softw. Tools Technol. Transfer 1–22 (2021)
16. Kober, J., Bagnell, J.A., Peters, J.: Reinforcement learning in robotics: a survey. Int. J. Robot. Res. **32**(11), 1238–1274 (2013)
17. Kwiatkowska, M., Norman, G., Parker, D.: PRISM 4.0: verification of probabilistic real-time systems. In: Gopalakrishnan, G., Qadeer, S. (eds.) CAV 2011. LNCS, vol. 6806, pp. 585–591. Springer, Heidelberg (2011). https://doi.org/10.1007/978-3-642-22110-1_47
18. Manna, Z., Pnueli, A.: A hierarchy of temporal properties. In: 6th Annual ACM Symposium on Principles of Distributed Computing, pp. 377–410 (1990)
19. Pnueli, A.: The temporal logic of programs. In: 18th Annual Symposium on Foundations of Computer Science, pp. 46–57 (1977)
20. Puterman, M.L.: Markov Decision Processes: Discrete Stochastic Dynamic Programming. Wiley, Hoboken (2014)
21. United States Department of Energy. Alternative fuels data center (2019). https://afdc.energy.gov/stations
22. Wolff, E.M., Topcu, U., Murray, R.M.: Robust control of uncertain Markov decision processes with temporal logic specifications. In: 51th IEEE Conference on Decision and Control, pp. 3372–3379 (2012)

HyperProb: A Model Checker for Probabilistic Hyperproperties

Oyendrila Dobe[1], Erika Ábrahám[2], Ezio Bartocci[3],
and Borzoo Bonakdarpour[1(✉)]

[1] Michigan State University, East Lansing, MI, USA
{dobeoyen,borzoo}@msu.edu
[2] RWTH-Aachen, Aachen, Germany
abraham@informatik.rwth-aachen.de
[3] Technische Universität Wien, Vienna, Austria
ezio.bartocci@tuwien.ac.at

Abstract. We present HyperProb, a model checker to verify probabilistic hyperproperties on Markov Decision Processes (MDP). Our tool receives as input an MDP expressed as a PRISM model and a formula in Hyper Probabilistic Computational Tree Logic (HyperPCTL). By restricting the domain of scheduler quantification to memoryless non-probabilistic schedulers, our tool exploits an SMT-based encoding to model check probabilistic hyperproperties in HyperPCTL. Furthermore, when the property is satisfied, the tool can provide a witness that can be used for synthesizing a DTMC that conforms with the specification.

1 Introduction

Stochastic phenomena appear in many systems. In computing systems that interact with the physical environment, the modeling of physical processes is usually probabilistic due to environmental uncertainties like thermal fluctuations, random message loss, and processor failure. Probabilistic models can be also used as approximations to analyze very complex deterministic physical processes.

Certain requirements of computing systems prescribe the behavior of the system as a whole – they *simultaneously* argue about different system executions and compare observations on them. Such requirements are called *hyperproperties* [3]. Hyperproperties can describe the requirements of probabilistic systems as well. They generally express probabilistic relations between multiple experiments. For example, in information-flow security, adding probabilities is motivated by establishing a connection between information theory and information flow across multiple traces. A prominent example is probabilistic schedulers that open up an opportunity for an attacker to set up a probabilistic covert channel. Or, *probabilistic causation* compares the probability of occurrence of an effect

This work is sponsored in part by the United States NSF SaTC-1813388 grant.

between scenarios where the cause is or is not present. Also, the goal of *quantitative information flow* is to measure the amount of information leaked about a secret by observing different runs of a program.

As a more concrete example, consider the MDP in Fig. 1b, we can express the property where a computation tree starting from a state labeled $h0$, reaches a state labeled $l1$ with probability at least 0.5 as the classical PCTL formula: $h0 \wedge \mathbb{P}(\Diamond l1) > 0.5$. But we cannot use PCTL to express a property where all pairs of computation trees, starting at states labeled $h0$ and $h1$ respectively, reach a state labeled $\ell1$ with equal probability. In a nondeterministic system, for all schedulers, the above property can be expressed using HyperPCTL [1,2] as follows:

$$\forall \hat{\sigma}. \; \forall \hat{s}(\hat{\sigma}). \; \forall \hat{s}'(\hat{\sigma}). \; \Big((h0_{\hat{s}} \wedge h1_{\hat{s}'}) \Rightarrow \big(\mathbb{P} \left(\Diamond \; \ell1_{\hat{s}} \right) = \mathbb{P} \left(\Diamond \; \ell1_{\hat{s}'} \right) \big) \Big)$$

In this paper, we introduce the tool HYPERPROB, a model checker for verifying probabilistic hyperproperties expressed in the temporal logic HyperPCTL [1,2] on Markov Decision Processes (MDP) given as a PRISM model [7]. HYPERPROB reduces the model checking problem to a satisfiability modulo theory (SMT) problem, implemented by the SMT-solver Z3 [4]. Furthermore, the tool may provide with the verdict of model checking accompanied by a witness or a counterexample represented as deterministic memoryless scheduler. A witness is provided when the probabilistic hyperproperty containing an existential quantifier over all the possible schedulers, holds, and it can be used to synthesize the induced discrete-time Markov chain (DTMC) satisfying the desired probabilistic hyperproperty. A counterexample is provided when the probabilistic hyperproperty containing a universal quantifier over all possible schedulers, does not hold, and it can be exploited to synthesize an adversarial attack that may violate the desired probabilistic hyperproperty.

This tool demonstration paper provides guide for potential users of HYPERPROB, focusing on the usage and implementation aspects of the tool. For details on theoretical and algorithmic aspects of HYPERPROB, we refer to [1,2]. Our implementation is available at: https://www.cse.msu.edu/tart/tools.

2   Input to the Tool

Input Modeling Language. The input model is provided as a high-level PRISM[1] program [7]. We illustrate the language here on a simple example shown in Fig. 1. This program takes a high-security input h and computes a low-security output ℓ. The execution steps are represented symbolically by probabilistic actions. For example, line 5 in Fig. 1a declares that action `alpha` can be executed if $\ell = 0$ and $h = 0$, and the action resets ℓ to the value 1 with probability 3/4, and to the value 2 with probability 1/4. Line 10 defines that $\ell = 0$ initially. Modeling each state explicitly yields the Markov decision process (MDP) depicted in Fig. 1b, where the state labeling with atomic propositions is defined in the lines 11–14

---

[1] https://www.prismmodelchecker.org/.

in Fig. 1a. For the given PRISM program, we use STORMpy to parse the model and to generate the underlying MDP.

```
1    mdp
2    module basic_mdp
3      h: [0..1]; // high input
4      ℓ: [0..2]; // low output
5      [alpha] (ℓ=0 & h=0) → 3/4: (ℓ'=1) + 1/4: (ℓ'=2);
6      [alpha] (ℓ=0 & h=1) → 2/3: (ℓ'=1) + 1/3: (ℓ'=2);
7      [beta]  (h=0) → 1/2: (ℓ'=1) + 1/2: (ℓ'=2);
8      [beta]  (h=1) → 1/2: (ℓ'=1) + 1/2: (ℓ'=2);
9      [tau]   (!ℓ=0) → 1: true;
10   endmodule
11   init  (ℓ=0) endinit    //initial states
12   label "h0" = (h=0);    //h0 label on s0
13   label "h1" = (h=1);    //h1 label on s1
14   label "ℓ1" = (ℓ=1);    //ℓ1 label on s2,s4
15   label "ℓ2" = (ℓ=2);    //ℓ2 label on s3,s5
```

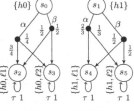

(b) MDP of the PRISM program in Fig 1a.

(a) PRISM model generating the MDP in Fig.1b

Fig. 1. An MDP and its corresponding PRISM program.

Specification Language: To protect the secret value h, there should be no probabilistic dependency between observations on the low variable ℓ and the value of h. For example, an attacker that chooses a scheduler that always takes action α from states s_0 and s_1 can learn whether or not $h = 0$ by observing the probability of obtaining $\ell = 1$ (or $\ell = 2$). Such properties, which compare observations on system execution when using different schedulers in different initial states are *probabilistic hyperproperties*. These properties, which should be model checked by HYPERPROB, can be specified in the temporal logic HyperPCTL [1]. We refer to [1] for a detailed description of HyperPCTL but show the tool's input grammar in Fig. 2. For example, the property that we expect from the MDP in Fig. 1b is that for any scheduler (*AS sched.*) and any two initial states $s1$ and $s2$ (*A s1. A s2.*) with different high input values ($h0(s1) \wedge h1(s2)$), the probability to reach the low value 1 from $s1$ ($P\ F\ \ell1(s1)$) is the same as from $s2$ ($P\ F\ \ell1(s2)$), and analogously for the low value 2:

$$AS\ sched.\ A\ s1.\ A\ s2.\ (h0(s1) \wedge h1(s2)) =>$$
$$(P\ F\ \ell1(s1) = P\ F\ \ell1(s2))\ \&\ (P\ F\ \ell2(s1) = P\ F\ \ell2(s2))$$

Note that in the above formula we use expressions of the form $a(s)$ to state that the atomic proposition a holds in the computation tree starting from the (quantified) state s. For this formula, our tool will provide a violation as output with a deterministic memoryless scheduler that would leak information to an attacker.

$$\varphi^{sched} ::= \text{"AS" NAME "." } \varphi^{state} \mid \text{"ES" NAME "." } \varphi^{state}$$

$$\varphi^{state} ::= \phi \mid \text{"A" NAME "." } \varphi^{state} \mid \text{"E" NAME "." } \varphi^{state}$$

$$\phi ::= \text{"t" } \mid \text{"f" } \mid \text{NAME "(" NAME ")" } \mid \text{"}\sim\text{" } \phi \mid$$
$$\phi \text{ "\&" } \phi \mid \phi \text{ "|" } \phi \mid \phi \text{ "=>" } \phi \mid \phi \text{ "<->" } \phi \mid c$$

$$c ::= p \text{ "<" } p \mid p \text{ "<=" } p \mid p \text{ "=" } p \mid p \text{ ">=" } p \mid p \text{ ">" } p$$

$$p ::= \text{"P" } \psi \mid p \text{ "+" } p \mid p \text{ "-" } p \mid p \text{ "." } p \mid \text{NUM}$$

$$\psi ::= \text{"(X" } \phi \text{ ")" } \mid \text{"(" } \phi \text{ "U" } \phi \text{ ")" } \mid$$
$$\text{"(" } \phi \text{ "U[" NUM "," NUM "]" } \phi \text{ ")" } \mid \text{"(F" } \phi \text{ ")"}$$

Fig. 2. Grammar defining HyperPCTL inputs to HYPERPROB, where the NUM token is a decimal number and NAME is a non-empty string.

3   Tool Structure and Usage

3.1   Implementation

HYPERPROB, is an optimized implementation of the algorithm presented in [1]. Given an MDP and a HyperPCTL property, it verifies if the given hyperproperty holds in the input MDP. Depending on the scheduler quantifier in the hyperproperty, if it holds, we get a witness to the property (in case of $\exists$) or if the hyperproperty does not hold, we get a counterexample in the model (in case of $\forall$). The witness or counterexample is defined by the actions chosen at each state to obtain the required DTMC.

The tool has been implemented using Python3 and depends on several python packages. Computer Arithmetic and Logic (CArL), is an open source C++ library for handling of complex mathematical computations and is needed by STORM. Carl-parser is an ANTLR based parser which is meant as an exten-

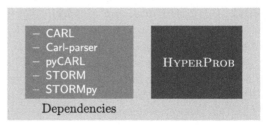

Fig. 3. Overview of the docker container with the tool and its dependencies

sion to CArL. pyCArL essentially provides python bindings for CArL and is a dependency for STORM. STORM is an academically developed probabilistic model checker. STORMpy is the python binding for STORM that we use to parse the input model. For the ease of usage, we have provided a docker image for the user. The image comes pre-installed with Ubuntu, all the required dependencies, and the tool. Docker makes it easier for the user to run the tool, as they do not have to install any of the dependencies mentioned above. The main advantage of docker is that running of the tool becomes independent of the operating system the user has. The overall view of the docker container can be seen in Fig. 3.

Inside the tool, as shown in Fig. 4, we first parse the model using STORMpy [9] to store them in an optimized way and for easy retrieval of the details of the model like labels, transitions, states, and actions. We, then, parse the input hyperproperty into a syntax tree that allows us to recursively encode the property in the next stages. Using the parsed model, we first encode all possible actions in each state as SMT constraints. Using the parsed model and the parsed property, we encode, as SMT constraints, both, the quantifier combinations by generating constraints that should be satisfied at all states (for $\forall$) or by at least one state (for $\exists$), and the semantic interpretation of the operators in the formula.

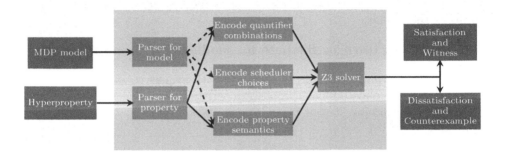

Fig. 4. Dataflow inside the tool

In the final step of the algorithm, we feed these constraints to the SMT solver Z3 [4]. If our scheduler quantifier is a $\exists$, and the constraints are satisfiable, the tool outputs a witness to the property, as a set of actions that should be chosen at each state of the model. If our scheduler quantifier is a $\forall$, and the constraints are unsatisfiable, the tool outputs a counterexample to the property as a set of actions that should be chosen at each state of the model. For all the other combinations of the scheduler quantifier and satisfiability, the tool returns a true/false but with no sequence of actions.

In our previous work [1], we present the HyperPCTL model checking algorithm for MDPs. HYPERPROB, incorporates additional optimizations whose impact is reflected in Table 1 (columns **N** referring to original implementation in [1], and **O** referring to the optimized implementation). In particular, instead of considering all possible state combinations when encoding a state formula for Z3, we consider only the relevant state combinations. For example, let us consider the scenario in Fig. 1 with six states, and its HyperPCTL specification as described in Sect. 2 with two state quantifiers. Our goal is to encode the atomic proposition $h0(s1)$. In the unoptimized version, this is encoded for 36 state combinations $((s_{0_1}, s_{0_2}), (s_{0_1}, s_{1_2}), \ldots, (s_{1_1}, s_{0_2}), \ldots, (s_{5_1}, s_{5_2}))$, since we have two copies of the MDP. However, in HYPERPROB, we consider the information that while encoding $h0(s1)$, only states of the second copy of the MDP are relevant. Hence, we encode it for just six state combinations, $((s_{0_1}, s_{0_2}), \ldots, (s_{0_1}, s_{5_2}))$. We keep the first state for the irrelevant copy as the first member of every state combination.

This not only reduces the number of constraints generated but also relaxes the constraints Z3 needed work on.

3.2   Usage

In order to use the tool, we will first need to ensure that our system has docker [5] installed in it. Then, download the *docker image* and create a container from it. Inside the container, all dependency packages are installed in the */opt* folder under the root directory. The main tool package is located in */home/HyperProb* folder under the root directory. We can add our model file anywhere in this folder. The tool can be run by invoking the **source.py** script with appropriate inputs in the format,

python source.py **file_path_for_model hyperproperty**

Here *file_path_for_model* refers to the file path with respect to */home/HyperProb* directory as base and the hyperproperty is written according to the grammar in Sect. 2. For example, if your file is */home/HyperProb/models/mdp.nm*, your command would be,

python source.py **models/mdp.nm hyperproperty**

The commands to replicate all our case studies have been placed under */home/HyperProb/benchmark_files/Experiments.txt*.

4   Evaluation

4.1   Case Studies

Side-Channel Timing Leaks. open a channel for attackers to infer the value of a secret by observing the execution time of a function. For example, the heart of the RSA public-key encryption algorithm is the modular exponentiation algorithm that computes $(a^b \mod n)$, where a is an integer representing the plaintext and b is the integer encryption key. A careless implementation can leak b through a probabilistic scheduling channel (see Fig. 5). This program is not secure since the two branches of the *if* have

```
1 void  mexp(){
2    c = 0; d = 1; i = k;
3    while (i >= 0){
4       i = i−1; c = c*2;
5       d = (d*d) % n;
6       if (b(i) = 1)
7          c = c+1;
8          d = (d*a) % n;
9       }
10 }
11 ***********
12 t = new Thread(mexp());
13 j = 0; m = 2 * k;
14 while (j < m & !t.stop) j++;
15 ***********
```

Fig. 5. Modular exponentiation.

different timing behaviors. Under a fair execution scheduler for parallel threads, an attacker thread can infer the value of b by running in parallel to a modular exponentiation thread and iteratively incrementing a counter variable until the other thread terminates (lines 12–14). To model this program by an MDP, we can use two nondeterministic actions for the two branches of the *if* statement, such that the choice of different schedulers corresponds to the choice of different bit configurations b(i) for the key b. This algorithm should satisfy the following property: the probability of observing a concrete value in the counter j should be independent of the bit configuration of the secret key b:

$$\forall \hat{\sigma}_1. \forall \hat{\sigma}_2. \forall \hat{s}(\hat{\sigma}_1). \forall \hat{s}'(\hat{\sigma}_2). \left(init_{\hat{s}} \wedge init_{\hat{s}'} \right) \Rightarrow \bigwedge_{\ell=0}^{m} \left(\mathbb{P}(\Diamond(j = \ell)_{\hat{s}}) = \mathbb{P}(\Diamond(j = \ell)_{\hat{s}'}) \right)$$

Another example of timing attack that can be implemented through a probabilistic scheduling side channel is password verification. It is typically implemented by comparing an input string with another confidential string (see Fig. 6). Also here, an attacker thread can measure the time necessary to break the loop, and use this information to infer the prefix of the input string matching the secret string.

```
1 int str_cmp(char * r){
2    char * s = 'Bg\$4\0';
3    i = 0;
4    while (s[i] != '\0'){
5       i++;
6       if (s[i]!=r[i]) return 0;
7    }
8    return 1;
9 }
```

Fig. 6. String comparison.

Scheduler-specific observational determinism policy (SSODP) [8] is a confidentiality policy in multi-threaded programs that defends against an attacker choosing an appropriate scheduler to control the set of possible traces. In particular, given any scheduler and two initial states that are indistinguishable with respect to a secret input (i.e., low-equivalent), any two executions from these two states should terminate in low-equivalent states with equal probability. Formally, given a proposition h representing a secret:

$$\forall \hat{\sigma}. \forall \hat{s}(\hat{\sigma}). \forall \hat{s}'(\hat{\sigma}). \left(h_{\hat{s}} \oplus h_{\hat{s}'} \right) \Rightarrow \bigwedge_{\ell \in L} \left(\mathbb{P}(\Diamond \ell_{\hat{s}}) = \mathbb{P}(\Diamond \ell_{\hat{s}'}) \right)$$

where $\ell \in L$ are atomic propositions that classify low-equivalent states and $\oplus$ is the exclusive-or operator. A stronger variation of this policy is that the executions are stepwise low-equivalent:

$$\forall \hat{\sigma}. \forall \hat{s}(\hat{\sigma}). \forall \hat{s}'(\hat{\sigma}). \left(h_{\hat{s}} \oplus h_{\hat{s}'} \right) \Rightarrow \mathbb{P}\Box \left(\bigwedge_{\ell \in L} \left((\mathbb{P}\bigcirc \ell_{\hat{s}}) = (\mathbb{P}\bigcirc \ell_{\hat{s}'}) \right) \right) = 1.$$

Probabilistic conformance describes how well a model and an implementation conform with each other with respect to a specification. As an example, consider a six-sided die. The probability to obtain one possible side of the die is 1/6. We would like to synthesize a protocol that simulates the six-sided die behavior only by repeatedly tossing a fair coin. We know that such an implementation exists [6], but our aim is to find such a solution automatically by modeling the die as a DTMC and by using an MDP to model all the possible coin-implementations

Table 1. Experimental results and comparison. **TA:** Timing attack. **PW:** Password leakage. **TS:** Thread scheduling. **PC:** Probabilistic conformance. **TO:** Timeout. **N:** Prototype presented in [1]. **O:** HyperProb, **SE:** SMT encoding. **SS:** SMT solving. #op: Formula size (number of operators). #st: Number of states. #tr: Number of transitions.

Case study		Running time(s)						#SMT variables		#op	#st	#tr
		SE		SS		Total						
		N	O	N	O	N	O	N	O			
TA	$m = 2$	5	2	<1	<1	5	2	8088	2520	14	24	46
	$m = 4$	114	18	20	1	134	19	50460	14940		60	136
	$m = 6$	1721	140	865	45	2586	185	175728	51184		112	274
	$m = 8$	12585	952	TO	426	TO	1378	388980	131220		180	460
PW	$m = 2$	5	2	<1	<1	6	3	8088	2520	14	24	46
	$m = 4$	207	26	40	1	247	27	68670	20230		70	146
	$m = 6$	3980	331	1099	41	5079	372	274540	79660		140	302
	$m = 8$	26885	2636	TO	364	TO	3000	657306	221130		234	514
TS	$h = (0,1)$	<1	<1	<1	<1	1	1	1379	441	28	7	13
	$h = (0,15)$	60	8	1607	<1	1667	8	34335	8085		35	83
	$h = (4,8)$	12	3	17	<1	29	3	12369	3087		21	48
	$h = (8,15)$	60	8	1606	<1	1666	8	34335	8085		35	83
	$h = (10,20)$	186	19	13707	1	13893	20	52695	13095		45	108
PC	$s = (0)$	277	10	1996	5	2273	15	21220	6780	44	20	188
	$s = (0,1)$	822	13	5808	5	6630	18	21220	6780		20	340
	$s = (0..2)$	1690	15	TO	5	TO	20	21220	6780		20	494
	$s = (0..3)$	4631	16	TO	7	TO	23	21220	6780		20	648
	$s = (0..4)$	7353	22	TO	21	TO	43	21220	6780		20	802
	$s = (0..5)$	10661	19	TO	61	TO	80	21220	6780		20	956
	$s = (0..6)$	13320	18	TO	41	TO	59	21220	6780		20	1110

with a given maximum number of states, including six absorbing final states to model the outcomes. In the MDP, we associate with the states, a set of possible nondeterministic actions, each of them choosing two states as successors with equal probability $1/2$. Then, each scheduler corresponds to a particular implementation. Our goal is to check whether there exists a scheduler that induces a DTMC over the MDP, such that repeatedly tossing a coin simulates die-rolling with equal probabilities for all possible outcomes:

$$\exists \hat{\sigma}.\forall \hat{s}(\hat{\sigma}).\exists \hat{s}'(\hat{\sigma}).\Big(init_{\hat{s}} \wedge init_{\hat{s}'} \Big) \;\Rightarrow\; \bigwedge_{\ell=1}^{6} \Big(\mathbb{P}(\Diamond(die = \ell)_{\hat{s}}) = \mathbb{P}(\Diamond(die = \ell)_{\hat{s}'}) \Big)$$

4.2   Results and Discussions

All of our experiments in Sect. 4.1 were run on a MacBook Pro with a 2.3 GHz quad-core i7 processor with 32 GB of RAM. The results are presented in Table 1.

For our first case study **TA**, described in Sect. 4.1, models and analyzes information leakage in the modular exponentiation algorithm. We experimented with up to four bits for the encryption key (hence, $m \in \{2, 4, 6, 8\}$). The specification checks whether there is a timing channel for all possible schedulers, which is the case for the implementation in `modexp`.

Our second case study **PW**, described in Sect. 4.1 handles the verification of password leakage through the string comparison algorithm. Here, we experimented with $m \in \{2, 4, 6, 8\}$.

In our third case study **TS**, described in Sect. 4.1, we assume two concurrent processes. The first process decrements the value of a secret h by 1 as long as the value is still positive, and after this it sets a low variable ℓ to 1. A second process just sets the value of the same low variable ℓ to 2. The two threads run in parallel; as long as none of them terminates. A fair scheduler chooses for each CPU cycle the next executing thread. This opens a probabilistic thread scheduling channel and leaks the value of h. We compare observations for executions with different secret values h_1 and h_2 (denoted as $h = (h_1, h_2)$). There is an interesting relation between the data for **TS**. Both the encoding and running time for the experiment is proportional to the higher value in the tuple h.

Our last case study **PC**, described in Sect. 4.1, is on probabilistic conformance. The input is a DTMC modeling a fair 6-sided die as well as an MDP whose actions model single fair coin tosses with two successor states each. We are interested in finding a scheduler that induces a DTMC which simulates the die outcomes using a fair coin. Given a fixed state space, we experiment with different numbers of actions. In particular, we started from the implementation in [6] and for the state space of the die section of the protocol, we added all the possible nondeterministic transitions from the first state to all the other states (denoted $s = 0$), from the first and second states to all the others ($s = 0, 1$), and, similarly scaled it stepwise to include transitions from all states to all others ($s = 0 \ldots 6$). Each time, we were not only able to satisfy the formula, but also obtain the witness corresponding to the scheduler satisfying the property.

In our previous prototypical implementation [1], due to encoding of all formula for all composed states, both the encoding as well as SMT solving time were significantly higher. Hence, we opted for a timeout for cases where the timing did not seem practically useful. For **TA**, **PW**, and **PC**, we used a timeout of 0000 s for the SMT solving.

5   Conclusion

We introduced HyperProb, a fully automated tool for model checking probabilistic hyperproperties expressed in the temporal logic HyperPCTL for DTMCs and as well as MDPs. HyperProb reduces the model checking problem to a satisfiability modulo theory (SMT) problem, implemented by the SMT-solver Z3 [4]. Furthermore, the tool may provide with the verdict of model checking, a witness or a counterexample represented as a deterministic memoryless scheduler. A witness is provided when the probabilistic hyperproperty contains an existential scheduler quantifier and it can be used to synthesize the induced discrete-time Markov chain (DTMC) satisfying the desired probabilistic hyper-property. The counterexample is provided when the probabilistic hyperproperty contains a universal scheduler quantifier and it can be exploited to synthesize an adversarial attack that may violate the desired probabilistic hyperproperty. We also provided detailed experimental results that evaluate the effectiveness of our tool.

References

1. Ábrahám, E., Bartocci, E., Bonakdarpour, B., Dobe, O.: Probabilistic hyperproper-ties with nondeterminism. In: Hung, D.V., Sokolsky, O. (eds.) ATVA 2020. LNCS, vol. 12302, pp. 518–534. Springer, Cham (2020). https://doi.org/10.1007/978-3-030-59152-6_29
2. Ábrahám, E., Bonakdarpour, B.: HyperPCTL: A temporal logic for probabilistic hyperproperties. In: Proceedings of QEST 2018, pp. 20–35 (2018)
3. Clarkson, M.R., Schneider, F.B.: Hyperproperties. J. Comput. Secur. **18**(6), 1157–1210 (2010)
4. de Moura, L.M., Bjørner, N.: Z3: an efficient SMT solver. In: Proceedings of TACAS 2008, pp. 337–340 (2008)
5. Docker. https://www.docker.com/get-started
6. Knuth, D., Yao, A.: Algorithms and complexity: new directions and recent results. In: The Complexity of Nonuniform Random Number Generation. Academic Press (1976)
7. Kwiatkowska, M., Norman, G., Parker, D.: PRISM 4.0: verification of probabilistic real-time systems. In: Gopalakrishnan, G., Qadeer, S. (eds.) CAV 2011. LNCS, vol. 6806, pp. 585–591. Springer, Heidelberg (2011). https://doi.org/10.1007/978-3-642-22110-1_47
8. Ngo, T.M., Stoelinga, M., Huisman, M.: Confidentiality for probabilistic multi-threaded programs and its verification. In: Proceedings of ESSoS 2013, pp. 107–122 (2013)
9. STORMpy. https://moves-rwth.github.io/stormpy/

The Probabilistic Termination Tool Amber

Marcel Moosbrugger[1]([⊠]) [iD], Ezio Bartocci[1] [iD], Joost-Pieter Katoen[2] [iD], and Laura Kovács[1] [iD]

[1] TU Wien, Vienna, Austria
marcel.moosbrugger@tuwien.ac.at
[2] RWTH Aachen University, Aachen, Germany

Abstract. We describe the AMBER tool for proving and refuting the termination of a class of probabilistic while-programs with polynomial arithmetic, in a fully automated manner. AMBER combines martingale theory with properties of asymptotic bounding functions and implements relaxed versions of existing probabilistic termination proof rules to prove/disprove (positive) almost sure termination of probabilistic loops. AMBER supports programs parameterized by symbolic constants and drawing from common probability distributions. Our experimental comparisons give practical evidence of AMBER outperforming existing state-of-the-art tools.

Keywords: Almost sure termination · Martingales · Asymptotic bounds

1 Introduction

Probabilistic programming obviates the need to manually provide inference methods and enables rapid prototyping [13]. Automated formal verification of probabilistic programs, however, is still in its infancy. Our tool AMBER provides a step towards solving this problem when it comes to automating the termination analysis of probabilistic programs, which is an active research topic [1, 6, 7, 9–12, 14, 16]. Probabilistic programs are almost-surely terminating (AST) if they terminate with probability 1 on all inputs. They are positively AST (PAST) if their expected runtime is finite [5]. We describe AMBER, a fully automated software artifact to prove/disprove (P)AST. Proving (P)AST is a notoriously difficult problem; in fact it is harder than proving traditional program termination [15]. AMBER supports the analysis of a class of polynomial probabilistic programs. Programs in the supported class consist of single loops whose body is a sequence of random assignments with acyclic variable dependencies. Moreover, AMBER's

This research was supported by the WWTF ICT19-018 grant ProbInG, the ERC Starting Grant SYMCAR 639270, ERC Consolidator Grant ARTIST 101002685, the ERC AdG Grant FRAPPANT 787914, the Austrian FWF project W1255-N23, and the SecInt Doctoral College funded by TU Wien.

M. Huisman et al. (Eds.): FM 2021, LNCS 13047, pp. 667–675, 2021.
https://doi.org/10.1007/978-3-030-90870-6_36

$bop \in \{+, -, *, **, /\}, cop \in \{>, <\}$

$dist \in \{$uniform, gauss, laplace, bernoulli, binomial, geometric, hypergeometric, exponential, beta, chi-squared, rayleigh$\}$

$\langle program \rangle ::= \langle i\_assign \rangle^* \text{ while } \langle poly \rangle \langle cop \rangle \langle poly \rangle : \langle rv\_assign \rangle^+ \langle v\_assign \rangle^+$

$\langle i\_assign \rangle ::= \langle var \rangle = \langle const \rangle \mid \langle var \rangle = \langle rv\_expr \rangle \qquad \langle rv\_assign \rangle ::= \langle var \rangle = \langle rv\_expr \rangle$

$\langle v\_assign \rangle ::= \langle var \rangle = \langle branches \rangle \qquad \langle rv\_expr \rangle ::= \text{RV}(\langle dist \rangle [, \langle const \rangle]^*)$

$\langle branches \rangle ::= \langle poly \rangle \mid \langle poly \rangle @ \langle const \rangle; \langle branches \rangle$

$\langle poly \rangle ::= p \in C[V] \qquad \langle sym \rangle ::= \text{[a-zA-Z][a-zA-Z0-9]}^* \qquad \langle var \rangle \text{ V} ::= \text{[a-zA-Z][a-zA-Z0-9]}^*$

$\langle const \rangle \text{ C} ::= n \in \mathbb{N} \mid \langle sym \rangle \mid - \langle const \rangle \mid \langle const \rangle \langle bop \rangle \langle const \rangle$

Fig. 1. The AMBER input syntax. $C[V]$ denotes the set of polynomials in V (program variables) with coefficients from C (constants). The power operator is '**'.

programming model supports programs parametrized by symbolic constants and drawing from common probability distributions. To automate termination analysis, AMBER automates relaxations of various existing martingale-based proof rules ensuring (non-)(P)AST [8] and combines symbolic computation with asymptotic bounding functions. AMBER certifies (non-)(P)AST without relying on user-provided templates/bounds over termination conditions. Our experiments demonstrate AMBER outperforming the state-of-the-art in the automated termination analysis of probabilistic programs (Sect. 3).

Related Work. The tools MGen [6] and LexRSM [1] use linear programming techniques to certify PAST and AST, respectively. The recent tools Absynth [20], KoAT2 [18] and ecoimp [2] can establish upper bounds on expected costs, therefore also on expected runtimes, and thus certify PAST. While powerful on respective AST/PAST domains, we note that none of the aforementioned tools support both proving and disproving (P)AST. AMBER is the first tool able to prove and disprove (P)AST. Our recent work introduces relaxations of existing proof rules for probabilistic (non-)termination together with automation techniques based on *asymptotic bounding functions* [19]. We utilize these proof rule relaxations in AMBER and extend the technique of asymptotic bounding functions to programs drawing from common probability distributions and including symbolic constants.

Contributions. This tool demonstration paper describes *what* AMBER can do and *how* it can be used for certifying (non-)(P)AST.

- We present AMBER, a fully automatic open-source software artifact[1] for certifying probabilistic (non-)termination (Sect. 2).
- We exhaustively compare AMBER to related tools and report on our experimental findings (Sect. 3).
- We provide a benchmark suite of 50 probabilistic programs as a publicly available repository of probabilistic program examples (Sect. 3).

---

[1] https://github.com/probing-lab/amber.

```
1   x = RV(gauss , 0, 1)
2   y = RV(gauss , 0, 1)
3   while x**2+y**2 < c:
4       s = RV(uniform , 1, 2)
5       t = RV(gauss , 0, 1)
6       x = x+s @1/2; x+2*s
7       y = y+x+t**2 @1/2; y-x-t**2
```
(a)

```
1   x = x0
2   while x > 0:
3       x = x+c @1/2; x-c
```
(b)

```
1   x = x0
2   while x > 0:
3       x = x+c @1/2+e; x-c
```
(c)

Fig. 2. Two programs supported by AMBER, with symbolic constants $c, x0, e \in \mathbb{R}^+$; Program 2a is PAST, program 2b is AST but not PAST and program 2c is not AST.

2   Usage and Components

Programming Model. AMBER supports analyzing the probabilistic termination behavior of a class of probabilistic programs involving polynomial arithmetic and drawing from common probability distributions, parameterized by symbolic constants which represent arbitrary real numbers. All symbolic constants are assumed to be positive. Negative constants can be modeled with the explicit use of "-". The grammar in Fig. 1 defines the input programs to AMBER. Inputs consist of an initialization part and a while-loop, whose guard is a polynomial inequality over program variables. The initialization part is a sequence of assignments either assigning (symbolic) constants or values drawn from probability distributions. Within the loop body, program variables are updated with either (i) a value drawn from a distribution or (ii) one of multiple polynomials over program variables with some probability. Additional to the structure imposed by the grammar in Fig. 1, input programs are required to satisfy the following *structural constraint: each variable updated in the loop body depends at most linearly on itself and at most polynomially on variables preceding.* On a high-level, this constraint enables the use of algebraic recurrence techniques for probabilistic termination analysis [19]. Despite the syntactical restrictions, most existing benchmarks on automated probabilistic termination analysis [19] and dynamic Bayesian networks [3] can be encoded in our programming language. Figure 2 shows three example programs for which AMBER is able to automatically infer the respective termination behavior.

Implementation and Usage. AMBER is implemented in `python3` and relies on the `lark-parser`[2] package to parse its input programs. Further, AMBER uses the `diofant`[3] package as its computer-algebra system. To compute closed-form expressions for statistical moments of monomials over program variables only depending on the loop counter, AMBER uses the tool `Mora` [4]. However, for efficient integration within AMBER, we reimplemented and adapted the `Mora` functionalities exploited by AMBER (`Mora v2`), in particular by employing dynamic

---

[2] https://github.com/lark-parser/lark.
[3] https://github.com/diofant/diofant.

programming to avoid redundant computations. Altogether, AMBER consists of ∼2000 lines of code. Figure 3 shows AMBER's output when run on the program from Fig. 2a. AMBER can be used through a Docker container [17] or installed locally. Detailed installation and usage instructions are available at https://github.com/probing-lab/amber.

Run with Docker. AMBER can be used through a Docker container [17] by running: `$ docker run -ti marcelmoosbrugger/amber`
AMBER can be run on our `2d_bounded_random_walk` benchmark with:
`$ ./amber benchmarks/past/2d_bounded_random_walk`

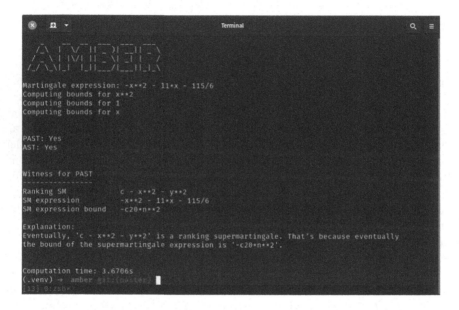

Fig. 3. The output of AMBER when run on the program from Fig. 2a.

Local Installation. First, clone the repository by running the following command in your terminal: `$ git clone git@github.com:probing-lab/amber.git`
Change directories to AMBER's root folder and make sure `python3.8` and the package manager `pip` are installed on your system. All required python packages can be installed by running `$ pip install -r requirements.txt`
Create an input program (see Sect. 2) and save it in the `benchmarks` folder for example with the file name `my-benchmark`. AMBER can now be run with respect to the input program `benchmarks/my-benchmark` with the following command:
`$ python ./amber.py --benchmarks benchmarks/my-benchmark`.

Components. Figure 4 illustrates AMBER's main components. AMBER uses four existing probabilistic termination proof rules [6,9,12,16] and their relaxations [19]. Additionally, AMBER extends the algorithms for these relaxations to further support drawing from common probability distributions and symbolic

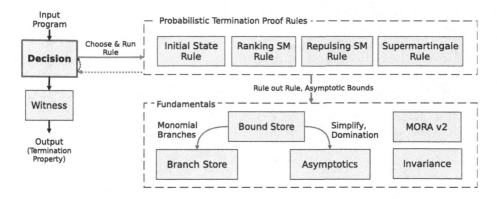

Fig. 4. Main components of AMBER and interactions between them.

constants (cf. Fig. 1). After parsing the input program, AMBER initializes the four proof rule relaxations and determines their applicability [19]. AMBER then executes applicable proof rules consecutively and reports the analysis result containing potential witnesses for (non-)(P)AST. The proof rule algorithms require the computation of asymptotic bounding functions which is implemented in the *Bound Store* component.

3   Evaluation

Experimental Setup. AMBER and our benchmarks, are publicly available at https://github.com/probing-lab/amber. The output of AMBER is an answer ("Yes", "No" or "Maybe") to PAST and AST, together with a potential witness. We took all 39 benchmarks from [19] and extended them by 11 new programs to test AMBER's capability to handle symbolic constants and drawing from probability distributions. The 11 new benchmarks are constructed from the 39 original programs, by adding noise drawn from common probability distributions and replacing concrete constants with symbolic ones. As such, we conduct experiments using a total of 50 challenging benchmarks, involving polynomial arithmetic, probability distributions and symbolic constants. Further, we compare AMBER not only against `Absynth` and `MGen` (as in [19]), but also evaluate AMBER in comparison to the recent tools `LexRSM` [1], `KoAT2` [18] and `ecoimp` [2]. Note that `MGen` can only certify PAST and `LexRSM` only AST. Moreover, the tools `Absynth`, `KoAT2` and `ecoimp` mainly aim to find upper bounds on expected costs. Tables 1, 2 and 3 summarize our experimental results, with benchmarks separated into *PAST* (Table 1), *AST but not PAST* (Table 2), and *not AST* (Table 3). Benchmarks marked with * are part of our 11 new examples. In every table, ✓ (✗) marks a tool (not) being able to certify the respective termination property. Moreover, NA symbolizes that a benchmark is out-of-scope for a tool, for instance, due to not supporting some distributions or polynomial arithmetic. All benchmarks have been run on a machine with a 2.6 GHz Intel i7 (Gen 10)

Table 1. 27 programs which are PAST.

Program	AMBER	Absynth	MGen	LexRSM	KoAT2	ecoimp	Program	AMBER	Absynth	MGen	LexRSM	KoAT2	ecoimp
2d_bounded_random_walk	✓	✗	NA	NA	✗	✗	linear_past_1	✓	✗	✗	✗	✗	✗
biased_random_walk_const	✓	✓	✓	✓	✓	✓	linear_past_2	✓	✗	NA	✗	✗	✗
biased_random_walk_exp	✓	✗	✓	✗	✗	✗	nested_loops	NA	✓	✗	✓	✓	✓
biased_random_walk_poly	✓	✗	✗	NA	✗	✗	polynomial_past_1	✓	✗	NA	NA	✗	✗
binomial_past	✓	✓	✓	✓	✓	✓	polynomial_past_2	✓	✗	NA	NA	✗	✗
complex_past	✓	✗	NA	NA	✗	✗	sequential_loops	NA	✓	✗	✓	✓	✓
consecutive_bernoulli_trails	✓	✓	✓	✓	✓	✓	tortoise_hare_race	✓	✓	✓	✓	✓	✓
coupon_collector_4	✓	✗	✓	✓	✓	✓	dependent_dist*	NA	NA	NA	NA	✗	✓
coupon_collector_5	✓	✗	✓	✓	✓	✓	exp_rw_gauss_noise*	✓	NA	NA	NA	NA	NA
dueling_cowboys	✓	✓	✓	✓	✓	✓	gemoetric_gaussian*	✓	NA	NA	NA	NA	NA
exponential_past_1	✓	NA	NA	NA	✗	NA	race_uniform_noise*	✓	✗	✓	✓	✗	✓
exponential_past_2	✓	NA	NA	NA	✗	NA	symb_2d_rw*	✓	✗	NA	NA	✗	✗
geometric	✓	✓	✓	✓	✓	✓	uniform_rw_walk*	✓	✓	✓	✓	✓	✓
geometric_exp	✗	✗	✗	✗	✗	✗	Total ✓	23	9	11	12	11	13

processor and 32 GB of RAM and finished within a timeout of 50 s, where most experiments terminated within a few seconds.

Experimental Analysis. AMBER successfully certifies 23 out of the 27 PAST benchmarks (Table 1). Although Absynth, KoAT2 and ecosimp can find expected cost upper bounds for large programs [2,18,20], they struggle on small programs whose termination is not known a priori. For instance, they struggle when a benchmark probabilistically "chooses" between two polynomials working against each other (one moving the program state away from a termination criterion and one towards it). Our experiments show that AMBER handles such cases successfully. MGen supports the continuous uniform distribution and KoAT2 the geometric distribution whose support is infinite. With these two exceptions, AMBER is the only tool supporting continuous distributions and distributions with infinite support. To the best of our knowledge, AMBER is the first tool certifying PAST supporting both discrete and continuous distributions as well as distributions with finite and infinite support. AMBER successfully certifies 12 benchmarks to be AST which are not PAST (Table 2). Whereas the LexRSM tool can certify non-PAST programs to be AST, such programs need to contain subprograms which are PAST [1]. The well-known example of symmetric_1D_random_walk, contained in our benchmarks, does not have a PAST subprogram. Therefore, the LexRSM tool cannot establish AST for it. In contrast, AMBER using the *Supermartingale Rule* can handle these programs. To the best of our knowledge, AMBER is the first tool capable of certifying non-AST for polynomial probabilistic programs involving drawing from distributions and symbolic constants. AMBER is also the first tool automating (non-)AST and (non-)PAST analysis in a unifying manner.

Table 2. 14 programs which are AST and not necessarily PAST.

Program	AMBER	LexRSM
fair_in_limit_random_walk	NA	NA
gambling	✓	✗
symmetric_2d_random_walk	✗	NA
symmetric_random_walk_constant_1	✓	✗
symmetric_random_walk_constant_2	✓	✗
symmetric_random_walk_exp_1	✓	✗
symmetric_random_walk_exp_2	✓	NA
symmetric_random_walk_linear_1	✓	✗
symmetric_random_walk_linear_2	✓	✗
symmetric_random walk_poly_1	✓	NA
symmetric_random_walk_poly_2	✓	NA
gaussian_rw_walk*	✓	NA
laplacian_noise*	✓	NA
symb_1d_rw*	✓	NA
Total ✓	12	0

Table 3. 9 programs which are not AST.

Program	AMBER
biased_random_walk_nast_1	✓
biased_random_walk_nast_2	✓
biased_random_walk_nast_3	✓
biased_random_walk_nast_4	✓
binomial_nast	✓
polynomial_nast	✗
binomial_nast_noise*	✓
symb_nast_1d_rw*	✓
hypergeo_nast*	✓
Total ✓	8

Experimental Summary. Tables 1, 2 and 3 demonstrate that (i) AMBER outperforms the state-of-the-art in certifying (P)AST, and (ii) AMBER determines (non-)(P)AST for programs with various distributions and symbolic constants.

4 Conclusion

We described AMBER, an open-source tool for analyzing the termination behavior for polynomial probabilistic programs, in a fully automatic way. AMBER computes asymptotic bounding functions and martingale expressions and is the first tool to prove and disprove (P)AST in a unifying manner. AMBER can analyze continuous, discrete, finitely- and infinitely supported distributions in polynomial probabilistic programs parameterized by symbolic constants. Our experimental comparisons give practical evidence that AMBER can (dis)prove (P)AST for a substantially larger class of programs than state-of-the-art tools.

References

1. Agrawal, S., Chatterjee, K., Novotný, P.: Lexicographic ranking supermartingales: an efficient approach to termination of probabilistic programs. Proc. of POPL **2**, 1–32 (2017). https://doi.org/10.1145/3158122

2. Avanzini, M., Moser, G., Schaper, M.: A modular cost analysis for probabilistic programs. Proc. of OOPSLA **4**, 1–30 (2020). https://doi.org/10.1145/3428240
3. Bartocci, E., Kovács, L., Stanković, M.: Analysis of bayesian networks via probsolvable loops. In: Pun, V.K.I., Stolz, V., Simao, A. (eds.) ICTAC 2020. LNCS, vol. 12545, pp. 221–241. Springer, Cham (2020). https://doi.org/10.1007/978-3-030-64276-1_12
4. Bartocci, E., Kovács, L., Stankovic, M.: Mora - automatic generation of moment-based invariants. In: Proceedings of TACAS (2020). https://doi.org/10.1007/978-3-030-45190-5
5. Bournez, O., Garnier, F.: Proving positive almost-sure termination. In: Giesl, J. (ed.) RTA 2005. LNCS, vol. 3467, pp. 323–337. Springer, Heidelberg (2005). https://doi.org/10.1007/978-3-540-32033-3_24
6. Chakarov, A., Sankaranarayanan, S.: Probabilistic program analysis with martingales. In: Sharygina, N., Veith, H. (eds.) CAV 2013. LNCS, vol. 8044, pp. 511–526. Springer, Heidelberg (2013). https://doi.org/10.1007/978-3-642-39799-8_34
7. Chatterjee, K., Fu, H., Goharshady, A.K.: Termination analysis of probabilistic programs through positivstellensatz's. In: Chaudhuri, S., Farzan, A. (eds.) CAV 2016. LNCS, vol. 9779, pp. 3–22. Springer, Cham (2016). https://doi.org/10.1007/978-3-319-41528-4_1
8. Chatterjee, K., Fu, H., Novotný, P.: Termination Analysis of Probabilistic Programs with Martingales. Foundations of Probabilistic Programming, pp. 221–258 (2020). https://doi.org/10.1017/9781108770750.008
9. Chatterjee, K., Novotný, P., Zikelic, D.: Stochastic invariants for probabilistic termination. In: Proceedings. of POPL (2017). https://doi.org/10.1145/3009837.3009873
10. Chen, J., He, F.: Proving almost-sure termination by omega-regular decomposition. In: Proceedings of PLDI (2020). https://doi.org/10.1145/3385412.3386002
11. Esparza, J., Gaiser, A., Kiefer, S.: Proving termination of probabilistic programs using patterns. In: Madhusudan, P., Seshia, S.A. (eds.) CAV 2012. LNCS, vol. 7358, pp. 123–138. Springer, Heidelberg (2012). https://doi.org/10.1007/978-3-642-31424-7_14
12. Ferrer Fioriti, L.L.M., Hermanns, H.: Probabilistic termination: soundness, completeness, and compositionality. In: Proceedings of POPL (2015). https://doi.org/10.1145/2676726.2677001
13. Ghahramani, Z.: Probabilistic machine learning and artificial intelligence. Nature **521**, 452–459 (2015). https://doi.org/10.1038/nature14541
14. Huang, M., Fu, H., Chatterjee, K.: New approaches for almost-sure termination of probabilistic programs. In: Ryu, S. (ed.) APLAS 2018. LNCS, vol. 11275, pp. 181–201. Springer, Cham (2018). https://doi.org/10.1007/978-3-030-02768-1_11
15. Kaminski, B.L., Katoen, J.P.: On the hardness of almost–sure termination. In: Italiano, G.F., Pighizzini, G., Sannella, D.T. (eds.) MFCS 2015. LNCS, vol. 9234, pp. 307–318. Springer, Heidelberg (2015). https://doi.org/10.1007/978-3-662-48057-1_24
16. McIver, A., Morgan, C., Kaminski, B.L., Katoen, J.P.: A new proof rule for almost-sure termination. Proc. of ACM Program. Lang. (2018). https://doi.org/10.1145/3158121
17. Merkel, D.: Docker: lightweight linux containers for consistent development and deployment. Linux J. **239**, 2 (2014)
18. Meyer, F., Hark, M., Giesl, J.: Inferring expected runtimes of probabilistic integer programs using expected sizes. In: TACAS 2021. LNCS, vol. 12651, pp. 250–269. Springer, Cham (2021). https://doi.org/10.1007/978-3-030-72016-2_14

19. Moosbrugger, M., Bartocci, E., Katoen, J.P., Kovács, L.: Automated termination analysis of polynomial probabilistic programs. In: ESOP 2021. LNCS, vol. 12648, pp. 491–518. Springer, Cham (2021). https://doi.org/10.1007/978-3-030-72019-3_18

20. Ngo, V.C., Carbonneaux, Q., Hoffmann, J.: Bounded expectations: resource analysis for probabilistic programs. In: Proceedings of PLDI (2018). https://doi.org/10.1145/3192366.3192394

Model Checking Collision Avoidance of Nonlinear Autonomous Vehicles

Rong Gu[(✉)], Cristina Seceleanu, Eduard Enoiu, and Kristina Lundqvist

Mälardalen University, Västerås, Sweden
{rong.gu,cristina.seceleanu,eduard.enoiu,kristina.lundqvist}@mdh.se

Abstract. Autonomous vehicles are expected to be able to avoid static and dynamic obstacles automatically, along their way. However, most of the collision-avoidance functionality is not formally verified, which hinders ensuring such systems' safety. In this paper, we introduce formal definitions of the vehicle's movement and trajectory, based on hybrid transition systems. Since formally verifying hybrid systems algorithmically is undecidable, we reduce the verification of nonlinear vehicle behavior to verifying discrete-time vehicle behavior overapproximations. Using this result, we propose a generic approach to formally verify autonomous vehicles with nonlinear behavior against reach-avoid requirements. The approach provides a UPPAAL timed-automata model of vehicle behavior, and uses UPPAAL STRATEGO for verifying the model with user-programmed libraries of collision-avoidance algorithms. Our experiments show the approach's effectiveness in discovering bugs in a state-of-the-art version of a selected collision-avoidance algorithm, as well as in proving the absence of bugs in the algorithm's improved version.

1 Introduction

Autonomous vehicles (AV), such as driverless cars and robots, are becoming increasingly promising, hence prompting a wide interest in industry and academia. Safety of vehicle operations is the most important concern, requiring these systems to move and act without colliding with static or dynamic objects (obstacles) in the environment, such as big rocks, humans, and other mobile machines. Algorithms like A* [21], Rapidly-exploring Random Tree (RRT) [17], and Theta* [5] are able to navigate the AV towards reaching their destinations, while avoiding static obstacles along the way. However, when encountering dynamic obstacles that could appear and move arbitrarily in the environment, these algorithms are not enough for collision avoidance, and have to be complemented by algorithms such as those based on dipole flow fields [23] or dynamic window approach [10], which are capable of circumventing dynamic obstacles.

Although many collision-avoidance algorithms are being proposed in recent years, few of them have been formally verified, despite the fact that formal verification is a very important tool for discovering problems in the early stage of algorithm design. In this paper, we consider two main challenges that can turn formal verification of AV models and their algorithms into a daunting task: (i)

© Springer Nature Switzerland AG 2021
M. Huisman et al. (Eds.): FM 2021, LNCS 13047, pp. 676–694, 2021.
https://doi.org/10.1007/978-3-030-90870-6_37

nonlinearity of the vehicle kinematics, and (ii) complexity and uncertainty of the environment where AV move. On the one hand, ordinary differential equations are used to describe the continuous dynamics and kinematics of the often non-linear vehicles. The trajectories formed by these vehicle models are consequently nonlinear, which is the nonlinearity that we consider throughout the paper. On the other hand, discrete decisions made by the vehicles' control systems influence the movement of vehicles. In the model-checking world, verification of these so-called *nonlinear hybrid systems* that combine nonlinear continuous kinematics and discrete control is undecidable [13,15]. In addition, AV that aim at tracking initially planned paths are inevitably diverted by their tracking errors caused by the inaccuracy of their sensors and actuators, and the disturbance from the complex environment. Dynamic obstacles are unpredictable before AV sense them. All these reasons render exhaustive model checking of models of nonlinear vehicles that move in an environment containing static obstacles and uncertain dynamic obstacles an unsolved problem.

In this paper, we solve this problem by addressing challenges (i) and (ii). First, we introduce *safe zones* of the trajectories formed by *controllable* nonlinear AV models, which overcomes challenge (i), as follows. If an AV's tracking error has a Lyapunov function, it is called *controllable* in this paper, and its deviation from the reference path is bounded [8]. The boundaries of tracking errors form the safe zone of the AV, assuming the reference path as the axis. As long as the dynamic obstacles do not intrude into these zones, the vehicles are guaranteed to be safe. Based on this observation, we reduce the verification of *controllable* AV's nonlinear trajectories to the verification of its piece-wise-continuous (PWC) reference trajectories, and further to the verification of discrete-time models of trajectories. The various vehicle dynamics and kinematics, together with the uncertain tracking errors are all subsumed by the safe zones, so the undecidable verification problem is simplified to a decidable one, without losing completeness.

Next, we solve challenge (ii) by leveraging the nondeterminism of timed automata in UPPAAL STRATEGO [6]. The initialization and movement of dynamic obstacles are modeled as timed automata, in which their positions etc. are nondeterministically initialized and updated. In this way, the vehicle model satisfies the *liveness* property only when it is able to reach the destination, and the *invariance* property if there is no collision happening under any circumstance. When multiple dynamic obstacles are involved, the state space of the model becomes large and the verification becomes computationally expensive or even unsolvable. Consequently, we also propose a way of reducing the state space by splitting the verification into multiple tractable phases.

Note that, our approach is orthogonal to the methods of controller synthesis (e.g., [7,9]). The latter targets the construction of motion plans that avoid static and dynamic obstacles, whereas our method can be used to verify the correctness of these methods, regardless of the path-planning and collision-avoidance algorithms considered. To summarize, our main contributions are:

1. A proven transformation of the verification of nonlinear vehicle trajectories to the verification of PWC trajectories and discrete-time trajectories.

2. A generic verification approach for model checking reach-avoid requirements of AV equipped with different collision-avoidance algorithms (Sect. 4).
3. An implementation of the approach in UPPAAL STRATEGO, and a demonstration showing the ability of the approach to discover bugs in a state-of-the-art collision-avoidance algorithm, and to prove the absence of bugs in an improved version of the same algorithm (Sect. 5).

Preliminaries. In this paper, we denote a vector x by $\vec{x}$, the module of $\vec{x}$ by $||\vec{x}||$, and multiplications between two scalars, and between a vector and a scalar by "$\times$". *Timed Automata* is a widely-used formalism for modeling real-time systems [4]. The UPPAAL model checker [16] uses an extension of the timed-automata language with a number of features such as constants, data variables, arithmetic operations, arrays, broadcast channels, urgent and committed locations. Properties that can be checked by UPPAAL are formalized in a simplified *timed computation tree logic* (TCTL) [3], which basically contains a decidable subset of *computation tree logic* (CTL) plus clock constraints. A branch of UPPAAL, named UPPAAL STRATEGO [6], supports calling external C-code functions written in libraries. This new feature enables us to treat the user-designed collision-avoidance algorithm as a black box in our model.

The remainder of the paper is organized as follows. In Sect. 2, we introduce the systems to be verified. In Sect. 3, we concretely define the movement and trajectories of AV and prove two theorems of transforming the verification of nonlinear vehicle trajectories to the verification of PWC trajectories and discrete-time trajectories. A detailed description of the verification approach and tool support is presented in Sect. 4, followed by experiments in Sect. 5. We compare our study to related work in Sect. 6, and conclude the paper in Sect. 7.

2   Problem Description

Vehicles that are capable to calculate paths to their destinations, which avoid collision with any obstacles in the environment, and follow them without human intervention, are called *autonomous vehicles* (AV). As depicted in Fig. 1, when the environment contains only static obstacles whose positions are already known by the AV, paths are calculated by the path planner inside the controller of the AV. Path planners are usually equipped with path-planning algorithms, e.g., Theta* [5] or RRT [17], which explore the map (M) to find a path that avoids the static obstacles and reaches the destination. The reference controller (g_r) uses

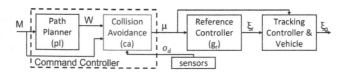

Fig. 1. The architecture of the controller of autonomous vehicles. The collision-avoidance module does not exist if the environment only contains static obstacles.

the output of the path planner and generates a trajectory of the state variables of the system, e.g., position and linear velocity of the vehicle, as a reference (ξ_r) for the tracking controller to follow. The tracking controller aims to produce an input to the vehicle to drive it to track the reference trajectory. The real trajectory (ξ_g) follows the reference path (ξ_r) with some tracking errors.

Since the dynamics and kinematics of a real AV are nonlinear, and tracking errors between the actual trajectory and reference trajectory exist inevitably, path planners do not guarantee the safety of AV driving. Moreover, formally verifying if the actual trajectories ever hit the static obstacles is an undecidable problem, due to the model-checking of nonlinear hybrid systems being undecidable [15]. Overapproximation is a method of linearizing the vehicle model, to facilitate verification. Fan et al. [8] propose a method that proves that, as long as the dynamics of tracking errors has a Lyapunov function, the tracking errors are bounded by a piece-wise constant value, which depends on the initial tracking error and the number of segments of the reference trajectory. Figure 2 shows an example of a reference trajectory and the boundary of tracking errors. Consequently, as long as the safe regions of AV (green color) do not overlap with the grey areas, the actual trajectory is guaranteed to be safe.

Fig. 2. The reference trajectory is solid black lines, and the actual trajectory is violet dotted lines. The initial area is blue and the goal area is yellow. The boundaries of tracking errors are green. Static obstacles are grey [8]. (Color figure online)

Due to this result, one can reduce the problem of verifying whether the actual trajectory (ξ_g) ever overlaps with obstacles, to a simplified problem of verifying whether the distance between the reference trajectory (ξ_r) and the obstacles is larger than the respective boundary of tracking error on each segment of ξ_r. In other words, the verification of nonlinear vehicle trajectories is reduced to the verification of their piece-wise-continuous reference trajectories. Although much simplified, the problem is still undecidable as long as the piece-wise-continuous trajectories are non-linear [8]. Moreover, when dynamic obstacles appear, the verification becomes intractable, because dynamic obstacles cannot be known completely before the AV encounters them. The controller must be additionally equipped with a collision-avoidance module that perceives the environment periodically, via sensors. Figure 1 shows such a controller. The path planner still calculates a path that avoids known static obstacles and goes to the destination. The path serves as input to the collision-avoidance module as a sequence of waypoints (positions of turning directions, denoted as W), as well as the information of the map (M) and dynamic obstacles (o_d). The command controller should meet the following two requirements, which are the focus of verification in this paper:

- Collision avoidance (invariance property): always circumventing the static and dynamic obstacles;
- Destination reaching (liveness property): always eventually reaching the goal area.

3   Definitions and Verification Reduction Theorems

In this section, we introduce the definitions of the important concepts used in this paper and the collision-avoidance verification theorems that eventually reduce the nonlinear trajectory verification to discrete-time trajectory verification. We denote AV and dynamic obstacles collectively by the term *agents*.

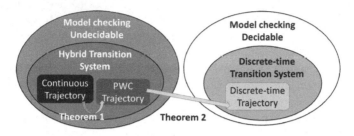

Fig. 3. Overall description of models and their decidability

First, let us establish an overall view of the different types of models that are used in this section. So far, we have stated that model-checking *liveness* properties (e.g., destination reaching) and *invariance* properties (e.g., collision avoidance) of nonlinear hybrid systems is undecidable. Note that hybrid systems are described by syntactic models with an underlying semantics defined as hybrid transition systems (HTS), used in the following definitions. As depicted in Fig. 3, the continuous trajectories of agents are modeled as HTS. By incorporating the tracking errors of agents, the continuous trajectories are simplified into piece-wise-continuous (PWC) trajectories. However, the verification of PWC trajectories is still undecidable, so we transform the PWC trajectories into discrete-time trajectories, whose verification is decidable. Furthermore, the two-step transformation from continuous trajectories to discrete-time trajectories is proved to preserve the *liveness* and *invariance* properties that we want to verify (Theorems 1 and 2).

3.1   Definitions of Maps, Agent States, and Trajectories

In this section, we first define the agent states and the map where agents move. Next, we define the command controllers and agent-state trajectories.

Definition 1 (Map). *A map is a 4-tuple $\mathcal{M} =< \mathcal{X}, \mathbf{O}_u, \mathcal{I}, \mathcal{G} >$, where (i) $\mathcal{X} \in \mathbb{R}^d$ is the moving space, with $d \in \{2, 3\}$ being the dimension of the map, (ii) $\mathbf{O}_u \subseteq \mathcal{X}$ is the unsafe area, (iii) $\mathcal{I} \subseteq \mathcal{X}$ is the initial area of AV, and (iv) $\mathcal{G} \subseteq \mathcal{X}$ is the goal area where the AV aims to go.*

An example of a map is illustrated in Fig. 2.

Definition 2 (Agent State). *Given a map $\mathcal{M} =< \mathcal{X}, \mathbf{O}_u, \mathcal{I}, \mathcal{G} >$, an agent state is a 5-tuple $\mathcal{S} =< \vec{p}, \vec{v}, \vec{a}, \theta, \omega >$, where (i) $\vec{p} \in \mathcal{X}$ is the position vector, (ii)*

$\vec{v}$ is the linear velocity vector, $||\vec{v}|| \in [0, V_{max}] \subset \mathbb{R}_{\geq 0}$, (iii) $\vec{a}$ is the acceleration vector, $||\vec{a}|| \in [A_{min}, A_{max}] \subset \mathbb{R}$, (iv) $\theta \in [-\pi, \pi] \subset \mathbb{R}$ is the heading, and (v) $\omega \in [\Omega_{min}, \Omega_{max}] \subset \mathbb{R}$ is the rotational velocity.

The agent states are states of AV and dynamic obstacles. Some elements in the tuple of agent states S evolve continuously and some are assumed to change instantaneously. We define the trajectories of the evolution of the agent states in Definition 4. Before that, we first define the controller of AV, where dynamic obstacles ($\mathbf{O}_d$) are instances of agent states S, as follows:

Definition 3 (Controller). *Given a map $\mathcal{M}$, and a set of dynamic obstacles $\mathbf{O}_d$, we define a command controller of AV as a 3-tuple $\mathcal{C} = < pl, ca, \Lambda >$, where (i) $pl : \mathcal{M} \longrightarrow \mathcal{W}$ is a path-planning function, $\mathcal{W} \subseteq \mathcal{X}$ is a set of waypoints, (ii) $ca : \mathcal{M} \times \mathcal{W} \times \mathbf{O}_d \longrightarrow \Lambda$ is a collision-avoidance function, and (iii) $\Lambda = \{ACC, BRK, TR^+, TR^-, STR\}$ is a set of commands.*

The commands are signals sent from the controllers to the actuators of the AV: ACC means acceleration, BRK means brake, TR^+ and TR^- mean turning counter-clockwise and clockwise, respectively, and STR means moving straightly at a constant speed. An example of the AV's controller architecture is shown in Fig. 1. When an AV starts to move, the transitions of its agent states form a trajectory, in which its position, linear velocity, and heading evolve continuously according to corresponding dynamic functions, whereas its acceleration and rotational velocity change discretely based on the commands.

Definition 4 (Continuous Trajectory). *Given an AV, whose command controller is $\mathcal{C} = < pl, ca, \Lambda >$, we define its movement by a hybrid transition system $< S, s_0, \Sigma, X, \rightarrow >$, where S is a set of states, s_0 is the initial state, $\Sigma \subseteq \Lambda$ is the alphabet, $X = X_d \cup X_c$ is a set of variables combining discrete variables in X_d and continuous variables in X_c, and $\rightarrow$ is a set of transitions defined by the following rules, with kinematic functions of the AV denoted by f:*

- *Delayed transitions: $< \vec{p}, \vec{v}, \vec{a}, \theta, \omega > \xrightarrow{\Delta t} < \vec{p'}, \vec{v'}, \vec{a'}, \theta', \omega' >$, where $t \in X_c$, $\vec{p'} = \vec{p} + \int_l^u \vec{v} dt$, $\vec{v'} = \vec{v} + \int_l^u \vec{a} dt$, $\vec{a'} = \vec{a}$, $\theta' = \theta + \int_l^u \omega dt$, $\omega' = \omega$, $l \in \mathbb{R}_{>0}$ and $u \in \mathbb{R}_{>0}$ are the upper and lower time bounds, respectively, and $\Delta t = u - l$;*
- *Instantaneous transitions: $< \vec{p}, \vec{v}, \vec{a}, \theta, \omega > \xrightarrow{cmd} < \vec{p'}, \vec{v'}, \vec{a'}, \theta', \omega' >$, where $\vec{p'} = \vec{p}$, $\vec{v'} = \vec{v}$, $\vec{a'} = ca(\vec{a}, cmd)$, $\theta' = \theta$, $\omega' = ca(\omega, cmd)$, $cmd \in \Sigma$.*

A run of the transition system defined above over a duration U is a *trajectory* of agent states, also described by the function $\xi : [0, U] \rightarrow S$. Henceforth, we name the agent-state trajectory as *trajectory* for brevity, and denote $\xi(t)$ as a point of ξ at time t, the projection of ξ on a dimension of an agent-state as $\xi \downarrow dimension$, e.g., positions on a trajectory are $\xi \downarrow \vec{p}$. The continuous variables of actual trajectories of agents are generated by their nonlinear kinematic functions, yet these variables are piece-wise-continuous (PWC) in reference trajectories (see Fig. 2). More specific, a reference trajectory ξ_r is a sequence of concatenated trajectory segments $\xi_{r,1} \frown \ldots \frown \xi_{r,k}$. The concatenating points $\{\vec{p}_i\}_{i=0}^k$ are the waypoints calculated by path-planners, where the discontinuity of the vehicle's heading θ happens. Therefore, the definition of agent movement on a reference trajectory changes as follows:

Definition 5 (Reference Trajectory). *Let us assume an AV, whose command controller is $\mathcal{C} = <pl, ca, \Lambda>$, and a PWC trajectory ξ_r of the AV, which is a sequence of trajectories $\xi_{r,1} \frown \ldots \frown \xi_{r,k}$ concatenated by a set of waypoints $\{\vec{P}_i\}_{i=0}^k$. Then, the AV's movement along the reference trajectory is a hybrid transition system similar to that of Definition 4, and its transitions are defined by the following rules:*

- *Delayed transitions on $\xi_r \downarrow \vec{p} \notin \{\vec{P}_i\}_{i=0}^k$: $<\vec{p}, \vec{v}, \vec{a}, \theta, \omega> \xrightarrow{\Delta t} <\vec{p}', \vec{v}', \vec{a}', \theta', \omega'>$, where $\vec{p}' = \vec{p} + (\vec{v} + \frac{\vec{a} \times \Delta t}{2}) \times \Delta t$, $\vec{v}' = \vec{v} + \vec{a} \times \Delta t$, $\vec{a}' = \vec{a}$, $\theta' = \theta$, $\omega' = 0$;*
- *Instantaneous transitions: $<\vec{p}, \vec{v}, \vec{a}, \theta, \omega> \xrightarrow{cmd} <\vec{p}', \vec{v}', \vec{a}', \theta', \omega'>$, where $\vec{p}' = \vec{p}$, $\vec{v}' = \vec{v}$, $\vec{a}' = ca(\vec{a}, cmd)$, $\theta' = \begin{cases} arctangent(\vec{P}_i, \vec{P}_{i+1}), & \text{if } \vec{p} \in \{\vec{P}_i\}_{i=0}^{k-1}, \\ \theta, & \text{if } \vec{p} \notin \{\vec{P}_i\}_{i=0}^{k-1} \end{cases}, \omega' = 0$*

Intuitively, when an agent is moving along its reference trajectory (ξ_r), its heading ($\xi_r \downarrow \theta$) remains unchanged before it arrives at a waypoint, which means the rotational velocity ($\xi_r \downarrow \omega$) is irrelevant and remains 0. Therefore, the reference trajectory is infeasible to be tracked exactly by the agents. Although the integration of $\xi_r \downarrow \vec{p}$ and $\xi_r \downarrow \vec{v}$ on delayed transitions is simplified to polynomial functions, the nonlinearity of $\xi_r \downarrow \vec{p}$ still renders undecidability. The trigonometric function in the definition also causes a computational difficulty when running verification. In practice, we use linear speed vector ($\vec{v}$) to describe both the linear speed and the orientation of the agent. The acceleration ($\xi_r \downarrow \vec{a}$) changes instantaneously based on the commands from the command controller. Last but not least, the trajectories of dynamic obstacles are similar to Definition 4, but without a well-defined controller. On their instantaneous transitions, accelerations and rotational velocities are changed arbitrarily within the valid ranges.

3.2   Collision-Avoidance Verification Reduction

We use ξ_r and ξ_g to denote the reference and actual trajectory of AV, respectively, and ξ_o for the actual trajectories of dynamic obstacles.

Fig. 4. A dynamic obstacle is at the red cross, while the current position of AV on the reference path is the yellow dot. The safety-critical area is dark green. (Color figure online)

Let $d(var_1, var_2)$ denote the distance between var_1 and var_2, e.g., $d(\vec{p}_i, \xi_j \downarrow \vec{p})$ is the distance from position $\vec{p}_i$ to trajectory $\xi_j \downarrow \vec{p}$, and $d(\xi_i \downarrow \vec{p}, \mathbf{O}_u)$ is the distance from trajectory $\xi_i \downarrow \vec{p}$ to static obstacles. For brevity, we omit the projection when using this notation, i.e., $d(\vec{p}_i, \xi_j \downarrow \vec{p}) = d(\vec{p}_i, \xi_j)$. Let $\xi(t_1, t_2)$ denote a segment of trajectory ξ between time points t_1 and t_2. The problem of verifying if AV hit static obstacles $\mathbf{O}_u$ is relatively simple, as $\mathbf{O}_u$ does not change. However, checking if AV hit moving obstacles is different and much harder, because both trajectories are formed dynamically while the agents are moving. Dynamic obstacles might meet an AV's reference trajectory, yet far enough from its current position (see Fig. 4). Therefore, we introduce the concept of *safety-critical segments*:

Definition 6 (Safety-Critical Segment). *Let C be the current time. Given a trajectory ξ, a time span of length $T \in \mathbb{R}_{>0}$, we define a safety-critical segment $sc(\xi)$ of ξ, as $\xi(C - T, C + T)^1$.*

The length of time-span T, so that the safety-critical area covers the actual current position of AV, can be delivered by design engineers with knowledge of vehicle dynamics, so this is not within the scope of this paper. Now, instead of checking if any part of the AV's entire trajectory (ξ_g) overlaps with a moving obstacle's trajectory (ξ_o), we check if the safety-critical segments of these two trajectories ($sc(\xi_g)$ and $sc(\xi_o)$) overlap.

Definition 7 (Collision-Avoidance Verification). *Given a map $\mathcal{M} = <\mathcal{X}, \mathbf{O}_u, \mathcal{I}, \mathcal{G}>$, a nonlinear AV, whose actual continuous trajectory is ξ_g, and a set of dynamic obstacles whose trajectories are in set Ξ_o, we say that the collision-avoidance verification of the AV's actual trajectory equates with verifying that condition $\xi_g \downarrow \vec{p} \cap \mathcal{G} \neq \varnothing \wedge \xi_g \downarrow \vec{p} \cap \mathbf{O}_u = \varnothing \wedge sc(\xi_g \downarrow \vec{p}) \cap sc(\xi_o \downarrow \vec{p}) = \varnothing$ holds, where $\xi_o \in \Xi_o$.*

Since model-checking ξ_g is undecidable, we prove next that its verification can be reduced to one over the PWC trajectory ξ_r that ξ_g tracks.

Theorem 1 (Non-linearity to PWC). *Assume the collision-avoidance verification condition of Definition 7, a position $\vec{p}_g \in \mathcal{G}$ whose distance to the closest boundary of $\mathcal{G}$ is B, and that the tracking errors of the AV have a Lyapunov function. Then, it follows that if the condition $\xi_r \downarrow \vec{p} \cap \{\vec{p}_g\} \neq \varnothing \wedge d(\xi_r, \mathbf{O}_u) > L \wedge d(sc(\xi_r), sc(\xi_o)) > L$, with $L \in \mathbb{R}_{>0}$ and $L \leq B$ holds, then the collision-avoidance condition of Definition 7 holds too.*

Proof. Based on Lemmas 2 and 3 proven by Fan et al. [8], if the tracking errors of the AV have a Lyapunov function, its ξ_g is bounded within a certain distance to its ξ_r. Let the distance be L, then $d(\xi_g, \xi_r) < L \leq B$. Hence, if $\xi_r \downarrow \vec{p} \cap \{\vec{p}_g\} \neq \varnothing$, then $\xi_g \downarrow \vec{p} \cap \mathcal{G} \neq \varnothing$. Since $d(\xi_r, \mathbf{O}_u) > L > d(\xi_g, \xi_r)$ and $d(sc(\xi_r), sc(\xi_o)) > L > d(\xi_g, \xi_r)$, then $\xi_g \downarrow \vec{p} \cap \mathbf{O}_u = \varnothing \wedge sc(\xi_g \downarrow \vec{p}) \cap sc(\xi_o \downarrow \vec{p}) = \varnothing$. $\square$

Note that these two problems are not equivalent. When the actual trajectory is not colliding with any obstacles, the distance from the reference trajectory to the obstacles could be less than L. The method of calculating L is not the concern of this paper. We refer the reader to literature [8] for details.

---

[1] When $C < T$, $sc(\xi) = \xi(0, C + T)$.

3.3   Discretization of Trajectories

Although the verification of nonlinear trajectories is simplified by Theorem 1, model-checking PWC trajectories is still difficult. PWC trajectories are described by hybrid systems, in which variables, e.g., $\vec{p}$ and $\vec{v}$, change continuously (specifically, $\vec{p}$ is nonlinear), whereas variables, e.g., θ, $\vec{a}$ and ω, change instantaneously (Definition 5). Unfortunately, the algorithmic verification of such model is undecidable [20]. To make the problem tractable, we discretize PWC trajectories into a discrete-time model, where the movement of agents (including AV and dynamic obstacles) is sampled synchronously:

Definition 8 (Discrete-Time Trajectory). *Given a PWC trajectory named ξ_r, whose concatenating points (waypoints) are $\{\vec{P}_i\}_{i=0}^k$, a discretized trajectory ξ_{rd} of ξ_r is a run of a corresponding discrete-time transition system $< D, d_0, \Pi, \rightarrow>$, where D is the set of states, d_0 is the initial state, $\Pi \subseteq \Lambda \cup \{sync\}$ is the set of labels consisting of controller commands and a label for synchronization with other discretized trajectories, and $\rightarrow$ is a transition relation, in which the instantaneous transitions of $\theta, \vec{a}$ and ω remain the same as defined in Definition 5, and the delayed transitions are sampled at the time points when $\Delta t = \varepsilon$, where $\varepsilon \in \mathbb{R}_{>0}$ is the granularity of sampling:*

- *if $\Delta t < \varepsilon$, $< \vec{p}, \vec{v}, \vec{a}, \theta, \omega >$ does not change,*
- *if $\Delta t = \varepsilon$, $< \vec{p}, \vec{v}, \vec{a}, \theta, \omega > \xrightarrow{\Delta t, sync} < \vec{p'}, \vec{v'}, \vec{a'}, \theta', \omega' >$, where $\theta' = \theta, \omega' = \omega, \vec{a'} = \vec{a}, \vec{v'} = \begin{cases} \vec{v} + \vec{a} \times \varepsilon, & \text{if } ||\vec{v} + \vec{a} \times \varepsilon|| < V_{max}, \\ \frac{\vec{v}}{||\vec{v}||} \times V_{max}, & \text{if } ||\vec{v} + \vec{a} \times \varepsilon|| \geq V_{max} \end{cases}, \vec{p'} = \begin{cases} \vec{P}_i, & \text{if } \vec{p} + (\vec{v} + \frac{\vec{a} \times \varepsilon}{2}) \times \varepsilon > \vec{P}_i, \\ \vec{p} + (\vec{v} + \frac{\vec{a} \times \varepsilon}{2}) \times \varepsilon, & \\ & \text{if } \vec{p} + (\vec{v} + \frac{\vec{a} \times \varepsilon}{2}) \times \varepsilon \leq \vec{P}_i \end{cases}$*

To denote if the position passes (resp., does not pass) the next waypoint, we use the syntactic sugar $>$ (resp., $\leq$). The algorithm of judging this is given in literature [12]. Intuitively, when the time interval Δt is less than a small period ε, the environment is not observed, so the trajectories of the agents are not sampled; when Δt reaches ε, the agent states are observed and sampled. When an agent reaches or passes its target waypoint in the current period ε, it stops at the waypoint until the next period comes when the new waypoint and heading are updated by the instantaneous transitions.

Dynamic obstacles do not have pre-computed waypoints but appear and move arbitrarily in the map. However, a reasonable obstacle would not change its direction too frequently, e.g., every sampling period. We design dynamic obstacles such that, initially, they choose their starting agent-states arbitrarily. Then, they keep moving for N sampling periods before choosing a new agent-state as a target. The straight path between the current and target positions is a reference trajectory that the dynamic obstacle tracks in the next N periods, and the tracking errors are also bounded.

The agents' accelerations and rotational velocities are assumed to be changing discretely in these definitions. If the assumption is violated in some applications, one can discretize these two variables in the same way as in the discretization of position and linear velocity. Next, we prove a theorem that reduces the verification of PWC reference trajectories to the one of discrete-time trajectories.

Theorem 2. *(PWC to discrete-time trajectories). Assume a map $\mathcal{M}$ =< $\mathcal{X}, \mathbf{O}_u, \mathcal{I}, \mathcal{G}$ >, a set of trajectories Ξ_o formed by dynamic obstacles, with the maximum linear velocity V, a reference trajectory ξ_r of an AV with concatenating points $\{\vec{P}_i\}_{i=0}^{k}$, whose safety-critical segment is $sc(\xi_r)$, and synchronized and discretized trajectories ξ_{rd} of ξ_r, and ξ_{od} of $\xi_o \in \Xi_o$ with a granularity of sampling $\varepsilon \le \frac{L}{||V||}$; here, $L = L_a + L_o$, where L_a is the tracking-error boundary of the AV, and L_o is the smallest tracking-error boundary among dynamic obstacles[2]. Then, if $\vec{p}_g \in \mathcal{G}$, and $\xi_{rd}\downarrow\vec{p} \cap \{\vec{p}_g\} \ne \varnothing \wedge d(\xi_{rd}, \mathbf{O}_u) > L \wedge d(sc(\xi_{od}), sc(\xi_r)) > L$, it follows that $\xi_r\downarrow\vec{p} \cap \{\vec{p}_g\} \ne \varnothing \wedge d(\xi_r, \mathbf{O}_u) > L \wedge d(sc(\xi_o), sc(\xi_r)) > L$.*

Proof. By substituting Δt in the delay transitions of Definition 5 with ε, we can see that $\xi_{rd}(\varepsilon)$ is a sampling of the reference trajectory $\xi_r(t)$ at the time points when $\Delta t = \varepsilon$. Hence, $\xi_{rd}\downarrow\vec{p} \subseteq \xi_r\downarrow\vec{p}$. Therefore, if $\xi_{rd}\downarrow\vec{p} \cap \{\vec{p}_g\} \ne \varnothing$, which means ξ_{rd} can reach $\vec{p}_g$, then $\xi_r\downarrow\vec{p} \cap \{\vec{p}_g\} \ne \varnothing$ as well.

Based on Definition 8, waypoints $\{\vec{P}_i\}_{i=0}^{k} \subseteq \xi_{rd}\downarrow\vec{p}$, where turning occurs. Therefore, if t_i and t_{i+1} are two consecutive sampling points of ξ_{rd}, the line segment connecting t_i and t_{i+1} must be on ξ_r, denoted by $\xi_{rd}(t_i, t_{i+1})$. Therefore, if $d(\mathbf{O}_u, \xi_{rd}(t_i, t_{i+1})) > L^3$, then the concatenation of $\{\xi_{rd}(t_i, t_{i+1})\}_{i=0}^{n-1}$, which is ξ_r, satisfies $d(\mathbf{O}_u, \xi_r) > L$.

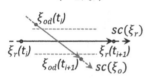

Fig. 5. The trajectory of a dynamic obstacle is red. The reference trajectory of AV is black. Dotted greens lines are the boundaries of tracking errors. (Color figure online)

For $\xi_o \in \Xi_o$, similarly, t_i and t_{i+1} are two consecutive sampling points. As depicted in Fig. 5, $\xi_o(t_i, t_{i+1})$ and $\xi_r(t_i, t_{i+1})$ are the segments of $sc(\xi_o)$ and $sc(\xi_r)$, respectively. Assume $d(sc(\xi_{od}), sc(\xi_r)) > L$, but $d(sc(\xi_o), sc(\xi_r)) \le L$, which means $d(\xi_{od}(t_i), \xi_r(t_i, t_{i+1})) > L$ and $d(\xi_{od}(t_{i+1}), \xi_r(t_i, t_{i+1})) > L$, but $d(\xi_o(t_i, t_{i+1}), \xi_r(t_i, t_{i+1})) \le L$, then $\xi_o(t_i, t_{i+1})$ and $\xi_r(t_i, t_{i+1})$ must be intersecting, and thus $d(\xi_o(t_i), \xi_o(t_{i+1})) > L$ (see Fig. 5). Based on Definition 8, $d(\xi_o(t_i), \xi_o(t_{i+1})) = ||(\vec{v} + \frac{\vec{a}\times\varepsilon}{2}) \times \varepsilon|| \le ||V|| \times \varepsilon$.

Therefore, $||V|| \times \varepsilon > L$, which contradicts the assumption $\varepsilon \le \frac{L}{||V||}$. Hence, if $d(sc(\xi_{od}), sc(\xi_r)) > L$, then $d(sc(\xi_o), sc(\xi_r)) > L$.   □

Based on Theorems 1 and 2, the reach-avoid verification of discretized trajectories is sufficient to entail that of nonlinear trajectories. The reach-avoid verification of discrete-time transition systems is decidable [13]. Therefore, the undecidable problem of model-checking nonlinear trajectories of agents is successfully simplified to a decidable one over discrete-time trajectories. In the next section, we introduce our approach of verifying the discrete-time models.

---

[2] When no dynamic obstacle is detected, L_o is zero.
[3] Computation of $d(\mathbf{O}_u, \xi_{rd}(t_i, t_{i+1}))$ is in a more detailed version of this paper [12].

4   Verification Approach and Tool Support

In our verification approach, we employ UPPAAL Timed Automata (UTA) [16] to build the discrete-time model of the agents, and UPPAAL STRATEGO as the model checker to execute the verification. The latest version of UPPAAL STRATEGO provides a function of calling external libraries. This function enables us to design a model for verification without knowing the implementation details of algorithms, hence modeling them as black boxes. Although UPPAAL STRATEGO is mainly designed for strategy synthesis of stochastic timed games, our approach only leverages its function of exhaustive model checking. The semantics of UTA is timed transition systems. When discretizing time in timed transition systems, one gets discrete-time transition systems, which can be used to model the discrete-time trajectory of agents (Definition 8). Our UTA templates are designed to act only at the end of each sampling period simultaneously, so within the sampling periods, nothing happens but only time elapses. Therefore, the semantics of our UTA templates is shown to be conservatively abstracted by the discrete-time transition semantics, with the discretizing step being equal to the sampling period of the discrete-time trajectories.

4.1   General Description of the Approach

Figure 6 shows the workflow of the verification approach. The input of the approach is the parameters of the agents (i.e., AV and dynamic obstacles) and their boundary of the tracking errors, as well as the environment (e.g., static obstacles). In Step 1, users provide their nonlinear vehicle models, which are for calculating the boundary of tracking errors. This module is the approach provided by Fan et al. [8], which is not the focus of this paper. We simply use the output of this approach in our models for verification. In Step 2, users configure the parameters of the approach, which are used for instantiating the UTA models. Parameters regulate the minimum and maximum values of the elements of agent states, e.g., linear velocity. The detailed specification of the parameters is in literature [12]. In Step 3, UTA templates of the discrete-time models are instantiated into UTA models based on the configured parameters. Note that the user-programmed collision-avoidance algorithm is embedded in the models as

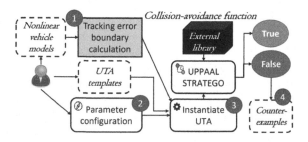

Fig. 6. The workflow of the verification approach

executable libraries, e.g., Dynamic-Link Libraries (DLL) in Windows, or Shared Object (SO) in Linux. After the instantiation of UTA, the model checker verifies the model by traversing its state space, calling the external libraries when necessary, and checking if the vehicle model avoids all obstacles and reaches the destination under all circumstances. If the verification result is "true", the algorithm is guaranteed to be correct under the current parameter configuration; otherwise, counter-examples are returned by the model checker for the users to debug their algorithm or change the configuration of the parameters (Step 4).

4.2   Design of the UTA Templates and CTL Properties

There are four UTA templates that are well designed to be reusable. The figures and the detailed description of the templates are in our technical report [12]. First, we overview the UTA templates:

- **AV Parameter Template.** Based on Definition 8, after being initialized, the AV parameters (e.g., position, speed) either stay unchanged or update their values at the end of the sampling periods, simultaneously. Therefore, we define this template for updating the AV parameters periodically. Instances of this template are parameters of AV, hence, users can add their parameters of AV simply by instantiating this template. The update of AV parameters are synchronized by the controller template.
- **AV Controller Template.** The AV controller template mainly accomplishes three jobs: initializing the AV parameters; invoking the UTA of AV parameters periodically; making decisions, such as turning at waypoints, or calling the external function of collision avoidance when seeing an obstacle.
- **Obstacle Initialization Template.** As depicted by its name, this template is responsible for initializing moving obstacles. For each parameter of the obstacle (e.g., position, speed), the template traverses the range of its value and nondeterministically chooses one to be the initial value of the parameter. Therefore, when running the exhaustive model checking in UPPAAL STRATEGO, all the values are enumerated and verified.
- **Obstacle Movement Template.** This template is for updating the obstacle's parameters periodically. At every end of the sampling period, the AV controller UTA invokes the AV parameter UTA as well as the obstacle movement UTA. In this way, sampling the AV and dynamic obstacles is synchronized at the same moments. Note that this template updates the acceleration and heading of the obstacle every N periods, $N > 1$. As aforementioned, reasonable obstacles do not change their direction and acceleration too frequently.

The CTL properties that formalize the reach-avoid requirement are as following:

- **Obstacle avoiding:** `A[]!collision`, where `collision` is a Boolean variable that is updated every sampling period. When the distances from the safety-critical segment of AV to any of the obstacles in the map is less than the boundaries of tracking errors, `collision` is turned to true, and remains *false* elsewhere. Therefore, this query asks: for *all* execution paths, is collision *always* avoided?

- **Destination reaching**: A<>controller.STOP, where STOP is a location in UTA of AV's controller. When controller goes to location *STOP*, it means that the AV has reached the destination. Therefore, this query asks: for *all* the execution paths of the model, does AV *eventually* reach the destination?

4.3   Reduction of the State Space of the UTA Model

To explore all the possible behaviors of dynamic obstacles, in the worst-case scenario, we would have to explore the entire map, and enumerate all possible values of linear speeds, rotational speeds, and headings of dynamic obstacles. This generates a huge state space of the model that can be infeasible to check. In this section, we introduce how to reduce the state space of the UTA model without damaging the completeness of the verification.

Reduction of Initial Values of Parameters. Even though the dynamic obstacles can appear at any positions in the map, some positions are too far away from the AV to be relevant at the current period, and some are too close to the AV to be possible to be avoided. Hence, we categorize positions into three classes, namely *safety-critical* area, *closest* area, and *valid* area. Figure 7 depicts these three kinds of areas. The safety-critical area is defined in Definition 6.

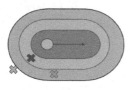

Fig. 7. The green arrow is the reference path. The green circle is the AV. The crosses are the dynamic obstacles, where red and grey ones are invalid positions, and the green cross is valid. (Color figure online)

Positions from which the distance to the safety-critical segment of the reference path is shorter than or equal to $V \times n \times \varepsilon$ is called *closest* area, where V is the velocity of the dynamic obstacle, ε is the sampling period, and $n \in \mathbb{N}$ is a coefficient whose value depends on the physical limitations of the AV. Obstacles appearing within the closest area are impossible to be avoided, so they should be excluded from the valid initial positions. Similarly, positions from which the distance to the safety-critical segment is greater than $V \times n \times \varepsilon$ and less than or equal to $V \times m \times \varepsilon$ are called *valid* area, where $m \in \mathbb{N}$ is a coefficient for calculating the detection period of sensors. Obstacles outside this area cannot enter the safety-critical area within the current detection period, so they should be excluded from the verification in this period.

Collision-avoidance algorithms can turn the AV to any angle, so any heading of the dynamic obstacles can be dangerous. Hence, the initial value of heading is within π to $-\pi$ and cannot be reduced, and same for the linear velocity.

Phased Verification. Another way of handling large state spaces is to split the verification into several phases, and in each phase, the state space is constrained under a solvable level. For example, when the traveling time of AV is long, the entire journey can be split into multiple sections. As long as the concatenating states between consecutive phases are unchanged, the logic conjunction of verification results of each phase implies the result throughout the entire verification.

5   Experimental Evaluation

The experiments are conducted on a server with Ubuntu 18.04, 48 CPU, and 256 GB memory. The verification is executed in UPPAAL 4.1.20-stratego-7[4] [6].

5.1   The Collision-Avoidance Algorithm to Be Verified

In the following experiments, we employ a state-of-the-art algorithm to demonstrate the ability of our verification approach. The algorithm is based on dipole flow fields [23], and calculates static flow fields for all objects in the map, and dynamic dipole fields for moving objects. When the AV starts to move, the static flow fields generate attractive forces along the reference path to draw the AV to move towards the closest waypoint. When it encounters a dynamic obstacle, dipole fields are generated dynamically and centered by these two moving objects. Magnetic moments are thus calculated in these dipole fields, which push the moving objects away from each other. Therefore, the AV could possibly deviate from its planned path when meeting dynamic obstacles, and thus, it might encounter some static obstacles that are not taken into account by the reference path. Static flow fields now generate repulsive forces surrounding these static obstacles and push the AV away from them. Formulas for calculating these fields and forces can be found in the literature [23]. This algorithm has not been comprehensively verified considering all possible scenarios of dynamic obstacles.

5.2   Verification Results

In this study, we verify the model containing a C-code library that implements this algorithm, by using our approach. We demonstrate how to find the potential problems of this newly-designed algorithm by using counter-examples returned from the approach, followed by verifying iteratively the improved version.

Experiment Design. We report in Table 1 several statistics relevant to the obtained results. For each scenario S, we vary the following aspects relevant in real scenarios: (i) WP representing the number of waypoints, (ii) TT that stands for the travelling time of AV, (iii) DO, the number of dynamic obstacles, and (iv) VA, the number of allowed velocities of dynamic obstacles. In scenarios S1 and S2, we use one phase of verification and one allowed velocity, which means that the dynamic obstacle can appear at any moment, always moving at the highest speed throughout the verification. S3 is similar to S1 but it prolongs the travelling time of the AV, and thus, the verification is split into three phases (S3.1–S3.3). In S4, the dynamic obstacle has three possible velocities, which means its velocity has three initial values and changes arbitrarily during the

---

[4] The models and external library: https://github.com/rgu01/FM2021.

verification. S5 increases the number of dynamic obstacles to 2, which means there could be at most 2 dynamic obstacles in the map at the same time. For each scenario S, we report the number of states (NOS) and the computation time (CT) needed to verify two requirements, namely obstacle avoiding and destination reaching (see Sect. 4.2 for details). These two values are useful indicators of our approach's performance dealing with various scenarios. All the dynamic obstacles are detected only when they get close to the AV, i.e., they are not foreknown by the AV.

Problems Discovered by Counter-Examples. Initially, the proposed collision-avoidance algorithm could not pass the reach-avoid verification in any of these scenarios, and we have discovered several problematic scenarios by analyzing the counter-examples returned from our approach:

Problematic Scenario 1. When there is only one dynamic obstacle whose maximum velocity is less than the maximum velocity of AV, the dipole flow fields generated by the algorithm sometimes draw the AV to the obstacle instead of pushing the obstacle away from it, until their distance is too short (see Fig. 8(a)). This happens because the magnetic moments could push or draw the moving objects. Here, we improve the algorithm by simply turning the direction of the magnetic moments before the AV and the dynamic obstacle get too close.

Table 1. Verification results of the improved version of the algorithm.

S	Environment		Obstacles		Avoiding Obstacles			Reaching Destination		
	WP	TT	DO	VA	NOS	CT	Result	NOS	CT	Result
S1	2	25	1	1	547,617	2.7 s	true	545,505	5.5 s	true
S2	6	25	1	1	411,747	1.8 s	true	411,168	3.6 s	true
S3	2	85	1	1	3,222,290	15.3 s	true	3,217,767	31.8	true
S3.1	1	30	1	1	1,532,082	7.4 s	true	1,527,811	15.7 s	true
S3.2	1	30	1	1	1,183,792	5.5 s	true	1,185,550	11.4 s	true
S3.3	1	25	1	1	506,416	2.4 s	true	504,406	4.7 s	true
S4	2	15	1	3	12,317,809	1.0 mins	true	12,498,924	2.1 mins	true
S5	2	15	2	1	1,398,011	7.6 s	false	226,896,902	43.2 mins	true

Problematic Scenario 2. When the dynamic obstacle and AV move directly towards each other, the dipole fields can only generate magnetic moments on the line of their moving directions, which drive the AV to its opposite direction but on the same line. When the dynamic obstacle keeps moving towards the same direction, the AV can only move backwards until its distance is longer than a certain value and turns 180° towards its next waypoint, which soon lets the AV get close to the dynamic obstacle again and turn backward (see Fig. 8(b)). According to the counter-examples, this scenario keeps happening iteratively until the AV stops at the boundary of the map, and is hit by the dynamic obstacle eventually. This is the so-called "livelock" scenario that was also discovered by Gu et al. [11]. To overcome this, we force the AV to turn slightly when its heading is opposite to a dynamic obstacle's heading.

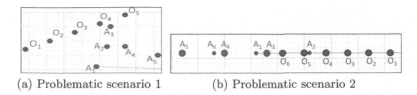

(a) Problematic scenario 1   (b) Problematic scenario 2

Fig. 8. Problematic scenarios discovered by counter-examples. AV's discretized trajectory is blue dots. The dynamic obstacle's discretized trajectory is red dots. AV's reference path is the green line. For differentiation, positions that are too close but belong to different time points are represented by small and large dots in scenario 2. A_n and O_m indicate the AV and obstacle, respectively, n and m are time points. (Color figure online)

Experimental Results. Although the improved algorithm passes the verification in S1-S4, our results suggest that it still cannot satisfy the obstacle-avoiding requirement in the last scenarios (S5) that contain more than one dynamic obstacle (see Table 1). Note that the destination-reaching property is still satisfied in S5, because the vehicle models are not designed to stop when a collision happens. The rationale of this design is that collisions do not necessarily stop a car from continuing moving. We want to see if the dipole-flow field algorithm can draw the vehicle to its destination anyway when it deviates from the planned paths. Counter-examples are found relatively fast in S5, even though it is more complicated than other scenarios. We leave the further improvement of the algorithm to deal with multiple agents as a future work. The experiments have demonstrated the approach's ability of discovering problems in the early stage of designing collision-avoidance algorithms, and proving the absence of errors in some scenarios for the improved version of the algorithm.

6   Related Work

Mitsch et al. [18] propose a method to verify safety properties of robots. Their method is based on hybrid system models and differential dynamic logic for theorem proving in KeYMaera. Abhishek et al. [1,2] also use KeYMaera for collision-avoidance verification. Their models consider the realistic geometrical shapes of vehicles, as well as the combination of maneuvers and braking. Heß et al. [14] propose a method to verify an autonomous robotic system during its operation, in order to cope with changing environments. Our work differs from the above studies in the following aspects: we prove that the reach-avoid verification of nonlinear vehicle models can be simplified to a decidable problem of verifying discrete-time models. In addition, our approach provides counter-examples that are useful to improve the algorithms.

Shokri-Manninen et al. [22] have proposed maritime games as a special case of Stochastic Priced Timed Games and modelled the autonomous navigation using UPPAAL STRATEGO. Their models do not consider the nonlinear kinematics of the vessels, and the options of maneuvers for collision-avoidance are limited.

O'Kelly et al. [19] have developed a verification tool, called APEX, and have investigated the combined action of a behavioral planner and state lattice-based motion planner to guarantee a safe vehicle trajectory. In contrast, our approach provides users a generic interface to verify their specific vehicle models equipped with their own collision-avoidance functions. This feature is beneficial to finding bugs in the early stage of designing new algorithms, or employing modified ones.

Although our work relies on the theorems proposed by Fan et al. [8], our work is orthogonal to theirs, that is, their work can be used for the initial construction of reference paths that avoid static obstacles, and our method can be used to verify the dynamic collision-avoidance function of moving obstacles.

7   Conclusion and Future Work

In this paper, we propose a verification approach to formally verify reach-avoid requirements of autonomous vehicles, assuming nonlinear trajectories of movement. We overcome the difficulty of verifying nonlinear hybrid vehicle trajectories by transforming the latter into discrete-time trajectories whose verification we prove sufficient to guarantee meeting the requirements of the original nonlinear ones. Moreover, we engage tool support (i.e., UPPAAL STRATEGO) that provides users a generic interface to configure and verify their own vehicle models equipped with different collision-avoidance algorithms. We show the abilities of our verification method by model checking a state-of-the-art collision-avoidance algorithm based on dipole flow fields, which discovers bugs not detectable by simulation or testing.

Some interesting directions of future work include: (i) exploring ways of handling complex vehicle models that represent more detailed kinematic features, and (ii) statistical verification of the cases where the distances between dynamic obstacles and AV are smaller than the tracking-error boundaries but collisions do not necessarily occur.

Acknowledgement. We acknowledge the support of the Swedish Knowledge Foundation via the profile DPAC - Dependable Platform for Autonomous Systems and Control, grant nr: 20150022, and via the synergy ACICS - Assured Cloud Platforms for Industrial Cyber-Physical Systems, grant nr. 20190038.

References

1. Abhishek, A., Sood, H., Jeannin, J.B.: Formal verification of braking while swerving in automobiles. In: Proceedings of the 23rd International Conference on Hybrid Systems: Computation and Control, pp. 1–11 (2020)
2. Abhishek, A., Sood, H., Jeannin, J.B.: Formal verification of swerving maneuvers for car collision avoidance. In: 2020 American Control Conference (ACC), pp. 4729–4736. IEEE (2020)
3. Alur, R., Courcoubetis, C., Dill, D.: Model-checking in dense real-time. Inf. Comput. **104**(1), 2–34 (1993)

4. Alur, R., Dill, D.L.: A theory of timed automata. Theoret. Comput. Sci. **126**, 183–235 (1994)
5. Daniel, K., Nash, A., Koenig, S., Felner, A.: Theta*: any-angle path planning on grids. J. Artif. Intell. Res. **39**, 533–579 (2010)
6. David, A., Jensen, P.G., Larsen, K.G., Mikučionis, M., Taankvist, J.H.: Uppaal stratego. In: Baier, C., Tinelli, C. (eds.) TACAS 2015. LNCS, vol. 9035, pp. 206–211. Springer, Heidelberg (2015). https://doi.org/10.1007/978-3-662-46681-0_16
7. DeCastro, J.A., Alonso-Mora, J., Raman, V., Rus, D., Kress-Gazit, H.: Collision-free reactive mission and motion planning for multi-robot systems. In: Bicchi, A., Burgard, W. (eds.) Robotics Research. SPAR, vol. 2, pp. 459–476. Springer, Cham (2018). https://doi.org/10.1007/978-3-319-51532-8_28
8. Fan, C., Miller, K., Mitra, S.: Fast and guaranteed safe controller synthesis for nonlinear vehicle models. In: Lahiri, S.K., Wang, C. (eds.) CAV 2020. LNCS, vol. 12224, pp. 629–652. Springer, Cham (2020). https://doi.org/10.1007/978-3-030-53288-8_31
9. Fan, C., Qin, Z., Mathur, U., Ning, Q., Mitra, S., Viswanathan, M.: Controller synthesis for linear system with reach-avoid specifications. IEEE Trans. Automatic Control (2021)
10. Fox, D., Burgard, W., Thrun, S.: The dynamic window approach to collision avoidance. IEEE Robot. Autom. Mag. **4**(1), 23–33 (1997)
11. Gu, R., Marinescu, R., Seceleanu, C., Lundqvist, K.: Formal verification of an autonomous wheel loader by model checking. In: Proceedings of the 6th Conference on Formal Methods in Software Engineering, pp. 74–83. ACM (2018)
12. Gu, R., Seceleanu, C., Enoiu, E.P., Lundqvist, K.: Formal verification of collision avoidance for nonlinear autonomous vehicle models. Technical report, Mälardalen University, April 2021
13. Henzinger, T.A., Kopke, P.W., Puri, A., Varaiya, P.: What's decidable about hybrid automata? J. Comput. Syst. Sci. **57**(1), 94–124 (1998)
14. Heß, D., Althoff, M., Sattel, T.: Formal verification of maneuver automata for parameterized motion primitives. In: 2014 IEEE/RSJ International Conference on Intelligent Robots and Systems, pp. 1474–1481. IEEE (2014)
15. Lafferriere, G., Pappas, G.J., Yovine, S.: A new class of decidable hybrid systems. In: Vaandrager, F.W., van Schuppen, J.H. (eds.) HSCC 1999. LNCS, vol. 1569, pp. 137–151. Springer, Heidelberg (1999). https://doi.org/10.1007/3-540-48983-5_15
16. Larsen, K.G., Pettersson, P., Yi, W.: Uppaal in a nutshell. Int. J. Softw. Tools Technol. Transfer **1**, 134–152 (1997)
17. LaValle, S.M.: Rapidly-exploring random trees: a new tool for path planning. Technical report, Computer Science Department, Iowa State University, October 1998
18. Mitsch, S., Ghorbal, K., Vogelbacher, D., Platzer, A.: Formal verification of obstacle avoidance and navigation of ground robots. Int. J. Robot. Res. **36**(12), 1312–1340 (2017)
19. O'Kelly, M., Abbas, H., Gao, S., Shiraishi, S., Kato, S., Mangharam, R.: Apex: autonomous vehicle plan verification and execution. In: SAE World Congress (2016)
20. Platzer, A.: Differential-algebraic dynamic logic for differential-algebraic programs. J. Log. Comput. **20**(1), 309–352 (2010)
21. Rabin, S.: Game programming gems, chapter a* aesthetic optimizations. Charles River Media (2000)

22. Shokri-Manninen, F., Vain, J., Waldén, M.: Formal verification of COLREG-based navigation of maritime autonomous systems. In: de Boer, F., Cerone, A. (eds.) SEFM 2020. LNCS, vol. 12310, pp. 41–59. Springer, Cham (2020). https://doi.org/10.1007/978-3-030-58768-0_3

23. Trinh, L., Ekström, M., Çürüklü, B.: Dipole flow field for dependable path planning of multiple agents. In: IEEE/RSJ International Conference on Intelligent Robots and Systems, September 2017

Industry Track Invited Papers

Formal Verification of Complex Data Paths: An Industrial Experience

Carl-Johan H. Seger$^{(\boxtimes)}$

Department of CSE, Chalmers University of Technology, Gothenburg, Sweden
secarl@chalmers.se

Abstract. After caches, most transistors in a modern microprocessor are devoted to wide data-paths. Due to performance and power requirements, these data-paths often use complex implementations of sophisticated algorithms. As Intel experienced in 1994, a bug in a data-path can be extremely expensive and thus needs to be avoided at almost any cost. At the same time, simulation based verification is extremely poor at verifying data-paths due to the vast data space and thus formal verification is almost a requirement. In this paper a retrospective is given of the formal verification of complex data-paths that took place at Intel from the mid 1990s until very recently. The technology that made the effort possible, the tools developed that made it feasible, and the methodology created that made it practical will all be discussed. Finally, a few examples that illustrates the approach will be presented as well as a concluding discussion on what the goal of using formal verification should be.

Keywords: Formal verification · Functional languages · Model checking · Symbolic trajectory evaluation · Circuit visualization

1 Introduction

In a modern microprocessor the second largest use of transistors is in wide data-paths. For example, floating point units, graphics units, machine learning TPUs, encryption or decryption units, signal processing units for radio and/or human interfaces, are all major consumers of "data-path transistors." These data-paths have several things in common. First, they tend to be quite wide; it is not uncommon to have several hundred bits wide data-paths. Second, since they are critical for the performance of the chip, they tend to use very sophisticated algorithms and even more complex implementation techniques. In particular, with the ever increasing emphasis on lowering the power consumption, they often have very complex power down/up circuits. A direct results of these characteristics is that

This work was partially supported by the Wallenberg Autonomous Systems and Software Program (WASP) funded by Knut and Alice Wallenberg Foundation, by a grant from the Swedish Foundation for Strategic Research (SSF) under the project Octopi (Ref. RIT17-0023), and by a generous donation from Intel corp.

M. Huisman et al. (Eds.): FM 2021, LNCS 13047, pp. 697–716, 2021.
https://doi.org/10.1007/978-3-030-90870-6_38

there is a significant risk for subtle bugs to creep into the designs. Added to this is the difficulty of verifying such circuits using traditional simulation. As a result we have the ingredients for a perfect storm. In 1994 Intel was hit by such an event when it was found that a bug in the Pentium FDIV sometimes made the processor compute the wrong answer. This bug caused Intel to take a $475 million charge against earnings [1]—or $850 million in today's dollars.

Although it might be tempting to think that the Pentium FDIV bug was an anomaly, there has been several "near misses" since then. For example, a formal verification effort of a graphics unit in 2012 [12] found over 200 bugs, and in 2015 an "even worse" bug than the Pentium FDIV bug was found during formal verification of a new floating point divider at Intel [private communication, Kaivola, 2015]. Similarly, during the formal verification of a new complex micro-controller in 2016 over 70 bugs in the data-path were discovered [private communication, Seger, 2016]. Of course, it is important to remember that the type of bugs we are talking about are not the "typos" that every design encounters and that are quite easy to find. Thus, it is almost always corner cases, settings of flags and other status results, or interactions between operations and power control circuitry that are the cause of these bugs.

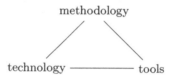

Fig. 1. Ingredients needed for practical formal verification.

In this paper we will provide a retrospective of the formal verification effort that started in 1995 at Intel and that ultimately led to the replacement of traditional simulation as a verification tool for most complex data-path circuits at Intel [11]. We will provide this retrospective by focusing on the three required aspects needed to make such verification possible, as shown in Fig. 1: the underlying technology needed, the tool environment enabling the deployment of the technology and finally the methodology that made the approach practical, repeatable and predictable. We will then conclude by illustrating these aspects by discussing a few concrete examples.

2   Technology

In order to carrying out an effective formal verification effort on a modern microprocessor design, a collection of technologies are needed since the complexity and size of the unit that is under verification prevents any single formal verification technique to handle it by itself. However, a critical part of any multi-technology approach is to ensure the different techniques actually "fit together." The literature (and practice!) is full of examples of formal verification efforts that are put together with various technologies/tools and only very vague hand-waving arguments are provided for their soundness. The reality though is that in a very complex environment with multiple technologies, there is a high chance that some corner case is not covered. There is nothing that reduces the confidence in a formal verification effort faster, than bugs discovered in a unit that had been "formally verified." Thus it is critical that the various technologies work seamlessly together and, as much as possible, prevent escapes.

In this section we will highlight a few of the key technologies that were used or were developed at Intel to enable the complete formal verification of some of the most complex data-paths in existence.

2.1 Symbolic Representations

The breakthroughs we have witnessed in model checking, and symbolic model checking in particular, in the last 30 years, have virtually all been based on two technologies: Ordered Binary Decision Diagrams (OBDDs) [5], or SAT solvers [13]. OBDDs were the first to arrive and for some types of problems, is still the reigning champion. In particular, for many compute intensive problems encountered when verifying complex data-paths, OBDDs are the most effective approach. However, there is an important proviso for this statement. OBDDs are often the most efficient approach **when there are no bugs**. The problem with OBDDs is that an error in the specification or even a rather trivial bug in the implementation, can make the OBDDs grow exponentially. On the other hand, methods based on SAT are often extremely efficient for buggy designs or specifications. It is only when the final complete verification needs to be done, the SAT approach sometimes suffers from very long run times. Thus a practical approach is always to use the SAT solver approach first and only switch to OBDDs when it appears that the design satisfies the specification.

2.2 Model Checking

Although there are many model checking approaches described in the literature [6], one of the most effective for verification of complex data-paths is Symbolic Trajectory Evaluation (STE) [15]. The basic idea in STE is to model the values in a design as a lattice. A typical approach is to use the lattice shown in Fig. 2 for a single wire and extend the lattice to a crossproduct lattice to model all the wires in the design.

Fig. 2. Basic node value lattice.

By using a very simple linear temporal logic with only simple predicates, conjunction, domain constraints, and a next time operator, there is a unique weakest sequence of lattice points for every formula in the logic. If we use Boolean expressions over some set of Boolean variables for the domain constraints, we can encode a large number of simple trajectory logic formula very concisely. By using a symbolic circuit simulator that operates over this partially symbolic lattice domain, we can very effectively determine the validity of a trajectory formula of the form $A \rightarrow C$, where A (the antecedent) represents the assumptions we make about the circuit values and C (the consequent) represents what we hope the circuit will guarantee given the assumptions in A. The STE algorithm works equally well with OBDDs as with SAT solvers.

Experience has shown that STE scales well to very large and complex designs [16]. Part of the reason for this is that the complexity of the verification is more determined by the complexity of the formula to be verified, rather than the complexity of the design being verified. In addition, since STE uses a lattice structure, the number of Boolean variables needed, and thus to a large extent the complexity of the verification effort, is often vastly smaller than what a traditional symbolic simulator or traditional symbolic model checker would require. In fact, clever encodings of conditions to be verified using a few Boolean variables to represent well chosen points in the lattice structure, enable formal verification of very large designs.

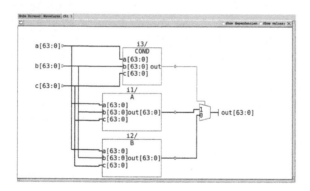

Fig. 3. Common circuit using speculation.

However, the use of lattice structure for modeling has also another important benefit. A common situation encountered in high performance designs is situations like the one depicted in Fig. 3. Here a choice between two different results is decided by some condition circuit, named COND. To speed up the design, both A and B are computed while the condition is evaluated. Now if the property we are currently verifying is such that we know that COND will evaluate to 1, then the simulation of all the circuits in B is unnecessary. Worse, it may even cause an OBDD based STE run to fail, since the OBDDs computed inside B may be so large the simulation is aborted. Since the only requirement of the symbolic simulator is that it respects the information ordering in the lattice[1], we can abstract the simulation of B by simply making all the wires inside B X. If the verification goes through successfully even with this abstraction of the simulator, then the theory of STE guarantees that the verification would have gone through without the abstraction in an ideal world in which there was no limit on the size of the OBDDs.

Although this type of "weakening" of internal wires is very useful and often critical to making a verification to go through, it has a major drawback—every node inside B that needs to be weakened to X must be explicitly mentioned. If the circuit is changed slightly so that the nodes change name, the effort of determining these wire names will need to be repeated. Effectively, weakening nodes by name makes the verification run very fragile to changes in the design. Fortunately, there is a nice extension to the weakening approach described above. Instead of weakening named nodes at some specific time, one can instead weaken any node for which the size of the OBDD is over some threshold. This "dynamic weakening" turns out to be one of the most effective techniques we developed for OBDD based STE and is a corner stone in making formal verification scripts robust and maintainable [11].

2.3   Theorem Proving

Although STE is a very high capacity model checking algorithm, in particular in conjunction with dynamic weakening, for many computations performed by complex data-paths, it is still insufficient. For these types of designs, we need to break down the verification effort into multiple smaller verification tasks. As mentioned earlier, the complexity of STE depends largely on the complexity of the property being checked. Consequently, breaking down a complex property into smaller ones is almost always beneficial when using STE. The difficulty with this approach is that we must ensure that the combined successful verification of all the smaller properties indeed implies the satisfaction of the original "big" property. In other words, we need to reason about collections of properties. Furthermore, this reasoning is unlikely to be possible using fully automated approaches, like OBDDs or SAT, since if it could, then the STE run for the complete property would likely have been possible. As a result, we move into the domain of theorem proving and reasoning based on the syntax of the formulae. Fortunately, there is a set of sound and complete inference rules for STE [8, 18]. This provides a solid foundation for breaking down a complex STE property into a collection of smaller, and likely much easier to verify, STE properties.

In addition to theorem proving for decomposing an STE property, we also need to verify bit-level properties against more abstract domains. For example, we may need to verify that a high-level reference model for floating point addition based on bit-vectors satisfies the IEEE 754 standard [3]. However, the IEEE 754 standard is stated in terms of real numbers. For such reasoning, the full machinery of a general purpose theorem prover is needed. At the same time,

---

[1] Technically speaking the simulator must be monotonic with respect to the lattice.

it is critical that this verification is tied closely to the actual verification at the circuit level.

In practice, there are broadly five types of reasoning that are needed when verifying complex data-paths.

1. Sequential composition: Used to break down a complex computation/specification into a sequence of smaller operations.
2. Parallel composition: Primarily used to verify SIMD type of operations, i.e., when a single control drives a collection of (almost) identical compute units that all perform the same computation on independent data.
3. Case splitting: Used to break down a complex property into more restrictive properties. Useful in particular for OBDD based STE runs since each case may be verified using a different variable ordering for the OBDD variables.
4. Induction over infinite streams: Used to transform a specification written in terms of stream transformers into an inductive proof with a base case and an inductive step.
5. Specification reasoning: A catch-all for reasoning about a specification to show that it has some desired property. Often bridging between specifications written in terms of abstract entities, e.g., real numbers, and reference models written in terms of bit-vectors.

2.4   Specifications

So far we have not discussed "what" to verify. There are broadly three types of properties:

1. high-level reference models,
2. low-level functional or relational properties, and
3. metamorphic properties.

A high-level reference model is simply a design written to make its correctness as easy as possible to determine. One can view a reference model as a version 0 implementation for which the only requirement is that the answer should be correct for all inputs and the model should be as easy as possible to reason about in a theorem prover. For many computations, a high-level reference model is typically quite easy to write in a handful of lines. Even more complex specifications, e.g., floating point addition, have reference models that are quite small (10s of lines).

A major benefit of high-level reference models is that they can be proven correct against an abstract specification once and for all and then be used in formal verifications against many types of implementations of this operation. For example, some of the high-level reference models developed for various operations at Intel have stayed essentially unmodified for more than 15 years [11].

Low-level properties are often needed for verifying one-of-a-kind design features; in particular control-oriented blocks. Here the specification can either be functional or relational. A functional specification simply provides the answer the design should compute for all inputs whereas a relational specification only specifies that some relation should hold between the inputs and outputs.

There are several problems with low-level specifications. First, they often end up being created from reverse engineering of the design, and thus provide very little value. Second, they depend often directly on detailed design decisions in the implementation and thus changes to the design often invalidates the verification—even if the change would not break the complete computation. Finally, because they rely so heavily on the design, they are very difficult to re-use for other designs.

Although, one tries to avoid low-level properties as much as possible, it is unfortunately not always possible to avoid them completely. One approach to limit the drawbacks of such properties is to isolate them to a particular part of the verification so that when the design changes or the verification script needs to be moved to a new design, most of the re-work can be focused on that one design-dependent part.

Finally, a major difficulty for some complex data-path computations is the inherent difficulty to even capture the specifications. For example, when verifying the instruction-length decoder (ILD) in the original PentiumPro [16], we encountered this difficulty. Intuitively, the ILD reads a cache line of instructions and computes the start and end of each x86 instruction. Given the complexity of the x86 architecture, writing a specification for the ILD is a major undertaking and one that is difficult to ascertain its correctness. Added to this is the difficulty in specifying how this computation should be repeated over all the bytes in the cache line that may contain anywhere from 1 to 15 instructions depending on the length of the individual instructions.

We solved this problem by splitting the verification into two parts: verifying that an instruction that starts at byte 0 is decoded correctly and that an instruction that starts at byte i is determined to have the same length as it would have if it had started at byte 0. The second is an example of a metamorphic property, or as we often called them, a self-consistency property.

What is interesting with metamorphic properties is that they often trigger subtle boundary case design flaws. In addition, they can often be verified before a full specification has been created thus reducing the average "age" of these bugs. At the same time, these properties are often quite challenging in practice since they often depend on establishing some invariant(s) of the design.

3   Tools

Although the technology discussed in the previous section is critical to make the formal verification of complex data-paths possible, practical tools are needed to make it feasible. In fact, a complete environment in which designs can be imported, specifications can be written and manipulated, verification runs can be controlled and failures debugged is needed. For the verification effort discussed in this paper, the VOSS[2] system provided all this. The key to the VOSS system was the interface language FL. In this section we will discuss how the VOSS system, and FL in particular, grew to meet the needs of the formal verification effort at Intel.

3.1   Model Import

In order to ensure that the formal verification effort was connected to the design, VOSS imported the Register Transfer Level (RTL) model through a separate compiler. This compiler changed over the years as Intel moved from an in-house RTL language to the industry language SystemVerilog [2]. There were two major aspects that this compiler needed to satisfy. First, it had to handle very large RTL models (up to million lines) efficiently. Second, the semantic given to a design by the compiler had to match the semantics given to the same design by other tools. At Intel, this was achieved through two mechanisms. First, the formal verification model used the same compiler as the formal equivalence verification (FEV) tools (for a long time the FEV tools were also based on VOSS), which ensured the connection to the schematic model was solid. To ensure that the simulation model matched the formal verification model, an extensive Lint [9] like tool was used to ensure only "well defined constructs" were allowed in the RTL model. These well defined constructs were selected rather carefully and tested on many tools to minimize the possibility that the formal tools gave a model a different semantics than other tools[3].

3.2   Scripting and Implementation Language

Originally FL was simply designed as a scripting language for controlling the STE engine in a combined theorem-proving and STE system [10] and was basically a simple, untyped, functional language with OBDDs and STE built-in. However, it became clear early that FL could be extended much further. To reduce the number of bugs the user writes, the language first became strongly typed with an effective type inference engine. As time went on, the type system and the type checker became more and more powerful to the point that it today equals even advanced modern functional languages.

The actual FL interpreter is written in C and, for efficiency reasons, a fairly large number of functions are implemented in C and built in to the system. For general programs, FL implements a compilation system based on a set of fixed combinators and graph reduction [17]. Although FL's implementation is not terribly efficient, the use of many built in, and highly optimized, functions make the system quite snappy in practice.

What sets FL apart from other functional languages is the tight integration of ordered binary decision diagrams (OBDDs) [5] into the language.

---

[2] The system was renamed Forte and the interface language renamed reFlect inside Intel, but we will use the original names VOSS and FL to avoid confusion.

[3] An interesting outcome of this testing was a rather large set of bug reports created for both in-house as well as external vendor tools.

All Boolean expressions in FL are maintained as OBDDs. Hence, it is very easy to compare complex Boolean expressions and to combine them in different ways. To illustrate some simple examples, consider the following FL session[4]:

```
: VARS "a b c[3:0] d[3:0]";
a::bool
: b::bool
: c::bool list
: d::bool list
: : let ex1 = NOT (a AND b);
ex1::bool
: let ex2 = NOT a OR NOT b;
ex2::bool
: let ex3 = NOT a XOR b;
ex3::bool
: ex1 == ex2;
T
it::bool
: ex1 == ex3;
F
it::bool
:
```

where we declared some Boolean variables: a and b as well as two lists of Boolean variables c and d and defined three Boolean expressions ex1, ex2, and ex3. Finally, we compared the expressions:

The use of Boolean expressions in functions can be illustrated by defining a **greater** function that takes two list of Boolean expressions and treat them as bit-vectors (big-endian).

```
: letrec greater (u:us) (v:vs) =
     u AND NOT v OR (u = v) AND (greater us vs)
 /\    greater [] [] = F;
greater::(bool list)->(bool list)->bool
:
```

Here we used pattern matching in the definition of the function to walk down the two lists (a better implementation would check for unequal lengths of the lists).

The combination of high-order functions and recursive functions, allow us to define many useful building blocks. For example, for most model checking algorithms or symbolic reachability computations, a greatest fixpoint operation is often needed. In FL, a greatest fixpoint function can be defined as:

```
: letrec Gfp fn cur =
     let new = cur OR (fn cur) in
     (new == cur) => cur | Gfp fn new
;
Gfp::(bool->bool)->bool->bool
:
```

Here we used OBDDs to represent the sets and thus the canonicity of the OBDDs to determine when a fix point has been reached[5]. A least fixpoint can be defined similarly. This type of high-order functions can then be used for many formal verification algorithms.

---

[4] The examples were created in VossII [14], the open-source version of Voss.

[5] Note the syntax for if-then-else is *cond* => *then-expr* | *else-expr*.

3.3   Specification Language

Although the above functionality illustrated the usefulness of having OBDDs as
first class objects, there is an extension of their usage in FL that significantly
enhances the system, namely that symbolic Boolean expressions can be used as a
condition in an if-then-else statement. In particular, the control of recursion can
be done through symbolic expressions. Effectively, FL programs can be symbolically evaluated. However, there are some restrictions. The most visible restriction
is that integers need to be replaced with the built-in bitvectors representation.
As an example, consider the following sequence of functions.

```
: letrec factorial n =
    (n <= '1) => int2bv 1
             | n*(factorial (n - '1))
;
factorial::bv->bv
: // Scalar input
factorial '5;
<F,T,T,T,T,F,F,F>
it::bv
: // Symbolic input
factorial ((variable "c") => '3 | '4);
<F,c',c',c,c,F>
it::bv
: let v = bv_variable "a[6:0]";
v::bv
: let test = v > '0 AND
             (factorial v) <= (v*v + '10);
test::bool
: enumerate_examples 20 (depends v) test;

a[6:0]=0x1
a[6:0]=0x2
a[6:0]=0x3
a[6:0]=0x4
:
```

Finally, an example of a (partial) high-level reference model for floating point
addition might be written as:

```
": let num_fp_add sfp1 sfp2 =
    val (sgn1,exp1,mant1) = destr_NUM sfp1 in
    val (sgn2,exp2,mant2) = destr_NUM sfp2 in
    let emin = min exp1 exp2 in
    let a1 = mant1 * '2 ** (exp1-emin) in
    let a2 = mant2 * '2 ** (exp2-emin) in
    let m1 = sgn1 => '-1*a1 | a1 in
    let m2 = sgn2 => '-1*a2 | a2 in
    let sum = m1 + m2 in
    let res_sgn = sum < '0 in
    let res_frac = res_sgn => '-1*sum | sum in
    let res_exp = emin in
    NUM res_sgn res_exp res_frac
;
num_fp_add::sfp->sfp->sfp
:
```

3.4   Term Language

As we already highlighted in the technology section, an important part of any
formal verification effort of complex data-paths is the need to combine many
smaller properties, and their corresponding verification runs, into the high-level
desired property. For this, theorem proving technology is needed.

The traditional approach to theorem proving, at least in the LCF style [7], is to embed some logic as an abstract data type in the metalanguage. However, this means that there are effectively two languages that have to be understood: the language of the logic and the metalanguage used to manipulate and control the theorem prover. To avoid this, the Voss system used reflection [4]. In other words, one can write programs in FL that manipulate other FL programs. As a result, the same function that is used to run the STE engine to verify some property can automatically become a data object for which inference rules can be used to combine it with other FL expressions. As a result, the user of the theorem prover only needs to be aware of a single language and there is no overhead in performing the underlying model checking.

3.5   Visualization

When formal verification is attempted on large industrial designs, a critical observation is that most of the time will not be spent in running a successful verification, but rather in debugging failing ones. As a result, an absolutely critical part of the Voss system was an extensive circuit visualization system. This involved both statically (the structure of the design) as well as dynamically (the behavior of the design in response to some stimulae). To give a flavor how this part of the system worked, we will illustrate a typical debugging session through a few screen shots.

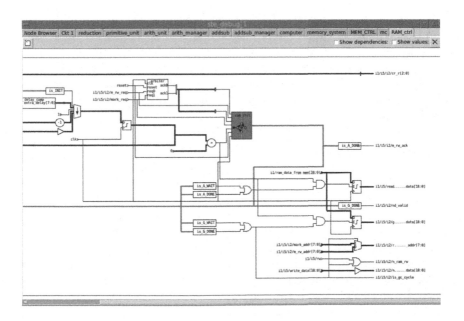

Fig. 4. Visualization of circuit.

First, we visualize the circuit hierarchically, from the top-level hierarchy and selectively down to an area of interest. Note that the generation of schematics is completely automatic and no manual intervention is needed. In Fig. 4 we show part of a larger circuit. The visualization is (almost) instantaneous and thus one can very rapidly drill down to relevant circuits.

Of course, we also need to visualize how the signals change and thus a waveform viewer is also available. A small part of a long counter example is shown in Fig. 5.

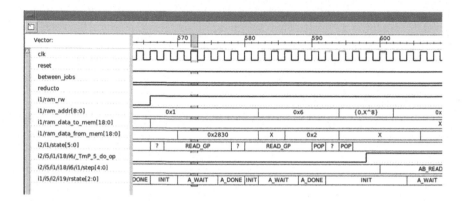

Fig. 5. Waveform viewer after (scalar) STE run.

To ease the debugging even further, the time line on the waveform viewer can be frozen and the values on all visible nodes annotated with their value at the frozen time.

Finally, custom visualization procedures can be written and connected to the simulation and visualization system.. For example, visualization of finite state machines or visualization of data structures represented in a RAM are powerful debugging tools.

4   Methodology

In order to have a practical formal verification approach that actually can be deployed in an industrial setting, it is not sufficient with technology and tools implementing the technology. A practical methodology is equally important. Over the years, a five-stage methodology was created at Intel that made verification of complex data-paths efficient, predictable, and reproducible. In this section we will go through the five stages and discuss the main steps in each stage. Although we describe the stages as being sequential, in practice there is significant iterations between the stages.

4.1   Wiggling

A modern industrial design is not only extremely complex but also often rather poorly documented. As a result, the first task of a formal verification engineer is to get his/her head around the design. Basically, get the design to do some simple operations, identify the relevant inputs, outputs, and major internal state machines. All of this requires reading the RTL code. However, that only provides a static view of the design. In order to gain a better understanding of the behavior of the design, simple simulation is always needed. This is the main focus during the wiggling phase. For STE based verification, this is often referred to X-chasing, since input and internal state signals that are not assigned values during the simulation will remain unknown ("X"). Thus the common activity is chasing the X's on the output to where they originate being it a forgotten control input, an internal state machine or a forgotten feedback loop.

In the process of doing this simulation, one important activity is to create an abstract interface description of the design. In other words, rather than mentioning node names explicitly, abstract names for relevant signals (and their timing behavior) are created. These abstractions provide a "circuit-API" an isolates many design specific features to this interface. This helps greatly later in handling regression runs on modified RTL or reuse on different designs.

4.2 Scalar Verification

The next major phase is started when the outputs can be driven to non-X values and involves simulating simple inputs. For example, for a floating point adder one may try to simulate $1.0 + 3.3$ to ensure the environment has been set up properly and that the circuit behaves as expected. Although this seems trivial and very few bugs in the design are found during this phase, it often reveals misunderstandings of the control signals and allows these misunderstandings to be clarified very quickly. As in the wiggling phase, the circuit visualization environment is absolutely critical during this phase.

At the same time as these simple examples are run, the specification is gradually refined and made more complete. Although this could, in theory, have been done earlier, in practice it is first during this phase many boundary conditions are being considered and the specifications extended to cover them.

4.3 Symbolic Verification

In this phase, the simple scalar values are being replaced with symbolic inputs. One can look at this phase as the one that finally performs serious formal verification. To make the process efficient, this symbolic verification is started by using the SAT based STE engine, since there will likely still be many bugs or errors in the specification and/or the design. Since SAT based STE is far better at finding bugs in a bug-rich environment, it is the preferred method here. As the symbolic verification progresses, however, a switch to OBDD based STE often takes place.

Once most "simple" bugs are dealt with, the emphasis of the verification effort switches to complexity management. This may involve case splits, OBDD variable ordering, symbolic indexing for arrays or similar structures, dynamic weakening, etc. If none of these approaches are sufficient, structural decomposition may be needed and the verification broken up into several smaller verification efforts.

Of course, the goal of this stage is to find any and all bugs in the design. As a result, whenever an STE run fails, the failure set is captured. Contrary to many symbolic model checkers, STE provides more than just a simple counter-example. The most common is that an OBDD representing all failure cases is returned. This allows the user to probe the answer in different ways. For example, ask the system to compute "forcing" values, i.e., values that must have specific values for the failure to occur, or asking for multiple counter examples to ease the effort in root causing the bug.

In practice, this phase is the one in which most design bugs are found and certainly the one in which most subtle bugs are discovered.

4.4   Theorem Proving

Once the symbolic verification phase is over, the verification engineer is left with a (often very large) collection of properties and verification scripts that all successfully run to completion. However, there are two aspects of these results that potentially may lead to false verification: are the specifications correct and did the proof decomposition actually cover all cases?

To increase the confidence in the specifications, theorem proving, or more precisely, proof based analysis of the specifications is needed. Here a theorem proving system is used to reason about the specification(s) and, typically, is used to relate the specification to a more abstract specification. For example, if the specification is a reference model for floating point addition, like the one at the end of Sect. 3.3, we may want to verify that if we map the inputs to reals and add them together as reals we get the same answer as converting the result of the function to a real. Although this type of specification verification is non-trivial, it is a one-time cost if the reference model can be re-used for a long time and it provides high confidence in the reference models.

Since any practical formal verification effort will likely result in a large number of verification runs, it is very easy to forget some case. Formal verification of the verification composition removes this potential problem. An interesting point here is that because of the reflection mechanism in the VOSS system, the theorem proving actually is used to establish that the programs that were run did indeed cover all cases – not that our intent of the decomposition was correct. Thus, by proving the correctness of the compositions of the various verification scripts we also eliminate bugs in the verification scripts.

It should be pointed out that the theorem proving phase will not directly find bugs in the design. However, it is not uncommon to find holes in the verification script that, when finally run, trigger bugs in the design.

4.5   Regression

Although it might be tempting to think the verification effort is completed once the theorem proving has completed, this is far from the case. For formal verification to be of real value, it needs to be done throughout the design effort. As a result, the design which we are trying to verify correct will be continuously changing; new features will be added, better algorithms implemented, implementation choices will be changed when timing, power or area constraints make earlier decisions suboptimal etc. The immediate consequent of this "alive" design is that the formal verification effort needs to be repeated many times on slightly different RTL models. This regression activity can quickly overwhelm a formal verification team unless the proof effort from day one is structured with regression in mind. More specifically, this means that both the tools and methodology should be optimized for failing cases, not the successful verification cases. In hindsight, this should be obvious, but came as a surprise when we originally tried to deploy the STE based formal verification approach. The second major learning from regression work was the importance of separating the design-specific and the design-independent parts of the proofs. That way needed changes are isolated to a few files.

As a side note, a lesson we learned was also that making a proof effort robust for regression also eased the effort of porting the proof to a new design that implemented the same, or at least similar, functionality.

5   Examples

In this section we will highlight some of the main lessons obtained in verifying a few typical data-path designs.

5.1   Floating Point Unit

IEEE 754 floating point arithmetic is a very good target for STE based verification for several reasons. First, there is a specification for what the operations should do and the specification has been unchanging for many years. Second, it is an effort with very high return-on-the-investment since a bug in such unit could be extremely costly. Finally, since the performance of a processor on floating point numbers is a critical aspect, a modern high-performance floating point unit is extremely complex and thus will almost certainly contain a number of subtle bugs.

Over time, we developed two distinct types of verification approaches for floating point instructions: behavioral and structural. Below we will discuss each approach on some representative verifications of a 5k latches and 80k gates design.

In the behavioral approach we wrote a high-level reference model against which all verification was done. The actual verification relied usually heavily on decomposing the input space and dynamic weakening. To ensure the correctness of the high-level reference model, theorem proving was used to relate it to a more "mathematical" domain. To verify all versions of floating point add/subtract operations for all rounding modes and all formats took approximately three person months. In addition, the theorem proving of the correctness of the reference model took an additional month. What is interesting is that this reference model, and its associated high-level correctness proof, was used essentially unchanged for many years afterwards on several generations of processors.

The structural approach to verification was needed for multiplication, division, mod, and square root. There were two reasons for this. First, both OBDD based and SAT based STE cannot handle non-trivial multiplication circuits. As a result, a structural decomposition was needed. The other operations are all iterative. As a result, the verification needed to be broken down into a base case and an induction case. Both of these then required some effort in the theorem prover to link the pieces together to establish the desired high-level verification result. Just verifying the divider took approximately three months in total: two months doing the STE model checking and one month to prove the verification decomposition correct. The proof was fairly robust for regression, but was a complete throw away for the next generation processor.

5.2   Complete Micro-controller ISA Verification

Our next example was the complete formal verification of a fairly complex and high-performance micro-controller. An unusual aspect of this verification was that the specification was already given. There was both a detailed English document for the instruction set architecture (ISA) as well as a very exact C++ model that was used for the software development for the micro-controller. The latter, in particular, was meant to be an exact definition of the ISA. Converting the C++ model to an FL reference model was a surprisingly easy task, primarily due to the extensive capabilities in FL to re-define and overload operators. In the end, the FL high-level model looked almost identical to the C++ model with only minor syntactic differences.

When doing reference model verification, the process is as follows. First an abstract (ISA) level state representation is created. Second, a specification is created that defines the update function on the abstract state. As already mentioned, these two items were already existing in the C++ model and only had to be translated into FL syntax. Next, a function ϕ, mapping from an abstract state to a sequence of values on some collection of wires in the design, had to be created. This mapping is then used to verify commutativity, i.e., that for every transition in the abstract state space from a state s to $N(s)$, where N is the next state function, we have $\phi(N(s)) \sqsubseteq Sim(\phi(s))$, where Sim is the behavior of the design as determined by the symbolic simulator and the ordering is the lattice ordering. Developing the mapping function ϕ is not overly difficult, but fairly time consuming and is created almost entirely during the wiggling and scalar simulation phase.

If this is all that is needed, the formal verification of the design could have been completed in a month or so. However, we wanted a complete correctness proof. In particular, we needed to make sure that an instruction was executed correctly no matter which instruction(s) preceded it and which instruction(s) succeeded it. As a result, we needed to find an invariant that could be assumed to hold before the instruction entered the machine and we could verify still holding after the instruction left the machine. In addition, we also had to verify that the invariant was true after the machine was reset. Finding such invariants are difficult and quite time consuming. A very valuable tool here was the ability to run longer sequences of instructions and, using FL's ability to get simulation values and automatically extract patterns and relations. However, this was a tedious task.

The formal verification was the sole verification done on the design and thus completeness was of essence. In the end, about 70 bugs were found. What is interesting is that only slightly more than half were found in the design. The remaining ones were in the specification. In many ways this illustrates the main benefit of formal verification. Ensuring that the model used for software development and the actual hardware behaves the same. As a curiosity, the unmasking of one bug caused the English description, the C++ model, and the RTL model all to be changed since they all had different interpretations on what should happen, none of which ultimately were correct!

As bugs were found, the design engineers fixed them and the formal verification was redone. In many cases the first few attempts at fixing a bug failed. Either by not fixing the problem (rare) or creating a new failure. These bug fixing bugs are not included in the total bug count. A major productivity boost was both that the turnaround time for re-verifying a proposed fixed design was of the order of hours or at most a day. Also, the failure traces we could provide were extremely short which enabled the design engineers to focus only on the problem and not having to wade through a lot of irrelevant simulation data.

6   Discussion

As the experience at Intel has shown, a formal verification approach based on STE aimed at complex data-paths is both feasible and effective. In fact, it is likely the longest sustained formal verification effort in industry, going on for over twenty years.

Although confidentiality agreements make it impossible to provide collected data on the efficacy of the approach, the experience at Intel was that formal verification of complex data-paths provided at least three main advantages:

1. The designs that had been formally verified were much cleaner by the time first silicon arrived, even when the formal verification had not been completed.
2. Replacing traditional simulation with formal verification led to an increase in productivity in the verification team and an actual head-count reduction.
3. Formal verification enabled designs that were far "riskier." In fact some algorithms that ended up in the chips would never had been considered without a formal verification's stamp of approval.

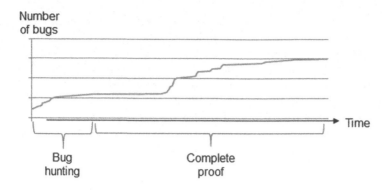

Fig. 6. Bugs found over time.

A discussion that is almost as old as formal verification is what the goal of the formal verification effort should be. Should the aim be for "bug hunting" or "complete verification?" The argument for bug hunting is usually that formal verification is very good at rapidly finding obscure "Friday the 13th" bugs and bug hunting can be done by every design engineer. As a result, bug hunting will rapidly pay for itself. On the other hand, the argument for complete verification is that it is only when *all* corner cases have been explored will you find the really difficult bugs. In addition, if one uses formal verification for bug hunting, one likely still has to create a full simulation environment including all the coverage infrastructure. Thus, bug hunting ends up being "in addition to" rather than "instead of." At Intel this debate went on for many years (it probably still is ongoing). However, for data-paths the evidence was pretty clear. Full proof should be the ultimate goal. But, the debate is likely pointless, since the right answer is probably that formal verification should be used for both bug hunting and full verification. To illustrate this point, in Fig. 6 we have plotted the number of bugs found during one major formal verification effort. It is interesting to see how many bugs were found very rapidly in the beginning, basically during the wiggling, scalar simulation, and early days of the symbolic verification. However, there was then a major lull in bug finding. There were two reasons for this. First, the remaining bugs were much more difficult to find and were almost all related to subtle unintended interactions between particular instructions. Second, during this time the work on finding the invariant was the focus. At the same time, it is telling how many more bugs were found once the invariant was in place and the focus again was on complete verification. In conclusion, about 2/3 of the bugs were not found until the goal was full verification, confirming that in verifying complex data-paths, the majority of bugs occur in obscure corner cases and in particular in unintended interactions between instructions (often power saving related!).

Acknowledgements. The work discussed in this paper was the result of many people's efforts. With the danger of omitting some that should have been mentioned, we would like to highlight (in no particular order): Randy Bryant, Dereck Beatty, John O'Leary, Robert Jones, Tom Melham, Mark Aagaard, Roope Kaivola, Jim Grundy, Jin Yang, and Jeremy Casas.

References

1. Intel corporation annual report (1994). https://www.intel.com/content/www/us/en/history/history-1994-annual-report.html
2. 2017 - IEEE standard for SystemVerilog - unified hardware design, specification, and verification language (2017). https://standards.ieee.org/standard/1800-2017.html
3. IEEE standard for floating-point arithmetic. IEEE Std 754–2019 (Revision of IEEE 754–2008), pp. 1–84 (2019)
4. Aagaard, M.D., Jones, R.B., Seger, C.J.H.: Lifted-FL: a pragmatic implementation of combined model checking and theorem proving. In: Bertot, Y., Dowek, G., Théry, L., Hirschowitz, A., Paulin, C. (eds.) TPHOLs 1999. LNCS, vol. 1690, pp. 323–340. Springer, Heidelberg (1999). https://doi.org/10.1007/3-540-48256-3_22
5. Bryant, R.E.: Graph-based algorithms for boolean function manipulation. IEEE Trans. Comput. **100**(8), 677–691 (1986)
6. Clarke, E.M., Henzinger, T.A., Veith, H., Bloem, R.: Handbook of model checking, vol. 10. Springer (2018). https://doi.org/10.1007/978-3-319-10575-8
7. Gordon, M.J., Milner, A.J.: Edinburgh LCF. A mechanised logic of computation (1979)
8. Hazelhurst, S., Seger, C.-J.: A simple theorem prover based on symbolic trajectory evaluation and BDD's. IEEE Trans. Comput.-Aided Des. Integr. Circ. Syst. **14**(4), 413–422 (1995)
9. Johnson, S.C.: Lint, a C program checker. Bell Telephone Laboratories Murray Hill (1977)
10. Joyce, J.J., Seger, V.: Linking BDD-based symbolic evaluation to interactive theorem-proving. In: 30th ACM/IEEE Design Automation Conference, pp. 469–474. IEEE (1993)
11. Kaivola, R., et al.: Replacing testing with formal verification in Intel CoreTM i7 processor execution engine validation. In: Bouajjani, A., Maler, O. (eds.) CAV 2009. LNCS, vol. 5643, pp. 414–429. Springer, Heidelberg (2009). https://doi.org/10.1007/978-3-642-02658-4_32
12. KiranKumar, V.A., Gupta, A., Ghughal, R.: Symbolic trajectory evaluation: the primary validation vehicle for next generation Intel processor graphics FPU. In: 2012 Formal Methods in Computer-Aided Design (FMCAD), pp. 149–156. IEEE (2012)
13. Prasad, M.R., Biere, A., Gupta, A.: A survey of recent advances in sat-based formal verification. Int. J. Softw. Tools Technol. Transfer **7**(2), 156–173 (2005)
14. Seger, C.-J.: The VossII hardware verification suite (2020). https://github.com/TeamVoss/VossII
15. Seger, C.-J.H., Bryant, R.E.: Formal verification by symbolic evaluation of partially-ordered trajectories. Formal Methods Syst. Des. **6**(2), 147–189 (1995)
16. Seger, C.J.H., et al.: An industrially effective environment for formal hardware verification. IEEE Trans. Comput.-Aided Des. Integr. Circ. Syst. **24**(9), 1381–1405 (2005)

17. Turner, D.A.: A new implementation technique for applicative languages. Softw. Pract. Exper. **9**(1), 31–49 (1979)
18. Zhu, Z., Seger, C.-J.: The completeness of a hardware inference system. In: Dill, David L. (ed.) CAV 1994. LNCS, vol. 818, pp. 286–298. Springer, Heidelberg (1994). https://doi.org/10.1007/3-540-58179-0_62

Some Lessons Learned in the Industrialization of Formal Methods for Financial Algorithms

Grant Olney Passmore[1,2]([⊠])

[1] Imandra Inc., Austin, USA
grant@imandra.ai
[2] Clare Hall, University of Cambridge, Cambridge, UK
https://www.cl.cam.ac.uk/~gp351

1 Extended Abstract

At Imandra Inc. we have pioneered the application of formal methods to financial algorithms [3]. After nearly a decade of R&D and business development, our Imandra automated reasoning system is now in mainstream use at major financial firms such as Goldman Sachs, Itiviti and OneChronos. In these settings, Imandra is relied upon for the design, verification, ongoing auditing and calibration of global financial infrastructure such as trading venues (exchanges and dark pools), smart order routers and FIX connectivity between trading systems.

Getting to this point, however, was not an easy road. When we began, we faced a collection of simultaneous challenges, including:

1. Nearly all financial practitioners we spoke to (and attempted to sell Imandra to) had not heard of formal methods. The very idea that code could be automatically mathematically analyzed in a manner fundamentally different from 'testing' was initially a hard sell.
2. To win the hearts and minds of users, we needed to find highly specialized niches and industrial pain points in which we could deliver fully automated solutions which "just worked" and saved our clients time and money. These products had to be easily usable by relevant stakeholders without them needing to understand the underlying technology, but should also in an 'opt in' fashion expose them to enough underlying concepts so they may gain intuitive familiarity with key ideas of formal methods along the way.

While working to address these challenges, we've learned many lessons. These include:

1. **Build generic but sell predictable**: Imandra is a general purpose proof assistant which can be used for basically any algorithm analysis task [2]. However, depending on the nature of the task, different levels of user interaction may be required. The fully automated products we build (cf. 2 above) should be built on top of Imandra, specializing its application to restricted classes of

© Springer Nature Switzerland AG 2021
M. Huisman et al. (Eds.): FM 2021, LNCS 13047, pp. 717–721, 2021.
https://doi.org/10.1007/978-3-030-90870-6_39

problems with predictably exploitable problem structure. Though this can be more challenging than developing a disparate collection of bespoke automated reasoning tools (not to mention the fact that it requires having a generic proof assistant upon which to work in the first place), it has the major strategic advantage that all analyses done by the various specialized tools share a common language and logic, and can be combined with each other and enhanced within a single framework. From the user perspective, as they gain familiarity with the results of one tool, they are gaining intuition relevant to the underpinnings of another. Moreover, as their intuition grows, they may suggest other application areas in which we can build compelling products (this has happened many times). This stable incremental growth in understanding of a single generic substrate helps tremendously in our technology becoming "sticky" in an industrial setting.

2. **Shared interactive representation is paramount**: All systems and properties we analyze should be translatable into a common representation which users can explore and interrogate. We have developed such a representation at the core of Imandra which we call a *region decomposition* [1,3]. A region decomposition is a compact symbolic representation of an algorithm's state-space given by a finite collection of disjoint 'regions' or 'cells'. Each region contains three key pieces of data: (a) a collection of constraints on the system input, (b) an invariant result symbolically specifying the system's output when the region constraints are met, and (c) a sample-point generator for synthesizing sample points which satisfy the region constraints. Region decompositions may be computed with respect to varying levels of abstraction (by specifying a *basis* or *vocabulary*) and side-conditions (e.g., "compute all regions of behavior in which this algorithm will send a reject message to the client"). This representation naturally facilitates interactive graphical displays such as Voronoi diagrams (cf. Fig. 3) and event graphs (cf. Fig. 1).

3. **Counterexamples are just as important as proofs (if not more so)**: In the formal world, there is perhaps nothing more beautiful than a completed and elegant proof. But most real systems have flaws most of the time. In our experience, the biggest time sink in formal methods lies in trying to prove false goals. The more we can do to automatically refute false goals, the more quickly we can improve our systems and specifications to the point that their correctness proofs exist at all and have a hope of being constructed.

Just as our tools make it possible to prove a design correct, they must also make it possible to prove a design incorrect by efficiently finding concrete (and elegant) counterexamples. These counterexamples should be expressed both in the language and the run-time of the system being analyzed.

In Imandra, we've done this by making counterexamples "first class". All verification goals may be analyzed for the existence of counterexamples, and if found, the counterexamples are reflected in the run-time as first-class values which may be computed with and run through the executable formal models. This unified computational environment for formal models, proofs and counterexamples facilitates rapid triage, investigation, problem isolation and model refinement.

As users are getting accustomed to our tools and designing their systems, they are regularly making mistakes and learning from the counterexamples presented to them. This further helps them gain assurance in both the tools and their system designs and specifications, long before their systems are ready to be proved correct.

As the systems being analyzed mature and evolve, concrete counterexamples often correspond to deep issues connected to new features and modifications. These counterexamples can save users from major mistakes, and help facilitate an efficient design dialogue until all counterexamples are eliminated. In our experience, users can typically "sell" the use of formal methods to management much more effectively by showing counterexamples which saved them from major blunders than they can by showing them proofs.

In this talk, we shall discuss these lessons with an eye towards open problems and the future (Fig. 2).

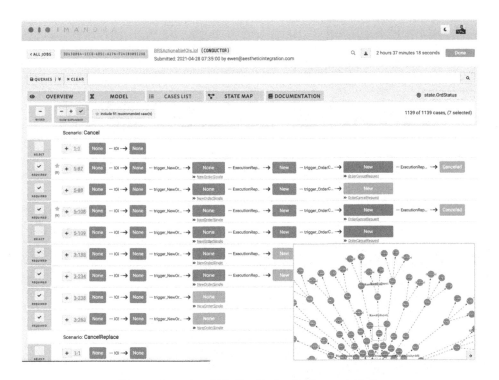

Fig. 1. Imandra IPL Studio for FIX connectivity

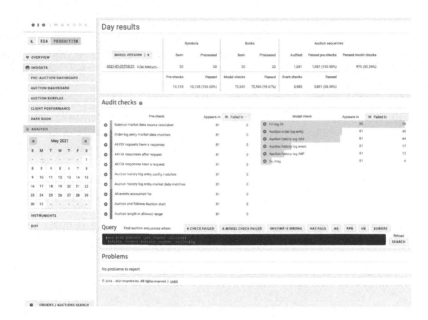

Fig. 2. Imandra auditor for trading venues

Fig. 3. Region decomposition of an exchange's pricing function

Acknowledgements. This talk reflects joint work with our incredible team at Imandra Inc., including Denis Ignatovich, David Aitken, Matt Bray, Simon Cruanes, Elijah Kagan, Konstantin Kanishev, Ewen Maclean and Nicola Mometto.

References

1. Imandra Inc.: Imandra: interactive online documentation (2021). https://docs. imandra.ai/
2. Passmore, G., et al.: The imandra automated reasoning system (system description). In: Peltier, N., Sofronie-Stokkermans, V. (eds.) Automated Reasoning, pp. 464–471. Springer International Publishing, Cham (2020)
3. Passmore, G.O., Ignatovich, D.: Formal verification of financial algorithms. In: de Moura, L. (ed.) Automated Deduction - CADE 26, pp. 26–41. Springer International Publishing, Cham (2017)

Industry Track

Two Decades of Formal Methods in Industrial Products at BTC Embedded Systems

Tino Teige[✉], Andreas Eggers, Karsten Scheibler, Matthias Stasch,
Udo Brockmeyer, Hans J. Holberg, and Tom Bienmüller

BTC Embedded Systems AG, Oldenburg, Germany
{tino.teige,andreas.eggers,karsten.scheibler,matthias.stasch,
udo.brockmeyer,hans.j.holberg,tom.bienmueller}@btc-es.de
http://www.btc-es.de

Abstract. Over the last two decades, we at BTC Embedded Systems
have collected experience with various applications of formal methods
in our products together with our industrial partners and customers. In
this paper, we give an overview of these fields of applications.

1 Introduction

BTC Embedded Systems was founded in 1999 in Oldenburg, Germany, as a spin-off of the OFFIS institute. We started with an ambitious goal: To make complex and powerful mathematical verification and test methods from academia available for real-life industrial projects [1]. Today, BTC is a world-wide operating tool provider for testing and verification solutions for the development of embedded systems and software mainly in the automotive domain, with more than 160 employees and with subsidiaries in the USA, Japan, China, and Romania.

Over the years we learned, on the one hand, that such "magic rocket-science technology" with all its countless applications actually attracts large interest in industry. On the other hand, a loose coupling of rocket-science academic tools for expert users was not the key to our success. Moreover, to convince customers to use formal methods in their projects, it is equally important to design an easy-to-use tool for non-expert users that focus on solving the problem of the customer in a "push-button" manner. Thus, one of our top priorities is to make formal methods available in the most user-friendly way.

To keep pace with the recent academic trends, we maintain a strong academic network, e.g. with the universities of Oldenburg, Freiburg, and Oxford, and participate in large international research projects[1]. In doing so, the focus of our industrial research is always driven by finding solutions for the problems of our customers: for us, research is not an end in itself but must always be a means to an end. With this mission statement in mind, we were able to contribute to

---

[1] More details can be found at https://www.btc-es.de/en/company/research.html.

© Springer Nature Switzerland AG 2021
M. Huisman et al. (Eds.): FM 2021, LNCS 13047, pp. 725–729, 2021.
https://doi.org/10.1007/978-3-030-90870-6_40

the success of our customers during the last two decades[2]. The maturity and effectiveness of BTC verification solutions compared to academic tools are also recognized by the academic world [8]. In [6], we give some more insights into our customer-centric development process for the application of formal methods.

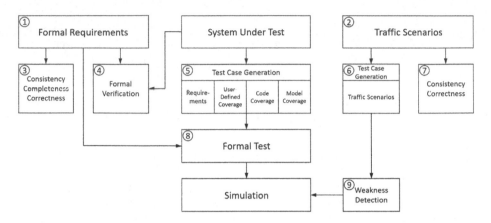

Fig. 1. Fields of application of formal methods within BTC products

2   Formal Methods in BTC Products

In this section, we present the application of formal methods in our test and verification tools: the specification languages, the backend solving tools, and, finally, the use cases based upon formal methods – with (i) referring to Fig. 1.

Specification Languages. By our long-standing cooperation with our customers, we designed an intuitive ① graphical specification language for the formalization of natural-language requirements based on a temporal trigger-action relationship called *universal pattern* (UP) [7], which is easy to use for non-expert users. Scenario-based virtual testing will play a key role in the validation of autonomous driving systems, for which we developed an intuitive ② *graphical traffic scenario* language [3]. Figure 2 shows examples for both.

Backend Solving Tools. Most of the analysis tasks shown in Fig. 1 can be reduced to the *state reachability problem.* In our products, we employ a diverse set of state-of-the-art *model checking* tools like iSAT3 [4], CBMC [5], and some other BDD and SAT-based solvers – in particular, to deal with *floating-point* code efficiently. The progress of the SMT community is also of special interest for us, in particular whether promising SMT solvers can be integrated into our products in the future [2]. We further employ *non-exhaustive analysis methods* based on random sampling and mathematical optimization like genetic algorithms or swarm intelligence. Moreover, for some special adaptive control problem, as explained later on, we use techniques from control theory like *model predictive control.*

---

[2] Some selected success stories of our customers can be found at https://www.btc-es. de/en/company/references.html.

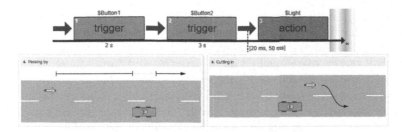

Fig. 2. A UP describing that if button 1 is pressed for 2 s and thereafter button 2 is pressed for 3 s then the light is swichted on within 20 ms to 50 ms (top), and a traffic scenario specifying a passing-by maneuver followed by a cut-in (bottom).

Fields of Applications. The most prominent use case of our customers is ⑤ *automatic test case generation* for the system under test (SUT), in particular to achieve a high level of code and model coverage. But also test cases derived from the requirements or from user-defined coverage goals are of increasing interest. For that use case, random sampling and model checking are currently the most successful techniques, though recent experiments suggest that also optimization algorithms could be a very promising complement.

The classical ④ *formal verification* problem, i.e. whether the model or code satisfies the formal specification, is handled by the aforementioned model checkers. Due to the well-known state-space explosion problem of model checking that might occur at customer site, our tool suite also provides a more scalable though incomplete simulation-based testing approach, called ⑧ *formal test*: executable monitors are automatically derived from the formal requirements that judge the SUT when simulated using manual or automatically derived test cases.

In a very early design stage, namely before system development starts, it is of utmost importance to ensure a high quality of the system requirements. Our products support that effort by automatic ③ *consistency*, i.e. whether no contradiction exists within the set of requirements, *completeness*, i.e. whether no requirement was missed, and *correctness* checks, i.e. whether the requirements actually express the intended behavior [7]. The algorithmic core of this requirement analysis use case is based on model checking technology.

For the use case of scenario-based testing, we follow a similar approach. Specified traffic scenarios can be checked for ⑦ *consistency*, i.e. whether the abstract traffic scenario is concretizable, and *correctness*, i.e. whether the scenario specification expresses the intended traffic situation. For that purpose, we implemented a special scenario-concretization solver derived from iSAT3 [3].

To actually test the autonomous system within the simulation using, e.g., formal test, ⑥ *test case generation* from traffic scenarios calls for a special treatment: the autonomous and complex behavior of the SUT can hardly be predicted a priori since any howsoever small detail in the concrete virtual simulation environment like slope of the road or conditions of illumination potentially influences internal decision making of the SUT. Therefore, the actual behavior of the surrounding traffic needs to be adapted reactively during simulation according to the behavior of the SUT, in order to successfully execute the scenario specification. For solving that complex control task, we combined techniques from control theory like model predictive control and from model checking.

One of the most challenging problems in scenario-based testing is to find critical edge cases of an abstract traffic scenario, i.e. preferably the most critical concrete scenario execution matching it. Given some criticality metrics like time-to-collision, we conduct ⑨ *weakness detection*, realized by optimization algorithms, to find the most critical concrete scenario instance within the space of variation parameters (like velocities or distances) of the abstract traffic scenario.

3   Conclusion

Formal methods play an essential role in what we do: from specification languages with clear formal semantics that allow e.g. the precise translation into observer code, via model checkers and solvers that allow finding even the most obscure corner cases that would be overlooked by humans and that are unlikely to be detected by mere random guessing, to mixtures with approximative methods like our formal test that combines the scalability of a simulation-based method with the precision of a formal requirements specification. The key to success from our experience is that these methods must be embedded into and surrounded by intuitive tools and processes that are easy to use and understand. Formalisms must be precise without being unneccessarily complex, tools must be powerful without being overly hard to use, and results must be translated back to the problem space of the user such that they can be understood and assessed correctly depending on their context. No easy task, but certainly one remaining interesting and challenging for decades to come.

Acknowledgments. We would like to thank all our colleagues for their various contributions to the tools which we briefly discussed in this paper.

References

1. Bienmüller, T., Damm, W., Wittke, H.: The STATEMATE verification environment. In: Emerson, E.A., Sistla, A.P. (eds.) CAV 2000. LNCS, vol. 1855, pp. 561–567. Springer, Heidelberg (2000). https://doi.org/10.1007/10722167_45
2. Mentel, L., Scheibler, K., Winterer, F., Becker, B., Teige, T.: Benchmarking SMT solvers on automotive code. In: MBMV (2021)
3. Scheibler, K., Eggers, A., Teige, T., Walz, M., Bienmüller, T., Brockmeyer, U.: Solving constraint systems from traffic scenarios for the validation of autonomous driving. In: SC² (2019)
4. Scheibler, K., et al.: Accurate ICP-based floating-point reasoning. In: FMCAD (2016)
5. Schrammel, P., Kroening, D., Brain, M., Martins, R., Teige, T., Bienmüller, T.: Incremental bounded model checking for embedded software. Formal Aspects Comput. **29**(5), 911–931 (2017). https://doi.org/10.1007/s00165-017-0419-1

6. Teige, T.: The power of focus: how to optimize a model checker for embedded software (2020). https://www.btc-es.de/en/blog/the-power-of-focus-how-to-optimize-a-model-checker-for-embedded-software.html
7. Teige, T., Meincke, W., Brockmeyer, U.: Applying automated formal CCC checks for complex systems development. In: Embedded World Conference (2021)
8. Westhofen, L., Berger, P., Katoen, J.P.: Benchmarking software model checkers on automotive code. In: Lee, R., Jha, S., Mavridou, A., Giannakopoulou, D. (eds.) NFM 2020. LNCS, vol. 12229, pp. 133–150. Springer, Cham (2020). https://doi.org/10.1007/978-3-030-55754-6_8

Formal Analysis of Neural Network-Based Systems in the Aircraft Domain

Panagiotis Kouvaros[1], Trent Kyono[2], Francesco Leofante[1(✉)],
Alessio Lomuscio[1], Dragos Margineantu[2], Denis Osipychev[2], and Yang Zheng[1]

[1] Imperial College London, London, UK
f.leofante@imperial.ac.uk
[2] Boeing Research and Technology, Seattle, USA

Abstract. Neural networks are being increasingly used for efficient decision making in the aircraft domain. Given the safety-critical nature of the applications involved, stringent safety requirements must be met by these networks. In this work we present a formal study of two neural network-based systems developed by Boeing. The VENUS verifier is used to analyse the conditions under which these systems can operate safely, or generate counterexamples that show when safety cannot be guaranteed. Our results confirm the applicability of formal verification to the settings considered.

Keywords: Trustworthy AI · Formal verification · Neural networks

1 Introduction

Neural Networks (NN) have achieved impressive breakthroughs across several domains of science – see [20] for a comprehensive catalogue of success stories. Although being versatile and efficient, neural networks are known be susceptible to adversarial perturbations [10,27], i.e., imperceptible modifications to their inputs can lead to unexpected, and often inexplicable, consequences on the outputs produced by the network. This lack of reliability and transparency has hindered a wider adoption of neural networks in safety and security-critical settings.

Verification of neural networks (VNN) offers a promising solution to alleviate this problem. Since its inception, the field of VNN has experienced an impressive growth, with several methods and tools being developed for different classes of neural architectures and specifications [29]. In this paper, we consider two neural network-based industrial systems developed by Boeing for the DARPA Assured Autonomy programme and present results pertaining to their formal verification.

Work partly supported by the DARPA Assured Autonomy programme (FA8750-18-C-0095). The views, opinions and/or findings expressed are those of the author and should not be interpreted as representing the official views or policies of the Department of Defense or the U.S. Government. Approved for Public Release, Distribution Unlimited.

© Springer Nature Switzerland AG 2021
M. Huisman et al. (Eds.): FM 2021, LNCS 13047, pp. 730–740, 2021.
https://doi.org/10.1007/978-3-030-90870-6_41

Specifically, the VENUS verification toolkit [6] is used to analyse *local robustness* properties [16,25] of *(i.)* an object detection system trained for open category detection and *(ii.)* a neural controller trained to assist landing in non-towered airports. VENUS is used to identify the conditions under which these systems satisfy local robustness or generate counterexamples that comprehensively show the circumstances under which safety cannot be guaranteed.

Related Work. In recent years, there has been a large amount of work on reasoning on safety of neural networks. Formal verification for neural networks concerns checking whether a network satisfies an input/output specification defining the set of possible inputs and the set of admissible outputs, respectively.

Efficient methods exist to check this property for different classes of neural architectures, e.g., [2,4–6,12,17,24,26,28]. While an exhaustive review of existing approaches is outside the scope of this paper, we remark that only some methods are *complete*, i.e., if a counterexample exists, these approaches are guaranteed to find it. In contrast, *incomplete* approaches are normally based on various forms of convex relaxations of the network, and they can be conservative and thus fail to find some counterexamples. Despite considerable achievements in the field, the verification problem remains challenging for industry-scale networks. Indeed, the problem is known to be NP-complete [16], thereby motivating a very active area of research to improve the scalability of neural network verification.

An also recent body of work concerns the verification of closed-loop and cyber-physical systems equipped with learned controllers – see, e.g., [1,14,15,30]. Verification at this level typically entails checking richer specifications pertaining to the systems' temporal evolutions. Since verification over specifications expressed in standard temporal logics, such as LTL and CTL [13], is often undecidable [1], verification procedures in this context are typically restricted to checking *bounded* specifications which express properties concerning only a bounded number of execution steps.

2   Network Verification with the Venus Toolkit

VENUS is a state-of-the-art sound and complete verification toolkit for ReLU-based feed-forward neural networks. In this section, we give a formal description of the verification problem tackled by VENUS and an outline of the procedure in VENUS to solve it. We begin with the definition of feed-forward neural networks.

Feed-Forward ReLU Networks. A *feed-forward neural network* (FFNN) is a vector-valued function $\mathbf{f} \colon \mathbb{R}^m \to \mathbb{R}^n$ that composes a sequence of $k > 1$ *layers*, where each layer $\mathbf{f}^{(i)}$ is the composition of an input transformation and a non-linear *activation* function. In *linear* layers, $\mathbf{f}^{(i)}(\mathbf{x}^{(i-1)}) \triangleq \mathsf{act}^{(i)}(\mathbf{W}^{(i)}\mathbf{x}^{(i-1)} + \mathbf{b}^{(i)})$, where $\mathbf{x}^{(i-1)}$, $i > 0$, is the input to the i-th layer, $\mathbf{x}^{(0)}$ is the input to the network, $\mathsf{act}^{(i)}$ is the activation function of the i-th layer, and $z^{(i)} = \mathbf{W}^{(i)}\mathbf{x}^{(i-1)} + \mathbf{b}^{(i)}$ is the vector of *pre-activations* of the layer which is the affine transformation of the previous layer's output for a weight matrix $\mathbf{W}^{(i)}$ and a bias vector $\mathbf{b}^{(i)}$. In *convolutional* layers, $\mathbf{f}^{(i)}$ computes the convolution between

$\mathbf{x}^{(i-1)}$ a learned kernel. VENUS focuses on the Rectified Linear Unit (ReLU) activation function, $\mathsf{ReLU}(\mathbf{z}^{(i)}) \triangleq \max(0, \mathbf{z}^{(i)})$, $i > 0$, where the maximum function is applied element-wise on $\mathbf{z}^{(i)}$.

Verification Problem. Given a feed-forward neural network, VENUS answers positively or negatively as to whether the output of the network for every input within a linearly definable set[1] of inputs is contained within a linearly definable set of outputs. Formally, we have:

Definition 1 (Verification problem). *Given a FFNN $f \colon \mathbb{R}^m \to \mathbb{R}^n$, a linearly definable set of inputs $\mathcal{X} \subset \mathbb{R}^m$ and a linearly definable set of outputs $\mathcal{Y} \subset \mathbb{R}^n$, the verification problem concerns determining whether $\forall \mathbf{x} \in \mathcal{X} \colon \mathbf{f}(\mathbf{x}) \in \mathcal{Y}$.*

Among the many instantiations of the above verification problem, the *local adversarial robustness problem* is perhaps the most studied [16,25]. Answering the local adversarial robustness problem requires establishing whether all images within a norm-ball of a given image are classified equivalently by f, and can be instantiated by setting $\mathcal{X} = \{\mathbf{x}' \mid \|\mathbf{x} - \mathbf{x}'\|_p \leq \epsilon\}$ and $\mathcal{Y} = \{\mathbf{y} \mid \forall i \neq c \colon y_i < y_c\}$ for a given image $\mathbf{x}$ with class label c, perturbation radius $\epsilon \geq 0$ and norm $\|\cdot\|_p$.

Verification with VENUS. VENUS implements a verification method whereby the verification problem is translated into a Mixed Integer Linear Program (MILP). An MILP is an optimisation problem whereby an objective function is sought to be maximised subject to a set of linear constraints over real-valued and integer variables. The feasibility status of the MILP program associated with a verification problem, i.e., whether there is an assignment to the variables of the MILP that satisfies all constraints, has a strict correspondence to the satisfaction of the verification problem: the verification problem is satisfied if and only if its MILP program has no feasible solution. VENUS makes use of the big-M method [3,23] to translate the verification problem into MILP and relies on GUROBI [11] as solving back-end. In addition, VENUS implements a number of methods that aim at reducing the search space of feasible solutions that needs to be considered by GUROBI, including dependency analysis and input domain splitting [6].

3   Neural Network-Based Systems for the Aircraft Domain

In this section, we present our main results pertaining to the verification of two neural network-based industrial systems developed by Boeing. First we will focus on verifying the robustness of a high-dimensional image classifier for open object detection. Then, we will consider the verification of a landing assistant for non-towered airports.

---

[1] A linearly definable set is a set that can be expressed as a finite set of linear constraints over real-valued and integer variables.

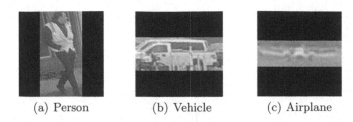

| (a) Person | (b) Vehicle | (c) Airplane |

Fig. 1. Sample images in the data set for open-category detection.

3.1 Object Detection with Open Categories

Problem Description. In real-world applications, a neural network classifier is likely to encounter novel obstacles (i.e., open categories), such as novel types of ground vehicles and static objects. It is desirable that the classifier is able to detect these novel objects without previous training on the objects thereof while producing only a small number of false alarms, i.e., an alarm on the detection of a novel object even though the object is not novel. The classifier should also have a certain robustness against adversarial perturbations on its input. The following study is concerned with providing risk-bounded assurance against open category instances for an image classification system developed by Boeing.

Data Set and Neural Network Classifier. For this problem, Boeing has created a labelled data set that includes contiguous image sequences as aircraft approach novel obstacles or conditions. In particular, the data set contains three classes of objects: *ground vehicle*, *person*, and *airplane*. Figure 1 shows three sample images in each category. Each image has three channels, with 255×255 pixels in each channel. The image input is thus expressed as a three-dimensional matrix with a high dimension $255 \times 255 \times 3$. Boeing has also trained a large convolutional neural network (CNN) with roughly 10^5 neurons using two categories (vehicle and person) as the training set. The other category (i.e., airplane) is used as open objects for the neural network to test its performance of detecting novel objects.

The architecture of this large CNN model has two convolutional layers of 16 and 32 filters respectively (size 5×5 and 3×3, respectively), followed by one global average pooling layer, two fully connected layers with 128 and 2 neurons respectively, and one final softmax layer. The softmax layer normalizes the output into the interval $[0, 1]$ such that its outputs add up to one. The activation function in each layer is the standard ReLU operator. Therefore, the CNN model maps an image input $x \in \mathbb{R}^{255 \times 255 \times 3}$ to an output $y \in \mathbb{R}^2$ and classifies x using the following logic: if $y_1 \geq t_1$, it outputs the label *"vehicle"* with confidence y_1; if $y_2 \geq t_2$, it outputs the label *"person"* with confidence y_2; otherwise, it reports the input image as a novel object. The thresholds t_1 and t_2 were carefully chosen to balance the false alarm rate of (20%) and the overall prediction error rate (30%).

Table 1. Numerical results via Venus on randomly selected 20 images

Radius ϵ	Robust		Non-robust		Time-out (7200 s)
	Number	Avg time (s)	Number	Avg time (s)	
1.0×10^{-4}	20	2500	0	—	0
1.0×10^{-3}	6	2720	2	4850	12
1.0×10^{-2}	0	—	10	4200	10

Robustness Verification Setup. We aim to verify the local robustness of the above CNN against adversarial perturbations on the image input. Formally, given a correctly classified image x_0 (person, vehicle, or open object) and a perturbation radius $\epsilon > 0$, we would like to certify

$$\text{for all } x \text{ s.t. } \|x - x_0\|_\infty \leq \epsilon \text{ we have } f(x) = f(x_0), \tag{1}$$

or to identify a counterexample $\hat{x}$ to falsify the condition above. In (1), $f(\cdot)$ denotes the CNN model. If (1) is true, then the neural network is certified to be locally robust for the image input x_0 against any adversarial perturbation up to ϵ. Otherwise, a counterexample can be found which can be used to augment the training set to improve the robustness of the model. Note that (1) is a particular instantiation of the verification problem in Sect. 2.

Extension of Venus *and Numerical Results:* The images in this case study have a very high dimension, i.e., $x \in \mathbb{R}^{255 \times 255 \times 3}$, similar to the dimension of those in Imagenet [9]. We note that most existing complete robustness verifiers only test their verification performance on standard benchmarks, such as the MNIST dataset [19] or the CIFAR10 dataset [18], where the images have a much lower dimension ($28 \times 28 \times 1$ and $32 \times 32 \times 3$, respectively). In addition, the CNN model is large (approximately 10^5 neurons) as compared to the standard models considered in neural network verification. As a consequence, Venus could not efficiently generate the MILP encoding of the robustness verification problem (1), either because of memory issues or because of exceeding the time consumption limit (see below). To overcome this, we have improved Venus's implementation by exploiting the special structure of CNNs, i.e., that the value of a neuron depends only on a small subset of the neurons in the previous layers, to obtain a much more scalable MILP encoding method.

For the numerical experiments, we used a machine with an Intel Core i9 9900X 3.5 GHz 10-core CPU, 128 GB RAM running Fedora 30 with Linux kernel 5.3. We randomly selected 20 images from the data set that are correctly classified by the CNN model. We then used the extended version of Venus to solve the robustness verification problem (1) with a timeout limit of 7200 s. To test the robustness of the CNN model, we varied the perturbation radius from 1.0×10^{-4} to 1.0×10^{-2}. Table 1 lists the results. We can see that the CNN model is robust with respect to the small perturbation (1.0×10^{-4}); in this case Venus could return a positive certificate within 1 h. Concerning the bigger perturbation radii, the CNN model becomes less robust; in this case VENUS could identify concrete counterexamples for 10 images out of 20 within 7200 s. In particular, VENUS identified a counterexample for the "vehicle" image shown in Fig. 1(b) for $\epsilon = 10^{-2}$. This counterexample fooled the CNN to classify it an open object. Finally, we note that since VENUS is a complete verifier the robustness of the CNN can by certified w.r.t the rest of the images by increasing the timeout.

3.2 Collision Avoidance for Landing at Non-towered Airports

Problem Description. Automated collision avoidance has become an essential component of every autonomous system. Whilst the safety of commercial aviation relies on centralized guidance from Air Traffic Control (ATC), private aviation must rely on onboard systems, especially when operating at non-towered airports. To prevent collisions, the regulator requires all vehicles to maintain a minimum safe horizontal separation which is advised via ATC commands, a set of rules defined in the pilot's handbook and the airport-specific traffic pattern.

This case study poses the collision avoidance problem as a data-driven detection problem. The goal is to detect the collisions when approaching landing by analysing the dynamic state of the airplane (Agent) and another vehicle (Intruder). The detection is done via an ML-based inference model trained on the previous (simulated) experience. A *positive* detection triggers the rejection of the landing and makes the Agent go for another landing approach. This rejection guarantees safe separation in the vertical space.

Simulation Environment. Boeing developed a lightweight Python simulation integrated with the OpenAI GYM framework [7] to facilitate the study of the problem described above. The surrogate environment simulates a 2D collision avoidance problem that mimics the real task (on the ground collision avoidance for the aircraft landing). The environment simulates the movements of multiple Intruder vehicles on a $10 \times 10\,\mathrm{km}^2$. The Agent has to either continue the automated landing or reject it to provide minimal horizontal separation. The environment incorporates a probabilistic behaviour model for the Intruder and the use of scripted configuration files: the former allows to randomize the trajectory of the Intruder vehicle and simulate a violation of the traffic rules; the latter enables quick reconfiguring of simulated scenarios.

The surrogate simulation imitates the dynamics of both the Agent and the Intruder vehicles selected for the experiment. All ground vehicles are represented by a simplistic dynamic model (mass-less Dubin's car). Each vehicle uses a base class that takes control inputs in form of steering and acceleration commands in return for its updated position and speed. For the Agent vehicle, we simulate the dynamics of a single-engine turboprop Cessna 208 Grand Caravan. The aircraft control is different from 2D car-like dynamics and does not have conventional brakes, acceleration, and steering. The effectiveness of the controls depends on the aircraft's altitude, airspeed, etc. A PID-based waypoint controller provides low-level control for the Agent and Intruders. The controller defines trajectories

Table 2. Robustness results for safe configurations and collision configurations.

ϵ	Safe configurations				Collision configurations			
	Robust	Avg time (s)	Not robust	Avg time(s)	Robust	Avg time (s)	Not robust	Avg time(s)
0.05	50	0.09	0	–	48	0.11	2	0.33
0.1	50	0.09	0	–	48	0.10	2	0.38
0.2	50	0.08	0	–	48	0.10	2	0.39
0.5	50	0.08	0	–	48	0.11	2	0.39
1	50	0.08	0	–	47	0.10	3	0.33
1.5	50	0.07	0	–	45	0.11	5	0.37

as lists of waypoints to be followed and adds a controlled level of noise to the controller state to make trajectories more natural.

Neural Network Classifier. The rejection action is commanded by a pre-trained neural network classification model that predicts the probability of collision between the Agent and Intruder vehicles projected on a 2D surface. The network is fully-connected and is trained using data gathered from the simulator. Each data sample represents a state vector that captures the position, heading and speed of the Agent and the Intruder vehicles. Samples are labelled either as 0 or 1, depending on whether the simulation run from which they were gathered resulted in a collision or not. The neural network has 8 input neurons, 2 hidden layers with 128 nodes each and ReLU activations, and 1 output neuron that uses a Sigmoid activation to produce a continuous collision probability within $[0, 1]$.

To evaluate the performance of the system, Boeing developed a run-time rejection system that utilizes the neural network to predict the probability of collision and compares this with a predefined threshold λ to command the rejection. The runtime system evaluates the chance of collision with each Intruder vehicle on the ground individually, and triggers a rejection if the inference model predicts a probability greater than λ for any Intruder.

Robustness Analysis. We conducted a formal analysis of the neural classifier to assess its local robustness against adversarial perturbations. Formally, given an input x_0 and a perturbations radius $\epsilon > 0$, we check if for all x such that $\|x - x_0\|_\infty \le \epsilon$ it holds that $f(x) \diamond \lambda^2$, where $f(\cdot)$ denotes the network trained by Boeing and $\diamond \in \{\ge, \le\}$ depending on whether the initial input x_0 belonged to a collision trajectory or not. Intuitively, the inference model should always compute prediction probabilities that are $\ge \lambda$ (resp. $\le \lambda$) for inputs x in the vicinity of an x_0 for which a collision happened (resp. did not happen).

We collected 50 samples from the simulator for which the neural network correctly predicted collision and 50 for which collisions did not occur. Table 2 reports our results for a rejection threshold of $\lambda = 0.75$. The inference model appears to be robust for perturbations up to $\varepsilon = 1.5$ for inputs that belong to a

---

[2] Note that VENUS does not support the Sigmoid function used in the output layer; we therefore use its inverse to compute the preimage of λ and compare this value with the pre-activation value of the output node.

safe trajectory, i.e., the model consistently predicted low collision probabilities for the perturbations considered. However decisions appear to be less robust in the other case; we hypothesise this is because of the fact that increasing ϵ may effectively create input configurations for which rejection commands should not be triggered. In all cases, VENUS was able to solve the verification problem within less than a second.

Analysing Sensitivity to Single Inputs. Our previous analysis considered adversarial perturbations that are allowed to modify all input components at the same time. This corresponds to a scenario where all sensors of the Agent vehicle are subject to failure. However, more realistic failures may involve only a subset of the sensors; moreover, different sensor failures may have different consequences on the final prediction of the inference model.

To investigate this, we carry out a formal analysis where the inference model is verified against a variation of the local robustness property previously used. Namely, we apply adversarial ϵ-bounded perturbations to a single input component at the time and verify robustness in the resulting scenario. Similarly to the previous experiments, we sampled 50 instances for which collisions were flagged in the simulator and tested increasing per-

Table 3. Sensitivity analysis results for perturbations applied to single input components and perturbation radius $\epsilon = 1$.

Component	Not robust	Avg time (s)
x_E	1	0.25
y_E	1	0.26
θ_E	1	0.26
s_E	1	0.25
x_I	1	0.24
y_I	1	0.24
θ_I	1	0.26
s_I	3	0.29

turbation radii. Table 3 reports sample results obtained for $\epsilon = 1$. Our analysis helped us identify that predictions seem to be comparably less robust to perturbations applied to the input component related to the speed of the Intruder vehicle. This can be explained by the fact that changes in speed may create scenarios where the Intruder proceeds slowly and thus collisions can be avoided. Again, VENUS was able to solve all verification queries within less than a second.

4   Conclusions and Outlook

We considered two neural network-based industrial systems developed by Boeing and showed how formal verification can be used to provide assurance guarantees for said systems. The VENUS verification toolkit was successfully employed to formally analyse the behaviour of these models, providing proofs of safety or counterexamples to show when safety could not be guaranteed. Despite promising results, several challenges remain for the wider application of formal methods to neural network-based industrial systems.

Scalability is admittedly the biggest challenge in this arena, as industrial applications often require checking neural models that contain hundreds of thousands parameters, if not millions. While recent efforts in VNN have contributed to impressive scalability improvements – especially as far as incomplete verification methods are concerned [21,22] – more work still needs to be done to address industrial-scale problems. This need becomes even more evident when verification is performed at system level, i.e., when the neural network-based system is considered in its entirety and closed-loop behaviours are analysed.

Another important direction where the expertise of the formal methods community may be determinant is that of formalising *richer specifications* beyond local adversarial robustness, especially in the case of perception systems such as the one studied in Sect. 3. Recent developments in VNN have addressed new specifications, such as robustness against semantic perturbations that can alter, e.g., saturation or contrast in an image [17], and geometric perturbations that apply transformations such as rotations to input images [5].

We conclude by highlighting that safe deployment of neural network-based systems will also require *runtime assurance methods* that are able to detect anomalous behaviour during execution. Different proposals have been made within the formal verification community, see, e.g., [8]; however several interesting open questions remain in this domain.

References

1. Akintunde, M., Botoeva, E., Kouvaros, P., Lomuscio, A.: Formal verification of neural agents in non-deterministic environments. In: Proceedings of the 19th International Conference on Autonomous Agents and Multi-Agent Systems (AAMAS20), pp. 25–33. IFAAMAS (2020)
2. Akintunde, M., Kevorchian, A., Lomuscio, A., Pirovano, E.: Verification of RNN-based neural agent-environment systems. In: Proceedings of the 33rd AAAI Conference on Artificial Intelligence (AAAI19), pp. 6006–6013. AAAI Press (2019)
3. Anderson, R., Huchette, J., Ma, W., Tjandraatmadja, C., Vielma, J.: Strong mixed-integer programming formulations for trained neural networks. Mathe. Programm., 1–37 (2020)
4. Bak, S., Tran, H.-D., Hobbs, K., Johnson, T.T.: Improved geometric path enumeration for verifying ReLU neural networks. In: Lahiri, S.K., Wang, C. (eds.) CAV 2020. LNCS, vol. 12224, pp. 66–96. Springer, Cham (2020). https://doi.org/10.1007/978-3-030-53288-8_4
5. Balunovic, M., Baader, M., Singh, G., Gehr, T., Vechev, M.: Certifying geometric robustness of neural networks. In: NeurIPS19, pp. 15287–15297 (2019)
6. Botoeva, E., Kouvaros, P., Kronqvist, J., Lomuscio, A., Misener, R.: Efficient verification of neural networks via dependency analysis. In: Proceedings of the 34th AAAI Conference on Artificial Intelligence (AAAI20), pp. 3291–3299. AAAI Press (2020)
7. Brockman, G., et al.: OpenAI Gym. arXiv preprint **1606**, 01540 (2016)
8. Cheng, C., Nührenberg, G., Yasuoka, H.: Runtime monitoring neuron activation patterns. In: Proceedings of the Design, Automation & Test in Europe Conference & Exhibition (DATE19), pp. 300–303. IEEE (2019)
9. Deng, J., Dong, W., Socher, R., Li, L., Li, K., Fei-Fei, L.: ImageNet: a large-scale hierarchical image database. In: Proceedings of the 2009 IEEE Conference on Computer Vision and Pattern Recognition (CVPR09), pp. 248–255. IEEE (2009)

10. Goodfellow, I., Shlens, J., Szegedy, C.: Explaining and harnessing adversarial examples. arXiv preprint arXiv:1412.6572 (2014)
11. Gu, Z., Rothberg, E., Bixby, R.: Gurobi optimizer reference manual (2020). http://www.gurobi.com
12. Henriksen, P., Lomuscio, A.: Efficient neural network verification via adaptive refinement and adversarial search. In: Proceedings of the 24th European Conference on Artificial Intelligence (ECAI20), pp. 2513–2520. IOS Press (2020)
13. Huth, M.A., Ryan, M.: Logic in Computer Science: Modelling and Reasoning about Systems. Cambridge University Press (2000)
14. Ivanov, R., Carpenter, T., Weimer, J., Alur, R., Pappas, G., Lee, I.: Verifying the safety of autonomous systems with neural network controllers. ACM Trans. Embed. Comput. Syst. **20**(1), 7:1–7:26 (2021)
15. Johnson, T., et al.: ARCH-COMP20 category report: artificial intelligence and neural network control systems (AINNCS) for continuous and hybrid systems plants. In: Proceedings of the 7th International Workshop on Applied Verification of Continuous and Hybrid Systems (ARCH20), pp. 107–139. EasyChair (2020)
16. Katz, G., Barrett, C., Dill, D.L., Julian, K., Kochenderfer, M.J.: Reluplex: an efficient SMT solver for verifying deep neural networks. In: Majumdar, R., Kunčak, V. (eds.) CAV 2017. LNCS, vol. 10426, pp. 97–117. Springer, Cham (2017). https://doi.org/10.1007/978-3-319-63387-9_5
17. Kouvaros, P., Lomuscio, A.: Formal verification of CNN-based perception systems. arXiv preprint arXiv:1811.11373 (2018)
18. Krizhevsky, A., Hinton, G.: Learning multiple layers of features from tiny images (2009)
19. LeCun, Y.: The MNIST database of handwritten digits. http://yann.lecun.com/exdb/mnist/ (1998)
20. LeCun, Y., Bengio, Y., Hinton, G.: Deep learning. Nature **521**(7553), 436–444 (2015)
21. Li, L., Qi, X., Xie, T., Li, B.: SoK: certified robustness for deep neural networks. arXiv preprint arXiv:2009.04131 (2020)
22. Liu, C., Arnon, T., Lazarus, C., Barrett, C., Kochenderfer, M.: Algorithms for verifying deep neural networks. arXiv preprint arXiv:1903.06758 (2019)
23. Lomuscio, A., Maganti, L.: An approach to reachability analysis for feed-forward ReLU neural networks. arXiv preprint arXiv:1706.07351 (2017)
24. Narodytska, N., Kasiviswanathan, S., Ryzhyk, L., Sagiv, M., Walsh, T.: Verifying properties of binarized deep neural networks. arXiv preprint arXiv:1709.06662 (2017)
25. Pulina, L., Tacchella, A.: An abstraction-refinement approach to verification of artificial neural networks. In: Touili, T., Cook, B., Jackson, P. (eds.) CAV 2010. LNCS, vol. 6174, pp. 243–257. Springer, Heidelberg (2010). https://doi.org/10.1007/978-3-642-14295-6_24
26. Singh, G., Gehr, T., Mirman, M., Püschel, M., Vechev, M.: Fast and effective robustness certification. In: Advances in Neural Information Processing Systems (NeurIPS18), pp. 10802–10813 (2018)
27. Szegedy, C., et al.: Intriguing properties of neural networks. In: Proceedings of the 2nd International Conference on Learning Representations (ICLR14) (2014)
28. Tran, H.-D., Bak, S., Xiang, W., Johnson, T.T.: Verification of deep convolutional neural networks using ImageStars. In: Lahiri, S.K., Wang, C. (eds.) CAV 2020. LNCS, vol. 12224, pp. 18–42. Springer, Cham (2020). https://doi.org/10.1007/978-3-030-53288-8_2

29. VNN-COMP: Verification of Neural Networks Competition (VNN-COMP20) (2020). https://sites.google.com/view/vnn20/vnncomp. Accessed 23 Mar 2021
30. Xiang, W.H., Rosenfeld, J., Johnson, T.: Reachable set estimation and safety verification for piecewise linear systems with neural network controllers. In: 2018 Annual American Control Conference (ACC), pp. 1574–1579. AACC (2018)

Formal Verification of Consensus in the Taurus Distributed Database

Song Gao[1,2(✉)], Bohua Zhan[1,2], Depeng Liu[1,2], Xuechao Sun[1,2], Yanan Zhi[3], David N. Jansen[1], and Lijun Zhang[1,2,4]

[1] State Key Laboratory of Computer Sciences, Institute of Software, Chinese Academy of Sciences, Beijing, China
gaos@ios.ac.cn
[2] University of Chinese Academy of Sciences, Beijing, China
[3] Huawei, Shenzhen, China
[4] Institute of Intelligent Software, Guangzhou, China

Abstract. Distributed database services are an increasingly important part of cloud computing. They are required to satisfy several key properties, including consensus and fault tolerance. Given the highly concurrent nature of these systems, subtle errors can arise that are difficult to discover through traditional testing methods. Formal verification can help in discovering bugs and ensuring correctness of these systems. In this paper, we apply formal methods to specify and verify an industrial distributed database, Taurus, which uses a combination of several fundamental protocols, including Multi-Version Concurrency Control and Raft-based Cluster Management. TLA$^+$ is used to model an abstraction of the system and specify its properties. The properties are verified using the TLC model checker, as well as by theorem proving using the TLA proof system (TLAPS). We show that model checking is able to reproduce a bug in Taurus that was found during testing. But our most significant result is twofold: we successfully verified an abstract model of Taurus, and convinced our industrial partners of the usefulness of formal methods to industrial systems.

Keywords: Formal verification · Distributed consensus · TLA$^+$

1 Introduction

In recent years, formal methods have found increasing application in industry. One successful case is the use of the TLA$^+$ model checker in verifying distributed protocols by Amazon [9,10] and Microsoft [7]. Model checking has the advantage that it is mostly automatic. However, it also faces inherent state space explosion problems, making it difficult to apply to industrial-sized models. Verification by theorem proving, which is supported in the TLA proof system (TLAPS), offers

This work is based on a joint project with Huawei, together with colleagues in Huawei. Zhi currently works at TEG, Tencent.

M. Huisman et al. (Eds.): FM 2021, LNCS 13047, pp. 741–751, 2021.
https://doi.org/10.1007/978-3-030-90870-6_42

an alternative that is less automatic but more expressive, applicable to more complex systems and properties.

Distributed databases form an important part of services such as cloud computing. Traditional databases are designed to meet very high standards, often stated as ACID (atomicity, consistency, isolation, durability) properties. Distributed databases are required to meet the same standards. In particular, we are concerned with issues like consensus (necessary for atomicity and consistency) and fault tolerance (necessary for isolation and durability). Taurus [1] is a cloud database providing distributed access, designed by the technology company Huawei. In order to achieve both consensus and fault tolerance, Taurus combines several protocols, including Multi-Version Concurrency Control (MVCC) and Raft-based Cluster Management, into a coherent system. The protocols have to be modified in order to work together properly, and various optimizations increase their complexity. This raises the likelihood of human errors. Indeed, Huawei has discovered many abnormal scenarios including process crashes and loss of data during network transmission. Many of these errors are extremely difficult to discover or reproduce using traditional testing methods. On the other hand, extremely high confidence in the correctness and robustness of the database system is necessary before it can be launched into service.

In this work, we present a formal high-level model of the Taurus database using the specification language TLA$^+$ [5]. We also specify in TLA$^+$ *safety* properties that the model should satisfy. We then verify these properties using both model checking and theorem proving. In addition, we reproduce and analyze a bug using the TLC model checker. For the models and properties we considered, the system is shown to be correct. That is, it satisfies the main consensus properties, and its fault tolerance mechanisms are also functional. Moreover, the model itself and the process of creating it have value: our project partners acknowledge that they benefited from this process, as it improved their understanding of the system in multiple places.

This paper is organised as follows. First, we describe the structure and key components of Taurus in Sect. 2. In Sect. 3, we present the formal specification and verification of the system. In Sect. 4 we discuss challenges faced and lessons learned during the project. Finally, we review related work in Sect. 5 and conclude in Sect. 6.

2   Taurus Distributed Database

Taurus is a distributed database system designed to be highly extensible and reliable. It consists physically of three parts: SQL nodes, Storage nodes and cluster management (Fig. 1).

The database is accessed through its SQL nodes. There is a single PSN (Primary SQL Node), and the other SQL nodes are RSNs (Replica SQL Nodes). The PSN accepts both READ and WRITE transactions from users and generates redologs, i.e. the operation logs of WRITE transactions. In contrast, RSNs only accept READ transactions and do not generate redologs. The data is divided

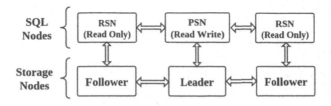

Fig. 1. The structure of Taurus with two RSNs

into pages, and stored in a distributed manner across Storage nodes. Thanks to the SQL nodes, Taurus also can interpret the SQL language, as well as keep snapshots of the database. Every transaction should start from a snapshot and once it commits, a new snapshot will be generated.

Storage nodes provide persistent storage for data. They run a Raft-based [11] consensus algorithm. In normal operation there is one Leader node, which handles all change requests. The Leader receives and stores redologs from the PSN, and generates the correct version of data pages as replies to PSN requests. It informs Followers about updated pages and sends them periodic heartbeat messages. When an RSN receives a request for a page, it first checks with the PSN whether it has the required version. If not, it asks the Storage for that version. In this way, we maintain distributed consensus between the PSN and all RSNs.

Leader election and membership changes are under the control of cluster management. There has to be a Leader among the Storage nodes to receive and broadcast the redologs to the other nodes. An election occurs when a Follower has not received a heartbeat message within a certain timeout, indicating that the Leader has failed or lost contact. Such nodes become Candidates and ask for votes. The Candidate that receives a majority wins the election and becomes the Leader in the new term. Election can fail if no candidate wins a majority, and multiple rounds may be necessary to eventually elect a Leader.

3   Approach

3.1   Specifying the System with TLA$^+$

TLA$^+$ [5] is a high-level formal specification language for modelling programs and systems, especially concurrent and distributed systems. Its logical foundation is ZF Set Theory and the Temporal Logic of Actions (TLA) [4].

The TLA$^+$ specification of the Taurus distributed database is composed of several modules. First, there are three modules specifying the Storage nodes (323 lines), PSN (489 lines) and RSN (340 lines), respectively. These three modules specify the initial states and transitions of the respective nodes. Further, there are two main modules for Distributed Consensus (DC, 460 lines) and Cluster Management (CM, 530 lines), which import the required node modules and

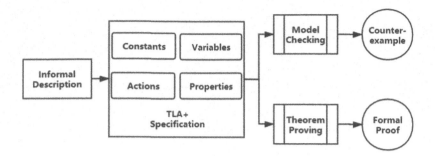

Fig. 2. Framework of formal verification with TLA$^+$

compose them to form the system specification (Fig. 2). Overall, our specifications have around 2.1k lines in TLA$^+$.[1]

The overall TLA$^+$ specification has the form $Spec \triangleq Init \land \Box[Next]_{vars}$. *Init* is the conjunction of the initial state formulas of the module; together they describe an empty database. An action is expressed as a formula, describing the relation between the values of variables before and after it. *Next* is the disjunction of all action specifications for reading data, writing data, sending messages etc. In the following example, *CommitTx* describes the action of PSN committing a transaction labelled t. It first confirms that transaction t is active and finished before the action. Variables with a prime indicate state variables after the action, thus the following lines say the action removes t from the set of active transactions, and appends a message into the channel from PSN to Storage.

$$CommitTx(t) \triangleq \text{LET } msg == [type \mapsto redolog, value \mapsto ...]$$
$$\text{IN } \land\ t \in ActiveTx \qquad\qquad \backslash * \ t \text{ is active}$$
$$\land\ operationLeft(t) = 0 \qquad \backslash * \ and \ finished$$
$$\land\ ActiveTx' == ActiveTx - \{t\} \qquad \backslash * \ remove \ t$$
$$...\ ... \qquad\qquad\qquad\qquad \backslash * \ lines \ omitted$$
$$\land\ Ch\_P2S\_Redo' == Append(Ch\_P2S\_Redo, msg)$$

Communication between modules is specified using the classic channel model. For each kind of message and each pair of sender and receiver, there is a FIFO array maintaining the list of messages sent. The sender adds entries to the end of the array, and the receiver retrieves the entries starting from the beginning. For example, in the *CommitTx* action, messages sent from PSN to Storage are appended to the end of the FIFO array Ch_P2S_Redo. From the Storage side, there is a corresponding action of receiving messages by popping entries from the head of the same array.

---

[1] The specifications are available at https://iscasmc.ios.ac.cn/?page_id=2148.

3.2   Properties of Interest

The Taurus distributed database is required to satisfy consensus and fault tolerance properties. Many of these properties can be stated as *safety,* and in fact *invariant,* properties. From extensive discussions with engineers involved in building Taurus, we extracted 11 properties of the DC and CM modules that the domain experts considered important for the overall correctness of the system.

We show one of them as an example. The invariant property *NumberOfLeader* for Storage nodes states that in the Raft-based consensus algorithm, there is at most one Leader node at any time. It can be formulated in TLA^+ as follows:

$$NumberOfLeader \triangleq \forall i, j \in StorageIDs :$$
$$(i \neq j) \Rightarrow \bigvee StorageStatus[i] \neq \text{LEADER}$$
$$\bigvee StorageStatus[j] \neq \text{LEADER} \quad ,$$

where *StorageIDs* is the set of IDs of all Storage nodes, and the value of *Storage-Status* is in the set $\{\text{LEADER}, \text{FOLLOWER}, \text{CANDIDATE}\}$. By adding the temporal operator $\square$ before *NumberOfLeader*, we assert that *NumberOfLeader* must always remain true during the execution of the system.

Besides *NumberOfLeader*, the properties include:

- Every page can only be written by at most one transaction at any time.
- If changes in a page have not been committed by a transaction, other transactions cannot read this page.
- Every page in the buffer of the PSN should be its latest version.
- During clearing the buffer of the PSN, every page in it should be lock-free.

There are other properties about snapshots of the database, etc.

3.3   Model Checking with TLC

The default model checker TLC is an explicit-state model checker and simulator that can check both *safety* and *liveness* properties for executable TLA^+ specifications. It analyzes a finite instance of a TLA^+ specification and checks whether the desired properties hold in every execution of that instance.

We apply model checking to verify properties of DC and CM modules on small configurations. This requires instantiating the parameters in the models with concrete values to make the model finite:[2]

- DC module: we instantiate one PSN node, two RSN nodes, and one Storage node. We assume that the status of each node is normal and does not change. We also fix the number of database transactions to be at most three.

---

[2] The configurations are available at https://iscasmc.ios.ac.cn/?page_id=2148.

- CM module: we instantiate one PSN node, two RSN nodes, and three Storage nodes. We investigate the process of nodes leaving and joining the network and the resulting leader election process in Storage nodes.

We model-checked 10 properties for DC and 1 for CM using the TLC model checker. Model checking automatically explores the state space of systems. The relevant configurations are: TLC version 2.09 of 10 March 2017, on a computer with Intel® i5-7300HQ CPU and 8 GB memory. All 11 properties are verified without finding errors, indicating that the high-level model of the system satisfies these properties on the given configurations.

We consider four metrics for the performance of model checking: CPU time, diameter (maximum depth) of the reachability graph, the total number of examined states and the number of distinct states (the cardinality of the set of reachable vertices of the state-graph). Verifying the 10 properties for DC took 805 s to explore 7,551,852 distinct states, reaching diameter 52 and 36,077,757 states overall. By comparison, verifying the single property of the CM module took 913 s to explore 17,603,935 distinct states, reaching diameter 70 and 22,672,361 states overall.

3.4 Fault Injection Analysis

During the project, a non-trivial severe bug was found through testing. Our coauthor in Huawei led the team that found the bug. Due to the high complexity of the database, this took almost a week of extensive testing. The bug was caused by a coding error instead of a fault in design, therefore it would not occur in our original high-level TLA$^+$ specification of the system.

We are able to simulate the bug within our model, in a way similar to fault injection. The coding bug is triggered only when the PSN visits a page generated from a Storage node, and an old version of the page instead of the newest version is delivered to the PSN. This could result in data inconsistency. Thus we wrote a modified version of the specification where the related key parameter was set to an incorrect, lower value than requested by the PSN. After that, we ran the TLC model checker over the properties in the modified specification, and it showed that the property *PSNBuffer* (every page in the buffer of the PSN should be its latest version) does not hold. The error trace for this violation is still too complicated. We simplified the property to another invariant, *ConsistReq*, which mentioned only the variables related to the bug.

Figure 3 shows the error trace reported by TLC for the violation of invariant *ConsistReq*. It has a depth of 22 steps, which indicates that the error hides deeply. All of the variables during the steps from initialization to the violation are recorded in the error trace. It helped the engineering team to understand what happened in the system from a high-level view.

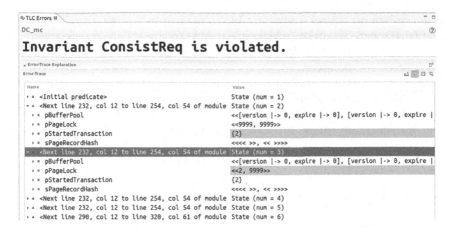

Fig. 3. Screenshot of the error Trace for *ConsistReq*

3.5 Theorem Proving with TLAPS

Theorem proving is a powerful method for verifying properties of systems. Instead of attempting to traverse the potentially very large state space of the system, it uses logical deduction to reason about the TLA$^+$ formulas directly. If a property is proved, it is guaranteed to hold for any configuration of the system. TLA Proof System (TLAPS) is a proof assistant for properties written in TLA$^+$. The TLA$^+$ proof is usually declarative and hierarchical. The latter helps to organise large scale proofs. It provides a consistent abstraction over several back-end verifiers, including Z3, CVC4, Zenon and Isabelle.

We have written machine-checked proofs for 10 out of 11 properties. The last property is too complicated to be proved at this time, but we believe it is still possible to prove it given enough time and effort. For instance, in order to check the *NumberOfLeader* property, we first write a theorem

THEOREM $Spec \Rightarrow \Box NumberOfLeader$,

where *Spec* equals $Init \land \Box [Next]_{vars}$. Our goal is to write a TLA$^+$ proof for this theorem, which means the specification implies the property. Usually we have to find a suitable inductive invariant *Inv*, and prove:

(i) $Init \Rightarrow Inv$ (ii) $Inv \land [Next]_{vars} \Rightarrow Inv'$ (iii) $Inv \Rightarrow NumberOfLeader$.

It turns out that *NumberOfLeader* itself is an inductive invariant of the system (the same holds for the other nine properties that we proved). Hence we set *Inv* to be *NumberOfLeader*, then prove the first two subgoals. These can be decomposed further (most importantly by considering the transitions case-by-case), until TLA$^+$ is able to finish the proof automatically. We conclude with a few tips for theorem proving with TLAPS:

- Reformulate properties containing TLA$^+$ operators that are poorly supported in TLAPS, e.g. ENABLED, which represents the condition that a certain transition can be executed. We replace them with equivalent TLA$^+$ formulas without these operators.
- In proofs by cases, TLAPS can provide its own decomposition suggestions, but sometimes it is helpful to specify custom ways to split the cases.
- Make full use of *TypeInvariant* (the TLA$^+$ way to express type correctness) and auxiliary theorems, especially when proving properties about partial orders between data changes. These auxiliary theorems help to prove that properties such as *NumberOfLeader* is inductive.

4 Lessons and Challenges

4.1 Total Effort

The size of our TLA$^+$ specifications for Taurus is 2142 lines of code in total. In contrast, the machine-checked proofs for the 10 properties have 3070 lines, which makes our ratio of proof-to-specification around 1.43 to 1. One reason for our relatively low ratio is likely that TLA$^+$ specifications usually spend extra lines for aligned conjunction and disjunction lists and for ease of reading.

It took a whole year to complete this work. More precisely, 2 months for investigating various tools for verifying distributed systems, 2 months for an exhaustive survey of the design and implementation of Taurus, 4 months for writing the specifications, 1 month for model checking experiments and 3 months for theorem proving. In total, it required approximately 3 person-years.

4.2 Why TLA$^+$ Was Chosen

We investigated a number of tools for formally verifying a model of the Taurus distributed database system, and at last we decided to use TLA$^+$ because:

  i. TLA$^+$ is designed for concurrent and distributed systems and algorithms, and is simple to learn for engineers, especially with the help of its companion language PlusCal, a C-styled alternative for pseudo-code.
 ii. There are some industrial uses of TLA$^+$ in verifying distributed databases. The successful examples in Amazon [9,10] removed doubts about suitability of TLA$^+$ and encouraged Huawei to try it in verifying its own products.
iii. TLA$^+$ has both a model checker and a proof system. In practice, model checking is more attractive for engineers than theorem proving, because it is fully automatic, so it is easier to learn and use, and usually is enough to find most bugs at a small scale.

4.3 Challenges and Limitations

Many challenges were encountered in our work because of the approach we adopted and the limitations of TLA$^+$. We would like to share our experience with the community and hope that it can help with further applications of formal methods in industry.

Level of Abstraction. It is always hard to decide the proper level of abstraction with which to specify the system. This requires experience and understanding of which parts of the design are most vulnerable to errors. For example, during the project we investigated the implementation of Remote Procedure Calls among different nodes in detail, but chose to simply abstract these as messages and FIFO channels in the TLA$^+$ specification. This is because the mechanism of RPCs is already well-understood and unlikely to go wrong. The abstraction makes it easier to specify and verify the system, but also means verification would miss errors in actual implementation like the one in Sect. 3.4.

Properties to Check. It is not difficult to write formulas in TLA$^+$ to describe the properties thanks to its high expressiveness, but it turns out to be a challenge to figure out what properties to check. After we finished our specifications together with the engineers, we were a bit lost for not knowing what to check.

We received inspiration from the TLA$^+$ verification of Paxos [6] and Raft [11], and found properties that should also hold in our model as starting point. We then encouraged the engineers to figure out some critical mechanisms that they were not fully confident in. With their answers we could then easily find the related variables and write formulas to describe the properties.

Limitations of TLA$^+$. During this work we felt some limitations of TLA$^+$, and would welcome further progress and improvement in the following areas:

i. TLAPS does not support reasoning about *liveness* properties, which currently can only be checked by model checking.
ii. TLAPS poorly supports some operators such as ENABLED and CHOOSE.
iii. The known limitation of model checking, the problem of state space explosion, remains in TLC model checker.

5   Related Work

5.1   Formal Verification of Distributed Protocols

A lot of effort has been made to develop tools for formal verification of distributed protocols, including interactive verification frameworks Verdi [14], IronFleet [3], domain specific language PSync [2] with its related tools and multi-modal verification tool Ivy [8,13]. Many of them use Raft and Paxos protocols as case studies, and proved a variety of safety and liveness properties.

Compared to the above work, we focus on specific safety properties that our domain experts found to be of most concern. We do not consider liveness properties. We chose TLA$^+$ since it is widely used and relatively easy to learn (as discussed in Sect. 4.2). The model that we verify is large compared to most published works using TLA$^+$. For example, the basic Raft TLA$^+$ specification [11] has 485 lines while ours has about 2.1k.

5.2   Verifying Distributed Systems Using TLA$^+$

Amazon [9,10] has applied TLA$^+$ to its complex distributed systems such as S3 and DynamoDB and found several subtle but serious bugs using model checking. Moreover, the engineering team of CosmosDB [7,12], Microsoft's distributed database service, have been using TLA$^+$ to specify the core algorithms and protocols and model-check them for correctness. The uses of TLA$^+$ in Amazon and Microsoft apply model checking only, while in our work we further write machine-checked proofs for the desired properties to compensate the limitations of model checking.

6   Conclusion

We have presented the application of TLA$^+$ to formally specify and verify a real-world distributed database system. We wrote TLA$^+$ specifications to model our target system and the properties that it should satisfy. We successfully checked all of the properties using model checking on small configurations of the system, and also wrote machine-checked proofs for all but one of these properties. Finally, we simulated and analysed a bug with the help of the TLC model checker. Overall, this is a successful application of formal verification to lift a distributed database to the expected quality level.

Acknowledgements. We would like to thank the anonymous reviewers for their valuable suggestions and comments about this paper. Work supported in part by the Guangdong Science and Technology Department (Grant No. 2018B010107004).

References

1. Depoutovitch, A., et al.: Taurus database: how to be fast, available, and frugal in the cloud. In: Proceedings of the 2020 ACM SIGMOD International Conference on Management of Data, pp. 1463–1478. ACM (2020)
2. Drăgoi, C., Henzinger, T., Zufferey, D.: PSYNC: a partially synchronous language for fault-tolerant distributed algorithms. In: POPL, pp. 400–415. ACM (2016)
3. Hawblitzel, C., et al.: IronFleet: proving practical distributed systems correct. In: SOSP, pp. 1–17. ACM (2015)
4. Lamport, L.: The temporal logic of actions. TOPLAS **94** 16(3), 872–923 (1994)
5. Lamport, L.: Specifying Systems, vol. 388. Addison-Wesley, Boston (2002)
6. Lamport, L.: Byzantizing Paxos by refinement. In: Peleg, D. (ed.) DISC 2011. LNCS, vol. 6950, pp. 211–224. Springer, Heidelberg (2011). https://doi.org/10.1007/978-3-642-24100-0_22
7. Lamport, L.: Industrial use of TLA$^+$ (2018). https://lamport.azurewebsites.net/tla/industrial-use.html. Accessed 1 May 2021
8. McMillan, K.L., Padon, O.: Ivy: a multi-modal verification tool for distributed algorithms. In: Lahiri, S.K., Wang, C. (eds.) CAV 2020. LNCS, vol. 12225, pp. 190–202. Springer, Cham (2020). https://doi.org/10.1007/978-3-030-53291-8_12

9. Newcombe, C.: Why Amazon chose TLA+. In: Ait Ameur, Y., Schewe, K.D. (eds.) Abstract State Machines, Alloy, B, TLA, VDM, and Z. ABZ 2014. Lecture Notes in Computer Science, vol. 8477, pp. 25–39. Springer, Heidelberg (2014). https:// doi.org/10.1007/978-3-662-43652-3_3

10. Newcombe, C., Rath, T., Fan, Z., Munteanu, B., Brooker, M., Deardeuff, M.: How Amazon web services uses formal methods. Commun. ACM **58**(4), 66–73 (2015)

11. Ongaro, D., Ousterhout, J.: In search of an understandable consensus algorithm. In: USENIX Annual Technical Conference, pp. 305–319. USENIX Association (2014)

12. Shukla, D.: High-level TLA+ specifications for the five consistency levels offered by Azure CosmosDB (2018). https://github.com/Azure/azure-cosmos-tla. Accessed 1 May 2021

13. Taube, M., et al.: Modularity for decidability of deductive verification with applications to distributed systems. In: PLDI, pp. 190–202. ACM (2018)

14. Wilcox, J.R., et al.: Verdi: a framework for implementing and formally verifying distributed systems. In: PLDI, pp. 357–368. ACM (2015)

Combined Online Checking and Control Synthesis: A Study on a Vehicle Platoon Testbed

Jiawan Wang, Lei Bu$^{(\boxtimes)}$, Shaopeng Xing, Yuming Wu, and Xuandong Li

State Key Laboratory of Novel Software Technology, Nanjing University,
Nanjing, China
bulei@nju.edu.cn

Abstract. Vehicle platoon systems are typical safety-critical cyber-physical systems (CPS), and are designed for safe and efficient transportation. However, vehicles' complex dynamics and uncertain runtime environment make it difficult to apply conventional offline model checking methods to ensure their safety. To address this challenge, we propose an online safety assurance framework for CPS, conducting combined online model checking and control synthesis in well-scheduled cycles. In each cycle, we conduct (1) a quick online formal verification on systems' coarse-grained hybrid automata (HA) models, as a fault prediction mechanism; (2) for potential risks, an accurate optimal control synthesis on systems' fine-grained HA models. Furthermore, we develop a robotic vehicle platoon testbed, and implement our framework on it. We conduct a series of evaluations, and experimental results show that the systems' safety and efficiency are significantly enhanced by our framework.

1 Introduction

Cyber-physical systems (CPS) [1] tightly integrate discrete computational processes and continuous physical components, exhibiting inherently hybrid and dynamic behaviors. Nowadays, CPS can be found in various safety-critical areas, such as automotive, aerospace, healthcare, and infrastructure. Robots, autonomous vehicles, implantable medical devices, and intelligent buildings are all typical CPS, where a failure may cause severe damage to human life and property. Thus, formal safety assurance is important to these systems.

However, it is challenging to ensure the safety of CPS at design time. Large uncertainties exist during CPS operations, and could potentially lead to failures. For one thing, CPS are often deployed in intrinsically unpredictable physical environment. For another, distributed sub-CPS could exchange data online by communication networks. Since these parameters are all unpredictable until runtime, conventional offline model checking [2] is infeasible for many CPS. Therefore, there is a need for online methods to handle uncertainties and prevent failures during CPS operations.

This work is supported in part by the Leading-edge Technology Program of Jiangsu Natural Science Foundation (No. BK20202001).

M. Huisman et al. (Eds.): FM 2021, LNCS 13047, pp. 752–762, 2021.
https://doi.org/10.1007/978-3-030-90870-6_43

To study the online safety of CPS, we set up an indoor robotic vehicle testbed, including sub-systems, such as wheeled robotic cars, wayside sensors, and a wayside control center, connected by wired and wireless communication networks. Then, we construct a vehicle platoon scenario on our testbed.

Automated vehicle platoon requires strings of vehicles to drive together with ideal inter-vehicle distances. It could increase road capacity and reduce fuel consumption, due to decreased inter-vehicle distances [3]. However, a smaller inter-vehicle distance not only leads to higher traffic and fuel efficiency, but also higher risks of collision; and safety is the prerequisite to achieve any potential efficiency benefits. How to maintain a small inter-vehicle distance with formal safety guarantees is key to vehicle platoon. Thus, after our testbed is constructed, we further analyze the main challenges in vehicle platoon into the following two points, and propose our solutions:

1. Vehicles' dynamics are complex, including both continuous and discrete ones. The composition of multiple vehicles further enlarges their state space. Besides, their received wayside data and runtime environment are highly uncertain (e.g., real-time road conditions and front vehicle's behaviors). All these together make the offline model checking of such system inapplicable. Therefore, instead of checking the system at design-time, we conduct online model checking for platooning vehicles: building online models for vehicles, and verifying safety properties for their time-bounded short-run behaviors.
2. Once a potential collision is reported after online checking, the next challenging thing is to synthesize suitable control commands for vehicles. For a vehicle with collision risks, braking with its maximum braking power may avoid collisions, but it usually causes low transport efficiency, un-smooth vehicle behavior, and even potential danger to the onboard passengers. Therefore, instead of braking immediately, we synthesize optimal control commands for risky vehicles in the form of acceleration profiles.

In sum, we propose an online safety assurance framework for CPS and apply it to platooning vehicles. Combined online model checking and control synthesis are conducted in well-scheduled cycles to ensure complete runtime safety. In each cycle, coarse-grained linear hybrid automata (HA) [4] models and fine-grained nonlinear HA models are built online for vehicles. To ensure vehicles' safety in the short-run future, time-bounded verification of the target safety property is conducted on coarse-grained models. For potential risks, we then synthesize safe and optimal control commands on vehicles' fine-grained models.

In this work, we deploy this framework on our testbed, applying a formal time-bounded HA reachability verification tool BACH [5] and an optimal HA control synthesis tool CDH [6] in it. Evaluations show significant enhancement in system safety and efficiency after the deployment of our framework.

2 Robotic Vehicle Testbed and Platoon Scenario

2.1 Robotic Vehicle Testbed

As shown in Fig. 1, instead of software-based vehicle simulators running in virtual driving environment, we construct a robotic vehicle testbed. It consists of a rounded rectangle magnetic track with three wayside ultra-wideband (UWB) anchors, four-wheeled CVTECH A8 robotic cars, and a laptop (Intel Core i7 2.20 GHz and 16 GB RAM) with a ZigBee module as a wayside control center.

Each robotic car is equipped with motors, magnetic sensors, a UWB tag for position measurement, a grating sensor for speed measurement, a ZigBee module for wireless communication, and a Samsung board for control. Cars' top speed is limited to 55 cm/s. Wayside UWB anchors receive pulses emitted by UWB tags on cars, and measure their distances with cars. Thus, three UWB anchors enable real-time locating for cars running in three-dimensional space.

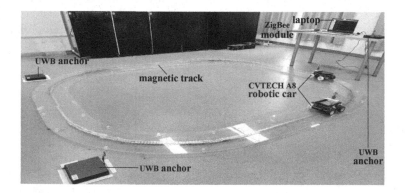

Fig. 1. A picture of the wheeled robotic vehicle testbed

2.2 Vehicle Platoon Scenario

In the vehicle platoon scenario on our testbed, two robotic cars are programmed to run along the magnetic track according to sensed magnetic information.

Vehicle Dynamics. The car ahead keeps cruising at 10 cm/s. The following car plans its movements by its current mode, emergency brake intervention speed ($vebi$), and movement authority (MA)[1]. $vebi$ is calculated by function $f_{MA}(x)$:

$$vebi = f_{MA}(x) = \sqrt{(2 * a_{mbd} * (MA - x))} \qquad (1)$$

where x denotes its position and a_{mbd} denotes its maximum braking deceleration, which is 10 cm/s^2 here. The conditions and dynamics inside all three modes are given below:

---

[1] MA indicates the allowable travel distance for a vehicle by specifying its end-of-authority point [7]. Once a vehicle moves beyond its MA, a collision may occur.

- **Acceleration (AC)**: If its current speed is lower than $(vebi - 20$ cm/s$)$, it enters acceleration mode, accelerating at 5 cm/s^2.
- **Emergency Braking (EB)**: If its current speed exceeds $vebi$, it enters EB mode, braking with a_{mbd}.
- **Cruise Control (CC)**: Otherwise, it stays in CC mode with random accelerations within $[-5, 5]$ cm/s^2.

Communication Topology. As shown in Fig. 2, there is wireless bi-directional communication between robotic cars and the wayside control center to exchange car speed and MA data, supported by onboard and wayside ZigBee modules. There is also wired communication between an UWB anchor and the wayside control center. Besides, all UWB anchors could receive pulses from each other.

Safety Property. In order to avoid collision in this highly interconnected platoon system with dynamic robotic cars, the following car's position should never reach its MA, formally written as "$x <$ MA". Once we can prove that this safety property holds, the safety of the platoon can be formally guaranteed.

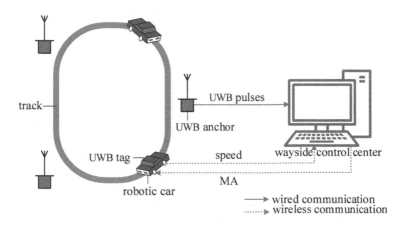

Fig. 2. Communication topology of the robotic vehicle platoon scenario

3   Periodically Online Safety Assurance Framework

To assure the safety of this scenario, we give our online safety assurance framework in Fig. 3. It performs online model checking and control synthesis for the running vehicle in scheduled cycles. In each cycle, we (1) concretize vehicle's online HA model by runtime parameters, (2) check whether any unsafe behavior will occur in the short-run future by time-bounded online reachability verification, (3) and once finding any potential risk, synthesize control commands online with safety guarantees, and feedback such commands to the vehicle.

3.1   Online Modeling

In this framework, we build online HA models periodically to handle runtime uncertainties. According to the vehicle dynamics introduced in Sect. 2.2 and monitored real-time parameters, we build a coarse-grained HA model for efficient online verification, and a fine-grained HA model for accurate control synthesis.

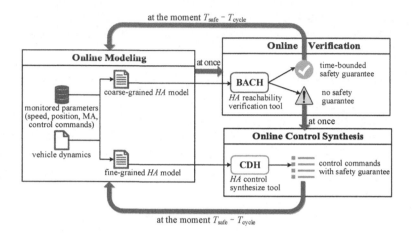

Fig. 3. Online and periodical safety assurance framework

For the coarse-grained model, as shown in Fig. 4(a), there is only one mode called RUN, modeling the vehicle's continuous dynamics. Variables 'x', 'v', and 't' are used to denote the vehicle's current position, speed, and execution time, and are initialized by vehicle's monitored real-time position, speed, and 0. There is also a timer variable, denoted as '$clock$', such that speed can be discretely updated every '$\triangle t$' time by jumping edges labeled AC, CC, and EB. Jumping conditions on edges are set by the vehicle's mode conditions described in Sect. 2.2, comparing its current speed 'v' with its emergency brake intervention speed computed by function $f_{\mathrm{MA}}(x)$ in Eq. 1.

For the fine-grained model in Fig. 4(b), there are additional variables '$vebi$' and 'a' to denote real-time emergency brake intervention speed and acceleration speed. Except the INIT mode to initialize variables, there are three modes, AC, CC, and EB, as described in Sect. 2.2, denoting that the vehicle's speed should be accelerated, approximately maintained, and decelerate respectively.

Comparing the coarse-grained model with the fine-grained model, there exist two major differences. (1) In the coarse-grained one, the computation of speed 'v' and emergency brake intervention speed '$vebi$' are conducted every '$\triangle t$' time by jumping edges; but conducted continuously in the fine-grained one as vehicle's original dynamics. So is the comparison between v and $vebi$ for checking jumping conditions, which is also discretely conducted in the coarse-grained one, but continuously in the fine-grained one. For example, once its real-time speed reaches real-time $vebi$ in the fine-grained model, it jumps to the mode EB at once. Besides, the dynamics are nonlinear in the fine-grained model, but, as a benefit of discretization abstraction, linear in the coarse-grained one. (2) The fine-grained model covers the vehicle's original behavior, but includes additional nondeterminism. The condition of CC mode is enlarged from $v \in [vebi - 20, vebi]$ to $v \in [vebi - 25, vebi]$, partial overlapping with the condition of AC mode, in order to provide additional space for optimal control synthesis.

3.2 Combined Online Verification and Control Synthesis

As shown in Fig. 3, in each cycle, we conduct time-bounded online verification for short-run fault prediction, and optimal control synthesis as a timely remedial measure for predicted faults.

We apply BACH, a time-bounded reachability checker for HA [5,8], to coarse-grained HA models, checking whether the target safety property, "$x < $ MA", always holds in the following bounded time. The tool BACH conducts path-oriented formal reachability verification by linear programming, and is chosen here for its efficiency in linear HA. If BACH returns safe, it means that in the following bounded time, this safety property always holds and no collision happens. If BACH returns unsafe, potential collisions might happen in the near future; thus, we conduct online control synthesis at once.

We apply CDH, a HA optimal control synthesis tool [6], to fine-grained HA models, synthesizing control commands in the form of acceleration profiles for the vehicle. CDH supports the generation of feasible and piecewise optimal control inputs for given control tasks in arbitrary nonlinear and nondeterministic HA. We apply CDH with a safety task that must be satisfied, which is "$x < $ MA" always hold before the end of the next verification and control cycle. Meanwhile, we can apply CDH with optional optimization tasks to realize other goals such as lower fuel cost and smoother vehicle behavior.

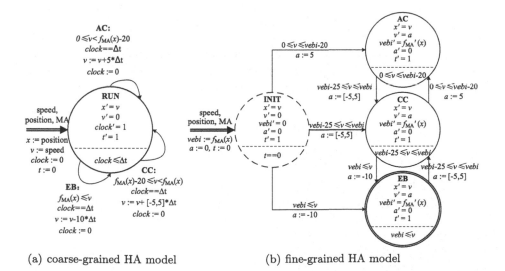

(a) coarse-grained HA model   (b) fine-grained HA model

Fig. 4. Online vehicle models with different granularity

3.3   Assignment Scheduling

The assignment of verification and control cycles are well-scheduled in our framework, such that the runtime safety for vehicles' complete execution can be ensured. We give an illustrative example for our assignment scheduling in Fig. 5.

T_{safe} denotes the valid scope of the safety guarantee obtained in each cycle, i.e., the bounded time given to BACH. T_{cycle} denotes the maximum time required for one online model checking cycle, i.e., the maximum execution time for BACH and CDH. A cycle starts if there is only T_{cycle} time left before the expiration of last cycle's safety guarantee.

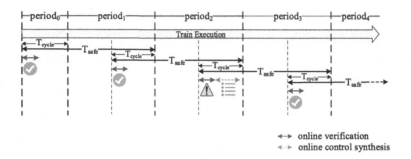

Fig. 5. An example of online model checking cycles

As shown in Fig. 5, we divide the vehicle's complete execution into multiple periods. Except for the first one denoted as $period_0$, which is a window period with length T_{cycle}, all other periods have the same length of $T_{safe} - T_{cycle}$. For $period_{i+1}$, its safety guarantee is obtained in $period_i$, either by the verification process or the control synthesis process. For example, the online verification process in $period_1$ returns safe, so we are assured that the whole $period_2$ is safe. While in $period_2$, the online verification process warns that the vehicle might be unsafe in the following T_{safe} scope. Thus, the control synthesis process is then performed, generating safe commands for the vehicle to execute during $period_3$.

4   Deployment and Evaluations

4.1   Framework Deployment

We deployed our framework on the vehicle platoon testbed, implementing periodical online model checking and control synthesis in the wayside control center. In our evaluation scene, when the car behind starts to move at an initial speed of 15 cm/s, the front one is 100 cm ahead of it.

In our experience, the control center typically accomplishes the online modeling and verification processes in 0.14–0.16 s by BACH, and the control synthesis process in 0.5–0.7 s by CDH in such scenarios. Considering the data transfer rate

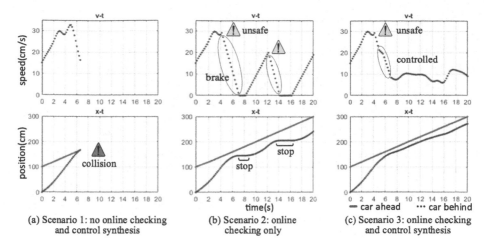

(a) Scenario 1: no online checking
and control synthesis

(b) Scenario 2: online
checking only

(c) Scenario 3: online checking
and control synthesis

Fig. 6. Vehicle's behavior in different scenarios with our framework deployment (Color figure online)

and the message size in our ZigBee network, the delay of wireless communication is very short, typically 0.015–0.03 s. Thus, we set the maximum execution time for an online model checking cycle (i.e. T_{cycle}) as 1 s, and the valid scope for each cycle's model checking (i.e. T_{safe}) as 3 s. Besides, except for the requisite safety task, an optimization task to maximize the car's moving distance was also given to CDH.

4.2 Framework Evaluation

During the evaluation, we aim to study whether the car's safety and the transport efficiency are improved by our online checking and control synthesis framework. Our evaluation is designed with three phases, applying none of, part of, and the full of our framework respectively. We plot the speed-time (v–t) graph and position-time (x–t) graph for all three phases in Fig. 6(a)–(c). The behavior of the car ahead is given in red lines and the following car in blue dots.

Scenario 1. In this scenario, neither the online checking nor the control synthesis module of our framework was deployed. As shown in Fig. 6(a), a dangerous rear-end collision happened after 6.6 s when the car behind running at a speed higher than 15 cm/s. Although the car behind started to conduct emergent braking since $t = 5.2$ s, it was already too late to prevent the collision.

Scenario 2. In this scenario, the modeling and verification module of our framework was applied, but the control module was not. As shown in Fig. 6(b), BACH fired the collision alarm in the third cycle of checking (conducted during $t = [4, 4.2)$ s)[2]. The car behind braked immediately and stopped at $t = 7.2$ s. As shown in its x-t graph, the collision that happened in scenario 1 was avoided.

---

[2] As $T_{cycle} = 1$, the length of one period is 2 s accordingly.

After BACH obtained a short-run safety guarantee in the fifth checking cycle during $[8.0, 8.2)$ s, the following car began to move again by its control logic. Unfortunately, during $[12.0, 12.2)$ s, BACH predicted another risk, and the following car braked again. After that, it did not move until $t = 16.2$ s. Two potential collisions were successfully avoided, due to well-scheduled checking cycles and BACH's efficient performance on linear HA. However, two emergency brakes are applied accordingly, and the car behind stopped completely on the track twice, which is neither comfortable for passengers nor efficient for transportation.

Scenario 3. Different from scenario 2, in scenario 3, control synthesis was conducted after BACH's warnings. As shown in Fig. 6(c), after BACH fired the alarm during $[4, 4.2)$ s, the car behind slowed down and CDH synthesized control commands for the car to execute in the next period $t = [5.0, 7.0)$ s. During the next period, the car's speed first decreased by 1.1 cm/s^2 for 0.8 s, then 1.3 cm/s^2 for 0.6 s, and finally 1.5 cm/s^2 for another 0.8 s. After that, it was reported safe by BACH and continued to move by its control logic.

We can see that, instead of braking urgently and stopping completely, with the help of efficient online control synthesis, the car behind never stopped. It kept moving on the track and also kept a safe distance from the car ahead. Thus, both the safety and efficiency of the running system are enhanced substantially.

5   Related Work

Online Verification and Control for CPS. Online reachability model checking has been recently proposed as a formal CPS fault prediction tool. Study [8] performs online reachability analysis for CPS by path-oriented bounded model checking (BMC). Several other works conduct reachable sets computation online. For linear systems, online reachability computation is conducted by flowpipe construction in [9], and by instantiating a pre-computed offline reachable set with a concrete recent state in [10]. For nonlinear systems, online reachability computation can be performed after decomposition of original system dynamics [11].

In terms of CPS control, conventional gradient-based methods are efficient [12,13], but require differentiable system dynamics. For non-differentiable CPS, sampling-based methods have achieved considerable success [14], but with no optimality guarantee. A robust model predictive control approach based on Monte Carlo simulation and rejection-sampling is proposed in [15], but with limited ability in complex control missions. An optimal control approach based on derivative-free optimization is proposed in [6], where complex control problems can be efficiently solved in a divide-and-conquer manner.

This work proposes a combined framework to ensure CPS runtime safety in scheduled cycles, combining both online verification and control synthesis. Periodically online verification works as a short-run fault prediction tool and control synthesis works as a remedial measure for predicted faults. Online verification solution in [8] and control synthesis solution in [6] are applied in this work.

Formal Verification and Control for Vehicle Platoon. Several works try to verify safety properties for platooning vehicles formally. Study [16] decomposes platooning vehicles into small components and verifies safety properties by SAL toolkit tool. Studies [17,18] model vehicle dynamics by timed automata and verify safety properties by model checker UPPAAL [19]. It is hard for these offline methods to build accurate vehicle models at design time and conduct precise verification.

There are extensive works on vehicle platoon control, involving both lateral and longitudinal control. Since cars move along a single track in our testbed, only longitudinal control is considered in this work. In general, existing longitudinal control methods mainly include proportional integral derivative (PID) based ones [20], sliding mode control (SMC) based ones [21], model predictive control (MPC) based ones [22], and consensus control based ones [3].

Different from the works above, the combined safety assurance framework proposed in this work is an online one to handle runtime uncertainties. Accurate parameters, like vehicle speed, position, and MA, are updated precisely in each online checking cycle. However, it is worth mentioning that our vehicle platoon testbed is a simplified one. Many interesting elements, such as multi-lane vehicle platoon and vehicle-to-vehicle (V2V) communication, have not been considered yet in this work. How to construct a more complex vehicle platoon testbed with these elements and implement our framework on it, will be our future work.

6   Conclusion

In this work, we proposed an online safety assurance framework for CPS, conducting combined online model checking and control synthesis in cycles. These cycles are well-scheduled, such that we can ensure runtime safety for systems' complete execution. In each cycle, efficient reachability verification on coarse-grained models is conducted for short-run fault prediction, and optimal control synthesis on fine-grained models is conducted for potential faults. We built an indoor robotic vehicle platoon testbed and deployed our framework on it. Evaluations showed a significant enhancement in traffic safety and efficiency.

References

1. Lee, E.A., Seshia, S.A.: Introduction to Embedded Systems: A Cyber-Physical Systems Approach. MIT Press (2017)
2. Clarke, E.M., Grumberg, O., et al.: Model Checking. MIT Press (2018)
3. Di Bernardo, M., Salvi, A., Santini, S.: Distributed consensus strategy for platooning of vehicles in the presence of time-varying heterogeneous communication delays. IEEE Trans. Intell. Transp. Syst. **16**(1), 102–112 (2014)
4. Henzinger, T.A.: The theory of hybrid automata. In: Inan, M.K., Kurshan, R.P. (eds.) Verification of Digital and Hybrid Systems, pp. 265–292. Springer, Heidelberg (2000). https://doi.org/10.1007/978-3-642-59615-5_13d
5. Bu, L., Li, Y., Wang, L., Li, X.: Bach: bounded reachability checker for linear hybrid automata. In: FMCAD, pp. 1–4 (2008)
6. Xing, S., Wang, J., Bu, L., et al.: Approximate optimal hybrid control synthesis by classification-based derivative-free optimization. In: HSCC, pp. 1–11 (2021)

7. Pascoe, R.D., Eichorn, T.N.: What is communication-based train control? IEEE Veh. Technol. Mag. **4**(4), 16–21 (2009)
8. Bu, L., Wang, Q., Ren, X., et al.: Scenario-based online reachability validation for cps fault prediction. IEEE Trans. Comput. Aided Des. Integr. Circuits Syst. **39**(10), 2081–2094 (2019)
9. Johnson, T.T., Bak, S., Caccamo, M., Sha, L.: Real-time reachability for verified simplex design. ACM Trans. Embed. Comput. Syst. **15**(2), 1–27 (2016)
10. Chen, X., Sankaranarayanan, S.: Model predictive real-time monitoring of linear systems. In: RTSS, pp. 297–306. IEEE (2017)
11. Chen, X., Sankaranarayanan, S.: Decomposed reachability analysis for nonlinear systems. In: RTSS, pp. 13–24. IEEE (2016)
12. Axelsson, H., Wardi, Y., Egerstedt, M., Verriest, E.: Gradient descent approach to optimal mode scheduling in hybrid dynamical systems. J. Optim. Theory Appl. **136**(2), 167–186 (2008)
13. Gonzalez, H., Vasudevan, R., Kamgarpour, M., et al.: A descent algorithm for the optimal control of constrained nonlinear switched dynamical systems. In: HSCC, pp. 51–60. ACM (2010)
14. Branicky, M.S., Curtiss, M.M., Levine, J.A., et al.: RRTs for nonlinear, discrete, and hybrid planning and control. In: CDC, pp. 657–663. IEEE (2003)
15. Farahani, S.S., Raman, V., Murray, R.M.: Robust model predictive control for signal temporal logic synthesis. IFAC **48**(27), 323–328 (2015)
16. El-Zaher, M., Contet, J.-M., Gruer, P., et al.: Compositional verification for reactive multi-agent systems applied to platoon non collision verification. Stud. Inform. Univ. **10**(3), 119–141 (2012)
17. Mallozzi, P., Sciancalepore, M., Pelliccione, P.: Formal verification of the on-the-fly vehicle platooning protocol. In: Crnkovic, I., Troubitsyna, E. (eds.) SERENE 2016. LNCS, vol. 9823, pp. 62–75. Springer, Cham (2016). https://doi.org/10.1007/978-3-319-45892-2_5
18. Peng, C., Bonsangue, M.M., Xu, Z.: Model checking longitudinal control in vehicle platoon systems. IEEE Access **7**, 112 015–112 (2019)
19. Behrmann, G., David, A., Larsen, K.G.: A tutorial on UPPAAL. In: Bernardo, M., Corradini, F. (eds.) SFM-RT 2004. LNCS, vol. 3185, pp. 200–236. Springer, Heidelberg (2004). https://doi.org/10.1007/978-3-540-30080-9_7
20. Knights, V.A., Gacovski, Z., Deskovski, S., Petrovska, O.: Guidance and control system for platoon of autonomous mobile robots. J. Electr. Eng. **6**, 281–288 (2018)
21. Xiao, L., Gao, F.: Practical string stability of platoon of adaptive cruise control vehicles. IEEE Trans. Intell. Transp. Syst. **12**(4), 1184–1194 (2011)
22. Graffione, S., Bersani, C., Sacile, R., Zero, E.: Model predictive control of a vehicle platoon. In: SoSE, pp. 513–518. IEEE (2020)

Formally Guaranteed Tight Dynamic Future Occupancy of Autonomous Vehicles

Yousaf Rahman$^{(\boxtimes)}$, Md Tawhid Bin Waez, and Yuming Niu

Ford Motor Company, Dearborn, USA
yrahman@ford.com

Abstract. Autonomous Vehicles (AVs) must be able to navigate complex traffic environments without collisions with other traffic participants. Formal methods can be used to guarantee collision avoidance by using reachability analysis techniques to verify if a planned trajectory is safe or unsafe. To prevent the formal collision avoidance system from being overly conservative, a tight reachable set of the AV must be calculated. Computing the tight reachable set of an AV is a difficult and computationally expensive process. Motion primitives are used to provide tight dynamic future occupancy of autonomous systems. Motion primitives are short segments of trajectories that are precomputed along with their reachable sets. By replacing a reference trajectory with a sequence of motion primitives, the computational requirements during vehicle operation can be greatly reduced. In this paper, we provide a treatment on motion primitives, and develop an algorithm to match motion primitives to a reference trajectory in a computationally efficient manner.

1 Introduction

A common industrial practice is dividing the development of an Automotive Safety Integrity Level (ASIL) system into two parts: An ASIL rated runtime monitor and the actual system as a Quality Management (QM) system. Motion planning is an extremely complicated, safety-critical, and core system for automated driving. Thus, formal methods-based runtime monitor or formal methods-based collision avoidance system would be highly desired but challenging to develop. A core capability of runtime monitor for motion planner or collision avoidance system is collision checking of the ego vehicles current and future occupancy with the similar occupancy of the other obstacles. From formal verification perspective, we can view collision checking as searching for the overlapping or conjunction of *formal ego future occupancy* and *formal future occupancy of other road participants* including road boundaries [1–3]. In the last several years, we have seen a great progress on real-time capable solutions for calculating formal future occupancy of other road participants [4], to our best knowledge, no real-time work on calculating formal future occupancy of the ego vehicle exist.

© Springer Nature Switzerland AG 2021
M. Huisman et al. (Eds.): FM 2021, LNCS 13047, pp. 763–775, 2021.
https://doi.org/10.1007/978-3-030-90870-6_44

A *tight prediction* is a key to achieve improve drivability. For calculating the future occupancy of the ego vehicle, using the exact techniques of calculating formal future occupancy of other road participants would produce too conservative reachable sets to drive. Compared to the other road participants, we have the knowledge of the intended trajectory of the motion planner, and we know the disturbances and sensor noise of the ego vehicle. Thus, developing much accurate future occupancy for ego vehicle could be feasible.

A common industrial practice to calculate the future occupancy of the ego vehicle is mostly creating a tube by repeatedly placing the exact bounding box (of the ego vehicle) one after another along the intended trajectory. The problem for such static and non-formal methods is not considering the disturbances and sensor noise that could cause enough deviation to have collision during execution of the intended trajectory by the ego vehicle. On the other hand, using larger bounding box would provide poor drivability. Therefore, we need dynamic formal reachable sets to achieve both formal guarantee and improved drivability.

One of the ways to use real-time dynamic reachable set by matching precomputed reachable sets of *motion primitives* [5]. A motion primitive is a short (typically < 1 s) precomputed trajectory that can approximate a reference trajectory. In operation, several motion primitives are combined to replace a reference trajectory with a close approximation. This process has two main benefits. First, the reachable set used for the AV is tight and therefore will lead to a less conservative collision avoidance system without losing the formal guarantee of collision avoidance. Secondly, since the motion primitives and their reachable sets are all precomputed, the computational cost of such an approach is relatively smaller than other approaches. In general, AV software stack, e.g., planning module, runs at 100 ms loop time. To finish all tasks, such as local path planning, behavior planning, and path selection, within 100 ms is a really challenging task. So, this brings a very challenging requirement to motion primitive matching, which has to be finished within a fraction of a second (typically $\approx$50 ms) in order to meet the overall real-time requirement. Using a motion primitive-based approach to trajectory following has two main challenges. The first obstacle is the large size of the motion primitive database required to accurately track trajectories. Typically, a database of over 100,000 motion primitives is used. Secondly, a second algorithm must be developed to match motion primitives to the reference trajectory. This matching must be done in a computationally efficient manner and the matched motion primitives must closely approximate the reference trajectory to prevent unnecessary deviations from the desired reference trajectory.

In a research collaboration, Ford R&A and Althoff et al. implemented a formal methods-based comprehensive collision avoidance framework for the autonomous vehicle's planning module [6]. The framework integrated two major parts of formal methods-based collision avoidance system with the planning module of Apollo. The first part is *formal collision checking*: A trajectory $Traj$ generated by the motion planner is formally safe if formal future ego (vehicle) reachable set (if follows $Traj$) does not overlap formal road boundaries [7] and also does not overlap formal future reachable sets of other road participants [8]. The remaining part of the framework is to have a formally guaranteed *fail-safe trajectory* at each time step [9,10]. The motion primitive database is created offline prior to vehicle operation. Figure 1 shows the steps required to construct the motion primitive database. Figure 2 shows how motion primitives are used for collision checking during vehicle operation.

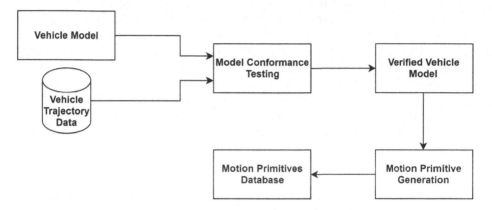

Fig. 1. Method for creating the motion primitive database. The database consists of the motion primitives and their reachable sets.

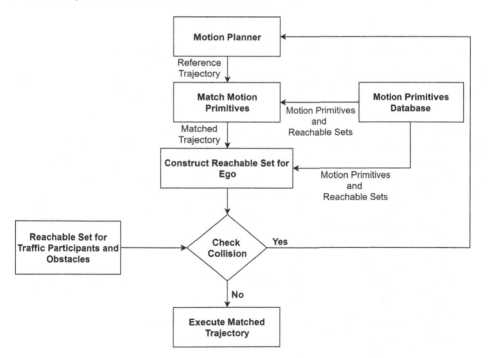

Fig. 2. Collision checking framework.

One functional requirement for such a collision avoidance framework is to operate within the execution cycle (e.g., 100 ms for Apollo 3.0) of the planning module to monitor each generated trajectory. While all the modules of this formal *collision avoidance system* were showing solid theoretical base and promising computation time, the collaboration could not find a promising real-time capable tight ego future occupancy calculation mechanism. Calculating the reachable set of the whole reference trajectory using hybrid reachability analysis would take several hours for each scenario, which is obviously infeasible for use in an autonomous vehicle. We are solving this problem pragmatically by proposing a computationally efficient formally guaranteed tight dynamic future occupancy of the ego vehicle for given trajectories. Our contribution enables a real-time formal methods-based comprehensive collision avoidance framework.

In this paper, we demonstrate a real-time capable motion primitive matching algorithm having negligible deviation, which is so small that we can extend the reachable sets with the maximal bound of the gap (between the reference trajectory and matched trajectory) to preserve both the formal guarantee and drivability. In Sect. 2, we present the problem definition, while in Sect. 4 discusses matching Motion Primitives to a desired trajectory. In Sect. 5, we show examples of motion primitive matching for turns and lane change trajectories. Finally, Sect. 6 concludes the paper.

2   Problem Definition

For formal guarantees of collision avoidance, the reachable set of the ego vehicle and nearby traffic participants must be calculated. For other traffic participants a low cost (computationally speaking) method [4] can be used. However, these methods generally over estimates the reachable set, and if also used for the ego vehicle would result in an overly conservative collision avoidance system. A tight computation of the reachable set for the ego vehicle during vehicle operation is often computationally infeasible. Therefore, a simplification is required. For the ego vehicle, a path planning algorithm has presumably planned the next several seconds of the route. By creating a database of discrete motion primitives with precomputed reachable sets *before vehicle operation*, and matching the motion primitives to the reference trajectory *during vehicle operation*, calculation of the ego vehicle reachable set is greatly simplified. The critical task is then to have

- An extensive database of motion primitives that can cover many different driving scenarios.
- A motion primitive matching algorithm that can match the motion primitives in the database to the reference trajectory in real-time.

The tight reachable sets of the matched motion primitives are then used to check for possible collisions.

2.1   Vehicle Model

We use a four state bicycle model [11] for the vehicle dynamics to create the motion primitive database, as shown below.

$$\dot{x} = v\cos(\theta),$$
$$\dot{y} = v\sin(\theta),$$
$$\dot{\theta} = \frac{v}{L_H}\delta, \tag{1}$$
$$\dot{v} = \alpha,$$

where x and y are the positions of the vehicle in an inertial reference frame, θ is the heading angle of the vehicle w.r.t. the inertial reference frame, and v is the absolute velocity of the vehicle, α is the longitudinal acceleration of the vehicle, L_H is the wheelbase of the vehicle, and δ is the steering angle of the vehicle. This simple model allows for computation of optimal motion primitives [12].

3 Motion Primitives

The motion primitive database was generated using the algorithm from [12]. The initial size of the bounds on disturbances, actuators, and sensor noise are given in Table 1. The algorithm first attempts to calculate a motion primitive that can reach the end point of the reference trajectory in the presence of the noise and disturbances, given the actuator constraints. If no such controller is found, the algorithm systematically reduces the size of the bounds on disturbances and noise iteratively until either a controller that can achieve the motion primitive is found or the bounds are decreased beyond a threshold. Table 2 shows the properties of the motion primitive database.

Table 1. Initial bounds on disturbances, noise, and actuators.

State/Input	Bounds
x	$[-0.2, 0.2]$ m
y	$[-0.2, 0.2]$ m
θ	$[-0.02, 0.02]$ rad
v	$[-0.2, 0.2]$ m/s
α_d	$[-2, 2]$ m/s^2
δ_d	$[-0.08, 0.08]$ rad

Table 2. Properties of the motion primitive database.

Parameter	Value
Motion primitive length	0.2 s
Velocity range	$[1.0, 15.0]$ m/s
Velocity discretization	0.25 m/s
Acceleration range	$[-3.0, 3.0]$ m/s^2
Acceleration discretization	0.2 m/s^2
Curvature range	$[0, 0.08]$ m^{-1}
Curvature discretization	0.001 m^{-1}
Maximum lateral acceleration	0.185 g

The primary advantage of using motion primitives to replace the reference trajectory is that the tight reachable set of the motion primitives is precomputed and stored. This enables a tight calculation of the reachable set of the AV during vehicle operation in a computationally efficient manner. To replace the reference trajectory, a matching algorithm selects motion primitives from its database that closely resemble the reference trajectory. If the matched motion primitives closely follow the reference trajectory, the followed trajectory can be formally guaranteed to be safe, whilst not deviating significantly from the reference trajectory.

4   Motion Primitive Matching

In this section, we present an algorithm developed for the purpose of motion primitive matching. This task involves selecting from a database of motion primitives for entries that when stitched together can closely approximate a reference trajectory. The algorithm searches the database for entries that have closest acceleration and curvature to the average acceleration and curvature of the section of the reference trajectory. The algorithm is described in Algorithm 1.

Algorithm 1: Algorithm to match motion primitives to planned trajectory $x_{\text{traj}}([0, T])$

$\texttt{MatchMotionPrimitive}(x_{traj}([0, T]), L, T_s, database)$

1 $v_0 \leftarrow v_{\text{traj}}(0),\ \theta_0 \leftarrow \theta_{\text{traj}}(0),\ \alpha_c \leftarrow 0,\ \kappa_c \leftarrow 0$
2 $N_{\text{seg}} \leftarrow \lceil \frac{T}{L} \rceil$
   for $k \leftarrow 1, N_{seg}$ **do**
3      $v_{\text{f}} \leftarrow v_{\text{traj}}(k \times L)$
4      $\alpha_{\text{s}} \leftarrow \text{CalcSegmentAcceleration}(v_0, v_{\text{f}}, L)$
5      $\alpha_{\text{m}} \leftarrow \text{CalcMatchedAcceleration}(\alpha_{\text{s}}, \alpha_{\text{c}}, database)$
6      $\alpha_{\text{c}} \leftarrow \alpha_{\text{s}} - \alpha_{\text{m}}$
7      $\theta_{\text{f}} \leftarrow \theta_{\text{traj}}(k \times L)$
8      $d_{\text{seg}} \leftarrow \text{CalcSegmentDistance}(x_{\text{seg}}, y_{\text{seg}})$
9      $\kappa_{\text{s}} \leftarrow \text{CalcSegmentCurvature}(\theta_0, \theta_{\text{f}}, d_{\text{seg}})$
10     $\kappa_{\text{m}} \leftarrow \text{CalcMatchedCurvature}(\kappa_{\text{s}}, \kappa_{\text{c}}, database)$
11     $\kappa_{\text{c}} \leftarrow \kappa_{\text{s}} - \kappa_{\text{m}}$
12     $x_{\text{m}}(k) \leftarrow \text{CreateTrajectorySegment}(v_0, \alpha_{\text{m}}, \kappa_{\text{m}}, T_{\text{s}})$
13     $v_0 \leftarrow v_{\text{f}},\ \theta_0 \leftarrow \theta_{\text{f}}$
   end
   return x_{m}

The segment acceleration is calculated as follows.

$$\alpha_{\text{s}} = \frac{v_{\text{f}} - v_0}{L}, \tag{2}$$

where v_0 is the velocity at the start of the trajectory, v_f is the velocity at the end of the section, and L is the time duration of the section. In this paper, we use $L = 0.2\,s$. Next, the algorithm searches the database that has the closest value of α as α_s. The difference in the matched acceleration α_m and the segment acceleration α_s is used as a correction in the next step, to prevent incremental drift in the case of mismatched motion primitives.

$$\alpha_m = \alpha_c + \arg\min_{\alpha_d}|\alpha_s - \alpha_d(v_0)|, \tag{3}$$

where $\alpha_d(v_0)$ is the discrete set of accelerations in *database* at the initial velocity v_0. The segment curvature is calculated as follows.

$$\kappa_s = \frac{\theta_f - \theta_0}{d_{seg}}, \tag{4}$$

where θ_0 is the orientation at the start of the section, θ_f is the orientation at the end of the trajectory section, and d_{seg} is given by

$$d_{seg} = \sum_{(k-1)\times L}^{k\times L} \sqrt{(x(i) - x(i - 1))^2 + (y(i) - y(i - 1))^2}. \tag{5}$$

Next, the algorithm searches the database that has the closest value of κ as κ_s. The difference in the matched curvature κ_m and the segment curvature κ_s is used as a correction in the next step, to prevent incremental drift in the case of mismatched motion primitives.

$$\kappa_m = \kappa_c + \arg\min_{\kappa_d}|\kappa_s - \kappa_d(\alpha_m, v_0)|, \tag{6}$$

where $\kappa_d(\alpha_m, v_0)$ is the discrete set of curvatures in *database* at the matched acceleration α_m and initial velocity v_0.

5   Examples

In this section, we show 3 examples of motion primitive matching using the proposed algorithm. In all examples, the algorithm was run using MATLAB R2020a on a system with an Intel i7-6820HQ 2.7 GHz processor and 32 GB of DDR3 1600 MHz memory. In the first example, the AV is making a right turn at 18 mph and with a turn radius of 20 m. Figure 3 shows the reference trajectory and the trajectory of the matched motion primitives. Figure 4 shows the curvature of the reference trajectory and the matched motion primitives. The figures show matching performance with both motion primitives of length 0.2 s and 1 s. The matched trajectory more closely matches the reference trajectory when shorter motion primitives are used to approximate the reference trajectory. In this example, the algorithm took 29 ms to match the trajectory when using 0.2 s motion primitives and 25 ms when using 1 s motion primitives.

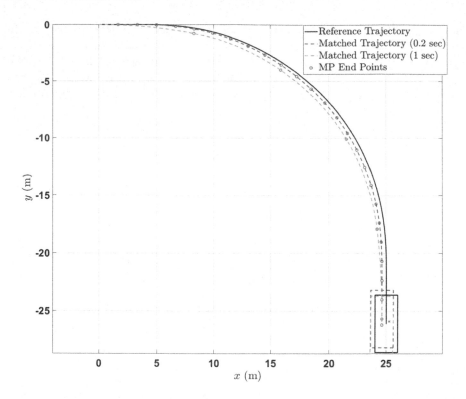

Fig. 3. Reference trajectory and the trajectory of the matched motion primitives

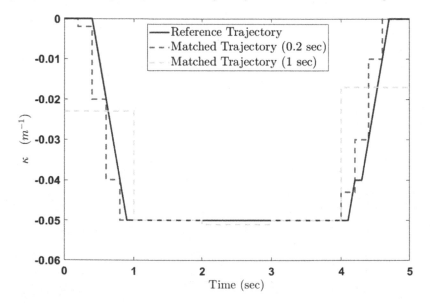

Fig. 4. Curvature of the reference trajectory and the trajectory of the matched motion primitives

In the next example, the AV is making a right lane change at 30 mph. Figure 5 shows the reference trajectory and the trajectory of the matched motion primitives. Figure 6 shows the curvature of the reference trajectory and the matched motion primitives. Figure 7 shows the acceleration of the reference trajectory and the matched motion primitives. The figures show matching performance with both motion primitives of length 0.2 s and 1 s. The matched trajectory more closely matches the reference trajectory when shorter motion primitives are used to approximate the reference trajectory. In this example, the algorithm took 30 ms to match the trajectory when using both 0.2 s and 1 s motion primitives.

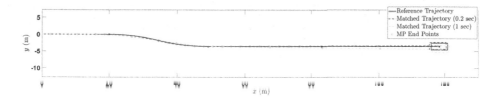

Fig. 5. Reference trajectory and the trajectory of the matched motion primitives

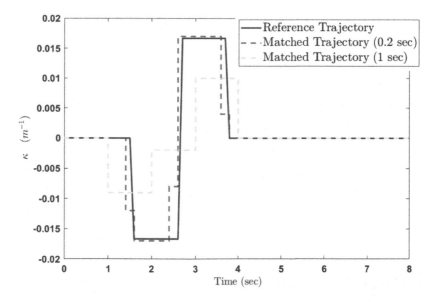

Fig. 6. Curvature of the reference trajectory and the trajectory of the matched motion primitives

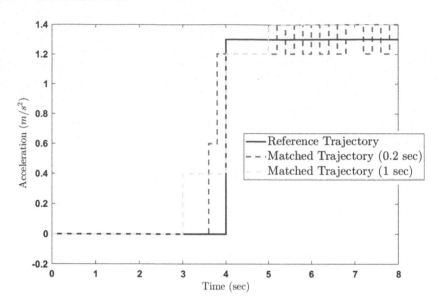

Fig. 7. Acceleration of the reference trajectory and the trajectory of the matched motion primitives

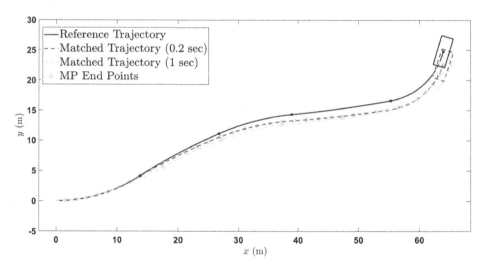

Fig. 8. Reference trajectory and the trajectory of the matched motion primitives

In the next example, the AV is driving on a rural road at 18 mph and alternatively accelerating and decelerating as it approaches curves in the road. Figure 8 shows the reference trajectory and the trajectory of the matched motion primitives. Figure 9 shows the curvature of the reference trajectory and the matched motion primitives. Figure 10 shows the acceleration of the reference trajectory and the matched motion primitives. The figures show matching performance

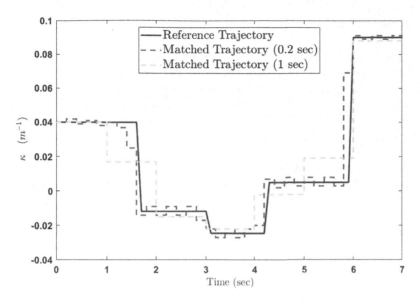

Fig. 9. Curvature of the reference trajectory and the trajectory of the matched motion primitives

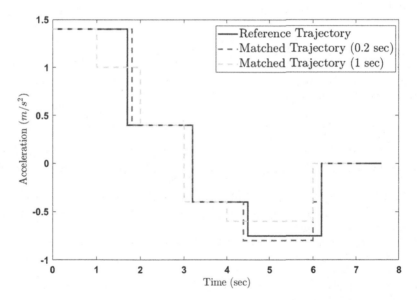

Fig. 10. Acceleration of the reference trajectory and the trajectory of the matched motion primitives

with both motion primitives of length 0.2 s and 1 s. The matched trajectory more closely matches the reference trajectory when shorter motion primitives are used to approximate the reference trajectory. In this example, the algorithm took 29 ms to match the trajectory when using 0.2 s motion primitives and 27 ms when using 1 s motion primitives.

6   Conclusion

In this paper, we presented an efficient method to match motion primitives having precomputed formal reachable sets to achieve reference trajectory tracking for autonomous vehicles and also to calculate ego future occupancy. The primary advantage of using precomputed motion primitives is that tight reachable sets can be used for future occupancy, without expensive computation during vehicle operation. This precomputed small reachable sets and their matching mechanism during vehicle operation may reduce computation time by several magnitudes. However, before this proposed method of this paper, there was no real-time capable formal motion primitive matching algorithm exist to our best knowledge. Our contribution allows us to implement a formal collision avoidance system for the planning modules to guarantee system safety, without being exceedingly conservative. The method presented uses the average curvature and acceleration of segments of the reference trajectory to match motion primitives. The benefit of using a simple approach is the relatively light computational requirements to match motion primitives. The algorithm returns good matching performance, as demonstrated by several examples.

References

1. Althoff, M., Dolan, J.M.: Online verification of automated road vehicles using reachability analysis. IEEE Trans. Rob. **30**(4), 903–918 (2014)
2. Pek, C., Koschi, M., Althoff, M.: An online verification framework for motion planning of self-driving vehicles with safety guarantees. In: AAET - Automatisiertes und vernetztes Fahren (2019)
3. Luckcuck, M., Farrell, M., Dennis, L.A., Dixon, C., Fisher, M.: Formal specification and verification of autonomous robotic systems: a survey. ACM Comput. Surv. (CSUR) **52**(5), 1–41 (2019)
4. Koschi, M., Althoff, M.: SPOT: a tool for set-based prediction of traffic participants. In: 2017 IEEE Intelligent Vehicles Symposium (IV), pp. 1686–1693. IEEE (2017)
5. Hess, D., Althoff, M., Sattel, T.: Formal verification of maneuver automata for parameterized motion primitives. In: Proceedings of the IEEE/RSJ International Conference on Intelligent Robots and Systems (2014)
6. Wang, X., Rettinger, A.K., Waez, M.T.B., Althoff, M.: Coupling apollo with the CommonRoad motion planning framework. In: FISITA World Congress (2020)
7. Pek, C., Rusinov, V., Manzinger, S., Üste, M.C., Althoff, M.: CommonRoad drivability checker: simplifying the development and validation of motion planning algorithms. In: Proceedings of the IEEE Intelligent Vehicles Symposium (2020). https://doi.org/10.1109/IV47402.2020.9304544
8. Koschi, M., Althoff, M.: SPOT: a tool for set-based prediction of traffic participants. In: Proceedings of the IEEE Intelligent Vehicles Symposium (2017). https://doi.org/10.1109/IVS.2017.7995951
9. Magdici, S., Althoff, M.: Fail-safe motion planning of autonomous vehicles. In: Proceedings of the 19th International IEEE Conference on Intelligent Transportation Systems, pp. 452–458 (2016)

10. Pek, C., Althoff, M.: Computationally efficient fail-safe trajectory planning for self-driving vehicles using convex optimization. In: Proceedings of the IEEE International Conference on Intelligent Transportation Systems (2018)
11. Rajamani, R.: Vehicle Dynamics and Control. Springer, Boston (2011). https://doi.org/10.1007/978-1-4614-1433-9
12. Schürmann, B., Althoff, M.: Guaranteeing constraints of disturbed nonlinear systems using set-based optimal control in generator space. IFAC-PapersOnLine **50**(1), 11515–11522 (2017)

Divide et Impera: Efficient Synthesis of Cyber-Physical System Architectures from Formal Contracts

César Augusto R. dos Santos[1,2]([✉]), Tom Schrijvers[2], Amr Hany Saleh[1], and Mike Nicolai[1]

[1] Siemens Digital Industries Software, Leuven, Belgium
[2] KU Leuven, Leuven, Belgium
cesar.augusto@siemens.com

Abstract. Generative Engineering is a new paradigm for the development of cyber-physical systems. Rather than developing a single, increasingly more detailed model of a system, multiple architectural variants are computationally generated and evaluated, which would be prohibitively expensive to do by hand. Existing synthesis approaches are geared towards finding one solution fast, but this makes them less effective for generative engineering where we are interested in enumerating many or all solutions. The common approach in generative engineering is to compute a new verification problem per generated architecture, despite all being variants of the same verification problem. This makes the tools unable to exploit commonalities and they end up doing much of the same verification work over and over again.

Our work addresses this inefficiency in the synthesis of *all* correct-by-construction logical architectures of a system with a simple but effective approach. We create only one parameterized verification problem per use case, and, by exploiting the assumption mechanism of SMT solvers, we can very efficiently and incrementally check each generated architecture.

Our experimental evaluation demonstrates that this approach is orders of magnitude faster than the typical synthesis approach.

Keywords: Generative engineering · Contract-based design · Cyber-physical systems

1 Introduction

Many industrial systems are succumbing under the weight of their own complexity. Innovation is becoming increasingly risky, and architectural innovation in particular has actually decreased over time [11].

Architecture, in the context of this paper, refers to the set of components and the connections between those components that form a particular implementation of the system. The system architecture [12] is defined early in the

© Springer Nature Switzerland AG 2021
M. Huisman et al. (Eds.): FM 2021, LNCS 13047, pp. 776–787, 2021.
https://doi.org/10.1007/978-3-030-90870-6_45

design process, and its formulation is often a manual process with limited feedback. Feedback on the quality of the architecture only arrives later, once detailed models are available.

If the architecture turns out to be suboptimal, or even infeasible, then a redesign is necessary. Not only does the system architecture have to be changed, but also all the models that are derived from it. Such redesign cycles are expensive, so architectures tend to closely follow older designs that were proven to work [11].

To allow for architectural innovation, engineers need methodologies and tools that allow them to efficiently explore many candidate designs early in the design process. Accomplishing this is the goal of the computational design synthesis field (a.k.a. Generative Engineering), where tools like Siemens Simcenter Studio [2] computationally synthesize all correct-by-construction architectures directly from a system model.

One major issue with existing approaches is that they are inefficient when it comes to enumerating all solutions: they translate each architecture to a separate variant of the same verification problem. This leads to a lot of redundant verification work and prevents the exploitation of commonalities. Architectures can be generated extremely efficiently with the right encoding, so we want to minimize as much as possible the cost of verification. The more architectures to explore, the cheaper verification needs to be.

Contributions. The goal of this work is to develop a synthesis methodology, targeted at generative engineering, that enumerates all valid architectures of a system as efficiently as possible. We accomplish this through the following contributions:

1. We introduce a methodology that efficiently synthesizes all correct-by-construction architectures of a system, from formal contracts written in Linear Temporal Logic (LTL) [6] with arithmetic, through the incremental application of a single parametric encoding of the verification problem per use case.
2. We evaluate our methodology on three use cases, and show that it is orders of magnitude faster than the naive synthesis approach.
3. We also evaluate our methodology on a range of solvers, and contrast the efficiency of our approach with the solvers' internal $\exists\forall$ reasoning, and show that our approach is faster as well.

2   Background

Before explaining our methodology, it is important to first understand the typical industrial design process. While the steps may vary between companies, they can be summarized into 4 phases: requirements, functions, logical and physical. To illustrate that process, we use a Redundant Sensor example adapted from OCRA [1].

The first phase of the design process focuses on requirement gathering. We assume that requirements are translated into formal specifications by an expert.

After gathering requirements, the next step is to figure out which functions the system must implement and to map those to the components which form the system implementation. The outcome is a hierarchical *system model*, as depicted in Fig. 1.

In this case the system is divided into two Sensors, which measure the environment; a Selector component, which handles error correction in the presence of failures; and two different types of monitors (a Variance Monitor and a Difference Monitor) which attempt to detect sensor failures based on the temporal variance and absolute difference of the sensor outputs, respectively. All the monitors have a cardinality $[n : m]$ (lower and upper bound on the number of allowed instances) that is variable, because we do not know a priori how many we will need to achieve a functioning system.

Once the system model is defined, we create the *logical architecture* for the system. A logical architecture specifies in an abstract manner the set of components that constitute the system implementation and how they are connected. Figure 2 shows one of the possible logical architectures of the system.

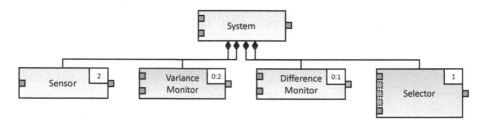

Fig. 1. The system model for the Redundant Sensors use case. The allowed number of instance per component is annotated in their top-right corners. Some ports of the selector have a dotted outline to indicate that they are optional.

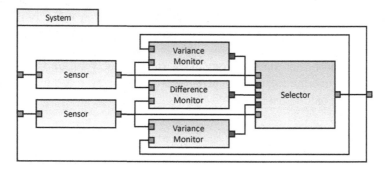

Fig. 2. One possible architecture for the Redundant Sensors use case. We want to know if there are others that also lead to working solutions, particularly with fewer monitors.

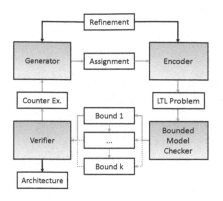 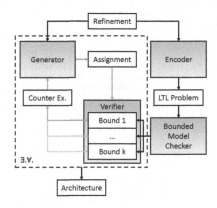

Fig. 3. The usual synthesis pipeline. The purple arrows indicate the synthesis loop per generated architecture. (Color figure online)

Fig. 4. Our synthesis pipeline, note the shorter loop. The generator and verifier can be merged with an ∃∀ encoding.

With the logical architecture in place, the next phase is to create one or more *detailed physical models* of the system, e.g. simulation models. These allow the engineers to evaluate the quality of the architecture and redo the design if it is suboptimal or infeasible.

Our methodology changes the last two steps. Instead of manually developing one or more logical architectures and corresponding models, we synthesize these automatically from the system model. In the next section we explain how this is accomplished.

3   Methodology

Our synthesis methodology is structured around a pipeline, shown in Fig. 4. The basic idea is adapted from Simcenter Studio al. [2] and an extension of previous work [15]. Figure 3 shows the typical synthesis approach for contrast.

Our methodology starts from the system model, which defines which components are available, what their interfaces are, and how many of them may appear in the system. In our methodology, the problem is defined as a set of contracts, one for each component (including the system itself), and a refinement specification that defines the structure of the system model. See Fig. 5 for the contract of the Redundant Sensor example.

Each contract defines the interface of the component and one or more viewpoints, which are independent sets of requirements comprised of the assumptions the component makes about its environment and which guarantees it provides under those assumptions. The refinement specification and the associated contracts are encoded into a generation problem and a verification problem. These two problems are encoded only once per use case, and then enter a loop (marked in purple). The loop works as follows:

```
 1  contract System:
 2    ports:
 3      in::Int[-15:15] reading [2]
 4      in::Bool fail1
 5      in::Bool fail2
 6      out::Int[-15:15] output
 7    viewpoint r_system_error:
 8      assumptions:
 9        !fail1 and !fail2
10        always (abs(reading - next(reading)) <= max_variance)
11        always (!(fail1 and fail2))
12        always ((fail1 or fail2) implies then (!fail1 and !fail2))
13      guarantees:
14        always (abs(reading - next(output)) <= max_sys_error)
15
16  refinement::System system:
17    components:
18      Sensor sensor [2]
19      VarMonitor vm [0:2]
20      DiffMonitor dm [0:1]
21      Selector selector [1]
22
23  contract Sensor:
24    ports:
25      in::Int[-15:15] input
26      in::Bool fail
27      out::Int[-15:15] output [1:2]
28    viewpoint r_nominal:
29      always (!fail implies (abs(input - output) <= max_sensor_error))
30
31  contract VarMonitor:
32    ports:
33      in::Int[-15:15] input
34      in::Int[-15:15] last
35      out::Bool valid
36    viewpoint r_isolate:
37      always (valid == (abs(input - last) <= 2*max_sensor_error + 1))
38
39  contract DiffMonitor:
40    ports:
41      in::Int[-15:15] in1
42      in::Int[-15:15] in2
43      out::Bool valid
44    viewpoint r_isolate:
45      always (valid == (abs(in1 - in2) <= 2*max_sensor_error))
46
47  contract Selector:
48    ports:
49      in::Int[-15:15] sensor1
50      in::Int[-15:15] sensor2
51      in::Bool vm1 [0:1]
52      in::Bool vm2 [0:1]
53      in::Bool dm [0:1]
54      out::Int[-15:15] output [1:3]
55    viewpoint r_select:
56      always (dm implies next(output) = (sensor1 + sensor2) / 2)
57      always ((!dm and !vm1 and vm2) implies next(output) == sensor2)
58      always ((!dm and !vm2 and vm1) implies next(output) == sensor1)
59      always (((!dm and !vm1 and !vm2) or (!dm and vm1 and vm2))
60              implies next(output) == output)
```

Fig. 5. The contracts for the Redundant Sensor use case.

Generation. Is there a set of components (an ensemble) and a set of connections that connects all the ports in that ensemble? If so, create that *architecture* and go to Verification. If not, terminate.

Verification. Does that architecture lead to a counter-example to the contract refinement? If not, save it, add constraints to prevent the architecture from being generated again, and loop back to Generation. If it is a counter-example, discard the architecture, add additional constraints to block all architectures that would lead to the same counter-example, and loop back to Generation.

We use Counter-Example Guided Inductive Synthesis (CEGIS) to guide the search [3]. When the verifier produces a counter-example, we take the bound-unrolled verification formula and replace each attribute and port variable with their respective values in the counter-example. Because the formula is parametric, the only remaining free variables are the boolean component and connection variables. By adding a negation of this formula to the generator, no other assignment to the component and connection variables that would lead to the same assignment of the port and attribute variables (the counter-example) is allowed.

Alternatively, the Generation step and the Verification step can be merged into a single problem using an $\exists \forall$ encoding and an $\exists \forall$ capable solver. This allows requirements to directly guide the search without an external CEGIS loop. In the next section we explain how these two steps are encoded.

4   Encodings

Generation. The goal of Generation is to compute sets of component instances and sets of connections between ports of those instances. The encoding for Generation is shown below:

$$\textbf{for } c \in \mathbb{C}\colon \textbf{assert } \sum_{i=1}^{\lceil c \rceil} c_i \geq \lfloor c \rfloor \tag{1}$$

$$\textbf{for } c \in \mathbb{C}, 1 < i \leq \lceil c \rceil\colon \textbf{assert } c_i \to c_{i-1} \tag{2}$$

$$\textbf{for } c.p \in \mathbb{P}, i \leq \lceil c \rceil\colon \textbf{assert } \lfloor c.p \rfloor \times c_i \leq \sum \mathbb{Q}_{c_i.p} \leq \lceil c.p \rceil \times c_i \tag{3}$$

We use $\mathbb{C}$ to refer to the set of all components in the system, c to refer to a particular component, $\lfloor c \rfloor$ to refer to the lower cardinality of component c, and $\lceil c \rceil$ to refer to the upper cardinality of component c. To refer to a component *instance*, we use c_i, where $i \in \mathbb{N}$. The presence of component instances in the system is modeled as $\lceil c \rceil$ boolean variables for each c. Equation 1 constrains the number of component instances of each component to be within the bounds of its cardinality. Equation 2 enforces an ordering on the component instance variables.

We use $\mathbb{P}$ to refer to the set of all ports in the system, $c.p$ to refer to a particular port, $\lfloor c.p \rfloor$ to refer to the lower cardinality of port $c.p$, and $\lceil c.p \rceil$ to refer to the upper cardinality of port $c.p$. $c_i.p$ refers to the port of a component instance c_i. We use $\mathbb{Q}$ to refer to the set of all possible connections between ports, and $\mathbb{Q}_{c_i.p}$ to the subset of possible connections involving port $c_i.p$. Each possible connection $a_i.x \triangleright b_j.y \in \mathbb{Q}$ is modeled as a boolean variable. A connection is possible if the two ports have opposite directions and the same type.

For each port $c_i.p$, we require that the number of times it connects to other ports is within the cardinality of $c.p$ and we multiply the cardinality by c_i to ensure that the port cannot be connected when the corresponding instance is not present. Symmetry breaking constraints are elided for space reasons.

The output of Generation is an assignment to the instance and connection variables. Each assignment is passed as assumptions to Verification.

Verification. The goal of Verification is to filter out ensembles or architectures that do not follow the system requirements. It is based on the contract refinement check ($\preceq$) of the contract meta-theory of Benveniste et al. [5]. The encoding for Verification is shown below:

$$\textbf{for } a_i.x \triangleright b_j.y \in \mathbb{Q}: \textbf{ assert } a_i.x \triangleright b_j.y \rightarrow a_i.x = b_j.y \qquad (4)$$

$$\textbf{assert } A_s \wedge (\bigwedge_{c \in \mathbb{C} \setminus \{s\}, i \leq \lceil c \rceil} c_i \rightarrow G_{c_i}) \rightarrow G_s \qquad (5)$$

$$\textbf{for } c \in \mathbb{C} \setminus \{s\}, i \leq \lceil c \rceil: \textbf{ assert } A_s \wedge (\bigwedge_{o \in \mathbb{C} \setminus \{s,c\}, j \leq \lceil o \rceil} o_j \rightarrow G_{o_j}) \rightarrow A_{c_i} \qquad (6)$$

We use s to refer to the system instance, A_{c_i} to refer to the assumptions of c projected to instance c_i, and G_{c_i} to refer to the guarantees. Each port instance $c_i.p$ is modeled as a variable of the type defined for port $c.p$.

Equation 4 enforces that if a particular connection is present, the connected ports must have the same values. Equation 5 enforces that the composition of the component instances (according to their presence) alongside the system assumptions implies the system guarantees. Finally, Eq. 6 enforces that for every component instance, its assumptions are implied by the assumptions of the system and the composition of all the other component instances.

Verification needs to hold for all possible states. It can be merged with Generation by encoding the problem in first-order logic, and using an $\exists \forall$ capable solver. This avenue was previously explored in CONDEnSe [15]. We support this merged configuration as well, but we found performance to be suboptimal. Instead, we encode the negation of the refinement constraints, and check for unsatisfiability, i.e. that the solver cannot find a counter-example. We use CEGIS [3] to add additional constraints to the Generation step as we verify each architecture, to prevent the generation architectures that would lead to the same counter-example.

We apply a time bounded, LTL satisfiability check with a user-defined bound k. Constraints are unrolled for all $i \in [1, k]$ *once*. Because the encoding is parametric and accepts the generated architectures as assumptions, we can check all unrollings very efficiently as they are encoded only once but executed many times.

5   Evaluation

Because other synthesis tools work very differently, a direct comparison is difficult, so we focus on evaluating the best way to synthesize with our encoding. We evaluate our work on 3 use cases: The running Redundant Sensors example, an XOR circuit built out of NAND gates, and a 4-bit adder circuit.

We contrast 3 different synthesis approaches: a) using an external verifier; b) using our one-time parametric encoding; and c) using an $\exists\forall$ encoding.

We run approach a) using only our fastest supported SMT solver for architecture generation and fastest supported LTL verifier (nuXmv [7]) configured for bounded model checking. For approaches b) and c) we use 3 different SMT solvers with $\exists\forall$ capabilities: Yices2 [9], Z3 [13] and CVC4 [4].

The following tables show the results for each use case and for each solver. The first row, Yices2+nuXmv, shows the naive approach with an external verifier, generating a new problem each time and without CEGIS. The other rows show our approach (generate and verify, GV) on a variety of solvers, and the variant using $\exists\forall$ reasoning (EF). Unlike Z3 and CVC4, Yices2 exposes its model generalization API, so we can take advantage of this to show how many architectures it explores in the EF case. GV (Yices2+) is a special case which combines our approach with Yices2's model generalization API.

Columns G. Archs and V. Archs are the number of generated and verified architectures, respectively. The total time includes the overhead of extracting the counter-example, processing it, and encoding it back to the generator, which can be substantial due to our Python implementation.

Our tests were executed on a laptop with a 4 core Intel i7-8650U CPU clocked at 2 GHz, 16 GB of RAM, running Ubuntu 20.04. Tests had a 1 h time limit (Tables 1, 2 and 3).

We can see from the results that our approach combined with the model extraction capabilities of Yices2 gives the best results, computing all the solutions to all 3 problems in a few seconds. The EF encodings using Z3 had very poor results, while CVC4 did well in the boolean circuit use-cases but timed-out in the Redundant Sensors use-case.

Table 1. Comparison of different synthesis approaches for the Redundant Sensor use-case.

Approach	G. Archs	V. Archs	G. Time (s)	V. Time (s)	Total (s)
Yices2+nuXmv	13985	48	116.25	2664.55	2797.40
GV (Yices2+)	2977	48	1.73	6.05	**8.59**
GV (Yices2)	2980	48	2.01	8.37	54.94
GV (Z3)	4432	48	17.37	77.49	638.85
GV (CVC4)	3191	48	15.74	542.46	646.68
EF (Yices2)	4580	48	5.40	122.47	132.28
EF (Z3)	0	0	3600.0	–	TIMEOUT
EF (CVC4)	0	0	3600.0	–	TIMEOUT

Table 2. Comparison of different synthesis approaches for a NAND-based XOR circuit

Approach	G. Archs	V. Archs	G. Time (s)	V. Time (s)	Total (s)
Yices2+nuXmv	7705	32	27.09	218.49	250.96
GV (Yices2+)	147	32	0.18	0.07	**0.27**
GV (Yices2)	141	32	0.19	0.10	0.77
GV (Z3)	142	32	0.45	0.69	5.09
GV (CVC4)	172	32	16.46	0.80	18.17
EF (Yices2)	509	32	0.43	0.32	0.87
EF (Z3)	32	32	27.29	–	27.37
EF (CVC4)	32	32	5.19	–	5.20

Table 3. Comparison of different synthesis approaches for a 4bit adder circuit.

Approach	G. Archs	V. Archs	G. Time (s)	V. Time (s)	Total (s)
Yices2+nuXmv	43725	0	1465.91	2132.95	TIMEOUT
GV (Yices2+)	2333	16	5.24	5.27	**11.11**
GV (Yices2)	2280	16	6.66	7.31	51.53
GV (Z3)	1613	16	26.59	25.15	250.51
GV (CVC4)	304	16	274.81	119.31	400.37
EF (Yices2)	3837	16	8.18	13.31	24.14
EF (Z3)	0	0	3600.0	–	TIMEOUT
EF (CVC4)	16	16	59.85	–	59.91

6   Related Work

There are many different methodologies and tools for synthesis, requirement verification and design exploration of hybrid systems and sub-problems thereof.

It would not be feasible to do the entire field justice, so we chose to focus on the closest related works.

Nuzzo et al. The work of Nuzzo et al. [14] was the main inspiration for our work, where the same contract meta-theory is applied to the synthesis of an electric power system (EPS). We follow their idea of splitting the problem into separate viewpoints, but Nuzzo et al. manually encode the generation and verification problems for their use case, while our approach is use-case agnostic.

Simcenter Studio. Simcenter Studio [2] was the inspiration for our Generation encoding. Simcenter Studio focuses on the efficient but separate generation of ensembles and architectures, with the verification and evaluation of the candidates being entirely user-defined. This has the advantage of wide industry applicability. Engineers can specify and evaluate the requirements in the way that is most natural to their domain, but it precludes the requirements from participating in the search, leading to the generation of many spurious candidates.

Contract-Based Synthesis Tools. Requirements in our approach are modeled in the contract meta-theory of Benveniste et al. [5], because it is highly modular and agnostic of the underlying logic of the contracts. There are many tools that support the same Assume/Guarantee style of contracts that we use, and three in particular also support synthesis: CONDEnSe [15], OCRA [8] and PyCo [10].

CONDEnSe was our previous attempt at a contract-based synthesis tool, but it lacked the features that were introduced in this work, namely: LTL support, component-level instantiation, CEGIS, and symmetry breaking.

OCRA is mainly a contract verification tool, and its input language served as one of the inspirations for ours. OCRA's 2.0 release added synthesis support, but it falls on the user to make their model parametric. OCRA does not handle the instantiation of connections itself which means there is no built-in symmetry breaking support and that it is possible to make the problem unbounded.

The PyCo tool of Iannopollo et al. [10] has some similarities to our approach in that it also focuses on synthesis of architectures from a library of components annotated with contracts. It uses very different encodings however, and focuses on finding a single, optimal architecture. As in our naive case, it generates a new verification problem for each candidate solution which it then sends to nuXmv, but with a CEGIS loop. As shown by our results, the cost of running nuXmv on each generated architecture is substantial. The tool also lacks support for arithmetic.

7   Conclusions and Future Work

In this paper we presented a synthesis methodology, targeted at generative engineering, that enumerates all valid architectures of a system as efficiently as possible. To do so, we adapted the general synthesis framework of Simcenter Studio to support contract-based verification, and use it to guide the search.

Our encodings allow us to efficiently verify each generated architecture on a single, unrolled refinement verification problem, leading to substantially better performance than the common synthesis approach. Our solution supports both CEGIS and ∃∀ reasoning to guide the generation of architectures towards valid solutions, and we were surprised to find that the ∃∀ support in existing SMT solvers was suboptimal for synthesis problems of this type, with Yices 2 being a standout exception, beating all other solvers.

There are two main areas of future work for this project: 1) more expressive specification logics, and 2) optimization.

Supporting more expressive logics is possible via various reductions to LTL.

When it comes to optimization, the naive solution is to restrict each new solution to be better in some metric than the last valid solution until no more solutions exist. It is worthwhile exploring if there is a better approach, taking advantage of a solver with direct optimization support. One major challenge is how to handle objectives that require simulation to evaluate (e.g. fuel consumption).

References

1. OCRA examples. https://ocra.fbk.eu/pmwiki.php?n=Main.Examples (2021). Accessed 05 May 2021
2. Simcenter Studio. https://www.plm.automation.siemens.com/global/en/products/simcenter/simcenter-studio.html (2021). Accessed 03 Sept 2021
3. Abate, A., David, C., Kesseli, P., Kroening, D., Polgreen, E.: Counterexample guided inductive synthesis modulo theories. In: Chockler, H., Weissenbacher, G. (eds.) CAV 2018. LNCS, vol. 10981, pp. 270–288. Springer, Cham (2018). https://doi.org/10.1007/978-3-319-96145-3_15
4. Barrett, C., et al.: CVC4. In: Gopalakrishnan, G., Qadeer, S. (eds.) CAV 2011. LNCS, vol. 6806, pp. 171–177. Springer, Heidelberg (2011). https://doi.org/10.1007/978-3-642-22110-1_14
5. Benveniste, A., et al.: Contracts for system design (2018)
6. Biere, A., Biere, A., Heule, M., van Maaren, H., Walsh, T.: Handbook of Satisfiability, vol. 185, Frontiers in Artificial Intelligence and Applications (2009)
7. Cavada, R., et al.: The nuXmv symbolic model checker. In: CAV, pp. 334–342 (2014)
8. Cimatti, A., Dorigatti, M., Tonetta, S.: OCRA: a tool for checking the refinement of temporal contracts. In: Proceedings of the 28th IEEE/ACM International Conference on Automated Software Engineering, ASE 2013, pp. 702–705 (2013)
9. Dutertre, B.: Yices 2.2. In: Biere, A., Bloem, R. (eds.) CAV 2014. LNCS, vol. 8559, pp. 737–744. Springer, Cham (2014). https://doi.org/10.1007/978-3-319-08867-9_49
10. Iannopollo, A., Tripakis, S., Sangiovanni-Vincentelli, A.L.: Constrained synthesis from component libraries. In: FACS (2016)
11. Kellari, D., Crawley, E.F., Cameron, B.G.: Architectural decisions in commercial aircraft from the DC-3 to the 787. J. Aircr. 55(2), 792–804 (2018)
12. Micouin, P.: Model-Based Systems Engineering: Fundamentals and Methods. Control, Systems and Industrial Engineering Series, Wiley, Hoboken (2014)

13. de Moura, L., Bjørner, N.: Z3: an efficient SMT solver. In: Ramakrishnan, C.R., Rehof, J. (eds.) TACAS 2008. LNCS, vol. 4963, pp. 337–340. Springer, Heidelberg (2008). https://doi.org/10.1007/978-3-540-78800-3_24

14. Nuzzo, P., et al.: A contract-based methodology for aircraft electric power system design. IEEE Access **2**, 1–25 (2014)

15. Ribeiro dos Santos, C.A., Hany Saleh, A., Schrijvers, T., Nicolai, M.: CONDEnSe: contract based design synthesis. In: 2019 ACM/IEEE 22nd International Conference on Model Driven Engineering Languages and Systems (MODELS), pp. 250–260 (2019)

Apply Formal Methods in Certifying the SyberX High-Assurance Kernel

Wenjing Xu[1], Yongwang Zhao[2](✉), Chengtao Cao[1],
Jean Raphael Ngnie Sighom[3], Lei Wang[1], Zhe Jiang[4], and Shihong Zou[4,5]

[1] School of Computer Science and Engineering, Beihang University, Beijing, China
[2] School of Cyber Science and Technology, College of Computer Science and
Technology, Zhejiang University, Hangzhou, China
`zhaoyw@zju.edu.cn`
[3] Zhejiang Wonsec Technology Co., Ltd., Hangzhou, China
[4] Yuanxin Information Technology Group Co., Ltd., Beijing, China
[5] Beijing University of Posts and Telecommunications, Beijing, China

Abstract. SyberX is an operating system microkernel used for safety
and security-critical applications, such as avionics and unmanned vehicles. In this paper, we present an effective approach to apply formal
methods in the development and security evaluation high-assurance level
of the SyberX based on Common Criteria (CC) methodology. To achieve
the evaluation under the CC at evaluation assurance level 5 augmented
(EAL5+), where "+" is applying formal methods compliant to the
highest evaluation assurance level, several partners from industry and
academia have contributed to this effort. Our work provides a standardized formal specification, security analysis as well as formal verification
proofs of the SyberX system. All results have been formalized in the
Isabelle/HOL theorem prover. During the verification and code review,
we find a total of 5 bugs, all confirmed and fixed by developers.

Keywords: Formal methods · High-assurance · SyberX · Common
criteria · Isabelle/HOL

1 Introduction

Software evaluation is commonly seen as a powerful method for ensuring high
software quality and reliability particularly when it is applied in security-critical
domains. Traditional methods of simulation and testing are not sufficient enough
to ensure the correctness of a system. This leads to the use of formal methods,
which are mathematically based techniques for specification, development and
verification of systems, both hardware and software. Formal methods can help
to eliminate errors early in the design process, ensures the correctness and provides sufficient evidence. The Common Criteria (CC) are a widely recognized international standard for computer security. There are seven Evaluation Assurance

This work has been supported in part by the National Natural Science Foundation of
China (NSFC) under the Grant No.61872016 and supported by the Academic Excellence Foundation of BUAA for PhD Students.

M. Huisman et al. (Eds.): FM 2021, LNCS 13047, pp. 788–798, 2021.
https://doi.org/10.1007/978-3-030-90870-6_46

Levels (EALs) defined in Common Criteria from EAL1 to EAL7, where EAL7 is the highest evaluation assurance level. EALs are a measure of assurance quality. For the high-level evaluations (5 to 7), it requires some degree of formalism in development to demonstrate that the appropriate level of assurance has been met. The CC certificate needs to use formal methods to build the different specifications of the product, starting from its security requirements down to its implementation.

An increasingly important trend in the design of real-time and embedded systems is the integration of components with different levels of criticality onto a common hardware platform. A mixed-criticality system (MCS) is one that has two or more distinct levels (for example safety-critical, mission-critical and non-critical). At the same time, these platforms are migrating from single cores to multi-cores and, in the future, many-core architectures [1]. This type of many-core MCS is the focal interest of the SyberX project[1]. It is designed to balance the conflicting requirements of security isolation, safety and efficient resource sharing.

Operating system (OS) kernels and hypervisors form the backbone of safety-critical software systems. Hence, it is highly desirable to verify the correctness of these programs formally [10]. Previous research efforts have shown that it is feasible to formally prove the functional correctness of OS kernels [3,5–7,11,12].

In this paper, we discuss the experiences of applying formal methods with regard to CC's highest evaluation assurance level. We present an extensible architecture for building the highest security assurance of any commercial microkernel operating system. We also present a realistic case study of the SyberX kernel to illustrate the application of our methodology. This work is developed and verified in Isabelle/HOL[2]. The main goal of our work is to elucidate the evaluation of SyberX under CC evaluation assurance level 5 augmented with security policy modeling.

Because our work adopted formal methods, the implementation must comply with the CC requirements. Since the CC standard has emphasized the use formal method especially for evaluation assurance level 6 and above. Therefore, the development of the security policy model, functional specification, and design specification require a large set of formal proof as well as mapping correspondence among them (see Fig. 2). Basically, once the CC certificate expires, the product has to undergo through an evaluation maintenance. Thus, the formal model shall be suitable and well adapted in case any changes are required. The security policy model in this paper represents the security policies of SyberX and it is a formal model (see Sect. 4.2), a parameterized model that can be reusable with strong support for extensibility. Functional specification is corresponding to the functional specifications formally described using Isabelle/HOL. The security properties demonstrated on the security policy model are formally preserved down to the functional specification by the model instantiation and instantiation proofs. The functional specification of SyberX can be refined to a design specification using stepwise refinement. The refinement process formally proves a correlation between the representations of the functional specification and the design specification. Certainly, code-to-spec review can be reflected among the formal model of the design specification and the concrete implementation to show the correspondence.

---

[1] http://www.syberos.com/.

[2] The sources are available at https://lvpgroup.github.io/SyberX/.

This paper is organized as follows: the preliminaries of this paper are described in Sect. 2. Section 3 presents an overview of our methodology. In Sect. 4, we present a realistic case study of the SyberX kernel to illustrate the application of our methodology. Finally, lessons learned and conclusions are summarized in Sect. 5.

2   SyberX

SyberX is a microkernel operating system that supports different types of virtual machines (VM) such as bare-metal applications, Linux, robot operating system (ROS), etc. It is mainly used in mixed-criticality systems, which allows applications of different criticality levels, such as real-time control, intelligence computing, etc., to coexist and interact on the same hardware platform. SyberX's kernel contains only about 3,500 lines of C code. This minimizes the trusted computing base and has enabled us to verify SyberX's functional correctness and security properties using formal methods.

SyberX mainly has the following features: strictly isolate and allocate resources, resources are statically partitioned and assigned at instantiation time; provide a scheduling mechanism compatible with real-time and non-real-time VMs; provide a communication mechanism between VMs to achieve secure inter-VM communication; supervise configured security attributes to detect and intercept illegal operations.

The architecture of SyberX is shown in Fig. 1.

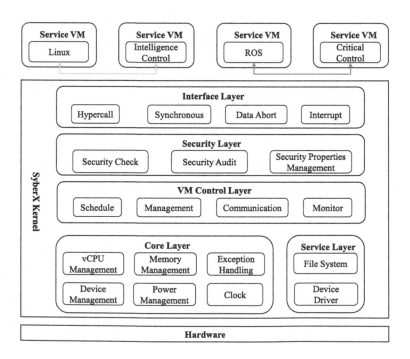

Fig. 1. Architecture of SyberX

The core layer provides resource abstraction and management functions, including virtual CPU management, memory management, exception handling, and clock functions. The control layer mainly provides scheduling, communication and other functions to the upper virtual machine. It includes functions such as scheduling, management, communication and monitoring. The security layer is mainly responsible for security functions. The application interface layer mainly provides the interactive interface between VM and SyberX.

SyberX's idea of resource access control is mainly embodied in the control of VM memory, port communication between VMs, interrupts, and CPU core access. SyberX uses a static memory allocation strategy to restrain each VM's access to memory. SyberX statically configures the communication ports between VMs and specifies that only VMs with valid ports in the configuration can use communication interfaces between VMs to interact at runtime. In terms of security management, SyberX deserves privileged VMs to modify configuration information. When other ordinary VMs try to modify file or memory space where the virtual machine's security attribute configuration is located through a hypercall, the system will reject the request.

3 Methodology in Isabelle/HOL

We present a formal specification framework for a high-assurance microkernel. This framework is based on the Common Criteria's methodology [4] that requires formal methods to prove that a product implements the claimed security level. The framework is shown in Fig. 2. Those specifications are development and security analysis based on stepwise refinement with respect to the EAL7 of CC certification.

The security properties formalize the security objectives in CC and are represented as information-flow security properties, e.g. *noninterference, nonleakage* and *noninfluence*. The security policy model (SPM) formalizes the security functional requirements of a microkernel. The functional specification (FSP) is the formal specification of security functions in this work. The Target of Evaluation design specification (TDS) is the design specification of concrete microkernel implementations. Finally, the implementation representation in CC is the C source code of the microkernel. We apply three refinement approaches in this work to show the correspondence among specifications, i.e. model instantiation, step-wise refinement, and informal code-to-spec review.

3.1 Specifications

This specification consists of three parts: security policy model, functional specification, Target of Evaluation (TOE) design specification.

The proposed security policy model is a generic model for information security, including a state machine-based execution model and the security configuration. It is a parameterized security model with security policies of microkernels, which means the kernel components are defined as abstract types. Unwinding specifications is a common proof strategy for reducing such specifications to a set of conditions that must hold for specific actions. It provides a basis for

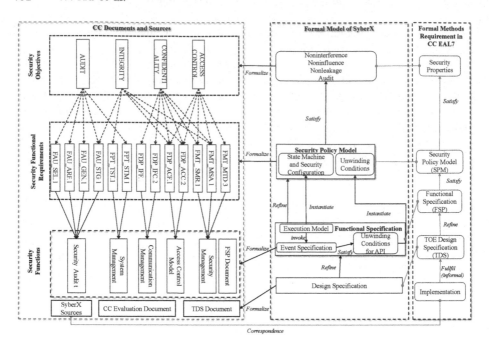

Fig. 2. Framework

practical methods for verifying systems that have noninterference policies [9]. In general, we provide unwinding conditions and prove a theory of intransitive noninterference policies. In the mechanized implementation, we develop a formal specification for the security policy model in Isabelle/HOL. It is created by *locales*. Locales are Isabelle's approach for dealing with parametric theories. Locales may be instantiated by assigning concrete data to parameters, and the resulting instantiated declarations are added to the current context. This is called locale interpretation.

The functional specification defined a high-level informal description of the microkernel external interface and the behavior of system security functions. It describes a safety function using logical predicates to relate its pre-condition and its post-condition. See Sect. 4.2 for more details.

In CC standard, the TOE design specification of the system is described in terms of sub-systems and modules. This is another important part of the requirements of a microkernel that is modeled in this work. We use State Monad [2], which is an abstraction that allows structuring programs generically and a state monad supports a purely functional model of computation with side effects, constructors to formally model functionalities related to all TOE security functions interfaces. The design specification refines functional specifications for the security function and contains more explicit detailed descriptions than functional specifications. In our method, the design specification describes the specification of the security function according to the design document and actual code implementation; compare to functional specification which is just an abstract implementation of the behavior of the system and formalized using a nondeterministic state monad.

3.2 Verification

To ensure the representation correspondence between models, we describe the refinement process corresponding to model development (Fig. 2), and also present the security proofs of the refinement.

Model Instantiation. The abstract specification of security policy model is instantiated by functional specification, and the instantiation is an interpretation of the security policy model (see Sect. 4.3). In particular, the parameters of security policy model are substituted with specific parameters. After instantiation proof, we prove the concrete unwinding conditions for each functional specification. Then we conclude the satisfaction of the noninfluence property on the functional specification. Thus, the functional specification satisfies security properties.

Refinement. To prove refinement between an abstract and a concrete specification, we use a hoare triple of State Monad, which denoted $\{P\}\ a\ \{Q\}$ on a monadic operator a, pre-condition P and post-condition Q. The pre-condition P is a function of type $s \Rightarrow bool$ and the post-condition Q is a function of type $r \Rightarrow s \Rightarrow bool$. Their meaning is defined as follows: $\{P\}\ f\ \{Q\} \equiv \forall s.\ P\ s \longrightarrow (\forall (r,s') \in \text{fst}\ (f\ s).\ Q\ r\ s')$. Then, let ω_a denote the abstract specification, let ω_c represent the design specification and we define the map α from concrete to abstract state variables as a map $\alpha : S_c \rightarrow S_a$ from concrete to abstract states. The possible result state of the execution of a specification ω in state s is denoted as $\mathcal{E}_{(\omega, s)}$. We use function $\mathfrak{R}$ to extract the return value from a abstract state. In general, such property of refinement can be expressed in the following form:

lemma *FSP-to-TDS-refinement*: $\bigwedge s'.\ \{\lambda s.\ s' = \alpha_s\}\ \omega_c\ \{\lambda r\ s.\ \alpha_s = \mathcal{E}_{(\omega_a, s')} \wedge \mathfrak{R}_{\omega_a} = r\ \}$

This lemma establishes equivalence between functional specification and a subset of the behavior modeled in a design specification. It means functional specification is refined by design specification if with the same initial state and input actions, execution of design specification yields a subset of the external states yielded by executing functional specification. After completing all refinement proofs, we have the design specification is a refinement of the functional specification.

From model instantiation and refinement proof, we can conclude if the design specification is a refinement of the functional specification and whether the design specification satisfies the security properties.

4 Application to the SyberX Kernel

4.1 Security Target

The security target is the security specification of the product. It is the main document of a CC evaluation used as a reference for the claimed security. The main goal of this document is to describe the efforts done by the developer to protect the assets of the product. Security target contains a set of security objectives, security functional requirements, and security functions. As shown in Fig. 2, it claimed 4 security objectives: *access_control*, *confidentiality*, *integrity* and *audit*. Security functional requirements define the security behavior of the SyberX and are necessary to meet the security objectives. We selected suitable security functional requirements from CC Part 2 for SyberX combined with the threats with regards to the risk analysis. The security functions of SyberX are implementation of security functional requirements.

4.2   Formalizing Specification

Security Policy Model. In this respect, we use noninterference [9] from our previous work [12] and extend its infrastructure to support a formal theorem foundation for security policy model about information flow security of SyberX Kernel. The information-flow security of our framework uses a state machine to represent the system model. The state machine is defined as follows: A state machine, $M = \langle S, A, s0, step \rangle$ is a tuple, where S is a set of states, A is a set of actions, $step$ is the state-transition function and $s0$ is the initial state. The $step(s, a)$ is denoted as $\varphi_{(s,a)}$ that means the system state transits from s to s' after executing action a. Domains ($\mathcal{D}$) represent the protection components in a system, i.e. processes or partitions, and actions are invoked by a set of domains. We use $u \rightsquigarrow v$ to denote a domain u can interfere with v if information is allowed to flow from u to v, which means that v can observe the effects of u's action. The equivalence relation $\sim$ on states defined by *vpep* and $s \sim d \sim t$ means that states s and t are identical for domain d, which is to say states s and t are indistinguishable for domain d. We use Φ to represent audit information of system and an audit policy is defined by a function $audit(a)$. The reachability of a state s is marked as $reachable(s)$ (denoted as $\mathcal{R}(s)$). Based on the above definitions, we define security model $SM = \langle M; \mathcal{D}; domain; interferes; vpeq; audit; access\_control; \Phi \rangle$, with assumptions as follows: 1) $\forall s\ t\ r\ d.\ s{\sim}d{\sim}t \wedge t{\sim}d{\sim}r \longrightarrow s{\sim}d{\sim}r$; 2) $\forall s\ d.\ s \sim d \sim s$; 3) $\forall s\ t\ d.\ s \sim d \sim t \longrightarrow t \sim d \sim s$; 4) $\forall d.\ d \rightsquigarrow d$; 5) $\forall s\ a.\ \mathcal{R}(s) \longrightarrow (\exists\ s'.\ s' = \varphi_{(s,a)})$; 6)$\forall s\ a\ t\ .\ audit(a) \wedge t = \varphi_{(s,a)} \longrightarrow (\exists\ a'.\ a' = \Phi_{(t,a)})$.

Functional Specification. As demonstrated in Fig. 2, the system consists of several functional modules: access control, communication management, security management, audit, and system management. The abstract level describes what the system does without saying how it is done, it simply specifies the functional behavior that is expected from the system. We design formal functional specifications based on semi-formal functional descriptions and we formally describe the functional specifications of all interfaces (15 interfaces) for SyberX kernel. For example, one security function of virtual machine management that getting the virtual machine's id by name is shown as follows. The semi-formal functional specification is illustrated in the left part, which is defined in the CC document of functional specification. The right part shows the formal specification in Isabelle/HOL of this function.

```
procedure shyper vm getvmid
  (vmname    : in String,
  RETURN_CODE: out RETURN_CODE_TYPE)
  is
error
  when (vmname does not identify an
  existing) =>
  RETURN_CODE := INVALID_PARAM;
normal
  RETURN_CODE := NO_ERROR;
end shyper vm getvmid;
```

definition *getvmid* :: *state* ⇒ *vm-name* ⇒ *state*
× *vm-id option* **where** *getvmid s name* ≡ *let*
nl=List.map (λ*x*.(*name x*)) (*vm s*);
idx = *find-index* (λ*x*.(*x=name*)) *nl*;
a = (|*res*=*T-VM*,*sub=idx*,*event=hvc*,*flag=True*|)
in if idx <(*length nl*) *then*
    (*audit-event s a, Some idx*)
  else
    (*audit-event s* (*a*(|*flag*:=*False*|)),*None*)

Design Specification. In our model, the design specification (TDS) describes the computational behavior of SyberX, refining the specification of the system functions in terms of algorithms. SyberX subsystem modules include memory, interrupt, communication, security management, etc., as detailed in design specification document. The number of design function definitions is as follows.

Modules	# of definition	Modules	# of definition	Modules	# of definition
Memory	14	CPU	6	VCPU	6
VM	33	Interrupt	13	Communication	6
Hypercall	10	Security	14	Schedule	1

For instance, consider the function *interrupt_vm_register* for VM interrupt register. The design level of description is that this function calls *interrupt_arch_conflict* to determine that the interrupt has been registered and then set the interrupt status and return value. We write its specification through the document of the design specification. Then, we conduct a precise and complete code-to-spec review required by CC certification. The formal design specification and C code are shown as follows.

```
bool interrupt_vm_register(struct vm *
    vm, u64 id) {
    ...
    if (interrupt_arch_conflict(
    interrupt_glb_bitmap, id)) {
    WARNING(...);
    return false;
    }

    interrupt_arch_vm_register(vm,id);
    bitmap_set(vm->int_bitmap, id);
    bitmap_set(interrupt_glb_bitmap,id);

    return true;
}
```

definition *interrupt-vm-register*:: *State* ⇒ *vm*
⇒ *u64* ⇒ (*State, bool*) *nondet-monad*
where *interrupt-vm-register s vm′ id* ≡
  let b = *Interrupt-glb-bitmap* (*read-glb-int s*)

in if interrupt-arch-conflict b id then
    return False
  else do
      interrupt-arch-vm-register s vm′ id;
    bitmap-set s (*int-bitmap vm′*) *id*;
    bitmap-set s b id;
    return True
  od

4.3 Verification

Since the execution model of SyberX is an instance of the security policy model, the first part of the security proof is the instantiation proof. To assure the correctness of the instantiation, the assumptions (1)–(6) of the security model have been proven on the specification. The parameters are substituted with specific parameters of SyberX, such as the state transition function φ is instantiated as the *exec-event* function, and the interference relation in the security model is instantiated as function *interference*, which is determined by the static configuration of system. The interpretation of instantiating the SM locale is as follows.

interpretation *SM s0 exec-event domain interference vpeq audit access_control* Φ.

Then, we display the unwinding conditions on events (UCE), i.e. satisfaction of local respect and step consistency. We defined a set of concrete conditions for events. The satisfaction of the concrete conditions of one event implies that the event satisfies the UCEs. After proving concrete unwinding conditions of each event, we inductively prove the unwinding conditions of the execution model of SyberX Kernel. Furthermore, we conclude the satisfaction of the security property on the functional specification.

To prove SyberX's design specification is a refinement of functional specification based on Sect. 3.2, we require to write an equivalence function to establish the correspondence between the design-level data structures and the abstract-level states. We provide the refinement process described in the previous sections formally proves that the security functions are correctly implemented by design specification. It includes some lemmas that are a concrete instance of lemma **FSP**-to-**TDS**-refinement.

4.4 Results

The work is carried out by a total effort of roughly 10 person-months (PM), we use 3,426 lines of code (LOC) to develop formal specifications and 244 lemmas/theorems are proven in Isabelle/HOL using 4,100 lines of proof (LOP) to ensure the security. The statistics for the effort and size of the specification and proofs are shown as follows.

Item	Specification		Proof		PM
	# of type/definition	LOC	# of lemma/theorem	LOP	
Security Model	25	130	92	900	2
FSP	183	1163	64	≈ 2200	4
TDS	135	2056	68	≈ 1000	4
Total	343	3426	224	≈ 4100	10

These formal specifications do not capture the full functional correctness of SyberX, but provide an effective approach to rapidly explore potential interface designs and expose subtle bugs in complex system implementations. During the verification and code review, we found in total five critical bugs, all have been confirmed and fixed by the developers. Those bugs are described as follow: 1) there was an index boundary issue when allocating heap space; 2) During the VM startup process, the byte length allocated to the CPU's initialization was incorrect; 3) The context was incorrect when the VM's startup activity on the CPU was completed; 4) the VM communication sender and receiver were out of range; 5) A null pointer appeared in the virtual CPU pool management function.

5   Discussion and Conclusion

Discussion. Our efforts to verify SyberX were guided by two motives. First, we hope to continue to works toward the long-sought goal of a safe and reliable SyberX kernel. For the reasons given above, formal methods are used to model and verify crucial properties, with a focus on the functional level. Second, we expect to find the best design and verification methodologies and provide sufficient evidence for the certification of SyberX that can be used to build a provably reliable and secure system. However, the application of CC evaluation requirements in a practice industrial setting is challenging because there are some challenges to deal with: how to ensure the correspondence between an informal description of security target and formal model; how to represent the concept of refinement between two formal models. In this paper, we have described an application of formal methods based on the CC methodology that has seen increasing attention from different industrial practitioners to address the challenge of security evaluation of SyberX. We hope that our work encourages researchers and industrial practitioners to choose integrating formal methods in certifying the high-assurance evaluation process and motivates more research on certification practice using formal methods for the complete chain of a CC evaluation.

Related Work. Noninterference has been used in a range of formally verified security properties that constrain information flows in a system [9]. It is used to formally specify and verify confidentiality and integrity properties of a wide variety of systems, such as OS kernels ([3,6,11]). We extend our previous work [12] to support a formal model for security policy model about information flow security. Moreover, we have been studied previous formal efforts about separation kernels, including the verification of seL4 [8] and PikeOS [11], to help us find an appropriate methodology to verify SyberX.

Conclusion. We presented a practical approach to the development of formal models for SyberX kernels based on Common Criteria. We applied our methodology to all security-relevant parts of the SyberX kernel and provided formal proof for the correspondence between security policy model, functional specification, and design specification. During the verification and code review, five bugs have been found. In future work, we intend to extend the implementation specifications of SyberX. Moreover, we hope to study a method to achieve automatic verification of the refinement of design specification and source code.

References

1. Burns, A., Davis, R.: Mixed criticality systems-a review. Dept. Comput. Sci. Univ. York Tech. Rep. 1–69 (2013)
2. Cock, D., Klein, G., Sewell, T.: Secure microkernels, state monads and scalable refinement. In: Mohamed, O.A., Muñoz, C., Tahar, S. (eds.) TPHOLs 2008. LNCS, vol. 5170, pp. 167–182. Springer, Heidelberg (2008). https://doi.org/10.1007/978-3-540-71067-7_16
3. Gu, R., et al.: Certikos: an extensible architecture for building certified concurrent *os* kernels. In: 12th *USENIX* Symposium on Operating Systems Design and Implementation (*OSDI*), pp. 653–669 (2016)
4. Herrmann, D.S.: Using the Common Criteria for IT Security Evaluation. Auerbach Publications, Boston (2002)
5. Klein, G.: Operating system verification an overview. Sadhana **34**(1), 27–69 (2009)
6. Klein, G., et al.: Comprehensive formal verification of an OS microkernel. ACM Trans, Comput. Syst. (TOCS) **32**(1), 2 (2014)
7. Klein, G., et al.: Sel4: formal verification of an OS kernel. In: Proceedings of the ACM SIGOPS 22nd Symposium on Operating Systems Principles, pp. 207–220. ACM (2009)
8. Klein, G., Sewell, T., Winwood, S.: Refinement in the formal verification of the sel4 microkernel. In: Hardin, D. (eds) Design and Verification of Microprocessor Systems for High-Assurance Applications, pp. 323–339. Springer (2010). https://doi.org/10.1007/978-1-4419-1539-9_11
9. Nelson, L., Bornholt, J., Krishnamurthy, A., Torlak, E., Wang, X.: Noninterference specifications for secure systems. ACM SIGOPS Operating Syst. Rev. **54**(1), 31–39 (2020)
10. Neumann, P.G., Robinson, L., Levitt, K.N., Boyer, R., Saxena, A.: A provably secure operating system. Stanford Research Inst Menlo Park Calif. Tech. Rep. (1975)
11. Verbeek, F., et al.: Formal API specification of the PikeOS separation kernel. In: Havelund, K., Holzmann, G., Joshi, R. (eds.) NFM 2015. LNCS, vol. 9058, pp. 375–389. Springer, Cham (2015). https://doi.org/10.1007/978-3-319-17524-9_26
12. Zhao, Y., Sanán, D., Zhang, F., Liu, Y.: Refinement-based specification and security analysis of separation kernels. IEEE Trans. Dependable Secure Comput. **16**(1), 127–141 (2019)

Author Index